PHILIP'S

STREET
ATLAS

UNRIVALLED
DET...
BES...
AT...

C000107980

NAVIGATOR®
LINCOLNSHIRE

NORTH LINCOLNSHIRE AND **NORTH EAST LINCOLNSHIRE**

www.philips-maps.co.uk

Published by Philip's a division of
Octopus Publishing Group Ltd
www.octopusbooks.co.uk
Carmelite House,
50 Victoria Embankment,
London EC4Y 0DZ
An Hachette UK Company
www.hachette.co.uk

First edition 2022
LINDA

ISBN 978-1-84907-571-8

© Philip's 2022

This product includes
mapping data licensed
from Ordnance Survey®
with the permission of
the Controller of
Her Majesty's Stationery Office.
© Crown copyright 2022. All rights
reserved. Licence number 100011710.

CONTENTS

III Key to map symbols

IV Key to map pages

VI Route planning

X Major administrative and Postcode boundaries

1 Street maps at 1¾ inches to 1 mile

178 Street maps at 3½ inches to 1 mile

234 Street map of Lincoln city centre
at 7 inches to 1 mile

235 Index of towns, villages, streets, hospitals,
industrial estates, railway stations, schools,
shopping centres, universities and places of interest

STREET ATLAS

UNRIVALLED
DETAIL FROM THE
BEST-SELLING
ATLAS RANGE

NAVIGATOR
LINCOLNSHIRE

NORTH LINCOLNSHIRE AND NORTH EAST LINCOLNSHIRE

CONTENTS

Key to map symbols

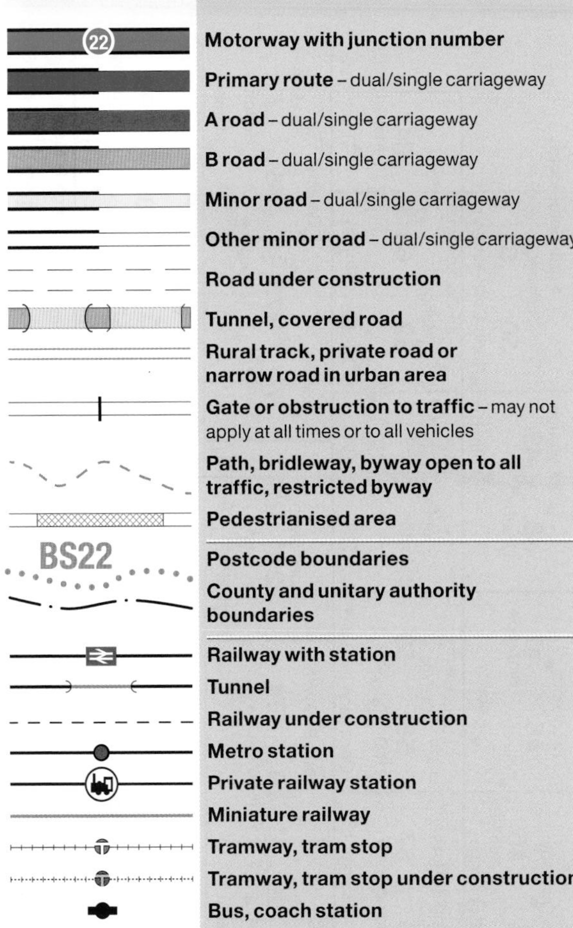

Motorway with junction number	
Primary route – dual/single carriageway	
A road – dual/single carriageway	
B road – dual/single carriageway	
Minor road – dual/single carriageway	
Other minor road – dual/single carriageway	
Road under construction	
Tunnel, covered road	
Rural track, private road or narrow road in urban area	
Gate or obstruction to traffic – may not apply at all times or to all vehicles	
Path, bridleway, byway open to all traffic, restricted byway	
Pedestrianised area	
BS22	Postcode boundaries
	County and unitary authority boundaries
Railway with station	
Tunnel	
Railway under construction	
Metro station	
Private railway station	
Miniature railway	
Tramway, tram stop	
Tramway, tram stop under construction	
Bus, coach station	

◆	Ambulance station
◆	Coastguard station
◆	Fire station
◆	Police station
✚	Accident and Emergency entrance to hospital
H	Hospital
✛	Place of worship
i	Information centre
P	Shopping centre, parking
P&R PO	Park and Ride, Post Office
Å ⛟	Camping site, caravan site
▸ ✕	Golf course, picnic site
Church ROMAN FORT	Non-Roman antiquity, Roman antiquity
Univ	Important buildings, schools, colleges, universities and hospitals
	Woods, built-up area
River Medway	Water name
	River, weir
	Stream
	Canal, lock, tunnel
	Water
	Tidal water
58 87 246	Adjoining page indicators and overlap bands – the colour of the arrow and band indicates the scale of the adjoining or overlapping page (see scales below)

The dark grey border on the inside edge of some pages indicates that the mapping does not continue onto the adjacent page

The small numbers around the edges of the maps identify the 1-kilometre National Grid lines

Abbreviations

Acad	Academy	Meml	Memorial
Allot Gdns	Allotments	Mon	Monument
Cemy	Cemetery	Mus	Museum
C Ctr	Civic centre	Obsy	Observatory
CH	Club house	Pal	Royal palace
Coll	College	PH	Public house
Crem	Crematorium	Recn Gd	Recreation ground
Ent	Enterprise	Resr	Reservoir
Ex H	Exhibition hall	Ret Pk	Retail park
Ind Est	Industrial Estate	Sch	School
IRB Sta	Inshore rescue boat station	Sh Ctr	Shopping centre
Inst	Institute	TH	Town hall / house
Ct	Law court	Trad Est	Trading estate
L Ctr	Leisure centre	Univ	University
LC	Level crossing	W Twr	Water tower
Liby	Library	Wks	Works
Mkt	Market	YH	Youth hostel

Enlarged maps only

	Railway or bus station building
	Place of interest
	Parkland

The map scale on the pages numbered in green is 1¾ inches to 1 mile
2.76 cm to 1 km • 1:36206

0	½ mile	1 mile	1½ miles	2 miles
0	500m 1 km	1½ km	2km	

The map scale on the pages numbered in blue is 3½ inches to 1 mile
5.52 cm to 1 km • 1:18103

0	¼ mile	½ mile	¾ mile	1 mile
0	250m 500m	750m	1km	

The map scale on the pages numbered in red is 7 inches to 1 mile
11.04 cm to 1 km • 1:9051

0	220yds	440yds	660yds	½ mile
0	125m 250m	375m	500m	

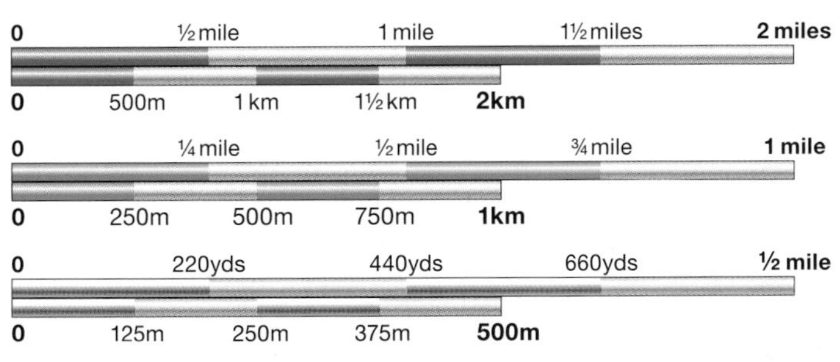

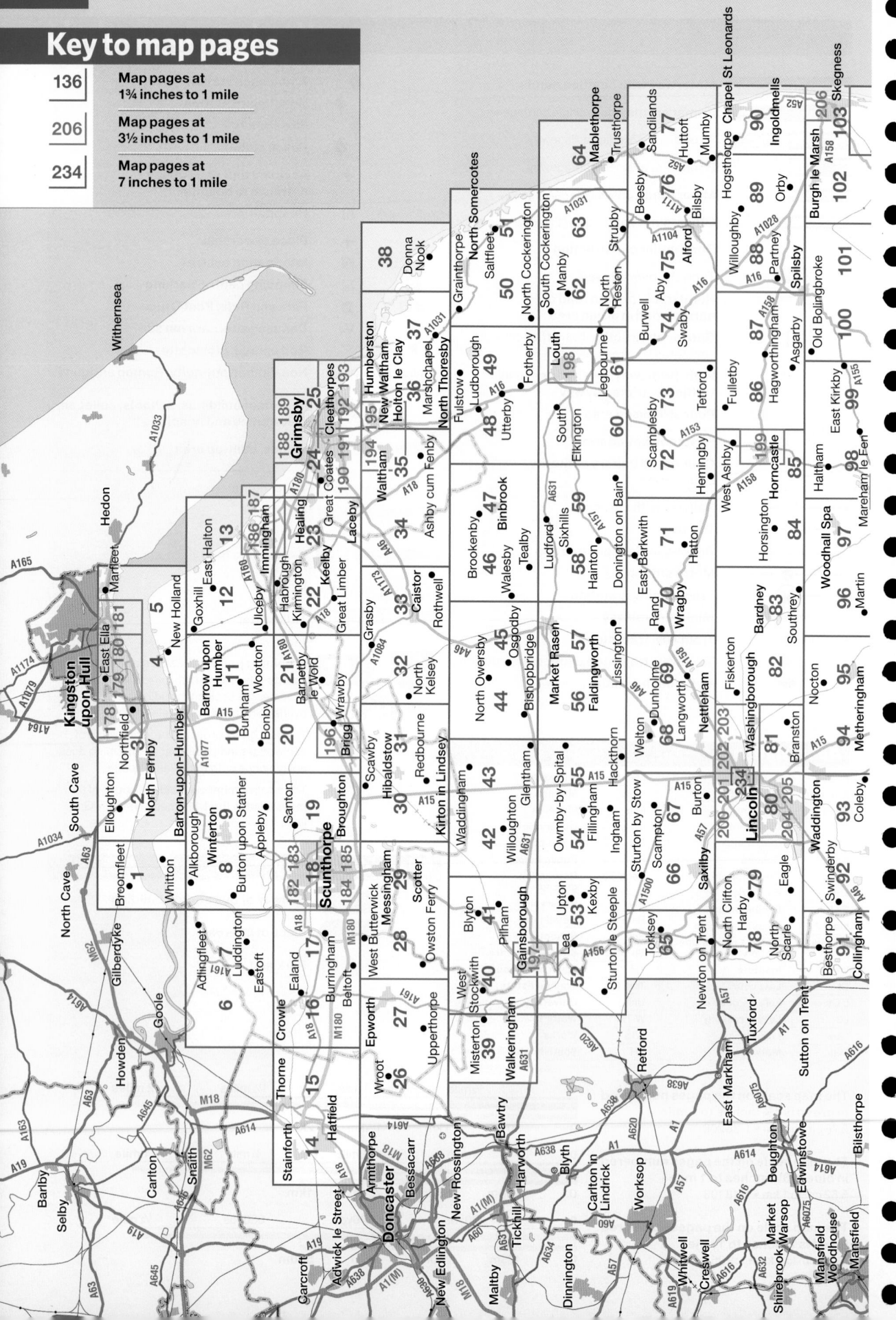

IV

Key to map pages

136	Map pages at 1¾ inches to 1 mile
206	Map pages at 3½ inches to 1 mile
234	Map pages at 7 inches to 1 mile

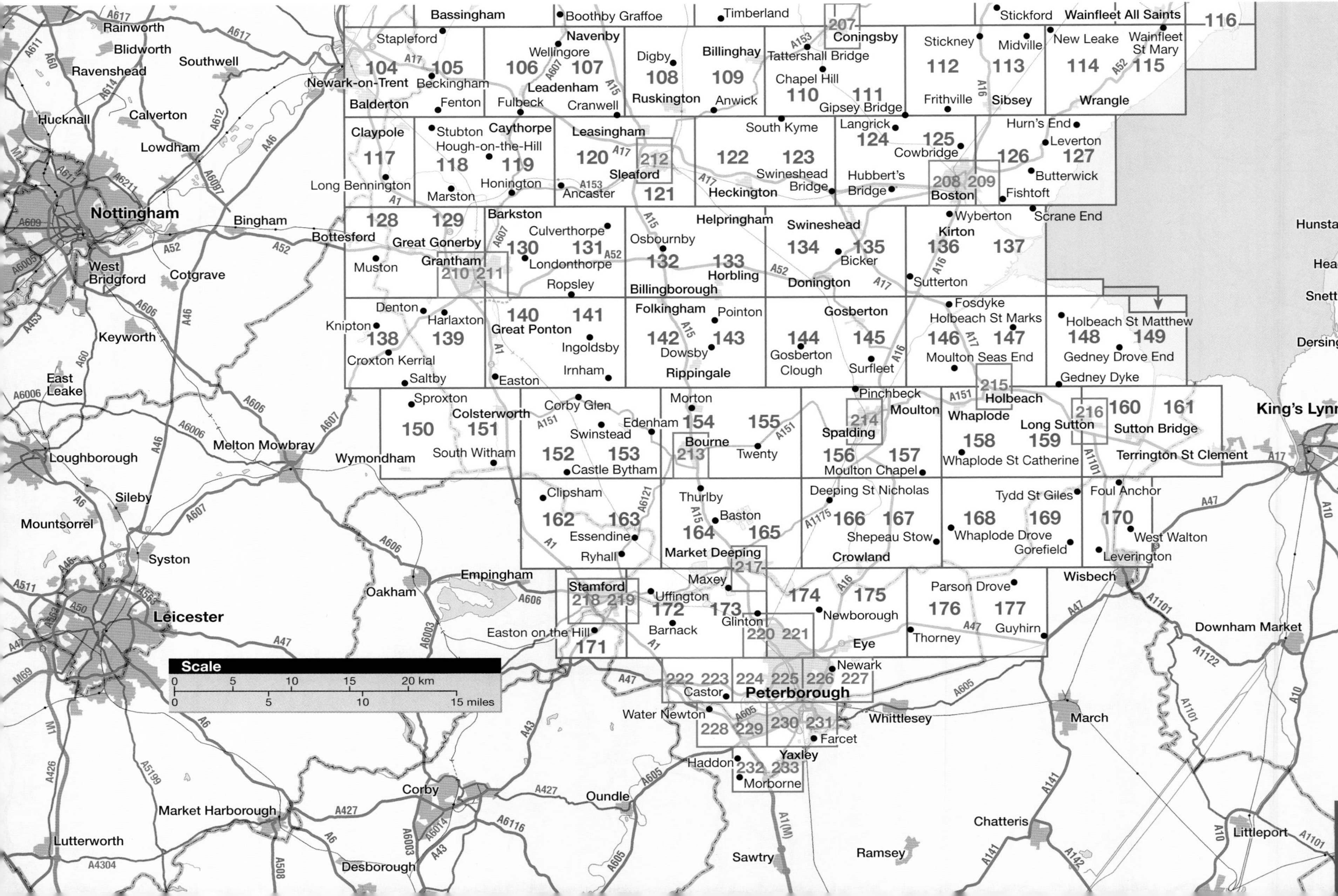

King's Lynn

Nottingham

Leicester

Peterborough

Stamford

Wisbech

March

Downham Market

Littleport

Chatteris

Ramsey

Oundle

Corby

Melton Mowbray

Grantham

Sleaford

Boston

Newark-on-Trent

Bingham

Loughborough

Market Harborough

Hunstanton
Heacham
Snettisham
Dersingham

Wainfleet All Saints
Wainfleet St Mary
New Leake
Wrangle
Stickford
Midville
Sibsey
Hurn's End
Leverton
Butterwick
Fishtoft
Scrane End
Holbeach St Matthew
Gedney Drove End
Gedney Dyke
Holbeach St Marks
Fosdyke
Moulton Seas End
Long Sutton
Sutton Bridge
Terrington St Clement
West Walton
Leverington
Foul Anchor
Tydd St Giles
Whaplade Drove
Gorefield
Guyhirn
Parson Drove
Thorney
Whittlesey
Farcet
Yaxley
Morborne
Haddon
Castor
Water Newton
Sawtry

Stickney
Frithville
Cowbridge
Wyberton
Kirton
Sutterton
Holbeach St Marks
Holbeach
Whaplode
Whaplode St Catherine
Whaplode Drove
Shepeau Stow
Newborough
Eye
Glinton
Maxey
Uffington
Barnack
Ryhall
Essendine
Easton on the Hill
Empingham
Oakham

Coningsby
Tattershall Bridge
Chapel Hill
Gipsey Bridge
Langrick
Hubbert's Bridge
Swineshead
Bicker
Donington
Gosberton
Surfleet
Gosberton Clough
Pinchbeck
Moulton
Moulton Chapel
Crowland
Thorney

Timberland
Billinghay
Anwick
South Kyme
Swineshead Bridge
Heckington
Helpringham
Horbling
Pointon
Dowsby
Rippingale
Twenty
Bourne
Baston
Thurlby
Market Deeping
Deeping St Nicholas
Deeping St James

Boothby Graffoe
Navenby
Wellingore
Leadenham
Fulbeck
Cranwell
Leasingham
Ruskington
Digby
Osbournby
Billingborough
Folkingham
Ingoldsby
Irnham
Morton
Edenham
Swinstead
Castle Bytham
Clipsham
Essendine

Bassingham
Stapleford
Balderton
Claypole
Long Bennington
Fenton
Marston
Stubton
Hough-on-the-Hill
Caythorpe
Honington
Barkston
Culverthorpe
Londonthorpe
Ropsley
Great Ponton
Easton
Colsterworth
Corby Glen
Swinstead

Newark-on-Trent
Bottesford
Great Gonerby
Harlaxton
Denton
Muston
Knipton
Croxton Kerrial
Saltby
Sproxton
Sproxton
South Witham
Wymondham

Rainworth
Blidworth
Southwell
Calverton
Lowdham
Ravenshead
Hucknall
West Bridgford
Keyworth
Cotgrave
East Leake
Sileby
Syston
Mountsorrel

Scale

0 5 10 15 miles

0 5 10 15 20 km

VI
Route planning
Scale
0 5 10 km
0 1 2 3 4 5 6 miles
North Lincolnshire
HUMBER
Humber Bridge
Kingston upon Hull
Goole
Scunthorpe
Gainsborough
Lincoln
Doncaster
RETFORD
Brigg
Barton-upon-Humber
Barrow upon Humber
Cottingham
Anlaby
Hessle
North Ferriby
South Cave
North Cave
Gilberdyke
Thorne
Hatfield
Stainforth
Crowle
Epworth
Messingham
Scotter
Kirton in Lindsey
Broughton
Winterton
Hibaldstow
Bawtry
Harworth
Tickhill
Blyth
Beckingham
Walkeringham
Tuxford
Ollerton
Boughton
Saxilby
Nettleham
Waddington
North Hykeham
Collingham
Bassingham
Sutton on Trent
Faldingworth
Washingborough
Metheringham
Laughton Woods
Doncaster Sheffield Airport
Read's Island
Redcliff Channel

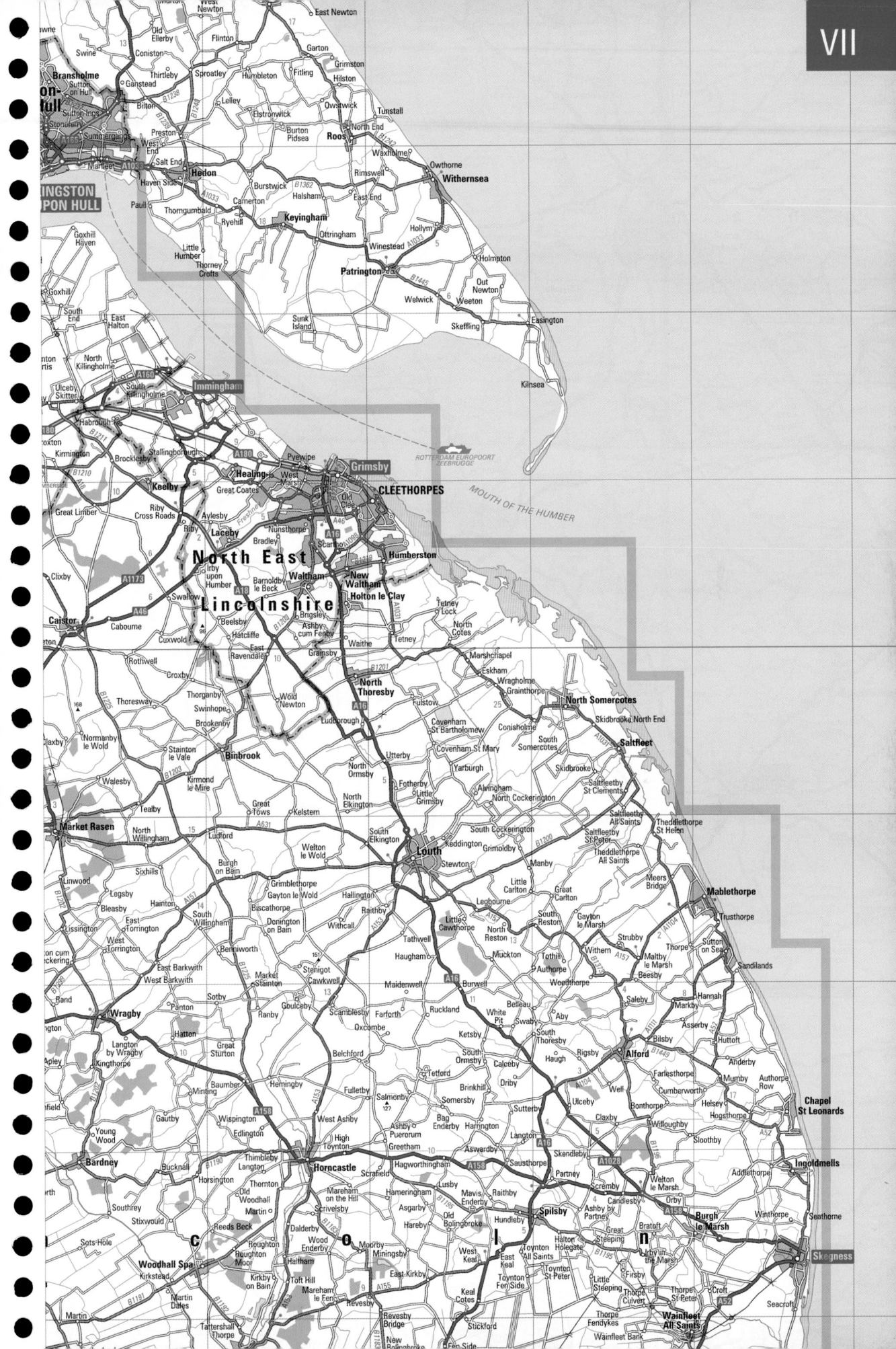
East Newton
Garton
Grimston
Hilston
Tunstall
Flinton
Old Ellerby
Swine
Coniston
Bransholme
Sutton on Hull
Thirtleby
Ganstead
Sproatley
Humbleton
Fitling
Lelley
Bilton
Elstronwick
Owstwick
Sutton Ings
Stoneferry
Summergangs
Preston
West End
Burton Pidsea
Roos
North End
Salt End
Marfleet
Hedon
Waxholme
Owthorne
Withernsea
Haven Side
Burstwick
Rimswell
Halsham
East End
Paull
Thorngumbald
Camerton
Ryehill
Keyingham
Ottringham
Hollym
Winestead
Holmpton
Little Humber
Thorney Crofts
Patrington
Out Newton
Welwick
Weeton
Easington
Skeffling
Sunk Island
Kilnsea
KINGSTON UPON HULL
Goxhill Haven
Goxhill
South End
East Halton
North Killingholme
South Killingholme
Immingham
Ulceby Skitter
Habrough
Kirmington
Brocklesby
Stallingborough
Pyewipe
Grimsby
Healing
West Marsh
Keelby
Great Coates
CLEETHORPES
Old Clee
Great Limber
Riby Cross Roads
Aylesby
Riby
Laceby
Nunsthorpe
Bradley
Scartho
Humberston
ROTTERDAM EUROPOORT
ZEEBRUGGE
MOUTH OF THE HUMBER
North East
Lincolnshire
Clixby
Irby upon Humber
Barnoldby le Beck
Waltham
New Waltham
Holton le Clay
Swallow
Caistor
Cabourne
Beelsby
Brigsley
Ashby cum Fenby
Tetney Lock
North Cotes
Tetney
Cuxwold
Hatcliffe
Waithe
East Ravendale
Grainsby
Marshchapel
Rothwell
Eskham
Wragholme
Grainthorpe
Croxby
North Thoresby
Thoresway
Thorganby
Swinhope
Wold Newton
Fulstow
North Somercotes
Skidbrooke North End
Brookenby
Ludborough
Covenham St Bartholomew
Conisholme
Claxby
Normanby le Wold
Stainton le Vale
Binbrook
Covenham St Mary
South Somercotes
Saltfleet
Utterby
Yarburgh
Skidbrooke
Walesby
Kirmond le Mire
North Ormsby
Fotherby
Little Grimsby
Alvingham
North Cockerington
Saltfleetby St Clements
Tealby
Great Tows
Kelstern
North Elkington
Saltfleetby All Saints
Theddlethorpe St Helen
Market Rasen
North Willingham
Ludford
South Elkington
South Cockerington
Saltfleetby St Peter
Theddlethorpe All Saints
Welton le Wold
Louth
Keddington
Grimoldby
Stewton
Manby
Sixhills
Burgh on Bain
Linwood
Grimblethorpe
Gayton le Wold
Hallington
Little Carlton
Great Carlton
Meers Bridge
Mablethorpe
Legsby
Hainton
Biscathorpe
Raithby
Legbourne
Bleasby
South Willingham
Donington on Bain
Little Cawthorpe
South Reston
Gayton le Marsh
Trusthorpe
Lissington
East Torrington
Withcall
North Reston
West Torrington
Tathwell
Strubby
Withern
Thorpe
Maltby le Marsh
Sutton on Sea
Benniworth
Haugham
Muckton
Tothill
Sandilands
East Barkwith
West Barkwith
Stenigot
Authorpe
Beesby
Market Stainton
Cawkwell
Maidenwell
Burwell
Woodthorpe
Rand
Sotby
Saleby
Hannah
Panton
Wragby
Ranby
Goulceby
Scamblesby
Farforth
Ruckland
Belleau
Markby
White Pit
Swaby
Aby
Oxcombe
Asserby
Hatton
Langton by Wragby
Great Sturton
Ketsby
South Thoresby
Bilsby
Huttoft
Apley
Kingthorpe
Belchford
South Ormsby
Calceby
Haugh
Rigsby
Alford
Anderby
Tetford
Farlesthorpe
Mumby
Authorpe Row
Baumber
Minting
Hemingby
Brinkhill
Driby
Well
Cumberworth
Chapel St Leonards
Fulletby
Salmonby
Somersby
Ulceby
Bonthorpe
Helsey
Hogsthorpe
Gautby
Wispington
Edlington
West Ashby
Ashby Puerorum
Bag Enderby
Harrington
Sutterby
Claxby
Willoughby
Young Wood
High Toynton
Greetham
Langton
Sloothby
Bardney
Thimbleby
Langton
Horncastle
Aswardby
Skendleby
Bucknall
Scrafield
Hagworthingham
Sausthorpe
Ingoldmells
Addlethorpe
Horsington
Thornton
Mareham on the Hill
Hameringham
Lusby
Mavis Enderby
Raithby
Partney
Scremby
Welton le Marsh
Old Woodhall
Candlesby
Orby
Southrey
Scrivelsby
Asgarby
Hareby
Old Bolingbroke
Hundleby
Spilsby
Ashby by Partney
Winthorpe
Seathorne
Stixwould
Martin
Burgh le Marsh
Reeds Beck
Dalderby
Bratoft
Great Steeping
Sots Hole
Roughton
Wood Enderby
Moorby
Halton Holegate
Skegness
Roughton Moor
Miningsby
West Keal
East Keal
Toynton All Saints
Irby in the Marsh
Woodhall Spa
Haltham
Kirkstead
Kirkby on Bain
Toft Hill
East Kirkby
Toynton Fen Side
Toynton St Peter
Little Steeping
Firsby
Croft
Mareham le Fen
Revesby
Thorpe Culvert
Thorpe St Peter
Martin Dales
Keal Cotes
Seacroft
Martin
Tattershall Thorpe
Revesby Bridge
Stickford
Thorpe Fendykes
Wainfleet All Saints
Wainfleet Bank
New Bolingbroke
Fen Side

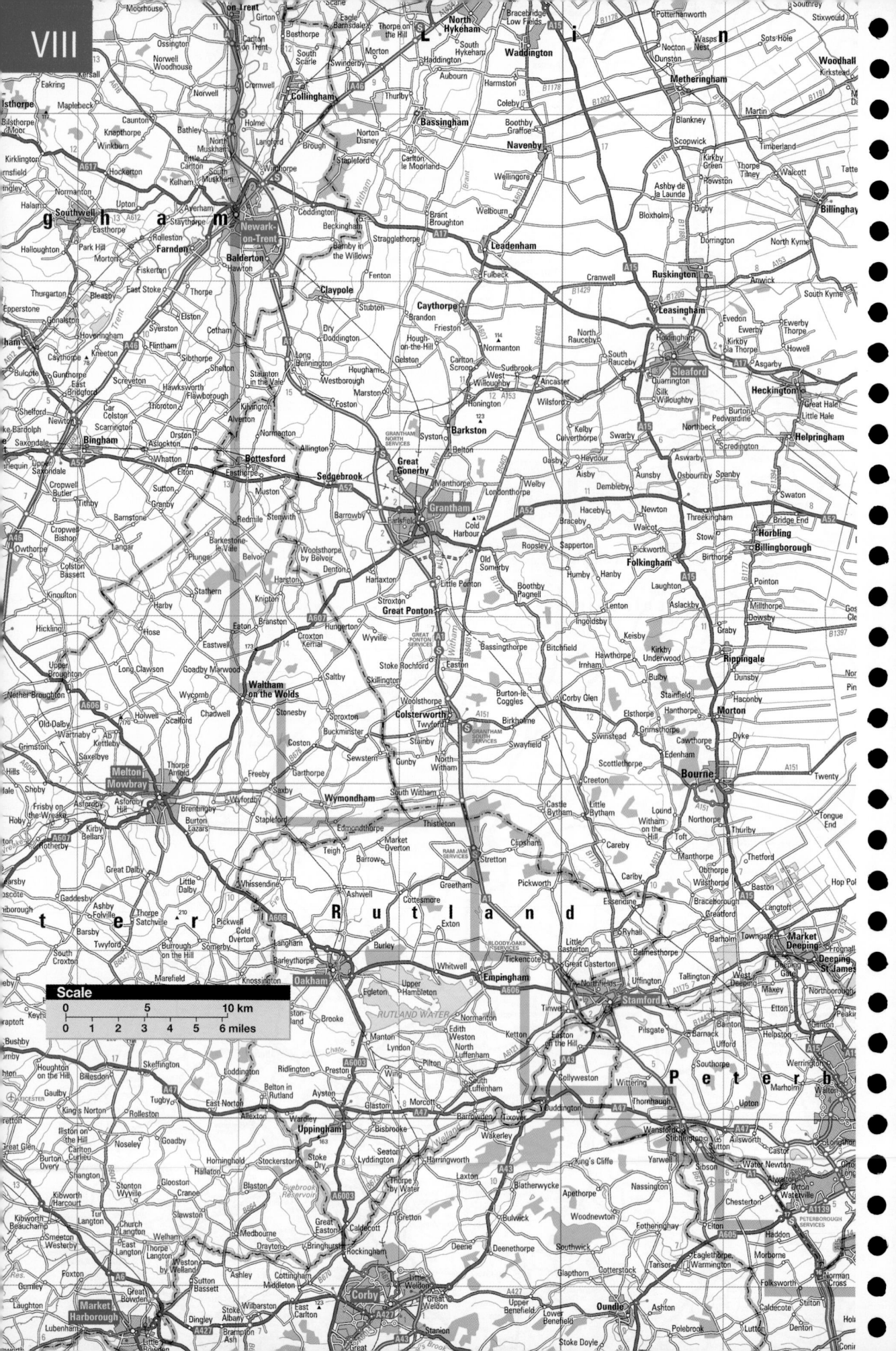
Scale
0
5
10 km
0
1
2
3
4
5
6 miles
R u t l a n d
Newark-on-Trent
Grantham
Sleaford
Melton Mowbray
Oakham
Stamford
Bourne
Market Deeping
Corby
Market Harborough
Southwell
Collingham
Bassingham
Navenby
Leadenham
Waddington
North Hykeham
Metheringham
Woodhall
Billinghay
Ruskington
Leasingham
Heckington
Helpringham
Horbling
Billingborough
Folkingham
Rippingale
Morton
Caythorpe
Claypole
Barkston
Great Gonerby
Sedgebrook
Bottesford
Bingham
Farndon
Balderton
Great Ponton
Colsterworth
Waltham on the Wolds
Wymondham
Empingham
Uppingham
Oundle
Deeping St James
Rutland Water
Eyebrook Reservoir

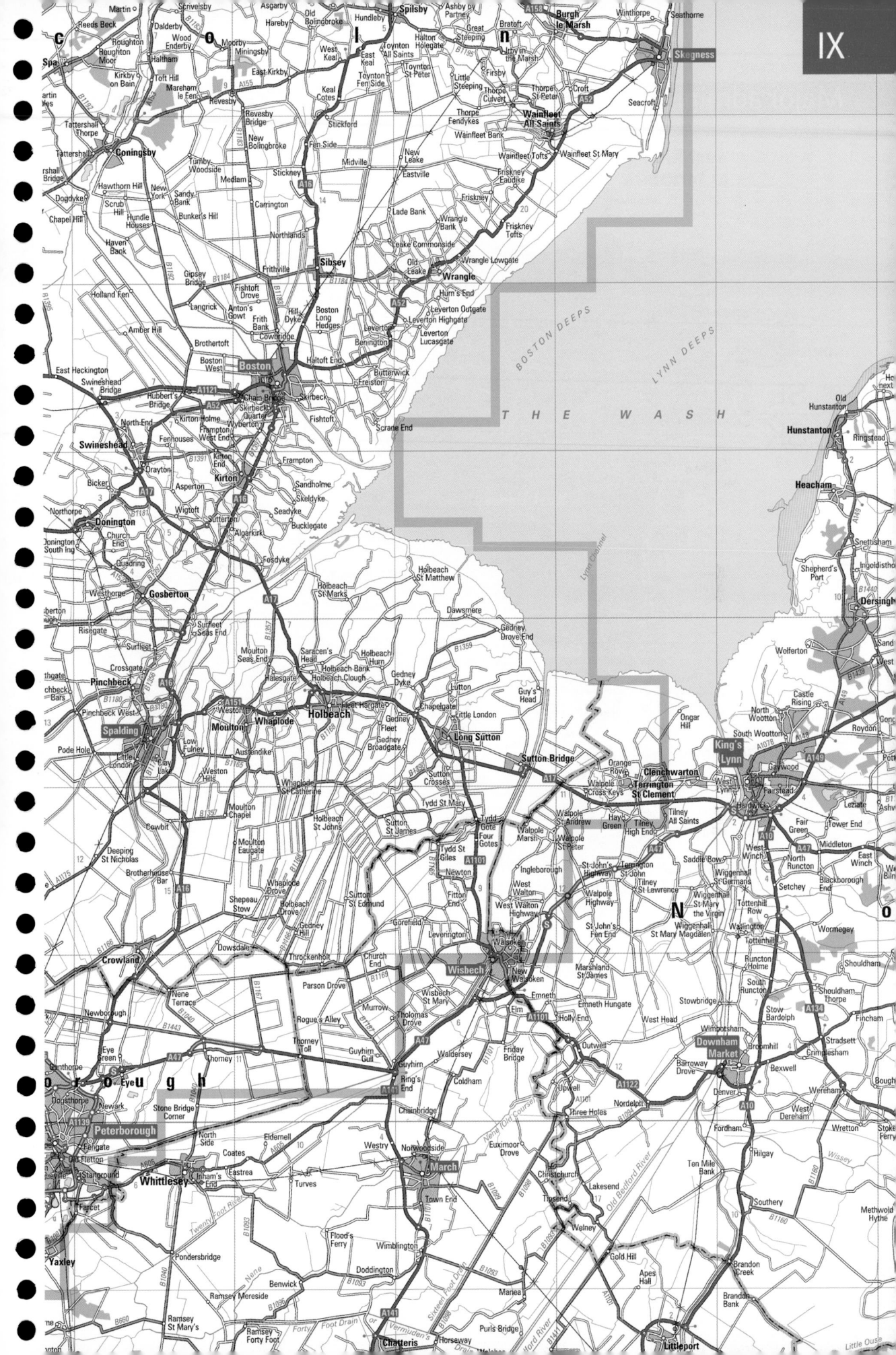
IX
Martin
Scrivelsby
Asgarby
Old Bolingbroke
Hundleby
Spilsby
Ashby by Partney
A158
Burgh le Marsh
Winthorpe
Seathorne
Reeds Beck
Dalderby
Hareby
Great Steeping
Bratoft
Skegness
Roughton
Wood Enderby
Moorby
Miningsby
West Keal
East Keal
Toynton All Saints
Halton Holegate
Irby in the Marsh
Roughton Moor
Haltham
East Kirkby
Toynton St Peter
Firsby
Kirkby on Bain
Toft Hill
Mareham le Fen
A155
Toynton Fen Side
Little Steeping
Thorpe Culvert
Thorpe St Peter
Croft
Revesby
Keal Cotes
Seacroft
Revesby Bridge
Stickford
Thorpe Fendykes
Wainfleet All Saints
Tattershall Thorpe
Coningsby
Tattershall
New Bolingbroke
Fen Side
Wainfleet Bank
New Leake
Wainfleet Tofts
Wainfleet St Mary
Tumby Woodside
Midville
Medlam
Stickney
Eastville
Friskney Eaudike
Dogdyke
Hawthorn Hill
New York
Sandy Bank
A16
Friskney
Scrub Hill
Carrington
Lade Bank
Chapel Hill
Hundle Houses
Bunker's Hill
Wrangle Bank
Friskney Tofts
Northlands
Haven Bank
Leake Commonside
Frithville
Sibsey
Old Leake
Wrangle Lowgate
Wrangle
Gipsey Bridge
Fishtoft Drove
Holland Fen
Langrick
Anton's Gowt
Hilldyke
Boston Long Hedges
Hurn's End
Leverton Outgate
Leverton Highgate
Frith Bank
Leverton
Leverton Lucasgate
Amber Hill
Cowbridge
Benington
Brothertoft
BOSTON DEEPS
LYNN DEEPS
Haltoft End
East Heckington
Boston West
Boston
Butterwick
Swineshead Bridge
Freiston
A1121
Chain Bridge
Hubbert's Bridge
Skirbeck
A52
Skirbeck Quarter
Fishtoft
North End
Kirton Holme
Wyberton
Frampton West End
Scrane End
T H E W A S H
Swineshead
Fenhouses
Kirton End
Frampton
Drayton
Kirton
Bicker
Asperton
Sandholme
Skeldyke
A17
Northorpe
Wigtoft
Seadyke
Donington
Sutterton
Bucklegate
Church End
Algarkirk
Donington South Ing
Quadring
Fosdyke
Westhorpe
Gosberton
Holbeach St Marks
Holbeach St Matthew
Lynn Channel
Surfleet Seas End
Dawsmere
Risegate
Gedney Drove End
Surfleet
Moulton Seas End
Crossgate
Saracen's Head
Holbeach Hurn
Pinchbeck
Holbeach Bank
Halesgate
Holbeach Clough
Gedney Dyke
Lutton
Guy's Head
A151
Fleet Hargate
Pinchbeck West
Weston
Whaplode
Holbeach
Gedney
Chapelgate
Little London
Spalding
Moulton
Fleet
Long Sutton
Ongar Hill
Gedney Broadgate
Pode Hole
Low Fulney
Austendike
Sutton Bridge
Little London
Weston Hills
Sutton Crosses
Orange Row
Clenchwarton
Walpole Cross Keys
Terrington St Clement
Whaplode St Catherine
Tydd St Mary
Moulton Chapel
Holbeach St Johns
Sutton St James
Tydd Gote
Four Gotes
Walpole St Andrew
Hay Green
Tilney High End
Tilney All Saints
Cowbit
Walpole Marsh
Walpole St Peter
Moulton Eaugate
Tydd St Giles
A1101
Deeping St Nicholas
Newton
Ingleborough
St John's Highway
Terrington St John
Brotherhouse Bar
Whaplode Drove
Fitton End
West Walton
Tilney St Lawrence
Sutton St Edmund
Walpole Highway
Shepeau Stow
Holbeach Drove
West Walton Highway
St John's Fen End
Gedney Hill
Gorefield
Leverington
Walsoken
Marshland St James
B1166
Dowsdale
Crowland
Throckenholt
Church End
Wisbech
New Walsoken
Parson Drove
Nene Terrace
Wisbech St Mary
Emneth
Emneth Hungate
Murrow
Newborough
Rogue's Alley
Tholomas Drove
Elm
Holly End
West Head
Eye Green
Thorney Toll
A47
Friday Bridge
Outwell
Guyhirn Gull
Waldersey
Thorney
Gunthorpe
Guyhirn
Ring's End
Coldham
Upwell
Nordelph
Eye
Dogsthorpe
Newark
Stone Bridge Corner
A141
Chainbridge
Three Holes
Peterborough
A1139
North Side
Eldernell
Fengate
Nene (Old Course)
Euximoor Drove
Old Fletton
Westry
Norwoodside
Coates
Eastrea
March
Stanground
Whittlesey
Inham's End
Christchurch
Lakesend
Turves
Town End
Farcet
Tipsend
Old Bedford River
Twenty Foot River
Welney
Yaxley
Flood's Ferry
Wimblington
Pondersbridge
Gold Hill
Doddington
Benwick
Apes Hall
Sixteen Foot Drain
Manea
Ramsey Mereside
Ramsey St Mary's
Ramsey Forty Foot
Forty Foot Drain
Vermuden's Drain
Purls Bridge
Chatteris
Horseway
Littleport
Little Ouse
Old Hunstanton
Hunstanton
Ringstead
Heacham
Snettisham
Shepherd's Port
Ingoldisthorpe
Dersingham
Wolferton
Castle Rising
North Wootton
South Wootton
Roydon
King's Lynn
Gaywood
A149
A148
A1076
West Lynn
Fairstead
Hardwick
Leziate
Fair Green
Tower End
Middleton
West Winch
North Runcton
East Winch
Saddle Bow
Wiggenhall St Germans
Wiggenhall St Mary the Virgin
Blackborough End
Setchey
Tottenhill Row
Watlington
Tottenhill
Wiggenhall St Mary Magdalen
Wormegay
Runcton Holme
Shouldham
South Runcton
Shouldham Thorpe
Stowbridge
Stow Bardolph
Fincham
Wimbotsham
Downham Market
Broomhill
Stradsett
Crimplesham
Barroway Drove
Bexwell
Denver
Wereham
West Dereham
Fordham
Wretton
Hilgay
Wissey
Ten Mile Bank
Southery
Methwold Hythe
Brandon Creek
Brandon Bank
A10
A1122
N
o
c
o
l
n
o
r
o
u
g
h

Major administrative and Postcode boundaries

Legend:
- County and unitary authority boundaries
- District boundaries
- Postcode boundaries
- Area covered by this atlas

Scale
0 10 20 km
0 5 10 15 miles

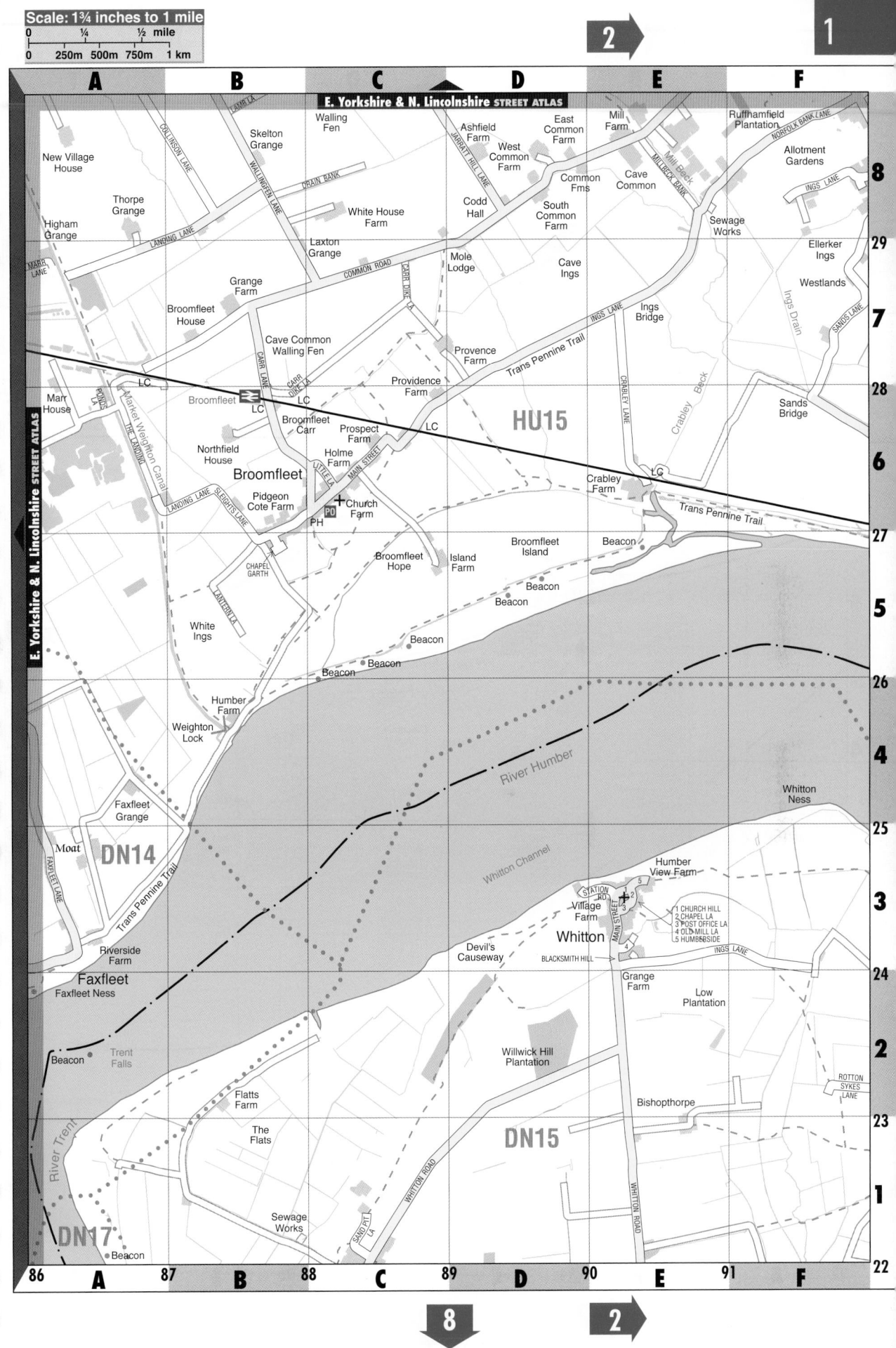
Scale: 1¾ inches to 1 mile
E. Yorkshire & N. Lincolnshire STREET ATLAS
Broomfleet
Whitton
Faxfleet
HU15
DN14
DN15
DN17
River Humber
River Trent
Whitton Channel
Trans Pennine Trail
Market Weighton Canal
Walling Fen
Skelton Grange
New Village House
Thorpe Grange
Higham Grange
White House Farm
Laxton Grange
Grange Farm
Broomfleet House
Cave Common Walling Fen
Ashfield Farm
West Common Farm
East Common Farm
Mill Farm
Ruffhamfield Plantation
Allotment Gardens
Codd Hall
Common Fms
Cave Common
South Common Farm
Sewage Works
Mole Lodge
Cave Ings
Ellerker Ings
Westlands
Ings Bridge
Ings Drain
Provence Farm
Providence Farm
Marr House
Northfield House
Broomfleet Carr
Prospect Farm
Holme Farm
Pidgeon Cote Farm
Church Farm
Crabley Farm
Crabley Beck
Sands Bridge
Broomfleet Hope
Island Farm
Broomfleet Island
Beacon
White Ings
Humber Farm
Weighton Lock
Faxfleet Grange
Moat
Riverside Farm
Faxfleet Ness
Trent Falls
Whitton Ness
Humber View Farm
Village Farm
Devil's Causeway
Grange Farm
Low Plantation
Willwick Hill Plantation
Bishopthorpe
Flatts Farm
The Flats
Sewage Works
1 CHURCH HILL
2 CHAPEL LA
3 POST OFFICE LA
4 OLD MILL LA
5 HUMBERSIDE
BLACKSMITH HILL
COLLINSON LANE
LAMB LA
WALLINGFEN LANE
DRAIN BANK
LANDING LANE
MARR LANE
COMMON ROAD
CARR DIKE LA
JARRATT HILL LANE
MILLBECK BANK
Mill Beck
NORFOLK BANK LANE
INGS LANE
SANDS LANE
CARR LANE
PONDS LA
THE LANDING
LITTLE LA
MAIN STREET
SLEIGHTS LANE
CHAPEL GARTH
LANTERN LA
CRABLEY LANE
FAXFLEET LANE
STATION RD
WHITTON ROAD
SAND PIT LA
ROTTON SYKES LANE
LC
PH
PO

2
8
2

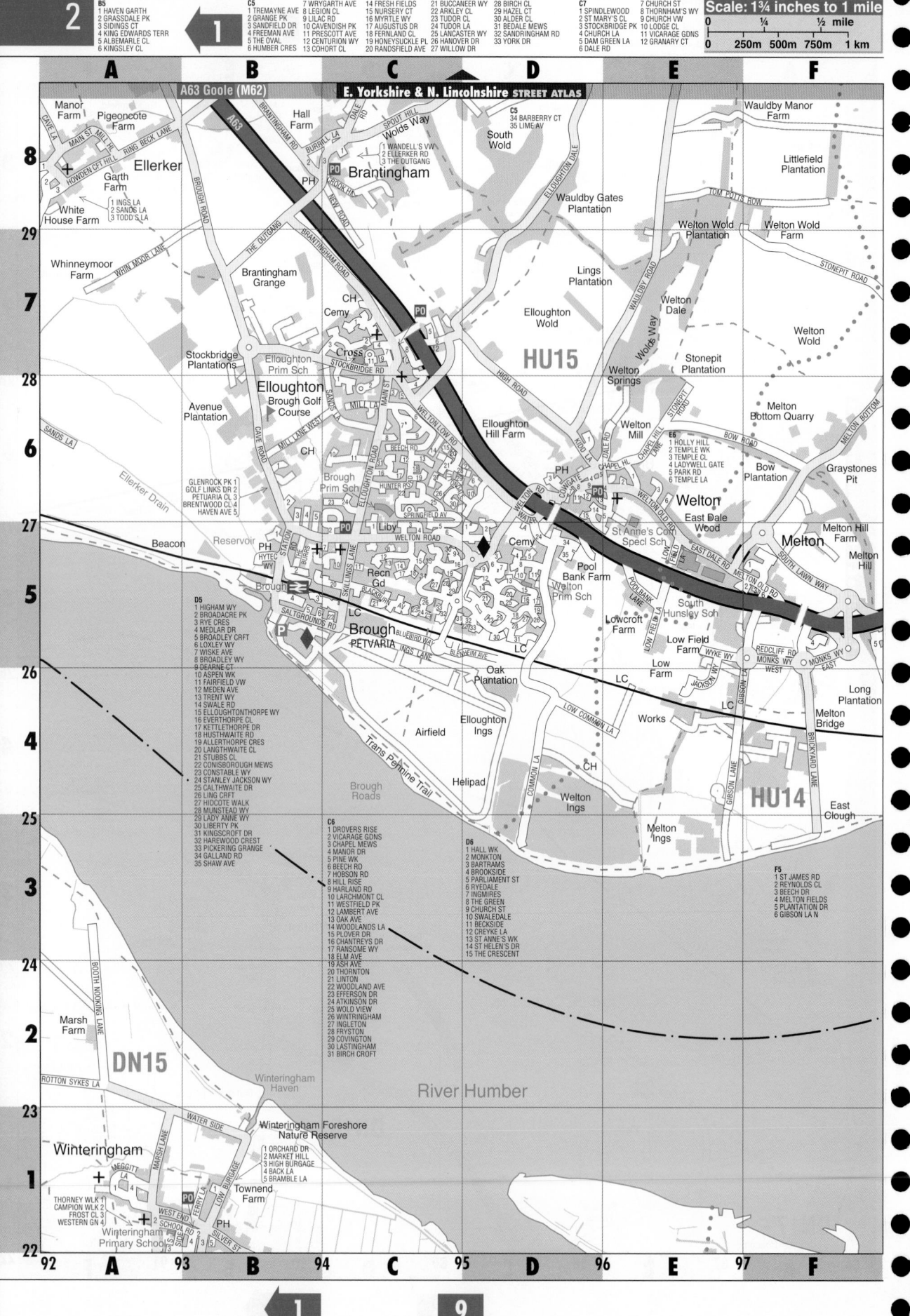

Scale: 1¾ inches to 1 mile

E. Yorkshire & N. Lincolnshire STREET ATLAS

B7
1 NORTHDALE PK
2 WAULDBY VW
3 WOOD VW
4 THE GREEN
5 WESTERDALE
6 MEADOW WLK

7 THE SPINNEY
8 CROWTHER WY
9 WELTON WOLD VW
10 DALE CL
11 DOWER RISE
12 PRIORY CL
13 HOLGATE PL

14 CHANTRY WAY E
15 SYKES CL
16 CHANTRY WY
17 ON HILL
18 ST MICHAEL'S MT
19 GALLANDS CL
20 HOLGATE PL

21 ST MARYS WALK

C7
1 ST BARNABAS DR
2 EASENBY CL
3 THE PADDOCK
4 BEECH GR
5 GREENACRES
6 STYLES CRFT
7 WOODSIDE

B6
1 WEST FIELD LA
2 QUEENSBURY WY
3 KEMP RD
4 HUMBER VW
5 HUMBERDALE CL
6 COPPER BEECH CL
7 WEST LEYS PK
8 GRANGE PK

A5
1 GREENWAYS
2 THE PADDOCK
3 WOODGATES MOUNT
4 CROFT PK
5 MOUNT VW
6 SWANLAND GARTH
7 WOODLANDS RISE
8 THE RISE
9 WEST PARKLANDS DR
10 PARKLANDS DR
11 PARKLANDS CRES
12 ASTON HALL DR
13 WOODGATES CL
14 SPINNEY CROFT CL
15 ROXTON HALL DR
16 WHITE HOUSE MEWS
17 TURNER'S LA
18 ASHDALE PK
19 WHITE HOUSE GARTH

E4
1 WEST HILL
2 CLIFF TOP LA
3 CLIFF HOUSE DR
4 SOUTHFIELD
5 ST MARYS CL
6 THE COACHINGS
7 RIVERSIDE CT
8 BLUEBELL GDNS
9 PARKLANDS MEWS

F4
1 VAUGHAN RD
2 DANES DR
3 BANNISTER CL
4 ALL SAINTS CL
5 DYKES CL
6 CASTLE WY
7 BEACON CL

Major labels: A164 Beverley, E. Yorkshire & N. Lincolnshire STREET ATLAS, HU10, HU13, HU14, DN18, West Ella, Kirk Ella, Anlaby, Hessle, Northfield, South Field, Swanland, North Ferriby, BARTON-UPON-HUMBER, Barton Waterside, River Humber, Humber Bridge, 178, Kingston Rd, Springfield Way, Boothferry Road, Wolds Way.

A4
1 SANDS CT
2 READING ROOM YARD
3 SCHOOL LA
4 WOOD DR
5 NUNBURNHOLME AVE
6 BEECH DR
7 CHURCH AVE
8 WILSON CL
9 TRIANGLE DR
10 ELMTREE AVE
11 COLLIER CL
12 EAST MOUNT
13 THE TRIANGLE
14 PARKFIELD AVE
15 WEST VW
16 SELWYN AVE
17 THE RIDINGS
18 DERWENT AVE
19 THE PICKERINGS
20 OLD POND PL
21 SOUTHFIELD DR
22 REDCLIFF DR
23 HIGHFIELD WY

E1
1 BARRACLOUGH'S LA
2 ROPERY LA
3 STABLE LA
4 HAVEN RD
5 VICTORIA DR
6 COUNCIL TERR
7 CASTLEDYKE W
8 FLEETGATE
9 OVERTON CT
10 PONDS WY
11 WESTERN DR
12 MALTBY LA
13 REGENCY CT
14 BIRCH WOOD CL
15 VAGARTH CL
16 WEST ACRIDGE
17 RIVERBANK RISE
18 PLOVER CT
19 RAMBLERS LA

20 LAPWING WY
21 SANDPIPER WY
22 WARBLERS CL
23 BITTERN RD
24 GODSANDER CL
25 KINGFISHER CL
26 BIRCH GDNS
27 Castledyke Prim Sch

28 PONDS WY
29 SHADWELL RISE
30 PINE PK
31 MILL VW
32 CLAPSON'S LA
33 HEWSON'S LA
34 DUNCAN DR
35 COTTINGHAM CT
36 ST PETER'S CT

F1
1 TRINITY WK
2 VICTORY WY
3 HARRIER RD
4 NURSERY CL
5 QUEEN'S AVE
6 SEDGE CL
7 GREENWAY
8 NEWPORT ST
9 WHISTON WY
10 TREECE GDNS
11 FINKLE LA
12 EAST GR
13 SOUTERGATE
14 WILLOW DR
15 EAST ACRIDGE
16 BRAMLEY CL
17 FRANKLIN MEWS
18 THE RUSHES
19 FENLAND CT
20 ST. PETERS ORCHARD
21 TYSON CL
22 Barton St Peters CE Prim Sch
23 LOWER MEADOWS

10   4

3

Scale: 1¾ inches to 1 mile

0 ¼ ½ mile
0 250m 500m 750m 1 km

A B C D E F

E. Yorkshire & N. Lincolnshire STREET ATLAS

179

180 A1079 Beverley (A1174)

HU5

HU2

8

CH HOTHAM RD S WESTLANDS RD WOLD ROAD CALVERT RD ROSEDALE GR KIRKLANDS ROAD BROOKLANDS RD PERTH ST NEWSTEAD ST WHARNCLIFFE THORESBY ST BELVOIR ST PRINCES AV POTS
Kingston Road WILLERBY ROAD Sch LOMOND ROAD Liby Cemy PERTH STRERET WELBECK ST SPRING BANK WEST SUNNY BANK Chy Acad East GREEN LA SCOTT ST HU2
REDCLIFFE DR NELSON RD HELMSLEY GROVE Spring Bank W SPRING BANK WEST Coll HYDE RD STANLEY ST Theatre PROSPECT ST ALBION ST GEORGE ST A165

East Ella West Park Sports Gd

29 SPRINGFIELD WY HULL RD COLVILLE AV EELA DR B1231 ANLABY ROAD L Ctr Liby St Stephen's CARR LA Sh PO

7 HU10 MEAD WK Liby A1105 ANLABY ROAD A1105 A1079 CASTLE ST Mus
Hull Road BELGRAVE DRIVE WESTFIELD ROAD PICKERING ROAD BOOTHFERRY RD WHEELER ST PLANE ST SELBY STREET HU3 GT THORNTON ST ADELAIDE ST A63 Hotel
Anlaby Park Sports Ctr NORTH RD GREEK ST GLASGOW ST ST GEORGE'S RD CAVILL PL WALKER ST Kingston St Dock

28 ELGAR RD Sch ASKEW AVENUE HAYTON GR EAST GROVE NEWINGTON ST Liby HESSLE ROAD English St Hull Arena Victoria Pier Locks
BOOTHFERRY ROAD Acad Allot Gdns Sch COLTMAN ST WOODCOCK ST JACKSON ST Chy

6 A1105 BOOTHFERRY ROAD Acad Pickering Park HESSLE RD A1106 Witty Street GOULTON ST Albert Dock HU1
TAUNTON RD ASHBY RD GOWER RD COLTMAN RD RIVER GR Liby Bsns Pk WEST DOCK ST

27 SALTASH RD BETHUNE AVE CAMPION AV GRAHAM AVE WILTSHIRE RD FREIGHTLINER ROAD
TILBURY RD HESSLE ROAD Gipsyville Priory Bridge St Andrews Quay
FIRST LANE HULL RD SUMMERGROVES WAY HU4 CLIVE SULLIVAN WAY Trans Pennine Trail

5 Mast Priory Park A63 P&R
Waterside Business Park

CLIVE SULLIVAN WY

26 179 180

4

25

3 New Holland Pier New Holland Mere

Fairfield Pit Nature Reserve New Holland
24 LC OXMARSH LANE OXMARSH LANE Summercroft Farm
New Holland CE Methodist Prim Sch New Holland
Barrow Haven Reedbed Nature Reserve LINCOLN CASTLE WAY

2 Pasture Wharf Nature Reserve Oxford Grange Farm MARSH LANE New Holland
Chy Sailing Club WEST MARSH LA Barrow Haven MARSH LANE BARROW ROAD

23 WEST MARSHLANE Barrow Haven PH Hann Farm
Windmill The Castles (Motte & Baileys) DN19 Field Farm Leys Farm
1 PASTURE RD N Mill Farm WEST HANN LANE Coulbeck Farm EAST HANN LANE
1 2 ARDENT RD Castle Farm West Hann Farm B1206 Mill Farm
3 PASTURE RD S Spring Farm The Beck NEW HOLLAND RD Barrow Hann
4 ANTELOPE RD West Marsh Farm Barrow Blow Wells Nature Reserve FALKLAND WAY

22 DN18

04 A 05 B 06 C 07 D 08 E 09 F

E2
1 SCHOOL LA
2 WENTWORTH CR
3 FULFORD CRES
4 WESTBURN AVE
5 MORGAN WY
6 GLENEAGLES CRES
7 ALBERT ST
8 MOUNT PL
9 PEPLOE LA
10 PEPLOE CRES
11 DANESGATE
12 SCHOOL LA

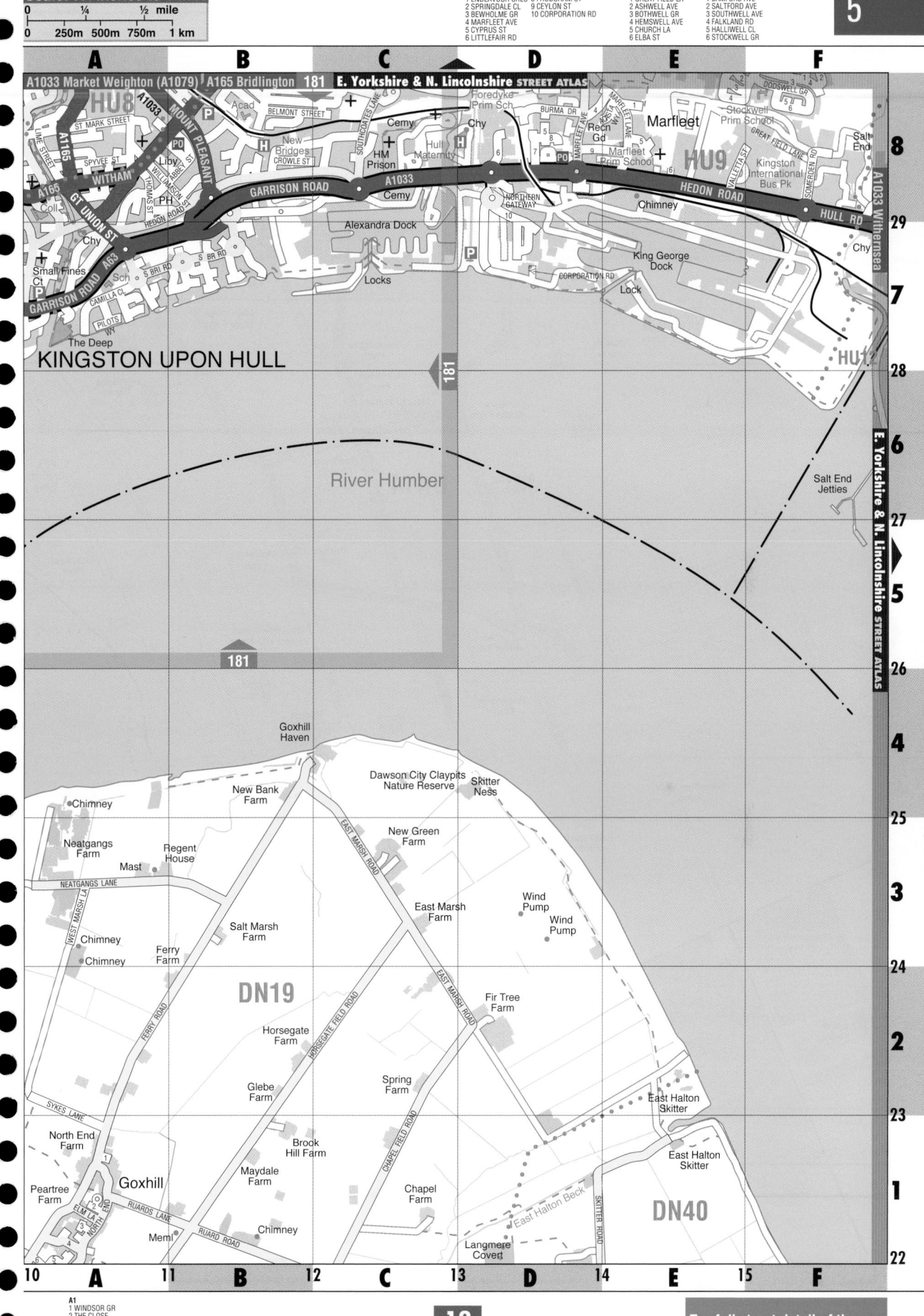

D8
1 ENDEAVOUR CRES
2 SPRINGDALE CL
3 BEWHOLME GR
4 MARFLEET AVE
5 CYPRUS ST
6 LITTLEFAIR RD

7 DELHI ST
8 FRODSHAM ST
9 CEYLON ST
10 CORPORATION RD

E8
1 GREAT FIELD LA
2 ASHWELL AVE
3 BOTHWELL GR
4 HEMSWELL AVE
5 CHURCH LA
6 ELBA ST

F8
1 BAMFORD AVE
2 SALTFORD AVE
3 SOUTHWELL AVE
4 FALKLAND RD
5 HALLIWELL CL
6 STOCKWELL GR

7 TOWER HOUSE LA

A1033 Market Weighton (A1079)   A165 Bridlington   181   E. Yorkshire & N. Lincolnshire STREET ATLAS

A   B   C   D   E   F

HU8

ST MARK STREET

WITHAM

A1033

MOUNT PLEASANT

Acad

BELMONT STREET

New Bridges CROWLE ST

Cemy

HM Prison

SOUTHCOATES LANE

Foredyke Prim Sch

Chy

Hull Maternity

Burma Dr

Recn Gd

Marfleet Prim School

Marfleet

Stockwell Prim School

HU9

Salt End

8

Liby

PH

Chy

GT UNION ST

Coll

A65

A1065

SPYVEE ST

WILLIAMSON ST

ABBEY ST

THOMAS ST

HEDON ROAD

GARRISON ROAD   A1033   Cemy

Northern Gateway

PO

HEDON ROAD

Chimney

HULL RD

A1033 Withernsea

29

Small Fines Ct

GARRISON ROAD   A65

CAMILLA CL

PILOTS WY

S BRI RD

S BRI RD

BR RD

Alexandra Dock

Locks

CORPORATION RD

King George Dock

Lock

Chy

HU1

7

The Deep

KINGSTON UPON HULL

181

28

River Humber

6

Salt End Jetties

27

E. Yorkshire & N. Lincolnshire STREET ATLAS

181

5

26

4

Goxhill Haven

Chimney

New Bank Farm

Dawson City Claypits Nature Reserve

Skitter Ness

25

Neatgangs Farm

Regent House

Mast

New Green Farm

EAST MARSH ROAD

NEATGANGS LANE

WEST MARSH LA

Chimney

Ferry Farm

Chimney

Salt Marsh Farm

East Marsh Farm

Wind Pump

Wind Pump

3

24

DN19

Horsegate Farm

HORSEGATE FIELD ROAD

FERRY ROAD

Fir Tree Farm

EAST MARSH ROAD

2

Glebe Farm

Spring Farm

CHAPEL FIELD ROAD

East Halton Skitter

23

North End Farm

SYKES LANE

Brook Hill Farm

Maydale Farm

East Halton Skitter

DN40

1

Peartree Farm

ELM LA

RUARDS LANE

RUARD ROAD

Goxhill

Meml

Chimney

Chapel Farm

East Halton Beck

SKITTER ROAD

Langmere Covert

22

10   A   11   B   12   C   13   D   14   E   15   F

A1
1 WINDSOR GR
2 THE CLOSE
3 FARROWS POND
4 MILL LA
5 MEADOW CL
6 WILLOW LA

12

For full street detail of the highlighted area see page 181.

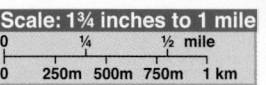

A161 Goole
GOOLE RD

E. Yorkshire & N. Lincolnshire STREET ATLAS

E. Yorkshire & N. Lincolnshire STREET ATLAS

Couper Farm

Goole Hall

Bankside Farm

Goole Mill Windmill (dis)

Parker House Farm

Causeway Farm

PARK ST

A161

DUNMIRES LANE

NEW LANE

SWINEFLEET ROAD

KING'S CAUSEWAY

BOG GATE

Field House

Charity Farm

Ash Tree Farm

Goole Grange Farm

Narrow Farm

Oak Tree Farm

Ivy Lodge Farm

Croft Farm

College Farm

Park Farm

Goole Fields

Goole Fields Farm

Nova Scotia Farm

Readingate Farm

Common Farm

Mount Pleasant Farm

Croft Farm

READING GATE

PLODINGERS LANE

MARGRAVE LANE

Low West Moor Field

Moor Fields

High West Moor Field

Mawgre Farm

Low East Moor Field

MOORFIELDS LA

High East Moor Field

OLD LANE

Highfields Farm

DN14

Bankside Farm

QUAY LANE

QUART LANE

Reednees Grange

OLD LANE GATE

Pasture Farm

Moorend Farm

Park Grounds Farm

Swinefleet Warping Drain

CROSSMOOR BANK

CROSSMOOR BANK

Yoke Fleet Farm

Swinefleet and Reedness Moor

Ousefleet Moor

SANDBY

Goole Moors

NEW ROAD

Reedness Moor

READING GATE

Moors Farm

OLD LANE GATE

Wigtoft Moor

Whitgift Moor

HIGHFIELDS LA

Eastoft Moor

Swinefleet Moor Farm

Red House Farm

OLD LANE GATE

Swinefleet and Reedness Waste or Moors

Easingwold House

Thorne Waste or Moors

Rainsbutt Moor

Eastoft Carr

CROWLE ROAD

Wilf Pitts

Crowle Waste or Moors

Rainsbutt Chicken Farm

DN17

Eastoft Grange

Slate House Farm

Crowle Moor Nature Reserve

Cottage Farm

West Ings

Ribbon Row

MOOR BOTTOM RD

NORTHMOOR RD

NORTHMOOR ROAD

RAINSBUTT ROAD

The Warpings

GOOLE RD

A161

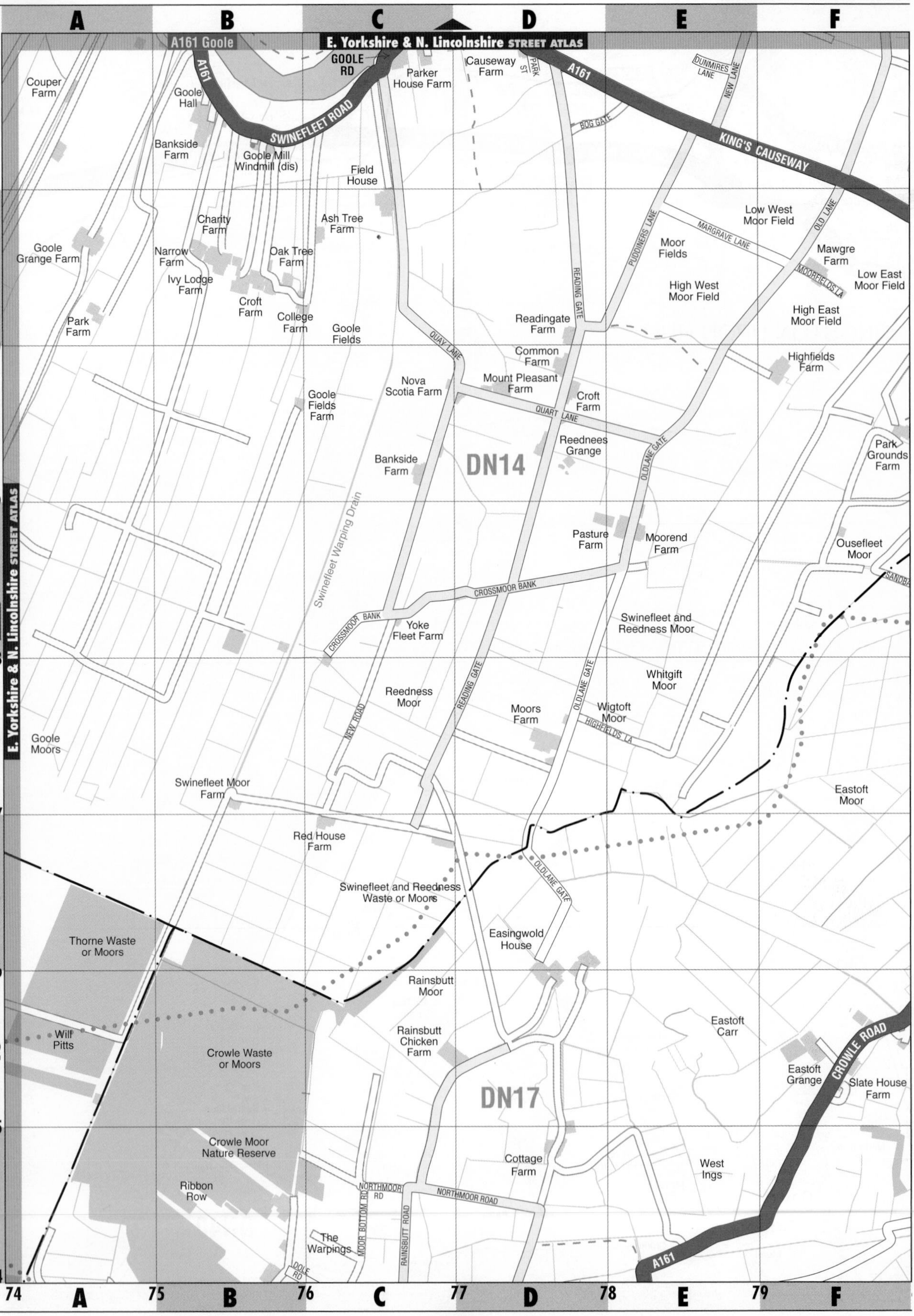

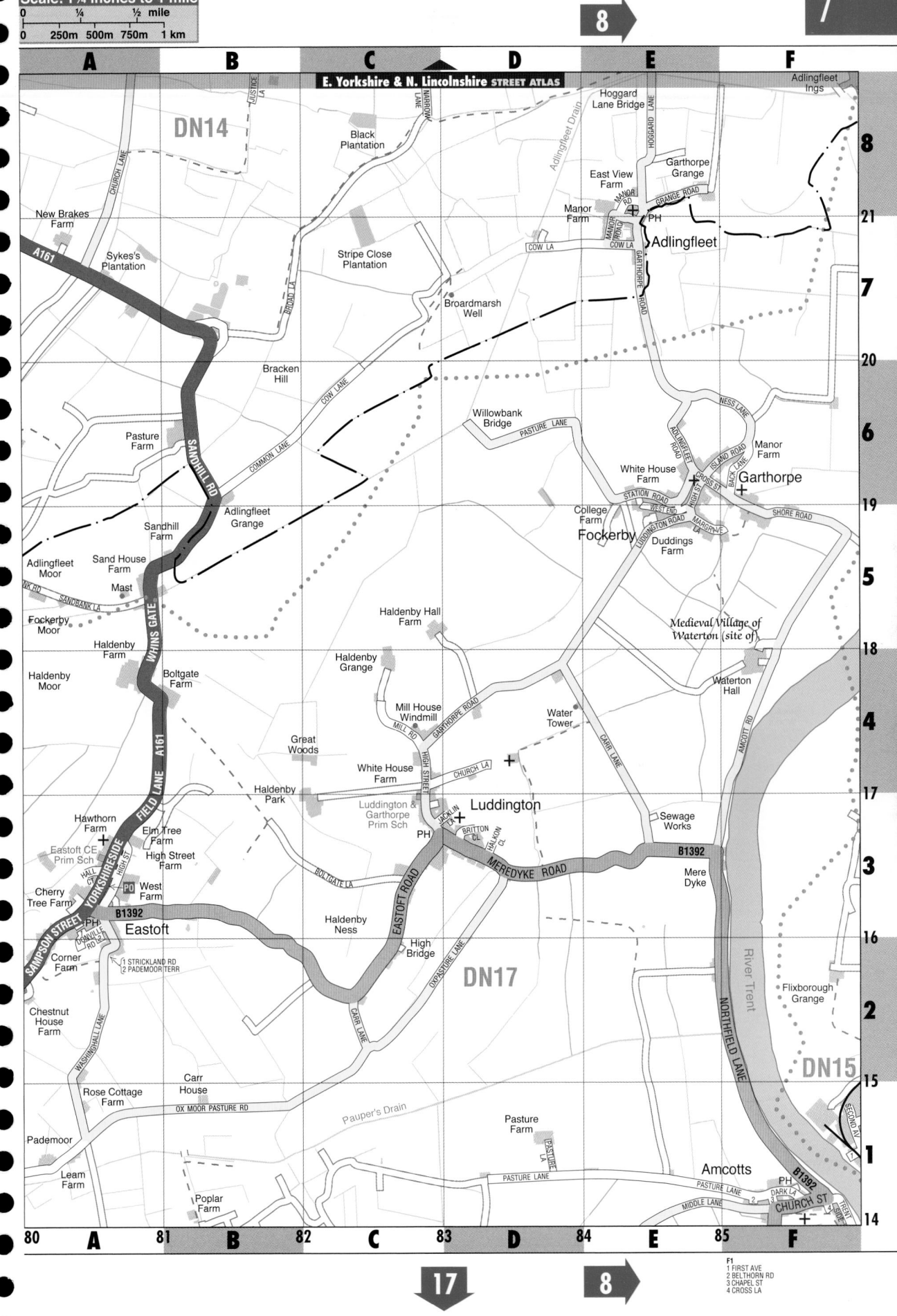

E. Yorkshire & N. Lincolnshire STREET ATLAS

DN14

New Brakes Farm

Sykes's Plantation

A161

CHURCH LANE

BROAD LA

JUSTICE LA

NARROW LANE

Black Plantation

Stripe Close Plantation

Broardmarsh Well

Hoggard Lane Bridge

HOGGARD LANE

Adlingfleet Ings

Adlingfleet Drain

East View Farm

Garthorpe Grange

MANOR RD

Manor Farm

GRANGE ROAD

PH

COW LA

COW LA

MANOR ROAD

GARTHORPE ROAD

Adlingfleet

21

7

Pasture Farm

SANDHILL RD

Bracken Hill

COW LANE

COMMON LANE

Willowbank Bridge

PASTURE LANE

NESS LANE

ADLINGFLEET ROAD

White House Farm

CROSS ST

ISLAND ROAD

BACK ROAD

Manor Farm

Garthorpe

20

6

19

Adlingfleet Moor

Sand House Farm

Sandhill Farm

Mast

Adlingfleet Grange

WHINS GATE

SANDBANK LA

NK RD

College Farm

STATION ROAD

WEST END

LUDDINGTON ROAD

Fockerby

MARGRAVE

HIGH ST

Duddings Farm

SHORE ROAD

5

Fockerby Moor

Haldenby Farm

Haldenby Moor

Boltgate Farm

A161

FIELD LANE

Haldenby Hall Farm

Haldenby Grange

Mill House Windmill

MILL RD

GARTHORPE ROAD

Water Tower

Medieval Village of Waterton (site of)

Waterton Hall

AMCOTT RD

18

4

Haldenby Park

Great Woods

White House Farm

HIGH STREET

CHURCH LA

CARR LANE

17

Hawthorn Farm

Eastoft CE Prim Sch

Elm Tree Farm

High Street Farm

HIGH ST

YORKSHIRESIDE

Cherry Tree Farm

PD

West Farm

PH

B1392

CONVILLE RD LCL

Eastoft

SAMPSON STREET

Corner Farm

1 STRICKLAND RD
2 PADEMOOR TERR

BOLTGATE LA

EASTOFT ROAD

Haldenby Park

Luddington & Garthorpe Prim Sch

JACK LN

PH

BRITTON CL

THALKON CL

Luddington

MEREDYKE ROAD

Sewage Works

B1392

Mere Dyke

Flixborough Grange

River Trent

NORTHFIELD LANE

16

3

Chestnut House Farm

WASHINGHALL LANE

Haldenby Ness

High Bridge

OXPASTURE LANE

DN17

2

Rose Cottage Farm

Carr House

OX MOOR PASTURE RD

CARR LANE

Pauper's Drain

Pasture Farm

PASTURE LA

DN15

15

Pademoor

Leam Farm

Poplar Farm

Pasture Farm

PASTURE LANE

MIDDLE LANE

Amcotts

PH

DARK LA

CHURCH ST

B1392

FRONT LANE

SECOND AV

1

14

F1
1 FIRST AVE
2 BELTHORN RD
3 CHAPEL ST
4 CROSS LA

7 1

Scale: 1¾ inches to 1 mile

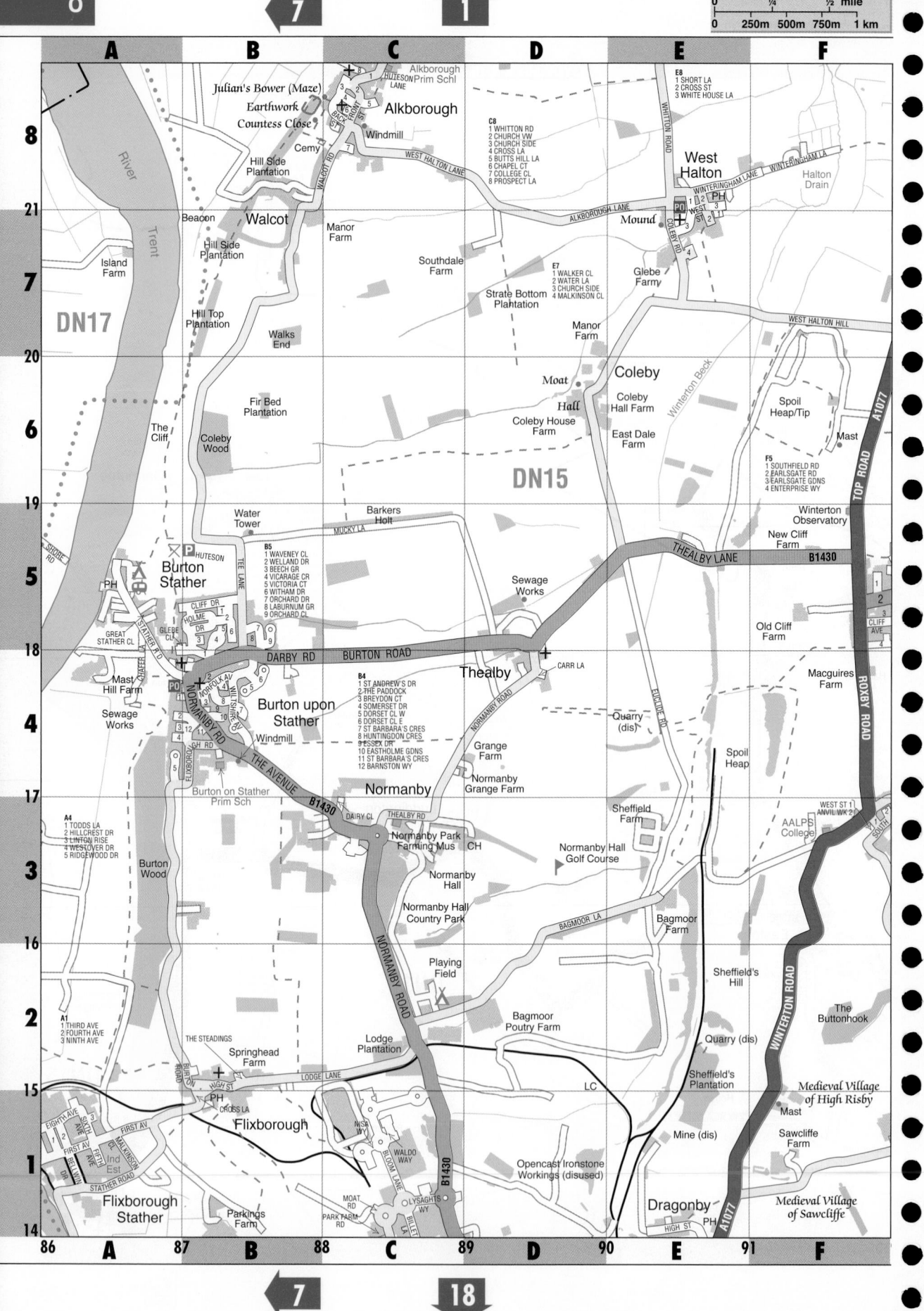
Alkborough
Julian's Bower (Maze)
Earthwork
Countess Close
Windmill
Cemy
Alkborough Prim Schl
Hill Side Plantation
Walcot
Beacon
Manor Farm
Island Farm
River Trent
DN17
Hill Top Plantation
Walks End
Southdale Farm
Strate Bottom Plantation
West Halton
Halton Drain
Mound
Glebe Farm
Manor Farm
Moat
Hall
Coleby
Coleby Hall Farm
Coleby House Farm
East Dale Farm
Winterton Beck
Spoil Heap/Tip
Mast
DN15
Fir Bed Plantation
The Cliff
Coleby Wood
Water Tower
Barkers Holt
Winterton Observatory
New Cliff Farm
Burton Stather
Sewage Works
THEALBY LANE
B1430
Old Cliff Farm
Great Stather CL
Mast Hill Farm
Thealby
Macguires Farm
Burton upon Stather
Windmill
Quarry (dis)
Grange Farm
Normanby Grange Farm
Spoil Heap
Burton on Stather Prim Sch
Normanby
Sheffield Farm
AALPS College
Normanby Park Farming Mus
Normanby Hall Golf Course
Burton Wood
Normanby Hall
Normanby Hall Country Park
Bagmoor Farm
Playing Field
Sheffield's Hill
The Buttonhook
Bagmoor Poutry Farm
Quarry (dis)
Springhead Farm
Lodge Plantation
Sheffield's Plantation
Medieval Village of High Risby
Flixborough
Mine (dis)
Sawcliffe Farm
Opencast Ironstone Workings (disused)
Flixborough Stather
Parkings Farm
Dragonby
Medieval Village of Sawcliffe
TOP ROAD
ROXBY ROAD
WINTERTON ROAD
NORMANBY ROAD
A1077
C8 1 WHITTON RD 2 CHURCH VW 3 CHURCH SIDE 4 CROSS LA 5 BUTTS HILL LA 6 CHAPEL CT 7 COLLEGE CL 8 PROSPECT LA
E8 1 SHORT LA 2 CROSS ST 3 WHITE HOUSE LA
E7 1 WALKER CL 2 WATER LA 3 CHURCH SIDE 4 MALKINSON CL
F5 1 SOUTHFIELD RD 2 EARLSGATE RD 3 EARLSGATE GDNS 4 ENTERPRISE WY
B5 1 WAVENEY CL 2 WELLAND DR 3 BEECH GR 4 VICARAGE CR 5 VICTORIA CT 6 WITHAM DR 7 ORCHARD DR 8 LABURNUM GR 9 ORCHARD CL
B4 1 ST ANDREW'S DR 2 THE PADDOCK 3 BREYDON CT 4 SOMERSET DR 5 DORSET CL W 6 DORSET CL E 7 ST BARBARA'S CRES 8 HUNTINGDON CRES 9 ESSEX DR 10 EASTHOLME GDNS 11 ST BARBARA'S CRES 12 BARNSTON WY
A4 1 TODDS LA 2 HILLCREST DR 3 LINTON RISE 4 WESTOVER DR 5 RIDGEWOOD DR
A1 1 THIRD AVE 2 FOURTH AVE 3 NINTH AVE

7 18

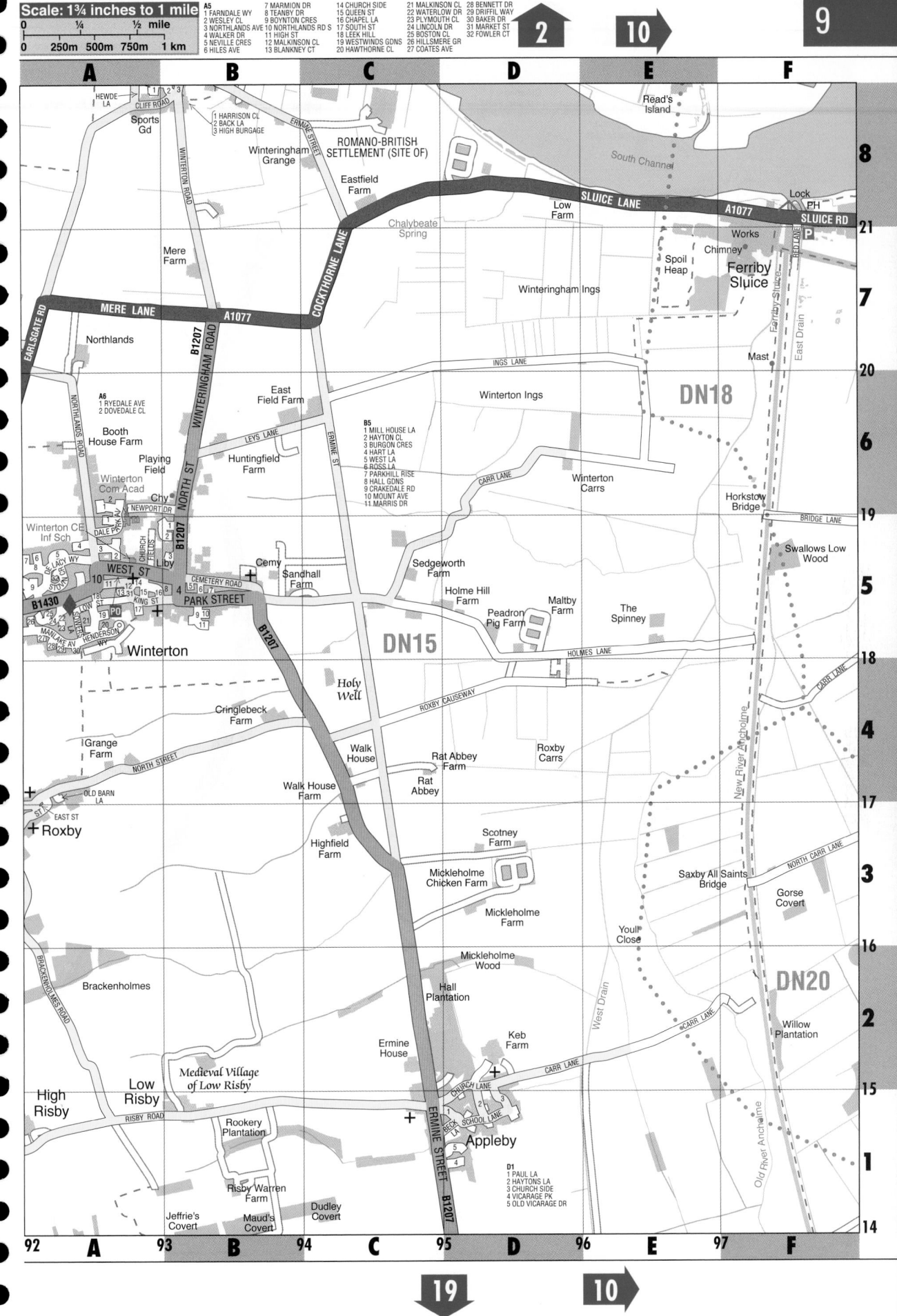

Scale: 1¾ inches to 1 mile

0   ¼   ½   mile
0   250m   500m   750m   1 km

A5
1 FARNDALE WY
2 WESLEY CL
3 NORTHLANDS AVE
4 WALKER DR
5 NEVILLE CRES
6 HILES AVE

7 MARMION DR
8 TEANBY DR
9 BOYNTON CRES
10 NORTHLANDS RD S
11 HIGH ST
12 MALKINSON CL
13 BLANKNEY CT

14 CHURCH SIDE
15 QUEEN ST
16 CHAPEL LA
17 SOUTH ST
18 LEEK HILL
19 WESTWINDS GDNS
20 HAWTHORNE CL

21 MALKINSON CL
22 WATERLOW DR
23 PLYMOUTH CL
24 LINCOLN DR
25 BOSTON CL
26 HILLSMERE GR
27 COATES AVE

28 BENNETT DR
29 DRIFFIL WAY
30 BAKER DR
31 MARKET ST
32 FOWLER CT

A6
1 RYEDALE AVE
2 DOVEDALE CL

B5
1 MILL HOUSE LA
2 HAYTON CL
3 BURGON CRES
4 HART LA
5 WEST LA
6 ROSS LA
7 PARKHILL RISE
8 HALL GDNS
9 CRAKEDALE RD
10 MOUNT AVE
11 MARRIS DR

1 HARRISON CL
2 BACK LA
3 HIGH BURGAGE

D1
1 PAUL LA
2 HAYTONS LA
3 CHURCH SIDE
4 VICARAGE PK
5 OLD VICARAGE DR

DN18
DN15
DN20

ROMANO-BRITISH SETTLEMENT (SITE OF)

Read's Island
South Channel
Sluice Lane
A1077
Sluice Rd
Lock PH
Ferriby Sluice
Works
Chimney
Spoil Heap
Winteringham Grange
Eastfield Farm
Low Farm
Chalybeate Spring
Mere Farm
Mere Lane   A1077
Northlands
Booth House Farm
Playing Field
Winterton Com Acad
Winterton CE Inf Sch
Winterton
Winteringham Ings
Winterton Ings
Winterton Carrs
Horkstow Bridge
Bridge Lane
Swallows Low Wood
East Field Farm
Huntingfield Farm
Leys Lane
Ermine St
Carr Lane
Sedgeworth Farm
Holme Hill Farm
Maltby Farm
Peadron Pig Farm
The Spinney
Cemetery Road
Cemy
Sandhall Farm
Park Street
Holmes Lane
Holy Well
Roxby Causeway
Cringlebeck Farm
Walk House
Rat Abbey Farm
Rat Abbey
Roxby Carrs
North Street
Grange Farm
Old Barn La
East St
Roxby
Walk House Farm
Highfield Farm
Mickleholme Chicken Farm
Scotney Farm
Youll Close
Saxby All Saints Bridge
Gorse Covert
North Carr Lane
Brackenholmes
Mickleholme Farm
Mickleholme Wood
Hall Plantation
Willow Plantation
Carr Lane
Ermine House
Keb Farm
Medieval Village of Low Risby
High Risby
Low Risby
Risby Road
Rookery Plantation
Church Lane
School Lane
Appleby
Risby Warren Farm
Jeffrie's Covert
Maud's Covert
Dudley Covert
West Drain
New River Ancholme
Old River Ancholme
East Drain
Ferriby Sluice
Red Lane
Hewde La
Cliff Road
Sports Gd
Winterton Road
Cockthorne Lane
Earlsgate Rd
B1207
North St
Northlands Road
B1430
B1207
Ermine Street

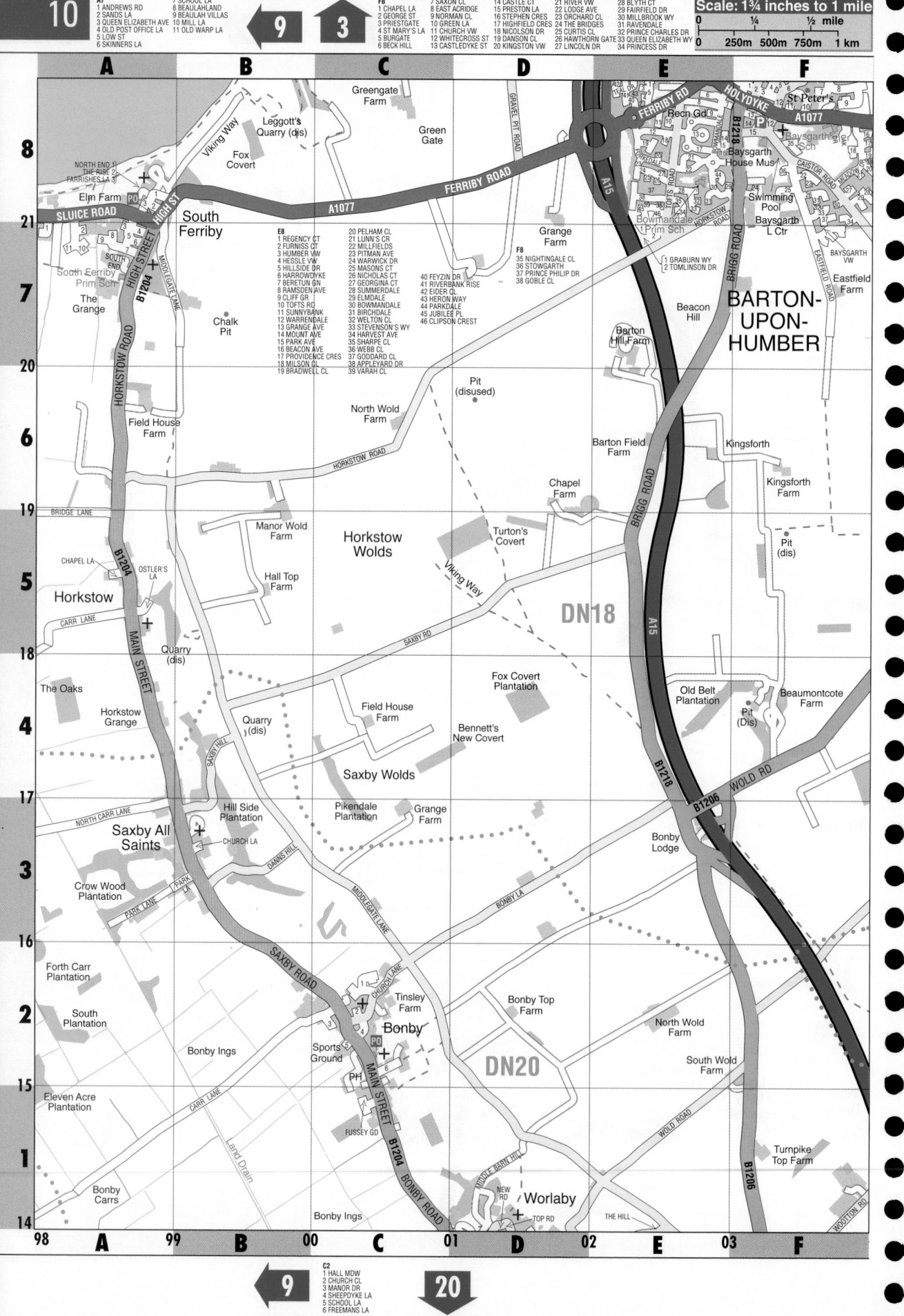

A7
1 ANDREWS RD
2 SANDS LA
3 QUEEN ELIZABETH AVE
4 OLD POST OFFICE LA
5 LOW ST
6 SKINNERS LA
7 SCHOOL LA
8 BEAULAHLAND
9 BEAULAH VILLAS
10 MILL LA
11 OLD WARP LA

9
3

F8
1 CHAPEL LA
2 GEORGE ST
3 PRIESTGATE
4 ST MARY'S LA
5 BURGATE
6 BECK HILL

7 SAXON CL
8 EAST ACRIDGE
9 NORMAN CL
10 GREEN LA
11 CHURCH VW
12 WHITECROSS ST
13 CASTLEDYKE ST

14 CASTLE CT
15 PRESTON LA
16 STEPHEN CRES
17 HIGHFIELD CRES
18 NICOLSON DR
19 DANSON CL
20 KINGSTON VW

21 RIVER VW
22 LODGE AVE
23 ORCHARD CL
24 THE BRIDGES
25 CURTIS CL
26 HAWTHORN GATE
27 LINCOLN DR

28 BLYTH CT
29 FAIRFIELD DR
30 MILLBROOK WY
31 RAVENDALE
32 PRINCE CHARLES DR
33 QUEEN ELIZABETH WY
34 PRINCESS DR

E8
1 REGENCY CT
2 FURNISS CT
3 HUMBER VW
4 HESSLE VW
5 HILLSIDE DR
6 HARROWDYKE
7 BERETUN GN
8 RAMSDEN AVE
9 CLIFF GR
10 TOFTS RD
11 SUNNYBANK
12 WARRENDALE
13 GRANGE AVE
14 MOUNT AVE
15 PARK AVE
16 BEACON AVE
17 PROVIDENCE CRES
18 MILSON CL
19 BRADWELL CL

20 PELHAM CL
21 LUNN'S CR
22 MILLFIELDS
23 PITMAN AVE
24 WARWICK DR
25 MASONS CT
26 NICHOLAS CT
27 GEORGINA CT
28 SUMMERDALE
29 ELMDALE
30 BOWMANDALE
31 BIRCHDALE
32 WELTON CL
33 STEVENSON'S WY
34 HARVEST AVE
35 SHARPE CL
36 WEBB CL
37 GODDARD CL
38 APPLEYARD DR
39 VARAH CL

40 FEYZIN DR
41 RIVERBANK RISE
42 EIDER CL
43 HERON WAY
44 PARKDALE
45 JUBILEE PL
46 CLIPSON CREST

F8
35 NIGHTINGALE CL
36 STOWGARTH
37 PRINCE PHILIP DR
38 GOBLE CL

1 GRABURN WY
2 TOMLINSON DR

BARTON-
UPON-
HUMBER

9
20

C2
1 HALL MDW
2 CHURCH CL
3 MANOR DR
4 SHEEPDYKE LA
5 SCHOOL LA
6 FREEMANS LA

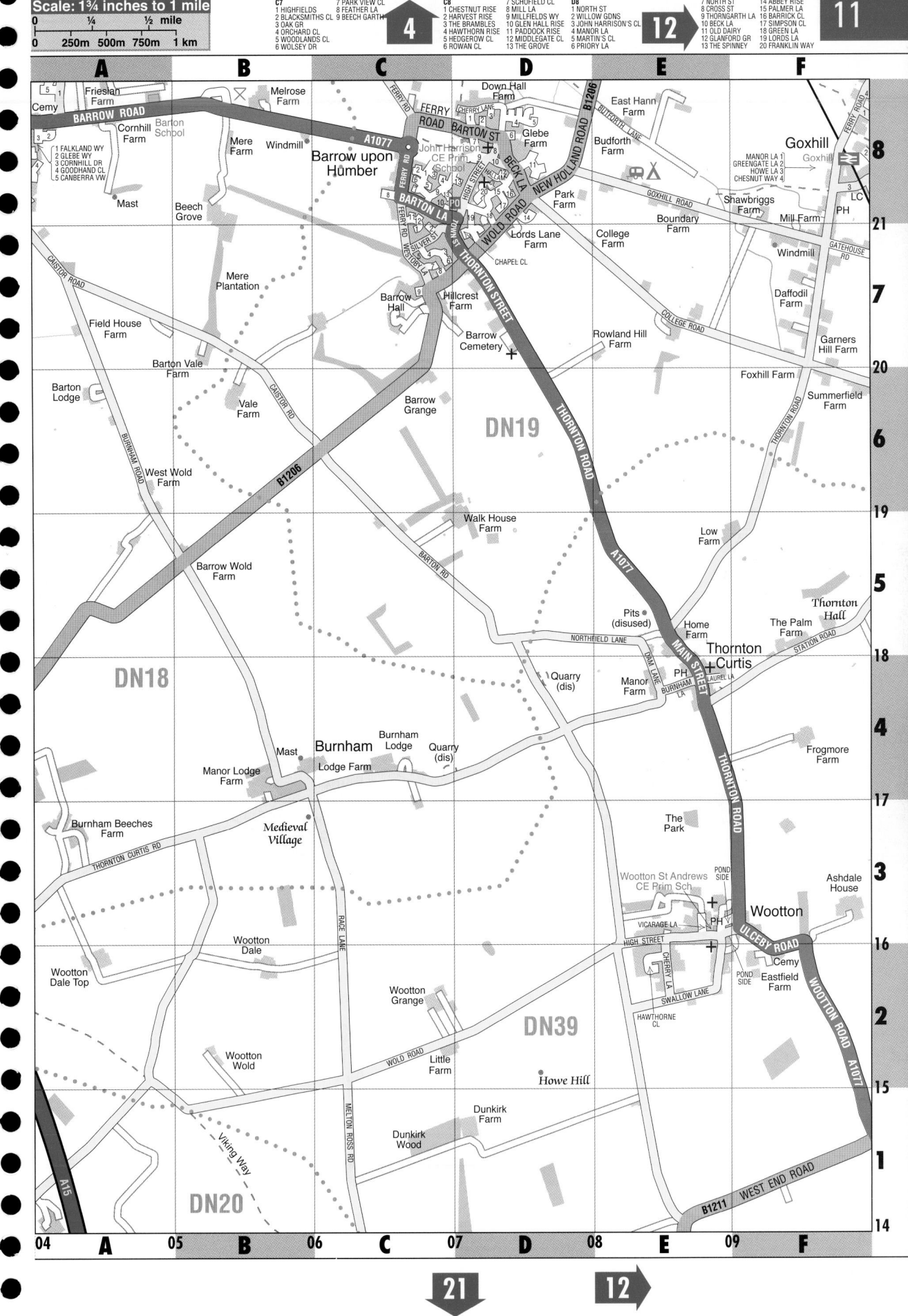

Scale: 1¾ inches to 1 mile

0   ¼   ½   mile
0 250m 500m 750m 1 km

C7
1 HIGHFIELDS
2 BLACKSMITHS CL
3 OAK GR
4 ORCHARD CL
5 WOODLANDS CL
6 WOLSEY DR
7 PARK VIEW CL
8 FEATHER LA
9 BEECH GARTH

C8
1 CHESTNUT RISE
2 HARVEST RISE
3 THE BRAMBLES
4 HAWTHORN RISE
5 HEDGEROW CL
6 ROWAN CL
7 SCHOFIELD CL
8 MILL LA
9 MILLFIELDS WY
10 GLEN HALL RISE
11 PADDOCK RISE
12 MIDDLEGATE CL
13 THE GROVE

D8
1 NORTH ST
2 WILLOW GDNS
3 JOHN HARRISON'S CL
4 MANOR LA
5 MARTIN'S CL
6 PRIORY LA
7 NORTH ST
8 CROSS ST
9 THORNGARTH LA
10 BECK LA
11 OLD DAIRY
12 GLANFORD GR
13 THE SPINNEY
14 ABBEY RISE
15 PALMER LA
16 BARRICK CL
17 SIMPSON CL
18 GREEN LA
19 LORDS LA
20 FRANKLIN WAY

4

12

11

Friesian Farm
Cemy
BARROW ROAD
A1077
Cornhill Farm
Barton School
Melrose Farm

1 FALKLAND WY
2 GLEBE WY
3 CORNHILL DR
4 GOODHAND CL
5 CANBERRA VW

Mast

Mere Farm
Windmill
Beech Grove

Mere Plantation

DN18

Field House Farm

Barton Vale Farm

Barton Lodge

Vale Farm

CAISTOR ROAD

BURNHAM ROAD

West Wold Farm

B1206
Barrow Wold Farm

Barton School
Barrow upon Humber
John Harrison CE Prim School
BARTON LA
SILVER ST
FERRY RD
FERRY ROAD
WEST DY
Barrow Hall
Hillcrest Farm

Barrow Cemetery

Barrow Grange

BARTON RD

Walk House Farm

DN19

Down Hall Farm
CHERRY LANE
FERRY ROAD
BARTON ST
BECK LA
Glebe Farm
WOLD ROAD
NEW HOLLAND ROAD
B1206
East Hann Farm
BUTTERFIELD LANE
Budforth Farm

Park Farm
Lords Lane Farm
CHAPEL CL
College Farm
Boundary Farm
GOXHILL ROAD
Shawbriggs Farm

Rowland Hill Farm
COLLEGE ROAD

THORNTON STREET
THORNTON ROAD
A1077

Low Farm

Pits (disused)

Home Farm
MAIN STREET
Thornton Curtis
NORTHFIELD LANE
DAM LANE
BURNHAM LA
PH
LAUREL LA

Manor Farm
Quarry (dis)

Goxhill
MANOR LA 1
GREENGATE LA 2
HOWE LA 3
CHESTNUT WAY 4
LC
PH
Mill Farm
GATEHOUSE RD
Windmill

Daffodil Farm

Garners Hill Farm

Foxhill Farm
Summerfield Farm

Thornton Hall
The Palm Farm
STATION ROAD

Frogmore Farm

Burnham
Burnham Lodge
Quarry (dis)
Lodge Farm
Mast
Manor Lodge Farm

Burnham Beeches Farm

THORNTON CURTIS RD

Medieval Village

RACE LANE

Wootton Dale

Wootton Dale Top

MELTON ROSS RD

THORNTON ROAD
ULCEBY ROAD

The Park

Wootton St Andrews CE Prim Sch
POND SIDE
VICARAGE LA
PH
High Street
CHERRY LA
SWALLOW LANE
HAWTHORNE CL
POND SIDE

Wootton
Ashdale House

Cemy
Eastfield Farm

WOOTTON ROAD
A1077

DN39

Wootton Grange

Wootton Wold

WOLD ROAD

Little Farm

Howe Hill

Dunkirk Wood

Dunkirk Farm

A15

DN20

Viking Way

B1211   WEST END ROAD

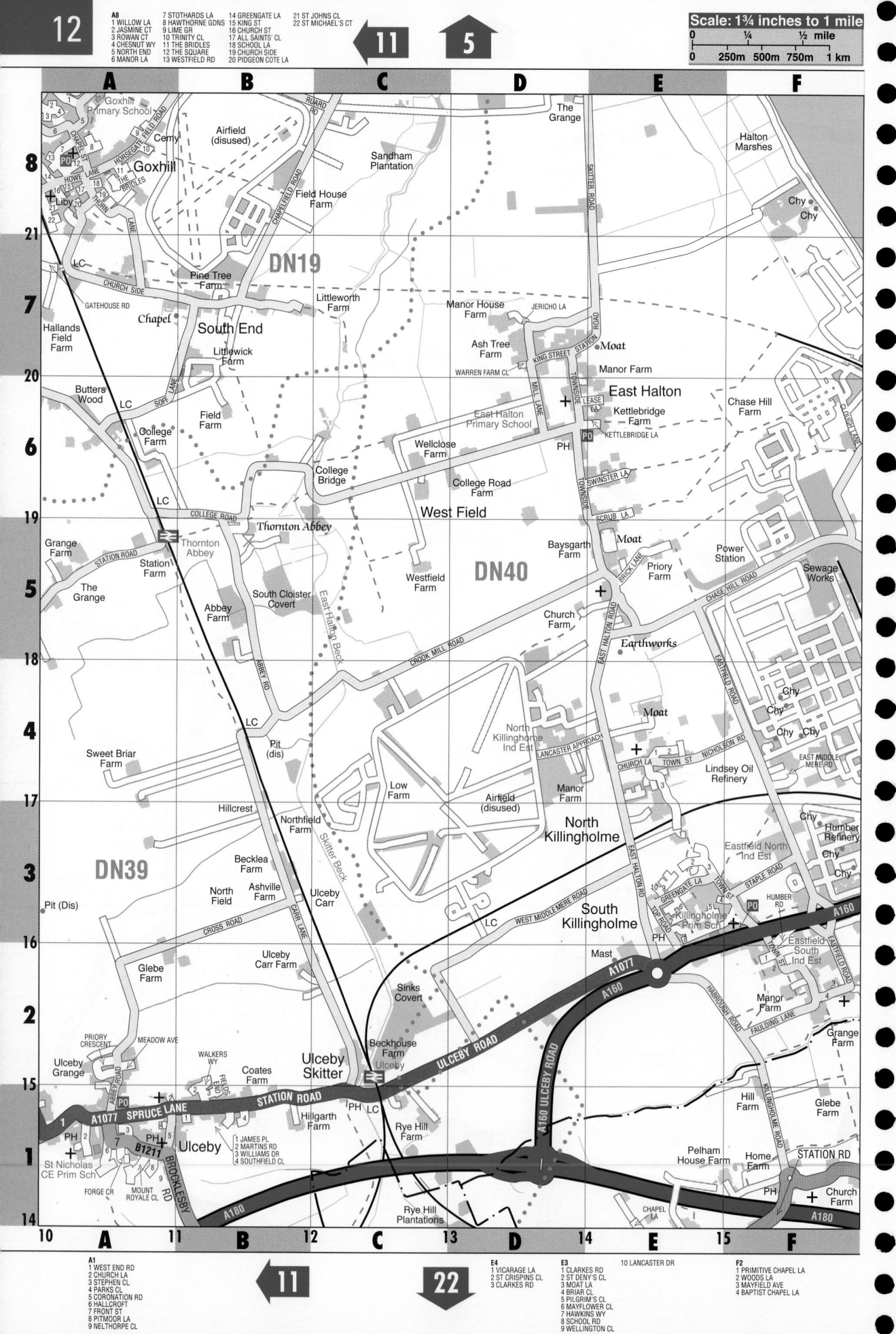

12

A8
1 WILLOW LA
2 JASMINE CT
3 ROWAN CT
4 CHESNUT WY
5 NORTH END
6 MANOR LA

7 STOTHARDS LA
8 HAWTHORNE GDNS
9 LIME GR
10 TRINITY CL
11 THE BRIDLES
12 THE SQUARE
13 WESTFIELD RD

14 GREENGATE LA
15 KING ST
16 CHURCH ST
17 ALL SAINTS' CL
18 SCHOOL LA
19 CHURCH SIDE
20 PIDGEON COTE LA

21 ST JOHNS CL
22 ST MICHAEL'S CT

11

5

Scale: 1¾ inches to 1 mile
0   ¼   ½   mile
0   250m   500m   750m   1 km

A   B   C   D   E   F

Scale: 1¾ inches to 1 mile

0   ¼   ½ mile
0 250m 500m 750m 1 km

E. Yorkshire & N. Lincolnshire STREET ATLAS

8
21
7
20
6
19
5
18
4
17
3
16
2
15
1
14

A   B   C   D   E   F

Foulholme
Sands

Cherry
Cobb Sands

CHERRY COBB SANDS RD

HAVEN RD

Oil
Terminal

LC

CHURCH LANE

HAVEN ROAD

Killingholme
Haven
Pits Nature
Reserve

Killingholme
Marshes

Mast

Sewage
Works

STATION ROAD

LC

Killingholme
High Lighthouse

Burkinshaw's
Covert

EAST MIDDLE MERE ROAD

ROSPER ROAD

LC

MARSH LANE

Oil
Refineries

LC

DN40

HUMBER
RD

South
Killingholme
Haven

187

Immingham
Dock

186

Chy

HUMBER ROAD

A160

A1173

Houlton's
Covert

MANBY ROAD

WEST HAVEN WY

LC

LC

Water
Tower

WEST RIVERSIDE

SOUTHERN WY

SOUTHERN ROAD

SEVEN QUAY RD

GRESLEY WAY

ROBINSON ROAD

LC

LC

LC

East End
Farm

186

Immingham
Golf Course

Manby Road
By Pass

Football
Gd

CH

STANSFIELD GDNS

WOODSIDE AV

WASHDYKE LANE

CHURCH LANE

MANBY RD

BATTERY ST

WORSLEY RD

SPRINGWY

P

Sports
Ground

Chimney

LC

Chimney

Cemy

Recn
Gd

MILL LANE

PILGRIMS WY

SONIA CREST

ROYAL DR

CLIFTON CH

RUESTONE LANE

Sch

PARK

Liby

P

Acad

PRINCESS ST

PH

WINSLOW RD

KINGS RD

KINGS RD

QUEENS RD

A1173

LAPORTE ROAD

Humber
Bank
Factories

DN41

Luxmore
Farm

B1210

HABROUGH RD

HUME
BRAE

Sch

PO

PH

PELHAM ROAD

MARGARET ST

P

Acad

PILGRIM AVENUE

ALBOT RD

HADLEIGH RD

CORFE
WALK

Immingham

A1173

Spoil
Heap

NETHERLANDS WY

EUROPA WY

KILN LANE

Kiln Lane
Ind Est

LC

HOBSON WAY

16   17   18   19   20   21

A   B   C   D   E   F

For full street detail of the highlighted area see pages 186 & 187.

186   23   187   187

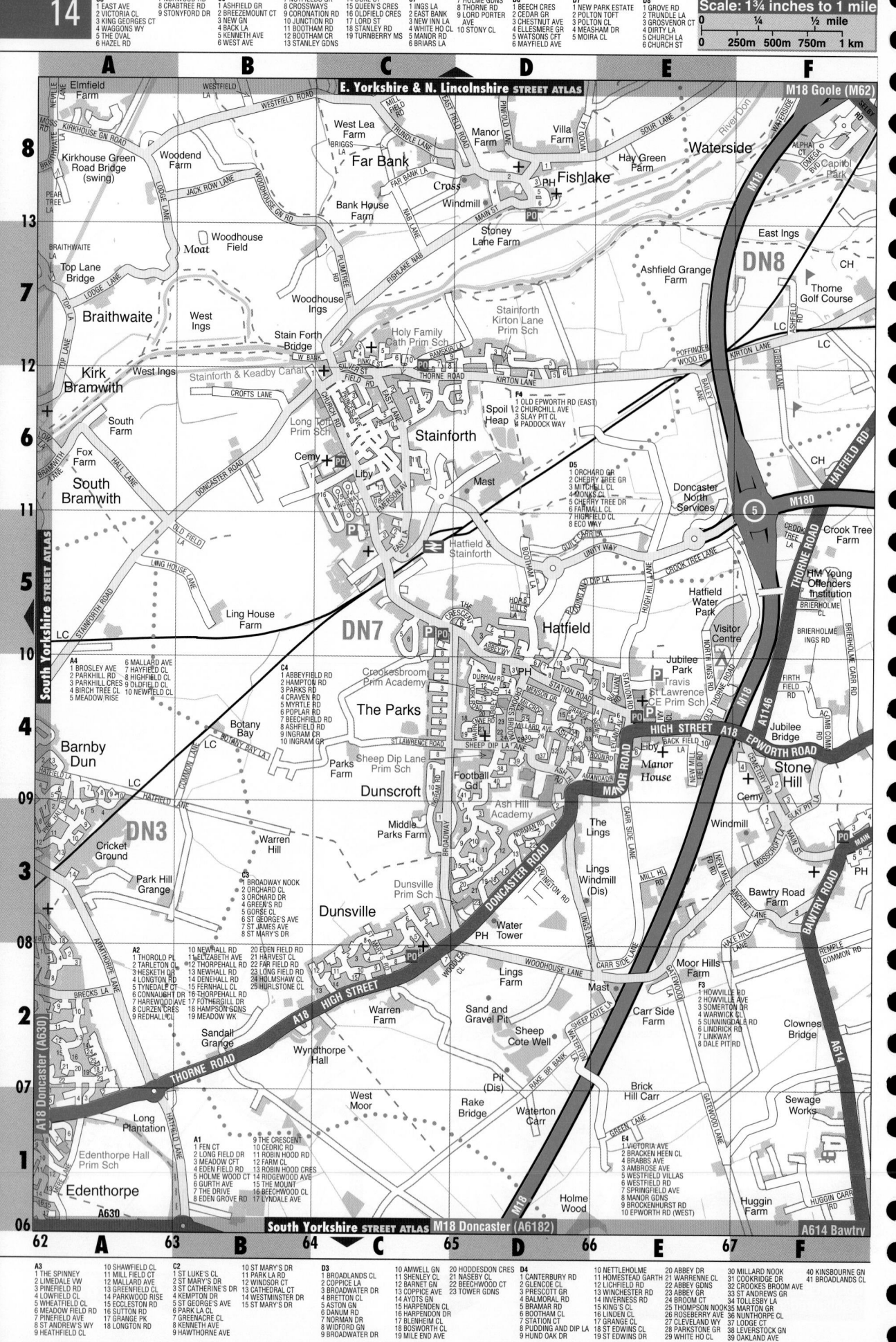

14

C5
1 EAST AVE
2 VICTORIA AVE
3 KING GEORGES CT
4 WAGGONS WY
5 THE OVAL
6 HAZEL RD

7 NORWOOD RD
8 CRABTREE RD
9 STONYFORD DR

C6
1 ASHFIELD GR
2 BREEZEMOUNT CT
3 NEW GN
4 BACK LA
5 KENNETH AVE
6 WEST AVE

7 NUTFIELDS GR
8 CROSSWAYS
9 CORONATION AVE
10 JUNCTION RD
11 BOOTHAM RD
12 BOOTHAM CR
13 STANLEY GDNS

14 DUKE ST
15 QUEEN'S CRES
16 OLDFIELD CRES
17 LORD ST
18 STANLEY RD
19 TURNBERRY MS

C7
1 INGS LA
2 EAST BANK
3 NEW INN LA
4 WHITE HO CL
5 MANOR RD
6 BRIARS LA

7 HOLME GDNS
8 THORNE RD
9 LORD PORTER AVE
10 STONY CL

D6
1 BEECH CRES
2 CEDAR GR
3 CHESTNUT AVE
4 ELLESMERE GR
5 WATSONS CFT
6 MAYFIELD AVE

D7
1 NEW PARK ESTATE
2 POLTON TOFT
3 POLTON CL
4 MEASHAM CL
5 MOIRA CL

D8
1 GROVE RD
2 TRUNDLE LA
3 GROSVENOR CT
4 DIRTY LA
5 CHURCH LA
6 CHURCH ST

Scale: 1¾ inches to 1 mile
0   ¼   ½   mile
0 250m 500m 750m 1 km

DN8

DN7

DN3

A4
1 BROSLEY AVE
2 PARKHILL RD
3 PARKHILL CRES
4 BIRCH TREE CL
5 MEADOW RISE
6 MALLARD AVE
7 HAYFIELD CL
8 HIGHFIELD CL
9 OLDFIELD CT
10 NEWFIELD CL

C4
1 ABBEYFIELD RD
2 HAMPTON RD
3 PARKS RD
4 CRAVEN RD
5 MYRTLE RD
6 POPLAR RD
7 BEECHFIELD RD
8 ASHFIELD RD
9 INGRAM CR
10 INGRAM GR

A2
1 THOROLD PL
2 TARLETON CL
3 HESKETH DR
4 LONGTON RD
5 TYNEDALE CT
6 CONNAUGHT DR
7 HAREWOOD AVE
8 CURZEN CRES
9 REDHALL CL
10 NEWHALL RD
11 ELIZABETH AVE
12 THORPEHALL RD
13 NEWHALL RD
14 DENEHALL RD
15 FERNHALL CL
16 THORPEHALL RD
17 FOTHERGILL DR
18 HAMPSON GDNS
19 MEADOW WK
20 EDEN FIELD RD
21 HARVEST CL
22 FAR FIELD RD
23 LONG FIELD RD
24 HOLMSHAW CL
25 HURLSTONE CL

C3
1 BROADWAY NOOK
2 ORCHARD CL
3 ORCHARD DR
4 GREEN'S RD
5 GORSE CL
6 ST GEORGE'S AVE
7 ST JAMES AVE
8 ST MARY'S DR

F4
1 OLD EPWORTH RD (EAST)
2 CHURCHILL AVE
3 SLAY PIT CL
4 PADDOCK WAY

D5
1 ORCHARD GR
2 CHERRY TREE GR
3 MITCHELL CL
4 MONKS CL
5 CHERRY TREE DR
6 FARNALL CL
7 HIGHFIELD CL
8 ECO WAY

A1
1 FEN CT
2 LONG FIELD DR
3 MEADOW CT
4 EDEN FIELD RD
5 HOLME MEAD AVE
6 GURTH AVE
7 THE DRIVE
8 EDEN GROVE RD
9 THE CRESCENT
10 CEDRIC RD
11 ROBIN HOOD AVE
12 FARM CL
13 ROBIN HOOD CRES
14 RIDGEWOOD AVE
15 THE MOUNT
16 BEECHWOOD CL
17 LYNDALE AVE

F3
1 HOWVILLE RD
2 HOWVILLE AVE
3 SOMERTON DR
4 WARWICK CL
5 SUNNINGDALE RD
6 LINDRICK CL
7 LINKWAY
8 DALE PIT RD

E4
1 VICTORIA AVE
2 BRACKEN HEEN CL
3 BRABBS AVE
4 AMBROSE AVE
5 WESTFIELD VILLAS
6 WESTFIELD CL
7 SPRINGFIELD AVE
8 MANOR GDNS
9 BROCKENHURST RD
10 EPWORTH RD (WEST)

A3
1 THE SPINNEY
2 LIMEDALE VW
3 PINEFIELD RD
4 LOWFIELD CL
5 WHEATFIELD CL
6 MEADOW FIELD RD
7 PINEFIELD AVE
8 ST ANDREW'S WY
9 HEATHFIELD CL
10 SHAWFIELD CL
11 MILL FIELD CT
12 MALLARD AVE
13 EGGLESTONE RISE
14 ECCLESTON RD
15 RASKELF RD
16 SUTTON RD
17 GRANGE PK

C2
1 ST LUKE'S CL
2 ST MARY'S CL
3 ST CATHERINE S DR
4 KEMPTON DR
5 ST GEORGE'S AVE
6 PARK LA CL
7 GREENACRE CL
8 KENNETH AVE
9 HAWTHORNE AVE

B
1 ST MARY'S DR
2 PARK LA RD
3 WINDSOR CT
4 CATHEDRAL CT
5 WESTMINSTER DR
6 ST MARY'S DR

D3
1 BROADLANDS CL
2 COPPICE LA
3 BROADWATER DR
4 BRETTON CL
5 ASTON GN
6 DANUM RD
7 NORMAN DR
8 WIDFORD CL
9 BOSWORTH CL
10 MILE END AVE

C
1 AMWELL GN
2 SHENLEY CL
3 BARNET GN
4 PRESCOTT GR
5 AYOTS GN
6 HARPENDEN CL
7 HAREFIELD RD
8 BLENHEIM CL
9 PUDDING AND DIP LA
10 OAK OAK DR

D4
1 CANTERBURY CL
2 GLENGOE CL
3 PRESCOTT GR
4 BALMORAL AVE
5 BRAMAR RD
6 BOOTHAM CL
7 STATION CT
8 ST EDWINS CL
9 ST EDWINS DR

E
10 NETTLEHOLME
11 HOMESTEAD GARTH
12 LICHFIELD RD
13 WINCHESTER RD
14 INVERNESS RD
15 KING'S CL
16 LINDEN CL
17 GRANGE CL
18 ST EDWINS CL
19 ST EDWINS DR

F
20 HODDESDON CRES
21 NASEBY CL
22 BEECHWOOD CT
23 TOWER GDNS

20 ABBEY DR
21 WARRENNE CL
22 ABBEY GDNS
23 ABBEY GR
24 BROOM CT
25 THOMPSON NOOK
26 ROSEBERRY AVE
27 CLEVELAND WY
28 PARKSTONE GR
29 WHITE HO CL

30 MILLARD NOOK
31 COOKRIDGE CT
32 CROOKES BROOM AVE
33 ST ANDREWS GR
34 TOLLESBY LA
35 MARTON GR
36 NUNTHORPE CL
37 LODGE CT
38 LEVERSTOCK GN
39 OAKLAND AVE

40 KINSBOURNE CL
41 BROADLANDS CL

E. Yorkshire & N. Lincolnshire STREET ATLAS

(Map content — area covering Thorne, Hatfield Chase, Hatfield Woodhouse, with locations including Canal Side, Wike Well End, Tudworth Green Farm, Bearswood Grove, Cherry Tree Farm, Hatfield Woodhouse, Remple Lane Farm, Sewage Works, Pit (disused), Masts, Woodhouse Grange Farm, Red House Farm, H M Prison Moorland, Lindholme Hall, Hatfield Moors, White Bridge Farm, Moor Farm, The Cottage on the Moor, Hollin Bridge, Brier Hills Farm, Brier Hills, Bull Moors, Stoupers Gate Farm, Dale Mount, Drain House, Levels Farm, High Levels, Low Levels, Works, Lindholme Grange, Roe Carr, West Carr, West Carr Houses, Lindholme Lake, Don Farm, Good Cop Farm, Park Farm, Pump House Farm, Plains House Farm, Elder House, Elder Glen Farm, Crow Tree Farm, Crow Tree, Severals Farm, Bank House Farm, Tithe Farm, Grove House, Sandhill Farm, Red House Farm, Haines Farm, Whitaker's Plantations, Nun Moors, South Moors or Sand Moors, Tween Bridge Moors, Thorne Waste or Moors, Causeway Farm, Moorland House Farm, Nunmoors Farm, Moors Farm, Buildings Farm, Old Laith House, Bradholme Farm, Double Bridges Farm, Wykewell Bridge, Moor's Bridge, Maud's Bridge, Water Tower, Red Mile Farm, Thorne South, Thorne North)

Roads: A614 Snaith (A1041), A1146, A614, A18, M180, Tudworth Road, High Levels Bank, Low Levels Bank, Green Bank, Clay Bank Road, Double Bridges Road, Sandtoft Road, Cross Road, Moor Dike Road, Lindholme Bank Road, Stainforth Moor Road, Plains Lane, Moor Lane, Idle Bank, Stone Hill, Hollin Br La, East Common Road, Bull Moor Road, Vulcan Wy, Stanhurst Lane, Moor Owners Road, Thorne Waste Drain Road

Areas: DN8, DN7, DN9

Sheffield & South Yorkshire Navigation, High Bridge Road, Stainforth & Keadby Canal, Boating Dyke

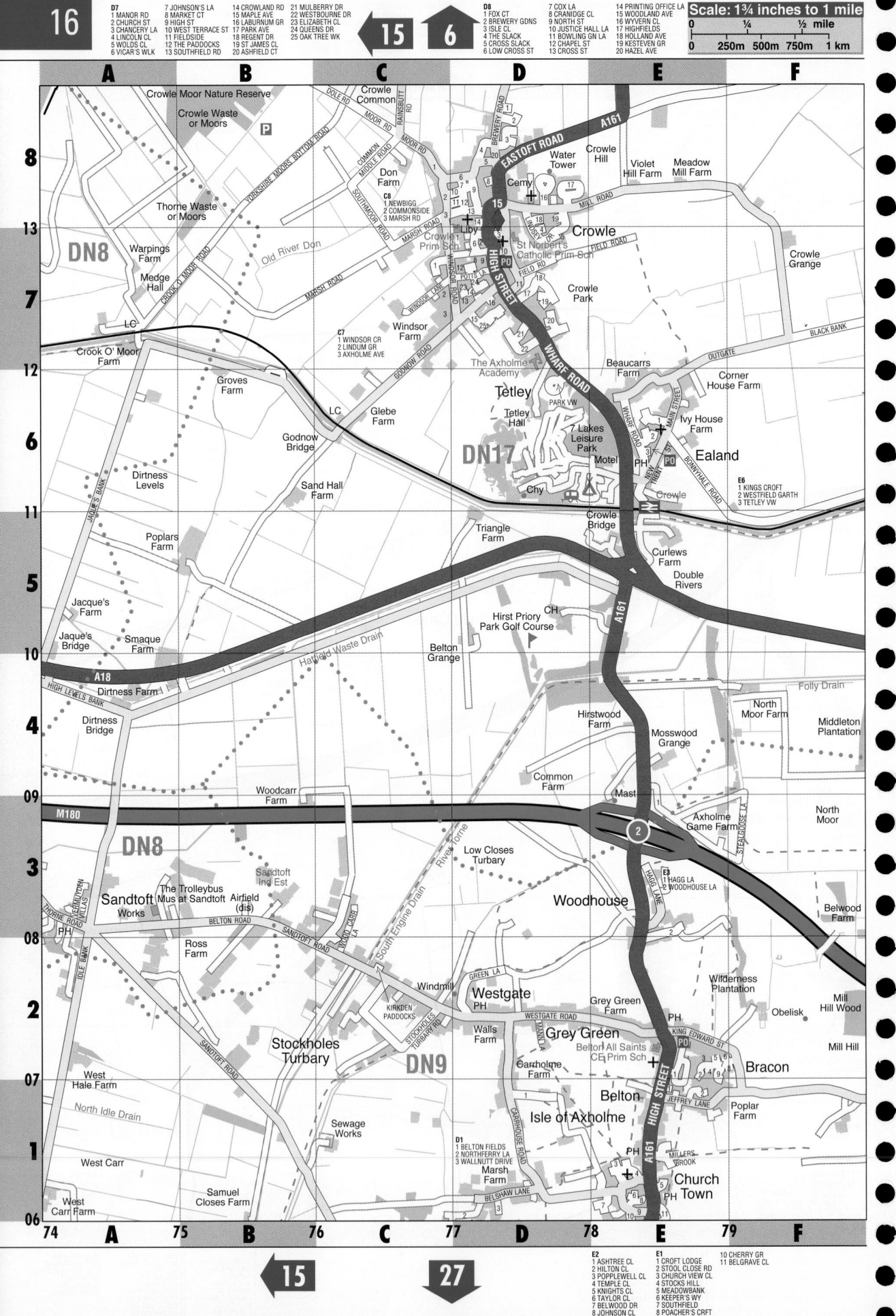

15
6

D7
1 MANOR RD
2 CHURCH ST
3 CHANCERY LA
4 LINCOLN CL
5 WOLDS CL
6 VICAR'S WLK

7 JOHNSON'S LA
8 MARKET CT
9 HIGH ST
10 WEST TERRACE ST
11 FIELDSIDE
12 THE PADDOCKS
13 SOUTHFIELD RD

14 CROWLAND RD
15 MAPLE AVE
16 LABURNUM GR
17 PARK AVE
18 REGENT DR
19 ST JAMES CL
20 ASHFIELD CT

21 MULBERRY DR
22 WESTBOURNE DR
23 ELIZABETH CL
24 QUEENS DR
25 OAK TREE WK

D8
1 FOX CT
2 BREWERY GDNS
3 ISLE CL
4 THE SLACK
5 CROSS SLACK
6 LOW CROSS ST

7 COX LA
8 CRANIDGE CL
9 NORTH ST
10 JUSTICE HALL LA
11 BOWLING GRN LA
12 CHAPEL ST
13 CROSS ST

14 PRINTING OFFICE LA
15 WOODLAND AVE
16 WYVERN CL
17 HIGHFIELDS
18 HOLLAND AVE
19 KESTEVEN GR
20 HAZEL AVE

Scale: 1¾ inches to 1 mile

| 0 | ¼ | ½ mile |
| 0 250m 500m 750m 1 km |

Map labels:

Crowle Moor Nature Reserve
Crowle Waste or Moors
Thorne Waste or Moors
Crowle Common
Crowle Hill
Water Tower
Violet Hill Farm
Meadow Mill Farm
Don Farm
Cemy
C8
1 NEWBIGG
2 COMMONSIDE
3 MARSH RD
Crowle Prim Sch
Liby
15
PO
St Norbert's Catholic Prim Sch
Crowle
Crowle Grange
DN8
Warpings Farm
Medge Hall
Old River Don
Crowle Park
Crook O' Moor Farm
LC
Windsor Farm
C7
1 WINDSOR CR
2 LINDUM GR
3 AXHOLME AVE
Beaucarrs Farm
Corner House Farm
BLACK BANK
OUTGATE
Groves Farm
Glebe Farm
The Axholme Academy
Tetley
Tetley Hall
7 Lakes Leisure Park
Ivy House Farm
Main Street
Ealand
Godnow Bridge
DN17
Motel
PH
PO
E6
1 KINGS CROFT
2 WESTFIELD GARTH
3 TETLEY VW
Dirtness Levels
Sand Hall Farm
Chy
Crowle Bridge
Crowle
Poplars Farm
Triangle Farm
Curlews Farm
Double Rivers
Jacque's Farm
Smaque Farm
Hatfield Waste Drain
Belton Grange
Hirst Priory Park Golf Course
CH
A161
Jacque's Bridge
Dirtness Farm
HIGH LEVELS BANK
A18
Hirstwood Farm
Mosswood Grange
North Moor Farm
Middleton Plantation
Folly Drain
Dirtness Bridge
Woodcarr Farm
Common Farm
Mast
North Moor
M180
Axholme Game Farm
STEALGOOSE LA
Sandtoft
DN8
River Torne
Low Closes Turbary
2
E3
1 HAGG LA
2 WOODHOUSE LA
HAGG LANE
The Trolleybus Mus at Sandtoft
Sandtoft Ind Est
Airfield (dis)
Woodhouse
Belwood Farm
Ross Farm
BELTON ROAD
SANDTOFT ROAD
WOOD LA
South Engine Drain
GREEN LA
Wilderness Plantation
Mill Hill Wood
West Hale Farm
Windmill
KIRKDEN PADDOCKS
STOCKHOLES TURBARY RD
Westgate
PH
WESTGATE ROAD
Grey Green Farm
PH
Obelisk
Mill Hill
Stockholes Turbary
Walls Farm
MANN LA
Grey Green
KING EDWARD ST
PO
West Carr
DN9
Carrholme Farm
Belton All Saints CE Prim Sch
Bracon
THORNE ROAD
VERMUYDEN HILLAS
IDLE BANK
North Idle Drain
Sewage Works
CARRHOUSE ROAD
Belton
Isle of Axholme
JEFFREY LANE
HIGH STREET
Poplar Farm
West Carr Farm
Samuel Closes Farm
D1
1 BELTON FIELDS
2 NORTHFERRY LA
3 WALLNUTT DRIVE
Marsh Farm
BELSHAW LANE
PH
A161
MILLERS BROOK
Church Town
PH

E2
1 ASHTREE CL
2 HILTON CL
3 POPPLEWELL CL
4 TEMPLE CL
5 KNIGHTS CL
6 TAYLOR CL
7 BELWOOD DR
8 JOHNSON CL
9 BRACON CL

E1
1 CROFT LODGE
2 STOOL CLOSE RD
3 CHURCH VIEW CL
4 STOCKS HILL
5 MEADOWBANK
6 KEEPER'S WY
7 SOUTHFIELD
8 POACHER'S CRFT
9 CHURCHTOWN

10 CHERRY GR
11 BELGRAVE CL

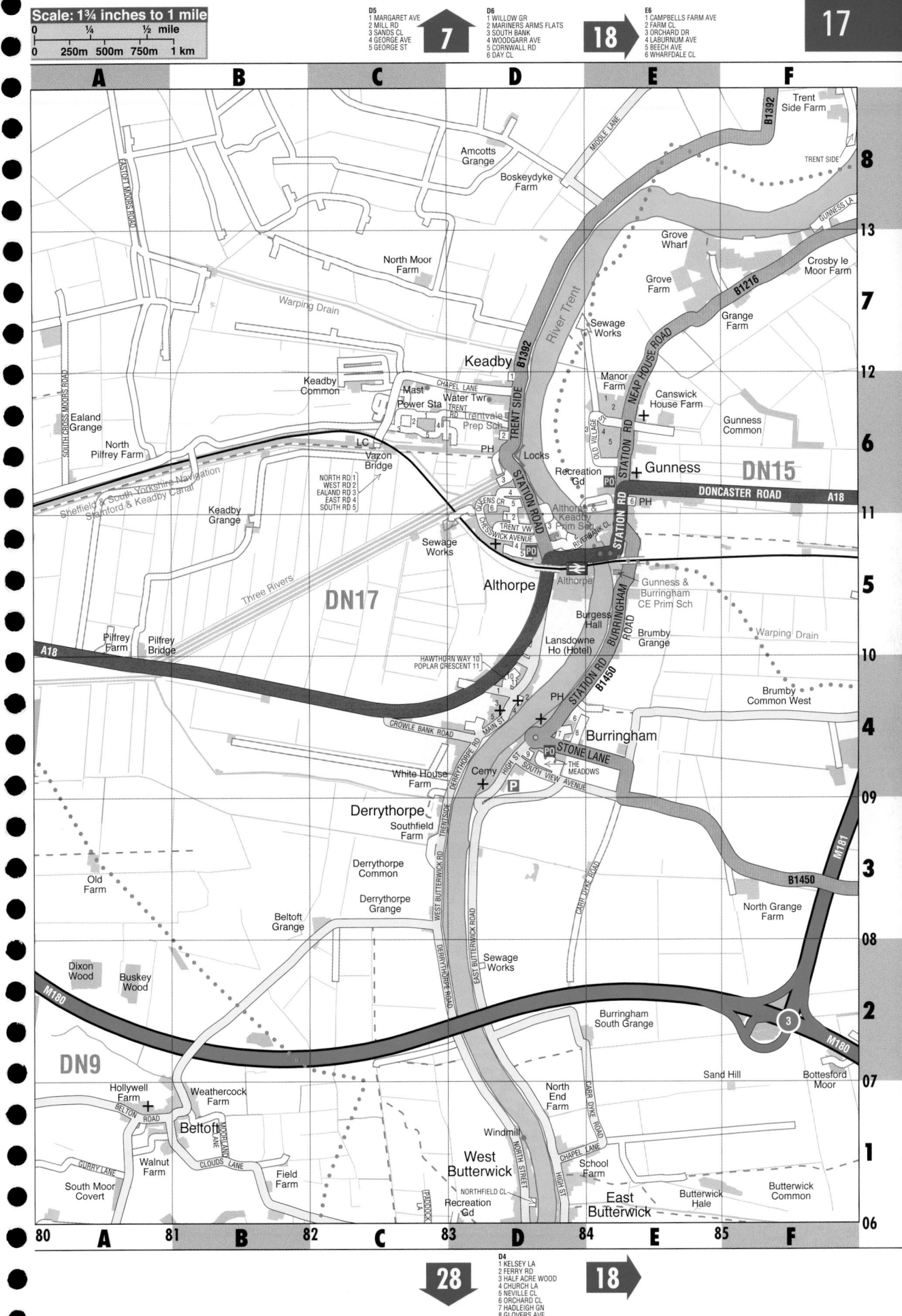

D5
1 MARGARET AVE
2 MILL RD
3 SANDS CL
4 GEORGE AVE
5 GEORGE ST

7

D6
1 WILLOW GR
2 MARINERS ARMS FLATS
3 SOUTH BANK
4 WOODGARR AVE
5 CORNWALL RD
6 DAY CL

18

E6
1 CAMPBELLS FARM AVE
2 FARM CL
3 ORCHARD DR
4 LABURNUM AVE
5 BEECH AVE
6 WHARFDALE CL

28

18

D4
1 KELSEY LA
2 FERRY RD
3 HALF ACRE WOOD
4 CHURCH LA
5 NEVILLE CL
6 ORCHARD CL
7 HADLEIGH GN
8 GLOVERS AVE
9 PASTURE AVE

Scale: 1¾ inches to 1 mile
0   ¼   ½   mile
0   250m   500m   750m   1 km

| | A | B | C | D | E | F |

River Trent
Neap House
Park Ings Farm
Foxhills Plantation
Park Ings
Industrial Park
Foxhills Ind Park
Snowdonia Av
Ferry Rd West
Ferry Road West
B1216
B1430
Normanby Road
Cupola Wy
Billet La
Park Farm Road
St Vincent's Av
Works
Phoenix Parkway
A1077
Mannaberg Wy
Winterton Road
A1077
A1029
ROMANO-BRITISH SETTLEMENT
Crosby Warren
Opencast Ironstone Workings (disused)
Spoil Heap
Works
Mast
Hargreaves Ind Est
Bessemer Way
Warren Road
DN15
SCUNTHORPE
Chy
Chimney
Frodingham
Steel Works
Sorrel Wy
Speedwell
Hilton Av
Hebden Road
Fairfield Road
Berkeley Ind Est
Retail Park
Burn Rd
A1077
A18
Doncaster Road
Moors Rd
Minster Rd
Lodge
Kingsway
CH
Football Gd
Frodingham Viaduct
Brumby Common West
Brumby Wood Lane
Sports Gd
Crosby Prim Sch
Theodore Road
Crosby
Berkeley Jun & Inf Sch
Collinson Av
Doncaster Road
Newland Dr
Cliff Gardens
Church Lane
Sports Hall
North Lincs Mus
Vicarage Gdns
Scunthorpe
Frodingham Inf Sch
Cty Ct
Theatre
Mary St
Cole St
Station Rd
Rowland Road
Neville Rd
Cottage Beck Road
Brumby Hall
Sports Ground
Civic Centre
Brumby
Midland Ind Est
Lilac Ave
East Common Lane
Sports Gd
Cemy
Cemy
Ashby Rd
Warwick Rd
Northampton Rd
Colin Rd
Lincoln Rd
Midland Road
Brigg Road
B1501
M181
M180
Brumby Common
Brumby Common Lane
Brumby Grove
Nature Reserve
Bristol Road
Plymouth Road
North Lindsey College
John Leggott Sixth Form Coll
Sports H
West Common Lane
Hamilton Way
Lloyds Av
Glanville Ave
Peveril Ave
Glover Rd
Westcliff
Carisbrooke Manor
Lichfield Ave
Scott Av
Chapman Av
Westcliff Prim Sch
Manor Park
Bridges Road
Dryden Road
Whitfield Rd
Woodclose Rd
Belvedere
Herrick Rd
Frances Rd
Priory Rd
Abbey Road
Dean Rd
Old Brumby St
Riversdale Rd
Kingston Rd
Gloucester Ave
West Street Gardens
Ashby Road
A159
A18
Fowler Rd
Healey Rd
Warley Rd
Burghley Rd
Grange La North
Grange Ind Est
A1029
Ind Est
Dunlop Rd
St Bede's Catholic Sch
Acad
Liby
Queensway
Superstore
Retail Pk
Ashby Broadway
Ashby Link
Ashby
Lancaster Rd
Rochdale Rd
Copse Rd
Churchfield Rd
Milton Rd
Cornwall Rd
B1501
B1450
Derwent
Manifold Rd
Burringham Road
B1450
Warp Farm
Ashby Decoy
CH
PH
Riddings
Acad
Manby Rd
Recn Gd
Oakfield Prim Sch
Bottesford Rd
Shipton Rd
Grange Lane South
Somervell Rd
Crowberry Dr
Wisteria Wy
DN16
Yaddlethorpe
DN17
Chy
Scotter Road South
Greenhoe Ind Est
Sunningdale Rd
Enderby Rd
Leys Farm Jun Sch
Chancel Road
B1501
Liby
Caistor Av
York Av
Recn Gd
Timberland
Holme Valley Prim Sch
PH
Holme Hall Golf Course
CH
Grange Farm
South Park Rd
Holyoake Rd
L Ctr
Park Ave
Frank Ave
The Dales
Moorwell Road
Newdowns Farm
Southfield Farm
Messingham Road
Jacklins App Rd
Bottesford Jun & Inf Sch
Valley Rd
St Peter's Av
Cambridge Av
Holme La
Holme Hall Avenue
Bottesford
Holme Wood
Holme Hall
Aspen Farm
Holme Lane
Bottesford Moor Farm
Snake Plantation
Moor Road
North Moor Lane
Endcliffe Av
Ellison Av
Bottesford Beck

For full street detail of the highlighted area see pages 182, 183, 184 and 185.

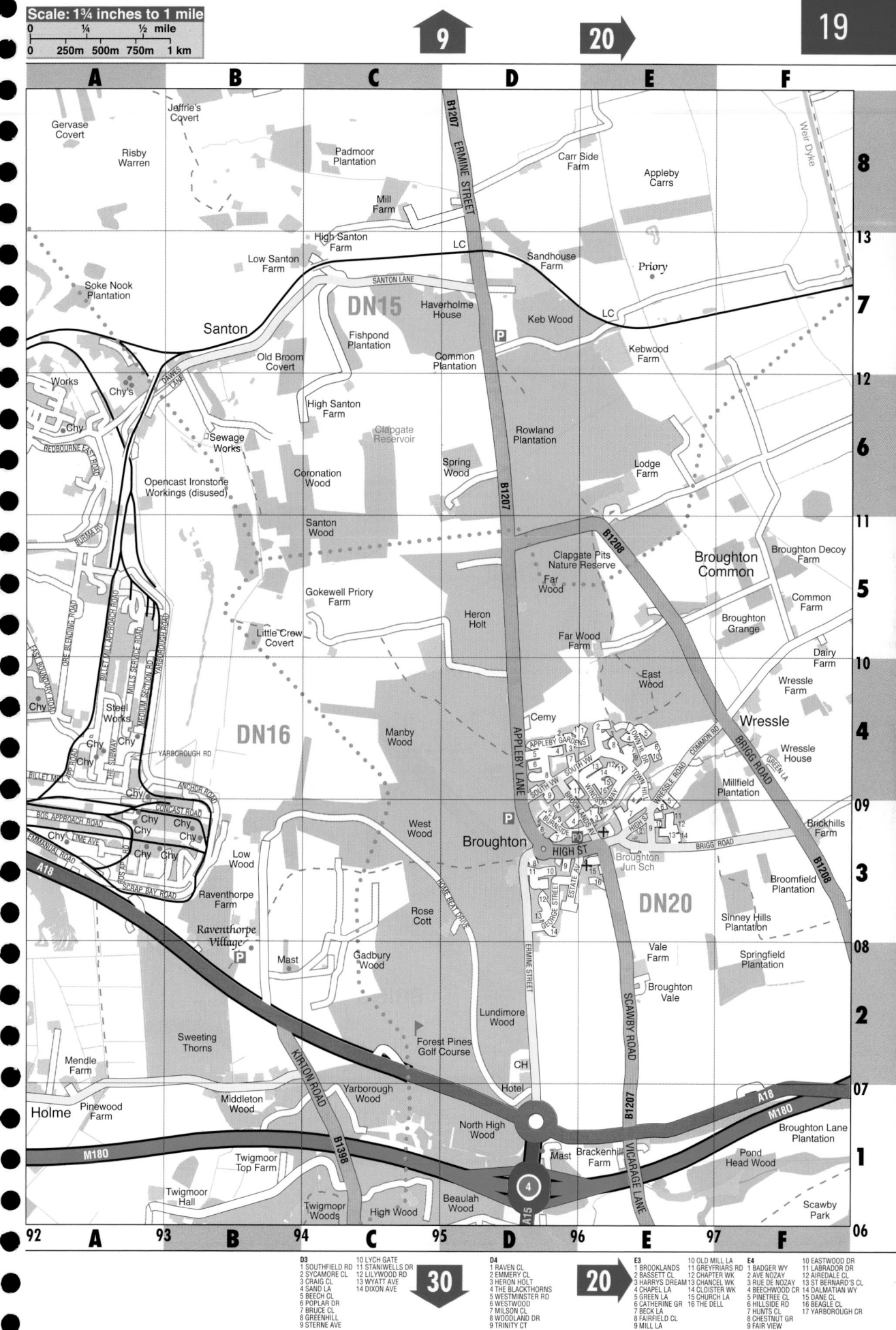

A   B   C   D   E   F

Gervase Covert

Jaffrie's Covert

Risby Warren

Padmoor Plantation

Carr Side Farm

Appleby Carrs

Weir Dyke

8

13

B1207

ERMINE STREET

Mill Farm

High Santon Farm

LC

Sandhouse Farm

Priory

7

Low Santon Farm

SANTON LANE

Soke Nook Plantation

DN15

Haverholme House

Keb Wood

LC

Santon

Old Broom Covert

Fishpond Plantation

Common Plantation

P

Kebwood Farm

12

Works

Chy's

Chy

DAWES LANE

Sewage Works

High Santon Farm

Clapgate Reservoir

Rowland Plantation

Lodge Farm

6

REDBOURNE EASTROAD

BURMA RD

Opencast Ironstone Workings (disused)

Coronation Wood

Spring Wood

B1207

B1208

11

Santon Wood

Clapgate Pits Nature Reserve

Far Wood

Broughton Common

Broughton Decoy Farm

5

Gokewell Priory Farm

Heron Holt

Far Wood Farm

Broughton Grange

Common Farm

Little Crew Covert

East Wood

Dairy Farm

10

Chy

Steel Works

YARBOROUGH RD

DN16

Manby Wood

Cemy

Wressle

Wressle House

Wressle Farm

4

Chy Chy Chy

Chy

ANCHOR ROAD

Chy Chy

APPLEBY LANE

BRIGG ROAD

COMMON RD

Millfield Plantation

GREEN LA

Chy Chy

BOS APPROACH ROAD

Low Wood

West Wood

P

Broughton

BRIGG ROAD

Brickhills Farm

09

A18

Raventhorpe Farm

Rose Cott

HIGH ST

Broughton Jun Sch

DN20

Broomfield Plantation

B1208

3

Raventhorpe Village

P

Mast

Gadbury Wood

HOME BEAT DRIVE

ERMINE STREET

GEORGE STREET

Sinney Hills Plantation

Vale Farm

Springfield Plantation

08

Mendle Farm

Sweeting Thorns

Forest Pines Golf Course

Lundimore Wood

CH

Broughton Vale

SCAWBY ROAD

2

Holme

Pinewood Farm

Middleton Wood

KIRTON ROAD

Yarborough Wood

Hotel

North High Wood

A18

M180

Broughton Lane Plantation

07

M180

B1398

Twigmoor Top Farm

Beaulah Wood

Mast

Brackenhill Farm

VICARAGE LANE

B1207

Pond Head Wood

Scawby Park

1

Twigmoor Hall

Twigmoor Woods

High Wood

A15

4

92   A   93   B   94   C   95   D   96   E   97   F   06

D3
1 SOUTHFIELD RD
2 SYCAMORE CL
3 CRAIG CL
4 SAND LA
5 BEECH CL
6 POPLAR DR
7 BRUCE CL
8 GREENHILL
9 STERNE AVE
10 LYCH GATE
11 STANIWELLS DR
12 LILYWOOD RD
13 WYATT AVE
14 DIXON AVE

D4
1 RAVEN CL
2 EMMERY CL
3 HERON HOLT
4 THE BLACKTHORNS
5 WESTMINSTER RD
6 WESTWOOD
7 MILSON CL
8 WOODLAND DR
9 TRINITY CT

E3
1 BROOKLANDS
2 BASSETT CL
3 HARRYS DREAM
4 CHAPEL LA
5 GREEN LA
6 CATHERINE GR
7 BECK LA
8 FAIRFIELD CL
9 MILL LA
10 OLD MILL LA
11 GREYFRIARS RD
12 CHAPTER WK
13 CHANCEL WK
14 CLOISTER WK
15 CHURCH LA
16 THE DELL

E4
1 BADGER WY
2 AVE NOZAY
3 RUE DE NOZAY
4 BEECHWOOD CR
5 PINETREE CL
6 HILLSIDE RD
7 HUNTS CL
8 CHESTNUT GR
9 FAIR VIEW
10 EASTWOOD DR
11 LABRADOR DR
12 AIREDALE CL
13 ST BERNARD'S CL
14 DALMATIAN WY
15 DANE CL
16 BEAGLE CL
17 YARBOROUGH CR

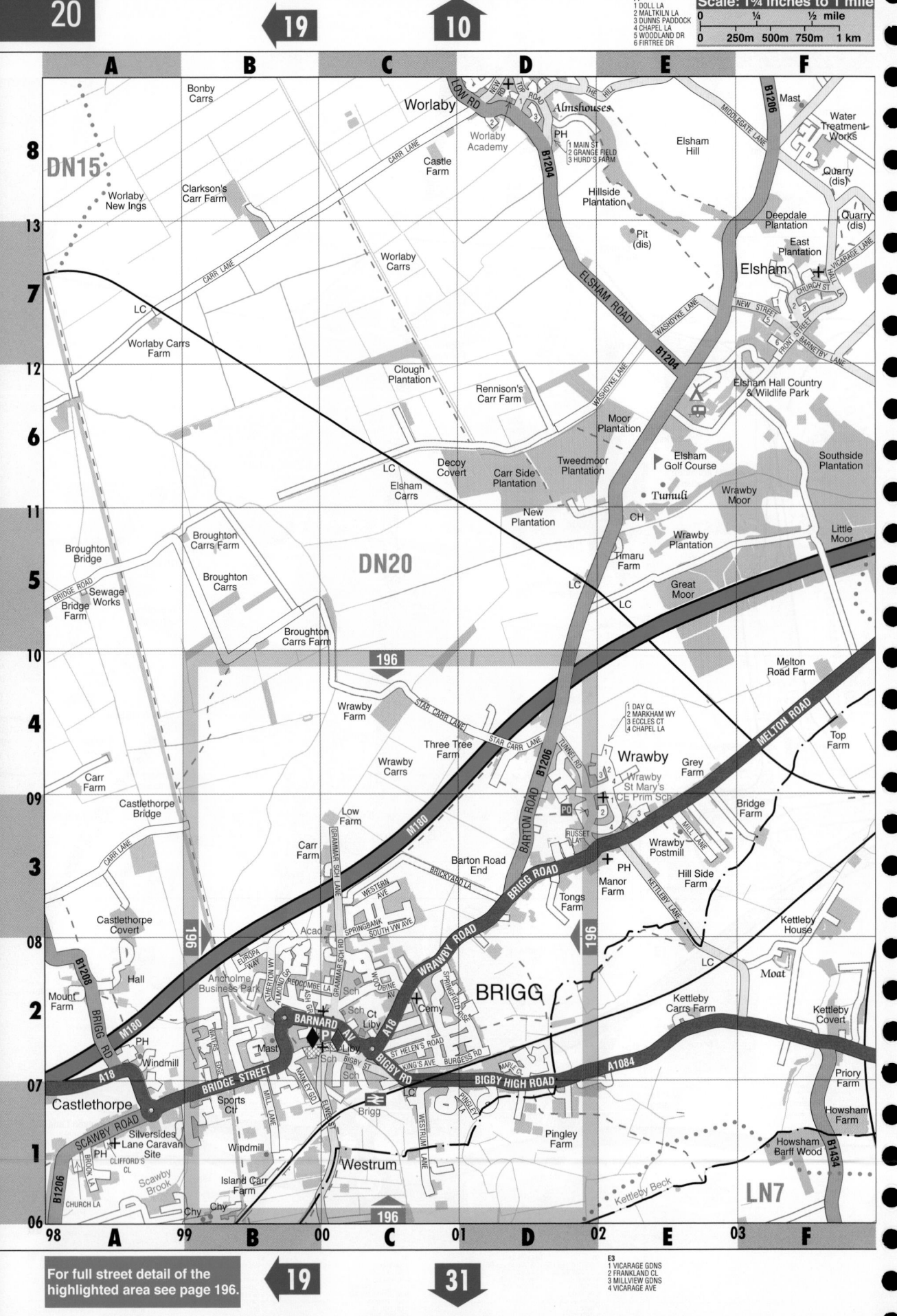

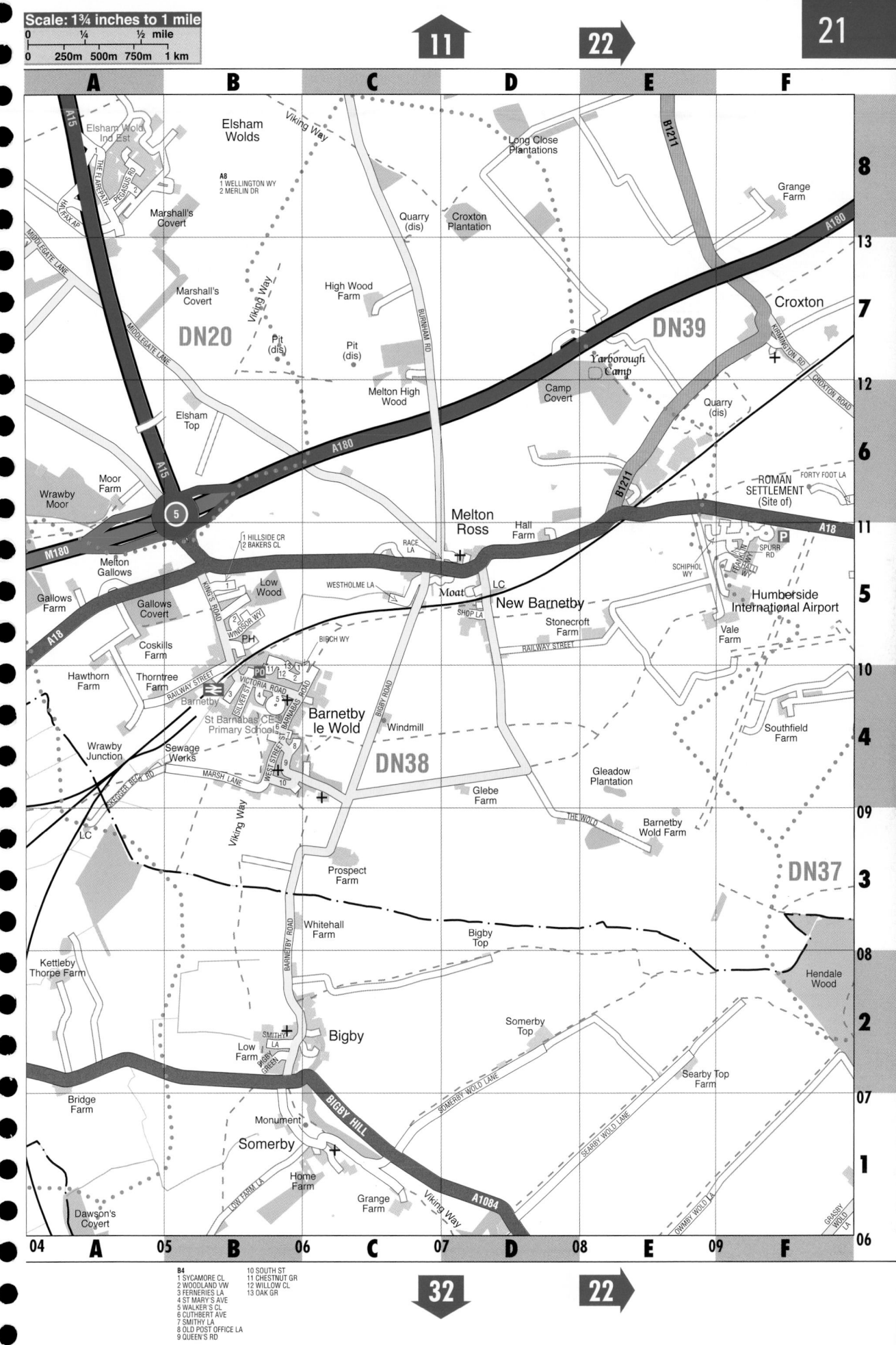

Scale: 1¾ inches to 1 mile

0   ¼   ½ mile
0 250m 500m 750m 1 km

11

22

A   B   C   D   E   F

A15
Elsham Wold Ind Est
THE FLAREPATH
HALIFAX AP
PEGASUS RD
Elsham Wolds

Viking Way
Long Close Plantations
B1211

A8
1 WELLINGTON WY
2 MERLIN DR

Grange Farm

Marshall's Covert
Quarry (dis)
Croxton Plantation
A180

8

13

Marshall's Covert
High Wood Farm
Croxton
7

VIKING WAY
DN20
Pit (dis)
Pit (dis)
Melton High Wood
BURNHAM RD
DN39
Yarborough Camp
KIRMINGTON RD
CROXTON ROAD
12

Elsham Top
A180
Camp Covert
6

MIDDLEGATE LANE
Moor Farm
A15
Quarry (dis)
ROMAN SETTLEMENT (Site of)
FORTY FOOT LA
A18
11

Wrawby Moor
5
Melton Ross
Hall Farm
B1211
P
SPURR RD
SCHIPHOL WY
Humberside International Airport
5

Gallows Farm
Melton Gallows
RACE LA
1 HILLSIDE CR
2 BAKERS CL
WESTHOLME LA
LC
Moat
SHOP LA
New Barnetby
Stonecroft Farm
Vale Farm

M180
Gallows Covert
KINGS ROAD
Low Wood
1
WINDSOR WY
2
PH
BIRCH WY
RAILWAY STREET
10

Coskills Farm
A18
Hawthorn Farm
Thorntree Farm
VICTORIA ROAD
PO
11
13
12
BIGBY ROAD
Southfield Farm
4

Barnetby
St Barnabas CE Primary Schools
SILVER ST
4
5
6
3
Barnetby le Wold
Windmill
Gleadow Plantation
DN37
DN38

Wrawby Junction
SKEGGER BECK RD
Sewage Works
MARSH LANE
WEST STREET
7
8
9
10
Glebe Farm
THE WOLD
Barnetby Wold Farm
3

LC
VIKING WAY
BARNETBY ROAD
Prospect Farm
09

Kettleby Thorpe Farm
Whitehall Farm
Bigby Top
Hendale Wood
08

SMITHY LA
Bigby
Somerby Top
Searby Top Farm
2

Low Farm
BIGBY GREEN
SOMERBY WOLD LANE
SEARBY WOLD LANE
07

Bridge Farm
BIGBY HILL
Monument
OWMBY WOLD LA
GRASSY WOLD LA
1

Dawson's Covert
Somerby
Home Farm
Grange Farm
Viking Way
A1084

04   A   05   B   06   C   07   D   08   E   09   F   06

B4
1 SYCAMORE CL
2 WOODLAND VW
3 FERNERIES LA
4 ST MARY'S AVE
5 WALKER'S CL
6 CUTHBERT AVE
7 SMITHY LA
8 OLD POST OFFICE LA
9 QUEEN'S RD
10 SOUTH ST
11 CHESTNUT GR
12 WILLOW CL
13 OAK GR

32

22

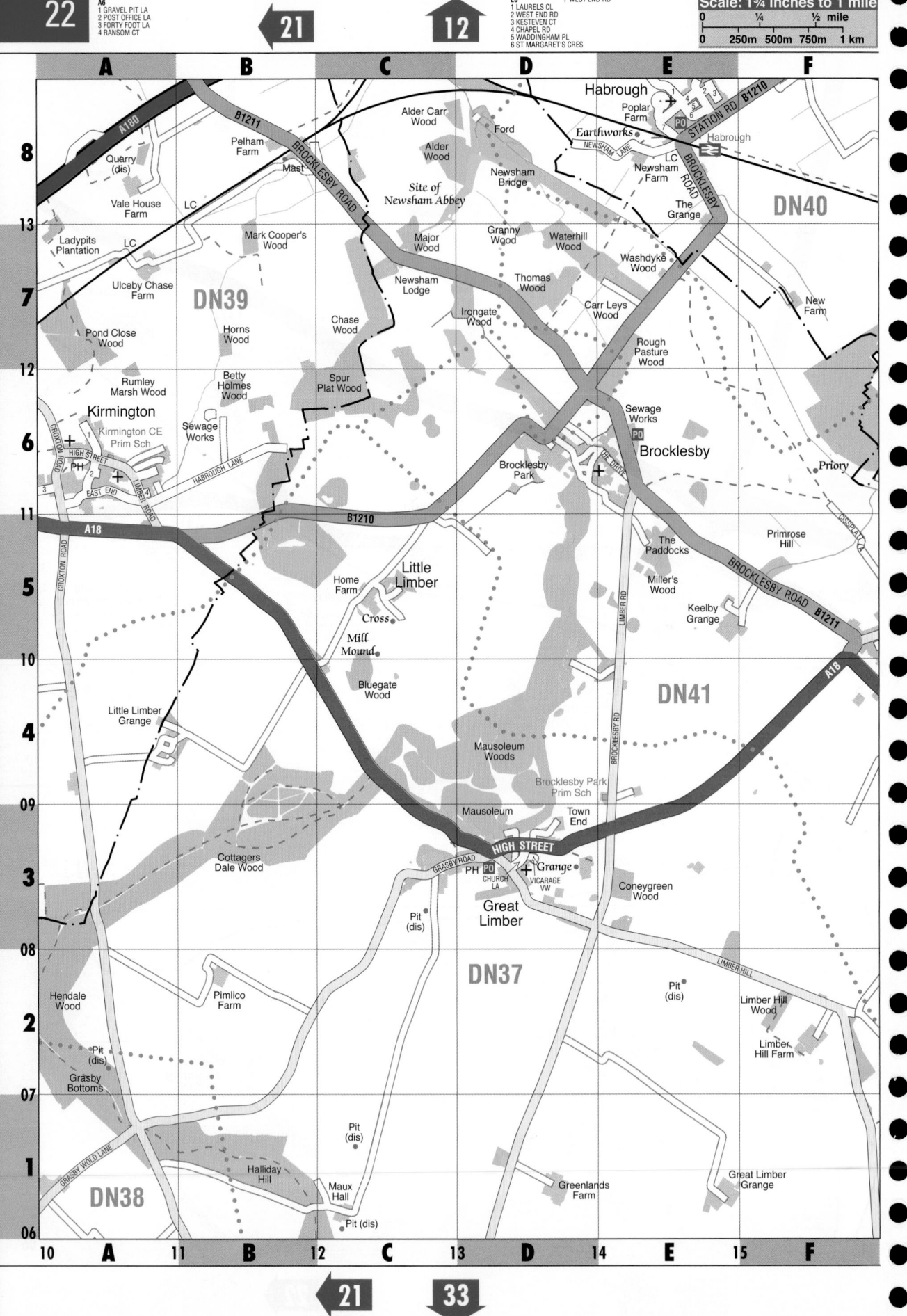

22

A6
1 GRAVEL PIT LA
2 POST OFFICE LA
3 FORTY FOOT LA
4 RANSOM CT

E8
1 LAURELS CL
2 WEST END RD
3 KESTEVEN CT
4 CHAPEL RD
5 WADDINGHAM PL
6 ST MARGARET'S CRES

7 WEST END RD

21

12

Scale: 1¾ inches to 1 mile

0   ¼   ½   mile
0   250m   500m   750m   1 km

A   B   C   D   E   F

Habrough

Poplar Farm

Earthworks

STATION RD   B1210

Habrough

DN40

8

Quarry (dis)

Vale House Farm

Pelham Farm

Mast

LC

BROCKLESBY ROAD

B1211

A180

Alder Carr Wood

Ford

Alder Wood

Newsham Bridge

NEWSHAM LANE

Newsham Farm

LC

The Grange

13

Ladypits Plantation

LC

Mark Cooper's Wood

Site of Newsham Abbey

Major Wood

Granny Wood

Waterhill Wood

Washdyke Wood

BROCKLESBY ROAD

7

Ulceby Chase Farm

DN39

Horns Wood

Chase Wood

Newsham Lodge

Thomas Wood

Irongate Wood

Carr Leys Wood

Rough Pasture Wood

New Farm

12

Pond Close Wood

Rumley Marsh Wood

Betty Holmes Wood

Spur Plat Wood

Sewage Works

6

Kirmington

Kirmington CE Prim Sch

HIGH STREET

PH

EAST END

CROXTON ROAD

LIMBER ROAD

HABROUGH LANE

Sewage Works

Brocklesby Park

THE DRIVE

Sewage Works

Brocklesby

PO

Priory

CISSPLAT LA

11

A18

CROXTON ROAD

B1210

The Paddocks

Miller's Wood

Keelby Grange

Primrose Hill

BROCKLESBY ROAD   B1211

5

Home Farm

Little Limber

Cross

Mill Mound

LIMBER RD

A18

10

Bluegate Wood

DN41

4

Little Limber Grange

Mausoleum Woods

Brocklesby Park Prim Sch

09

Cottagers Dale Wood

Mausoleum

Town End

GRASBY ROAD

HIGH STREET

PH PO

CHURCH LA

Grange

VICARAGE VW

Coneygreen Wood

3

Pit (dis)

Great Limber

DN37

LIMBER HILL

08

Hendale Wood

Pimlico Farm

Pit (dis)

Limber Hill Wood

2

Pit (dis)

GRASBY WOLD LANE

Limber Hill Farm

07

Grasby Bottoms

1

DN38

Halliday Hill

Maux Hall

Pit (dis)

Greenlands Farm

Great Limber Grange

06

Pit (dis)

10   11   12   13   14   15

A   B   C   D   E   F

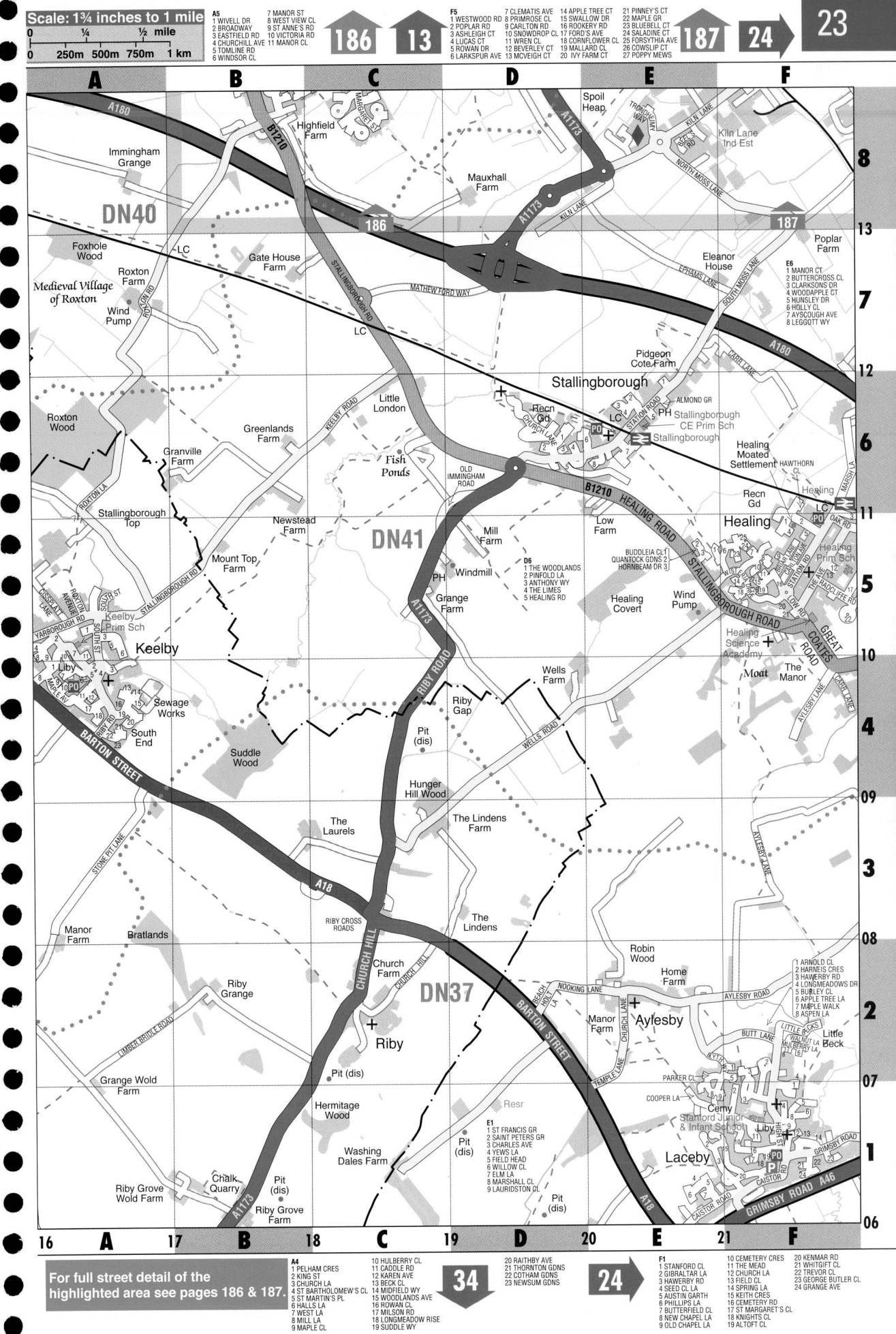

Scale: 1¾ inches to 1 mile

0   ¼   ½ mile
0   250m 500m 750m 1 km

186 13   187 24   23

A5
1 WIVELL DR
2 BROADWAY
3 EASTFIELD RD
4 CHURCHILL AVE
5 TOMLINE RD
6 WINDSOR CL
7 MANOR ST
8 WEST VIEW CL
9 ST ANNE'S RD
10 VICTORIA RD
11 MANOR CL

F5
1 WESTWOOD RD
2 POPLAR RD
3 ASHLEIGH CT
4 LUCAS CT
5 ROWAN DR
6 LARKSPUR AVE
7 CLEMATIS AVE
8 PRIMROSE CL
9 CARLTON RD
10 SNOWDROP CL
11 WREN CL
12 BEVERLEY CT
13 MCVEIGH CT
14 APPLE TREE CT
15 SWALLOW DR
16 ROOKERY RD
17 FORD'S AVE
18 CORNFLOWER CL
19 MALLARD CL
20 IVY FARM CT
21 PINNEY'S CT
22 MAPLE GR
23 CEDAR CT
24 SALADINE CT
25 FORSYTHIA AVE
26 COWSLIP CT
27 POPPY MEWS

E6
1 MANOR CT
2 BUTTERCROSS CL
3 CLARKSONS DR
4 WOODAPPLE CL
5 HUNSLEY DR
6 HOLLY CL
7 AYSCOUGH AVE
8 LEGGOTT WY

D6
1 THE WOODLANDS
2 PINFOLD LA
3 ANTHONY WY
4 THE LIMES
5 HEALING RD

A180
B1210
Highfield Farm
MARGARET'S RD
Mauxhall Farm
Spoil Heap
TRONDHEIM WAY
BECK'S RD
KILN LANE
Kiln Lane Ind Est
NORTH MOSS LANE

DN40
Immingham Grange
Foxhole Wood
Roxton Farm
LC
Gate House Farm
A1173
KILN LANE
Eleanor House
EPHAMS LANE
SOUTH MOSS LANE
Poplar Farm
A180
186   187

Medieval Village of Roxton
Wind Pump
ROXTON RD
STALLINGBOROUGH RD
MATHEW FORD WAY
LC
Pidgeon Cote Farm
CARR LANE
13

Roxton Wood
Greenlands Farm
KEELBY ROAD
Little London
OLD IMMINGHAM ROAD
Fish Ponds
Stallingborough
Recn Gd
CHURCH LANE
LC
PH
PO
Stallingborough CE Prim Sch
STATION ROAD
ALMOND GR
Stallingborough
Healing Moated Settlement
HAWTHORN CL
Healing
LC
12

Granville Farm
DOSSOR LA
Stallingborough Top
Newstead Farm
DN41
Mill Farm
Windmill
PH
Grange Farm
A1173
Low Farm
BUDDLEIA CL 1
QUANTOCK GDNS 2
HORNBEAM DR 3
Healing Covert
Wind Pump
HEALING ROAD
STALLINGBOROUGH ROAD
Recn Gd
PO
OAK RD
Healing Prim Sch
STATION RD
Healing
6

Mount Top Farm
STALLINGBOROUGH RD
ROXTON LA
ROXTON AVENUE RD
SOUTH ST
Keelby
Keelby Prim Sch
Healing Science Academy
Moat
The Manor
GREAT COATES ROAD
RADCLIFFE RD
AYLESBY LANE
CARR LANE
11

YARBOROUGH RD
MAPLE AV
Liby
PO
Sewage Works
South End
Suddle Wood
Riby Gap
Pit (dis)
RIBY ROAD
Wells Farm
WELLS ROAD
10

BARTON STREET
Hunger Hill Wood
The Lindens Farm
09

STONE PIT LANE
The Laurels
A18
The Lindens
AYLESBY LANE
3

Manor Farm
Bratlands
Riby Grange
LIMBER BRIDGE ROAD
CHURCH HILL
RIBY CROSS ROADS
Church Farm
CHURCH HILL
DN37
Robin Wood
Home Farm
AYLESBY ROAD
08

Grange Wold Farm
Riby
Pit (dis)
BARTON STREET
BECK HOLE LA
NOOKING LANE
Manor Farm
CHURCH LANE
TEMPLE LANE
Aylesby
BUTT LANE
LITTLE BECKS
WALNUT LA
MULBERRY LA
Little Beck
2

Hermitage Wood
Resr
E1
1 ST FRANCIS GR
2 SAINT PETERS GR
3 CHARLES AVE
4 YEWS LA
5 FIELD HEAD
6 WILLOW CL
7 ELM LA
8 MARSHALL CL
9 LAURIDSTON CL
PARKER CL
COOPER LA
Cemy
Stanford Junior & Infant School
Liby
07

Washing Dales Farm
Pit (dis)
Laceby
PO
P
CAISTOR RD
GRIMSBY ROAD A46
1

Riby Grove Wold Farm
Chalk Quarry
Pit (dis)
A1173
Riby Grove Farm
Pit (dis)
A18
CAISTOR ROAD
GRIMSBY ROAD A46
06

For full street detail of the highlighted area see pages 186 & 187.

34   24

A4
1 PELHAM CRES
2 KING ST
3 CHURCH LA
4 ST BARTHOLOMEW'S CL
5 ST MARTIN'S PL
6 HALLS LA
7 WEST LA
8 MILL LA
9 MAPLE CL
10 HULBERRY CL
11 CADDLE RD
12 KAREN AVE
13 BECK CL
14 MIDFIELD WY
15 WOODLANDS AVE
16 ROWAN CL
17 MILSON RD
18 LONGMEADOW RISE
19 SUDDLE WY
20 RAITHBY AVE
21 THORNTON GDNS
22 COTHAM GDNS
23 NEWSUM GDNS

F1
1 STANFORD CL
2 GIBRALTAR LA
3 HAWERBY RD
4 SEED CL LA
5 AUSTIN GARTH
6 PHILLIPS LA
7 BUTTERFIELD CL
8 NEW CHAPEL LA
9 OLD CHAPEL LA
10 CEMETERY CRES
11 THE MEAD
12 CHURCH LA
13 FIELD CL
14 SPRING LA
15 KEITH CRES
16 CEMETERY RD
17 ST MARGARET'S CL
18 KNIGHTS CL
19 ALTOFT CL
20 KENMAR RD
21 WHITGIFT CL
22 TREVOR CL
23 GEORGE BUTLER CL
24 GRANGE AVE

A 16 B 17 C 18 D 19 E 20 F 21

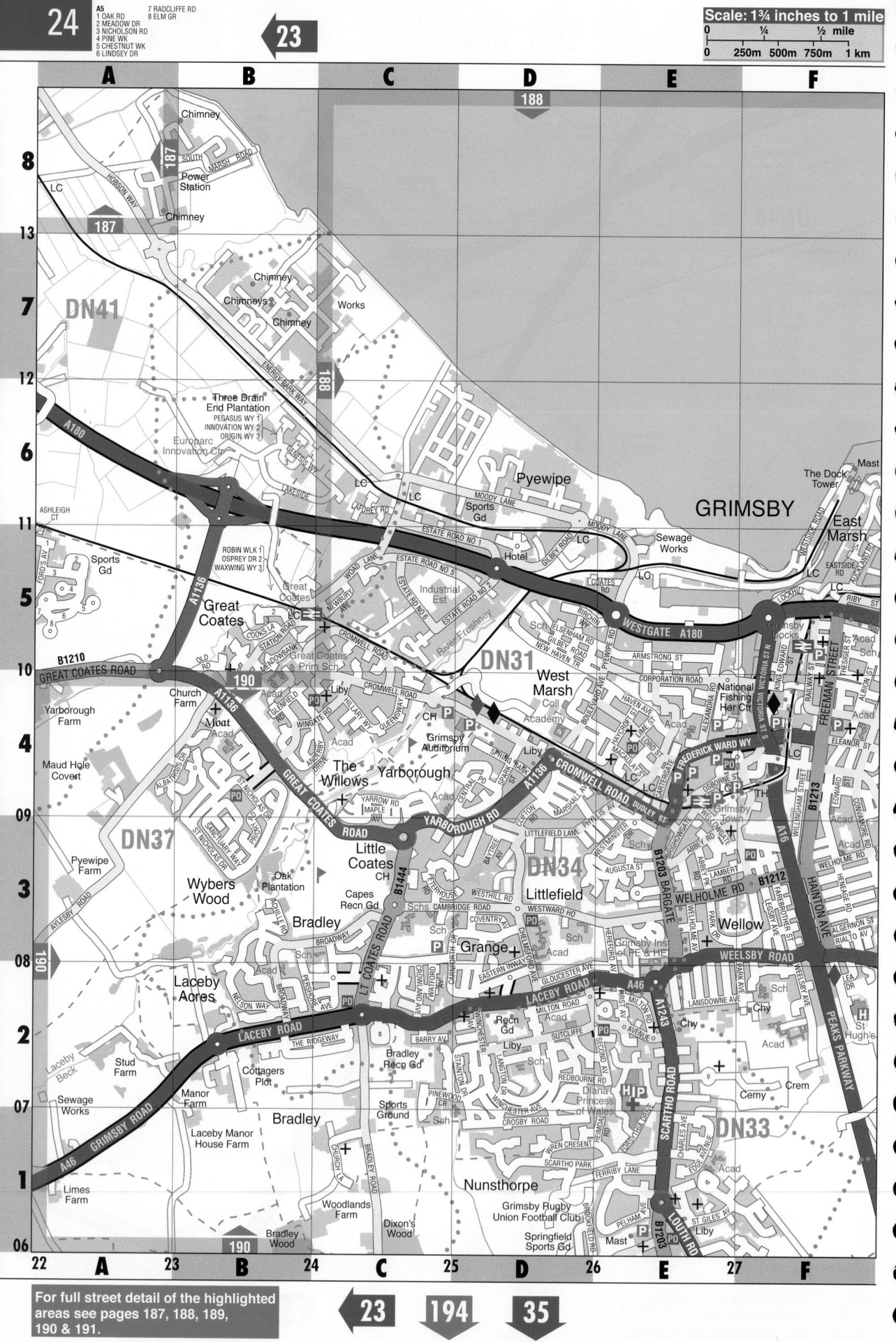
GRIMSBY
Great Coates
West Marsh
Pyewipe
The Willows
Yarborough
Little Coates
Littlefield
Grange
Bradley
Wybers Wood
Laceby Acres
Nunsthorpe
Wellow
East Marsh
DN41
DN37
DN31
DN34
DN33
A180
A1136
A46
A16
A1243
B1210
B1444
B1203
B1212
B1213
GREAT COATES ROAD
LACEBY ROAD
GRIMSBY ROAD
CROMWELL ROAD
YARBOROUGH RD
WESTGATE
WEELSBY ROAD
SCARTHO ROAD
PEAKS PARKWAY
HAINTON AVE
FREEMAN STREET
BARGATE
WELHOLME RD
LOUTH RD
National Fishing Her Ctr
Grimsby Auditorium
Grimsby Docks
Grimsby Town
Diana Princess of Wales
Grimsby Inst of FE & HE
Grimsby Rugby Union Football Club
Springfield Sports Gd
The Dock Tower
Europarc Innovation Ctr
Three Drain End Plantation
Power Station
Sewage Works
Industrial Est
Oak Plantation
Capes Recn Gd
Bradley Recn Gd
Sports Ground
Laceby Manor House Farm
Limes Farm
Woodlands Farm
Dixon's Wood
Bradley Wood
Stud Farm
Manor Farm
Cottagers Plot
Pyewipe Farm
Maud Hole Covert
Yarborough Farm
Church Farm
St Hugh's
Crem
Cemy

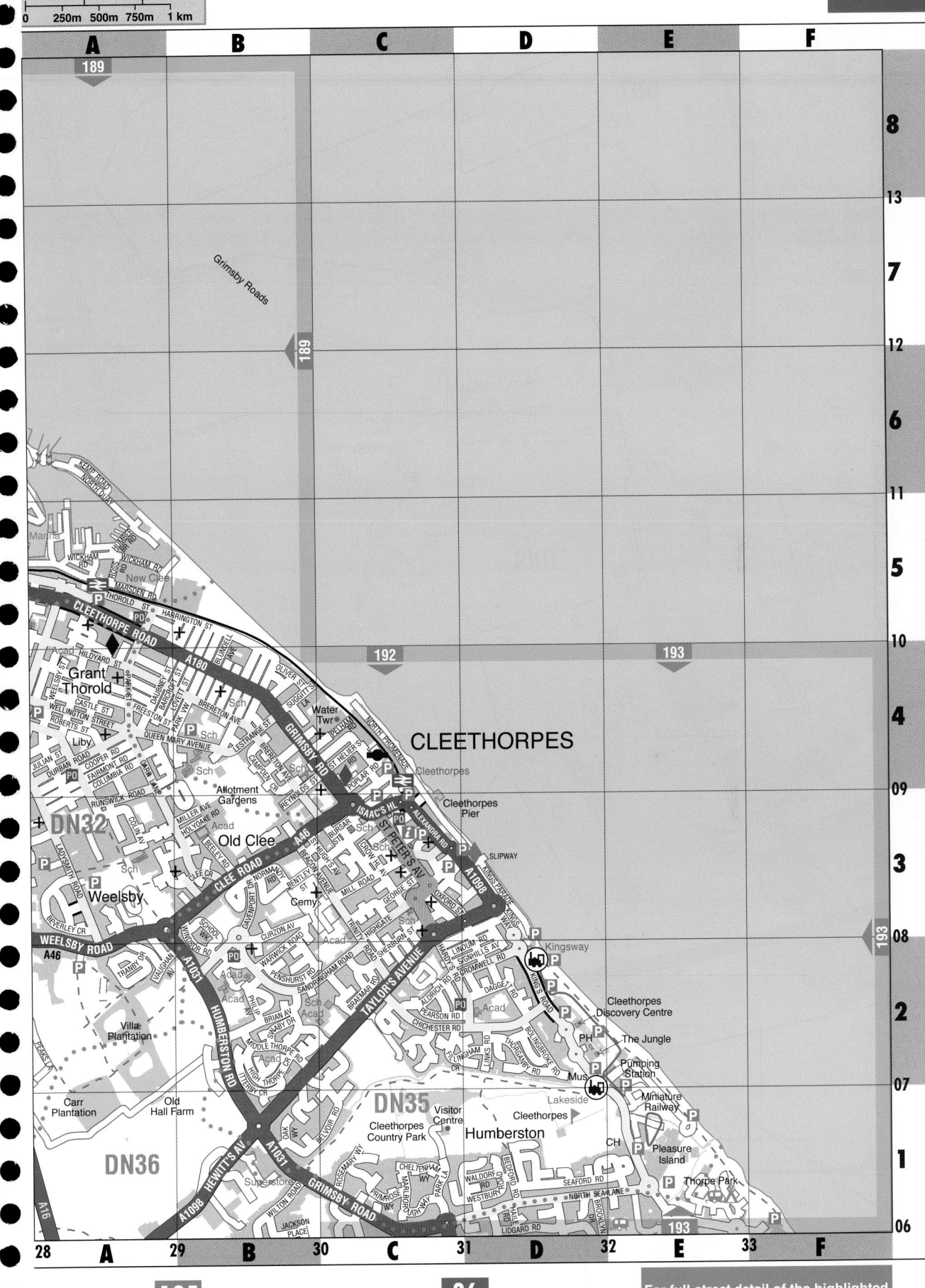

Scale: 1¾ inches to 1 mile

0   ¼   ½   mile
0   250m 500m 750m 1 km

189

8

13

7

Grimsby Roads

189

12

6

11

5

10

Marsh

North Quay

KENT ROAD

WICKHAM RD

Wickham RD

New Clee

MARSDEN RD

THOROLD ST

HARRINGTON ST

CLEETHORPE ROAD

192

193

10

Acad HILDYARD ST

Grant
Thorold

A180

BLUNDELL

OLIVER ST

SUGGITTS LA

North Promenade

4

Welsby

Castle St

Freeston St

BRERETON AVE

Water
Twr

PELHAM

CLEETHORPES

WELLINGTON STREET

ROBERTS ST

Sch

GRIMSBY RD

St Helen's

Cleethorpes

09

JULIAN ST

DURBAN RD

COOPER RD

FAIRMONT RD

COLUMBIA RD

Liby

PO

Sch

Queen Mary Avenue

Sch

LESTRANGE ST

CAMPDEN

REYNOLDS ST

POPLAR RD

ISAAC'S HL

ALEXANDRA RD

Cleethorpes
Pier

DN32

RUNSWICK ROAD

Allotment
Gardens

MILLER AVE

HOLYOAKE RD

Acad

BURSAR

Sch

ST PETER'S AV

PO

SLIPWAY

3

LADYSMITH ROAD

COLIN AV

Old Clee

A46

BEECK RD

BENTLEY ST

KINGS PARADE RD

A1098

Weelsby

BEVERLEY CR

Sch

CLEE CR

CLEE ROAD

DAVENPORT RD

NORMAN

Cemy

MILL ROAD

GEORGE ST

OXFORD ST

WEELSBY ROAD

A46

WINDSOR RD

VAUGHAN

TRANBY

SCHOOL
WK

WARWICK RD

CURZON AV

TRINITY

HIGHGATE

Sch

Acad

SHERBURN ST

08

193

A1031

PO

Acad

PENSHURST RD

SANDRINGHAM ROAD

BRAGMAN RD

TAYLOR'S AVENUE

ALDRICH RD

BROMWELL RD

SIGNHILLS AV

KING'S ROAD

Kingsway

P

2

HUMBERSTON ROAD

PHILIP

BRIAN AV

SNABY DR

MIDDLE THORPE

ACAD

Acad

Sch

PEARSON RD

CHICHESTER RD

DAGGETT RD

Acad

BOLINGBROKE RD

Cleethorpes
Discovery Centre

PH

The Jungle

Villa
Plantation

HIGH THORPE CR

ITTERBY CR

LINGHAM RD

THORGANBY RD

Mus

Pumping
Station

07

Carr
Plantation

Old
Hall Farm

OAK
WY

BELVOIR RD

DN35

Visitor
Centre

Cleethorpes
Country Park

Lakeside

Cleethorpes

Humberston

CH

Miniature
Railway

A1037

HEWITT'S AV

WILTON ROAD

GRIMSBY ROAD

ROSEMARY WY

PRIMROSE
WY

CHELTENHAM
WY

MARLBORO
WY

PARK LA

WALDORF
RD

WESTBURY
RD

BEDFORD RD

SEAFORD RD

Pleasure
Island

Thorpe Park

P

1

DN36

A1098

A16

Superstores

JACKSON
PLACE

LIDGARD RD

NORTH SEA LANE

BROKLYN
RD

193

06

28   A   29   B   30   C   31   D   32   E   33   F

195

36

For full street detail of the highlighted
areas see pages 189, 192 & 193.

A8
1 CUNNINGHAM RD
2 GIBSON RD
3 HAMPDEN CR
4 VARSITY CL

15

A   B   C   D   E   F

DN7

H M PRISON
Lindholme

Hatfield
Moors

P
PO
LANCASTER DR
BLENHEIM RD
WELLINGTON RD
MILLS DR
LINCOLN RD

CANBERRA AVE
MOOR DIKE RD

Canberra
Farm

Roe
Carr

Sand &
Gravel Pit

Moor
Bank

Wroot
Acres

River Torne

Chestnut
Farm

Poor
Piece

Ellerholme
Farm

Tunnel
Pits Bridge

ACRES LANE

P

South Yorkshire STREET ATLAS

River Torne

Candy
Farm

Sewage
Works

Fieldside
Farm

Wroot

MOOR LANE

Chester Cottage
Farm

Greenfield
Farm

Brook House
Farm

Woodside

Tunnel
Pits Farm

COMMON LANE

POLES BANK

IDLE BANK

God's
Cross

FIRTH LA 1
PINE TREE CL 2

PO
PH

HIGH ST

Eastfield
Farm

Aucklands
Farm

Long
Plantation

Wroot Travis Charity
CE Prim Sch

WOODSIDE LANE

Woodside
Farm

WATER BANK

CANDY
BANK

DN9

Thatch Carr
Farm

FIELD LANE

South Engine Drain

Carr
Side

NAN SAMPSON BANK

Thatch Carr
Plantation

Field House
Farm

Sand
Pit

Thorn
Cottage Farm

Greenholme
Bank Farm

Blaxton
Common

Ninescores
Farm

THATCH CARR BANK

Wroot
Grange

THORN BANK

LEVELS LANE

NINESCORES LANE

Charity
Farm

Birds Wood
Nature Reserve

Peat
Carr

Misson
Bank

PEAT CARR BANK

NINESCORES
LANE

COVE ROAD

Finningley
Grange
Farm

WROOT ROAD

Whin
Covert

MISSON BANK

Bull Hassocks
Farm

West Carr
Farm

BANK END ROAD

Old Bank
End Farm

Bank
End

Bull
Hassocks

IDLE BANK

B1396

SANDERSON'S BANK

DONCASTER ROAD

FIFTYEIGHTS
RD

LC

Beech Hill
Farm

Levels
Farm

LC

SPRINGS ROAD

BROOMSTON LANE

CROFT ROAD

DN10

PH

LC

LC

Warping Drain

Misson
Springs Farm

Newlands
Farm

LOW DEEPS LA

Springs
Farm

Levels
Farm

CHAPEL BAULK

IDLE BANK

BROOMSTON LANE

68   A   69   B   70   C   71   D   72   E   73   F

39

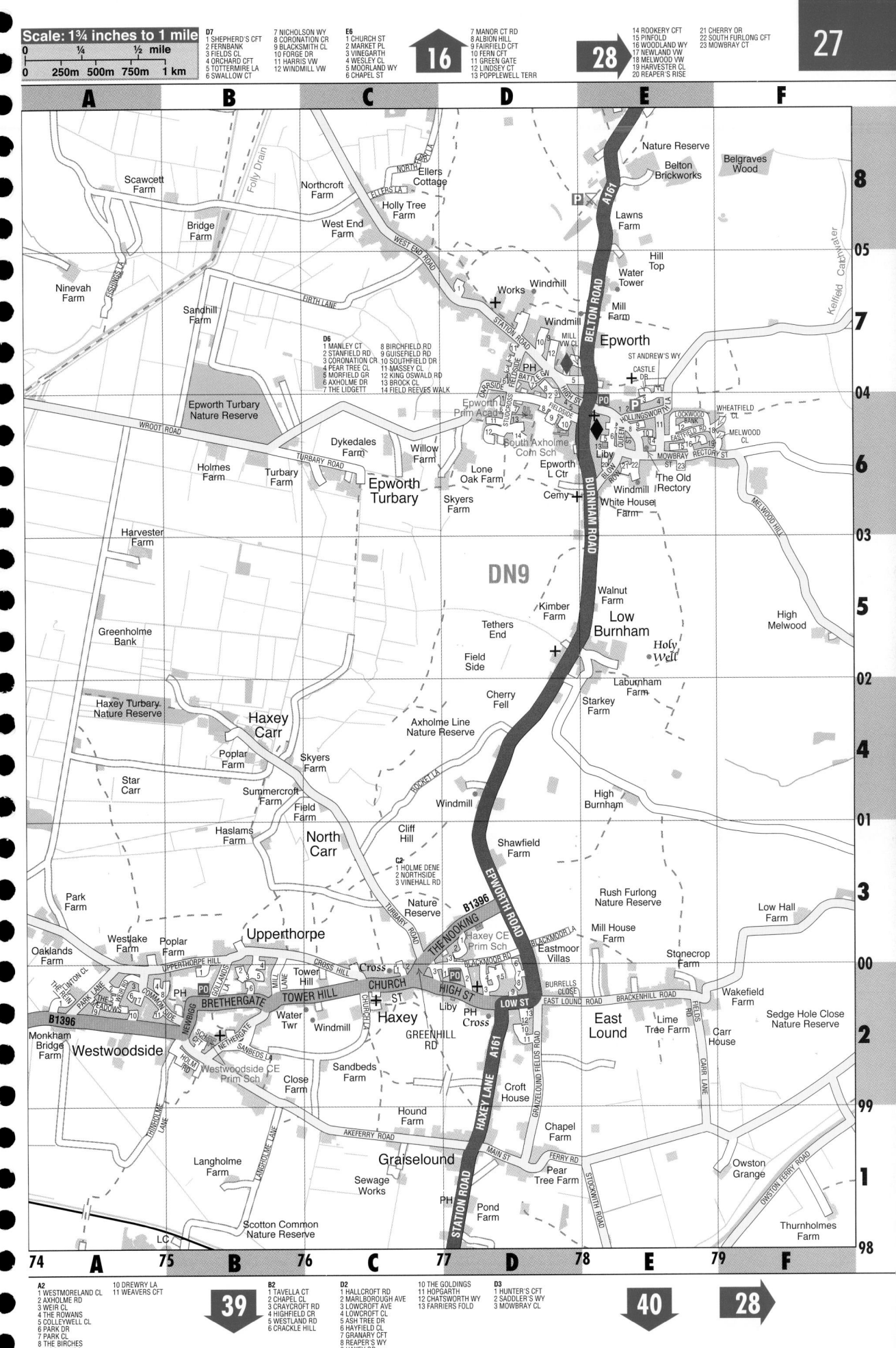

Scale: 1¾ inches to 1 mile

0 ¼ ½ mile
0 250m 500m 750m 1 km

16
28
39
40
28

D7
1 SHEPHERD'S CFT
2 FERNBANK
3 FIELDS CL
4 ORCHARD CFT
5 TOTTERMIRE LA
6 SWALLOW CT

7 NICHOLSON WY
8 BLACKSMITH CL
9 BLACKSMITH CL
10 FORGE DR
11 HARRIS VW
12 WINDMILL VW

E6
1 CHURCH ST
2 MARKET PL
3 VINEGARTH
4 WESLEY CL
5 MOORLAND WY
6 CHAPEL ST

7 MANOR CT RD
8 ALBION HILL
9 FAIRFIELD CFT
10 FERN CFT
11 GREEN GATE
12 LINDSEY CT
13 POPPLEWELL TERR

14 ROOKERY CFT
15 PINFOLD
16 WOODLAND WY
17 NEWLAND WY
18 NEWLAND VW
19 MELWOOD VW
20 REAPER'S RISE

21 CHERRY OR
22 SOUTH FURLONG CFT
23 MOWBRAY CT

D6
1 MANLEY CT
2 STANFIELD RD
3 CORONATION CR
4 PEAR TREE CL
5 MORFIELD GR
6 AXHOLME DR
7 THE LIDGETT

8 BIRCHFIELD RD
9 GUISEFIELD RD
10 SOUTHFIELD DR
11 MASSEY CL
12 KING OSWALD RD
13 BROCK CL
14 FIELD REEVES WALK

C2
1 HOLME DENE
2 NORTHSIDE
3 VINEHALL RD

A2
1 WESTMORELAND CL
2 AXHOLME RD
3 WEIR CL
4 THE ROWANS
5 COLLEYWELL CL
6 PARK DR
7 PARK CL
8 THE BIRCHES
9 MOORLANDS

10 DREWRY LA
11 WEAVERS CFT

B2
1 TAVELLA CT
2 CHAPEL CL
3 CRAYCROFT AVE
4 HIGHFIELD CR
5 WESTLAND RD
6 CRACKLE HILL

D2
1 HALLCROFT RD
2 MARLBOROUGH AVE
3 LOWCROFT AVE
4 LOWCROFT CL
5 ASH TREE DR
6 HAYFIELD CL
7 GRANARY CFT
8 REAPER'S WY
9 HAXEY GR

10 THE GOLDINGS
11 HOPGARTH
12 CHATSWORTH WY
13 FARRIERS FOLD

D3
1 HUNTER'S CFT
2 SADDLER'S WY
3 MOWBRAY CL

DN9

17

D8
1 FARM LA
2 THE CROFT
3 SCHOOL LA
4 PARKLANDS
5 CHRISTOPHERS MDW

Scale: 1¾ inches to 1 mile

0 ¼ ½ mile
0 250m 500m 750m 1 km

A B C D E F

Sealings Wood

Clouds Lane Farm

CLOUDS LA

WEST ST

CARR LANE

PARK VIEW TERR 1
ULYETT LA 2

West Butterwick CE Prim Sch

NORTH ST

HIGH STREET

East Butterwick

PO

SAND ROAD

Sewage Works

West Butterwick

MESSINGHAM ROAD

Bonito Farm

Highfield Farm

Common Farm

Glebe Farm

Hollywood Farm

SOUTH STREET

Poplar Grove Farm

West Grange

South Field Drain

River Trent

Ings Farm

Sand House Farm

8

05

7

04

Newlands

Messingham Ings

DN17

Trentings Farm

Black Bank Farm

6

03

Barlings Farm

Barlings House Farm

NORTH CARR ROAD

NEWLANDS LANE

DARNHOLME CRESCENT

PADDOCK LANE

Newlands Farm

CARR DYKE BK

South Ewster Livery Farm

CARR DYKE BANK

Walnut Tree Farm

Susworth PH

Castle House Farm

Middlemoor Farm

5

02

Priory (remains of)

DN9

Kelfield Grange

Cote House Farm

Glebe Farm

Melwood Park

Low Melwood Farm

Moat

Riverdale Farm

BLACKDYKES ROAD

Kelfield

Drainhead Farm

Grove Farm

South Ings

Tuetoes Hills

P

SUSWORTH ROAD

4

01

Mount Pleasant Farm

EPWORTH RD MELLWOOD VW

Owston Ferry

GAUTRY LANE

Ings Farm

Kelfield Grange

South Carr

Warren Farm

Cemy

St Martins CE Prim Sch

BAGSBY ROAD

Windmill Farm

EAST FERRY ROAD

3

New Farm

BURNHAM ROAD

1 CROFT S LA
2 MARKET PL
3 SANDARS CL

Ferry Barrier Bank

Hardwick Grange Farm

EAST LOUND RD

CHURCH ST

War Meml

NORTH STREET

The Old Smithy & Heritage Centre

00

Castle Hill Motte & Bailey

HIGH STREET

PO

SILVER ST

SOUTH STREET

HIGH STREET

East Ferry

Pin Hill

Hardwick Hill

Scotton Common

Laughton Woods

STATION ROAD

Chimney

2

Windmill

DN21

Redgate Farm

99

Lady Croft Farm

Laughton Lodge

Whitestone Farm

1

EASTFERRY ROAD

Jenny Hurn

Hornsey Hill

HORNSEY HILL ROAD

Jerry's Bog

98

MEYNELL ST

80 A 81 B 82 C 83 D 84 E 85 F

A3
1 CHURCH WK
2 BURNHAM SQ
3 GASHOUSE LA
4 CHURCH CRES
5 TEMPERTON'S LA
6 SOMERBY DR
7 ST MARTINS PARK
8 BLUEBELL COURT

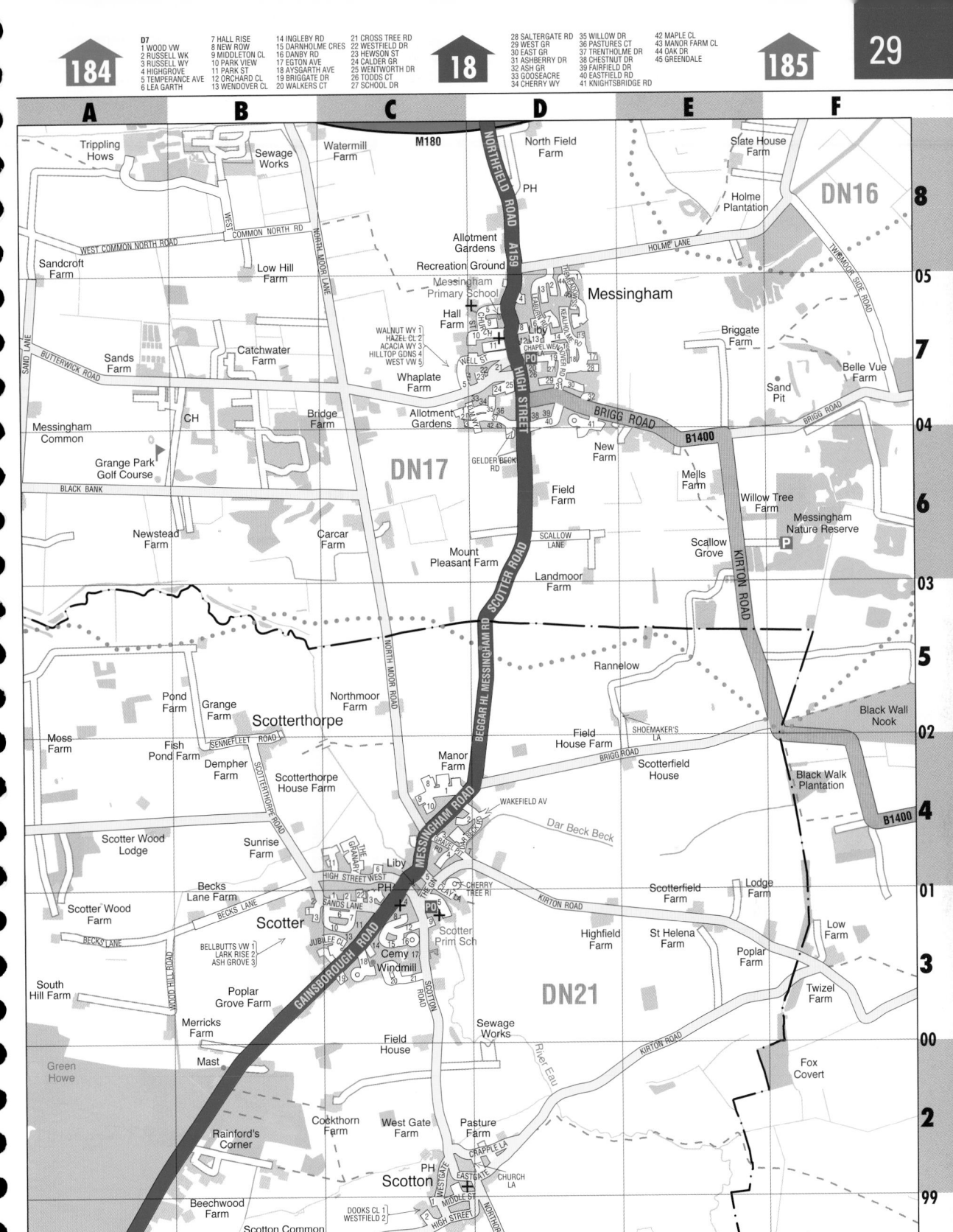

↑ 184
↑ 18
↑ 185

D7
1 WOOD VW
2 RUSSELL WK
3 RUSSELL WY
4 HIGHGROVE
5 TEMPERANCE AVE
6 LEA GARTH
7 HALL RISE
8 NEW ROW
9 MIDDLETON CL
10 PARK VIEW
11 PARK ST
12 ORCHARD CL
13 WENDOVER CL
14 INGLEBY RD
15 DARNHOLME CRES
16 DANBY RD
17 EGTON AVE
18 AYSGARTH AVE
19 BRIGGATE DR
20 WALKERS CT
21 CROSS TREE RD
22 WESTFIELD DR
23 HEWSON ST
24 CALDER GR
25 WENTWORTH DR
26 TODDS CT
27 SCHOOL DR
28 SALTERGATE RD
29 WEST GR
30 EAST GR
31 ASHBERRY DR
32 ASH GR
33 GOOSEACRE
34 CHERRY WY
35 WILLOW DR
36 PASTURES CT
37 TRENTHOLME DR
38 CHESTNUT DR
39 FAIRFIELD DR
40 EASTFIELD RD
41 KNIGHTSBRIDGE RD
42 MAPLE CL
43 MANOR FARM CL
44 OAK DR
45 GREENDALE

↓ 41
↓ 42
→ 30

C3
1 BRAMLEY GR
2 CEDAR CL
3 POPLAR GR
4 HOBB LA
5 LINDHOLME
6 WAKERLEY RD
7 BEECHWOOD DR
8 ORCHARD AVE
9 CHURCH LA
10 ROOKLANDS
11 PINETREE AVE
12 ST PETER'S RD
13 CHESTNUT CL
14 ST PETER'S GR
15 ST ASTLEY CRES
16 CECIL CL
17 REVILL CL
18 CHARLES AVE
19 SOUTHCLIFFE RD
20 MILL CRES
21 WESTCLIFFE RD
22 CROWN GDNS

C4
1 ELIZABETH CL
2 BARNES GR
3 FRANKLIN RD
4 COLINS WY
5 RIVERSIDE
6 EMINSON CL
7 BARLINGS CL
8 CORDEAUX CL
9 JOHNSON DR
10 EDGAR CL
11 WAGGONERS CL

E8
1 VICARAGE LA
2 OLD VICARAGE PK
3 MANOR DR
4 ST MARTIN'S RD
5 ST JOAN'S DR
6 ST JAMES'S RD

8 COACH HOUSE GDNS
9 CHURCH ST
10 CHAPEL LA
11 INGRAM GDNS
12 BEECHWOOD DR
13 OLD MANOR DR

F7
1 WALNUT DR
2 ST HYBALD'S GR
3 SWANNACKS VW
4 SUTTON PL

F8
1 PARK LA
2 THE ROOKERY
3 MILL CROFT
4 MEADOW VALE
5 OAK AVE
6 CEDAR CL

7 WILLOW GR
8 LARCH GR
9 KINGS CT
10 LIDGETT CL

Scale: 1¾ inches to 1 mile
0   ¼   ½   mile
0   250m 500m 750m 1 km

A B C D E F

DN16
Scotch Wood
Gull Ponds
Twigmoor Woods
High Wood
Top Farm
Scawby
Scawby Hall
Cemy
B1207

Bowers Wood
Manton Warren
Moor Farm
Messingham Lane
Scawby Academy
Windmill
WEST STREET
PO
PH

Twigmoor Grange
Black Hoe Plantation
Greetwell Hall Farm
Greetwell
Welburn Plantation
Sturton
MAIN ST
Sewage Works
Sturton Lane
Brigg Road
Gainsborough Lane
Mill Lane

Broom Plantation
BRIGG ROAD
Greetwell Hall
Aldham Plantation
Scawby Grange
Railway Plantation
New Farm

DN17
KIRTON ROAD
Stonepit Wood
Staniwells Farm
DN20
Station Farm
STATION ROAD
REDBOURNE ROAD
B1206
B1207

Middle Manton
Settlement
Manton Lane

Manor Farm
Newlands Farm
America Wood
B1398
PH
WEST STREET
Grange Farm

Manton
South Farm
SAND LANE
Cleatham Hall
Cliff Farm
PO

E5
1 WOODS MDW
2 COTTAGE CL
3 PELHAM VW
4 HUNTS LA
5 BECK SIDE
6 BARNSIDE
7 CHURCH ST
8 FORD LA
9 STATION RD
10 COCKETTS LA
11 DICKINSON CL
12 RUSHTONS WY
13 EAST ST
14 OLD SCHOOL DR
15 MEADOW CT
16 ST ALBANS CL
17 CHAPEL CT
18 ANDREW PADDOCK
19 FOX COVERT

Cleatham Hall Farm
Tumulus
Quarry Fields Farm
Quarry (dis)
Old Home Farm
Wood Home Farm
MILL ROAD

B1400
GAINSTHORPE ROAD WEST
GAINSTHORPE ROAD EAST
Medieval Village of Gainsthorpe

MANTON ROAD
PH
Chy
Gainsthorpe Farm

Cleatham
New Cleatham House Farm
CLEATHAM ROAD
Quarry (dis)
DN21
Northwood Farm
Stonepit Plantation
Redbourne
B1206

Mount Pleasant Farm
Kirton Tunnel
ST GEORGE'S CT 1
ST ANDREW'S CL 2
PARK LA 3
SCHOOL LA 4
CARR LANE

KIRTON ROAD
Low Farm
NORTH CLIFF ROAD
1 BECK LA
2 VICARAGE LA
3 THE FALCONERS

Sweet Hills
Mast
Northcliff Farm
HIGH STREET
PH
Hall

Station Farm
Kirton Lindsey
STATION ROAD
Grange Farm
Redbourne Park

Mount Pleasant Windmill
B1398
Kirton in Lindsey
REDBOURNE MERE
A15
Springcliff Farm

Ings Farm
Liby
KING EDWARD ST
REDBOURNE MERE
B1206
Cemy
PH
INGS ROAD
Huntcliff School
TH
PO
Cliff Farm
Pyewipe House

1 MILL LA
2 BIRCHAM CR
3 LINCOLN CR
4 FUSILIER WAY

Sewage Works
Moat
Manor Farm
30
CLAY LANE
Kirton Lindsey Prim Sch
B1398
Mast
CORK LANE
B1400

B1
1 ORCHARD CL
2 HIGHFIELD DR
3 EAST DALE DR
4 WHITEWELL CL
5 GROVE ST
6 DARWIN ST
7 CHURCH ST
8 SUNNY HLL
9 SPA HLL
10 UNICORN ROW
11 GEORGE ST
12 SYLVESTER ST
13 MARCH ST
14 TORKSEY ST
15 TURNER ST
16 ST ANDREW'S ST
17 OLD SCHOOL YD
18 HIGH ST
19 WESLEY ST
20 WRAY ST
21 CORNWALL ST
22 TRAIN GATE
23 WEST CROSS ST
24 EAST CROSS ST
25 DUNSTAN HILL
26 SOUTH CLIFF RD
27 PARK HILL
28 DUNSTAN VILLAS
29 CORNWALL ST
30 LOWFIELD CL
31 GAINSBOROUGH RD
32 FAIRFIELDS
33 BROOKES CL
34 ENDELL DR
35 MARKET PL
36 LANES END
37 ...

B2
1 RICHDALE AVE
2 WEST-DALE CRES
3 SOUTH-DALE CL
4 NORTH-DALE CT
5 BEECHCROFT DR
6 DARWIN ST
7 BOWLING GREEN GDNS
8 BARLEY CL
9 MILLSTONE CL

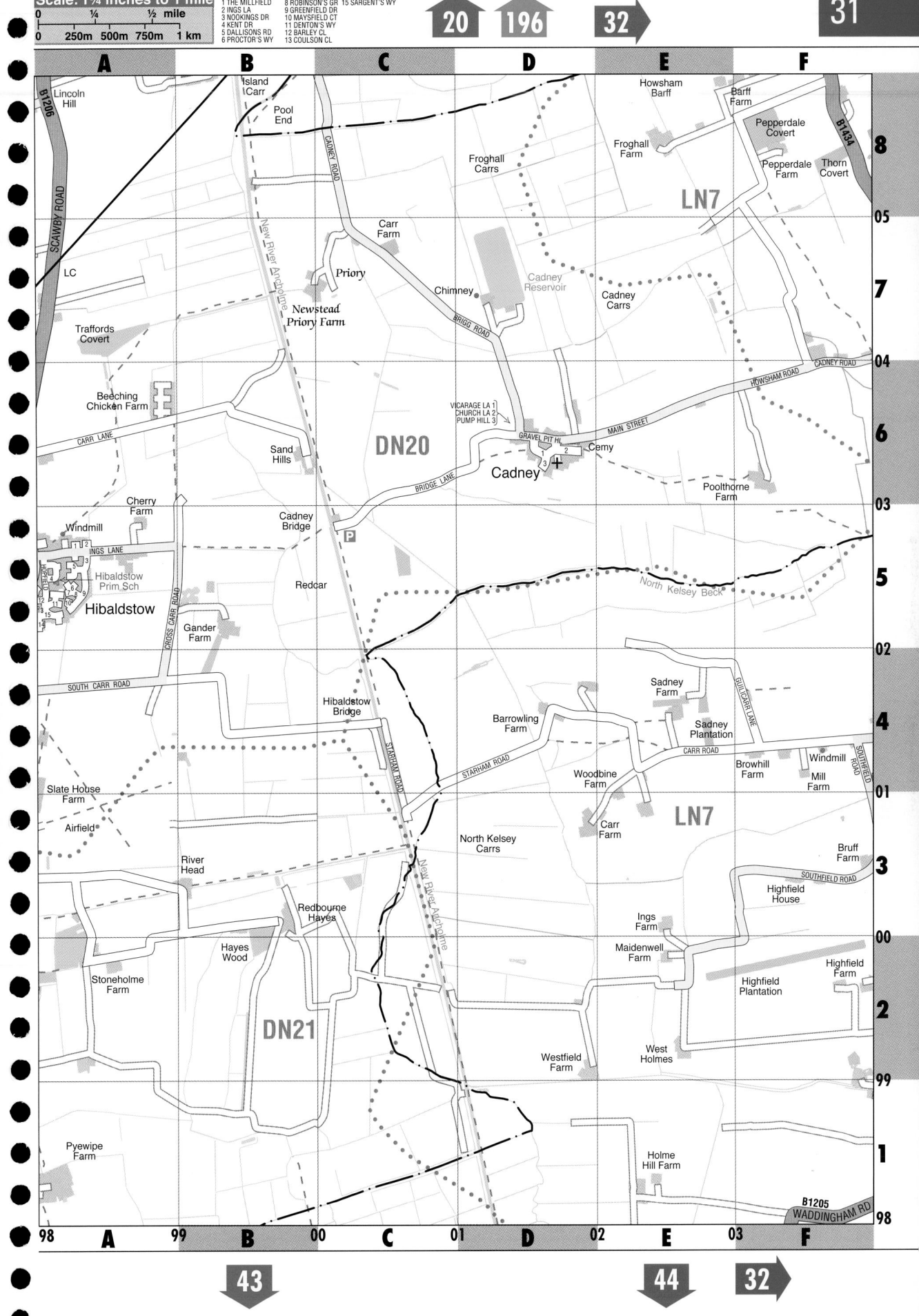
Scale: 1¾ inches to 1 mile
0 ¼ ½ mile
0 250m 500m 750m 1 km
A5
1 THE MILLFIELD
2 INGS LA
3 NOOKINGS DR
4 KENT DR
5 DALLISONS RD
6 PROCTOR'S WY
7 COX'S CT
8 ROBINSON'S GR
9 GREENFIELD DR
10 MAYSFIELD CT
11 DENTON'S WY
12 BARLEY CL
13 COULSON CL
14 WILLOUGHBY RD
15 SARGENT'S WY
20
196
32
A B C D E F
Lincoln Hill
B1206
SCAWBY ROAD
LC
Island Carr
Pool End
CADNEY ROAD
Froghall Carrs
Howsham Barff
Froghall Farm
Barff Farm
Pepperdale Covert
B1434
Pepperdale Farm
Thorn Covert
LN7
New River Ancholme
Carr Farm
Priory
Newstead Priory Farm
Chimney
Cadney Reservoir
Cadney Carrs
BRIGG ROAD
Traffords Covert
Beeching Chicken Farm
CARR LANE
Sand Hills
DN20
VICARAGE LA 1
CHURCH LA 2
PUMP HILL 3
GRAVEL PIT HL
MAIN STREET
HOWSHAM ROAD
CADNEY ROAD
Cemy
Cadney
BRIDGE LANE
Poolthorne Farm
Cherry Farm
Windmill
INGS LANE
HOPFIELD
Hibaldstow Prim Sch
Hibaldstow
Cadney Bridge
P
Redcar
North Kelsey Beck
CROSS CARR ROAD
Gander Farm
SOUTH CARR ROAD
Hibaldstow Bridge
STARHAM ROAD
Barrowling Farm
Sadney Farm
GUILICARR LANE
Sadney Plantation
CARR ROAD
Woodbine Farm
Browhill Farm
Windmill
Mill Farm
SOUTHFIELD ROAD
Slate House Farm
Airfield
River Head
North Kelsey Carrs
Carr Farm
LN7
Bruff Farm
SOUTHFIELD ROAD
Highfield House
Redbourne Hayes
Ings Farm
Maidenwell Farm
Hayes Wood
Stoneholme Farm
Highfield Farm
Highfield Plantation
DN21
West Holmes
Westfield Farm
Pyewipe Farm
Holme Hill Farm
B1205
WADDINGHAM RD
8 05 7 04 6 03 5 02 4 01 3 00 2 99 1 98
98 99 00 01 02 03
43
44
32

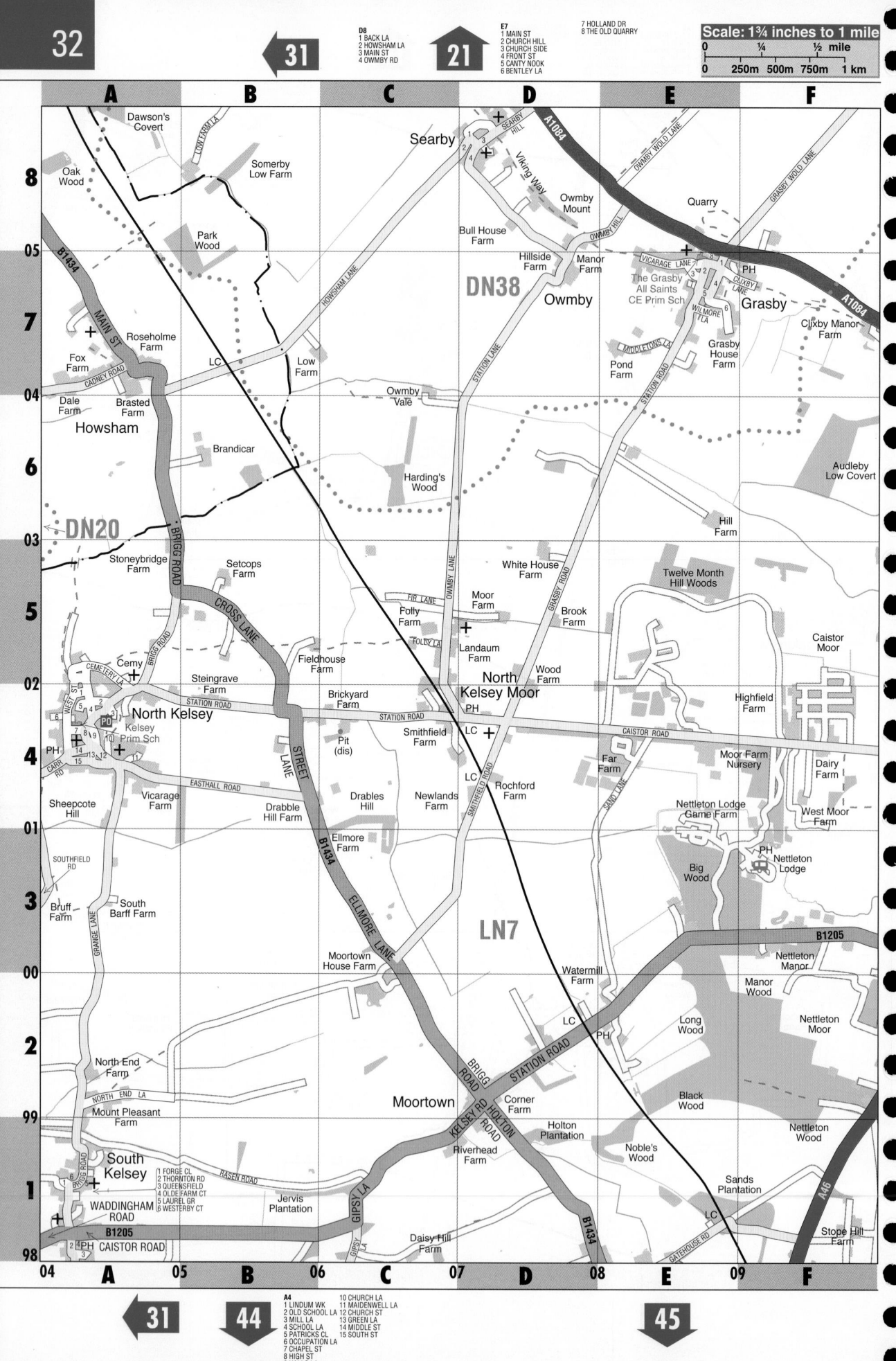
31
21
D8
1 BACK LA
2 HOWSHAM LA
3 MAIN ST
4 OWMBY RD
E7
1 MAIN ST
2 CHURCH HILL
3 CHURCH SIDE
4 FRONT ST
5 CANTY NOOK
6 BENTLEY LA
7 HOLLAND DR
8 THE OLD QUARRY
Scale: 1¾ inches to 1 mile
0 ¼ ½ mile
0 250m 500m 750m 1 km
A B C D E F
8 05 7 04 6 03 5 02 4 01 3 00 2 99 1 98
04 05 06 07 08 09
Dawson's Covert
Low Farm La
Somerby Low Farm
Searby
Searby Hill
A1084
Ownby Wold Lane
Grasby Wold Lane
Oak Wood
Viking Way
Ownby Mount
Quarry
Park Wood
Bull House Farm
Ownby Hill
B1434
Hillside Farm
Manor Farm
Vicarage Lane
PH
DN38
The Grasby All Saints CE Prim Sch
Clixby Lane
Grasby
Howsham Lane
Owmby
Wilmore La
Main St
Roseholme Farm
Clixby Manor Farm
Fox Farm
Cadney Road
LC
Low Farm
Middletons La
Grasby House Farm
Pond Farm
Station Lane
Station Road
Owmby Vale
Dale Farm
Brasted Farm
Howsham
Brandicar
Harding's Wood
Audleby Low Covert
DN20
Brigg Road
Hill Farm
Stoneybridge Farm
Setcops Farm
White House Farm
Twelve Month Hill Woods
Grasby Road
Ownby Lane
Fir Lane
Moor Farm
Cross Lane
Folly Farm
Brook Farm
Caistor Moor
Folly La
Landaum Farm
Fieldhouse Farm
Cemetery La
Cemy
Wood Farm
Steingrave Farm
North Kelsey Moor
Highfield Farm
West St
Brickyard Farm
Station Road
North Kelsey
PO
Smithfield Farm
Kelsey Prim Sch
Caistor Road
Pit (dis)
Street Lane
Moor Farm Nursery
Carr Rd
Far Farm
Dairy Farm
Easthall Road
Rochford Farm
Sand Lane
Smithfield Road
Sheepcote Hill
Vicarage Farm
Drabble Hill Farm
Drables Hill
Newlands Farm
Nettleton Lodge Game Farm
West Moor Farm
Ellmore Farm
Southfield Rd
Nettleton Lodge
Big Wood
Bruff Farm
South Barff Farm
Ellmore Lane
Grange Lane
LN7
B1205
Moortown House Farm
Nettleton Manor
Watermill Farm
Manor Wood
Long Wood
Nettleton Moor
North End Farm
Brigg Road
Station Road
North End La
Moortown
Corner Farm
Black Wood
Mount Pleasant Farm
Kelsey Rd
Holton Road
Holton Plantation
Nettleton Wood
Riverhead Farm
Noble's Wood
South Kelsey
1 FORGE CL
2 THORNTON RD
3 QUEENSFIELD
4 OLDE FARM CT
5 LAUREL GR
6 WESTERBY CT
Rasen Road
Sands Plantation
A46
Waddingham Road
Jervis Plantation
Gipsy La
B1434
Stope Hill Farm
Caistor Road
Daisy Hill Farm
Gatehouse Rd
A4
1 LINDUM WK
2 OLD SCHOOL LA
3 MILL LA
4 SCHOOL LA
5 PATRICKS CL
6 OCCUPATION LA
7 CHAPEL ST
8 HIGH ST
9 HALLS LA
10 CHURCH LA
11 MAIDENWELL LA
12 CHURCH ST
13 GREEN LA
14 MIDDLE ST
15 SOUTH ST
31
44
45

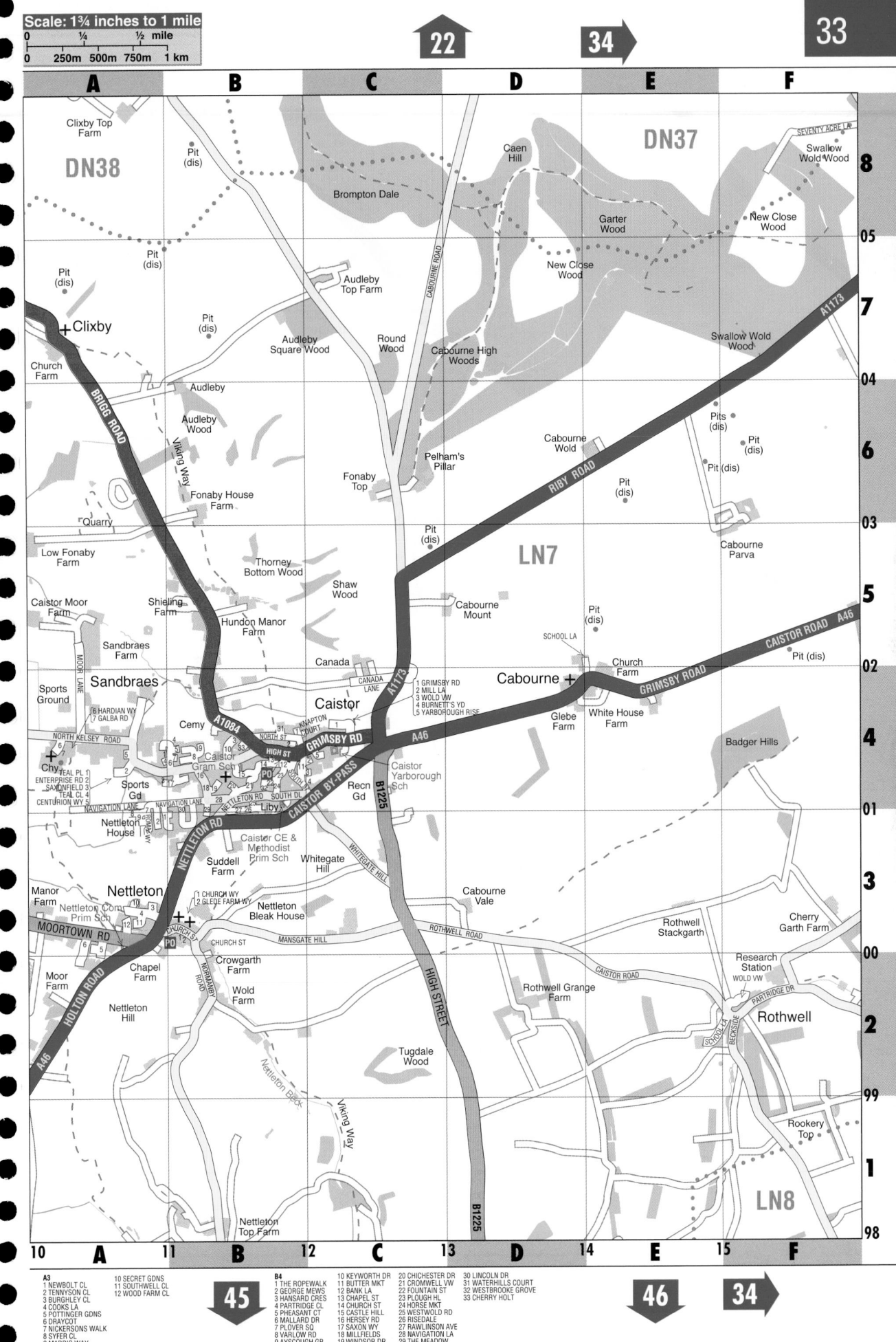
Scale: 1¾ inches to 1 mile
0 ¼ ½ mile
0 250m 500m 750m 1 km
22
34
A B C D E F
DN38
DN37
LN7
LN8
Clixby Top Farm
Pit (dis)
Brompton Dale
Caen Hill
Garter Wood
Swallow Wold Wood
SEVENTY ACRE LA
New Close Wood
Audleby Top Farm
Clixby
Church Farm
Audleby Square Wood
Round Wood
Cabourne High Woods
CABOURNE ROAD
Swallow Wold Wood
A1173
Audleby
Audleby Wood
BRIGG ROAD
Viking Way
Pits (dis)
Cabourne Wold
Pelham's Pillar
Fonaby Top
Fonaby House Farm
RIBY ROAD
Quarry
Low Fonaby Farm
Thorney Bottom Wood
Shaw Wood
Cabourne Parva
Caistor Moor Farm
Shieling Farm
Hundon Manor Farm
Cabourne Mount
Sandbraes Farm
MOOR LANE
SCHOOL LA
CAISTOR ROAD
A46
Canada
CANADA LANE
Church Farm
Cabourne
GRIMSBY ROAD
Sports Ground
Sandbraes
1 GRIMSBY RD
2 MILL LA
3 WOLD VW
4 BURNETT'S YD
5 YARBOROUGH RISE
Caistor
Glebe Farm
White House Farm
6 HARDIAN WY
7 GALBA RD
Cemy
A1084
KNAPTON COURT
NORTH ST
HIGH ST
GRIMSBY RD
NORTH KELSEY ROAD
Badger Hills
Chy
Caistor Gram Sch
Caistor Yarborough Sch
TEAL PL 1
ENTERPRISE RD 2
SAXONFIELD 3
TEAL CL 4
CENTURION WY 5
Sports Gd
Recn Gd
B1225
NAVIGATION LANE
NETTLETON RD
SOUTH DL
CAISTOR BY-PASS
Liby
Nettleton House
ROMAN WY
Caistor CE & Methodist Prim Sch
Suddell Farm
Whitegate Hill
WHITEGATE HILL
Manor Farm
Nettleton
1 CHURCH WY
2 GLEDE FARM WY
Nettleton Bleak House
Cabourne Vale
Nettleton Com Prim Sch
Rothwell Stackgarth
Cherry Garth Farm
MOORTOWN RD
CHURCH ST
MANSGATE HILL
ROTHWELL ROAD
Moor Farm
Chapel Farm
Crowgarth Farm
NORMANBY ROAD
Research Station
WOLD VW
PARTRIDGE DR
Rothwell Grange Farm
Wold Farm
Nettleton Hill
HOLTON ROAD
HIGH STREET
Rothwell
SCHOOL LA
BECKSIDE
Tugdale Wood
Nettleton Beck
Rookery Top
Nettleton Top Farm
8 05 7 04 6 03 5 02 4 01 3 00 2 99 1 98
10 11 12 13 14 15
A3
1 NEWBOLT CL
2 TENNYSON CL
3 BURGHLEY CL
4 COOKS LA
5 POTTINGER GDNS
6 DRAYCOT
7 NICKERSONS WALK
8 SYFER CL
9 MARRIS WAY
10 SECRET GDNS
11 SOUTHWELL CL
12 WOOD FARM CL
45
B4
1 THE ROPEWALK
2 GEORGE MEWS
3 HANSARD CRES
4 PARTRIDGE CL
5 PHEASANT CT
6 MALLARD DR
7 PLOVER SQ
8 VARLOW RD
9 AYSCOUGH GR
10 KEYWORTH DR
11 BUTTER MKT
12 BANK LA
13 CHAPEL ST
14 CHURCH ST
15 CASTLE HILL
16 HERSEY RD
17 SAXON WY
18 MILLFIELDS
19 WINDSOR DR
20 CHICHESTER DR
21 CROMWELL VW
22 FOUNTAIN ST
23 PLOUGH HL
24 HORSE MKT
25 WESTWOLD RD
26 RISEDALE
27 RAWLINSON AVE
28 NAVIGATION LA
29 THE MEADOW
30 LINCOLN DR
31 WATERHILLS COURT
32 WESTBROOKE GROVE
33 CHERRY HOLT
46
34

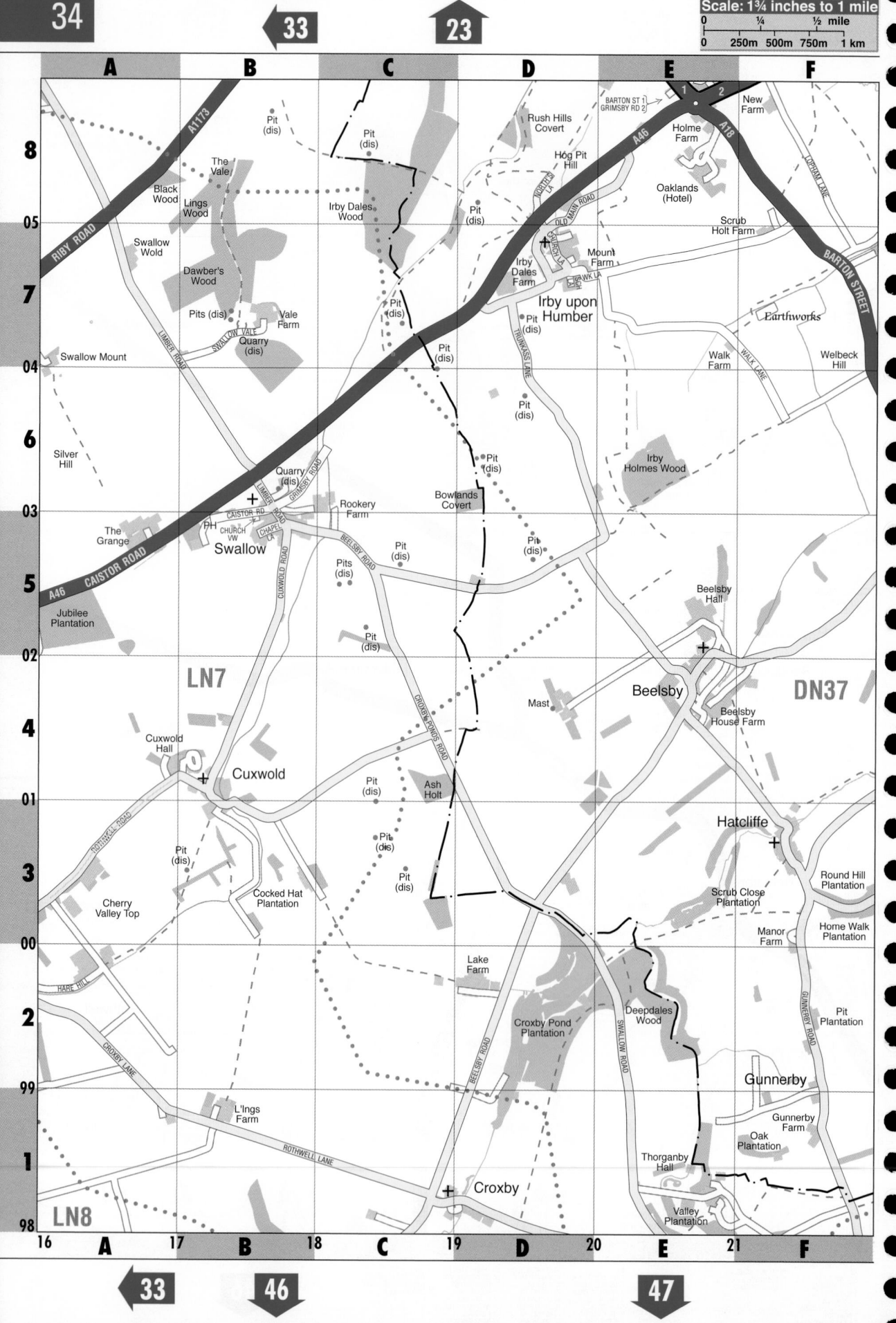

Scale: 1¾ inches to 1 mile

0   ¼   ½ mile
0 250m 500m 750m 1 km

A   B   C   D   E   F

8
05
7
04
6
03
5
02

LN7

4
01
3
00
2
99
1
98

LN8

16   17   18   19   20   21

A   B   C   D   E   F

RIBY ROAD
A1173
A46 CAISTOR ROAD

Black Wood
Swallow Wold
Lings Wood
The Vale
Dawber's Wood
Pit (dis)
Pit (dis)
Irby Dales Wood
Pits (dis)
Vale Farm
Quarry (dis)
Swallow Vale
LIMBER ROAD
Swallow Mount
Silver Hill
Quarry (dis)
GRIMSBY ROAD
Rookery Farm
The Grange
PH
CHURCH VW
CAISTOR RD
CHAPEL LA
Swallow
Jubilee Plantation
CUXWOLD ROAD
BEELSBY ROAD
Pits (dis)
Pit (dis)
Pit (dis)
Pit (dis)
Pit (dis)
Pit (dis)
Pit (dis)
Pit (dis)
Bowlands Covert

Rush Hills Covert
Hog Pit Hill
NORTH LA
OLD BARN ROAD
A46
Irby Dales Farm
CHURCH LA
HAWK LA
Mount Farm
Irby upon Humber
TRUNKASS LANE
Pit (dis)
Walk Farm
WALK LANE
Irby Holmes Wood

BARTON ST 1
GRIMSBY RD 2
Holme Farm
New Farm
A46
A18
Oaklands (Hotel)
Scrub Holt Farm
BARTON STREET
DEPBAM LANE
Earthworks
Welbeck Hill

Beelsby Hall
Beelsby
Mast
Beelsby House Farm

DN37

Hatcliffe
Scrub Close Plantation
Round Hill Plantation
Home Walk Plantation
Manor Farm
GUNNERBY ROAD
Pit Plantation
Gunnerby

Cuxwold Hall
Cuxwold
ROTHWELL ROAD
Pit (dis)
Cherry Valley Top
Cocked Hat Plantation
CROXBY POND ROAD
Ash Holt
Pit (dis)
Pit (dis)
Pit (dis)

Lake Farm
BEELSBY ROAD
SWALLOW ROAD
Croxby Pond Plantation
Deepdales Wood

HARE HILL
CROXBY LANE
L'Ings Farm
ROTHWELL LANE
Croxby
Thorganby Hall
Valley Plantation
Oak Plantation
Gunnerby Farm

33   23
33   46   47

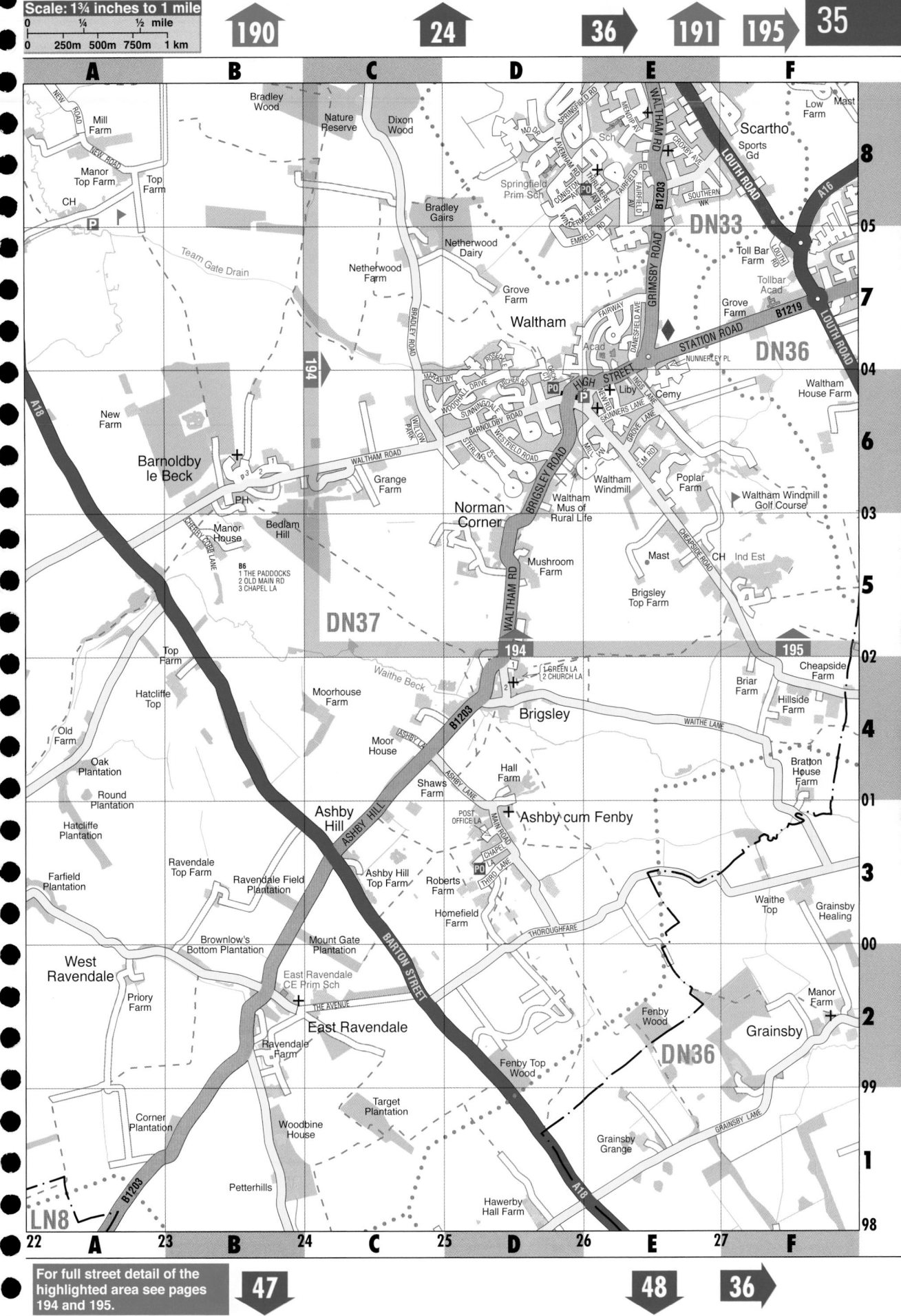

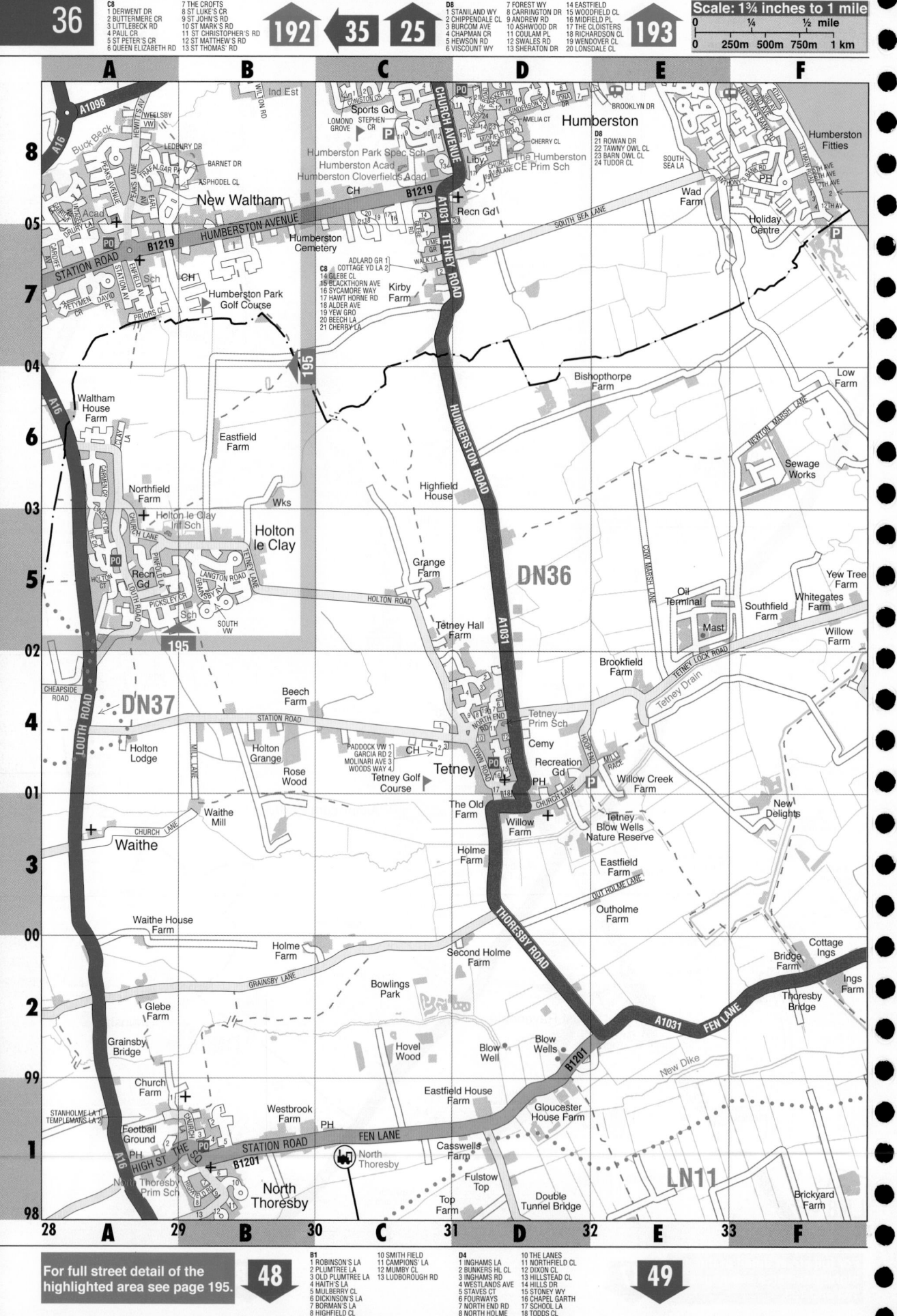
C8
1 DERWENT DR
2 BUTTERMERE CR
3 LITTLEBECK RD
4 PAUL CR
5 ST PETER'S CR
6 QUEEN ELIZABETH RD
7 THE CROFTS
8 ST LUKE'S CR
9 ST JOHN'S RD
10 ST MARK'S RD
11 ST CHRISTOPHER'S RD
12 ST MATTHEW'S RD
13 ST THOMAS' RD
192
35
25
D8
1 STANILAND WY
2 CHIPPENDALE CL
3 BURCOM AVE
4 CHAPMAN CR
5 HEWSON RD
6 VISCOUNT WY
7 FOREST WY
8 CARRINGTON DR
9 ANDREW RD
10 ASHWOOD DR
11 COULAM PL
12 SWALES RD
13 SHERATON DR
14 EASTFIELD
15 WOODFIELD CL
16 MIDFIELD PL
17 THE CLOISTERS
18 RICHARDSON CL
19 WENDOVER CL
20 LONSDALE CL
193
Scale: 1¾ inches to 1 mile
0 ¼ ½ mile
0 250m 500m 750m 1 km
A B C D E F
8
05
7
04
6
03
5
02
4
01
3
00
2
99
1
98
Ind Est
Sports Gd
Humberston
Humberston Park Spec Sch
Humberston Acad
Humberston Cloverfields Acad
The Humberston CE Prim Sch
D8
21 ROWAN DR
22 TAWNY OWL CL
23 BARN OWL CL
24 TUDOR CL
Humberston Fitties
New Waltham
HUMBERSTON AVENUE
STATION ROAD
B1219
A1098
A16
A1031
CHURCH AVENUE
TETNEY ROAD
SOUTH SEA LANE
Wad Farm
Holiday Centre
Recn Gd
Humberston Cemetery
C8
14 GLEBE CL
15 BLACKTHORN AVE
16 SYCAMORE WAY
17 HAWTHORNE RD
18 ALDER AVE
19 YEW GRO
20 BEECH LA
21 CHERRY LA
ADLARD GR 1
COTTAGE YD LA 2
Kirby Farm
Humberston Park Golf Course
195
Bishopthorpe Farm
Low Farm
Waltham House Farm
Eastfield Farm
HUMBERSTON ROAD
NEWTON MARSH LANE
Sewage Works
Highfield House
Northfield Farm
Holton le Clay Inf Sch
Wks
Holton le Clay
Grange Farm
DN36
COW MARSH LANE
Yew Tree Farm
Oil Terminal
Southfield Farm
Whitegates Farm
Mast
Willow Farm
HOLTON ROAD
Tetney Hall Farm
LANGTON ROAD
PICKSLEY CR
SOUTH VW
TETNEY LOCK ROAD
Brookfield Farm
Tetney Drain
CHEAPSIDE ROAD
DN37
Beech Farm
STATION ROAD
LOUTH ROAD
Tetney Prim Sch
Cemy
Holton Lodge
MILL LANE
Holton Grange
Rose Wood
PADDOCK VW 1
GARCIA RD 2
MOLINARI AVE 3
WOODS WAY 4
Tetney Golf Course
Tetney
Recreation Gd
Willow Creek Farm
The Old Farm
Willow Farm
CHURCH LANE
Waithe Mill
Waithe
Tetney Blow Wells Nature Reserve
New Delights
Holme Farm
Eastfield Farm
OUT HOLME LANE
Outholme Farm
THORESBY ROAD
Waithe House Farm
Holme Farm
Second Holme Farm
Cottage Ings
Bridge Farm
GRAINSBY LANE
Bowlings Park
Ings Farm
Thoresby Bridge
Glebe Farm
A1031 FEN LANE
Grainsby Bridge
Hovel Wood
Blow Well
Blow Wells
B1201
New Dike
Church Farm
Eastfield House Farm
STANHOLME LA 1
TEMPLEMANS LA 2
Football Ground
Westbrook Farm
Gloucester House Farm
PH
FEN LANE
HIGH ST
THE SQ
STATION ROAD
North Thoresby
Casswells Farm
North Thoresby Prim Sch
Fulstow Top
LN11
North Thoresby
Top Farm
Double Tunnel Bridge
Brickyard Farm
28 29 30 31 32 33
For full street detail of the highlighted area see page 195.
48
B1
1 ROBINSON'S LA
2 PLUMTREE LA
3 OLD PLUMTREE LA
4 HAITH'S LA
5 MULBERRY CL
6 DICKINSON'S LA
7 BORMAN'S LA
8 HIGHFIELD CL
9 MARFLEET CRES
10 SMITH FIELD
11 CAMPIONS' LA
12 MUMBY CL
13 LUDBOROUGH RD
D4
1 INGHAMS LA
2 BUNKERS HL CL
3 INGHAMS RD
4 WESTLANDS AVE
5 STAVES CT
6 FOURWAYS
7 NORTH END RD
8 NORTH HOLME
9 NORTH END CRES
10 THE LANES
11 NORTHFIELD CL
12 DIXON CL
13 HILLSTEAD CL
14 HILLS DR
15 STONEY WY
16 CHAPEL GARTH
17 SCHOOL LA
18 TODDS CL
19 NORTH HOLME
49

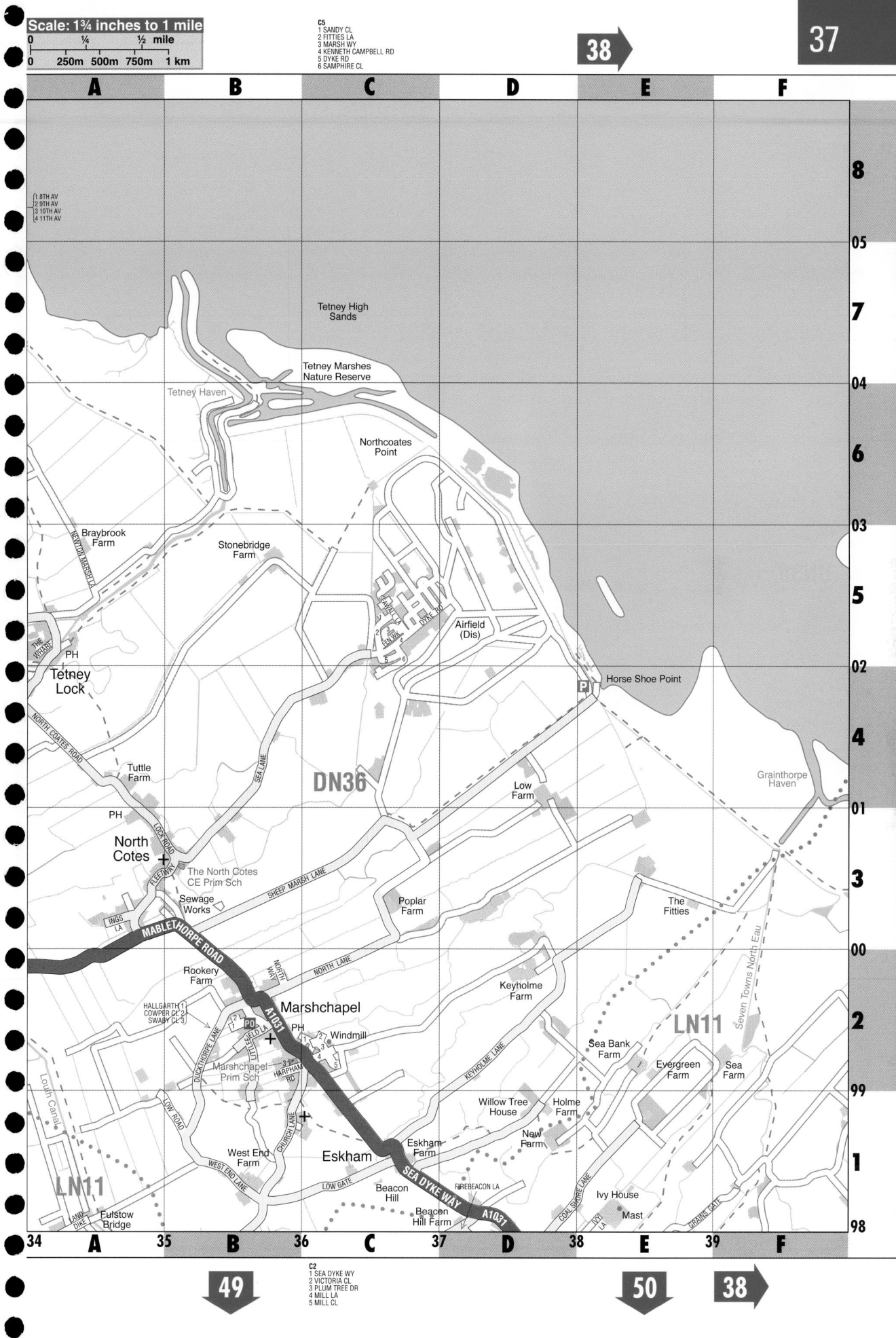

Scale: 1¾ inches to 1 mile

0   ¼   ½ mile
0   250m 500m 750m 1 km

C5
1 SANDY CL
2 FITTIES LA
3 MARSH WY
4 KENNETH CAMPBELL RD
5 DYKE RD
6 SAMPHIRE CL

38 ➤

1 8TH AV
2 9TH AV
3 10TH AV
4 11TH AV

Tetney High Sands

Tetney Marshes Nature Reserve

Tetney Haven

Northcoates Point

Braybrook Farm

Stonebridge Farm

Airfield (Dis)

THE WASH

PH

Tetney Lock

P Horse Shoe Point

NORTH COATES ROAD

Tuttle Farm

Low Farm

Grainthorpe Haven

DN36

SEA LANE

PH

LOCK ROAD

North Cotes

FLEETWAY

The North Cotes CE Prim Sch

SHEEP MARSH LANE

Poplar Farm

The Fitties

Sewage Works

INGS LA

MABLETHORPE ROAD

NORTH WAY

NORTH LANE

Keyholme Farm

LN11

Rookery Farm

A1031

Marshchapel

KEYHOLME LANE

Sea Bank Farm

Seven Towns North Eau

HALLGARTH 1
COWPER CL 2
SWABY CL 3

PO

DUCKTHORPE LANE

LITTLE LA

PH

Windmill

Evergreen Farm

Sea Farm

Marshchapel Prim Sch

HARPHAM RD

Willow Tree House

Holme Farm

Louth Canal

LOW ROAD

CHURCH LANE

West End Farm

Eskham Farm

New Farm

COAL SHORE LANE

Ivy House

Mast

Eskham

SEA DYKE WAY

LN11

WEST END LANE

LOW GATE

Beacon Hill

FIREBEACON LA

A1031

IVY LA

GRAINS GATE

LAND DIKE

Fulstow Bridge

Beacon Hill Farm

49

C2
1 SEA DYKE WY
2 VICTORIA CL
3 PLUM TREE DR
4 MILL LA
5 MILL CL

50

38 ➤

A   B   C   D   E   F

8
05
7
04
6
03
5
02
4
01
3
00
2
99
1
98

34   35   36   37   38   39

Scale: 1¾ inches to 1 mile

0   ¼   ½ mile

0   250m 500m 750m 1 km

A   B   C   D   E   F

8

05

7

04

6

03

North Sea

DN36

5

02

4

01

Somercotes
Haven

3

DANGER
AREA

Seven Towns South Eau

Donna Nook
National Nature Reserve

00

Stonebridge

P ⨉

Porter's
Sluice

Donna
Nook

2

Pye's
Farm

LN11

Laramie

Sprakes
Farm

COASTGUARD RD

Wells
Farm

MARSH LANE

99

Porter's
Marsh

Marsh
Grange

Fivehundred
Acres

1

Sewage
Works

Poplar
Farm

ARK RD

Holmes
Farm

98

HOLMES LA

40   A   41   B   42   C   43   D   44   E   45   F   46

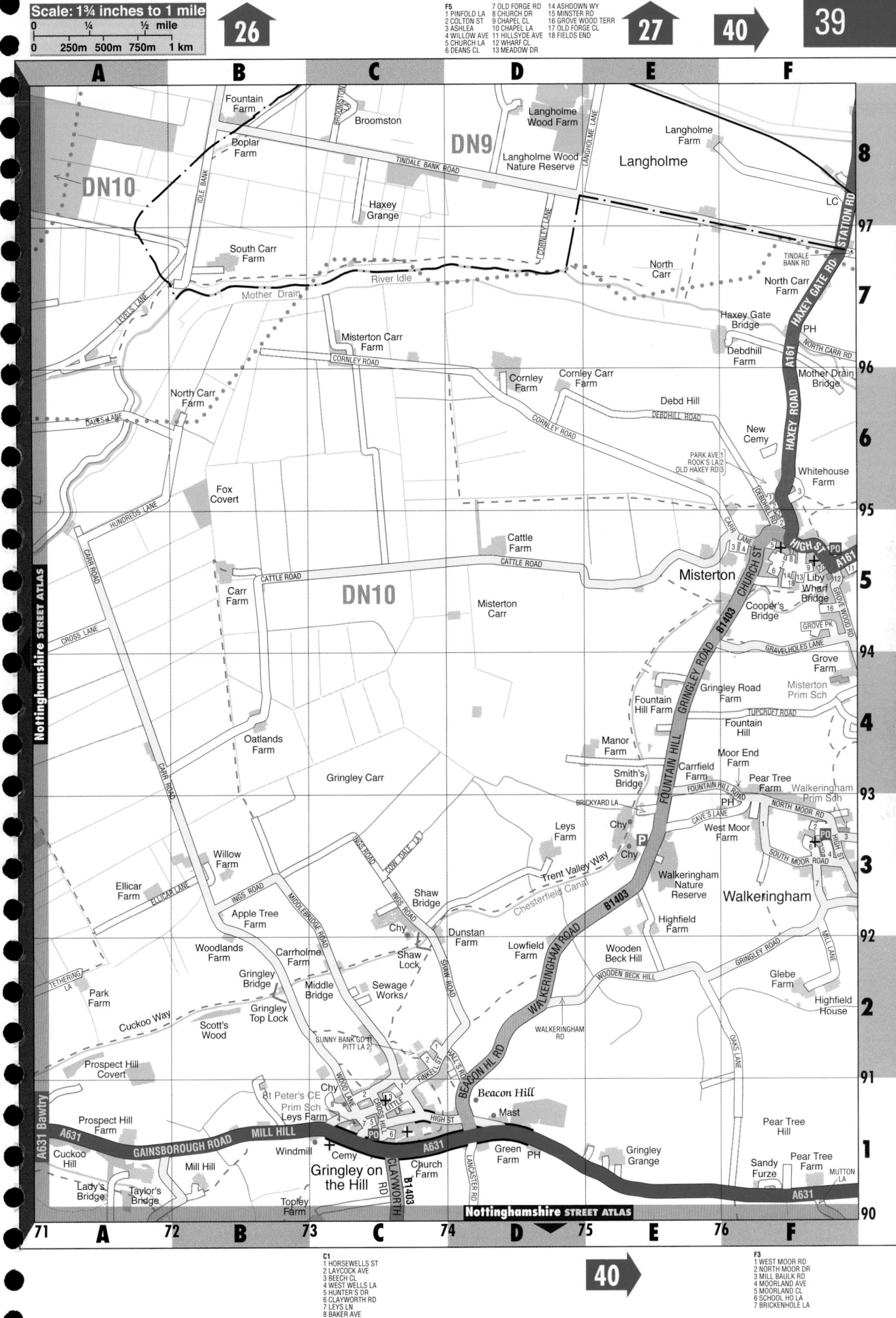
Scale: 1¾ inches to 1 mile
0 ¼ ½ mile
0 250m 500m 750m 1 km
26
F5
1 PINFOLD LA
2 COLTON ST
3 ASHLEA
4 WILLOW AVE
5 CHURCH LA
6 DEANS CL
7 OLD FORGE RD
8 CHURCH DR
9 CHAPEL CL
10 CHAPEL LA
11 HILLSYDE AVE
12 WHARF CL
13 MEADOW DR
14 ASHDOWN WY
15 MINSTER RD
16 GROVE WOOD TERR
17 OLD FORGE CL
18 FIELDS END
27
40
39
A
B
C
D
E
F
Fountain Farm
Broomston
BROOMSTON
Langholme Wood Farm
LANGHOLME LANE
Langholme Farm
Langholme
DN9
Poplar Farm
TINDALE BANK ROAD
Langholme Wood Nature Reserve
DN10
IDLE BANK
Haxey Grange
CORNLEY LANE
LC
STATION RD
South Carr Farm
North Carr
TINDALE BANK RD
River Idle
Mother Drain
North Carr Farm
LEVELS LANE
Haxey Gate Bridge
HAXEY GATE RD
PH
Misterton Carr Farm
NORTH CARR RD
CORNLEY ROAD
Debdhill Farm
A161
Cornley Farm
Cornley Carr Farm
Mother Drain Bridge
North Carr Farm
Debd Hill
DEBDHILL ROAD
HAXEY ROAD
DALES LANE
CORNLEY ROAD
New Cemy
PARK AVE 1
ROOK'S LA 2
OLD HAXEY RD 3
Whitehouse Farm
Fox Covert
DEBDHILL RD
HUNDREDS LANE
CARR LANE
Cattle Farm
HIGH ST
PO
CARR ROAD
CATTLE ROAD
CATTLE ROAD
Misterton
CHURCH ST
Carr Farm
DN10
Liby
Wharf Bridge
Misterton Carr
Cooper's Bridge
GROVE WOOD RD
B1403
GROVE PK
CROSS LANE
GRAVELHOLES LANE
GRINGLEY ROAD
Grove Farm
Fountain Hill Farm
Gringley Road Farm
Misterton Prim Sch
TUPCROFT ROAD
Fountain Hill
Oatlands Farm
Manor Farm
Moor End Farm
Carrfield Farm
Smith's Bridge
Pear Tree Farm
FOUNTAIN HILL
Gringley Carr
CARR ROAD
FOUNTAIN HILL ROAD
Walkeringham Prim Sch
BRICKYARD LA
PH
NORTH MOOR RD
CAVE'S LANE
Leys Farm
Chy
West Moor Farm
INGS ROAD
COW DALE LA
P
Chy
PO
HIGH ST
Willow Farm
Trent Valley Way
SOUTH MOOR ROAD
Walkeringham Nature Reserve
Ellicar Farm
ELLICAR LANE
INGS ROAD
Shaw Bridge
Chesterfield Canal
Walkeringham
MIDDLEBRIDGE ROAD
Apple Tree Farm
B1403
Highfield Farm
INGS ROAD
Chy
Dunstan Farm
WALKERINGHAM ROAD
MILL LANE
Woodlands Farm
Carrholme Farm
Shaw Lock
Lowfield Farm
Wooden Beck Hill
GRINGLEY ROAD
SHAW ROAD
WOODEN BECK HILL
Glebe Farm
TETHERING LA
Gringley Bridge
Park Farm
Middle Bridge
Sewage Works
Highfield House
Gringley Top Lock
WALKERINGHAM RD
Cuckoo Way
Scott's Wood
SUNNY BANK GD 1
PITT LA 2
OAKS LANE
HALL'S RD
BEACON HL RD
Prospect Hill Covert
FINKELL ST
WOOD LANE
Beacon Hill
Chy
St Peter's CE Prim Sch
LITTLE LA
CROSS HILL
Mast
Pear Tree Hill
Leys Farm
HIGH ST
A631 Bawtry
Prospect Hill Farm
A631
MILL HILL
PO
GAINSBOROUGH ROAD
A631
Green Farm
PH
Gringley Grange
Windmill
Cemy
Church Farm
LANCASTER RD
Sandy Furze
Pear Tree Farm
MUTTON LA
Cuckoo Hill
Mill Hill
Gringley on the Hill
CLAYWORTH RD
B1403
A631
Lady's Bridge
Taylor's Bridge
Topley Farm
Nottinghamshire STREET ATLAS
8
97
7
96
6
95
5
94
4
93
3
92
2
91
1
90
71
72
73
74
75
76
C1
1 HORSEWELLS ST
2 LAYCOCK AVE
3 BEECH CL
4 WEST WELLS LA
5 HUNTER'S DR
6 CLAYWORTH RD
7 LEYS LN
8 BAKER AVE
40
F3
1 WEST MOOR RD
2 NORTH MOOR DR
3 MILL BAULK RD
4 MOORLAND AVE
5 MOORLAND CL
6 SCHOOL HO LA
7 BRICKENHOLE LA

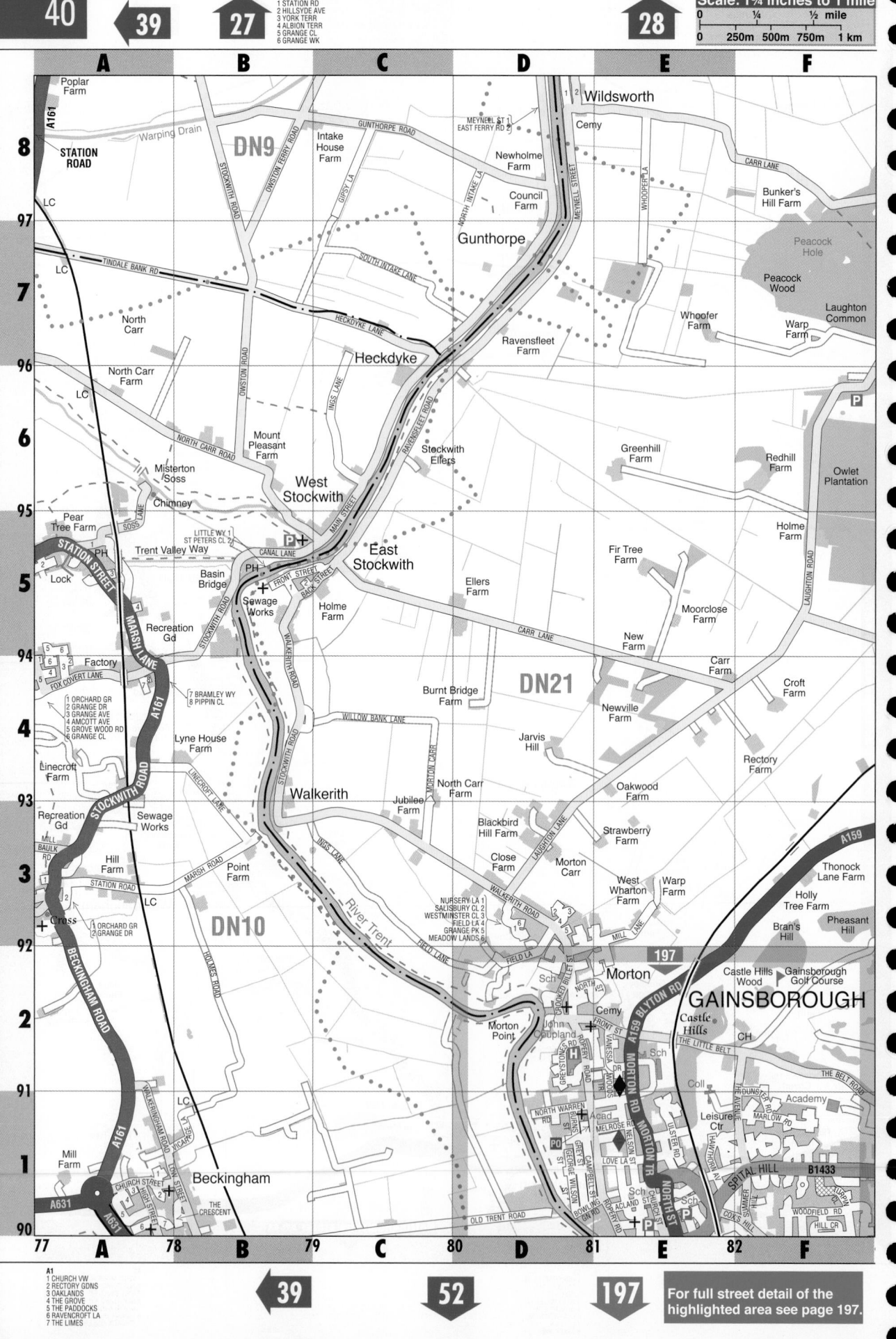

40

39

27

A5
1 STATION RD
2 HILLSYDE AVE
3 YORK TERR
4 ALBION TERR
5 GRANGE CL
6 GRANGE WK

28

Scale: 1¾ inches to 1 mile
0   ¼   ½ mile
0   250m 500m 750m 1 km

A   B   C   D   E   F

8

97

7

96

6

95

5

94

4

93

3

92

2

91

1

90

Poplar
Farm

A161

STATION
ROAD

LC

LC

TINDALE BANK RD

North
Carr

LC

North Carr
Farm

DN9

STOCKWITH ROAD

OWSTON FERRY ROAD

GUNTHORPE ROAD

GIPSY LA

Intake
House
Farm

SOUTH INTAKE LANE

HECKOYKE LANE

Heckdyke

INGS LANE

RAVENSFLEET ROAD

MEYNELL ST 1
EAST FERRY RD 2

Wildsworth

Cemy

MEYNELL STREET

WHOOPER LA

CARR LANE

Newholme
Farm

Council
Farm

Gunthorpe

Ravensfleet
Farm

Bunker's
Hill Farm

Peacock
Hole

Peacock
Wood

P

Whoofer
Farm

Laughton
Common

Warp
Farm

North Carr
Road

Misterton
Soss

Chimney

SOSS LANE

Mount
Pleasant
Farm

West
Stockwith

MAIN STREET

Stockwith
Ellers

Greenhill
Farm

Redhill
Farm

Owlet
Plantation

LC

Pear
Tree Farm

STATION STREET

PH

Lock

MARSH LANE

Recreation
Gd

1 ORCHARD GR
2 GRANGE DR
3 GRANGE AVE
4 AMCOTT AVE
5 GROVE WOOD RD
6 GRANGE CL

Factory

FOX COVERT LANE

A161

LITTLE WY 1
ST PETERS CL 2

Trent Valley Way

P

CANAL LANE

Basin
Bridge

PH

FRONT STREET

BACK STREET

Sewage
Works

East
Stockwith

Holme
Farm

Ellers
Farm

CARR LANE

Fir Tree
Farm

Moorclose
Farm

New
Farm

Holme
Farm

LAUGHTON ROAD

Carr
Farm

Croft
Farm

Linecroft
Farm

Lyne House
Farm

7 BRAMLEY WY
8 PIPPIN CL

LINECROFT LANE

WALKERITH ROAD

WILLOW BANK LANE

Burnt Bridge
Farm

MORTON CARR

DN21

Newville
Farm

Oakwood
Farm

Rectory
Farm

Recreation
Gd

STOCKWITH ROAD

Sewage
Works

MARSH ROAD

Point
Farm

Hill
Farm

STATION ROAD

LC

MILL
BAULK
RD

INGS LANE

Walkerith

Jubilee
Farm

North Carr
Farm

River Trent

WALKERITH ROAD

LAUGHTON LANE

Jarvis
Hill

Blackbird
Hill Farm

Close
Farm

Morton
Carr

Strawberry
Farm

West
Wharton
Farm

Warp
Farm

A159

Thonock
Lane Farm

Holly
Tree Farm

Pheasant
Hill

Bran's
Hill

BECKINGHAM ROAD

A161

HOLMES ROAD

DN10

Cross

1 ORCHARD GR
2 GRANGE DR

FIELD LANE

NURSERY LA 1
SALISBURY CL 2
WESTMINSTER CL 3
FIELD LA 4
GRANGE PK 5
MEADOW LANDS 6

FIELD LA

197

Morton

Castle Hills
Wood

Gainsborough
Golf Course

GAINSBOROUGH

Mill
Farm

WALKERINGHAM ROAD

VICAR LN

LON STREET

LC

Beckingham

THE
CRESCENT

A631

A631

CHURCH STREET
HIGH STREET

OLD TRENT ROAD

Morton
Point

CROOKED BILLET RD

John
Coupland

Cemy

NORTH ST

FRONT ST

JEFFERY ROAD

A159 BLYTON RD

MORTON RD

Castle
Hills

CH

THE LITTLE BELT

THE BELT ROAD

Coll

Academy

SPITAL HILL

B1433

Leisure
Ctr

MARLOW RD

HAWTHORN

SUMMER

WOODFIELD RD

HILL CR

H

Acad

PO

NORTH WARREN
RD

BURNS

GREY ST

GEORGE ST

ST

BOWLING GN RD

LOVE LA

MELROSE
RD

NELSON ST

CAROLGATE

RUFFORD RD

ACLAND
ST

ULSTER ST

NORTH ST

CHURCH ST

Sch

Sch

Sch

P

COX'S HILL

A1
1 CHURCH VW
2 RECTORY GDNS
3 OAKLANDS
4 THE GROVE
5 THE PADDOCKS
6 RAVENCROFT LA
7 THE LIMES

77   78   79   80   81   82

39

52

197

For full street detail of the
highlighted area see page 197.

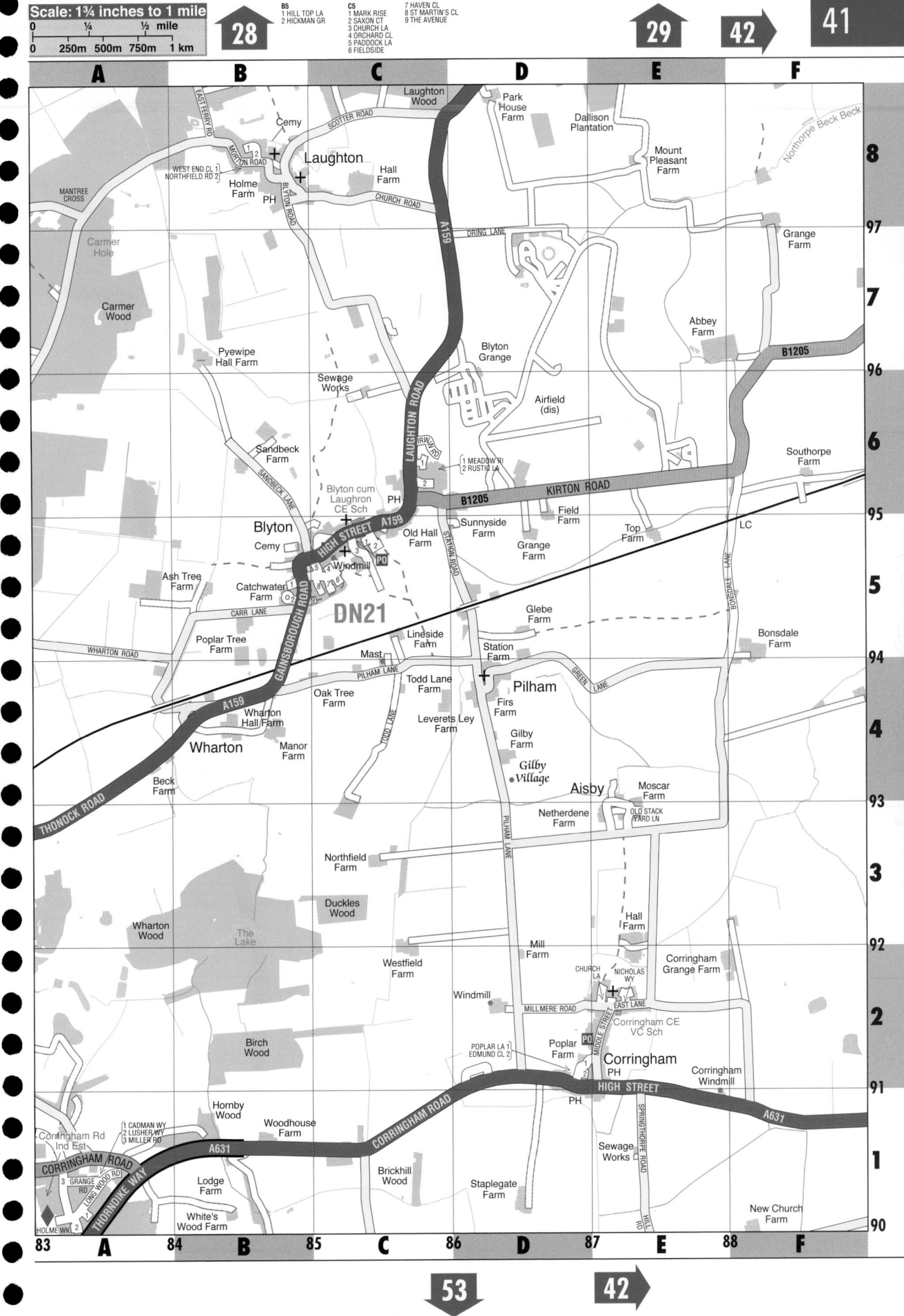
Scale: 1¾ inches to 1 mile
0 ¼ ½ mile
0 250m 500m 750m 1 km
28
B5
1 HILL TOP LA
2 HICKMAN GR
C5
1 MARK RISE
2 SAXON CT
3 CHURCH LA
4 ORCHARD CL
5 PADDOCK LA
6 FIELDSIDE
7 HAVEN CL
8 ST MARTIN'S CL
9 THE AVENUE
29
42
A
B
C
D
E
F
Laughton Wood
Park House Farm
Dallison Plantation
Mount Pleasant Farm
Northorpe Beck Beck
EAST FERRY RD
Cemy
SCOTTER ROAD
Laughton
MORTON ROAD
WEST END CL 1
NORTHFIELD RD 2
Holme Farm
PH
BLYTON ROAD
Hall Farm
CHURCH ROAD
MANTREE CROSS
A159
DRING LANE
Grange Farm
Carmer Hole
Carmer Wood
Abbey Farm
Pyewipe Hall Farm
Blyton Grange
B1205
Sewage Works
LAUGHTON ROAD
Airfield (dis)
IRWIN RD
Sandbeck Farm
1 MEADOW RI
2 RUSTIC LA
Southorpe Farm
SANDBECK LANE
Blyton cum Laughton CE Sch
PH
B1205
KIRTON ROAD
Field Farm
Blyton
HIGH STREET
A159
Sunnyside Farm
Old Hall Farm
STATION ROAD
Top Farm
LC
Cemy
Windmill
PO
Grange Farm
Ash Tree Farm
Catchwater Farm
GAINSBOROUGH ROAD
DN21
Glebe Farm
BONSDALE LANE
CARR LANE
Lineside Farm
Bonsdale Farm
Poplar Tree Farm
WHARTON ROAD
Mast
Station Farm
PILHAM LANE
Todd Lane Farm
GREEN LANE
Pilham
Oak Tree Farm
A159
Wharton Hall Farm
Firs Farm
Leverets Ley Farm
TODD LANE
Wharton
Manor Farm
Gilby Farm
Gilby Village
Beck Farm
Aisby
Moscar Farm
THONOCK ROAD
Netherdene Farm
OLD STACK YARD LN
PILHAM LANE
Northfield Farm
Duckles Wood
Hall Farm
Wharton Wood
The Lake
Mill Farm
Corringham Grange Farm
Westfield Farm
CHURCH LA
NICHOLAS WY
Windmill
MILL MERE ROAD
EAST LANE
Corringham CE VC Sch
MIDDLE STREET
Birch Wood
PO
Poplar Farm
POPLAR LA 1
EDMUND CL 2
Corringham
PH
Corringham Windmill
HIGH STREET
PH
A631
Hornby Wood
1 CADMAN WY
2 LUSHER WY
3 MILLER RD
Woodhouse Farm
CORRINGHAM ROAD
Corringham Rd Ind Est
CORRINGHAM ROAD
A631
Sewage Works
SPRINGTHORPE ROAD
GRANGE RD
LONG WOOD RD
THORNDIKE WAY
Lodge Farm
Brickhill Wood
Staplegate Farm
White's Wood Farm
HOLME WK
New Church Farm
HILL RD
8
97
7
96
6
95
5
94
4
93
3
92
2
91
1
90
83
84
85
86
87
88
53
42

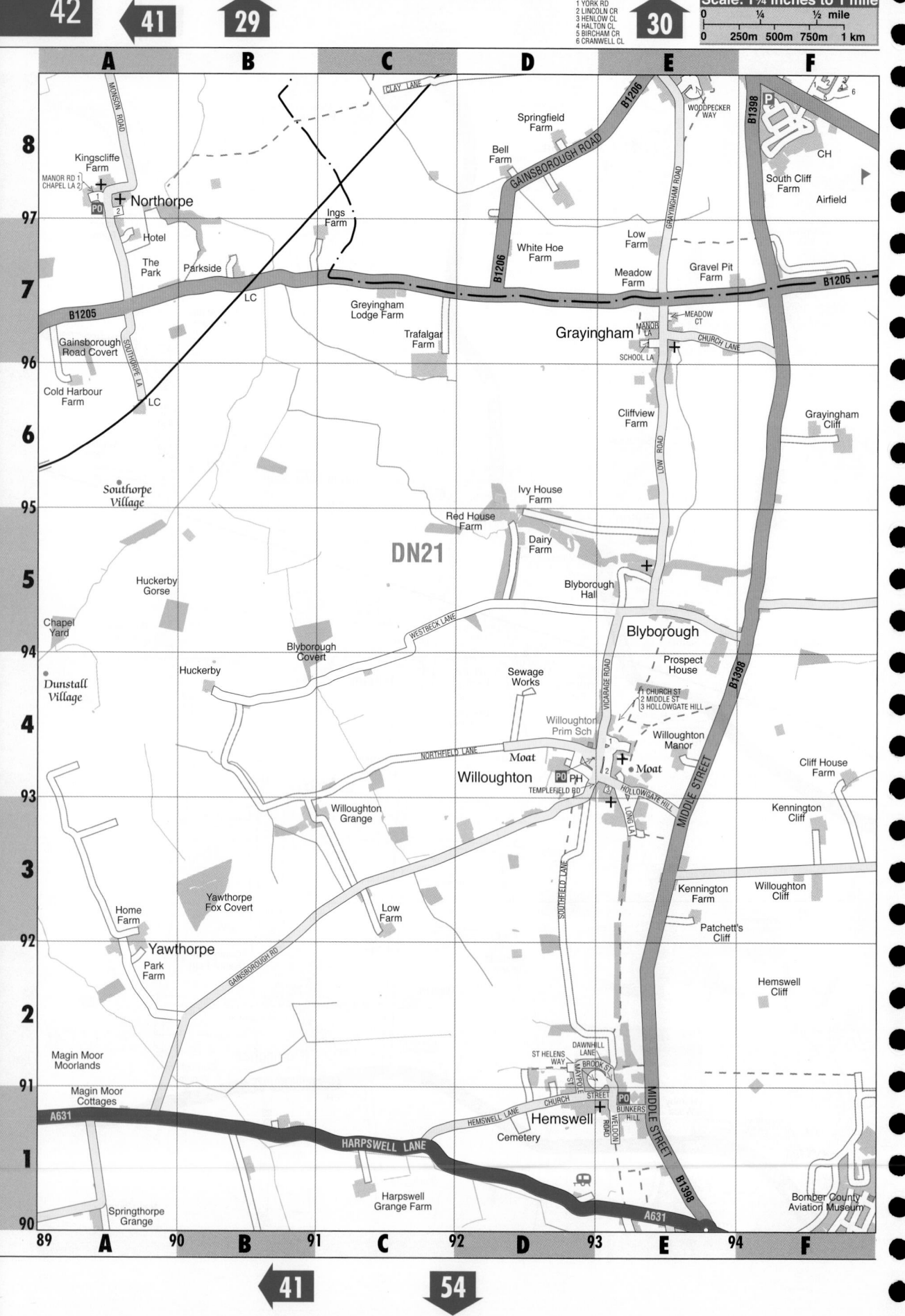

F8
1 YORK RD
2 LINCOLN CR
3 HENLOW CL
4 HALTON CL
5 BIRCHAM CR
6 CRANWELL CL

Scale: 1¾ inches to 1 mile
0   ¼   ½   mile
0   250m   500m   750m   1 km

MONSON ROAD

A B C D E F

8

Kingscliffe Farm
MANOR RD 1
CHAPEL LA 2
PO
Northorpe
Hotel

CLAY LANE

Springfield Farm
Bell Farm

GAINSBOROUGH ROAD
B1206
WOODPECKER WAY

CH

South Cliff Farm
Airfield

B1398

P

97

The Park
Parkside

Ings Farm

White Hoe Farm

Low Farm
Meadow Farm

Gravel Pit Farm

B1205

7

B1205
SOUTHORPE LA
LC

Greyingham Lodge Farm

Trafalgar Farm

Grayingham
MANOR LA
SCHOOL LA

LOW ROAD
GRAYINGHAM ROAD

MEADOW CT
CHURCH LANE

96

Gainsborough Road Covert

Cold Harbour Farm
LC

Cliffview Farm

Grayingham Cliff

6

95

Southorpe Village

Huckerby Gorse

Ivy House Farm

Red House Farm

Dairy Farm

DN21

Blyborough Hall

5

Chapel Yard

Huckerby

Blyborough Covert

Blyborough
1 CHURCH ST
2 MIDDLE ST
3 HOLLOWGATE HILL

Prospect House

B1398

94

Dunstall Village

Sewage Works

Willoughton Prim Sch

Willoughton Manor

Cliff House Farm

4

NORTHFIELD LANE
Moat
Willoughton
PO PH
TEMPLEFIELD RD

VICARAGE ROAD

Moat

HOLLOWGATE HILL
LONG LA
MIDDLE STREET

Kennington Cliff

93

Willoughton Grange

Low Farm

SOUTHFIELD LANE

Kennington Farm

Willoughton Cliff

3

Home Farm

Yawthorpe Fox Covert

Patchett's Cliff

92

Yawthorpe
Park Farm

GAINSBOROUGH RD

Hemswell Cliff

2

Magin Moor Moorlands

ST HELENS WAY
DAWNHILL LANE
MAYPOLE ST
BROOK ST

91

Magin Moor Cottages

A631

HEMSWELL LANE
CHURCH STREET
WELDON RD
Hemswell
PO
BUNKERS HILL

MIDDLE STREET

HARPSWELL LANE

Cemetery

B1398

1

Springthorpe Grange

Harpswell Grange Farm

A631

Bomber County Aviation Museum

90

89 A 90 B 91 C 92 D 93 E 94 F

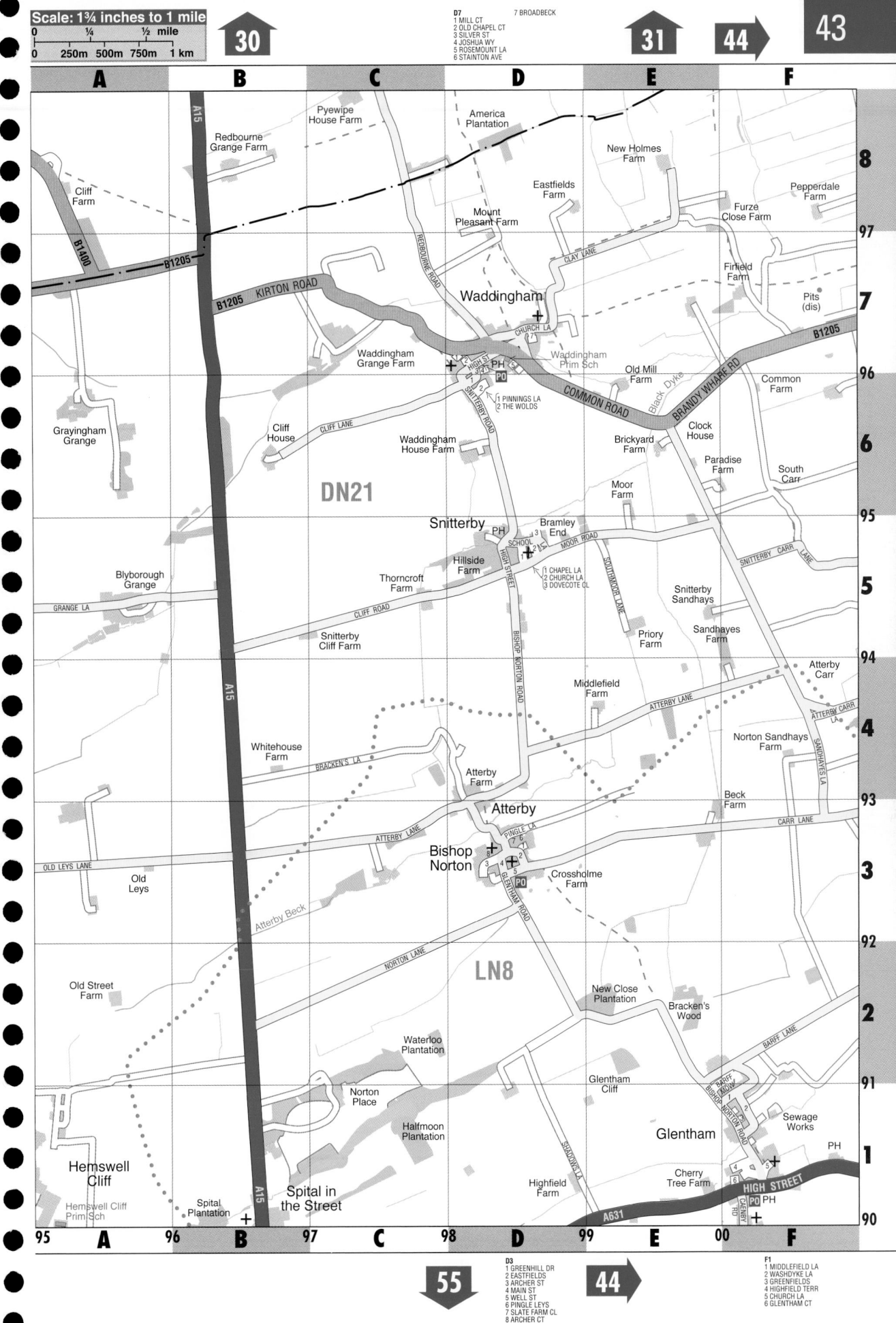

D7
1 MILL CT
2 OLD CHAPEL CT
3 SILVER ST
4 JOSHUA WY
5 ROSEMOUNT LA
6 STAINTON AVE

7 BROADBECK

Cliff Farm

B1400

Redbourne Grange Farm

Pyewipe House Farm

America Plantation

New Holmes Farm

Eastfields Farm

Pepperdale Farm

Mount Pleasant Farm

Furze Close Farm

Firfield Farm

B1205 KIRTON ROAD

REDBOURNE ROAD

CLAY LANE

Waddingham

Pits (dis)

B1205

CHURCH LA

Waddingham Prim Sch

Old Mill Farm

Common Farm

Waddingham Grange Farm

HIGH ST
PH
PO

1 PINNINGS LA
2 THE WOLDS

COMMON ROAD

Black Dyke

BRANDY WHARF RD

Grayingham Grange

Cliff House

CLIFF LANE

Waddingham House Farm

Brickyard Farm

Clock House

Paradise Farm

South Carr

DN21

SNITTERBY ROAD

Moor Farm

Snitterby

PH
SCHOOL

Bramley End

1 CHAPEL LA
2 CHURCH LA
3 DOVECOTE CL

MOOR ROAD

SNITTERBY CARR LANE

Blyborough Grange

Thorncroft Farm

Hillside Farm

HIGH STREET

SOUTHMOOR LANE

Snitterby Sandhays

GRANGE LA

CLIFF ROAD

Sandhayes Farm

Snitterby Cliff Farm

BISHOP NORTON ROAD

Priory Farm

Atterby Carr

ATTERBY CARR LA

Whitehouse Farm

BRACKEN'S LA

Middlefield Farm

ATTERBY LANE

Norton Sandhays Farm

SANDHAYES LA

Atterby Farm

Beck Farm

Atterby

CARR LANE

OLD LEYS LANE

ATTERBY LANE

PINGLE LA

Bishop Norton

GLENTHAM ROAD

Crossholme Farm

Old Leys

Atterby Beck

PO

LN8

NORTON LANE

Old Street Farm

New Close Plantation

Bracken's Wood

BARFF LANE

Waterloo Plantation

Glentham Cliff

BARFF MDW

BISHOP NORTON ROAD

Norton Place

Halfmoon Plantation

Sewage Works

CHERRY RD

PH

Glentham

SHADDOCK LA

Hemswell Cliff

A15

Spital Plantation

Spital in the Street

Highfield Farm

Cherry Tree Farm

HIGH STREET

PO PH

Hemswell Cliff Prim Sch

A631

D3
1 GREENHILL DR
2 EASTFIELDS
3 ARCHER ST
4 MAIN ST
5 WELL ST
6 PINGLE LEYS
7 SLATE FARM CL
8 ARCHER CT

F1
1 MIDDLEFIELD LA
2 WASHDYKE LA
3 GREENFIELDS
4 HIGHFIELD TERR
5 CHURCH LA
6 GLENTHAM CT

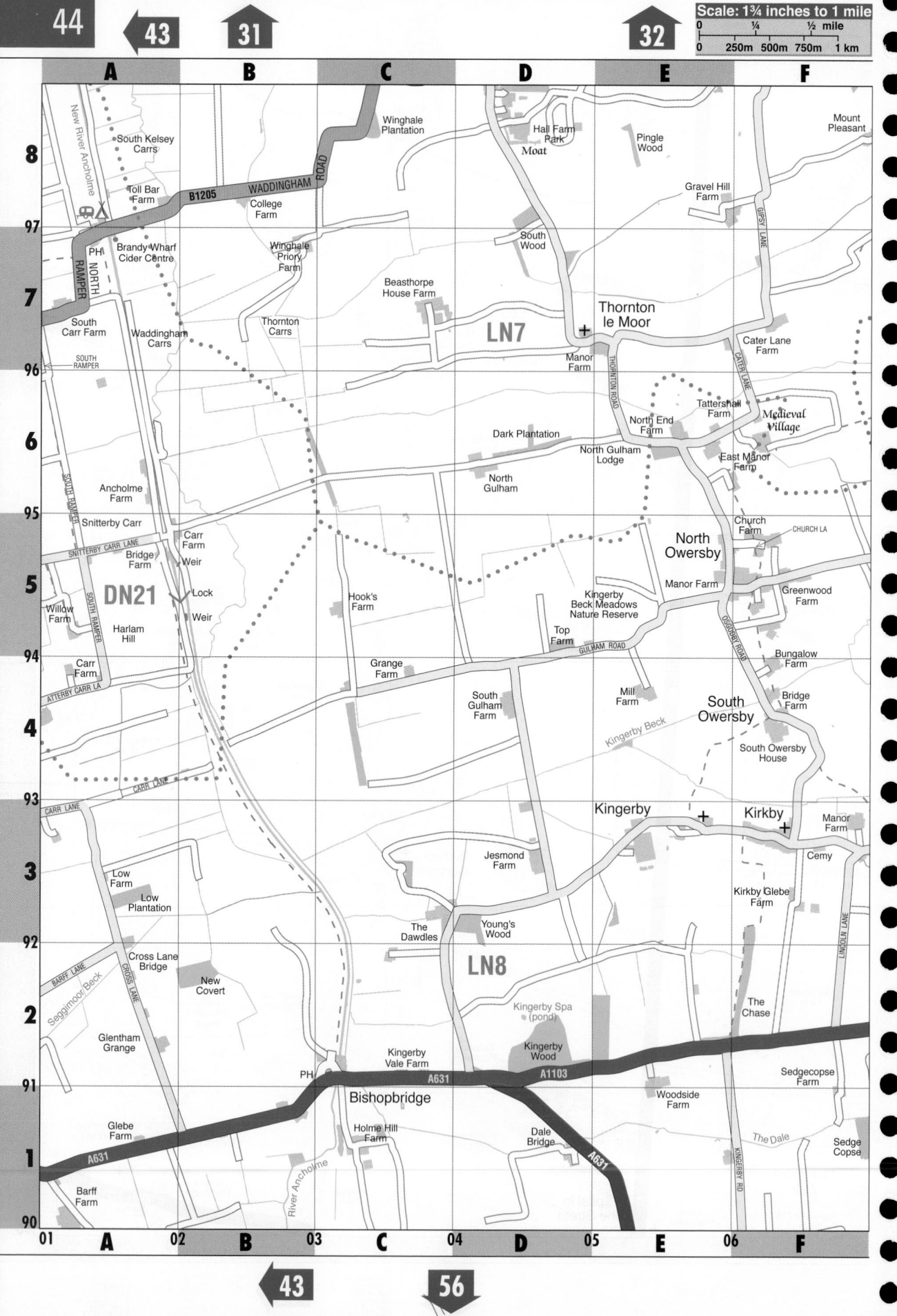

43
31
32
Scale: 1¾ inches to 1 mile
0 ¼ ½ mile
0 250m 500m 750m 1 km
A B C D E F
8 97 7 96 6 95 5 94 4 93 3 92 2 91 1 90
01 02 03 04 05 06
New River Ancholme
South Kelsey Carrs
Toll Bar Farm
B1205 WADDINGHAM ROAD
College Farm
Winghale Plantation
Hall Farm Park
Moat
Pingle Wood
Mount Pleasant
Gravel Hill Farm
GIPSY LANE
South Wood
PH
Brandy Wharf Cider Centre
NORTH RAMPER
Winghale Priory Farm
Beasthorpe House Farm
Thornton le Moor
South Carr Farm
Waddingham Carrs
Thornton Carrs
LN7
Manor Farm
Cater Lane Farm
SOUTH RAMPER
THORNTON ROAD
CATER LANE
Tattershall Farm
Medieval Village
North End Farm
Dark Plantation
North Gulham Lodge
East Manor Farm
North Gulham
Ancholme Farm
SOUTH RAMPER
Snitterby Carr
Carr Farm
Church Farm
CHURCH LA
North Owersby
SNITTERBY CARR LANE
Bridge Farm
Weir
Lock
Weir
DN21
Hook's Farm
Kingerby Beck Meadows Nature Reserve
Manor Farm
Greenwood Farm
Willow Farm
Harlam Hill
SOUTH RAMPER
Top Farm
GULHAM ROAD
OSGODBY ROAD
Carr Farm
ATTERBY CARR LA
Grange Farm
Bungalow Farm
South Gulham Farm
Mill Farm
Bridge Farm
South Owersby
Kingerby Beck
South Owersby House
CARR LANE
CARR LANE
Kingerby
Kirkby
Manor Farm
Jesmond Farm
Cemy
Low Farm
Low Plantation
Kirkby Glebe Farm
The Dawdles
Young's Wood
LN8
Cross Lane Bridge
BARFF LANE
CROSS LANE
Seggimoor Beck
New Covert
LINCOLN LANE
Kingerby Spa (pond)
The Chase
Glentham Grange
Kingerby Wood
Kingerby Vale Farm
PH
A631
A1103
Sedgecopse Farm
Bishopbridge
Woodside Farm
Glebe Farm
Holme Hill Farm
Dale Bridge
The Dale
A631
A631
Sedge Copse
River Ancholme
KINGERBY RD
Barff Farm
43
56

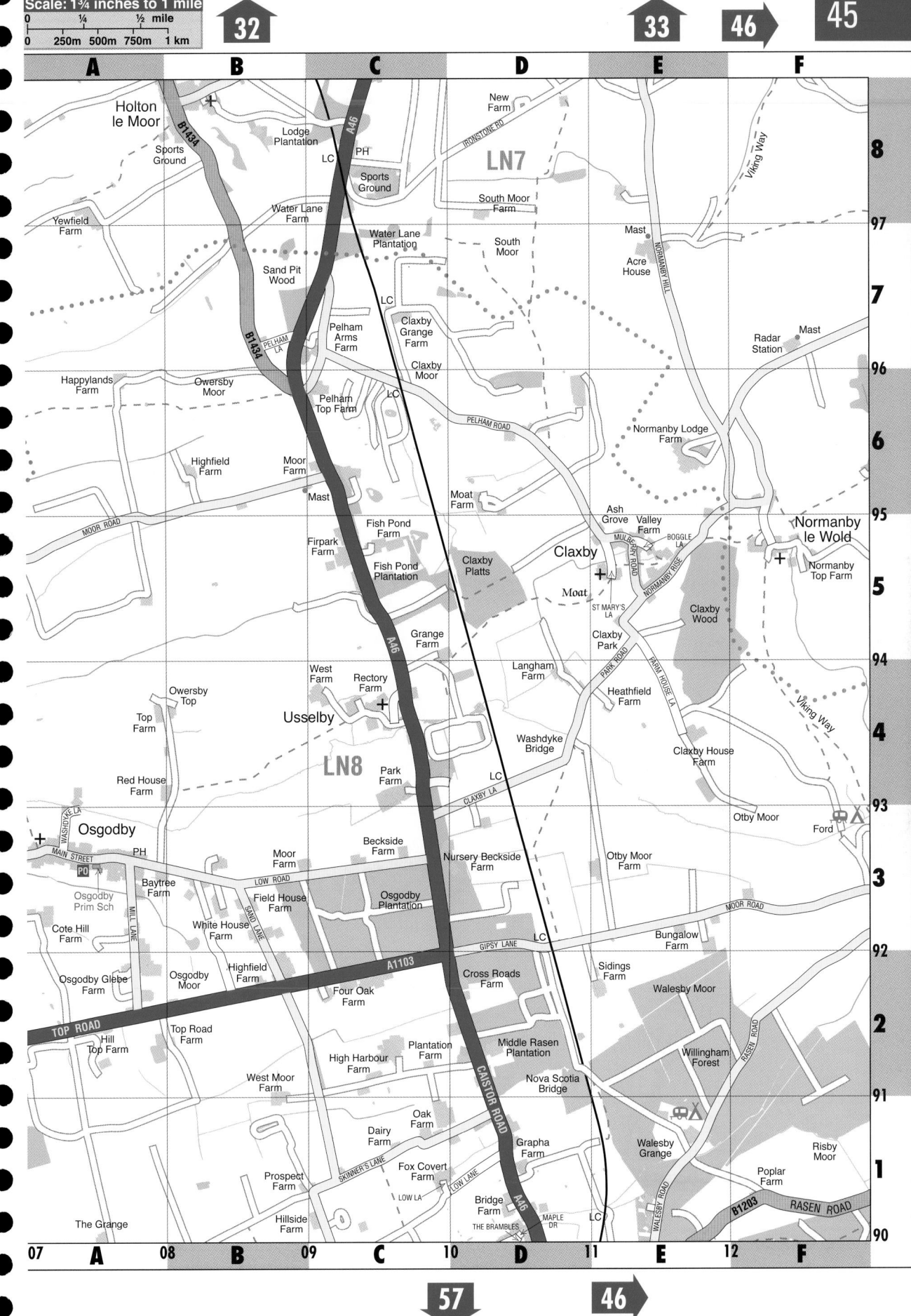
A
B
C
D
E
F
Holton le Moor
B1434
Sports Ground
Lodge Plantation
A46
LC
PH
Sports Ground
IRONSTONE RD
New Farm
LN7
South Moor Farm
Viking Way
8
97
Yewfield Farm
Water Lane Farm
Water Lane Plantation
South Moor
Mast
Acre House
NORMANBY HILL
Sand Pit Wood
7
LC
Pelham Arms Farm
PELHAM LA
Claxby Grange Farm
Claxby Moor
Radar Station
Mast
Happylands Farm
Owersby Moor
Pelham Top Farm
LC
PELHAM ROAD
96
Normanby Lodge Farm
6
Highfield Farm
Moor Farm
Mast
Moat Farm
MOOR ROAD
Ash Grove
Valley Farm
95
Normanby le Wold
Firpark Farm
Fish Pond Farm
Fish Pond Plantation
Claxby Platts
Claxby
MULBERRY ROAD
BOGGLE LA
NORMANBY RISE
Normanby Top Farm
Moat
ST MARY'S LA
Claxby Wood
5
Grange Farm
A46
Claxby Park
PARK ROAD
FARM HOUSE LA
94
West Farm
Rectory Farm
Langham Farm
Heathfield Farm
Owersby Top
Top Farm
Usselby
Viking Way
Washdyke Bridge
Claxby House Farm
4
LN8
Park Farm
LC
CLAXBY LA
Red House Farm
93
Otby Moor
Ford
Osgodby
WASHDYKE LA
MAIN STREET
PH
PO
Osgodby Prim Sch
Moor Farm
Beckside Farm
Nursery Beckside Farm
Otby Moor Farm
3
LOW ROAD
Baytree Farm
Field House Farm
Osgodby Plantation
MOOR ROAD
Cote Hill Farm
MILL LANE
White House Farm
SAND LANE
LC
GIPSY LANE
Bungalow Farm
92
Osgodby Glebe Farm
Osgodby Moor
Highfield Farm
A1103
Cross Roads Farm
Sidings Farm
Walesby Moor
Four Oak Farm
TOP ROAD
Hill Top Farm
Top Road Farm
Middle Rasen Plantation
RASEN ROAD
2
Plantation Farm
High Harbour Farm
Willingham Forest
West Moor Farm
CAISTOR ROAD
Nova Scotia Bridge
91
Oak Farm
Dairy Farm
Grapha Farm
Walesby Grange
Risby Moor
Prospect Farm
SKINNER'S LANE
Fox Covert Farm
LOW LANE
LOW LA
1
Poplar Farm
WALESBY ROAD
B1203
RASEN ROAD
Bridge Farm
A46
LC
The Grange
Hillside Farm
THE BRAMBLES
MAPLE DR
90
07
08
09
10
11
12

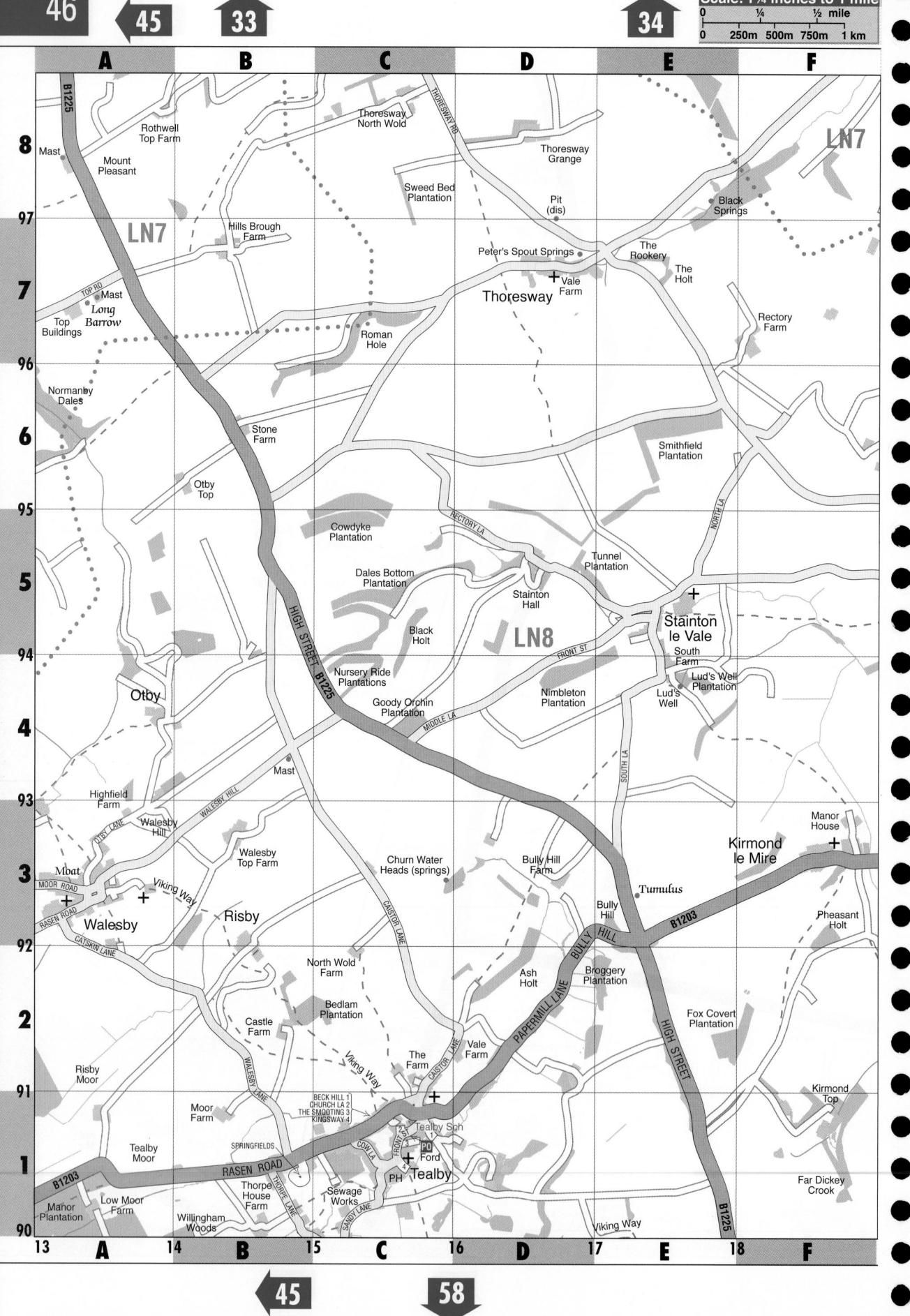

Scale: 1¾ inches to 1 mile

0   ¼   ½ mile
0 250m 500m 750m 1 km

A   B   C   D   E   F

8

B1225

Mast

LN7

Rothwell
Top Farm

Mount
Pleasant

Thoresway
North Wold

Sweed Bed
Plantation

Thoresway
Grange

Pit
(dis)

Black
Springs

LN7

97

Hills Brough
Farm

Peter's Spout Springs

The
Rookery

The
Holt

7

TOP RD

Mast

Long
Barrow

Top
Buildings

Roman
Hole

Thoresway

Vale
Farm

Rectory
Farm

96

Normanby
Dales

Stone
Farm

Smithfield
Plantation

6

Otby
Top

RECTORY LA

NORTH LA

95

Cowdyke
Plantation

Dales Bottom
Plantation

Tunnel
Plantation

5

Stainton
Hall

Stainton
le Vale

HIGH STREET

B1225

Black
Holt

LN8

South
Farm

Lud's Well
Plantation

94

Otby

Nursery Ride
Plantations

FRONT ST

Nimbleton
Plantation

Lud's
Well

Goody Orchin
Plantation

MIDDLE LA

4

Mast

93

Highfield
Farm

WALESBY HILL

Manor
House

Kirmond
le Mire

Walesby
Hill

OTBY LANE

Walesby
Top Farm

Churn Water
Heads (springs)

Bully Hill
Farm

SOUTH LA

Pheasant
Holt

3

Moat

Viking Way

Risby

Tumulus

Bully
Hill

B1203

MOOR ROAD

Walesby

CAISTOR LANE

BULLY HILL

RASEN ROAD

CATSKIN LANE

North Wold
Farm

Ash
Holt

Broggery
Plantation

Fox Covert
Plantation

2

Castle
Farm

Bedlam
Plantation

PAPERMILL LANE

HIGH STREET

Kirmond
Top

WALESBY LANE

Risby
Moor

Viking Way

The
Farm

Vale
Farm

CAISTOR LANE

Moor
Farm

BECK HILL 1
CHURCH LA 2
THE SMOOTING 3
KINGSWAY 4

1

B1203

Tealby
Moor

SPRINGFIELDS

RASEN ROAD

THORPE LANE

Tealby Sch

FRONT ST

COW LA

PO
Ford

PH

Tealby

Far Dickey
Crook

B1225

Manor
Plantation

Low Moor
Farm

Thorpe
House
Farm

Willingham
Woods

SANDY LANE

Sewage
Works

Viking Way

90

13   A   14   B   15   C   16   D   17   E   18   F

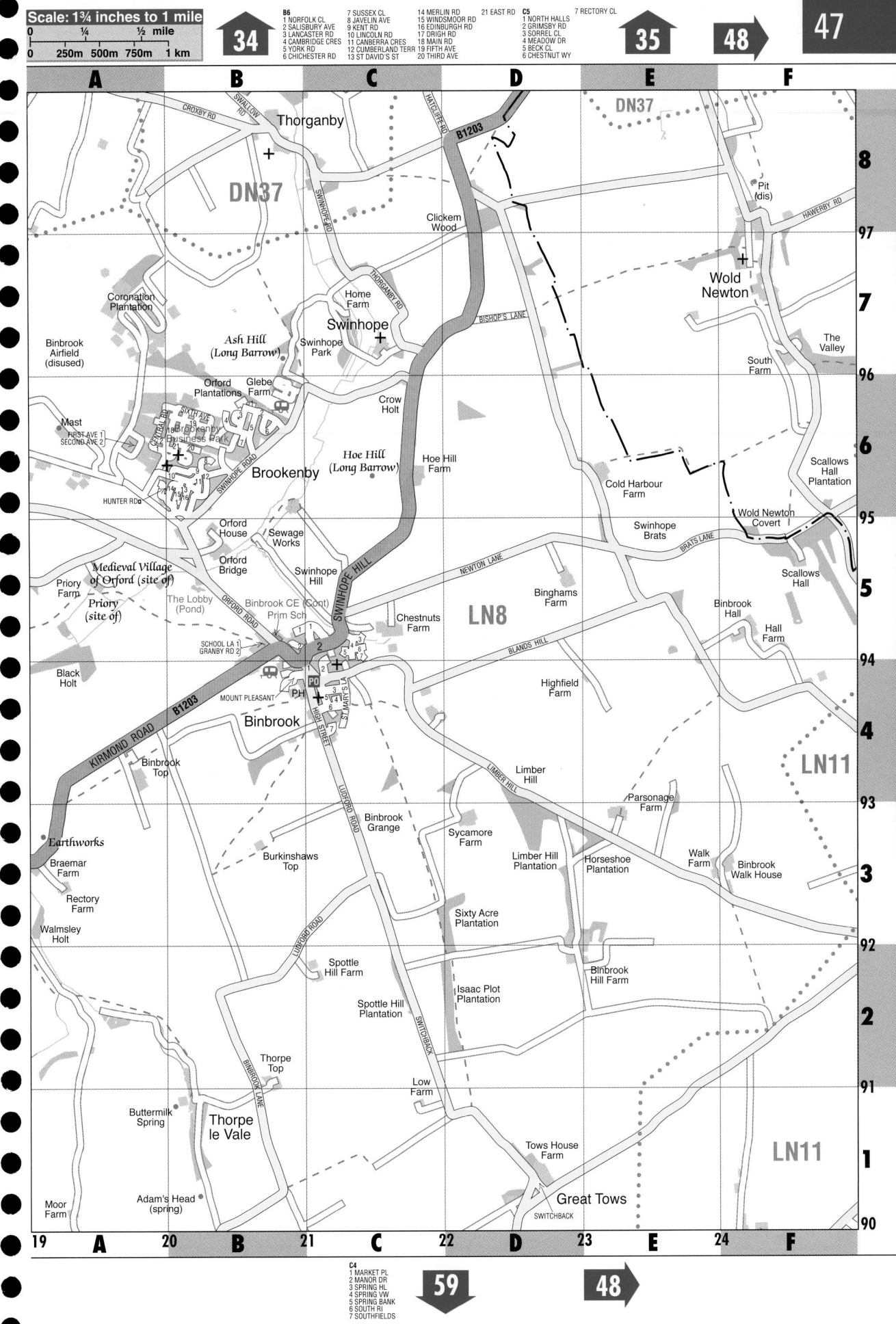

B6
1 NORFOLK CL
2 SALISBURY AVE
3 LANCASTER RD
4 CAMBRIDGE CRES
5 YORK RD
6 CHICHESTER RD

7 SUSSEX CL
8 JAVELIN AVE
9 KENT RD
10 LINCOLN RD
11 CANBERRA CRES
12 CUMBERLAND TERR
13 ST DAVID'S ST

14 MERLIN RD
15 WINDSMOOR RD
16 EDINBURGH RD
17 DRIGH RD
18 MAIN RD
19 FIFTH AVE
20 THIRD AVE

21 EAST RD

C5
1 NORTH HALLS
2 GRIMSBY RD
3 SORREL CL
4 MEADOW DR
5 BECK CL
6 CHESTNUT WY

7 RECTORY CL

DN37

DN37

Thorganby

CROXBY RD

SWALLOW RD

SWINHOPE RD

B1203

HATCLIFFE RD

Pit
(dis)

HAWERBY RD

Wold
Newton

Clickem
Wood

THORGANBY RD

BISHOP'S LANE

Home
Farm

Swinhope

South
Farm

The
Valley

Coronation
Plantation

Ash Hill
(Long Barrow)

Swinhope
Park

Binbrook
Airfield
(disused)

Orford
Plantations

Glebe
Farm

Crow
Holt

Mast

SIXTH AVE

Brookenby
Business Park

FIRST AVE 1
SECOND AVE 2

CENTRAL RD

SWINHOPE RD

Brookenby

HUNTER RD

Hoe Hill
(Long Barrow)

Hoe Hill
Farm

Scallows
Hall
Plantation

Cold Harbour
Farm

Wold Newton
Covert

Swinhope
Brats

BRATS LANE

Scallows
Hall

Orford
House

Sewage
Works

Swinhope
Hill

SWINHOPE HILL

NEWTON LANE

Binghams
Farm

Binbrook
Hall

Medieval Village
of Orford (site of)

Orford
Bridge

Priory
Farm

Priory
(site of)

The Lobby
(Pond)

ORFORD ROAD

Binbrook CE (Cont)
Prim Sch

Chestnuts
Farm

LN8

Hall
Farm

Black
Holt

SCHOOL LA 1
GRANBY RD 2

BLANDS HILL

Highfield
Farm

B1203

KIRMOND ROAD

MOUNT PLEASANT

PH

P.O.

Binbrook

MARKET LA

HIGH STREET

LN11

Binbrook
Top

LIMBER HILL

Limber
Hill

Parsonage
Farm

Walk
Farm

Binbrook
Walk House

Earthworks

Braemar
Farm

Burkinshaws
Top

LUDFORD ROAD

Binbrook
Grange

Sycamore
Farm

Limber Hill
Plantation

Horseshoe
Plantation

Rectory
Farm

Walmsley
Holt

Spottle
Hill Farm

Sixty Acre
Plantation

Binbrook
Hill Farm

BINBROOK LANE

Spottle Hill
Plantation

Isaac Plot
Plantation

SWITCHBACK

Thorpe
Top

Buttermilk
Spring

Thorpe
le Vale

Low
Farm

Tows House
Farm

LN11

Moor
Farm

Adam's Head
(spring)

Great Tows

SWITCHBACK

C4
1 MARKET PL
2 MANOR DR
3 SPRING HL
4 SPRING VW
5 SPRING BANK
6 SOUTH RI
7 SOUTHFIELDS

59

48

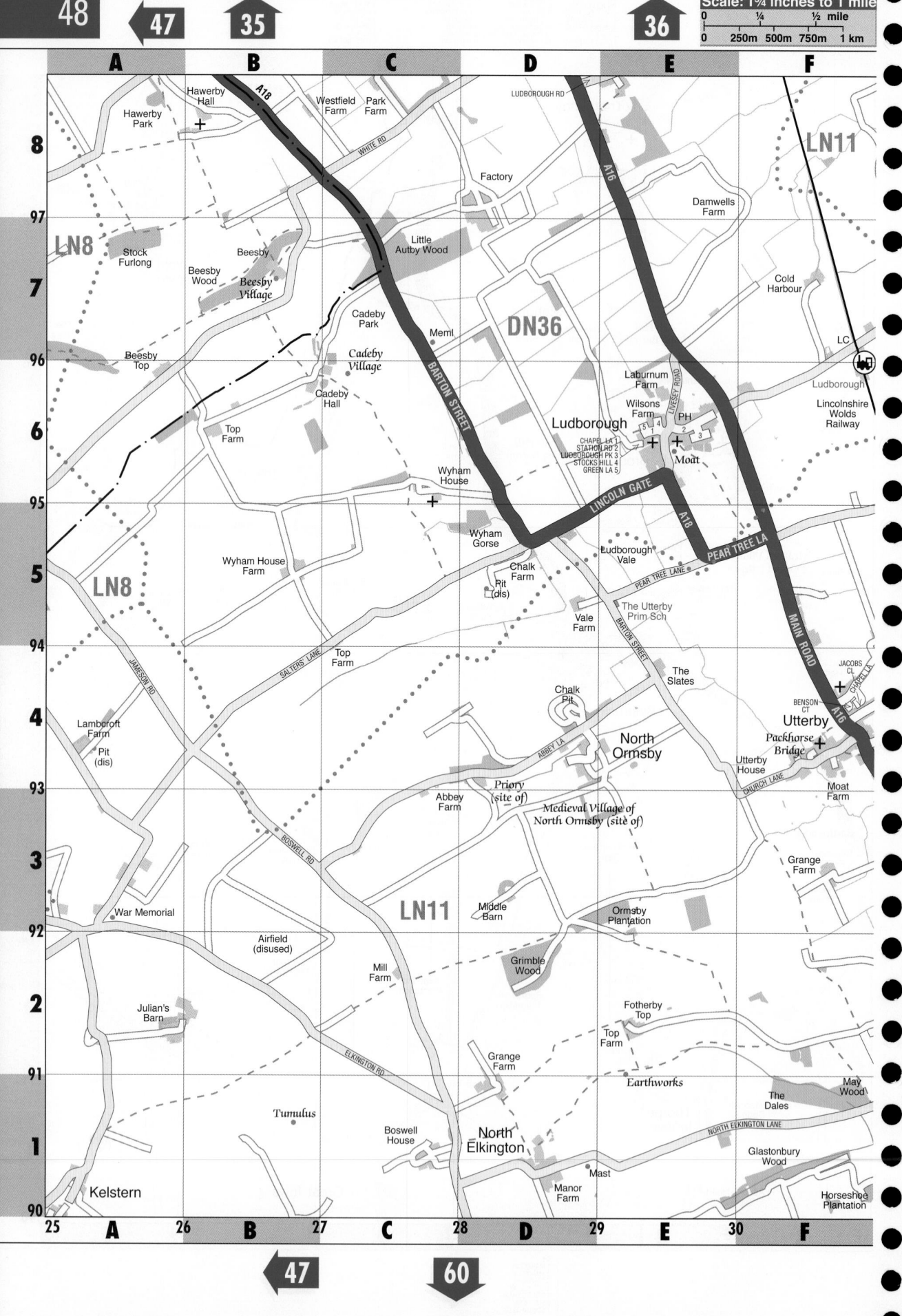

A   B   C   D   E   F

8

Hawerby
Hall
Hawerby
Park
Westfield
Farm
Park
Farm
LUDBOROUGH RD
A18
WHITE RD
A16
LN11

97

LN8
Stock
Furlong
Beesby
Little
Autby Wood
Factory
Damwells
Farm

7

Beesby
Wood
Beesby
Village
Cadeby
Park
DN36
Cold
Harbour

96

Beesby
Top
Cadeby
Village
Meml
Ludborough
LC
Ludborough
Lincolnshire
Wolds
Railway

6

Top
Farm
Cadeby
Hall
BARTON STREET
Laburnum
Farm
Wilsons
Farm
LIVESEY ROAD
PH
Ludborough
CHAPEL LA 1
STATION RD 2
LUDBOROUGH PK 3
STOCKS HILL 4
GREEN LA 5
Moat

95

Wyham
House
LINCOLN GATE
A18
Wyham
Gorse
Ludborough
Vale
PEAR TREE LA

5

LN8
Wyham House
Farm
Chalk
Farm
Pit
(dis)
PEAR TREE LANE
MAIN ROAD
JACOBS
CL

94

SALTERS LANE
Top
Farm
Vale
Farm
The Utterby
Prim Sch
The
Slates
A16
CHAPEL LA

4

JAMESON RD
Lamboroft
Farm
Pit
(dis)
Chalk
Pit
ABBEY LA
North
Ormsby
BENSON
CT
Utterby
Packhorse
Bridge
Utterby
House

93

BOSWELL RD
Abbey
Farm
Priory
(site of)
Medieval Village of
North Ormsby (site of)
CHURCH LANE
Moat
Farm

3

War Memorial
LN11
Middle
Barn
Ormsby
Plantation
Grange
Farm

92

Airfield
(disused)
Mill
Farm
Grimble
Wood
Fotherby
Top
Top
Farm
Earthworks

2

Julian's
Barn
ELKINGTON RD
Grange
Farm
May
Wood

91

Tumulus
Boswell
House
North
Elkington
NORTH ELKINGTON LANE
The
Dales
Glastonbury
Wood

1

Kelstern
Manor
Farm
Mast
Horseshoe
Plantation

90

25   A   26   B   27   C   28   D   29   E   30   F

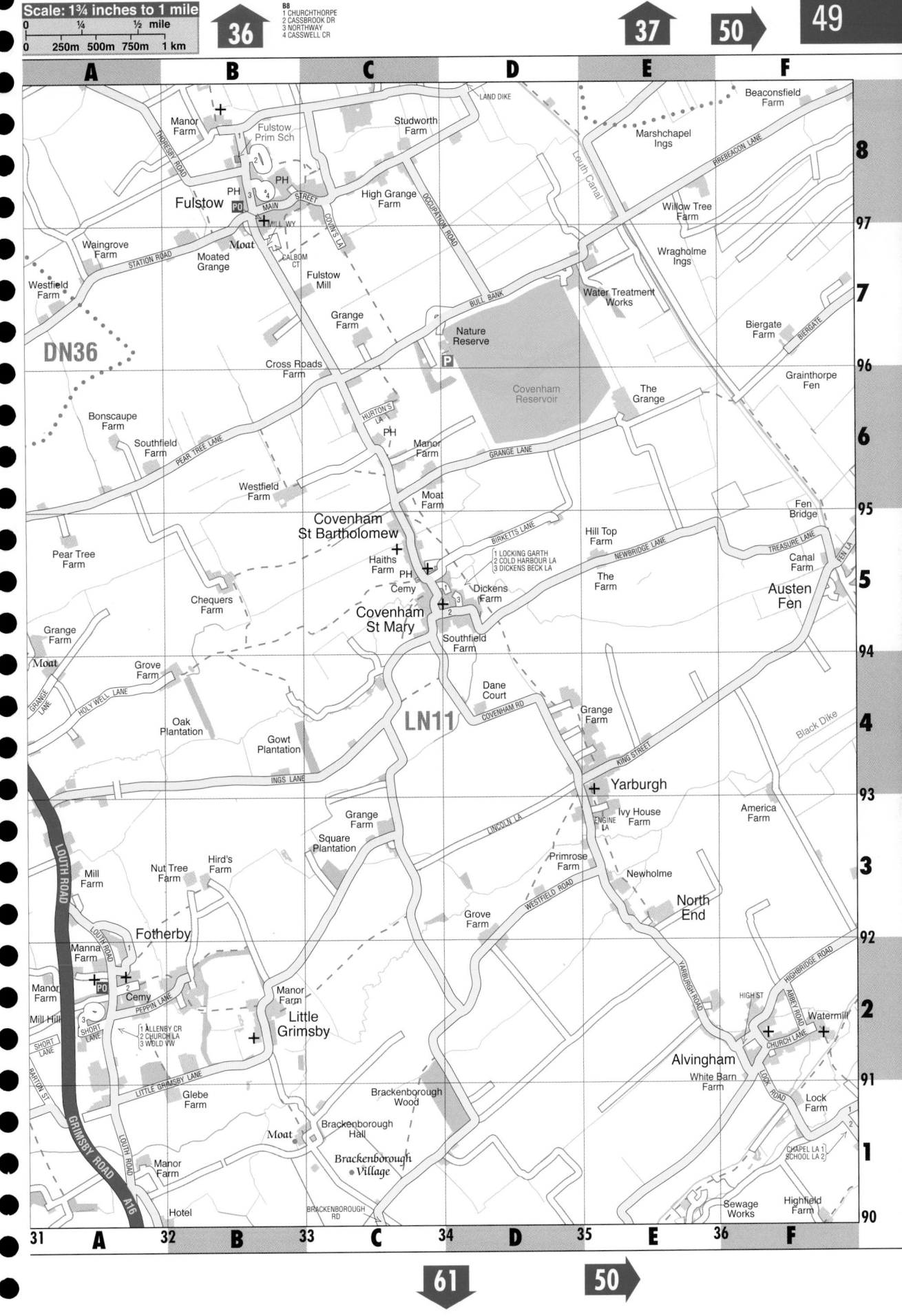

Scale: 1¾ inches to 1 mile

0   ¼   ½ mile
0   250m 500m 750m 1 km

36

B8
1 CHURCHTHORPE
2 CASSBROOK DR
3 NORTHWAY
4 CASSWELL CR

37   50   49

A   B   C   D   E   F

8

LAND DIKE

Beaconsfield Farm

Manor Farm

Fulstow Prim Sch

Studworth Farm

Marshchapel Ings

PREBEACON LANE

PH

PH

Fulstow

High Grange Farm

Louth Canal

97

Willow Tree Farm

PO

MAIN STREET

MILL WY

COUR'S LA

OCCUPATION ROAD

Wragholme Ings

Waingrove Farm

STATION ROAD

Moat

Moated Grange

CALBOM CT

Fulstow Mill

7

BULL BANK

Water Treatment Works

Biergate Farm

BIERGATE

Westfield Farm

DN36

Grange Farm

Cross Roads Farm

Nature Reserve

P

96

Covenham Reservoir

Grainthorpe Fen

6

Bonscaupe Farm

Southfield Farm

PEAR TREE LANE

HURTON'S LA

PH

Westfield Farm

Manor Farm

GRANGE LANE

The Grange

95

Fen Bridge

Moat Farm

BIRKETTS LANE

Hill Top Farm

NEWBRIDGE LANE

TREASURE LANE

FEN LA

Pear Tree Farm

Covenham St Bartholomew

Haiths Farm

PH

Cemy

1 LOCKING GARTH
2 COLD HARBOUR LA
3 DICKENS BECK LA

Canal Farm

Austen Fen

5

The Farm

Chequers Farm

Covenham St Mary

1
2
3

Dickens Farm

Grange Farm

Moat

Southfield Farm

94

Grove Farm

HOLY WELL LANE

GRANGE LANE

LN11

Dane Court

COVENHAM RD

Grange Farm

4

Oak Plantation

Gowt Plantation

KING STREET

Black Dike

INGS LANE

Yarburgh

93

LINCOLN LA

Ivy House Farm

America Farm

Grange Farm

Square Plantation

ENGINE LA

Mill Farm

Nut Tree Farm

Hird's Farm

Primrose Farm

WESTFIELD ROAD

Newholme

North End

3

Fotherby

LOUTH ROAD

Grove Farm

YARBURGH ROAD

HIGHBRIDGE ROAD

92

Manna Farm

PO

Cemy

PEPPIN LANE

Manor Farm

Little Grimsby

HIGH ST

ABBEY ROAD

CHURCH LANE

Watermill

2

Manor Farm

Mill Hill

SHORT LANE

1 ALLENBY CR
2 CHURCH LA
3 WOLD VW

Alvingham

White Barn Farm

LOCK ROAD

SHORT LANE

BARTON ST

LITTLE GRIMSBY LANE

Glebe Farm

Brackenborough Wood

Lock Farm

91

GRIMSBY ROAD

A16

Moat

Brackenborough Hall

CHAPEL LA 1
SCHOOL LA 2

LOUTH ROAD

Manor Farm

Brackenborough Village

BRACKENBOROUGH RD

Sewage Works

Highfield Farm

90

Hotel

31   A   32   B   33   C   34   D   35   E   36   F

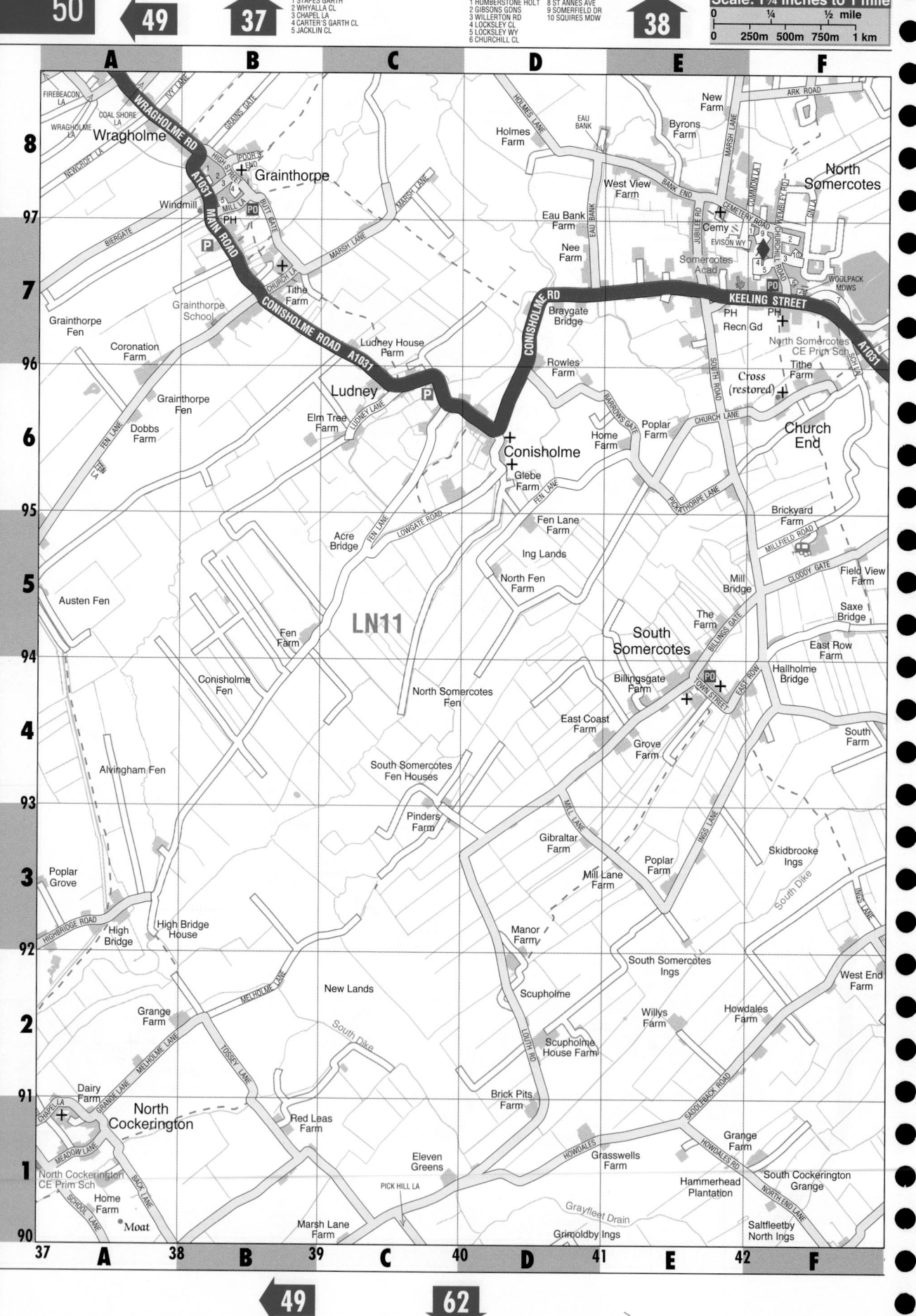

B8
1 STAPES GARTH
2 WHYALLA CL
3 CHAPEL LA
4 CARTER'S GARTH CL
5 JACKLIN CL

F7
1 HUMBERSTONE HOLT
2 GIBSONS GDNS
3 WILLERTON RD
4 LOCKSLEY CL
5 LOCKSLEY WY
6 CHURCHILL CL

7 KEELING ST
8 ST ANNES AVE
9 SOMERFIELD DR
10 SQUIRES MDW

Scale: 1¾ inches to 1 mile
0   ¼   ½ mile
0 250m 500m 750m 1 km

Wragholme
Grainthorpe
North Somercotes
Ludney
Conisholme
Church End
South Somercotes
North Cockerington

LN11

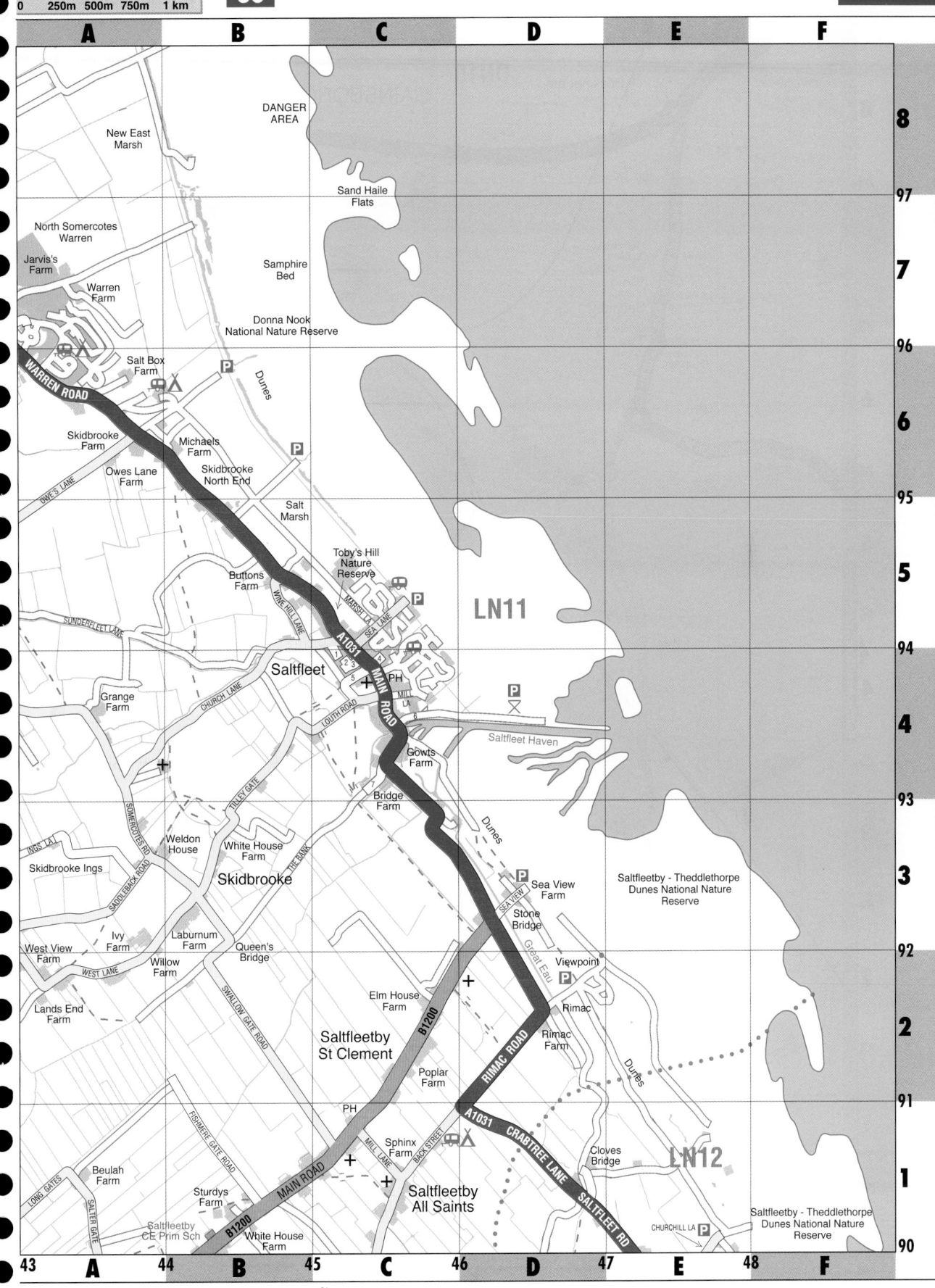

Scale: 1¾ inches to 1 mile

0   ¼   ½   mile

0   250m 500m 750m 1 km

38

8

97

7

96

6

95

5

94

4

93

3

92

2

91

1

90

A   B   C   D   E   F

DANGER AREA

New East Marsh

Sand Haile Flats

North Somercotes Warren

Samphire Bed

Jarvis's Farm

Donna Nook National Nature Reserve

Warren Farm

WARREN ROAD

Salt Box Farm

Dunes

P

Skidbrooke Farm

Michaels Farm

OWES LANE

Owes Lane Farm

Skidbrooke North End

P

Salt Marsh

SUNDERELEET LANE

Buttons Farm

Toby's Hill Nature Reserve

LN11

WIRE HILL LANE

MARSH LA

SEA LANE

P

Saltfleet

A1031

1 2 3

4

5

MAIN ROAD

PH

MILL LA

P

CHURCH LANE

Grange Farm

LOUTH ROAD

6

Saltfleet Haven

Gowts Farm

TILLEY GATE

THE BANK

Bridge Farm

Dunes

Weldon House

SOMERCOTES RD

White House Farm

Skidbrooke

P

Sea View Farm

Saltfleetby - Theddlethorpe Dunes National Nature Reserve

INGS LA

Skidbrooke Ings

SADDLEBACK ROAD

Ivy Farm

Laburnum Farm

Queen's Bridge

Stone Bridge

SEA VIEW

West View Farm

WEST LANE

Willow Farm

SWALLOW GATE ROAD

Viewpoint

P

Lands End Farm

Elm House Farm

B1200

Great Eau

Rimac

Saltfleetby St Clement

RIMAC ROAD

Rimac Farm

Poplar Farm

Dunes

FISHMERE GATE ROAD

PH

MILL LANE

A1031

CRABTREE LANE

Cloves Bridge

LN12

SALTFLEET RD

LONG GATES

SALTER GATE

Beulah Farm

Sphinx Farm

BACK STREET

Saltfleetby All Saints

Sturdys Farm

Saltfleetby CE Prim Sch

B1200

MAIN ROAD

White House Farm

CHURCHILL LA

P

Saltfleetby - Theddlethorpe Dunes National Nature Reserve

43   A   44   B   45   C   46   D   47   E   48   F

63

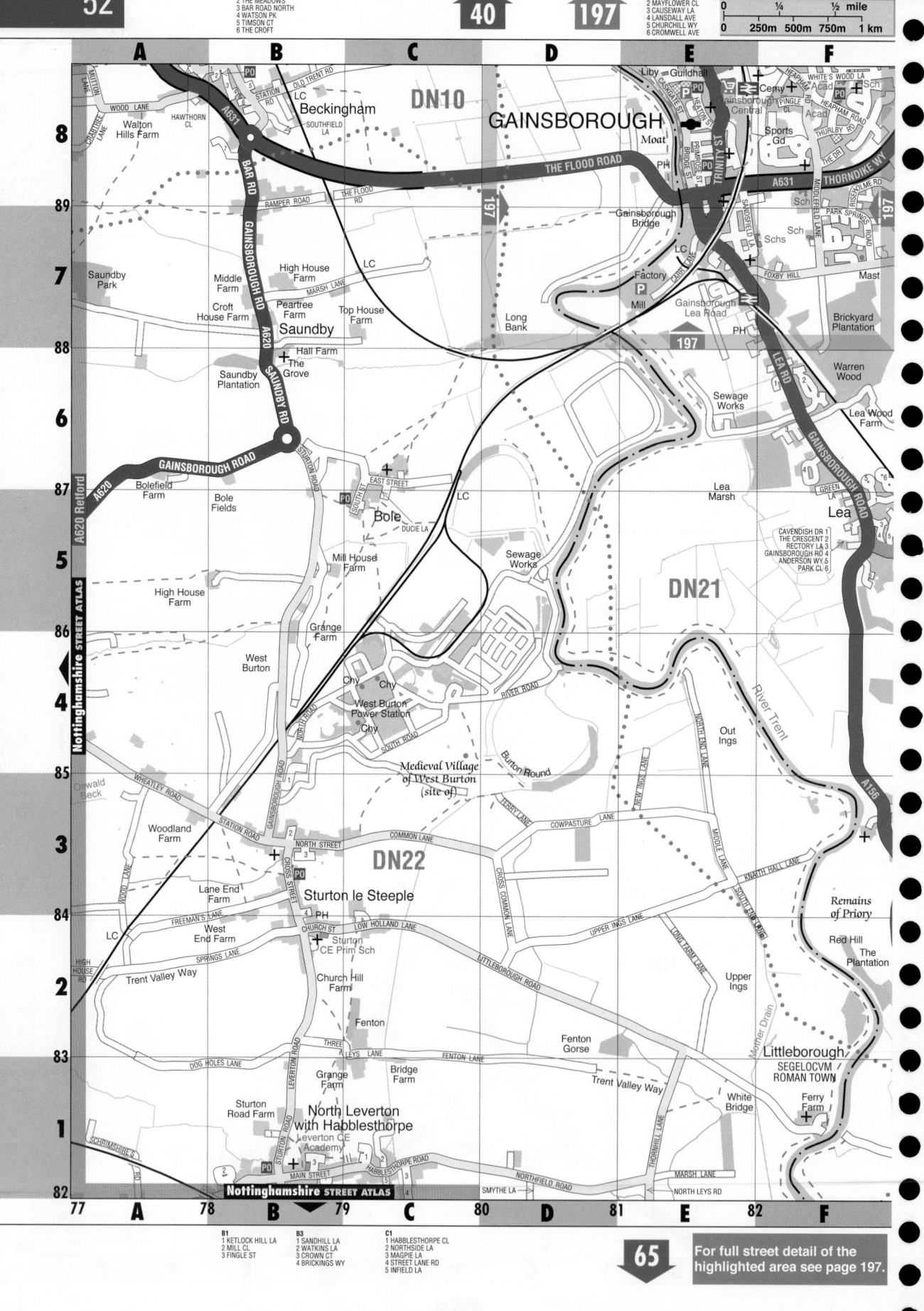

Scale: 1¾ inches to 1 mile
0   ¼   ½ mile
0 250m 500m 750m 1 km

B8
1 HIGH ST
2 THE MEADOWS
3 BAR ROAD NORTH
4 WATSON PK
5 TIMSON CT
6 THE CROFT
7 BAR ROAD SOUTH
8 THE ROTUNDA

F6
1 COPPER BEECH CL
2 MAYFLOWER CL
3 CAUSEWAY LA
4 LANSDALL AVE
5 CHURCHILL WY
6 CROMWELL AVE

40

197

DN10

GAINSBOROUGH

Beckingham

THE FLOOD ROAD

RAMPER ROAD

THE FLOOD RD

Saundby Park

Middle Farm

High House Farm

Croft House Farm

Peartree Farm

Saundby

Top House Farm

Hall Farm

The Grove

Saundby Plantation

Moat

Gainsborough Central

Gainsborough Bridge

Long Bank

Factory

Mill

Gainsborough Lea Road

Sewage Works

Warren Wood

Lea Wood Farm

GAINSBOROUGH ROAD

Bolefield Farm

Bole Fields

East Street

Lea Marsh

Lea

Bole

DUCIE LA

Mill House Farm

High House Farm

Grange Farm

Sewage Works

DN21

West Burton

Chy   Chy

West Burton Power Station

Chy

River Road

Out Ings

River Trent

Medieval Village of West Burton (site of)

Burton Round

Wheatley Road

Oswald Beck

Woodland Farm

Cowpasture Lane

North Street

DN22

Common Lane

Remains of Priory

Red Hill The Plantation

Lane End Farm

Sturton le Steeple

West End Farm

Sturton CE Prim Sch

Low Holland Lane

Upper Ings Lane

Upper Ings

Trent Valley Way

Church St

Church Hill Farm

Springs Lane

LITTLEBOROUGH ROAD

Fenton

Fenton Gorse

Fenton Lane

Littleborough

SEGELOCVM ROMAN TOWN

Dog Holes Lane

Three Leys Lane

Grange Farm

Bridge Farm

Trent Valley Way

White Bridge

Ferry Farm

Sturton Road Farm

North Leverton with Habblesthorpe

Leverton CE Academy

HABBLESTHORPE ROAD

NORTHFIELD ROAD

SMYTHE LA

MARSH LANE

NORTH LEYS RD

SCHRIMSHIRE'S RD

CAVENDISH DR 1
THE CRESCENT 2
RECTORY LA 3
GAINSBOROUGH RD 4
ANDERSON WY 5
PARK CL 6

B1
1 KETLOCK HILL LA
2 MILL CL
3 FINGLE ST

B3
1 SANDHILL LA
2 WATKINS LA
3 CROWN CT
4 BRICKINGS WY

C1
1 HABBLESTHORPE CL
2 NORTHSIDE LA
3 MAGPIE LA
4 STREET LANE RD
5 INFIELD LA

65

For full street detail of the highlighted area see page 197.

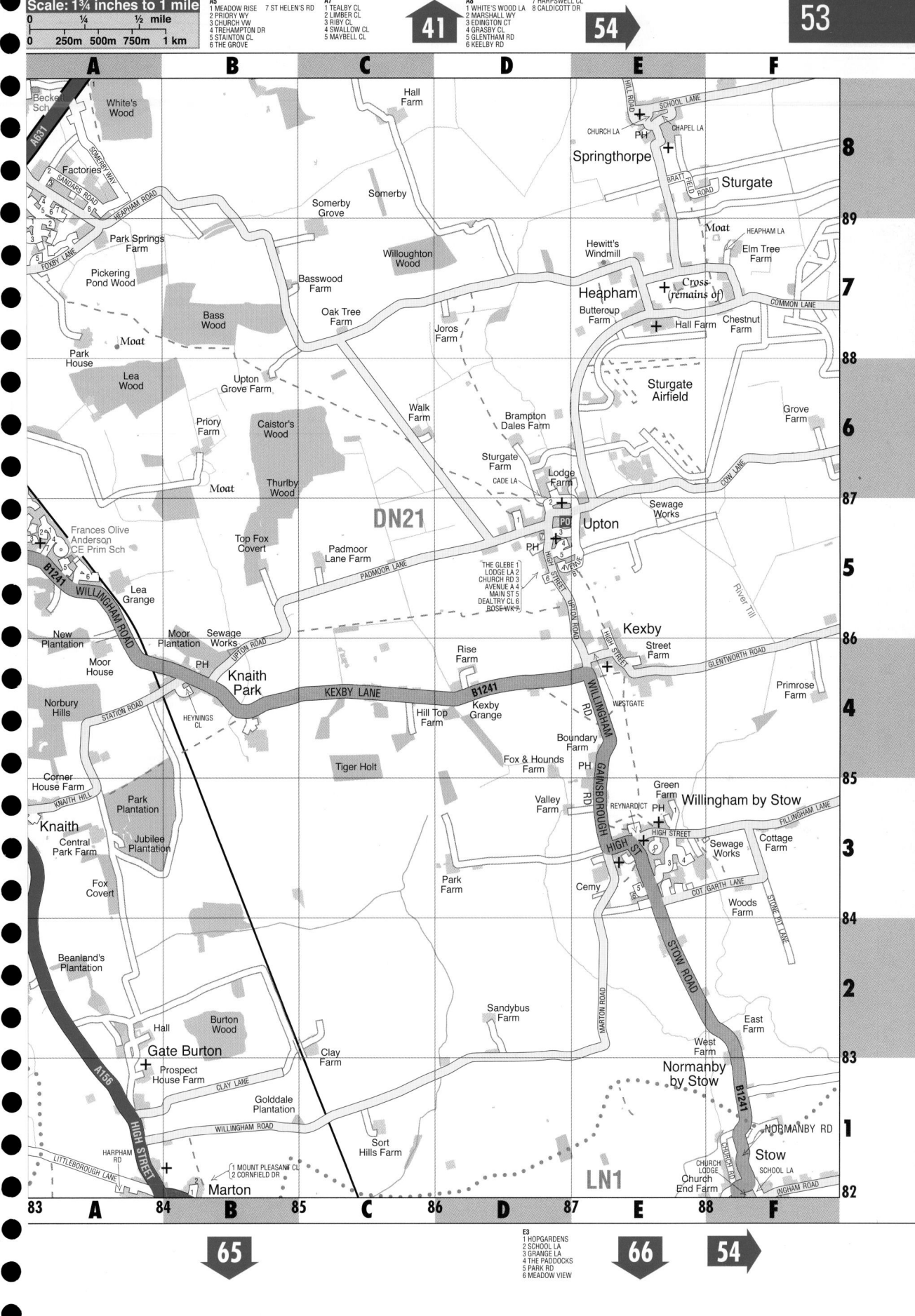
Scale: 1¾ inches to 1 mile
0 ¼ ½ mile
0 250m 500m 750m 1 km
A5
1 MEADOW RISE
2 PRIORY WY
3 CHURCH VW
4 TREHAMPTON DR
5 STAINTON CL
6 THE GROVE
7 ST HELEN'S RD
A7
1 TEALBY CL
2 LIMBER CL
3 RIBY CL
4 SWALLOW CL
5 MAYBELL CL
41
A8
1 WHITE'S WOOD LA
2 MARSHALL WY
3 EDINGTON CT
4 GRASBY CL
5 GLENTHAM RD
6 KEELBY RD
7 HARPSWELL CL
8 CALDICOTT DR
54
A
B
C
D
E
F
8
89
7
88
6
87
5
86
4
85
3
84
2
83
1
82
Beckett Sch
White's Wood
A631
Factories
SOMERBY WAY
SANDARS ROAD
HEAPHAM ROAD
FOXBY LANE
Park Springs Farm
Pickering Pond Wood
Moat
Park House
Lea Wood
Bass Wood
Hall Farm
Somerby
Somerby Grove
Willoughton Wood
Basswood Farm
Oak Tree Farm
Upton Grove Farm
Priory Farm
Caistor's Wood
Thurlby Wood
Moat
Walk Farm
Joros Farm
Brampton Dales Farm
Sturgate Farm
Lodge Farm
CADE LA
DN21
HILL ROAD
SCHOOL LANE
CHURCH LA
PH
CHAPEL LA
Springthorpe
BRATT FIELD ROAD
Sturgate
Moat
HEAPHAM LA
Hewitt's Windmill
Elm Tree Farm
Heapham
Cross (remains of)
COMMON LANE
Buttercup Farm
Hall Farm
Chestnut Farm
Sturgate Airfield
Grove Farm
COW LANE
Sewage Works
Upton
PO
PH
HIGH STREET
AVENUE
THE GLEBE 1
LODGE LA 2
CHURCH RD 3
AVENUE A 4
MAIN ST 5
DEALTRY CL 6
ROSE WK 7
River Till
Frances Olive Anderson CE Prim Sch
Top Fox Covert
Padmoor Lane Farm
PADMOOR LANE
B1241
WILLINGHAM ROAD
Lea Grange
New Plantation
Moor Plantation
Sewage Works
UPTON ROAD
Moor House
PH
Knaith Park
KEXBY LANE
B1241
Rise Farm
Kexby
HIGH STREET
Street Farm
GLENTWORTH ROAD
UPTON ROAD
Norbury Hills
STATION ROAD
HEYNINGS CL
Hill Top Farm
Kexby Grange
WILLINGHAM RD
WESTGATE
Primrose Farm
Boundary Farm
Fox & Hounds Farm
PH
Tiger Holt
Corner House Farm
KNAITH HILL
Park Plantation
Knaith
Central Park Farm
Jubilee Plantation
Valley Farm
GAINSBOROUGH RD
REYNARD CT
Green Farm
PH
Willingham by Stow
FILLINGHAM LANE
HIGH STREET
HIGH ST
Sewage Works
Cottage Farm
Fox Covert
Park Farm
Cemy
COT GARTH LANE
Woods Farm
STONE PIT LANE
Beanland's Plantation
STOW ROAD
MARTON ROAD
Sandybus Farm
Hall
Burton Wood
Gate Burton
Prospect House Farm
Clay Farm
CLAY LANE
A156
HIGH STREET
Golddale Plantation
East Farm
West Farm
Normanby by Stow
B1241
NORMANBY RD
WILLINGHAM ROAD
Sort Hills Farm
HARPHAM RD
LITTLEBOROUGH LANE
1 MOUNT PLEASANT CL
2 CORNFIELD DR
Marton
LN1
Stow
CHURCH LODGE
CHURCH RD
Church End Farm
SCHOOL LA
INGHAM ROAD
83
84
85
86
87
88
65
E3
1 HOPGARDENS
2 SCHOOL LA
3 GRANGE LA
4 THE PADDOCKS
5 PARK RD
6 MEADOW VIEW
66
54

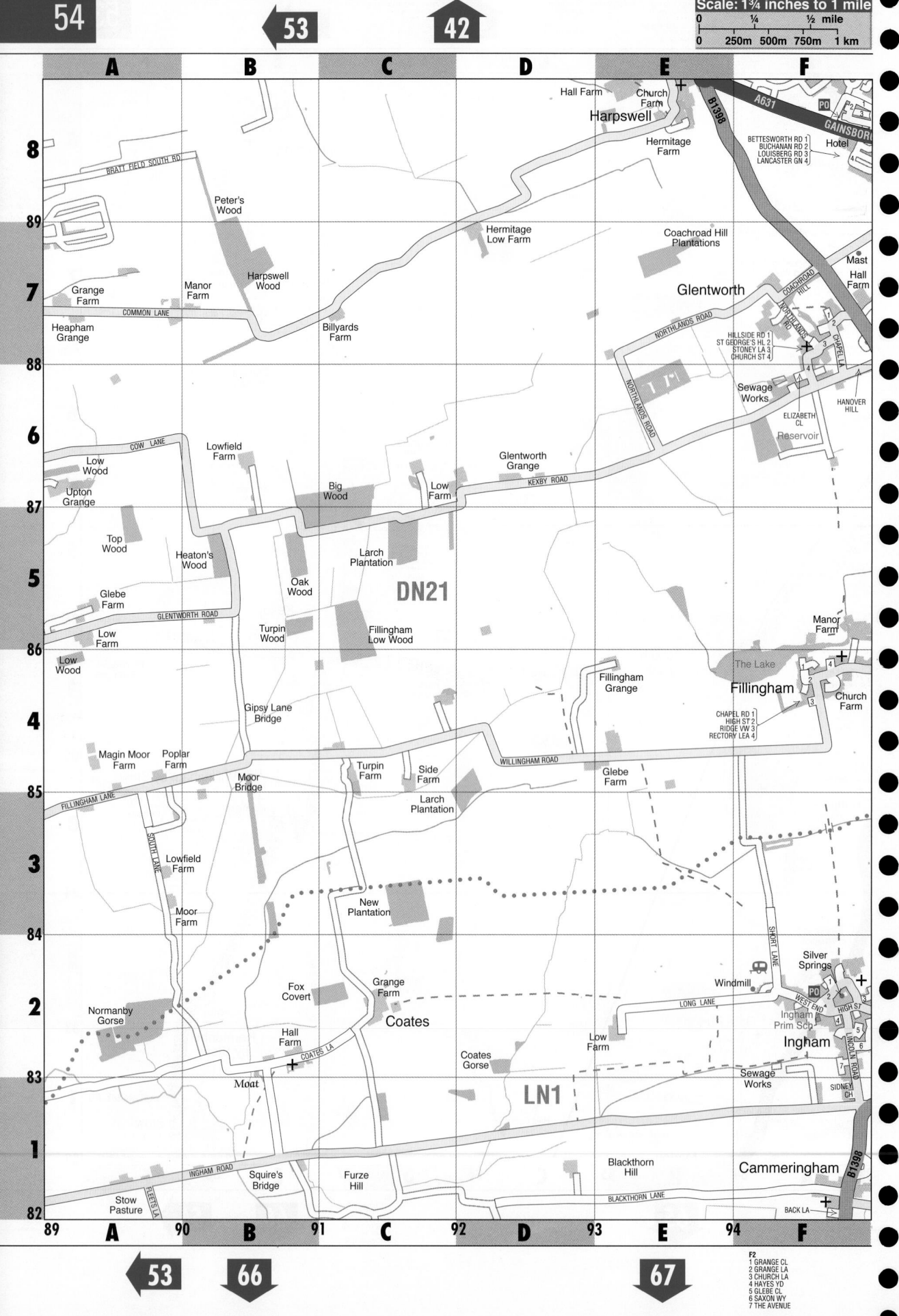

53
42

Scale: 1¾ inches to 1 mile

0   ¼   ½   mile
0 250m 500m 750m 1 km

A   B   C   D   E   F

8

Hall Farm   Church Farm   P.O.
Harpswell
Hermitage Farm

BRATT FIELD SOUTH RD

GAINSBORO
A631
B1398
BETTESWORTH RD 1
BUCHANAN RD 2
LOUISBERG RD 3
LANCASTER GN 4
Hotel

89

Peter's Wood   Hermitage Low Farm   Coachroad Hill Plantations

Mast Hall Farm

7

Grange Farm   Manor Farm   Harpswell Wood   Glentworth
COMMON LANE

Heapham Grange   Billyards Farm
HILLSIDE RD 1
ST GEORGE'S HL 2
STONEY LA 3
CHURCH ST 4

COACHROAD HILL
NORTHLANDS RD
CHAPEL LA

88

NORTHLANDS ROAD
Sewage Works
HANOVER HILL
ELIZABETH CL
Reservoir

6

COW LANE   Lowfield Farm
Low Wood   Glentworth Grange
Upton Grange   Big Wood   Low Farm   KEXBY ROAD

87

Top Wood   Heaton's Wood   Larch Plantation
Glebe Farm   Oak Wood   DN21
Low Farm   GLENTWORTH ROAD   Turpin Wood   Fillingham Low Wood

Manor Farm

86

Low Wood   The Lake
Fillingham Grange   Fillingham

CHAPEL RD 1
HIGH ST 2
RIDGE VW 3
RECTORY LEA 4
Church Farm

4

Gipsy Lane Bridge
Magin Moor Farm   Poplar Farm   Moor Bridge   Turpin Farm   Side Farm   WILLINGHAM ROAD   Glebe Farm

85

FILLINGHAM LANE   Larch Plantation
SOUTH LANE
Lowfield Farm

SHORT LANE

3

New Plantation

84

Silver Springs
Windmill   P.O.
WEST END   HIGH ST
LONG LANE

Moor Farm

2

Normanby Gorse   Fox Covert   Grange Farm
Coates   Ingham Prim Sch
Ingham
LINCOLN ROAD

Hall Farm   COATES LA   Low Farm   Sewage Works   SIDNEY CH

83

Moat   Coates Gorse   LN1

1

INGHAM ROAD   Squire's Bridge   Furze Hill   Blackthorn Hill   Cammeringham
Stow Pasture   BLACKTHORN LANE   BACK LA

B1398

82

89   A   90   B   91   C   92   D   93   E   94   F

53
66
67

F2
1 GRANGE CL
2 GRANGE LA
3 CHURCH LA
4 HAYES YD
5 GLEBE CL
6 SAXON WY
7 THE AVENUE

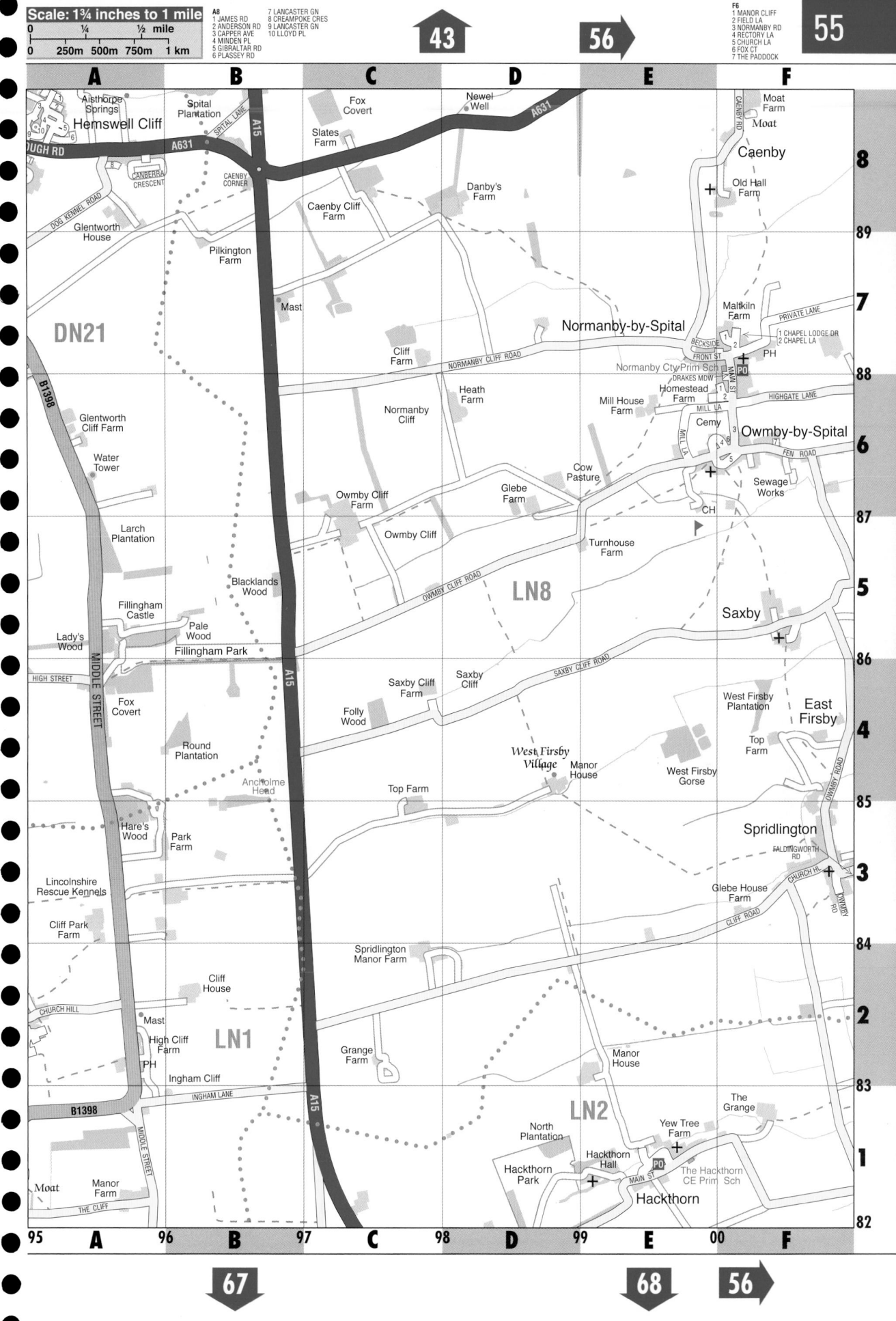
Scale: 1¾ inches to 1 mile
0 ¼ ½ mile
0 250m 500m 750m 1 km
A8
1 JAMES RD
2 ANDERSON RD
3 CAPPER AVE
4 MINDEN PL
5 GIBRALTAR RD
6 PLASSEY RD
7 LANCASTER GN
8 CREAMPOKE CRES
9 LANCASTER GN
10 LLOYD PL
43
56
F6
1 MANOR CLIFF
2 FIELD LA
3 NORMANBY RD
4 RECTORY LA
5 CHURCH LA
6 FOX CT
7 THE PADDOCK
Aisthorpe Springs
Hemswell Cliff
Spital Plantation
Fox Covert
Newel Well
Moat Farm
Moat
Caenby
Slates Farm
CAENBY CORNER
CANBERRA CRESCENT
Danby's Farm
Old Hall Farm
Caenby Cliff Farm
Glentworth House
Pilkington Farm
Mast
Maltkiln Farm
PRIVATE LANE
Normanby-by-Spital
1 CHAPEL LODGE DR
2 CHAPEL LA
DN21
Cliff Farm
NORMANBY CLIFF ROAD
Normanby Cty Prim Sch
PH
Heath Farm
Mill House Farm
Homestead Farm
HIGHGATE LANE
Normanby Cliff
Glentworth Cliff Farm
Cemy
Owmby-by-Spital
Water Tower
FEN ROAD
Cow Pasture
Sewage Works
Owmby Cliff Farm
Glebe Farm
CH
Larch Plantation
Owmby Cliff
Turnhouse Farm
Blacklands Wood
OWMBY CLIFF ROAD
LN8
Fillingham Castle
Saxby
Lady's Wood
Pale Wood
Fillingham Park
HIGH STREET
MIDDLE STREET
Saxby Cliff Farm
Saxby Cliff
SAXBY CLIFF ROAD
West Firsby Plantation
East Firsby
Fox Covert
Folly Wood
Top Farm
Round Plantation
West Firsby Village
Manor House
West Firsby Gorse
Ancholme Head
Top Farm
OWMBY ROAD
Hare's Wood
Park Farm
Spridlington
FALDINGWORTH RD
Lincolnshire Rescue Kennels
CHURCH HL
Glebe House Farm
Cliff Park Farm
CLIFF ROAD
Spridlington Manor Farm
Cliff House
CHURCH HILL
Mast
High Cliff Farm
LN1
Grange Farm
Manor House
PH
Ingham Cliff
INGHAM LANE
B1398
A15
A631
The Grange
LN2
Yew Tree Farm
North Plantation
Hackthorn Hall
Hackthorn Park
PO
MAIN ST
The Hackthorn CE Prim Sch
Hackthorn
Moat
Manor Farm
THE CLIFF
67
68
56

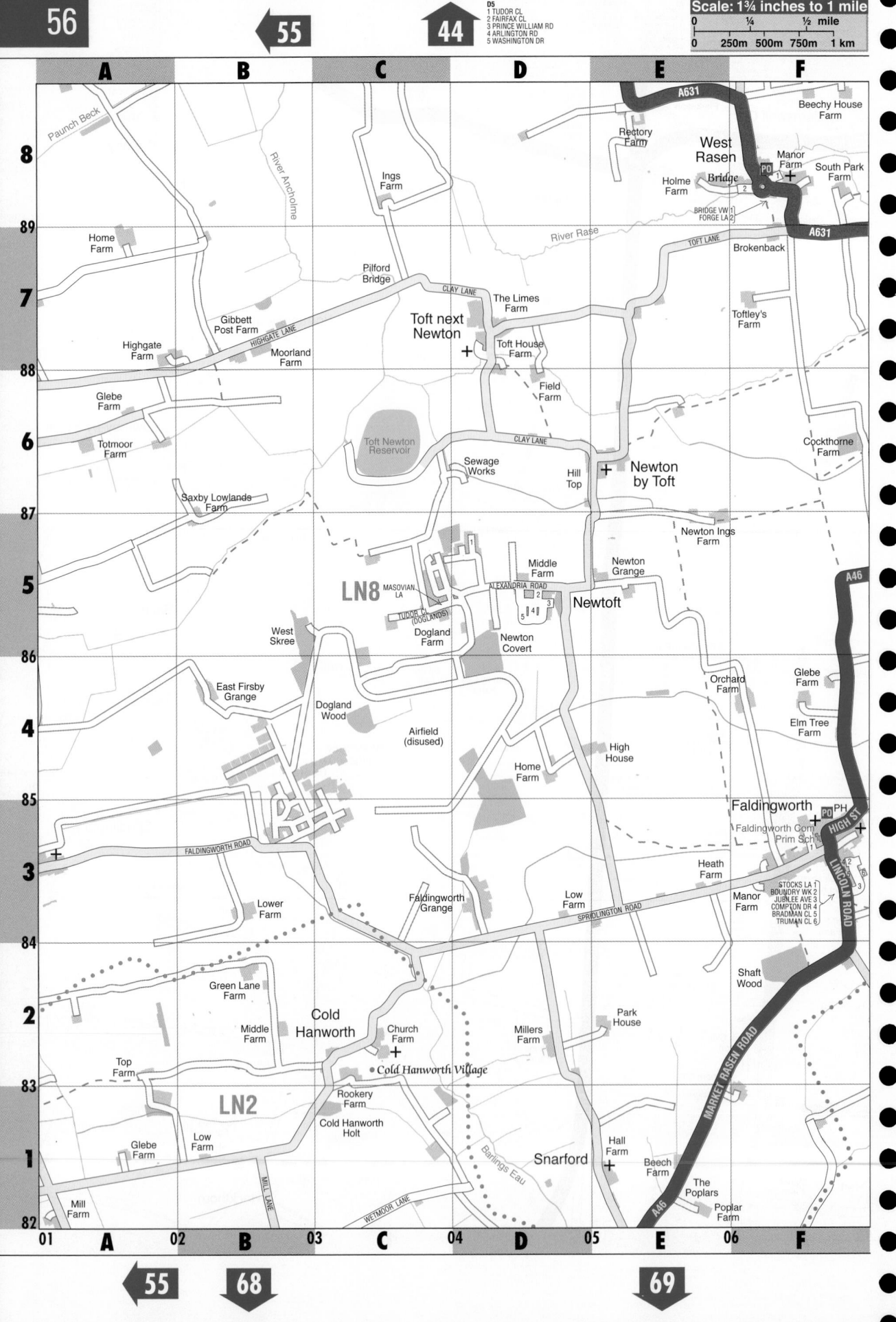

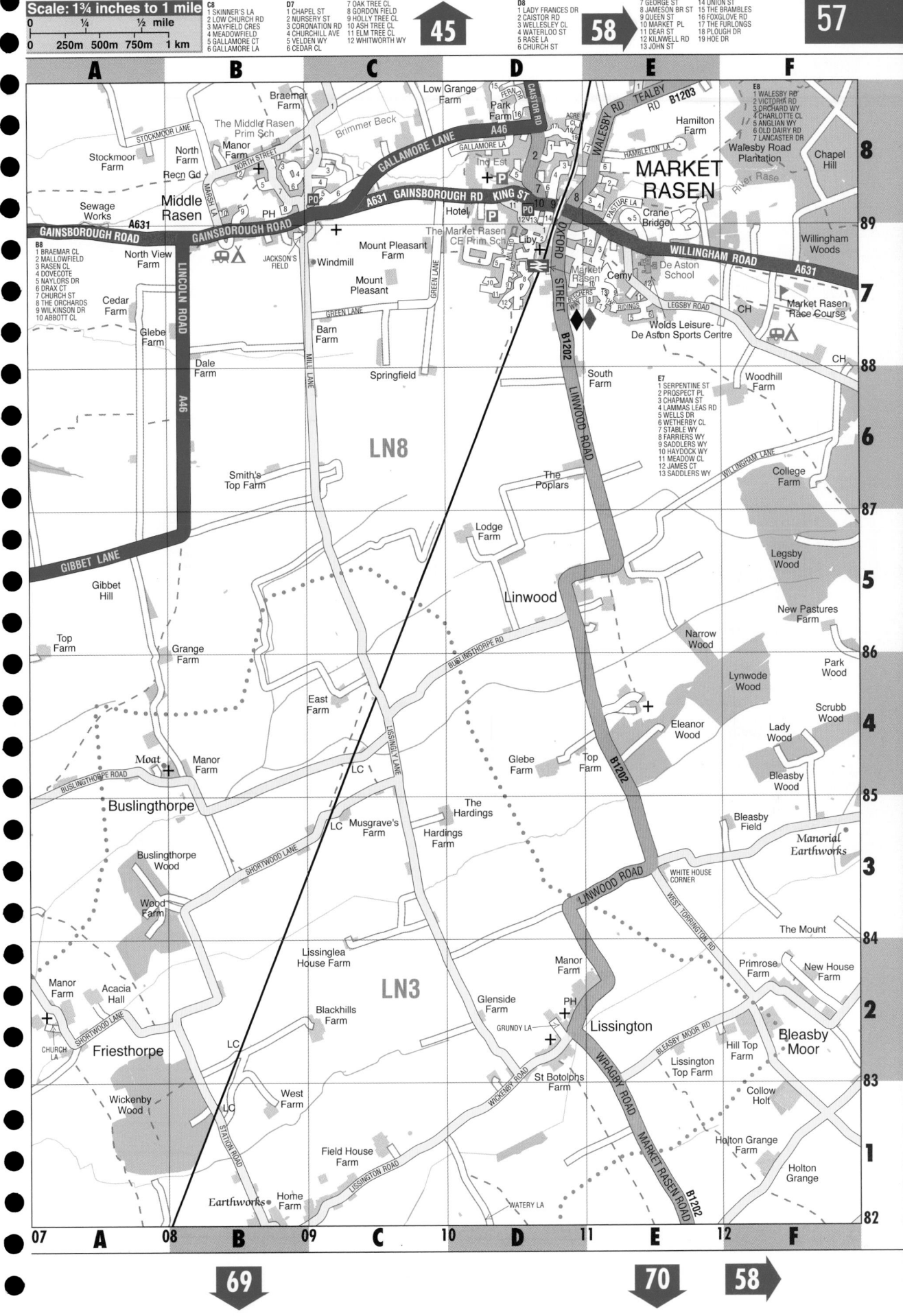
Scale: 1¾ inches to 1 mile
0 ¼ ½ mile
0 250m 500m 750m 1 km
C8
1 SKINNER'S LA
2 LOW CHURCH RD
3 MAYFIELD CRES
4 MEADOWFIELD
5 GALLAMORE CT
6 GALLAMORE LA
D7
1 CHAPEL ST
2 NURSERY ST
3 CORONATION RD
4 CHURCHILL AVE
5 VELDEN WY
6 CEDAR CL
7 OAK TREE CL
8 GORDON FIELD
9 HOLLY TREE CL
10 ASH TREE CL
11 ELM TREE CL
12 WHITWORTH WY
45
D8
1 LADY FRANCES DR
2 CAISTOR RD
3 WELLESLEY CL
4 WATERLOO ST
5 RASE LA
6 CHURCH ST
58
7 GEORGE ST
8 JAMESON BR ST
9 QUEEN ST
10 MARKET PL
11 DEAR ST
12 KILNWELL RD
13 JOHN ST
14 UNION ST
15 THE BRAMBLES
16 FOXGLOVE RD
17 THE FURLONGS
18 PLOUGH DR
19 HOE DR
A
B
C
D
E
F
E8
1 WALESBY RD
2 VICTORIA RD
3 ORCHARD WY
4 CHARLOTTE CL
5 ANGLIAN WY
6 OLD DAIRY RD
7 LANCASTER DR
Braemar Farm
Low Grange Farm
Park Farm
CAISTOR RD
WALESBY RD
TEALBY RD
B1203
Hamilton Farm
The Middle Rasen Prim Sch
Brimmer Beck
STOCKMOOR LANE
GALLAMORE LANE
A46
GALLAMORE LA
HAMBLETON LA
Walesby Road Plantation
Chapel Hill
Stockmoor Farm
North Farm
Manor Farm
NORTH STREET
Ind Est
MARKET RASEN
River Rase
Recn Gd
Sewage Works
Middle Rasen
MARSH LA
PH
PO
A631
GAINSBOROUGH RD
KING ST
Hotel
PASTURE LA
Crane Bridge
GAINSBOROUGH ROAD
A631
The Market Rasen CE Prim Sch
Liby
OXFORD STREET
Willingham Woods
B8
1 BRAEMAR CL
2 MALLOWFIELD
3 RASEN CL
4 DOVECOTE
5 NAYLORS DR
6 DRAX CT
7 CHURCH ST
8 THE ORCHARDS
9 WILKINSON DR
10 ABBOTT CL
North View Farm
JACKSON'S FIELD
Windmill
Mount Pleasant Farm
MILL RD
WILLINGHAM ROAD
De Aston School
Market Rasen
Cemy
A631
LINCOLN ROAD
Mount Pleasant
GREEN LANE
Cedar Farm
BEECHERS WAY
THE RIDINGS
LEGSBY ROAD
CH
Market Rasen Race Course
Glebe Farm
Barn Farm
B1202
Wolds Leisure-De Aston Sports Centre
CH
Dale Farm
Springfield
South Farm
E7
1 SERPENTINE ST
2 PROSPECT PL
3 CHAPMAN ST
4 LAMMAS LEAS RD
5 WELLS DR
6 WETHERBY CL
7 STABLE WY
8 FARRIERS WY
9 SADDLERS WY
10 HAYDOCK WY
11 MEADOW CL
12 JAMES CT
13 SADDLERS WY
Woodhill Farm
MILL LANE
A46
LN8
LINWOOD ROAD
College Farm
WILLINGHAM LANE
Smith's Top Farm
The Poplars
Lodge Farm
Legsby Wood
GIBBET LANE
Gibbet Hill
Linwood
New Pastures Farm
Narrow Wood
Top Farm
Grange Farm
BUSLINGTHORPE RD
Park Wood
Lynwode Wood
East Farm
Scrubb Wood
Eleanor Wood
Lady Wood
Moat
Manor Farm
LC
Glebe Farm
Top Farm
B1202
BUSLINGTHORPE ROAD
Bleasby Wood
Buslingthorpe
LISSINGLY LANE
The Hardings
Bleasby Field
LC
Musgrave's Farm
Hardings Farm
Manorial Earthworks
Buslingthorpe Wood
SHORTWOOD LANE
LINWOOD ROAD
WHITE HOUSE CORNER
Wood Farm
WEST TORRINGTON RD
The Mount
Lissinglea House Farm
Manor Farm
Primrose Farm
New House Farm
LN3
Manor Farm
Acacia Hall
Blackhills Farm
Glenside Farm
PH
Lissington
Bleasby Moor
GRUNDY LA
SHORTWOOD LANE
CHURCH LA
Friesthorpe
LC
BLEASBY MOOR RD
Hill Top Farm
Lissington Top Farm
WICKENBY ROAD
St Botolphs Farm
WRAGBY ROAD
Collow Holt
Wickenby Wood
LC
West Farm
STATION ROAD
Holton Grange Farm
Field House Farm
LISSINGTON ROAD
MARKET RASEN ROAD
Holton Grange
Earthworks
Home Farm
WATERY LA
B1202
8
89
7
88
6
87
5
86
4
85
3
84
2
83
1
82
07
08
09
10
11
12
69
70
58

57 46

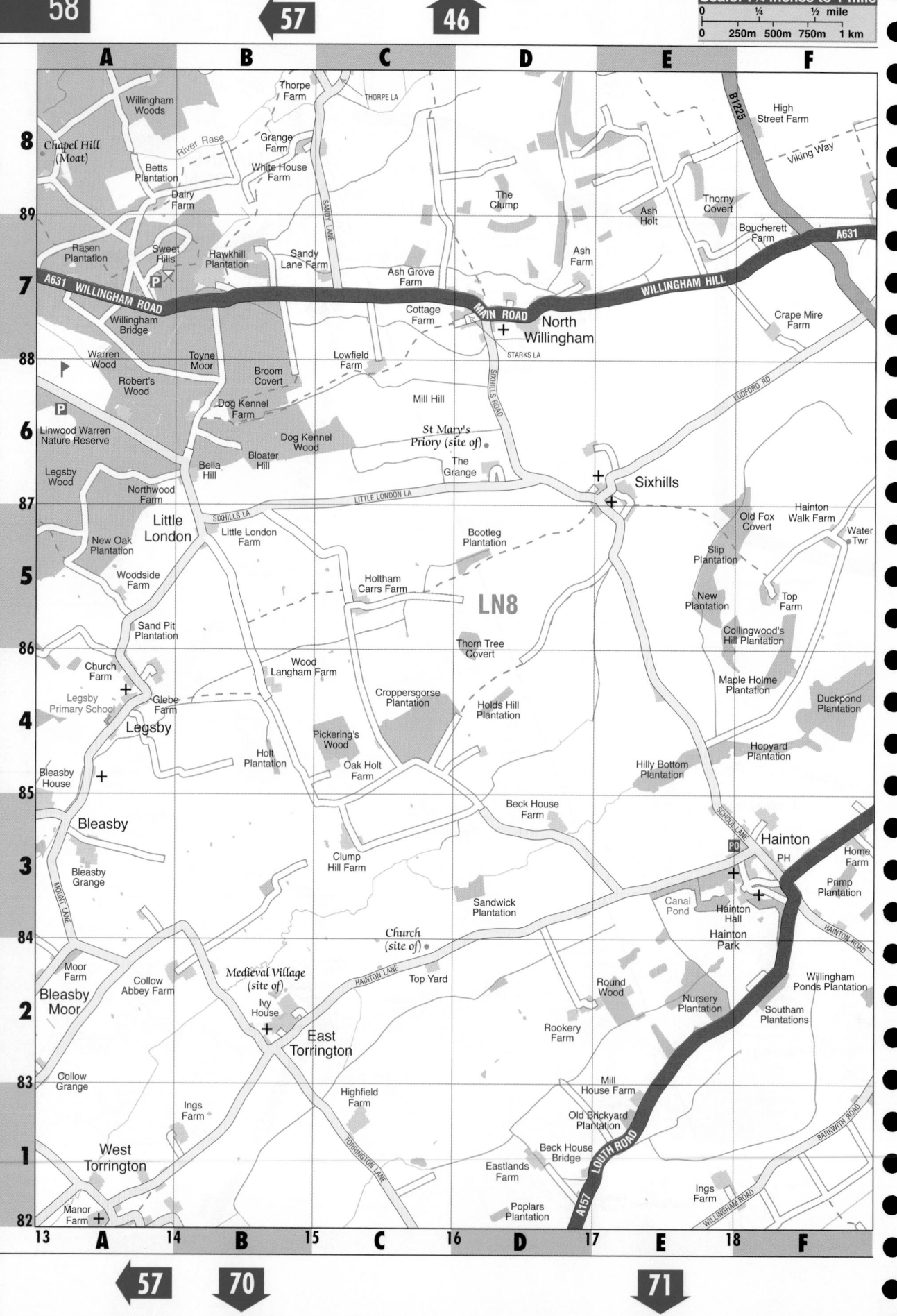

Scale: 1¾ inches to 1 mile
0 ¼ ½ mile
0 250m 500m 750m 1 km
Chapel Hill (Moat)
Willingham Woods
Thorpe Farm
THORPE LA
River Rase
Grange Farm
White House Farm
Betts Plantation
Dairy Farm
SANDY LANE
High Street Farm
B1225
Viking Way
The Clump
Ash Holt
Thorny Covert
Boucherett Farm
A631
Rasen Plantation
Sweet Hills
Hawkhill Plantation
Sandy Lane Farm
Ash Grove Farm
Ash Farm
A631 WILLINGHAM ROAD
WILLINGHAM HILL
MAIN ROAD
Cottage Farm
North Willingham
Crape Mire Farm
Willingham Bridge
STARKS LA
Warren Wood
Toyne Moor
Lowfield Farm
Broom Covert
Robert's Wood
SIXHILLS ROAD
LUDFORD RD
Mill Hill
Dog Kennel Farm
Linwood Warren Nature Reserve
Dog Kennel Wood
St Mary's Priory (site of)
Bloater Hill
Bella Hill
The Grange
Legsby Wood
Sixhills
Northwood Farm
LITTLE LONDON LA
SIXHILLS LA
Little London
Little London Farm
Bootleg Plantation
Old Fox Covert
Hainton Walk Farm
Water Twr
New Oak Plantation
Slip Plantation
Woodside Farm
Holtham Carrs Farm
LN8
New Plantation
Top Farm
Sand Pit Plantation
Thorn Tree Covert
Collingwood's Hill Plantation
Church Farm
Wood Langham Farm
Maple Holme Plantation
Legsby Primary School
Glebe Farm
Croppersgorse Plantation
Holds Hill Plantation
Duckpond Plantation
Legsby
Pickering's Wood
Hopyard Plantation
Holt Plantation
Oak Holt Farm
Bleasby House
Hilly Bottom Plantation
Beck House Farm
Bleasby
SCHOOL LANE
Hainton
PO
PH
Home Farm
Bleasby Grange
Clump Hill Farm
Canal Pond
Hainton Hall
Primp Plantation
MOUNT LANE
Sandwick Plantation
Hainton Park
HAINTON ROAD
Church (site of)
Moor Farm
Collow Abbey Farm
Medieval Village (site of)
HAINTON LANE
Top Yard
Round Wood
Willingham Ponds Plantation
Bleasby Moor
Ivy House
Nursery Plantation
Southam Plantations
East Torrington
Rookery Farm
Collow Grange
Mill House Farm
Ings Farm
Highfield Farm
Old Brickyard Plantation
West Torrington
TORRINGTON LANE
Beck House Bridge
A157 LOUTH ROAD
BARKWITH ROAD
Eastlands Farm
Ings Farm
Manor Farm
Poplars Plantation
WILLINGHAM ROAD
A B C D E F
89 88 87 86 85 84 83 82
8 7 6 5 4 3 2 1
13 14 15 16 17 18

57 70 71

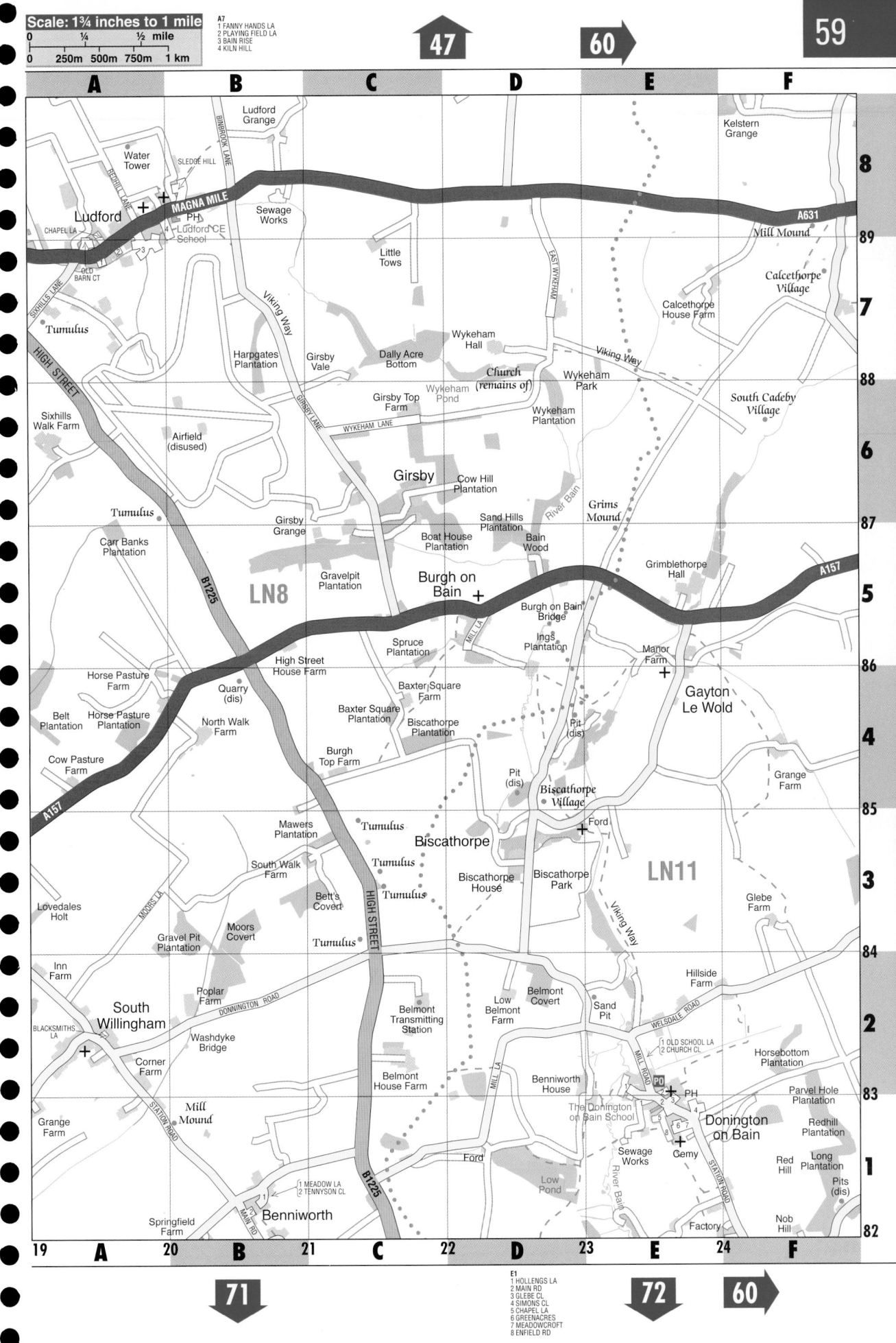
Scale: 1¾ inches to 1 mile
0 ¼ ½ mile
0 250m 500m 750m 1 km
A7
1 FANNY HANDS LA
2 PLAYING FIELD LA
3 BAIN RISE
4 KILN HILL
47
60
A B C D E F
Ludford Grange
Kelstern Grange
Water Tower
SLEDGE HILL
BINBROOK LANE
REDHILL LANE
Ludford
MAGNA MILE
PH
Ludford CE School
CHAPEL LA
OLD BARN CT
Sewage Works
Little Tows
A631
Mill Mound
Calcethorpe Village
Calcethorpe House Farm
EAST WYKEHAM
SIXHILLS LANE
Tumulus
Viking Way
HIGH STREET
Harpgates Plantation
Girsby Vale
Dally Acre Bottom
Wykeham Hall
Church (remains of)
Wykeham Park
Wykeham Pond
Girsby Top Farm
GIRSBY LANE
WYKEHAM LANE
Wykeham Plantation
South Cadeby Village
Sixhills Walk Farm
Airfield (disused)
Girsby
Cow Hill Plantation
River Bain
Grims Mound
Tumulus
Girsby Grange
Sand Hills Plantation
Boat House Plantation
Bain Wood
Carr Banks Plantation
Grimblethorpe Hall
A157
B1225
LN8
Gravelpit Plantation
Burgh on Bain
Burgh on Bain Bridge
MILL LA
Ings Plantation
Spruce Plantation
Manor Farm
High Street House Farm
Horse Pasture Farm
Quarry (dis)
Baxter Square Farm
Gayton Le Wold
Belt Plantation
Horse Pasture Plantation
North Walk Farm
Baxter Square Plantation
Biscathorpe Plantation
Pit (dis)
Cow Pasture Farm
Burgh Top Farm
Pit (dis)
Grange Farm
A157
Biscathorpe Village
Mawers Plantation
Tumulus
Ford
Biscathorpe
LN11
South Walk Farm
Tumulus
Biscathorpe House
Biscathorpe Park
Lovedales Holt
MOORS LA
Bett's Covert
Tumulus
HIGH STREET
Viking Way
Glebe Farm
Gravel Pit Plantation
Moors Covert
Tumulus
Inn Farm
Hillside Farm
Poplar Farm
Belmont Covert
South Willingham
DONINGTON ROAD
Belmont Transmitting Station
Low Belmont Farm
Sand Pit
WELSDALE ROAD
BLACKSMITHS LA
Washdyke Bridge
1 OLD SCHOOL LA
2 CHURCH CL
Horsebottom Plantation
Corner Farm
MILL ROAD
MILL LA
Belmont House Farm
Benniworth House
PO
PH
Parvel Hole Plantation
Grange Farm
Mill Mound
STATION ROAD
The Donington on Bain School
Donington on Bain
Redhill Plantation
Sewage Works
Cemy
Ford
Red Hill
Long Plantation
1 MEADOW LA
2 TENNYSON CL
B1225
Low Pond
River Bain
STATION ROAD
Pits (dis)
MAIN RD
Benniworth
Springfield Farm
Factory
Nob Hill
8 89 7 88 6 87 5 86 4 85 3 84 2 83 1 82
19 A 20 B 21 C 22 D 23 E 24 F
71
E1
1 HOLLENGS LA
2 MAIN RD
3 GLEBE CL
4 SIMONS CL
5 CHAPEL LA
6 GREENACRES
7 MEADOWCROFT
8 ENFIELD RD
72
60

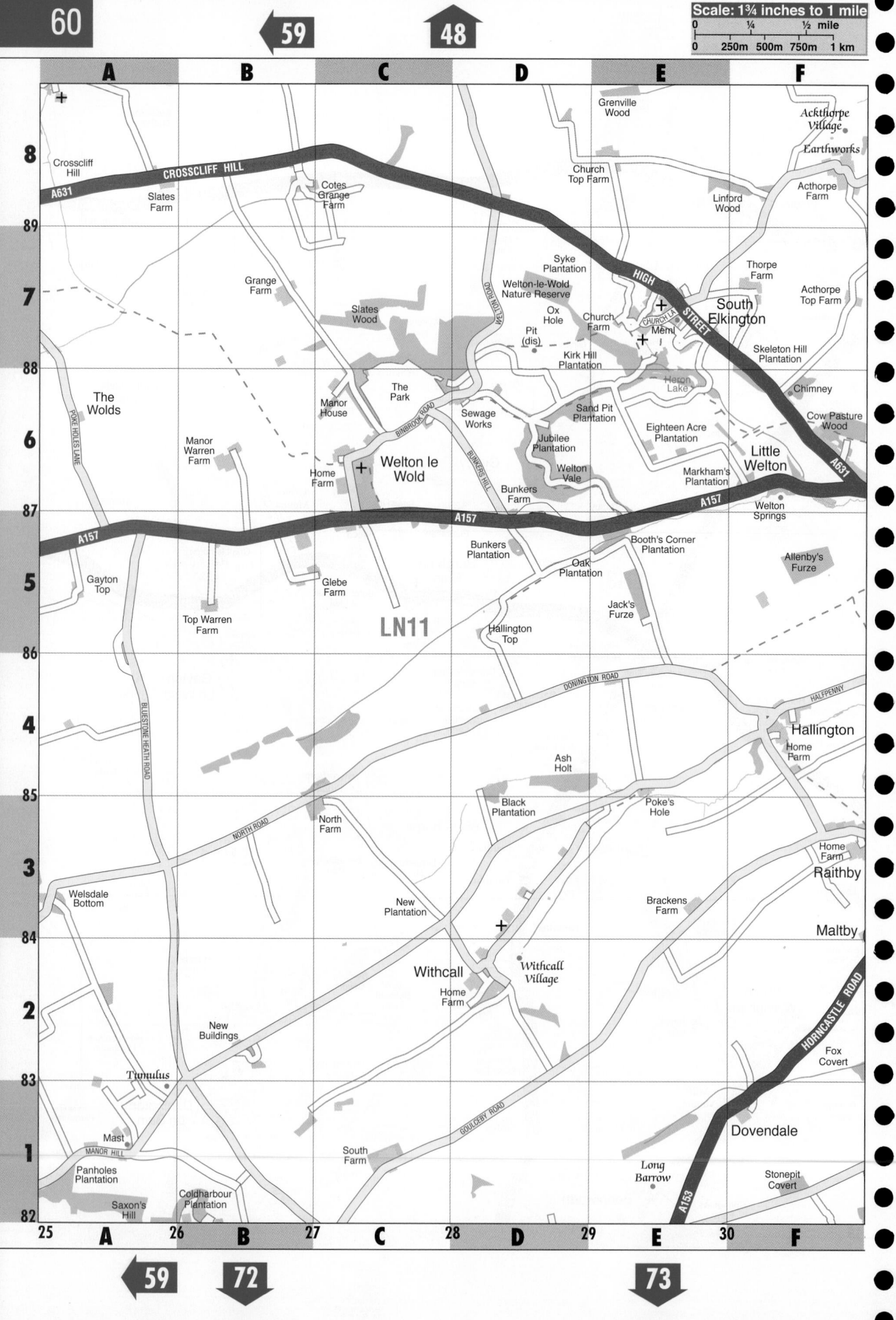

Scale: 1¾ inches to 1 mile

| 0 | ¼ | ½ | mile |

| 0 | 250m | 500m | 750m | 1 km |

59
48

A B C D E F

8 Crossliff Hill
CROSSCLIFF HILL
A631
Slates Farm
Cotes Grange Farm
Grenville Wood
Ackthorpe Village
Earthworks
Church Top Farm
Acthorpe Farm
Linford Wood
Acthorpe Top Farm

89
Grange Farm
Syke Plantation
Thorpe Farm

7
Slates Wood
Welton-le-Wold Nature Reserve
Ox Hole
Church Farm
HIGH STREET
South Elkington
CHURCH LA
Meml
Pit (dis)
Kirk Hill Plantation
Skeleton Hill Plantation

88
The Wolds
Manor House
The Park
Sewage Works
Sand Pit Plantation
Heron Lake
Chimney

6
PYKE HOLES LANE
Manor Warren Farm
BINBROOK ROAD
Jubilee Plantation
Eighteen Acre Plantation
Cow Pasture Wood
BUNKERS HILL
Welton le Wold
Home Farm
Welton Vale
Markham's Plantation
Little Welton
A631

87
A157
Bunkers Farm
A157
Welton Springs

5
A157
Gayton Top
Glebe Farm
Bunkers Plantation
Oak Plantation
Booth's Corner Plantation
Allenby's Furze

86
Top Warren Farm
LN11
Hallington Top
Jack's Furze
DONINGTON ROAD

4
BLUESTONE HEATH ROAD
Ash Holt
HALFPENNY
Hallington
Home Farm

85
NORTH ROAD
North Farm
Black Plantation
Poke's Hole
Home Farm

3
Welsdale Bottom
Raithby

84
New Plantation
Brackens Farm
Maltby

2
New Buildings
Withcall
Home Farm
Withcall Village
HORNCASTLE ROAD

83
Tumulus
GOULCEBY ROAD
Fox Covert

1
Mast
MANOR HILL
Panholes Plantation
South Farm
Dovendale
Long Barrow
Stonepit Covert

82
Saxon's Hill
Coldharbour Plantation
A153

25 A 26 B 27 C 28 D 29 E 30 F

59
72
73

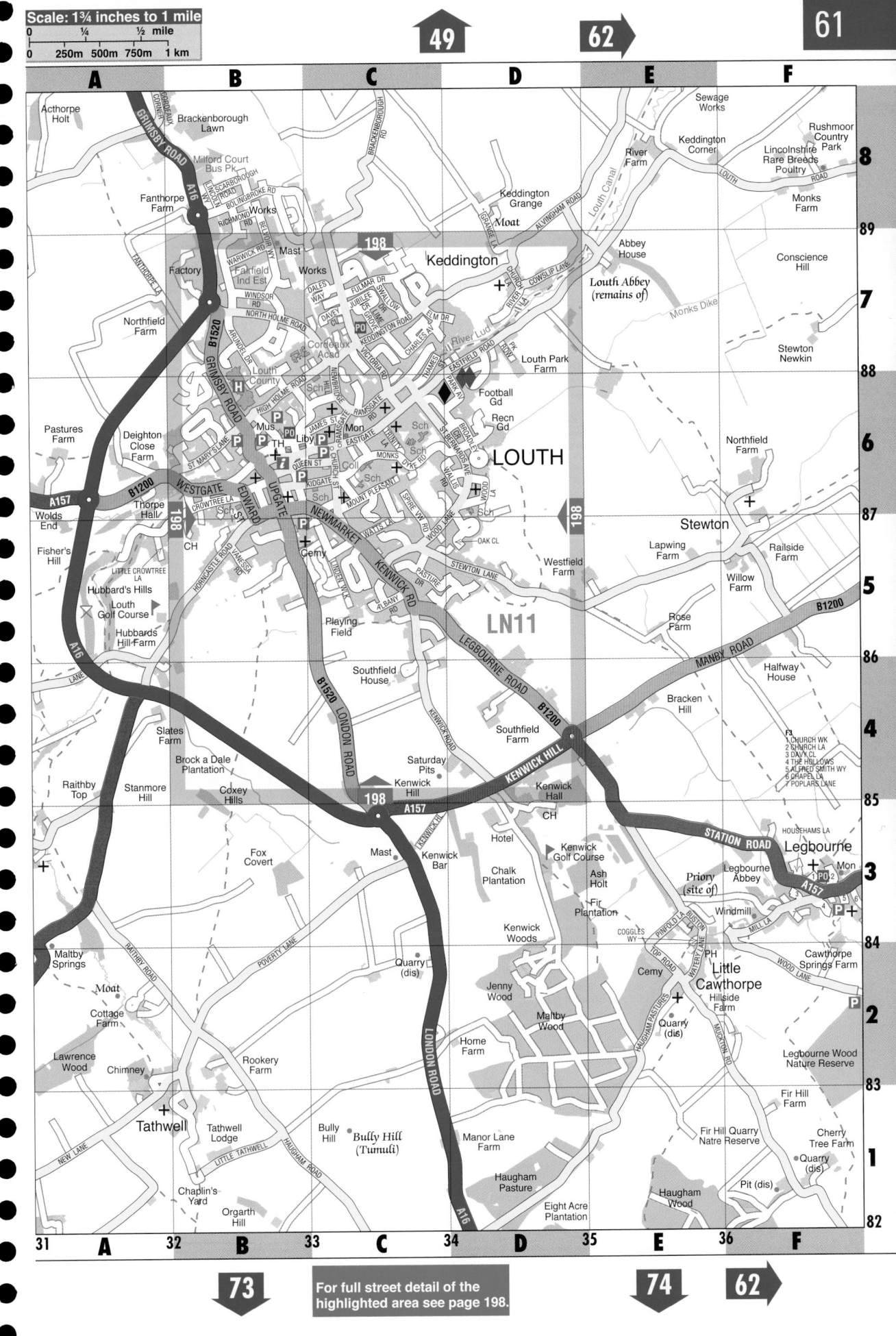

Scale: 1¾ inches to 1 mile

0   ¼   ½   mile
0 250m 500m 750m 1 km

49   62

A   B   C   D   E   F

Acthorpe Holt
Brackenborough Lawn
Sewage Works
Keddington Corner
Rushmoor Country Park
Lincolnshire Rare Breeds Poultry   8

Milford Court Bus Pk
River Farm
Monks Farm

Fanthorpe Farm
A16
SCARBOROUGH ROAD
BOLINGBROKE RD
RICHMOND RD
Works
Keddington Grange
Moat
ALVINGHAM ROAD
Louth Canal
Abbey House   89

Factory
WARWICK RD
Fairfield Ind Est
WINDSOR RD
NORTH HOLME ROAD
Mast
DALES WAY
Works
198
FULMAR DR
SWALLOW
JUBILEE CR
GROUP LANE
ELM DR
Keddington
GRANGE LA
CHURCH
RIVER Lud
COWSLIP LANE
Louth Abbey (remains of)
Conscience Hill
Monks Dike   7

Northfield Farm
FANTHORPE LA
BEVLOR WY
ARUNDEL DR
DAVEY CL
PO
VICTORIA RD
CHARLES AV
ELM DR
EASTFIELD ROAD
PARK RD
Louth Park Farm
Stewton Newkin   88

Pastures Farm
GRIMSBY ROAD
B1520
Cordeaux Acad
Louth County Sch
H
NEWBRIDGE
RAWSGATE RD
JAMES ST
TRINITY
ST BERNARDS AVE
BROAD
Football Gd
Northfield Farm   6

Deighton Close Farm
A157
B1200
Thorpe Hall
WESTGATE
EDWARD ST
CROWTREE LA
UPGATE
P
PO
P TH
P Mus
Liby
P
P
QUEEN ST
KIDGATE
Mon
MONKS
Sch
Coll
Sch
DYKE
Sch
WALLIS
WOOD LA
Sch
LOUTH
Recn Gd
Stewton   87

Wolds End
Fisher's Hill
LITTLE CROWTREE LA
Hubbard's Hills
Louth Golf Course
Hubbards Hill Farm
CH
HORNCASTLE ROAD
VANESSA
P
Cemy
MOUNT PLEASANT
SPIRE VW RD
OAK CL
198
Lapwing Farm
Willow Farm
Railside Farm   B1200   5

Raithby Top
Stanmore Hill
Slates Farm
B1520
LONDON ROAD
KENWICK RD
ALBANY RD
Playing Field
PASTURE DR
STEWTON LANE
Westfield Farm
LN11
Rose Farm
MANBY ROAD
Halfway House   86

Southfield House
KENWICK ROAD
Southfield Farm
LEGBOURNE ROAD
B1200
Bracken Hill   4

F3
1 CHURCH WK
2 CHURCH LA
3 DAVY CL
4 THE HOLLOWS
5 ALFRED SMITH WY
6 CHAPEL LA
7 POPLARS LANE

Brock a Dale Plantation
Coxey Hills
Saturday Pits
Kenwick Hill
198
A157
KENWICK HILL
Kenwick Hall
CH
STATION ROAD
HOUSEHAMS LA
Legbourne   85

A16
BAITHBY ROAD
Fox Covert
Mast
Kenwick Bar
LEGBOURNE RD
Hotel
Chalk Plantation
Kenwick Golf Course
Ash Holt
Fir Plantation
Priory (site of)
COGGLES WY
PINFOLD LA
BUSTON
Windmill
Legbourne Abbey
A157
PO
MILL LA
P   3

Maltby Springs
Moat
POVERTY LANE
Quarry (dis)
Kenwick Woods
Jenny Wood
Maltby Wood
Home Farm
HAUGHAM PASTURES
TOP LANE
PH
Cemy
MUCKTON RD
Little Cawthorpe
Quarry (dis)
Hillside Farm
WOOD LANE
Cawthorpe Springs Farm
Legbourne Wood Nature Reserve
P   2

Cottage Farm
Lawrence Wood
Chimney
NEW LANE
Rookery Farm
Fir Hill Farm   83

Tathwell
Tathwell Lodge
LITTLE TATHWELL
HAUGHAM ROAD
Bully Hill
Bully Hill (Tumuli)
Manor Lane Farm
Fir Hill Quarry Natre Reserve
Cherry Tree Farm
Quarry (dis)   1

Chaplin's Yard
Orgarth Hill
LONDON ROAD
A16
Haugham Pasture
Eight Acre Plantation
Haugham Wood
Pit (dis)   82

31   A   32   B   33   C   34   D   35   E   36   F

73   74   62

For full street detail of the highlighted area see page 198.

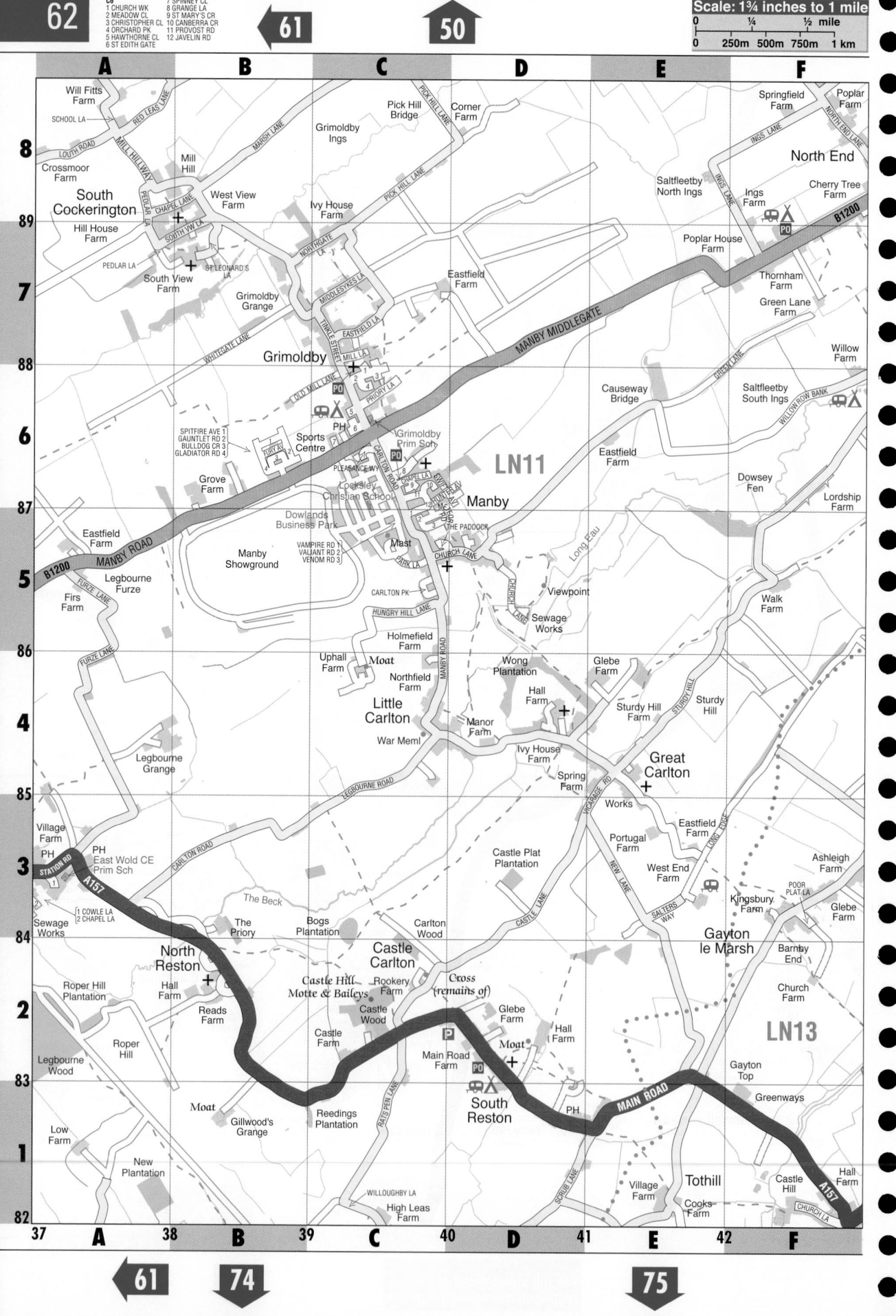

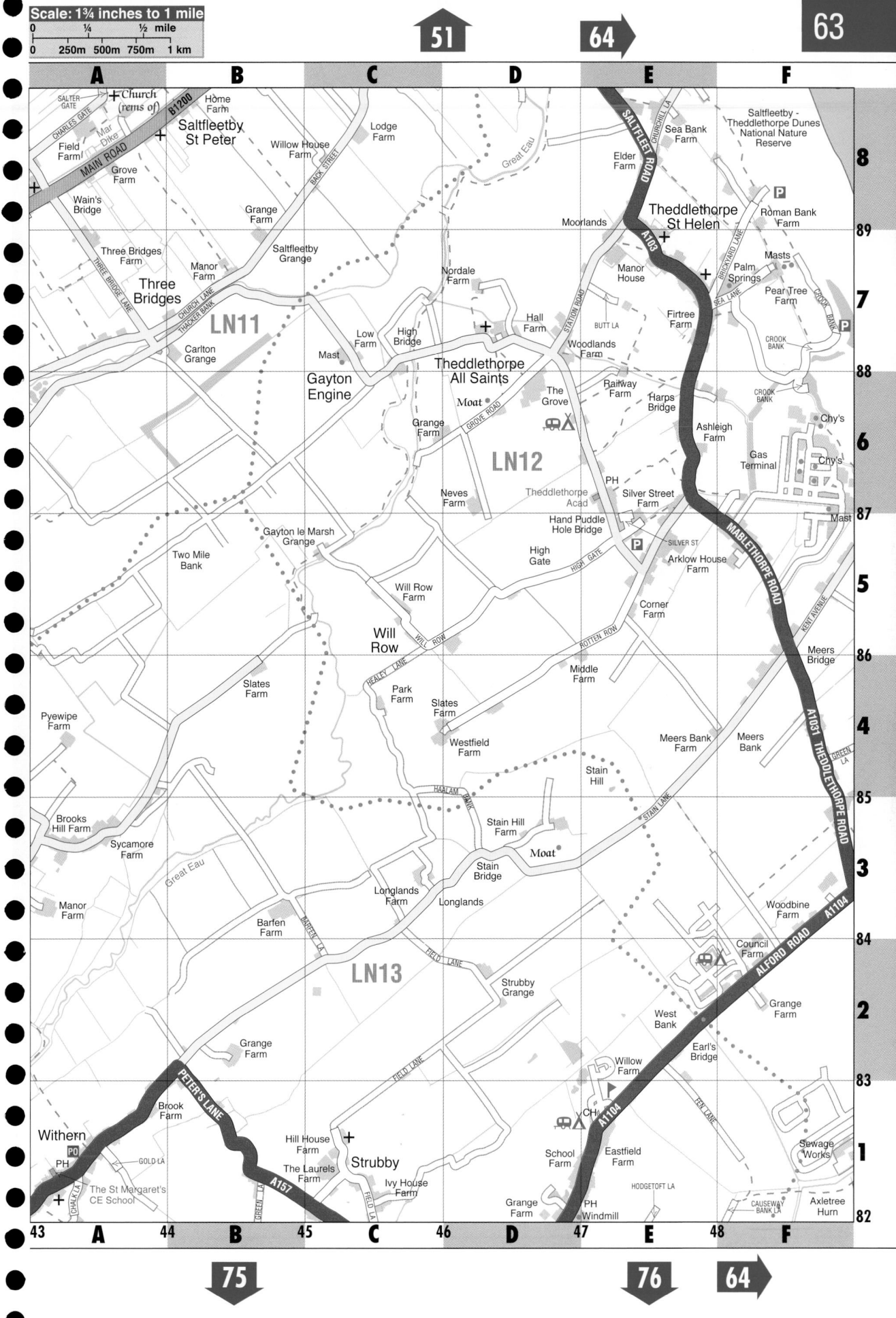
Scale: 1¾ inches to 1 mile
51
64
Saltfleetby St Peter
Home Farm
Lodge Farm
Willow House Farm
Field Farm
Grove Farm
Wain's Bridge
Grange Farm
Three Bridges Farm
Saltfleetby Grange
Manor Farm
Three Bridges
LN11
Carlton Grange
Mast
Gayton Engine
Low Farm
High Bridge
Nordale Farm
Theddlethorpe All Saints
Hall Farm
Woodlands Farm
Moat
Grange Farm
The Grove
LN12
Neves Farm
Theddlethorpe Acad
Hand Puddle Hole Bridge
High Gate
Gayton le Marsh Grange
Two Mile Bank
Will Row Farm
Will Row
Park Farm
Slates Farm
Westfield Farm
Pyewipe Farm
Brooks Hill Farm
Sycamore Farm
Manor Farm
Great Eau
Barfen Farm
Longlands Farm
Longlands
Stain Bridge
Stain Hill Farm
Stain Hill
LN13
Strubby Grange
Grange Farm
Brook Farm
Withern
PH
The St Margaret's CE School
Hill House Farm
The Laurels Farm
Strubby
Ivy House Farm
Grange Farm
School Farm
Eastfield Farm
Windmill
Willow Farm
Sea Bank Farm
Elder Farm
Saltfleetby - Theddlethorpe Dunes National Nature Reserve
Theddlethorpe St Helen
Roman Bank Farm
Moorlands
Manor House
Masts
Palm Springs
Pear Tree Farm
Firtree Farm
Railway Farm
Harps Bridge
Ashleigh Farm
Chy's
Gas Terminal
Silver Street Farm
Mast
Arklow House Farm
Corner Farm
Middle Farm
Meers Bridge
Meers Bank Farm
Meers Bank
Woodbine Farm
Council Farm
Grange Farm
West Bank
Earl's Bridge
Sewage Works
Axletree Hurn
SALTFLEET ROAD
MABLETHORPE ROAD
A1031 THEDDLETHORPE ROAD
ALFORD ROAD A1104
PETER'S LANE
A157
75
76
64

B5
1 CAMBRIDGE RD N
2 LINKS AVE
3 CAMBRIDGE RD S
4 IVEL GR
5 WHITEHEAD CL
6 IVEL CL

63

Scale: 1¾ inches to 1 mile

0   ¼   ½   mile

0   250m   500m   750m   1 km

A B C D E F

8

89

7

88

6

87

Saltfleetby - Theddlethorpe Dunes National Nature Reserve

North End Farm

MEERS BANK

CROOK BANK

PH

KENT AVE

MEERS BANK

P

The Seal Sanctuary & Nature Centre

5

POPLAR AVE 1
CHALFONT AVE 2

86

QUEBEC ROAD

GOLF ROAD

P

PO

P

A4
1 THE FAIRWAY
2 THE DRIVE
3 FALDOS WY
4 GOLF RD
5 LYLE CL
6 THE GREEN
7 EAGLE CL
9 PETER CHAMBERS WY
10 TUPLIN RD

The Dunes Family Entertainment Centre

4

GREEN LANE

Station Sports Ctr

PO

i

Fun Fair

Mon

IRB Station

Mablethorpe Prim Acad

Liby

Olde Curiosity Mus

85

HIGH STREET

VICTORIA RD

Mablethorpe Hall

Moat

ALFORD ROAD

A1104

PH

Art Gall

The Tennyson High School

MABLETHORPE

SEAHOLME ROAD

C3
1 QUEENS PK CL
2 NEWSTEAD RD
3 DYMOKE CL
4 BROOKE DR
5 DYMOKE RD
6 ARDEN CL

3

LN12

CHURCH LANE

PH

Seahaven Springs

84

SEAHOLME ROAD

AQUA DR 1
MARIAN AVE 2
MEDINA GD 3
CHAMPION WY 4

Masts

Masts

SUTTON RD

C2
1 MILL FIELD
2 CAMPLING WY
3 BARTON CL
4 AUBREY PARKER CL
5 PARKINSON'S WY
6 JAMES AVE
7 ST PETER'S LA
8 BRAY AVE
9 ETON RD

2

Poplar Farm

Trusthorpe

Bourne Farm

NORTH ROAD

MILE LANE

83

Bambers Farm

Bamber's Bridge

Elder Farm

Bridge Farm

A52

TRUSTHORPE ROAD

ASHLEIGH CLOSE

WHITBY STREET

Crossing Farm

Sewage Works

MAIN STREET

1 PARK RD E
2 CROMER AVE
3 HIGH ST
4 PROMENADE
5 YORK RD

1

Thorpe Farm

Trusthorpe Hall

Boswell Farm

FEN LA

82

Thorpe

49 **A** 50 **B** 51 **C** 52 **D** 53 **E** 54 **F** 55

A3
1 ORCHARD WY
2 ORCHARD CL
3 CHURCH RD
4 MALBOROUGH DR
5 OAKHAM AVE
6 WINCHESTER DR
7 CHELTENHAM WY

63

76

B3
1 HAWTHORN DR
2 MAYFLOWER WY
3 TRENCHARD RD
4 NELSON RD
5 STANLEY AVE
6 MAXWELL DR
7 KENSINGTON GDNS
8 STRAND CL
9 TOWER CL

10 HARLEQUIN DR
11 MARIAN AVE
12 HARRIS BOULEVARD
13 ELM AVE
14 KING ST
15 MARINA RD
16 ANCASTER RD
17 RIPON PL
18 VYNER CL
19 FOXE END

20 KNOWLE ST
21 PARK AVE
22 PARRY RD
23 THE BOULEVARD
24 GROSVENOR RD
25 RUTLAND ROAD

B4
1 LONG ACRE
2 ST ANDREWS RD
3 SHERWOOD RD
4 RUGBY RD
5 MALVERN RD
6 HARROW RD
7 REPTON RD
8 QUEENSWAY
9 SOMERSBY AVE

10 FITZWILLIAM ST
11 WELLINGTON AVE
12 CHAUCER AVE
13 RUSKIN RD
14 KINGSLEY RD
15 CHARLES WRIGHT CL
16 TENNYSON RD
17 TENNYSON AVE
18 HIGH ST
19 ADMIRALTY RD

20 STATION RD
21 ALEXANDRA RD
22 ALEXANDRA PK

77

C1
1 HALL LEAS DR
2 TRUSTHORPE RD
3 HIGHGATE CL
4 HIGHFIELD AVE
5 OUNDLE RD
6 UPPINGHAM RD
7 WILLOUGHBY RD
8 MARINE AVE
9 HARDING CL

C1
10 RICHMOND RD
11 ST JAMES CT
12 HIGHGATE LA

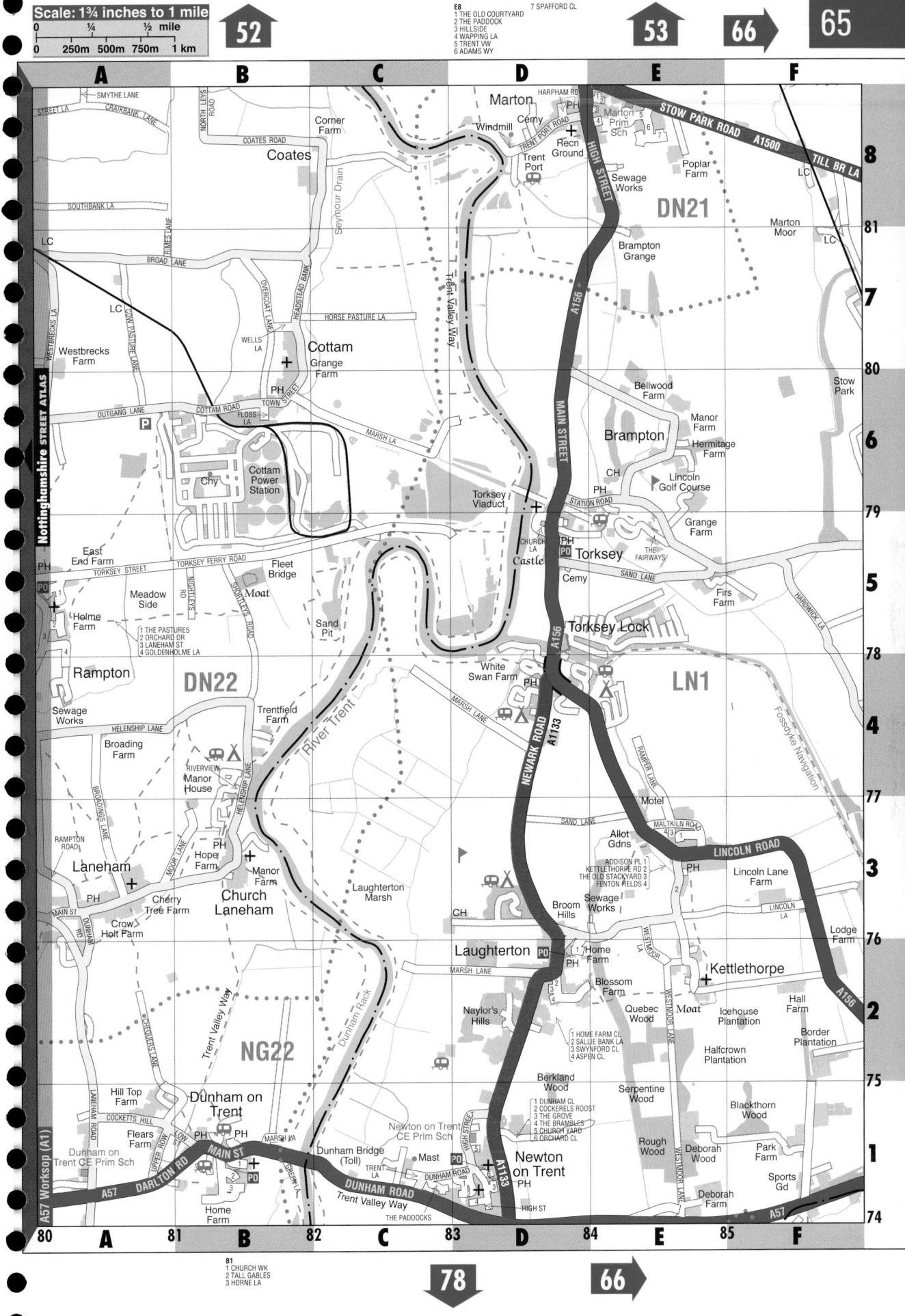

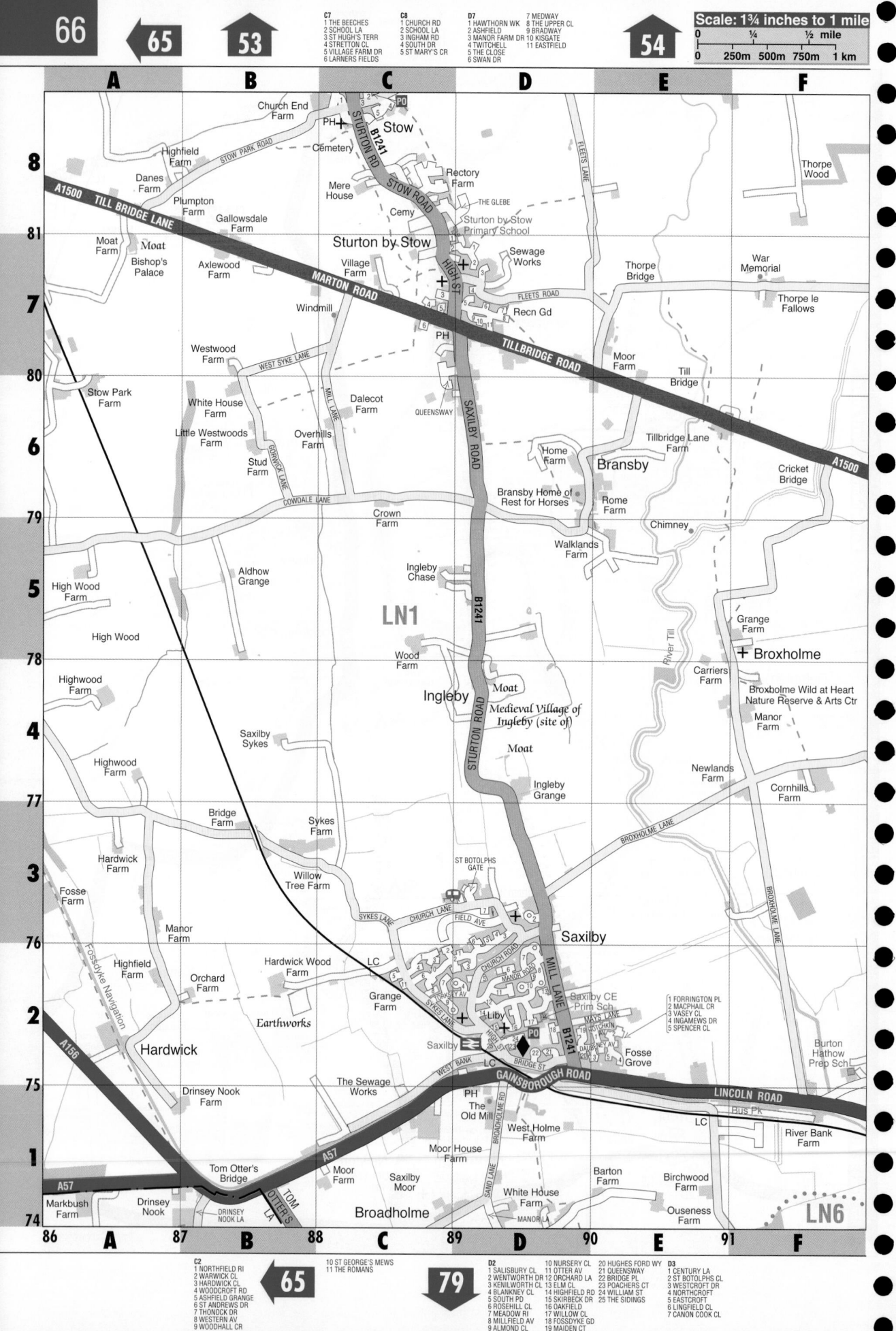

Church End
Farm
Church End
Farm
PH
Stow
Cemetery
Highfield
Farm
STOW PARK ROAD
Danes
Farm
A1500 TILL BRIDGE LANE
Plumpton
Farm
Gallowsdale
Farm
Moat
Farm
Moat
Bishop's
Palace
Axlewood
Farm
MARTON ROAD
Village
Farm
Windmill
WEST SYKE LANE
Westwood
Farm
Mere
House
Cemy
Sturton by Stow
Rectory
Farm
THE GLEBE
Sturton by Stow
Primary School
STOW ROAD
HIGH ST
Sewage
Works
FLEETS LANE
FLEETS ROAD
Thorpe
Bridge
Moor
Farm
Thorpe le
Fallows
War
Memorial
Thorpe
Wood
TILLBRIDGE ROAD
A1500
Recn Gd
PH
PH
MILL LANE
White House
Farm
Dalecot
Farm
Queensway
SAXILBY ROAD
Little Westwoods
Farm
Overhills
Farm
GORNICK LANE
Stud
Farm
COWDALE LANE
Stow Park
Farm
Crown
Farm
Home
Farm
Bransby
Bransby Home of
Rest for Horses
Tillbridge Lane
Farm
Rome
Farm
Cricket
Bridge
Till
Bridge
Aldhow
Grange
LN1
Ingleby
Chase
B1241
Walklands
Farm
Chimney
River Till
Grange
Farm
High Wood
Farm
High Wood
Wood
Farm
Ingleby
Moat
Medieval Village of
Ingleby (site of)
Moat
Broxholme
Carriers
Farm
Broxholme Wild at Heart
Nature Reserve & Arts Ctr
Highwood
Farm
Saxilby
Sykes
STURTON ROAD
Ingleby
Grange
Newlands
Farm
Manor
Farm
Cornhills
Farm
Highwood
Farm
Bridge
Farm
Sykes
Farm
BROXHOLME LANE
BROXHOLME LANE
Fosse
Farm
Hardwick
Farm
Willow
Tree Farm
St Botolphs
Gate
SYKES LANE
CHURCH LANE
FIELD AVE
Saxilby
Fossdyke Navigation
Manor
Farm
Highfield
Farm
Orchard
Farm
Hardwick Wood
Farm
LC
CHURCH ROAD
MANOR ROAD
MILL LANE
Saxilby CE
Prim Sch
1 FORRINGTON PL
2 MACPHAIL CR
3 VASEY CL
4 INGAMEWS DR
5 SPENCER CL
A156
Earthworks
Grange
Farm
SYKES LANE
MARKSEY AVE
Liby
MAYS LANE
PO
B1241
Fosse
Grove
Burton
Hathow
Prep Sch
Hardwick
Saxilby
LC
WEST BANK
BRIDGE ST
GAINSBOROUGH ROAD
DAUBNEY AV
LINCOLN ROAD
Bus Pk
LC
River Bank
Farm
Drinsey Nook
Farm
The Sewage
Works
PH The
Old Mill
BROADHOLME RD
West Holme
Farm
SAND LANE
LC
A57
Tom Otter's
Bridge
A57
A57
TOM OTTER'S
Moor
Farm
Moor House
Farm
Saxilby
Moor
White House
Farm
Barton
Farm
Birchwood
Farm
Ouseness
Farm
LN6
Markbush
Farm
Drinsey
Nook
DRINSEY
NOOK LA
TOM OTTER'S LA
Broadholme
MANOR LA

65

79

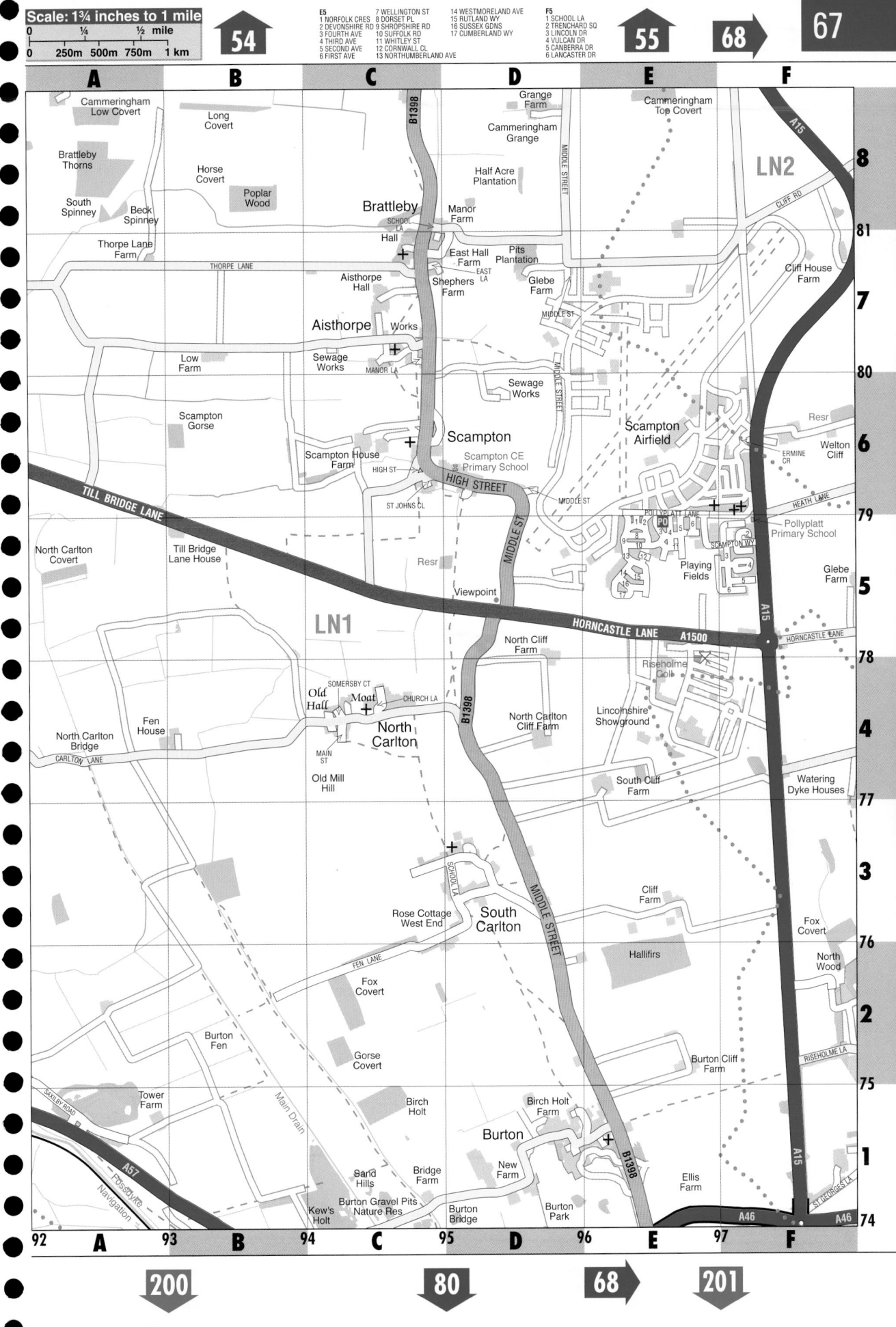
Scale: 1¾ inches to 1 mile
0 ¼ ½ mile
0 250m 500m 750m 1 km
54
E5
1 NORFOLK CRES
2 DEVONSHIRE RD
3 FOURTH AVE
4 THIRD AVE
5 SECOND AVE
6 FIRST AVE
7 WELLINGTON ST
8 DORSET PL
9 SHROPSHIRE RD
10 SUFFOLK RD
11 WHITLEY ST
12 CORNWALL CL
13 NORTHUMBERLAND AVE
14 WESTMORELAND AVE
15 RUTLAND WY
16 SUSSEX GDNS
17 CUMBERLAND WY
F5
1 SCHOOL LA
2 TRENCHARD SQ
3 LINCOLN DR
4 VULCAN DR
5 CANBERRA DR
6 LANCASTER DR
55
68
A B C D E F
Cammeringham Low Covert
Long Covert
Grange Farm
Cammeringham Grange
Cammeringham Top Covert
A15
LN2
Brattleby Thorns
Horse Covert
Poplar Wood
Half Acre Plantation
MIDDLE STREET
CLIFF RD
South Spinney
Beck Spinney
Brattleby
SCHOOL LA
Hall
Manor Farm
Thorpe Lane Farm
THORPE LANE
East Hall Farm
Pits Plantation
EAST LA
Aisthorpe Hall
Shephers Farm
Glebe Farm
Cliff House Farm
B1398
MIDDLE ST
Aisthorpe
Works
Low Farm
Sewage Works
MANOR LA
Sewage Works
Scampton Gorse
Scampton
Scampton House Farm
HIGH ST
Scampton CE Primary School
HIGH STREET
Scampton Airfield
Resr
ERMINE CR
Welton Cliff
TILL BRIDGE LANE
ST JOHNS CL
MIDDLE ST
POLLYPLATT LANE
PO
HEATH LANE
Pollyplatt Primary School
SCAMPTON WY
North Carlton Covert
Till Bridge Lane House
Resr
Playing Fields
Glebe Farm
Viewpoint
LN1
HORNCASTLE LANE
A1500
HORNCASTLE LANE
North Cliff Farm
Riseholme Golf
SOMERSBY CT
Old Hall
Moat
CHURCH LA
Fen House
North Carlton
North Carlton Cliff Farm
Lincolnshire Showground
North Carlton Bridge
CARLTON LANE
MAIN ST
Old Mill Hill
South Cliff Farm
Watering Dyke Houses
SCHOOL LA
Cliff Farm
Rose Cottage West End
South Carlton
MIDDLE STREET
Fox Covert
Hallifirs
North Wood
FEN LANE
Fox Covert
Burton Fen
Gorse Covert
Burton Cliff Farm
RISEHOLME LA
Tower Farm
SAXILBY ROAD
Main Drain
Birch Holt
Birch Holt Farm
Burton
A57
Fossdyke Navigation
Sand Hills
Bridge Farm
New Farm
Ellis Farm
ST GEORGES LA
Kew's Holt
Burton Gravel Pits Nature Res
Burton Bridge
Burton Park
A46
A46
8 81 7 80 6 79 5 78 4 77 3 76 2 75 1 74
92 93 94 95 96 97
200
80
68
201

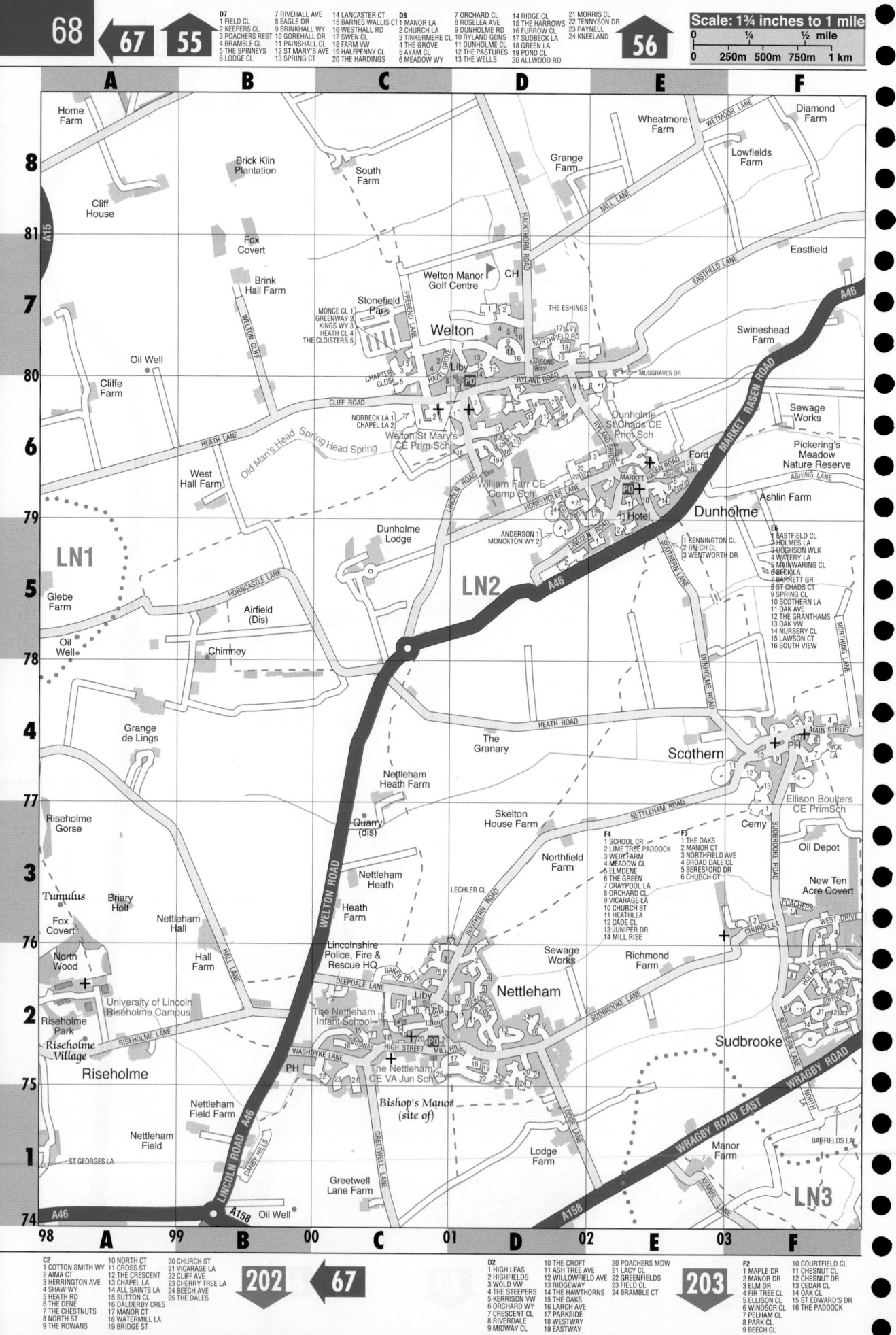

D7
1 FIELD CL
2 KEEPERS CL
3 POACHERS REST
4 BRAMBLE CL
5 THE SPINNEYS
6 LODGE CL

7 RIVEHALL AVE
8 EAGLE DR
9 BRINKHALL WY
10 GOREHALL DR
11 PAINSHALL CL
12 ST MARY'S AVE
13 SPRING CT

14 LANCASTER CT
15 BARNES WALLIS CT
16 WESTHALL RD
17 SWEN CL
18 FARM VW
19 HALFPENNY CL
20 THE HARDINGS

D6
1 MANOR LA
2 CHURCH LA
3 TINKERMERE CL
4 THE GROVE
5 AYAM CL
6 MEADOW WY

7 ORCHARD CL
8 ROSELEA AVE
9 DUNHOLME RD
10 RYLAND GDNS
11 DUNHOLME CL
12 THE PASTURES
13 THE WELLS

14 RIDGE CL
15 THE HARROWS
16 FURROW CL
17 SUDBECK LA
18 GREEN LA
19 POND CL
20 ALLWOOD RD

21 MORRIS CL
22 TENNYSON DR
23 PAYNELL
24 KNEELAND

LN1

LN2

LN3

C2
1 COTTON SMITH WY
2 AIMA CT
3 HERRINGTON AVE
4 SHAW WY
5 HEATH RD
6 THE DENE
7 THE CHESTNUTS
8 NORTH ST
9 THE ROWANS

10 NORTH CT
11 CROSS ST
12 THE CRESCENT
13 CHAPEL LA
14 ALL SAINTS LA
15 SUTTON CL
16 DALDERBY CRES
17 MANOR CT
18 WATERMILL LA
19 BRIDGE ST

20 CHURCH ST
21 VICARAGE LA
22 CLIFF AVE
23 CHERRY TREE LA
24 BEECH AVE
25 THE DALES

D2
1 HIGH LEAS
2 HIGHFIELDS
3 WOLD VW
4 THE STEEPERS
5 KERRISON VW
6 ORCHARD WY
7 CRESCENT CL
8 RIVERDALE
9 MIDWAY CL

10 THE CROFT
11 ASH TREE AVE
12 WILLOWFIELD AVE
13 RIDGEWAY
14 THE HAWTHORNS
15 THE OAKS
16 LARCH AVE
17 PARKSIDE
18 WESTWAY
19 EASTWAY

20 POACHERS MDW
21 LACY CL
22 GREENFIELDS
23 FIELD CL
24 BRAMBLE CT

F2
1 MAPLE DR
2 MANOR CT
3 ELM DR
4 FIR TREE CL
5 ELLISON CL
6 WINDSOR CL
7 PELHAM CL
8 PARK CL
9 BEECH CL

10 COURTFIELD CL
11 CHESNUT CL
12 CHESNUT DR
13 CEDAR CL
14 OAK CL
15 ST EDWARD'S CL
16 THE PADDOCK

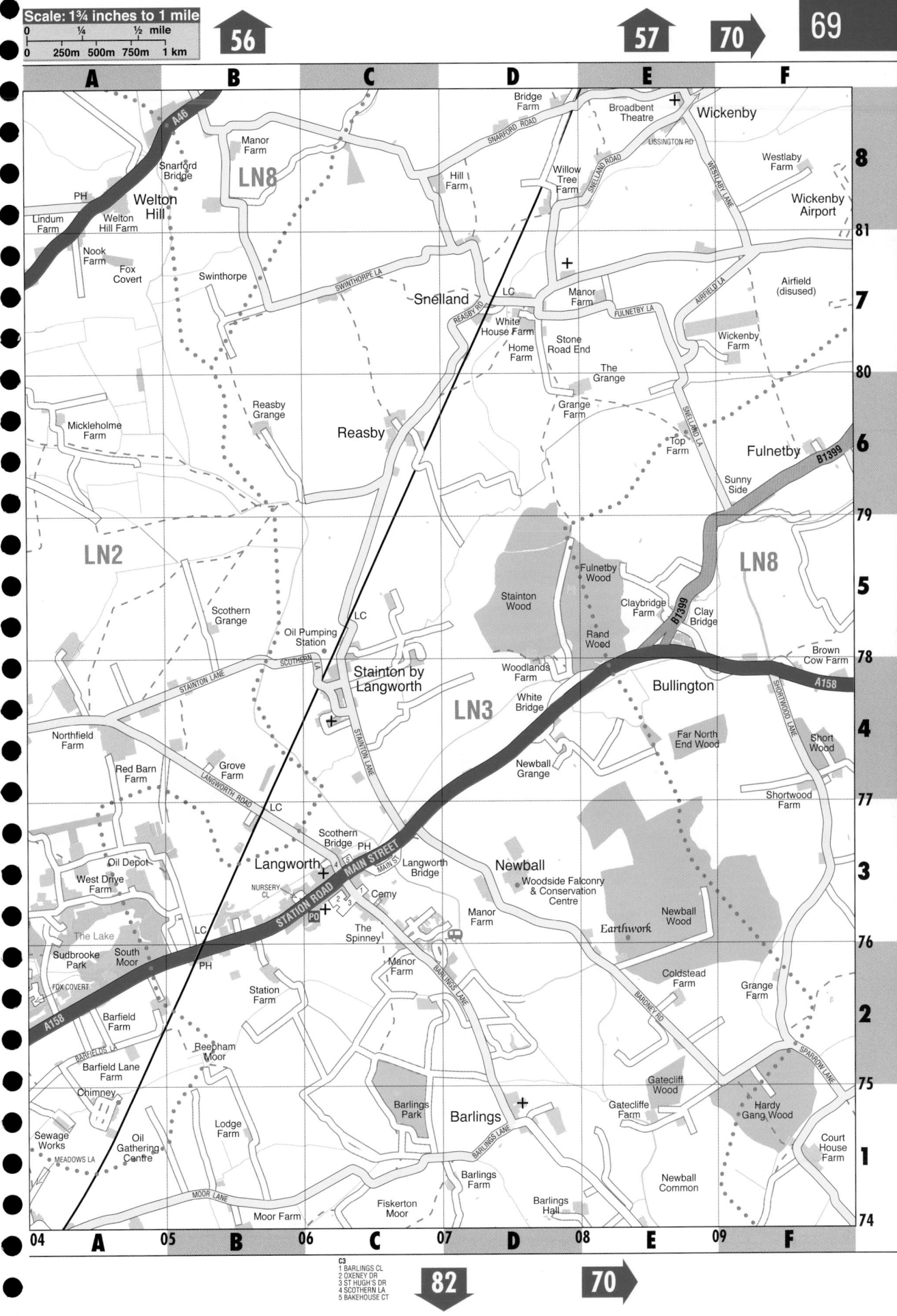

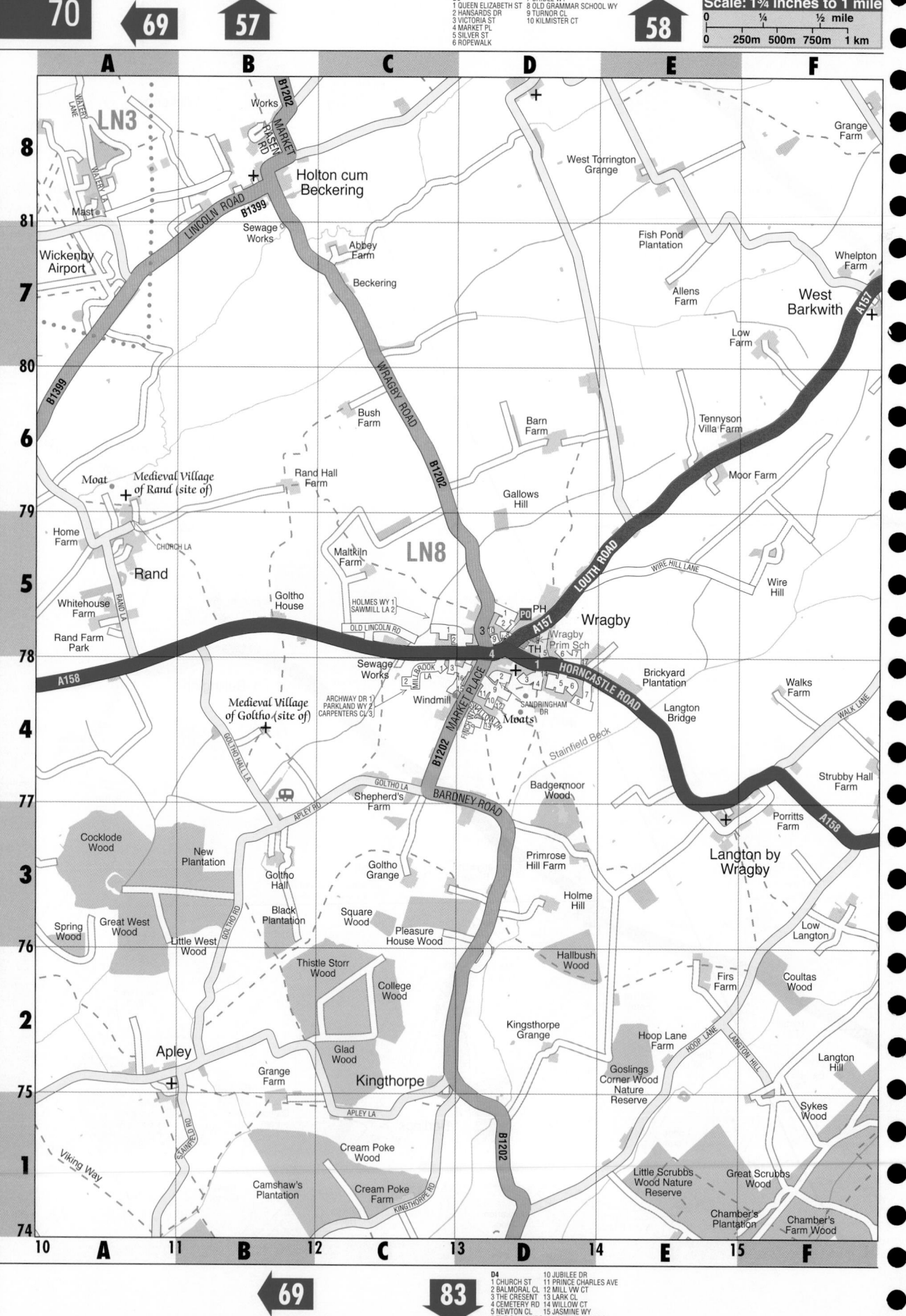

Scale: 1¾ inches to 1 mile

58 59 72

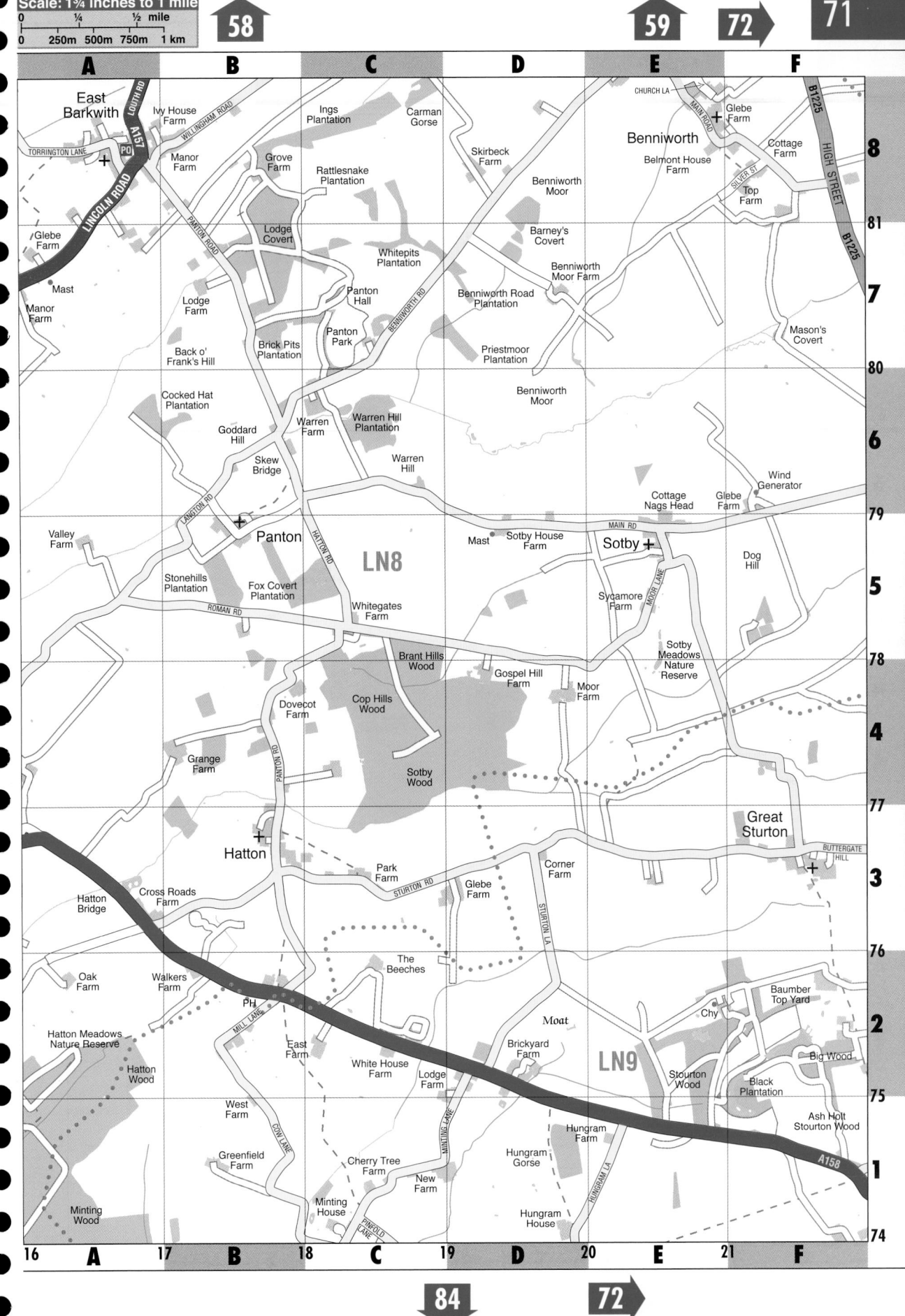
A
B
C
D
E
F
East Barkwith
Ivy House Farm
Ings Plantation
Carman Gorse
Benniworth
Glebe Farm
Cottage Farm
Belmont House Farm
Top Farm
Skirbeck Farm
Benniworth Moor
Manor Farm
Grove Farm
Rattlesnake Plantation
Glebe Farm
Lodge Covert
Barney's Covert
Whitepits Plantation
Benniworth Moor Farm
Mast
Manor Farm
Lodge Farm
Panton Hall
Benniworth Road Plantation
Mason's Covert
Panton Park
Brick Pits Plantation
Back o' Frank's Hill
Priestmoor Plantation
Benniworth Moor
Cocked Hat Plantation
Warren Hill Plantation
Goddard Hill
Warren Farm
Skew Bridge
Warren Hill
Wind Generator
Cottage Nags Head
Glebe Farm
Valley Farm
Panton
Mast
Sotby House Farm
Sotby
LN8
Dog Hill
Stonehills Plantation
Fox Covert Plantation
Sycamore Farm
Whitegates Farm
Brant Hills Wood
Sotby Meadows Nature Reserve
Gospel Hill Farm
Moor Farm
Dovecot Farm
Cop Hills Wood
Grange Farm
Sotby Wood
Great Sturton
Hatton
Park Farm
Corner Farm
Hatton Bridge
Cross Roads Farm
Glebe Farm
The Beeches
Oak Farm
Walkers Farm
PH
Baumber Top Yard
Chy
Moat
Hatton Meadows Nature Reserve
East Farm
Brickyard Farm
LN9
Big Wood
Hatton Wood
White House Farm
Lodge Farm
Stourton Wood
Black Plantation
West Farm
Hungram Farm
Ash Holt Stourton Wood
Greenfield Farm
Hungram Gorse
Cherry Tree Farm
New Farm
Minting Wood
Minting House
Hungram House
TORRINGTON LANE
LOUTH RD
A157
PO
LINCOLN ROAD
WILLINGHAM ROAD
PANTON ROAD
BENNIWORTH RD
CHURCH LA
MAIN ROAD
SILVER ST
B1225
HIGH STREET
LANGTON RD
HATTON RD
MAIN RD
MOOR LANE
ROMAN RD
PANTON RD
STURTON RD
STURTON LA
BUTTERGATE HILL
MILL LANE
COW LANE
MINTING LANE
HUNGRAM LA
PINFOLD LANE
A158
8
81
7
80
6
79
5
78
4
77
3
76
2
75
1
74
16
17
18
19
20
21

84 72

71
59
60

Scale: 1¾ inches to 1 mile

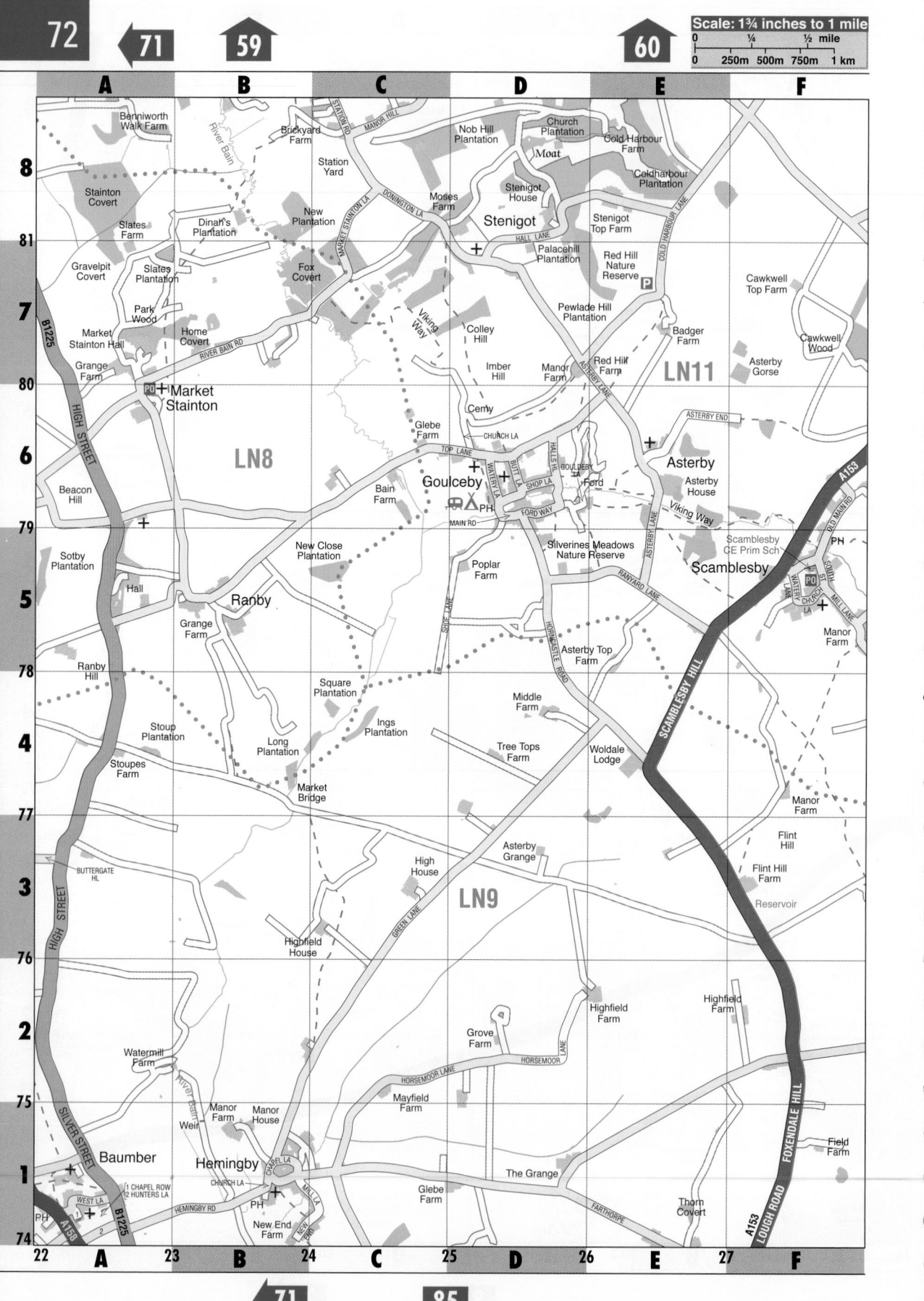

0 ¼ ½ mile
0 250m 500m 750m 1 km
A B C D E F
Benniworth Walk Farm
Brickyard Farm
Station Yard
Nob Hill Plantation
Church Plantation
Cold Harbour Farm
Moat
Coldharbour Plantation
Stainton Covert
Stenigot House
Moses Farm
Stenigot
Stenigot Top Farm
New Plantation
Slates Farm
Dinah's Plantation
Gravelpit Covert
Slates Plantation
Fox Covert
Palacehill Plantation
Red Hill Nature Reserve
Cawkwell Top Farm
Park Wood
Market Stainton Hall
Home Covert
Viking Way
Colley Hill
Pewlade Hill Plantation
Badger Farm
Cawkwell Wood
Grange Farm
Imber Hill
Manor Farm
Red Hill Farm
LN11
Asterby Gorse
Market Stainton
Cemy
Glebe Farm
LN8
Asterby
Asterby House
Goulceby
Beacon Hill
Bain Farm
Ford
PH
Sotby Plantation
New Close Plantation
Poplar Farm
Silverines Meadows Nature Reserve
Scamblesby CE Prim Sch
Scamblesby
Hall
Ranby
Grange Farm
Manor Farm
Asterby Top Farm
Ranby Hill
Square Plantation
Middle Farm
Stoup Plantation
Ings Plantation
Long Plantation
Tree Tops Farm
Woldale Lodge
Stoupes Farm
Market Bridge
Manor Farm
Flint Hill
Asterby Grange
High House
Flint Hill Farm
LN9
Reservoir
Highfield House
Highfield Farm
Highfield Farm
Grove Farm
Watermill Farm
Mayfield Farm
Manor Farm
Manor House
Weir
Field Farm
Baumber
Hemingby
The Grange
Glebe Farm
Thorn Covert
New End Farm
1 CHAPEL ROW
2 HUNTERS LA
B1225
HIGH STREET
SILVER STREET
A158
A153
SCAMBLESBY HILL
FOXENDALE HILL
LOUGH ROAD
RIVER BAIN RD
MARKET STAINTON LA
DONINGTON LA
STATION RD
MANOR HILL
HALL LANE
COLD HARBOUR LANE
ASTERBY LANE
ASTERBY END
TOP LANE
CHURCH LA
WATERY LA
BUTT LA
SHOP LA
HALLS HL
GOULCEBY LA
FORD WAY
MAIN RD
ASTERBY LANE
RANYARD LANE
SHOE LANE
HORNCASTLE ROAD
GREEN LANE
HORSEMOOR LANE
FARTHORPE
HEMINGBY RD
CHAPEL LA
CHURCH LA
MILL LA
NEW END
WEST LA
BUTTERGATE HL
OLD MAIN RD
SOUTH ST
MILL LANE
CHURCH LA
WATERY LANE
River Bain
8 81 7 80 6 79 5 78 4 77 3 76 2 75 1 74
22 23 24 25 26 27

71
85

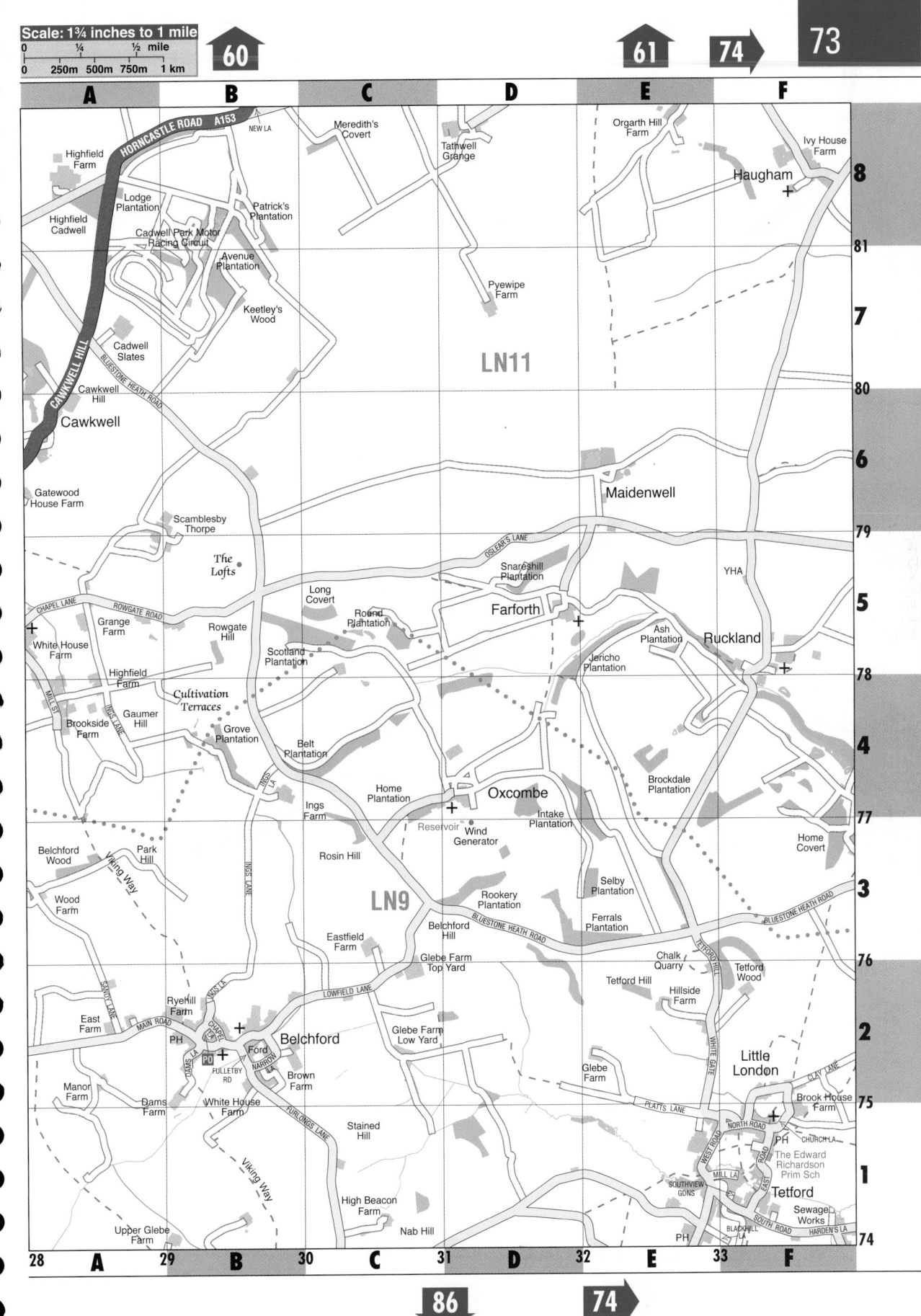

Scale: 1¾ inches to 1 mile

| 0 | ¼ | ½ | mile |

| 0 | 250m | 500m | 750m | 1 km |

60   61   74

86   74

Map labels:

HORNCASTLE ROAD A153
NEW LA
Highfield Farm
Highfield Cadwell
Lodge Plantation
Patrick's Plantation
Meredith's Covert
Tathwell Grange
Orgarth Hill Farm
Ivy House Farm
Haugham
Cadwell Park Motor Racing Circuit
Avenue Plantation
Keetley's Wood
Cadwell Slates
Pyewipe Farm
LN11
CAWKWELL HILL
BLUESTONE HEATH ROAD
Cawkwell Hill
Cawkwell
Gatewood House Farm
Maidenwell
Scamblesby Thorpe
The Lofts
OSLEAR'S LANE
Snareshill Plantation
YHA
CHAPEL LANE
ROWGATE ROAD
Long Covert
Round Plantation
Farforth
Ash Plantation
Ruckland
Grange Farm
Rowgate Hill
Scotland Plantation
Jericho Plantation
White House Farm
Highfield Farm
Cultivation Terraces
Grove Plantation
Belt Plantation
MILL ST
INGS LANE
Brookside Farm
Gaumer Hill
Home Plantation
Oxcombe
Intake Plantation
Brockdale Plantation
Home Covert
Ings Farm
Reservoir
Wind Generator
Belchford Wood
Park Hill
VIKING WAY
Rosin Hill
Selby Plantation
Wood Farm
INGS LA
LN9
Rookery Plantation
BLUESTONE HEATH ROAD
Ferrals Plantation
BLUESTONE HEATH ROAD
Eastfield Farm
Belchford Hill
Chalk Quarry
Tetford Wood
Glebe Farm Top Yard
Tetford Hill
Hillside Farm
TETFORD HILL
East Farm
MAIN ROAD
SANDY LANE
Ryehill Farm
LOWFIELD LANE
Belchford
Glebe Farm Low Yard
PH
CHAPEL LA
CROSS LA
PO
Ford
NARROW LA
FULLETBY RD
Brown Farm
Glebe Farm
WHITE GATE
Little London
CLAY LANE
Manor Farm
Dams Farm
White House Farm
FURLONGS LANE
Stained Hill
PLATTS LANE
Brook House Farm
NORTH ROAD
PH
CHURCH LA
VIKING WAY
High Beacon Farm
Nab Hill
WEST ROAD
MILL LA
EAST ROAD
SOUTHVIEW GDNS
The Edward Richardson Prim Sch
Tetford
Upper Glebe Farm
SOUTH ROAD
PH
BLACKHILL
Sewage Works
HARDEN'S LA

Grid references (right edge): 8, 81, 7, 80, 6, 79, 5, 78, 4, 77, 3, 76, 2, 75, 1, 74

Grid references (bottom): 28, 29, 30, 31, 32, 33

Column letters: A, B, C, D, E, F

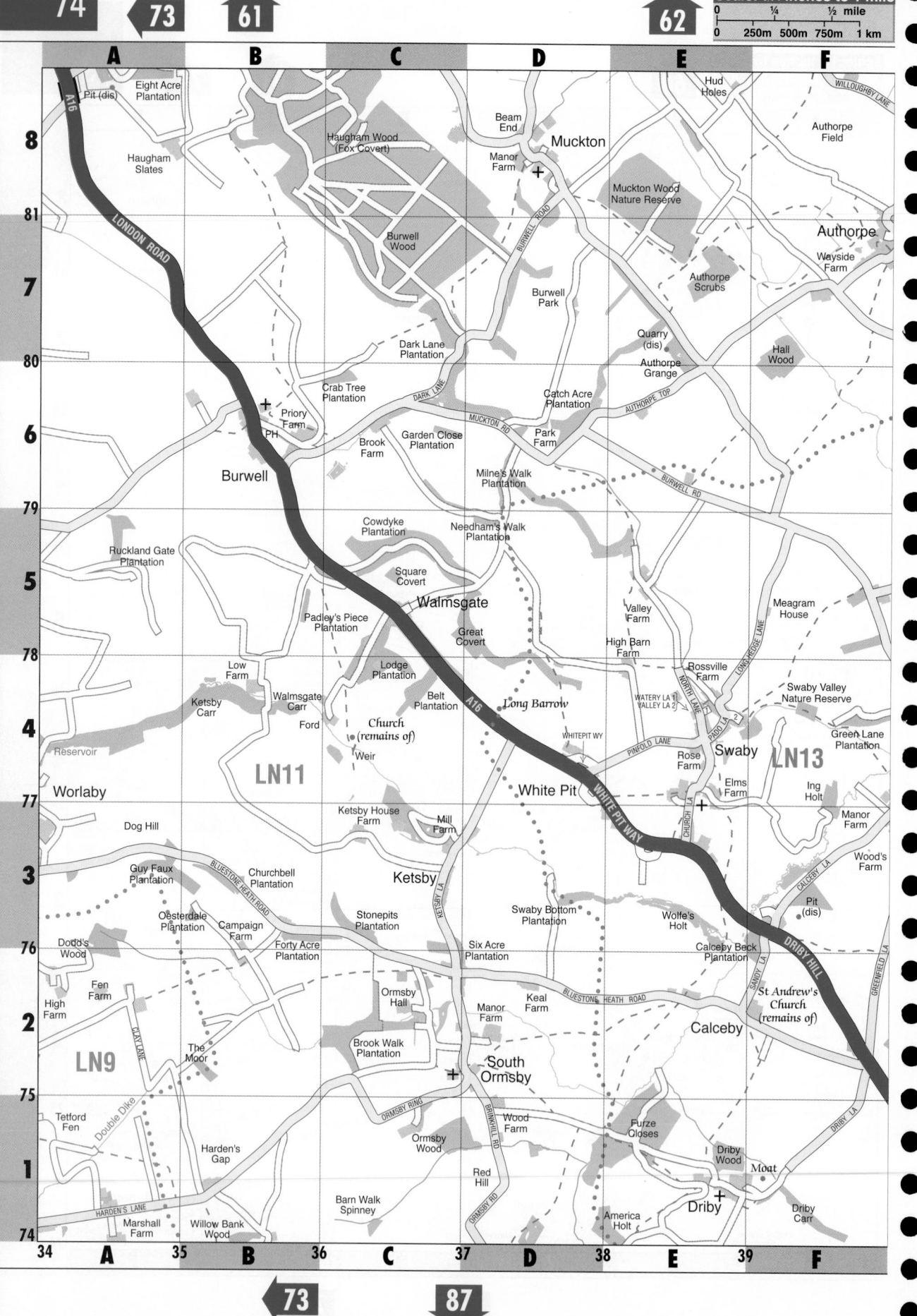

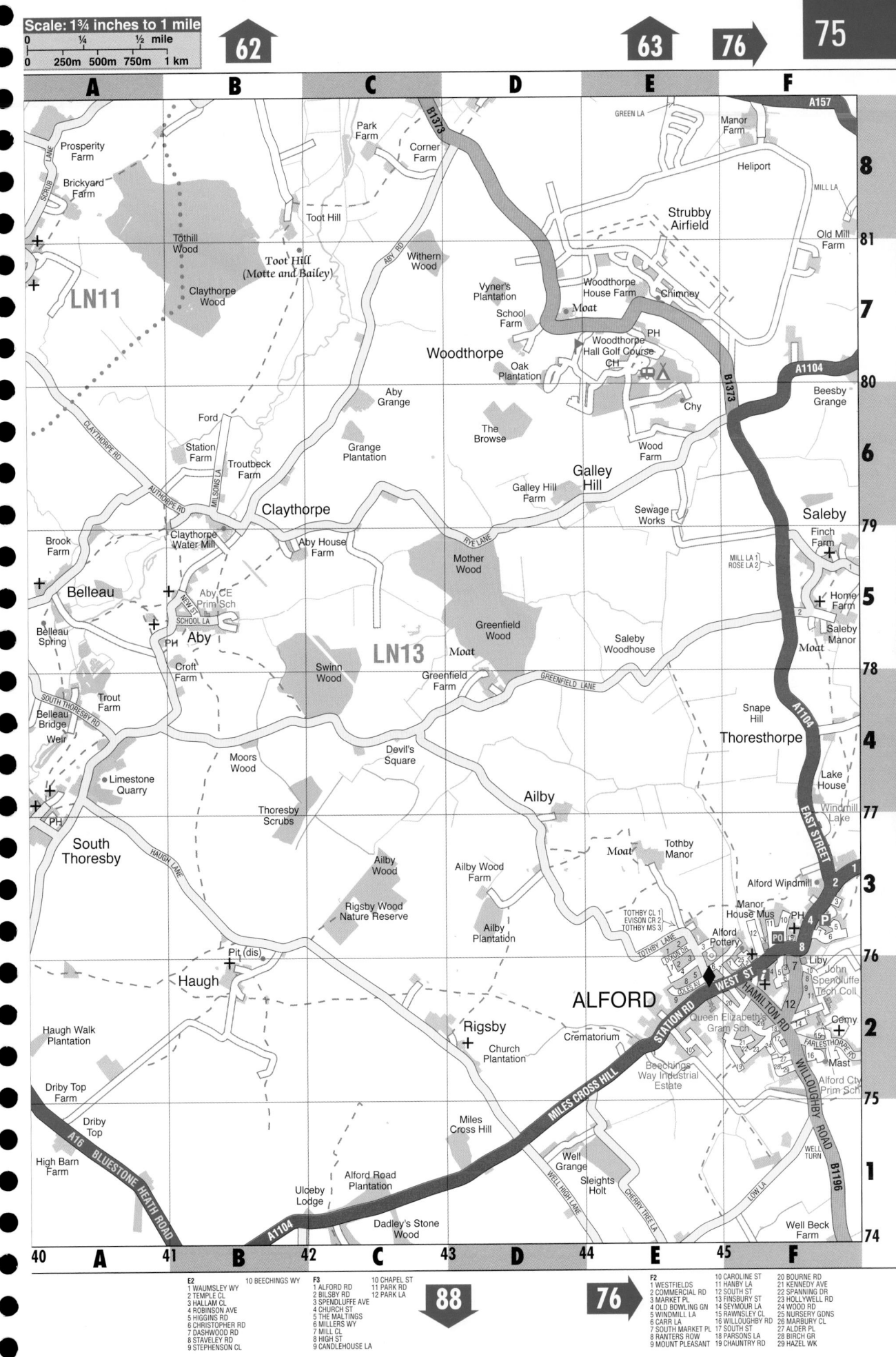

A   B   C   D   E   F

LN11

Prosperity Farm
Brickyard Farm
Tothill Wood
Toot Hill
Park Farm
Corner Farm
B1373
Withern Wood
Aby Rd
Toot Hill (Motte and Bailey)
Claythorpe Wood

Green La
Manor Farm
Heliport
Strubby Airfield
A157

8

81

Vyner's Plantation
School Farm
Moat
Woodthorpe House Farm
Chimney
Woodthorpe
Woodthorpe Hall Golf Course
PH
CH
Oak Plantation
Chy

7

Ford
Station Farm
Troutbeck Farm
Aby Grange
Grange Plantation
The Browse
Wood Farm
B1373
A1104
Beesby Grange

80

Claythorpe
Claythorpe Water Mill
Aby House Farm
Galley Hill Farm
Galley Hill
Sewage Works
Saleby
Finch Farm

6

Brook Farm
Rye Lane
Mother Wood

79

Belleau
Belleau Spring
Aby CE Prim Sch
SCHOOL LA
PH
Aby
Greenfield Wood
Moat
Saleby Woodhouse
Mill La 1
Rose La 2
Home Farm
Saleby Manor
Moat

5

Croft Farm
Swinn Wood
LN13
Greenfield Farm
Greenfield Lane

Trout Farm
Belleau Bridge Weir
SOUTH THORESBY RD
Moors Wood
Devil's Square
Snape Hill
A1104
Thoresthorpe

4

78

South Thoresby
HAUGH LANE
Thoresby Scrubs
Ailby
Lake House
Windmill Lake
EAST STREET

77

Limestone Quarry
PH
Ailby Wood
Ailby Wood Farm
Moat
Tothby Manor
Alford Windmill
1
2
3

3

Haugh Walk Plantation
Pit (dis)
Haugh
Rigsby Wood Nature Reserve
Ailby Plantation
Tothby Cl 1
Evison Cr 2
Tothby Ms 3
TOTHBY LANE
Manor House Mus
Alford Pottery
PH
P
PO
Liby
John Spendluffe Tech Coll

76

ALFORD
WEST ST
STATION RD
HAMILTON RD
Cemy
Mast
FARLESTHORPE RD

2

Driby Top Farm
Driby Top
Rigsby
Church Plantation
Crematorium
Queen Elizabeth Gram Sch
WILLOUGHBY ROAD
Alford Cty Prim Sch

75

High Barn Farm
A16
BLUESTONE HEATH ROAD
Ulceby Lodge
Alford Road Plantation
Miles Cross Hill
MILES CROSS HILL
Well Grange
Sleights Holt
WELL HIGH LANE
CHERRY TREE LA
WELL TURN
B1196

1

A1104
Dadley's Stone Wood
Well Beck Farm

74

40   A   41   B   42   C   43   D   44   E   45   F

E2
1 WAUMSLEY WY
2 TEMPLE CL
3 HALLAM CL
4 ROBINSON AVE
5 HIGGINS RD
6 CHRISTOPHER RD
7 DASHWOOD RD
8 STAVELEY RD
9 STEPHENSON CL
10 BEECHINGS WY

F3
1 ALFORD RD
2 BILSBY RD
3 SPENDLUFFE AVE
4 CHURCH ST
5 THE MALTINGS
6 MILLERS WY
7 MILL CL
8 HIGH ST
9 CANDLEHOUSE LA
10 CHAPEL ST
11 PARK RD
12 PARK LA

F2
1 WESTFIELDS
2 COMMERCIAL RD
3 MARKET PL
4 OLD BOWLING GN
5 WINDMILL LA
6 CARR LA
7 SOUTH MARKET PL
8 RANTERS ROW
9 MOUNT PLEASANT
10 CAROLINE ST
11 HANBY LA
12 SOUTH ST
13 FINSBURY ST
14 SEYMOUR LA
15 RAWNSLEY CL
16 WILLOUGHBY RD
17 SOUTH ST
18 PARSONS LA
19 CHAUNTRY RD
20 BOURNE RD
21 KENNEDY AVE
22 SPANNING DR
23 HOLLYWELL RD
24 WOOD RD
25 NURSERY GDNS
26 MARBURY CL
27 ALDER PL
28 BIRCH GR
29 HAZEL WK

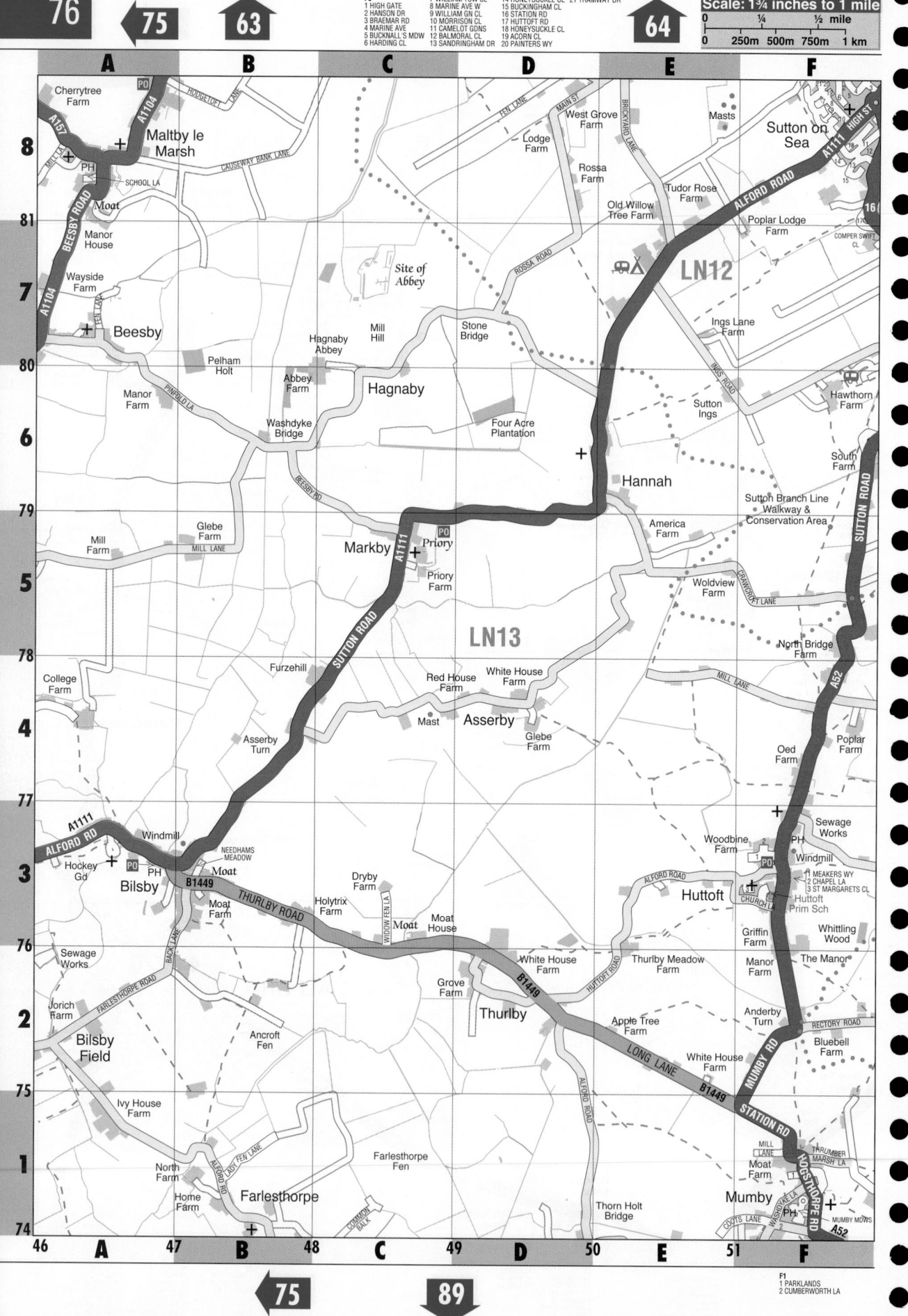

Sandilands, Anderby, Anderby Creek, LN12, LN13, PE24

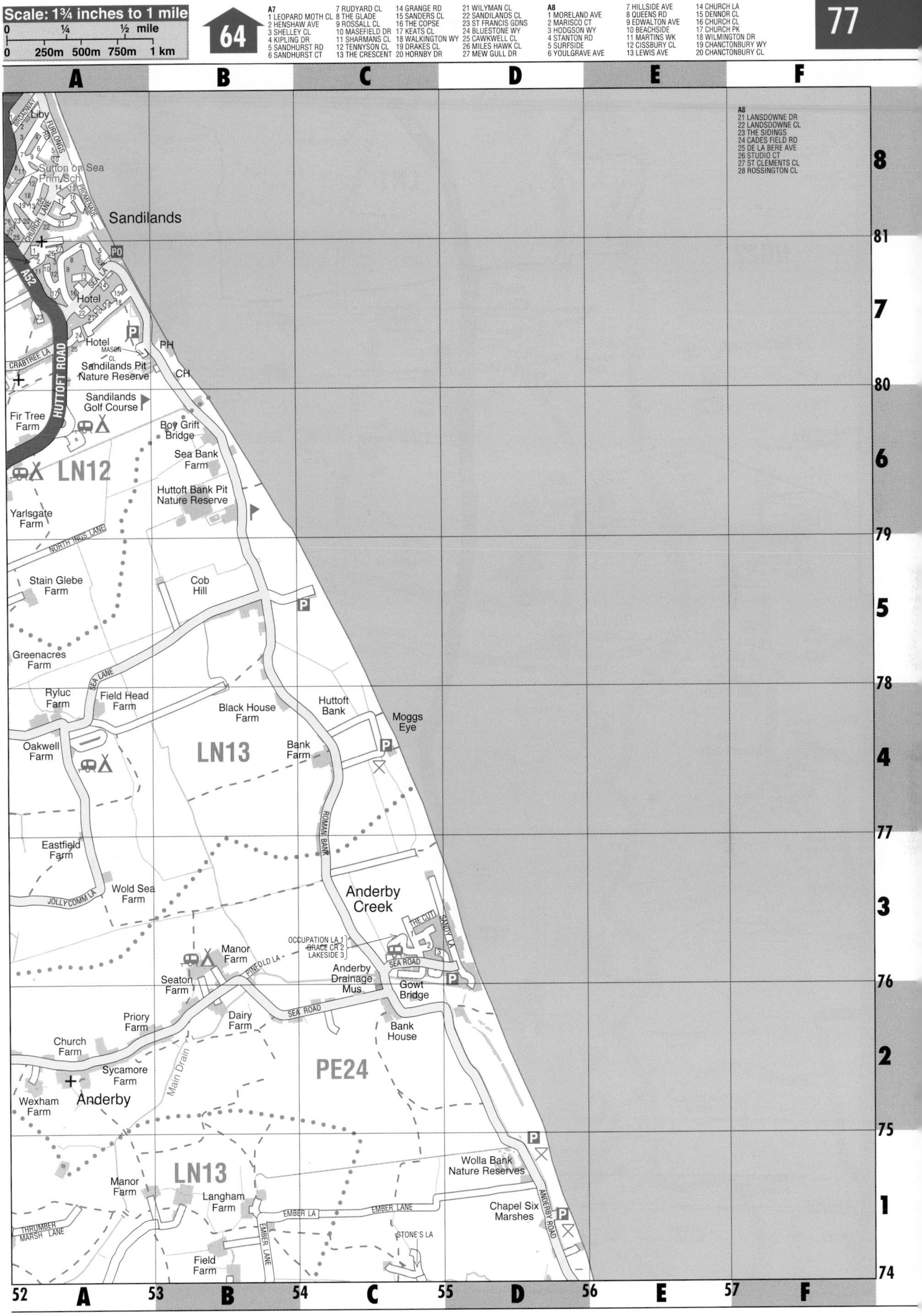

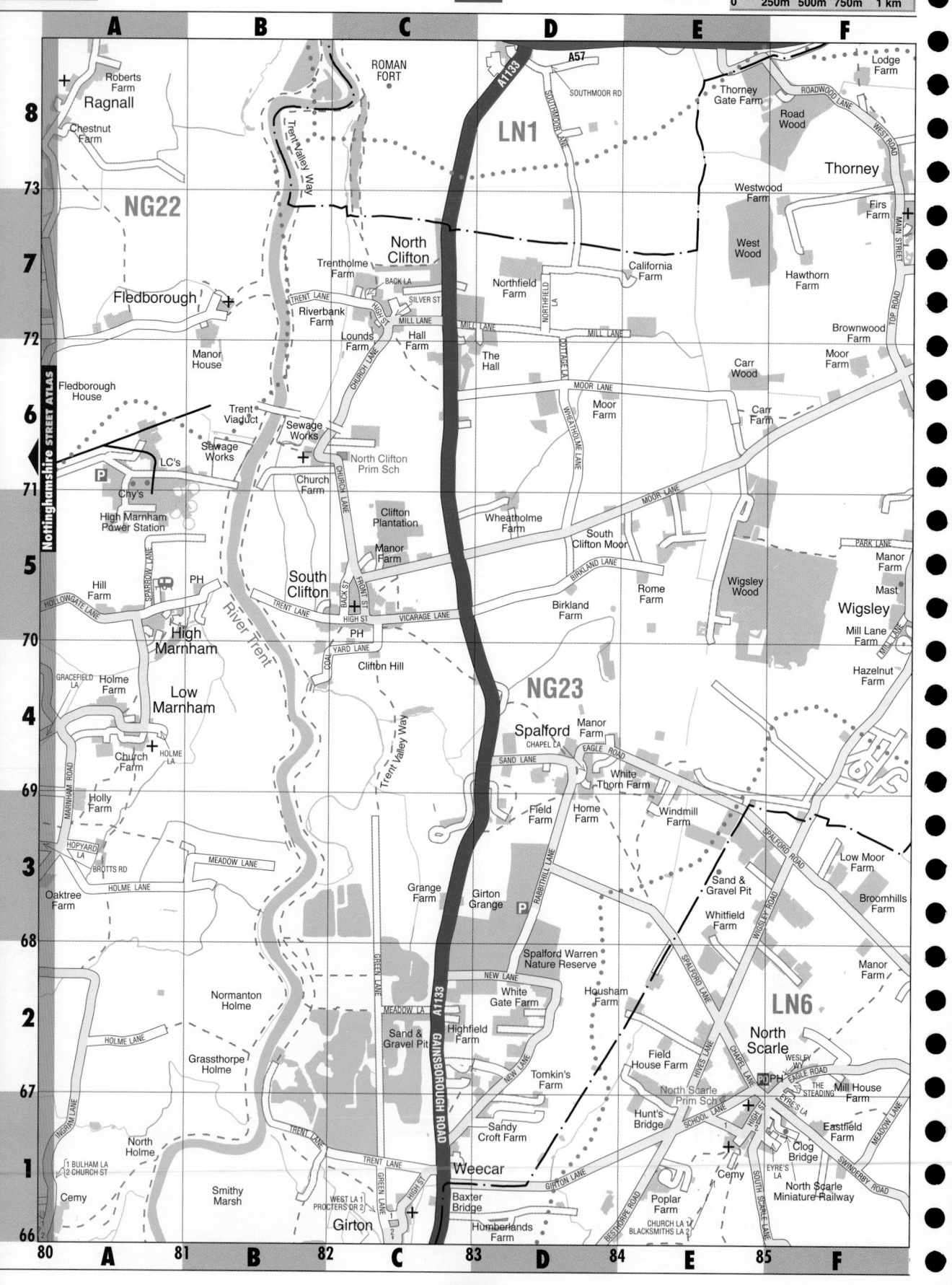

Scale: 1¾ inches to 1 mile

| 0 | ¼ | ½ mile |
| 0 | 250m | 500m | 750m | 1 km |

Nottinghamshire STREET ATLAS

A **B** **C** **D** **E** **F**

Roberts Farm
+ Ragnall
Chestnut Farm
8

ROMAN FORT
LN1
A57
SOUTHMOOR RD
Thorney Gate Farm
Lodge Farm
ROADWOOD LANE
Road Wood
WEST ROAD
Thorney

73

NG22
Trent Valley Way
Westwood Farm
West Wood
Firs Farm
MAIN STREET

7
Trentholme Farm
North Clifton
BACK LA
SILVER ST
Northfield Farm
NORTHFIELD LA
California Farm
Hawthorn Farm

Fledborough +
Riverbank Farm
HIGH ST
MILL LANE
Lounds Farm
Hall Farm
MILL LANE
COTTAGE LA
MILL LANE
Brownwood Farm

72
Manor House
CHURCH LANE
The Hall
Moor Farm

Fledborough House
Trent Viaduct
Sewage Works
Sewage Works
Moor LANE
Moor Farm
Carr Wood
Carr Wood
Moor Farm

6
Trent Viaduct
+ North Clifton Prim Sch
WHEATHOLME LANE
Carr Farm

P
LC's
Church Farm
CHURCH LANE
Clifton Plantation
Wheatholme Farm
MOOR LANE
PARK LANE
Manor Farm

71
Chy's
High Marnham Power Station
Manor Farm
South Clifton Moor
Rome Farm
Wigsley Wood
Mast
Wigsley

5
Hill Farm
SPARROW LANE
PH
TRENT LANE
South Clifton
FRONT ST
BACK ST
Manor Farm
BIRKLAND LANE
Mill Lane Farm

HOLLOWGATE LANE
HIGH ST
+ VICARAGE LANE
PH
Birkland Farm
Hazelnut Farm

70
River Trent
COAL YARD LANE
Clifton Hill
NG23

4
GRACEFIELD LA
Holme Farm
High Marnham
Low Marnham
HOLME LA
Trent Valley Way
Spalford
Manor Farm
CHAPEL LA
EAGLE ROAD
White Thorn Farm

69
Church Farm
Holly Farm
SAND LANE
Field Farm
Home Farm
Windmill Farm
Low Moor Farm

3
HOPYARD LA
BROTTS RD
MEADOW LANE
MARNHAM ROAD
HOLME LANE
GREEN LANE
RABBITHILL LANE
Grange Farm
Girton Grange
P
SPALFORD ROAD
WIGSLEY ROAD
Sand & Gravel Pit
Whitfield Farm
Broomhills Farm

68
Oaktree Farm
Spalford Warren Nature Reserve
Manor Farm

2
Normanton Holme
MEADOW LA
A1133
NEW LANE
White Gate Farm
Housham Farm
LN6
North Scarle
WESLEY WY
EAGLE ROAD

67
HOLME LANE
Grassthorpe Holme
Sand & Gravel Pit
Highfield Farm
NEW LANE
Tomkin's Farm
Field House Farm
RIVES LANE
CHAPEL LANE
P PH
North Scarle Prim Sch
THE STEADING
Mill House Farm

1
INGRAM LANE
North Holme
TRENT LANE
Sandy Croft Farm
SCHOOL LANE
Hunt's Bridge
HIGH ST
EYRE'S LA
Eastfield Farm
SWINDERBY ROAD
MEADOW LANE

1 BULHAM LA
2 CHURCH ST
Cemy
Smithy Marsh
WEST LA 1
PROCTERS DR 2
GREEN LANE
HIGH ST
Weecar
Baxter Bridge
GIRTON LANE
BESTHORPE ROAD
Poplar Farm
Cemy
EYRE'S LA
Clog Bridge
North Scarle Miniature Railway

66
Cemy
Girton
+
Humberlands Farm
GAINSBOROUGH ROAD
CHURCH LA 1
BLACKSMITHS LA 2
SOUTH SCARLE LANE

A 80 **B** 81 **C** 82 **D** 83 **E** 84 85 **F**

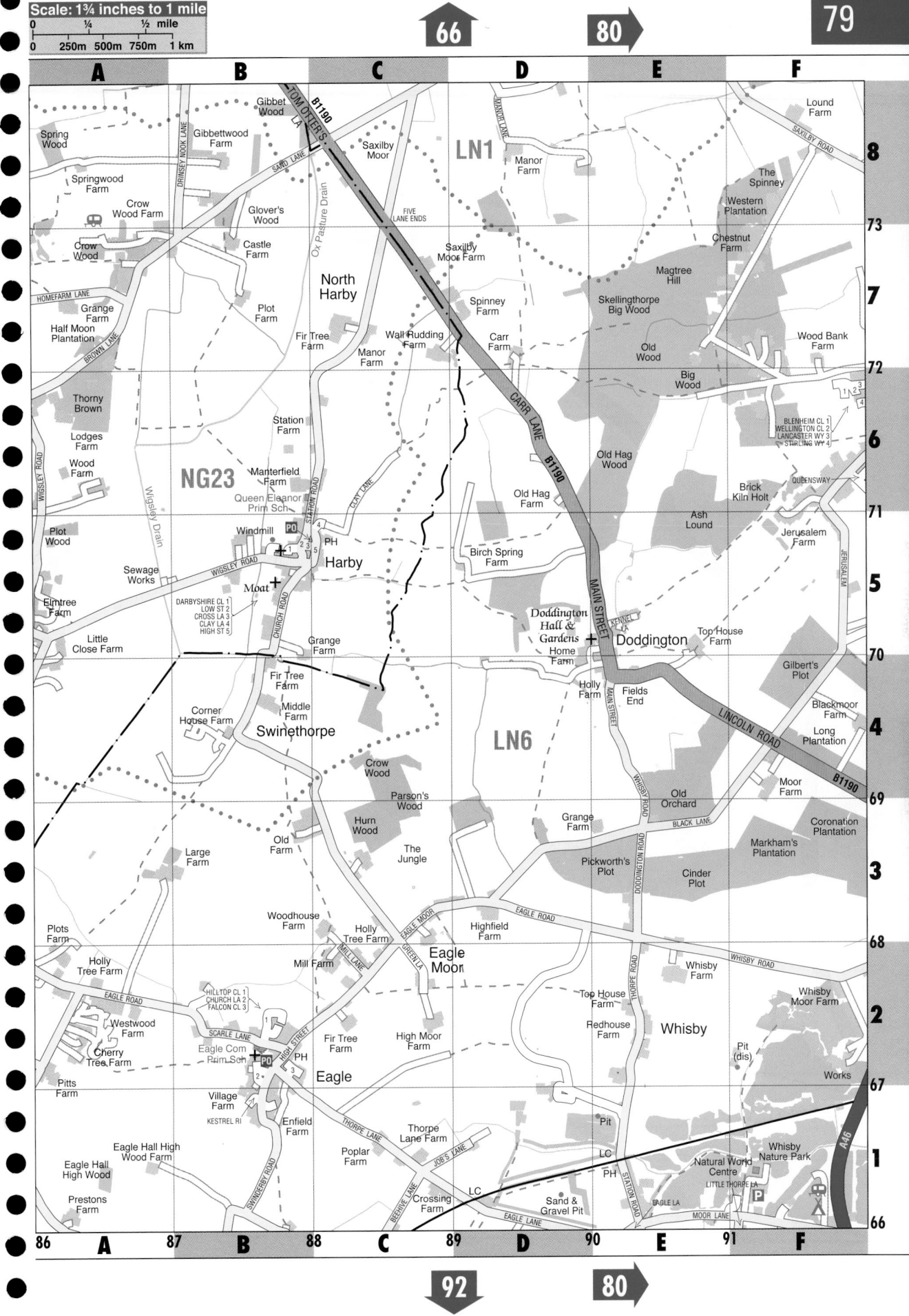
Scale: 1¾ inches to 1 mile
0 ¼ ½ mile
0 250m 500m 750m 1 km
66
80
A B C D E F
Spring Wood
Springwood Farm
Crow Wood Farm
Crow Wood
Gibbet Wood
Gibbettwood Farm
DRINSEY NOOK LANE
SAND LANE
TOM OTTER'S LA
B1190
Saxilby Moor
LN1
MANOR LANE
Manor Farm
Lound Farm
SAXILBY ROAD
The Spinney
Western Plantation
Glover's Wood
Castle Farm
Ox Pasture Drain
FIVE LANE ENDS
Saxilby Moor Farm
Chestnut Farm
Magtree Hill
Skellingthorpe Big Wood
HOMEFARM LANE
Grange Farm
Half Moon Plantation
BROWN LANE
Plot Farm
North Harby
Fir Tree Farm
Manor Farm
Wall Rudding Farm
Spinney Farm
Carr Farm
Old Wood
Wood Bank Farm
Big Wood
Thorny Brown
Lodges Farm
Wood Farm
WIGSLEY ROAD
Station Farm
CARR LANE
B1190
BLENHEIM CL 1
WELLINGTON CL 2
LANCASTER WY 3
STIRLING WY 4
Old Hag Wood
NG23
Wigsley Drain
Manterfield Farm
Queen Eleanor Prim Sch
CLAY LANE
STATION ROAD
Old Hag Farm
Brick Kiln Holt
QUEENSWAY
Ash Lound
Jerusalem Farm
JERUSALEM
Plot Wood
Windmill
PO
PH
Harby
Sewage Works
WIGSLEY ROAD
Moat
Birch Spring Farm
MAIN STREET
Elmtree Farm
DARBYSHIRE CL 1
LOW ST 2
CROSS LA 3
CLAY LA 4
HIGH ST 5
CHURCH ROAD
Doddington Hall & Gardens
KENNEL LA
Doddington
Top House Farm
Little Close Farm
Grange Farm
Home Farm
Gilbert's Plot
Fir Tree Farm
Holly Farm
Fields End
Middle Farm
Blackmoor Farm
Corner House Farm
Swinethorpe
LN6
LINCOLN ROAD
Long Plantation
Crow Wood
Parson's Wood
Moor Farm
B1190
Hurn Wood
Old Orchard
WHISBY ROAD
Grange Farm
BLACK LANE
Coronation Plantation
Old Farm
The Jungle
Large Farm
Pickworth's Plot
DODDINGTON ROAD
Markham's Plantation
Cinder Plot
Woodhouse Farm
Holly Tree Farm
EAGLE MOOR
Highfield Farm
EAGLE ROAD
Plots Farm
MILL LANE
GREEN LA
Eagle Moor
Holly Tree Farm
Mill Farm
WHISBY ROAD
Whisby Farm
EAGLE ROAD
HILLTOP CL 1
CHURCH LA 2
FALCON CL 3
Top House Farm
THORPE ROAD
Whisby Moor Farm
Westwood Farm
SCARLE LANE
HIGH STREET
Fir Tree Farm
High Moor Farm
Redhouse Farm
Whisby
Cherry Tree Farm
Eagle Com Prim Sch
PO
PH
Pit (dis)
Pitts Farm
Eagle
Works
Village Farm
KESTREL RI
Enfield Farm
THORPE LANE
Thorpe Lane Farm
Pit
A46
Eagle Hall High Wood Farm
SWINDERBY ROAD
JOB'S LANE
Poplar Farm
LC
Whisby Nature Park
Eagle Hall High Wood
PH
Natural World Centre
LITTLE THORPE LA
Prestons Farm
BEEHIVE LANE
Crossing Farm
LC
Sand & Gravel Pit
STATION ROAD
EAGLE LA
MOOR LANE
EAGLE LANE
P
8
73
7
72
6
71
5
70
4
69
3
68
2
67
1
66
86 A 87 B 88 C 89 D 90 E 91 F
92
80

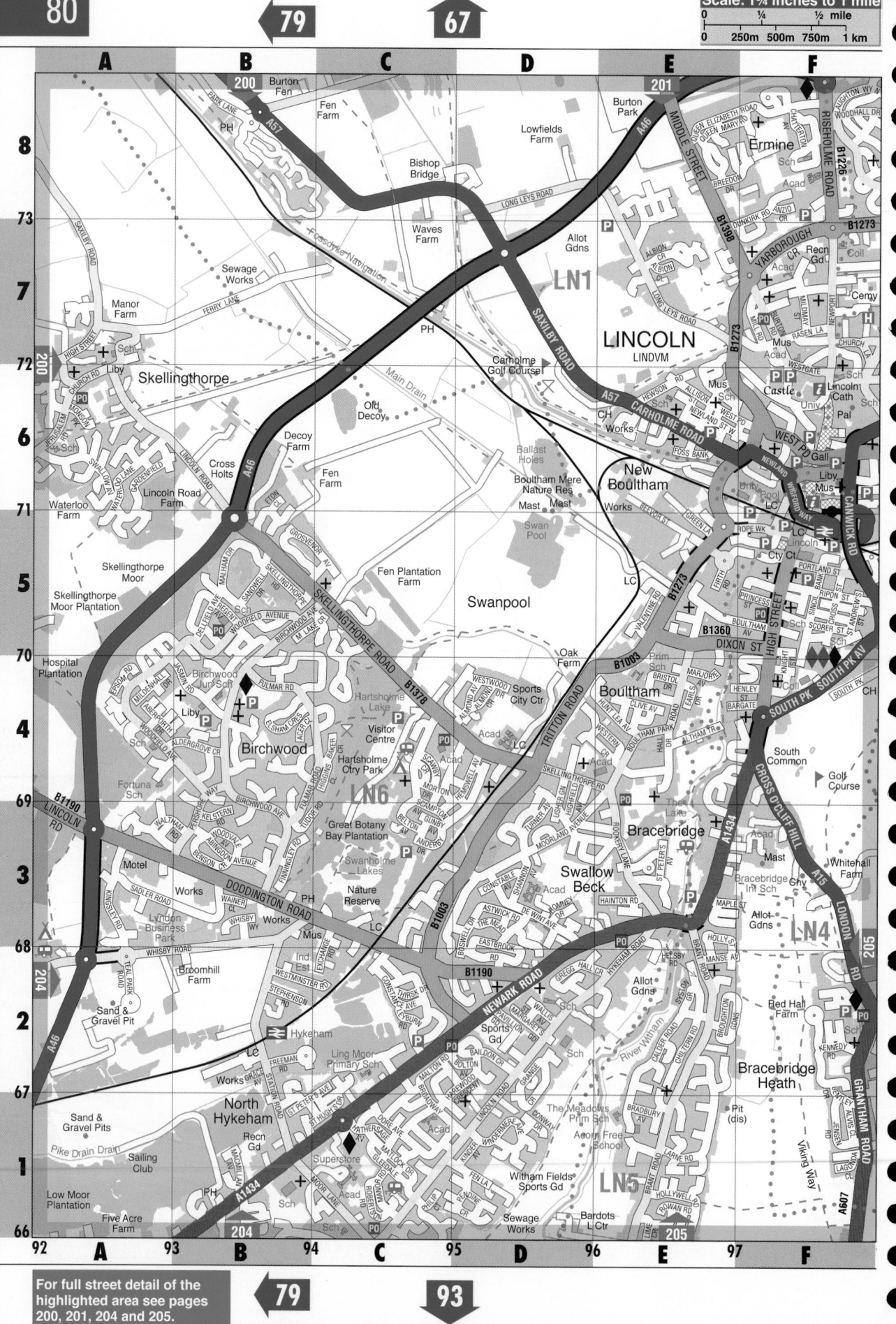

79   67

Scale: 1¾ inches to 1 mile
0   ¼   ½   mile
0   250m   500m   750m   1 km

79   93

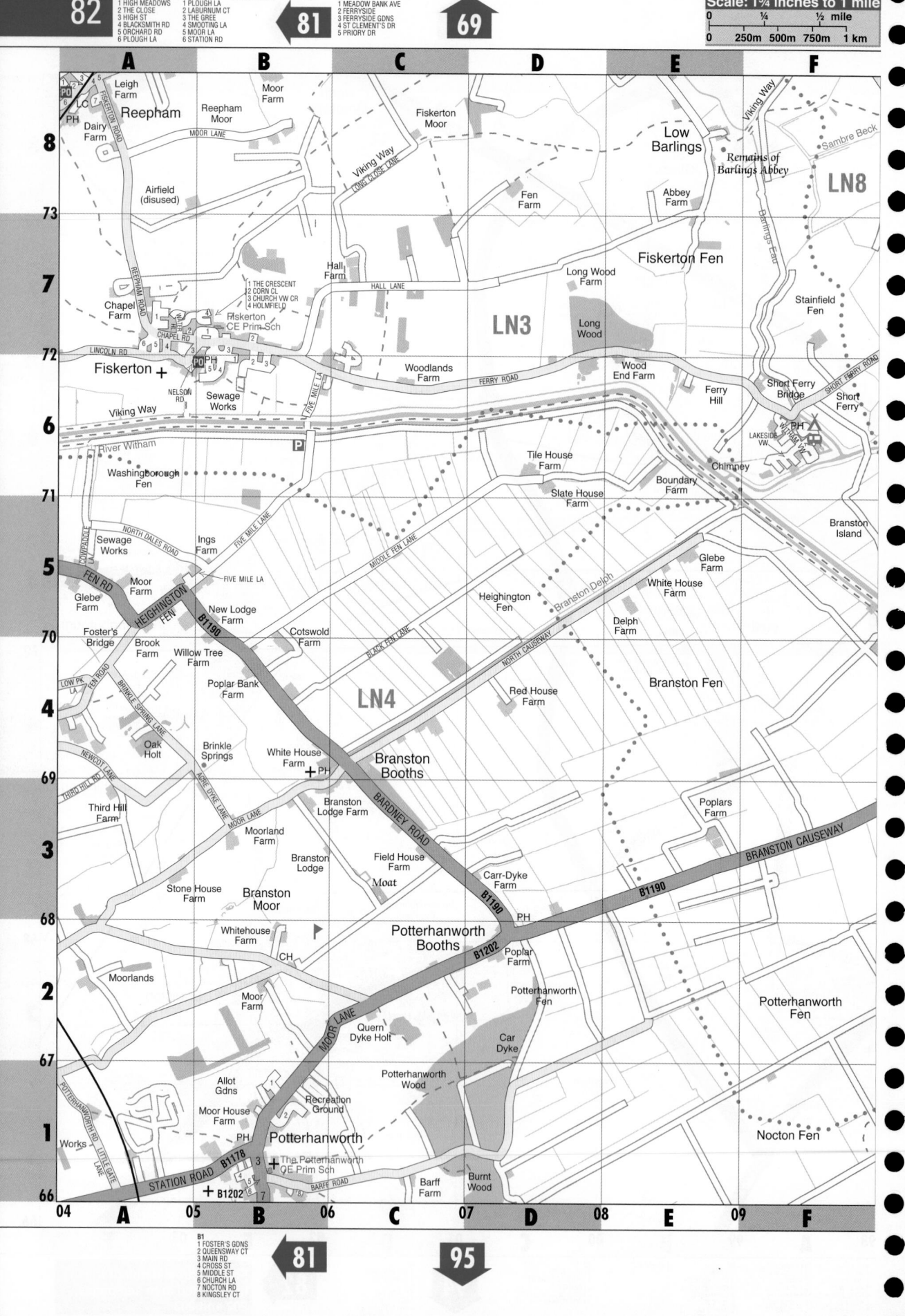

A7
1 HIGH MEADOWS
2 THE CLOSE
3 HIGH ST
4 BLACKSMITH RD
5 ORCHARD RD
6 PLOUGH LA

A8
1 PLOUGH LA
2 LABURNUM CT
3 THE GREE
4 SMOOTING LA
5 MOOR LA
6 STATION RD

7 MEADOW CL

B6
1 MEADOW BANK AVE
2 FERRYSIDE
3 FERRYSIDE GDNS
4 ST CLEMENT'S DR
5 PRIORY DR

Scale: 1¾ inches to 1 mile

0   ¼   ½ mile
0   250m   500m   750m   1 km

A **B** **C** **D** **E** **F**

Leigh Farm
Reepham
Moor Farm
Reepham Moor
Fiskerton Moor
Low Barlings
Remains of Barlings Abbey
LN8

PO
LC
PH
Dairy Farm
Airfield (disused)
MOOR LANE
Fen Farm
Abbey Farm
Sambre Beck

8

Chapel Farm
Hall Farm
HALL LANE
Long Wood Farm
Fiskerton Fen
Stainfield Fen

73

1 THE CRESCENT
2 CORN CL
3 CHURCH VW CR
4 HOLMFIELD
Fiskerton CE Prim Sch
LN3
Long Wood

7

Fiskerton
CHAPEL RD
PH
PO
Woodlands Farm
FERRY ROAD
Wood End Farm
Ferry Hill
Short Ferry Bridge
Short Ferry

72

LINCOLN RD
NELSON RD
Viking Way
FIVE MILE LA
Sewage Works
PH
LAKESIDE VW
WITHAM VW

6

River Witham
P
Washingborough Fen
Tile House Farm
Boundary Farm
Chimney

71

Sewage Works
NORTH DALES ROAD
Ings Farm
FIVE MILE LANE
MIDDLE FEN LANE
Slate House Farm
Branston Island

5

FEN RD
Moor Farm
HEIGHINGTON FEN
B1190
New Lodge Farm
FIVE MILE LA
Branston Delph
Glebe Farm
White House Farm

Glebe Farm
Foster's Bridge
Brook Farm
Willow Tree Farm
Cotswold Farm
BLACK FEN LANE
Heighington Fen
NORTH CAUSEWAY
Delph Farm

70

LOW PK LA
FEN ROAD
Oak Holt
Poplar Bank Farm
LN4
Red House Farm
Branston Fen

4

NEWCOT LANE
Brinkle Springs
BRINKLE SPRING LANE
White House Farm
PH
Branston Booths
BARDNEY ROAD
Poplars Farm

69

THIRD HILL RD
Third Hill Farm
ACRE DYKE LANE
MOOR LANE
Moorland Farm
Branston Lodge Farm
Field House Farm
Moat
B1190

3

Stone House Farm
Branston Lodge
Branston Moor
Carr-Dyke Farm
PH
BRANSTON CAUSEWAY

Whitehouse Farm
CH
Potterhanworth Booths
B1202
Poplar Farm

68

Moorlands
Moor Farm
MOOR LANE
Potterhanworth Fen
Potterhanworth Fen

2

Quern Dyke Holt
Car Dyke

67

POTTERHANWORTH RD
LITTLEGATE LANE
Allot Gdns
Moor House Farm
Recreation Ground
Potterhanworth Wood
Nocton Fen

1

Works
PH
Potterhanworth
B1178
The Potterhanworth
QE Prim Sch
B1202
STATION ROAD
BARFF ROAD
Barff Farm
Burnt Wood

66

04 **A** **05** **B** **06** **C** **07** **D** **08** **E** **09** **F**

B1
1 FOSTER'S GDNS
2 QUEENSWAY CT
3 MAIN RD
4 CROSS ST
5 MIDDLE ST
6 CHURCH LA
7 NOCTON RD
8 KINGSLEY CT

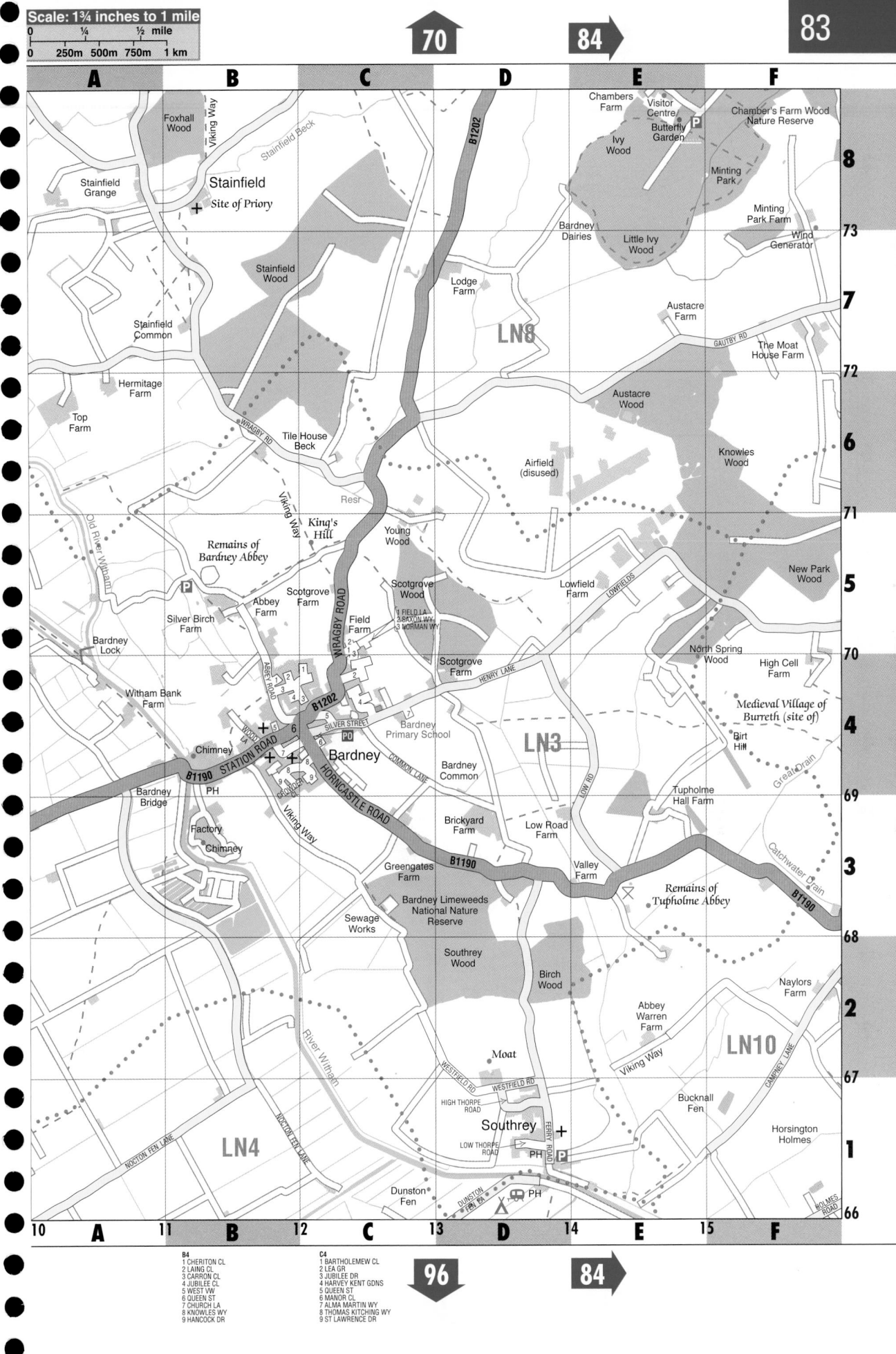

Scale: 1¾ inches to 1 mile

0   ¼   ½   mile
0   250m 500m 750m 1 km

70
84

A   B   C   D   E   F

8
73
7
72
6
71
5
70
4
69
3
68
2
67
1
66

10   11   12   13   14   15

Foxhall Wood
Viking Way
Stainfield Grange
Stainfield
+ Site of Priory
Stainfield Beck
B1202

Chambers Farm
Visitor Centre
Butterfly Garden
Ivy Wood
Chamber's Farm Wood Nature Reserve
Minting Park
Minting Park Farm
Wind Generator

Stainfield Wood
Lodge Farm
Bardney Dairies
Little Ivy Wood

LN8

Austacre Farm
GAUTBY RD
The Moat House Farm

Stainfield Common
WRAGBY RD
Tile House Beck

Austacre Wood

Knowles Wood

Hermitage Farm
Top Farm
Viking Way
Resr
King's Hill
Young Wood
Airfield (disused)

Old River Witham
Remains of Bardney Abbey
Scotgrove Farm
Scotgrove Wood
Lowfield Farm
LOWFIELDS
New Park Wood

Bardney Lock
P
Silver Birch Farm
Abbey Farm
Field Farm
1 FIELD LA
2 SAXON WY
3 NORMAN WY
Scotgrove Farm
North Spring Wood
High Cell Farm

Witham Bank Farm
ABBEY ROAD
WRAGBY ROAD
B1202
SILVER STREET
1
2
3
4
5
6
7
HENRY LANE
Medieval Village of Bureth (site of)
Birt Hill

Bardney Lock
Chimney
STATION ROAD
B1190
PH
PO
Bardney
Bardney Primary School
COMMON LANE
LN3
LOW RD
Tupholme Hall Farm
Great Drain

Bardney Bridge
Factory
Chimney
CROWDER
Viking Way
HORNCASTLE ROAD
Bardney Common
Brickyard Farm
Low Road Farm
Valley Farm
Remains of Tupholme Abbey
Catchwater Drain
B1190

Greengates Farm
B1190
Sewage Works
Bardney Limeweeds National Nature Reserve
Southrey Wood
Birch Wood
Naylors Farm

River Witham
Moat
Abbey Warren Farm
Viking Way
LN10

NOOTON FEN LANE
LN4
NOOTON FEN LANE
WESTFIELD RD
WESTFIELD RD
HIGH THORPE ROAD
Southrey
FERRY ROAD
+
Bucknall Fen
Horsington Holmes

LOW THORPE ROAD
PH
P
Dunston Fen
DUNSTON FEN RD
PH
HOLMES ROAD

B4
1 CHERITON CL
2 LAING CL
3 CARRON CL
4 JUBILEE CL
5 WEST VW
6 QUEEN ST
7 CHURCH LA
8 KNOWLES WY
9 HANCOCK DR

C4
1 BARTHOLEMEW CL
2 LEA GR
3 JUBILEE DR
4 HARVEY KENT GDNS
5 QUEEN ST
6 MANOR CL
7 ALMA MARTIN WY
8 THOMAS KITCHING WY
9 ST LAWRENCE DR

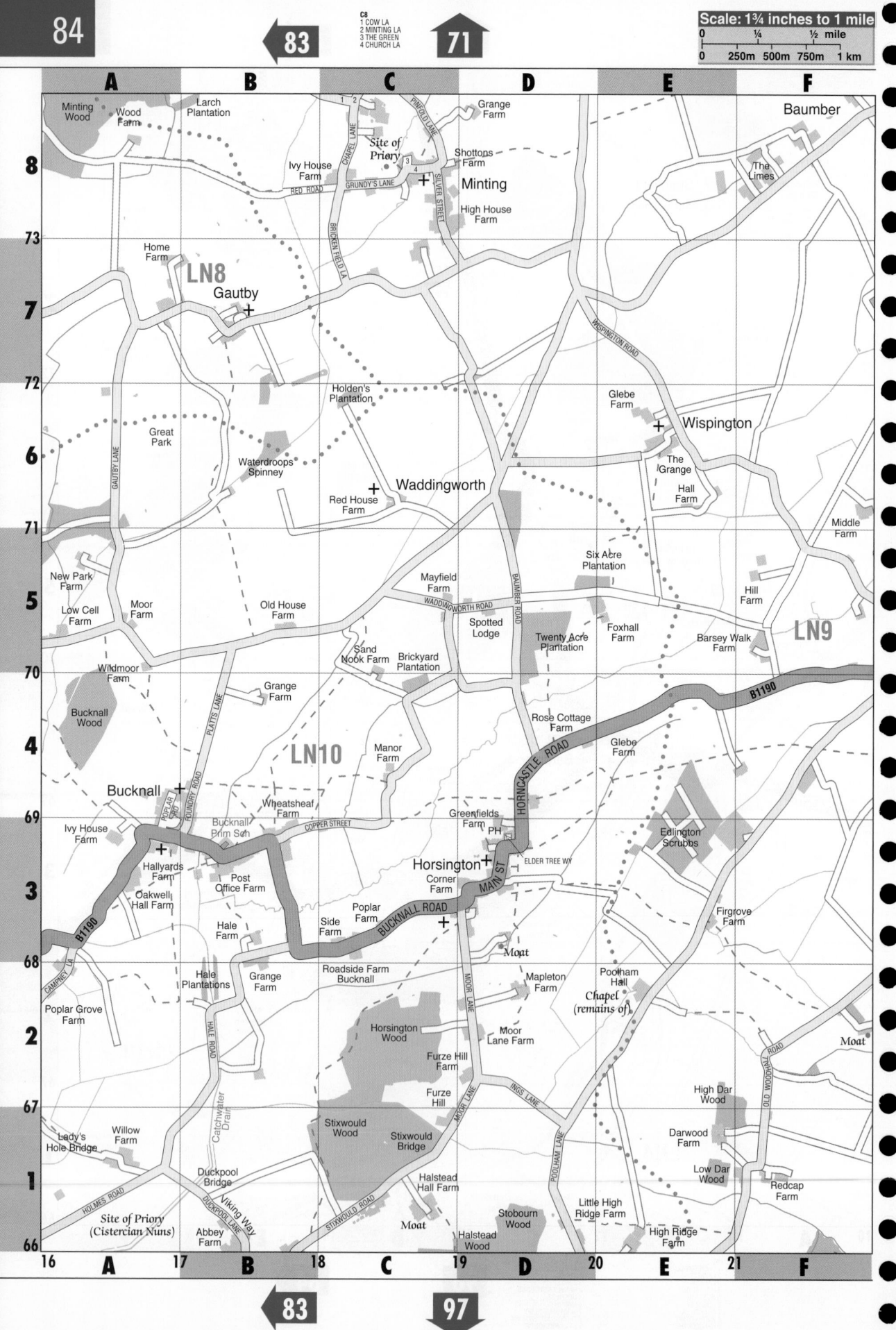

Scale: 1¾ inches to 1 mile

0   ¼   ½   mile
0   250m 500m 750m 1 km

C8
1 COW LA
2 MINTING LA
3 THE GREEN
4 CHURCH LA

83

71

83

97

A   B   C   D   E   F

8

73

7

72

6

71

5

70

4

69

3

68

2

67

1

66

16   A   17   B   18   C   19   D   20   E   21   F

Minting Wood
Wood Farm
Larch Plantation
Chapel Lane
Site of Priory
Grange Farm
Baumber
The Limes
Ivy House Farm
Grundy's Lane
RED ROAD
Shottons Farm
Minting
Silver Street
High House Farm
Home Farm
LN8
Gautby
BRACKEN FIELD LA
Wispington Road
Holden's Plantation
Glebe Farm
Wispington
GAUTBY LANE
Great Park
Waterdroops Spinney
The Grange
Hall Farm
Middle Farm
Red House Farm
Waddingworth
Six Acre Plantation
New Park Farm
Mayfield Farm
Hill Farm
Low Cell Farm
Moor Farm
Old House Farm
WADDINGWORTH ROAD
BAUMBER ROAD
Spotted Lodge
Twenty Acre Plantation
Foxhall Farm
Barsey Walk Farm
LN9
Sand Nook Farm
Brickyard Plantation
Wildmoor Farm
PLATTS LANE
Grange Farm
Rose Cottage Farm
B1190
Glebe Farm
Bucknall Wood
LN10
Manor Farm
HORNCASTLE ROAD
FOUNDRY ROAD
Bucknall
POPLAR
Wheatsheaf Farm
Greenfields Farm
Edlington Scrubbs
Ivy House Farm
Bucknall Prim Sch
COPPER STREET
PH
ELDER TREE WY
Hallyards Farm
Post Office Farm
Horsington
MAIN ST
Firgrove Farm
B1190
Oakwell Hall Farm
Corner Farm
BUCKNALL ROAD
CAMPNEY LA
Hale Farm
Side Farm
Poplar Farm
Moat
Mapleton Farm
Poolham Hall
Moat
Poplar Grove Farm
HALE ROAD
Hale Plantations
Grange Farm
Roadside Farm Bucknall
MOOR LANE
Moor Lane Farm
Chapel (remains of)
POOLHAM ROAD
OLD WOODHALL ROAD
Catchwater Drain
Horsington Wood
Furze Hill Farm
INGS LANE
High Dar Wood
Furze Hill
POOLHAM LANE
Darwood Farm
HOLMES ROAD
Lady's Hole Bridge
Willow Farm
Duckpool Bridge
Viking Way
Stixwould Wood
Stixwould Bridge
Stoboum Wood
Little High Ridge Farm
Low Dar Wood
Redcap Farm
DUCKPOOL LANE
Site of Priory (Cistercian Nuns)
Abbey Farm
STIXWOULD ROAD
Moat
Halstead Hall Farm
Halstead Wood
High Ridge Farm

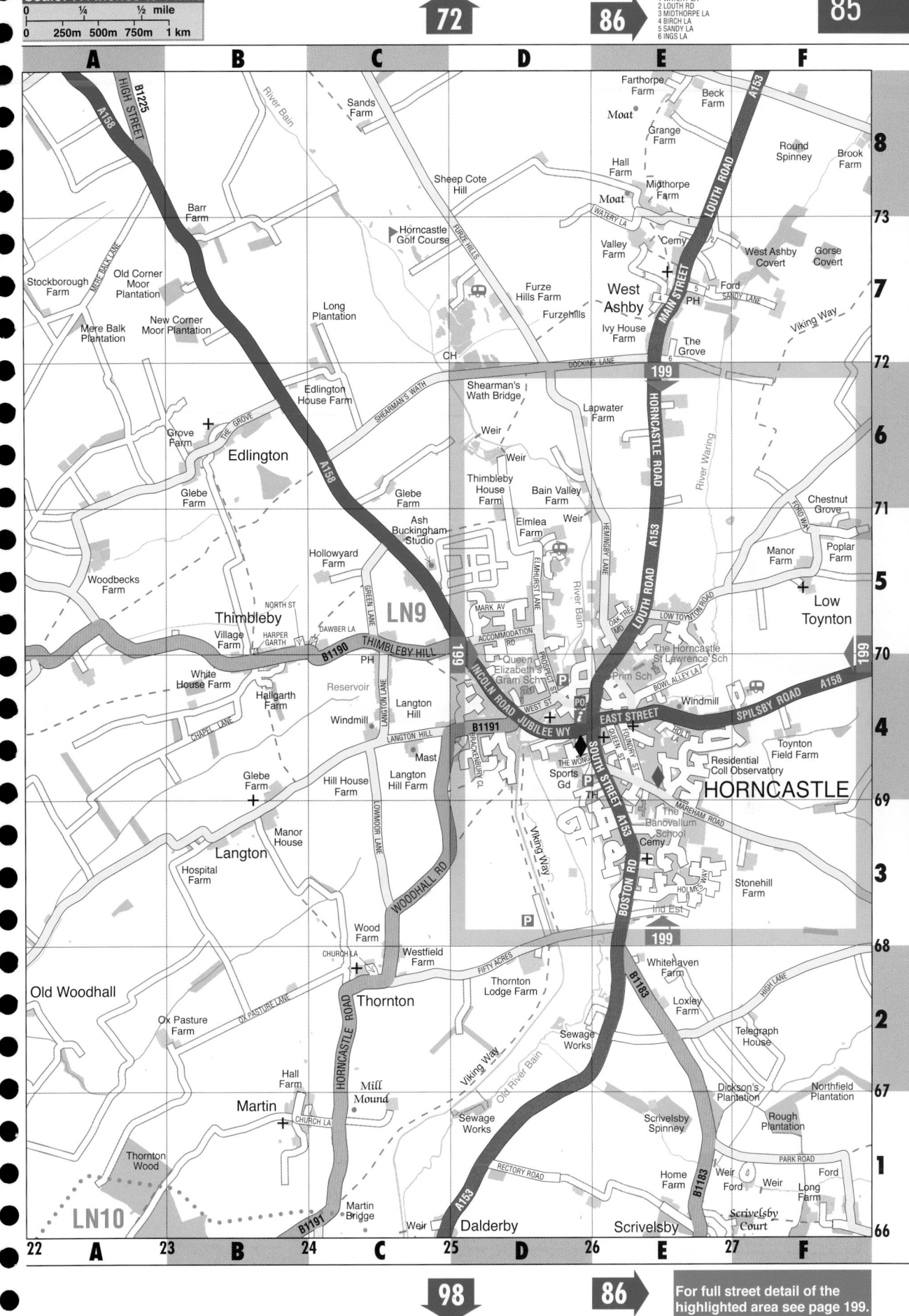

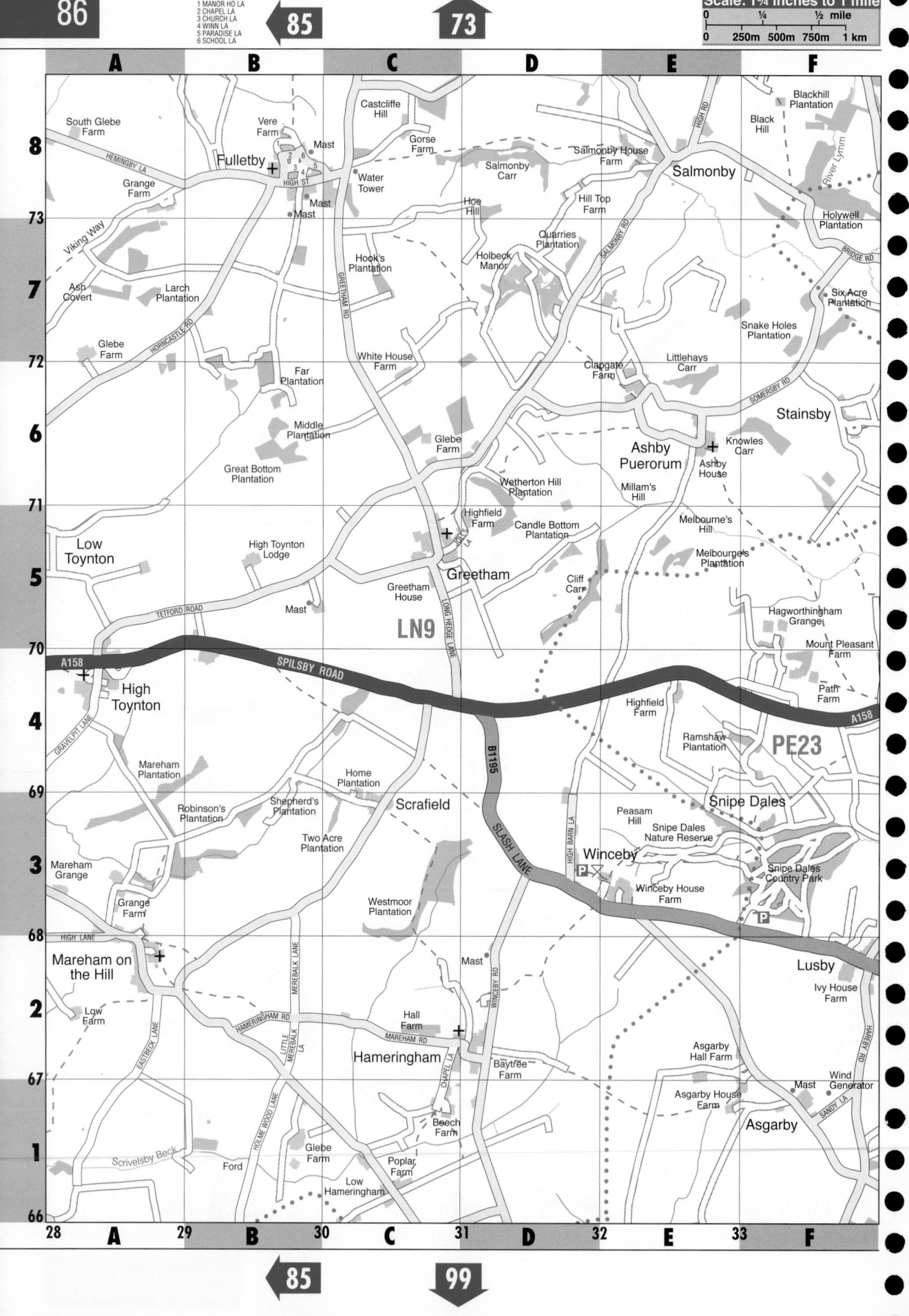
B8
1 MANOR HO LA
2 CHAPEL LA
3 CHURCH LA
4 WINN LA
5 PARADISE LA
6 SCHOOL LA
85
73
Scale: 1¾ inches to 1 mile
0 ¼ ½ mile
0 250m 500m 750m 1 km
A B C D E F
South Glebe Farm
Vere Farm
Fulletby
Mast
Castcliffe Hill
Gorse Farm
Water Tower
Salmonby House Farm
Salmonby Carr
Salmonby
Blackhill Plantation
Black Hill
River Lymn
HEMINGBY LA
Grange Farm
HIGH ST
Mast
Hoe Hill
Hill Top Farm
Holywell Plantation
Viking Way
Hook's Plantation
Quarries Plantation
Holbeck Manor
SALMONBY RD
BRIDGE RD
HIGH RD
Ash Covert
Larch Plantation
GREETHAM RD
Six Acre Plantation
Snake Holes Plantation
Glebe Farm
HORNCASTLE RD
White House Farm
Clapgate Farm
Littlehays Carr
Far Plantation
SOMERSBY RD
Stainsby
Middle Plantation
Glebe Farm
Ashby Puerorum
Knowles Carr
Ashby House
Great Bottom Plantation
Wetherton Hill Plantation
Millam's Hill
Highfield Farm
Candle Bottom Plantation
Melbourne's Hill
Low Toynton
High Toynton Lodge
JOLLS LA
Melbourne's Plantation
Greetham
Cliff Carr
Greetham House
Mast
TETFORD ROAD
LONG HEDGE LANE
LN9
Hagworthingham Grange
Mount Pleasant Farm
A158
SPILSBY ROAD
High Toynton
Path Farm
Highfield Farm
A158
GRAVELPIT LANE
Ramshaw Plantation
PE23
B1195
Mareham Plantation
Home Plantation
Scrafield
Robinson's Plantation
Shepherd's Plantation
Peasam Hill
Snipe Dales
Snipe Dales Nature Reserve
Two Acre Plantation
SLASH LANE
HIGH BARN LA
Winceby
Mareham Grange
Snipe Dales Country Park
Winceby House Farm
Grange Farm
Westmoor Plantation
HIGH LANE
MEREBALK LANE
Mast
Mareham on the Hill
Lusby
Ivy House Farm
WINCEBY RD
Low Farm
HAMERINGHAM RD
Hall Farm
MAREHAM RD
EASTBECK LANE
LITTLE MEREBALK LA
Hameringham
Baytree Farm
Asgarby Hall Farm
HAREBY RD
CHAPEL LA
Mast
Wind Generator
Asgarby House Farm
HOLME WOOD LANE
SANDY LA
Beech Farm
Asgarby
Scrivelsby Beck
Glebe Farm
Ford
Poplar Farm
Low Hameringham
8
73
7
72
6
71
5
70
4
69
3
68
2
67
1
66
28 29 30 31 32 33
85
99

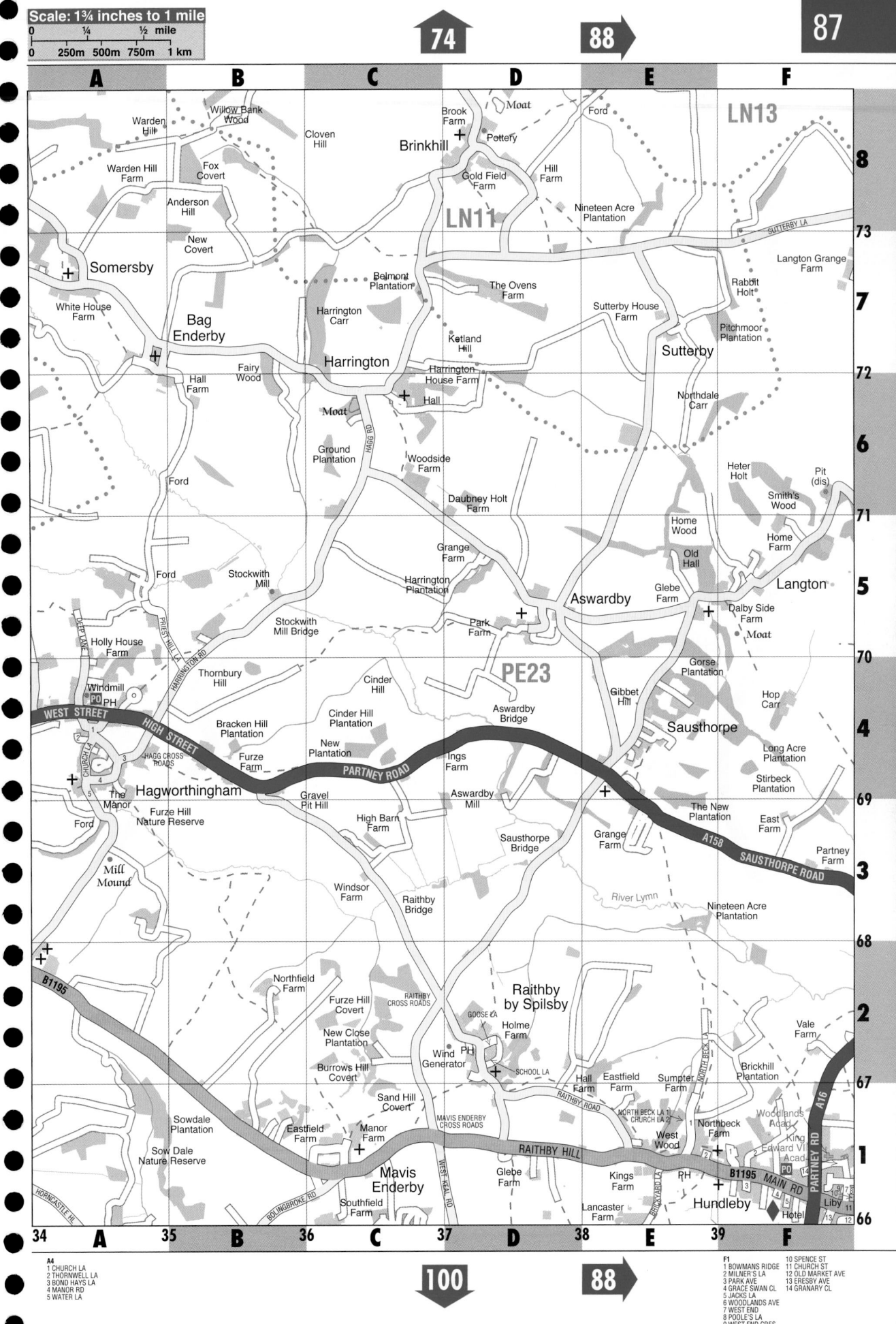
87
Scale: 1¾ inches to 1 mile
0 ¼ ½ mile
0 250m 500m 750m 1 km
74
88
A B C D E F
Warden Hill
Willow Bank Wood
Cloven Hill
Brook Farm
Moat
Ford
LN13
Brinkhill
Pottery
Warden Hill Farm
Fox Covert
Gold Field Farm
Hill Farm
Anderson Hill
LN11
Nineteen Acre Plantation
SUTTERBY LA
New Covert
Somersby
Langton Grange Farm
Belmont Plantation
The Ovens Farm
Rabbit Holt
White House Farm
Bag Enderby
Harrington Carr
Sutterby House Farm
Pitchmoor Plantation
Ketland Hill
Sutterby
Fairy Wood
Harrington
Harrington House Farm
Hall Farm
Hall
Northdale Carr
Moat
HAGG RD
Ground Plantation
Woodside Farm
Heter Holt
Pit (dis)
Ford
Daubney Holt Farm
Smith's Wood
Home Wood
Home Farm
Grange Farm
Old Hall
Ford
Stockwith Mill
Harrington Plantation
Glebe Farm
Langton
Aswardby
DEEP LANE
Holly House Farm
PRIEST HILL LA
Stockwith Mill Bridge
Park Farm
Dalby Side Farm
Moat
HARRINGTON RD
Thornbury Hill
Cinder Hill
PE23
Gorse Plantation
Windmill
PO PH
Gibbet Hill
Hop Carr
WEST STREET
Cinder Hill Plantation
Aswardby Bridge
HIGH STREET
Bracken Hill Plantation
Sausthorpe
CHURCH LA
HAGG CROSS ROADS
New Plantation
Ings Farm
Long Acre Plantation
Furze Farm
PARTNEY ROAD
Stirbeck Plantation
Hagworthingham
The Manor
Gravel Pit Hill
Aswardby Mill
The New Plantation
East Farm
Furze Hill Nature Reserve
High Barn Farm
Ford
Grange Farm
Sausthorpe Bridge
A158
Partney Farm
SAUSTHORPE ROAD
Mill Mound
Windsor Farm
Raithby Bridge
River Lymn
Nineteen Acre Plantation
B1195
Northfield Farm
Raithby by Spilsby
Furze Hill Covert
RAITHBY CROSS ROADS
GOOSE LA
New Close Plantation
Holme Farm
Vale Farm
Wind Generator
PH
NORTH BECK LA
Burrows Hill Covert
SCHOOL LA
Brickhill Plantation
Hall Farm
Eastfield Farm
Sumpter Farm
Sand Hill Covert
RAITHBY ROAD
Sowdale Plantation
Eastfield Farm
Manor Farm
MAVIS ENDERBY CROSS ROADS
NORTH BECK LA 1
CHURCH LA 2
Northbeck Farm
Woodlands Acad
A16
West Wood
King Edward VI Acad
Sow Dale Nature Reserve
RAITHBY HILL
PO
HORNCASTLE RD
Mavis Enderby
WEST KEAL RD
Glebe Farm
Kings Farm
PH
B1195 MAIN RD
PARTNEY RD
BOLINGBROKE RD
Southfield Farm
BRICKYARD LA
Lancaster Farm
Hundleby
Hotel
Liby
8 73 7 72 6 71 5 70 4 69 3 68 2 67 1 66
34 35 36 37 38 39
100
88
A4
1 CHURCH LA
2 THORNWELL LA
3 BOND HAYS LA
4 MANOR RD
5 WATER LA
F1
1 BOWMANS RIDGE
2 MILNER'S LA
3 PARK AVE
4 GRACE SWAN CL
5 JACKS LA
6 WOODLANDS AVE
7 WEST END
8 POOLE'S LA
9 WEST END CRES
10 SPENCE ST
11 CHURCH ST
12 OLD MARKET AVE
13 ERESBY AVE
14 GRANARY CL

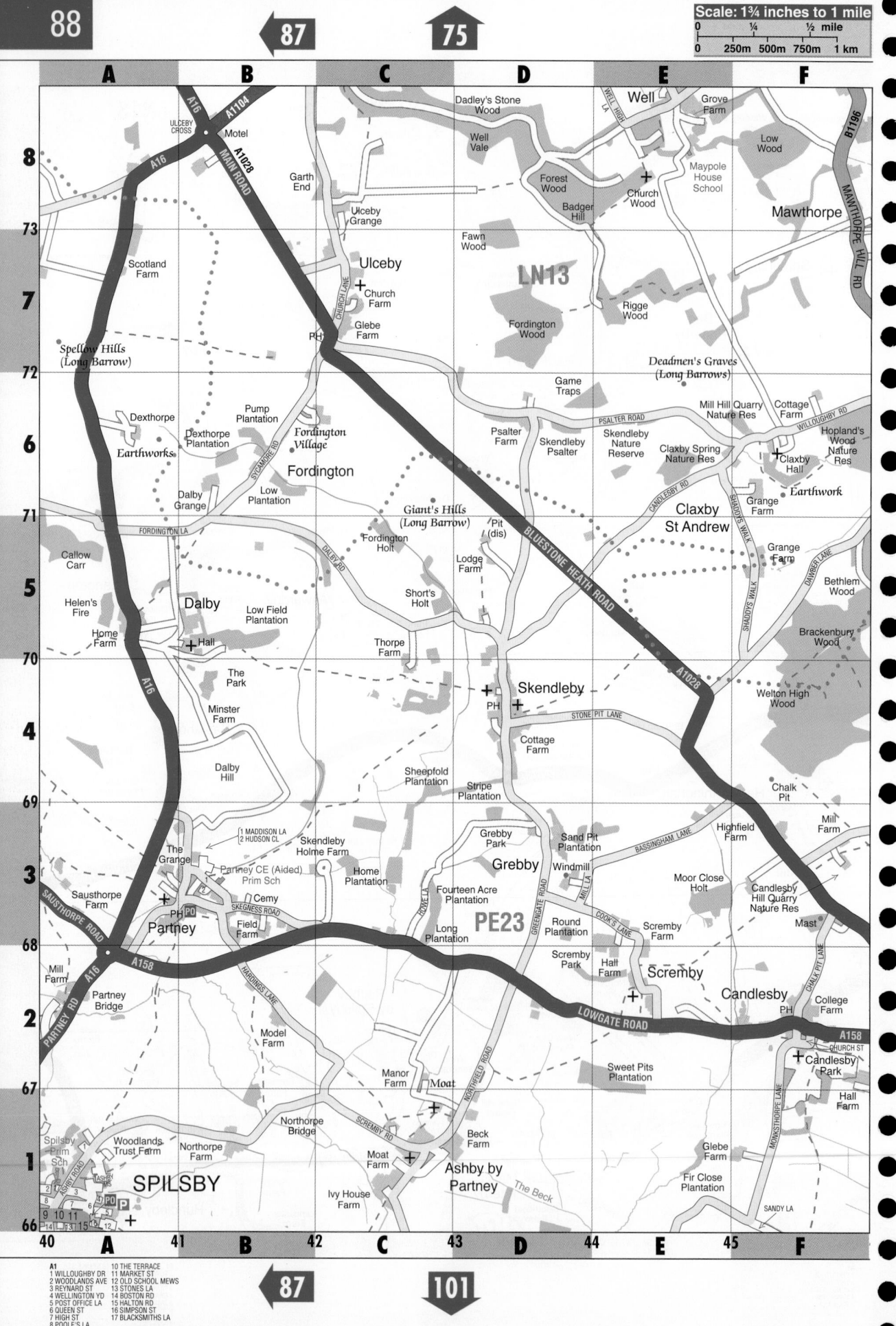

Scale: 1¾ inches to 1 mile

0   ¼   ½   mile
0 250m 500m 750m 1 km

A   B   C   D   E   F

8

Dadley's Stone Wood

Well
Grove Farm

Well Vale

Low Wood

73

ULCEBY CROSS

Motel

Garth End

Forest Wood

Church Wood

Maypole House School

Mawthorpe

Badger Hill

Ulceby Grange

7

Scotland Farm

Ulceby

Fawn Wood

LN13

Church Farm

Rigge Wood

72

Spellow Hills (Long Barrow)

Glebe Farm

Deadmen's Graves (Long Barrows)

Fordington Wood

Game Traps

Mill Hill Quarry Nature Res

Cottage Farm

6

Dexthorpe

Pump Plantation

Fordington Village

PSALTER ROAD

Hopland's Wood Nature Res

Dexthorpe Plantation

Psalter Farm

Skendleby Psalter

Skendleby Nature Reserve

Claxby Spring Nature Res

Claxby Hall

Earthworks

Earthwork

Fordington

Grange Farm

Dalby Grange

Low Plantation

71

Callow Carr

FORDINGTON LA

Giant's Hills (Long Barrow)

Claxby St Andrew

Grange Farm

Fordington Holt

Pit (dis)

Bethlem Wood

5

Helen's Fire

Dalby

Short's Holt

Lodge Farm

BLUESTONE HEATH ROAD

Brackenbury Wood

Home Farm

Low Field Plantation

Thorpe Farm

70

Hall

The Park

Skendleby

Welton High Wood

PH

4

Minster Farm

Stone Pit Lane

Dalby Hill

Cottage Farm

Chalk Pit

69

Sheepfold Plantation

Stripe Plantation

Highfield Farm

Mill Farm

1 MADDISON LA
2 HUDSON CL

The Grange

Skendleby Holme Farm

Grebby Park

Sand Pit Plantation

BASSINGHAM LANE

3

Sausthorpe Farm

Partney CE (Aided) Prim Sch

Home Plantation

Grebby

Windmill

Moor Close Holt

Candlesby Hill Quarry Nature Res

Cemy

SKEGNESS ROAD

Fourteen Acre Plantation

PE23

Round Plantation

Scremby Farm

Mast

PH PO

Partney

Field Farm

Long Plantation

68

Mill Farm

A158

HARDINGS LANE

Scremby Park

Half Farm

Scremby

Candlesby

PH

College Farm

Partney Bridge

LOWGATE ROAD

A158

CHURCH ST

2

Model Farm

Sweet Pits Plantation

Candlesby Park

67

Manor Farm

Moat

Hall Farm

Northorpe Bridge

SCREMBY RD

Beck Farm

Glebe Farm

1

Spilsby Prim Sch

Woodlands Trust Farm

Northorpe Farm

Moat Farm

Ashby by Partney

Fir Close Plantation

SPILSBY

Ivy House Farm

The Beck

SANDY LA

66

40 A 41 B 42 C 43 D 44 E 45 F

A1
1 WILLOUGHBY DR
2 WOODLANDS AVE
3 REYNARD ST
4 WELLINGTON YD
5 POST OFFICE LA
6 QUEEN ST
7 HIGH ST
8 POOLE'S LA
9 CHURCH ST
10 THE TERRACE
11 MARKET ST
12 OLD SCHOOL MEWS
13 STONES LA
14 BOSTON RD
15 HALTON RD
16 SIMPSON ST
17 BLACKSMITHS LA

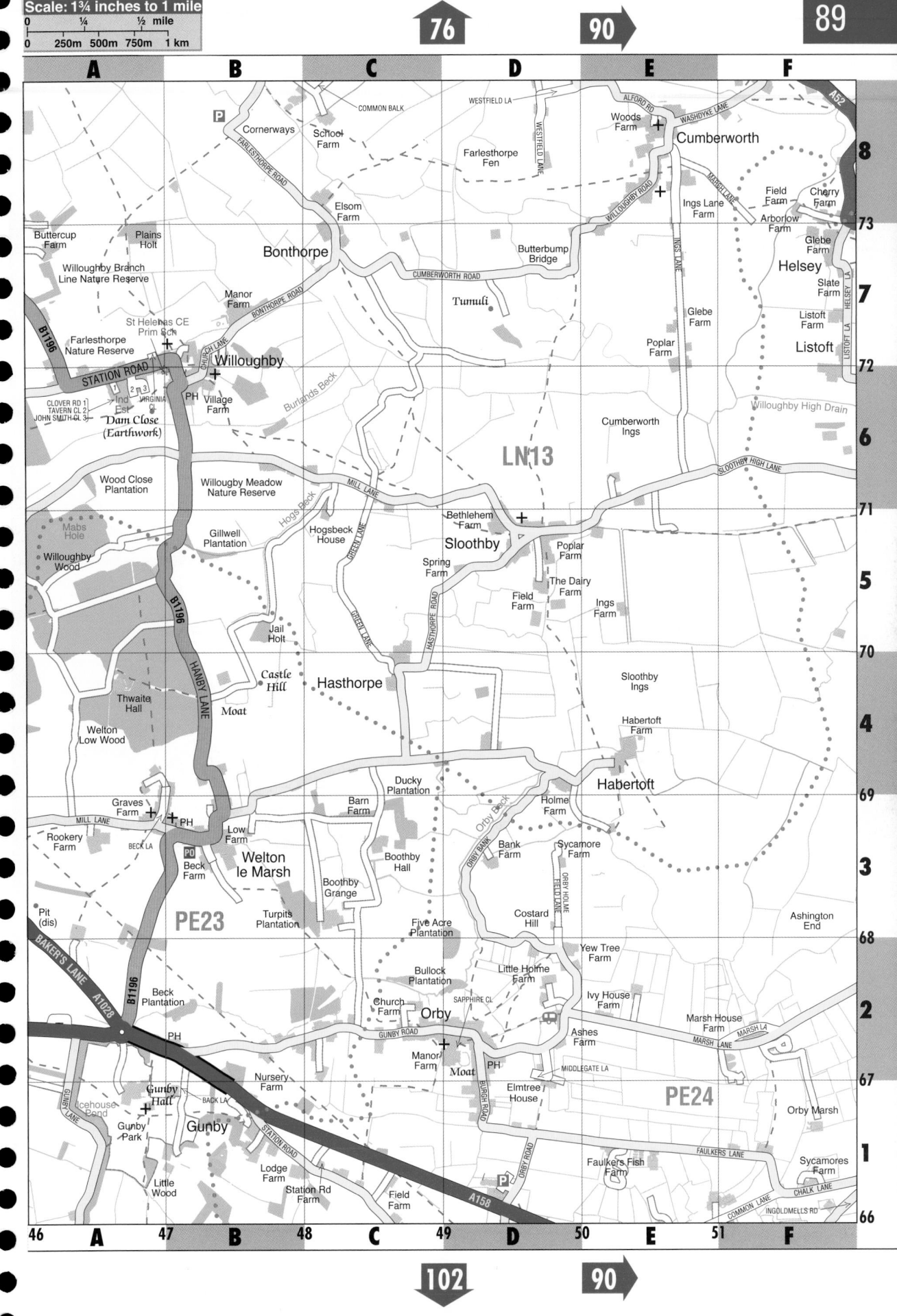
Scale: 1¾ inches to 1 mile
0 ¼ ½ mile
0 250m 500m 750m 1 km
76
90
A B C D E F
COMMON BALK
WESTFIELD LA
ALFORD RD
WASHDYKE LANE
A52
Cornerways
School Farm
Woods Farm
Cumberworth
FARLESTHORPE ROAD
Farlesthorpe Fen
WESTFIELD LANE
MARSH LANE
Field Farm
Cherry Farm
Elsom Farm
WILLOUGHBY ROAD
Ings Lane Farm
Arborlow Farm
Buttercup Farm
Plains Holt
Bonthorpe
Butterbump Bridge
Glebe Farm
Helsey
Willoughby Branch Line Nature Reserve
CUMBERWORTH ROAD
INGS LANE
Slate Farm
Manor Farm
Tumuli
HELSEY LA
BONTHORPE ROAD
Glebe Farm
Listoft Farm
B1196
St Helenas CE Prim Sch
Farlesthorpe Nature Reserve
CHURCH LANE
Willoughby
Poplar Farm
Listoft
LISTOFT LA
STATION ROAD
PH
Village Farm
Burlands Beck
CLOVER RD 1
TAVERN CL 2
JOHN SMITH CL 3
Ind Est
VIRGINIA CL
Dam Close (Earthwork)
Willoughby High Drain
Cumberworth Ings
LN13
SLOOTHBY HIGH LANE
Wood Close Plantation
Willougby Meadow Nature Reserve
MILL LANE
Hogs Beck
Bethlehem Farm
Mabs Hole
Gillwell Plantation
Hogsbeck House
Sloothby
Poplar Farm
Willoughby Wood
GREEN LANE
Spring Farm
The Dairy Farm
Field Farm
Ings Farm
Jail Holt
HASTHORPE ROAD
Castle Hill
Hasthorpe
Sloothby Ings
Thwaite Hall
HANBY LANE
Moat
Welton Low Wood
Habertoft Farm
Ducky Plantation
Habertoft
Graves Farm
Barn Farm
Holme Farm
Orby Beck
MILL LANE
PH
Rookery Farm
BECK LA
Low Farm
Welton le Marsh
Boothby Hall
Bank Farm
Sycamore Farm
ORBY BANK
PO
Beck Farm
Boothby Grange
ORBY HOLME FIELD LANE
Pit (dis)
PE23
Turpits Plantation
Five Acre Plantation
Costard Hill
Ashington End
BAKER'S LANE
Yew Tree Farm
Bullock Plantation
Little Holme Farm
A1028
B1196
Beck Plantation
Church Farm
SAPPHIRE CL
Orby
Ivy House Farm
Marsh House Farm
MARSH LA
PH
GUNBY ROAD
Ashes Farm
MARSH LANE
Manor Farm
Moat
PH
MIDDLEGATE LA
Nursery Farm
Gunby Hall
BACK LA
BURGH ROAD
Elmtree House
PE24
GUNBY LANE
Icehouse Pond
Orby Marsh
Gunby Park
Gunby
STATION ROAD
Faulkers Fish Farm
FAULKERS LANE
Little Wood
Lodge Farm
ORBY ROAD
Sycamores Farm
Station Rd Farm
P
Field Farm
A158
CHALK LANE
COMMON LANE
INGOLDMELLS RD
8
73
7
72
6
71
5
70
4
69
3
68
2
67
1
66
46 47 48 49 50 51
102
90

B7
1 JUBILEE CL
2 THAMES MD DR
3 THAMES CL
4 THAMES CR
5 STONES CL
6 CARSON CL
7 TAVERN LA
8 GOODWIN DR
9 MILL LANE CL

D7
1 SOUTH CR
2 PALMA CT
3 CROWN AVE
4 CONNAUGHT DR
5 SWALLOW CL
6 JUBILEE PAR
7 WARWICK RD
8 PRINCE AVE
9 FAIRBURN CL
10 REGINA WLK
11 ELLIOTT WY
12 ELIZABETH DR
13 PARKSIDE DR
14 WILTON AVE
15 BEACH AVE
16 BUCKINGHAM DR
17 ELIZABETH CT
18 ELIZABETH CL
19 SEA RD
20 CHURCH MDW DR
21 CHAPEL FARM DR
22 BROCKS CL
23 CHURCH FARM CL
24 CHURCH LA
25 WEST VIEW CL
26 FAIRFIELD AVE
27 ANDREW AVE
28 BEATRICE WY
29 WELL VALE DR
30 TYLERS CL
31 AMERY WY
32 WATERSIDE WY
33 ANCASTER MEWS
34 ROWAN CT

Scale: 1¾ inches to 1 mile

LN13
Mickleberry Hill
Hawnby House Farm
Lowgate Farm
Chapel Pit Nature Res
LANDSEER AVE 1
CHAPEL CL 2
ACACIA AVE 3
Nelson Villa
St Leonards Dr
Chapel Point
ROMAN BANK
Ivy House Farm
Field Farm
Chapman's Farm
Croft Farm
Willow Farm
Sundial Farm
Sycamore Farm
Chapel St Leonards
1 LINDUM GR
2 THE PULLOVER
3 SUNNINGDALE DR
4 SUNNINGDALE CL
5 SANDY LA
6 THE GREEN
7 VINE RD
Hogsthorpe Com Prim Sch
Mill Hill
Orchard Farm
Hogsthorpe
Church Farm
Sewage Works
Chapel St Leonards Prim Sch
EASTVIEW CL
GRASMERE AVE
Loft's Bridge
Moat Farm
Drain Farm
Common Farm
Stone Bridge
A52
Beeches Farm
THE CEDARS
TRUNCH LANE
Wyche Farm
Slackholme End
Slackholme House Farm
PE24
Hope Farm
D4
1 OLD CHURCH RD
2 CHURCH LA
3 CHAPEL RD
Abbey Farm
Hardy's Animal Farm
Vickers Point
Bridge Farm
Welbourne Farm
1 CHERRYTREE AVE
2 COOPER AVE
3 ROMAN BANK
4 RYMAC CR
Red Gowt
North Drain
Ingoldmells Prim Sch
Ingoldmells
BJ's Leisure World
Addlethorpe
Wilcox Farm
Grange Farm
Fantasy Island
Ingoldmells Point
1 POINT RD
2 CORONATION RD
3 BANK DR
4 CENTRAL AVE
Manor Farm
Bridge End
Skegness Motor Racing Stadium
Whitehouse Farm
Poplar Farm
Sewage Works
PE25
Funcoast World
Fir Tree Farm
Cottage Farm
Teapot Hall
Corner Farm
Factory
Addlethorpe Mill
Valetta Farm
Illinois Farm
Ashington End
Oak Farm
Cherry Tree Farm
Field House Farm
Lincolnshire Coast Light Railway
Skegness Water Leisure Park
ROMAN BANK
Marsh View Farm
Bristol Farm
Black House Farm
Skegness (Ingoldmells) Aerodrome
Nettle Hill Farm
CHALK LA
WINTHORPE WY
ELM DR
SEATHORNE CR
A52

D3
1 MAYFIELD DR
2 STACEY CL
3 FESTIVAL AVE
4 WINDSOR CR
5 DOUGLAS AVE
6 ELMWOOD DR
7 LIME GR
8 OAK CL
9 HAWTHORN WY

E3
1 QUEENSWAY
2 HIGH ST
3 HERLYN CR
4 BURCHNALL DR
5 LAURA CT
6 ELIZABETH CR

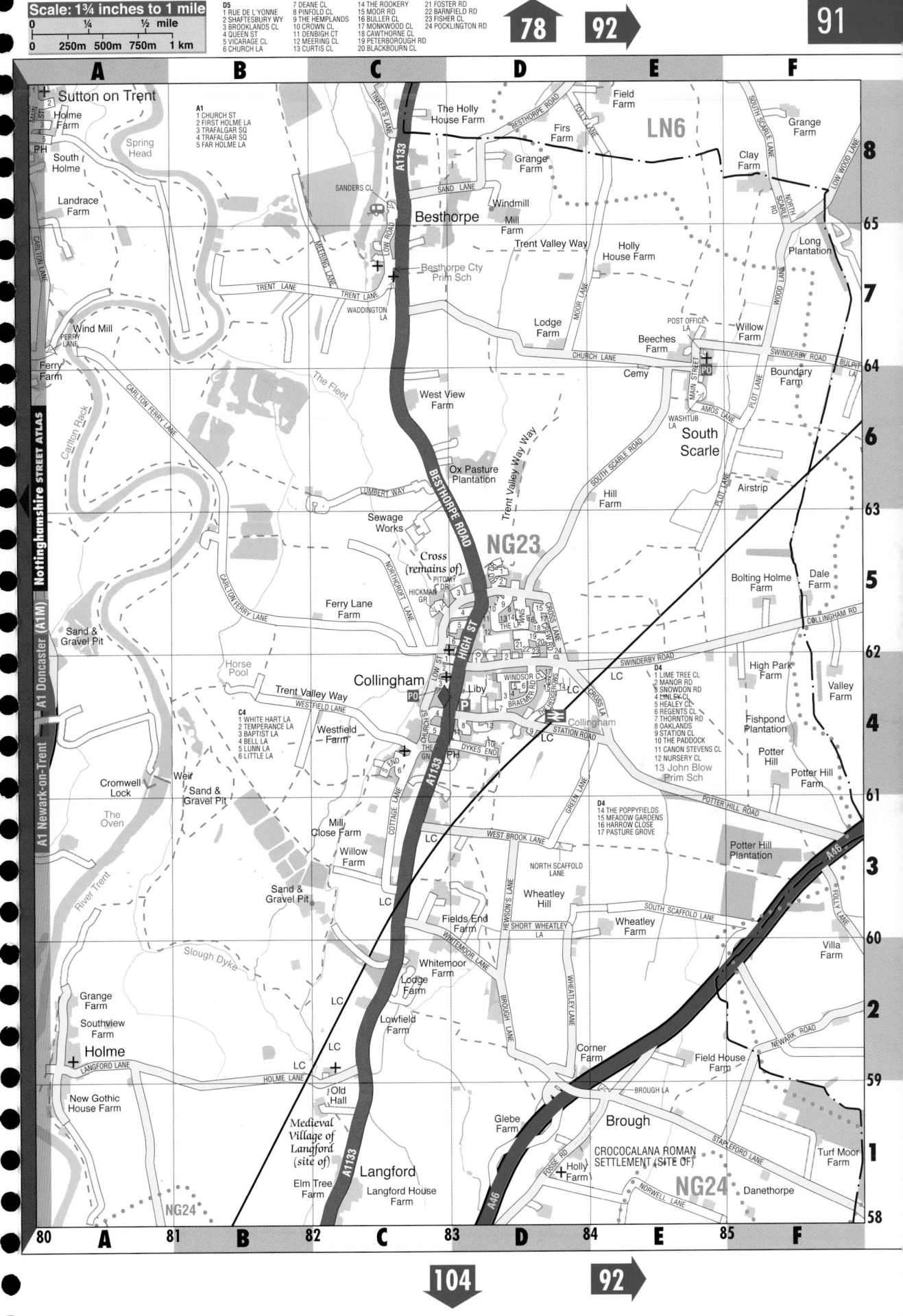

Scale: 1¾ inches to 1 mile

0   ¼   ½ mile
0 250m 500m 750m 1 km

78   92

D5
1 RUE DE L'YONNE
2 SHAFTESBURY WY
3 BROOKLANDS CL
4 QUEEN ST
5 VICARAGE CL
6 CHURCH LA

7 DEANE CL
8 PINFOLD CL
9 THE HEMPLANDS
10 CROWN CL
11 DENBIGH CT
12 MEERING CL
13 CURTIS CL

14 THE ROOKERY
15 MOOR RD
16 BULLER CL
17 MONKWOOD CL
18 CAWTHORNE CL
19 PETERBOROUGH RD
20 BLACKBOURN CL

21 FOSTER RD
22 BARNFIELD RD
23 FISHER CL
24 POCKLINGTON RD

A1
1 CHURCH ST
2 FIRST HOLME LA
3 TRAFALGAR SQ
4 TRAFALGAR SQ
5 FAR HOLME LA

Nottinghamshire STREET ATLAS

A1 Doncaster (A1M)

A1 Newark-on-Trent

Sutton on Trent
Holme Farm
South Holme
Spring Head
Landrace Farm
Wind Mill
Ferry Farm
FERRY LANE
Carlton Rack
CARLTON FERRY LANE
The Fleet
CARLTON FERRY LANE
Sand & Gravel Pit
Horse Pool
Ferry Lane Farm
NORTHCROFT LANE
Trent Valley Way
WESTFIELD LANE
Westfield Farm
Cromwell Lock
Weir
Sand & Gravel Pit
The Oven
River Trent
Slough Dyke
Grange Farm
Southview Farm
Holme
LANGFORD LANE
New Gothic House Farm
HOLME LANE
Medieval Village of Langford (site of)
Elm Tree Farm
Langford

MEERING LANE
TRENT LANE
TRENT LANE
WADDINGTON LA
SANDERS CL
LOW ROAD
A1133
TINKER'S LANE
Besthorpe
SAND LANE
Windmill
Mill Farm
Besthorpe Cty Prim Sch
West View Farm
LUMBER WAY
BESTHORPE ROAD
Ox Pasture Plantation
Sewage Works
Cross (remains of)
HICKMAN GR
PITOMY DR
NG23
C4
1 WHITE HART LA
2 TEMPERANCE LA
3 BAPTIST LA
4 BELL LA
5 LUNN LA
6 LITTLE LA
Collingham
PO
CHURCH LANE
COTTAGE LANE
THE PH
GN
LOW ST
HIGH ST
Liby
P
Windsor
BRAEMAR RD
WEDGEWOOD
LOW ST
DYKES END
A1133
Mill Close Farm
Willow Farm
Sand & Gravel Pit
LC
LC
LC
LC
Old Hall
Langford House Farm
A1133

The Holly House Farm
BESTHORPE ROAD
Firs Farm
Grange Farm
Trent Valley Way
Holly House Farm
Lodge Farm
MOOR LANE
CHURCH LANE
Beeches Farm
Cemy
MAIN STREET
WASHTUB LA
South Scarle
Hill Farm
SOUTH SCARLE ROAD
Trent Valley Way Way
AMOS LANE
PLOT LANE
SWINDERBY ROAD
LC
SWINDERBY ROAD
LC
LC
Collingham
STATION ROAD
LC
D4
1 LIME TREE CL
2 MANOR RD
3 SNOWDON RD
4 LINLEY CL
5 HEALEY CL
6 REGENTS CL
7 THORNTON RD
8 OAKLANDS
9 STATION CL
10 THE PADDOCK
11 CANON STEVENS CL
12 NURSERY CL
13 JOHN BLOW Prim Sch
D4
14 THE POPPYFIELDS
15 MEADOW GARDENS
16 HARROW CLOSE
17 PASTURE GROVE
GREEN LANE
WEST BROOK LANE
NORTH SCAFFOLD LANE
HEWSON'S LANE
SHORT WHEATLEY LA
Wheatley Hill
Wheatley Farm
SOUTH SCAFFOLD LANE
POTTER HILL ROAD
WATERMOOR LANE
BROUGH LANE
WHEATLEY LANE
Fields End Farm
Whitemoor Farm
Lodge Farm
Lowfield Farm
Corner Farm
Glebe Farm
BROUGH LA
Brough
FOSSE RD
Holly Farm
CROCOCALANA ROMAN SETTLEMENT (SITE OF)
STAPLEFORD LANE
NG24
NORWELL LANE
Danethorpe

LN6
Field Farm
FOTY LA
Clay Farm
Grange Farm
LOW WOOD LANE
NORTH SCARLE RD
SOUTH SCARLE LANE
Long Plantation
Willow Farm
POST OFFICE LA
PO
Boundary Farm
BULPHET LA
Airstrip
Bolting Holme Farm
Dale Farm
COLLINGHAM RD
High Park Farm
Valley Farm
Fishpond Plantation
Potter Hill
Potter Hill Farm
POTTER HILL ROAD
Potter Hill Plantation
A46
FOLLY LANE
Villa Farm
NEWARK ROAD
Field House Farm
Turf Moor Farm
NG24

80   A   81   B   82   C   83   D   84   E   85   F

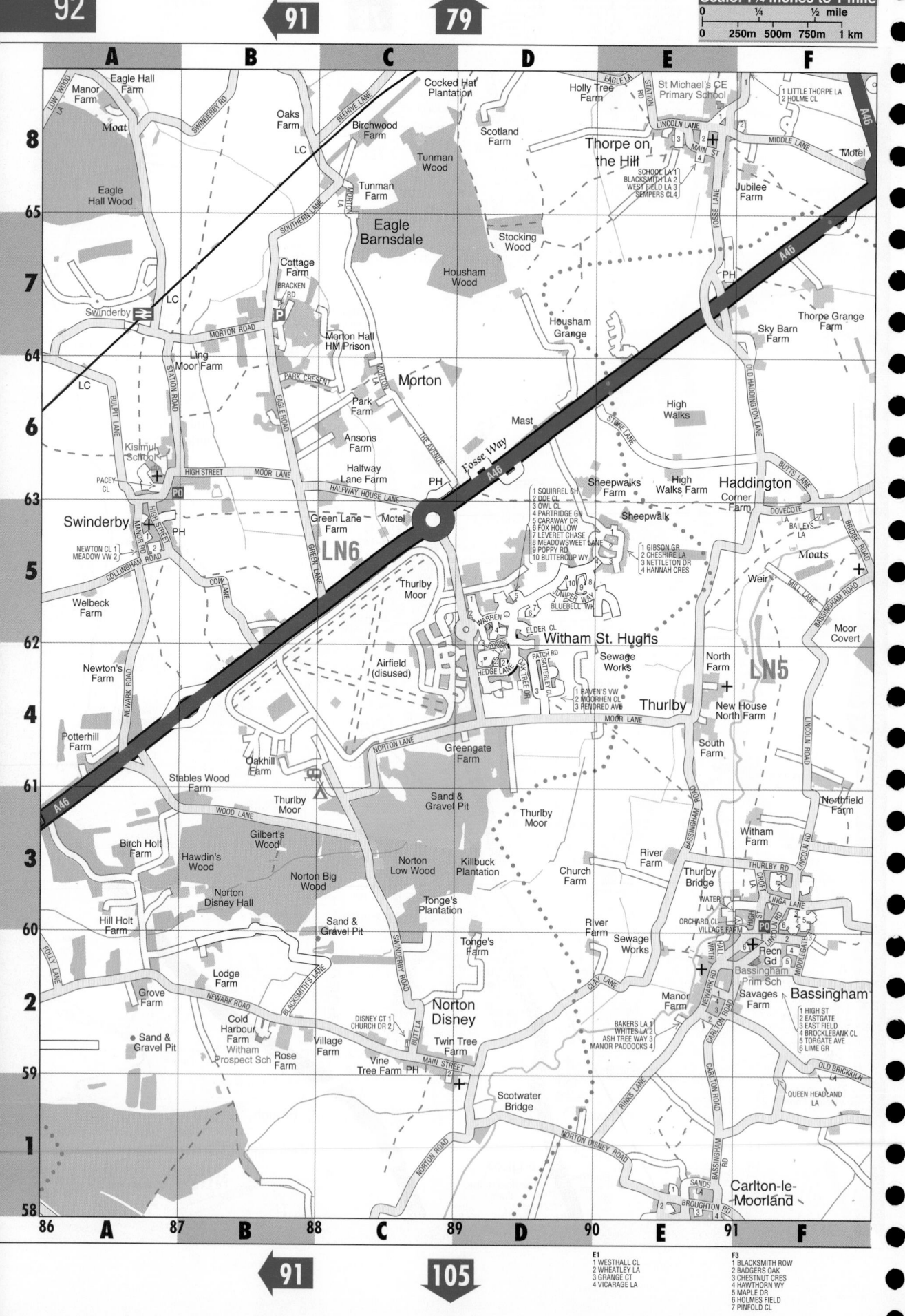

A   B   C   D   E   F

8

Manor Farm
Eagle Hall Farm
Moat
Oaks Farm
Birchwood Farm
Cocked Hat Plantation
Holly Tree Farm
St Michael's CE Primary School
1 LITTLE THORPE LA
2 HOLME CL
Motel

SWINDERBY RD
BEEHIVE LANE
LC
Tunman Wood
Scotland Farm
Thorpe on the Hill
LINCOLN LANE
MIDDLE LANE
A46

65

Eagle Hall Wood
SOUTHERN LANE
Tunman Farm
Eagle Barnsdale
Stocking Wood
SCHOOL LA 1
BLACKSMITH LA 2
WEST FIELD LA 3
SEMPERS CL4
Jubilee Farm
FOSSE LANE

7

LOW WOOD LA
Cottage Farm
BRACKEN RD
P
Housham Wood
Housham Grange
PH
Thorpe Grange Farm
Sky Barn Farm
OLD HADDINGTON LANE
BUTTS LANE

64

Swinderby
LC
Ling Moor Farm
MORTON ROAD
Merton Hall HM Prison
PARK CRESENT
Morton
Mast
High Walks
High Walks Farm
Haddington
Corner Farm
DOVECOTE LA
BAILEYS LA
Moats
BRIDGE ROAD

6

LC
BULPIT LANE
STATION ROAD
EAGLE ROAD
Park Farm
Ansons Farm
THE AVENUE
Fosse Way
A46
STONE LANE
Sheepwalks Farm
High Walks
Sheepwalk
Weir
MILL LANE
BASSINGHAM ROAD
Moor Covert

63

Kismul School
PACEY CL
PO
HIGH STREET
MOOR LANE
Halfway Lane Farm
HALFWAY HOUSE LANE
PH
1 SQUIRREL CH
2 DOE CL
3 OWL CL
4 PARTRIDGE GN
5 CARAWAY DR
6 FOX HOLLOW
7 LEVERET CHASE
8 MEADOWSWEET LANE
9 POPPY RD
10 BUTTERCUP WY
1 GIBSON GR
2 CHESHIRE LA
3 NETTLETON DR
4 HANNAH CRES

5

Swinderby
MANOR RD
PH
NEWTON CL 1
MEADOW VW 2
COLLINGHAM ROAD
COW LANE
GREEN LANE
Green Lane Farm
Motel
LN6
JUNIPER WAY
BLUEBELL WK
North Farm
LN5

Welbeck Farm
NEWARK ROAD
Thurlby Moor
WARREN
ELDER CL
Witham St. Hughs
Sewage Works

62

Newton's Farm
Airfield (disused)
HEDGE LANE
OAK TREE DR
PATCH RD
BUTTERLEY CL
1 RAVEN'S VW
2 MOORHEN CL
3 PENDRED AVE
Thurlby
New House North Farm
LINCOLN ROAD

4

Potterhill Farm
Oakhill Farm
NORTON LANE
Greengate Farm
MOOR LANE
South Farm

61

Stables Wood Farm
Thurlby Moor
WOOD LANE
Sand & Gravel Pit
Thurlby Moor
River Farm
Witham Farm
Northfield Farm
BASSINGHAM ROAD

3

Birch Holt Farm
Hawdin's Wood
Gilbert's Wood
Norton Big Wood
Norton Low Wood
Killbuck Plantation
Church Farm
Thurlby Bridge
THURLBY RD
CROFT
LINGA LANE

Hill Holt Farm
Norton Disney Hall
SWINDERBY ROAD
Tonge's Plantation
WATER LA
ORCHARD CL
VILLAGE FARM
HIGH ST
Bassingham Prim Sch

60

FOLLY LANE
Sand & Gravel Pit
Tonge's Farm
River Farm
Sewage Works
Recn Gd
NEWARK RD
CARLTON ROAD
MIDDLE ST
Bassingham

2

Grove Farm
NEWARK ROAD
BLACKSMITH'S LANE
Lodge Farm
Norton Disney
DISNEY CT 1
CHURCH RD 2
BUTT LA
Manor Farm
Savages Farm
1 HIGH ST
2 EASTGATE
3 EAST FIELD
4 BROCKLEBANK CL
5 TORGATE AVE
6 LIME GR

Sand & Gravel Pit
Cold Harbour Farm
Witham Prospect Sch
Village Farm
Rose Farm
Vine Tree Farm PH
MAIN STREET
Twin Tree Farm
BAKERS LA 1
WHITES LA 2
ASH TREE WAY 3
MANOR PADDOCKS 4
OLD BRICKKILN

59

Scotwater Bridge
RINKS LANE
QUEEN HEADLAND LA

1

NORTON DISNEY ROAD
BASSINGHAM RD
SANDS

Carlton-le-Moorland

58

86   A   87   B   88   C   89   D   90   E   91   F

E1
1 WESTHALL CL
2 WHEATLEY LA
3 GRANGE CT
4 VICARAGE LA

F3
1 BLACKSMITH ROW
2 BADGERS OAK
3 CHESTNUT CRES
4 HAWTHORN WY
5 MAPLE DR
6 HOLMES FIELD
7 PINFOLD CL

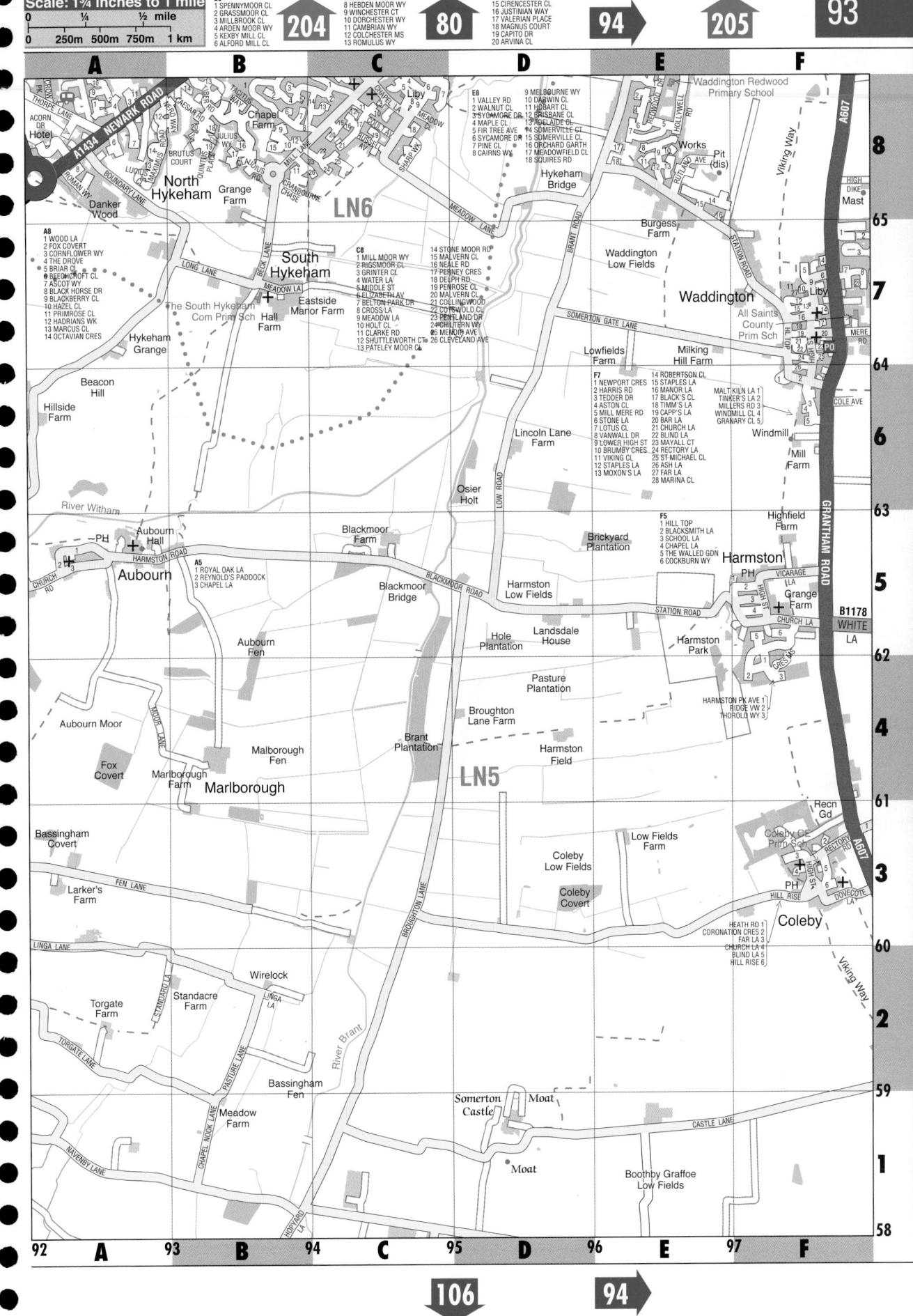

Scale: 1¾ inches to 1 mile

0   ¼   ½ mile
0 250m 500m 750m 1 km

204   80   94   205

B8
1 SPENNYMOOR CL
2 GRASSMOOR CL
3 MILLBROOK CL
4 ARDEN MOOR WY
5 KEXBY MILL CL
6 ALFORD MILL CL

7 LADD'S MILL CL
8 HEBDEN MOOR WY
9 WINCHESTER CT
10 DORCHESTER WY
11 CAMBRIAN WY
12 COLCHESTER MS
13 ROMULUS WY

14 MAPPLETON
15 CIRENCESTER CL
16 JUSTINIAN WAY
17 VALERIAN PLACE
18 MAGNUS COURT
19 CAPITO DR
20 ARVINA CL

E8
1 VALLEY RD
2 WALNUT CL
3 SYCAMORE DR
4 MAPLE CL
5 FIR TREE AVE
6 SYCAMORE DR
7 PINE CL
8 CAIRNS WY

9 MELBOURNE WY
10 DARWIN CL
11 HOBART CL
12 BRISBANE CL
13 ADELAIDE CL
14 SOMERVILLE CL
15 SOMERVILLE CL
16 ORCHARD GARTH
17 MEADOWFIELD CL
18 SQUIRES RD

C8
1 MILL MOOR WY
2 RIGSMOOR CL
3 GRINTER CL
4 WATER LA
5 MIDDLE ST
6 ELIZABETH AV
7 BELTON PARK DR
8 CROSS LA
9 MEADOW LA
10 HOLT CL
11 CLARKE RD
12 SHUTTLEWORTH CT
13 PATELEY MOOR CL

14 STONE MOOR RD
15 MALVERN CL
16 NEALE RD
17 PERNEY CRES
18 DELPH RD
19 PENROSE CL
20 MALVERN CL
21 COLLINGWOOD
22 COTSWOLD CL
23 PENTLAND DR
24 CHILTERN WY
25 MENDIP AVE
26 CLEVELAND AVE

F7
1 NEWPORT CRES
2 HARRIS RD
3 TEDDER DR
4 ASTON CL
5 MILL MERE RD
6 STONE LA
7 LOTUS CL
8 VANWALL DR
9 LOWER HIGH ST
10 BRUMBY CRES
11 VIKING CL
12 STAPLES LA
13 MOXON'S LA

14 ROBERTSON CL
15 STAPLES LA
16 MANOR LA
17 BLACK'S CL
18 TIMM'S LA
19 CAPP'S LA
20 BAR LA
21 CHURCH LA
22 BLIND LA
23 MAYALL CT
24 RECTORY LA
25 ST MICHAEL CL
26 ASH LA
27 FAR LA
28 MARINA CL

MALT KILN LA 1
TINKER'S LA 2
MILLERS RD 3
WINDMILL CL 4
GRANARY CL 5

F5
1 HILL TOP
2 BLACKSMITH LA
3 SCHOOL LA
4 CHAPEL LA
5 THE WALLED GDN
6 COCKBURN WY

A8
1 WOOD LA
2 FOX COVERT
3 CORNFLOWER WY
4 THE DROVE
5 BRIAR CL
6 BEECHCROFT CL
7 ASCOT WY
8 BLACK HORSE DR
9 BLACKBERRY CL
10 HAZEL CL
11 PRIMROSE CL
12 HADRIANS WK
13 MARCUS CL
14 OCTAVIAN CRES

A5
1 ROYAL OAK LA
2 REYNOLD'S PADDOCK
3 CHAPEL LA

HARMSTON PK AVE 1
RIDGE VW 2
THOROLD WY 3

HEATH RD 1
CORONATION CRES 2
FAR LA 3
CHURCH LA 4
BLIND LA 5
HILL RISE 6

Waddington Redwood Primary School

THORPE LANE
CROFT LANE
ACORN DR
Hotel
A1434 NEWARK ROAD
ROMAN WY
BOUNDARY LANE
CAESAR RD
TACITUS WAY
JULIUS WY
BRUTUS ST
HADRIANS ROAD
QUINTUS WAY
PLACE
CLINTON RD
CRANBOURNE CHASE
MILL LANE
CHURCH LA
RUSSELL AVE
SHARP WK
MEADOW CL
Chapel Farm
Liby
LN6
North Hykeham
Danker Wood
Grange Farm
Hykeham Bridge
Works
Pit (dis)
RUTLAND AVE
FENWOOD DR
HOLLYWELL RD
Viking Way
A607
HIGH DIKE Mast

South Hykeham
LONG LANE
BECK LANE
MEADOW LA
The South Hykeham Com Prim Sch
Hall Farm
Eastside Manor Farm
Hykeham Grange
Burgess Farm
Waddington Low Fields
Waddington
All Saints County Prim Sch
Liby
MERE RD
NICOLE AVE

Beacon Hill
Hillside Farm
Lowfields Farm
Milking Hill Farm
SOMERTON GATE LANE
BRANT ROAD
STATION ROAD
GRANTHAM ROAD
Windmill
Mill Farm

River Witham
Lincoln Lane Farm
LOW ROAD
Osier Holt
Brickyard Plantation
Highfield Farm

PH
Aubourn Hall
HARMSTON ROAD
Aubourn
CHURCH RD
MOOR LANE
Blackmoor Farm
Blackmoor Bridge
BLACKMOOR ROAD
Blackmoor Bridge
Harmston Low Fields
STATION ROAD
Harmston
PH
VICARAGE LA
Grange Farm
CHURCH LA
B1178
WHITE LA

Aubourn Fen
Hole Plantation
Landsdale House
Harmston Park
CRES

Fox Covert
Marlborough Farm
Malborough Fen
Marlborough
LN5
Pasture Plantation
Broughton Lane Farm
Brant Plantation
Harmston Field

Aubourn Moor
Low Fields Farm
Coleby CE Prim Sch
Recn Gd
A607

Bassingham Covert
Larker's Farm
FEN LANE
Coleby Low Fields
Coleby Covert
Coleby
HILL RISE
HIGH ST
DOVECOTE LA
RECTORY RD
PH

LINGA LANE
Wirelock
Standacre Farm
LINGA LA
STANDARD LA
Viking Way

Torgate Farm
TORGATE LANE
PASTURE LANE
CHAPEL NOOK LANE
River Brant
Bassingham Fen
Meadow Farm
NAVENBY LANE
HOPYARD LA

Somerton Castle
Moat
Moat
CASTLE LANE
Boothby Graffoe Low Fields

8
65
7
64
6
63
5
62
4
61
3
60
2
59
1
58

92 A 93 B 94 C 95 D 96 E 97 F

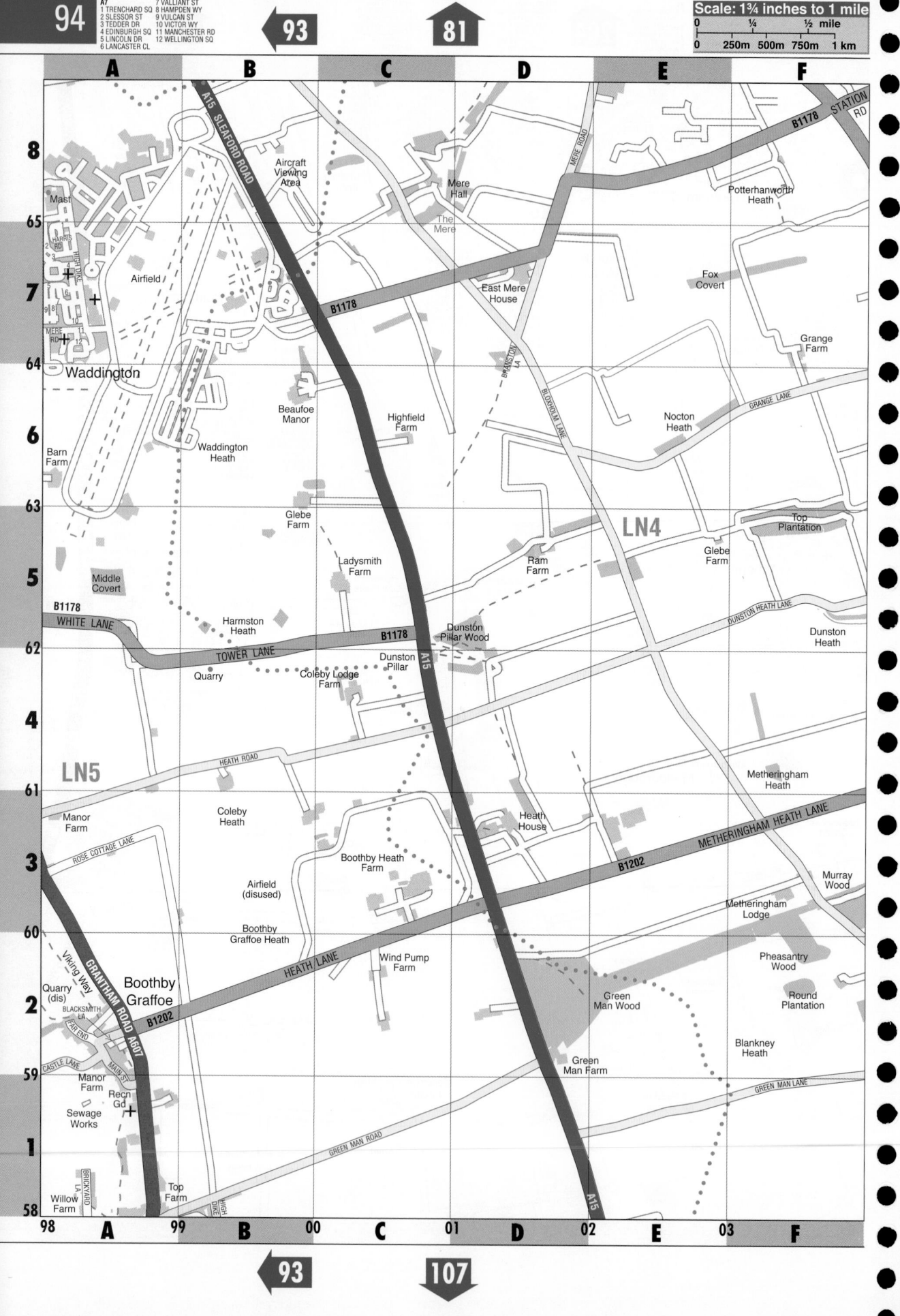

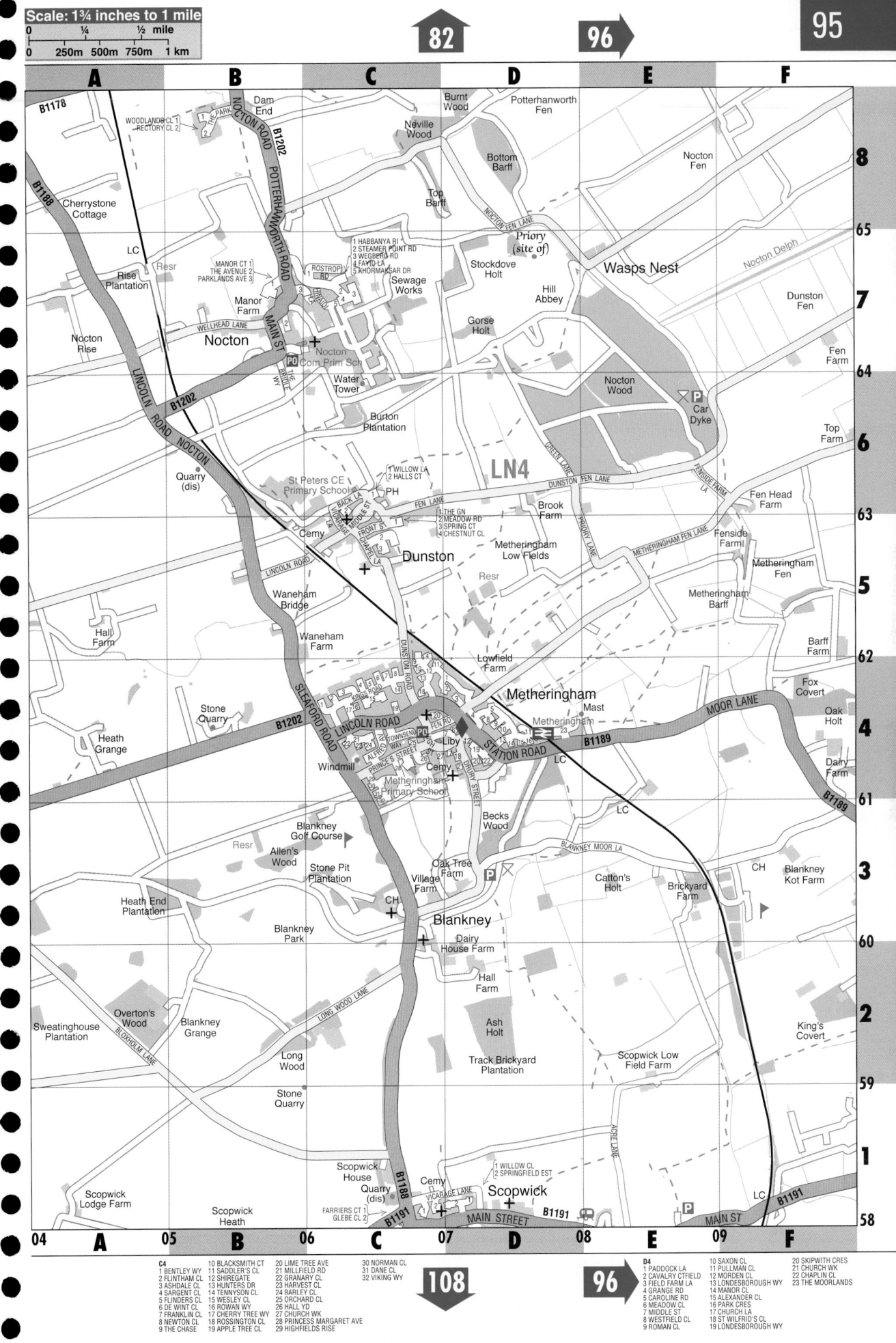

B1178

B1188

Cherrystone
Cottage

LC

Rise
Plantation

Resr

Nocton
Rise

LINCOLN ROAD

B1202 NOCTON

Quarry
(dis)

Hall
Farm

Heath
Grange

Windmill

SLEAFORD ROAD
B1202

Sweatinghouse
Plantation

BLOXHOLM LANE

Overton's
Wood

Blankney
Grange

Scopwick
Lodge Farm

THE PARK

NOCTON ROAD

B1202

POTTERHANWORTH ROAD

MAIN ST

Dam
End

WOODLAND CL 1
RECTORY CL 2

MANOR CT 1
THE AVENUE 2
PARKLANDS AVE 3

ROSTROP
RD

Manor
Farm

Nocton

WELLHEAD LANE

PO

Nocton
Com Prim Sch

Water
Tower

Burton
Plantation

St Peters CE
Primary School

Cemy

BACK LA

VICARAGE LA

MIDDLE ST

FRONT ST

Waneham
Bridge

Waneham
Farm

Stone
Quarry

Allen's
Wood

Heath End
Plantation

Blankney
Park

Blankney
Golf Course

Resr

Stone Pit
Plantation

Long
Wood

CH

Stone
Quarry

LONG WOOD LANE

1 HABBANYA RI
2 STEAMER POINT RD
3 WEGBERG RD
4 FAYID LA
5 KHORMAKSAR DR

Sewage
Works

1 WILLOW LA
2 HALLS CT

PH

Neville
Wood

Burnt
Wood

Bottom
Barff

Top
Barff

Gorse
Holt

FEN LANE

DUNSTON ROAD

1 THE GN
2 MEADOW RD
3 SPRING CT
4 CHESTNUT CL

Dunston

Metheringham
Low Fields

Resr

Lowfield
Farm

LINCOLN ROAD

KINGS RD

ALFRED ST

PRINCE'S STREET

TOWNSEND

FEN RD

PO

Metheringham
Primary School

Libv

Cemy

DRURY STREET

STATION ROAD

Oak Tree
Farm

Village
Farm

P

CH

Blankney

Dairy
House Farm

Hall
Farm

Ash
Holt

Becks
Wood

Metheringham

Mast

Metheringham

B1189

LC

LC

Blankney
Moor La

BLANKNEY MOOR LA

Catton's
Holt

Brickyard
Farm

Track Brickyard
Plantation

Scopwick Low
Field Farm

Potterhanworth
Fen

Stockdove
Holt

Hill
Abbey

Priory
(site of)

Nocton
Wood

GREEN LANE

LN4

DUSTON FEN LANE

Brook
Farm

PRIORY LANE

METHERINGHAM FEN LANE

Metheringham
Barff

MOOR LANE

B1189

Wasps Nest

Nocton Delph

Dunston
Fen

Fen
Farm

Car
Dyke

P

FENSIDE FARM
LA

Top
Farm

Fen Head
Farm

Fenside
Farm

Metheringham
Fen

Barff
Farm

Fox
Covert

Oak
Holt

Dairy
Farm

Blankney
Kot Farm

CH

B1188

King's
Covert

Scopwick
House
Quarry
(dis)

FARRIERS CT 1
GLEBE CL 2

Cemy

VICARAGE LANE

B1191

MAIN STREET

1 WILLOW CL
2 SPRINGFIELD EST

Scopwick

B1191

ACRE LANE

P

Scopwick
Heath

LC

B1191

MAIN ST

8

65

7

64

6

63

5

62

4

61

3

60

2

59

1

58

C4
1 BENTLEY WY
2 FLINTHAM CL
3 ASHDALE CL
4 SARGENT CL
5 FLINDERS CL
6 DE WINT CL
7 FRANKLIN CL
8 NEWTON CL
9 THE CHASE

10 BLACKSMITH CT
11 SADDLER'S CL
12 SHIREGATE
13 HUNTERS DR
14 TENNYSON CL
15 WESLEY CL
16 ROWAN WY
17 CHERRY TREE WY
18 ROSSINGTON CL
19 APPLE TREE CL

20 LIME TREE AVE
21 MILLFIELD RD
22 GRANARY CL
23 HARVEST CL
24 BARLEY CL
25 ORCHARD CL
26 HALL YD
27 CHURCH WK
28 PRINCESS MARGARET AVE
29 HIGHFIELDS RISE

30 NORMAN CL
31 DANE CL
32 VIKING WY

D4
1 PADDOCK LA
2 CAVALRY CTFIELD
3 FIELD FARM LA
4 GRANGE RD
5 CAROLINE RD
6 MEADOW CL
7 MIDDLE ST
8 WESTFIELD CL
9 ROMAN CL

10 SAXON CL
11 PULLMAN CL
12 MORDEN CL
13 LONDESBOROUGH WY
14 MANOR CL
15 ALEXANDER CL
16 PARK CRES
17 CHURCH LA
18 ST WILFRIO'S CL
19 LONDESBOROUGH WY

20 SKIPWITH CRES
21 CHURCH WK
22 CHAPLIN CL
23 THE MOORLANDS

95
83

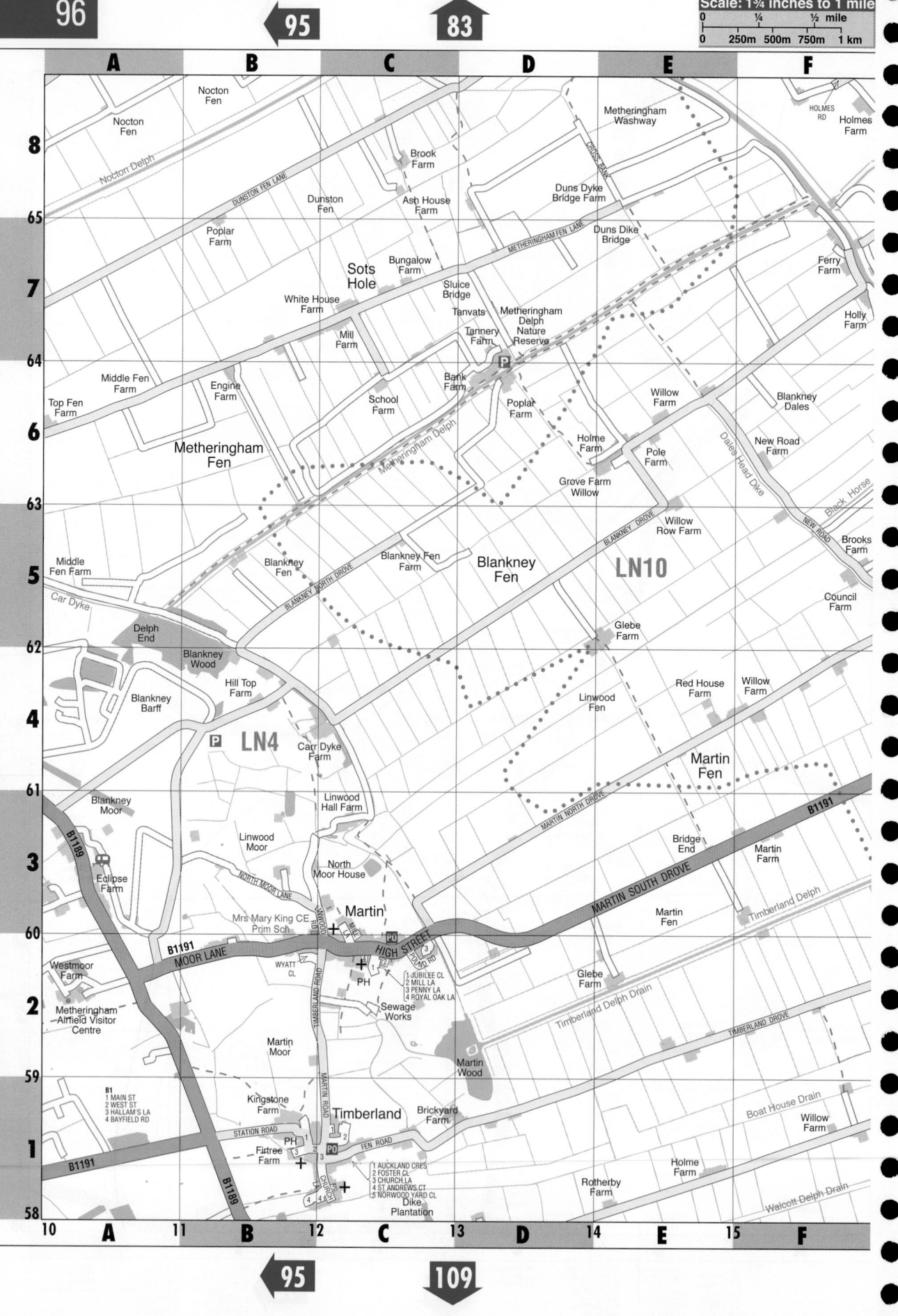
Scale: 1¾ inches to 1 mile
0 ¼ ½ mile
0 250m 500m 750m 1 km
A B C D E F
8
65
7
64
6
63
5
62
4
61
3
60
2
59
1
58
10 11 12 13 14 15
Nocton Fen
Nocton Fen
Nocton Delph
DUNSTON FEN LANE
Poplar Farm
Dunston Fen
Brook Farm
Ash House Farm
Metheringham Washway
CROSS BANK
Duns Dyke Bridge Farm
Duns Dike Bridge
METHERINGHAM FEN LANE
HOLMES RD
Holmes Farm
Ferry Farm
Holly Farm
Sots Hole
Bungalow Farm
White House Farm
Sluice Bridge
Tanvats
Metheringham Delph Nature Reserve
Tannery Farm
Mill Farm
Middle Fen Farm
Top Fen Farm
Engine Farm
School Farm
Bank Farm
Poplar Farm
Willow Farm
Blankney Dales
Metheringham Fen
Metheringham Delph
Holme Farm
Pole Farm
New Road Farm
Dales Head Dike
Grove Farm Willow
Black Horse
NEW ROAD
Brooks Farm
Willow Row Farm
BLANKNEY DROVE
Middle Fen Farm
Blankney Fen
Blankney Fen Farm
Blankney Fen
LN10
BLANKNEY NORTH DROVE
Car Dyke
Council Farm
Delph End
Blankney Wood
Glebe Farm
Hill Top Farm
Blankney Barff
Red House Farm
Willow Farm
Linwood Fen
LN4
Carr Dyke Farm
Martin Fen
Blankney Moor
Linwood Hall Farm
MARTIN NORTH DROVE
B1191
B1189
Linwood Moor
Bridge End
Martin Farm
Eclipse Farm
North Moor House
NORTH MOOR LANE
MARTIN SOUTH DROVE
Timberland Delph
Martin
Martin Fen
Mrs Mary King CE Prim Sch
LINWOOD RD
MILL LA
PO
B1191
MOOR LANE
HIGH STREET
POND RD
Westmoor Farm
WYATT CL
PH
1 JUBILEE CL
2 MILL LA
3 PENNY LA
4 ROYAL OAK LA
Glebe Farm
Metheringham Airfield Visitor Centre
TIMBERLAND ROAD
Sewage Works
Timberland Delph Drain
TIMBERLAND DROVE
Martin Moor
Martin Wood
B1
1 MAIN ST
2 WEST ST
3 HALLAM'S LA
4 BAYFIELD RD
Kingstone Farm
MARTIN ROAD
Timberland
Brickyard Farm
Boat House Drain
Willow Farm
STATION ROAD
PH
FEN ROAD
Fírtree Farm
B1191
B1189
CHURCH
1 AUCKLAND CRES
2 FOSTER CL
3 CHURCH LA
4 ST ANDREWS CT
5 NORWOOD YARD CL
Holme Farm
Rotherby Farm
Walcott Delph Drain
Dike Plantation

95
109

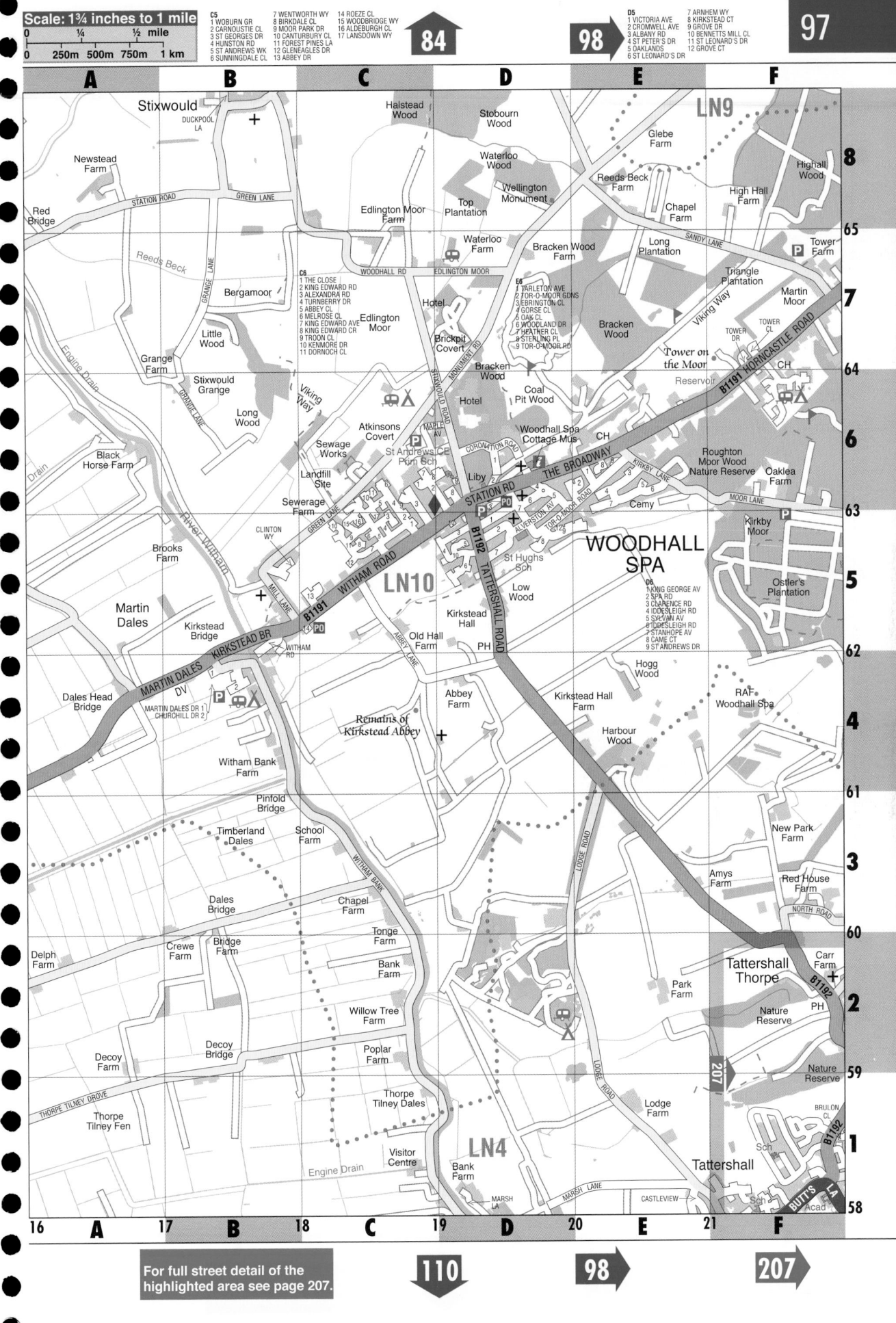

Scale: 1¾ inches to 1 mile

0   ¼   ½   mile
0   250m 500m 750m 1 km

84

98

C5
1 WOBURN GR
2 CARNOUSTIE CL
3 ST GEORGES DR
4 HUNSTON RD
5 ST ANDREWS WK
6 SUNNINGDALE CL
7 WENTWORTH WY
8 BIRKDALE CL
9 MOOR PARK DR
10 CANTURBURY CL
11 FOREST PINES LA
12 GLENEAGLES DR
13 ABBEY DR
14 ROEZE CL
15 WOODBRIDGE WY
16 ALDEBURGH CL
17 LANSDOWN WY

D5
1 VICTORIA AVE
2 CROMWELL AVE
3 ALBANY RD
4 ST PETER'S DR
5 OAKLANDS
6 ST LEONARD'S DR
7 ARNHEM WY
8 KIRKSTEAD CT
9 GROVE DR
10 BENNETTS MILL CL
11 ST LEONARD'S DR
12 GROVE CT

C6
1 THE CLOSE
2 KING EDWARD RD
3 ALEXANDRA RD
4 TURNBERRY DR
5 ABBEY CL
6 MELROSE CL
7 KING EDWARD AVE
8 KING EDWARD CR
9 TROON CL
10 KENMORE DR
11 DORNOCH CL

E6
1 TARLETON AVE
2 TOR-O-MOOR GDNS
3 EBRINGTON CL
4 GORSE CL
5 OAK CL
6 WOODLAND DR
7 HEATHER CL
8 STERLING PL
9 TOR-O-MOOR RD

D6
1 KING GEORGE AV
2 SPA RD
3 CLARENCE RD
4 IDDESLEIGH RD
5 SILVAN AV
6 IDDESLEIGH RD
7 STANHOPE AV
8 CAME CT
9 ST ANDREWS DR

Stixwould
LN9
Newstead Farm
Red Bridge
Halstead Wood
Stobourn Wood
Waterloo Wood
Wellington Monument
Reeds Beck Farm
Glebe Farm
Highall Wood
High Hall Farm
Edlington Moor Farm
Top Plantation
Bracken Wood Farm
Chapel Farm
Tower Farm
Bergamoor
Little Wood
Grange Farm
Stixwould Grange
Long Wood
Edlington Moor
Hotel
Waterloo Farm
Brickpit Covert
Bracken Wood
Long Plantation
Triangle Plantation
Martin Moor
Tower on the Moor
Viking Way
B1191 HORNCASTLE ROAD
Black Horse Farm
Atkinsons Covert
Sewage Works
St Andrews CE Prim Sch
Landfill Site
Hotel
Coal Pit Wood
Woodhall Spa Cottage Mus
Roughton Moor Wood Nature Reserve
Oaklea Farm
Reservoir
Brooks Farm
Sewerage Farm
Liby
THE BROADWAY
STATION RD
Kirkby Lane
Cemy
Kirkby Moor
Martin Dales
CLINTON WY
LN10
B1192
St Hughs Sch
WOODHALL SPA
Ostler's Plantation
Kirkstead Bridge
KIRKSTEAD BR
Old Hall Farm
Low Wood
Kirkstead Hall
Dales Head Bridge
MARTIN DALES
WITHAM RD
B1191
Abbey Farm
PH
Kirkstead Hall Farm
Hogg Wood
RAF Woodhall Spa
Remains of Kirkstead Abbey
TATTERSHALL ROAD
Harbour Wood
Witham Bank Farm
Pinfold Bridge
School Farm
New Park Farm
Timberland Dales
Dales Bridge
Chapel Farm
LODGE ROAD
Amys Farm
Red House Farm
NORTH ROAD
Crewe Farm
Bridge Farm
Tonge Farm
Delph Farm
Bank Farm
Park Farm
Tattershall Thorpe
Carr Farm
B1192
PH
Willow Tree Farm
Nature Reserve
Decoy Farm
Decoy Bridge
Poplar Farm
207
Nature Reserve
Thorpe Tilney Drove
Thorpe Tilney Dales
Lodge Farm
BRULON CL
Thorpe Tilney Fen
Visitor Centre
LN4
Bank Farm
Tattershall
Engine Drain
MARSH LA
MARSH LANE
CASTLEVIEW
BUTT'S LA

110
98
207

For full street detail of the highlighted area see page 207.

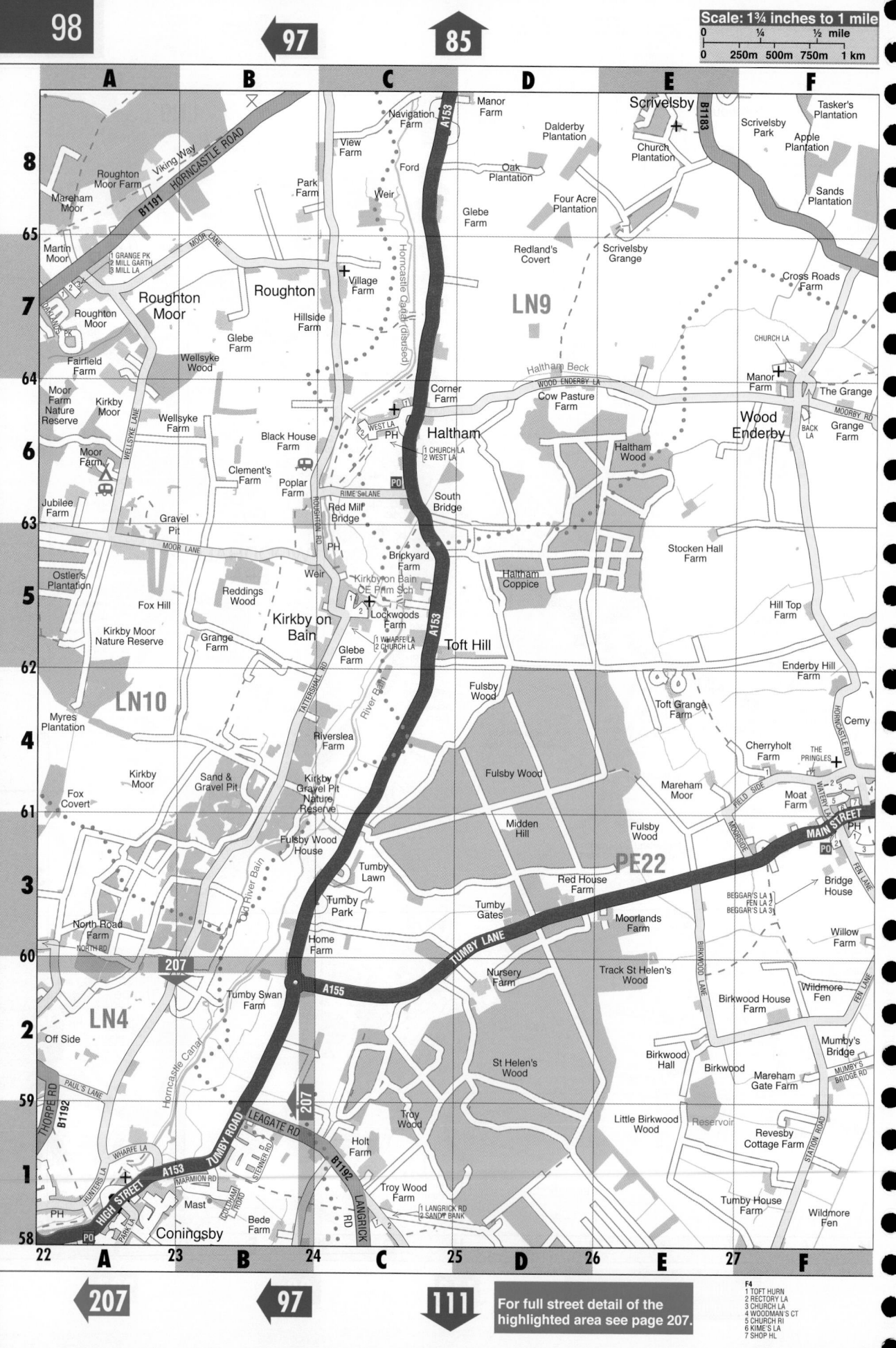

97

85

A   B   C   D   E   F

8

Mareham
Moor

Roughton
Moor Farm

Viking Way

HORNCASTLE ROAD

B1191

MOOR LANE

Navigation
Farm

View
Farm

Park
Farm

Ford

Weir

A153

Manor
Farm

Dalderby
Plantation

Oak
Plantation

Glebe
Farm

Four Acre
Plantation

Scrivelsby

B1183

Church
Plantation

Scrivelsby
Park

Tasker's
Plantation

Apple
Plantation

Sands
Plantation

65

Martin
Moor

OAK LANE

1 GRANGE PK
2 MILL GARTH
3 MILL LA

Roughton
Moor

Roughton

Roughton
Moor

Glebe
Farm

Hillside
Farm

Village
Farm

LN9

Redland's
Covert

Scrivelsby
Grange

CHURCH LA

Cross Roads
Farm

7

Fairfield
Farm

WELLSYKE LANE

Wellsyke
Wood

Black House
Farm

Corner
Farm

Haltham Beck

WOOD ENDERBY LA

Cow Pasture
Farm

Manor
Farm

MOORBY RD

BACK LA

The Grange

Grange
Farm

Wood
Enderby

64

Moor
Farm
Nature
Reserve

Kirkby
Moor

Wellsyke
Farm

WEST LA

PH

Haltham

1 CHURCH LA
2 WEST LA

Haltham
Wood

6

Moor
Farm

Jubilee
Farm

Clement's
Farm

Poplar
Farm

RIME S LANE

PO

South
Bridge

Haltham
Coppice

Stocken Hall
Farm

Hill Top
Farm

63

Gravel
Pit

MOOR LANE

ROUGHTON RD

PH

Red Mill
Bridge

Brickyard
Farm

5

Ostler's
Plantation

Fox Hill

Weir

Reddings
Wood

Kirkby on Bain
CE Prim Sch

Kirkby on
Bain

Lockwoods
Farm

1 WHARFE LA
2 CHURCH LA

A153

Toft Hill

Haltham
Coppice

Enderby Hill
Farm

62

Kirkby Moor
Nature Reserve

Grange
Farm

Glebe
Farm

River Bain

Fulsby
Wood

Toft Grange
Farm

Cemy

LN10

Myres
Plantation

TATTERSHALL RD

Riverslea
Farm

Fulsby Wood

Mareham
Moor

HORNCASTLE RD

Cherryholt
Farm

THE
PRINGLES

4

Kirkby
Moor

Sand &
Gravel Pit

Kirkby
Gravel Pit
Nature
Reserve

Midden
Hill

Fulsby
Wood

Moat
Farm

WATERY LA

FIELD SIDE

MOORSIDE

61

Fox
Covert

Old River Bain

Fulsby Wood
House

PE22

FEN LANE

MAIN STREET

PH

PO

3

North Road
Farm

NORTH RD

Tumby
Lawn

Tumby
Park

Tumby
Gates

Red House
Farm

Moorlands
Farm

BEGGAR'S LA 1
FEN LA 2
BEGGAR'S LA 3

Bridge
House

Willow
Farm

60

207

A155

Home
Farm

TUMBY LANE

Nursery
Farm

Track St Helen's
Wood

BIRKWOOD LANE

FEN LANE

Birkwood House
Farm

Wildmore
Fen

2

LN4

Off Side

PAUL'S LANE

Tumby Swan
Farm

207

St Helen's
Wood

Birkwood
Hall

Birkwood

Mareham
Gate Farm

MUMBY'S
BRIDGE RD

Mumby's
Bridge

59

Thorpe RD

B1192

Horncastle Canal

WHARFE LA

LEAGATE RD

207

Troy
Wood

STATION ROAD

Little Birkwood
Wood

Reservoir

Revesby
Cottage Farm

1

HUNTER'S LA

A153

HIGH STREET

TUMBY ROAD

MARMION RD

STEINER RD

COTTMAN ROAD

Mast

Bede
Farm

Holt
Farm

B1192

LANGRICK RD

Troy Wood
Farm

1 LANGRICK RD
2 SAND BANK

Tumby House
Farm

Wildmore
Fen

58

PH

PARK LA

PO

Coningsby

22   A   23   B   24   C   25   D   26   E   27   F

For full street detail of the
highlighted area see page 207.

F4
1 TOFT HURN
2 RECTORY LA
3 CHURCH LA
4 WOODMAN'S CT
5 CHURCH RI
6 KIME'S LA
7 SHOP HL

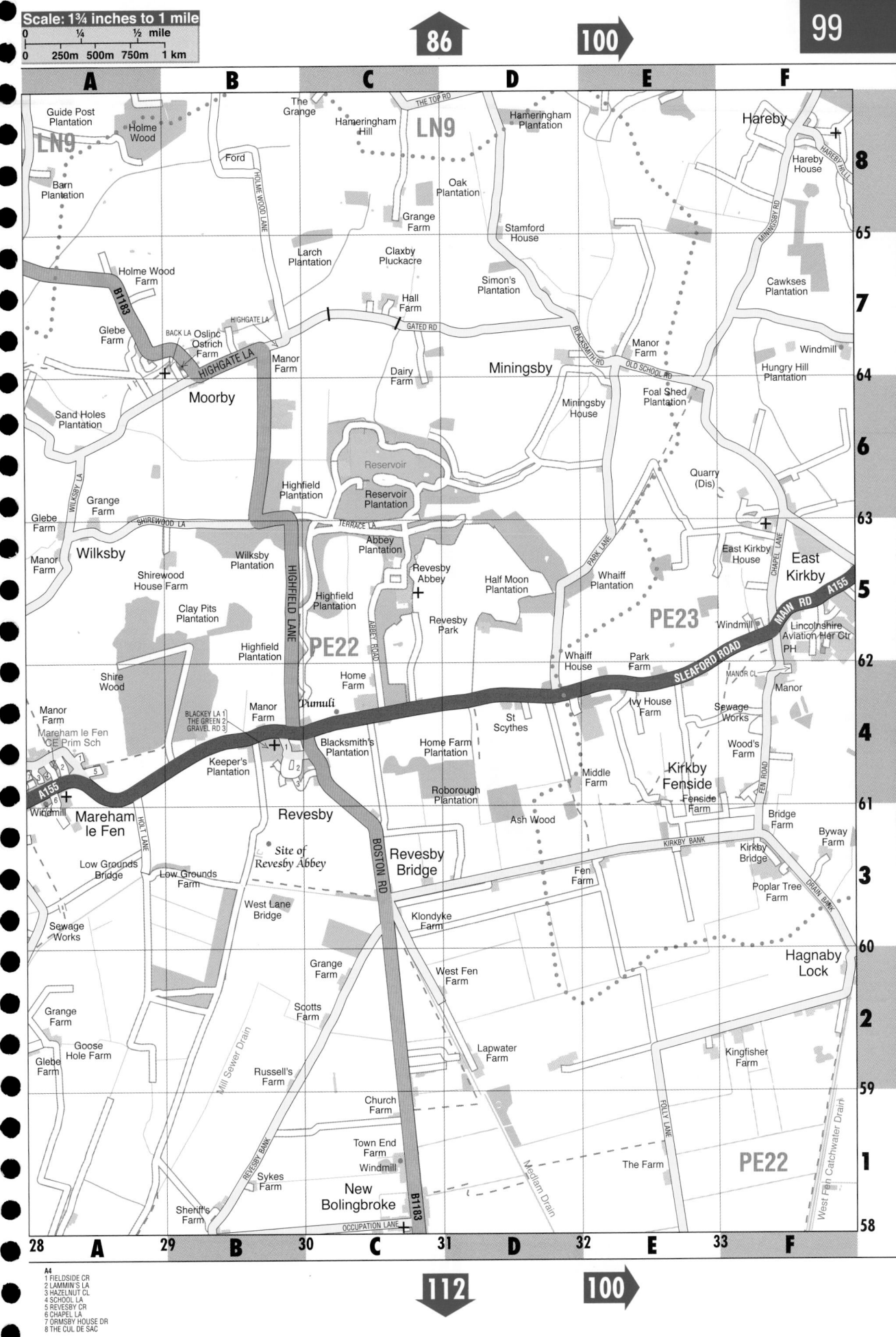

Scale: 1¾ inches to 1 mile

A B C D E F

Guide Post Plantation
Holme Wood
The Grange
Hameringham Hill
LN9
Hameringham Plantation
Hareby
Hareby House
LN9
Ford
Barn Plantation
Oak Plantation
Stamford House
Cawkses Plantation
8
65
Holme Wood Farm
Larch Plantation
Grange Farm
Simon's Plantation
HIGHGATE LA
Hall Farm
GATED RD
Miningsby
Manor Farm
Windmill
7
B1183
Glebe Farm
BACK LA Oslinc Ostrich Farm
HIGHGATE LA
Manor Farm
Dairy Farm
Hungry Hill Plantation
Moorby
Claxby Pluckacre
Miningsby House
Foal Shed Plantation
64
Sand Holes Plantation
HOLME WOOD LANE
BLACKSMITH RD
OLD SCHOOL RD
6
Glebe Farm
Grange Farm
Reservoir
Reservoir Plantation
Quarry (Dis)
63
Manor Farm
WILKSBY LA
SHIREWOOD LA
Highfield Plantation
TERRACE LA
Abbey Plantation
Whaiff Plantation
East Kirkby House
East Kirkby
Wilksby
Wilksby Plantation
Revesby Abbey
Half Moon Plantation
PE23
Windmill
Lincolnshire Aviation Her Ctr
A155
5
Shirewood House Farm
HIGHFIELD LANE
Highfield Plantation
Revesby Park
Whaiff House
Park Farm
SLEAFORD ROAD
MAIN RD
PH
62
Clay Pits Plantation
ABBEY ROAD
PE22
Home Farm
St Scythes
Ivy House Farm
Manor
MANOR CL
Shire Wood
Highfield Plantation
Tumuli
Manor Farm
Home Farm Plantation
Middle Farm
Sewage Works
Wood's Farm
4
Manor Farm
BLACKEY LA 1
THE GREEN 2
GRAVEL RD 3
Blacksmith's Plantation
Kirkby Fenside
FEN ROAD
61
Mareham le Fen CE Prim Sch
A155
Keeper's Plantation
Roborough Plantation
Fenside Farm
Bridge Farm
Byway Farm
Windmill
HOLT LANE
Mareham le Fen
Revesby
Ash Wood
KIRKBY BANK
Kirkby Bridge
DRAIN BANK
Poplar Tree Farm
Low Grounds Bridge
Low Grounds Farm
Site of Revesby Abbey
BOSTON RD
Revesby Bridge
Fen Farm
Hagnaby Lock
60
3
West Lane Bridge
Klondyke Farm
Sewage Works
Grange Farm
West Fen Farm
Kingfisher Farm
2
Grange Farm
REVESBY BANK
Scotts Farm
Lapwater Farm
FOLLY LANE
59
Goose Hole Farm
Russell's Farm
MILL SEWER DRAIN
Church Farm
The Farm
PE22
Glebe Farm
Town End Farm
Windmill
MEDLAM DRAIN
1
Sykes Farm
New Bolingbroke
B1183
WEST FEN CATCHWATER DRAIN
Sheriff's Farm
OCCUPATION LANE
58

28 A 29 B 30 C 31 D 32 E 33 F

A4
1 FIELDSIDE CR
2 LAMMIN'S LA
3 HAZELNUT CL
4 SCHOOL LA
5 REVESBY CR
6 CHAPEL LA
7 ORMSBY HOUSE DR
8 THE CUL DE SAC

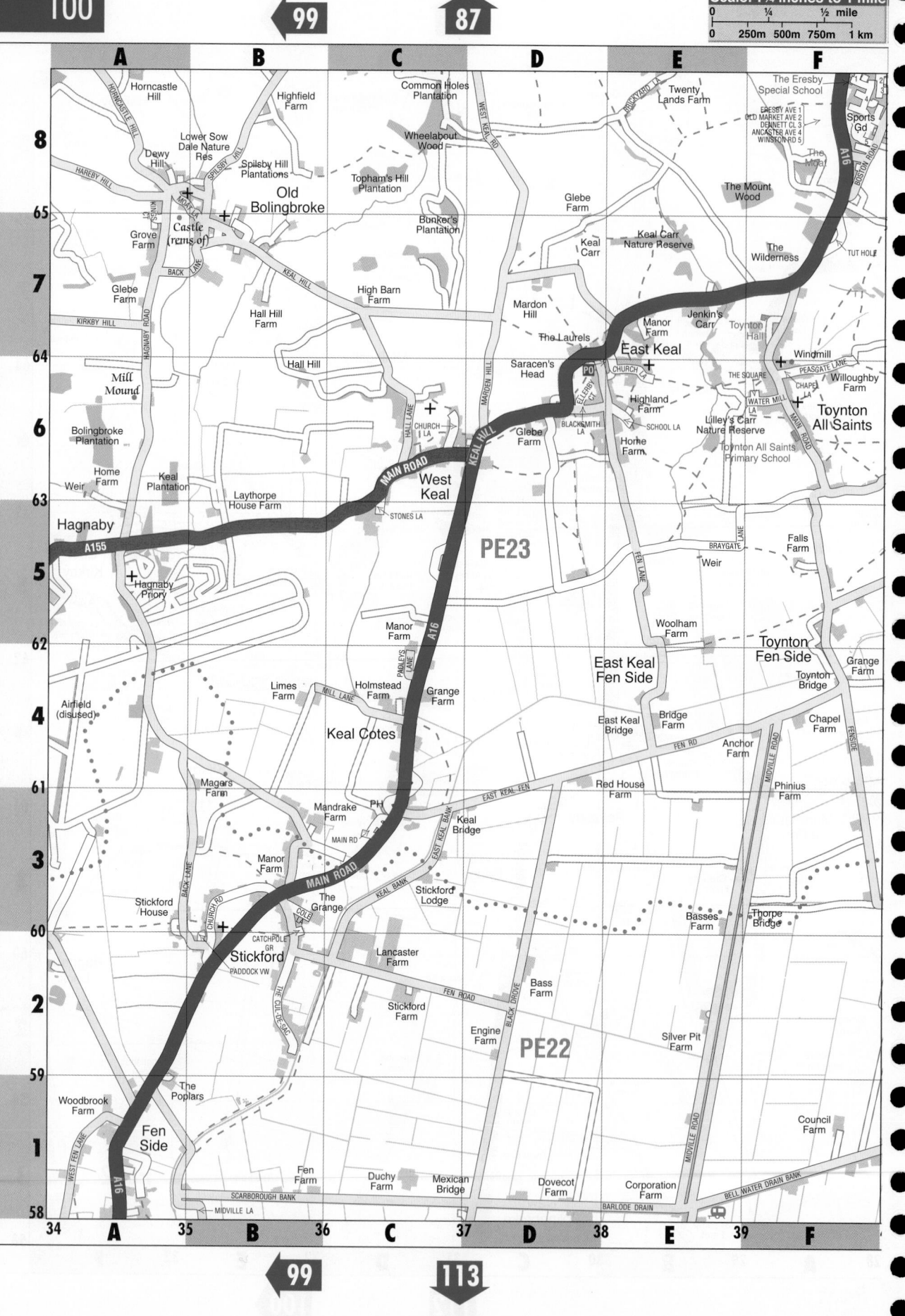

Scale: 1¾ inches to 1 mile

| 0 | ¼ | ½ mile |

| 0 | 250m | 500m | 750m | 1 km |

Horncastle Hill
Highfield Farm
Common Holes Plantation
Twenty Lands Farm
The Eresby Special School
ERESBY AVE 1
OLD MARKET AVE 2
DENNETT CL 3
ANCASTER AVE 4
WINSTON RD 5
Sports Gd
The Moat

Lower Sow Dale Nature Res
Dewy Hill
Spilsby Hill Plantations
Wheelabout Wood
Topham's Hill Plantation
Glebe Farm
The Mount Wood
The Wilderness
TUT HOLE

Old Bolingbroke
Castle (rems of)
Grove Farm
Bunker's Plantation
Keal Carr
Keal Carr Nature Reserve
Jenkin's Carr
Toynton Hall

Glebe Farm
Hall Hill Farm
High Barn Farm
Mardon Hill
The Laurels
Manor Farm
East Keal
Windmill
Peasgate Lane
Willoughby Farm

Kirkby Hill
Hall Hill
Saracen's Head
Church La
The Square
Chapel
Toynton All Saints

Mill Mound
Church La
Glebe Farm
Blacksmith La
Highland Farm
School La
Water Mill
Lilley's Carr Nature Reserve

Bolingbroke Plantation
Home Farm
Weir
Keal Plantation
Laythorpe House Farm
West Keal
Horne Farm
Toynton All Saints Primary School

Hagnaby
A155
Stones La
PE23
Weir
Woolham Farm
Toynton Fen Side
Falls Farm

Hagnaby Priory
Manor Farm
East Keal Fen Side
Grange Farm

Airfield (disused)
Limes Farm
Mill Lane
Holmstead Farm
Grange Farm
East Keal Bridge
Bridge Farm
Anchor Farm
Chapel Farm
Toynton Bridge
Grange Farm

Keal Cotes
East Keal Fen
Red House Farm
Phinius Farm

Magers Farm
Mandrake Farm
PH
Main Rd
Keal Bridge
Midville Road

Manor Farm
Back Lane
Church Rd
The Grange
Cole La
Keal Bank
Stickford Lodge
Basses Farm
Thorpe Bridge

Stickford House
Catchpole Gr
Paddock Vw
Stickford
Lancaster Farm
Bass Farm

The Cul-de-Sac
Stickford Farm
Fen Road
Black Drove
Engine Farm
PE22
Silver Pit Farm
Council Farm

Woodbrook Farm
The Poplars
Fen Side
Fen Farm
Duchy Farm
Mexican Bridge
Dovecot Farm
Corporation Farm

West Fen Lane
A16
Scarborough Bank
Midville La
Barlode Drain
Bell Water Drain Bank

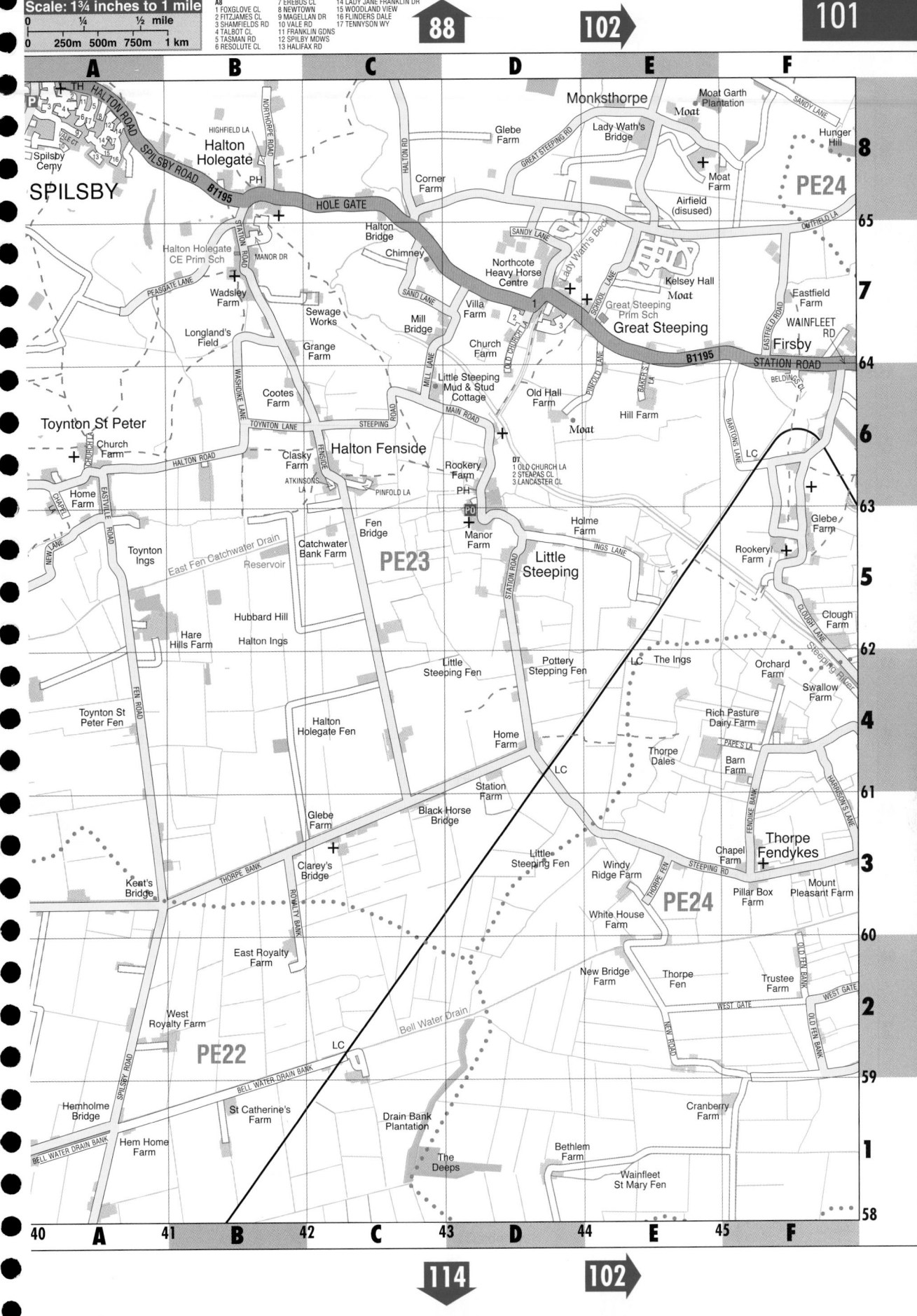
Scale: 1¾ inches to 1 mile
0 ¼ ½ mile
0 250m 500m 750m 1 km
A8
1 FOXGLOVE CL
2 FITZJAMES CL
3 SHAMFIELDS RD
4 TALBOT CL
5 TASMAN RD
6 RESOLUTE CL
7 EREBUS CL
8 NEWTOWN
9 MAGELLAN DR
10 VALE RD
11 FRANKLIN GDNS
12 SPILBY MDWS
13 HALIFAX RD
14 LADY JANE FRANKLIN DR
15 WOODLAND VIEW
16 FLINDERS DALE
17 TENNYSON WY
88
102
A B C D E F
SPILSBY
Spilsby Cemy
HALTON ROAD
SPILSBY ROAD
B1195
HIGHFIELD LA
NORTHORPE ROAD
Halton Holegate
PH
HOLE GATE
HALTON RD
Glebe Farm
Corner Farm
Monksthorpe
Moat Garth Plantation
Moat
Lady Wath's Bridge
GREAT STEEPING RD
SANDY LANE
Hunger Hill
Moat Farm
Airfield (disused)
PE24
OUTFIELD LA
STATION ROAD
MANOR DR
Halton Holegate CE Prim Sch
PEASGATE LANE
Wadsley Farm
Halton Bridge
Chimney
SAND LANE
Sewage Works
Mill Bridge
Villa Farm
Northcote Heavy Horse Centre
Lady Wath's Beck
SCHOOL LANE
Kelsey Hall
Moat
Eastfield Farm
EASTFIELD ROAD
WAINFLEET RD
Great Steeping Prim Sch
Great Steeping
Firsby
STATION ROAD
BELDINGS CL
Longland's Field
Grange Farm
Church Farm
OLD CHURCH LA
PINFOLD LANE
BAKER'S LA
WASHDIKE LANE
MILL LANE
Little Steeping Mud & Stud Cottage
Cootes Farm
Old Hall Farm
Hill Farm
Moat
MAIN ROAD
Toynton St Peter
Church Farm
CHURCH LA
TOYNTON LANE
STEEPING ROAD
Halton Fenside
BARTONS LANE
LC
HALTON ROAD
Clasky Farm
FENSIDE
ATKINSONS LA
PINFOLD LA
Rookery Farm
PH
D7
1 OLD CHURCH LA
2 STEAPAS CL
3 LANCASTER CL
Home Farm
CHAPEL LA
EASTVILLE ROAD
PO
Manor Farm
Fen Bridge
Holme Farm
Glebe Farm
NEW LANE
Toynton Ings
East Fen Catchwater Drain
Reservoir
Catchwater Bank Farm
PE23
STATION ROAD
Little Steeping
INGS LANE
Rookery Farm
Hubbard Hill
Hare Hills Farm
Halton Ings
CLOUGH LANE
Clough Farm
Steeping River
Little Steeping Fen
Pottery Stepping Fen
LC
The Ings
Orchard Farm
Swallow Farm
FEN ROAD
Toynton St Peter Fen
Halton Holegate Fen
Rich Pasture Dairy Farm
Home Farm
PAPE'S LA
Thorpe Dales
Barn Farm
LC
Station Farm
HARRISON'S LANE
FENDIKE BANK
Black Horse Bridge
Glebe Farm
Thorpe Fendykes
Little Steeping Fen
Chapel Farm
Windy Ridge Farm
THORPE FEN
STEEPING RD
Clarey's Bridge
THORPE BANK
Kent's Bridge
ROYALTY BANK
PE24
Pillar Box Farm
Mount Pleasant Farm
White House Farm
East Royalty Farm
OLD FEN BANK
New Bridge Farm
Thorpe Fen
Trustee Farm
WEST GATE
WEST GATE
West Royalty Farm
Bell Water Drain
PE22
LC
NEW ROAD
OLD FEN BANK
BELL WATER DRAIN BANK
SPILSBY ROAD
Hemholme Bridge
St Catherine's Farm
Cranberry Farm
Drain Bank Plantation
Hem Home Farm
BELL WATER DRAIN BANK
The Deeps
Bethlem Farm
Wainfleet St Mary Fen
8 65 7 64 6 63 5 62 4 61 3 60 2 59 1 58
40 41 42 43 44 45
114
102

← 101   ⬆ 89

E7
1 CHURCH HILL
2 OLD CHAPEL LA
3 EAST END
4 BARNACK EST
5 WALLS AVE
6 CHAPMAN AVE
7 THE PADDOCKS
8 DAWSON DR
9 HOLDEN DR
10 CUMBERLIDGE CL
11 BEAUMONT CL
12 PARKERS CL
13 VENABLES CL
14 JOHNSON WY
15 Burgh le Marsh Mus

Scale: 1¾ inches to 1 mile
0   ¼   ½   mile
0 250m 500m 750m 1 km

E8
1 CLAREMONT RD
2 KENNETH AVE
3 MARKET CL
4 JACKSONS LA
5 CHURCH ST
6 BREWERY PL
7 MARKET PL
8 CERVANTES CT
9 BISHOP TOZER CL
10 DOUGLAS CL

Grid columns: A 46 · 47 B · 48 C · 49 D · 50 E · 51 F

Grid rows: 8 · 65 · 7 · 64 · 6 · 63 · 5 · 62 · 4 · 61 · 3 · 60 · 2 · 59 · 1 · 58

PE23

Place names and features:
Grange Farm, Buttoncap Holt, Moat, Elmstead Farm, White Gate Farm, Bratoft, Manor Farm, White House Farm, North Road, Gravel Pits Lane, Gatrum Farm, Woody Nook Farm, Kirks Farm, Common Lane, Pear Tree Farm, Burgh Common, Motel, Willow Lodge, A158, Orby Road, West End, Doubledays La 1, Windmill Dr 2, St Peter's Cl 3, Elm Cr 4, Windmill, PO, PH, High Street, Libry, St Michaels Farm, Ingoldmells Road, St Peter & St Paul CE Prim School, St Pauls Cl 1, Ash Cl 2, Linden Dr 3, Lime Cl 4, Hall Lane, Windmill, Burgh le Marsh, Summergates La, Mill Hill Farm, Millfield Rd, Wildshed Lane, Heath's Meadow Nature Reserve, Green La, Ings Lane, Wainfleet Road, Bratoft Corner, Long Plantation, Bratoft End, Church Farm, Peartree Farm, B1195, Manor Farm, Irby in the Marsh, Wainfleet Road, Lincoln Farm, Oxlands Lane, Wongs Lane, Coldwater Lane, End House Farm, Ings Lane, Croft End, High Lane, Low Lane, Billgate Lane, Jock Hedge, Lloyds Farm, Blands Farm, Catchwater Drain, PE23, The Ings, Grove House Farm, Hollytrees Farm, The Hollies, Home Farm, Mast, LC, PE24, New House Farm, Croft Lane, Low Road, Rivulet House, Millhill Bridge, Mill Hill Farm, The Hundreds, Washdike Lane, Meml, Croft, Church La, Clough La, Clough Bridge, Tip Lane, Lymn Bank, Lymn Bank Farm, White House Farm, Spilsby Road, Corn Lane, Firsby Clough, Sycamore Cl, Monson Farm, PH, Oak Bridge, Pinchbeck Lane, Church Lane, Warth's Bridge, Thorpe St Peter, Station Road, LC, Holly Farm, Thorpe Culvert, PH, Thorpe Fen, Leaver Gate, Culvert Road, Thorpe Culvert, Old Hall Farm, Moat, B1195, Green La, Wedland Lane, PH, Wainfleet Road, Florence Farm, Poplar Farm, Works, Bank House, Croft Road, Croft Bank, Manor House Farm, Primrose Farm, Crown Farm, Havenhouse, West Gate, Lady La, Watson Farm, King Street, Wainfleet Common, Back La, Church Farm, Crow's Bridge, Grows La, Collison Gate, Brewster Lane, LC, Wainfleet All Saints, Cemy, Tower Tree Farm, Waincroft Close, New England, Whiteheads Farm, Lady Lane, Green La, Wainfleet Bank, Maxeys La, Mill La, Washdike Lane, Wainfleet Magdalen CE/Meth Sch, Magdalen Rd, Wainfleet, Skegness Road, Riverside Farm, Wainfleet St Mary Fen, Church Lane, Old Fen Bank, Low Grounds, Low Road, Hall Gate, Queen's Est, Vicarage La, Bateman's Brewery, Magdalen Mus, High St, Station Road, Libry, Dovecote La, Merrifield's Farm, White House Farm, Windsor Farm, Low Farm, Boston Rd, B1195, A52

← 101   ⬆ 115

D1
1 ST JOHN ST
2 PATTEN AVE
3 RUMBOLD LA
4 ALL SAINTS CL
5 SILVER ST
6 BARTON RD
7 COLLEGE CL
8 HAVEN SIDE
9 BETHLEM CRES
10 TINDALL WY
11 ST MICHAEL'S LA
12 THE PADDOCKS

D2
1 BEES CR
2 STANLEY CL
3 HILL FIELD
4 HASTINGS DR
5 NEW END
6 MOUNT PLEASANT
7 BARKHAM ST
8 WINCHESTER RD

E2
1 CROFT BANK
2 BATEMANS CT
3 CROFT CL
4 MILL CL
5 SKEGNESS GDNS
6 MAWSON GDNS
7 MERRIFIELD RD

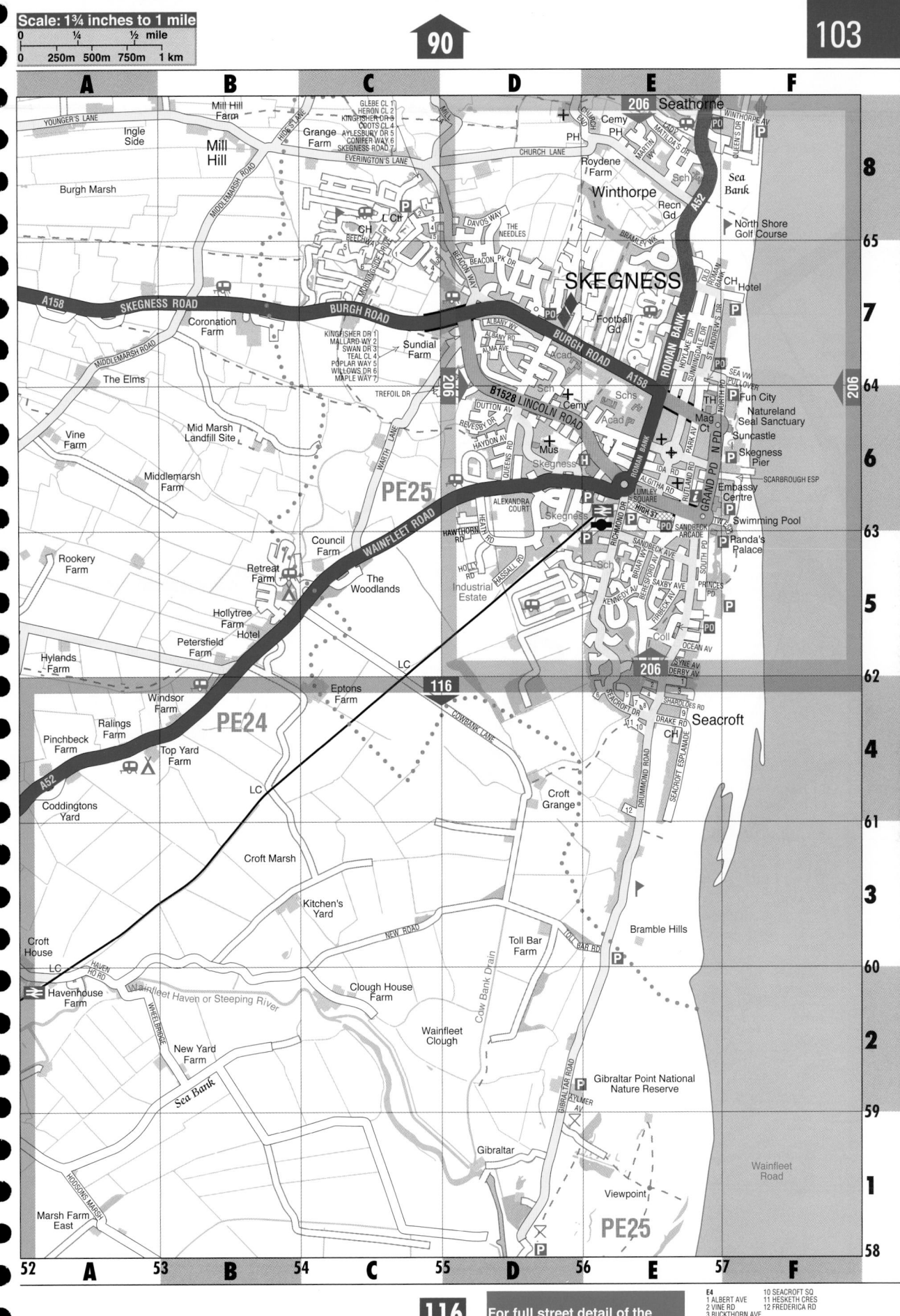

A   B   C   D   E   F

Younger's Lane

Ingle Side

Mill Hill Farm

Mill Hill

Grange Farm

Glebe Cl 1
Heron Cl 2
Kingfisher Dr 3
Coots Cl 4
Aylesbury Dr 5
Conifer Way 6
Skegness Road

206 Seathorne

WINTHORPE AV

Cemy

PH

8

Burgh Marsh

Everington's Lane

CH

L Ctr

Church Lane

DAVOS WAY

THE NEEDLES

BEACON PK DR

BEACON WAY

Roydene Farm

Winthorpe

Recn Gd

Sch

Sea Bank

North Shore Golf Course

65

A158

SKEGNESS ROAD   BURGH ROAD

Coronation Farm

Sundial Farm

KINGFISHER DR 1
MALLARD WY 2
SWAN DR 3
TEAL CL 4
POPLAR WAY 5
WILLOWS DR 6
MAPLE WAY 7

TREFOIL DR

206

Albany Rd
Albany Rd
Alma Ave

BURGH ROAD

SKEGNESS

Football Gd

PO

A158

ROMAN BANK

CH Hotel

7

The Elms

Middlemarsh Road

Mid Marsh Landfill Site

B1528 LINCOLN ROAD

DUTTON AV

REVESBY DR
HAYDON AV

Cemy

Acad

Schs

Sch

Schs

SEA VW
PULLOVER

Fun City
Natureland Seal Sanctuary

206

64

Vine Farm

Middlemarsh Farm

WARTH LANE

QUEENS RD

Mus

Skegness

H

Skegness Pier

Scarbrough Esp

6

Rookery Farm

PE25

WAINFLEET ROAD

Council Farm

Retreat Farm

The Woodlands

ALGITHA RD

Alexandra Court

Skegness

HAWTHORN RD

HEATH RD

HASSALL RD

HOLLY RD

BRIAR RD
SAXBY AVE

SANDBECK AVE

Sandbeck Arcade

LUMLEY SQUARE

SOUTH PD

Embassy Centre

Swimming Pool

Randa's Palace

63

Hylands Farm

Hollytree Farm Hotel

Petersfield Farm

LC

Industrial Estate

KENNEDY AV

FORBECK AV

PRINCES PD

Sch

PO

5

A52

PE24

Windsor Farm

Eptons Farm

116

COWBANK LANE

LC

Coll

OCEAN AV

206

TYNE AV
DERBY AV

62

Pinchbeck Farm

Ralings Farm

Top Yard Farm

LC

Croft Grange

SEACROFT DR

DRAKE RD

SHARLOES RD

CH

Seacroft

DRUMMOND ROAD

SEACROFT ESPLANADE

4

Coddingtons Yard

Croft Marsh

Kitchen's Yard

NEW ROAD

Toll Bar Farm

TOLL BAR RD

Bramble Hills

61

Croft House

LC

HAVEN HO RD

WHEEL BRIDGE

Wainfleet Haven or Steeping River

Cow Bank Drain

Clough House Farm

P

3

Havenhouse Farm

New Yard Farm

Sea Bank

Wainfleet Clough

GIBRALTAR ROAD

AYLMER AV

Gibraltar Point National Nature Reserve

60

59

Marsh Farm East

HODSONS MARSH RD

Gibraltar

Viewpoint

PE25

Wainfleet Road

2

1

58

52   A   53   B   54   C   55   D   56   E   57   F

116   For full street detail of the highlighted area see page 206.

E4
1 ALBERT AVE
2 VINE RD
3 BUCKTHORN AVE
4 NORWOOD RD
5 PRECINCT CRES
6 BAYES RD
7 GREEN LA
8 LINKS CRES
9 SEA FRONT RD
10 SEACROFT SQ
11 HESKETH CRES
12 FREDERICA RD

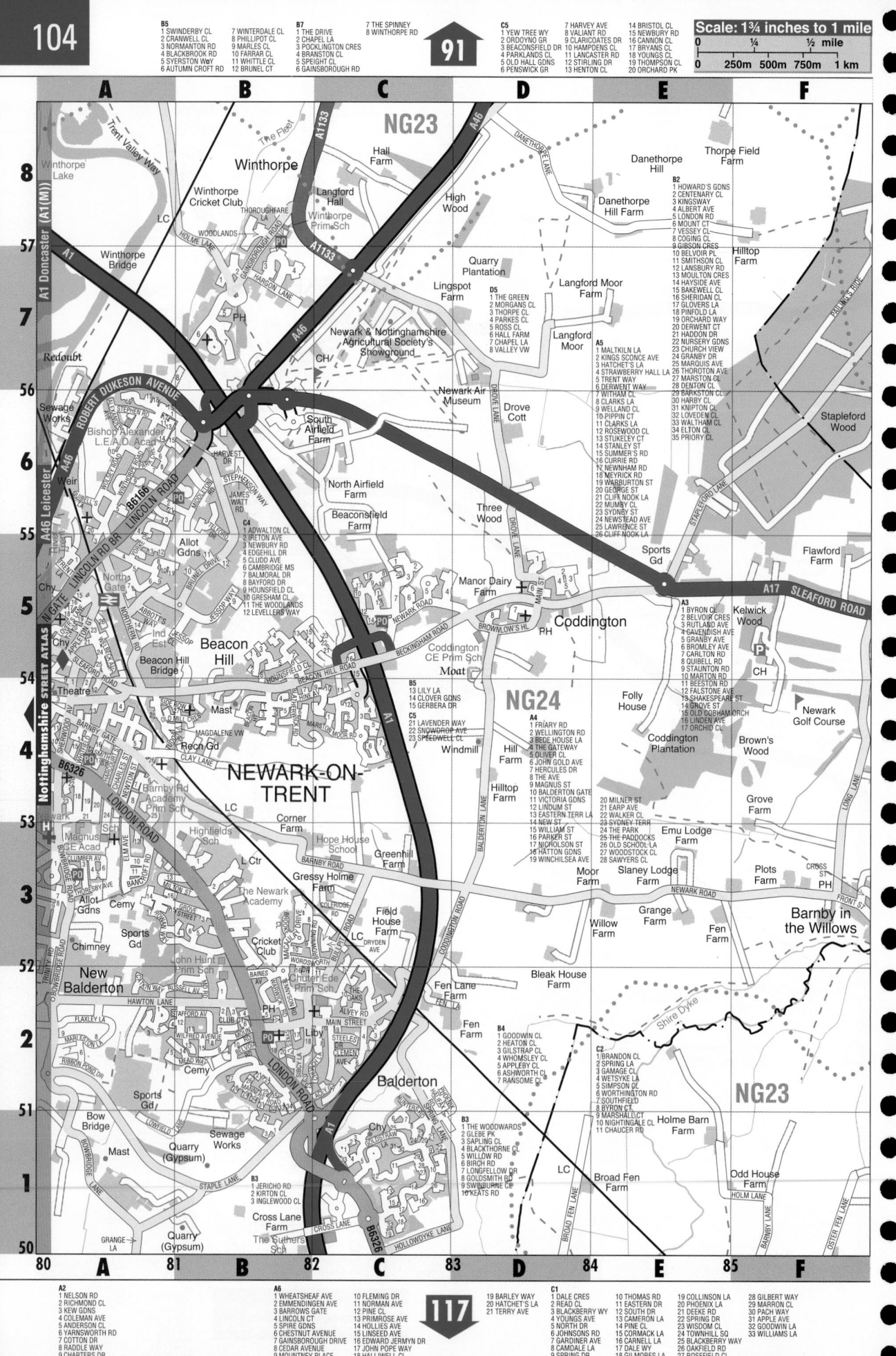

B5
1 SWINDERBY CL
2 CRANWELL CL
3 NORMANTON RD
4 BLACKBROOK CL
5 SYERSTON WAY
6 AUTUMN CROFT RD

7 WINTERDALE CL
8 PHILLIPOT CL
9 MARLES CL
10 FARRAR CL
11 WHITTLE CL
12 BRUNEL CT

B7
1 THE DRIVE
2 CHAPEL LA
3 POCKLINGTON CRES
4 BRANSTON CL
5 SPEIGHT CL
6 GAINSBOROUGH RD

7 THE SPINNEY
8 WINTHORPE RD

C5
1 YEW TREE WY
2 ORDOVNO GR
3 BEACONSFIELD DR
4 PARKLANDS CL
5 OLD HALL GDNS
6 PENSWICK GR

7 HARVEY AVE
8 VALIANT RD
9 CLARICOATES DR
10 HAMPOENS CL
11 LANCASTER RD
12 STIRLING DR
13 HENTON CL

14 BRISTOL CL
15 NEWBURY RD
16 CANNON CL
17 BRYANS CL
18 BRYANS CL
19 THOMPSON CL
20 ORCHARD PK

NG23

Winthorpe

Winthorpe Lake

Trent Valley Way

The Fleet

Hall Farm

Winthorpe Cricket Club

Langford Hall

Winthorpe Prim Sch

High Wood

Danethorpe Hill

Thorpe Field Farm

Danethorpe Hill Farm

B2
1 HOWARD'S GDNS
2 CENTENARY CL
3 KINGSWAY
4 ALBERT AVE
5 LONDON RD
6 MOUNT CL
7 VESSEY CL
8 COGING CL
9 GIBSON CRES
10 BELVOIR PL
11 SMITHSON CL
12 LANSBURY RD
13 MOULTON CRES
14 HAYSIDE AVE
15 BAKEWELL CL
16 SHERIDAN CL
17 GLOVERS LA
18 PINFOLD LA
19 ORCHARD WAY
20 DERWENT CT
21 HADDON DR
22 NURSERY GDNS
23 CHURCH VIEW
24 GRANBY DR
25 MARQUIS AVE
26 THOROTON AVE
27 MARSTON CL
28 DENTON CL
29 BARKSTON CL
30 HARBY CL
31 KNIPTON CL
32 LOWDEN CL
33 WALTHAM CL
34 ELTON CL
35 PRIORY CL

Hilltop Farm

Stapleford Wood

Winthorpe Bridge

A1 Doncaster (A1(M))

Redoubt

Sewage Works

Weir

A46 Leicester

Bishop Alexander L.E.A.D. Acad

North Gate

Beacon Hill

Beacon Hill Bridge

Allot Gdns

Lingspot Farm

Langford Moor Farm

Langford Moor

Quarry Plantation

Newark & Nottinghamshire Agricultural Society's Showground

Newark Air Museum

South Airfield Farm

North Airfield Farm

Beaconsfield Farm

Three Wood

Drove Cott

Drove Lane

D5
1 THE GREEN
2 MORGANS CL
3 THORPE CL
4 PARKES CL
5 ROSS CL
6 HALL FARM
7 CHAPEL LA
8 VALLEY VW

A5
1 MALTKILN LA
2 KINGS SCONCE AVE
3 HATCHET'S LA
4 STRAWBERRY HALL LA
5 TRENT WAY
6 DERWENT WAY
7 WITHAM CL
8 CLARKS LA
9 WELLAND CL
10 PIPPIN CT
11 CLARKS LA
12 ROSEWOOD CL
13 STUKELEY CL
14 STANLEY ST
15 SUMMER'S RD
16 CURRIE RD
17 NEWNHAM RD
18 MEYRICK RD
19 WARBURTON ST
20 GEORGE ST
21 CLIFF NOOK LA
22 MUMBY CL
23 SYDNEY ST
24 NEWSTEAD AVE
25 LAWRENCE ST
26 CLIFF NOOK LA

Flawford Farm

Sports Gd

Kelwick Wood

A3
1 BYRON CL
2 BELVOIR CRES
3 RUTLAND AVE
4 CAVENDISH AVE
5 GRANBY AVE
6 BROMLEY AVE
7 CARLTON RD
8 QUIBELL RD
9 MARTON RD
10 BEESTON RD
11 FALSTONE AVE
12 SHAKESPEARE ST
13 GROVE ST
14 OLD OGBHAM ORCH
15 LINDEN AVE
16 LINDEN AVE
17 ORCHID CL

Newark Golf Course

Manor Dairy Farm

Coddington CE Prim Sch

Moat

Coddington

Brownlow's Hl

NG24

B5
13 LILY LA
14 CLOVER GDNS
15 GERBERA DR

C5
21 LAVENDER WAY
22 SNOWDROP AVE
23 SPEEDWELL CL

Windmill

Hill Farm

Hilltop Farm

Folly House

Coddington Plantation

Brown's Wood

Grove Farm

C4
1 ADWALTON CL
2 IRETON AVE
3 NEWBURY RD
4 EDGEHILL DR
5 CLUDD AVE
6 CAMBRIDGE MS
7 BALMORAL DR
8 BAYFORD DR
9 HOUNSFIELD CL
10 GRESHAM CL
11 THE WOODLANDS
12 LEVELLERS WAY

NEWARK-ON-TRENT

A4
1 FRIARY RD
2 WELLINGTON RD
3 BEDE HOUSE LA
4 THE GATEWAY
5 OLIVER CL
6 JOHN GOLD AVE
7 HERCULES DR
8 THE AVE
9 MAGNUS ST
10 BALDERTON GATE
11 VICTORIA GDNS
12 LINDUM ST
13 EASTERN TERR LA
14 NEW ST
15 WILLIAM ST
16 PARKER ST
17 NICHOLSON ST
18 HATTON GDNS
19 WINCHILSEA AVE

20 MILNER ST
21 EARP AVE
22 WALKER ST
23 SYDNEY TERR
24 THE PARK
25 THE PADDOCKS
26 OLD SCHOOL LA
27 WOODSTOCK CL
28 SAWYERS CL

Emu Lodge Farm

Plots Farm

Magnus CE Acad

New Balderton

Corner Farm

Hope House School

Greenhill Farm

Gressy Holme Farm

The Newark Academy

Field House Farm

Moor Farm

Slaney Lodge Farm

Grange Farm

Barnby in the Willows

Fen Farm

Willow Farm

Fen Lane Farm

Bleak House Farm

Fen Farm

Shire Dyke

B4
1 GOODWIN CL
2 HEATON CL
3 GILSTRAP CL
4 WHOMSLEY CL
5 APPLEBY CL
6 ASHWORTH CL
7 RANSOME CL

C2
1 BRANDON CL
2 SPRING LA
3 GAMAGE CL
4 WETSYKE LA
5 SIMPSON CL
6 WORTHINGTON RD
7 SOUTHFIELD
8 BYRON CT
9 MARSHALL CL
10 NIGHTINGALE CL
11 CHAUCER RD

NG23

Balderton

B3
1 THE WOODWARDS
2 GLEBE PK
3 SAPLING CL
4 BLACKTHORNE CL
5 WILLOW RD
6 BIRCH RD
7 LONGFELLOW DR
8 GOLDSMITH RD
9 SWINBURNE CB
10 KEATS RD

Holme Barn Farm

Broad Fen Farm

Bow Bridge

Sports Gd

Chimney

Quarry (Gypsum)

Sewage Works

Odd House Farm

Cross Lane Farm

Quarry (Gypsum)

The Suthers

A2
1 NELSON RD
2 RICHMOND CL
3 KEW GDNS
4 COLEMAN AVE
5 ANDERSON CL
6 YARNSWORTH RD
7 COTTON DR
8 RADDLE WAY
9 CHARTERS DR

A6
1 WHEATSHEAF AVE
2 EMMENDINGEN AVE
3 BARROWS GATE
4 LINCOLN CT
5 SPIRE GDNS
6 CHESTNUT AVENUE
7 GAINSBOROUGH DRIVE
8 CEDAR AVENUE
9 MOUNTNEY PLACE

10 FLEMING DR
11 NORMAN AVE
12 PINE CL
13 PRIMROSE AVE
14 HOLLIES AVE
15 LINSEED AVE
16 EDWARD JERMYN DR
17 JOHN POPE WAY
18 HALLIWELL CL

19 BARLEY WAY
20 HATCHET'S LA
21 TERRY AVE

C1
1 DALE CRES
2 READ CL
3 BLACKBERRY WY
4 YOUNGS AVE
5 NORTH DR
6 JOHNSONS RD
7 GARDINER AVE
8 CAMDALE LA
9 SPRING DR

10 THOMAS RD
11 EASTERN DR
12 SOUTH DR
13 CAMERON LA
14 PINE CL
15 CORMACK LA
16 CARNELL LA
17 DALE WY
18 GILMORES LA

19 COLLINSON LA
20 PHOENIX LA
21 DEEKE RD
22 SPRING DR
23 WISDOM CL
24 TOWNHILL SQ
25 BLACKBERRY WAY
26 OAKFIELD RD
27 ROSEFIELD CL

28 GILBERT CL
29 MARRON CL
30 PACH WAY
31 APPLE AVE
32 GOODWIN LA
33 WILLIAMS LA

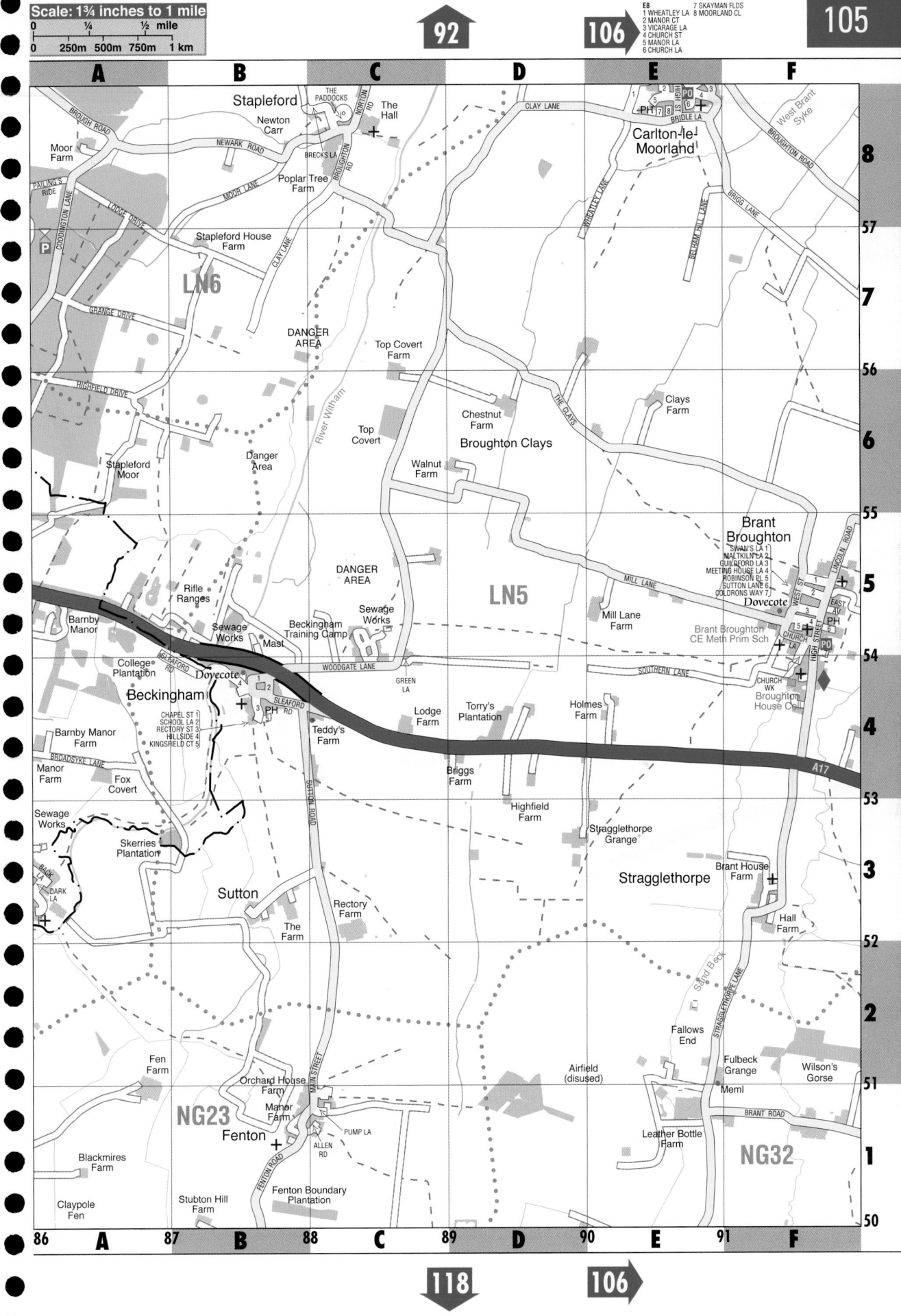

Scale: 1¾ inches to 1 mile

0   ¼   ½   mile
0   250m 500m 750m 1 km

92

106

E8
1 WHEATLEY LA
2 MANOR CT
3 VICARAGE LA
4 CHURCH ST
5 MANOR LA
6 CHURCH LA
7 SKAYMAN FLDS
8 MOORLAND CL

A   B   C   D   E   F

8
57
7
56
6
55
5
54
4
53
3
52
2
51
1
50

Stapleford
Newton Carr
The Hall
THE PADDOCKS
NEWARK ROAD
Moor Farm
BROUGH ROAD
PAILING'S RIDE
CODDINGTON LANE
LODGE DRIVE
P
BRECKS LA
NORTON RD
BROUGHTON RD
MOOR LANE
Poplar Tree Farm
CLAY LANE
Stapleford House Farm
LN6
GRANGE DRIVE
HIGHFIELD DRIVE

CLAY LANE
Carlton-le-Moorland
PH
BRIDLE LA
WHEATLEY LANE
BELTHAM HILL LANE
BRIGG LANE
BROUGHTON ROAD
West Brant Syke
PO
1 2
3
4
5
6
7 8

DANGER AREA
Top Covert Farm
Chestnut Farm
Broughton Clays
THE CLAYS
Clays Farm
River Witham
Stapleford Moor
Danger Area
Top Covert
Walnut Farm
DANGER AREA
LN5
MILL LANE
Brant Broughton
LINCOLN ROAD
SWAN'S LA 1
MALTKILN LA 2
GUILDFORD LA 3
MEETING HOUSE LA 4
ROBINSON PL 5
SUTTON LANE 6
GOLDRONS WAY 7
WEST ST
EAST AV
HIGH STREET
Dovecote
PH
PO
Brant Broughton CE Meth Prim Sch
CHURCH
WK
Broughton House Coll

Rifle Ranges
Barnby Manor
Sewage Works
SLEAFORD RD
Dovecote
College Plantation
Beckingham
CHAPEL ST 1
SCHOOL LA 2
RECTORY ST 3
HILLSIDE 4
KINGSFIELD CT 5
SLEAFORD RD
PH
Beckingham Training Camp
Mast
WOODGATE LANE
Sewage Works
GREEN LA
Mill Lane Farm
SOUTHERN LANE
CHURCH WK

Barnby Manor Farm
BROADSYKE LANE
Manor Farm
Fox Covert
Teddy's Farm
Lodge Farm
Torry's Plantation
Holmes Farm
Briggs Farm
A17

Sewage Works
BACK LA
DARK LA
Skerries Plantation
Highfield Farm
Stragglethorpe Grange
Brant House Farm
Stragglethorpe
Hall Farm
Sutton
MAIN STREET
FENTON ROAD
Rectory Farm
The Farm
Sand Beck
STRAGGLETHORPE LANE

Fen Farm
Orchard House Farm
Manor Farm
NG23
Fenton
PUMP LA
ALLEN RD
Airfield (disused)
Fallows End
Meml
Fulbeck Grange
Leather Bottle Farm
BRANT ROAD
Wilson's Gorse
NG32

Blackmires Farm
Claypole Fen
Stubton Hill Farm
Fenton Boundary Plantation

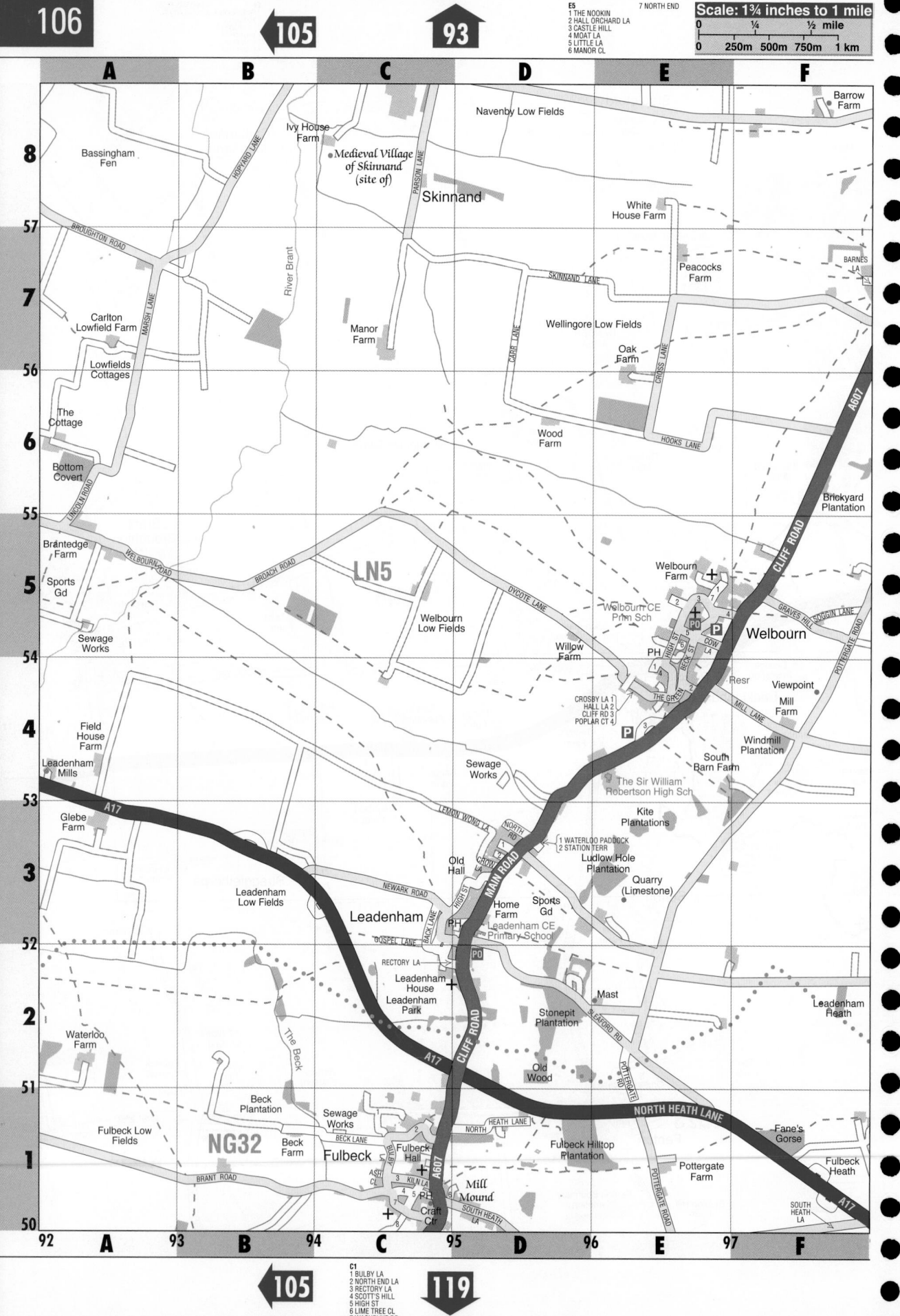

105
93
E5
1 THE NOOKIN
2 HALL ORCHARD LA
3 CASTLE HILL
4 MOAT LA
5 LITTLE LA
6 MANOR CL
7 NORTH END
Scale: 1¾ inches to 1 mile
0
¼
½ mile
0
250m
500m
750m
1 km
A
B
C
D
E
F
8
57
7
56
6
55
5
54
4
53
3
52
2
51
1
50
92
93
94
95
96
97
Barrow Farm
Navenby Low Fields
Ivy House Farm
Medieval Village of Skinnand (site of)
Bassingham Fen
HOPYARD LANE
PARSON LANE
Skinnand
White House Farm
BROUGHTON ROAD
River Brant
SKINNAND LANE
Peacocks Farm
BARNES LA
MARSH LANE
Carlton Lowfield Farm
Manor Farm
Wellingore Low Fields
CARR LANE
Oak Farm
CROSS LANE
Lowfields Cottages
The Cottage
Wood Farm
HOOKS LANE
A607
Bottom Covert
LINCOLN ROAD
Brickyard Plantation
Brantedge Farm
WELBOURN ROAD
BROACH ROAD
LN5
CLIFF ROAD
Welbourn Farm
Sports Gd
DYCOTE LANE
Welbourn CE Prim Sch
GRAVES HILL
SOGGIN LANE
Welbourn Low Fields
PO
P
Welbourn
POTTERGATE ROAD
Sewage Works
Willow Farm
PH
HIGH ST
BECK ST
COW LA
Resr
Viewpoint
THE GREEN
CROSBY LA 1
HALL LA 2
CLIFF RD 3
POPLAR CT 4
Mill Farm
MILL LANE
Field House Farm
Windmill Plantation
Leadenham Mills
South Barn Farm
Sewage Works
The Sir William Robertson High Sch
Glebe Farm
A17
Kite Plantations
LEMON WONG LA
NORTH RD
1 WATERLOO PADDOCK
2 STATION TERR
Ludlow Hole Plantation
Old Hall
CROW LA
MAIN ROAD
Leadenham Low Fields
NEWARK ROAD
Quarry (Limestone)
HIGH ST
Home Farm
Sports Gd
Leadenham
BACK LANE
PH
Leadenham CE Primary School
GOSPEL LANE
RECTORY LA
PO
Leadenham House
Mast
Leadenham Park
Leadenham Heath
Stonepit Plantation
SLEAFORD RD
Waterloo Farm
The Beck
CLIFF ROAD
A17
Old Wood
POTTERGATE RD
NORTH HEATH LANE
Beck Plantation
Sewage Works
HEATH LANE
NORTH
Fane's Gorse
Fulbeck Low Fields
NG32
Beck Farm
BECK LANE
Fulbeck
BULBY LA
Fulbeck Hall
Fulbeck Hilltop Plantation
Pottergate Farm
Fulbeck Heath
BRANT ROAD
ASH CL
KILN LA
A607
Mill Mound
POTTERGATE ROAD
PH
Craft Ctr
SOUTH HEATH LA
SOUTH HEATH LA
A17
A
B
C
D
E
F
105
119
C1
1 BULBY LA
2 NORTH END LA
3 RECTORY LA
4 SCOTT'S HILL
5 HIGH ST
6 LIME TREE CL
7 WASHDYKE RD
8 SUDTHORPE HILL

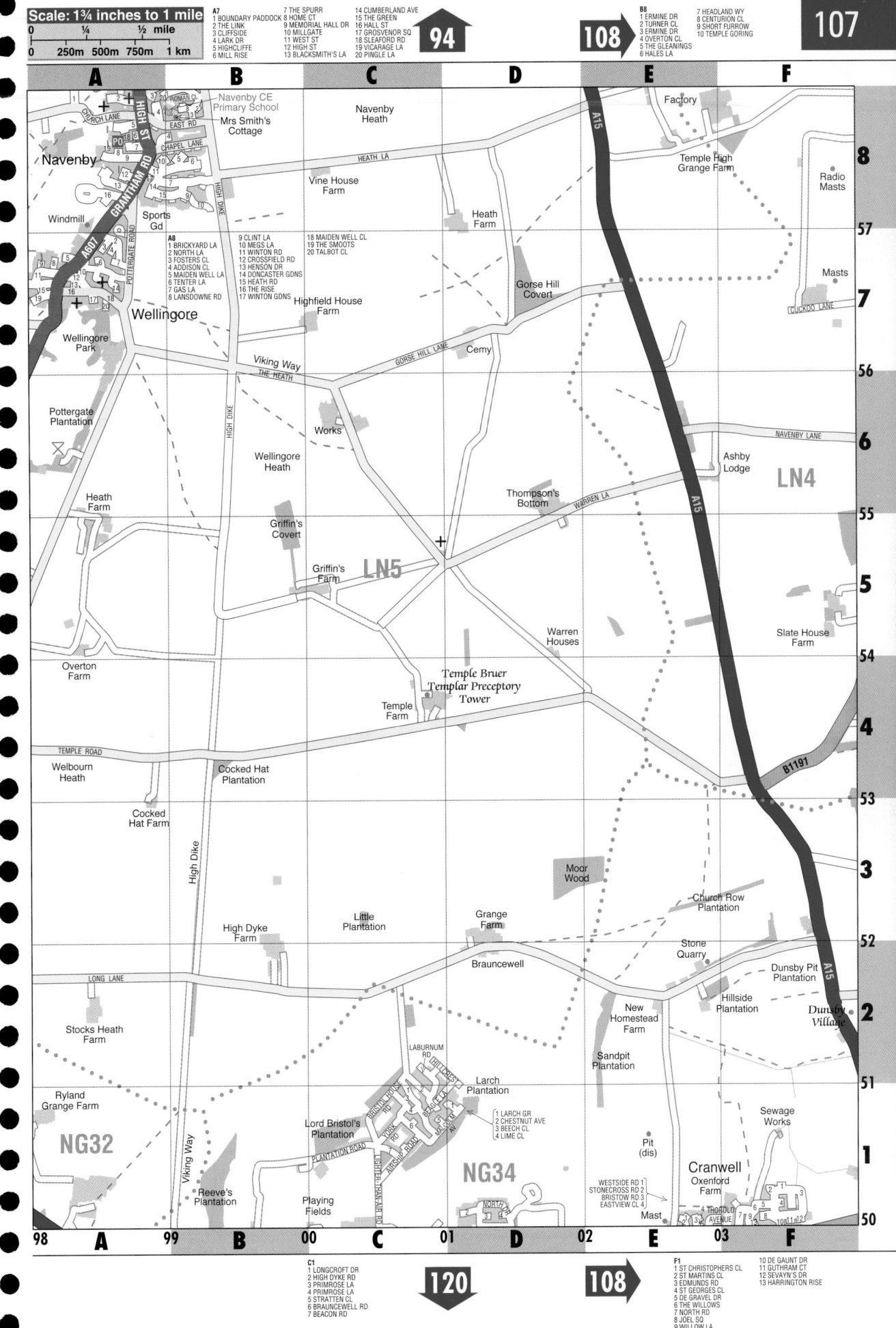

A7
1 BOUNDARY PADDOCK
2 THE LINK
3 CLIFFSIDE
4 LARK DR
5 HIGHCLIFFE
6 MILL RISE
7 THE SPURR
8 HOME CT
9 MEMORIAL HALL DR
10 MILLGATE
11 WEST ST
12 HIGH ST
13 BLACKSMITH'S LA
14 CUMBERLAND AVE
15 THE GREEN
16 HALL ST
17 GROSVENOR SQ
18 SLEAFORD RD
19 VICARAGE LA
20 PINGLE LA

B8
1 ERMINE DR
2 TURNER CL
3 ERMINE DR
4 OVERTON CL
5 THE GLEANINGS
6 HALES LA
7 HEADLAND WY
8 CENTURION CL
9 SHORT FURROW
10 TEMPLE GORING

A B C D E F

8

Navenby CE
Primary School

Mrs Smith's
Cottage

Navenby
Heath

Factory

ROMAN CL
EAST RD
CHURCH LANE
HIGH ST
CHAPEL LANE
PO

Navenby

HEATH LA

Temple High
Grange Farm

Radio
Masts

57

Windmill

GRANTHAM RD
A607
POTTERGATE ROAD

Sports
Gd

HIGH DIKE

Vine House
Farm

Heath
Farm

Masts

Gorse Hill
Covert

7

A8
1 BRICKYARD LA
2 NORTH LA
3 FOSTERS CL
4 ADDISON CL
5 MAIDEN WELL LA
6 TENTER LA
7 GAS LA
8 LANSDOWNE RD
9 CLINT LA
10 MEGS LA
11 WINTON RD
12 CROSSFIELD RD
13 HENSON DR
14 DONCASTER GDNS
15 HEATH RD
16 THE RISE
17 WINTON GDNS
18 MAIDEN WELL CL
19 THE SMOOTS
20 TALBOT CL

Highfield House
Farm

CUCKOO LANE

Wellingore

Viking Way
THE HEATH

GORSE HILL LANE

Cemy

56

Wellingore
Park

Pottergate
Plantation

Works

Navenby Lane

LN4

6

HIGH DIKE

Wellingore
Heath

Thompson's
Bottom

Ashby
Lodge

WARREN LA

A15

55

Heath
Farm

Griffin's
Covert

Griffin's
Farm

LN5

Warren
Houses

Slate House
Farm

5

Overton
Farm

Temple Bruer
Templar Preceptory
Tower

54

Temple
Farm

B1191

4

TEMPLE ROAD

Welbourn
Heath

Cocked Hat
Plantation

53

Cocked
Hat Farm

HIGH DIKE

Moor
Wood

Church Row
Plantation

3

High Dyke
Farm

Little
Plantation

Grange
Farm

Stone
Quarry

Dunsby Pit
Plantation

A15

52

LONG LANE

Brauncewell

Hillside
Plantation

Dunsby
Village

2

Stocks Heath
Farm

New
Homestead
Farm

Sandpit
Plantation

Viking Way

Ryland
Grange Farm

NG32

LABURNUM RD
LITTLECREST
BRISTOL HOUSE
YORK
BEECH LA
MALCOLM
AV

Larch
Plantation

1 LARCH GR
2 CHESTNUT AVE
3 BEECH CL
4 LIME CL

Pit
(dis)

Sewage
Works

Cranwell

1

Lord Bristol's
Plantation

NG34

WESTSIDE RD 1
STONECROSS RD 2
BRISTOW RD 3
EASTVIEW CL 4

Oxenford
Farm

Reeve's
Plantation

PLANTATION ROAD
LOTHER TANGAR RD
AIRSHIRE ROAD

Playing
Fields

NORTH

THOROLD
AVENUE

Mast

50

98 A 99 B 00 C 01 D 02 E 03 F

C1
1 LONGCROFT DR
2 HIGH DYKE RD
3 PRIMROSE LA
4 PRIMROSE LA
5 STRATTEN CL
6 BRAUNCEWELL RD
7 BEACON RD

F1
1 ST CHRISTOPHERS CL
2 ST MARTINS CL
3 EDMUNDS RD
4 ST GEORGES CL
5 DE GRAVEL DR
6 THE WILLOWS
7 NORTH RD
8 JOEL SQ
9 WILLOW LA
10 DE GAUNT DR
11 GUTHRAM CT
12 SEVAYN'S DR
13 HARRINGTON RISE

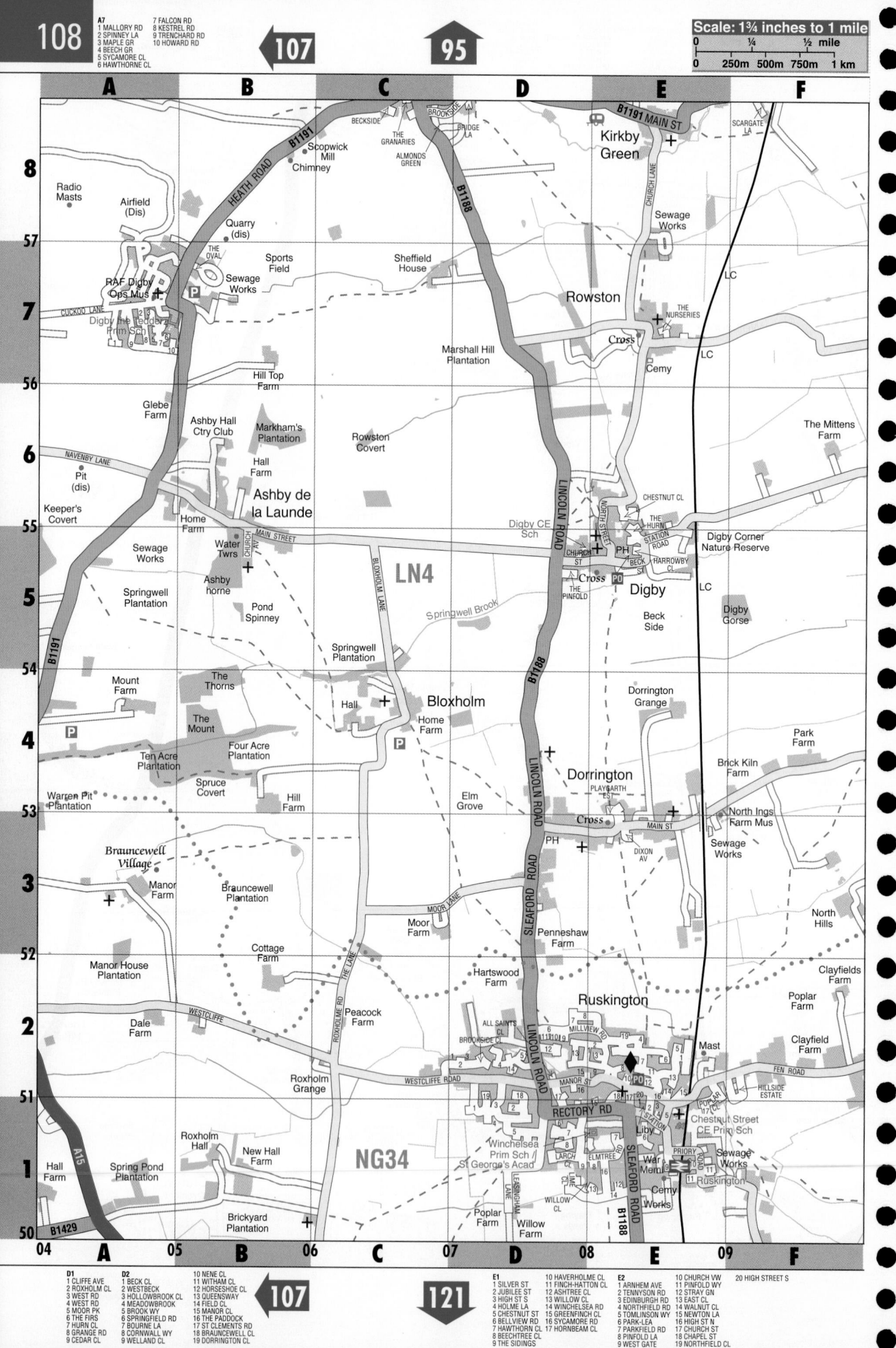

Scale: 1¾ inches to 1 mile

A7
1 MALLORY RD
2 SPINNEY LA
3 MAPLE GR
4 BEECH GR
5 SYCAMORE CL
6 HAWTHORNE CL
7 FALCON RD
8 KESTREL RD
9 TRENCHARD RD
10 HOWARD RD

D1
1 CLIFFE AVE
2 ROXHOLM CL
3 WEST RD
4 WEST RD
5 MOOR PK
6 THE FIRS
7 HURN CL
8 GRANGE RD
9 CEDAR CL

D2
1 BECK CL
2 WESTBECK
3 HOLLOWBROOK CL
4 MEADOWBROOK
5 BROOK WY
6 SPRINGFIELD RD
7 BOURNE LA
8 CORNWALL WY
9 WELLAND CL

10 NENE CL
11 WITHAM CL
12 HORSESHOE CL
13 QUEENSWAY
14 FIELD CL
15 MANOR CL
16 THE PADDOCK
17 ST CLEMENTS RD
18 BRAUNCEWELL CL
19 DORRINGTON CL

E1
1 SILVER ST
2 JUBILEE ST
3 HIGH ST S
4 HOLME LA
5 CHESTNUT ST
6 BELLVIEW RD
7 HAWTHORN CL
8 BEECHTREE CL
9 THE SIDINGS

10 HAVERHOLME CL
11 FINCH-HATTON CL
12 ASHTREE CL
13 WILLOW CL
14 WINCHELSEA RD
15 GREENFINCH CL
16 SYCAMORE RD
17 HORNBEAM CL

E2
1 ARNHEM AVE
2 TENNYSON RD
3 EDINBURGH RD
4 NORTHFIELD RD
5 TOMLINSON WY
6 PARK-LEA
7 PARKFIELD RD
8 PINFOLD LA
9 WEST GATE

10 CHURCH VW
11 PINFOLD WY
12 STRAY GN
13 EAST CL
14 WALNUT CL
15 NEWTON LA
16 HIGH ST N
17 CHURCH ST
18 CHAPEL ST
19 NORTHFIELD CL

20 HIGH STREET S

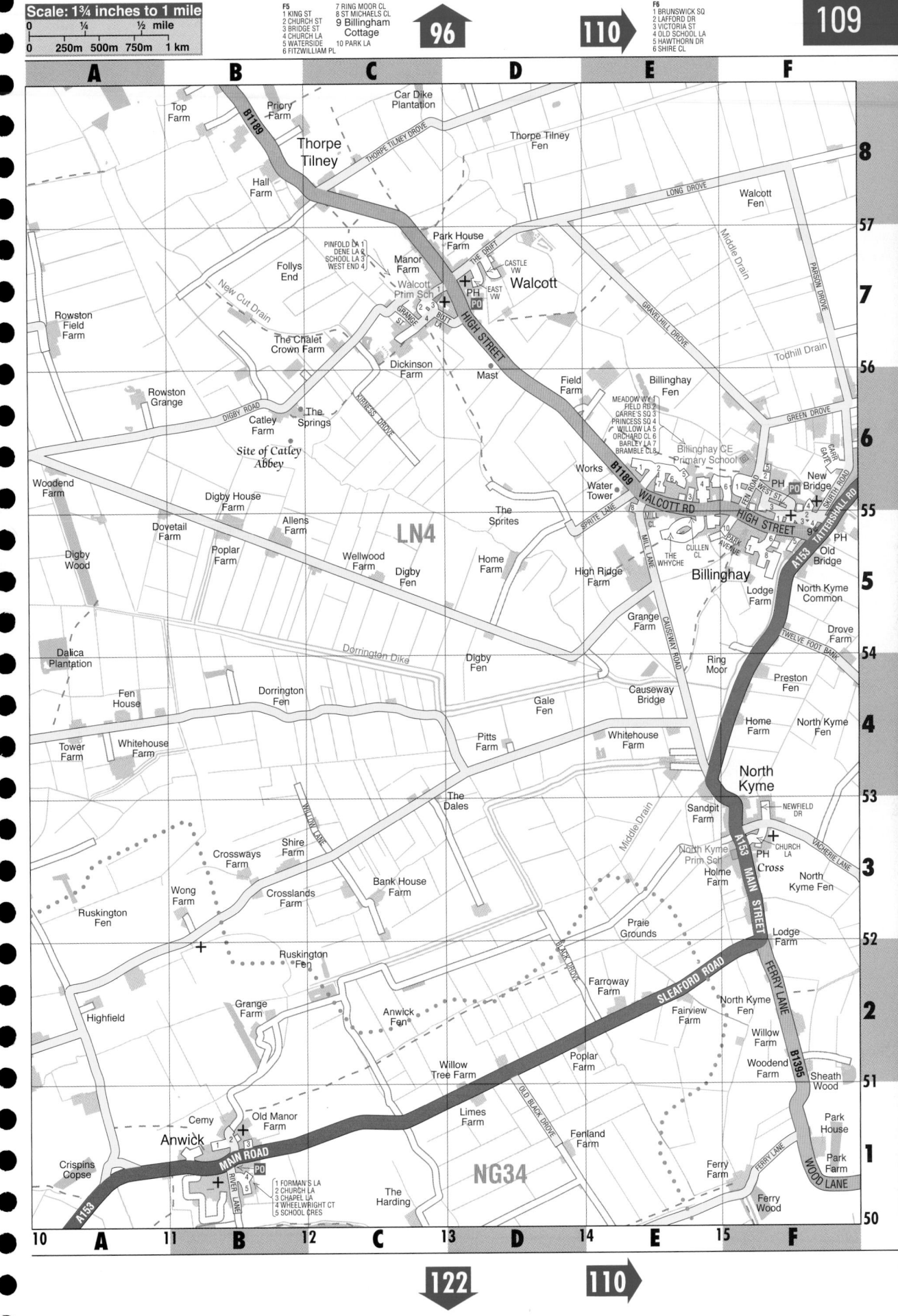

Scale: 1¾ inches to 1 mile

0   ¼   ½ mile
0   250m   500m   750m   1 km

F5
1 KING ST
2 CHURCH ST
3 BRIDGE ST
4 CHURCH LA
5 WATERSIDE
6 FITZWILLIAM PL

7 RING MOOR CL
8 ST MICHAELS CL
9 Billingham
  Cottage
10 PARK LA

96

110

F6
1 BRUNSWICK SQ
2 LAFFORD DR
3 VICTORIA ST
4 OLD SCHOOL LA
5 HAWTHORN DR
6 SHIRE CL

A   B   C   D   E   F

Top Farm
Priory Farm
B1189
Car Dike Plantation
Thorpe Tilney
Thorpe Tilney Fen
8
Hall Farm
Long Drove
Walcott Fen
57
Follys End
New Cut Drain
Park House Farm
THE DRIFT
CASTLE VW
Manor Farm
Walcott
7
Rowston Field Farm
PINFOLD LA 1
DENE LA 4
SCHOOL LA 3
WEST END 4
Walcott Prim Sch
PH
PO
EAST VW
GRANGE ST
HIGH STREET
Gravelhill Drive
Middle Drain
Parson Drove
The Chalet
Crown Farm
Dickinson Farm
Mast
BIXIT LA
Field Farm
Billinghay Fen
Green Drove
Todhill Drain
56
Rowston Grange
Digby Road
Catley Farm
The Springs
Kirkness Drove
MEADOW WY 1
FIELD RD 2
CARRE'S SQ 3
PRINCESS SQ 4
WILLOW LA 5
ORCHARD CL 6
BARLEY LA 7
BRAMBLE CL 8
Billinghay CE Primary School
CARR GATE
New Bridge
6
Site of Catley Abbey
Digby House Farm
LN4
Works
Water Tower
B1189
PH
PO
SHORT RD
TATTERSHALL RD
55
Woodend Farm
Dovetail Farm
Poplar Farm
Allens Farm
Wellwood Farm
Digby Fen
The Sprites
Home Farm
High Ridge Farm
WALCOTT RD
SPRITE LANE
MILL CL
THE WHYCHE
CULLEN CL
PARK AVENUE
HIGH STREET
A153
Old Bridge
PH
Billinghay
5
Digby Wood
Grange Farm
MILL LANE
CAUSEWAY ROAD
Ring Moor
Lodge Farm
North Kyme Common
Old Bridge
Drove Farm
54
Dalica Plantation
Fen House
Dorrington Fen
Dorrington Dike
Digby Fen
Gale Fen
Causeway Bridge
TWELVE FOOT BANK
Preston Fen
Home Farm
North Kyme Fen
4
Tower Farm
Whitehouse Farm
Pitts Farm
Whitehouse Farm
North Kyme
53
The Dales
Middle Drain
Sandpit Farm
NEWFIELD DR
A153
CHURCH LA
VACHERIE LANE
Crossways Farm
Shire Farm
Bank House Farm
North Kyme Prim Sch
PH
Holme Farm
Cross
North Kyme Fen
3
Wong Farm
Crosslands Farm
NELSON LANE
BLACK DROVE
MAIN STREET
Ruskington Fen
Ruskington Fen
Praie Grounds
Farroway Farm
Lodge Farm
52
Grange Farm
Highfield
Anwick Fen
SLEAFORD ROAD
Fairview Farm
North Kyme Fen
FERRY LANE
Willow Farm
Woodend Farm
B1395
Sheath Wood
2
Willow Tree Farm
OLD BLACK DROVE
Poplar Farm
Fenland Farm
Park House
51
Crispins Copse
Cemy
Old Manor Farm
Anwick
MAIN ROAD
RIVER LANE
PO
Limes Farm
The Harding
NG34
Ferry Farm
Ferry Lane
WOOD LANE
Park Farm
1
A153
1 FORMAN'S LA
2 CHURCH LA
3 CHAPEL LA
4 WHEELWRIGHT CT
5 SCHOOL CRES
Ferry Wood
50

10   A   11   B   12   C   13   D   14   E   15   F

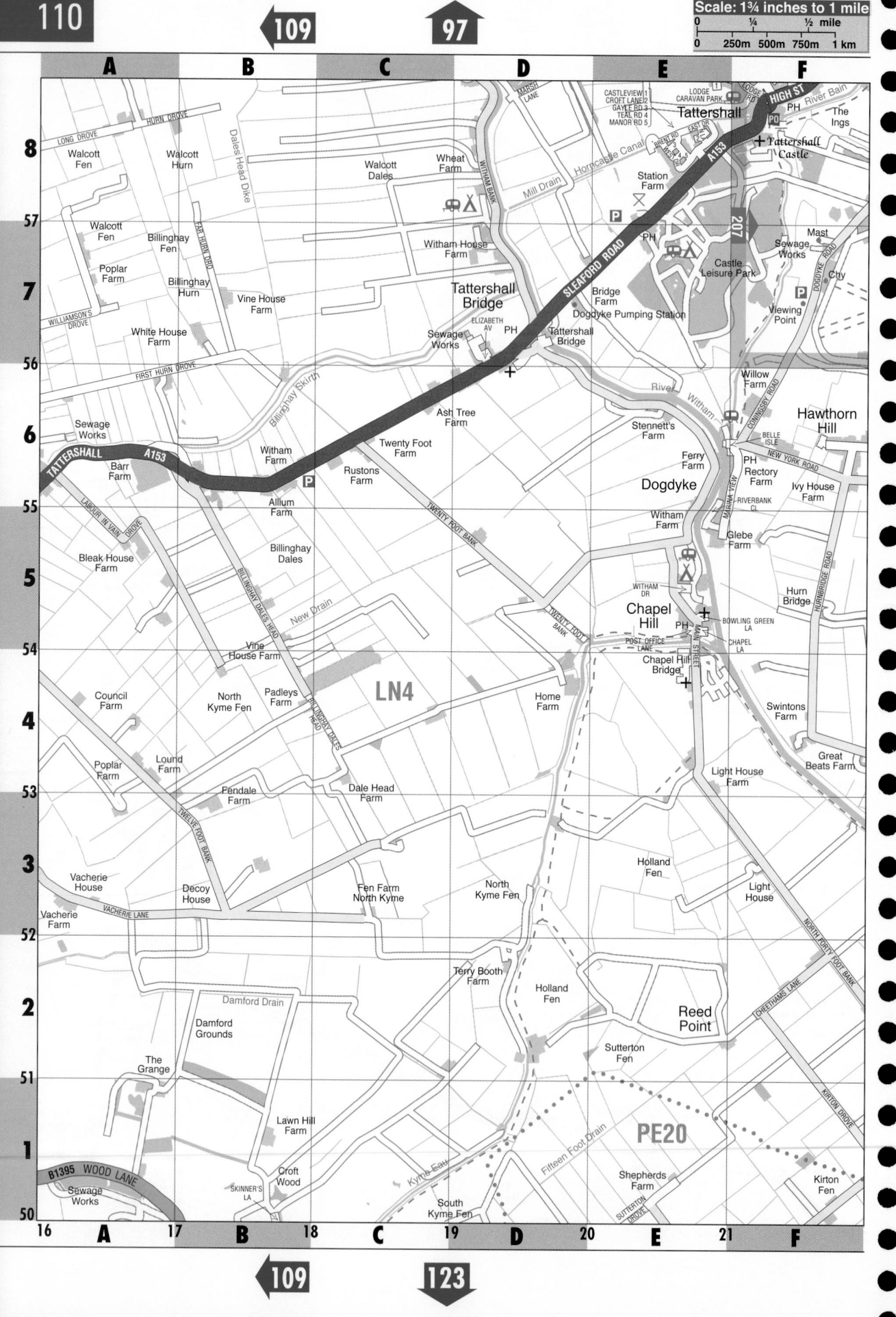

109
97

Scale: 1¾ inches to 1 mile

0   ¼   ½   mile
0 250m 500m 750m 1 km

A   B   C   D   E   F

Long Drove
Hurn Drove
Walcott Fen
Walcott Hurn
Dales Head Dike
Walcott Dales
Wheat Farm
Marsh Lane
Witham Bank
Horncastle Canal

CASTLEVIEW 1
CROFT LANE 2
GAYLE RD 3
TEAL RD 4
MANOR RD 5

LODGE CARAVAN PARK
BRENT RD
EAST DR
LODGE RD
HIGH ST
River Bain
The Ings
PO
PH
Tattershall

8

Walcott Fen
Billinghay Fen
Poplar Farm
Billinghay Hurn
Vine House Farm
Witham House Farm
Mill Drain
Station Farm
A153
Tattershall Castle
Sewage Works
Mast

57

7

White House Farm
Williamson's Drove
Tattershall Bridge
Sewage Works
ELIZABETH AV
PH
Tattershall Bridge
Bridge Farm
Dogdyke Pumping Station
PH
Castle Leisure Park
Chy
Viewing Point
207
DOGDYKE ROAD

First Hurn Drove
Billinghay Skirth
SLEAFORD ROAD

56

6

Sewage Works
Tattershall
A153
Barr Farm
Witham Farm
Twenty Foot Farm
Ash Tree Farm
Stennett's Farm
River Witham
Willow Farm
Hawthorn Hill
BELLE ISLE
NEW YORK ROAD
CONINGSBY ROAD

Labour in Vain Drove
Rustons Farm
Allium Farm

55

5

Bleak House Farm
Billinghay Dales
Twenty Foot Bank
Ferry Farm
PH Rectory Farm
Dogdyke
Ivy House Farm
MARINA VIEW
RIVERBANK CL
Witham Farm
Glebe Farm
Hurn Bridge
HUMBERBRIDGE ROAD

Billinghay Dales Head
New Drain
Vine House Farm

54

4

Council Farm
North Kyme Fen
Padleys Farm
LN4
Twenty Foot Bank
WITHAM DR
Chapel Hill
POST OFFICE LANE
PH
BOWLING GREEN LA
CHAPEL LA
Swintons Farm
MAIN STREET

Billinghay Dales Head

53

3

Poplar Farm
Lound Farm
Fendale Farm
Dale Head Farm
Home Farm
Chapel Hill Bridge
Light House Farm
Great Beats Farm

Twelve Foot Bank

52

2

Vacherie House
Decoy House
Fen Farm North Kyme
North Kyme Fen
Holland Fen
Light House
NORTH FORTY FOOT BANK
CHEETHAMS LANE

Vacherie Farm
VACHERIE LANE

51

1

The Grange
Damford Drain
Damford Grounds
Terry Booth Farm
Holland Fen
Reed Point
Sutterton Fen
KIRTON DROVE

Lawn Hill Farm
Kyme Eau

50

Sewage Works
B1395 WOOD LANE
SKINNER'S LA
Croft Wood
South Kyme Fen
Fifteen Foot Drain
SUTTERTON DROVE
PE20
Shepherds Farm
Kirton Fen

16   A   17   B   18   C   19   D   20   E   21   F

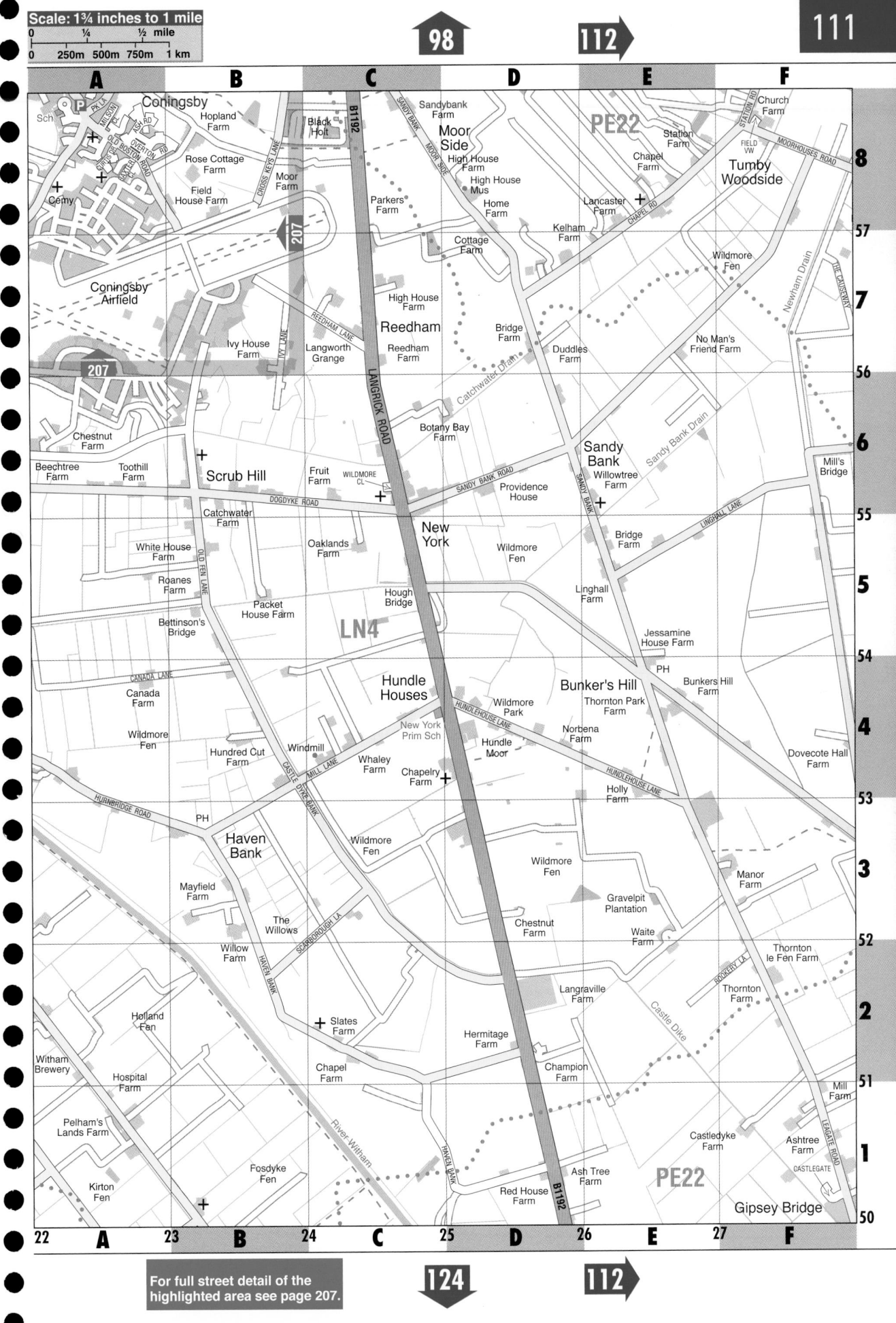

A   B   C   D   E   F

Coningsby

Sch   P

Hopland Farm

Black Holt

Sandybank Farm

Moor Side

PE22

Church Farm

Station Farm

Rose Cottage Farm

Moor Farm

High House Farm

Chapel Farm

Tumby Woodside

8

Field House Farm

High House Mus

Lancaster Farm

Kelham Farm

Cemy

Parkers Farm

Home Farm

57

Coningsby Airfield

Reedham Lane

High House Farm

Cottage Farm

Bridge Farm

Duddles Farm

Wildmore Fen

No Man's Friend Farm

7

207

Ivy House Farm

Langworth Grange

Reedham

Reedham Farm

56

Chestnut Farm

Botany Bay Farm

Sandy Bank

Sandy Bank Drain

Mill's Bridge

6

Beechtree Farm

Toothill Farm

Scrub Hill

Fruit Farm

WILDMORE CL

Willowtree Farm

Catchwater Farm

Dogdyke Road

Sandy Bank Road

Providence House

Bridge Farm

Linghall Lane

55

White House Farm

Oaklands Farm

New York

Wildmore Fen

5

Roanes Farm

OLD FEN LANE

Packet House Farm

Hough Bridge

Linghall Farm

Bettinson's Bridge

LN4

Jessamine House Farm

54

CANADA LANE

Canada Farm

Hundle Houses

Wildmore Park

Bunker's Hill

PH

Bunkers Hill Farm

4

Wildmore Fen

Hundred Cut Farm

Windmill

New York Prim Sch

HUNDLEHOUSE LANE

Hundle Moor

Thornton Park Farm

Norbena Farm

Dovecote Hall Farm

CASTLE DYKE BANK

MILL LANE

Whaley Farm

HUNDLEHOUSE LANE

53

HURNBRIDGE ROAD

PH

Haven Bank

Chapelry Farm

Holly Farm

Manor Farm

3

Mayfield Farm

Wildmore Fen

Wildmore Fen

Gravelpit Plantation

Thornton le Fen Farm

52

The Willows

Chestnut Farm

Waite Farm

ROOKERY LA

Thornton Farm

HAVEN BANK

SCARBOROUGH LA

Langraville Farm

Castle Dike

2

Willow Farm

Holland Fen

Slates Farm

Hermitage Farm

Champion Farm

Mill Farm

51

Witham Brewery

Hospital Farm

Chapel Farm

River Witham

Castledyke Farm

Ashtree Farm

LEGATE ROAD

1

Pelham's Lands Farm

Ash Tree Farm

PE22

CASTLEGATE

Kirton Fen

Fosdyke Fen

HAVEN BANK

Red House Farm

B1192

Gipsey Bridge

50

22   A   23   B   24   C   25   D   26   E   27   F

For full street detail of the highlighted area see page 207.

124   112

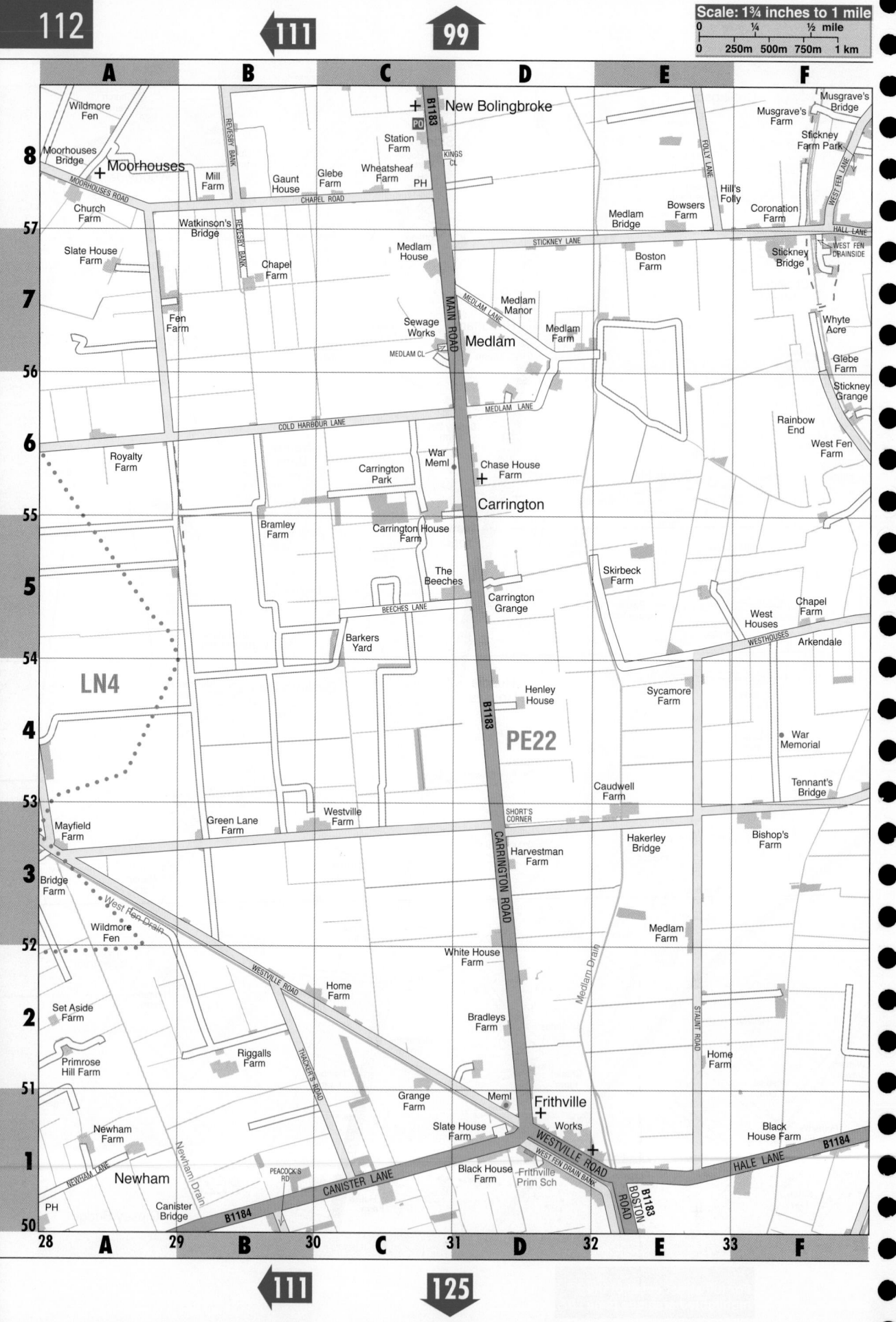

← 111
↑ 99

Scale: 1¾ inches to 1 mile

0   ¼   ½ mile
0 250m 500m 750m 1 km

A   B   C   D   E   F

8
Wildmore Fen
Moorhouses Bridge
+ Moorhouses
Mill Farm
Gaunt House
Glebe Farm
Wheatsheaf Farm
Station Farm
+ B1183
PO
New Bolingbroke
KINGS CL
PH
Musgrave's Farm
Musgrave's Bridge
Stickney Farm Park
FOLLY LANE
Hill's Folly
Coronation Farm
WEST FEN LANE
HALL LANE

MOORHOUSES ROAD
Church Farm
Watkinson's Bridge
CHAPEL ROAD
Medlam Bridge
Bowsers Farm
STICKNEY LANE

57

REVESBY BANK

7
Slate House Farm
Chapel Farm
Fen Farm
Medlam House
MAIN ROAD
MEDLAM LANE
Medlam Manor
Medlam Farm
Medlam
Boston Farm
WEST FEN DRAINSIDE
Stickney Bridge
Whyte Acre
Glebe Farm

56
Sewage Works
MEDLAM CL
MEDLAM LANE
Stickney Grange
Rainbow End
West Fen Farm

6
COLD HARBOUR LANE
Royalty Farm
War Meml
Carrington Park
Chase House Farm +
Carrington

55
Bramley Farm
Carrington House Farm
Skirbeck Farm

5
The Beeches
BEECHES LANE
Carrington Grange
West Houses
Chapel Farm
WESTHOUSES
Arkendale

54
Barkers Yard
Henley House
Sycamore Farm

LN4

4
B1183
PE22
Caudwell Farm
War Memorial
Tennant's Bridge

53
Mayfield Farm
Green Lane Farm
Westville Farm
SHORT'S CORNER
Hakerley Bridge
Bishop's Farm

3
Bridge Farm
West Fen Drain
Harvestman Farm
CARRINGTON ROAD
MEDLAM DRAIN

52
Wildmore Fen
WESTVILLE ROAD
White House Farm
Medlam Farm

2
Set Aside Farm
Home Farm
THACKER'S ROAD
Bradleys Farm
STAUNT ROAD
Home Farm

Primrose Hill Farm
Riggalls Farm
Grange Farm
Meml
Frithville
+ Works
Black House Farm
B1184

51
Newham Farm
Newham Drain
Slate House Farm
WESTVILLE ROAD
+
HALE LANE

1
NEWHAM LANE
Newham
PEACOCK'S RD
CANISTER LANE
Black House Farm
WEST FEN DRAIN BANK
Frithville Prim Sch
B1183 BOSTON ROAD

50
PH
Canister Bridge
B1184

28   A   29   B   30   C   31   D   32   E   33   F

← 111
↓ 125

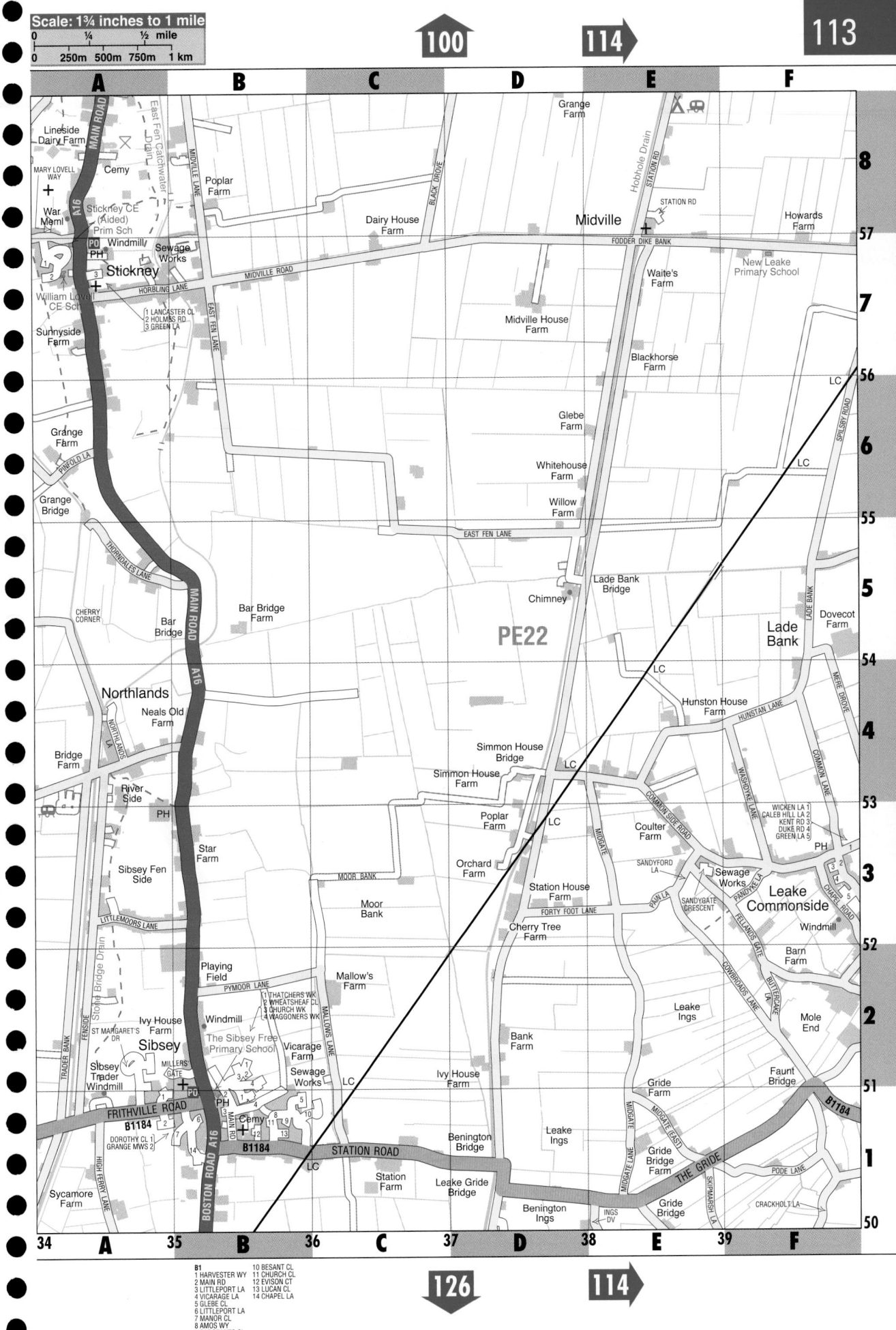

B1
1 HARVESTER WY
2 MAIN RD
3 LITTLEPORT LA
4 VICARAGE LA
5 GLEBE CL
6 LITTLEPORT LA
7 MANOR CL
8 AMOS WY
9 SARGEANTS CL
10 BESANT CL
11 CHURCH CL
12 EVISON CT
13 LUCAN CL
14 CHAPEL LA

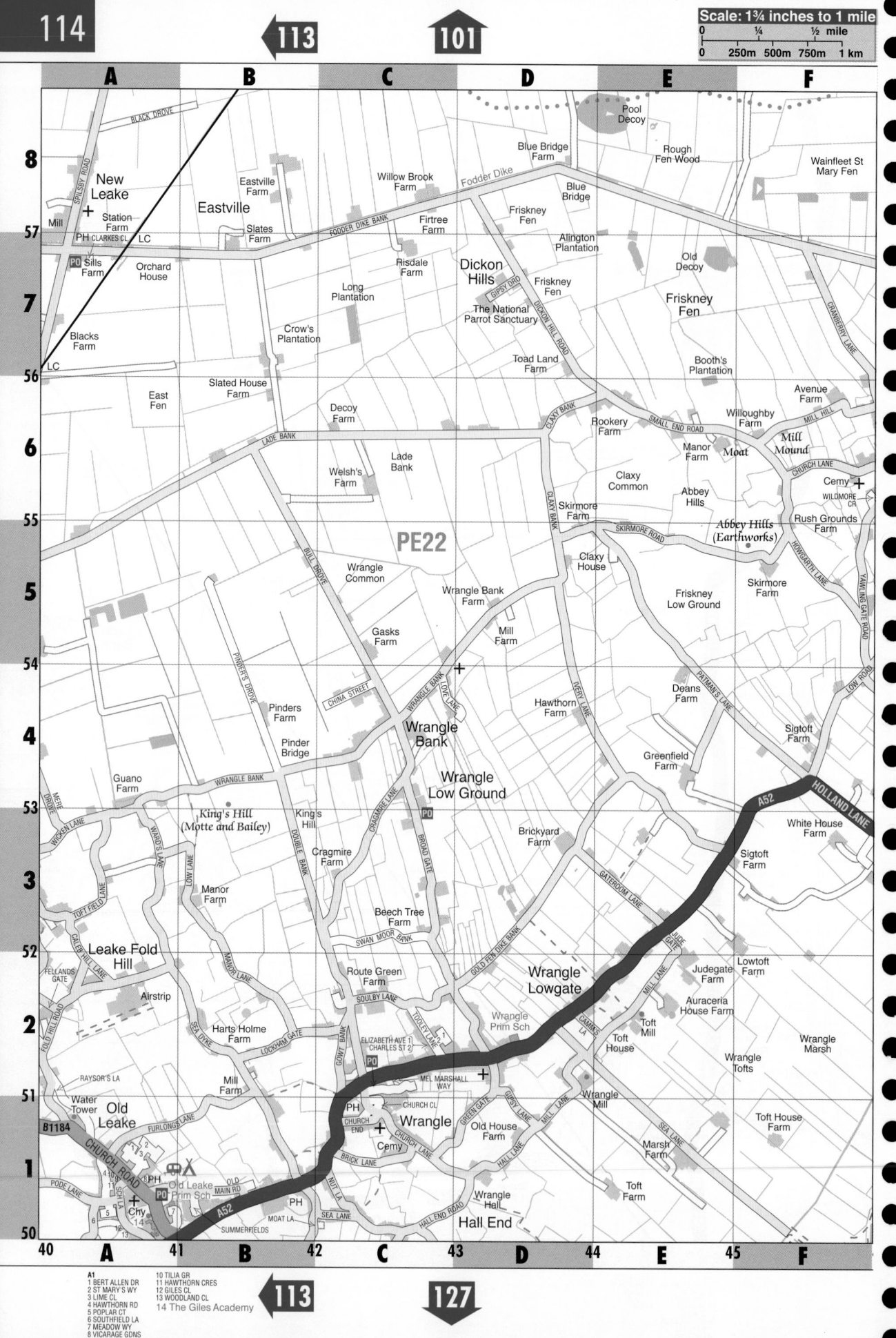

Scale: 1¾ inches to 1 mile

0   ¼   ½ mile
0 250m 500m 750m 1 km

A1
1 BERT ALLEN DR
2 ST MARY'S WY
3 LIME CL
4 HAWTHORN RD
5 POPLAR CT
6 SOUTHFIELD LA
7 MEADOW WY
8 VICARAGE GDNS
9 LIME WALK
10 TILIA GR
11 HAWTHORN CRES
12 GILES CL
13 WOODLAND CL
14 The Giles Academy

Scale: 1¾ inches to 1 mile

102
116

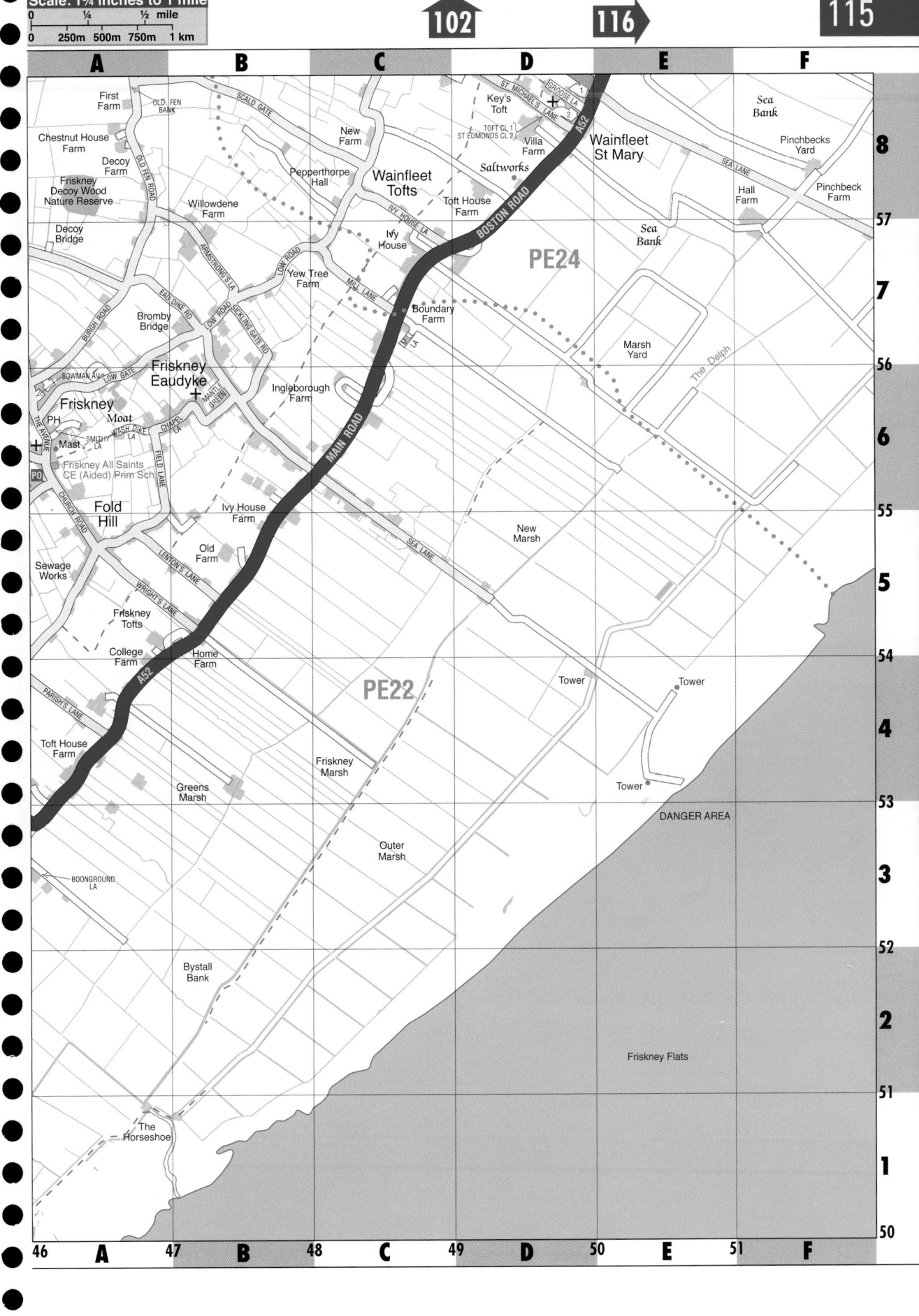
0 ¼ ½ mile
0 250m 500m 750m 1 km
A B C D E F
First Farm
OLD FEN BANK
SCALD GATE
Chestnut House Farm
Decoy Farm
Friskney Decoy Wood Nature Reserve
Decoy Bridge
OLD FEN ROAD
Willowdene Farm
Pepperthorpe Hall
New Farm
Wainfleet Tofts
Key's Toft
ST MICHAEL'S LANE
GROOSE LA
TOFT CL
ST EDMONDS CL
Villa Farm
Saltworks
Wainfleet St Mary
Sea Bank
Pinchbecks Yard
SEA LANE
Pinchbeck Farm
Hall Farm
Toft House Farm
IVY HOUSE LA
Ivy House
BOSTON ROAD
A52
PE24
ARMSTRONG'S LA
LOW ROAD
Yew Tree Farm
MILL LANE
Boundary Farm
MILL LA
Marsh Yard
The Delph
BURGH ROAD
EAU DIKE RD
Bromby Bridge
SICKLING GATE RD
BOWMAN AV
LOW GATE
Friskney Eaudyke
MANTLE GREEN
Ingleborough Farm
Friskney
Moat
PH
THE AVENUE
SMITHY LA
WASH DIKE LA
CHAPEL LA
Mast
Friskney All Saints CE (Aided) Prim Sch
PO
FIELD LANE
MAIN ROAD
CHURCH ROAD
Fold Hill
Ivy House Farm
Old Farm
LENTON'S LANE
New Marsh
SEA LANE
Sewage Works
WRIGHT'S LANE
Friskney Tofts
College Farm
Home Farm
PE22
Tower
Tower
PARISH'S LANE
Toft House Farm
Friskney Marsh
Greens Marsh
Tower
DANGER AREA
BOONGROUND LA
Outer Marsh
Bystall Bank
Friskney Flats
The Horseshoe
8 57 7 56 6 55 5 54 4 53 3 52 2 51 1 50
46 47 48 49 50 51

102
103
206

E8
1 ALBERT AVE
2 VINE RD
3 BUCKTHORN AVE
4 NORWOOD RD
5 PRECINCT CRES
6 BAYES RD
7 GREEN LA
8 LINKS CRES
9 SEA FRONT RD
10 SEACROFT SQ
11 HESKETH CRES
12 FREDERICA RD

Scale: 1¾ inches to 1 mile
0   ¼   ½   mile
0   250m   500m   750m   1 km

Windsor Farm
Ralings Farm
Pinchbeck Farm
CROFT BANK
A52
Top Yard Farm
Coddingtons Yard
A52
LC
LC
COWBANK LA
PE25
Seacroft
SEACROFT DRIVE
SHARDLOES RD
DRAKE RD
DRUMMOND ROAD
SEACROFT ESPLANADE
CH
Croft Grange
Croft Marsh
Bramble Hills
Kitchen's Yard
Bramble Hills
NEW ROAD
TOLL BAR ROAD
Toll Bar Farm
Cow Bank Drain
Croft House
LC
Croft Marsh Lane
Havenhouse
Havenhouse Farm
WHEELBRIDGE
Wainfleet Haven or Steeping River
Clough House Farm
Wainfleet Clough
P
Gibralter Point National Nature Reserve
New Yard Farm
Sea Bank
AYLMER AVE
P
PE24
Gibraltar
GIBRALTAR ROAD
Viewpoint
Wainfleet Road
Marsh Farm East
103
P
Gibraltar Point Visitor Centre
Gibraltar Point
Outmarsh Yard
Wainfleet Harbour
Wainfleet Sand
Inner Knock
Sea Lane
Wainfleet Swatchway
DANGER AREA

A B C D E F
8 61 7 60 6 59 5 58 4 57 3 56 2 55 1 54
52 A 53 B 54 C 55 D 56 E 57 F 58

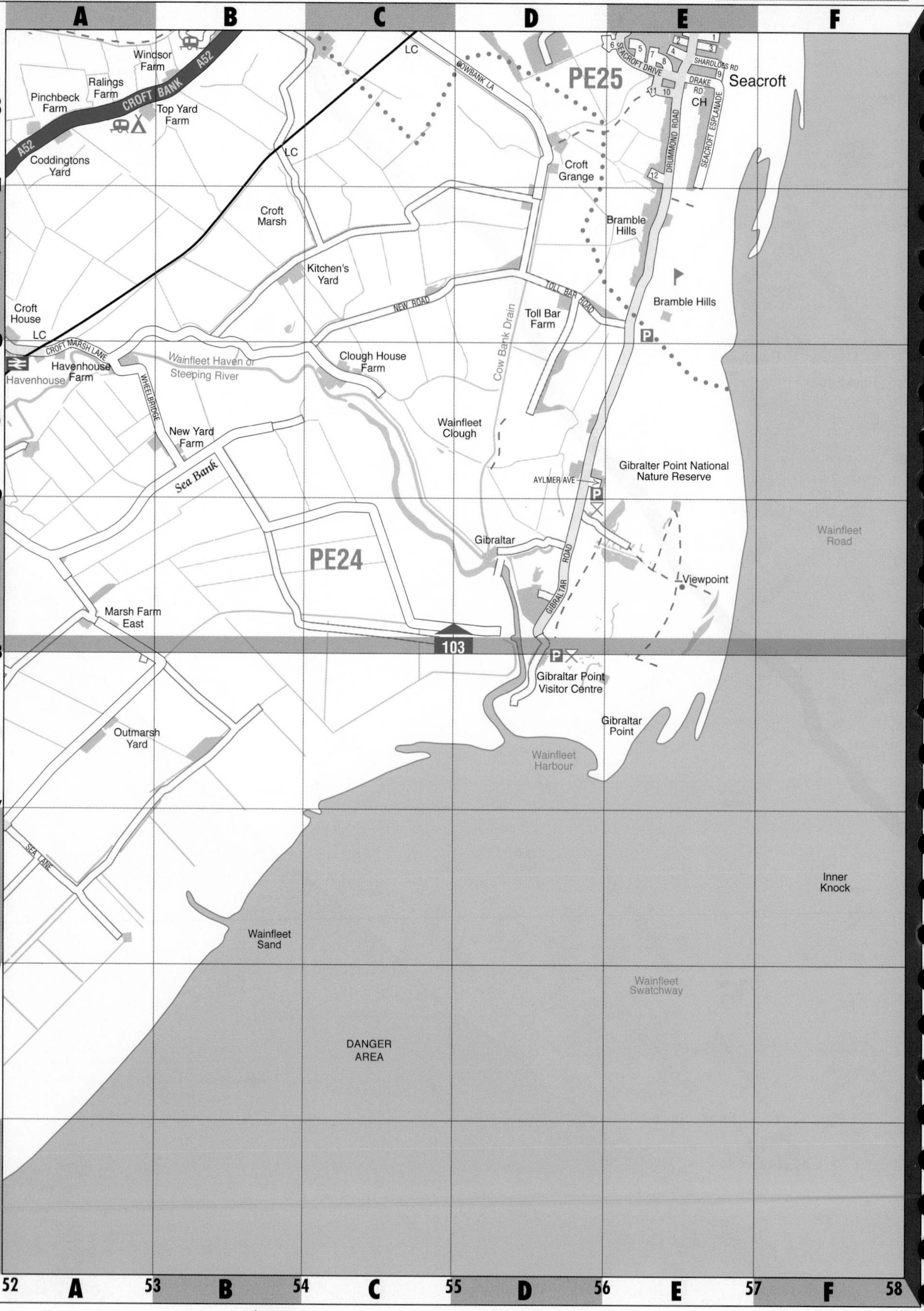

115

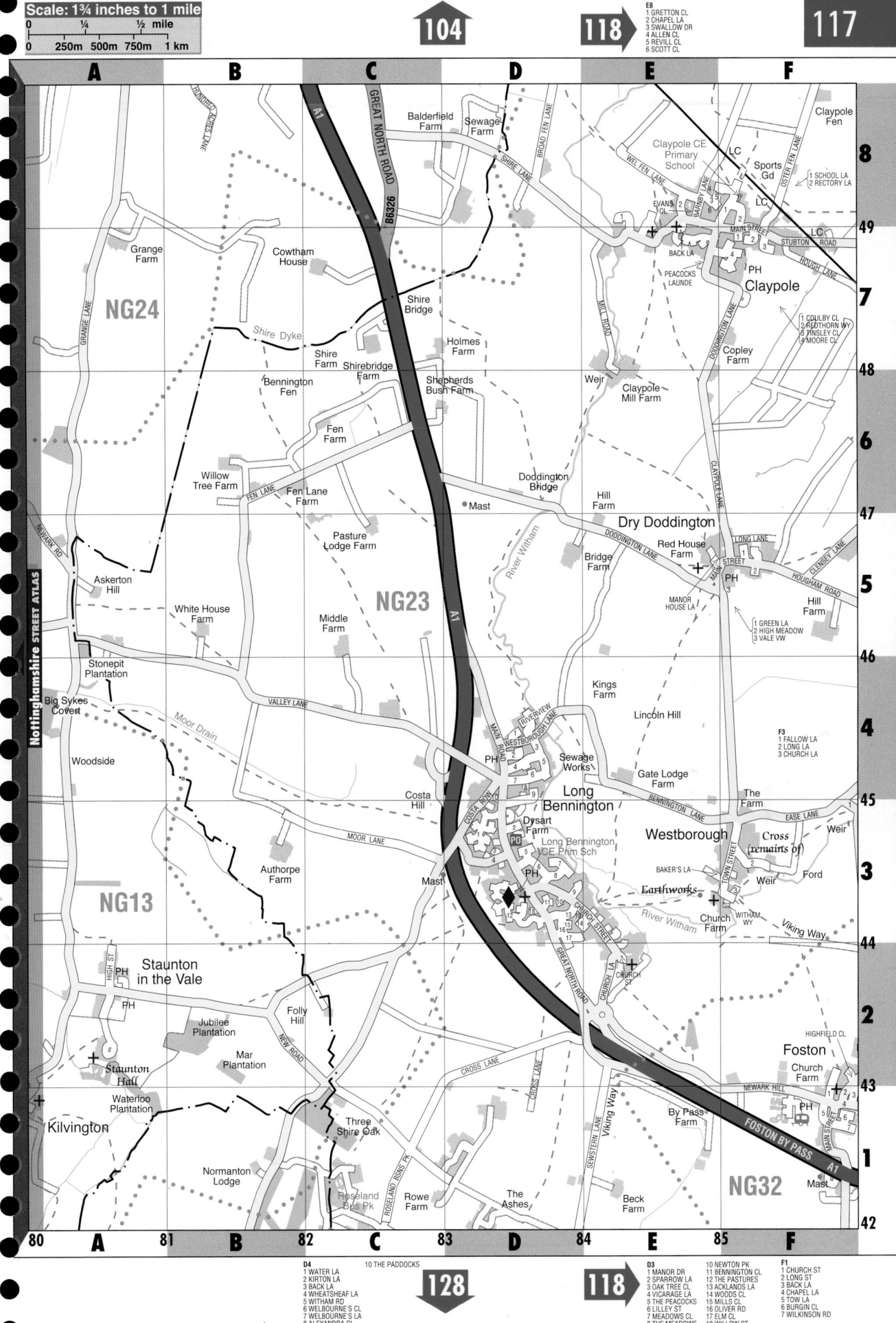

Scale: 1¾ inches to 1 mile

0   ¼   ½ mile
0   250m 500m 750m 1 km

104

118

117

E8
1 GRETTON CL
2 CHAPEL LA
3 SWALLOW DR
4 ALLEN CL
5 REVILL CL
6 SCOTT CL

A B C D E F

Nottinghamshire STREET ATLAS

8

49

7

48

6

47

5

46

4

45

3

44

2

43

1

42

NG24

Grange
Farm

Cowtham
House

Balderfield
Farm

Sewage
Farm

Claypole CE
Primary
School

Sports
Gd

LC

LC

1 SCHOOL LA
2 RECTORY LA

EVANS
CL

BACK LA

PEACOCKS
LAUNDE

PH

Claypole

1 COULBY CL
2 REDTHORN WY
3 TINSLEY CL
4 MOORE CL

Claypole
Fen

STUBTON
ROAD

Copley
Farm

Shire Dyke

Shire
Bridge

Shire
Farm

Shirebridge
Farm

Holmes
Farm

Shepherds
Bush Farm

Weir

Claypole
Mill Farm

Bennington
Fen

Fen
Farm

Doddington
Bridge

Hill
Farm

Dry Doddington

Willow
Tree Farm

Fen Lane
Farm

Mast

River Witham

Red House
Farm

LONG LANE

CLENSEY LANE

HOUGHAM ROAD

PH

Hill
Farm

1 GREEN LA
2 HIGH MEADOW
3 VALE VW

Pasture
Lodge Farm

Bridge
Farm

MANOR
HOUSE LA

NG23

White House
Farm

Middle
Farm

Kings
Farm

Lincoln Hill

Askerton
Hill

Stonepit
Plantation

VALLEY LANE

Gate Lodge
Farm

The
Farm

F3
1 FALLOW LA
2 LONG LA
3 CHURCH LA

Big Sykes
Covert

Moor Drain

RIVERVIEW

WESTBOROUGH LANE

PH

Sewage
Works

Long
Bennington

BENNINGTON LANE

EASE LANE

Weir

Westborough

Cross
(remains of)

Woodside

Costa
Hill

MOOR LANE

COSTA ROAD

MAIN ROAD

Dysart
Farm

PO

Long Bennington
CE Prim Sch

PH

BAKER'S LA

Earthworks

TOWN STREET

Ford

Weir

WITHAM
WY

Church
Farm

River Witham

Viking Way

NG13

Authorpe
Farm

Mast

CHURCH STREET

CHURCH LA

CHURCH
ST

Staunton
in the Vale

HIGH ST

PH

PH

Folly
Hill

NEW ROAD

Jubilee
Plantation

Mar
Plantation

GREAT NORTH ROAD

Foston

HIGHFIELD CL

Church
Farm

PH

NEWARK HILL

Staunton
Hall

Waterloo
Plantation

Kilvington

Three
Shire Oak

Normanton
Lodge

Roseland
Bsn Pk

Rowe
Farm

CROSS LANE

CROSS LANE

SEWSTERN LANE

VIKING WAY

The
Ashes

By Pass
Farm

Beck
Farm

FOSTON BY PASS

A1

NG32

Mast

80 81 82 83 84 85

A B C D E F

128

118

D4
1 WATER LA
2 KIRTON LA
3 BACK LA
4 WHEATSHEAF LA
5 WITHAM RD
6 WELBOURNE'S CL
7 WELBOURNE'S LA
8 ALEXANDRA CL
9 WINTER'S LA

10 THE PADDOCKS

E3
1 MANOR DR
2 SPARROW LA
3 OAK TREE LA
4 VICARAGE LA
5 THE PEACOCKS
6 LILLEY ST
7 MEADOWS CL
8 THE MEADOWS
9 DRURY PK

10 NEWTON PK
11 BENNINGTON CL
12 THE PASTURES
13 ACKLANDS LA
14 WOODS CL
15 MILLS CL
16 OLIVER RD
17 ELM CL
18 WILLOW CT
19 BRAMBLE CL

F1
1 CHURCH ST
2 LONG ST
3 BACK LA
4 CHAPEL LA
5 TOW LA
6 BURGIN CL
7 WILKINSON RD

117 105

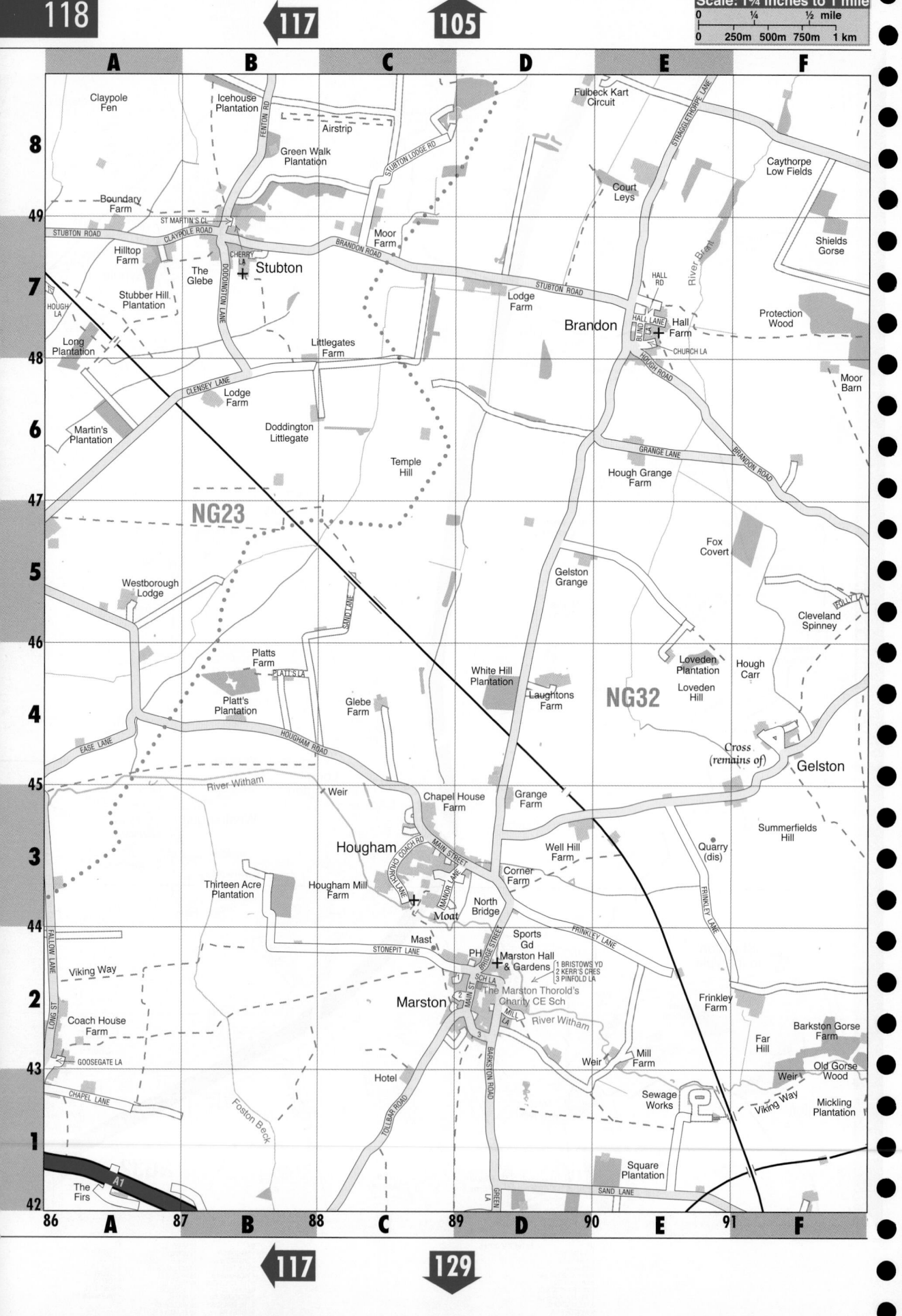
Scale: 1¾ inches to 1 mile
Claypole Fen
Icehouse Plantation
Airstrip
Green Walk Plantation
Fulbeck Kart Circuit
Boundary Farm
Hilltop Farm
Stubton
The Glebe
Stubber Hill Plantation
Moor Farm
Court Leys
Caythorpe Low Fields
Shields Gorse
Lodge Farm
Brandon
Hall Farm
Protection Wood
Long Plantation
Littlegates Farm
Lodge Farm
Martin's Plantation
Doddington Littlegate
Temple Hill
Moor Barn
Hough Grange Farm
NG23
Fox Covert
Westborough Lodge
Gelston Grange
Cleveland Spinney
Platts Farm
Platt's Plantation
White Hill Plantation
Laughtons Farm
Loveden Plantation
Loveden Hill
Hough Carr
NG32
Glebe Farm
Cross (remains of)
Gelston
River Witham
Weir
Chapel House Farm
Grange Farm
Hougham
Well Hill Farm
Quarry (dis)
Summerfields Hill
Thirteen Acre Plantation
Hougham Mill Farm
Corner Farm
North Bridge
Moat
Mast
Sports Gd
PH
Marston Hall & Gardens
1 BRISTOWS YD
2 KERR'S CRES
3 PINFOLD LA
The Marston Thorold's Charity CE Sch
Viking Way
Marston
Frinkley Farm
Coach House Farm
River Witham
Mill Farm
Weir
Barkston Gorse Farm
Far Hill
Old Gorse Wood
Hotel
Sewage Works
Viking Way
Mickling Plantation
Foston Beck
Square Plantation
The Firs
A1
STUBTON ROAD
CLAYPOLE ROAD
ST MARTIN'S CL
CHERRY LA
FENTON RD
DODDINGTON LANE
STUBTON LODGE RD
BRANDON ROAD
STUBTON ROAD
STRAGGLETHORPE LANE
HALL RD
HALL LANE
BLIND LA
CHURCH LA
HOUGH ROAD
HOUGH LA
CLENSEY LANE
GRANGE LANE
BRANDON ROAD
SAND LANE
FOLLY LA
PLATT'S LA
EASE LANE
HOUGHAM ROAD
COACH RD
MAIN STREET
CHURCH LANE
MANOR LANE
STONEPIT LANE
BRIDGE STREET
SCH LA
MAIN ST
MILL LA
FRINKLEY LANE
FALLOW LANE
LONG ST
GOOSEGATE LA
CHAPEL LANE
TOLLBAR ROAD
BARKSTON ROAD
GREEN LA
SAND LANE
River Brant
A B C D E F
86 87 88 89 90 91
49 48 47 46 45 44 43 42
8 7 6 5 4 3 2 1

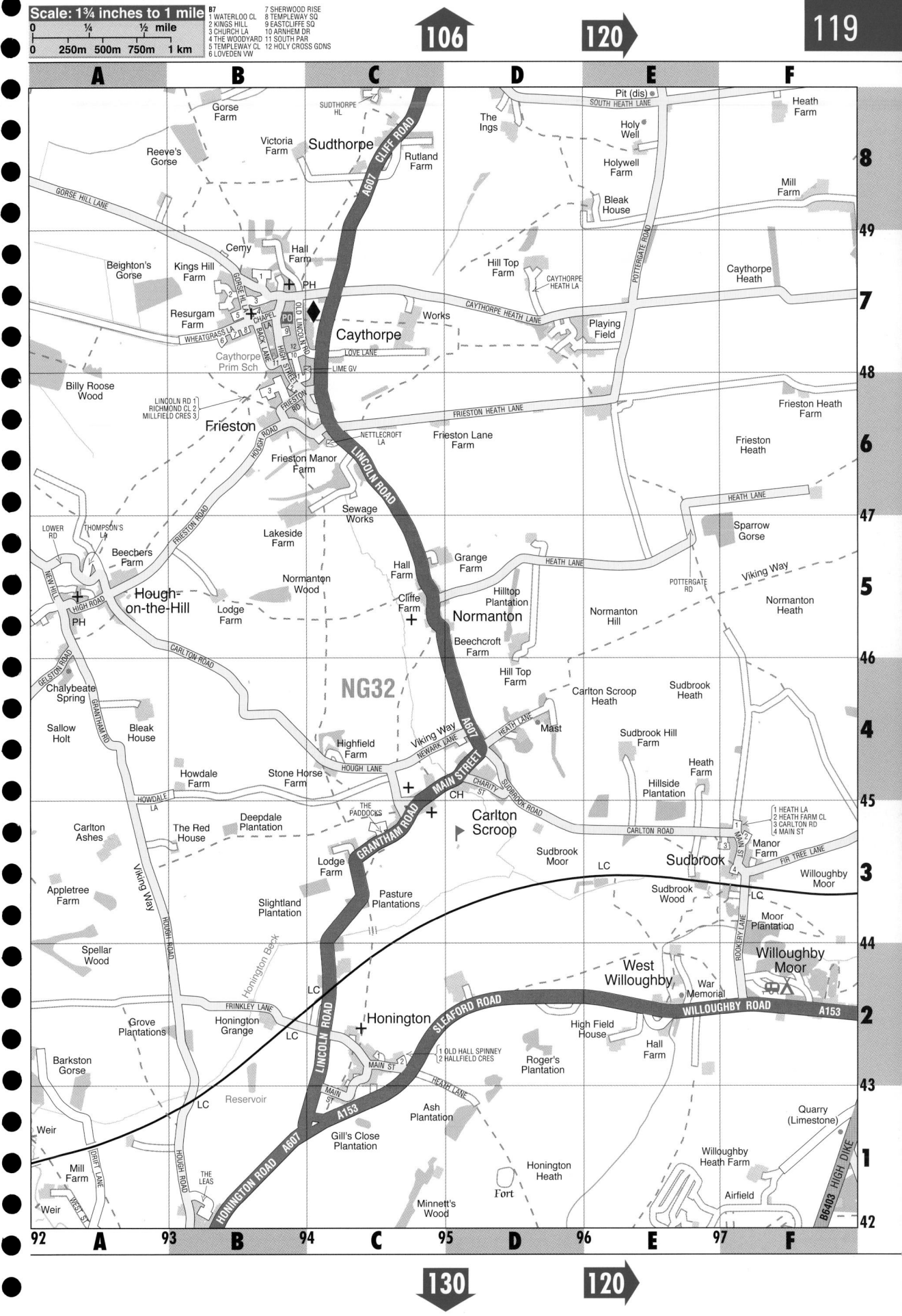
Scale: 1¾ inches to 1 mile
0 ¼ ½ mile
0 250m 500m 750m 1 km
B7
1 WATERLOO CL
2 KINGS HILL
3 CHURCH LA
4 THE WOODYARD
5 TEMPLEWAY CL
6 LOVEDEN VW
7 SHERWOOD RISE
8 TEMPLEWAY SQ
9 EASTCLIFFE SQ
10 ARNHEM DR
11 SOUTH PAR
12 HOLY CROSS GDNS
106
120
130
Sudthorpe
Caythorpe
Frieston
Hough-on-the-Hill
Normanton
Carlton Scroop
Sudbrook
West Willoughby
Willoughby Moor
Honington
NG32
A607 CLIFF ROAD
LINCOLN ROAD
GRANTHAM ROAD
MAIN STREET
SLEAFORD ROAD
WILLOUGHBY ROAD
A153
HONINGTON ROAD
B6403 HIGH DIKE
GORSE HILL LANE
SOUTH HEATH LANE
POTTERGATE ROAD
CAYTHORPE HEATH LANE
FRIESTON HEATH LANE
HEATH LANE
CARLTON ROAD
SUDBROOK ROAD
HOUGH LANE
NEWARK LANE
HOWDALE LA
HOUGH ROAD
GRANTHAM RD
GELSTON ROAD
FRINKLEY LANE
FIR TREE LANE
ROOKERY LANE
DRIFT LANE
WEST ST
Viking Way
1 HEATH LA
2 HEATH FARM CL
3 CARLTON RD
4 MAIN ST
1 OLD HALL SPINNEY
2 HALLFIELD CRES
LINCOLN RD 1
RICHMOND CL 2
MILLFIELD CRES 3
Gorse Farm
Reeve's Gorse
Victoria Farm
Rutland Farm
The Ings
Pit (dis)
Holy Well
Holywell Farm
Heath Farm
Mill Farm
Bleak House
Beighton's Gorse
Kings Hill Farm
Cemy
Hall Farm
Resurgam Farm
Caythorpe Prim Sch
Hill Top Farm
Works
Playing Field
Caythorpe Heath
Billy Roose Wood
Frieston Lane Farm
Frieston Heath Farm
Frieston Heath
Frieston Manor Farm
Sewage Works
Lakeside Farm
Beechers Farm
Normanton Wood
Lodge Farm
Grange Farm
Hilltop Plantation
Sparrow Gorse
Normanton Hill
Normanton Heath
Beechcroft Farm
Chalybeate Spring
Sallow Holt
Bleak House
Carlton Scroop Heath
Sudbrook Heath
Mast
Highfield Farm
Howdale Farm
Stone Horse Farm
Sudbrook Hill Farm
Hillside Plantation
Carlton Ashes
The Red House
Deepdale Plantation
Sudbrook Moor
Manor Farm
Willoughby Moor
Appletree Farm
Slightland Plantation
Pasture Plantations
Sudbrook Wood
Moor Plantation
Spellar Wood
War Memorial
Grove Plantations
Honington Grange
High Field House
Hall Farm
Roger's Plantation
Barkston Gorse
Reservoir
Ash Plantation
Gill's Close Plantation
Quarry (Limestone)
Weir
Mill Farm
Willoughby Heath Farm
Honington Heath
Fort
Airfield
Minnett's Wood
Honington Beck
A B C D E F
92 93 94 95 96 97
42 43 44 45 46 47 48 49
1 2 3 4 5 6 7 8

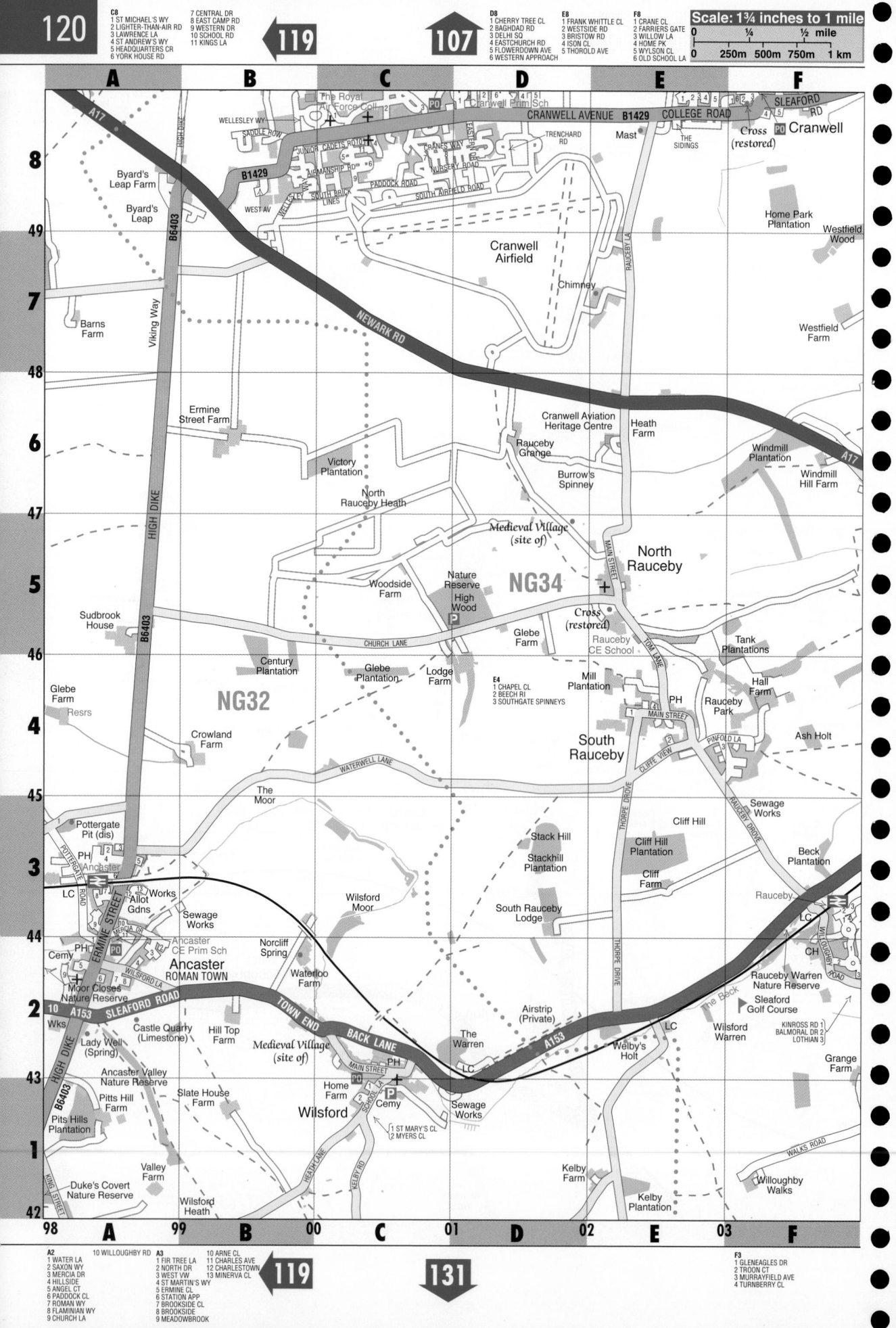

119   107

C8
1 ST MICHAEL'S WY
2 LIGHTER-THAN-AIR RD
3 LAWRENCE LA
4 ST ANDREW'S WY
5 HEADQUARTERS CR
6 YORK HOUSE RD
7 CENTRAL DR
8 EAST CAMP RD
9 WESTERN DR
10 SCHOOL RD
11 KINGS LA

D8
1 CHERRY TREE CL
2 BAGHDAD RD
3 DELHI SQ
4 EASTCHURCH RD
5 FLOWERDOWN AVE
6 WESTERN APPROACH

E8
1 FRANK WHITTLE CL
2 WESTSIDE RD
3 BRISTOW RD
4 ISON CL
5 THOROLD AVE

F8
1 CRANE CL
2 FARRIERS GATE
3 WILLOW LA
4 HOME PK
5 WYLSON CL
6 OLD SCHOOL LA

Scale: 1¾ inches to 1 mile

0   ¼   ½   mile
0 250m 500m 750m 1 km

A B C D E F

A17

The Royal
Air Force Coll

Cranwell Prim Sch

SLEAFORD RD

CRANWELL AVENUE B1429 COLLEGE ROAD

Cross (restored)   Cranwell

8

Byard's
Leap Farm

WEST AV

TRENCHARD RD

Mast

THE SIDINGS

Home Park
Plantation

Westfield
Wood

Byard's
Leap

B1429

SADDLE ROW

JUNIOR CADETS ROAD

AIRMANSHIP RD

NURSERY ROAD

PADDOCK ROAD

SOUTH BRICK
LINES

SOUTH AIRFIELD ROAD

49

B6403

Cranwell
Airfield

RAUCEBY LA

Westfield
Farm

7

Barns
Farm

Viking Way

NEWARK RD

Chimney

A17

48

Ermine
Street Farm

Cranwell Aviation
Heritage Centre

Heath
Farm

Windmill
Plantation

6

HIGH DIKE

Victory
Plantation

Rauceby
Grange

Burrow's
Spinney

Windmill
Hill Farm

47

North
Rauceby Heath

Medieval Village
(site of)

MAIN STREET

North
Rauceby

5

Sudbrook
House

B6403

Woodside
Farm

Nature
Reserve
High
Wood

NG34

Cross
(restored)

Rauceby
CE School

TOM LANE

Tank
Plantations

Glebe
Farm

CHURCH LANE

Glebe
Farm

Resrs

Century
Plantation

Glebe
Plantation

Lodge
Farm

E4
1 CHAPEL CL
2 BEECH RI
3 SOUTHGATE SPINNEYS

Mill
Plantation

Hall
Farm

PH

Rauceby
Park

46

NG32

MAIN STREET

4

Crowland
Farm

WATERWELL LANE

South
Rauceby

PINFOLD LA

Ash Holt

CLIFFE VIEW

45

The
Moor

Stack Hill

Cliff Hill

Sewage
Works

Beck
Plantation

3

Pottergate
Pit (dis)

PH
Ancaster

Wilsford
Moor

Stackhill
Plantation

Cliff Hill
Plantation

THORPE DRIVE

RAUCEBY DRIVE

Rauceby

LC

Works
Allot
Gdns

Cliff
Farm

CH

LC

Ancaster
CE Prim Sch

Norcliff
Spring

South Rauceby
Lodge

ERMINE STREET

Sewage
Works

Raceby Warren
Nature Reserve

44

PH

Cemy

PO

Waterloo
Farm

Airstrip
(Private)

The Beck

Sleaford
Golf Course

WILLOUGHBY ROAD

Ancaster
ROMAN TOWN

The
Warren

LC

Welby's
Holt

KINROSS RD 1
BALMORAL DR 2
LOTHIAN 3

Moor Closes
Nature Reserve

A153

SLEAFORD ROAD

TOWN END

BACK LANE

A153

Wilsford
Warren

2

Wks

Lady Well
(Spring)

Castle Quarry
(Limestone)

Hill Top
Farm

Medieval Village
(site of)

MAIN STREET

PH

Sewage
Works

Grange
Farm

HIGH DIKE

Ancaster Valley
Nature Reserve

Home
Farm

PO

Cemy

43

B6403

Pitts Hill
Farm

Slate House
Farm

Wilsford

1 ST MARY'S CL
2 MYERS CL

WALKS ROAD

1

Pits Hills
Plantation

SCHOOL LANE

Kelby
Farm

Willoughby
Walks

KING STREET

HEATH LANE

KELBY RD

Duke's Covert
Nature Reserve

Valley
Farm

Wilsford
Heath

Kelby
Plantation

42

98 A 99 B 00 C 01 D 02 E 03 F

119   131

A2
1 WATER LA
2 SAXON WY
3 MERCIA DR
4 HILLSIDE
5 ANGEL CT
6 PADDOCK CL
7 ROMAN WY
8 FLAMINIAN WY
9 CHURCH LA
10 WILLOUGHBY RD

A3
1 FIR TREE LA
2 NORTH DR
3 WEST VW
4 ST MARTIN'S WY
5 ERMINE CL
6 STATION APP
7 BROOKSIDE CL
8 BROOKSIDE
9 MEADOWBROOK
10 ARNE CL
11 CHARLES AVE
12 CHARLESTOWN
13 MINERVA CL

F3
1 GLENEAGLES DR
2 TROON CT
3 MURRAYFIELD AVE
4 TURNBERRY CL

Scale: 1¾ inches to 1 mile

0 ¼ ½ mile
0 250m 500m 750m 1 km

B7
1 THE MALTINGS
2 CHAPEL LA
3 LINCOLN RD
4 THE SQUARE
5 SPRING LA
6 ST ANDREW'S CRES

7 MANOR CL
8 WANSBECK RD
9 GORSE LA
10 JUNIPER CL
11 ST JOHN'S CL
12 FLAXWELL WY
13 ROOKERY LA

14 SLEAFORD RD

B8
1 LINCOLN RD
2 THE LINK
3 DEAN CL
4 KIRKDALE CL
5 LILBURN CL
6 ROBERTSON AVE

7 RUSSELL RD
8 THE GREEN
9 JESSOP CL

108
122
132
122
212

For full street detail of the highlighted area see page 212.

121
109

Scale: 1¾ inches to 1 mile

0 ¼ ½ mile
0 250m 500m 750m 1 km

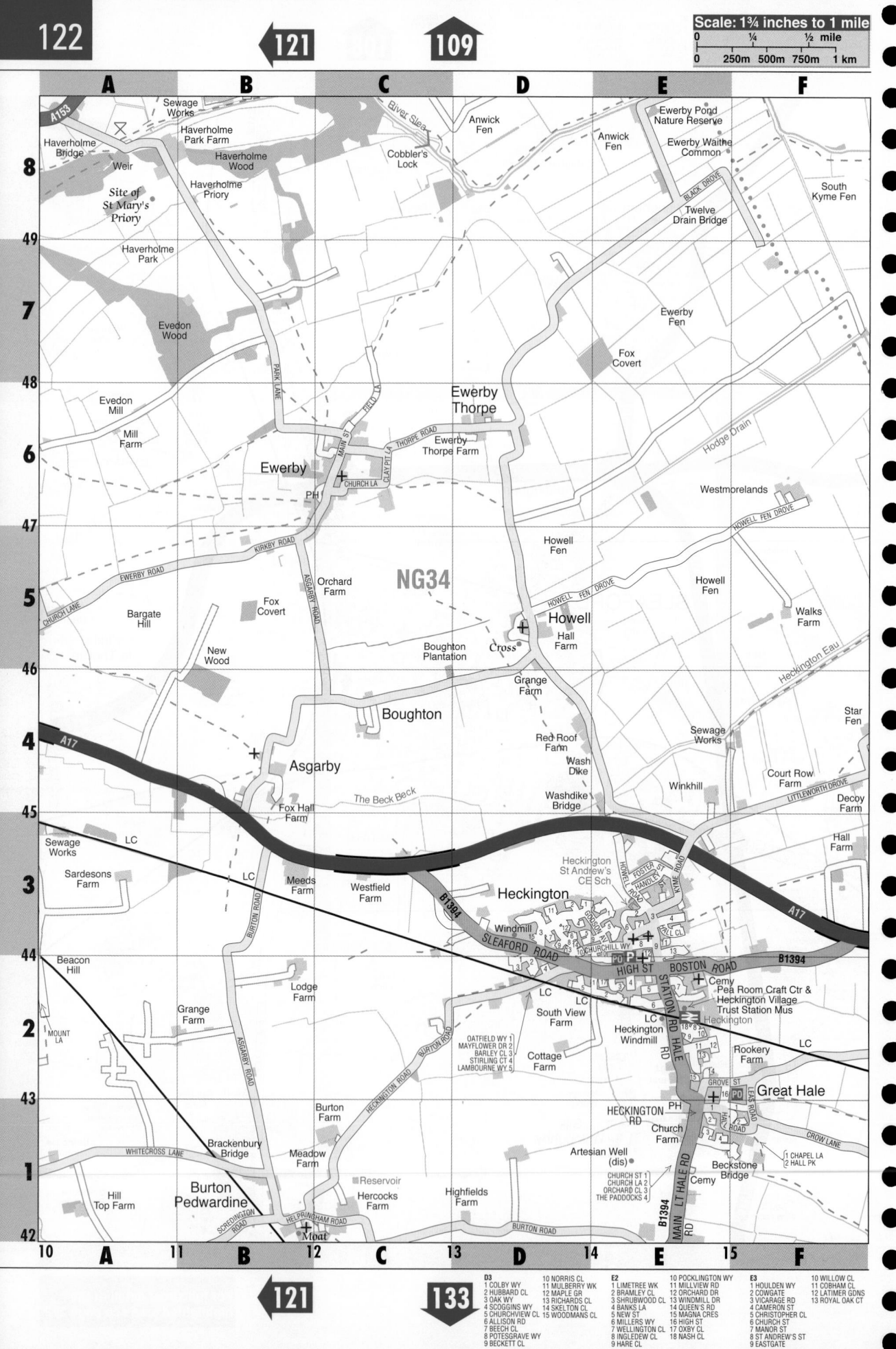

A **B** **C** **D** **E** **F**

A153

Sewage Works

Haverholme Bridge

Weir

Site of St Mary's Priory

Haverholme Park Farm

Haverholme Wood

Haverholme Priory

Anwick Fen

Cobbler's Lock

River Slea

Anwick Fen

Ewerby Pond Nature Reserve

Ewerby Waithe Common

BLACK DROVE

South Kyme Fen

Haverholme Park

Evedon Wood

Twelve Drain Bridge

Evedon Mill

Mill Farm

PARK LANE

FIELD LA

MAIN ST

Ewerby

CLAY PIT LA

CHURCH LA

PH

THORPE ROAD

Ewerby Thorpe

Ewerby Thorpe Farm

Ewerby Fen

Fox Covert

Hodge Drain

Westmorelands

Ewerby Road

KIRKBY ROAD

ASGARBY ROAD

Orchard Farm

Howell Fen

Howell

Cross

Hall Farm

Howell Fen

HOWELL FEN DROVE

Walks Farm

NG34

Bargate Hill

Fox Covert

New Wood

Boughton Plantation

Grange Farm

Boughton

Red Roof Farm

Wash Dike

Sewage Works

Winkhill

Heckington Eau

Star Fen

A17

CHURCH LANE

BURTON ROAD

Asgarby

Fox Hall Farm

The Beck Beck

Washdike Bridge

FOSTER ST

HANDLEY

KYME ROAD

Court Row Farm

LITTLEWORTH DROVE

Decoy Farm

Hall Farm

Sewage Works

Sardesons Farm

LC

LC

Meeds Farm

Westfield Farm

B1394

Heckington St Andrew's CE Sch

Heckington

THE PADDOCKS

SLEAFORD ROAD

CHURCHILL WY

HIGH ST

P

BOSTON ROAD

A17

B1394

Beacon Hill

MOUNT LA

Grange Farm

Lodge Farm

ASGARBY ROAD

HECKINGTON ROAD

BURTON ROAD

LC

South View Farm

OATFIELD WY 1
MAYFLOWER DR 2
BARLEY CL 3
STIRLING CT 4
LAMBOURNE WY 5

Cottage Farm

LC

LC

STATION RD

HALE RD

LC

Heckington Windmill

Cemy

Pea Room Craft Ctr & Heckington Village Trust Station Mus

Heckington

GROVE ST

PO

Rookery Farm

Great Hale

LC

Brackenbury Bridge

WHITECROSS LANE

SCREDINGTON ROAD

Burton Pedwardine

Meadow Farm

Hercocks Farm

Reservoir

HELPRINGHAM ROAD

Moat

Highfields Farm

BURTON ROAD

HECKINGTON RD

Artesian Well (dis)

CHURCH ST 1
CHURCH LA 2
ORCHARD CL 3
THE PADDOCKS 4

Church Farm

PH

MAIN LT HALE RD

LEAN ROAD

Cemy

B1394

PO

HALE ROAD

CROW LANE

Beckstone Bridge

1 CHAPEL LA
2 HALL PK

Hill Top Farm

10 11 12 13 14 15

A **B** **C** **D** **E** **F**

121
133

D3
1 COLBY WY
2 HUBBARD CL
3 OAK WY
4 SCOGGINS WY
5 CHURCHVIEW CL
6 ALLISON RD
7 BEECH CL
8 POTESGRAVE WY
9 BECKETT CL

10 NORRIS CL
11 MULBERRY WK
12 MAPLE GR
13 RICHARDS CL
14 SKELTON CL
15 WOODMANS CL

E2
1 LIMETREE WK
2 BRAMLEY CL
3 SHRUBWOOD CL
4 BANKS LA
5 NEW ST
6 MILLERS WY
7 WELLINGTON CL
8 INGLEDEW CL
9 HARE CL

10 POCKLINGTON WY
11 MILLVIEW RD
12 ORCHARD DR
13 WINDMILL DR
14 QUEEN'S RD
15 MAGNA CRES
16 HIGH ST
17 OXBY CL
18 NASH CL

E3
1 HOULDEN WY
2 COWGATE
3 VICARAGE RD
4 CAMERON ST
5 CHRISTOPHER CL
6 CHURCH ST
7 MANOR ST
8 ST ANDREW'S ST
9 EASTGATE

10 WILLOW CL
11 COBHAM CL
12 LATIMER GDNS
13 ROYAL OAK CT

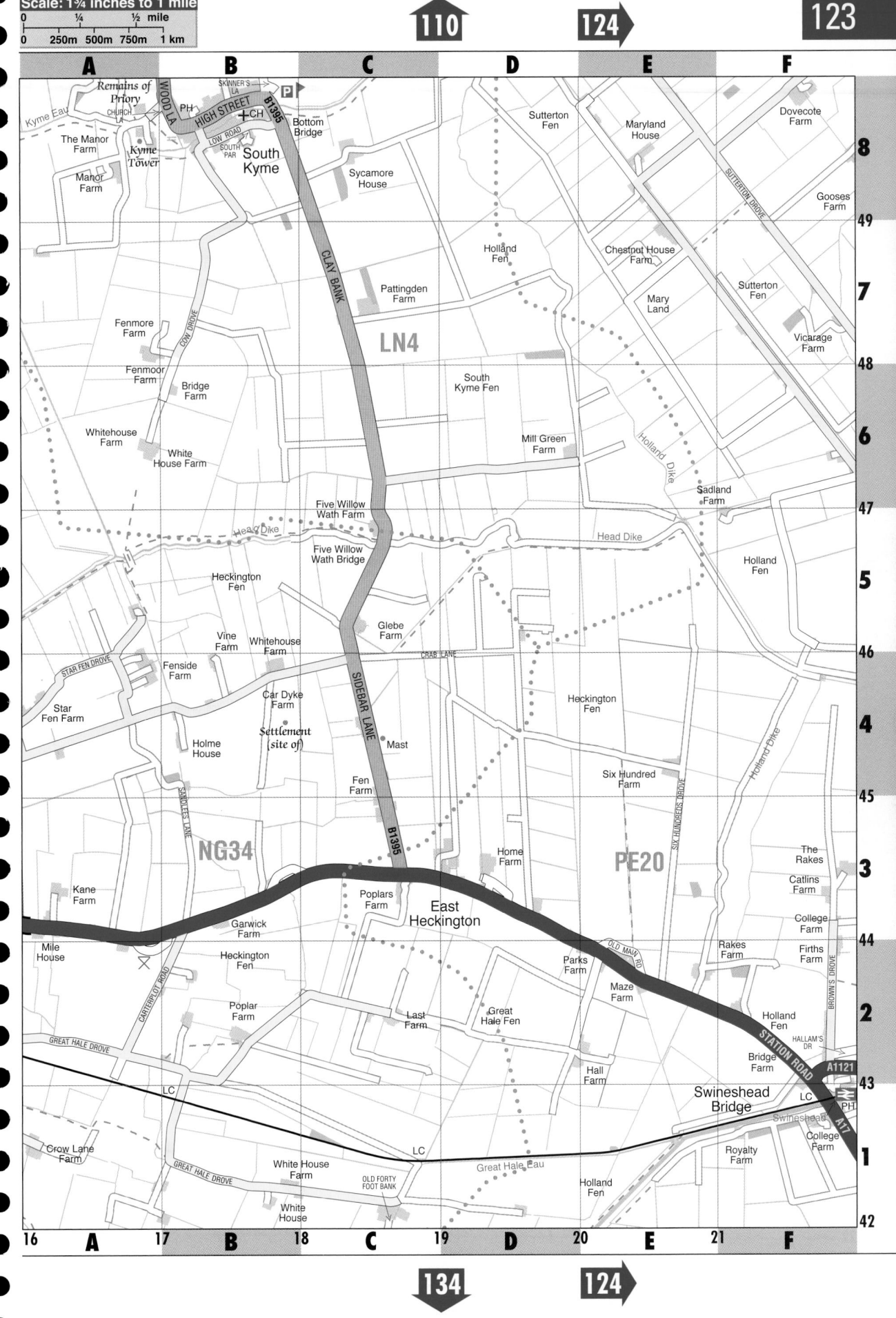

Scale: 1¾ inches to 1 mile

0   ¼   ½ mile
0 250m 500m 750m 1 km

110

124

Remains of
Priory

CHURCH
LA.

Kyme Eau

The Manor
Farm

Kyme
Tower

Manor
Farm

PH

WOOD LA

SKINNER'S
LA

HIGH STREET

CH

P

B1395

LOW ROAD

SOUTH
PAR

Bottom
Bridge

South
Kyme

Sycamore
House

COW DROVE

Fenmore
Farm

Fenmoor
Farm

Bridge
Farm

Whitehouse
Farm

White
House Farm

CLAY BANK

Pattingden
Farm

LN4

Holland
Fen

South
Kyme Fen

Mill Green
Farm

Sutterton
Fen

Maryland
House

Chestnut House
Farm

Mary
Land

SUTTERTON DROVE

Dovecote
Farm

Gooses
Farm

Sutterton
Fen

Vicarage
Farm

Head Dike

Five Willow
Wath Farm

Five Willow
Wath Bridge

Heckington
Fen

Head Dike

Holland
Dike

Sadland
Farm

Holland
Fen

Vine
Farm

Whitehouse
Farm

Glebe
Farm

CRAB LANE

Heckington
Fen

STAR FEN DROVE

Fenside
Farm

Car Dyke
Farm

Settlement
(site of)

SIDEBAR LANE

Mast

Six Hundred
Farm

Holland
Dike

Star
Fen Farm

Holme
House

Fen
Farm

B1395

SANDTOES LANE

NG34

Kane
Farm

Garwick
Farm

Poplars
Farm

East
Heckington

PE20

The
Rakes

Catlins
Farm

College
Farm

Mile
House

Heckington
Fen

OLD MAIN RD

Parks
Farm

Rakes
Farm

Firths
Farm

CARTERPLOT ROAD

Poplar
Farm

Last
Farm

Great
Hale Fen

Maze
Farm

Holland
Fen

Bridge
Farm

BROWN'S DROVE

STATION ROAD

HALLAM'S
DR

A1121

GREAT HALE DROVE

LC

Hall
Farm

Swineshead
Bridge

LC

Swineshead

PH

A17

Crow Lane
Farm

GREAT HALE DROVE

White House
Farm

OLD FORTY
FOOT BANK

LC

Great Hale Eau

Holland
Fen

Royalty
Farm

College
Farm

White
House

134

124

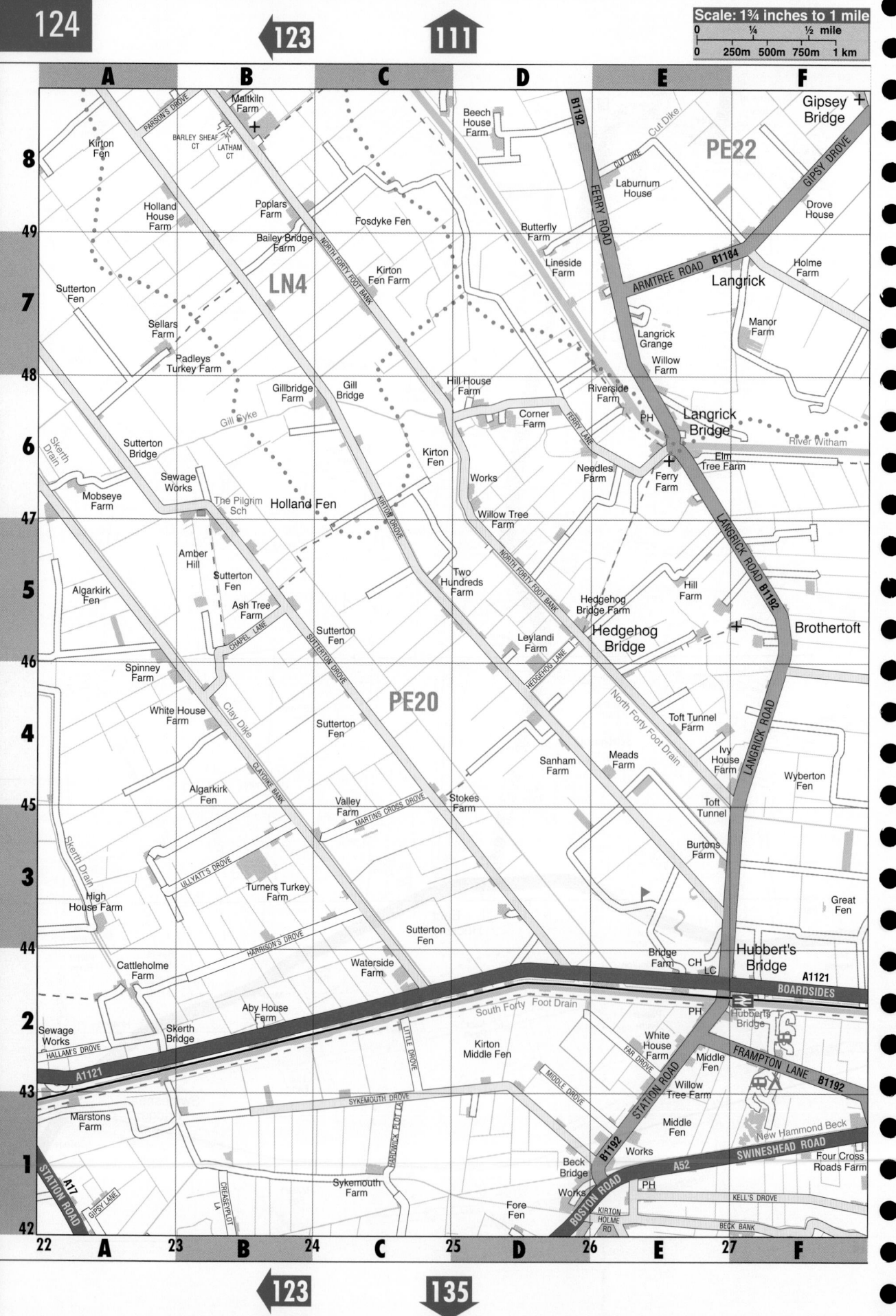
123
111
Scale: 1¾ inches to 1 mile
0 ¼ ½ mile
0 250m 500m 750m 1 km
Kirton Fen
Maltkiln Farm
Barley Sheaf Ct
Latham Ct
Parson's Drove
Beech House Farm
Gipsey Bridge
PE22
Cut Dike
Gipsy Drove
Ferry Road
B1192
Laburnum House
Holland House Farm
Poplars Farm
Fosdyke Fen
Bailey Bridge Farm
Butterfly Farm
Drove House
North Forty Foot Bank
Kirton Fen Farm
Lineside Farm
Armtree Road
B1184
Langrick
Holme Farm
LN4
Sutterton Fen
Manor Farm
Sellars Farm
Langrick Grange
Padleys Turkey Farm
Willow Farm
Gillbridge Farm
Gill Bridge
Hill House Farm
Riverside Farm
Gill Syke
Corner Farm
Ferry Lane
PH
Langrick Bridge
Skerth Drain
Sutterton Bridge
River Witham
Kirton Fen
Elm Tree Farm
Needles Farm
Ferry Farm
Sewage Works
Works
Mobseye Farm
The Pilgrim Sch
Holland Fen
Willow Tree Farm
Kirton Drove
Langrick Road
Amber Hill
Two Hundreds Farm
Algarkirk Fen
Sutterton Fen
Hedgehog Bridge Farm
Hill Farm
Ash Tree Farm
Hedgehog Bridge
Brothertoft
Chapel Lane
Sutterton Fen
Leylandi Farm
Hedgehog Lane
Spinney Farm
Sutterton Drove
PE20
North Forty Foot Drain
White House Farm
Clay Dike
Toft Tunnel Farm
Sutterton Fen
Sanham Farm
Meads Farm
Ivy House Farm
Wyberton Fen
Algarkirk Fen
Claydike Bank
Valley Farm
Martins Cross Drove
Stokes Farm
Toft Tunnel
Burtons Farm
Ullyatt's Drove
Turners Turkey Farm
High House Farm
Great Fen
Harrison's Drove
Sutterton Fen
Bridge Farm
CH
LC
Hubbert's Bridge
Cattleholme Farm
Waterside Farm
A1121
Boardsides
Aby House Farm
South Forty Foot Drain
PH
Hubbert's Bridge
Sewage Works
Skerth Bridge
Little Drove
Kirton Middle Fen
White House Farm
Middle Fen
Frampton Lane
Hallam's Drove
Far Drove
Middle Drove
Willow Tree Farm
Station Road
Sykemouth Drove
Marstons Farm
Middle Fen
New Hammond Beck
Works
Swineshead Road
A52
Four Cross Roads Farm
Beck Bridge
Hardwick Plot La
Sykemouth Farm
Works
Boston Road
PH
Station Road
A17
Gipsy Lane
Creaseyplot La
Fore Fen
Kirton Holme Rd
Kell's Drove
Beck Bank
A B C D E F
8 49 7 48 6 47 5 46 4 45 3 44 2 43 1 42
22 23 24 25 26 27

123
135

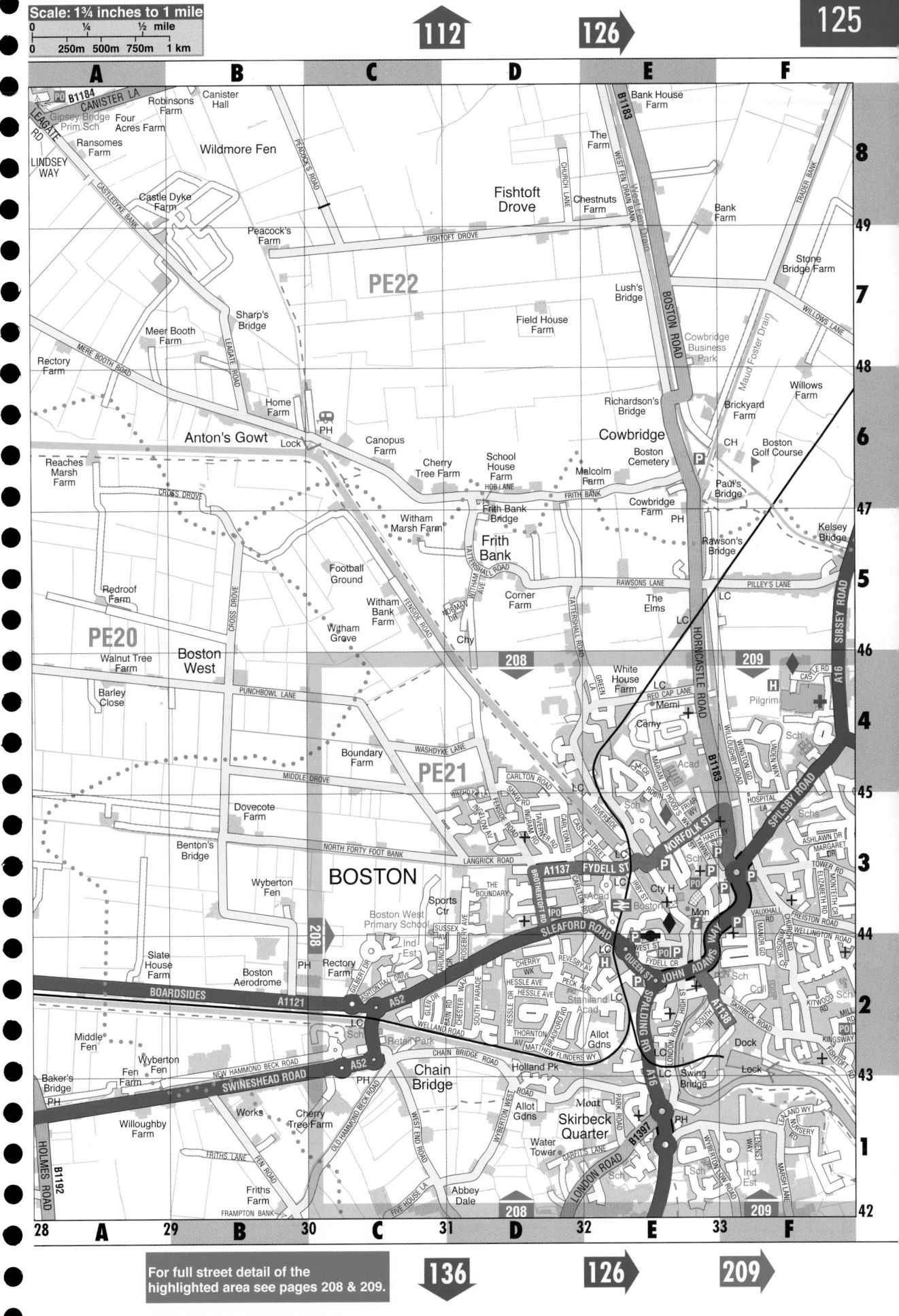

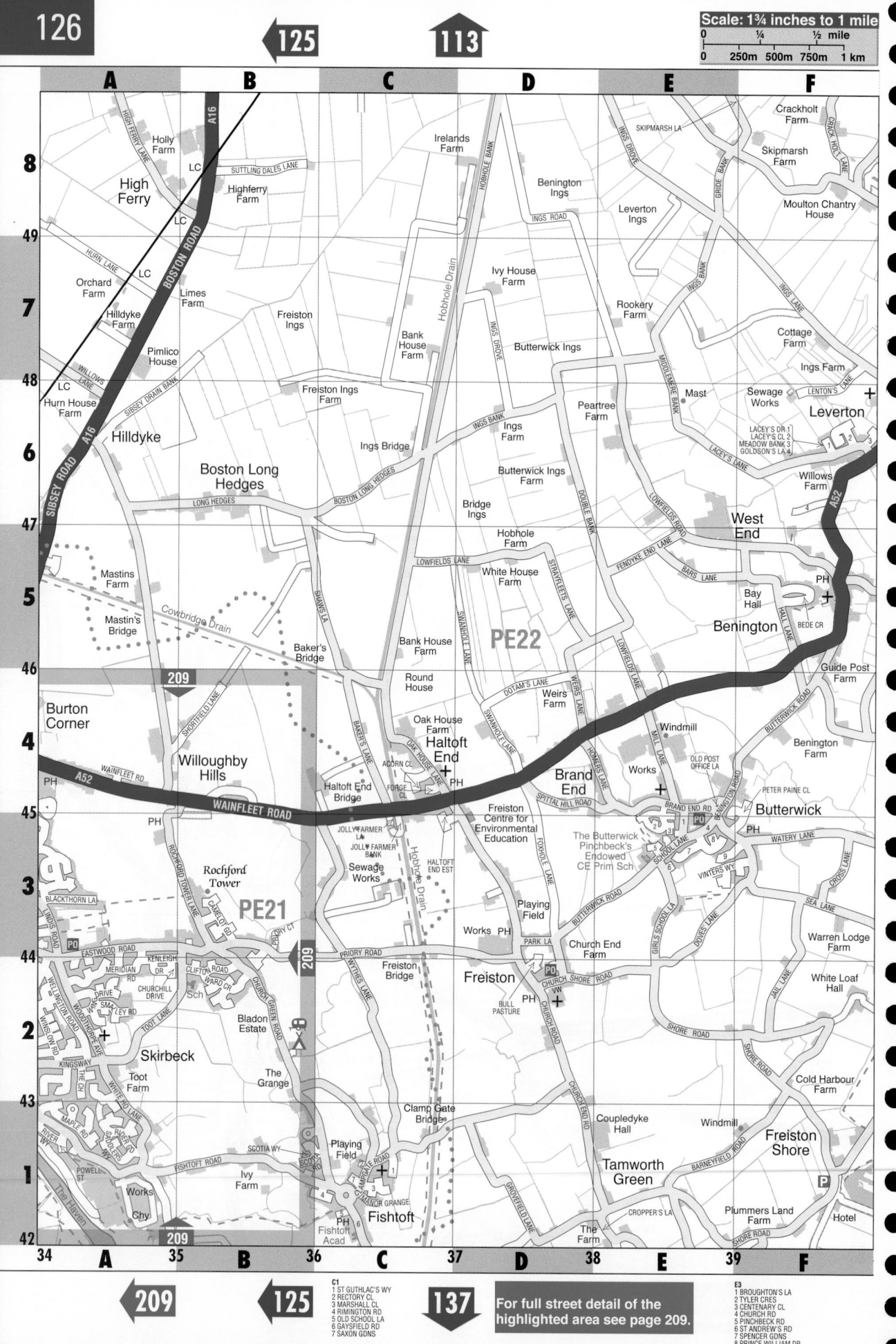

126

125

113

Scale: 1¾ inches to 1 mile

0   ¼   ½ mile
0   250m 500m 750m 1 km

A   B   C   D   E   F

8

49

7

48

6

47

5

46

4

45

3

44

2

43

1

42

34   A   35   B   36   C   37   D   38   E   39   F

High Ferry
Holly Farm
High Ferry
Highferry Farm
LC
SUTTLING DALES LANE
BOSTON ROAD
A16
Orchard Farm
Hilldyke Farm
Limes Farm
HURN LANE
WILLOWS LANE
LC
LC
LC
Pimlico House
Hurn House Farm
A16
SIBSEY ROAD
Hilldyke
SIBSEY DRAIN BANK
Boston Long Hedges
LONG HEDGES
BOSTON LONG HEDGES
Freiston Ings
Freiston Ings Farm
Bank House Farm
Ings Bridge
INGS BANK
Ings Farm
Ings Bridge

Irelands Farm
HOBHOLE BANK
Benington Ings
INGS DROVE
Benington Ings
INGS ROAD
Ivy House Farm
Butterwick Ings
INGS DROVE
Peartree Farm
Butterwick Ings Farm
DOUBLE BANK
Bridge Ings
Hobhole Farm
LOWFIELDS LANE
White House Farm
STRAYFLEETS LANE
Bank House Farm
DOTAM'S LANE
SWANHOLE LANE
Weirs Farm
WEIRS LANE
Round House
Oak House Farm
Haltoft End
BAKER'S LANE
OAK HOUSE LANE
PH
AGORN CL
FORGE CL
Haltoft End Bridge
Freiston Centre for Environmental Education
FOXHOLE LANE
SPITTAL HILL ROAD
Brand End
FORGE CL
JOLLY FARMER LA
JOLLY FARMER BANK
Sewage Works
HOBHOLE DRAIN
HALTOFT END EST
Playing Field
Works PH
PARK LA
PRIORY ROAD
WYTHES LANE
Freiston Bridge
Freiston
PH
BULL PASTURE
VW

SKIPMARSH LA
GRIDE BANK
INGS DROVE
Leverton Ings
INGS BANK
Rookery Farm
MIDDLEMERE BANK
Mast
LACEY'S DR 1
LACEY'S CL 2
MEADOW BANK 3
GOLDSON'S LA 4
Sewage Works
LENTON'S LA
LACEY'S LANE
West End
FENDYKE END LANE
LOWFIELDS ROAD
LOWFIELDS LANE
BARS LANE
HALL LANE
Bay Hall
Benington
BEDE CR
Windmill
Works
OLD POST OFFICE LA
MILL LANE
BENINGTON ROAD
PETER PAINE CL
Brand End
BRAND END RD
PO
PH
The Butterwick Pinchbeck's Endowed CE Prim Sch
SCHOOL LANE
VINTERS WY
Butterwick
WATERY LANE
CROSS LANE
BUTTERWICK ROAD
GIRL'S SCHOOL LA
Church End Farm
JOYCE'S LANE
SEA LANE
Church Shore Road
SHORE ROAD
CHURCH END RD

Crackholt Farm
CRACK HOLL LANE
Skipmarsh Farm
Moulton Chantry House
Cottage Farm
INGS LANE
Ings Farm
Leverton
Willows Farm
A52
Guide Post Farm
BUTTERWICK ROAD
Benington Farm
Warren Lodge Farm
White Loaf Hall
Cold Harbour Farm
Freiston Shore
Hotel
P

PE22
PE21
A52
WAINFLEET RD
WAINFLEET ROAD
PH
PH
Burton Corner
Willoughby Hills
SHORTFIELD LANE
ROCHFORD TOWER LANE
Rochford Tower
CAMELOT
IVORY CT
209
BAKER'S LANE
Blackthorn La
BLACKTHORN LA
LEWIS ROAD
PO
EASTWOOD ROAD
MERIDIAN RD
KENLEIGH DR
CLIFTON ROAD
WARD CR
CHURCHILL DRIVE
Sch
CHURCH GREEN ROAD
WELLINGTON RD
WOODTHORPE AV
SM4
LEY RD
WINSOR RD
KINGSWAY
THE CH
Skirbeck
Toot Farm
WHITE LEY LANE
TOOT LANE
Bladon Estate
The Grange
MAPLE RD
RIVER WY
SALTER'S WY
POWELL ST
THE HAVEN
Works
Chy
FISHTOFT ROAD
SCOTIA WY
Ivy Farm
Playing Field
SCOTT RD
Clamp Gate Bridge
MANOR GRANGE
Fishtoft
Fishtoft Acad
PH
BLADON RD
CAMPGATE ROAD
GROVEFIELD LANE
CROPPER'S LA
Tamworth Green
Coupledyke Hall
Windmill
BARNEYFIELD ROAD
Plummers Land Farm
The Farm
SHORE ROAD

For full street detail of the highlighted area see page 209.

C1
1 ST GUTHLAC'S WY
2 RECTORY CL
3 MARSHALL CL
4 RIMINGTON RD
5 OLD SCHOOL LA
6 GAYSFIELD RD
7 SAXON GDNS

E3
1 BROUGHTON'S LA
2 TYLER CRES
3 CENTENARY CL
4 CHURCH RD
5 PINCHBECK RD
6 ST ANDREW'S RD
7 SPENCER GDNS
8 PRINCE WILLIAM DR
9 UPSALL RD

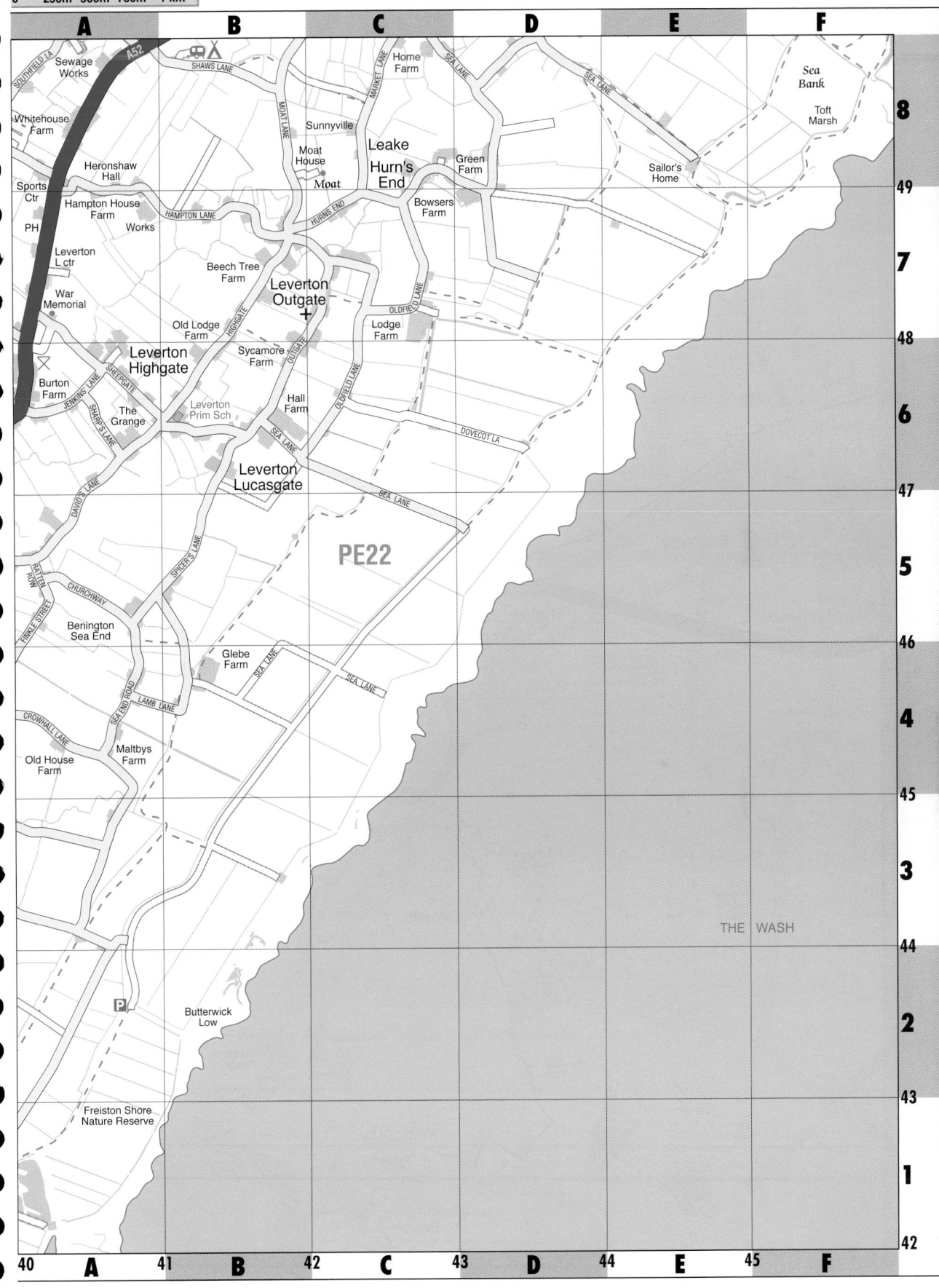

Scale:
0   ¼   ½   mile
0   250m 500m 750m 1 km

A **B** **C** **D** **E** **F**

SOUTHFIELD LA
A52
Sewage Works
Whitehouse Farm
Heronshaw Hall
Sports Ctr
PH
Hampton House Farm
Works
Leverton L ctr
War Memorial
Old Lodge Farm
Leverton Highgate
Burton Farm
JENKINS LANE
SHEEPGATE
The Grange
Leverton Prim Sch
SHARP'S LANE
DAVID'S LANE
PATTEN ROW
FINKLE STREET
CHURCHWAY
Benington Sea End
CROWHALL LANE
Old House Farm
Maltbys Farm
SEA END ROAD
LAMB LANE
SPICER'S LANE
Glebe Farm
SEA LANE
Butterwick Low
P
Freiston Shore Nature Reserve

SHAWS LANE
MOAT LANE
Sunnyville
Moat House
Moat
HAMPTON LANE
Beech Tree Farm
HIGHGATE
Leverton Outgate
OUTGATE
Sycamore Farm
Hall Farm
SEA LANE
Leverton Lucasgate

MARKET LANE
Home Farm
Leake Hurn's End
HURNS END
Lodge Farm
OLDFIELD LANE
Bowsers Farm
OLDFIELD LANE
DOVECOT LA
SEA LANE

SEA LANE
Green Farm

SEA LANE
Sailor's Home

Sea Bank
Toft Marsh

PE22

THE WASH

8
49
7
48
6
47
5
46
4
45
3
44
2
43
1
42

40 **A** 41 **B** 42 **C** 43 **D** 44 **E** 45 **F**

A5
1 NOTTINGHAM RD
2 LIME GR
3 WALNUT RD
4 HOOPERS CL
5 GRANBY DR
6 THE PADDOCKS

7 NORTH CRES
8 SILVERWOOD RD
9 KEEL DR
10 SCHOOL VW
11 SOUTH CRES
12 BELVOIR AVE
13 VINE CL

14 HOWITTS RD
15 RUTLAND LA
16 BEECH DR

A6
1 SPIRE VW
2 BEACON VW
3 WIMBISHTHORPE CL
4 BOWBRIDGE GDNS
5 WINTERBECK CL
6 TOLL BAR AVE

7 PINFOLD CL
8 RIVERSIDE WLK
9 WEST END CL
10 BOWBRIDGE LA
11 PINFOLD LA
12 FARMHOUSE CL
13 CHURCH VW

14 RIVERSIDE CL
15 ALBERT ST
16 CHAPEL ST
17 DEVON LA
18 ST MARY'S CL
19 BECKINGTHORPE DR
20 DAYBELL CL

21 WYGGESTON RD
22 WYGGESTON AVE

Scale: 1¾ inches to 1 mile
0   ¼   ½   mile
0   250m   500m   750m   1 km

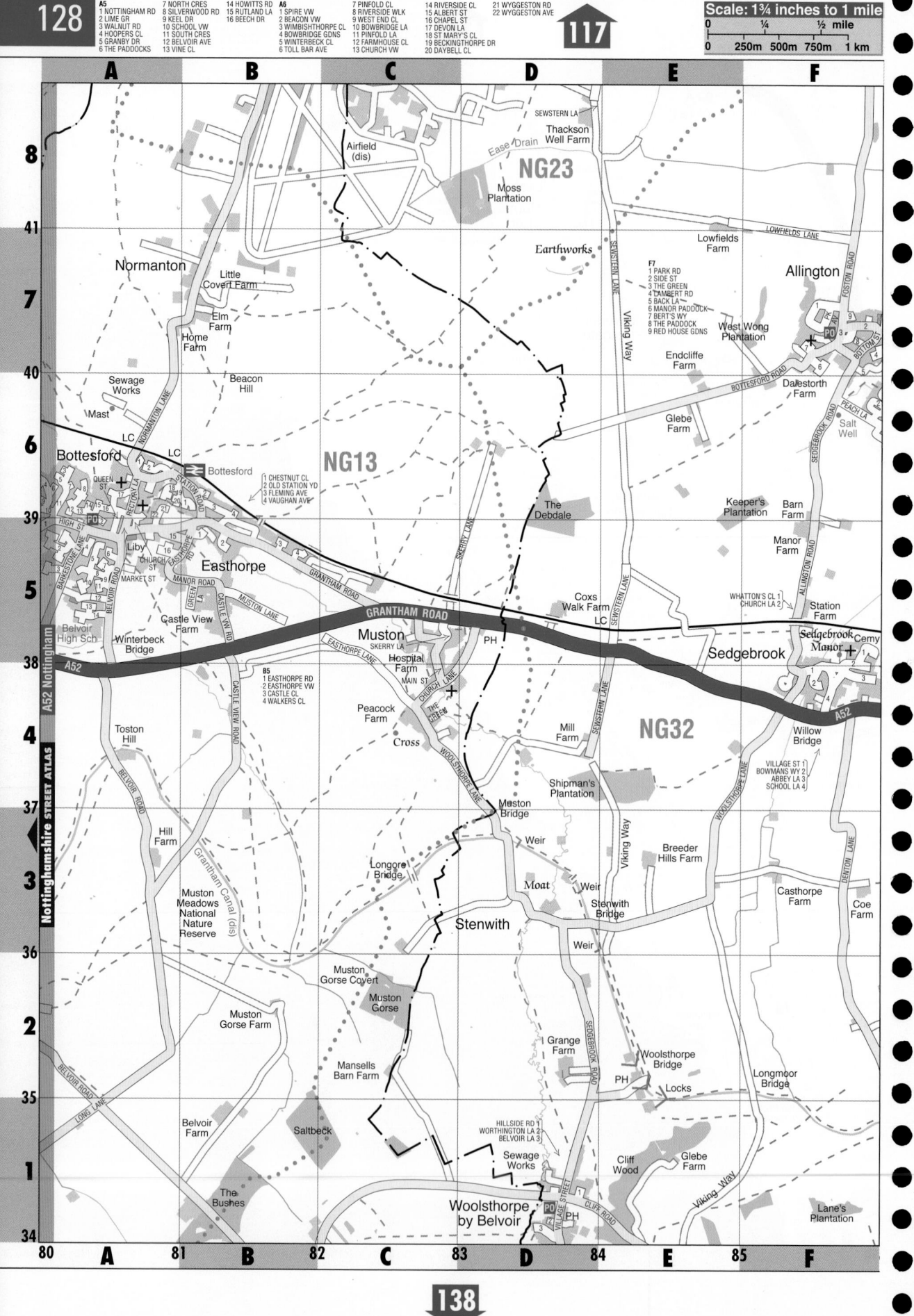

Nottinghamshire STREET ATLAS

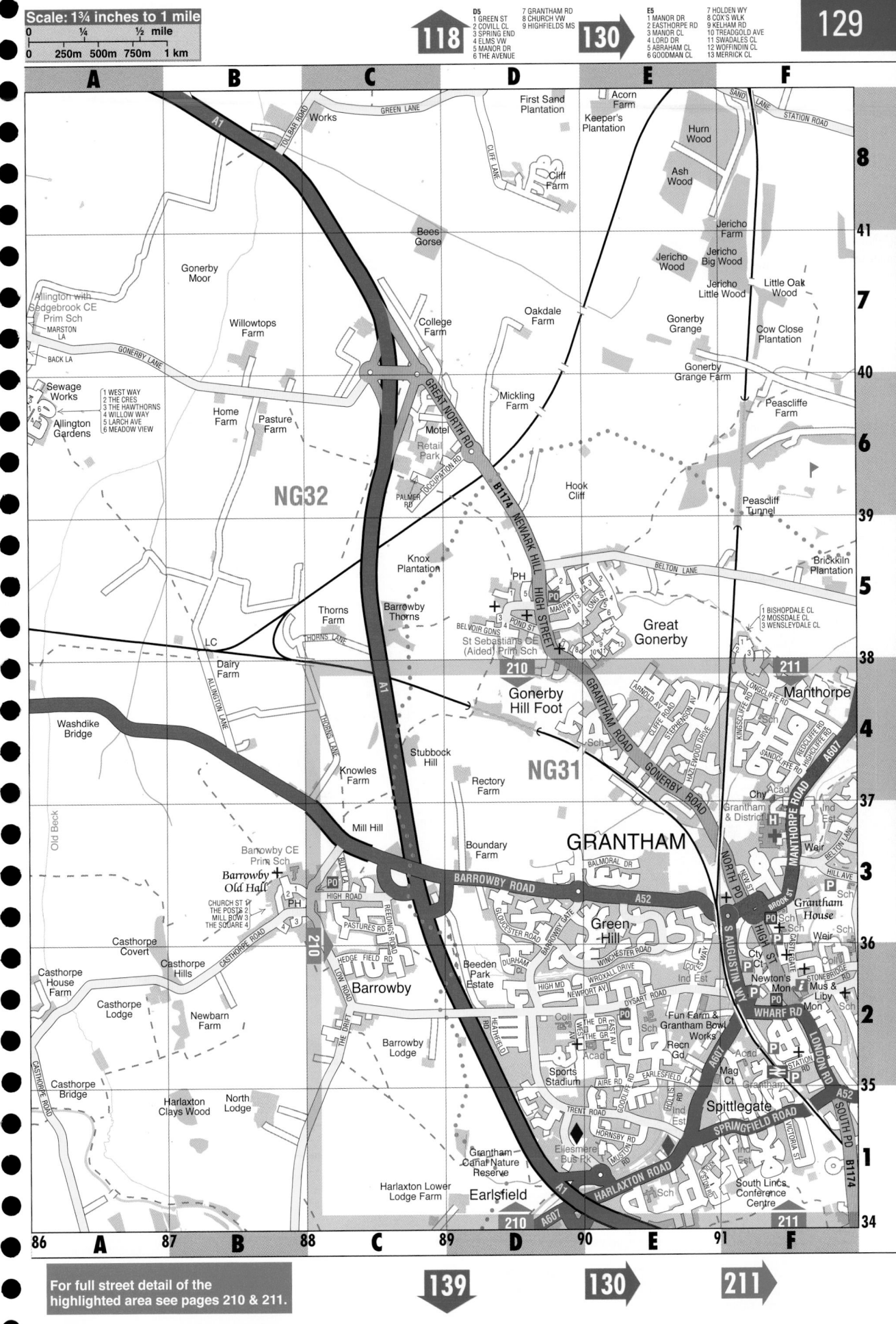

Scale: 1¾ inches to 1 mile
0 ¼ ½ mile
0 250m 500m 750m 1 km
118
D5
1 GREEN ST
2 COVILL CL
3 SPRING END
4 ELMS VW
5 MANOR DR
6 THE AVENUE
7 GRANTHAM RD
8 CHURCH VW
9 HIGHFIELDS MS
130
E5
1 MANOR DR
2 EASTHORPE RD
3 MANOR CL
4 LORD DR
5 ABRAHAM CL
6 GOODMAN CL
7 HOLDEN WY
8 COX'S WLK
9 KELHAM RD
10 TREADGOLD AVE
11 SWADALES CL
12 WOFFINDIN CL
13 MERRICK CL
129
A B C D E F
8
41
7
40
6
39
5
38
4
37
3
36
2
35
1
34
A1
Works
GREEN LANE
TOLLBAR ROAD
First Sand Plantation
Acorn Farm
Keeper's Plantation
SAND LANE
STATION ROAD
Hurn Wood
Ash Wood
CLIFF LANE
Cliff Farm
Bees Gorse
Jericho Farm
Jericho Wood
Jericho Big Wood
Jericho Little Wood
Little Oak Wood
Gonerby Moor
Allington with Sedgebrook CE Prim Sch
MARSTON LA
BACK LA
GONERBY LANE
Willowtops Farm
College Farm
Oakdale Farm
Gonerby Grange
Cow Close Plantation
Gonerby Grange Farm
Sewage Works
1 WEST WAY
2 THE CRES
3 THE HAWTHORNS
4 WILLOW WAY
5 LARCH AVE
6 MEADOW VIEW
Allington Gardens
Home Farm
Pasture Farm
GREAT NORTH RD
Motel
Retail Park
Mickling Farm
Peascliffe Farm
NG32
OCCUPATION RD
PALMER RD
B1174
NEWARK HILL
Hook Cliff
Peascliff Tunnel
Knox Plantation
BELTON LANE
Brickkiln Plantation
PH
PO
HIGH STREET
MARRATTS LA
LONG ST
Thorns Farm
Barrowby Thorns
POND ST
BELVOIR GDNS
St Sebastians CE (Aided) Prim Sch
Great Gonerby
1 BISHOPDALE CL
2 MOSSDALE CL
3 WENSLEYDALE CL
LC
THORNS LANE
Dairy Farm
210
211
Manthorpe
Gonerby Hill Foot
GRANTHAM ROAD
ARNOLD AV
CLIFFE ROAD
STEPHENSON AV
HAZLEWOOD DRIVE
LONGCLIFFE RD
KINGSCLIFFE RD
SANDCLIFFE RD
REDCLIFFE RD
HIGHCLIFFE RD
A607
Washdike Bridge
ALLINGTON LANE
THORNS LANE
Stubbock Hill
Sch
NG31
GONERBY ROAD
Knowles Farm
Rectory Farm
Chy
Acad
Grantham & District
H
Ind Est
MANTHORPE ROAD
BELTON LANE
Mill Hill
Old Beck
GRANTHAM
Weir
Barrowby CE Prim Sch
Boundary Farm
BALMORAL DR
NORTH PD
HILL AVE
Barrowby Old Hall
BUTT LA
BARROWBY ROAD
A52
NEW ST
BROOK ST
Grantham House
HIGH ROAD
CHURCH ST 1
THE POSTS 2
MILL ROW 3
THE SQUARE 4
PASTURES RD
REEDINGS ROAD
GLOUCESTER ROAD
BARROWBY GATE
Green Hill
S AUGUSTIN WY
HIGH ST
CASTLEGATE
Casthorpe Covert
CASTHORPE ROAD
HEDGE FIELD RD
Beeden Park Estate
DURHAM CL
WINCHESTER ROAD
COL WAY
Cty Ct
Coll
Casthorpe Hills
Casthorpe House Farm
LOW ROAD
Barrowby
WROXALL DRIVE
Ind Est
Newton's Mon
STONEBRIDGE
Mus & Liby
Casthorpe Lodge
HIGH MD
NEWPORT AV
DYSART ROAD
Mon
WHARF RD
Newbarn Farm
THE DRIFT
HEATHFIELD RD
WEST AV
THE DR
THE GR
EAST AV
Fun Farm & Grantham Bowl Works
Barrowby Lodge
Recn Gd
A607
Mag Ct
STATION RD
LONDON RD
CASTHORPE ROAD
Casthorpe Bridge
Sports Stadium
AIRE RD
GOODLIFF RD
EARLESFIELD LA
HOLLIS RD
Grantham
Harlaxton Clays Wood
North Lodge
TRENT ROAD
Ind Est
Spittlegate
SPRINGFIELD ROAD
VICTORIA ST
SOUTH PD
HORNSBY RD
Grantham Canal Nature Reserve
Ellesmere Bus Pk
MUSTON RD
HARLAXTON ROAD
B1174
South Lincs Conference Centre
Harlaxton Lower Lodge Farm
Earlsfield
86 87 88 89 90 91
139
130
211
For full street detail of the highlighted area see pages 210 & 211.

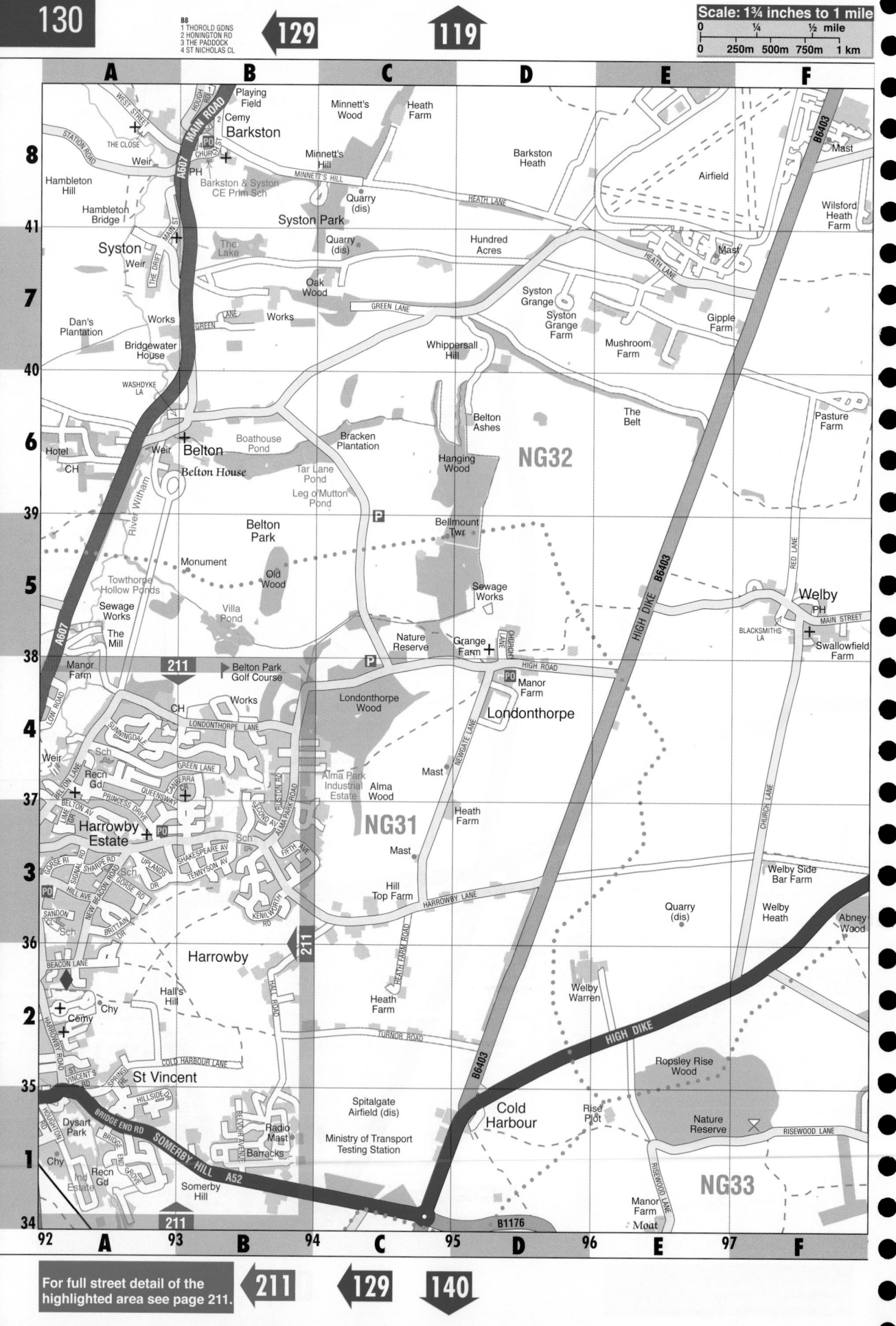

129
119

Scale: 1¾ inches to 1 mile

0 ¼ ½ mile
0 250m 500m 750m 1 km

A B C D E F

8

Playing Field
WEST STREET
THE CLOSE
Weir
Hambleton Hill
Hambleton Bridge
STATION ROAD
Cemy
Barkston
MAIN ROAD
PO
PH
Barkston & Syston CE Prim Sch
CHURCH ST
Minnett's Wood
Heath Farm
Minnett's Hill
Minnett's Hill
Barkston Heath
Airfield
Mast
B6403

41

Syston
A607
THE DRIFT
MAIN ST
Syston Park
The Lake
Quarry (dis)
Quarry (dis)
Hundred Acres
HEATH LANE
Mast
Wilsford Heath Farm

7

Dan's Plantation
Works
Bridgewater House
GREEN LANE
Oak Wood
Works
GREEN LANE
Syston Grange
Syston Grange Farm
Mushroom Farm
HEATH LANE
Gipple Farm
Mast

40

WASHDYKE LA
Whippersall Hill
Belton Ashes
The Belt
Pasture Farm

6

Hotel
CH
Weir
Belton
Belton House
River Witham
Boathouse Pond
Tar Lane Pond
Leg o' Mutton Pond
Bracken Plantation
Hanging Wood
NG32
B6403
RED LANE

39

Belton Park
P
Bellmount Twr

5

A607
Towthorpe Hollow Ponds
Monument
Old Wood
Villa Pond
Sewage Works
The Mill
Sewage Works
Nature Reserve
HIGH DIKE
Welby
PH
BLACKSMITHS LA
Swallowfield Farm

38

Manor Farm
211
Belton Park Golf Course
P
Londonthorpe Wood
Grange Farm
CHURCH LANE
HIGH ROAD
PO
Manor Farm

4

Low Road
CH
Works
LONDONTHORPE LANE
SUNNINGDALE
CANBERRA CR
Alma Park Industrial Estate
Alma Wood
Londonthorpe
NEWGATE LANE
Mast

37

Weir
BELTON LANE
Sch
Recn Gd
QUEENSWAY
GREEN LANE
PRINCESS DRIVE
Sch
PISTON RD
Harrowby Estate
PO
SECOND AVE
ALMA PARK ROAD
Sch
FIFTH AVE
Heath Farm
Mast

3

PO
GORSE RI
SIGNAL RD
SHARPE RD
HILL AVE
NEW BEACON ROAD
BRITTAIN DR
SANDON CL
UPLANDS DR
TENNYSON AV
SHAKESPEARE AV
Sch
KENILWORTH RD
Hill Top Farm
HARROWBY LANE
Welby Side Bar Farm
Quarry (dis)
Welby Heath
Abney Wood

36

BEACON LANE
Harrowby
211
HALL ROAD
Hall's Hill
HEATH FARM ROAD
Heath Farm
Welby Warren

2

HARROWBY ROAD
Cemy
St Vincent
COLD HARBOUR LANE
TURNOR ROAD
HIGH DIKE
Ropsley Rise Wood
Nature Reserve
RISEWOOD LANE

35

ST VINCENT'S RD
HILLSIDE DR
SPRING DR
Dysart Park
BRIDGE END RD
SOMERBY HILL
BELTON AVENUE
Spitalgate Airfield (dis)
B6403
Cold Harbour
Rise Plot
RISEWOOD LANE

1

HOUGH DR
Chy
Ind Estate
Recn Gd
BRIDGE END GROVE
Radio Mast
Barracks
A52
Somerby Hill
Ministry of Transport Testing Station
B1176
Manor Farm Moat
NG33

34

92 A 93 B 94 C 95 D 96 E 97 F

NG31

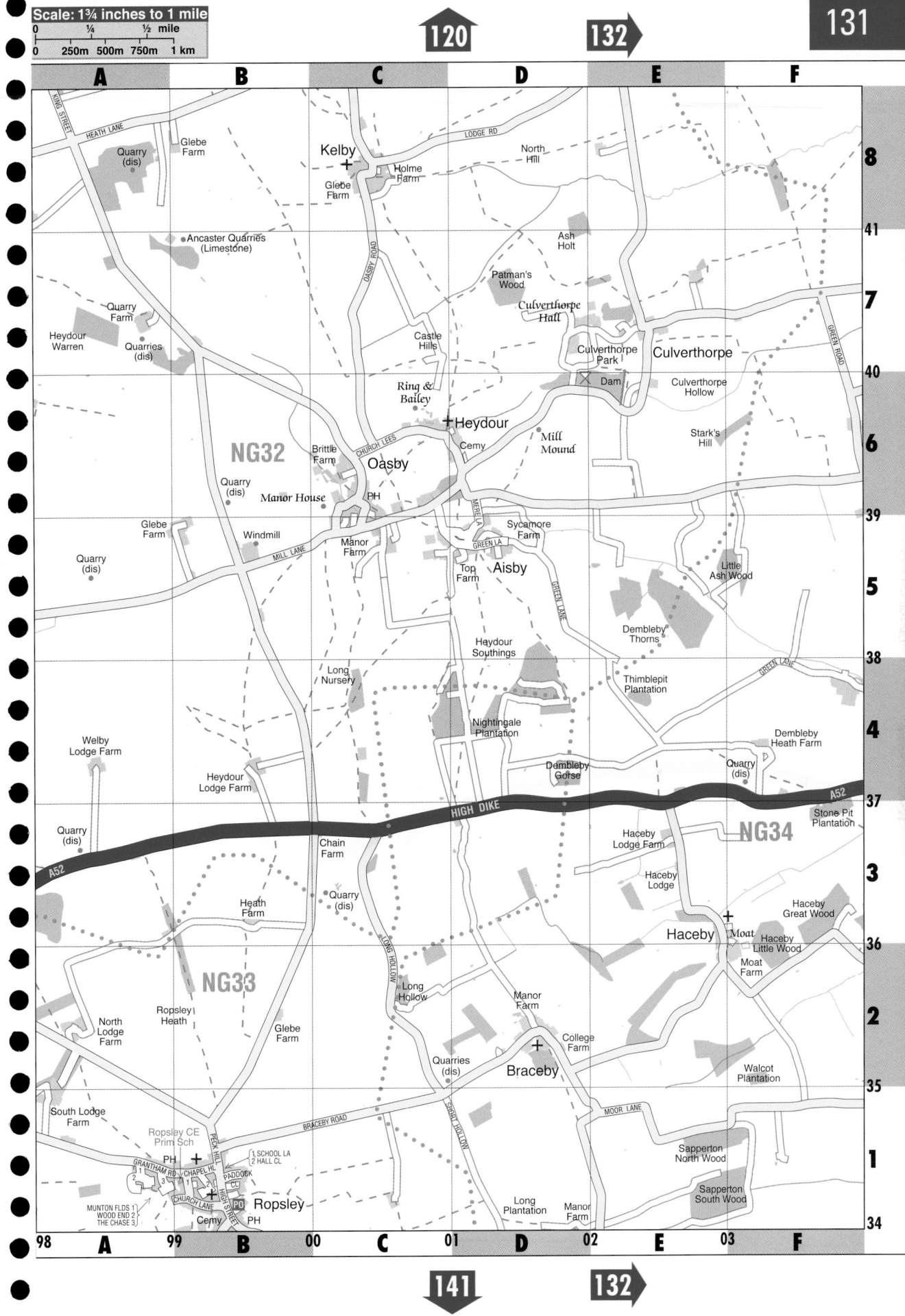

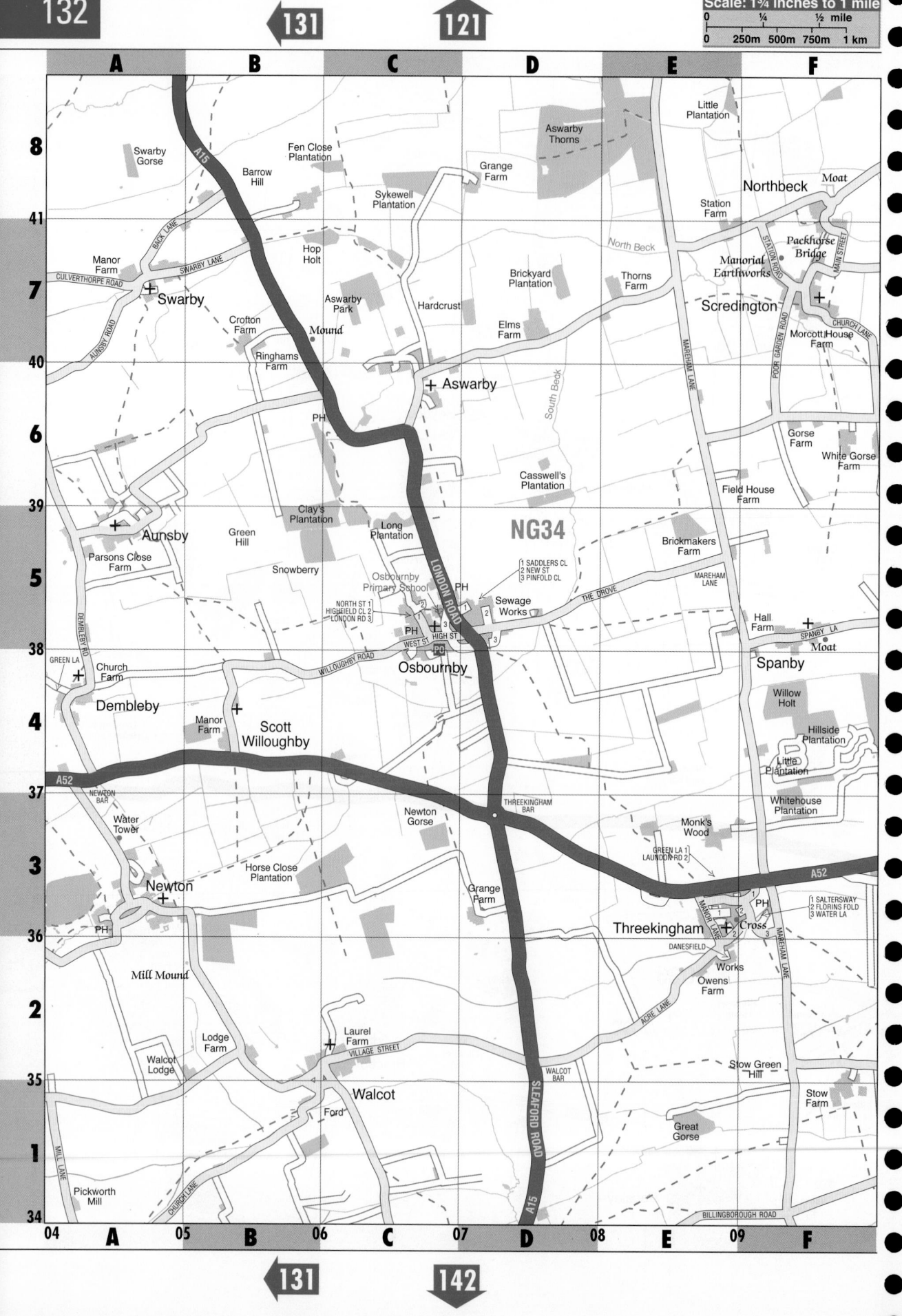

Scale: 1¾ inches to 1 mile

0   ¼   ½   mile
0 250m 500m 750m 1 km

131
121

A **B** **C** **D** **E** **F**

8

Swarby
Gorse

Fen Close
Plantation

Barrow
Hill

Aswarby
Thorns

Little
Plantation

Moat

41

Station
Farm

Northbeck

Manor
Farm

CULVERTHORPE ROAD

BACK LANE

SWARBY LANE

Hop
Holt

Sykewell
Plantation

Grange
Farm

North Beck

Manorial
Earthworks

Packhorse
Bridge

STATION ROAD

MAIN STREET

7

Swarby

Crofton
Farm

Aswarby
Park

Brickyard
Plantation

Thorns
Farm

Scredington

CHURCH LANE

Mound

Hardcrust

Morcott House
Farm

POOR GARDEN ROAD

40

AUNSBY ROAD

Ringhams
Farm

Aswarby

Elms
Farm

South Beck

MAREHAM LANE

6

PH

Casswell's
Plantation

Gorse
Farm

White Gorse
Farm

39

Clay's
Plantation

Long
Plantation

NG34

Field House
Farm

Green
Hill

Parsons Close
Farm

Snowberry

LONDON ROAD

Brickmakers
Farm

MAREHAM
LANE

5

Aunsby

Osbournby
Primary School

1 SADDLERS CL
2 NEW ST
3 PINFOLD CL

THE DROVE

PH

Hall
Farm

SPANBY LA

DEMBLEBY RD

NORTH ST 1
HIGHFIELD CL 2
LONDON RD 3

1
3
PH

Sewage
Works

Moat

38

GREEN LA

Church
Farm

PH
WEST ST
HIGH ST
2O

2
3

Osbournby

Spanby

4

Dembleby

Manor
Farm

Scott
Willoughby

Willow
Holt

Hillside
Plantation

WILLOUGHBY ROAD

Little
Plantation

37

A52

NEWTON
BAR

THREEKINGHAM BAR

Whitehouse
Plantation

Water
Tower

Newton
Gorse

Monk's
Wood

3

Horse Close
Plantation

GREEN LA 1
LAUNDON RD 2

A52

MANOR LANE

1 SALTERSWAY
2 FLORINS FOLD
3 WATER LA

Newton

Grange
Farm

Threekingham

PH
Cross

MAREHAM LANE

36

PH

DANESFIELD

Works

2

Mill Mound

ACRE LANE

Owens
Farm

Stow Green
Hill

Lodge
Farm

Laurel
Farm

VILLAGE STREET

SLEAFORD ROAD

Stow
Farm

35

Walcot
Lodge

Walcot

WALCOT
BAR

MILL LANE

CHURCH LANE

Ford

Great
Gorse

1

Pickworth
Mill

A15

BILLINGBOROUGH ROAD

34

04 **A** 05 **B** 06 **C** 07 **D** 08 **E** 09 **F**

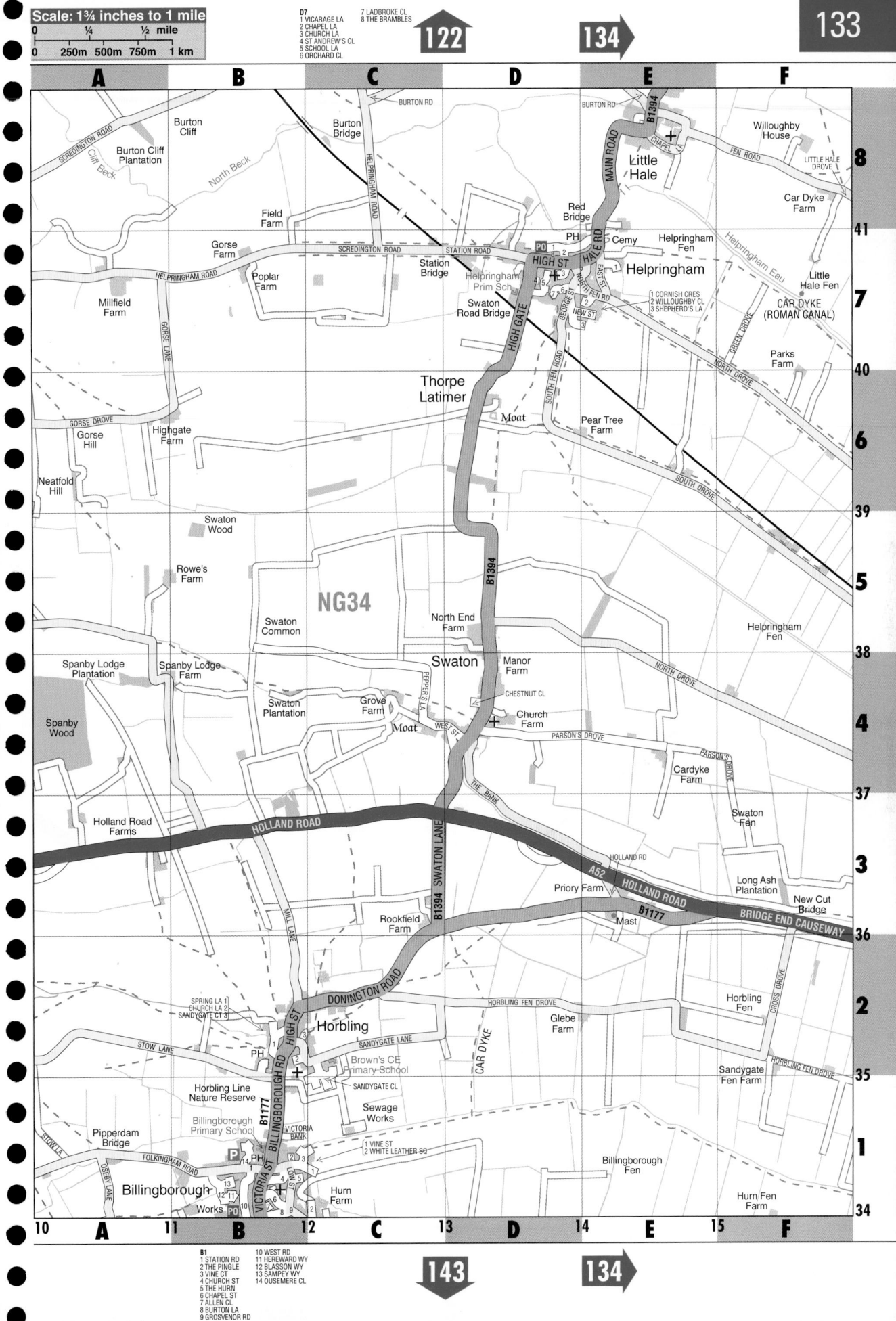

Scale: 1¾ inches to 1 mile
0 ¼ ½ mile
0 250m 500m 750m 1 km
D7
1 VICARAGE LA
2 CHAPEL LA
3 CHURCH LA
4 ST ANDREW'S CL
5 SCHOOL LA
6 ORCHARD CL
7 LADBROKE CL
8 THE BRAMBLES
122
134
Burton Cliff
Burton Cliff Plantation
Burton Bridge
Willoughby House
Little Hale
Field Farm
Red Bridge
Car Dyke Farm
Gorse Farm
Cemy
Helpringham Fen
Helpringham
Poplar Farm
Station Bridge
Helpringham Prim Sch
Little Hale Fen
Millfield Farm
Swaton Road Bridge
CAR DYKE (ROMAN CANAL)
1 CORNISH CRES
2 WILLOUGHBY CL
3 SHEPHERD'S LA
Parks Farm
Thorpe Latimer
Moat
Gorse Hill
Highgate Farm
Pear Tree Farm
Neatfold Hill
Swaton Wood
Rowe's Farm
NG34
Swaton Common
North End Farm
Helpringham Fen
Spanby Lodge Plantation
Spanby Lodge Farm
Swaton
Manor Farm
CHESTNUT CL
Swaton Plantation
Grove Farm
Church Farm
Spanby Wood
Cardyke Farm
Holland Road Farms
HOLLAND ROAD
Swaton Fen
Priory Farm
Long Ash Plantation
A52 HOLLAND ROAD
New Cut Bridge
BRIDGE END CAUSEWAY
Rookfield Farm
Mast
Horbling
Horbling Fen
Glebe Farm
SPRING LA 1
CHURCH LA 2
SANDYGATE CT 3
Brown's CE Primary School
SANDYGATE CL
Sandygate Fen Farm
Horbling Line Nature Reserve
Sewage Works
Billingborough Primary School
Pipperdam Bridge
VICTORIA BANK
1 VINE ST
2 WHITE LEATHER SQ
Billingborough Fen
Billingborough
Works
Hurn Farm
Hurn Fen Farm
B1
1 STATION RD
2 THE PINGLE
3 VINE CT
4 CHURCH ST
5 THE HURN
6 CHAPEL ST
7 ALLEN CL
8 BURTON LA
9 GROSVENOR RD
10 WEST RD
11 HEREWARD WY
12 BLASSON WY
13 SAMPEY WY
14 OUSEMERE CL
143
134

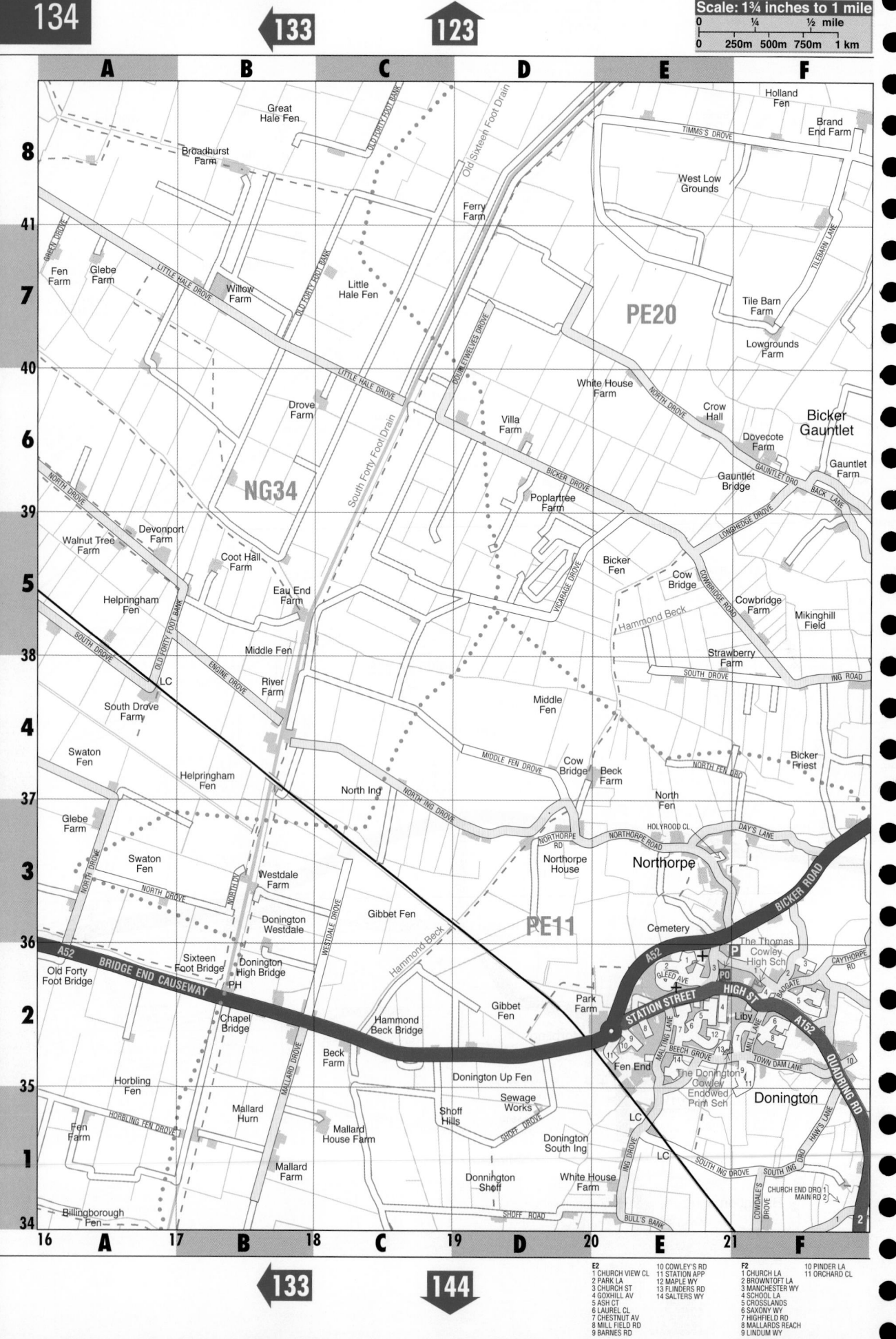

Scale: 1¾ inches to 1 mile

0   ¼   ½ mile
0   250m   500m   750m   1 km

A   B   C   D   E   F

8

41

7

40

6

39

5

38

4

37

3

36

2

35

1

34

16   A   17   B   18   C   19   D   20   E   21   F

PE20

NG34

PE11

Bicker
Gauntlet

Northorpe

Donington

Map labels:

Great Hale Fen
Broadhurst Farm
Holland Fen
Brand End Farm
West Low Grounds
Ferry Farm
Fen Farm
Glebe Farm
Willow Farm
Little Hale Fen
Tile Barn Farm
Lowgrounds Farm
Drove Farm
White House Farm
Crow Hall
Dovecote Farm
Villa Farm
Gauntlet Farm
Gauntlet Bridge
Walnut Tree Farm
Devonport Farm
Coot Hall Farm
Poplartree Farm
Bicker Fen
Cow Bridge
Cowbridge Farm
Mikinghill Field
Helpringham Fen
Eau End Farm
Middle Fen
River Farm
Strawberry Farm
South Drove Farm
Swaton Fen
Helpringham Fen
Middle Fen
Cow Bridge
Beck Farm
Bicker Priest
North Ing
North Fen
Glebe Farm
Swaton Fen
Holyrood Cl
Day's Lane
Northorpe House
Northorpe Road
Westdale Farm
Gibbet Fen
Donington Westdale
Cemetery
The Thomas Cowley High Sch
Old Forty Foot Bridge
Sixteen Foot Bridge
Donington High Bridge
Park Farm
Chapel Bridge
Hammond Beck Bridge
Beck Farm
Gibbet Fen
Fen End
Horbling Fen
Mallard Hurn
Donington Up Fen
Sewage Works
The Donington Cowley Endowed Prim Sch
Fen Farm
Mallard House Farm
Shoff Hills
Donington South Ing
White House Farm
Mallard Farm
Donnington Shoff
Billingborough Fen
Bull's Bank
LC
LC
LC
PH
A52
BRIDGE END CAUSEWAY
LITTLE HALE DROVE
NORTH DROVE
SOUTH DROVE
OLD FORTY FOOT BANK
SOUTH FORTY FOOT DRAIN
OLD SIXTEEN FOOT DRAIN
DONINGTWELVES DRIVE
VICARAGE DRIVE
BICKER DROVE
NORTH DROVE
LONGHEDGE DROVE
GAUNTLET DRO
COWBRIDGE ROAD
BACK LANE
TILEBARN LANE
TIMMS'S DROVE
BREED DROVE
ENGINE DROVE
MALLARD DRIVE
WESTDALE DRIVE
NORTH ING DROVE
MIDDLE FEN DROVE
SOUTH DROVE
ING ROAD
NORTH FEN DRO
HORBLING FEN DROVE
MALLARD DRIVE
SHOFF DRIVE
SHOFF ROAD
Hammond Beck
BICKER ROAD
QUADRING RD
HIGH ST
STATION STREET
A152
A52
ING DROVE
SOUTH ING DRIVE
SOUTH ING DRO
COWDALE'S DROVE
CHURCH END DRO
MAIN RD
CAYTHORPE RD
BADGATE
MALTING LANE
BEECH GROVE
TOWN DAM LANE
MILL LANE
HAN'S LANE
GLEED AVE
PO
P
Liby
Little Hale Drove

E2
1 CHURCH VIEW CL
2 PARK LA
3 CHURCH ST
4 GOXHILL AV
5 ASH CT
6 LAUREL CL
7 CHESTNUT AV
8 MILL FIELD RD
9 BARNES RD
10 COWLEY'S RD
11 STATION APP
12 MAPLE WY
13 FLINDERS RD
14 SALTERS WY

F2
1 CHURCH LA
2 BROWNTOFT LA
3 MANCHESTER WY
4 SCHOOL LA
5 CROSSLANDS
6 SAXONY WY
7 HIGHFIELD RD
8 MALLARDS REACH
9 LINDUM WY
10 PINDER LA
11 ORCHARD CL

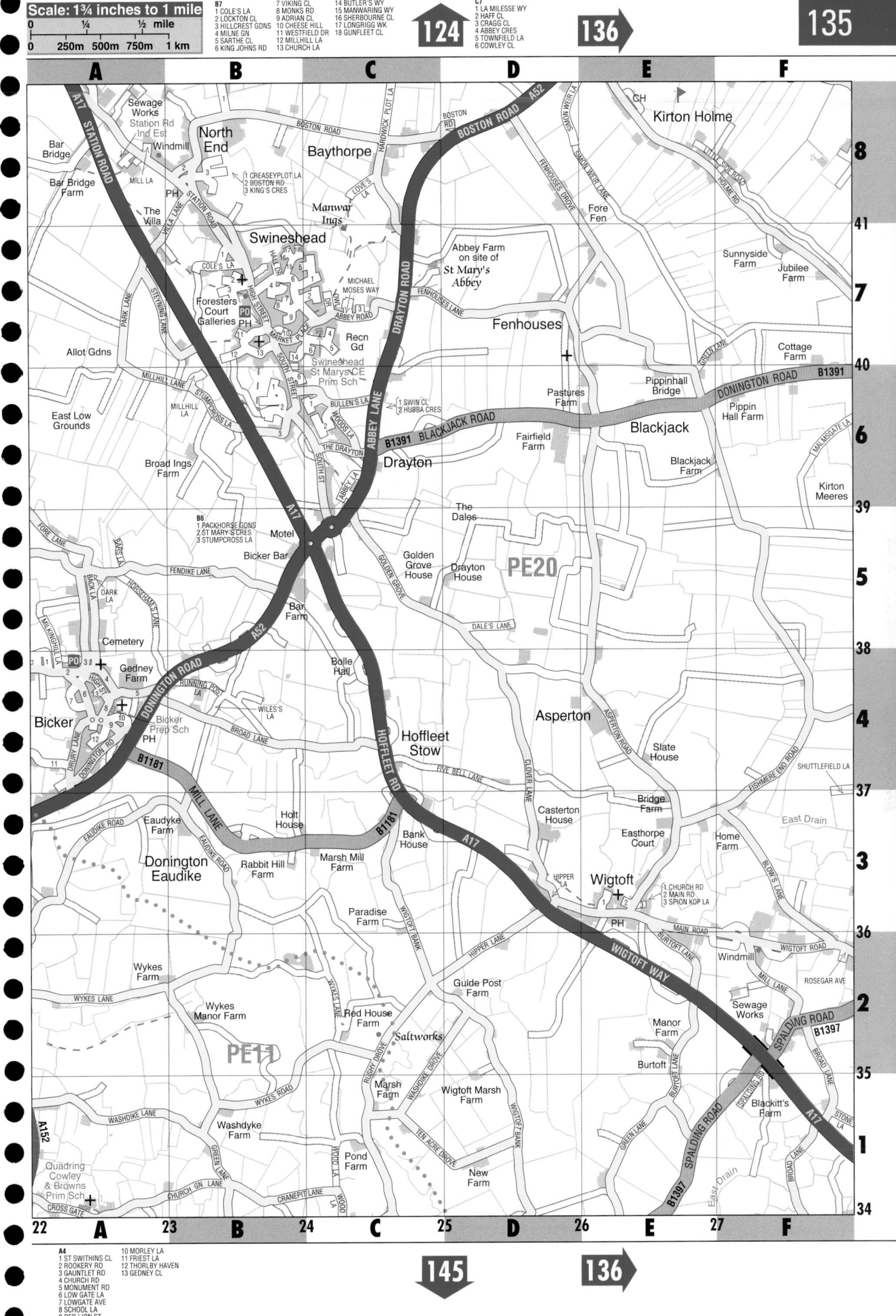

Scale: 1¾ inches to 1 mile

0   ¼   ½ mile
0   250m 500m 750m 1 km

◀ 124   136 ▶

B7
1 COLE'S LA
2 LOCKTON CL
3 HILLCREST GDNS
4 MILNE GN
5 SARTHE CL
6 KING JOHNS RD
7 VIKING CL
8 MONKS RD
9 ADRIAN CL
10 CHEESE HILL
11 WESTFIELD DR
12 MILLHILL LA
13 CHURCH LA
14 BUTLER'S WY
15 MANWARING WY
16 SHERBOURNE CL
17 LONGRIGG WK
18 GUNFLEET CL

C7
1 LA MILESSE WY
2 HAFF CL
3 CRAGG CL
4 ABBEY CRES
5 TOWNFIELD LA
6 COWLEY CL

B7 (under motel area)
1 PACKHORSE GDNS
2 ST MARY'S CRES
3 STUMPCROSS LA

A4
1 ST SWITHINS CL
2 ROOKERY RD
3 GAUNTLET RD
4 CHURCH RD
5 MONUMENT RD
6 LOW GATE LA
7 LOWGATE AVE
8 SCHOOL LA
9 RED LION ST
10 MORLEY LA
11 FRIEST LA
12 THORLBY HAVEN
13 GEDNEY CL

145   136 ▶

136

◄ **135**

▲ **125**

▲ **208**

Scale: 1¾ inches to 1 mile

0   ¼   ½ mile
0   250m   500m   750m   1 km

Map grid columns: A B C D E F (top), labeled 28 A 29 B 30 C 31 D 32 E 33 F (bottom)
Map grid rows: 8, 41, 7, 40, 6, 39, 5, 38, 4, 37, 3, 36, 2, 35, 1, 34

PE21
PE20

Place names and labels:

Lilley's Bridge, Old Hammond Beck, Orange House Farm, Frampton Bank, Silvertoft Lane, Slate House Farm, Holmes Farm, Holmes Road, Yew Tree Farm, Cherry Tree Farm, Whitebread Rd, Kirton Holme Road, Green La, B1391, Donington Road, Mathgate La, Washdike Road, Chapelgate, Multon Ings Lane, Badgers Lane, Church Gn Lane, Chapel Farm, Kirton End, Willoughby House, Willington Rd, Welcome Farm, Willington Road, West End Road, Bannister's La, Ralphs Lane, Fen Road, Five House Lane, Spotfield Lane, Mast, Frampton West End, Radio Mast, Frampton House Farm, Browns Farm, St Leodegar's, Millfield Lane West, Sewage Works, Millfield Lane East, Wyberton, London Road, Tytton Lane West, Tytton Lane East, Wells Pl, A16, B1397, Tytton Hall, PH, Sports Club, PO, Wyberton Prim Sch, Causeway, Solway Ave, Yarborough Rd, Wallace Way, Field Dr, Birch Cl, Low Rd, Wyberton Park, Streetway, Wybert's Castle (Earthwork), Blacks Farm, Baptist Farm, Heron Wy, Marsh La, Bittern Wy, Slippery Gowt La, Wyberton Lw Rd, Glosshill La, Green La, Bunkers Hill Lane, Church Rd, Rowdyke Road

Chestnut Farm, Drainside, Hill Lane, Meeres Lane, Minns Farm, Kirton Drain, Bungley Lane, Middlegate, Kirton Cemy, B1192, Church La, Vicarage Dr, Manor Rd, Laburnum Gdns, Government Offices, Church Mdws, Kirton Prim Sch, Liby, PO, 1 SENTANCE CRES, 2 FYSON WY, 3 SENTANCE CRES, 4 GROSVENOR RD, 5 WALNUT RD, 6 THE FAIRWAYS, 1 MIDDLEGATE RD WEST, 2 LENTON WY, Park's Farm, Horseshoe La, Keal Dr, 1 PEAR TREE RD, 2 FRANKS CL, 3 JACKSON DR, 4 CRAVEN AVE, 5 PELL'S DR, 6 STATION RD, 7 KIME MEWS, Middlegate Rd East, Catbridge Lane, Frampton, Catts Edyke Lane, Sandholme Lane, Manor Farm, Frampton Roads, Frampton Towns Drain, Thorniman Lane, Hall Lane

Fishmere End, Grange Farm, B1397, Aaron Way, Thorne Wy, Princess Rd, Drainside South, West Road, Kirton Drain, Kirton, Kirton Distribution Park, Beechtree Farm, Southfield Farm, Sandholme, Moat, Skeldyke Road, Eleven Acre La, Skeldyke, Bool Lane, Nibb's Lane, Silt Lane, Burton House, Hospital Farm, Bunkway Lane

Fishmere End Road, Cherry Holt La, Roper's Bridge Lane, Boston Road, Strugg's Hill, Christians Farm, Strugg's Hill Lane, Red Barn Lane, Colder Bridge, Archers La, Ivy House Farm, Dean's Farm, The Farm, Elms Farm, Crook Green Farm, Seadyke Road, Seadyke, Bucklegate, Slade Bridge, Slade House, Bucklegate Lane, Clough Rd, Lentons Farm, Hundred Acre Farm, Three Towns Drain, Slate House Farm, Recn Gd, Monarchs Rd, Sutterton, Hall Lane, Green Lane, Red Barn La, Rainwall's La

Spalding Road, PO, PH, The Fourfields CE Sch, Cerny, Algakirk, Church La, Spalding Rd, Endeavour Wy, Enterprise Park, Limes Farm, Station Road, Low Lane, Stone Lane, Waterbelly La, A16, A17, West Field Farm, Church Lane, Gells Farm, Work Dike Road, Pitcher Row La, Countwade Bridge, Mandike Road, Mandike Bridge, Five Towns Drain, Hill Six Acres, Bush Green La, Mill Lane, Roundlands, Woodlands Farm, White House Farm, Villa Farm, Little Farm, Fosdyke Villa, Low Mill Lane, Lamming's Marsh Farm, Pilton's La, Earl Marsh, Waterbelly La

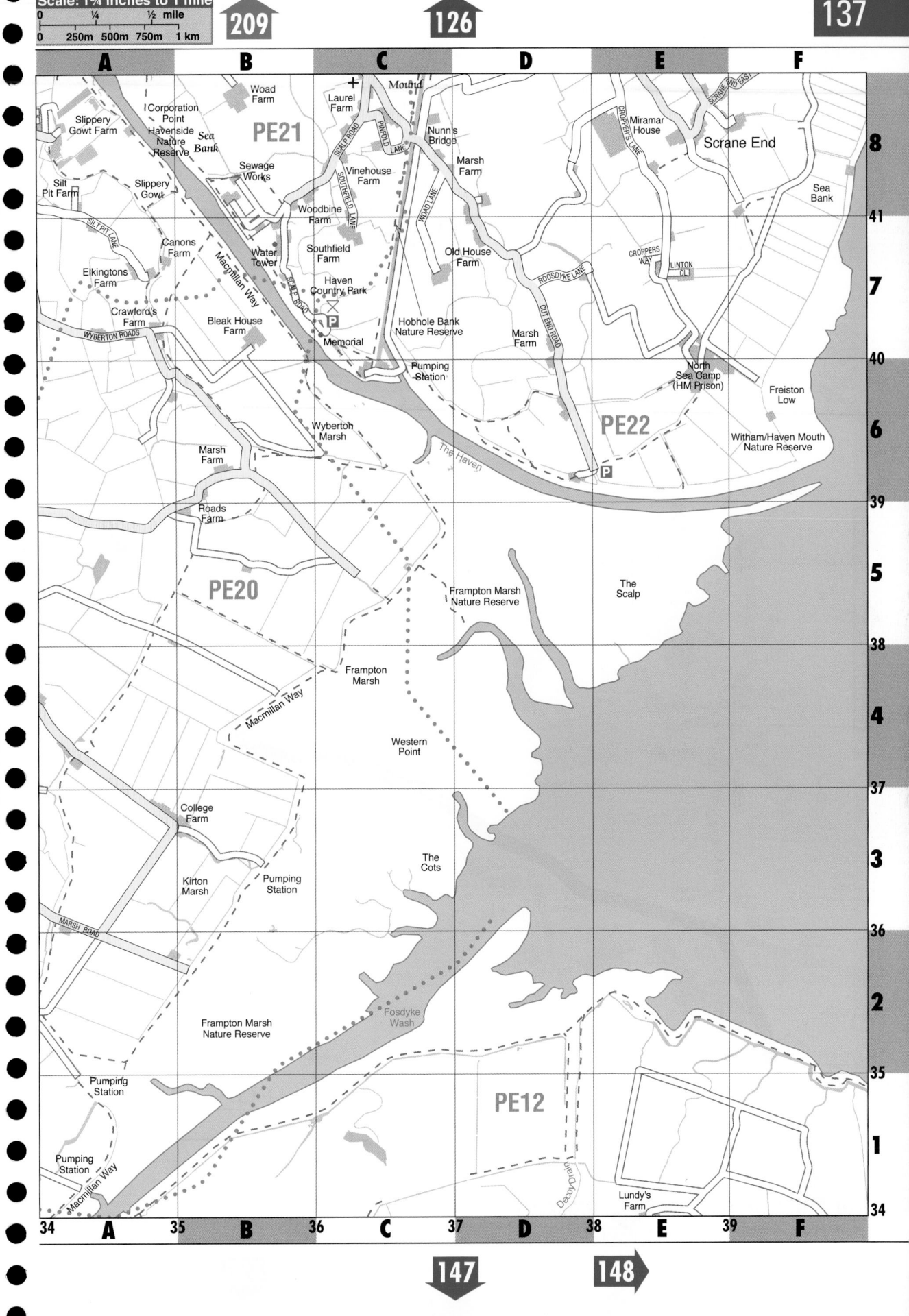

A   B   C   D   E   F

8
41
7
40
6
39
5
38
4
37
3
36
2
35
1
34

Slippery Gowt Farm
Corporation Point
Haverside Nature Reserve
Sea Bank
Woad Farm
PE21
Laurel Farm
Mound
Nunn's Bridge
Miramar House
SCRANE END EAST
Scrane End

Silt Pit Farm
Slippery Gowt
Sewage Works
Vinehouse Farm
Marsh Farm
CROPPER'S LANE
SILT PIT LANE
SCALP ROAD
PINFOLD LD
SOUTHFIELD LANE
WOAD LANE
Sea Bank

Canons Farm
Woodbine Farm
Macmillan Way
Water Tower
Southfield Farm
Old House Farm
CROPPERS WAY
LINTON CL

Elkingtons Farm
Crawford's Farm
Haven Country Park
ROOSDYKE LANE
CUT END ROAD

WYBERTON ROADS
Bleak House Farm
SCALP ROAD
P
Memorial
Hobhole Bank Nature Reserve
PE22

Marsh Farm

Pumping Station
Marsh Farm
North Sea Camp (HM Prison)
Freiston Low

Wyberton Marsh
The Haven
P
Witham/Haven Mouth Nature Reserve

Marsh Farm

Roads Farm

PE20
Frampton Marsh Nature Reserve
The Scalp

Frampton Marsh
Macmillan Way
Western Point

College Farm
The Cots

Kirton Marsh
Pumping Station

MARSH ROAD

Frampton Marsh Nature Reserve
Fosdyke Wash

Pumping Station

Pumping Station
Macmillan Way
PE12
Decoy Drain
Lundy's Farm

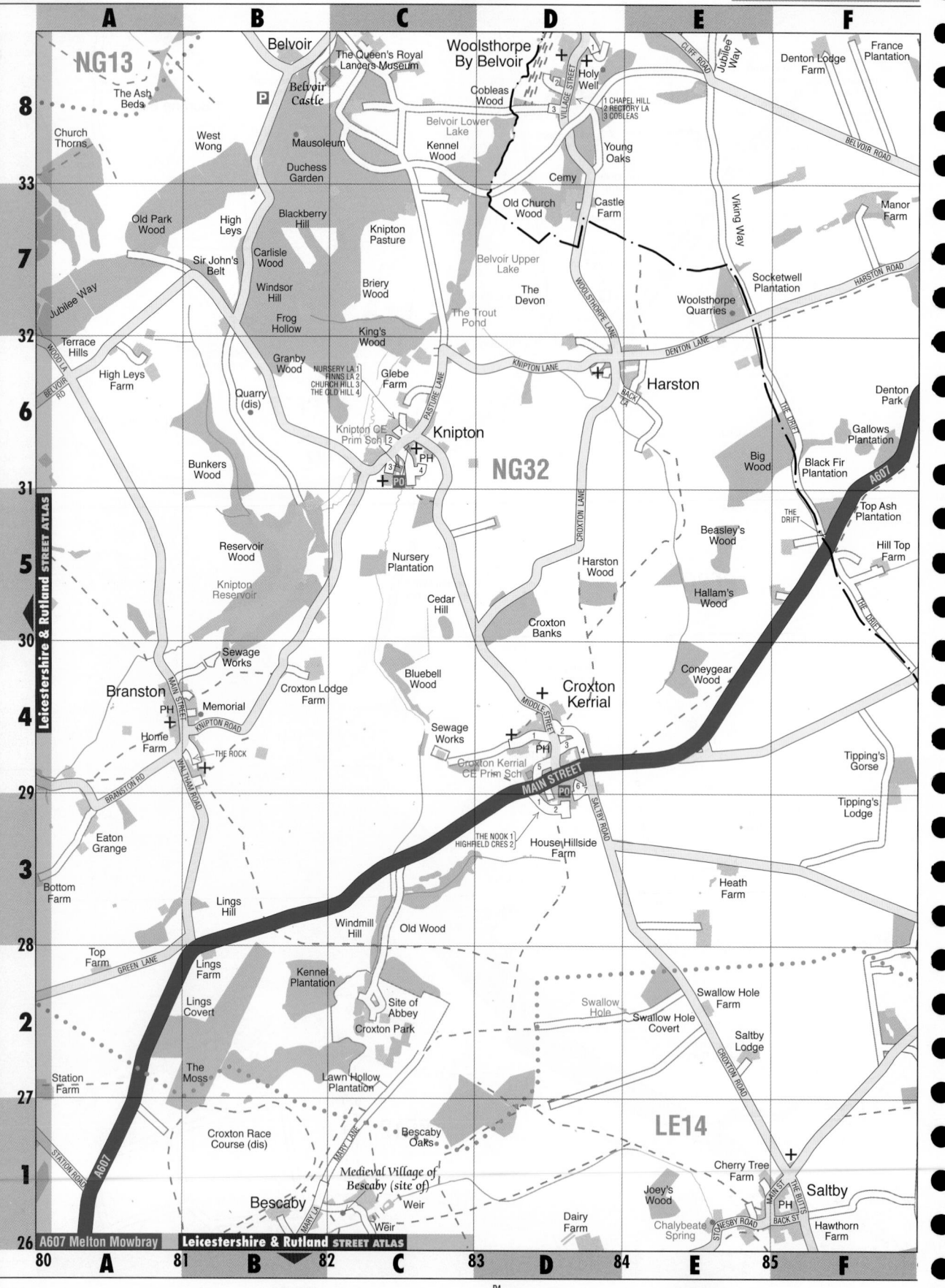

Scale: 1¾ inches to 1 mile

0   ¼   ½   mile
0   250m 500m 750m 1 km

A | **B** | **C** | **D** | **E** | **F**

NG13

The Ash Beds

Church Thorns

Belvoir

The Queen's Royal Lancers Museum

P

Belvoir Castle

Mausoleum

West Wong

Duchess Garden

Belvoir Lower Lake

Kennel Wood

Woolsthorpe By Belvoir

Cobleas Wood

Holy Well

1 CHAPEL HILL
2 RECTORY LA
3 COBLEAS

Denton Lodge Farm

France Plantation

Jubilee Way

BELVOIR ROAD

33

Old Park Wood

High Leys

Blackberry Hill

Knipton Pasture

Young Oaks

Cemy

Manor Farm

7

Sir John's Belt

Carlisle Wood

Windsor Hill

Briery Wood

Belvoir Upper Lake

The Devon

Old Church Wood

Castle Farm

Viking Way

Socketwell Plantation

Woolsthorpe Quarries

HARSTON ROAD

Jubilee Way

Terrace Hills

Frog Hollow

King's Wood

The Trout Pond

32

BELVOIR RD

WOODLA

High Leys Farm

Granby Wood

Quarry (dis)

Glebe Farm

NURSERY LA 1
FINNS LA 2
CHURCH HILL 3
THE OLD HILL 4

PASTURE LANE

Knipton Lane

KNIPTON LANE

DENTON LANE

Harston

BACK LA

Denton Park

6

Knipton CE Prim Sch

Knipton

PH

NG32

Gallows Plantation

THE DRIFT

Black Fir Plantation

A607

Bunkers Wood

Reservoir Wood

PO

Nursery Plantation

CROXTON LANE

Harston Wood

Beasley's Wood

THE DRIFT

Top Ash Plantation

Hill Top Farm

31

Knipton Reservoir

Cedar Hill

Croxton Banks

Hallam's Wood

THE DRIFT

5

Bluebell Wood

Sewage Works

Coneygear Wood

30

Branston

PH

Memorial

Sewage Works

Croxton Lodge Farm

Croxton Kerrial

MIDDLE STREET

PH

Tipping's Gorse

4

Home Farm

KNIPTON ROAD

THE ROCK

Croxton Kerrial CE Prim Sch

MAIN STREET

PO

SALTBY ROAD

Tipping's Lodge

29

BRANSTON RD

NN THAM ROAD

Eaton Grange

THE NOOK 1
HIGHFIELD CRES 2

House Hillside Farm

Heath Farm

3

Bottom Farm

Lings Hill

Windmill Hill

Old Wood

28

Top Farm

GREEN LANE

Lings Farm

Kennel Plantation

Swallow Hole

Swallow Hole Covert

Swallow Hole Farm

Saltby Lodge

2

Lings Covert

Site of Abbey

Croxton Park

MARY LANE

CROXTON ROAD

27

Station Farm

The Moss

Lawn Hollow Plantation

LE14

STATION ROAD

A607

Croxton Race Course (dis)

MARY LA

Bescaby Oaks

Cherry Tree Farm

Joey's Wood

MAIN ST

Saltby

1

Bescaby

Medieval Village of Bescaby (site of)

Weir

Weir

Dairy Farm

Chalybeate Spring

STONESBY ROAD

BACK ST

PH

THE BUTTS

Hawthorn Farm

26

A607 Melton Mowbray

Leicestershire & Rutland STREET ATLAS

80 | A | 81 | B | 82 | C | 83 | D | 84 | E | 85 | F

D4
1 CHAPEL LA
2 CHURCH LA
3 THORPES LA
4 TOP RD
5 SCHOOL LA
6 SHIRES ORCH
7 MILL LA

Leicestershire & Rutland STREET ATLAS

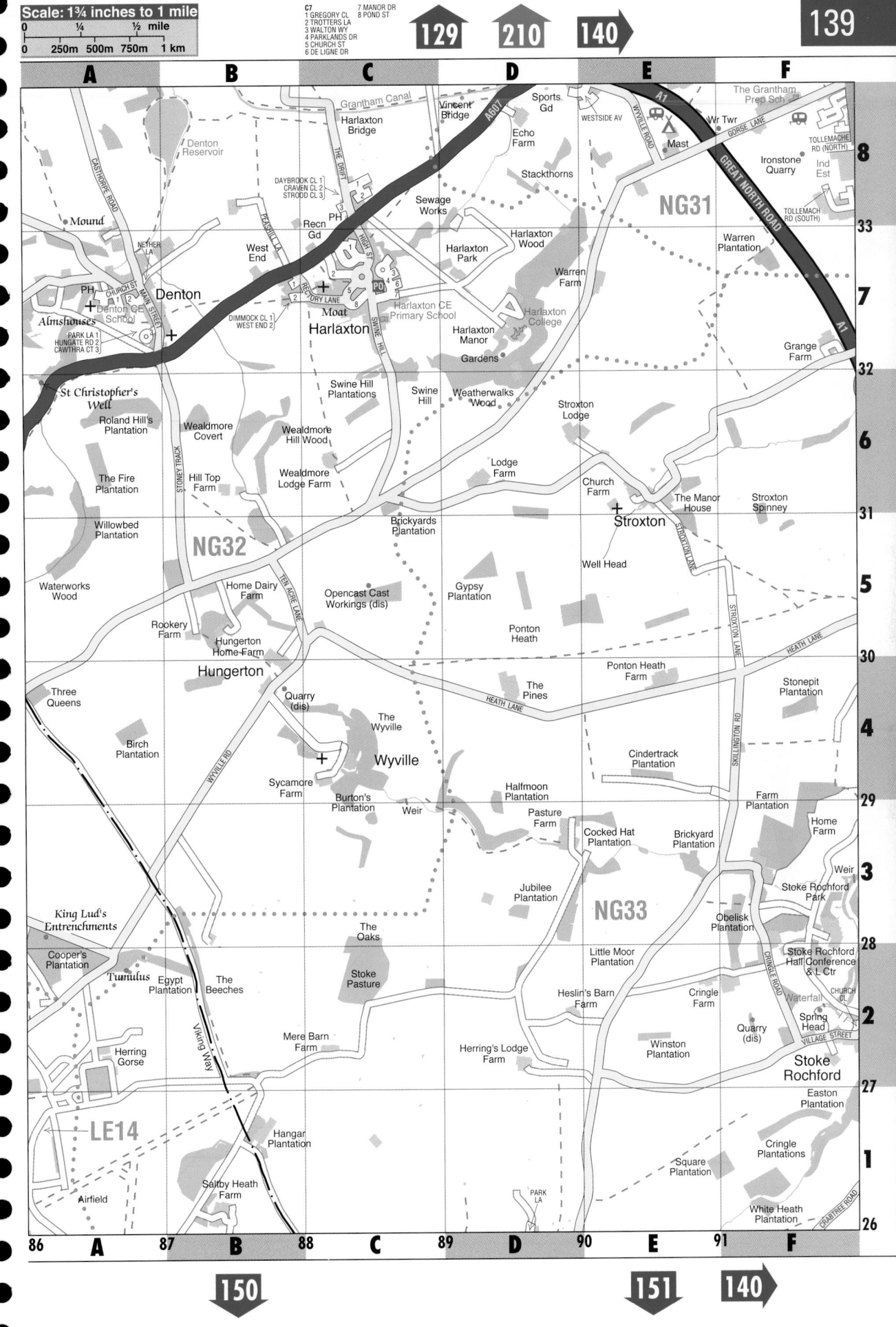

Scale: 1¾ inches to 1 mile

| 0 | ¼ | ½ mile |

| 0 | 250m | 500m | 750m | 1 km |

C7
1 GREGORY CL
2 TROTTERS LA
3 WALTON WY
4 PARKLANDS DR
5 CHURCH ST
6 DE LIGNE DR
7 MANOR DR
8 POND ST

129   210   140   139

A B C D E F

8
33
7
32
6
31
5
30
4
29
3
28
2
27
1
26

The Grantham Prep Sch

Grantham Canal

Denton Reservoir

Mound

NETHER LA

PH

Almshouses

Denton CE School

PARK LA 1
HUNGATE RD 2
CAWTHRA CT 3

St Christopher's Well

CHURCH ST
MAIN STREET

Denton

West End

Harlaxton Bridge

THE DRIFT

PEASHILL LA

DAYBROOK CL 1
CRAVEN CL 2
STROOD CL 3

Recn Gd

PH

HIGH ST

DIMMOCK CL 1
WEST END 2

RECTORY LANE

Moat

Harlaxton

PO

Harlaxton Park

Harlaxton CE Primary School

SWINE HILL

Vincent Bridge

A607

Sewage Works

Echo Farm

Stackthorns

Harlaxton Wood

Warren Farm

Harlaxton Manor

Harlaxton College

Gardens

Sports Gd

WESTSIDE AV

A1

WYVILLE ROAD

Mast

Wr Twr

GORSE LANE

GREAT NORTH ROAD

Ironstone Quarry

Warren Plantation

NG31

TOLLEMACHE RD (NORTH)

Ind Est

TOLLEMACHE RD (SOUTH)

Grange Farm

Roland Hill's Plantation

Wealdmore Covert

STONEY TRACK

Hill Top Farm

Wealdmore Hill Wood

Wealdmore Lodge Farm

Swine Hill Plantations

Swine Hill

Weatherwalks Wood

Lodge Farm

Stroxton Lodge

Church Farm

Stroxton

The Manor House

Stroxton Spinney

The Fire Plantation

Willowbed Plantation

NG32

Brickyards Plantation

Well Head

Waterworks Wood

Home Dairy Farm

TEN ACRE LANE

Opencast Cast Workings (dis)

Gypsy Plantation

Ponton Heath

STROXTON LANE

HEATH LANE

Rookery Farm

Hungerton Home Farm

Hungerton

Quarry (dis)

The Wyville

Ponton Heath Farm

Stonepit Plantation

SKILLINGTON RD

Three Queens

Birch Plantation

WYVILLE RD

Sycamore Farm

Wyville

Burton's Plantation

Weir

The Pines

Halfmoon Plantation

Pasture Farm

Cinderbrack Plantation

Farm Plantation

Home Farm

Weir

Cocked Hat Plantation

Brickyard Plantation

Stoke Rochford Park

King Lud's Entrenchments

Cooper's Plantation

Tumulus

Egypt Plantation

The Beeches

VIKING WAY

The Oaks

Stoke Pasture

Jubilee Plantation

NG33

Little Moor Plantation

Heslin's Barn Farm

Cringle Farm

Obelisk Plantation

CRINGLE ROAD

Stoke Rochford Hall Conference & L Ctr

Waterfall

CHURCH CL

Spring Head

VILLAGE STREET

Stoke Rochford

Herring Gorse

Mere Barn Farm

Herring's Lodge Farm

Winston Plantation

Quarry (dis)

LE14

Airfield

Hangar Plantation

Saltby Heath Farm

PARK LA

Square Plantation

Cringle Plantations

White Heath Plantation

CRABTREE ROAD

211
139
130

Scale: 1¾ inches to 1 mile

0   ¼   ½   mile
0   250m   500m   750m   1 km

A **B** **C** **D** **E** **F**

8

NG31

Whalebone Spinney

Water Works

Twentytwo Acre Plantation

33

Tumulus

Valley Plantation

Woodnook Farm

Griff's Plantation

Old Somerby

B1176

PO

Quarry (dis)

PH

GRANTHAM RD BOURNE ROAD

SCHOOL LA

THE PASTURES

CHURCH LA

ROPSLEY RD

7

Little Ponton

Weir

Woodnook

The Lodge

32

B1174

Adam's Well

Dalepond Plantation

GREAT NORTH RD

Park Farm

Woodnook Plantation

Farmstead Plantation

6

Valley Farm

River Witham

Ponton Park Wood

Poplar Farm

BRACKENBURY FIELDS

31

Gibbet Hill

Ford

HELL LANE

Boothby Great Wood

Dairy Farm

Brackenbury Farm

Great Wood Farm

Boothby Pagnell

MAIN STREET

SCHOOL LA

B1176

5

Great Ponton

Sewage Works

Great Ponton CE Prim Sch

DALLYGATE LANE

Ponton Great Wood

PONTON ROAD

Boothby Pagnell Manor House

Manor Farm

Boothby Hall

West Glen River

Heath Lane

PH

1 MILL LA
2 ARCHERS WY
3 THE TERRACE
4 CRINGLEWAY
5 ELLYSLANDE
6 BLUE HORSE CT

Quarry (Limestone)

B6403 HIGH DYKE

30

Lodge Farm

Quarry (dis)

Ermine Street Farm

Bassingthorpe New Plantation

NG33

4

Cringle Brook

A1

Lodge Plantation

PIT LANE

Pasture Farm

Lower Bassingthorpe

Sycamore Farm

Valley Farm

29

Mast

Air Shaft

Manor Farm

3

WASHDIKE LANE

Ford

Highdyke Farm

Stoke Tunnel

Bassingthorpe Spoil Bank

Bassingthorpe

Manor House

Moat

Hall Farm

Westby

28

Water Tower

Maiden Bower

Stoke Grange Farm

Stoke Park Wood

Westby

Lodge Farm

WESTBY ROAD

2

CH

River Witham

VILLAGE ST

PO

Church Farm

EASTON LANE

Post Office Plantation

Quarries (dis)

Park Farm

Old Park Farm

Stoke Park Wood

Old Park Wood

27

Easton Lodge

Easton Walled Garden

Home Farm

Easton

Easton Cold Store

Lownd Wood

1

Easton Park

Water Tower

PLANTING ROAD

BURTON LANE

B6403

Dumpling Farm

Sleight's Wood

BURTON LANE

26

CRABTREE RD

A1

Easton Farm

92   **A**   93   **B**   94   **C**   95   **D**   96   **E**   97   **F**

139
151
152

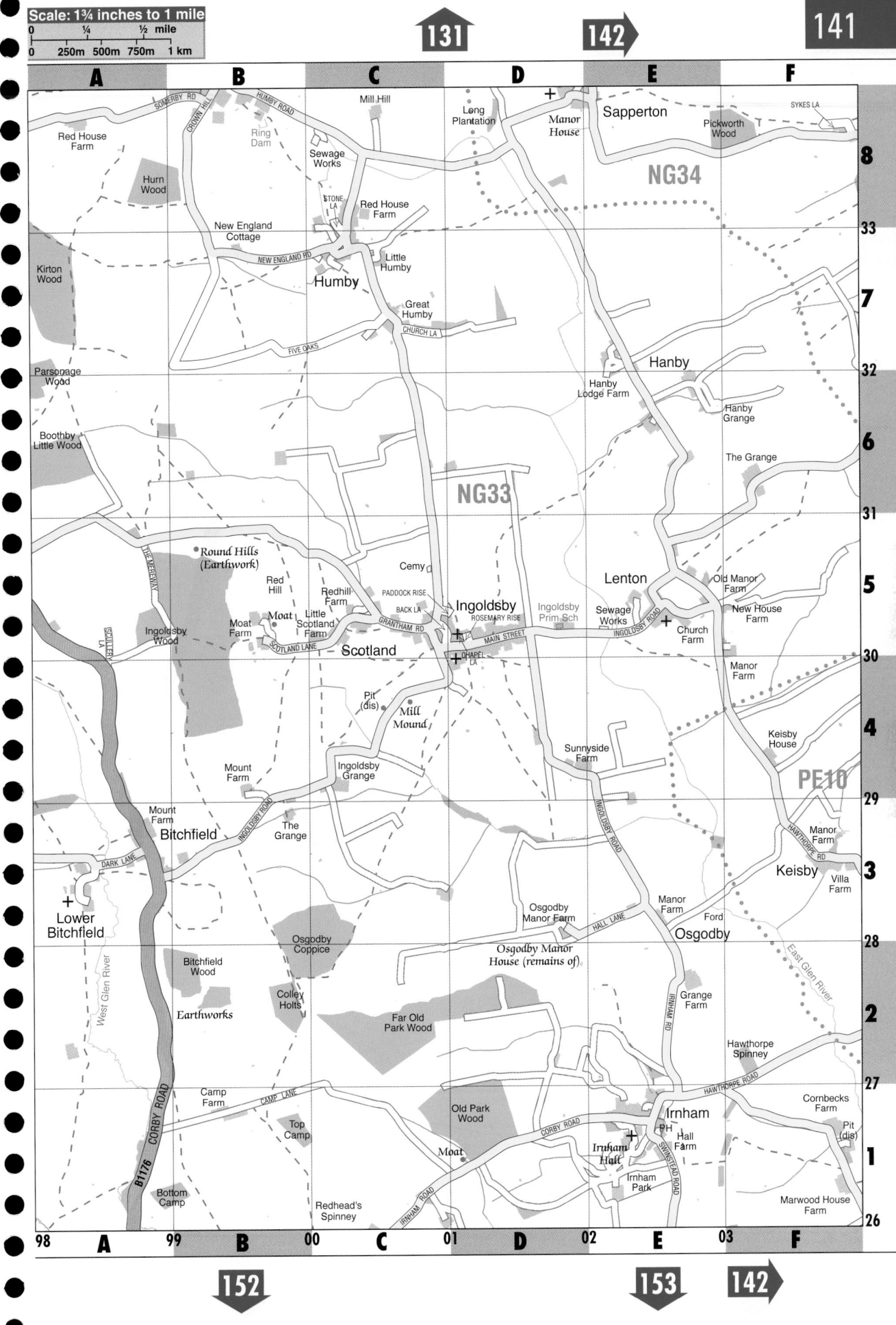
Scale: 1¾ inches to 1 mile
0 ¼ ½ mile
0 250m 500m 750m 1 km
131
142
A B C D E F
Red House Farm
Hurn Wood
Kirton Wood
Parsonage Wood
Boothby Little Wood
SOMERBY RD
CROWN HILL
HUMBY ROAD
Ring Dam
Mill Hill
Sewage Works
STONE LA
Red House Farm
New England Cottage
NEW ENGLAND RD
Little Humby
Humby
Great Humby
CHURCH LA
FIVE OAKS
Long Plantation
Manor House
Sapperton
Pickworth Wood
SYKES LA
NG34
Hanby
Hanby Lodge Farm
Hanby Grange
The Grange
NG33
Round Hills (Earthwork)
THE MEREWAY
Red Hill
Redhill Farm
Cemy
PADDOCK RISE
BACK LA
Ingoldsby
ROSEMARY RISE
Ingoldsby Prim Sch
Sewage Works
Lenton
Old Manor Farm
New House Farm
INGOLDSBY ROAD
Church Farm
Moat
Moat Farm
Little Scotland Farm
GRANTHAM RD
MAIN STREET
SCOTLAND LANE
Scotland
CHAPEL LA
Ingoldsby Wood
SCULLERY LA
Manor Farm
Pit (dis)
Mill Mound
Keisby House
Sunnyside Farm
Mount Farm
Ingoldsby Grange
PE10
Mount Farm
Bitchfield
INGOLDSBY ROAD
The Grange
INGOLDSBY ROAD
HAWTHORPE RD
Manor Farm
DARK LANE
Keisby
Villa Farm
Lower Bitchfield
Osgodby Manor Farm
HALL LANE
Manor Farm
Ford
Osgodby
Osgodby Coppice
Osgodby Manor House (remains of)
East Glen River
Bitchfield Wood
West Glen River
Colley Holts
Earthworks
Far Old Park Wood
IRNHAM RD
Grange Farm
Hawthorpe Spinney
HAWTHORPE ROAD
Camp Farm
CAMP LANE
Old Park Wood
Irnham
Cornbecks Farm
Top Camp
CORBY ROAD
PH
Hall Farm
Pit (dis)
CORBY ROAD
B1176
Moat
Irnham Hall
SWINSTEAD ROAD
Irnham Park
Bottom Camp
Redhead's Spinney
IRNHAM ROAD
Marwood House Farm
8 33 7 32 6 31 5 30 4 29 3 28 2 27 1 26
98 99 00 01 02 03
152
153
142

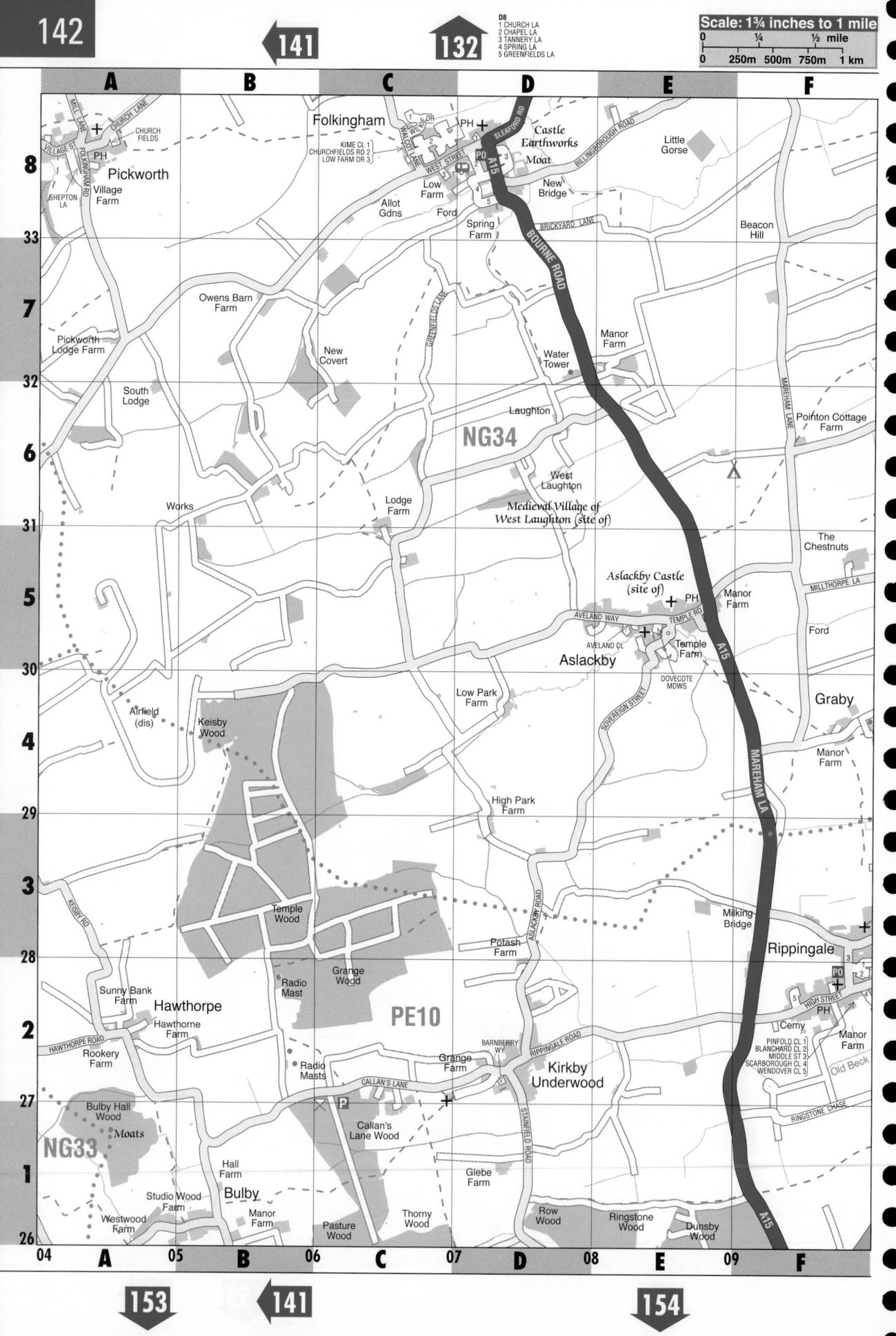

D8
1 CHURCH LA
2 CHAPEL LA
3 TANNERY LA
4 SPRING LA
5 GREENFIELDS LA

Scale: 1¾ inches to 1 mile
0   ¼   ½ mile
0 250m 500m 750m 1 km

A   B   C   D   E   F

8

Pickworth
Village Farm
PH
Shepton La
Village Farm
Church Lane
Church Fields
Mill Lane
Folkingham Road

Folkingham
Windsor
Waldot Lane
West Street
PH
Castle Earthworks
Moat
New Bridge
Billingborough Road
KIME CL 1
CHURCHFIELDS RD 2
LOW FARM DR 3
PO
A15
Low Farm
Ford
Allot Gdns
Spring Farm

Little Gorse

33

Beacon Hill

Brickyard Lane

7

Owens Barn Farm
Greenfields Lane
Bourne Road

Manor Farm

Pickworth Lodge Farm
New Covert
Water Tower

Mareham Lane

32

South Lodge
Laughton

NG34
West Laughton
Pointon Cottage Farm

6

Works
Lodge Farm
Medieval Village of West Laughton (site of)

The Chestnuts

31

Aslackby Castle (site of)
PH
Manor Farm
Millthorpe La

5

Aveland Way
Temple Rd
Ford
Aveland Cl
Temple Farm
A15

30

Aslackby
Dovecote Mdws

Graby

Airfield (dis)
Keisby Wood
Low Park Farm
Sovereign Street
Manor Farm

4

High Park Farm
Mareham La

29

3

Temple Wood
Aslackby Road
Milking Bridge

Rippingale

28

Potash Farm
PO
PH
High Street
3
2

Sunny Bank Farm
Hawthorpe
Radio Mast
Grange Wood
PE10
Barnberry Wy
Rippingale Road
Cemy
PINFOLD CL 1
BLANCHARD CL 2
MIDDLE ST 3
SCARBOROUGH CL 4
WENDOVER CL 5

2

Hawthorne Farm
Rookery Farm
Hawthorpe Road
Radio Masts
Grange Farm
Kirkby Underwood
Manor Farm
Old Beck

27

Bulby Hall Wood
Moats
Callan's Lane
Callan's Lane Wood
Stainfield Road
Ringstone Chase

NG33

Hall Farm
Bulby
Glebe Farm

1

Westwood Farm
Studio Wood Farm
Manor Farm
Pasture Wood
Thorny Wood
Row Wood
Ringstone Wood
Dunsby Wood
A15

26

04   A   05   B   06   C   07   D   08   E   09   F

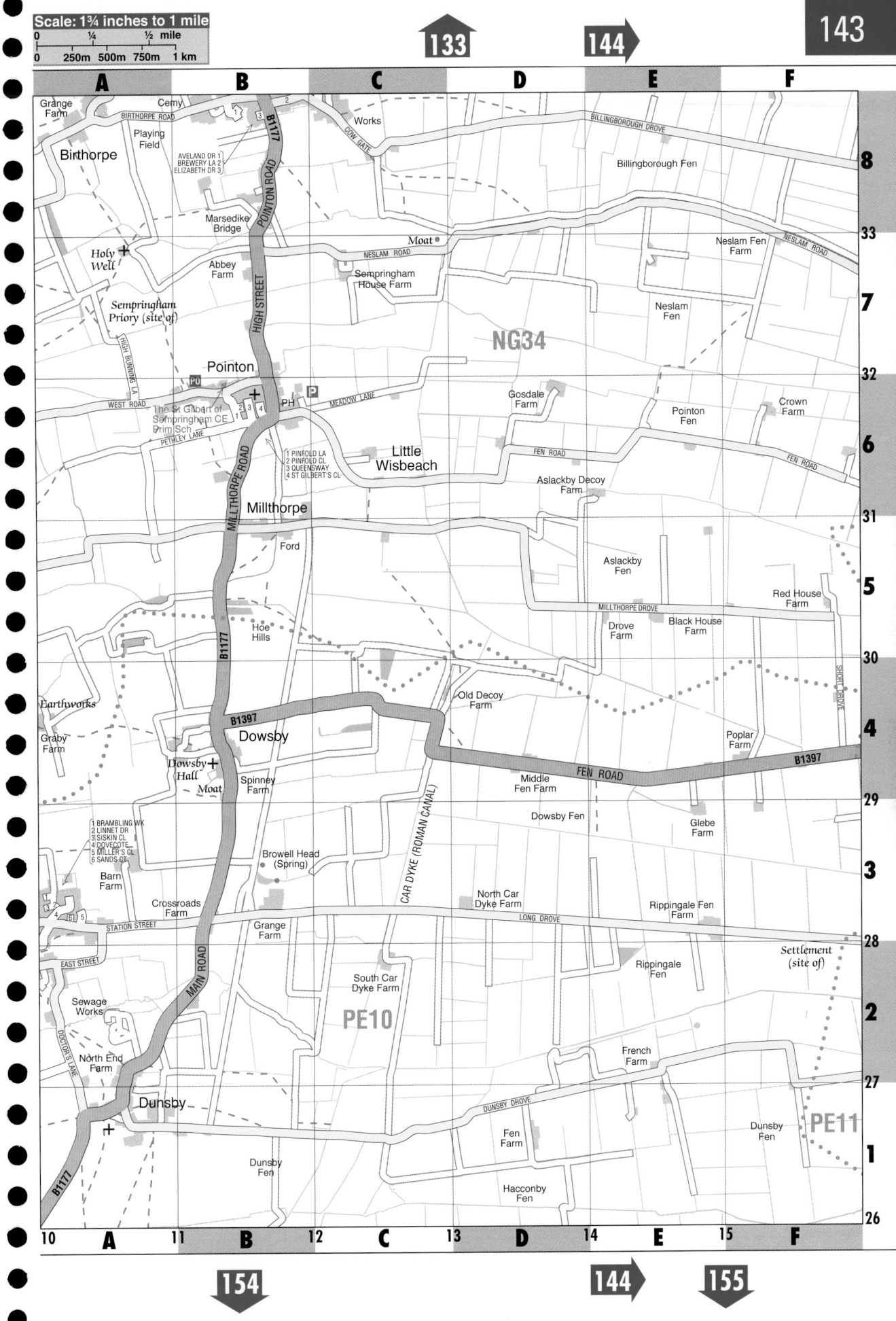

Scale: 1¾ inches to 1 mile
0 ¼ ½ mile
0 250m 500m 750m 1 km
133
144
A B C D E F
Grange Farm
Cemy
BIRTHORPE ROAD
Works
BILLINGBOROUGH DROVE
Playing Field
Birthorpe
AVELAND DR 1
BREWERY LA 2
ELIZABETH DR 3
B1177
COW GATE
POINTON ROAD
Billingborough Fen
Marsedike Bridge
Moat
NESLAM ROAD
Holy Well
Abbey Farm
Sempringham House Farm
Neslam Fen Farm
HIGH STREET
Sempringham Priory (site of)
Neslam Fen
NG34
HIGH BUNNING LA
Pointon
PH
MEADOW LANE
Gosdale Farm
Pointon Fen
Crown Farm
WEST ROAD
The St Gilbert of Sempringham CE Prim Sch
PETHLEY LANE
1 PINFOLD LA
2 PINFOLD CL
3 QUEENSWAY
4 ST GILBERT'S CL
Little Wisbeach
FEN ROAD
MILLTHORPE ROAD
Aslackby Decoy Farm
Millthorpe
Ford
Aslackby Fen
Red House Farm
MILLTHORPE DROVE
Drove Farm
Black House Farm
Hoe Hills
B1177
SHORT DROVE
Earthworks
Old Decoy Farm
B1397
Dowsby
Graby Farm
Poplar Farm
Dowsby Hall
Moat
Spinney Farm
Middle Fen Farm
FEN ROAD
B1397
Dowsby Fen
Glebe Farm
1 BRAMBLING WK
2 LINNET DR
3 SISKIN CL
4 DOVECOTE
5 MILLER'S CL
6 SANDS CT
Browell Head (Spring)
CAR DYKE (ROMAN CANAL)
Barn Farm
Crossroads Farm
North Car Dyke Farm
Rippingale Fen Farm
STATION STREET
Grange Farm
LONG DROVE
EAST STREET
Settlement (site of)
Rippingale Fen
MAIN ROAD
South Car Dyke Farm
Sewage Works
PE10
DOCTOR'S LANE
North End Farm
French Farm
Dunsby
DUNSBY DROVE
Fen Farm
Dunsby Fen
PE11
B1177
Dunsby Fen
Hacconby Fen
8 33 7 32 6 31 5 30 4 29 3 28 2 27 1 26
10 11 12 13 14 15
154
144
155

143 134

Scale: 1¾ inches to 1 mile

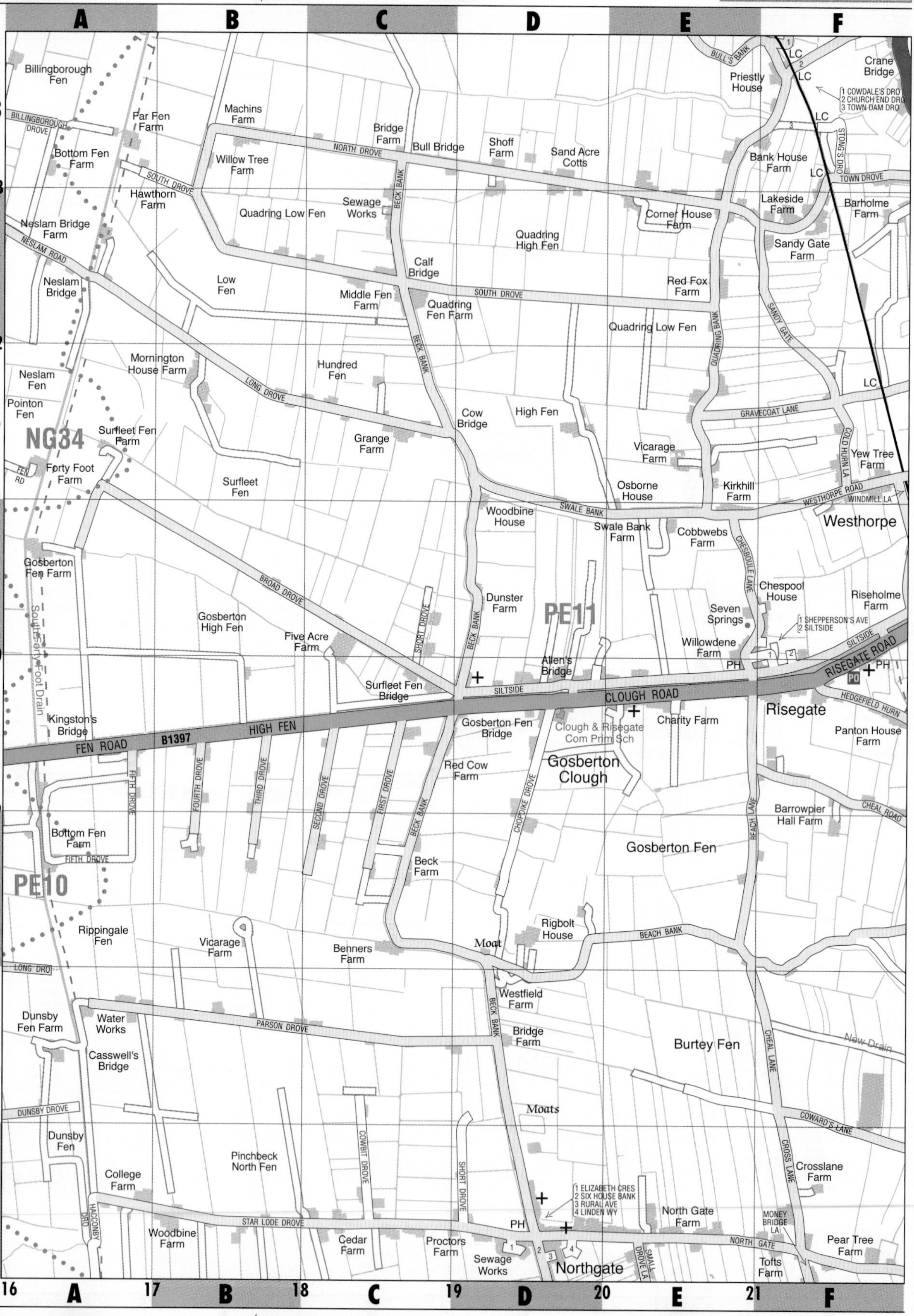

0 ¼ ½ mile
0 250m 500m 750m 1 km

A B C D E F

8
33
7
32
6
31
5
30
4
29
3
28
2
27
1
26

Billingborough Fen
Par Fen Farm
Machins Farm
Bridge Farm
Bull Bridge
Shoff Farm
Sand Acre Cotts
Priestly House
Crane Bridge
LC
1 COWDALE'S DRO
2 CHURCH END DRO
3 TOWN DAM DRO
Bank House Farm
Barholme Farm
Lakeside Farm
TOWN DROVE
STONG'S DRO
Bottom Fen Farm
NORTH DROVE
Willow Tree Farm
Quadring Low Fen
Sewage Works
BECK BANK
Hawthorn Farm
SOUTH DROVE
Quadring High Fen
Corner House Farm
Sandy Gate Farm
Neslam Bridge Farm
NESLAM ROAD
Low Fen
Calf Bridge
Red Fox Farm
Neslam Bridge
Middle Fen Farm
SOUTH DROVE
Quadring Fen Farm
Quadring Low Fen
SANDY GATE
QUADRING BANK
Neslam Fen
LONG DROVE
Hundred Fen
GRAVECOAT LANE
LC
Pointon Fen
Mornington House Farm
Cow Bridge
High Fen
Vicarage Farm
Yew Tree Farm
COLD HORN LA
NG34
Surfleet Fen Farm
Grange Farm
Osborne House
Kirkhill Farm
WESTHORPE ROAD
WINDMILL LA
FEN RD
Forty Foot Farm
Surfleet Fen
SWALE BANK
Woodbine House
Swale Bank Farm
Cobbwebs Farm
CHESRULE LANE
Westhorpe
BROAD DROVE
Gosberton Fen Farm
Gosberton High Fen
Five Acre Farm
SHORT DROVE
BECK BANK
Dunster Farm
PE11
Chespool House
Riseholme Farm
Seven Springs
1 SHEPPERSON'S AVE
2 SILTSIDE
SILTSIDE
South Forty Foot Drain
Surfleet Fen Bridge
Allen's Bridge
Willowdene Farm
PH
RISEGATE ROAD
PH
PO
Kingston's Bridge
SILTSIDE
CLOUGH ROAD
Risegate
HEDGEFIELD HURN
FEN ROAD B1397 HIGH FEN
Gosberton Fen Bridge
Charity Farm
Panton House Farm
Clough & Risegate Com Prim Sch
Gosberton Clough
PE10
Red Cow Farm
FIFTH DRIVE
FOURTH DRIVE
THIRD DRIVE
SECOND DROVE
FIRST DRIVE
BECK BANK
CHOPDYKE DROVE
BEACH LANE
Barrowpier Hall Farm
CHEAL ROAD
Bottom Fen Farm
FIFTH DROVE
Beck Farm
Gosberton Fen
Rippingale Fen
Vicarage Farm
Benners Farm
Moat
Rigbolt House
BEACH BANK
LONG DRO
Dunsby Fen Farm
Water Works
PARSON DROVE
Westfield Farm
Bridge Farm
Burtey Fen
CHEAL LANE
New Drain
Casswell's Bridge
BECK BANK
Moats
COWARD'S LANE
DUNSBY DROVE
CROSS LANE
Dunsby Fen
COWBIT DROVE
Pinchbeck North Fen
SHORT DROVE
1 ELIZABETH CRES
2 SIX HOUSE BANK
3 RURAL AVE
4 LINDEN WY
Crosslane Farm
College Farm
STAR LODE DROVE
Cedar Farm
Proctors Farm
PH
North Gate Farm
MONEY BRIDGE LA
Pear Tree Farm
HACCONBY DRO
Woodbine Farm
Sewage Works
Northgate
NORTH GATE
SMALL DROVE LA
Tofts Farm

16 17 18 19 20 21
A B C D E F

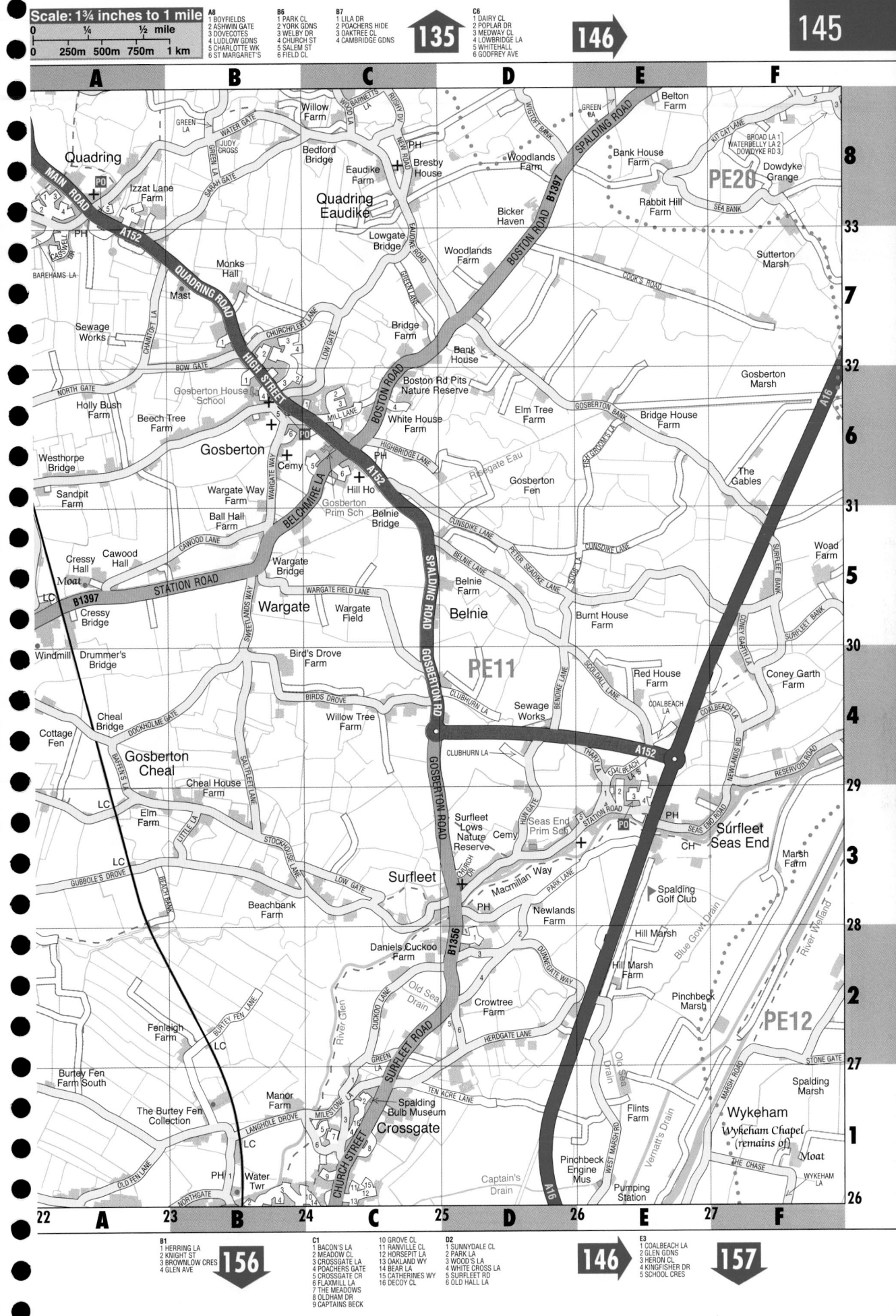

145
Scale: 1¾ inches to 1 mile
0 ¼ ½ mile
0 250m 500m 750m 1 km
A8
1 BOYFIELDS
2 ASHWIN GATE
3 DOVECOTES
4 LUDLOW GDNS
5 CHARLOTTE WK
6 ST MARGARET'S
B6
1 PARK CL
2 YORK GDNS
3 WELBY DR
4 CHURCH ST
5 SALEM ST
6 FIELD CL
B7
1 LILA DR
2 POACHERS HIDE
3 OAKTREE CL
4 CAMBRIDGE GDNS
135
C6
1 DAIRY CL
2 POPLAR DR
3 MEDWAY CL
4 LOWBRIDGE LA
5 WHITEHALL
6 GODFREY AVE
146
A B C D E F
Quadring
MAIN ROAD
A152
Izzat Lane Farm
PH
CASWELL DR
BAREHAMS LA
GREEN LA
WATER GATE
JUDY CROSS
GREEN LA
SARAH GATE
Willow Farm
WOOD LA
BARNETTS LA
RUSHY DV
Bedford Bridge
NEW ROAD
Eaudike Farm
Bresby House
Quadring Eaudike
Lowgate Bridge
EAUDIKE ROAD
GREEN LANE
WISTOFT BANK
GREEN LA
SPALDING ROAD
B1397
Woodlands Farm
Bicker Haven
Woodlands Farm
BOSTON ROAD
Belton Farm
Bank House Farm
Rabbit Hill Farm
PE20
KIT CAT LANE
BROAD LA 1
WATERBELLY LA 2
DOWDYKE RD 3
Dowdyke Grange
SEA BANK
Sutterton Marsh
COOK'S ROAD
Monks Hall
QUADRING ROAD
Mast
Sewage Works
CHAINTOFT LA
CHURCHFLEET LANE
LOW GATE
Bridge Farm
Bank House
BOW GATE
HIGH STREET
NORTH GATE
Gosberton House School
Holly Bush Farm
Beech Tree Farm
Boston Rd Pits Nature Reserve
White House Farm
MILL LANE
Gosberton
Cemy
PO
HIGHBRIDGE LANE
PH
Hill Ho
Elm Tree Farm
GOSBERTON BANK
Bridge House Farm
Gosberton Marsh
A16
Westhorpe Bridge
WARGATE WAY
BELCHMIRE LA
Gosberton Prim Sch
Risegate Eau
Gosberton Fen
FISHGROOM'S LA
The Gables
Sandpit Farm
Wargate Way Farm
Ball Hall Farm
Belnie Bridge
CUNSDIKE LANE
CUNSDIKE LANE
PETER SEADIKE LANE
Cressy Hall
Cawood Hall
CAWOOD LANE
Moat
Wargate Bridge
BELNIE LANE
Belnie Farm
SURFLEET BANK
Wood Farm
LC
B1397
STATION ROAD
Cressy Bridge
SWEETLANDS WAY
Wargate
WARGATE FIELD LANE
Wargate Field
SPALDING ROAD
Belnie
Burnt House Farm
SURFLEET BANK
CONEY GARTH LA
Windmill
Drummer's Bridge
Bird's Drove Farm
GOSBERTON RD
PE11
BENDIKE LANE
SCOLDALL LANE
Red House Farm
Coney Garth Farm
BIRDS DROVE
CLUBHURN LA
Sewage Works
COALBEACH LA
COALBEACH LA
Cheal Bridge
DOCKHOLME GATE
Cottage Fen
Willow Tree Farm
Gosberton Cheal
BAFFEN'S LA
CLUBHURN LA
THARY LA
COALBEACH LA
NEWLANDS RD
RESERVOIR ROAD
SALTFLEET LANE
Cheal House Farm
GOSBERTON ROAD
HUN GATE
STATION ROAD
Seas End Prim Sch
Elm Farm
LITTLE LA
Surfleet Lows Nature Reserve
Cemy
SEAS END ROAD
Surfleet Seas End
CH
Marsh Farm
STOCKHOUSE LANE
GUBBOLE'S DROVE
BEACH BANK
LOW GATE
Surfleet
CHURCH DR
Macmillan Way
PARK LANE
Spalding Golf Club
Beachbank Farm
PH
Newlands Farm
Blue Gowt Drain
River Welland
Hill Marsh
B1356
Daniels Cuckoo Farm
DUNNEGATE WAY
Hill Marsh Farm
Old Sea Drain
Crowtree Farm
Pinchbeck Marsh
River Glen
CUCKOO LANE
PE12
Fenleigh Farm
BURTEY FEN LANE
SURFLEET ROAD
HERDGATE LANE
STONE GATE
GREEN LA
Old Sea Drain
MARSH ROAD
Spalding Marsh
Burtey Fen Farm South
Manor Farm
TEN ACRE LANE
Spalding Bulb Museum
Flints Farm
Wykeham
Wykeham Chapel (remains of)
The Burtey Fen Collection
LANGHOLE DROVE
MILESTONE LA
Crossgate
Vernatt's Drain
Moat
THE CHASE
WYKEHAM LA
OLD FEN LANE
PH
Water Twr
CHURCH STREET
Pinchbeck Engine Mus
WEST MARSH RD
Captain's Drain
Pumping Station
NORTHGATE
8 33 7 32 6 31 5 30 4 29 3 28 2 27 1 26
22 23 24 25 26 27
B1
1 HERRING LA
2 KNIGHT ST
3 BROWNLOW CRES
4 GLEN AVE
156
C1
1 BACON'S LA
2 MEADOW CL
3 CROSSGATE LA
4 POACHERS GATE
5 CROSSGATE CR
6 FLAXMILL LA
7 THE MEADOWS
8 OLDHAM DR
9 CAPTAINS BECK
10 GROVE CL
11 RANVILLE CL
12 HORSEPIT LA
13 OAKLAND WY
14 BEAR LA
15 CATHERINES WY
16 DECOY CL
D2
1 SUNNYDALE CL
2 PARK LA
3 WOOD'S LA
4 WHITE CROSS LA
5 SURFLEET RD
6 OLD HALL LA
146
E3
1 COALBEACH LA
2 GLEN GDNS
3 HERON CL
4 KINGFISHER DR
5 SCHOOL CRES
157

Scale: 1¾ inches to 1 mile

0   ¼   ½   mile
0   250m   500m   750m   1 km

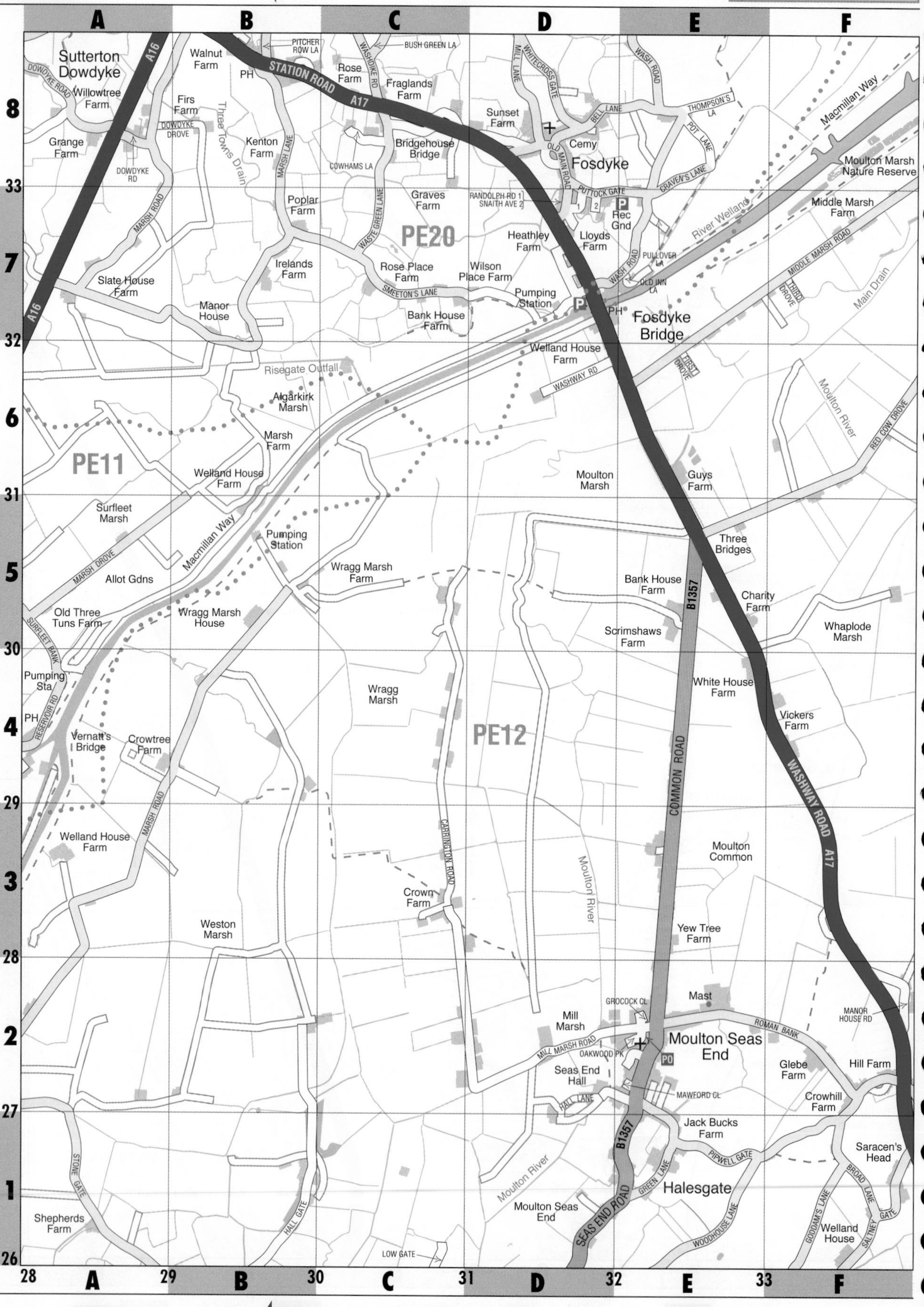

A   B   C   D   E   F

8

Sutterton Dowdyke

Willowtree Farm
Walnut Farm
PH
STATION ROAD
A17
Rose Farm
PITCHER ROW LA
BUSH GREEN LA
WASHDIKE RD
Fraglands Farm
MILL LANE
WHITECROSS GATE
WASH ROAD
Macmillan Way

Grange Farm
Firs Farm
DOWDYKE DROVE
Kenton Farm
COWHAMS LA
Bridgehouse Bridge
Sunset Farm
BELL LANE
Cemy
Fosdyke
THOMPSON'S LA
POT LANE
Moulton Marsh Nature Reserve

33

DOWDYKE RD
Three Towns Drain
MARSH LANE
WASTE GREEN LANE
Poplar Farm
Graves Farm
Heathley Farm
RANDOLPH RD 1
SNAITH AVE 2
Rec Gnd
Lloyds Farm
CRAVEN'S LANE
River Welland
Middle Marsh Farm

7

A16
Slate House Farm
Ireland's Farm
SMEETON'S LANE
Rose Place Farm
Wilson Place Farm
Welland House
PULLOVER
OLD INN LA
MIDDLE MARSH ROAD
THIRD DROVE
Main Drain

Manor House
Bank House Farm
Pumping Station
PH
Fosdyke Bridge
PE20
OLD MAIN ROAD
PUTTOCK GATE
P

32

Welland House Farm
WASHWAY RD
FIRST DROVE
Moulton River
RED COW DROVE

Risegate Outfall
Algarkirk Marsh

6

PE11
Marsh Farm
Moulton Marsh
Guys Farm

Welland House Farm
Surfleet Marsh
Macmillan Way

31

MARSH DROVE
Pumping Station
Three Bridges
B1357

5

Allot Gdns
Wragg Marsh Farm
Bank House Farm
Charity Farm
Whaplode Marsh

Old Three Tuns Farm
SURFLEET BANK
Wragg Marsh House
Scrimshaws Farm
White House Farm

30

Pumping Sta
PH
RESERVOIR RD
Wragg Marsh
PE12
Vickers Farm
WASHWAY ROAD
A17

4

Vernatt's Bridge
Crowtree Farm
MARSH ROAD
CARRINGTON ROAD
COMMON ROAD

29

Welland House Farm
Moulton Common

3

Crown Farm
Moulton River

28

Weston Marsh
Yew Tree Farm

2

Mill Marsh
GROCOCK CL
Mast
ROMAN BANK
MANOR HOUSE RD

MILL MARSH ROAD
OAKWOOD PK
Moulton Seas End
PO
Glebe Farm
Hill Farm

Seas End Hall
MAWFORD CL
Crowhill Farm

27

HALL LANE
Jack Bucks Farm
Saracen's Head

HALL GATE
B1357
PIPWELL GATE
BROAD LANE

1

Shepherds Farm
SEAS END ROAD
GREEN LANE
Halesgate
GOODLAN'S LANE
SALTNEY GATE

STONE GATE
Moulton Seas End
WOODHOUSE LANE
Welland House

26

28   A   29   B   30   C   31   D   32   E   33   F

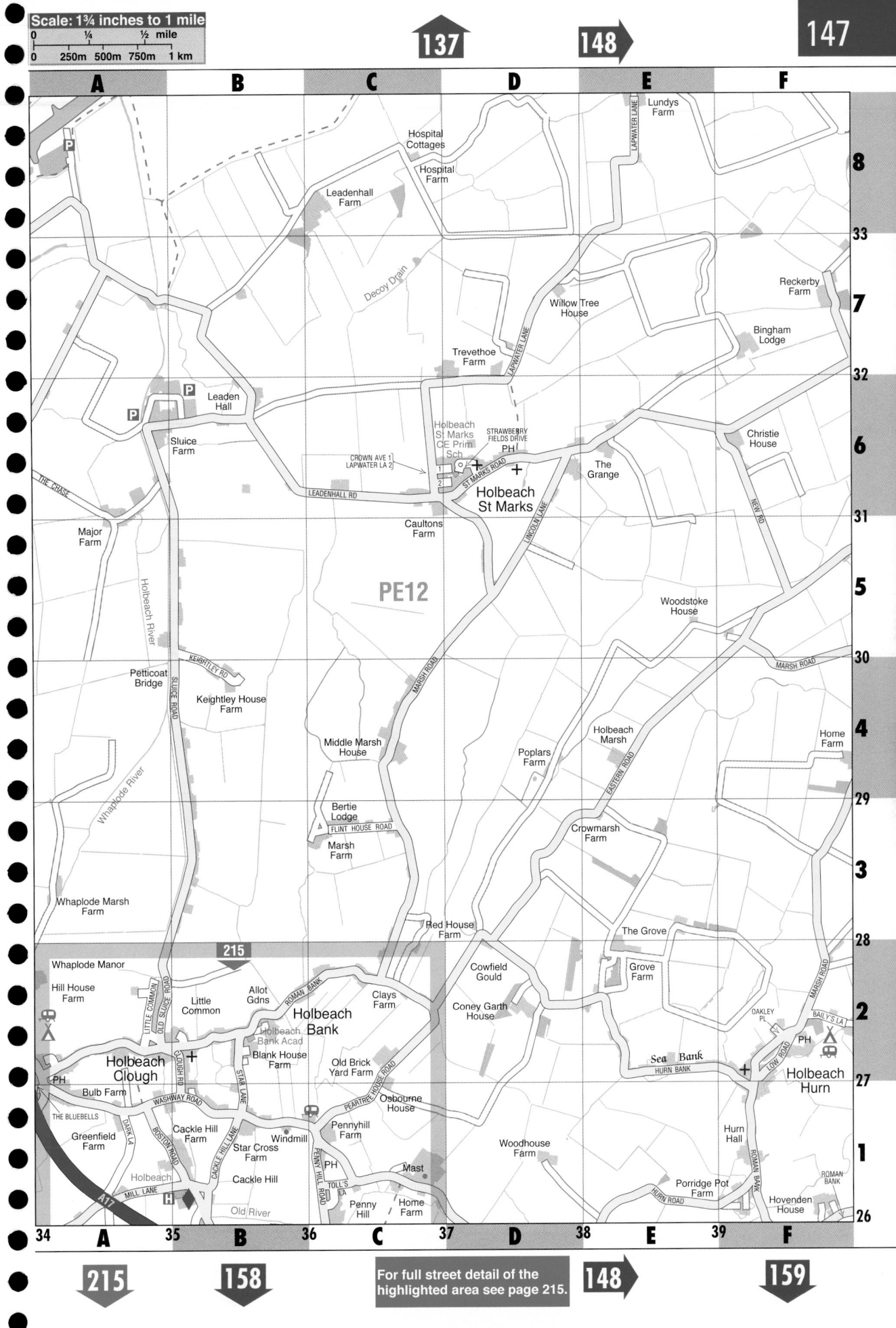

A   B   C   D   E   F

8
33
7
32
6
31
5
30
4
29
3
28
2
27
1
26

Hospital
Cottages

Hospital
Farm

Leadenhall
Farm

Decoy Drain

Willow Tree
House

LAPWATER LANE

Lundys
Farm

Reckerby
Farm

Bingham
Lodge

Trevethoe
Farm

Leaden
Hall

Holbeach
St Marks
CE Prim
Sch

CROWN AVE 1
LAPWATER LA 2

STRAWBERRY
FIELDS DRIVE
PH

Christie
House

Sluice
Farm

LEADENHALL RD

ST MARKS ROAD

Holbeach
St Marks

The Grange

NEW RD

THE CHASE

Caultons
Farm

LINCOLN LANE

Major
Farm

PE12

Woodstoke
House

MARSH ROAD

Holbeach River

KEIGHTLEY RD

SLUICE ROAD

Petticoat
Bridge

Keightley House
Farm

MARSH ROAD

Holbeach
Marsh

EASTERN ROAD

Home
Farm

Whaplode River

Middle Marsh
House

Poplars
Farm

Bertie
Lodge

FLINT HOUSE ROAD

Marsh
Farm

Crowmarsh
Farm

Whaplode Marsh
Farm

Red House
Farm

The Grove

MARSH ROAD

215

Whaplode Manor

Hill House
Farm

LITTLE COMMON

OLD SLUICE ROAD

Little
Common

ROMAN BANK

Allot
Gdns

Holbeach
Bank

Clays
Farm

Cowfield
Gould

Grove
Farm

OAKLEY PL

BAILY'S LA

Holbeach
Bank Acad

Blank House
Farm

Coney Garth
House

PH

CLOUGH RD

Holbeach
Clough

Old Brick
Yard Farm

PEARTREE HOUSE ROAD

Sea Bank

HURN BANK

LOW ROAD

Holbeach
Hurn

PH

Bulb Farm

WASHWAY ROAD

STAR LANE

Osbourne
House

BOSTON ROAD

THE BLUEBELLS

Greenfield
Farm

DARK LA

CACKLE HILL LANE

Cackle Hill
Farm

Windmill

PENNY HILL ROAD

Pennyhill
Farm

PH

Woodhouse
Farm

Hurn
Hall

ROMAN BANK

Holbeach

MILL LANE

A17

H

Star Cross
Farm

Cackle Hill

TOLL'S
LA

Mast

Penny
Hill

Home
Farm

Old River

Porridge Pot
Farm

HURN ROAD

ROMAN
BANK

Hovenden
House

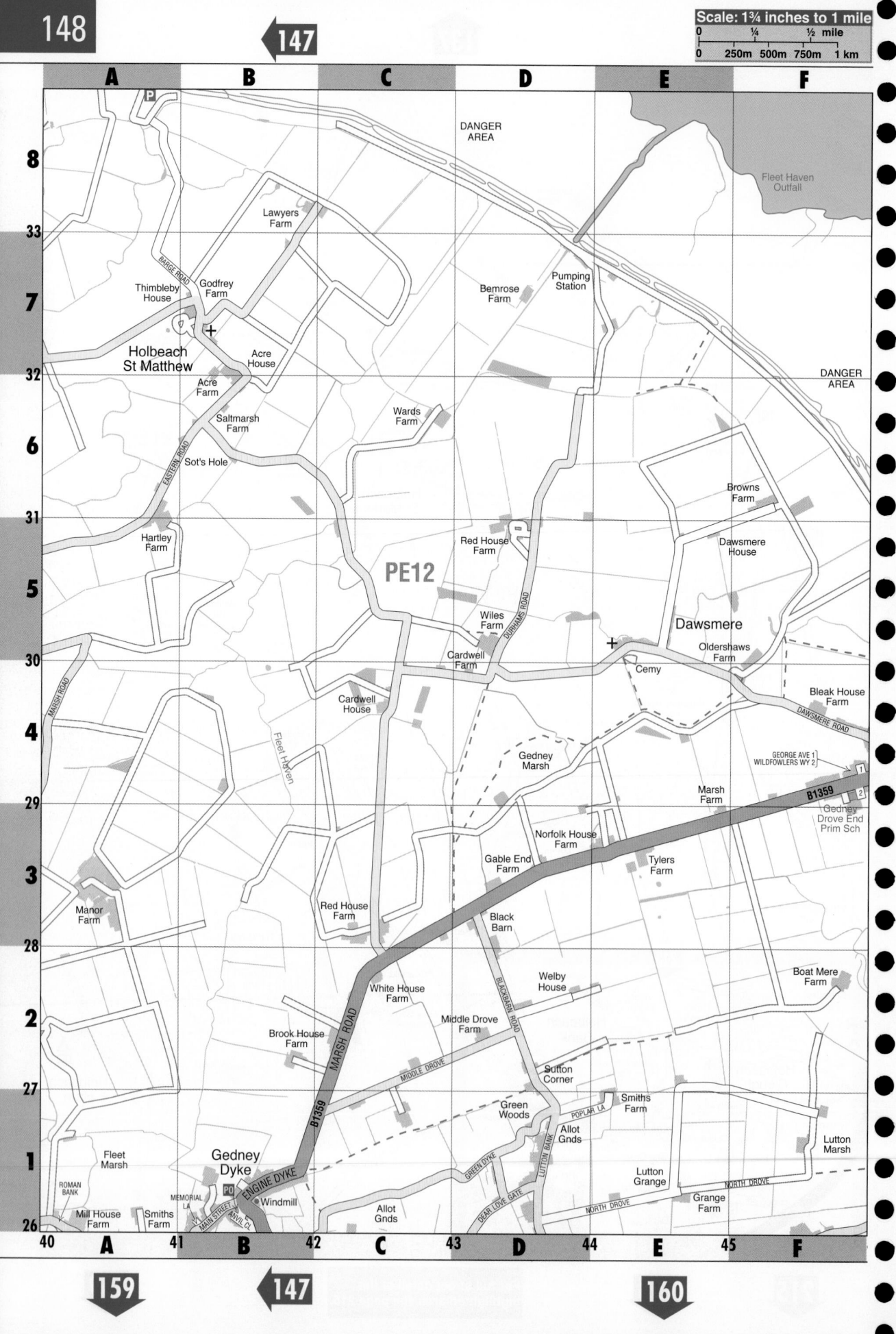

147

Scale: 1¾ inches to 1 mile

0   ¼   ½   mile
0 250m 500m 750m 1 km

DANGER
AREA

Fleet Haven
Outfall

Lawyers
Farm

BARGE ROAD

Godfrey
Farm

Thimbleby
House

Bemrose
Farm

Pumping
Station

Holbeach
St Matthew

Acre
House

DANGER
AREA

Acre
Farm

Saltmarsh
Farm

EASTERN ROAD

Wards
Farm

Sot's Hole

Browns
Farm

Hartley
Farm

Dawsmere
House

Red House
Farm

PE12

DURHAMS ROAD

MARSH ROAD

Wiles
Farm

Dawsmere

Oldershaws
Farm

Cardwell
Farm

Cemy

Cardwell
House

Bleak House
Farm

DAWSMERE ROAD

Fleet Haven

Gedney
Marsh

GEORGE AVE 1
WILDFOWLERS WY 2

Marsh
Farm

1

B1359

2

Gedney
Drove End
Prim Sch

Norfolk House
Farm

Gable End
Farm

Tylers
Farm

Manor
Farm

Red House
Farm

Black
Barn

Boat Mere
Farm

White House
Farm

BLACKBARN ROAD

Welby
House

Brook House
Farm

MARSH ROAD

Middle Drove
Farm

MIDDLE DROVE

Sutton
Corner

Smiths
Farm

POPLAR LA

Green
Woods

Allot
Gnds

LUTTON BANK

Lutton
Marsh

Fleet
Marsh

B1359

Gedney
Dyke

ENGINE DYKE

PO

Windmill

Allot
Gnds

GREEN DYKE

DEAR LOVE GATE

Lutton
Grange

NORTH DROVE

NORTH DROVE

Grange
Farm

ROMAN
BANK

MEMORIAL LA

MAIN STREET

ANVIL CL

Mill House
Farm

Smiths
Farm

Scale: 1¾ inches to 1 mile

0   ¼   ½   mile

0   250m 500m 750m 1 km

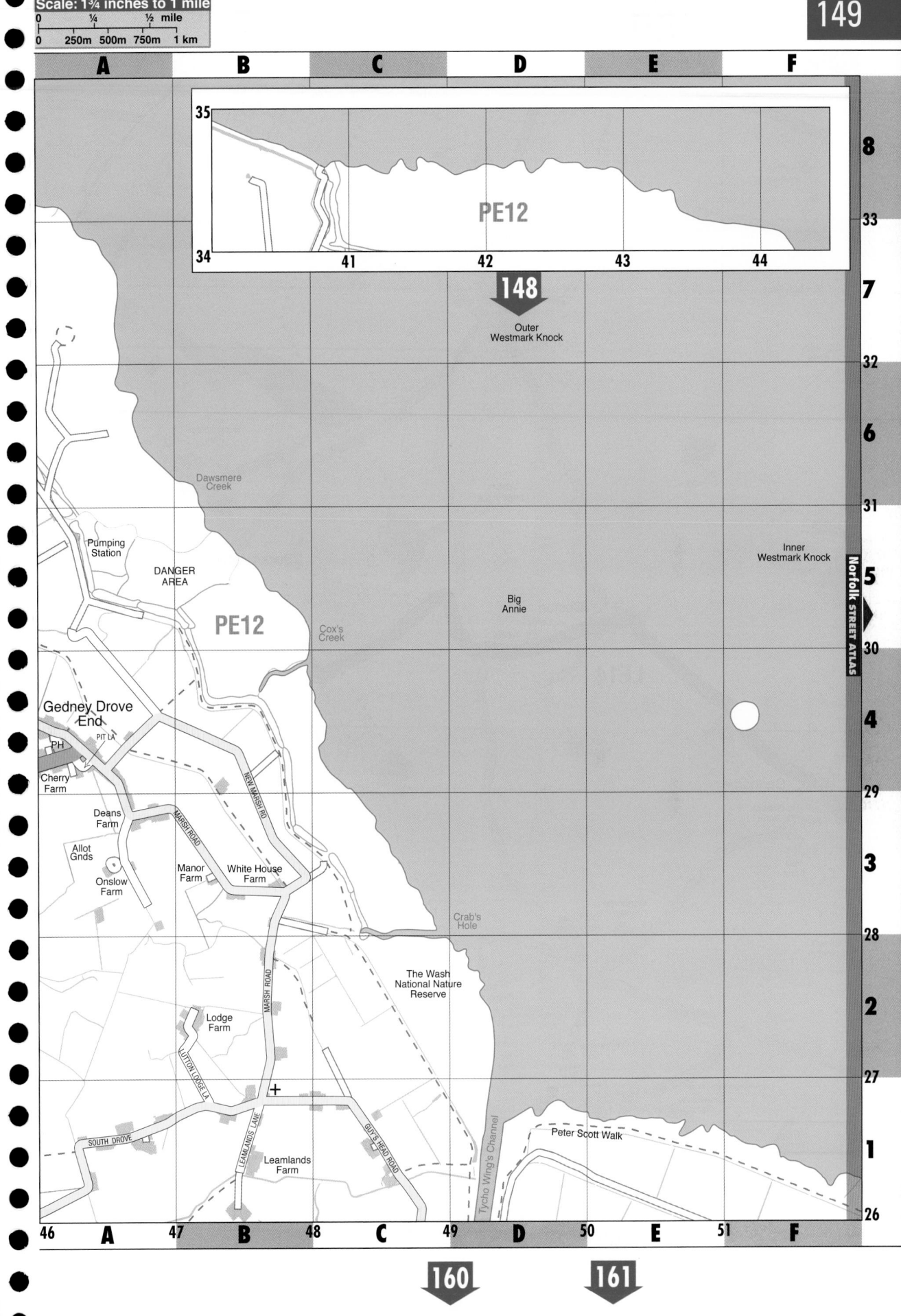

PE12

35

34   41   42   43   44

148

Outer
Westmark Knock

8

33

7

32

6

Dawsmere
Creek

31

Pumping
Station

Inner
Westmark Knock

DANGER
AREA

5

PE12

Cox's
Creek

Big
Annie

30

Gedney Drove
End

4

PH   PIT LA

Cherry
Farm

Deans
Farm

29

MARSH ROAD

NEW MARSH RD

Allot
Gnds

Manor
Farm

White House
Farm

3

Onslow
Farm

Crab's
Hole

28

The Wash
National Nature
Reserve

MARSH ROAD

2

Lodge
Farm

LUTTON LODGE LA

27

Peter Scott Walk

Tycho Wing's Channel

SOUTH DROVE

LEAMLANDS LANE

Leamlands
Farm

GUY'S HEAD ROAD

1

26

46   A   47   B   48   C   49   D   50   E   51   F

160   161

Norfolk STREET ATLAS

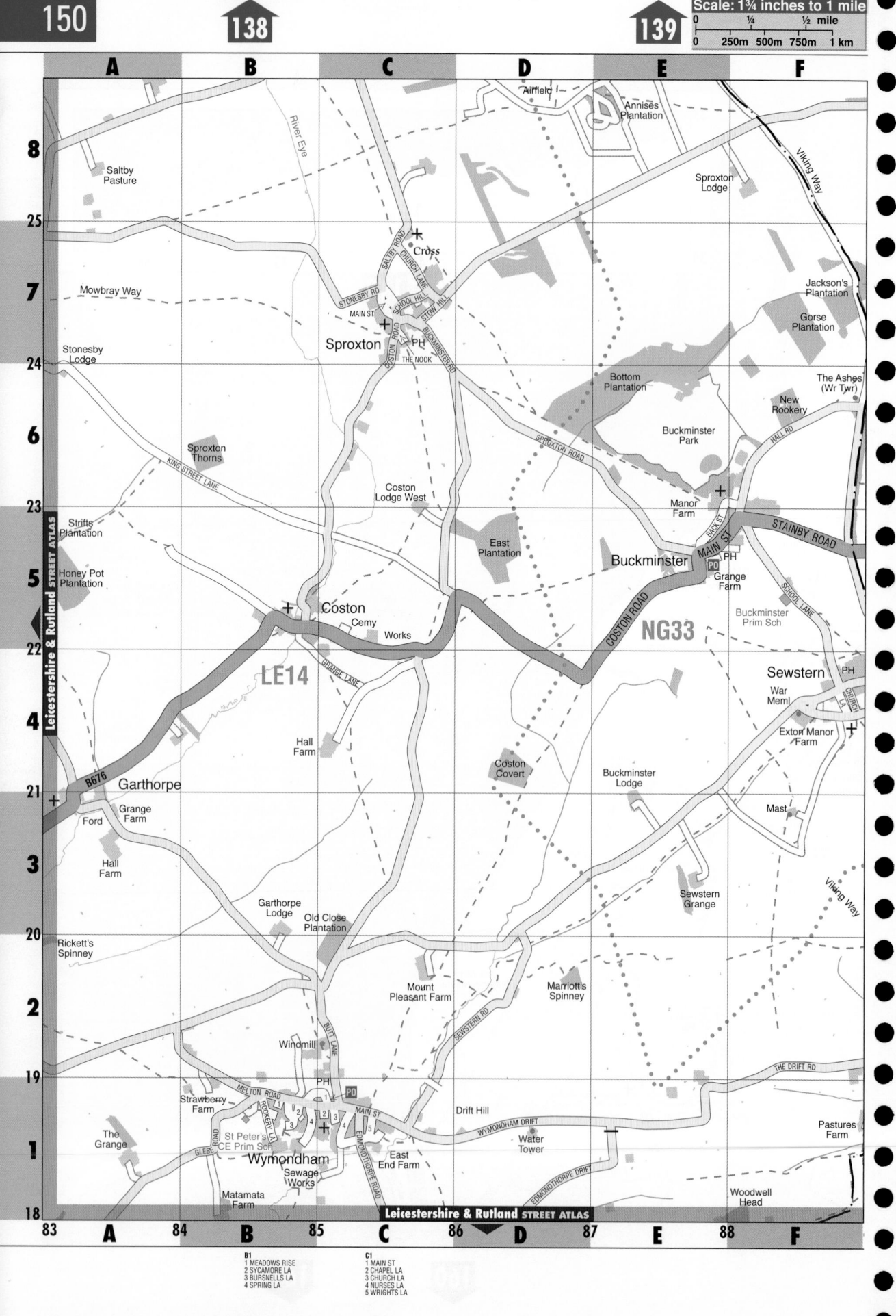

138

139

Scale: 1¾ inches to 1 mile

| 0 | ¼ | ½ mile |
| 0 | 250m | 500m | 750m | 1 km |

A B C D E F

8

25

7

24

6

23

5

22

4

21

3

20

2

19

1

18

Leicestershire & Rutland STREET ATLAS

Saltby
Pasture

River Eye

Airfield

Annises
Plantation

Sproxton
Lodge

Viking Way

Mowbray Way

Cross
SALTBY ROAD
CHURCH LANE
Stonesby Rd
SCHOOL HILL
Jackson's
Plantation

Gorse
Plantation

Stonesby
Lodge

MAIN ST
STOW HILL

Sproxton

PH
BUCKMINSTER RD
COSTON ROAD

THE NOOK

Bottom
Plantation

The Ashes
(Wr Twr)

New
Rookery

Sproxton
Thorns

KING STREET LANE

Sproxton Road

Buckminster
Park

HALL RD

Strifts
Plantation

Coston
Lodge West

Manor
Farm

BACK ST

STAINBY ROAD

Honey Pot
Plantation

East
Plantation

Buckminster

MAIN ST
PH
PO
Grange
Farm

SCHOOL LANE

Coston

GRANGE LANE

Cemy

Works

COSTON ROAD

NG33

Buckminster
Prim Sch

Sewstern

PH

LE14

War
Meml

CHURCH LA

Hall
Farm

Coston
Covert

Buckminster
Lodge

Exton Manor
Farm

B676

Garthorpe

Ford

Grange
Farm

Mast

Viking Way

Hall
Farm

Garthorpe
Lodge

Old Close
Plantation

Sewstern
Grange

Rickett's
Spinney

Mount
Pleasant Farm

Marriott's
Spinney

THE DRIFT RD

BUTT LANE

Windmill

SEWSTERN RD

MELTON ROAD

PH
PO

Strawberry
Farm

ROOKERY LA

MAIN ST

EDMONDTHORPE ROAD

Drift Hill

WYMONDHAM DRIFT

Water
Tower

Pastures
Farm

GLEBE ROAD

St Peter's
CE Prim Sch

Wymondham

East
End Farm

EDMONDTHORPE DRIFT

The
Grange

Sewage
Works

Matamata
Farm

Woodwell
Head

Leicestershire & Rutland STREET ATLAS

83 A 84 B 85 C 86 D 87 E 88 F

B1
1 MEADOWS RISE
2 SYCAMORE LA
3 BURSNELLS LA
4 SPRING LA

C1
1 MAIN ST
2 CHAPEL LA
3 CHURCH LA
4 NURSES LA
5 WRIGHTS LA

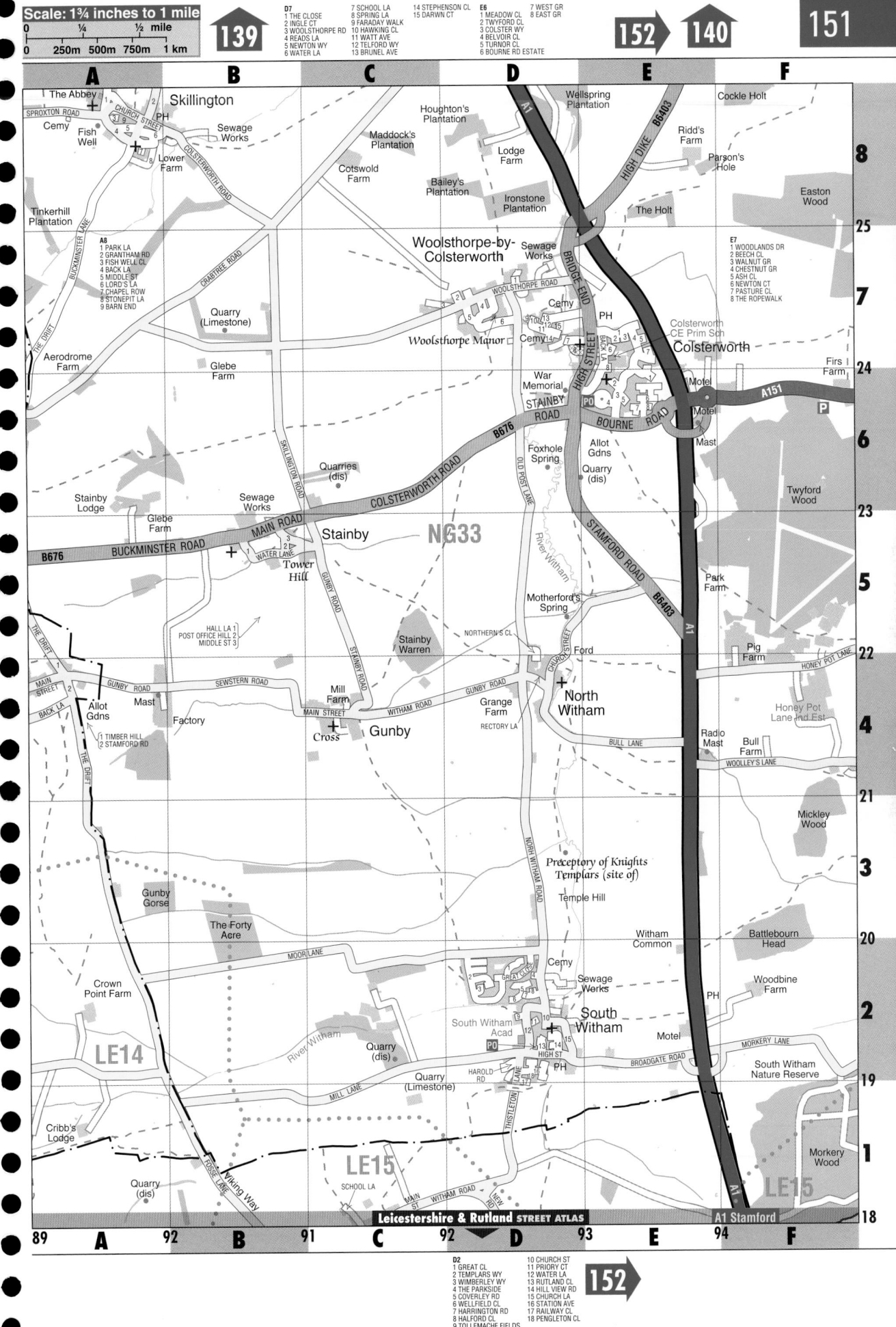

D7
1 THE CLOSE
2 INGLE CT
3 WOOLSTHORPE RD
4 READS LA
5 NEWTON WY
6 WATER LA

7 SCHOOL LA
8 SPRING LA
9 FARADAY WALK
10 HAWKING CL
11 WATT AVE
12 TELFORD WY
13 BRUNEL AVE

14 STEPHENSON CL
15 DARWN CT

E6
1 MEADOW CL
2 TWYFORD CL
3 COLSTER WY
4 BELVOIR CL
5 TURNOR CL
6 BOURNE RD ESTATE

7 WEST GR
8 EAST GR

E7
1 WOODLANDS DR
2 BEECH CL
3 WALNUT GR
4 CHESTNUT GR
5 ASH CL
6 NEWTON CT
7 PASTURE CL
8 THE ROPEWALK

A8
1 PARK LA
2 GRANTHAM RD
3 FISH WELL CL
4 BACK LA
5 MIDDLE ST
6 LORD'S LA
7 CHAPEL ROW
8 STONEPIT LA
9 BARN END

The Abbey
Skillington
Cemy
Fish Well
Lower Farm
SPROXTON ROAD
CHURCH STREET
PH
COLSTERWORTH ROAD
BUCKMINSTER LANE

Tinkerhill Plantation

Sewage Works

Cotswold Farm

Maddock's Plantation

Houghton's Plantation

Lodge Farm

Bailey's Plantation

Ironstone Plantation

Wellspring Plantation

Cockle Holt

Ridd's Farm

Parson's Hole

Easton Wood

HIGH DIKE
B6403

Woolsthorpe-by-Colsterworth

Sewage Works

WOOLSTHORPE ROAD

Cemy

PH

BRIDGE END

HIGH STREET

BACK LA

Colsterworth CE Prim Sch

Colsterworth

Motel

Firs Farm

A151

Quarry (Limestone)

CRABTREE ROAD

Aerodrome Farm

THE DRIFT

Glebe Farm

Woolsthorpe Manor

War Memorial

STAINBY ROAD

PO

BOURNE ROAD

Motel

Mast

P

Twyford Wood

Quarries (dis)

SKILLINGTON ROAD

COLSTERWORTH ROAD

B676

Foxhole Spring

OLD POST LANE

Allot Gdns

Quarry (dis)

Stainby Lodge

Glebe Farm

Sewage Works

MAIN ROAD

Stainby

NG33

River Witham

STAMFORD ROAD

B6403

A1

Park Farm

B676 BUCKMINSTER ROAD

Tower Hill

WATER LANE

GUNBY ROAD

HALL LA 1
POST OFFICE HILL 2
MIDDLE ST 3

Stainby Warren

Motherford's Spring

NORTHERN'S CL

Ford

CHURCH STREET

Pig Farm

HONEY POT LANE

THE DRIFT

MAIN STREET

BACK LA

Allot Gdns

Mast

SEWSTERN ROAD

GUNBY ROAD

STAINBY ROAD

Mill Farm

WITHAM ROAD

Grange Farm

GUNBY ROAD

RECTORY LA

North Witham

BULL LANE

Radio Mast

Bull Farm

WOOLLEY'S LANE

Honey Pot Lane Ind Est

Factory

1 TIMBER HILL
2 STAMFORD RD

Cross

Gunby

MAIN STREET

Mill Farm

Mickley Wood

Gunby Gorse

The Forty Acre

MOOR LANE

NORTH WITHAM ROAD

Preceptory of Knights Templars (site of)

Temple Hill

Witham Common

Battlebourn Head

Woodbine Farm

PH

Crown Point Farm

LE14

River Witham

South Witham Acad

GREAT CL

Cemy

Sewage Works

South Witham

Motel

MORKERY LANE

Quarry (dis)

PO

HIGH ST

PH

BROADGATE ROAD

South Witham Nature Reserve

Quarry (Limestone)

HAROLD RD

MILL LANE

THISTLETON LANE

A1

Morkery Wood

Cribb's Lodge

LE15

VIKING WAY

FOSSE LANE

Quarry (dis)

SCHOOL LA

MAIN ST WITHAM ROAD

NEW RD

LE15

D2
1 GREAT CL
2 TEMPLARS WY
3 WIMBERLEY WY
4 THE PARKSIDE
5 COVERLEY RD
6 WELLFIELD CL
7 HARRINGTON RD
8 HALFORD CL
9 TOLLEMACHE FIELDS

10 CHURCH ST
11 PRIORY CT
12 WATER LA
13 RUTLAND CL
14 HILL VIEW RD
15 CHURCH LA
16 STATION AVE
17 RAILWAY CL
18 PENGLETON CL

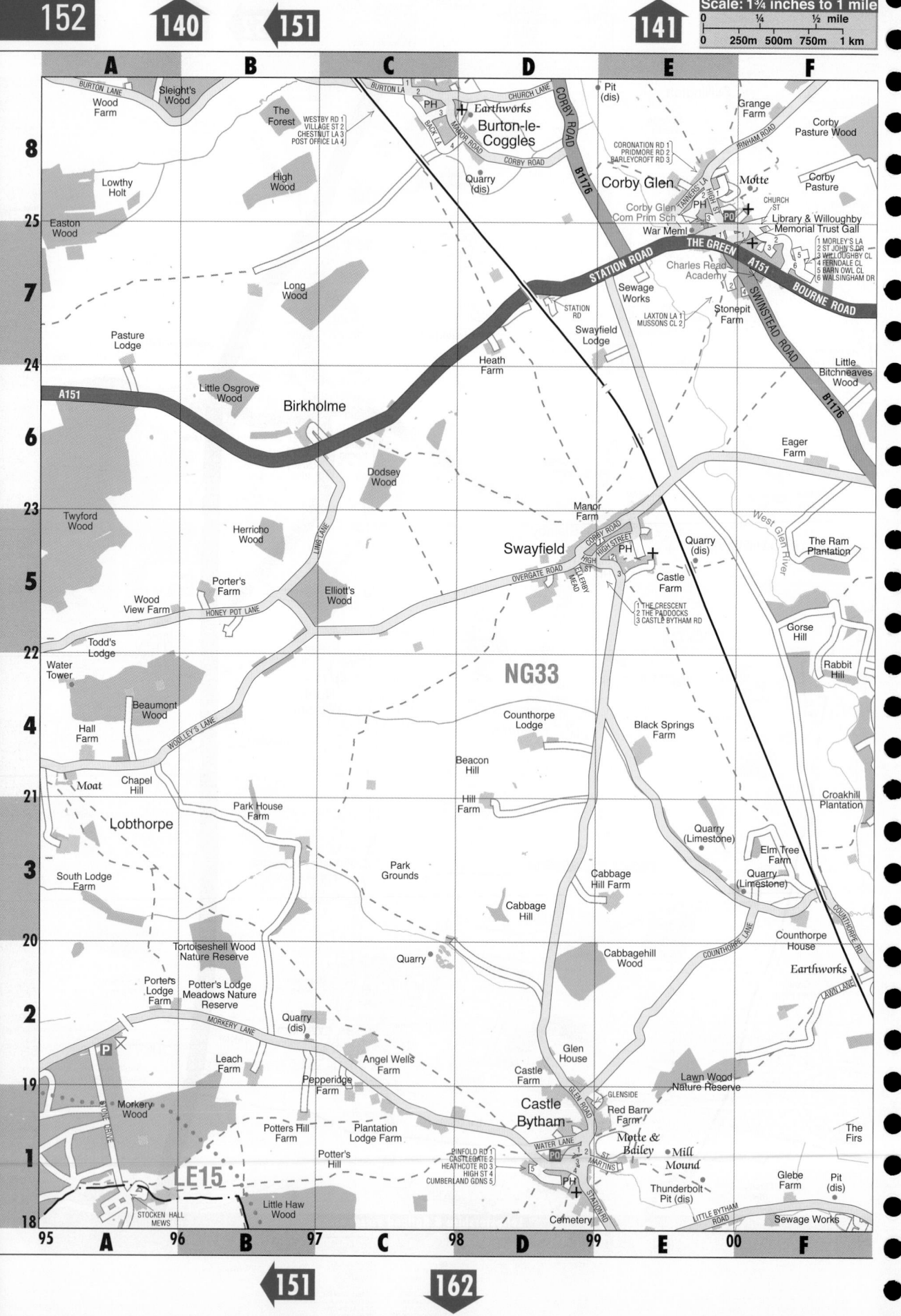

152

140

◄ 151

141

Scale: 1¾ inches to 1 mile

0   ¼   ½   mile
0   250m 500m 750m 1 km

A   B   C   D   E   F

8

Burton Lane
Wood Farm
Sleight's Wood
The Forest
WESTBY RD 1
VILLAGE ST 2
CHESTNUT LA 3
POST OFFICE LA 4
Burton La
PH
Earthworks
Burton-le-Coggles
Back La
Manor Road
Church Lane
Corby Road
B1176
Pit (dis)
Grange Farm
Corby Pasture Wood
CORONATION RD 1
PRIDMORE RD 2
BARLEYCROFT RD 3
Corby Glen
Motte
Corby Pasture

25

Lowthy Holt
High Wood
Quarry (dis)
Corby Glen Com Prim Sch
Tanners La
High St
Church St
Library & Willoughby Memorial Trust Gall
PO
War Meml
1 MORLEY'S LA
2 ST JOHN'S DR
3 WILLOUGHBY CL
4 FERNDALE CL
5 BARN OWL CL
6 WALSINGHAM DR

Easton Wood

7

Long Wood
Station Rd
STATION ROAD
Sewage Works
Charles Read Academy
Swayfield Lodge
LAXTON LA 1
MUSSONS CL 2
Stonepit Farm
THE GREEN
A151
BOURNE ROAD
SWINSTEAD ROAD

24

Pasture Lodge
Heath Farm
Little Bitchneaves Wood
B1176

A151

6

Little Osgrove Wood
Birkholme
Eager Farm

23

Twyford Wood
Dodsey Wood
Herricho Wood
Ling Lane
Manor Farm
Corby Road
High Street
PH
Quarry (dis)
West Glen River
The Ram Plantation

5

Porter's Farm
Elliott's Wood
Wood View Farm
Honey Pot Lane
Swayfield
Overgate Road
High St
Ellerby Mead
Castle Farm
1 THE CRESCENT
2 THE PADDOCKS
3 CASTLE BYTHAM RD
Gorse Hill

22

Todd's Lodge
Water Tower
Beaumont Wood
Worlley's Lane
NG33
Rabbit Hill

4

Hall Farm
Counthorpe Lodge
Black Springs Farm
Croakhill Plantation

21

Moat
Chapel Hill
Park House Farm
Beacon Hill
Hill Farm
Quarry (Limestone)

3

Lobthorpe
South Lodge Farm
Park Grounds
Cabbage Hill Farm
Quarry (Limestone)
Elm Tree Farm
Counthorpe Lane

20

Tortoiseshell Wood Nature Reserve
Quarry
Cabbage Hill
Cabbagehill Wood
Counthorpe House
Earthworks
Lawn Lane

2

Porters Lodge Farm
Potter's Lodge Meadows Nature Reserve
Quarry (dis)
Morkery Lane
Glen House
Castle Farm
Glen Lane
Lawn Wood Nature Reserve

19

P
Morkery Wood
Leach Farm
Pepperidge Farm
Angel Wells Farm
Glenside
Red Barn Farm
The Firs

1

LE15
Potters Hill Farm
Plantation Lodge Farm
Potter's Hill
PINFOLD RD 1
CASTLEGATE 2
HEATHCOTE RD 3
HIGH ST 4
CUMBERLAND GDNS 5
Water Lane
PO
Castle Bytham
St Martins
Stanford
PH
Motte & Bailey
Mill Mound
Thunderbolt Pit (dis)
Glebe Farm
Pit (dis)

18

Stocken Hall Mews
Little Haw Wood
Cemetery
Little Bytham Road
Sewage Works

95   A   96   B   97   C   98   D   99   E   00   F

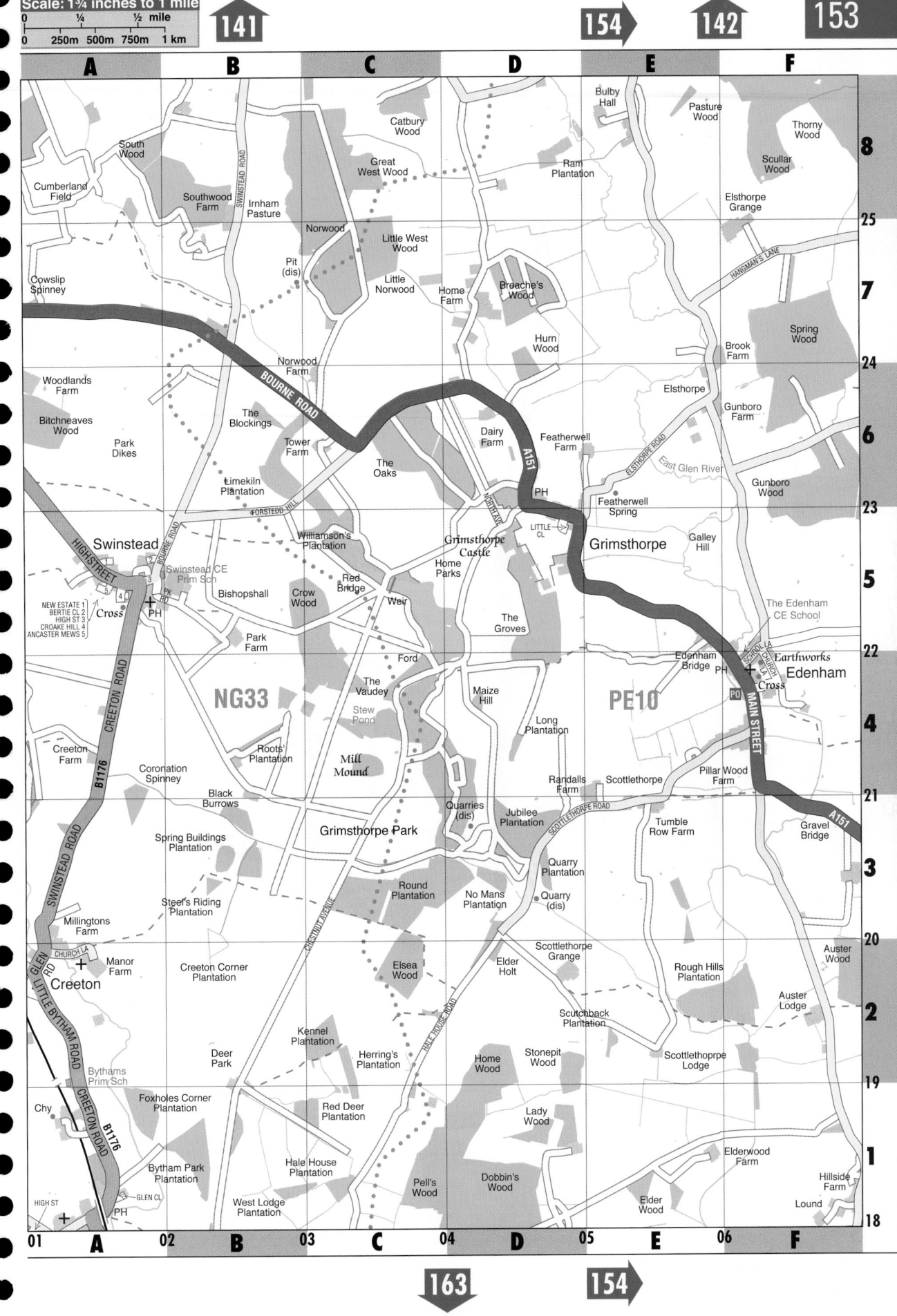

A   B   C   D   E   F

8
25
7
24
6
23
5
22
4
21
3
20
2
19
1
18

South Wood
Cumberland Field
Southwood Farm
Southwood
Irnham Pasture
Catbury Wood
Great West Wood
Ram Plantation
Bulby Hall
Pasture Wood
Thorny Wood
Scullar Wood
Elsthorpe Grange

Cowslip Spinney
Norwood
Little West Wood
Little Norwood
Home Farm
Breache's Wood
Hurn Wood
Hangman's Lane
Brook Farm
Spring Wood

Pit (dis)
Norwood Farm
BOURNE ROAD

Woodlands Farm
Bitchneaves Wood
Park Dikes
The Blockings
Tower Farm
The Oaks
Dairy Farm
Featherwell Farm
PH
Elsthorpe
Gunboro Farm
Gunboro Wood

Limekiln Plantation
FORSTEDD HILL
NORTH LA
Featherwell Spring
ELSTHORPE ROAD
East Glen River

Swinstead
HIGH STREET
Williamson's Plantation
Grimsthorpe Castle
LITTLE CL
Grimsthorpe
Galley Hill

Cross
NEW ESTATE 1
BERTIE CL 2
HIGH ST 3
CROAKE HILL 4
ANCASTER MEWS 5
PH
PK RD
Swinstead CE Prim Sch
Bishopshall
Crow Wood
Red Bridge
Home Parks
Weir
The Groves
The Edenham CE School

Park Farm
Ford
Edenham Bridge
PH
Earthworks
Edenham Cross
Edenham
SCHOOL LA
CHURCH LA
PO
MAIN STREET

NG33
The Vaudey
Stew Pond
Maize Hill
Long Plantation
PE10

Creeton Farm
CREETON ROAD
B1176
Coronation Spinney
Roots' Plantation
Mill Mound
Randalls Farm
Scottlethorpe
Pillar Wood Farm

Black Burrows
Quarries (dis)
Jubilee Plantation
SCOTTLETHORPE ROAD
Tumble Row Farm
Gravel Bridge
A151

Spring Buildings Plantation
Grimsthorpe Park
Quarry Plantation
Quarry (dis)
Rough Hills Plantation
Auster Wood

Steel's Riding Plantation
SWINSTEAD ROAD
Round Plantation
No Mans Plantation
Scottlethorpe Grange
Scutchback Plantation
Scottlethorpe Lodge
Auster Lodge

Millingtons Farm
CHURCH LA
Manor Farm
Creeton Corner Plantation
CHESTNUT AVENUE
Elsea Wood
Elder Holt
Stonepit Wood

Creeton
GLEN RD
LITTLE BYTHAM ROAD
Kennel Plantation
Herring's Plantation
HALL HOUSE ROAD
Home Wood
Lady Wood
Elderwood Farm

Bythams Prim Sch
Deer Park
Red Deer Plantation
Dobbin's Wood
Hillside Farm

Chy
CREETON ROAD
B1176
Foxholes Corner Plantation
Pell's Wood
Elder Wood
Lound

HIGH ST
GLEN CL
PH
Bytham Park Plantation
West Lodge Plantation
Hale House Plantation

01   02   03   04   05   06

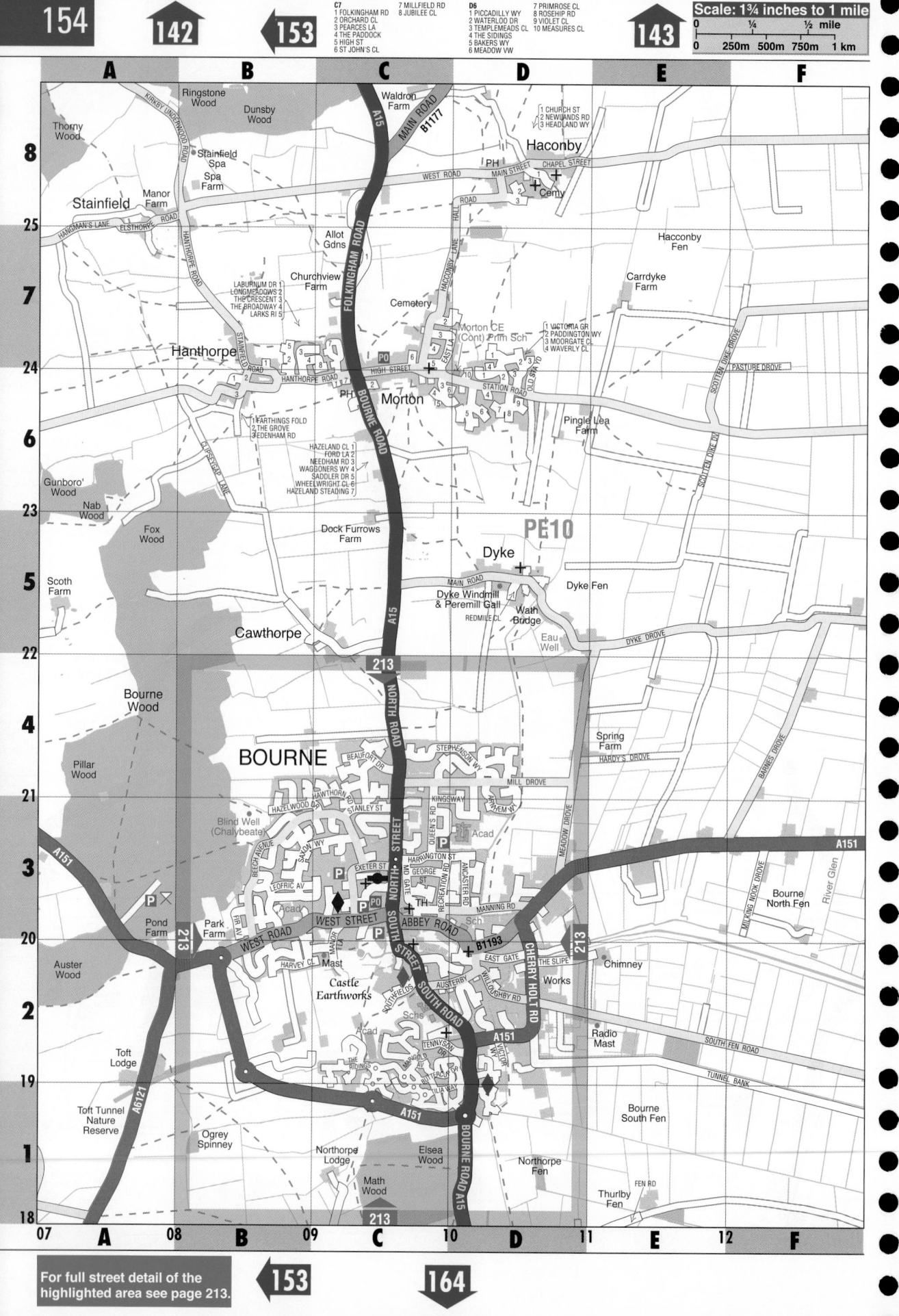

154
142
153
143

Scale: 1¾ inches to 1 mile
0   ¼   ½   mile
0   250m 500m 750m 1 km

C7
1 FOLKINGHAM RD
2 ORCHARD CL
3 PEARCES LA
4 THE PADDOCK
5 HIGH ST
6 ST JOHN'S CL

7 MILLFIELD RD
8 JUBILEE CL

D6
1 PICCADILLY WY
2 WATERLOO DR
3 TEMPLEMEADS CL
4 THE SIDINGS
5 BAKERS WY
6 MEADOW VW

7 PRIMROSE CL
8 ROSEHIP RD
9 VIOLET CL
10 MEASURES CL

A   B   C   D   E   F

Thorny Wood
Ringstone Wood
Dunsby Wood
Waldron Farm

MAIN ROAD
B1177

1 CHURCH ST
2 NEWLANDS RD
3 HEADLAND WY

Haconby

8

Stainfield Spa
Spa Farm

PH
WEST ROAD
MAIN STREET
CHAPEL STREET
Cemy

Stainfield
Manor Farm

HANGMAN'S LANE
ELSTHORPE ROAD
HANTHORPE ROAD
FOLKINGHAM ROAD

25

Allot Gdns

Hacconby Fen

7

LABURNUM DR 1
LONGMEADOWS 2
THE CRESCENT 3
THE BROADWAY 4
LARKS RI 5

Churchview Farm

Cemetery

HACCONBY LANE
HALL ROAD
EAST LA

Carrdyke Farm

SCOTTEN DIKE DROVE

Morton CE (Cont) Prim Sch

1 VICTORIA GR
2 PADDINGTON WY
3 MOORGATE CL
4 WAVERLY CL

24

Hanthorpe

STAINFIELD ROAD
HANTHORPE ROAD
PO
HIGH STREET

STATION ROAD
OLD STA RD

PASTURE DROVE

PH
BOURNE ROAD
Morton

6

1 FARTHINGS FOLD
2 THE GROVE
3 EDENHAM RD

Pingle Lea Farm

UPSHERP LANE
GIPSERP LANE

HAZELAND CL 1
FORD LA 2
NEEDHAM RD 3
WAGGONERS WY 4
SADDLER DR 5
WHEELWRIGHT CL 6
HAZELAND STEADING 7

PE10

Gunboro' Wood

23

Nab Wood

Dock Furrows Farm

Dyke

SCOTTEN DIKE DV

Fox Wood

Scoth Farm

5

Dyke Windmill & Peremill Gall
REDMILE CL
Wath Bridge

Dyke Fen

MAIN ROAD

A15
BOURNE ROAD

Eau Well

Cawthorpe

DYKE DROVE

22

213
NORTH ROAD

Bourne Wood

4

Pillar Wood

BOURNE

BEAUFORT DR
STEPHENSON WY

Spring Farm
HARDY'S DROVE

BARNES DROVE

21

HAZELWOOD
HAWTHORN
STANLEY ST
SAXON WY
MILL DROVE
KINGSWAY
MEADOW DROVE

A151

Blind Well (Chalybeate)

BEECH AVENUE
QUEEN'S RD
Acad

3

A151

HARRINGTON ST

ANCASTER RD
Bourne North Fen

MILKING NOOK DROVE
River Glen

EXETER ST
GEORGE ST
Acad
LEOFRIC AV
PO
TH
Sch
MANNING RD

213

Park Farm
FIR AV

Pond Farm
WEST ROAD
MANOR RD
WEST STREET
SOUTH STREET
ABBEY ROAD
EAST GATE
B1193
Chimney

20

A6121

HARVEY CL
Mast
Works
The Slipe

Auster Wood

2

Castle Earthworks

Acad
Schs
SOUTHFIELDS
AUSTERBY
WILLOUGHBY RD
CHERRY HOLT RD
A151
VICTOR WY

Radio Mast

SOUTH FEN ROAD

Toft Lodge

SOUTH ROAD
TENNYSON
THE RIDINGS
BITTERN
LILIA WY
BUTTERCUP

Bourne South Fen

TUNNEL BANK

19

Toft Tunnel Nature Reserve

Ogrey Spinney

Northorpe Lodge
Elsea Wood
Northorpe Fen

BOURNE ROAD A5

FEN RD
Thurlby Fen

1

Math Wood

213

18

07   A   08   B   09   C   10   D   11   E   12   F

For full street detail of the highlighted area see page 213.

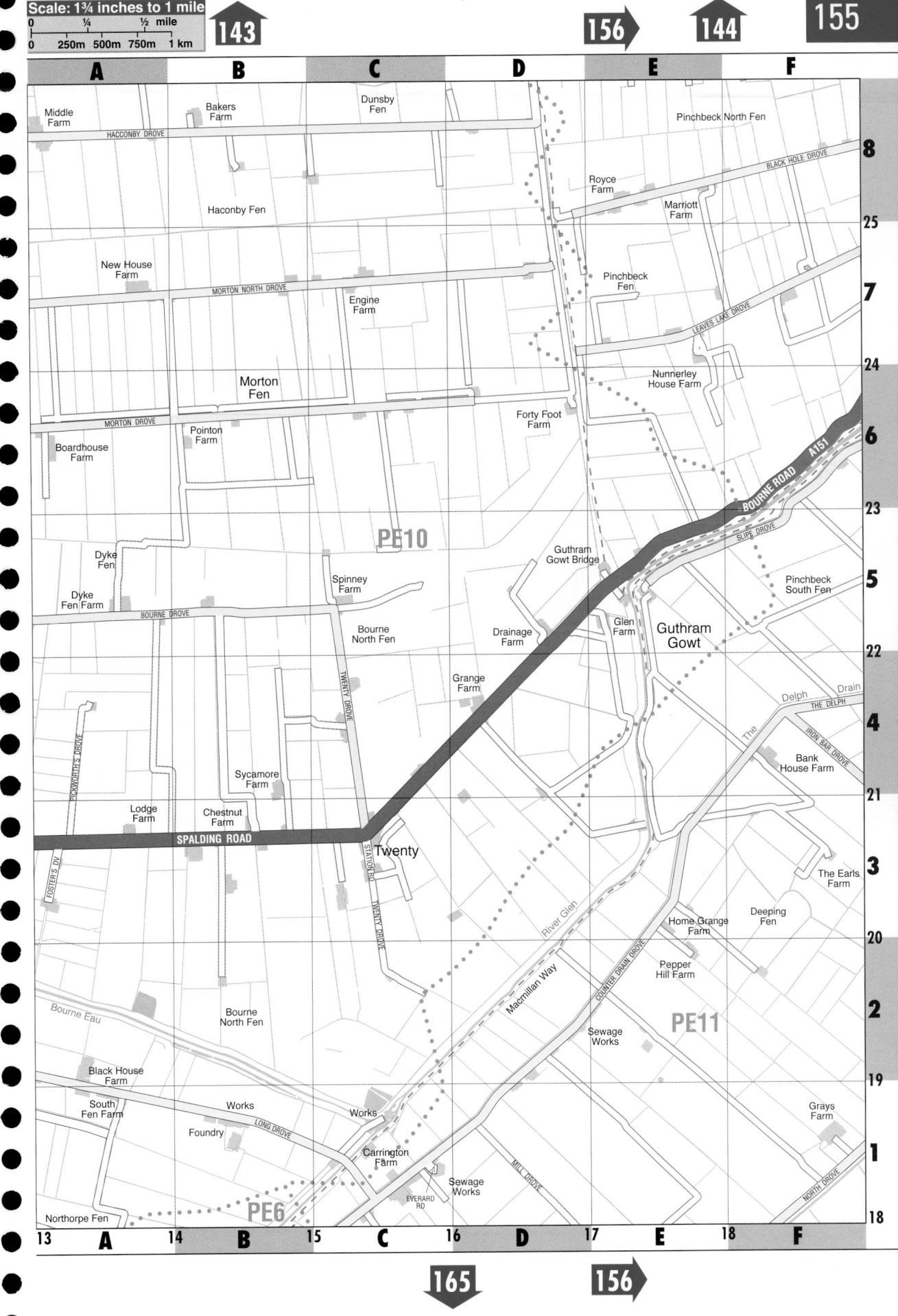

Scale: 1¾ inches to 1 mile

0   ¼   ½ mile
0   250m 500m 750m 1 km

143

156

144

155

A   B   C   D   E   F

Middle Farm

HACONBY DROVE

Bakers Farm

Dunsby Fen

Pinchbeck North Fen

BLACK HOLE DROVE

8

Royce Farm

Marriott Farm

25

Haconby Fen

New House Farm

MORTON NORTH DROVE

Pinchbeck Fen

LEAVES LAKE DROVE

7

Engine Farm

Morton Fen

Nunnerley House Farm

24

MORTON DROVE

Pointon Farm

Forty Foot Farm

6

Boardhouse Farm

BOURNE ROAD A151

PE10

SLIPE DROVE

23

Dyke Fen

Spinney Farm

Guthram Gowt Bridge

Pinchbeck South Fen

5

Dyke Fen Farm

BOURNE DROVE

Bourne North Fen

Drainage Farm

Glen Farm

Guthram Gowt

22

The Delph Drain

THE DELPH

The

IRON BAR DROVE

4

Grange Farm

TWENTY DROVE

Bank House Farm

21

PICKWORTH'S DROVE

Sycamore Farm

Lodge Farm

Chestnut Farm

The Earls Farm

3

SPALDING ROAD

STATION RD

Twenty

TWENTY DROVE

River Glen

Deeping Fen

FOSTER'S DV

Macmillan Way

COUNTER DRAIN DROVE

Home Grange Farm

20

Bourne Eau

Bourne North Fen

Pepper Hill Farm

PE11

2

Black House Farm

Sewage Works

19

South Fen Farm

Works

Works

Grays Farm

1

LONG DROVE

Foundry

Carrington Farm

MILL DROVE

NORTH DROVE

Northorpe Fen

PE6

EVERARD RD

Sewage Works

18

Scale: 1¾ inches to 1 mile
0 ¼ ½ mile
0 250m 500m 750m 1 km

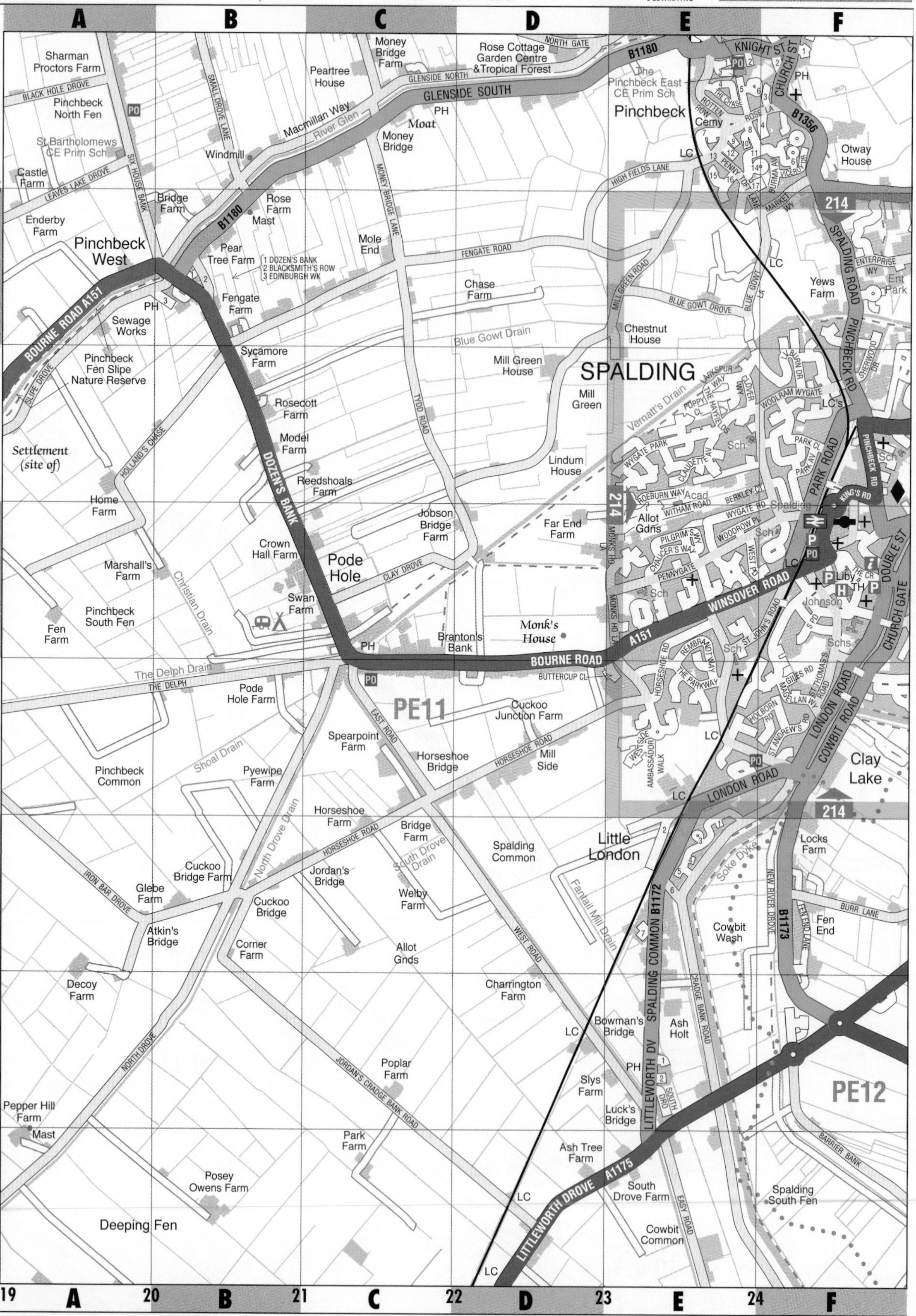

E8
1 WESTFIELD DR
2 GUILDHALL DR
3 FORGE CRES
4 PRIMROSE CRES
5 FENNELL RD
6 WAYET RD
7 LAXTON GDNS
8 WIMBERLEY WY
9 ORCHARD CL
10 HARPE CL
11 MOUNTBATTEN AVE
12 SOUTHGATE
13 CHERRY HOLT LA
14 KELLY CL
15 MAYFIELD CL
16 PENNYFIELD
17 VISCOUNT CL

F8
1 TOWN FARM CL
2 CHURCH WK
3 ST MARY'S AVE
4 ST MARY'S AVE
5 INDEPENDENCE DR
6 EDWINA AVE

Column letters: A B C D E F

Row numbers: 8 25 7 24 6 23 5 22 4 21 3 20 2 19 1 18

Sharman Proctors Farm
BLACK HOLE DROVE
Pinchbeck North Fen
St Bartholomews CE Prim Sch
Castle Farm
Enderby Farm
LEAVES LAKE DROVE
Pinchbeck West
BOURNE ROAD A151
SLIPE DROVE
Settlement (site of)
Home Farm
Marshall's Farm
Pinchbeck South Fen
Fen Farm
Pepper Hill Farm
Mast
Posey Owens Farm
Deeping Fen

Peartree House
Windmill
SMALL DROVE LANE
ST HOUSE BANK
Bridge Farm
B1180
Pear Tree Farm
Fengate Farm
PH
Sewage Works
Pinchbeck Fen Slipe Nature Reserve
HOLLAND'S CHASE
DOZEN'S BANK
Sycamore Farm
Rosecott Farm
Model Farm
Reedshoals Farm
Jobson Bridge Farm
Crown Hall Farm
Pode Hole
Swan Farm
PH
CHRISTIAN DRAIN
The Delph Drain
THE DELPH
Pode Hole Farm
Pinchbeck Common
Pyewipe Farm
SHOAL DRAIN
Glebe Farm
Cuckoo Bridge Farm
Atkin's Bridge
Decoy Farm
IRON BAR DROVE
NORTH DROVE

Money Bridge Farm
MACMILLAN WAY
River Glen
GLENSIDE SOUTH
PH
Moat
Money Bridge
Money Bridge
MONEY BRIDGE LANE
Rose Farm
Mast
Mole End
1 DOZEN'S BANK
2 BLACKSMITH'S ROW
3 EDINBURGH WK
TYDD ROAD
Clay Drove
CLAY DROVE
Branton's Bank
PH
B1180
PO
PE11
EAST ROAD
Spearpoint Farm
Horseshoe Bridge
Horseshoe Farm
Bridge Farm
Jordan's Bridge
Welby Farm
NORTH DROVE DRAIN
HORSESHOE ROAD
SOUTH DROVE DRAIN
Cuckoo Bridge
Corner Farm
Poplar Farm
Allot Gnds
JORDAN'S CRADGE BANK ROAD
Park Farm

GLENSIDE NORTH
NORTH GATE
Rose Cottage Garden Centre & Tropical Forest
B1180
The Pinchbeck East CE Prim Sch
FENGATE ROAD
Chase Farm
Blue Gowt Drain
Mill Green House
HIGH FIELDS LANE
MILL GREEN ROAD
Chestnut House
Lindum House
Far End Farm
Jobson Bridge Farm
Monk's House
BOURNE ROAD
BUTTERCUP CL
Cuckoo Junction Farm
Mill Side
HORSESHOE ROAD
Spalding Common
WEST ROAD
Little London
Charrington Farm
FANTAIL MILL DRAIN
Bowman's Bridge
Slys Farm
Luck's Bridge
Ash Tree Farm
A1175
South Drove Farm
LC
LITTLEWORTH DROVE

Pinchbeck
KNIGHT ST
CHURCH ST
PH
B1356
Cemy
BOTTEN ROW
MARKET WY
PENNY CL
LC
Otway House
214
SPALDING ROAD
PINCHBECK RD
Yews Farm
Ent Park
ENTERPRISE
BLUE GOWT DROVE
BLUE GOWT DRAIN
SPALDING
Mill Green
VERNATT'S DRAIN
WYGATE PARK
Acad
Allot Gdns
PILGRIM'S
214
MONKS RD
PARK ROAD
PINCHBECK RD
Sch
KING'S RD
DOUBLE ST
PO
Liby
TH
P
H
WINSOVER ROAD
Johnson
A151
HORSESHOE RD
THE PARKWAY
ST JOHN'S ROAD
LONDON ROAD
COWBIT ROAD
Clay Lake
214
PO
ST ANDREW'S RD
AMBASSADOR WALK
WESTSIDE
Locks Farm
BURR LANE
Fen End
SPALDING COMMON B1172
LITTLEWORTH DV
B1172
CRADGE BANK ROAD
Soke Dyke
Cowbit Wash
NEW RIVER DRIVE
B1173
FENLAND LANE
Ash Holt
PH
EASY ROAD
South Drove Farm
Cowbit Common
PE12
BARRIER BANK
Spalding South Fen
LITTLEWORTH DROVE A1175

E2
1 STENNETT AVE
2 FANTAIL CL

E3
1 CHEPSTOW CL
2 THE RACEGROUND
3 KEMPTON CL
4 ASCOT CL
5 SANDOWN CL
6 THE RAMPER
7 GOODFELLOWS RD

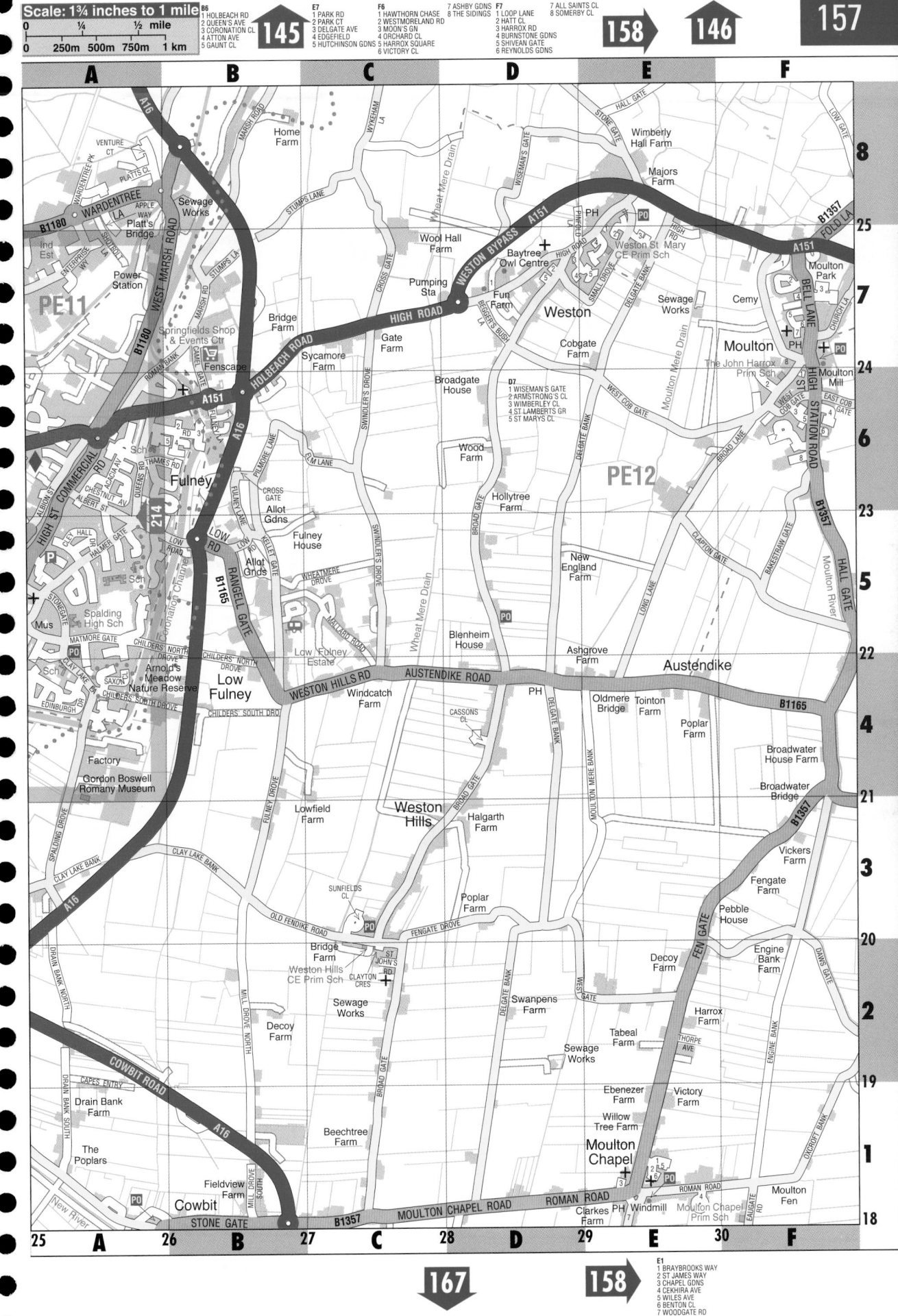

B6
1 HOLBEACH RD
2 QUEEN'S AVE
3 CORONATION CL
4 ATTON AVE
5 GAUNT CL

E7
1 PARK RD
2 PARK CT
3 DELGATE AVE
4 EDGEFIELD
5 HUTCHINSON GDNS

F6
1 HAWTHORN CHASE
2 WESTMORELAND RD
3 MOON'S GN
4 ORCHARD CL
5 HARROX SQUARE
6 VICTORY CL

7 ASHBY GDNS
8 THE SIDINGS

F7
1 LOOP LANE
2 HATT CL
3 HARROX RD
4 BURNSTONE GDNS
5 SHIVEAN GATE
6 REYNOLDS GDNS

7 ALL SAINTS CL
8 SOMERBY CL

145   158   146

167   158

E1
1 BRAYBROOKS WAY
2 ST JAMES WAY
3 CHAPEL GDNS
4 CEKHIRA AVE
5 WILES AVE
6 BENTON CL
7 WOODGATE RD

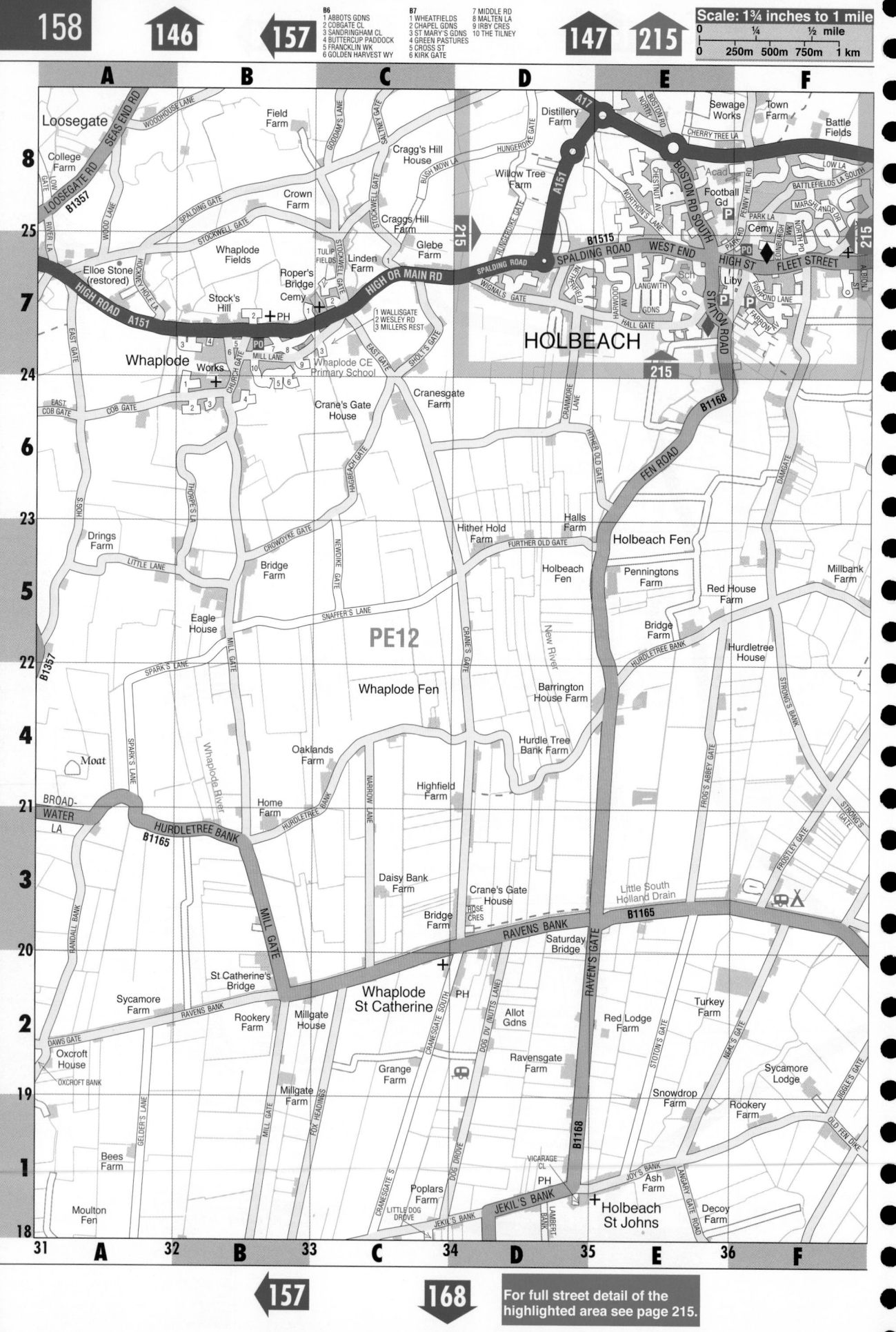

158
146
157
147
215

Scale: 1¾ inches to 1 mile
0   ¼   ½ mile
0   250m   500m   750m   1 km

B6
1 ABBOTS GDNS
2 COBGATE CL
3 SANDRINGHAM CL
4 BUTTERCUP PADDOCK
5 FRANCKLIN WK
6 GOLDEN HARVEST WY

B7
1 WHEATFIELDS
2 CHAPEL GDNS
3 ST MARY'S GDNS
4 GREEN PASTURES
5 CROSS ST
6 KIRK GATE

7 MIDDLE RD
8 MALTEN LA
9 IRBY CRES
10 THE TILNEY

A   B   C   D   E   F

Loosegate

College Farm

8

25

7

24

6

23

5

22

4

21

3

20

2

19

1

18

SEAS END RD
WOODHOUSE LANE
B1357
LOOSEGATE RD
WOOD LANE
LOW GATE
RIVER LA
HIGH ROAD
A151
EAST GATE
HOCKNEYHOLE LA
Elloe Stone (restored)

Whaplode
Works

Stock's Hill
Church Gate
PO
MILL LANE

EAST COB GATE
COB GATE

Field Farm
GODDAM'S LANE
SALTNEY GATE
STOCKWELL GATE
SPALDING GATE
Crown Farm
Whaplode Fields
Cragg's Hill House
BUSH MOW LA
Craggs Hill Farm
STOCKWELL GATE
TULIP FIELDS
Linden Farm
Glebe Farm
HIGH OR MAIN RD
Roper's Bridge Cemy
1 WALLISGATE
2 WESLEY RD
3 MILLERS REST
PH
Whaplode CE Primary School
Whaplode
SHOLL'S GATE
EAST GATE

Crane's Gate House
Cranesgate Farm
CRANMORE LANE
CROWOYKE GATE
HAGBECK GATE
NEWDIKE GATE

Drings Farm
LITTLE LANE
Bridge Farm
SNAFFER'S LANE
THORPE'S LA
S SQH
Eagle House
MILL GATE
SPARK'S LANE

PE12

Whaplode Fen

Moat
SPARK'S LANE
Whaplode River
Oaklands Farm
NARROW LANE
Home Farm
HURDLETREE BANK
Highfield Farm
Daisy Bank Farm

BROAD-WATER LA
B1357
B1165
HURDLETREE BANK
RANDALL BANK
MILL GATE

St Catherine's Bridge
Sycamore Farm
RAVENS BANK
DAWS GATE
Rookery Farm
Millgate House
GELDER'S LANE
Millgate Farm
Grange Farm
CRANESGATE S
FOX HEADINGS
MILL GATE

Oxcroft House
OXCROFT BANK

Bees Farm

Moulton Fen

Whaplode St Catherine
RAVENS BANK
Saturday Bridge
Allot Gdns
ROSE CRES
Crane's Gate House
Bridge Farm
PH
DOG DIKE DV
JEKIL'S LANE
DOG DROVE
Poplars Farm
LITTLE DOG DROVE
JEKIL'S BANK

Distillery Farm
A17
NORTHAM
HUNGERGATE GATE
A151
Willow Tree Farm
JUNGERGATE GATE
SPALDING ROAD
WIGNALS GATE
215

B1515
SPALDING ROAD
WEST END
Scb
HOLBEACH
LANGWITH GDNS
GOODWIN AV
HALL GATE
215
B1168

Cherry Tree La
BOSTON RD NORTH
CHESTNUT AV
NORTHOR'S LANE
Acad
Football Gd
P
High St
Liby
STATION ROAD
P P
PARROW

Sewage Works
Town Farm
LOW LA
Cemy
PARK LA
PENNY HILL RD
PARK RD
NORTH RD
FISH POND LANE
Battle Fields
Battlefields La South
MARSHLANDS RD
FLEET STREET
215
ALBION

Hither Hold Farm
FURTHER OLD GATE
CRANE'S GATE
Holbeach Fen
Halls Farm
HITHER OLD GATE
FEN ROAD
DAMGATE
Holbeach Fen
Penningtons Farm
Red House Farm
Bridge Farm
HURDLETREE BANK
Hurdletree House
Millbank Farm

Barrington House Farm
New River
Hurdle Tree Bank Farm
FROG'S ABBEY GATE
STRONG'S BANK

STRONG'S GATE
FROSTLEY GATE
Little South Holland Drain
B1165
Red Lodge Farm
STOTON'S GATE
Turkey Farm
NIGEL'S GATE
Snowdrop Farm
NIGGLE'S GATE
Sycamore Lodge
Rookery Farm
OLD FEN DIKE

RAVEN'S GATE
B1168
Ravensgate Farm
LAMBERT BANK
VICARAGE CL
PH
JEKIL'S BANK
Holbeach St Johns
JOY'S BANK
Ash Farm
LANGARY GATE ROAD
Decoy Farm

31   A   32   B   33   C   34   D   35   E   36   F

For full street detail of the highlighted area see page 215.

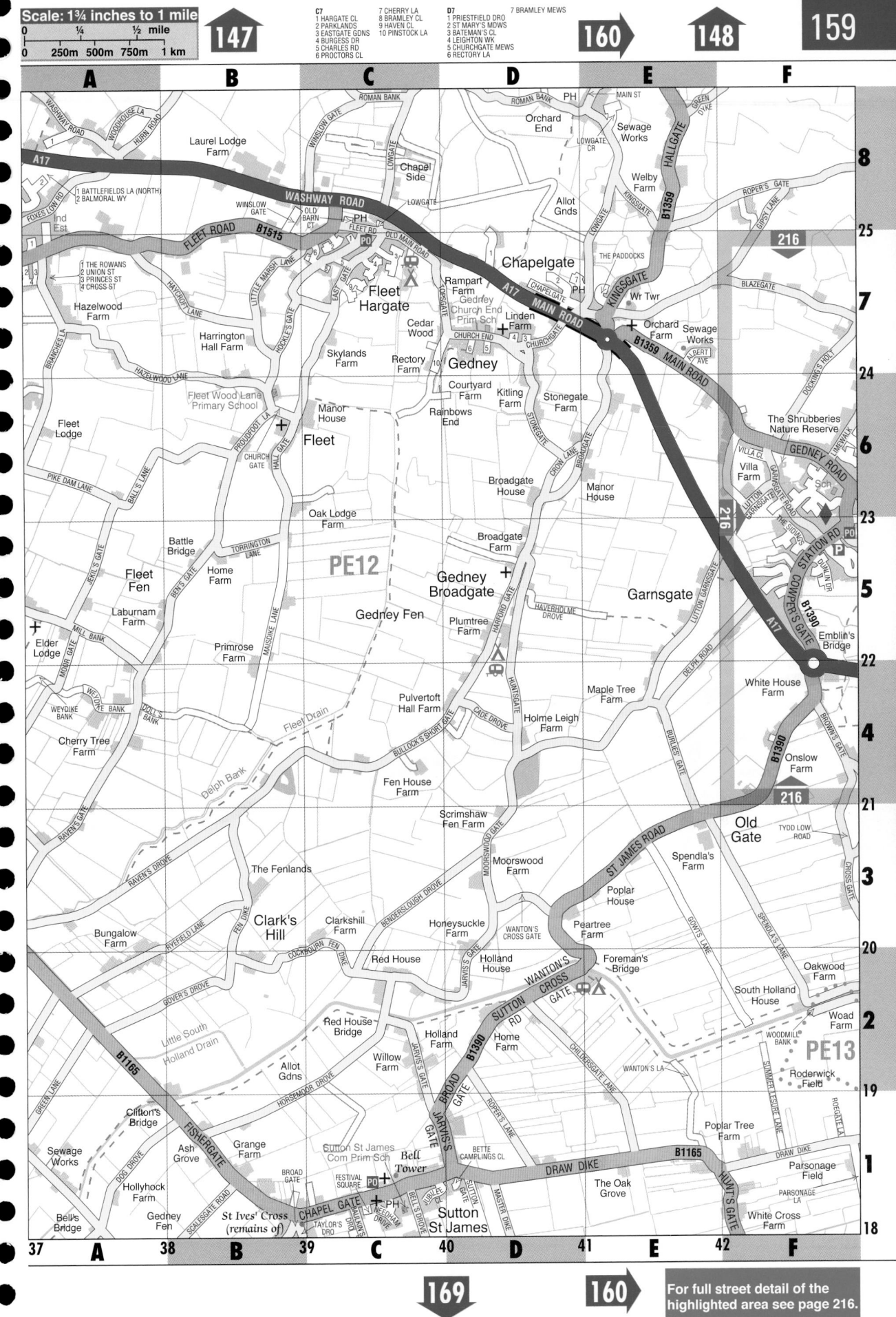

Scale: 1¾ inches to 1 mile

0   ¼   ½ mile
0 250m 500m 750m 1 km

147

160

148

159

C7
1 HARGATE CL
2 PARKLANDS
3 EASTGATE GDNS
4 BURGESS DR
5 CHARLES RD
6 PROCTORS CL

7 CHERRY LA
8 BRAMLEY CL
9 HAVEN CL
10 PINSTOCK LA

D7
1 PRIESTFIELD DRO
2 ST MARY'S MDWS
3 BATEMAN'S CL
4 LEIGHTON WK
5 CHURCHGATE MEWS
6 RECTORY LA

7 BRAMLEY MEWS

A   B   C   D   E   F

ROMAN BANK

WASHWAY ROAD

A17

Laurel Lodge Farm

WINSLOW GATE

LOWGATE

Chapel Side

ROMAN BANK

PH

Orchard End

MAIN ST

LOWGATE CR

Sewage Works

Welby Farm

HALLGATE

GREEN DYKE

8

1 BATTLEFIELDS LA (NORTH)
2 BALMORAL WY

FLEET ROAD   B1515

WINSLOW GATE

FLEET RD

OLD BARN CT

PH

PO

Old Main Road

Chapelgate

THE PADDOCKS

KINGSGATE

B1359

ROPER'S GATE

GIPSY LANE

216

25

Foxes Low Rd

Ind Est

1 THE ROWANS
2 UNION ST
3 PRINCES ST
4 CROSS ST

Hazelwood Farm

HAYCROFT LANE

LITTLE MARSH LANE

EAST GATE

CHAPELGATE

Fleet Hargate

Rampart Farm

Gedney Church End Prim Sch

Linden Farm

A17

MAIN ROAD

PH

Wr Twr

KINGSGATE

Orchard Farm

B1359

MAIN ROAD

ALBERT AVE

Sewage Works

BLAZEGATE

DUCKING'S HOLT

216

7

BRANCHES LA

HAZELWOOD LANE

Harrington Hall Farm

Skylands Farm

Cedar Wood

CHURCH END

Rectory Farm

10

Gedney

CHURCHGATE

VILLA CL

Villa Farm

GEDNEY ROAD

Sch

LIMEWALK

The Shrubberies Nature Reserve

24

Fleet Wood Lane Primary School

PROUDFOOT LA

CHURCH GATE

HALL GATE

Manor House

Fleet

Courtyard Farm

Rainbows End

Kitling Farm

Stonegate Farm

CRON LANE

BROADGATE

Manor House

GARNSGATE ROAD

LUTTON GARNSGATE

THE SIDINGS

STATION RD

PO

6

Fleet Lodge

PIKE DAM LANE

BALL'S LANE

TORRINGTON LANE

Oak Lodge Farm

PE12

Broadgate House

Broadgate Farm

216

P

DUNLOP DR

B1390

23

Battle Bridge

Home Farm

MASIOUNE LANE

Gedney Broadgate

HAVERHOLME DROVE

Manor House

Garnsgate

A17

COWPER'S GATE

Emblin's Bridge

22

JEVIL'S GATE

BEN'S GATE

Fleet Fen

Laburnam Farm

Gedney Fen

Plumtree Farm

HARFORD GATE

HUNTSGATE

Maple Tree Farm

DELPH ROAD

White House Farm

BROWN'S GATE

MILL BANK

MOOR GATE

Elder Lodge

Primrose Farm

Pulvertoft Hall Farm

Holme Leigh Farm

CADE DROVE

BURLEIS GATE

B1390

Onslow Farm

216

21

WEYDIKE BANK

WYKE BANK

DOLL'S BANK

Cherry Tree Farm

Fleet Drain

BULLOCK'S SHORT GATE

Fen House Farm

DELPH BANK

Scrimshaw Fen Farm

MOORSWOOD GATE

Moorswood Farm

ST JAMES ROAD

Spendla's Farm

Old Gate

TYDD LOW ROAD

CROSS GATE

3

RAVEN'S GATE

RAVEN'S DROVE

FEN DIKE

The Fenlands

Clarkshill Farm

BENDERSLOUGH DROVE

Honeysuckle Farm

WANTON'S CROSS GATE

Poplar House

Peartree Farm

GUNT'S LANE

SPENDLA'S LANE

20

RYEFIELD LANE

Clark's Hill

JARVIS'S GATE

COCKBURN FEN DIKE

Red House

Holland House

WANTON'S CROSS GATE

Foreman's Bridge

Oakwood Farm

South Holland House

WOODMILL BANK

PE13

2

GOVER'S DROVE

Bungalow Farm

HORSEMOOR DROVE

Red House Bridge

Willow Farm

Holland Farm

Home Farm

BROAD GATE

SUTTON RD

ROPER'S LANE

CHILDERSGATE LANE

WANTON'S LA

SUMMER LEISURE LANE

Roderwick Field

Woad Farm

ROEGATE LA

19

B1165

Little South Holland Drain

Allot Gdns

JARVIS'S GATE

B1390

DRAW DIKE

Poplar Tree Farm

GREEN LANE

Clifton's Bridge

FISHERGATE

Ash Grove

Grange Farm

Sutton St James Com Prim Sch

Bell Tower

BETTE CAMPLINGS CL

MASTER DIKE

B1165

DRAW DIKE

The Oak Grove

HUVT'S GATE

Poplar Tree Farm

DRAW DIKE

Parsonage Field

PARSONAGE LA

1

Sewage Works

DOG DROVE

Hollyhock Farm

Gedney Fen

SCALESGATE ROAD

CHAPEL GATE

FESTIVAL SQUARE

PO

PH

JUBILEE DRO

BELL'S DROVE

SUTTON GATE

Sutton St James

White Cross Farm

18

Bell's Bridge

St Ives' Cross (remains of)

TAYLOR'S DRO

NEEDHAM DROVE

FAULKNER'S

37   A   38   B   39   C   40   D   41   E   42   F

169

160

For full street detail of the highlighted area see page 216.

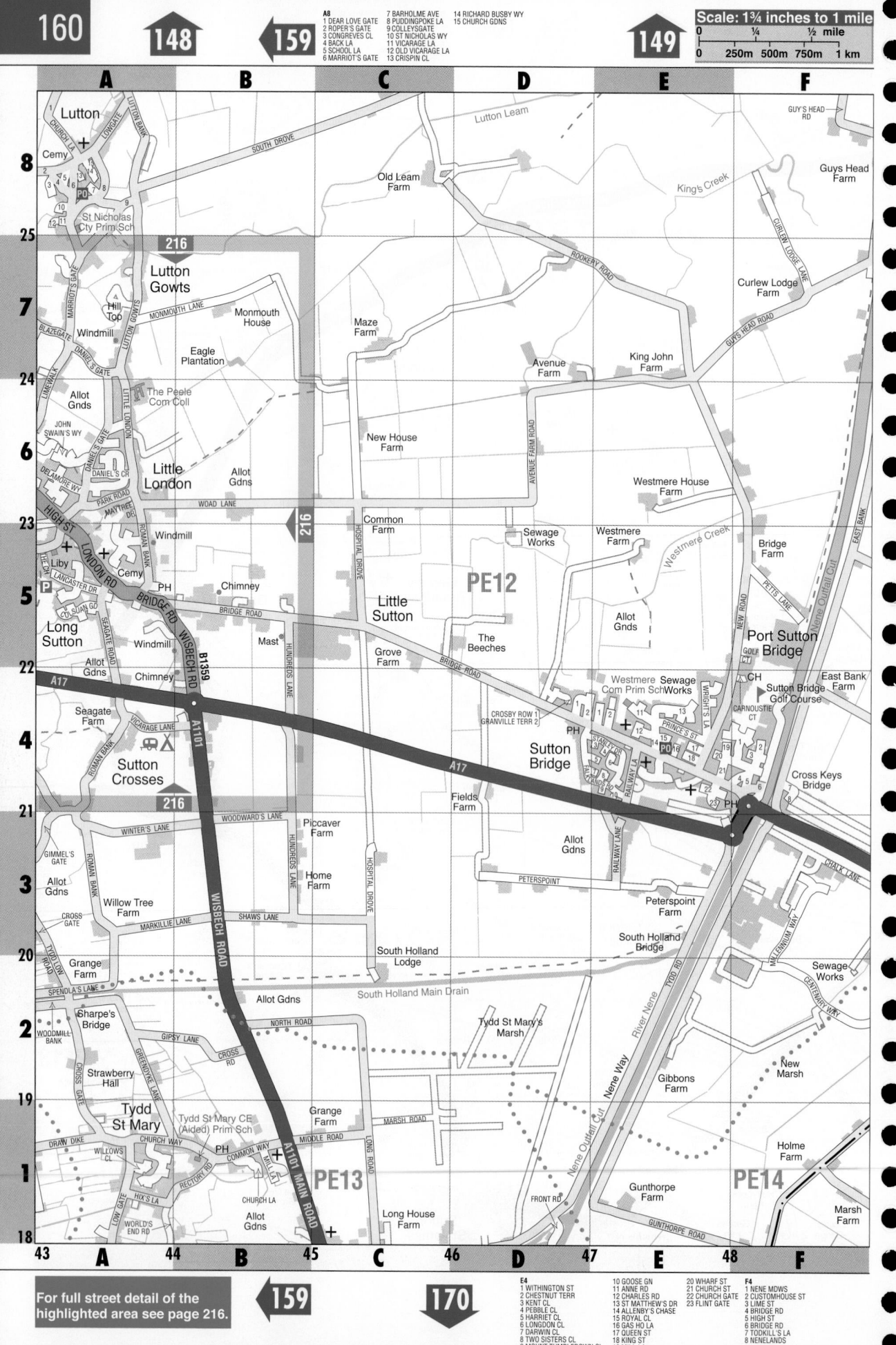

148
159
149

Scale: 1¾ inches to 1 mile
0   ¼   ½   mile
0   250m 500m 750m 1 km

A8
1 DEAR LOVE GATE
2 ROPER'S GATE
3 CONGREVES CL
4 BACK LA
5 SCHOOL LA
6 MARRIOT'S GATE
7 BARHOLME AVE
8 PUDDINGPOKE LA
9 COLLEYSGATE
10 ST NICHOLAS WY
11 VICARAGE LA
12 OLD VICARAGE LA
13 CRISPIN CL
14 RICHARD BUSBY WY
15 CHURCH GDNS

Lutton
Cemy
PO
St Nicholas
Cty Prim Sch
Lutton Leam
Old Leam Farm
King's Creek
GUY'S HEAD RD
Guys Head Farm

Lutton Gowts
216
Hill Top
Windmill
Monmouth Lane
Monmouth House
Eagle Plantation
Maze Farm
ROOKERY ROAD
Avenue Farm
King John Farm
Curlew Lodge Farm
CURLEW LODGE LANE

Marriot's Gate
Blazegate
Daniel's Gate
Allot Gnds
John Swain's Wy
Daniel's Gate
Little London
Daniel's Cr
Park Road
Maytree Dr
Woad Lane
Allot Gdns
The Peele Com Coll
Little London
New House Farm
AVENUE FARM ROAD
Westmere House Farm
GUYS HEAD ROAD

Delamore Wy
High St
London Rd
Cemy
Bridge Rd
Windmill
Chimney
Common Farm
Little Sutton
PE12
Sewage Works
Westmere Farm
Westmere Creek
Bridge Farm
NEW ROAD
PETTIS LANE
EAST BANK
Nene Outfall Cut

Liby
Lancaster Dr
Colsquar Gd
PH
Seagate Road
Windmill
Chimney
Bridge Road
Grove Farm
The Beeches
Allot Gnds
Port Sutton Bridge
GOLF CT
CH
Long Sutton
Wisbech Rd
B1359
Mast
Hundreds Lane
Hospital Drove
BRIDGE ROAD
Westmere Com Prim Sch
Sewage Works
CARNOUSTIE CT
East Bank Farm
Sutton Bridge Golf Course

A17
Allot Gdns
Seagate Farm
A1101
Vicarage Lane
Roman Bank
Crosby Row 1
Granville Terr 2
PH
PO
PH
Sutton Bridge
PRINCE'S ST
STANLEY DR
RAILWAY LA
Cross Keys Bridge

Sutton Crosses
216
WINTER'S LANE
Woodward's Lane
Piccaver Farm
Fields Farm
Allot Gdns
PETERSPOINT
RAILWAY LANE
CHALK LANE

Gimmel's Gate
Roman Bank
Allot Gdns
Hundreds Lane
Home Farm
Shaws Lane
South Holland Bridge
Peterspoint Farm
TYDD RD
MILLENNIUM WAY
Sewage Works

Cross Gate
Willow Tree Farm
Markillie Lane
South Holland Lodge
South Holland Bridge
River Nene
Nene Way
CENTENARY WAY

Tydd Low Rd
Grange Farm
Spendla's Lane
South Holland Main Drain
Tydd St Mary's Marsh
New Marsh

Woodmill Bank
Sharpe's Bridge
Gipsy Lane
North Road
Cross Rd
Allot Gdns
Gibbons Farm
Nene Outfall Cut

Cross Gate
Strawbery Hall
Greendyke Lane
Tydd St Mary
Tydd St Mary CE (Aided) Prim Sch
Church Way
PH
Grange Farm
Marsh Road
Middle Road
Long Road
Gunthorpe Farm
PE14
Holme Farm

Draw Dike
Willows Cl
Hix's La
Low Gate
World's End Rd
Rectory Rd
Common Way
Mill La
A1101 MAIN ROAD
Church La
Allot Gdns
PE13
Long House Farm
FRONT RD
GUNTHORPE ROAD
Marsh Farm

E4
1 WITHINGTON ST
2 CHESTNUT TERR
3 KENT CL
4 PEBBLE CL
5 HARRIET CL
6 LONGDON CL
7 DARWIN CL
8 TWO SISTERS CL
9 MOUNT TUMBLEDOWN CL
10 GOOSE GN
11 ANNE RD
12 CHARLES RD
13 ST MATTHEW'S DR
14 ALLENBY'S CHASE
15 ROYAL CL
16 GAS HO LA
17 QUEEN ST
18 KING ST
19 MILL LA
20 WHARF ST
21 CHURCH ST
22 CHURCH GATE
23 FLINT GATE

F4
1 NENE MDWS
2 CUSTOMHOUSE ST
3 LIME ST
4 BRIDGE RD
5 HIGH ST
6 BRIDGE RD
7 TODKILL'S LA
8 NENELANDS

A B C D E F

Norfolk STREET ATLAS

Peter Scott Walk

8

25

Head Lighthouse (Dis)

East Lighthouse (Dis)

P

River Nene

WEST BANK RD

7

Lighthouse Farm

Walkers Marsh

24

Nene Lodge Farm

Kamarad Farm

Wingland Marsh

Terrington Marsh

Nene Way

New Intake Farm

Bankside Farm

Sharpes Bank Farm

Burman Farm

FERN FARM LA

6

SLUICE ROAD

Clarks Farm

New Marsh Common

Fern House Farm

23

PE12

Grange Farm

Weatherall Farm

Grove Farm

Creek Farm

Myrobella Farm

5

HOSPITAL ROAD

Grange Farm

COCKETHOLE ROAD

Wingland Grange

PE34

Sycamore Farm

Bungalow Farm

LONG ROAD

22

White House Farm

ANCHOR ROAD

Middle Crown Farm

Home Farm

Tommyshop Farm

Bellmount

Sewage Works

4

Red House Farm

Old Common Marsh

NEW ROMAN BANK

Eversfield Farm

Bleak House Farm

GARNER'S LANE

GRANGE ROAD

Middle Crown Farm

MIDDLE ROAD

21

Orange Row

Allot Gdns

Crown Farm

New Inland Marsh

OLD ROMAN BANK

NEW ROMAN BANK

Emorsgate

BEACON HILL LANE

Emorsgate Farm

CHURCH BANK

3

A17

White House Farm

GRANGE ROAD

Poplar Tree Farm

Walpole Cross Keys

LOW RD

Spencer Farm

CRASKE LANE

BRUSH MEADOW LANE

Sea Newland Field

EMORSGATE

LOW LANE

CHAPEL ROAD

PH

Terrington St Clement

PH

SUTTON ROAD

Whitehouse Farm

LITTLE HOLME RD

STATION ROAD

SUTTON ROAD

Plumbs Farm

Dovecote Farm

MARGATE LANE

SEBMAN'S LANE

POPE'S LANE

WANTON LANE

WALCOTT STREET

PEDER ST

20

KING JOHN BANK

SUTTON ROAD

Walpole House

Poplar Farm

Bonnetts Farm

South Green

HAY GN RD (N)

EASTGATE LA S

MARKET LANE

Cockles Farm

LOVELL WY 1
HOWARD CL 2
SPRING GR 3
SUTTON RD 4

Lovell's Hall

A17 King's Lynn

2

EASTLANDS BANK

Crown Farm

Norfolk Cycle Way

STATION RD S

Station Farm

A17

19

PE14

Old Inclosed Marsh

Long Four Farm

EASTLANDS BANK

WISBECH ROAD

BUSTARDS BANK

MARKET LANE

Cherry Farm

Hankinson's Est

FENCE BANK

HAY GREEN RD (SOUTH)

HAY GREEN ROAD

Tuxhill Farm

TUXHILL ROAD

HAY GN RD

Experimental Husbandry Farm

MOAT ROAD

BULLOCK ROAD

1

GOOSE'S LANE

Highenden House

Feale Abbey

Hay Green

JANKIN LA

18

Norfolk STREET ATLAS

49 A 50 B 51 C 52 D 53 E 54 F

F3
1 ORANGE ROW RD
2 CHURCH BANK
3 ORANGE ROW
4 KING WILLIAM CL
5 WESLEY AVE
6 THE SALTINGS
7 BRELLOWS HILL
8 CAVE'S CL
9 WESLEY RD
10 MARSHLAND ST
11 WESLEY CL
12 FOLKES DR
13 COBBS HILL

E8
1 LITTLE BYTHAM RD
2 REGAL GDNS
3 BYTHAM HEIGHTS

Scale: 1¾ inches to 1 mile
0   ¼   ½ mile
0   250m 500m 750m   1 km

Stocken Park
HM Prison
Lady Wood
Little Haw Wood
Quarry (dis)
Glebe Farm
Meadows End

NG33

Chimney
Addah Wood
Clipsham Park Wood
School Farm
Belton Firs
Pillowsyke Holt
Lodge Farm

1 HESKETH CT
2 FLEETWOOD CT
3 WILSON CT
4 STOVE CT

Stretton Wood

BRADLEY LA 1
CHURCH LA 2
NEW RD 3
WEST ST 4

Clipsham Park
Quarry (dis)
New Wood
Holywell Hall

Moor Plantation
Clipsham
MAIN ST
The Quarries
Holywell Quarry
Holy Well

Stockton Lane Plantation
STRETTON ROAD
Manor Farm
Hill Top Farm
New Quarry House
HOLYWELL ROAD
Holywell Quarry
Mill Farm

PH
MANOR RD
BIDWELL LANE
New Quarry Plantation
Infield Holt
CLIPSHAM ROAD
CASTLE BYTHAM ROAD
CARLBY ROAD

LE15
Bidwell Farm
White's Plantation
Quarries (dis)
Pettywood Farm
Pattinson's Holt

Glebe Farm
Osbonall Wood
Clipsham Old Quarry (Limestone)
Quarry (dis)
Holywell Wood
Lincolnshire Gate
Robert's Field Nature Reserve

Big Pits Wood
Pickworth Great Wood
The Grange
Newell Wood
Clay Pit
Castle Dike

Greetham Wood Far
Quarry (dis)
NEWELL LANE

A1 Grantham
Quarry (dis)
Woolfox Wood
Church (remains of)
Pit (dis)

Airfield (dis)
Pickworth
Turnpole Wood

A1
The Coppice
THE PLAINS
CASTERTON LANE

Woolfox Depot
Taylor's Farm

Hardwick Wood
Pickworth Plain

CH
PE9
Rutland County Golf Course

North Road Spinney
Woodhead
East Wood

Horn Farm
PICKWORTH LANE
GREAT NORTH ROAD
Exeter Gorse
Woodhead Castle (site of)
PICKWORTH ROAD

Medieval Village of Horn (site of)
Little Oaks
Warren Plantation
Mounts Lodge

North Brook
Pug's Park Spinney
Bloody Oaks
Tickencote Warren

HORN LANE
Empingham Old Wood
Wing Plantations
Quarry (dis)

Horn Mill Spinney
Tickencote Laund
Quarry (dis)

A1

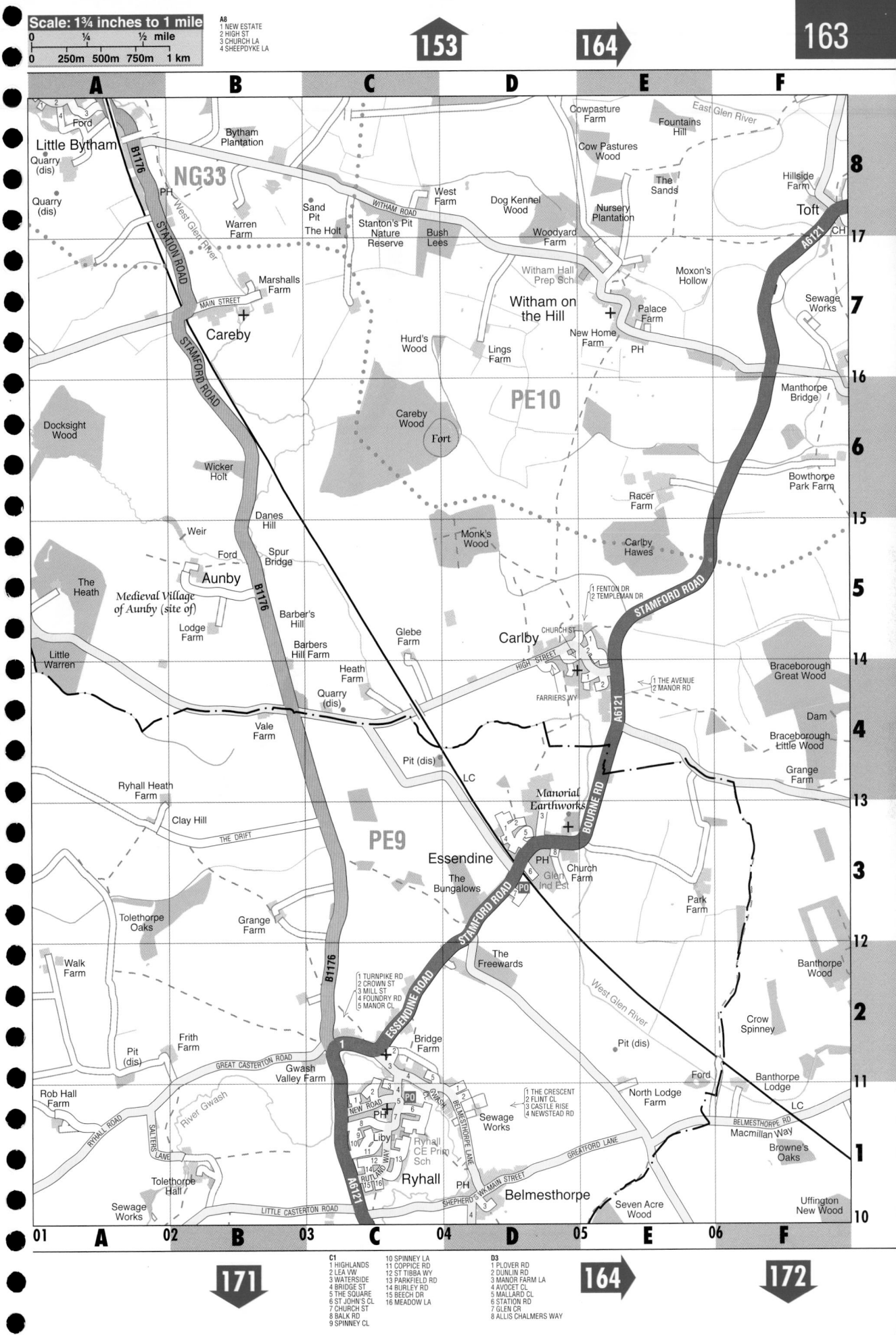
Scale: 1¾ inches to 1 mile
0 ¼ ½ mile
0 250m 500m 750m 1 km
A8
1 NEW ESTATE
2 HIGH ST
3 CHURCH LA
4 SHEEPDYKE LA
153
164
A B C D E F
Little Bytham
Ford
Quarry (dis)
Quarry (dis)
Bytham Plantation
B1176
NG33
PH
West Glen River
STATION ROAD
Warren Farm
Sand Pit
The Holt
WITHAM ROAD
Stanton's Pit Nature Reserve
West Farm
Bush Lees
Dog Kennel Wood
Cowpasture Farm
Cow Pastures Wood
Fountains Hill
East Glen River
The Sands
Nursery Plantation
Woodyard Farm
Hillside Farm
Toft
CH
A6121
Witham Hall Prep Sch
Moxon's Hollow
Sewage Works
Marshalls Farm
MAIN STREET
Careby
Witham on the Hill
Palace Farm
New Home Farm
PH
Hurd's Wood
Lings Farm
STAMFORD ROAD
PE10
Manthorpe Bridge
Docksight Wood
Careby Wood
Fort
Bowthorpe Park Farm
Wicker Holt
Racer Farm
Danes Hill
Weir
Monk's Wood
Carlby Hawes
Ford
Spur Bridge
Aunby
The Heath
Medieval Village of Aunby (site of)
1 FENTON DR
2 TEMPLEMAN DR
STAMFORD ROAD
Barber's Hill
Lodge Farm
Glebe Farm
CHURCH ST
Carlby
Little Warren
Barbers Hill Farm
HIGH STREET
Heath Farm
1 THE AVENUE
2 MANOR RD
Braceborough Great Wood
Quarry (dis)
FARRIERS WY
A6121
Dam
Vale Farm
Braceborough Little Wood
Pit (dis)
LC
Grange Farm
Ryhall Heath Farm
Manorial Earthworks
BOURNE RD
Clay Hill
THE DRIFT
PE9
Essendine
PH
The Bungalows
Church Farm
Glen Ind Est
PO
STAMFORD ROAD
Park Farm
Tolethorpe Oaks
Grange Farm
The Freewards
Banthorpe Wood
Walk Farm
B1176
1 TURNPIKE RD
2 CROWN ST
3 MILL ST
4 FOUNDRY RD
5 MANOR CL
ESSENDINE ROAD
West Glen River
Crow Spinney
Frith Farm
Pit (dis)
Bridge Farm
Pit (dis)
GREAT CASTERTON ROAD
Gwash Valley Farm
Ford
Banthorpe Lodge
Rob Hall Farm
River Gwash
NEW ROAD
PO
PH
GWASH
1 THE CRESCENT
2 FLINT CL
3 CASTLE RISE
4 NEWSTEAD RD
North Lodge Farm
LC
RYHALL ROAD
SALTERS LANE
Liby
Ryhall CE Prim Sch
BELMESTHORPE LANE
Sewage Works
BELMESTHORPE RD
Macmillan Way
Browne's Oaks
GREATFORD LANE
RUTLAND WAY
Ryhall
PH
MAIN STREET
SHEPHERD'S WK
A6121
Tolethorpe Hall
Sewage Works
LITTLE CASTERTON ROAD
Belmesthorpe
Seven Acre Wood
Uffington New Wood
8 17 7 16 6 15 5 14 4 13 3 12 2 11 1 10
01 02 03 04 05 06
171
C1
1 HIGHLANDS
2 LEA VW
3 WATERSIDE
4 BRIDGE ST
5 THE SQUARE
6 ST JOHN'S CL
7 CHURCH ST
8 BALK RD
9 SPINNEY CL
10 SPINNEY LA
11 COPPICE RD
12 ST TIBBA WY
13 PARKFIELD RD
14 BURLEY RD
15 BEECH DR
16 MEADOW LA
D3
1 PLOVER RD
2 DUNLIN RD
3 MANOR FARM LA
4 AVOCET CL
5 MALLARD CL
6 STATION RD
7 GLEN CR
8 ALLIS CHALMERS WAY
164
172

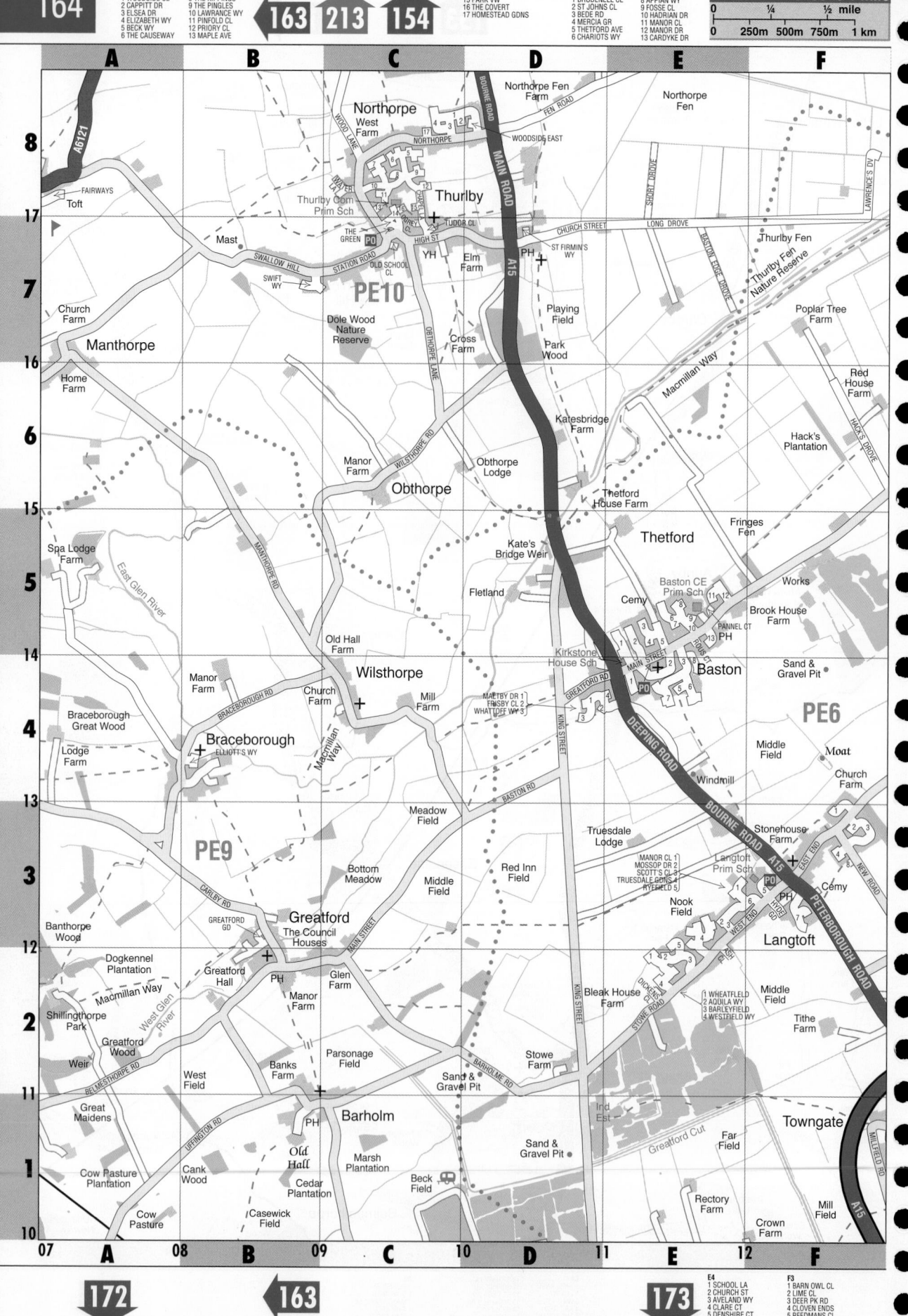

C8
1 WOODSIDE CL
2 CAPPITT DR
3 ELSEA DR
4 ELIZABETH WY
5 BECK WY
6 THE CAUSEWAY

7 VIKING WY
8 THE KIPPINGS
9 THE PINGLES
10 LAWRANCE WY
11 PINFOLD CL
12 PRIORY CL
13 MAPLE AVE

14 CROWN LA
15 PARK VW
16 THE COVERT
17 HOMESTEAD GDNS

E5
1 BRUDENELL CL
2 ST JOHNS CL
3 BEDE RD
4 MERCIA GR
5 THETFORD AVE
6 CHARIOTS WY

7 CAESAR CL
8 APPIAN WY
9 FOSSE CL
10 HADRIAN DR
11 MANOR CL
12 MANOR DR
13 CARDYKE DR

163 213 154

A6121
FAIRWAYS
Toft

Church Farm

Manthorpe

Home Farm

Mast

SWALLOW HILL

SWIFT WY

STATION ROAD

PE10

Northorpe
West Farm
Thurlby Com Prim Sch
THE GREEN
YH
HIGH ST
OLD SCHOOL CL
TUDOR CL
Thurlby
NORTHORPE
WATER ?
YH
Elm Farm
St FIRMIN'S WY
PH

Northorpe Fen Farm
Northorpe Fen
WOODSIDE EAST
FEN ROAD

CHURCH STREET
LONG DROVE
Thurlby Fen
Thurlby Fen Nature Reserve

BOURNE ROAD
A15

MAIN ROAD

SHORT DROVE
BASTON EDGE DROVE
LAWRENCE'S DV

Poplar Tree Farm

Dole Wood Nature Reserve

Cross Farm

Playing Field

Park Wood

Katesbridge Farm

Macmillan Way

Red House Farm

Hack's Plantation

HACK'S DRIVE

WILSTHORPE RD

ORTHORPE LANE

Manor Farm

Obthorpe

Obthorpe Lodge

Thetford House Farm

Thetford

Fringes Fen

Spa Lodge Farm

East Glen River

MANTHORPE RD

Old Hall Farm

Wilsthorpe

Kate's Bridge Weir

Fletland

Baston CE Prim Sch
Cemy
PANNEL CT
PH

Brook House Farm

Works

Sand & Gravel Pit

Manor Farm

Braceborough Great Wood

Lodge Farm

Braceborough
ELLIOTT'S WY

BRACEBOROUGH RD

Macmillan Way

Church Farm

Mill Farm

MALTBY DR 1
FRISBY CL 2
WHATTOFF WY 3

KING STREET

Kirkstone House Sch
MAIN STREET
PO
Baston

PE6

Middle Field

Moat

Church Farm

DEEPING ROAD

BOURNE ROAD A15

Windmill

Stonehouse Farm

PE9

CARLBY RD

GREATFORD GD

Meadow Field

Bottom Meadow

Middle Field

Red Inn Field

Truesdale Lodge

MANOR CL 1
MOSSOP DR 2
SCOTT'S CL 3
TRUESDALE GDNS 4
AVEFIELD 5

Langtoft Prim Sch
PO
Nook Field

EAST END
NEW ROAD
Cemy

PETERBOROUGH ROAD A15

Banthorpe Wood

Dogkennel Plantation

Macmillan Way

Shillingthorpe Park

Greatford Wood

West Glen River

Weir

BELMESTHORPE RD

Greatford Hall
PH

GREATFORD GD

Greatford
The Council Houses

Manor Farm

Glen Farm

MAIN STREET

Banks Farm

West Field

Parsonage Field

BARHOLME RD

Sand & Gravel Pit

Stowe Farm

STOWE ROAD

Bleak House Farm

1 WHEATFIELD
2 AQUILA WY
3 BARLEYFIELD
4 WESTFIELD WY

WEST END

DACK DR?

Langtoft

Middle Field

Tithe Farm

Great Maidens

Cow Pasture Plantation

UFFINGTON RD

Cank Wood

Old Hall
PH

Barholm

Marsh Plantation

Cedar Plantation

Casewick Field

Beck Field

Sand & Gravel Pit

Ind Est

Greatford Cut

Far Field

Towngate

MILLFIELD RD

Rectory Farm

Crown Farm

Mill Field

A15

172   163   173

E4
1 SCHOOL LA
2 CHURCH ST
3 AVELAND WY
4 CLARE CT
5 DENSHIRE CT
6 COLTON CL
7 CHESHAM DR
8 PADMORE PL

F3
1 BARN OWL CL
2 LIME CL
3 DEER PK RD
4 CLOVEN ENDS
5 REEDMANS CL
6 MANOR WY
7 THE RIDES
8 GIBBS CL

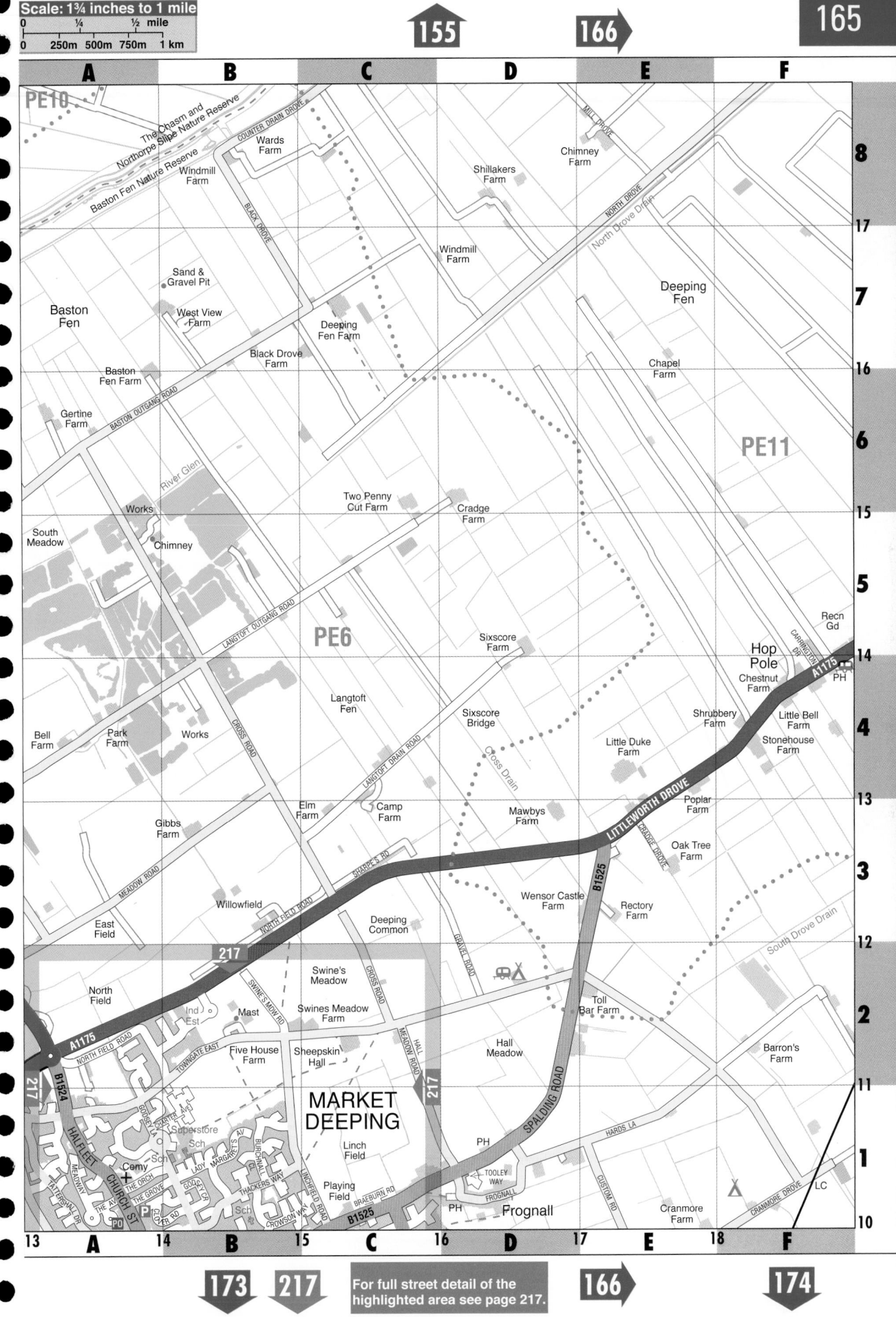

Scale: 1¾ inches to 1 mile

0   ¼   ½   mile
0   250m 500m 750m 1 km

155

166

165

PE10

The Chasm and Northorpe Slipe Nature Reserve

Baston Fen Nature Reserve

COUNTER DRAIN DROVE

Wards Farm

Windmill Farm

BLACK DROVE

Shillakers Farm

Chimney Farm

MILL DROVE

NORTH DROVE

North Drove Drain

Deeping Fen

Sand & Gravel Pit

Baston Fen

West View Farm

Deeping Fen Farm

Windmill Farm

Black Drove Farm

PE11

Chapel Farm

Baston Fen Farm

BASTON OUTGANG ROAD

Gertine Farm

River Glen

Works

Two Penny Cut Farm

Cradge Farm

LANGTOFT OUTGANG ROAD

South Meadow

Chimney

PE6

Sixscore Farm

Recn Gd

CARRINGTON DROVE

Hop Pole

A1175

PH

Langtoft Fen

Sixscore Bridge

Chestnut Farm

Shrubbery Farm

Little Bell Farm

Bell Farm

Park Farm

Works

CROSS ROAD

Cross Drain

Little Duke Farm

LITTLEWORTH DROVE

Stonehouse Farm

Poplar Farm

LANGTOFT DRAIN ROAD

Elm Farm

Camp Farm

Mawbys Farm

CRADGE DROVE

Oak Tree Farm

MEADOW ROAD

Gibbs Farm

Willowfield

NORTH FIELD ROAD

SHARPE'S RD

Deeping Common

Wensor Castle Farm

B1525

Rectory Farm

South Drove Drain

217

East Field

North Field

Swine's Meadow

CROSS ROAD

GRAVEL ROAD

Toll Bar Farm

Ind Est

Mast

Swines Meadow Farm

HALL MEADOW ROAD

Hall Meadow

Barron's Farm

A1175

NORTH FIELD ROAD

TOWNGATE EAST

Five House Farm

Sheepskin Hall

217

SPALDING ROAD

217

B1524

HALFLEET

CHURCH ST

Superstore

Sch

Cemy

THE ORCH

THACKERS WAY

LINCHFIELD ROAD

MARKET DEEPING

Linch Field

HARDS LA

CUSTOM RD

PH

PO

Playing Field

BRAEBURN RD

CROWSON WY

B1525

PH

Frognall

Prognall

Tooley Way

FROGNALL

Cranmore Farm

CRANMORE DROVE

LC

166

C6
1 WOODBANK
2 CORONATION AVE
3 CHAPPELL RD
4 BARLEY GR
5 HARVEST MEWS
6 HAYWAIN DR

7 FALLOW FIELDS
8 WHEATSHEAF CT
9 CORNFIELD CL
10 FARMHOUSE DR

← 165

↑ 156

Scale: 1¾ inches to 1 mile
0 ¼ ½ mile
0 250m 500m 750m 1 km

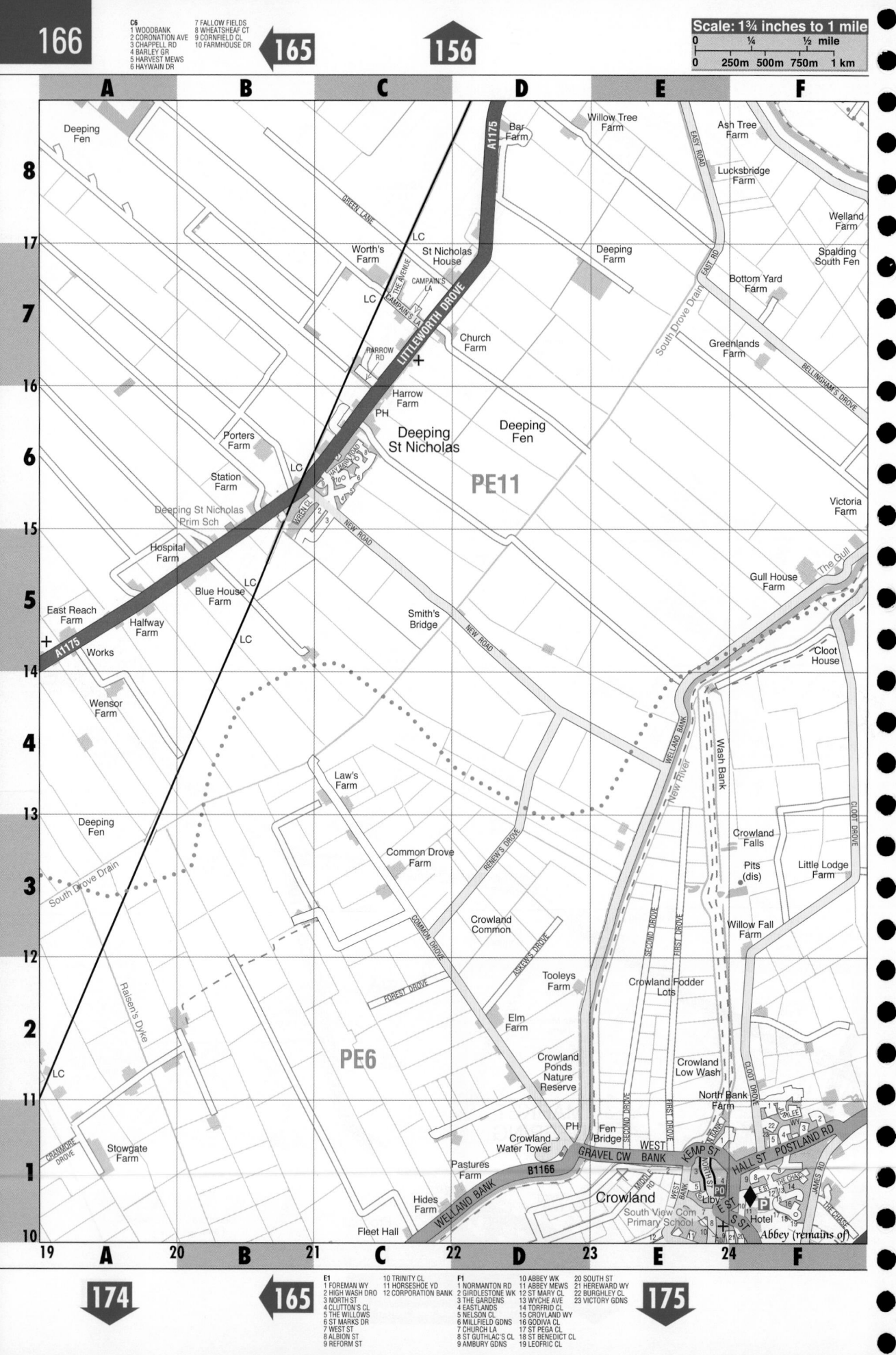

E1
1 FOREMAN WY
2 HIGH WASH DRO
3 NORTH ST
4 CLUTTON'S CL
5 THE WILLOWS
6 ST MARKS DR
7 WEST ST
8 ALBION ST
9 REFORM ST

10 TRINITY CL
11 HORSESHOE YD
12 CORPORATION BANK

F1
1 NORMANTON RD
2 GIRDLESTONE WK
3 THE GARDENS
4 EASTLANDS
5 NELSON CL
6 MILLFIELD GDNS
7 CHURCH LA
8 ST GUTHLAC'S CL
9 AMBURY GDNS

10 ABBEY WK
11 ABBEY MEWS
12 ST MARY CL
13 WYCHE AVE
14 TORFRID CL
15 CROYLAND WY
16 GODIVA CL
17 ST PEGA CL
18 ST BENEDICT CL
19 LEOFRIC CL

20 SOUTH ST
21 HEREWARD WY
22 BURGHLEY CL
23 VICTORY GDNS

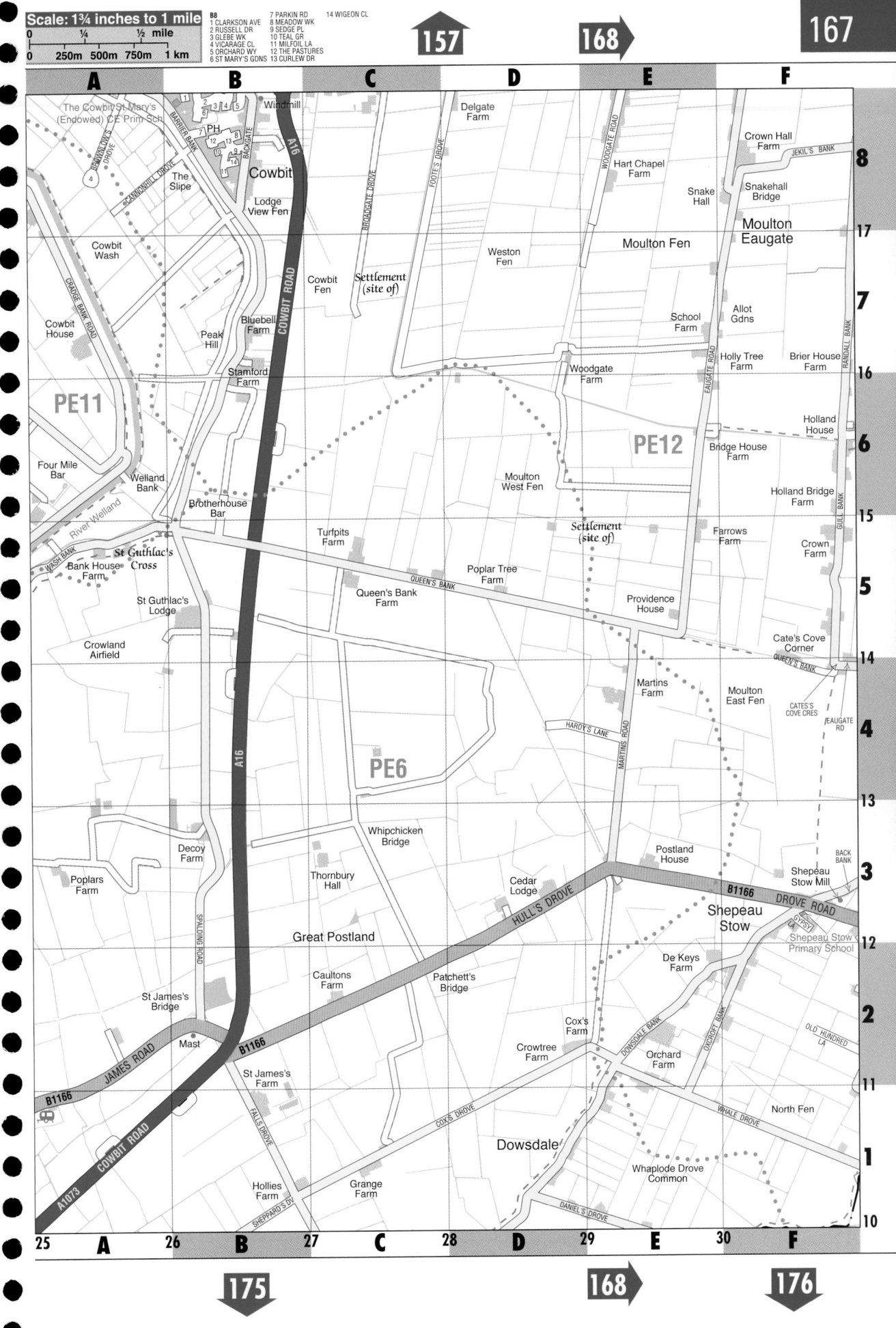

Scale: 1¾ inches to 1 mile

0   ¼   ½   mile
0   250m   500m   750m   1 km

B8
1 CLARKSON AVE
2 RUSSELL DR
3 GLEBE WK
4 VICARAGE CL
5 ORCHARD WY
6 ST MARY'S GDNS

7 PARKIN RD
8 MEADOW WK
9 SEDGE PL
10 TEAL GR
11 MILFOIL LA
12 THE PASTURES
13 CURLEW DR

14 WIGEON CL

157
168

A B C D E F

The Cowbit St Mary's
(Endowed) CE Prim Sch

Windmill

PH

Cowbit

Crown Hall
Farm

Jekil's Bank

The Slipe

Lodge
View Fen

Snake
Hall

Snakehall
Bridge

Moulton
Eaugate

8

Cowbit
Wash

Delgate
Farm

Hart Chapel
Farm

17

Cowbit
Fen

Weston
Fen

Settlement
(site of)

Moulton Fen

Peak
Hill

Bluebell
Farm

Cowbit
House

School
Farm

Allot
Gdns

7

PE11

Stamford
Farm

Woodgate
Farm

Holly Tree
Farm

Brier House
Farm

16

PE12

Bridge House
Farm

Holland
House

6

Four Mile
Bar

Welland
Bank

Moulton
West Fen

Holland Bridge
Farm

Brotherhouse
Bar

Settlement
(site of)

Farrows
Farm

15

River Welland

Turfpits
Farm

Poplar Tree
Farm

Crown
Farm

Wash Bank

St Guthlac's
Cross

Bank House
Farm

Queen's Bank

Providence
House

Cate's Cove
Corner

14

St Guthlac's
Lodge

Queen's Bank
Farm

Queen's Bank

CATE'S
COVE CRES

Crowland
Airfield

Martins
Farm

Moulton
East Fen

EAUGATE
RD

4

13

PE6

Whipchicken
Bridge

Postland
House

BACK
BANK

Shepeau
Stow Mill

3

Decoy
Farm

Thornbury
Hall

Cedar
Lodge

B1166

DROVE ROAD

Poplars
Farm

Shepeau
Stow

Shepeau Stow
Primary School

12

Great Postland

De Keys
Farm

St James's
Bridge

Caultons
Farm

Patchett's
Bridge

Cox's
Farm

Orchard
Farm

OLD HUNDRED
LA

2

Mast

B1166

Crowtree
Farm

North Fen

St James's
Farm

WHALE DROVE

11

B1166

COX'S DROVE

Dowsdale

Whaplode Drove
Common

1

COWBIT ROAD

Hollies
Farm

Grange
Farm

DANIEL'S DROVE

10

25 A 26 B 27 C 28 D 29 E 30 F

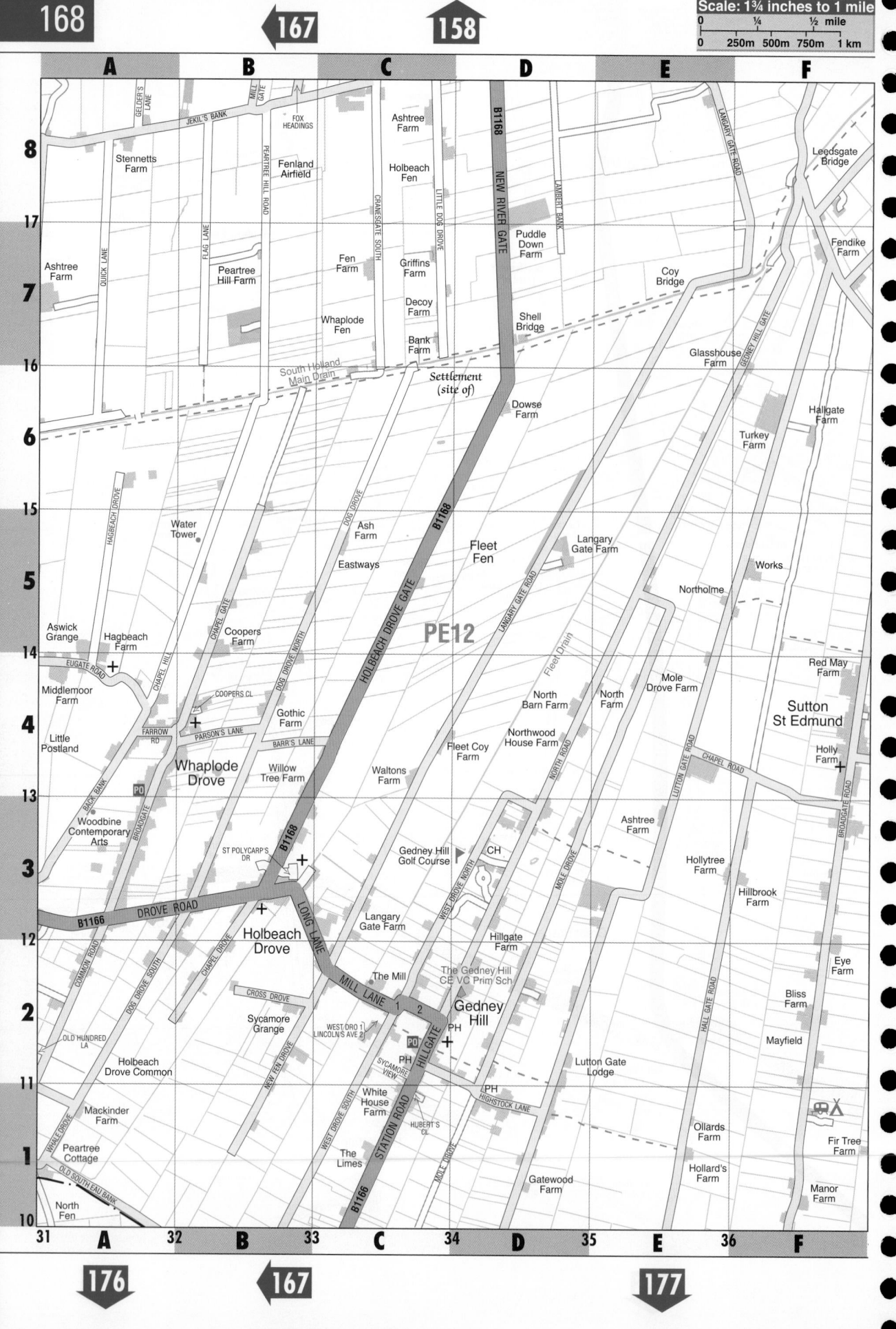

168

167

158

Scale: 1¾ inches to 1 mile
0   ¼   ½   mile
0   250m 500m 750m 1 km

A   B   C   D   E   F

8
17
7
16
6
15
5
14
4
13
3
12
2
11
1
10

31   A   32   B   33   C   34   D   35   E   36   F

GELDER'S LANE
JEKIL'S BANK
MILL GATE
FOX HEADINGS
Ashtree Farm
B1168
NEW RIVER GATE
LANGARY GATE ROAD
Leedsgate Bridge

Stennetts Farm
Fenland Airfield
Holbeach Fen
Puddle Down Farm
Fendike Farm

QUICK LANE
FLAG LANE
PEARTREE HILL ROAD
CRANESGATE SOUTH
LITTLE DOG DROVE
LAMBERT PARK
Coy Bridge

Ashtree Farm
Peartree Hill Farm
Fen Farm
Griffins Farm
Shell Bridge
Glasshouse Farm
GEDNEY HILL GATE
Hallgate Farm

Whaplode Fen
Decoy Farm
Bank Farm

South Holland Main Drain
Settlement (site of)
Dowse Farm
Turkey Farm

HAGBEACH DROVE
DOG DROVE
Ash Farm
B1168
Fleet Fen
Langary Gate Farm
Works

Water Tower
Eastways
Northolme
Red May Farm

Aswick Grange
Hagbeach Farm
CHAPEL GATE
Coopers Farm
HOLBEACH CHAPEL DROVE GATE
PE12
LANGARY GATE ROAD
Fleet Drain
Mole Drove Farm
Sutton St Edmund

EUGATE ROAD
CHAPEL HILL
DOG DROVE NORTH
COOPERS CL
Gothic Farm
North Barn Farm
North Farm
Holly Farm

Middlemoor Farm
FARROW RD
PARSON'S LANE
BARR'S LANE
Northwood House Farm
NORTH ROAD
LUTTON GATE ROAD
CHAPEL ROAD
BROADGATE ROAD

Little Postland
Whaplode Drove
Willow Tree Farm
Waltons Farm
Fleet Coy Farm
Ashtree Farm
Hollytree Farm

BACK BANK
BROADGATE
PO
B1168
St POLYCARP'S DR
Gedney Hill Golf Course
CH
MOLE DROVE
Hollybrook Farm

Woodbine Contemporary Arts
DROVE ROAD
B1166
LONG LANE
Langary Gate Farm
WEST DROVE NORTH
Hillgate Farm
Hillbrook Farm

Holbeach Drove
MILL LANE
The Mill
The Gedney Hill CE VC Prim Sch
HIGHGATE
Eye Farm

COMMON ROAD
DOG DROVE SOUTH
CHAPEL DROVE
CROSS DROVE
Sycamore Grange
WEST DRO 1 LINCOLN'S AVE 2
1 2
Gedney Hill
PH
Bliss Farm

OLD HUNDRED LA
NEW FEN DROVE
PO
SYCAMORE VIEW
HUBERT'S CL
Lutton Gate Lodge
HALL GATE ROAD
Mayfield

Holbeach Drove Common
WEST DROVE SOUTH
STATION ROAD
PH
HIGHSTOCK LANE

WHALE DROVE
Mackinder Farm
White House Farm
MOLE DROVE
Ollards Farm
Fir Tree Farm

Peartree Cottage
The Limes
Gatewood Farm
Hollard's Farm
Manor Farm

OLD SOUTH EAU BANK
North Fen
B1166

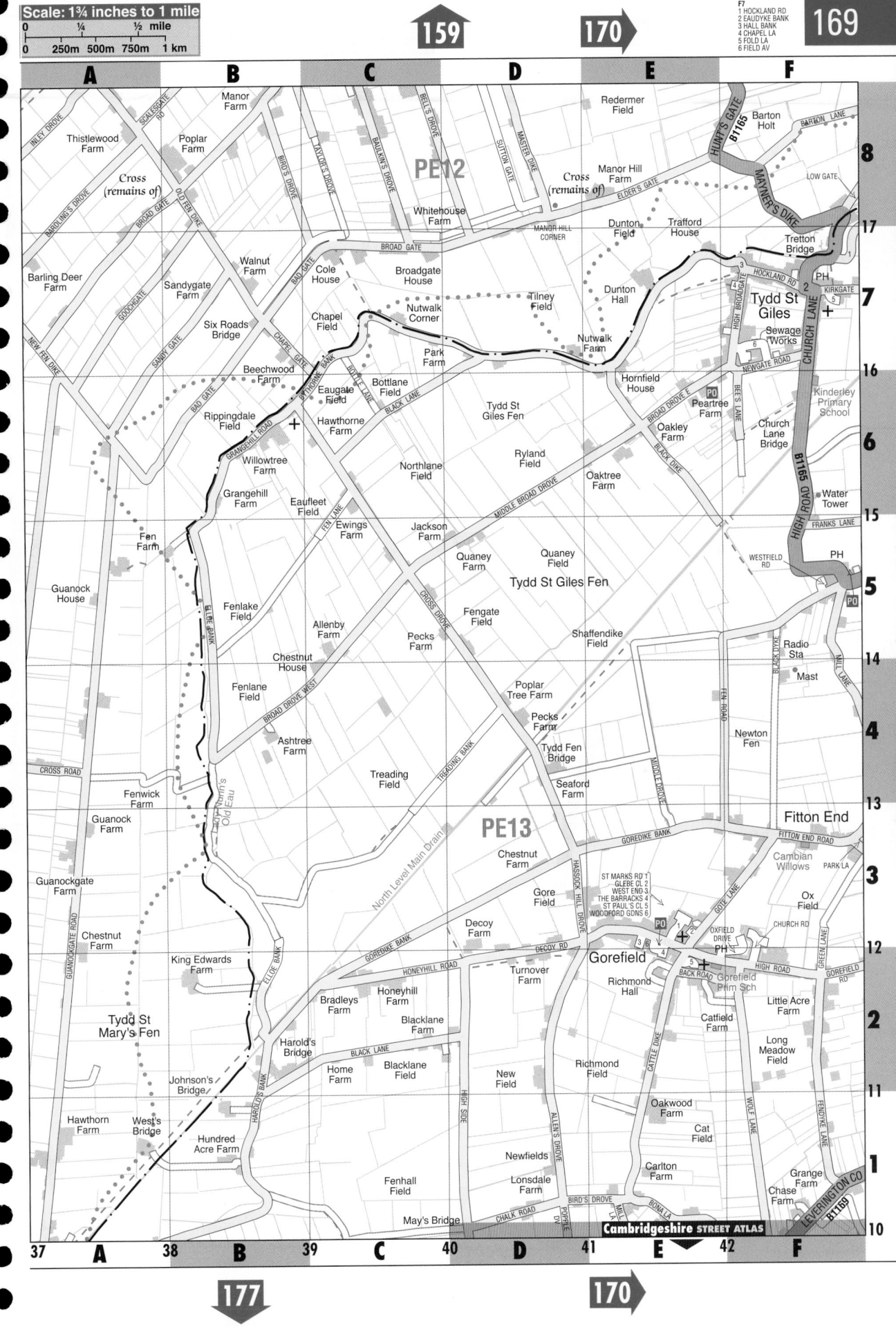

Scale: 1¾ inches to 1 mile

0   ¼   ½ mile
0 250m 500m 750m 1 km

159

170

F7
1 HOCKLAND RD
2 EAUDYKE BANK
3 HALL BANK
4 CHAPEL LA
5 FOLD LA
6 FIELD AV

169

A   B   C   D   E   F

PE12

Inley Drove
Thistlewood Farm
Manor Farm
Poplar Farm
Scalesgate Rd
Bird's Drove
Taylor's Drove
Baulking's Drove
Bell's Drove
Redermer Field
Barton Holt
Barton Lane
Hunt's Gate
B1165
Mayner's Dike

Imboling's Drove
Cross (remains of)
Broad Gate
Old Fen Dike
Goodgate
Walnut Farm
Master Dike
Sutton Gate
Elder's Gate
Cross (remains of)
Manor Hill Farm
Dunton Field
Trafford House
Low Gate

Barling Deer Farm
Sandygate Farm
Whitehouse Farm
Broad Gate
Manor Hill Corner
Tretton Bridge

8

17

Sandy Gate
New Fen Dike
Six Roads Bridge
Chapel Gate
Cole House
Broadgate House
Tilney Field
Dunton Hall
Hockland Rd
Tydd St Giles
High Broadgate
Kirkgate
Church Lane
PH

7

Beechwood Farm
Chapel Field
Nutwalk Corner
Park Farm
Nutwalk Farm
Newgate Road
Sewage Works

Rippingdale Field
Grangehill Road
Pithorne Bank
Eaugate Field
Bottlane Field
Hawthorne Farm
Black Lane
Bad Gate
Tydd St Giles Fen
Hornfield House
Broad Drove E
Peartree Farm
Oakley Farm
Bee's Lane
PO
Church Lane Bridge
Kinderley Primary School

16

Willowtree Farm
Grangehill Farm
Eaufleet Field
Fen Lane
Bottle Lane
Northlane Field
Ryland Field
Oaktree Farm
Middle Broad Drove
Black Dike
B1165
High Road
Water Tower

6

Fen Farm
Elloe Bank
Ewings Farm
Jackson Farm
Quaney Farm
Quaney Field
Franks Lane

15

Guanock House
Fenlake Field
Allenby Farm
Pecks Farm
Fengate Field
Tydd St Giles Fen
Shaffendike Field
Westfield Rd
PH
PO

5

Chestnut House
Fenlane Field
Ashtree Farm
Broad Drove West
Cross Drove
Treading Bank
Poplar Tree Farm
Pecks Farm
Radio Sta
Mast
Fen Road

14

Cross Road
Fenwick Farm
Treading Field
Tydd Fen Bridge
Seaford Farm
Newton Fen
Middle Drove

4

Guanock Farm
North Level Main Drain
PE13
Chestnut Farm
Goredike Bank
Fitton End
Fitton End Road
Cambian Willows
Park La

13

Guanockgate Farm
St Thorn's Old Eau
Gore Field
Hassock Hill Drove
ST MARKS RD 1
GLEBE CL 2
WEST END 3
THE BARRACKS 4
ST PAUL'S CL 5
WOODFORD GDNS 6
Gore Lane
Ox Field
Green Lane
Church Rd

3

Chestnut Farm
King Edwards Farm
Goredike Bank
Decoy Farm
Decoy Rd
PO
Gorefield
Oxfield Drive
PH
Gorefield Rd

12

Guanockgate Road
Ellloe Bank
Honeyhill Road
Bradleys Farm
Honeyhill Farm
Turnover Farm
Blacklane Farm
Richmond Hall
Back Road
Gorefield Prim Sch
High Road
Catfield Farm
Little Acre Farm

2

Tydd St Mary's Fen
Harold's Bridge
Home Farm
Black Lane
Blacklane Field
New Field
Richmond Field
Cattle Dike
Wolf Lane
Long Meadow Field

Johnson's Bridge
Harold's Bank
Oakwood Farm
Cat Field
Fendyke Lane

11

Hawthorn Farm
West's Bridge
Hundred Acre Farm
High Side
Allen's Drove
Newfields
Carlton Farm
Grange Farm
Chase Farm
Leverington Co

Fenhall Field
Lonsdale Farm
Bird's Drove
Popple Dro
Bona La
Mill La
B1169

1

May's Bridge
Chalk Road

10

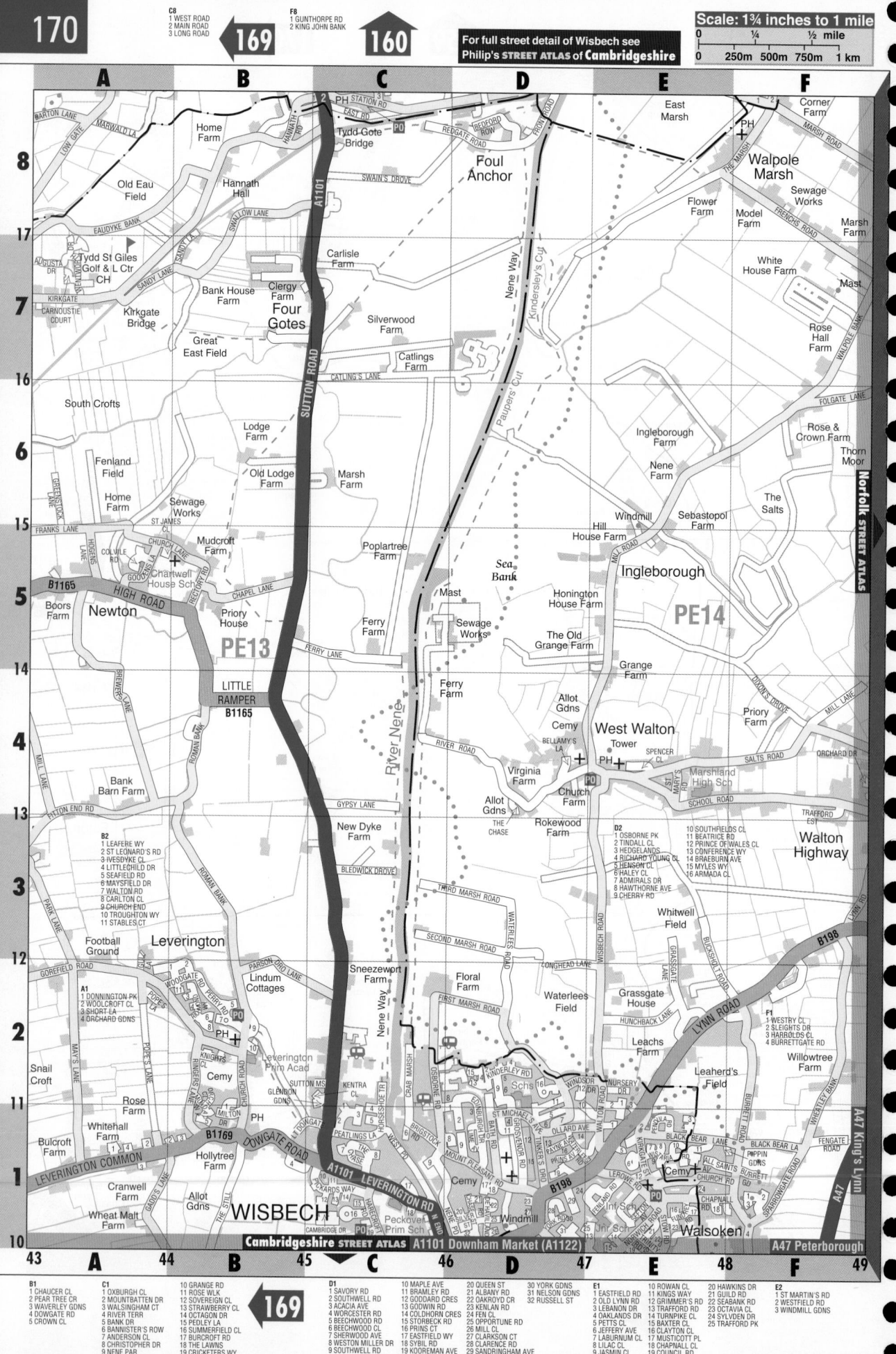

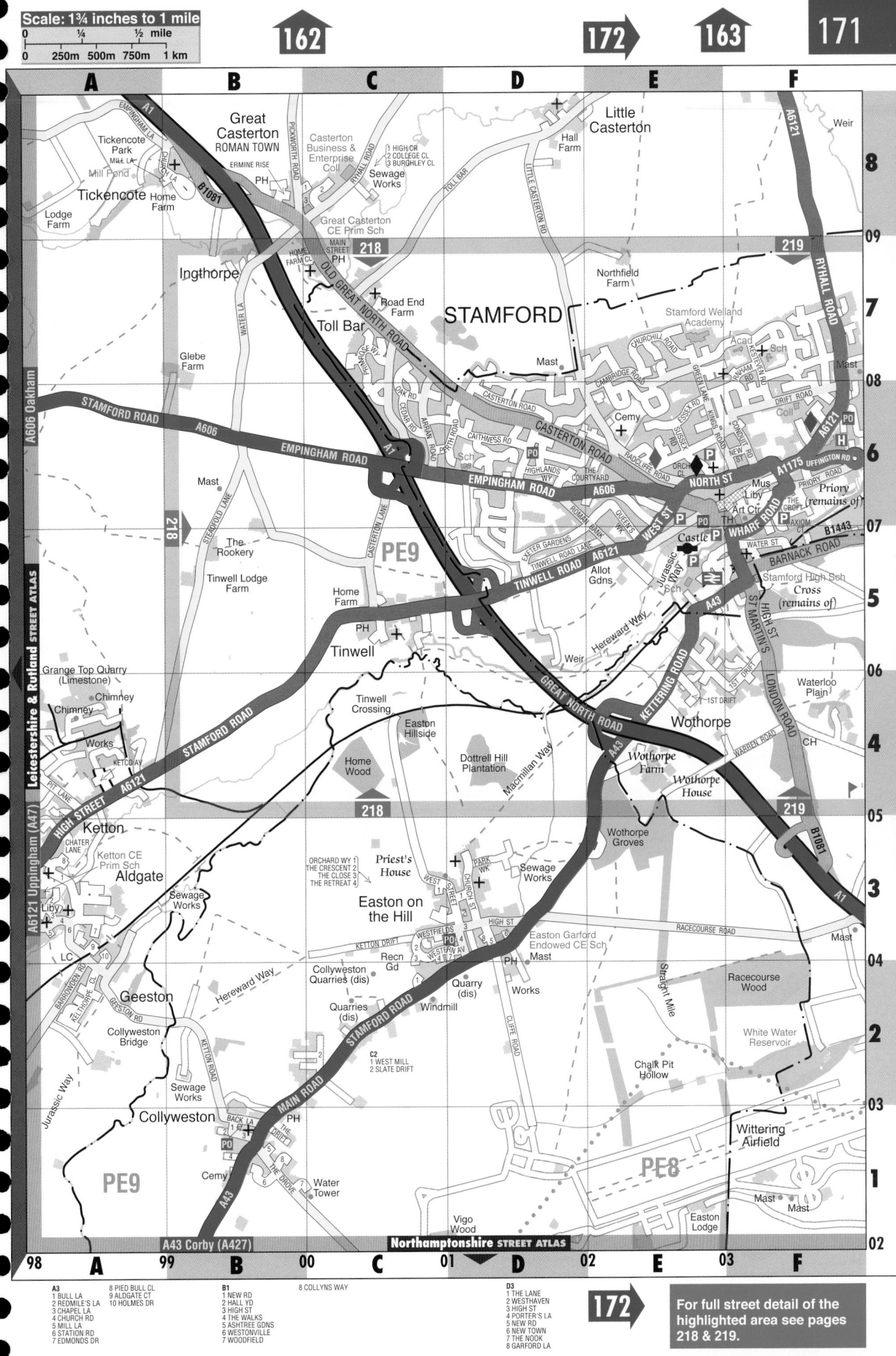

Scale: 1¾ inches to 1 mile

0   ¼   ½   mile
0 250m 500m 750m 1 km

162

172

163

171

A   B   C   D   E   F

8
09
7
08
6
07
5
06
4
05
3
04
2
03
1
02

Tickencote Park
Mill Pond
MILL LA
Home Farm
Lodge Farm
Tickencote
CHURCH LA
B1081
A1
ERMINE RISE
PH
Great Casterton
ROMAN TOWN
PICKWORTH ROAD
Casterton Business & Enterprise Coll
RYHALL ROAD
Sewage Works
A1 HIGH CR 2 COLLEGE CL 3 BURGHLEY CL
Great Casterton CE Prim Sch
Hall Farm
Little Casterton
LITTLE CASTERTON RD
TOLL BAR
Weir
A6121

A606 Oakham
Ingthorpe
EMPINGHAM LA
WATER LA
Toll Bar
OAK RD
CEDAR RD
ARRAN ROAD
Glebe Farm
HOME FARM CL
MAIN STREET
PH
218
Road End Farm
CLOSE RD
AVENUE
STAMFORD
Northfield Farm
219
Stamford Welland Academy
Mast
Acad
Sch
Mast

STAMFORD ROAD
A606
EMPINGHAM ROAD
A1
PENN ROAD
PENN ROAD
CAITHNESS RD
Sch
CASTERTON ROAD
Cemy
CHURCHILL ROAD
CAMBRIDGE ROAD
GREEN LANE
ESSEX RD
KINGS ROAD
SUSSEX RD
CONDUIT ROAD
KESTERTON RD
NEW ROAD
A1175
DRIFT ROAD
Coll
PO
H
A6121
UFFINGTON RD

Mast
STEADFOLD LANE
218
CASTERTON LANE
PE9
The Rookery
A1
Tinwell Lodge Farm
EMPINGHAM ROAD
A606
HIGHLANDS WY
THE COURTYARD
RADCLIFFE ROAD
PO
ORCH
NORTH ST
Mus Liby Art Ctr
Castle
WHARF ROAD
WATER ST
THE CROFT
MAXIOM
B1443
BARNACK ROAD
Priory (remains of)
PRIORY ROAD

Home Farm
PH
Tinwell
EXETER GARDENS
ROMAN BANK
QUEEN'S WK
WEST ST
P
PO
TINWELL ROAD LANE
TINWELL ROAD
A6121
Allot Gdns
Jurassic Way
Sch
A43
HIGH ST
ST MARTIN'S
Stamford High Sch
Cross (remains of)
WATER ST
ST DRIFT
LONDON ROAD

Grange Top Quarry (Limestone)
Chimney
Chimney
Works
KETTO LA
STAMFORD ROAD
A6121
Tinwell Crossing
Hereward Way
Weir
GREAT NORTH ROAD
KETTERING ROAD
Wothorpe
1ST DRIFT
WARREN ROAD
Waterloo Plain
CH

HIGH STREET
A6121 Uppingham (A47)
Ketton
CHATER LANE
Ketton CE Prim Sch
Aldgate
Sewage Works
Home Wood
Easton Hillside
Dottrell Hill Plantation
Macmillan Way
A43
Wothorpe Farm
Wothorpe House
219
B1081
A1

Liby
LC
BARROWDEN ROAD
KELTHORPE CL
Geeston
GEESTON RD
Hereward Way
Collyweston Quarries (dis)
Quarries (dis)
ORCHARD WY 1 THE CRESCENT 2 THE CLOSE 3 THE RETREAT 4
Priest's House
PARK WK
WEST STREET
CHURCH ST
Easton on the Hill
HIGH ST
WESTFIELDS
KETTON DRIFT
RECN GD
WESTERN AV
Easton Garford Endowed CE Sch
Mast
PH
Windmill
Quarry (dis)
Works
CLIFFE ROAD
STAMFORD ROAD
RACECOURSE ROAD
Mast
Straight Mile
Racecourse Wood
White Water Reservoir
Wothorpe Groves

Collyweston Bridge
KELLS LA
Sewage Works
KETTON RD
Collyweston
BACK LA
PH
PO
THE DRIFT
THE DROVE
Cemy
Water Tower
C2 1 WEST MILL 2 SLATE DRIFT
MAIN ROAD
Chalk Pit Hollow
Wittering Airfield
PE8

PE9
A43
A43 Corby (A427)
Vigo Wood
Northamptonshire STREET ATLAS
Mast
Easton Lodge
Mast

98   A   99   B   00   C   01   D   02   E   03   F

172

A3
1 BULL LA
2 REDMILE'S LA
3 CHAPEL LA
4 CHURCH RD
5 MILL LA
6 STATION RD
7 EDMONDS DR
8 PIED BULL CL
9 ALDGATE CT
10 HOLMES DR

B1
1 NEW RD
2 HALL YD
3 HIGH ST
4 THE WALKS
5 ASHTREE GDNS
6 WESTONVILLE
7 WOODFIELD
8 COLLYNS WAY

D3
1 THE LANE
2 WESTHAVEN
3 HIGH ST
4 PORTER'S LA
5 NEW RD
6 NEW TOWN
7 THE NOOK
8 GARFORD LA

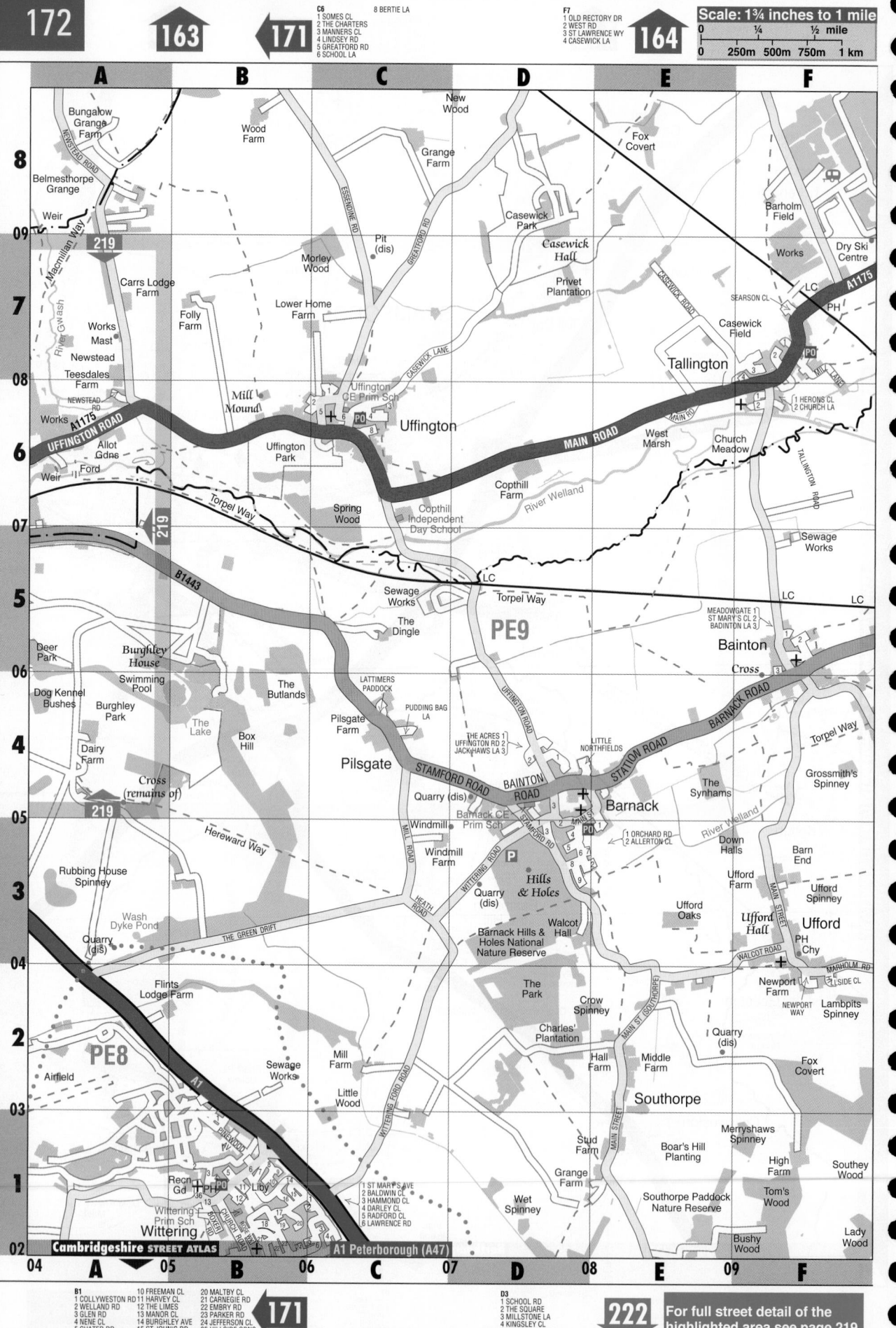

C6
1 SOMES CL
2 THE CHARTERS
3 MANNERS CL
4 LINDSEY RD
5 GREATFORD RD
6 SCHOOL LA

8 BERTIE LA

F7
1 OLD RECTORY DR
2 WEST RD
3 ST LAWRENCE WY
4 CASEWICK LA

Scale: 1¾ inches to 1 mile
0   ¼   ½   mile
0   250m 500m 750m 1 km

A   B   C   D   E   F

Bungalow
Grange
Farm

Wood
Farm

New
Wood

Fox
Covert

Barholm
Field

Dry Ski
Centre

8

Belmesthorpe
Grange

Grange
Farm

Casewick
Park

Works

Weir

219

Carrs Lodge
Farm

Morley
Wood

Pit
(dis)

Casewick
Hall

Privet
Plantation

LC

A1175

09

Folly
Farm

Lower Home
Farm

CASEWICK LANE

Searson CL

PH

7

Works
Mast

Newstead

Teesdales
Farm

Mill
Mound

Uffington
CE Prim Sch

PO

Uffington

Tallington

Casewick
Field

1 HERONS CL
2 CHURCH LA

MILL LANE

PO

08

NEWSTEAD
RD

Works

A1175

UFFINGTON ROAD

Allot
Gdns

Uffington
Park

MAIN ROAD

West
Marsh

Church
Meadow

TALLINGTON ROAD

6

Weir

Ford

Torpel Way

Spring
Wood

Copthill
Independent
Day School

Copthill
Farm

River Welland

Sewage
Works

07

219

B1443

Sewage
Works

The
Dingle

LC

Torpel Way

LC

LC

5

Deer
Park

Burghley
House

Swimming
Pool

The
Butlands

LATTIMERS
PADDOCK

PUDDING BAG
LA

PE9

MEADOWGATE 1
ST MARY'S CL 2
BADINTON LA 3

Bainton

06

Dog Kennel
Bushes

Burghley
Park

The
Lake

Box
Hill

Pilsgate
Farm

THE ACRES 1
UFFINGTON RD 2
JACK HAWS LA 3

LITTLE
NORTHFIELDS

BARNACK ROAD

Cross

05

Dairy
Farm

219

Cross
(remains of)

Pilsgate

STAMFORD ROAD

BAINTON
ROAD

STATION ROAD

Barnack

Barnack CE
Prim Sch

PO

1 ORCHARD RD
2 ALLERTON CL

The
Synhams

River Welland

Grossmith's
Spinney

4

Hereward Way

Quarry (dis)

MILL ROAD

Windmill

Windmill
Farm

HEATH ROAD

WITTERING ROAD

P

Quarry
(dis)

Hills
& Holes

STAMFORD RD

Down
Halls

Ufford
Farm

MAIN STREET

Barn
End

Ufford
Spinney

3

Rubbing House
Spinney

Wash
Dyke Pond

THE GREEN DRIFT

Barnack Hills &
Holes National
Nature Reserve

Walcot
Hall

Ufford
Oaks

Ufford
Hall

WALCOT ROAD

Ufford

PH
Chy

Quarry
(dis)

PE8

A1

Flints
Lodge Farm

Sewage
Works

Mill
Farm

WITTERING FORD ROAD

The
Park

Crow
Spinney

Charles'
Plantation

Hall
Farm

Middle
Farm

MAIN ST SOUTHORPE

Newport
Farm

NEWPORT
WAY

MARHOLM RD

LSIDE CL

Lambpits
Spinney

Fox
Covert

2

Airfield

Little
Wood

1 ST MARY'S AVE
2 BALDWIN CL
3 HAMMOND CL
4 DARLEY CL
5 RADFORD CL
6 LAWRENCE RD

Wet
Spinney

Stud
Farm

MAIN STREET

Boar's Hill
Planting

Southorpe

Merryshaws
Spinney

High
Farm

Tom's
Wood

Southey
Wood

1

Recn
Gd

PH
PO

Liby

Wittering
Prim Sch

CHURCH ST

FIXED RD

PINE WOODS

Grange
Farm

Southorpe Paddock
Nature Reserve

Bushy
Wood

Lady
Wood

Wittering

02

Cambridgeshire STREET ATLAS

A1 Peterborough (A47)

04   A   05   B   06   C   07   D   08   E   09   F

B1
1 COLLYWESTON RD
2 WELLAND RD
3 GLEN RD
4 NENE CL
5 CHATER RD
6 TOWNSEND RD
7 BROWNES RD
8 EXETER RD
9 HOLT CL
10 FREEMAN CL
11 HARVEY CL
12 THE LIMES
13 MANOR CL
14 BURGHLEY AVE
15 ST JOHN'S RD
16 ST MICHAEL'S RD
17 ST GEORGE'S RD
18 BROADHURST RD
19 NEWMAN CL
20 MALTBY CL
21 CARNEGIE RD
22 EMBRY RD
23 PARKER RD
24 JEFFERSON CL
25 HILLSIDE GDNS

171

D3
1 SCHOOL RD
2 THE SQUARE
3 MILLSTONE LA
4 KINGSLEY CL
5 BISHOPS WK
6 CANON DR
7 OWEN CL
8 SAXON RD
9 WHITMAN CL

222

For full street detail of the
highlighted area see page 219.

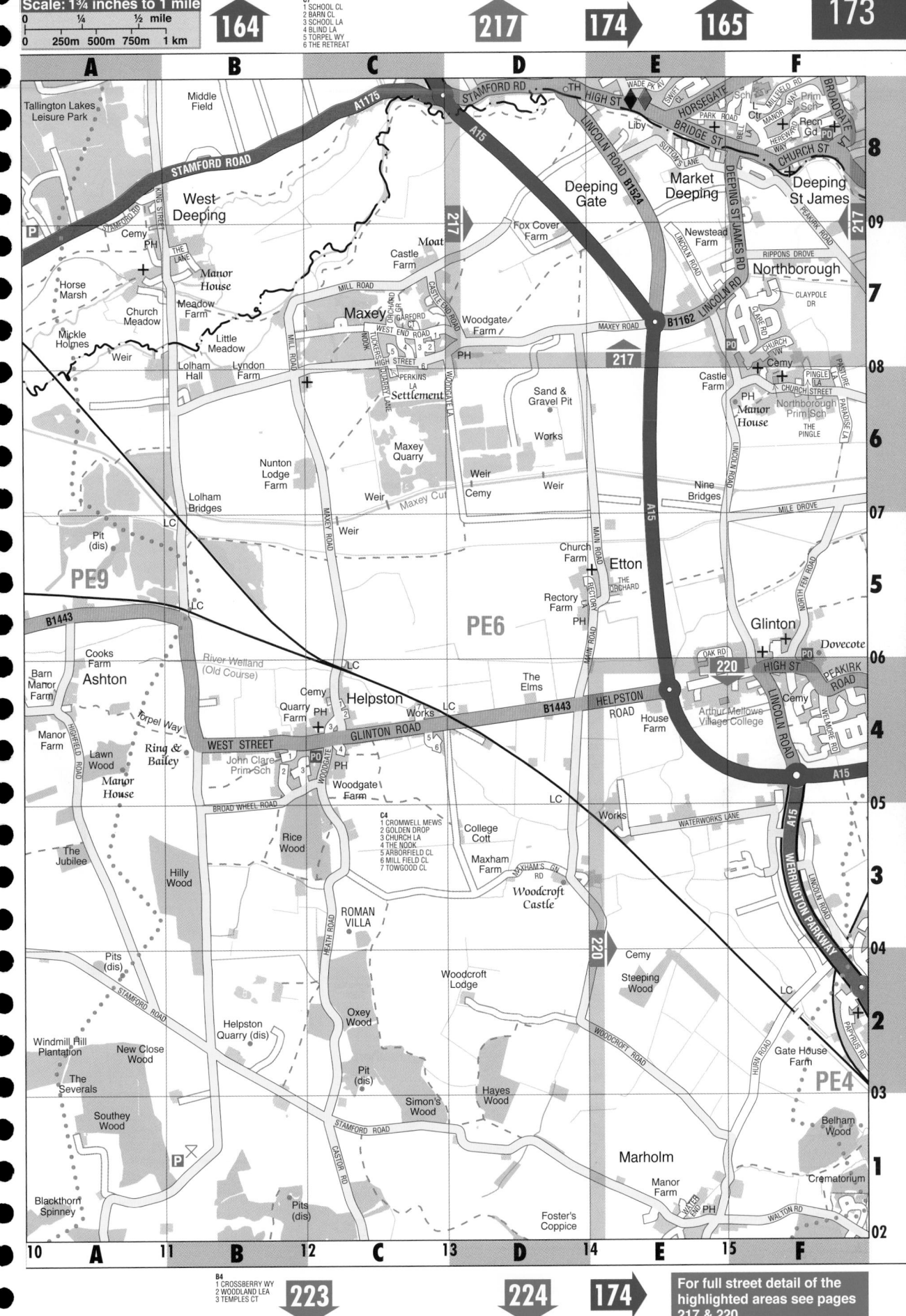
Scale: 1¾ inches to 1 mile
0 ¼ ½ mile
0 250m 500m 750m 1 km
164
C7
1 SCHOOL CL
2 BARN CL
3 SCHOOL LA
4 BLIND LA
5 TORPEL WY
6 THE RETREAT
217
174
165
A B C D E F
Tallington Lakes Leisure Park
Middle Field
A1175
STAMFORD ROAD
STAMFORD RD
A15
TH
HIGH ST
WADE PK AV
SWIFT CL
HORSEGATE
Sch
MILLFIELD RD
BROADGATE LA
Prim Sch
PARK ROAD
Ctr
MANOR WAY
Recn Gd
PO
Liby
BRIDGE ST
BELL LA
HEREWARD WAY
CHURCH ST
LINCOLN ROAD
B1524
SUTTON'S LANE
Market Deeping
DEEPING ST JAMES RD
Deeping St James
PEAKIRK ROAD
Deeping Gate
West Deeping
KING STREET
Cemy
PH
THE LANE
Manor House
Moat
Castle Farm
Fox Cover Farm
Newstead Farm
RIPPONS DROVE
Northborough
CLAYPOLE DR
Horse Marsh
Meadow Farm
MILL ROAD
ORCHARD GR
CASTLE END ROAD
Maxey
GARFORD CL
WEST END ROAD
Woodgate Farm
MAXEY ROAD
B1162
LINCOLN RD
CLARE RD
CHURCH WK
Church Meadow
Mickle Holmes
Little Meadow
NOOK
TUCKERS
HIGH STREET
Weir
Lolham Hall
Lyndon Farm
PERKINS LA
Settlement
QUARRY LANE
WOODGATE LA
Castle Farm
PINGLE LA
PASTURE LA
CHURCH STREET
Northborough Prim Sch
THE PINGLE
PARADISE LA
Sand & Gravel Pit
Works
Maxey Quarry
Nunton Lodge Farm
Lolham Bridges
Maxey Cut
Nine Bridges
MILE DROVE
LC
Pit (dis)
PE9
Church Farm
MAIN ROAD
Etton
THE ORCHARD
RECTORY LA
Rectory Farm
NORTH FEN ROAD
Glinton
Dovecote
B1443
PE6
River Welland (Old Course)
OAK RD
220
HIGH ST
PEAKIRK ROAD
Barn Manor Farm
Cooks Farm
Ashton
Quarry Farm
Helpston
The Elms
HELPSTON ROAD
House Farm
Arthur Mellows Village College
WELMORE RD
Manor Farm
Torpel Way
Ring & Bailey
WEST STREET
GLINTON ROAD
Lawn Wood
HIGHFIELD ROAD
John Clare Prim Sch
Manor House
Woodgate Farm
BROAD WHEEL ROAD
Rice Wood
C4
1 CROMWELL MEWS
2 GOLDEN DROP
3 CHURCH LA
4 THE NOOK
5 ARBORFIELD CL
6 MILL FIELD CL
7 TOWGOOD CL
College Cott
WATERWORKS LANE
The Jubilee
Hilly Wood
Maxham Farm
MAXHAM'S GN RD
Woodcroft Castle
WERRINGTON PARKWAY
ROMAN VILLA
HEATH ROAD
Cemy
Steeping Wood
Pits (dis)
Woodcroft Lodge
Helpston Quarry (dis)
Oxey Wood
WOODCROFT ROAD
HURN ROAD
Gate House Farm
PAPYRUS RD
Windmill Hill Plantation
New Close Wood
The Severals
Pit (dis)
Hayes Wood
PE4
Simon's Wood
STAMFORD ROAD
Belham Wood
Southey Wood
CASTOR RD
Marholm
Crematorium
Blackthorn Spinney
Pits (dis)
Manor Farm
WATER END
Foster's Coppice
WALTON RD
8 09 7 08 6 07 5 06 4 05 3 04 2 03 1 02
10 11 12 13 14 15
B4
1 CROSSBERRY WY
2 WOODLAND LEA
3 TEMPLES CT
223
224
174
For full street detail of the highlighted areas see pages 217 & 220.

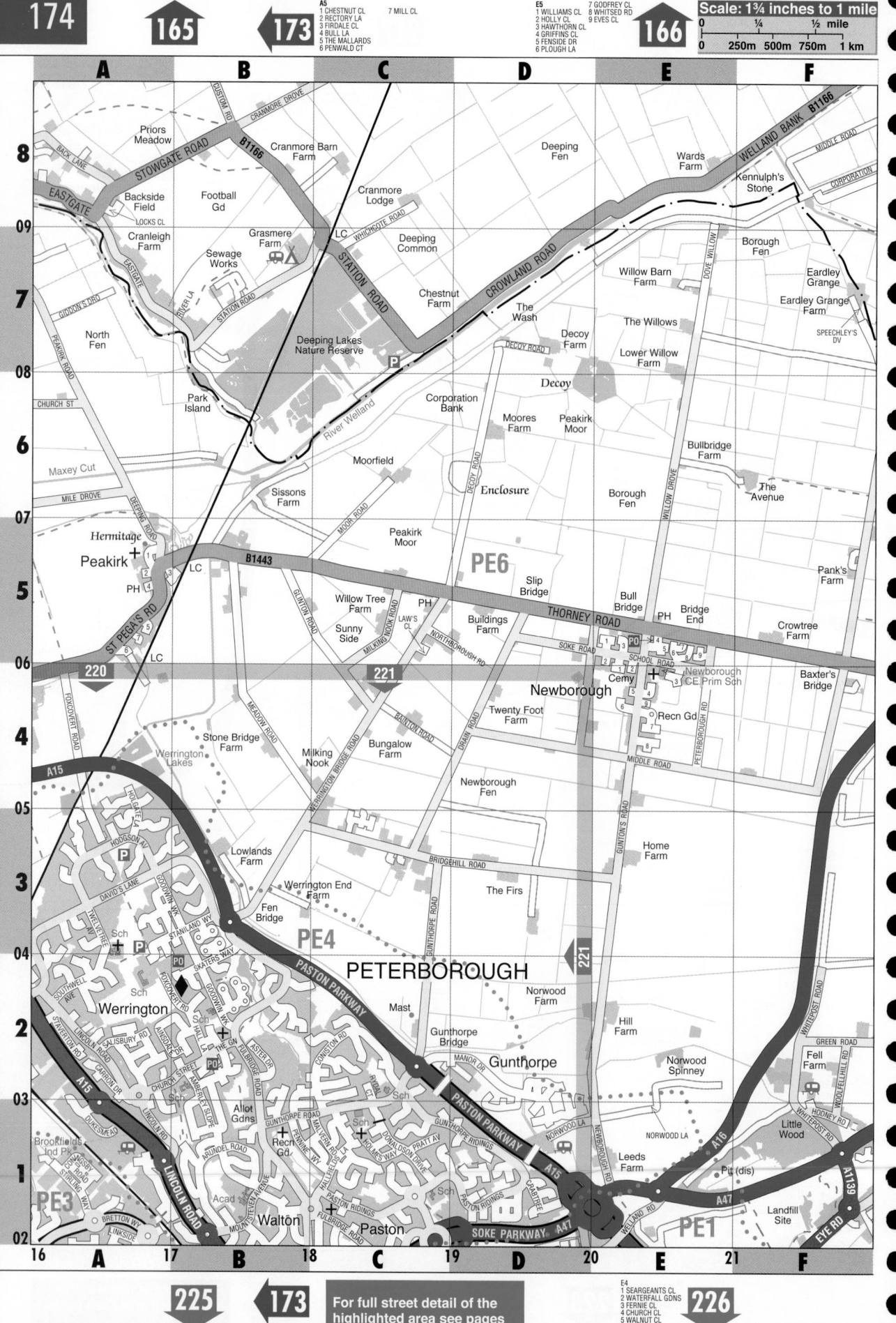

165
173
166

A5
1 CHESTNUT CL
2 RECTORY LA
3 FIRDALE CL
4 BULL LA
5 THE MALLARDS
6 PENWALD CT

7 MILL CL

E5
1 WILLIAMS CL
2 HOLLY CL
3 HAWTHORN CL
4 GRIFFINS CL
5 FENSIDE DR
6 PLOUGH LA

7 GODFREY CL
8 WHITSED RD
9 EVES CL

Scale: 1¾ inches to 1 mile

0   ¼   ½   mile
0   250m 500m 750m 1 km

Priors Meadow
BACK LANE
EASTGATE
STOWGATE ROAD
B1166
CUSTOM RD
CRANMORE DROVE
Cranmore Barn Farm
Cranmore Lodge
Deeping Fen
Wards Farm
WELLAND BANK B1166
Kennulph's Stone
MIDDLE ROAD
CORPORATION

Backside Field
Football Gd
LOCKS CL
Grasmere Farm
Sewage Works
WHICHCOTE ROAD
LC
Deeping Common
Borough Fen
DOVE WILLOW
Eardley Grange
Eardley Grange Farm

09
Cranleigh Farm
EASTGATE
Cranmore Lodge
CROWLAND ROAD
Willow Barn Farm
The Willows
SPEECHLEY'S DV

7
North Fen
GIDDON'S DRO
RIVER LA
STATION ROAD
STATION ROAD
Chestnut Farm
The Wash
Decoy Farm
Lower Willow Farm

CHURCH ST
Park Island
Deeping Lakes Nature Reserve
P
River Welland
DECOY ROAD
Decoy

08
DEEPING ROAD
Corporation Bank
Moores Farm
Peakirk Moor
Bullbridge Farm

6
Maxey Cut
Moorfield
Enclosure
Borough Fen
The Avenue

MILE DROVE
07
Sissons Farm
MOOR ROAD
Peakirk Moor
WILLOW DROVE
DECOY ROAD
Pank's Farm

Hermitage
Peakirk
PEAKIRK
B1443
Willow Tree Farm
PH
Buildings Farm
PE6
Slip Bridge
Bull Bridge
Bridge End
Crowtree Farm

5
PH
ST PEGA'S RD
GUNTON ROAD
Sunny Side
MILKING NOOK DROVE
LAW'S CL
NORTHBOROUGH RD
THORNEY ROAD
PH
SCHOOL ROAD
PO

06
220
LC
221
SOKE ROAD
PO
Cemy
Newborough CE Prim Sch
Baxter's Bridge
Newborough

MEADOW ROAD
BAINTON ROAD
BRAIN ROAD
Twenty Foot Farm
Recn Gd
MIDDLE ROAD
PETERBOROUGH ROAD

4
Stone Bridge Farm
Werrington Lakes
Milking Nook
Bungalow Farm
Newborough Fen
GUNTON'S ROAD
Home Farm

A15
WERRINGTON BRIDGE ROAD
Lowlands Farm
BRIDGEHILL ROAD

05
P
HODGSON AV
Werrington End Farm
The Firs

3
DAVID'S LANE
STANILAND WY
Fen Bridge
GUNTHORPE ROAD
221
PE4
Norwood Farm
Hill Farm
WHITEPOST ROAD
Fell Farm
GREEN ROAD

04
Sch
P
PO
SKATERS WAY
PASTON PARKWAY
PETERBOROUGH
Mast
Norwood Spinney

Werrington
SOUTHWELL AVE
Sch
GOODWIN WY
Gunthorpe Bridge
Gunthorpe
NORWOOD LA
A16
WOOLFELLHILL RD
HODNEY RD

03
LINCOLN RD
SALISBURY RD
CHURCH STREET
DUNSTON RD
FULBRIDGE RD
MANOR DR
A15
NORWOOD LA
Little Wood
WHITEPOST ROAD

STAVERTON RD
A15
Brookfields Ind Pk
DUKESMEAD
Allot Gdns
Recn Gd
GUNTHORPE RIDINGS
Leeds Farm
Pit (dis)
A1139
EYE RD

PE3
STIRLING WY
LINCOLN ROAD
Acad
Walton
Paston
PASTON RIDINGS
SOKE PARKWAY
A47
WELLAND RD
A47
PE1
Landfill Site

02
16   A   17   B   18   C   19   D   20   E   21   F

225
173

For full street detail of the highlighted area see pages 220 & 221.

E4
1 SEARGEANTS CL
2 WATERFALL GDNS
3 FERNIE CL
4 CHURCH CL
5 WALNUT CL
6 DAWSON CL
7 QUORN CL
8 REEDMACE CL
9 HARRIS CL

226

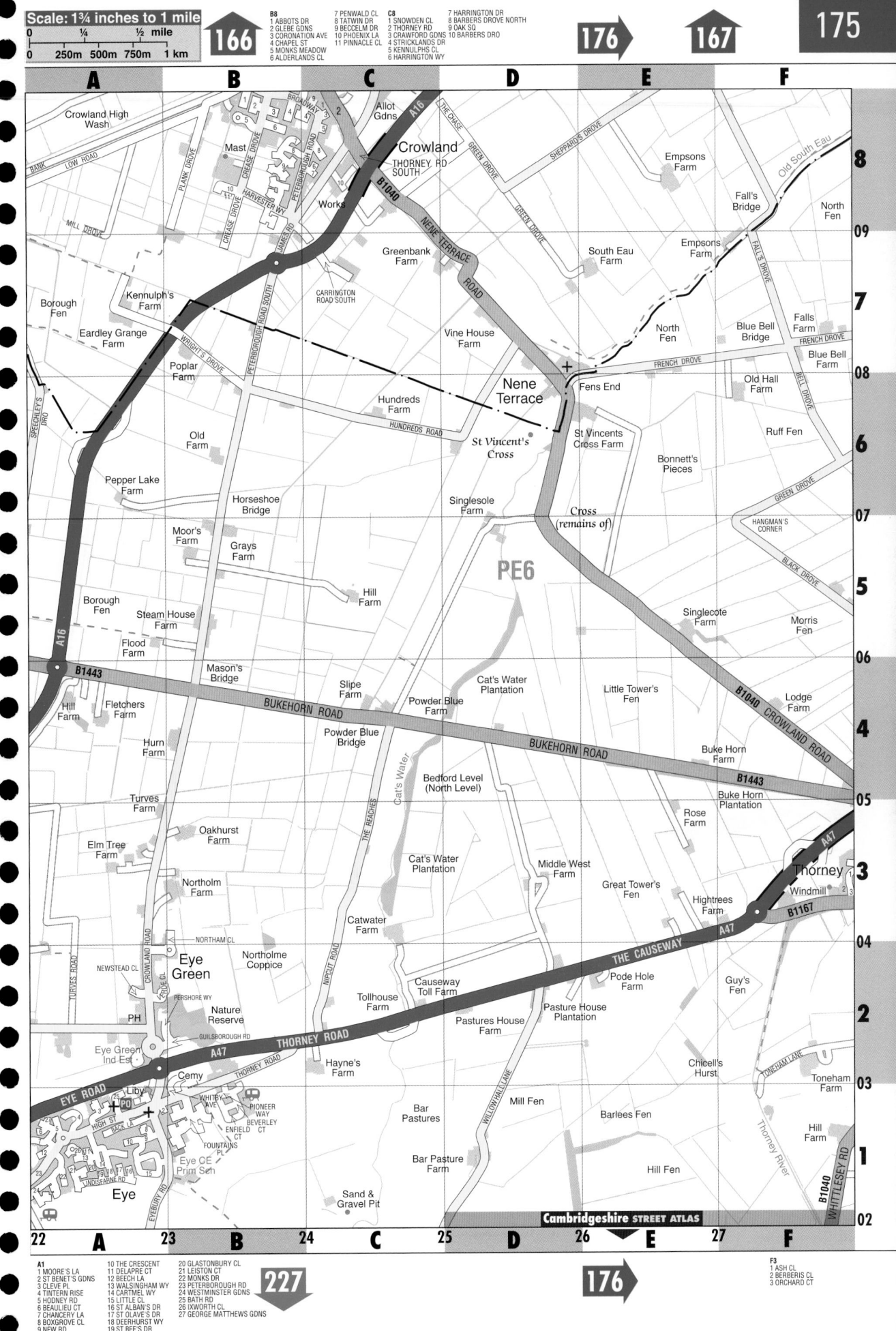

B8
1 ABBOTS DR
2 GLEBE GDNS
3 CORONATION AVE
4 CHAPEL ST
5 MONKS MEADOW
6 ALDERLANDS CL

7 PENWALD CL
8 TATWIN DR
9 BECCELM DR
10 PHOENIX LA
11 PINNACLE CL

C8
1 SNOWDEN CL
2 THORNEY RD
3 CRAWFORD GDNS
4 STRICKLANDS DR
5 KENNULPHS CL
6 HARRINGTON WY

7 HARRINGTON DR
8 BARBERS DROVE NORTH
9 OAK SQ
10 BARBERS DRO

A   B   C   D   E   F

Crowland High Wash

Allot Gdns

Mast

Crowland

THORNEY RD SOUTH

Works

Empsons Farm

Fall's Bridge

North Fen

BANK   LOW ROAD

MILL DROVE

PLANK DROVE

CREASE DROVE

PETERBOROUGH ROAD

JAMES RD

BROADWAY

NENE TERRACE ROAD

A16

B1040

THE CHASE

SHEPPARD'S DROVE

GREEN DROVE

GREEN DROVE

Greenbank Farm

South Eau Farm

Empsons Farm

Old South Eau

FALL'S DRIVE

09

Borough Fen

Kennulph's Farm

Eardley Grange Farm

Poplar Farm

CARRINGTON ROAD SOUTH

Vine House Farm

North Fen

Blue Bell Bridge

Falls Bridge

FRENCH DROVE

7

WRIGHT'S DROVE

PETERBOROUGH ROAD SOUTH

SPEECHLEY'S DRO

Old Farm

Hundreds Farm

Nene Terrace

FRENCH DROVE

Fens End

Old Hall Farm

Blue Bell Farm

BELL DRIVE

08

HUNDREDS ROAD

St Vincent's Cross

St Vincents Cross Farm

Ruff Fen

6

Pepper Lake Farm

Horseshoe Bridge

Singlesole Farm

Cross (remains of)

Bonnett's Pieces

Hangman's Corner

GREEN DROVE

07

Moor's Farm

Grays Farm

PE6

BLACK DROVE

5

Borough Fen

Steam House Farm

Hill Farm

Singlecote Farm

Morris Fen

Flood Farm

A16

Mason's Bridge

B1443

Slipe Farm

Powder Blue Farm

Cat's Water Plantation

Little Tower's Fen

B1040 CROWLAND ROAD

Lodge Farm

06

BUKEHORN ROAD

Hill Farm

Fletchers Farm

Powder Blue Bridge

BUKEHORN ROAD

Buke Horn Farm

B1443

4

Hurn Farm

Cat's Water

Bedford Level (North Level)

Rose Farm

Buke Horn Plantation

05

Turves Farm

Oakhurst Farm

THE REACHES

Cat's Water Plantation

Middle West Farm

A47

Thorney

Windmill

Elm Tree Farm

Northolm Farm

NORTHAM CL

Great Tower's Fen

Hightrees Farm

A47

B1167

3

Eye Green

Northolme Coppice

CROWLAND ROAD

NIPPUT ROAD

Catwater Farm

THE CAUSEWAY

Pode Hole Farm

Guy's Fen

TONEHAM LANE

04

NEWSTEAD CL

PERSHORE WY

Nature Reserve

GUILSBOROUGH RD

Tollhouse Farm

Causeway Toll Farm

Pasture House Plantation

Chicell's Hurst

Toneham Farm

2

PH

Eye Green Ind Est

A47

THORNEY ROAD

Pastures House Farm

WILLOW HALL LANE

Thorney River

Hill Farm

TURVES ROAD

EYEBURY RD

THORNEY ROAD

Cemy

Hayne's Farm

Mill Fen

Barlees Fen

WHITTLESEY RD

B1040

03

EYE ROAD

Liby

PO

WHITBY AVE

PIONEER WAY

BEVERLEY CT

ENFIELD CT

FOUNTAINS PL

BACK LA

HIGH ST

Bar Pastures

Hill Fen

Hill Farm

1

Eye OE Prim Sch

LANDISFARNE RD

Eye

Bar Pasture Farm

Sand & Gravel Pit

Hill Fen

02

22   A   23   B   24   C   25   D   26   E   27   F

A1
1 MOORE'S LA
2 ST BENET'S GDNS
3 CLEVE PL
4 TINTERN RISE
5 HODNEY RD
6 BEAULIEU CT
7 CHANCERY LA
8 BOXGROVE CL
9 NEW RD

10 THE CRESCENT
11 DELAPRE CT
12 BEECH LA
13 WALSINGHAM WY
14 CARTMEL WY
15 LITTLE CL
16 ST ALBAN'S DR
17 ST OLAVE'S DR
18 DEERHURST WY
19 ST BEE'S DR

20 GLASTONBURY CL
21 LEISTON CT
22 MONKS DR
23 PETERBOROUGH RD
24 WESTMINSTER GDNS
25 BATH RD
26 IXWORTH CL
27 GEORGE MATTHEWS GDNS

F3
1 ASH CL
2 BERBERIS CL
3 ORCHARD CT

Scale: 1¾ inches to 1 mile

0   ¼   ½   mile
0   250m 500m 750m 1 km

A   B   C   D   E   F

8

Avenue Farm

DOWSDALE BANK

North Fen

French Farm

09

French Farm

7

French Drove

Gothic Farm

Gothic House Farm

Grange Farm

New Cut Bridge

FRENCH DROVE

B1167

WEST DROVE SOUTH

B1166 STATION ROAD

MOLE DRIVE

COMMON RD

Lordship End

LITTLEWORTH DV

Allen's Bridge

New South Eau

Sycamore Farm

Malice Farm

Sutton St Edmund's Common

PE12

08

New South Eau

Ruff Fen

GREEN DROVE

Chestnut Farm

SCOLDING DROVE

North Fen

Lodge Farm

COMMON ROAD

6

Green Drove Farm

Morris Fen

Wrydelands Farm

ARCHERS DROVE

Gold Dike Farm

Wryde Croft

GOLD DIKE

07

5

Lodge Farm

Priests Farm

ENGLISH DROVE

Archer's Drove Farm

NEW CUT

Nutsgrove Farm

BLACK DROVE

06

CH

Little House Farm

Desford Farm

Fish Fen

PE6

SCOLDING DROVE

4

Lime Tree Farm

White Hart Farm

Earl's Fen

WALLACE'S DROVE

Wryde Plantation

Little Knarr Fen

Sewage Works

05

A47

STATION RD

Thorney Heritage Mus

Thorney

The Duke of Bedford Sch

Cobbler's Fen

East Wryde Farm

B1167

Wryde Plantation

3

WISBECH RD

1 PARK CL
2 PARK CRES
3 SMITHFIELD

Pigeons' Farm

Knarr Farm

Liby

Park House Sch

PO

04

WOODGATE LA

ROWLEY PL

B1167

Corner Farm

WISBECH ROAD

A47

Abbey House

Cemetery

Ashley Pool

High Lands

1

Park Farm

North Farm

Middle Knarr Fen

2

A2
1 WHITTLESEY RD
2 ST BOTOLPH'S WY
3 ST MARY'S CL
4 ST PETER'S WY
5 ASHLEY POOL LA
6 TONEHAM LA

South Farm

West Corner Farm

Rattlerow Farm

DAIRY DROVE

Glass House Farm

KNARR FEN ROAD

03

WHITTLESEY RD

B1040

Upper Knarr Fen

OLD KNARR FEN DROVE

Lower Knarr Fen

PE13

1

02

Hill Plantation

Cambridgeshire STREET ATLAS

28   A   29   B   30   C   31   D   32   E   33   F

A3
1 KINGSLINE CL
2 ASH CL
3 CHESTNUT DR
4 BEECH CL
5 GAS LA
6 THE MALTINGS
7 LAUREL DR
8 THE CAUSEWAY
9 CHURCH ST
10 ABBEY PL
11 THE GREEN
12 RUSSELL CL
13 TOPHAM CRES
14 SANDPIT RD
15 TAVISTOCK CL
16 BEDFORD CT

Scale: 1¾ inches to 1 mile

0 ¼ ½ mile
0 250m 500m 750m 1 km

168

169

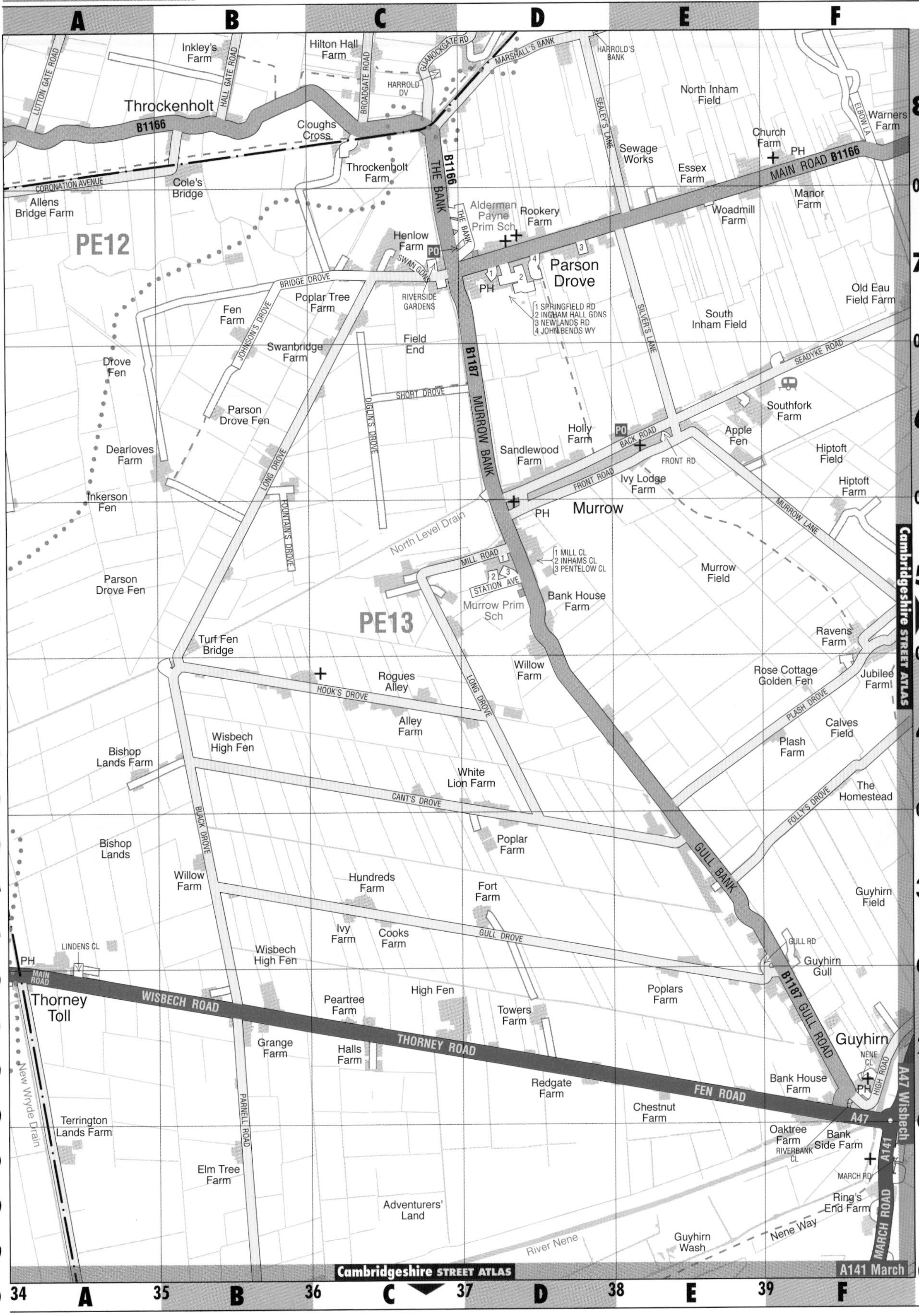

177

A B C D E F

Inkley's Farm
Hilton Hall Farm
QUANDONGATE RD
HALL GATE ROAD
BROADGATE ROAD
MARSHALL'S BANK
HARROLD'S BANK
North Inham Field
ELBOW LA
Warners Farm

8

Throckenholt
B1166
Cloughs Cross
HARROLD DV
THE BANK
B1166
Sewage Works
Church
PH
MAIN ROAD B1166

CORONATION AVENUE
Cole's Bridge
Throckenholt Farm
THE BANK
Essex Farm
Manor Farm

09

Allens Bridge Farm
Henlow Farm
SWAN GDNS
PO
Alderman Payne Prim Sch
Rookery Farm
SEALEY'S LANE
3
Woadmill Farm

PE12

7

Bridge Drove
Poplar Tree Farm
RIVERSIDE GARDENS
1 2
PH
Parson Drove
Old Eau Field Farm

Fen Farm
JOHNSON'S DROVE
Swanbridge Farm
Field End
1 SPRINGFIELD RD
2 INGHAM HALL GDNS
3 NEWLANDS RD
4 JOHN BENDS WY
SILVER'S LANE
South Inham Field

08

Drove Fen
DIGLIN'S DROVE
SHORT DROVE
B1187
MURROW BANK
SEADYKE ROAD
Southfork Farm

6

Parson Drove Fen
LONG DROVE
Holly Farm
Sandlewood Farm
PO
BACK ROAD
FRONT RD
Apple Fen
Hiptoft Field

Dearloves Farm
FOUNTAIN'S DROVE
FRONT ROAD
Ivy Lodge Farm
Hiptoft Farm

07

Inkerson Fen
North Level Drain
PH
Murrow
MURROW LANE

Parson Drove Fen
MILL ROAD
1 MILL CL
2 INHAMS CL
3 PENTELOW CL
Murrow Field

5

STATION AVE
1 2 3
Bank House Farm
Ravens Farm

Turf Fen Bridge
Murrow Prim Sch
Rose Cottage Golden Fen
Jubilee Farm

06

HOOK'S DROVE
Rogues Alley
LONG DROVE
Willow Farm
PLASH DROVE
Calves Field

4

Bishop Lands Farm
Wisbech High Fen
Alley Farm
Plash Farm

White Lion Farm
CANT'S DROVE
FOLLY'S DROVE
The Homestead

05

BLACK DROVE
Poplar Farm

3

Bishop Lands
Willow Farm
Hundreds Farm
Fort Farm
GULL BANK
Guyhirn Field

Ivy Farm
Cooks Farm
GULL DROVE
GULL RD
Guyhirn Gull

04

LINDENS CL
PH
Wisbech High Fen
Poplars Farm
B1187 GULL ROAD

MAIN ROAD
Thorney Toll
WISBECH ROAD
Peartree Farm
High Fen
Towers Farm
FEN ROAD
Guyhirn
NENE CL
PH
HIGH RD
A47 Wisbech

2

Grange Farm
Halls Farm
THORNEY ROAD
Redgate Farm
Bank House Farm

New Wryde Drain
PARNELL ROAD
Chestnut Farm
A47
Oaktree Farm
RIVERBANK CL
Bank Side Farm
A141

03

Terrington Lands Farm
Elm Tree Farm
MARCH RD
Ring's End Farm

1

Adventurers' Land
River Nene
Guyhirn Wash
Nene Way
MARCH ROAD

02

34 A 35 B 36 C 37 D 38 E 39 F

PE13

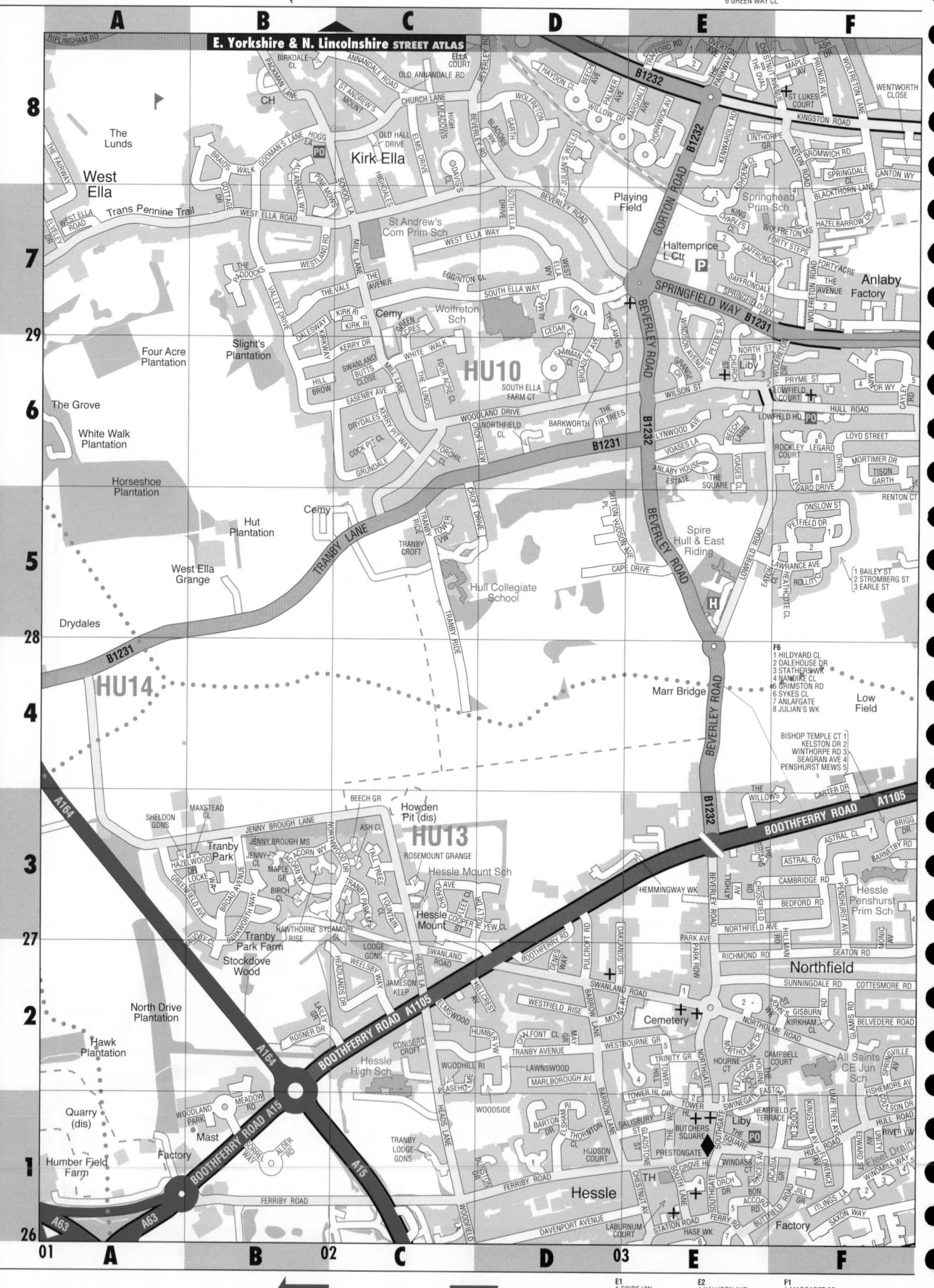

E6
1 NORTH DR
2 WILSON ST
3 WOLFRETON CT
4 RINGROSE LA

E7
1 CROMWELL CT
2 WOODHILL CL
3 NORWOOD CL
4 WAULDBY CL
5 WEETON WY

E8
1 COLLYNSON CL
2 SETTERWOOD GARTH
3 OAKDALE AV

F7
1 RAYWELL CL
2 PENWITH DR
3 ORCHARD CL
4 GLENHAM DR
5 WOLFRETON VILLAS
6 GREEN WAY CL

E. Yorkshire & N. Lincolnshire STREET ATLAS

E1
1 SPIRE VW
2 TOWER HILL MEWS
3 VICARAGE LA
4 CLOWES CT
5 FISHWICK AVE
6 CHAMPNEYS CLOSE
7 CASTLE WAY

E2
1 HALYCON AVE
2 NORTHOLME CL
3 WESTBOURNE AVE
4 THE CIRCLE
5 BRUNSWICK GR
6 ROBERT BARNETT CL

F1
1 MARGARET GR
2 BISHOP BLUNT CL
3 BISHOP KEMPTHORNE CL
4 BISHOP GURDON CL
5 CANON TARDREW CL

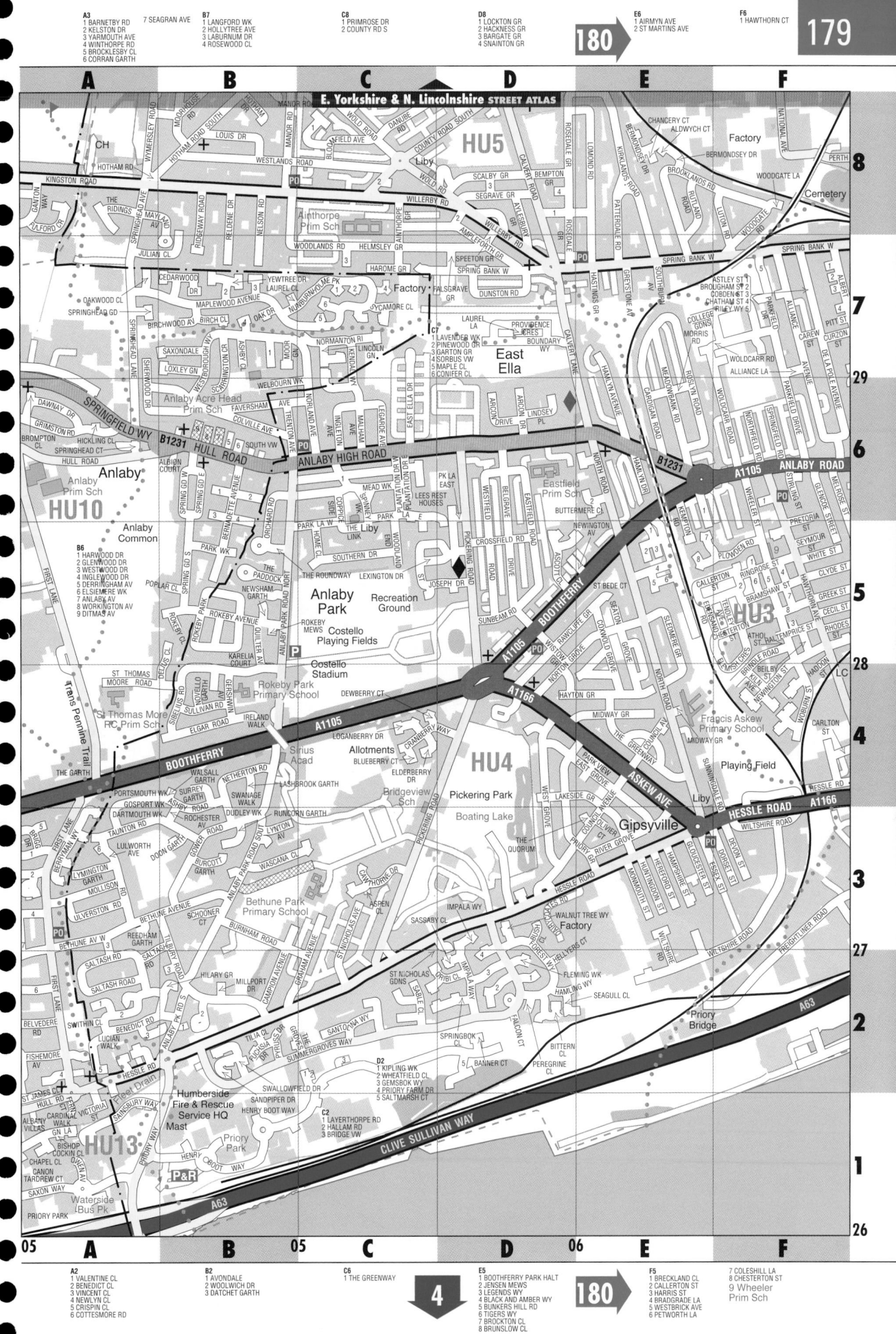

A3 1 BARNETBY RD 2 KELSTON DR 3 YARMOUTH AVE 4 WINTHORPE RD 5 BROCKLESBY CL 6 CORRAN GARTH 7 SEAGRAN AVE	**B7** 1 LANGFORD WK 2 HOLLYTREE AVE 3 LABURNUM DR 4 ROSEWOOD CL	**C8** 1 PRIMROSE DR 2 COUNTY RD S	**D8** 1 LOCKTON GR 2 HACKNESS GR 3 BARGATE GR 4 SNAINTON GR	**E6** 1 AIRMYN AVE 2 ST MARTINS AVE	**F6** 1 HAWTHORN CT

180 ▶

179

E. Yorkshire & N. Lincolnshire STREET ATLAS

A2 1 VALENTINE CL 2 BENEDICT CL 3 VINCENT CL 4 NEWLYN CL 5 CRISPIN CL 6 COTTESMORE RD	**B2** 1 AVONDALE 2 WOOLWICH DR 3 DATCHET GARTH	**C6** 1 THE GREENWAY	**E5** 1 BOOTHFERRY PARK HALT 2 JENSEN MEWS 3 LEGENDS WY 4 BLACK AND AMBER WY 5 BUNKERS HILL RD 6 TIGERS WY 7 BROCKTON CL 8 BRUNSLOW CL	**F5** 1 BRECKLAND CL 2 CALLERTON ST 3 HARRIS ST 4 BRADGADE LA 5 WESTBRICK AVE 6 PETWORTH CL 7 COLESHILL LA 8 CHESTERTON ST 9 WHEELER PRIM SCH	

◀ **4**   **180** ▶

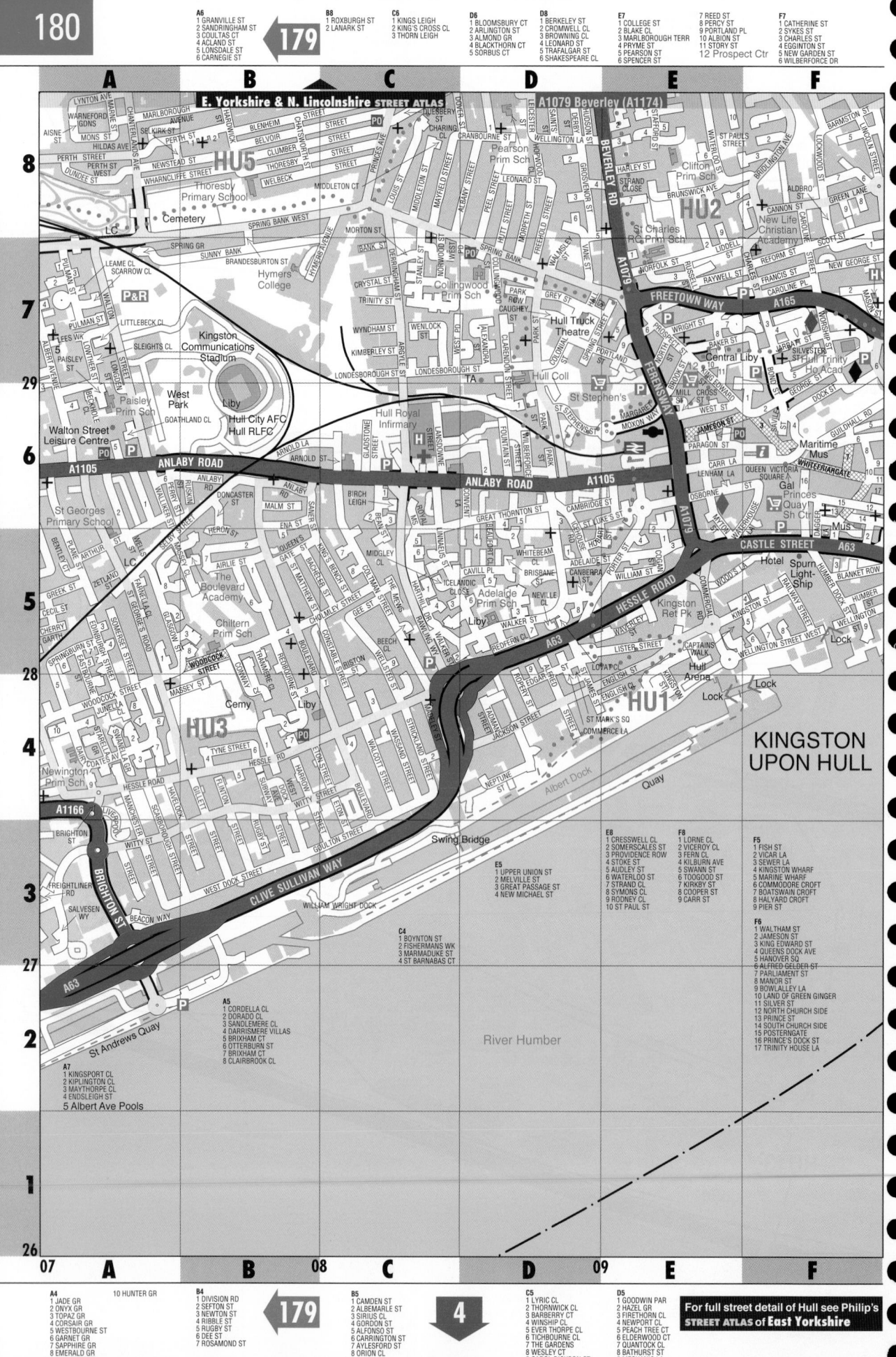

A6
1 GRANVILLE ST
2 SANDRINGHAM ST
3 COULTAS CT
4 ACLAND ST
5 LONSDALE ST
6 CARNEGIE ST

B8
1 ROXBURGH ST
2 LANARK ST

C6
1 KINGS LEIGH
2 KING'S CROSS CL
3 THORN LEIGH

D6
1 BLOOMSBURY CT
2 ARLINGTON ST
3 ALMOND GR
4 BLACKTHORN CT
5 SORBUS CT

D8
1 BERKELEY ST
2 CROMWELL CL
3 BROWNING ST
4 LEONARD ST
5 TRAFALGAR ST
6 SHAKESPEARE CL

E7
1 COLLEGE ST
2 BLAKE CL
3 MARLBOROUGH TERR
4 PRYME ST
5 PEARSON ST
6 SPENCER ST

7 REED ST
8 PERCY ST
9 PORTLAND PL
10 ALBION ST
11 STORY ST
12 PROSPECT CTR

F7
1 CATHERINE ST
2 SYKES ST
3 CHARLES ST
4 EGGINTON ST
5 NEW GARDEN ST
6 WILBERFORCE DR

E. Yorkshire & N. Lincolnshire STREET ATLAS

A1079 Beverley (A1174)

KINGSTON UPON HULL

E8
1 CRESSWELL CL
2 SOMERSCALES ST
3 PROVIDENCE ROW
4 STOKE ST
5 AUDLEY ST
6 WATERLOO ST
7 STRAND CL
8 SYMONS ST
9 RODNEY CL
10 ST PAUL ST

F8
1 LORNE CL
2 VICEROY CL
3 FERN CL
4 KILBURN AVE
5 SWANN ST
6 TOOGOOD ST
7 KIRKBY ST
8 COOPER ST
9 CARR ST

F5
1 FISH ST
2 VICAR LA
3 SEWER LA
4 KINGSTON WHARF
5 MARINE WHARF
6 COMMODORE CROFT
7 BOATSWAIN CROFT
8 HALYARD CROFT
9 PIER ST

F6
1 WALTHAM ST
2 JAMESON ST
3 KING EDWARD ST
4 QUEENS DOCK AVE
5 HANOVER SQ
6 ALFRED GELDER ST
7 PARLIAMENT ST
8 MANOR ST
9 BOWLALLEY LA
10 LAND OF GREEN GINGER
11 SILVER ST
12 NORTH CHURCH SIDE
13 PRINCE ST
14 SOUTH CHURCH SIDE
15 POSTERNGATE
16 PRINCE'S DOCK ST
17 TRINITY HOUSE LA

E5
1 UPPER UNION ST
2 MELVILLE ST
3 GREAT PASSAGE ST
4 NEW MICHAEL ST

C4
1 BOYNTON ST
2 FISHERMANS WK
3 MARMADUKE ST
4 ST BARNABAS CT

A5
1 CORDELLA CL
2 DORADO CL
3 SANDLEMERE CL
4 DARRISMERE VILLAS
5 BRIXHAM CT
6 OTTERBURN ST
7 BRIXHAM CT
8 CLAIRBROOK CL

A7
1 KINGSPORT CL
2 KIPLINGTON CL
3 MAYTHORPE CL
4 ENDSLEIGH ST
5 ALBERT AVE POOLS

A4
1 JADE GR
2 ONYX GR
3 TOPAZ GR
4 CORSAIR GR
5 WESTBOURNE ST
6 GARNET GR
7 SAPPHIRE GR
8 EMERALD GR
9 ST NECTAN GR

10 HUNTER GR

B4
1 DIVISION RD
2 SEFTON ST
3 NEWTON ST
4 RIBBLE ST
5 RUGBY ST
6 DEE ST
7 ROSAMOND ST

B5
1 CAMDEN ST
2 ALBEMARLE ST
3 SIRIUS CL
4 GORDON ST
5 ALFONSO ST
6 CARRINGTON ST
7 AYLESFORD ST
8 ORION CL

C5
1 LYRIC CL
2 THORNWICK CL
3 BARBERRY CT
4 WINSHIP CL
5 EVER THORPE CL
6 TICHBOURNE CL
7 THE GARDENS
8 WESLEY CT
9 CAROL DICKSON CL

D5
1 GOODWIN PAR
2 HAZEL GR
3 FIRETHORN CL
4 NEWPORT CL
5 PEACH TREE CT
6 ELDERWOOD CT
7 QUANTOCK CL
8 BATHURST ST
9 MECHANIC LA

179

4

For full street detail of Hull see Philip's STREET ATLAS of East Yorkshire

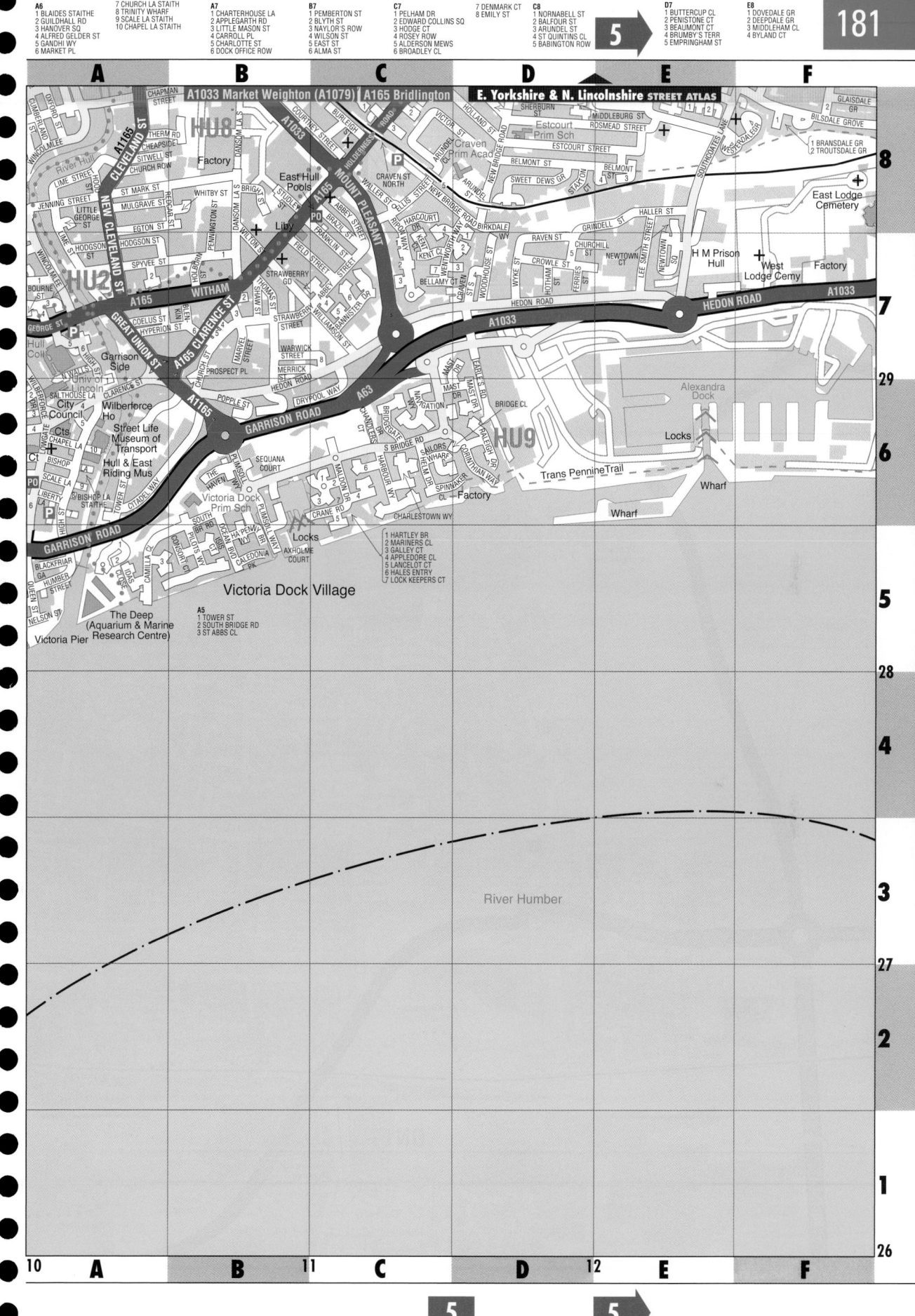
A6
1 BLAIDES STAITHE
2 GUILDHALL RD
3 HANOVER SQ
4 ALFRED GELDER ST
5 GANDHI WY
6 MARKET PL
7 CHURCH LA STAITH
8 TRINITY WHARF
9 SCALE LA STAITH
10 CHAPEL LA STAITH
A7
1 CHARTERHOUSE LA
2 APPLEGARTH RD
3 LITTLE MASON ST
4 CARROLL PL
5 CHARLOTTE ST
6 DOCK OFFICE ROW
B7
1 PEMBERTON ST
2 BLYTH ST
3 NAYLOR'S ROW
4 WILSON ST
5 EAST ST
6 ALMA ST
C7
1 PELHAM DR
2 EDWARD COLLINS SQ
3 HODGE CT
4 ROSEY ROW
5 ALDERSON MEWS
6 BROADLEY CL
7 DENMARK CT
8 EMILY ST
C8
1 NORNABELL ST
2 BALFOUR ST
3 ARUNDEL ST
4 ST QUINTINS CL
5 BABINGTON ROW
D7
1 BUTTERCUP CL
2 PENISTONE CT
3 BEAUMONT CT
4 BRUMBY'S TERR
5 EMPRINGHAM ST
E8
1 DOVEDALE GR
2 DEEPDALE GR
3 MIDDLEHAM CL
4 BYLAND CT
5
A1033 Market Weighton (A1079)
A165 Bridlington
E. Yorkshire & N. Lincolnshire STREET ATLAS
HU8
HU2
HU9
Factory
East Hull Pools
Liby
Estcourt Prim Sch
Craven Prim Acad
East Lodge Cemetery
H M Prison Hull
West Lodge Cemy
Factory
HEDON ROAD
A1033
WITHAM
A165
CLARENCE ST
GREAT UNION ST
NEW CLEVELAND ST
CLEVELAND ST
MOUNT PLEASANT
HOLDERNESS ROAD
A63
GARRISON ROAD
A1165
Garrison Side
Univ of Lincoln
City Council
Wilberforce Ho
Cts
Street Life Museum of Transport
Hull & East Riding Mus
Hull Coll
Alexandra Dock
Locks
Wharf
Trans Pennine Trail
Victoria Dock Prim Sch
Factory
Locks
Victoria Dock Village
The Deep (Aquarium & Marine Research Centre)
Victoria Pier
A5
1 TOWER ST
2 SOUTH BRIDGE RD
3 ST ABBS CL
1 HARTLEY BR
2 MARINERS CL
3 GALLEY CT
4 APPLEDORE CL
5 LANCELOT CT
6 HALES ENTRY
7 LOCK KEEPERS CT
1 BRANSDALE GR
2 TROUTSDALE GR
River Humber
A B C D E F
8 7 29 6 5 28 4 3 27 2 1 26
10 11 12
5
5

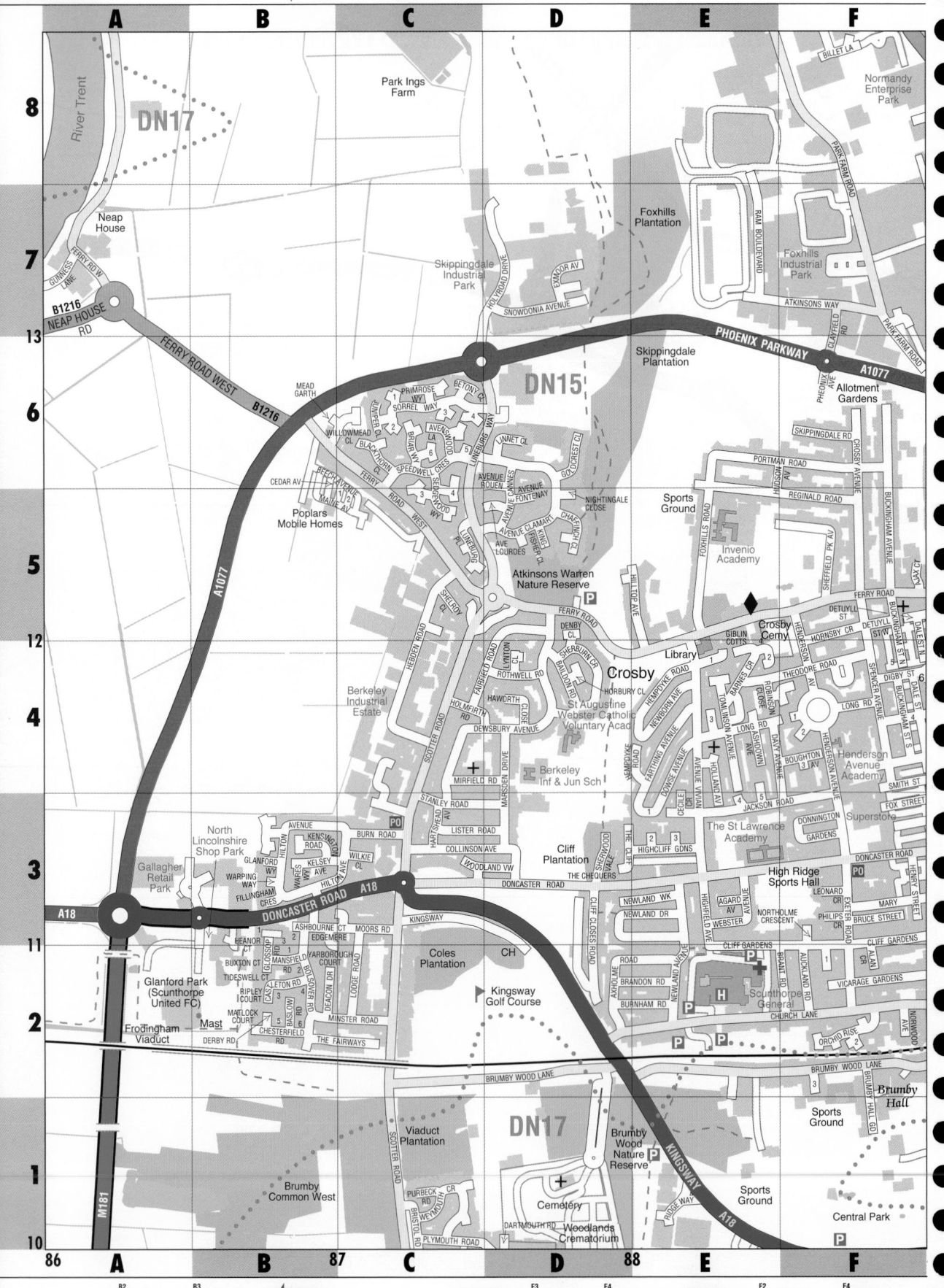

C5
1 ACACIA AVE
2 MAPLE AVE
3 PIPPIN CT
4 RUSSET CL

C6
1 POPPY CL
2 WOODALE CL
3 FLETCHER CL
4 COLTSFOOT CL
5 ST MARY'S CT
6 HERON CL

17

8

B2
1 TANSLEY CT
2 ALFRETON CT
3 HATHERSAGE CT
4 GRASSMOOR CT
5 EASTWOOD CT
6 BELPER CT

B3
1 BAKEWELL CT
2 ILKESTON CT
3 DRONFIELD CT

17

184

E3
1 JACKSON RD
2 DE ASTON SQ
3 CONWAY SQ
4 TOMLINSON AVE
5 ASHDOWN AVE

E4
1 LOCKWOOD CT
2 MALLALIEU CT
3 MARY SUMNER WY
4 KIRK CLOSE

18

F2
1 ERYHOLME CR
2 FUCHSIA CRFT
3 PAVILION GDNS

F4
1 LONG RD
2 HENDERSON CRES
3 EDWARDS RD
4 SHEFFIELD ST
5 BUCKINGHAM ST
6 Comm Ctr

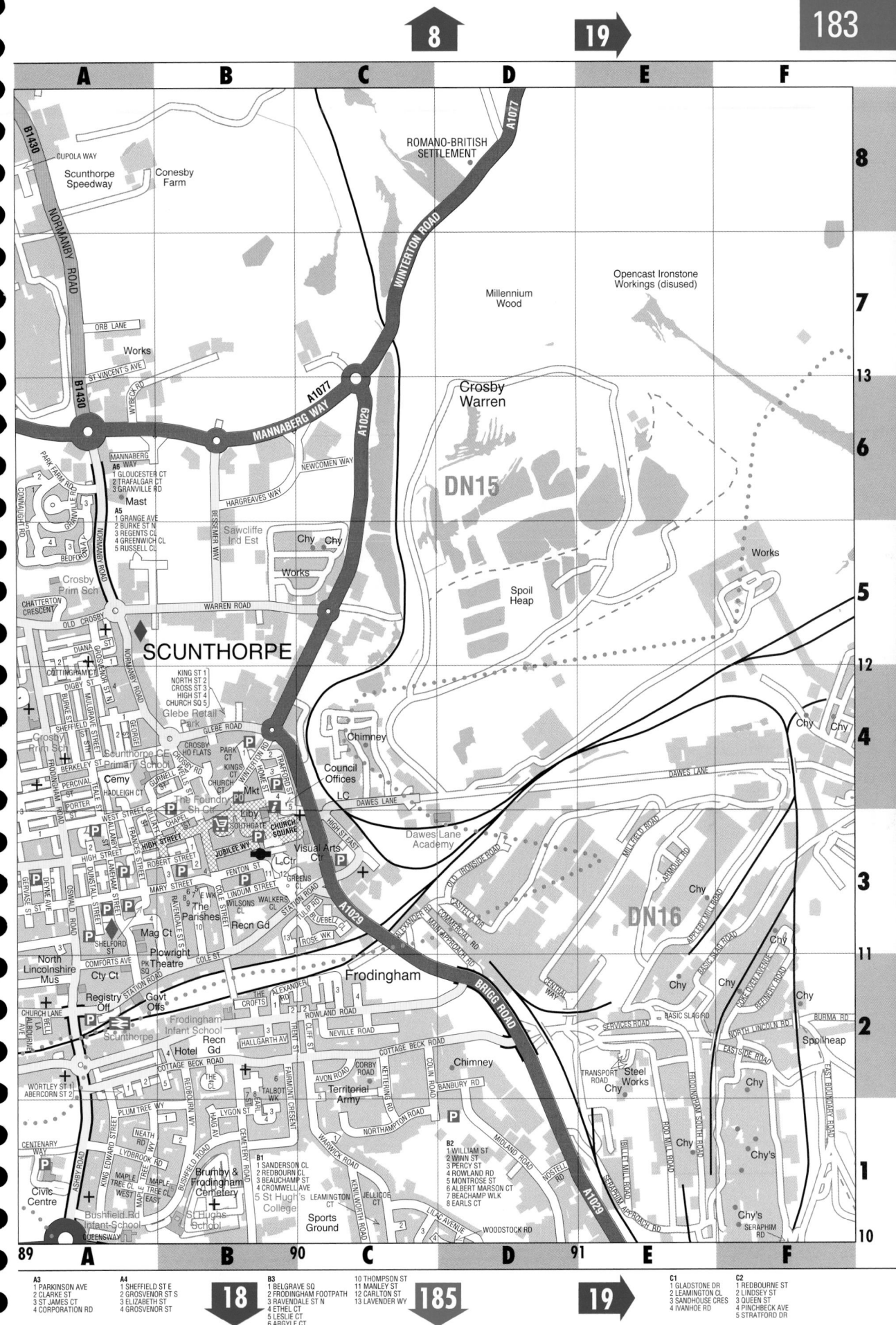

A B C D E F

8
7
13
6
5
12
4
3
11
2
1
10

SCUNTHORPE

B1430
CUPOLA WAY
Scunthorpe Speedway
Conesby Farm
NORMANBY ROAD
ROMANO-BRITISH SETTLEMENT
A1077
WINTERTON ROAD
Opencast Ironstone Workings (disused)
Millennium Wood
ORB LANE
Works
ST VINCENT'S AVE
MANNABERG WAY
A1077
A1029
Crosby Warren
DN15
MANNABERG WAY
A5 WAY
1 GLOUCESTER CT
2 TRAFALGAR CT
3 GRANVILLE RD
Mast
A5
1 GRANGE AVE
2 BURKE ST N
3 REGENTS CL
4 GREENWICH CL
5 RUSSELL CL
HARGREAVES WAY
BESSEMER WAY
NEWCOMEN WAY
Sawcliffe Ind Est
Chy Chy
Works
Works
Spoil Heap
PARK FARM RD
CONNAUGHT RD
PARK FARM RD
GRANARY
Crosby Prim Sch
Chatterton Crescent
OLD CROSBY
WARREN ROAD
WYBECK RD
BEDFORD
DIANA
COTTINGHAM RD
DIGBY
NORMANBY ROAD
GROSVENOR ST N
GEORGE
SHEFFIELD ST
MULGRAVE STREET
KING ST 1
NORTH ST 2
CROSS ST 3
HIGH ST 4
CHURCH SQ 5
Glebe Retail Park
CROSBY HO FLATS
GLEBE ROAD
PARK CT
KINGS
WINTERTON RD
CHURCH
TRAFFORD ST
Chimney
Council Offices
LC
DAWES LANE
Works
Chy Chy
Crosby Prim Sch
BERKELEY ST
PERCIVAL
HADLEIGH CT
Cemy
GURNELL ST
WELLS ST
Mkt
PD
Liby
SOUTHGATE
CHURCH SQUARE
Visual Arts Ctr
DAWES LANE
HIGH ST EAST
Dawes Lane Academy
OLD IRONSIDE ROAD
MILLFIELD ROAD
ASHMOUR RD
Chy
DN16
APPLEBY MILL ROAD
FRODINGHAM RD
PORTER ST
WALLENBY ST
FRANCES ST
HIGH STREET
CHAPEL
The Foundry Sh Ctr
JUBILEE WY
FENTON ST
LUNDUM STREET
L-Ctr
GREENS RD
EWART
STATION ROAD
TULIP RD
A1029
ALEXANDER RD
CASTELLA DR
COMMERCIAL RD
MAIN APPROACH RD
CENTRAL WAY
BASIC SLAG RD
COKE OVEN AVENUE
BASIC SLAG ROAD
NORTH LINCOLN RD
REFINERY ROAD
BURMA RD
EAST SIDE ROAD
EAST BOUNDARY ROAD
DEYNE AVE
GERVASE ST
OSWALD ROAD
DUNSTAL STREET
LANEHAM ST
ROBERT STREET
MARY STREET
COLE ST
COLE ST
RAVENDALE ST
WILSONS CL
WALKERS
BLUEBELL
ROSE WK
Recn Gd
13
The Parishes
Recn Gd
Mag Ct
SHELFORD ST
North Lincolnshire Mus
Cty Ct
COMFORTS AVE
PK Theatre
STATION ROAD
Plowright
Registry Off
Govt Offs
CHURCH LANE
MELBOURNE AVE
Scunthorpe
Hotel
Recn Gd
Frodingham Infant School
THE CROFTS
ALEXANDER RD
HALLGARTH AV
ROWLAND ROAD
NEVILLE ROAD
CLIFF ST
TRENT ST
Frodingham
COTTAGE BECK ROAD
COLIN ROAD
CORBY ROAD
KETTERING RD
BANBURY RD
Chimney
A1029
BRIGG ROAD
SERVICES ROAD
TRANSPORT ROAD
Steel Works
Chy
Spoilheap
Chy
WORTLEY 1
ABERCORN 2
Cottage Beck Road
THE CL
EARL
TALBOT WK
FAIRMONT CRESENT
AVON LANE
NORTHAMPTON ROAD
WARWICK ROAD
KENILWORTH ROAD
LILAC AVENUE
WOODSTOCK RD
MIDLAND ROAD
NOSTELL RD
SERACHIN APPROACH RD
FRODINGHAM SOUTH ROAD
BELLET MILL ROAD
FOOT MILL ROAD
Chy's
Chy
Chy's
SERAPHIM RD
CENTENARY WAY
Civic Centre
Bushfield Rd Infant School
KING EDWARD STREET
ASHBY ROAD
PLUM TREE WY
NEATH WY
LYOBROOK RD
MAPLE TREE CL WEST
MAPLE TREE CL EAST
LYGON ST
HAIG AV
CEMETERY ROAD
REDBOURN WAY
BUSHFIELD ROAD
HAG AV
Brumby & Frodingham Cemetery
St Hughs School
B1
1 SANDERSON CL
2 REDBOURN CL
3 BEAUCHAMP ST
4 CROMWELL AVE
5 St Hugh's Leamington College
JELLICOE CT
CARLTON CT
Sports Ground
B2
1 WILLIAM ST
2 WINN ST
3 PERCY ST
4 ROWLAND RD
5 MONTROSE ST
6 ALBERT MARSON CT
7 BEACHAMP WLK
8 EARLS CT
QUEENSWAY
GOVERNOR RD

A3
1 PARKINSON AVE
2 CLARKE ST
3 ST JAMES CT
4 CORPORATION RD

A4
1 SHEFFIELD ST E
2 GROSVENOR ST S
3 ELIZABETH ST
4 GROSVENOR ST

B3
1 BELGRAVE SQ
2 FRODINGHAM FOOTPATH
3 RAVENDALE ST N
4 ETHEL CT
5 LESLIE CT
6 ARGYLE CT
7 CROWSTON WK
8 KINSLEY WK
9 HINMAN WK

10 THOMPSON ST
11 MANLEY ST
12 CARLTON ST
13 LAVENDER WY

C1
1 GLADSTONE DR
2 LEAMINGTON CL
3 SANDHOUSE CRES
4 IVANHOE RD

C2
1 REDBOURNE ST
2 LINDSEY ST
3 QUEEN ST
4 PINCHBECK AVE
5 STRATFORD DR

C5
1 BETULA WY
2 CONIFER CL
3 ACER GR

C6
1 FOURTH AVE
2 THIRD AVE
3 SECOND AVE
4 SHAKESPEARE AVE
5 SIDNEY RD

C7
1 ROCHESTER CL
2 SALISBURY CL
3 ST ALBANS CL

D7
1 CANTERBURY CL
2 NEWBOLT AVE
3 LANDOR CL
4 KIPLING AVE
5 COVENTRY CL

D8
1 QUANTOCK CL
2 CLEVELAND CL
3 BARNSTAPLE RD

E6
1 BROWNING CL
2 MAVIS RD
3 MALLARD RD
4 KIPLING AVE
5 PHEASANT CL
6 SAXTON CL

F8
1 NORMAN CRES
2 GLANVILLE CRES
3 HAWTHORNE CRES
4 HAWTHORNE AVE

E3
1 WADDINGTON DR
2 THE OVAL
3 EDGBASTON AVE
4 HEADINGLEY AVE
5 JESMOND AVE
6 LOW LEYS RD

F3
1 PRINCESS ALEXANDRA CT
2 SOUTH RIDGE CR
3 AUSTIN CR
4 THORNHILL CR
5 KIRMAN CR

F4
1 HARROW GDNS
2 KEDDINGTO RD

F2
1 LEE FAIR GDNS
2 ST ANDREWS AVE

183

19

Brumby

Outwood Acad Brumby

Brumby Engineering College

Midland Industrial Estate

Rowmills Plantation

St Luke's Prim Sch

Grange Industrial Estate

Queensway Industrial Estate

Lincoln Gdns Prim Sch

St Bedes Cath Vol Acad

St Bernadettes Cath Primary Vol Acad

Ashby Link

Ashby Market

Ashby

Sunshine Hall

Recreation Ground

Superstore

Lakeside Retail Park

Lakeside Parkway

Brathill Farm

St Peter & St Paul CE Prim Sch

Brat Hill

E6
1 WHARFEDALE PL
2 SWALEDALE PL

1 GREBE MEWS
2 LAPWING WAY
3 CURLEW CFT
4 GARGANEY WK
5 SANDERLING WAY
6 PINTAIL CL
7 WIGEON WK
8 LINNET GARTH

Oakfield Primary School

Recreation Gd

Frederick Gough School

DN16

1 MIMOSA CT
2 SILVERBELL
3 SYCAMORE CRES

Recn Gd

Liby

Holme Hall Golf Course

Cherry Mount

Holme Valley Primary School

SCUNTHORPE

C5
1 MARSHFIELD RD
2 IRVINE RD

Bottesford

St John's Well

B3
1 ROSEWOOD WY
2 REPTON DR

Bottesford Inf Sch

Templar's Bath

Bottesford Jun Sch

Holme Wood

Holme Hall

CH

Aspen Farm

M180

M180

29

19

A B C D E F

8
7
16
6
5
15
4
14
3
2
1
13

Rosper Road Pools Nature Reserve
HUMBER ROAD
WEST HAVEN WAY
WEST HAVEN WY
WEST RIVERSIDE
Henderson Quay
Water Tower
Oil Storage Depot
A1173
Houlton's Covert
SOUTHERN WAY
WESTERN ACCESS ROAD
MINERAL QUAY ROAD
SEVEN QUAY ROAD
ALEXANDRA ROAD SOUTH
GRESLEY WAY
SOUTHOSBOURNE WAY
ALEXANDRA RD
ROBINSON RD
Works
MANBY ROAD
Pelham Industrial Estate
DN40
A1173
MIDDLEPLATT ROAD
Sports Ground
HALL PARK RD
Immingham Golf Course
Homestead Park
STANDISH LA 1
HINKLEY DR 2
WESTON GR 3
ATWOOD CL 4
1 CEDAR DR
2 MAPLE GR
3 OAKLANDS RD
Football Ground
Manby Hall Business Park
Mast
Mon
1 HUMBERVILLE RD
2 LARCH CL
3 TRENCHARD CL
Medieval Village of Immingham
WOODLANDS AVENUE
COPSE CL
WASHDYKE LANE
WINSLOW DRIVE
CHURCH LANE
ST ANDREWS
CH
STANSFIELD GDNS
MILL LANE
ST ANDREWS CT
PILGRIMS WAY
VIKING CL
Mon
MORTON
ROSS GDNS
Allerton Primary School
PARK CL
ASH TREE CL
SPIRE CL
BEECHWOOD
FENDYKE DR
HUMBERVILLE ROAD
HAWTHORN AV
WILLOW TREE CL
BATTERY ST
SPRING STREET
PELHAM ROAD
WORSLEY ROAD
HOLMES ST
HORACE ST
KINGS ROAD
A1173
KINGS ROAD
BROCK SQ
SAGBY AVE
VALDA WALK
Recreation Ground
CLIFTON CRESCENT
SONIA CREST
BRADFORD RD
ROBERT CL
TEALBY CL
ROYAL DRIVE
BLUESTONE LANE
ALLERTON DR
Hotel
Immingham L Ctr
KENNEDY WAY
Kennedy Way Shopping Ctr
Washdyke Retail Park
Civic Ctr
P
Mkt
Liby
PAMELA CLOSE
SACKVILLE RD
1 DEANE RD
2 SACKVILLE CL
3 WORSLEY CL
4 EATON RD
IMMINGHAM
Coomb Brigg's Prim Sch
ANCHOLME AVE 1
CALDER CL 2
STEEPING DR 3
AIRE CL 4
HABROUGH ROAD
B1210
PH
PO
THE ORCHARDS
HUME BRAE
HIGHLAND THORN
WINSLOW CL
ALDEN CL
PELHAM ROAD
THORNTON PL
MAYFLOWER AVE
CRAIKHILL AVE
CUSHMAN CR
MARGARET STREET
PRINCESS STREET
JASMINE CL
Swimming Pool
Oasis Academy
Cannon Peter Hall CE Prim Sch
Immingham Business Units
PILGRIM AVENUE
LYDFORD WALK
LULWORTH WALK
CARISBROOKE WALK
HARLECH WALK
NEWARK WALK
CORFE WK
HADLEIGH WALK
BLAIR WALK
LANGLEY WALK
NEWPORT WLK
BARNARD WALK
TALBOT RD
OAKHAM WALK
SURETON RD
INGS LANE
KENDAL RD
LYDFORD ROAD
Sports Gd
Immingham Museum
COLLIER RD 1
BREWSTER AV 2
THORNBURY RD 3
Eastfield Prim Academy
KISHORN CT 1
PERTH WY 2
TUMMEL CT 3
KINLOCH
Highfield Farm
GUERNSEY GR
ALDERNEY WY
ANGLESEY DR
SHETLAND WY
ARRAN CL
MULL WY
ORKNEY PL 1
FAIR ISLE RISE 2
LUNDY CT 3
STALLINGBOROUGH ROAD
A180
B1210
DN41
Mauxhall Farm
A1173
KILN LANE

17 A B 18 C D 19 E F

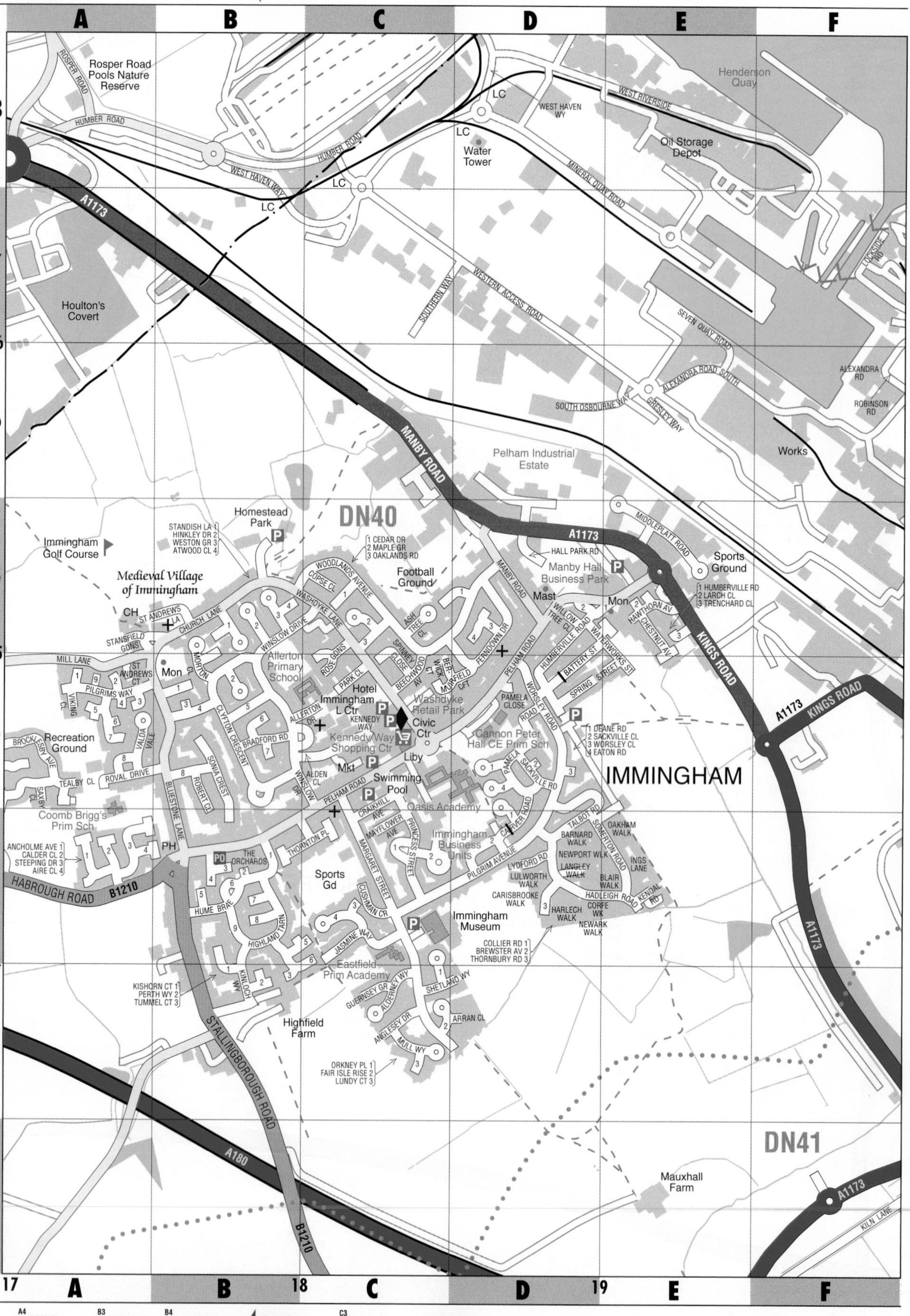

A4
1 MAIDEN CL
2 CLEVELAND CL
3 LYDIA CFT
4 HAZEL CFT
5 MILLHOUSE ST RISE
6 JACKSON MEWS
7 ANDREWS WY
8 HELEN CRES
9 PENNINE CL

B3
1 BLOSSOM WY
2 CLARENCE CL
3 LINDUM AVE
4 HIGHFIELD AVE
5 MACKENZIE PL
6 HUME BRAE
7 BOWMAN WY
8 HAMISH WK
9 JAMES WY

B4
1 HOLLINGSWORTH AVE
2 HOLBECK PL
3 BALFOUR PL
4 LANSDOWN RD
5 AINSWORTH RD
6 LEYDEN CL
7 CHILTON CL
8 STAINTON DR

C3
1 PRINCESS ST
2 ROUNDWAY
3 JAPONICA HL
4 MAGNOLIA RISE
5 PADDOCK CT
6 OBAN CT

23 **23**

13

A
B
C
D
E
F
8
7
16
6
5
15
4
3
14
2
1
13
20
21
22
Immingham Dock
EAST RIVERSIDE
Oil Storage Depot
EAST DOCK ROAD
LC
Oil Storage Depot
Chy
DN40
QUEENS RD
East Gate
A1173
LAPORTE ROAD
PRINCE EDWARD DRIVE
PRINCE HENRY DRIVE
QUEENS ROAD
Chimney
Works
Humber Bank Factories
Chimney
EUROPA WAY
SCANDINAVIAN WAY
NETHERLANDS WAY
EUROPA WAY
Kiln Lane Ind Est
Spoil Heap
KILN LANE
WORLDWIDE WAY
WORLDWIDE WAY
Kiln Lane Trading Est
TRONDHEIM WAY
OSBORNE RD
BEEL'S RD
Kiln Lane Ind Est
DN41
HOBSON WAY
South Marsh Road Ind Est
SOUTH MARSH ROAD
LC
NORTH MOSS LANE
SOUTH MARSH ROAD
Power Station
Chimney
Poplar Farm

23
24
24

24

River Humber

Works

Pyewipe

Chimney

Chimney
Works
Chimney

Water
Reclamation
Works

Sports
Ground

DN37

LC

GENESIS WY

LAKESIDE

LC

LC

ESTATE RD NO 4

ESTATE RD NO 3

Sports
Ground

MOODY LANE

DN31

Sewage
Works

A180

ENERGY PARK WAY

LAFOREY ROAD

WOLD LANE

Mast

ESTATE ROAD NO 1

Europa
Business
Park

ATHENA DR

1 APIAN WY
2 SAXON CT

APIAN WY

LC

MOODY LANE

GATE
WY

LC

WESTSIDE ROAD

NAVENSBY CL 1
ALLINGTON DR 2
RUSKINGTON CL 3

ESTATE ROAD NO 5

Hotel

GILBEY RD

ESTUARY WAY

Ventura
Business Park

ALEXANDRA
DOCK NORTH

SIBSEY
COURT

South Humberside
Industrial
Estate

ESTATE ROAD NO 6

ESTATE RD NO 7

Cherry Tree's
Business Park

ESTATE ROAD NO 2

HAVEN GDNS

Littlecoates
Prim Sch

Birch Way
Ind Est

BIRCHIN WAY

WEST
COATES
RD

Alexandra Dock

NEWBURY AV

Tintern
Walk

CROMWELL RD

NEWBURY AV

CRANWELL
DR

ESTATE RD NO 8

ELSENHAM ROAD

Pyewipe
Bungalows

PYEWIPE ROAD

BOULEVARD AV

WESTGATE

PINE
CL

BYLAND GR

The Willows

ST CHADS
GATE

West Marsh

HARLOW ST

GILBEY RD

HARGRAVE ST

DUNMOW

Beeson
Grove

BEESON ST

CHARLTON ST

ADAM SMITH ST

WATKIN
ST NORTH

ARMSTRONG ST

West Marsh
Ind Est

RENDEL ST

ALEXANDRA
ROAD

Alexandra
Ret Pk

FOUNTAINS
AV

MELROSE
WY

BUCKFAST CL

SALTERGATE

SOUTHLAND CT

NEW HAVEN TERRACE

A B C D E F

8
7
13
6
5
12
4

River Humber

Mast
Piers
The Dock Tower
Locks
Locks

GRIMSBY

3

KEMP ROAD
NORTH QUAY

Royal Dock
BROWN ST
WHARNCLIFFE RD
Fish Docks

11

FISH DOCK RD NORTH
WHARNCLIFFE RD NORTH
HUTTON RD

DN31

D1
1 CASSWELL CL
2 RUTLAND ST
3 MANSEL ST
4 SIDNEY ST

2

LC
Grimsby Marina

HUMBERSTONE BRIDGE ROAD

FARINGDON RD

Works

GRAFTON STREET
AUCKLAND RD
HUMBER BK.
WOMERSLEY RD

WICKHAM ROAD

WICKHAM ROAD
Works

DN32

LOOPHILL
EAST SIDE RD
RIBY SQ
LC
MURRAY STREET

RIBY STREET
ORWELL ST
MURRAY ST
ROBINSON LA.

New Clee

A180

A16 VICTORIA ST N

Grimsby Docks
The Caxton Theatre & Arts Ctr
CHURCH ST
TOMLINE ST
P PO
KENT ST
STRAND
Strand Com Sch
ALBERT PLACE

CLEETHORPE ROAD

STRAND
BATH ST
ST HILDA
BELPER ST
THOROLD STREET

MARSDEN ROAD

STIRLING ST

HARRINGTON STREET

DN35

High Point Ret Pk
PRINCE ALBERT GARD
P
P
FREEMAN ST
InShops Ctr
NELSON STREET
Victoria Retail Pk
DUNCOMBE GDNS

East Marsh
B1213
ALBION ST
ALBERT ST E
Ice House

VICTOR RD
BEDFORD ST
OXFORD STREET
SUFFOLK CT
SUSSEX CT
GUILDFORD ST
STANLEY
HAMILTON STREET
GRAFTON ST

WELLS ST

GRIMSBY ROAD
A180

SPENCER ST
GRANT ST
MONTAGUE ST
PELS ST
TAYLOR ST

PO

DALRINEY ST
BARCROFT ST
LOVETT ST
TIVERTON ST

BLUNDELL AVE

1

10

27 A B 28 C D 29 E F

191

25

192

25

A1
1 LOWER SPRING ST
2 CRESSEY ST
3 FOTHERBY ST
4 KING EDWARD ST

B1
1 BRIDGE ST NORTH
2 THESIGER ST
3 SERVICE RD NO 1
4 SERVICE RD NO 2
5 ALBERT ST WEST
6 GARIBALDI ST
7 ALBERT CL
8 THESIGER WLK
9 FREEMAN WAY

B2
1 STUART WORTLEY ST
2 MURRAY ST
3 ROWLANDSON ST
4 RAILWAY PL

C1
1 KESGRAVE ST
2 LEVINGTON ST
3 MILFORD CT
4 MANSFIELD CT
5 WORDSWORTH CT
6 MUNSTER CT
7 WINDSOR CT
8 WESLEY CT
9 BANBURY CT

10 BEXLEY CT
11 ARNOLD CT
12 ACTON CT
13 APPLEBY CT
14 TRINITY ST
15 WEELSBY ST
16 SALACON WY
17 BRADMAN CT
18 GRAFTON ST
19 NORFOLK CT

20 SURREY CT
21 MARLBOROUGH CL
22 DUKE ST
23 DERBY CL
24 GEORGE JANNEY CT

← 23
↑ 24
↑ 188

E8
1 SERVICE RD 21
2 SEVERN WY
3 SERVICE RD 22
4 DUNOON CT
5 SOLWAY CT
6 TRENT CT
7 TYNE WY
8 SERVICE RD 4
9 SERVICE RD 8
10 LOCKTON CT
11 SERVICE RD 25
12 GOATHLAND CT
13 SERVICE RD 5
14 SERVICE RD 6
15 SERVICE RD 3
16 SERVICE RD 15
17 SERVICE RD 2
18 SERVICE RD 1
19 SERVICE RD 20
20 ST CHAAS WK

F8
1 CROMWELL RD
2 PERKINS CL
3 SERVICE RD 7
4 SERVICE RD 19

B1210
Yarborough
Farm

DN41

Maud Hole
Covert

Moat

A1136
GREAT COATES ROAD

Wybers Wood
Prim Sch

John
Whitgift
Academy

SERVICE ROAD 24

Wybers Wood

Wybers
Wood

Pyewipe
Farm

DN37

Freshney Bog
Nature Reserve

D7
1 MINNOW CL
2 GRAYLING CL

The Willows

Liby
Willows
Prim Sch

Leisure
Centre

Great Grimsby
Golf Centre
Willow Park
Golf Club

River Freshney

CH

Little
Coates

Yarborough
Academy

YARBOROUGH ROAD

A1136

DN34

Grimsby
Golf Course

CH

B1444

FOXGLOVE GDNS 1
ST CATHERINES CT 2
DOWNING CL 3
FOX CL 4

Cambridge Road

Grange
Prim Sch

Grange

Oak
Plantation

Capes
Recreation
Ground

Western
Primary School

Bradley

Laceby Acres
Prim Academy

St Michael's

1 BRITANNIA CRES
2 MAXWELL CT
3 TRAFALGAR AVE

Carnforth
Cres

B1444

A46

Laceby
Acres

Collingwood

Rockingham
Crescent

Bradley
Rec Ground

Sports
Gd

LACEBY ROAD

Stud
Farm

HILMORE ROAD

MALTBY AVENUE

GRIMSBY ROAD

Sewage
Works

Laceby Beck

Manor
Farm

Cottagers
Plot

Laceby Manor
House Farm

Council
Farm

Bradley

DN33

GRIMSBY RD
A46

Limes
Farm

Woodlands
Farm

Bradley
Wood

Dixon's
Wood

← 23
↓ 35
↓ 194

D4
1 MOULTON CL
2 YARDLEY WY
3 BROADWAY
4 ORION WY
5 NELSON WY
6 HAMILTON CL
7 DEENE CL
8 VICTORY WY
9 ROCKINGHAM CT
10 EXETER CT
11 MANSON CL
12 SOVEREIGN CL

E4
1 BLAYDON GR
2 NEWBURY GR
3 WELBECK PL
4 SELBOURNE RD
5 THORNTON GR

F4
1 BARDNEY GDNS
2 WINSLOW GR
3 WINSLOW GR
4 GOXHILL GDNS
5 WILLOUGHBY GR
6 WICKENBY CL
7 WIRRAL AVE
8 FISKERTON CL
9 HIBALDSTOW CL

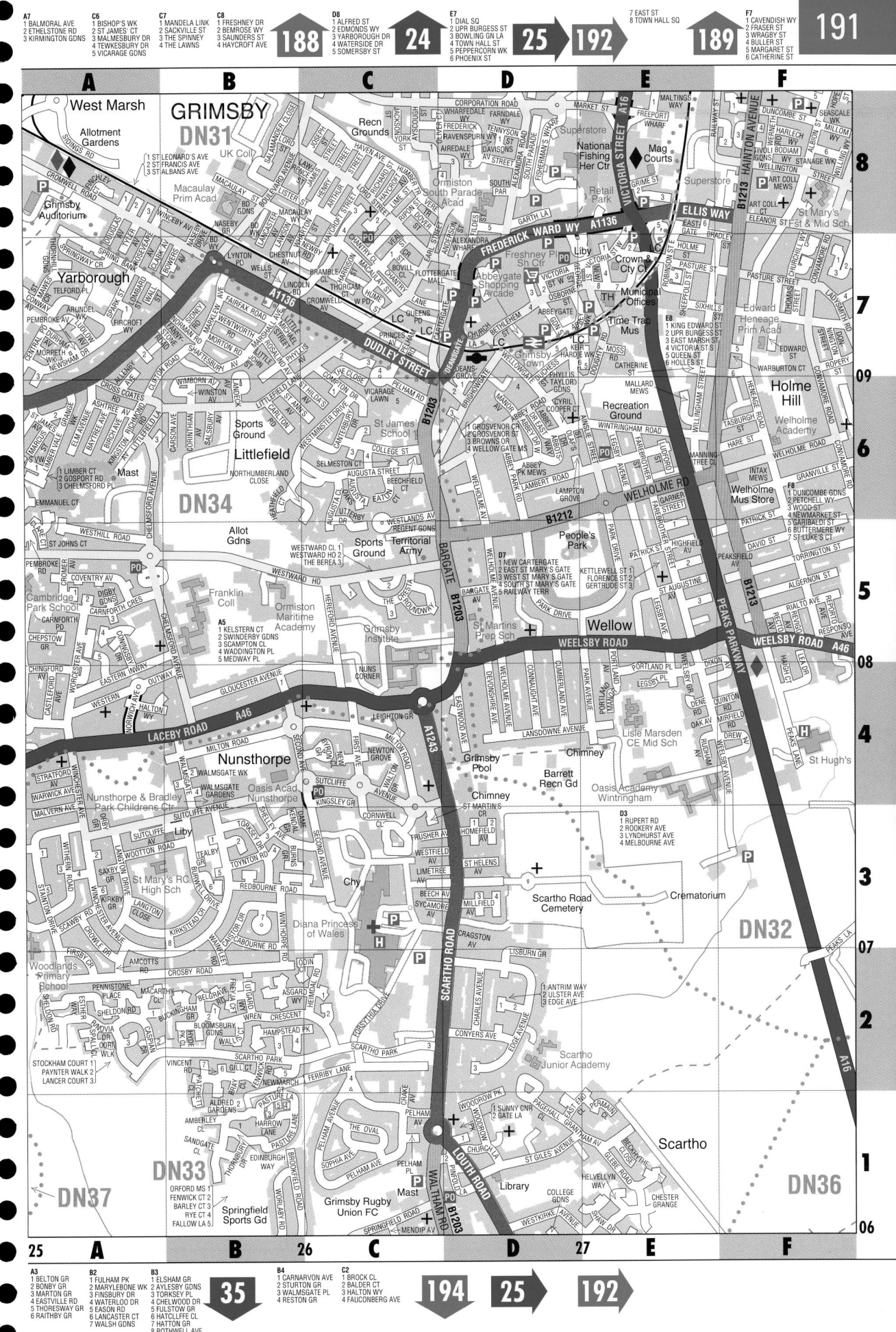

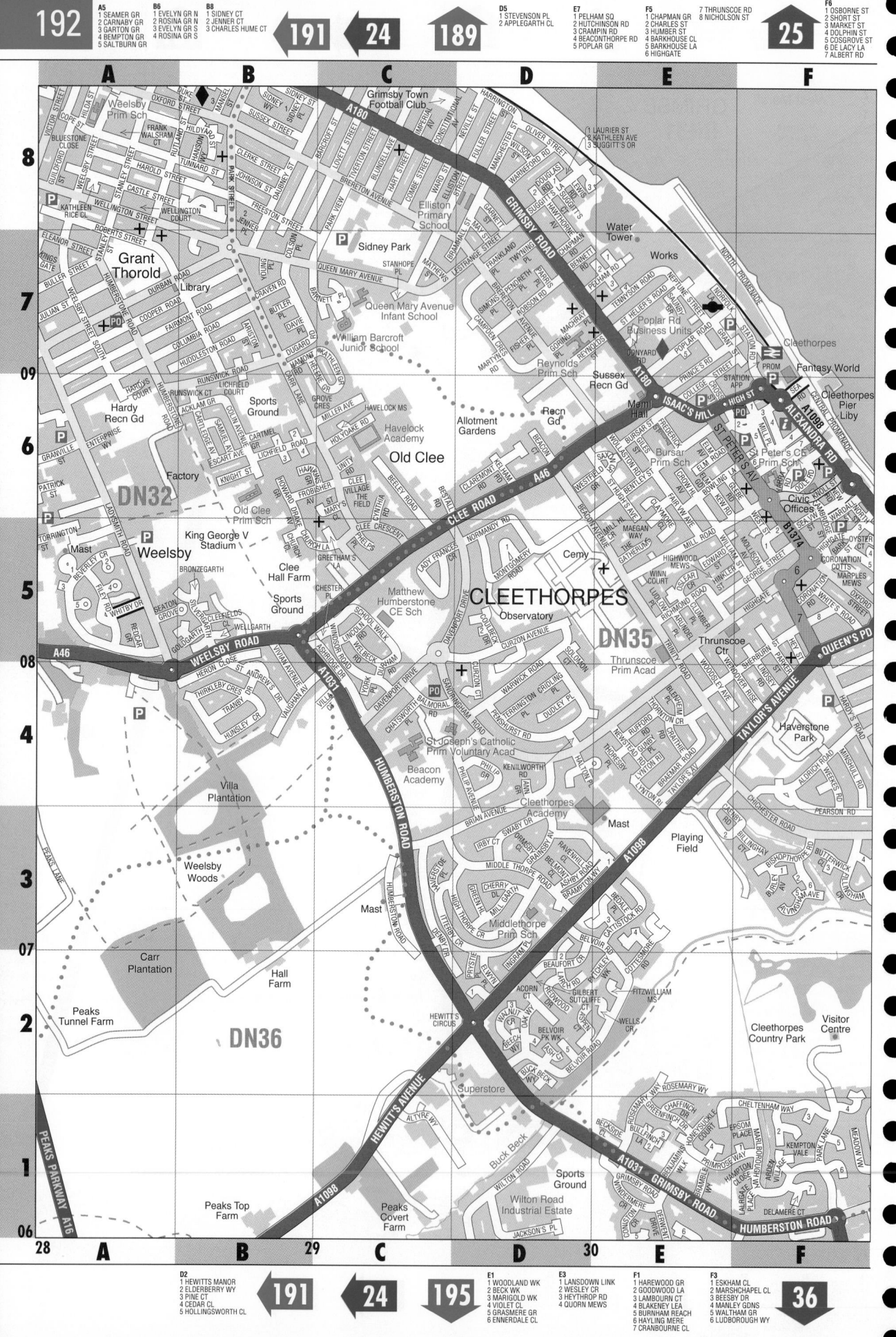

A5
1 SEAMER GR
2 CARNABY GR
3 GARTON GR
4 BEMPTON GR
5 SALTBURN GR

B6
1 EVELYN GR N
2 ROSINA GR N
3 EVELYN GR S
4 ROSINA GR S

B8
1 SIDNEY CT
2 JENNER CT
3 CHARLES HUME CT

191 24 189

D5
1 STEVENSON PL
2 APPLEGARTH CL

E7
1 PELHAM SQ
2 HUTCHINSON RD
3 CRAMPIN RD
4 BEACONTHORPE RD
5 POPLAR GR

F5
1 CHAPMAN GR
2 CHARLES ST
3 HUMBER ST
4 BARKHOUSE CL
5 BARKHOUSE LA
6 HIGHGATE

7 THRUNSCOE RD
8 NICHOLSON ST

25

F6
1 OSBORNE ST
2 SHORT ST
3 MARKET ST
4 DOLPHIN ST
5 COSGROVE ST
6 DE LACY LA
7 ALBERT RD

D2
1 HEWITTS MANOR
2 ELDERBERRY WY
3 PINE CT
4 CEDAR CL
5 HOLLINGSWORTH CL

191 24 195

E1
1 WOODLAND WK
2 BECK WK
3 MARIGOLD WK
4 VIOLET CL
5 GRASMERE GR
6 ENNERDALE CL

E3
1 LANSDOWN LINK
2 WESLEY CR
3 HEYTHROP RD
4 QUORN MEWS

F1
1 HAREWOOD GR
2 GOODWOOD LA
3 LAMBOURN CT
4 BLAKENEY LEA
5 BURNHAM REACH
6 HAYLING MERE
7 CRANBOURNE CL

F3
1 ESKHAM CL
2 MARSHCHAPEL CL
3 BEESBY DR
4 MANLEY GDNS
5 WALTHAM GR
6 LUDBOROUGH WY

36

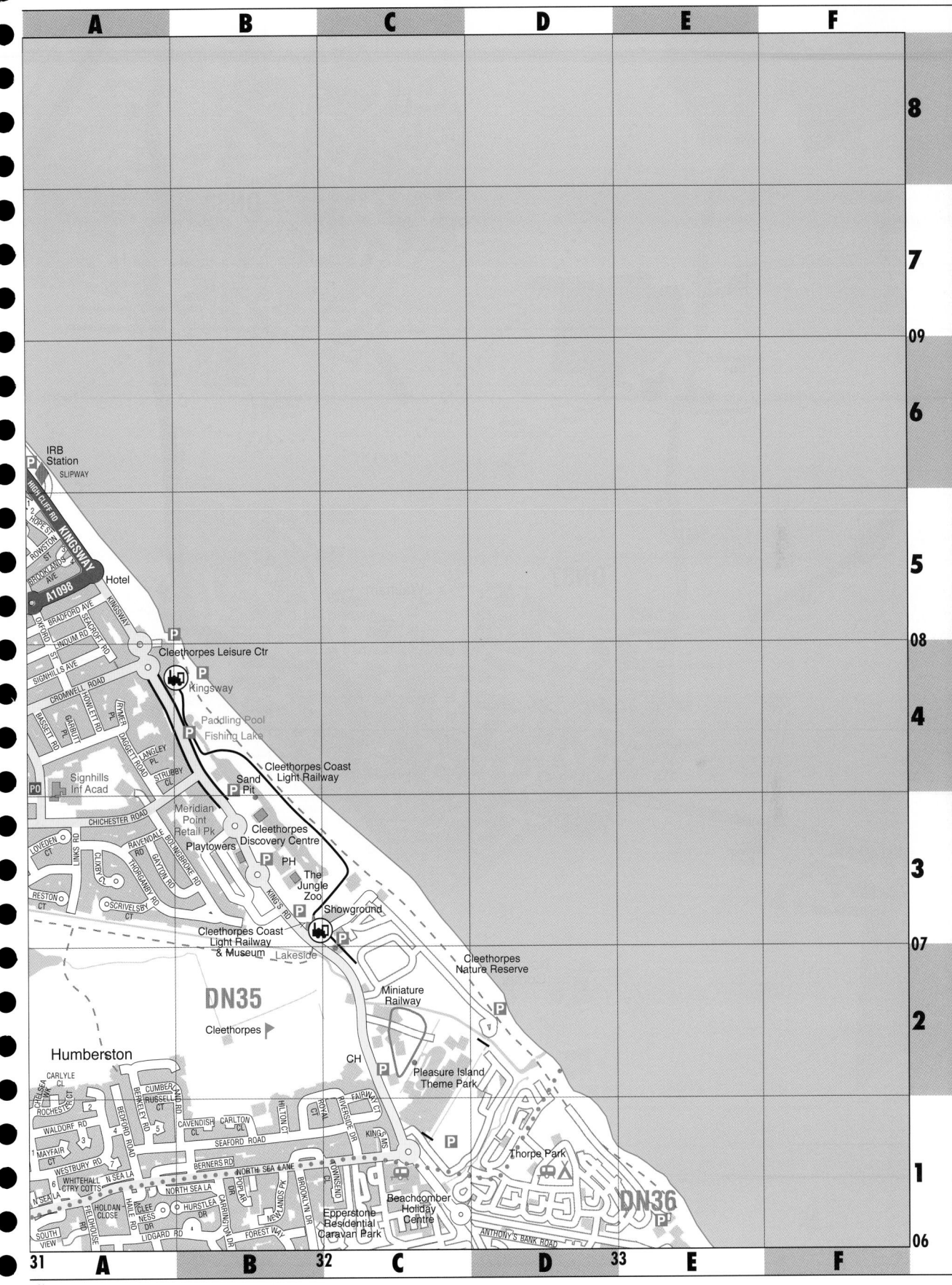

A5
1 SOUTH ST
2 BRIGHTON ST
3 SEGMERE ST
4 HAIGH ST

A B C D E F

8

7

09

6

5

08

4

3

07

2

1

06

IRB
Station
SLIPWAY

HIGH CLIFF RD
KINGSWAY
A1098
Hotel

Cleethorpes Leisure Ctr
Kingsway
Paddling Pool
Fishing Lake
Cleethorpes Coast
Light Railway
Sand
Pit
Meridian
Point
Retail Pk
Cleethorpes
Discovery Centre
Playtowers
PH
The
Jungle
Zoo
Showground
Cleethorpes Coast
Light Railway
& Museum
Lakeside
Cleethorpes
Nature Reserve

Signhills
Inf Acad
Signhills Ave
Cromwell Road

DN35
Cleethorpes
Humberston

Miniature
Railway
CH
Pleasure Island
Theme Park

North Sea Lane
Seaford Road
Epperstone
Residential
Caravan Park
Beachcomber
Holiday
Centre
Thorpe Park
DN36
ANTHONY'S BANK ROAD

A1
1 WESTPORT RD
2 WESTBURY PK
3 FAIRFIELD CT
4 WEYFORD RD
5 GROVENOR CT
6 WHITEHALL RD
7 KINGSTON CL

31 A B 32 C D 33 E F

C5
1 CORAL DR
2 PEACE HAVEN
3 CARDINAL CT
4 ALBERTINE CT
5 FOUNTAIN CL
6 SWEET BRIAR CL
7 WHEATFIELD DR
8 FRANCES CT
9 WRAY CL

D8
1 BAYSWATER PL 7 HORSESHOE CL
2 WELL VALE
3 MAYFIELD CL
4 CORNFIELD CL
5 SAGEFIELD CL
6 FOXTAIL CL

E7
1 CONISTON AVE
2 FLEETWOOD CL
3 BARBARA CL
4 WINDERMERE AVE
5 ORCHARD CFT
6 HEATHERDALE CL

E8
1 TONBRIDGE
2 GRAMPIAN WY
3 CHILTERN WY
4 LANCING WY
5 PURBECK RD
6 DOVEDALE DR

F8
1 GORDON GDNS
2 COLLEGE GDNS
3 LINDSEY RISE
4 HAWTHORNE AVE
5 LINWOOD AVE
6 WESTBOURNE GR

C4
1 DRURY CL
2 HARVEST CR
3 BARKWORTH CT
4 OLD FARM CT
5 LINDRICK WK
6 ASHBOURNE
7 CARNOUSTIE
8 SUNNINGDALE
9 BIRKDALE
10 GLENEAGLES
11 MUIRFIELD
12 MAYFAIR CR
13 CHESTNUT CL

E4
1 HIGH ST
2 CHURCH VW
3 CROSS ST
4 CHEESEMANS CL
5 MILL VW
6 ATKINSON LA
7 TANNERY CL

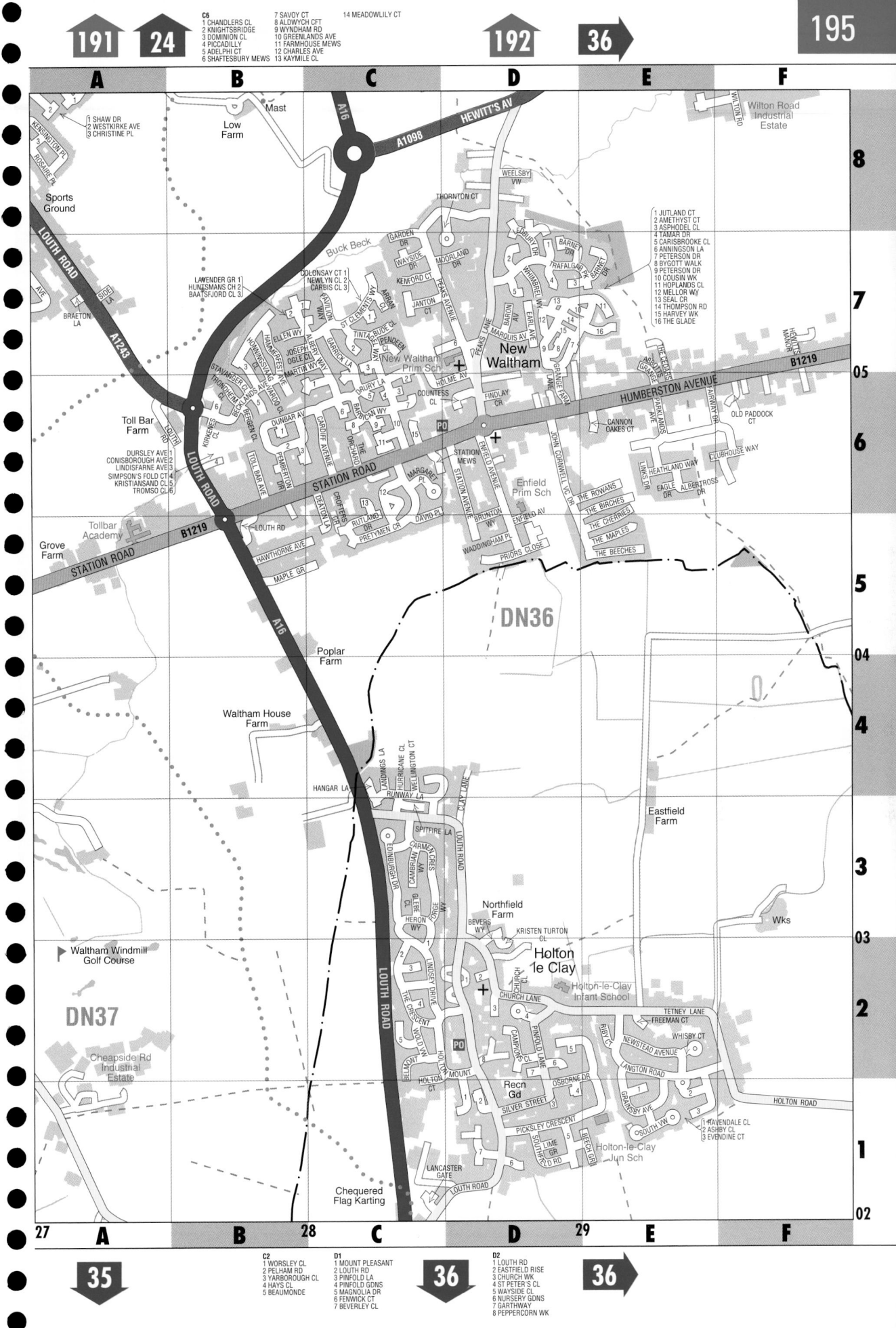
191
24
192
36
C6
1 CHANDLERS CL
2 KNIGHTSBRIDGE
3 DOMINION CL
4 PICCADILLY
5 ADELPHI CT
6 SHAFTESBURY MEWS
7 SAVOY CT
8 ALDWYCH CFT
9 WYNDHAM RD
10 GREENLANDS AVE
11 FARMHOUSE MEWS
12 CHARLES AVE
13 KAYMILE CL
14 MEADOWLILY CT
A
B
C
D
E
F
1 SHAW DR
2 WESTKIRKE AVE
3 CHRISTINE PL
KENSINGTON PL
ROSAIRE PL
Low Farm
Mast
A16
A1098
HEWITT'S AV
Wilton Road Industrial Estate
WILTON RD
8
Sports Ground
LOUTH ROAD
WEELSBY VW
THORNTON CT
Buck Beck
GARDEN DR
WAYSIDE DR
MOORLAND DR
KENFORD CT
JANTON CT
PEAKS AVENUE
LEDBURY DR
BARNET DR
TRAFALGAR PK
WHIMBREL WY
BARON AV
MARQUIS AV
EARL AVE
1 JUTLAND CT
2 AMETHYST CT
3 ASPHODEL CL
4 TAMAR DR
5 CARISBROOKE CL
6 ANNINGSON LA
7 PETERSON DR
8 BYGOTT WALK
9 PETERSON DR
10 COUSIN WK
11 HOPLANDS CL
12 MELLOR WY
13 SEAL CR
14 THOMPSON RD
15 HARVEY WK
16 THE GLADE
7
LAVENDER GR 1
HUNTSMANS CH 2
BAATSFJORD CL 3
COLONSAY CT 1
NEWLYN CL 2
CARBIS CL 3
BRAETON LA
SIDE LA
AVE
A1243
PAVILION WAY
ST CLEMENTS WY
ARRAN CL
BUDE CL
TINTAGEL WAY
PENDEEN CL
ELLEN WY
JOSEPH OGLE CL
ALBERY WAY
GARRICK LA
MARTIN WY
HAMMERFEST AVE
HONNINGSVAG CL
STAVANGER CL
TRONDHEIM CL
BECKLANDS AVE
VARDO CL
BERGEN CL
KIRKENES CL
New Waltham Prim Sch
New Waltham
PEAKS LANE
HOLME AV
COUNTESS CL
FINDLAY CR
GRANGE FARM LANE
ABBOTTS GRANGE
THE CEDARS
HEWITTS MANOR
B1219
05
HUMBERSTON AVENUE
FAIRWAY DR
PARKLANDS AVE
OLD PADDOCK CT
CANNON OAKES CT
Toll Bar Farm
LOUTH RD
DUNBAR AV
CARDIFF AVENUE
DRURY LA
BARBICAN WY
ORCHARD
THE
PO
DURSLEY AVE 1
CONISBOROUGH AVE 2
LINDISFARNE AVE 3
SIMPSON'S FOLD CT 4
KRISTIANSAND CL 5
TROMSO CL 6
TOLL BAR AVE
PEMBERTON DR
STATION ROAD
STATION MEWS
ENFIELD AVENUE
JOHN CORNWELL VC DR
MARGARET PL
6
HEATHLAND WAY
CLUBHOUSE WAY
LINKS DR
EAGLE DR
ALBERTROSS DR
Enfield Prim Sch
THE ROWANS
THE BIRCHES
THE CHERRIES
THE MAPLES
THE BEECHES
DEATON LA
CROFTERS GR
RUTLAND DR
PRETYMEN CR
DAVID PL
STATION AVENUE
BRUNTON WY
ENFIELD AV
WADDINGHAM PL
PRIORS CLOSE
Tollbar Academy
Grove Farm
B1219
STATION ROAD
LOUTH RD
HAWTHORNE AVE
MAPLE GR
5
DN36
A16
Poplar Farm
04
Waltham House Farm
4
LANDINGS LA
HURRICANE CL
WELLINGTON CT
HANGAR LA
RUNWAY LA
CLAY LANE
SPITFIRE LA
LOUTH ROAD
EDINBURGH DR
CAMBRIAN WY
CARMEN CRES
GLEBE CL
HERON WY
FORGE WAY
Eastfield Farm
3
Northfield Farm
BEVERS WY
KRISTEN TURTON CL
Wks
03
Waltham Windmill Golf Course
LOUTH ROAD
Holton le Clay
CHURCH CL
Holton-le-Clay Infant School
CHURCH LANE
TETNEY LANE
FREEMAN CT
DN37
LINDSEY DRIVE
THE CRESCENT
WOLD VW
2
RIBY CT
NEWSTEAD AVENUE
WHISBY CT
CAMPIONS CL
PINFOLD LANE
Cheapside Rd Industrial Estate
BELMONT
HOLTON MOUNT
HOLTON CT
LANGTON ROAD
OSBORNE DR
Recn Gd
SILVER STREET
GRAINSBY AVE
SOUTH VW
HOLTON ROAD
1 RAVENDALE CL
2 ASHBY CL
3 EVENDINE CT
PICKSLEY CRESCENT
SOUTHFIELD RD
LIME GR
BEECH GR
Holton-le-Clay Jun Sch
1
LANCASTER GATE
LOUTH ROAD
Chequered Flag Karting
02
27
28
29
C2
1 WORSLEY CL
2 PELHAM RD
3 YARBOROUGH CL
4 HAYS CL
5 BEAUMONDE
D1
1 MOUNT PLEASANT
2 LOUTH RD
3 PINFOLD LA
4 PINFOLD GDNS
5 MAGNOLIA DR
6 FENWICK CT
7 BEVERLEY CL
D2
1 LOUTH RD
2 EASTFIELD RISE
3 CHURCH WK
4 ST PETER'S CL
5 WAYSIDE CL
6 NURSERY GDNS
7 GARTHWAY
8 PEPPERCORN WK
35
36
36

20   20   20

F6
1 FRANKLAND CL
2 VICARAGE AVE
3 THE OLD STACK YD
4 DOVECOTE MEWS

F7
1 GILLIATTS CL
2 MARKHAM WY
3 ECCLES CT
4 CHAPEL LA

Map labels (A–F / 1–8 grid):

Wrawby Farm
Star Carr Lane
Three Tree Farm
Wrawby Carrs
B1206
M180
Wrawby
Low Farm
Bakersfield
Tunnel Road
Old Mill
College Farm
Russet La
Ashdale Farm
Carr La
Carr Farm
Grammar School Lane
DN20
Ivy House Farm
A18
Brigg Road
B1206
Manor Farm
Tongs Farm
Barton Road End
Highfield Rd
Elizabeth CT
Western Ave
Northern
Atkinsoy Ave
Poplar Dr
Horsted
Foxton Way
Sunningdale
Davy
Springbank
Highfield Ave
Grove
South View Ave
Recn Gd Playing Field
St Mary's Catholic Prim Voluntary Acad
The Vale Academy
Recreation Ground
St Helens
Brigg Prim Sch
School Yard Mews
Clover Court
1 WEST SQ
2 OLD SCHOOL CL
Football Gd
Wrawby Road
Europa Way
Atherton Way
Poppleton
Kingsgrove
Elm Wy
Ash Grove
Redcombe Lane
Dixon Cl
Preston Dr
Glebe Road
Hawthorn Ave
Central Square
Parade
Woodbine An
Churchill Avenue
BRIGG
Anfholme Business Park
Swimming Pool
Sewage Works
Birch Ave
Colton St
Sir John Nelthorpe School
North Lindsey Coll
Nicolgate La
Cerny
York Road
Eastfield Rd
St James Rd
Kingfisher Close
Mallard Way
Swift Dr
Island Carr Rd
Waters Edge
Mast
Anfholme Wy
BARNARD AVENUE
Springs Parade
P Liby
Chapel Lane
Wrawby St
PO
A18
BIGBY ROAD
A1084
Glanford Road
St Helen's Rd
O'Hanlon Ave
Yarborough Road
Kennedy Cl
Burgess Rd
Maple
Willowbrook
Bridge St
Demeter House
James St
Quest St
Bigby Street
Princes St
Albert Street
King's Avenue
St Johns Close
BRIDGE STREET
SCAWBY ROAD A18
Engine St
Mill Lane
Manley Gardens
Demeter House Sch
Elwes Street
BIGBY HIGH ROAD
A1084
Anfholme L Ctr
Sports Gd
Silversides Lane Caravan Site
Silversides La
River Midwo
Island Carr
Brigg
Tennyson Cl
The Spinney
LC
Pingley Mdw
Pingley Lane
The Copse
Garden Centre
New River Anfholme
Windmill
Island Carr Farm
Westrum
Westrum Lane
Pingley Farm
Bentley Farm
Chy Chy Chy

20   31   20

A3
1 THEMOORINGS
2 RIVERSIDE
3 THE NARROW BOATS
4 TEAL CL
5 MILL CL
6 MILLERS QUAY
7 ANCHORS WY

B3
1 FORRESTER ST
2 MARKET PL
3 CARY LA
4 ANCHORAGE ST
5 EXCHANGE PL
6 PARADISE PL

B4
1 BLUEBELL GR
2 BRAMBLE WY
3 KINGSWAY
4 CHERRY TREE AVE
5 LINDUM CRES

C3
1 MAGRATH CT
2 OLD COURTS RD
3 GRAMMAR SCHOOL RD S
4 CROSS ST
5 GARDEN ST
6 BIGBY RD
7 NEW ST
8 THE BOTTLINGS
9 ANCHOLME GDNS

D3
1 HEDGEROW LA
2 SPRINGFIELD RD

D4
1 WOLD VW
2 RIDGE VW
3 KETTLEBY VW
4 WELLBECK CL
5 WINSTON WY
6 CHAPEL WY

E3
1 SPRINGFIELD RISE
2 OAKFIELD CL
3 ASHDOWN CL

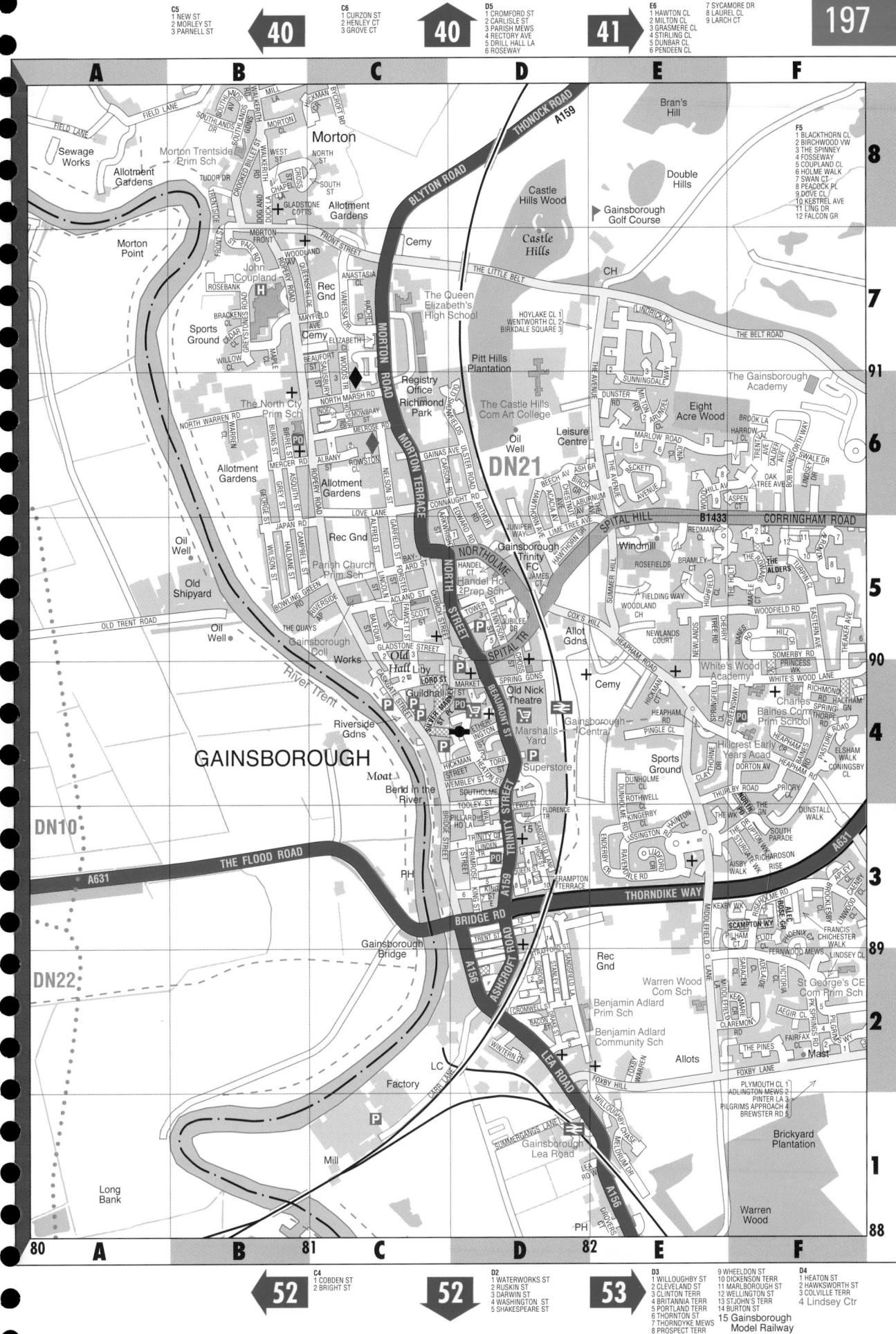

C5
1 NEW ST
2 MORLEY ST
3 PARNELL ST
◄ 40

C6
1 CURZON ST
2 HENLEY CT
3 GROVE CT
▲ 40

D5
1 CROMFORD ST
2 CARLISLE ST
3 PARISH MEWS
4 RECTORY AVE
5 DRILL HALL LA
6 ROSEWAY
▲

E6
1 HAWTON CL
2 MILTON CL
3 GRASMERE CL
4 FOSSEWAY
5 DUNBAR CL
6 PENDEEN CL

7 SYCAMORE DR
8 LAUREL CL
9 LARCH CT
41 ►

F5
1 BLACKTHORN CL
2 BIRCHWOOD VW
3 THE SPINNEY
4 FOSSEWAY
5 COUPLAND CL
6 HOLME WALK
7 SWAN CT
8 PEACOCK PL
9 DOVE CL
10 KESTREL AVE
11 LING DR
12 FALCON GR

C4
1 COBDEN ST
2 BRIGHT ST
◄ 52

D2
1 WATERWORKS ST
2 RUSKIN ST
3 DARWIN ST
4 WASHINGTON ST
5 SHAKESPEARE ST
▲ 52

D3
1 WILLOUGHBY ST
2 CLEVELAND ST
3 CLINTON TERR
4 BRITANNIA TERR
5 PORTLAND TERR
6 THORNTON ST
7 THORNDYKE MEWS
8 PROSPECT TERR

9 WHEELDON ST
10 DICKENSON TERR
11 MARLBOROUGH ST
12 WELLINGTON ST
13 ST JOHN'S TERR
14 BURTON ST

15 Gainsborough
Model Railway
53 ►

D4
1 HEATON ST
2 HAWKSWORTH ST
3 COLVILLE TERR
4 Lindsey Ctr

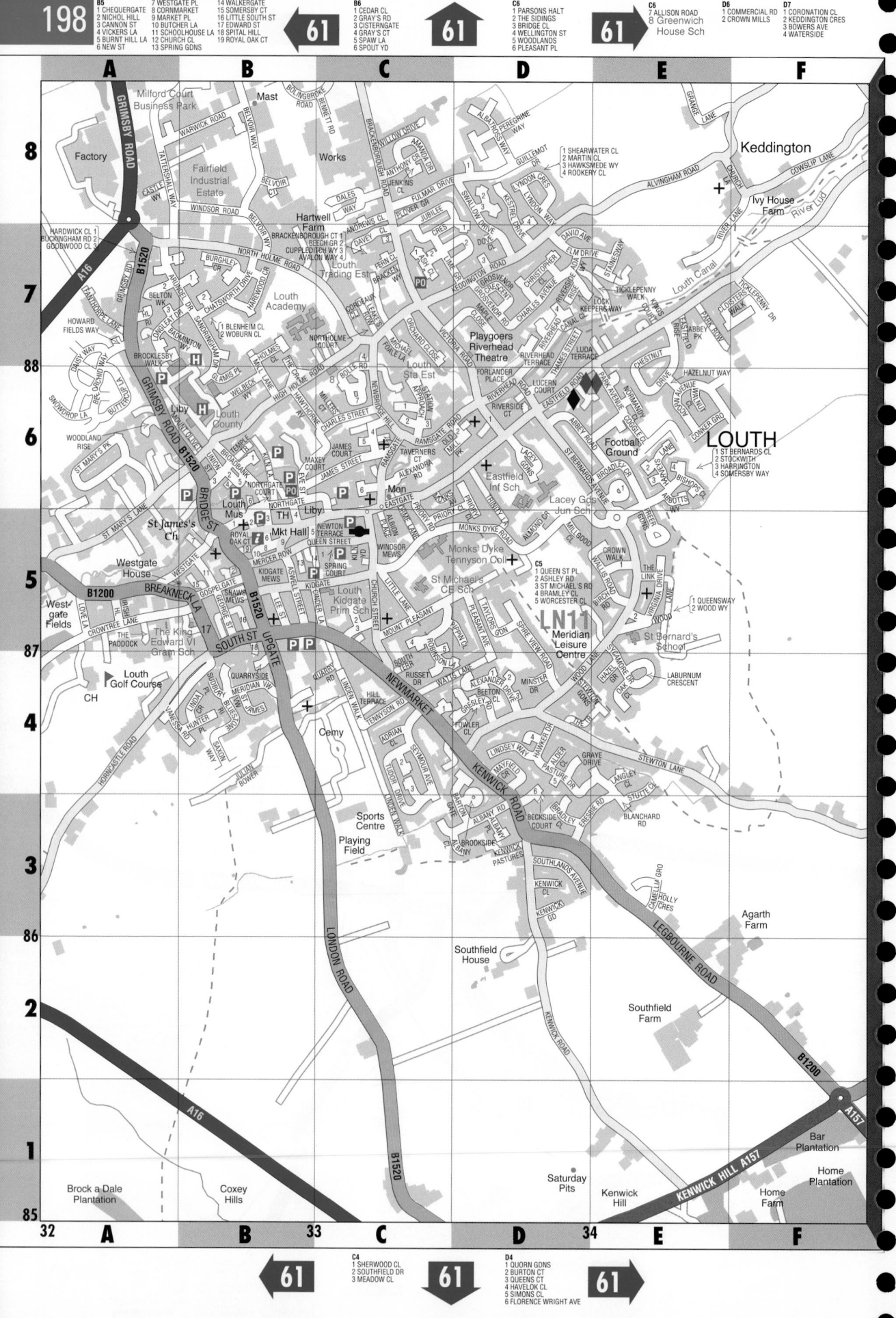

198
B5
1 CHEQUERGATE
2 NICHOL HILL
3 CANNON ST
4 VICKERS LA
5 BURNT HILL LA
6 NEW ST
7 WESTGATE PL
8 CORNMARKET
9 MARKET PL
10 BUTCHER LA
11 SCHOOLHOUSE LA
12 CHURCH CL
13 SPRING GDNS
14 WALKERGATE
15 SOMERSBY CT
16 LITTLE SOUTH ST
17 EDWARD ST
18 SPITAL HILL
19 ROYAL OAK CT
61
B6
1 CEDAR CL
2 GRAY'S RD
3 CISTERNGATE
4 GRAY'S CT
5 SPAW LA
6 SPOUT YD
61
C6
1 PARSONS HALT
2 THE SIDINGS
3 BRIDGE CL
4 WELLINGTON ST
5 WOODLANDS
6 PLEASANT PL
61
C6
7 ALLISON ROAD
8 Greenwich House Sch
D6
1 COMMERCIAL RD
2 CROWN MILLS
D7
1 CORONATION CL
2 KEDDINGTON CRES
3 BOWERS AVE
4 WATERSIDE
A
B
C
D
E
F
8
7
88
6
5
87
4
3
86
2
1
85
32
33
34
Milford Court Business Park
Mast
Factory
GRIMSBY ROAD
Fairfield Industrial Estate
Works
Hartwell Farm
Louth Trading Est
Louth Academy
Keddington
Ivy House Farm
River Lud
Louth Canal
ALVINGHAM ROAD
1 SHEARWATER CL
2 MARTIN CL
3 HAWKSMEDE WY
4 ROOKERY CL
HARDWICK CL 1
BUCKINGHAM RD 2
GOODWOOD CL 3
1 BLENHEIM CL
2 WOBURN CL
Playgoers Riverhead Theatre
Louth Sta Est
Louth County
Football Ground
LOUTH
1 ST BERNARDS CL
2 STOCKWITH
3 HARRINGTON
4 SOMERSBY WAY
Eastfield Inf Sch
Lacey Gds Jun Sch
Monks' Dyke Tennyson Coll
St Michael's CE Sch
St James's Ch
Louth Mus
TH
Liby
Mon
Mkt Hall
Westgate House
Westgate Fields
B1200
BREAKNECK LA
Louth Kidgate Prim Sch
The King Edward VI Gram Sch
SOUTH ST
UPGATE
B1520
C5
1 QUEEN ST PL
2 ASHLEY RD
3 ST MICHAEL'S RD
4 BRAMLEY CL
5 WORCESTER CL
LN11
Meridian Leisure Centre
1 QUEENSWAY
2 WOOD WY
St Bernard's School
LABURNUM CRESCENT
Louth Golf Course
CH
Cemy
NEWMARKET
KENWICK ROAD
STEWTON LANE
Sports Centre
Playing Field
LONDON ROAD
Agarth Farm
Southfield House
Southfield Farm
LEGBOURNE ROAD
A16
A157
Bar Plantation
Home Plantation
Home Farm
KENWICK HILL A157
Kenwick Hill
Saturday Pits
Brock a Dale Plantation
Coxey Hills
61
C4
1 SHERWOOD CL
2 SOUTHFIELD DR
3 MEADOW CL
61
D4
1 QUORN GDNS
2 BURTON CT
3 QUEENS CT
4 HAVELOK CL
5 SIMONS CL
6 FLORENCE WRIGHT AVE
61

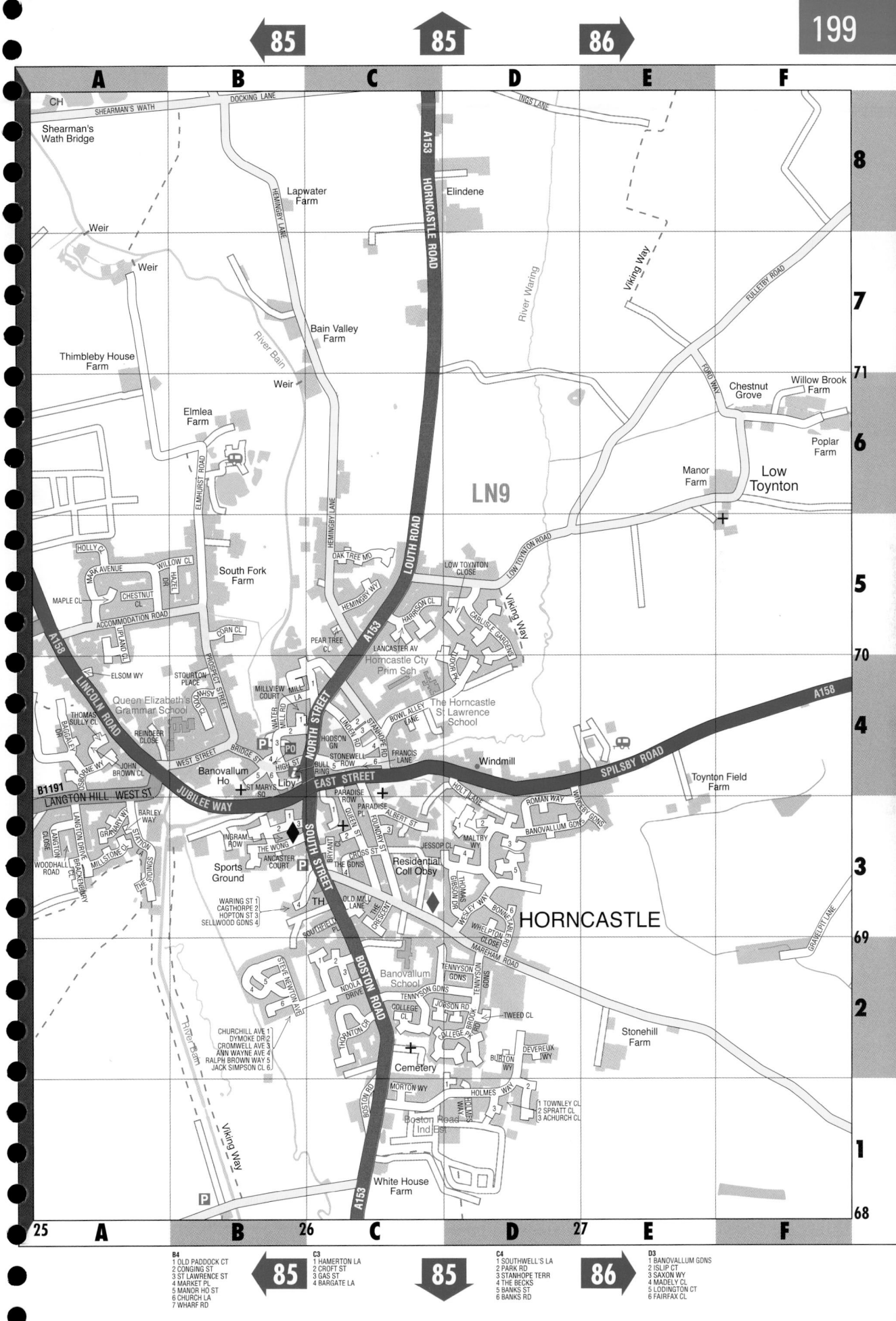

85 85 86

A B C D E F

8
7
71
6
5
70
4
69
2
1
68

CH
Shearman's Wath
Shearman's
Wath Bridge
Weir
Weir
Weir
Thimbleby House
Farm

DOCKING LANE
Lapwater
Farm
Elindene
INGS LANE

HEMINGBY LANE
Bain Valley
Farm
River Bain
Weir

Elmlea
Farm

HORNCASTLE ROAD
A153

River Waring

Viking Way

FULLETBY ROAD

FORD WAY
Chestnut
Grove
Willow Brook
Farm
Poplar
Farm
Manor
Farm
Low
Toynton

LN9

A158
Lincoln Road
B1191
Langton Hill WEST ST

ELMHURST ROAD
Holly Cl
MARK AVENUE
WILLOW CL
HAZEL
MAPLE CL
CHESTNUT CL
ACCOMMODATION ROAD
UPLAND CL
CORN CL
PROSPECT STREET
STOURTON PLACE
South Fork
Farm

HEMINGBY LANE
OAK TREE RD
HEMINGBY WY
LOUTH ROAD
A153
Low Toynton
Close

LOW TOYNTON ROAD

Viking Way
Viking Way

ELSOM WY
Queen Elizabeth's
Grammar School
THOMAS SULLY CL
BAGGALY
JOHN BROWN CL
WEST STREET
BRIDGE ST
St MARYS SQ
Banovallum
Ho
Liby

PEAR TREE CL
HARRISON CL
Lancaster Av
Horncastle Cty
Prim Sch
CARLISLE GARDENS

A153
NORTH STREET
MILL RD
WATER MILL RD
MILLVIEW COURT
LINDEN RD
HODSON GN
STONEWELL ROW
HIGH ST
BULL RING
STANHOPE RD
BOWL ALLEY LANE
FRANCIS LANE
The Horncastle
St Lawrence
School

Windmill
SPILSBY ROAD
A158
Toynton Field
Farm

EAST STREET
PARADISE ROW
QUEEN ST
ALBERT ST
PARADISE PL
FOUNDRY ST
HOLT LANE
ROMAN WAY
BANOVALLUM GDNS
WIGLEY GDNS

JUBILEE WAY
INGRAM ROW
THE WONG
ANCASTER COURT
SOUTH STREET
BRYANT
CROSS ST
THE GDNS
JESSOP CL
MALTBY WY
THOMAS GIBSON DR
SIBLEY WAY
BONNER
WHELPTON RD
CLOSE
Residential
Coll Obsy
HORNCASTLE

Sports
Ground
BARLEY WAY
LANGTON CLOSE
LANGTON DRIVE
GRANBY WY
STATION RD
MILLSTONE CL
BRACKENBURY
WOODHALL ROAD
THE SYMONDS
WARING ST 1
CAGTHORPE 2
HOPTON ST 3
SELLWOOD GDNS 4
TH
SOUTHFIELD PL
OLD MILL LANE
THE CRESCENT

STEVE NEWTON AVE
INDOLL CR
DRIVE
BOSTON DRIVE
THORNTON CR
Banovallum
School
TENNYSON GDNS
TENNYSON GDNS
COLLEGE CL
JOBSON RD
SINDS BROOK
TENNYSON
MAREHAM ROAD
Stonehill
Farm

CHURCHILL AVE 1
DYMOKE DR 2
CROMWELL AVE 3
ANN WAYNE AVE 4
RALPH BROWN WAY 5
JACK SIMPSON CL 6
River Bain
Viking Way
BOSTON ROAD
A153
COLLEGE PL
TWEED CL
DEVEREUX WY
BUXTON WY
Cemetery
MORTON WY
HOLMES WAY
HOLMES WAY
1 TOWNLEY CL
2 SPRATT CL
3 ACHURCH CL
Boston Road
Ind Est
White House
Farm

P
PO
P
P
P

25 A B 26 C D 27 E F

B4
1 OLD PADDOCK CT
2 CONGING ST
3 ST LAWRENCE ST
4 MARKET PL
5 MANOR HO ST
6 CHURCH LA
7 WHARF RD

C3
1 HAMERTON LA
2 PARK RD
3 GAS ST
4 BARGATE LA

C4
1 SOUTHWELL'S LA
2 PARK RD
3 STANHOPE TERR
4 THE BECKS
5 BANKS ST
6 BANKS RD

D3
1 BANOVALLUM GDNS
2 ISLIP CT
3 SAXON WY
4 MADELY CL
5 LODINGTON CT
6 FAIRFAX CL

85 85 86

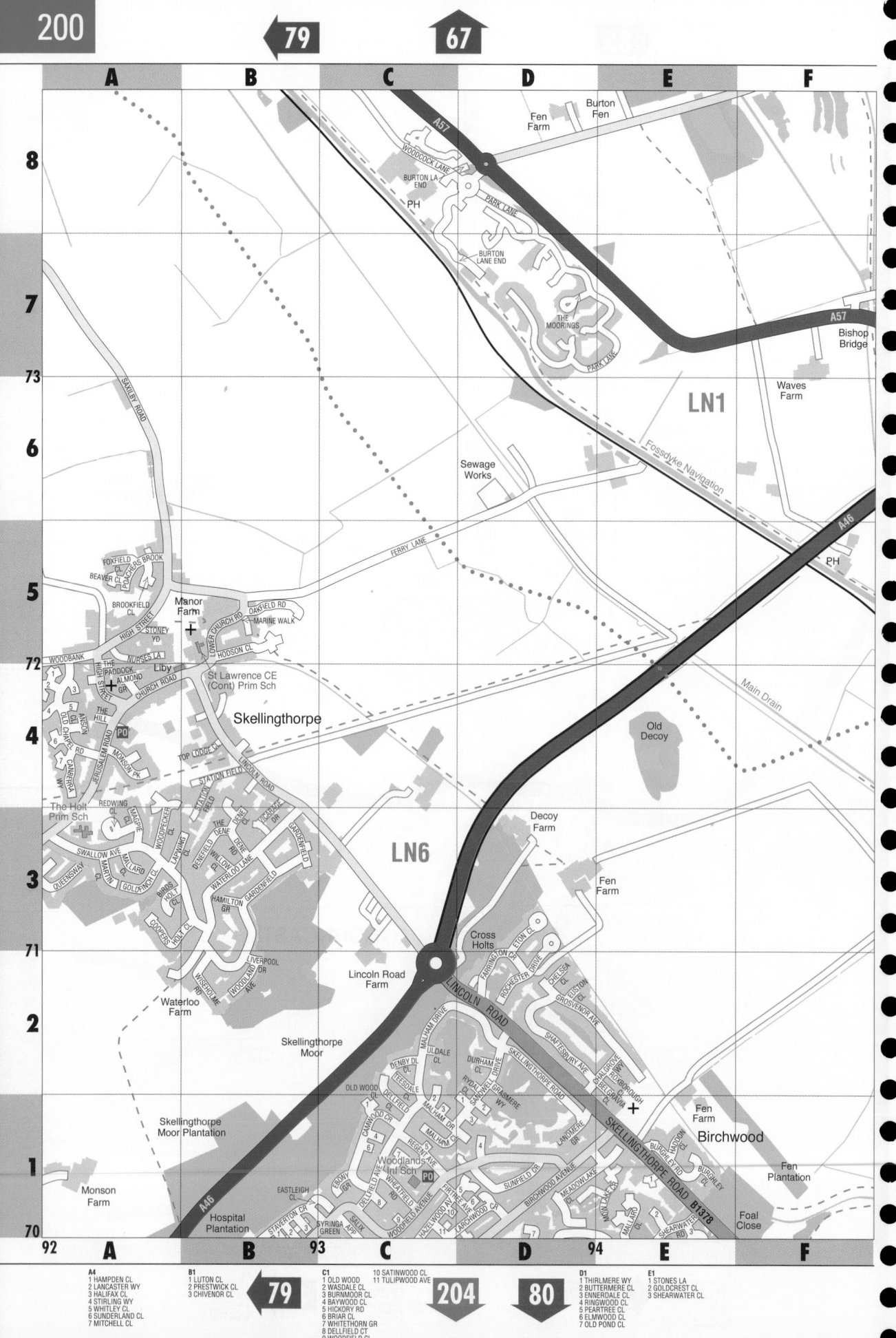

A4
1 HAMPDEN CL
2 LANCASTER WY
3 HALIFAX CL
4 STIRLING WY
5 WHITLEY CL
6 SUNDERLAND CL
7 MITCHELL CL

B1
1 LUTON CL
2 PRESTWICK CL
3 CHIVENOR CL

C1
1 OLD WOOD
2 WASDALE CL
3 BURNMOOR CL
4 BAYWOOD CL
5 HICKORY RD
6 BRIAR CL
7 WHITETHORN GR
8 DELLFIELD CT
9 WOODFIELD CL
10 SATINWOOD CL
11 TULIPWOOD AVE

D1
1 THIRLMERE WY
2 BUTTERMERE CL
3 ENNERDALE CL
4 RINGWOOD CL
5 PEARTREE CL
6 ELMWOOD CL
7 OLD POND CL

E1
1 STONES LA
2 GOLDCREST CL
3 SHEARWATER CL

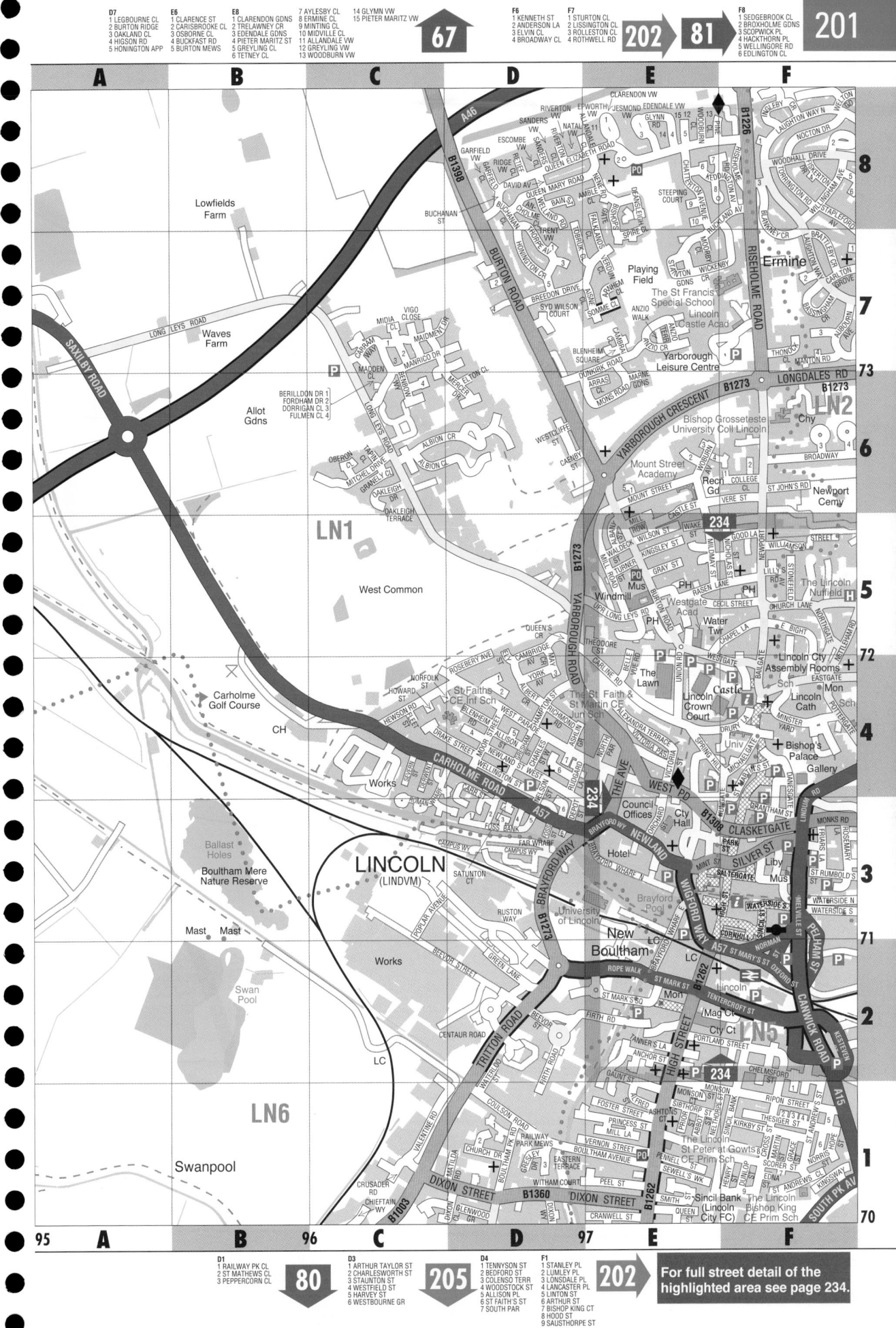
D7
1 LEGBOURNE CL
2 BURTON RIDGE
3 OAKLAND CL
4 HIGSON RD
5 HONINGTON APP
E6
1 CLARENCE ST
2 CARISBROOKE CL
3 OSBORNE CL
4 BUCKFAST RD
5 BURTON MEWS
E8
1 CLARENDON GDNS
2 TRELAWNEY CR
3 EDENDALE GDNS
4 PIETER MARITZ ST
5 GREYLING CL
6 TETNEY CL
7 AYLESBY CL
8 ERMINE CL
9 MINTING CL
10 MIDVILLE CL
11 ALLANDALE VW
12 GREYLING VW
13 WOODBURN VW
14 GLYMN VW
15 PIETER MARITZ VW
67
F6
1 KENNETH ST
2 ANDERSON LA
3 ELVIN CL
4 BROADWAY CL
F7
1 STURTON CL
2 LISSINGTON CL
3 ROLLESTON CL
4 ROTHWELL RD
202
81
F8
1 SEDGEBROOK CL
2 BROXHOLME GDNS
3 SCOPWICK PL
4 HACKTHORN PL
5 WELLINGORE RD
6 EDLINGTON CL
201
A B C D E F
8 7 73 6 5 72 4 3 71 2 1 70
Lowfields Farm
Waves Farm
Allot Gdns
LN1
West Common
Carholme Golf Course
Ballast Holes
Boultham Mere Nature Reserve
Mast
Swan Pool
LN6
Swanpool
LINCOLN
(LINDVM)
Works
Playing Field
The St Francis Special School
Lincoln Castle Acad
Yarborough Leisure Centre
Ermine
LN2
Bishop Grosseteste University Coll Lincoln
Mount Street Academy
Newport Cemy
The Lincoln Nuffield
Windmill
Westgate Acad
Water Twr
The Lawn
Castle
Lincoln Crown Court
Lincoln Cath
Bishop's Palace
Gallery
Lincoln City Assembly Rooms
Council Offices
City Hall
Hotel
University of Lincoln
Brayford Pool
New Boultham
LN5
The Lincoln St Peter at Gowts CE Prim Sch
Sincil Bank (Lincoln City FC)
The Lincoln Bishop King CE Prim Sch
YARBOROUGH ROAD
BURTON ROAD
RISEHOLME ROAD
CARHOLME ROAD
SAXILBY ROAD
LONG LEYS ROAD
YARBOROUGH CRESCENT
LONGDALES RD
BRAYFORD WAY
TRITTON ROAD
DIXON STREET
HIGH STREET
WIGFORD WAY
CANWICK ROAD
234
95 96 97
D1
1 RAILWAY PK CL
2 ST MATHEWS CL
3 PEPPERCORN CL
80
D3
1 ARTHUR TAYLOR ST
2 CHARLESWORTH ST
3 STAUNTON ST
4 WESTFIELD ST
5 HARVEY ST
6 WESTBOURNE GR
205
D4
1 TENNYSON ST
2 BEDFORD ST
3 COLENSO TERR
4 WOODSTOCK ST
5 ALLISON PL
6 ST FAITH'S ST
7 SOUTH PAR
F1
1 STANLEY PL
2 LUMLEY PL
3 LONSDALE PL
4 LANCASTER PL
5 LINTON ST
6 ARTHUR ST
7 BISHOP KING CT
8 HOOD ST
9 SAUSTHORPE ST
202
For full street detail of the highlighted area see page 234.

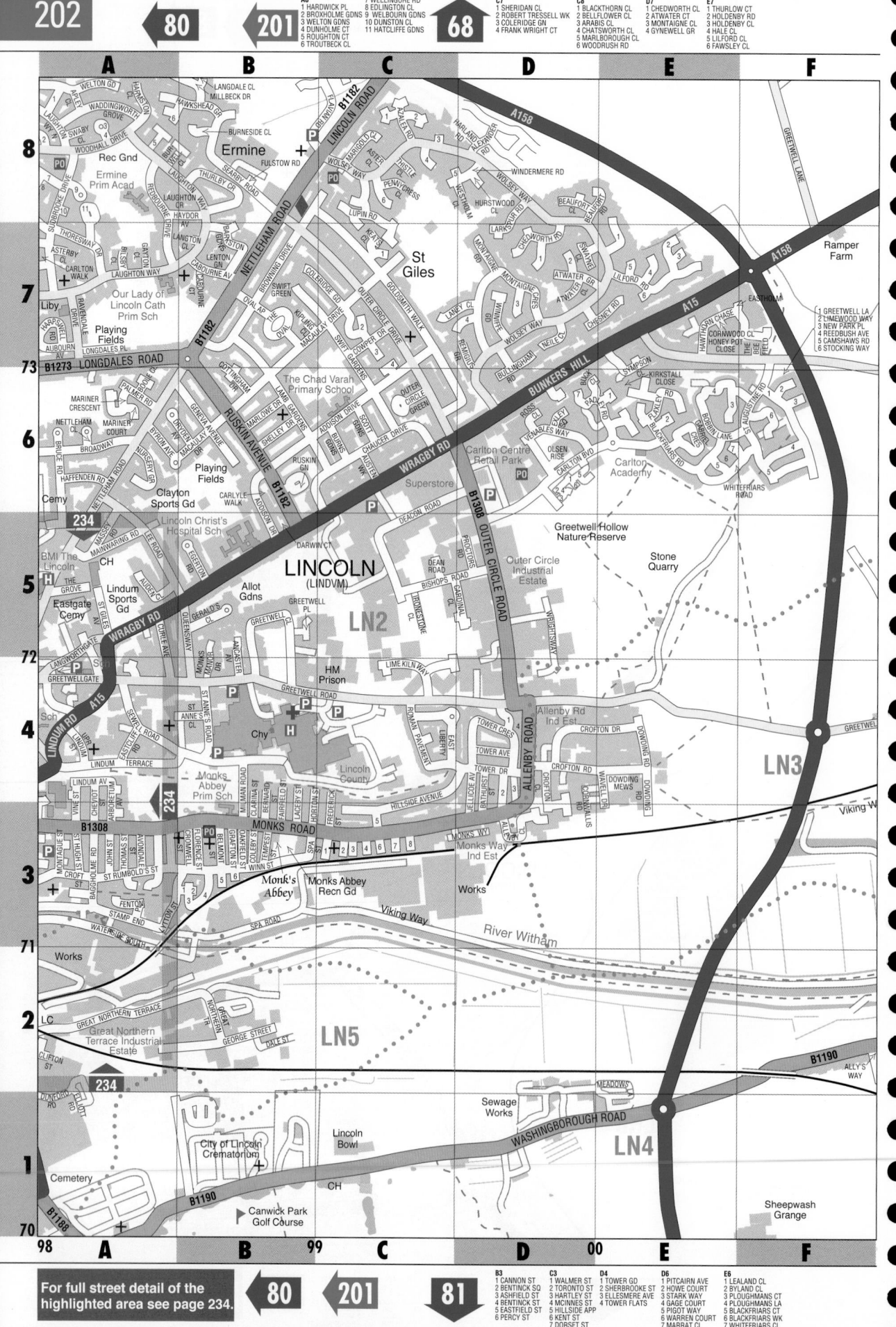

← 80
← 201
← 68

Grid labels: A B C D E F (top and bottom)

Row labels (left): 8 73 6 5 72 4 3 71 2 1 70

Map labels include:
Ermine, St Giles, LINCOLN (LINDVM), LN2, LN3, LN4, LN5, Bunkers Hill, Ramper Farm, Greetwell Hollow Nature Reserve, Stone Quarry, River Witham, Viking Way, Sewage Works, Lincoln Bowl, City of Lincoln Crematorium, Canwick Park Golf Course, Sheepwash Grange, Carlton Academy, Carlton Centre Retail Park, HM Prison, Lincoln County, Monk's Abbey, Monks Abbey Recn Gd, Great Northern Terrace Industrial Estate, Outer Circle Industrial Estate, Allenby Rd Ind Est, Monks Way Ind Est

For full street detail of the highlighted area see page 234.
← 80
← 201
81

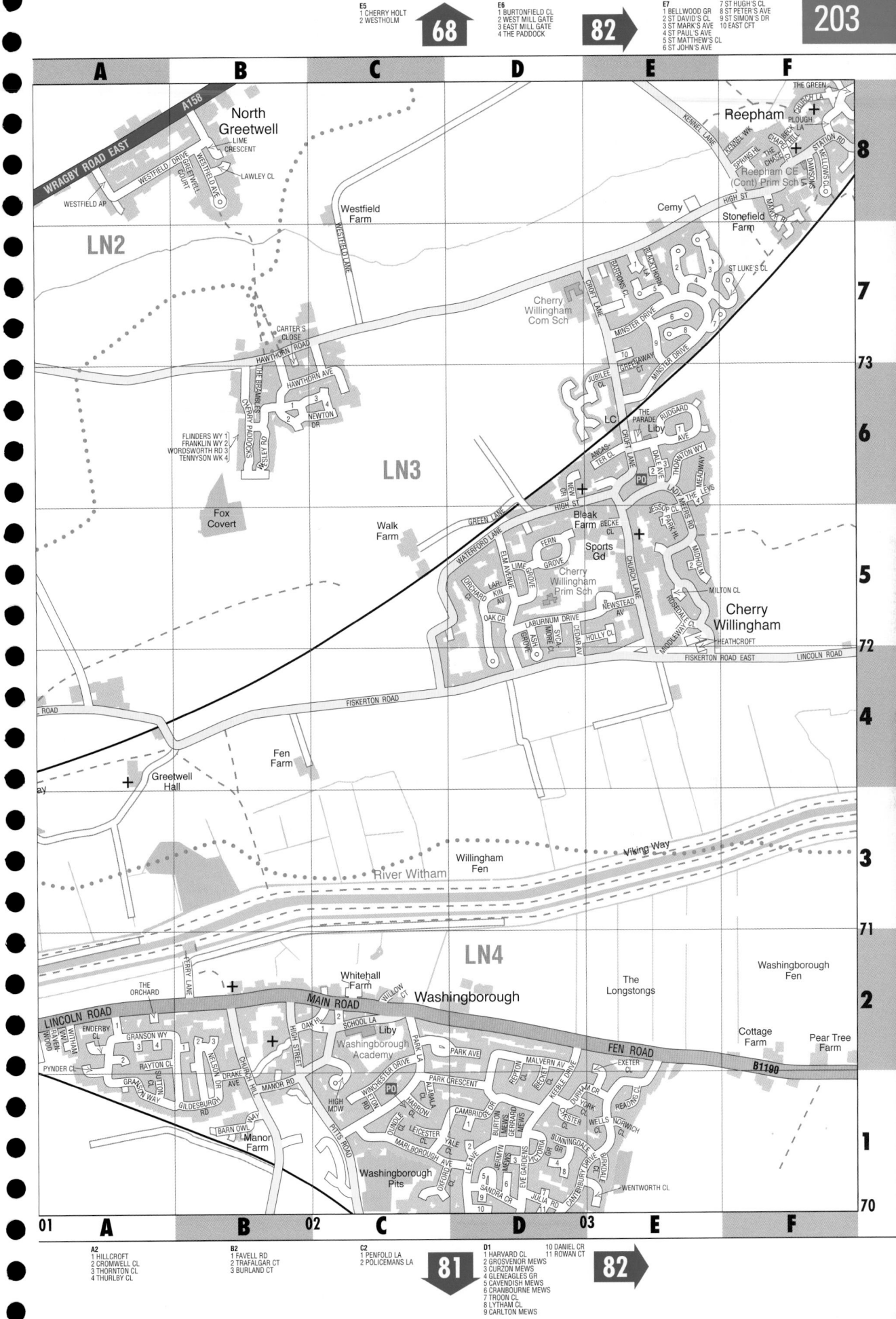

68

82

E5
1 CHERRY HOLT
2 WESTHOLM

E6
1 BURTONFIELD CL
2 WEST MILL GATE
3 EAST MILL GATE
4 THE PADDOCK

E7
1 BELLWOOD GR
2 ST DAVID'S CL
3 ST MARK'S AVE
4 ST PAUL'S AVE
5 ST MATTHEW'S CL
6 ST JOHN'S AVE

7 ST HUGH'S CL
8 ST PETER'S AVE
9 ST SIMON'S DR
10 EAST CFT

A158

WRAGBY ROAD EAST

North Greetwell

LIME CRESCENT

WESTFIELD AP

WESTFIELD DRIVE
GREENWELL COURT
WESTFIELD AVE

LAWLEY CL

LN2

Westfield Farm

WESTFIELD LANE

Reepham

THE GREEN
CHURCH LA
PLOUGH
CHAPEL HILL
KENNEL LANE
KENNEL WK
SPRING HL
THE CHASE
HIGH ST
STATION RD
WILLOWS CL
DAWSONS
MANOR RD

Reepham CE (Cont) Prim Sch

Cemy

Stonefield Farm

8

CARTER'S CLOSE

HAWTHORN ROAD

THE BRAMBLES
CHERRY PADDOCKS
KESTLEY RD

HAWTHORN AVE

NEWTON DR
1 2 3 4

FLINDERS WY 1
FRANKLIN WY 2
WORDSWORTH RD 3
TENNYSON WK 4

Fox Covert

LN3

Walk Farm

WATERFORD LANE
GREEN LANE

BLACKTHORN
CROFT LANE
BEHRONS CL
MINSTER DRIVE

Cherry Willingham Com Sch

St LUKE'S CL

JUBILEE CL
GREENAWAY CT
MINSTER DRIVE

LC
THE PARADE
PUDGARD
Liby
AVE

ANCASTER CL
CROFT LANE
DALE AVE
THORNTON WY
THE MEADWAY
THE LEVIS

7

73

6

NEW CL
HIGH ST
Bleak Farm
BECKE CL

JESSOP CL
PARK HL
LADY MEERS RD
MIDHOLM
ROSEDALE CL
MILTON CL

5

ELM AVENUE
LIME GROVE
LAR KIN CL
ORCHARD CL
FERN GROVE

Sports Gd

Cherry Willingham Prim Sch

CHURCH LANE
NEWSTEAD AV

Cherry Willingham

HEATHCROFT

OAK CR
LABURNUM DRIVE
MORE CL
ASH GROVE
SYCA
CEDAR AV
HOLLY CL

MIDDLEWAY

FISKERTON ROAD EAST
LINCOLN ROAD

72

ROAD

FISKERTON ROAD

Fen Farm

Greetwell Hall

WAY

Viking Way

River Witham

Willingham Fen

Washingborough Fen

3

71

LN4

THE ORCHARD

PERRY LANE

Whitehall Farm

MAIN ROAD

WILLOW CL

Washingborough

The Longstongs

Cottage Farm

Pear Tree Farm

2

LINCOLN ROAD
WITHAM
PYNDER CL
ENDERBY CL
GRANSON WY
RAYTON CL
GRANSON WAY
GILDESBURGH RD
BARN OWL WAY
NELSON DR
DRAKE AVE
BUTTON CL

HIGH STREET
CHURCH HL
MANOR RD

Manor Farm

SCHOOL LA
Liby
Washingborough Academy
PO
HIGH MDW
PITTS ROAD
Washingborough Pits

WINCHESTER RD
ETON RD
QUINTLE CL
ALABMA
HARROW
LEICESTER CL
MARLBOROUGH AVE
OXFORD CL

PARK LA
CAMBRIDGE
BURTON MEWS
GERRARD MEWS
YALE
LEE AVE
BERYM MEWS
EVE GARDENS
VICTORIA
SANDRA CR
JULIA RD

PARK AVE
PARK CRESCENT
REPTON CL
BECKET CL
CHESTER
SUNNINGDALE

MALVERN AV

KEEBLE DRIVE
DURHAM CR
YORK
WELLS
NORWICH CL
CANTERBURY DRIVE
BIRDALE
WENTWORTH CL

FEN ROAD

EXETER CL
READING CL

B1190

1

70

81

82

A2
1 HILLCROFT
2 CROMWELL CL
3 THORNTON CL
4 THURLBY CL

B2
1 FAVELL RD
2 TRAFALGAR CT
3 BURLAND CT

C2
1 PENFOLD LA
2 POLICEMANS LA

D1
1 HARVARD CL
2 GROSVENOR MEWS
3 CURZON MEWS
4 GLENEAGLES GR
5 CAVENDISH MEWS
6 CRANBOURNE MEWS
7 TROON CL
8 LYTHAM CL
9 CARLTON MEWS

10 DANIEL CR
11 ROWAN CT

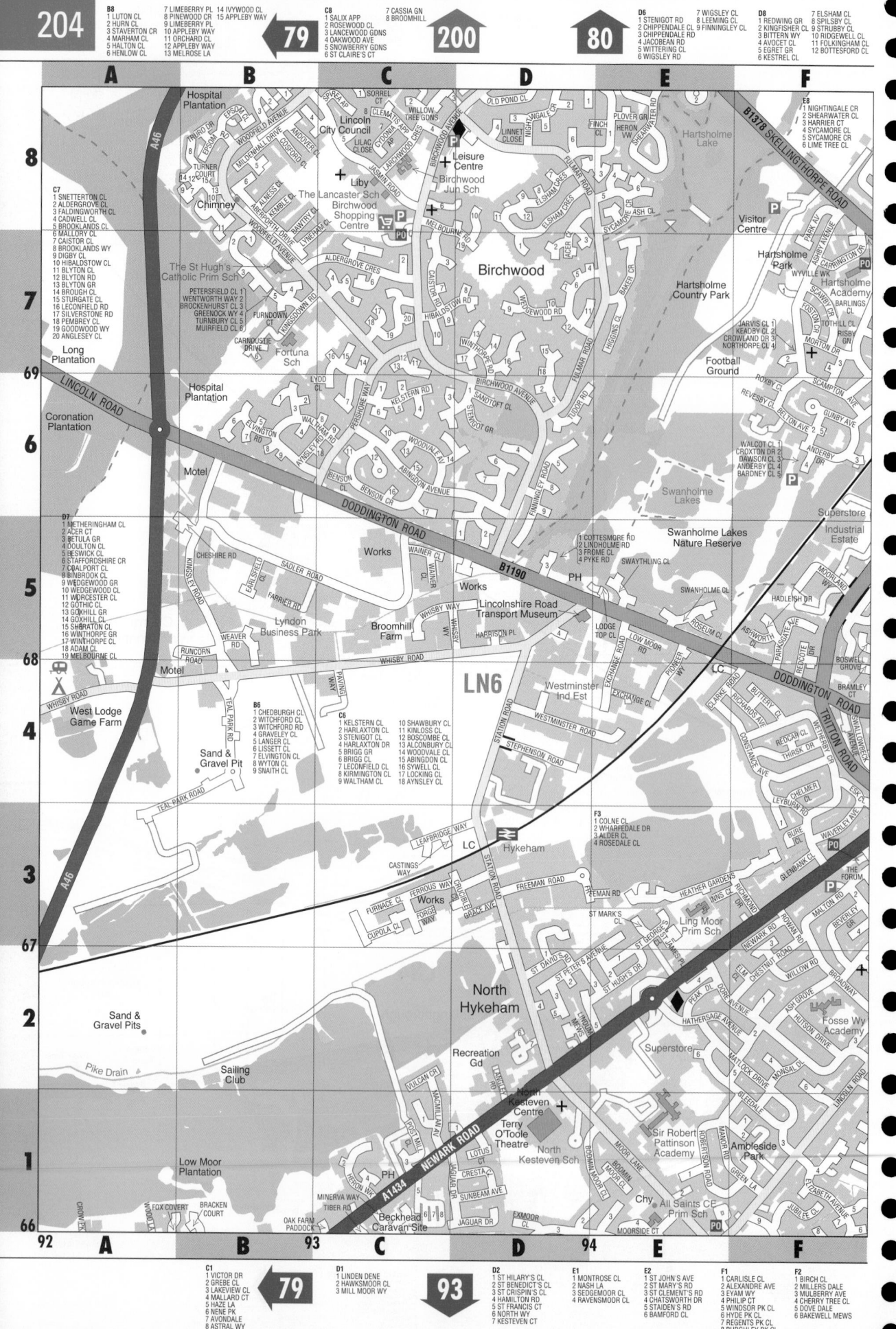

B8
7 LIMEBERRY PL 14 IVYWOOD CL
1 LUTON CL   8 PINEWOOD CR 15 APPLEBY WAY
2 HURN CL   9 LIMEBERRY PL
3 STAVERTON CR   10 APPLEBY WAY
4 MARHAM CL   11 ORCHARD CL
5 HALTON CL   12 APPLEBY WAY
6 HENLOW CL   13 MELROSE LA

79

C8
1 SALIX APP   7 CASSIA GN
2 ROSEWOOD CL   8 BROOMHILL
3 LANCEWOOD GDNS
4 OAKWOOD AVE
5 SNOWBERRY GDNS
6 ST CLAIRE'S CT

200

80

D6
1 STENIGOT RD   7 WIGSLEY CL
2 CHIPPENDALE CR   8 LEEMING CL
3 CHIPPENDALE RD   9 FINNINGLEY CL
4 JACOBEAN RD
5 WITTERING CL
6 WIGSLEY RD

D8
1 REDWING GR   7 ELSHAM CL
2 KINGFISHER CL   8 SPILSBY CL
3 BITTERN WY   9 STRUBBY CL
4 AVOCET CL   10 RIDGEWELL CL
5 EGRET GR   11 FOLKINGHAM CL
6 KESTREL CL   12 BOTTESFORD CL

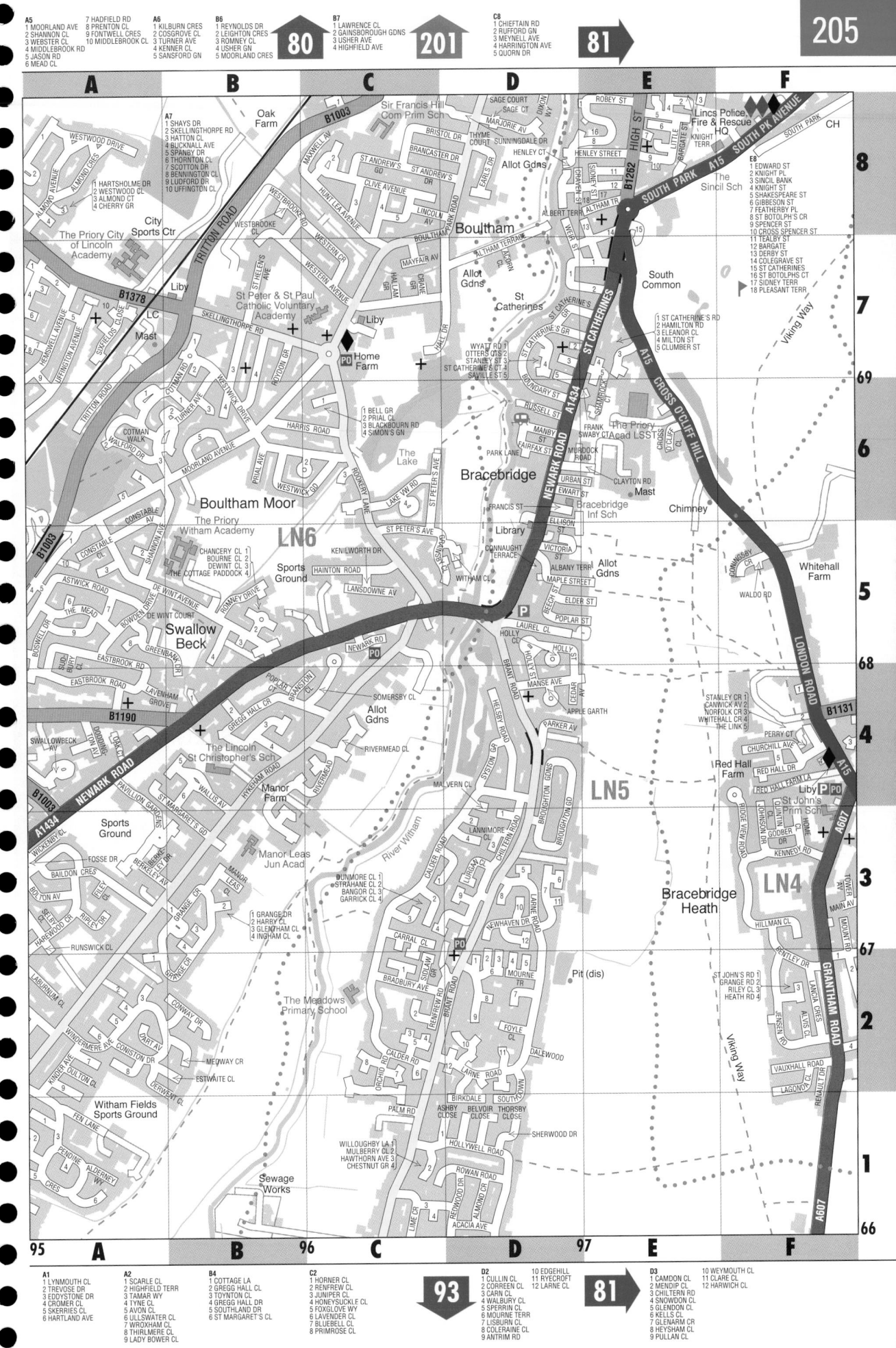

A5
1 MOORLAND AVE
2 SHANNON CL
3 WEBSTER CL
4 MIDDLEBROOK RD
5 JASON RD
6 MEAD CL

7 HADFIELD RD
8 PRENTON CL
9 FONTWELL CRES
10 MIDDLEBROOK CL

A6
1 KILBURN CRES
2 COSGROVE CL
3 TURNER AVE
4 KENNER CL
5 SANSFORD GN

B6
1 REYNOLDS DR
2 LEIGHTON CRES
3 ROMNEY CL
4 USHER GN
5 MOORLAND CRES

B7
1 LAWRENCE CL
2 GAINSBOROUGH GDNS
3 USHER AVE
4 HIGHFIELD AVE

C8
1 CHIEFTAIN RD
2 RUFFORD GN
3 MEYNELL AVE
4 HARRINGTON AVE
5 QUORN DR

80

201

81

A7
1 SHAYS DR
2 SKELLINGTHORPE RD
3 BUCKNALL AVE
4 SPANBY DR
5 THORNTON CL
6 SCOTTON DR
7 BENNINGTON CL
8 LUDFORD DR
9 LUDFORD CL
10 UFFINGTON CL

E8
1 EDWARD ST
2 KNIGHT PL
3 SINCIL BANK
4 KNIGHT ST
5 SHAKESPEARE ST
6 GIBBESON ST
7 FEATHERBY PL
8 ST BOTOLPH'S CR
9 SPENCER ST
10 CROSS SPENCER ST
11 TEALBY ST
12 BARGATE
13 DERBY ST
14 COLEGRAVE ST
15 ST CATHERINES
16 ST BOTOLPHS CT
17 SIDNEY TERR
18 PLEASANT TERR

1 ST CATHERINE'S RD
2 HAMILTON RD
3 ELEANOR CL
4 MILTON ST
5 CLUMBER ST

1 BELL GR
2 PRIAL CL
3 BLACKBOURN RD
4 SIMON'S GN

WYATT RD 1
OTTERS CT 2
STANLEY ST 3
ST CATHERINES GR 4
SAVILLE ST 5

STANLEY CR 1
CANNICK AV 2
NORFOLK CR 3
WHITEHALL AV 4
THE LINK 5

1 GRANGE DR
2 HARBY CL
3 GLENTHAM CL
4 INGHAM CL

DUNMORE CL 1
STRAHANE CL 2
BANGOR CL 3
GARRICK CL 4

ST JOHN'S RD 1
GRANGE RD 2
RILEY CL 3
HEATH RD 4

LN6

LN5

LN4

A1
1 LYNMOUTH CL
2 TREVOSE DR
3 EDDYSTONE DR
4 CROMER CL
5 SKERRIES CL
6 HARTLAND AVE

A2
1 SCARLE CL
2 HIGHFIELD TERR
3 TAMAR WY
4 TYNE CL
5 AVON CL
6 ULLSWATER CL
7 WROXHAM CL
8 THIRLMERE CL
9 LADY BOWER CL

B4
1 COTTAGE LA
2 GREGG HALL CL
3 TOYNTON CL
4 GREGG HALL DR
5 SOUTHLAND DR
6 ST MARGARET'S CL

C2
1 HORNER CL
2 RENFREW CL
3 JUNIPER CL
4 HONEYSUCKLE CL
5 FOXGLOVE WY
6 LAVENDER CL
7 BLUEBELL CL
8 PRIMROSE CL

D2
1 CULLIN CL
2 CORREEN CL
3 CARN CL
4 WALBURY CL
5 SPERRIN CL
6 MOURNE TERR
7 LISBURN CL
8 COLERAINE CL
9 ANTRIM RD

10 EDGEHILL
11 RYECROFT
12 LARNE CL

D3
1 CAMDON CL
2 MENDIP CL
3 CHILTERN RD
4 SNOWDON CL
5 GLENDON CL
6 KELLS CL
7 GLENARM CR
8 HEYSHAM CL
9 PULLAN CL

10 WEYMOUTH CL
11 CLARE CL
12 HARWICH CL

93

81

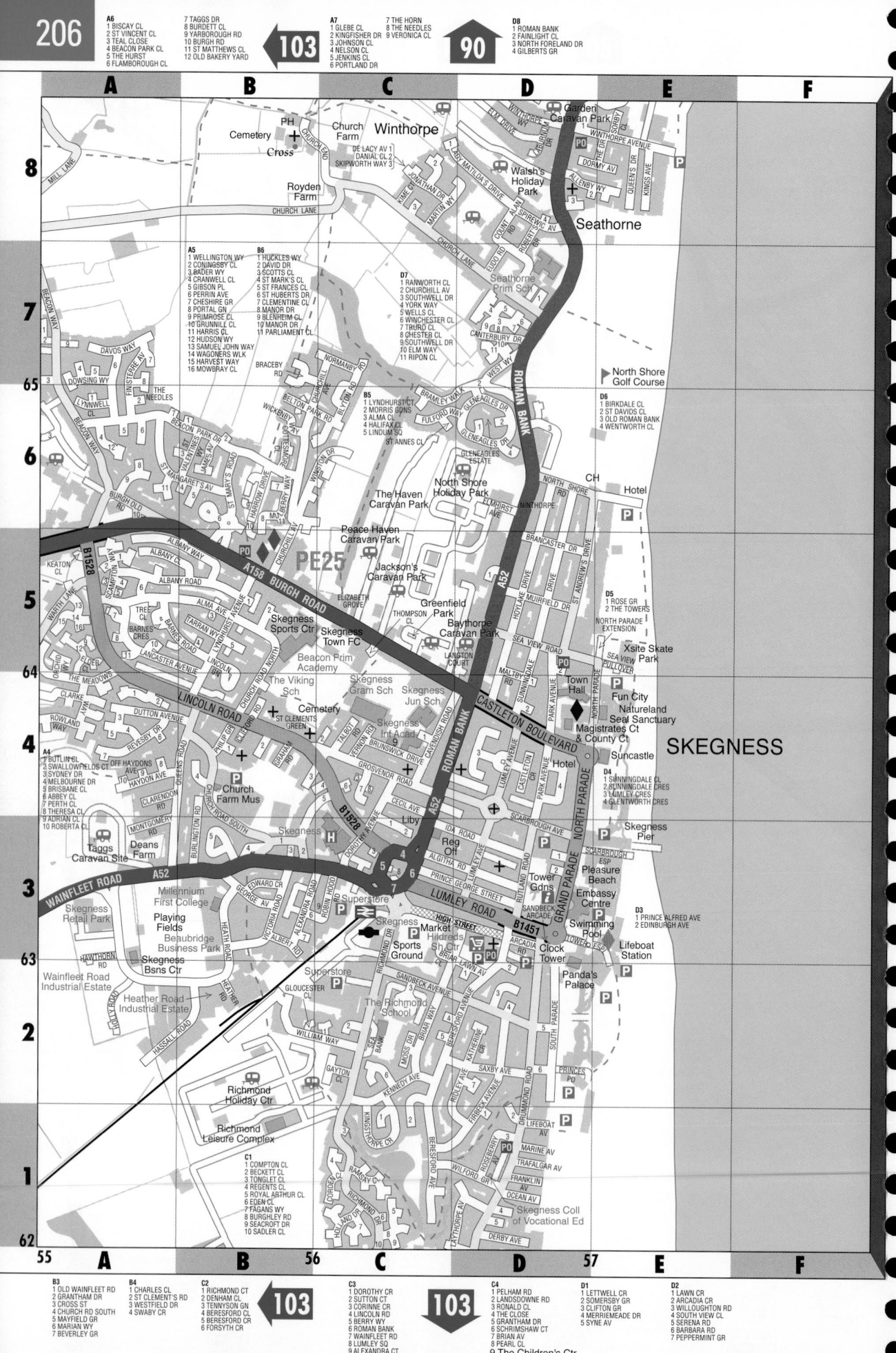

A6
1 BISCAY CL
2 ST VINCENT CL
3 TEAL CLOSE
4 BEACON PARK CL
5 THE HURST
6 FLAMBOROUGH CL

7 TAGGS DR
8 BURDETT CL
9 YARBOROUGH RD
10 BURGH RD
11 ST MATTHEWS CL
12 OLD BAKERY YARD

103

A7
1 GLEBE CL
2 KINGFISHER DR
3 JOHNSON CL
4 NELSON CL
5 JENKINS CL
6 PORTLAND DR

7 THE HORN
8 THE NEEDLES
9 VERONICA CL

90

D8
1 ROMAN BANK
2 FARNLIGHT CL
3 NORTH FORELAND DR
4 GILBERTS GR

SKEGNESS

PE25

Winthorpe

Seathorne

A5
1 WELLINGTON WY
2 CONINGSBY CL
3 BADER WY
4 CRANWELL CL
5 GIBSON PL
6 PERRIN AVE
7 CHESHIRE GR
8 PORTAL GN
9 PRIMROSE CL
10 GRUNNIL CL
11 HARRIS CL
12 HUDSON WY
13 SAMUEL JOHN WAY
14 WAGONERS WLK
15 HARVEST WAY
16 MOWBRAY CL

B6
1 HUCKLES WY
2 DAVID DR
3 SCOTTS CL
4 ST MARK'S CL
5 ST FRANCES CL
6 ST HUBERTS DR
7 CLEMENTINE CL
8 MANOR DR
9 BLENHEIM CL
10 MANOR DR 1
11 PARLIAMENT CL

D7
1 RANWORTH CL
2 CHURCHILL AV
3 SOUTHWELL CL
4 YORK WAY
5 WELLS CL
6 WINCHESTER CL
7 TRURO CL
8 CHESTER CL
9 SOUTHWELL DR
10 ELM WAY
11 RIPON CL

B5
1 LYNDHURST CT
2 MORRIS GDNS
3 ALMA CL
4 HALIFAX CL
5 LINDUM SQ

D6
1 BIRKDALE CL
2 ST DAVIDS CL
3 OLD ROMAN BANK
4 WENTWORTH CL

D5
1 ROSE GR
2 THE TOWERS

D4
1 SUNNINGDALE CL
2 SUNNINGDALE CRES
3 LUMLEY CRES
4 GLENTWORTH CRES

D3
1 PRINCE ALFRED AVE
2 EDINBURGH AVE

A4
1 BUTLIN CL
2 SWALLOWFIELDS CT
3 SYDNEY DR
4 MELBOURNE DR
5 BRISBANE CL
6 ABBEY CL
7 PERTH CL
8 THERESA CL
9 ADRIAN CL
10 ROBERTA CL

C1
1 COMPTON CL
2 BECKETT CL
3 TONGLET CL
4 REGENTS CL
5 ROYAL ARTHUR CL
6 EDEN CL
7 FAGANS WY
8 BURGHLEY RD
9 SEACROFT CL
10 SADLER CL

North Shore
Golf Course

B3
1 OLD WAINFLEET RD
2 GRANTHAM DR
3 CROSS ST
4 CHURCH RD SOUTH
5 MAYFIELD GR
6 MARIAN WY
7 BEVERLEY GR

B4
1 CHARLES CL
2 ST CLEMENT'S RD
3 WESTFIELD DR
4 SWABY CR

C2
1 RICHMOND CT
2 DENHAM CL
3 TENNYSON GN
4 BERESFORD CL
5 BERESFORD CR
6 FORSYTH CR

103

C3
1 DOROTHY CR
2 SUTTON CT
3 CORINNE GR
4 LINCOLN RD
5 BERRY WY
6 ROMAN BANK
7 WAINFLEET RD
8 LUMLEY SQ
9 ALEXANDRA CT

C4
1 PELHAM RD
2 LANDSDOWNE RD
3 RONALD CL
4 THE CLOSE
5 GRANTHAM DR
6 SCRIMSHAW CT
7 BRIAN AV
8 PEARL CL
9 The Children's Ctr

103

D1
1 LETTWELL CR
2 SOMERSBY GR
3 CLIFTON GR
4 MERRIEMEADE DR
5 SYNE AV

D2
1 LAWN CR
2 ARCADIA CR
3 WILLOUGHTON RD
4 SOUTH VIEW CL
5 SERENA RD
6 BARBARA RD
7 PEPPERMINT GR

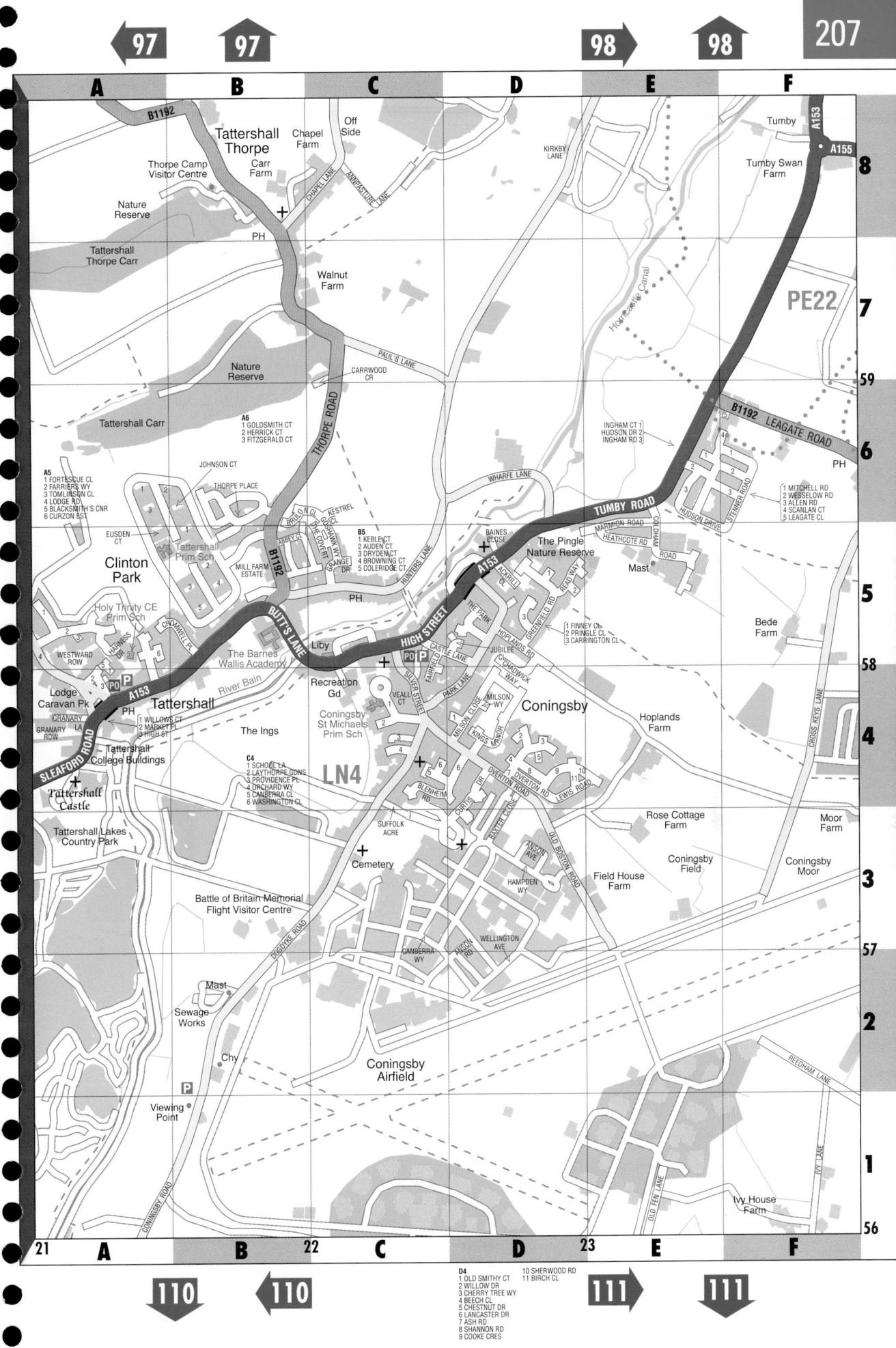

A B C D E F

8
7
59
6
5
58
4
3
57
2
1
56

B1192

Tattershall Thorpe

Chapel Farm

Off Side

Tumby

A153

A155

Tumby Swan Farm

Thorpe Camp Visitor Centre

Carr Farm

KIRKBY LANE

Nature Reserve

CHAPEL LANE

ANNS PASTURE LANE

PH

Tattershall Thorpe Carr

Walnut Farm

PE22

How Castle Canal

Nature Reserve

PAUL'S LANE

CARRWOOD CR

B1192 LEAGATE ROAD

Tattershall Carr

A6
1 GOLDSMITH CT
2 HERRICK CT
3 FITZGERALD CT

THORPE ROAD

INGHAM CT 1
HUDSON DR 2
INGHAM RD 3

STEINER ROAD

1 MITCHELL RD
2 WESSELOW RD
3 ALLEN RD
4 SCANLAN CT
5 LEAGATE CL

JOHNSON CT

THORPE PLACE

WHARFE LANE

TUMBY ROAD

HUDSON DRIVE

PH

A5
1 FORTESCUE CL
2 FARRIERS WY
3 TOMLINSON CL
4 LODGE RD
5 BLACKSMITH'S CNR
6 CURZON EST

EUSDEN CT

BRILON CT

KESTREL CL

GOSHAWK CL

THE COVERT

ABBEY CL

GRANGE DR

B5
1 KEBLE CT
2 AUDEN CT
3 DRYDEN CT
4 BROWNING CT
5 COLERIDGE CT

BAINES CLOSE

MARMION ROAD

HEATHCOTE RD

COLDHAM ROAD

The Pingle Nature Reserve

Mast

Bede Farm

Clinton Park

Tattershall Prim Sch

Holy Trinity CE Prim Sch

MILL FARM ESTATE

B1192

PH

HUNTERS LANE

HIGH STREET

A153

ACKRILL CL

THE PARK

GREENFIELD RD

HOPLANDS RD

READ WAY

1 FINNEY CL
2 PRINGLE CL
3 CARRINGTON CL

WESTWARD ROW

HARNESS DR

CROMWELL PL

BUTT'S LANE

The Barnes Wallis Academy

Liby

Recreation Gd

P P

CASTLE LANE

FAIRFIELD

JUBILEE

CHADWICK WAY

CROSS KEYS LANE

P

Lodge Caravan Pk

A153

PH

Tattershall

River Bain

The Ings

SILVER STREET

VEALL CT

Coningsby St Michaels Prim Sch

PARK LANE

MILSON CLOSE

MILSON WY

Coningsby

Hoplands Farm

GRANARY LA

GRANARY ROW

1 WILLOWS CT
2 MARKET PL
3 HIGH ST

KINGS MANOR

SLEAFORD ROAD

Tattershall College Buildings

LN4

C4
1 SCHOOL LA
2 LAYTHORPE GDNS
3 PROVIDENCE PL
4 ORCHARD WY
5 CANBERRA CL
6 WASHINGTON CL

BLENHEIM RD

CURTIS DR

OVERTON RD

OVERTON RD

LEWIS RD

11
10

Rose Cottage Farm

Moor Farm

Tattershall Castle

Tattershall Lakes Country Park

Cemetery

SUFFOLK ACRE

BAXTER CLOSE

ANSON AVE

OLD BOSTON ROAD

Field House Farm

Coningsby Field

Coningsby Moor

Coningsby

Battle of Britain Memorial Flight Visitor Centre

DOGDYKE ROAD

CANBERRA WY

ANSON RD

HAMPDEN WY

WELLINGTON AVE

Mast

Sewage Works

Chy

Coningsby Airfield

REEDHAM LANE

OLD FEN LANE

IVY LANE

P

Viewing Point

Ivy House Farm

D4
1 OLD SMITHY CT
2 WILLOW DR
3 CHERRY TREE WY
4 BEECH CL
5 CHESTNUT DR
6 LANCASTER DR
7 ASH RD
8 SHANNON RD
9 COOKE CRES
10 SHERWOOD RD
11 BIRCH CL

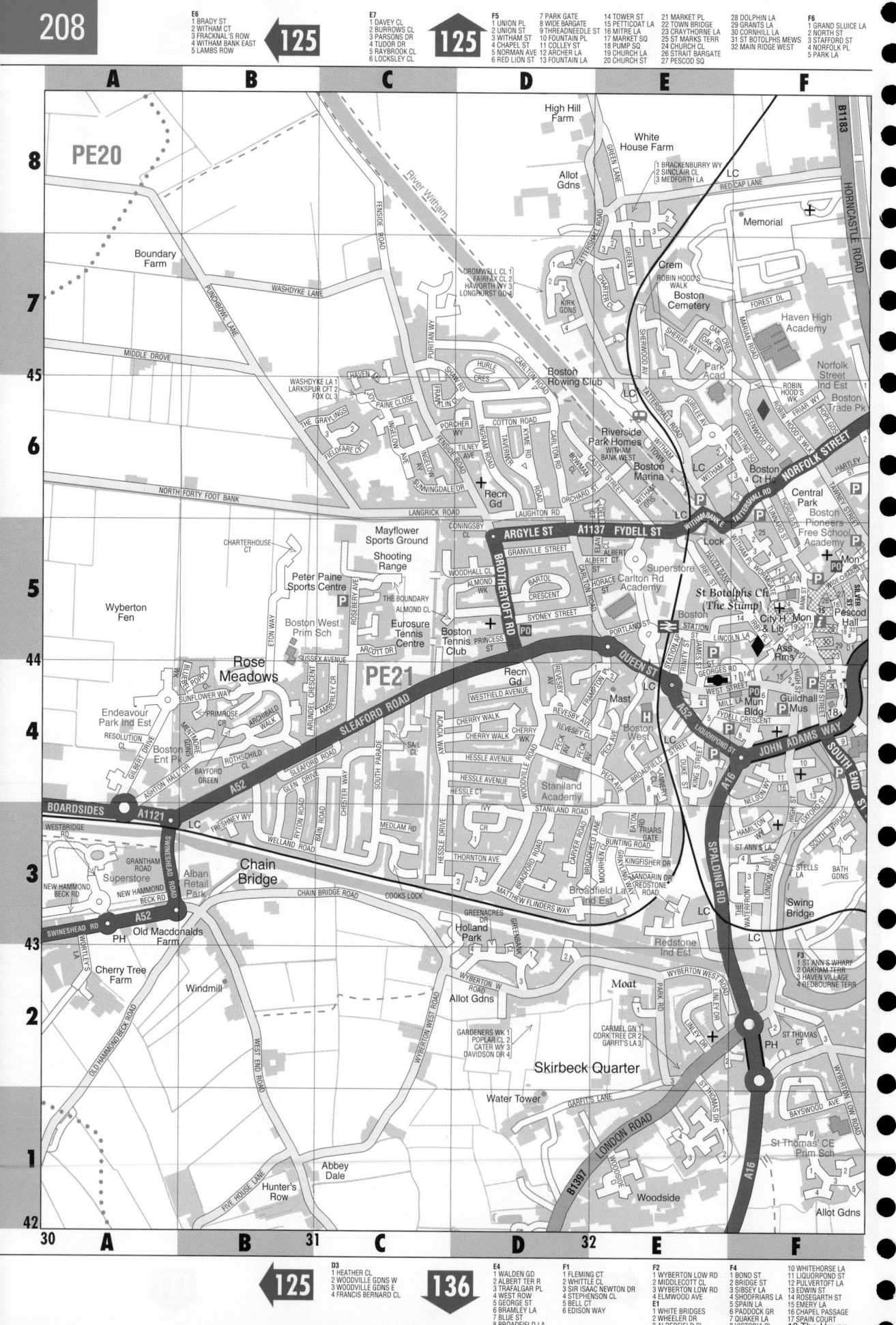

E6
1 BRADY ST
2 WITHAM CT
3 FRACKNAL'S ROW
4 WITHAM BANK EAST
5 LAMBS ROW

← 125

E7
1 DAVEY CL
2 BURROWS E
3 PARSONS DR
4 TUDOR CL
5 RAYBROOK CL
6 LOCKSLEY CL

125

F5
1 UNION PL
2 UNION ST
3 WITHAM ST
4 CHAPEL ST
5 NORMAN AVE
6 RED LION ST

7 PARK GATE
8 WIDE BARGATE
9 THREADNEEDLE ST
10 FOUNTAIN PL
11 COLLEY ST
12 ARCHER LA
13 FOUNTAIN LA

14 TOWER ST
15 PETTICOAT LA
16 MITRE LA
17 MARKET SQ
18 PUMP SQ
19 CHURCH LA
20 CHURCH ST

21 MARKET PL
22 TOWN BRIDGE
23 CRAYTHORNE LA
24 CHURCH CL
25 ST MARKS TERR
26 STRAIT BARGATE
27 PESCOD SQ

28 DOLPHIN LA
29 GRANTS LA
30 CORNHILL LA
31 ST BOTOLPHS MEWS
32 MAIN RIDGE WEST

F6
1 GRAND SLUICE LA
2 NORTH ST
3 STAFFORD ST
4 NORFOLK PL
5 PARK LA

D3
1 HEATHER CL
2 WOODVILLE GDNS W
3 WOODVILLE GDNS E
4 FRANCIS BERNARD CL

E4
1 WALDEN GD
2 ALBERT TER R
3 TRAFALGAR CL
4 WEST ROW
5 GEORGE ST
6 BRAMLEY LA
7 BLUE ST
8 BROADFIELD LA
9 NELSON WY

F1
1 FLEMING CT
2 WHITTLE CL
3 SIR ISAAC NEWTON DR
4 STEPHENSON CL
5 BELL CT
6 EDISON WAY

E1
1 WHITE BRIDGES
2 WHEELER DR
3 ALDERFIELD CL
4 WELLINGTONIA PARK

F2
1 WYBERTON LOW RD
2 MIDDLECOTT CL
3 WYBERTON LOW RD
4 ELMWOOD AVE
5 SPAIN LA
6 PADDOCK GR
7 QUAKER LA
8 VICTORIA PL
9 GREYFRIARS LA

F4
1 BOND ST
2 BRIDGE ST
3 SIBSEY LA
4 SHODFRIARS LA
5 EMERY LA

10 WHITEHORSE LA
11 LIQUORPOND ST
12 PULVERTOFT LA
13 EDWIN ST
14 ROSEGARTH ST
15 EMERY LA
16 CHAPEL PASSAGE
17 SPAIN COURT
18 The Haven

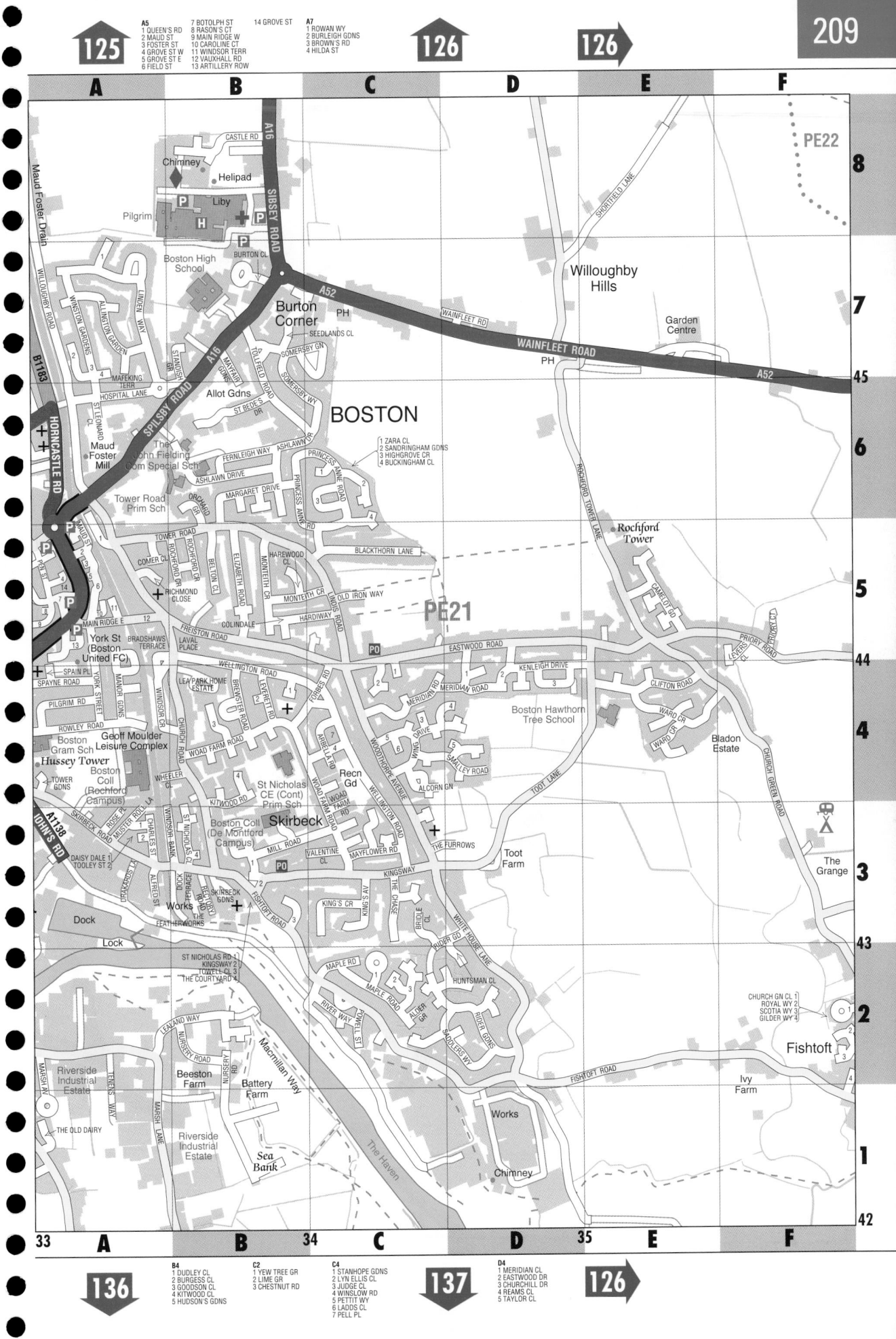

A5
1 QUEEN'S RD
2 MAUD ST
3 FOSTER ST
4 GROVE ST W
5 GROVE ST E
6 FIELD ST

7 BOTOLPH ST
8 RASON'S CT
9 MAIN RIDGE W
10 CAROLINE CT
11 WINDSOR TERR
12 VAUXHALL RD
13 ARTILLERY ROW

14 GROVE ST

A7
1 ROWAN WY
2 BURLEIGH GDNS
3 BROWN'S RD
4 HILDA ST

125   126   126

A · B · C · D · E · F

PE22

8

CASTLE RD

Chimney
Helipad
Liby
Pilgrim
Boston High School

Willoughby Hills

Garden Centre

7

Burton Corner
PH
Burton Cl
A52
WAINFLEET RD
Seedlands Cl
WAINFLEET ROAD
PH
A52

45

BOSTON

1 ZARA CL
2 SANDRINGHAM GDNS
3 HIGHGROVE CR
4 BUCKINGHAM CL

6

The John Fielding Com Special Sch
Tower Road Prim Sch

Rochford Tower

Rochford Tower Lane

5

PE21

BLACKTHORN LANE
OLD IRON WAY

York St (Boston United FC)
EASTWOOD ROAD

PO

44

Lea Park Home Estate
Boston Hawthorn Tree School
KENLEIGH DRIVE
CLIFTON ROAD

Bladon Estate

4

Geoff Moulder Leisure Complex
Boston Gram Sch
Hussey Tower
Boston Coll (Rochford Campus)

St Nicholas CE (Cont) Prim Sch
Recn Gd

TOOT LANE

The Grange

Skirbeck
Boston Coll (De Montford Campus)

Toot Farm

Works

The Featherworks

3

Dock
Lock

ST NICHOLAS RD 1
KINGSWAY 2
TOWELL CL 3
THE COURTYARD 4

Huntsman Cl

43

CHURCH GN CL 1
ROYAL WY 2
SCOTIA WY 3
GILDER WY 4

Fishtoft

2

Riverside Industrial Estate
Beeston Farm
Battery Farm
Macmillan Way
FISHTOFT ROAD

Ivy Farm

The Old Dairy
Riverside Industrial Estate
Sea Bank

Works

The Haven
Chimney

1

42

B4
1 DUDLEY CL
2 BURGESS CL
3 GOODSON CL
4 KITWOOD CL
5 HUDSON'S GDNS

C2
1 YEW TREE GR
2 LIME GR
3 CHESTNUT RD

C4
1 STANHOPE GDNS
2 LYN ELLIS CL
3 JUDGE CL
4 WINSLOW RD
5 PETTIT WY
6 LADDS CL
7 PELL PL

D4
1 MERIDIAN CL
2 EASTWOOD DR
3 CHURCHILL DR
4 REAMS CL
5 TAYLOR CL

E8
1 EMMINSON WY
2 KELHAM RD
3 THE HAVERLANDS
4 ORCHARD CL
5 MALVERN DR
6 MENDIP CL

F5
1 PORTSMOUTH CL
2 WESTMINSTER WY
3 ROBERTSON RD
4 CAMPBELL CL
5 ELY WY
6 RURO CL

F7
1 CEDARWOOD CL
2 BROOMWOOD CL
3 PALMWOOD CL
4 BIRCHWOOD CL
5 LILACWOOD DR
6 BRIARWOOD CL

7 ROWANWOOD DR
8 HOLLYWOOD DR

F8
1 VIVIAN CL
2 BEAUMONT DR
3 MALIM WY
4 PEACHWOOD CL
5 APPLEWOOD DR
6 BRAMBLEWOOD CL

7 ORANGAWOOD CL
8 OSTLER CL
9 COCHRAN CL

E5
1 CORFE CL
2 RIBER CL
3 TATTERSHALL CL
4 CAMARTHEN CL
5 BIRMINGHAM CL
6 CHICHESTER CL
7 NORWICH WY
8 HEREFORD WY
9 ROCHESTER DR
10 PETERBOROUGH CL
11 ROCHESTER DR

D5
1 SALISBURY CL
2 BLACKBURN CL
3 ST EDMUNDS CL
4 NEWCASTLE RD
5 ST ALBANS CL
6 CARLISLE CL
7 COVENTRY CL
8 CHESTER GDNS
9 WARWICK CL
10 BRADFORD CL

A5
1 RECTORY CL
2 CHURCH ST
3 CASTHORPE RD
4 CHAPEL LA
5 LAWSON LEAS
6 HIGHFIELDS
7 BERRYFIELD END
8 GRANGE PADDOCK

CHILTERN CL 1
CAMBRIAN CL 2
CHEVIOT CL 3
SWALLOW'S CL 4
KIMBERLEY TERR 5
LADYSMITH TERR 6

1 GRIMSTHORPE CL
2 DOVER CL
3 OAKHAM CL
4 MONMOUTH WAY
5 JAMESTON CL
6 BAMBURGH CL
7 SCARBOROUGH CL
8 DALTON CL

BRECON CL 1
GRAMPIAN WY 2
BRENDON CL 3

NEWARK VW 1
ST MAWES WAY 2
LEWES AVE 3
TAMWORTH CL 4
PEVERIL PL 5

D2
1 CHESTNUT GR
2 LARCH CL
3 SYCAMORE CT
4 HAWTHORNE CT

E2
1 CLYDE CT
2 LYMN CT
3 WELLAND CT
4 NENE CT
5 TAMAR CT
6 COLNE CT
7 STOUR CT
8 GANNET CT
9 FALCON CT

10 MALLARD CT
11 GRESLEY CT
12 STURROCK CT
13 IVATT CT
14 STIRLING CT
15 HICKLING CL
16 KINOULTON CT

E4
1 DERBY CL
2 WESTBOURNE PL
3 SHORWELL CL

F3
1 HODDER CL
2 BARNWELL TERR
3 HARLAXTON RD

129
A5
1 PROSPECT PL
2 ALBION RD
3 GLADSTONE TERR
4 BROWNDONS ST
5 BROAD ST
6 PREMIER CT

7 NORTH ST
8 BARROWBY RD
9 MOUNT ST
10 WONG ROW
11 WATERGATE
12 VINE ST
13 ALBION ST

14 SPIRE VIEW
15 STEEPLE LEAS

A7
1 DARLEY DALE CRES
2 WESTERDALE RD
3 HAWKSDALE CL

130
A8
1 WENSLEYDALE CL
2 HATCLIFFE CL
3 MEADOWDALE CRES
4 OAKDALE CL
5 FARNDALE CRES

130
E6
1 QUEENSWAY
2 EDINBURGH RD
3 WORDSWORTH RD
4 KIPLING CL

F6
1 ALMA PARK CL
2 SIXTH AVE
3 SEVENTH AVE
4 POLYGON WALK

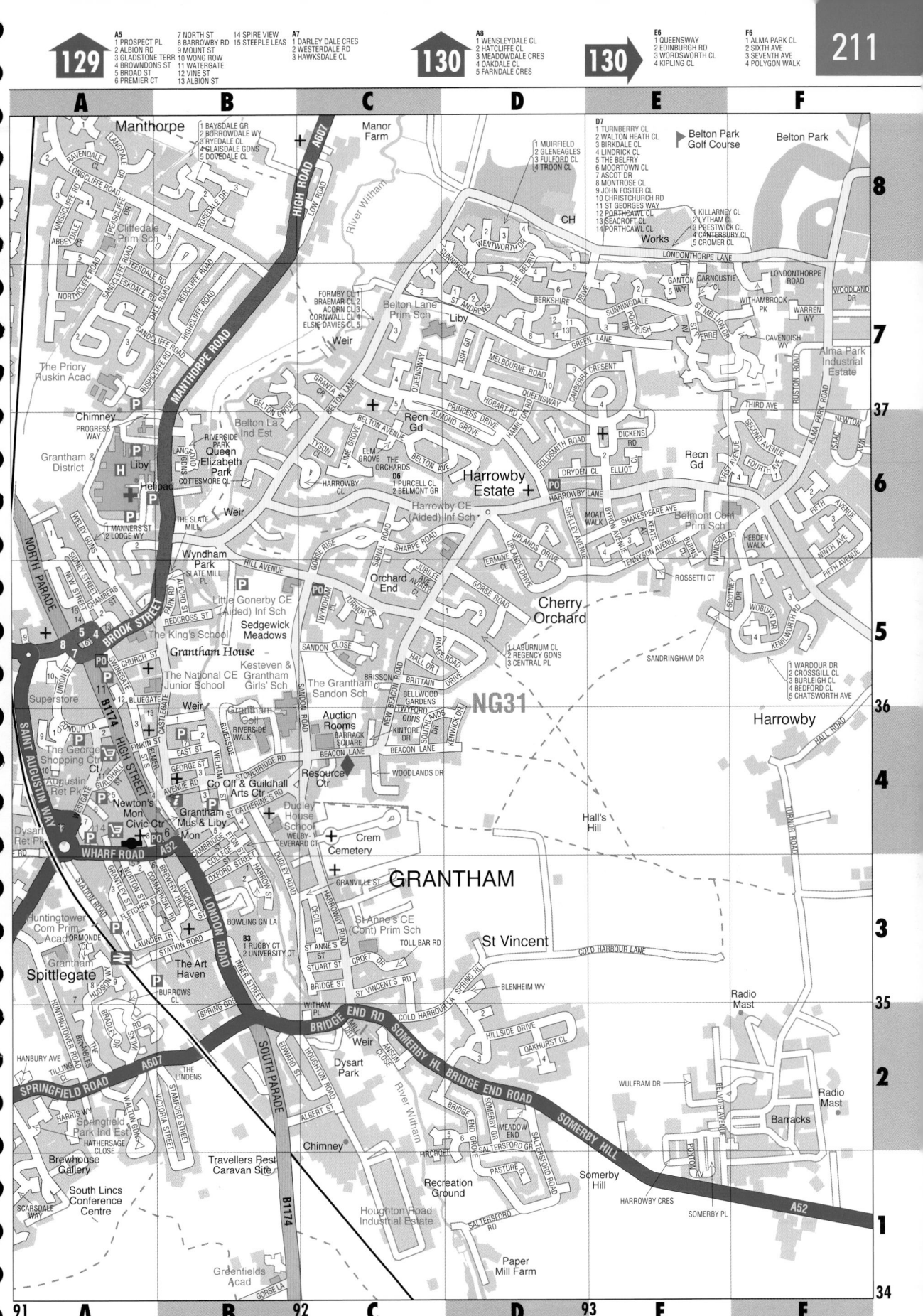

139
A3
1 ELTON ST
2 WILLIAM ST
3 RAILWAY TR
4 QUEEN ST
5 DIXON PL
6 ST JOHNS CT
7 HARDWICKE CL
8 ATLANTIC PL
9 MAYFLOWER MEWS

A4
1 THE GRANGE
2 MARKET PL
3 ELMER ST N
4 ST PETER'S HILL
5 GREENWOOD'S ROW
6 WELBY ST
7 STANTON ST
8 BATH ST
9 GREY FRIARS

B3
10 PRIORY COURT
11 KINGS WALK
12 GREAT NORTHERN COURT
13 RUSSELL READ ALMSHOUSES
14 Isaac Newton Sh Ctr

140
B4
1 MIDDLEMORE YD
2 AGNES ST
3 GROVE END RD
4 STONEMASONS CT
5 NEWTON ST
6 ST PETER'S HILL
7 WALLWORKS MEWS

130
D2
1 WELLINGTON DR
2 LANCASTER GDNS
3 HILLSIDE CRES
4 EASTWOOD DR
5 HOLLY CL
6 PRIMROSE WY

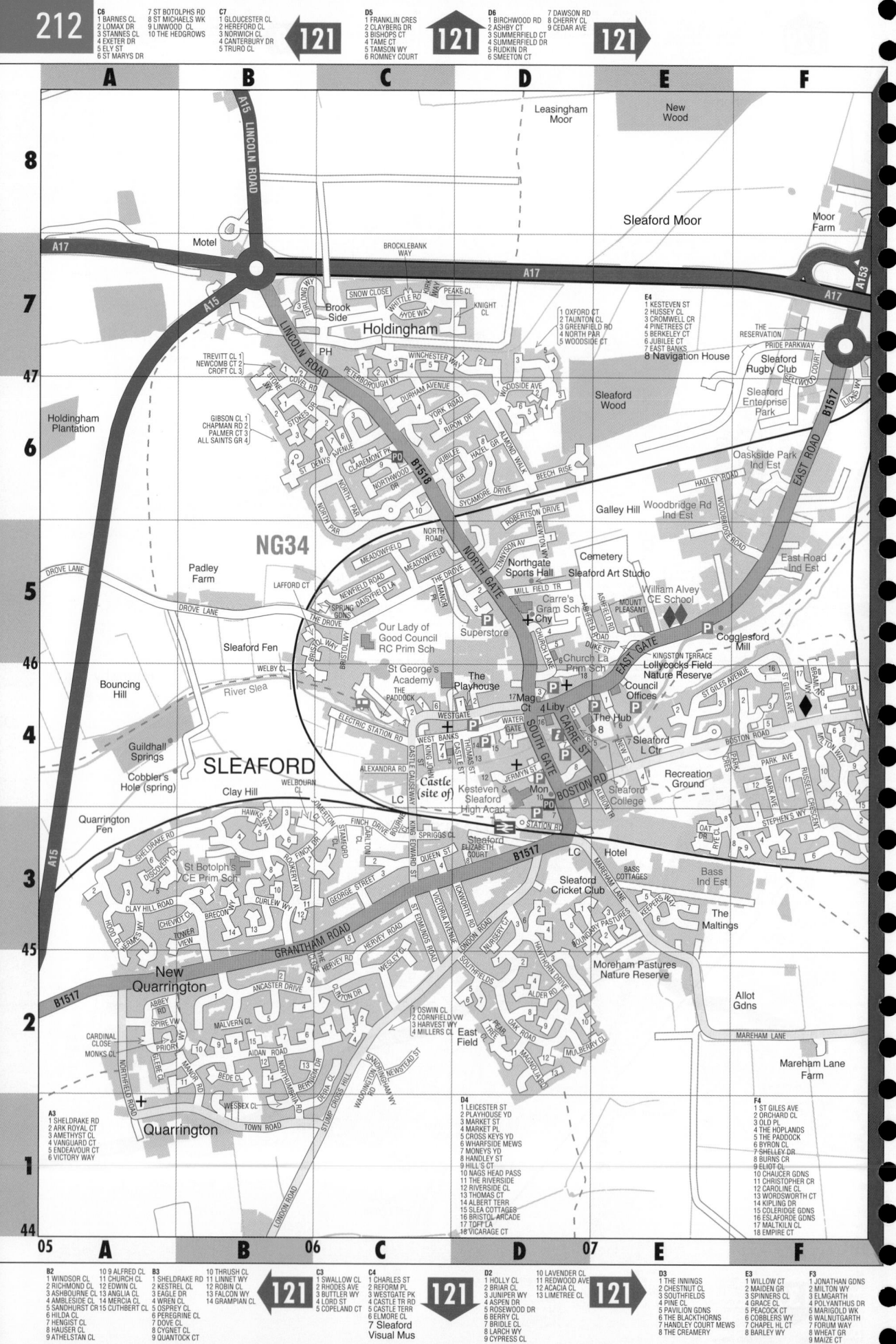

C6
1 BARNES CL
2 LOMAX DR
3 STANNES CL
4 EXETER DR
5 ELY ST
6 ST MARYS DR

7 ST BOTOLPHS RD
8 ST MICHAELS WK
9 LINWOOD CL
10 THE HEDGROWS

C7
1 GLOUCESTER CL
2 HEREFORD CL
3 NORWICH CL
4 CANTERBURY DR
5 TRURO CL

D5
1 FRANKLIN CRES
2 CLAYBERG DR
3 BISHOPS CT
4 TAME CT
5 TAMSON WY
6 ROMNEY COURT

D6
1 BIRCHWOOD RD
2 ASHBY CT
3 SUMMERFIELD CT
4 SUMMERFIELD DR
5 RUDKIN DR
6 SMEETON CT

7 DAWSON RD
8 CHERRY CL
9 CEDAR AVE

E4
1 KESTEVEN ST
2 HUSSEY CL
3 CROMWELL CR
4 PINETREES CT
5 BERKELEY CT
6 JUBILEE CL
7 EAST BANKS
8 Navigation House

A3
1 SHELDRAKE RD
2 ARK ROYAL CT
3 AMETHYST CL
4 VANGUARD CL
5 ENDEAVOUR CT
6 VICTORY WAY

D4
1 LEICESTER ST
2 PLAYHOUSE YD
3 MARKET ST
4 MARKET PL
5 CROSS KEYS YD
6 WHARFSIDE MEWS
7 MONEYS YD
8 HANDLEY ST
9 HILL'S CT
10 NAGS HEAD PASS
11 THE RIVERSIDE
12 RIVERSIDE CL
13 THOMAS CT
14 ALBERT TERR
15 SLEA COTTAGES
16 BRISTOL ARCADE
17 TOFT LA
18 VICARAGE CT

F4
1 ST GILES AVE
2 CHESTNUT CL
3 OLD PL
4 THE HOPLANDS
5 THE PADDOCK
6 BYRON CL
7 SHELLEY DR
8 BURNS CR
9 ELIOT CL
10 CHAUCER GDNS
11 CHRISTOPHER CR
12 CAROLINE CL
13 WORDSWORTH CT
14 KIPLING DR
15 COLERIDGE GDNS
16 ESLAFORDE GDNS
17 MALTKILN CL
18 EMPIRE CT

B2
1 WINDSOR CL
2 RICHMOND CL
3 ASHBOURNE CL
4 AMBLESIDE CL
5 SANDHURST CL
6 HILDA CL
7 HENGIST CL
8 HAUSER CL
9 ATHELSTAN CL

10 ALFRED CL
11 CHURCH CL
12 EDWIN CL
13 ANGLIA CL
14 MERCIA CL
15 CUTHBERT CL

B3
1 SHELDRAKE CL
2 KESTREL CL
3 EAGLE DR
4 WREN CL
5 OSPREY CL
6 PEREGRINE CL
7 DOVE CL
8 CYGNET CL
9 QUANTOCK CL

10 THRUSH CL
11 LINNET WY
12 ROBIN CL
13 FALCON WY
14 GRAMPIAN CL

C3
1 SWALLOW CL
2 RHODES AVE
3 BUTTLER WY
4 LORD ST
5 COPELAND ST

C4
1 CHARLES ST
2 REFORM PL
3 WESTGATE PK
4 CASTLE TR RD
5 CASTLE TERR
6 ELMORE CL
7 Sleaford Visual Mus

D2
1 HOLLY CL
2 BRIAR CL
3 JUNIPER WY
4 ASPEN DR
5 ROSEWOOD DR
6 BERRY CL
7 BRIDLE CL
8 LARCH WY
9 CYPRESS CL

10 LAVENDER CL
11 REDWOOD AVE
12 ACACIA CL
13 LIMETREE CL

D3
1 THE INNINGS
2 CHESTNUT CL
3 SOUTHFIELDS
4 PINE CL
5 PAVILION GDNS
6 THE BLACKTHORNS
7 HANDLEY COURT MEWS
8 THE CREAMERY

E3
1 WILLOW CT
2 MAIDEN GR
3 SPINNERS CL
4 GRACE CL
5 PEACOCK CT
6 COBBLERS WY
7 CHAPEL HL CT
8 BARLEY WY

F3
1 JONATHAN GDNS
2 MILTON WY
3 ELMGARTH
4 POLYANTHUS DR
5 MARIGOLD WK
6 WALNUTGARTH
7 FORUM WAY
8 WHEAT GR
9 MAIZE CL

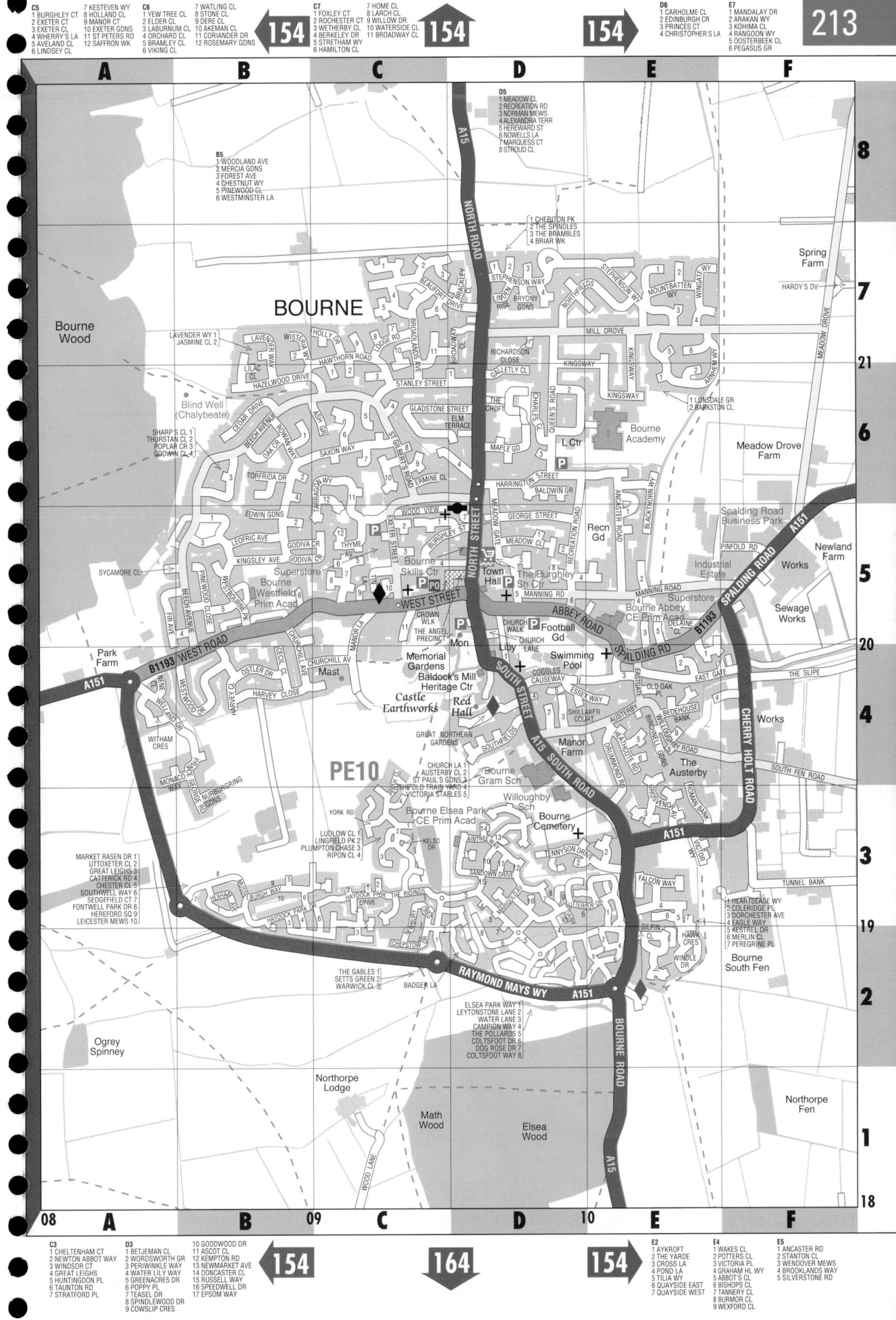

BOURNE

PE10

C5
1 BURGHLEY CT
2 EXETER CT
3 EXETER CL
4 WHERRY'S LA
5 AVELAND CL
6 LINDSEY CL
7 KESTEVEN WY
8 HOLLAND CL
9 MANOR CT
10 EXETER GDNS
11 ST PETERS RD
12 SAFFRON WK

C6
1 YEW TREE CL
2 ELDER CL
3 LABURNUM CL
4 ORCHARD DR
5 BRAMLEY CL
6 VIKING CL

B5
1 WOODLAND AVE
2 MERCIA GDNS
3 FOREST AVE
4 CHESTNUT WY
5 PINEWOOD CL
6 WESTMINSTER LA

B7
1 WATLING CL
2 STONE CL
3 DERE CL
4 AKEMAN CL

C7
1 FOXLEY CT
2 ROCHESTER CL
3 WETHERBY CL
4 BERKELEY DR
5 STRETHAM WY
6 HAMILTON CL

7 HOME CL
8 LARCH CL
9 WILLOW DR
10 WATERSIDE CL
11 BROADWAY CL

10 AKEMAN CL
11 CORIANDER DR
12 ROSEMARY GDNS

D5
1 MEADOW CL
2 RECREATION RD
3 NORMAN MEWS
4 ALEXANDRA TERR
5 HEREWARD ST
6 NOWELLS LA
7 MARQUESS CL
8 STROUD CL

D6
1 CARHOLME CL
2 EDINBURGH CR
3 PRINCES CT
4 CHRISTOPHER'S LA

E7
1 MANDALAY DR
2 ARAKAN WY
3 KOHIMA CL
4 RANGOON WY
5 OOSTERBEEK CL
6 PEGASUS GR

1 CHERITON PK
2 THE SPINDLES
3 THE BRAMBLES
4 BRIAR WK

C3
1 CHELTENHAM CT
2 NEWTON ABBOT WAY
3 WINDSOR CT
4 GREAT LEIGHS
5 HUNTINGDON PL
6 TAUNTON RD
7 STRATFORD PL

D3
1 BETJEMAN CL
2 WORDSWORTH GR
3 PERIWINKLE WAY
4 WATER LILY WAY
5 GREENACRES DR
6 POPPY PL
7 TEASEL DR
8 SPINDLEWOOD DR
9 COWSLIP CRES

10 GOODWOOD DR
11 ASCOT CL
12 KEMPTON RD
13 NEWMARKET AVE
14 DONCASTER CL
15 RUSSELL WAY
16 SPEEDWELL DR
17 EPSOM WY

E2
1 AYKROFT
2 THE YARDE
3 CROSS LA
4 POND LA
5 TILIA WY
6 QUAYSIDE EAST
7 QUAYSIDE WEST

E4
1 WAKES CL
2 POTTERS CL
3 VICTORIA PL
4 GRAHAM HL WY
5 ABBOT'S CL
6 BISHOPS CL
7 TANNERY CL
8 BURMOR CL
9 WEXFORD CL

E5
1 ANCASTER RD
2 STANTON CL
3 WENDOVER MEWS
4 BROOKLANDS WAY
5 SILVERSTONE RD

MARKET RASEN DR 1
UTTOXETER CL 2
GREAT LEIGHS 3
CATTERICK RD 4
CHESTER CL 5
SOUTHWELL WAY 6
SEDGEFIELD CT 7
FONTWELL PARK DR 8
HEREFORD SQ 9
LEICESTER MEWS 10

LUDLOW CL 1
LINGFIELD PK 2
PLUMPTON CHASE 3
RIPON CL 4

THE GABLES 1
SETTS GREEN 2
WARWICK CL 3

CHURCH LA 1
AUSTERBY CL 2
ST PAUL'S GDNS 3
THE OLD TRAIN YARD 4
VICTORIA STABLES 5

ELSEA PARK WAY 1
LEYTONSTONE LANE 2
WATER LANE 3
CAMPION WAY 4
THE POLLARDS 5
COLTSFOOT DR 6
DOG ROSE DR 7
COLTSFOOT WAY 8

1 HEARTSEASE WY
2 COLERIDGE PL
3 DORCHESTER AVE
4 EAGLE WAY
5 KESTREL DR
6 MERLIN CL
7 PEREGRINE PL

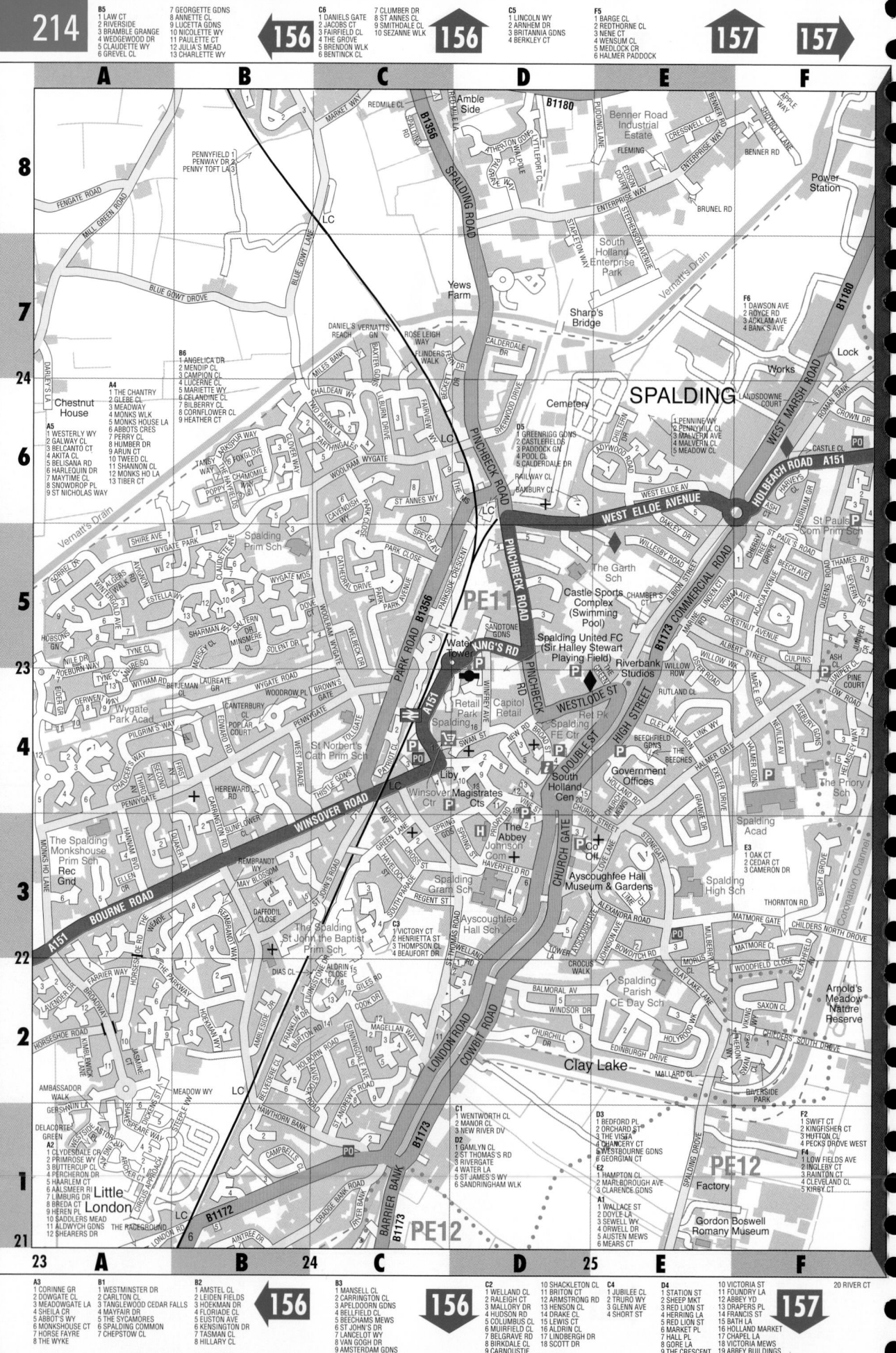
214
B5
1 LAW CT
2 RIVERSIDE
3 BRAMBLE GRANGE
4 WEDGEWOOD DR
5 CLAUDETTE WY
6 GREVEL CL
7 GEORGETTE GDNS
8 ANNETTE CL
9 LUCETTA GDNS
10 NICOLETTE WY
11 PAULETTE CT
12 JULIA'S MEAD
13 CHARLETTE WY
156
C6
1 DANIELS GATE
2 JACOBS CT
3 FAIRFIELD CL
4 THE GROVE
5 BRENDON WLK
6 BENTINCK CL
7 CLUMBER DR
8 ST ANNES CL
9 SMITHDALE CL
10 SEZANNE WLK
156
C5
1 LINCOLN WY
2 ARNHEM DR
3 BRITANNIA GDNS
4 BERKLEY CT
F5
1 BARGE CL
2 REDTHORNE CL
3 NENE CT
4 WENSUM CL
5 MEDLOCK CR
6 HALMER PADDOCK
157
157
A
B
C
D
E
F
8
7
6
5
4
3
2
1
Amble Side
B1180
Benner Road Industrial Estate
Power Station
South Holland Enterprise Park
Yews Farm
Sharp's Bridge
Vernatt's Drain
F6
1 DAWSON AVE
2 ROYCE RD
3 ACKLAM AVE
4 BANK'S AVE
Lock
Works
SPALDING
Cemetery
Chestnut House
A4
1 THE CHANTRY
2 GLEBE CL
3 MEADWAY
4 MONKS WLK
5 MONKS HOUSE LA
6 ABBOTS CRES
7 PERRY CL
8 HUMBER DR
9 ARUN CT
10 TWEED CL
11 SHANNON CL
12 MONKS HO LA
13 TIBER CT
A5
1 WESTERLY WY
2 GALWAY CL
3 BELCANTO CT
4 AKITA CL
5 BELISANA RD
6 HARLEQUIN DR
7 MAYTIME CL
8 SNOWDROP PL
9 ST NICHOLAS WAY
B6
1 ANGELICA DR
2 MENDIP CL
3 CAMPION CL
4 LUCERNE CL
5 MARIETTE WY
6 CELANDINE CL
7 BILBERRY CL
8 CORNFLOWER CL
9 HEATHER CT
D5
1 GREENRIGG GDNS
2 CASTLEFIELDS
3 PADDOCK GN
4 POOL CL
5 CALDERDALE DR
1 PENNINE WY
2 PENNYHILL CL
3 MALVERN AVE
4 MALVERN CL
5 MEADOW CL
WEST ELLOE AVENUE
HOLBEACH ROAD A151
WEST MARSH ROAD
PINCHBECK ROAD
SPALDING ROAD
Spalding Prim Sch
The Garth Sch
Castle Sports Complex (Swimming Pool)
Spalding United FC (Sir Halley Stewart Playing Field)
Riverbank Studios
St Pauls Com Prim Sch
PE11
Water Tower
KING'S RD
Retail Park
Capitol Retail
Spalding
Wygate Park Acad
St Norbert's Cath Prim Sch
Spalding FE Ctr
South Holland Cen
Government Offices
The Priory Sch
Spalding Acad
WINSOVER ROAD
Winsover Ctr
Liby
Magistrates Cts
The Abbey
Johnson Com
Co Off
Ayscoughfee Hall Museum & Gardens
Spalding High Sch
The Spalding Monkshouse Prim Sch
Rec Gnd
BOURNE ROAD
Spalding Gram Sch
Ayscoughfee Hall Sch
The Spalding St John the Baptist Prim Sch
E3
1 OAK CT
2 CEDAR CT
3 CAMERON DR
C3
1 VICTORY CT
2 HENRIETTA ST
3 THOMPSON CL
4 BEAUFORT DR
Coronation Channel
Spalding Parish CE Day Sch
Arnold's Meadow Nature Reserve
Clay Lake
LONDON ROAD
COWBIT ROAD
C1
1 WENTWORTH CL
2 MANOR CL
3 NEW RIVER DV
D2
1 GAMLYN CL
2 ST THOMAS'S RD
3 RIVERGATE
4 WATER LA
5 ST JAMES'S WY
6 SANDRINGHAM WLK
D3
1 BEDFORD PL
2 ORCHARD ST
3 THE VISTA
4 CHANCERY CT
5 WESTBOURNE GDNS
6 GEORGIAN CT
E2
1 HAMPTON CL
2 MARLBOROUGH AVE
3 CLARENCE GDNS
A1
1 WALLACE ST
2 DOYLE LA
3 SEWELL WY
4 ORWELL DR
5 AUSTEN MEWS
6 MEARS CT
F2
1 SWIFT CT
2 KINGFISHER CT
3 HUTTON CL
4 PECKS DROVE WEST
F4
1 LOW FIELDS AVE
2 INGLEBY CT
3 RAINTON CT
4 CLEVELAND CL
5 KIRBY CT
PE12
Factory
Gordon Boswell Romany Museum
A2
1 CLYDESDALE CR
2 PRIMROSE WY
3 BUTTERCUP CL
4 PERCHERON DR
5 HAARLEM CT
6 AALSMEER RI
7 LIMBURG DR
8 BREDA CT
9 HEREN PL
10 SADDLERS MEAD
11 ALDWYCH GDNS
12 SHEARERS DR
Little London
PE12
23
24
25
A3
1 CORINNE GR
2 DOWGATE CL
3 MEADOWGATE LA
4 SHEILA CR
5 ABBOT'S WY
6 MONKSHOUSE CT
7 HORSE FAYRE
8 THE WYKE
B1
1 WESTMINSTER DR
2 CARLTON CL
3 TANGLEWOOD CEDAR FALLS
4 MAYFAIR DR
5 THE SYCAMORES
6 SPALDING COMMON
7 CHEPSTOW CL
B2
1 AMSTEL CL
2 LEIDEN FIELDS
3 HOEKMAN DR
4 FLORIADE CL
5 EUSTON AVE
6 KENSINGTON DR
7 TASMAN CL
8 HILLARY CL
156
B3
1 MANSELL CL
2 CARRINGTON CL
3 APELDOORN GDNS
4 BELLFIELD CL
5 BEECHAMS MEWS
6 ST JOHN'S DR
7 LANCELOT WY
8 VAN GOGH DR
9 AMSTERDAM GDNS
156
C2
1 WELLAND CL
2 RALEIGH CT
3 MALLORY DR
4 HUDSON RD
5 COLUMBUS CL
6 MUIRFIELD CL
7 BELGRAVE RD
8 BIRKDALE CL
9 CARNOUSTIE
10 SHACKLETON CL
11 BRITON CT
12 ARMSTRONG RD
13 HENSON CL
14 DRAKE CL
15 LEWIS CT
16 ALDRIN CL
17 LINDBERGH DR
18 SCOTT DR
C4
1 JUBILEE CL
2 TRURO WY
3 GLENN AVE
4 SHORT ST
D4
1 STATION ST
2 SHEEP MKT
3 RED LION ST
4 HERRING LA
5 RED LION ST
6 MARKET PL
7 HALL PL
8 GORE LA
9 THE CRESCENT
10 VICTORIA ST
11 FOUNDRY LA
12 ABBEY YD
13 DRAPERS PL
14 FRANCIS ST
15 BATH LA
16 HOLLAND MARKET
17 CHAPEL LA
18 VICTORIA MEWS
19 ABBEY BUILDINGS
20 RIVER CT
157

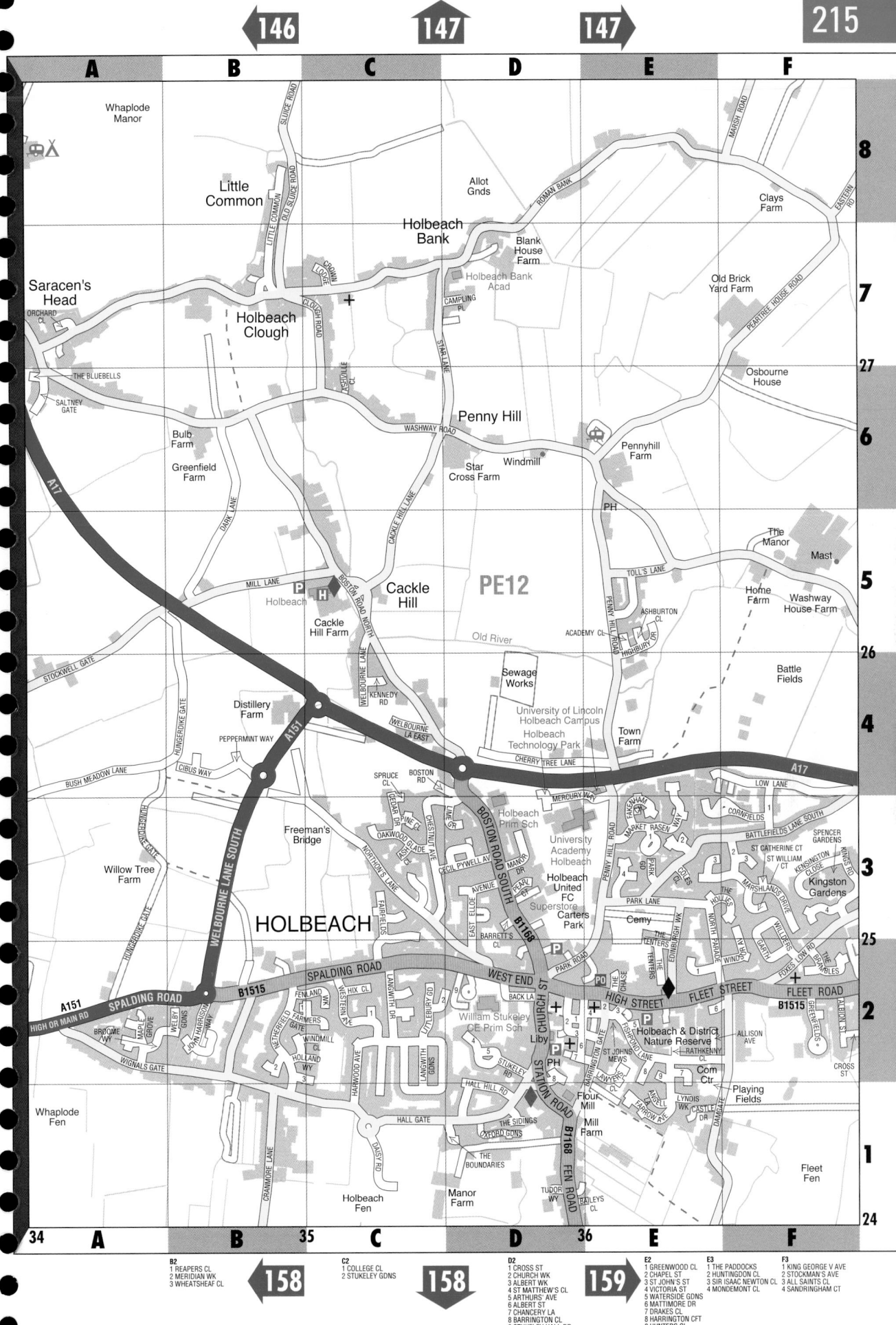

A B C D E F

8
7
27
6
5
26
4
3
25
2
1
24

Whaplode Manor

Little Common

Holbeach Bank

Allot Gnds

Clays Farm

Roman Bank

Blank House Farm

Old Brick Yard Farm

Holbeach Clough

Saracen's Head

ORCHARD CL

THE BLUEBELLS

SALTNEY GATE

Holbeach Bank Acad

CAMPLING PL

Osbourne House

Penny Hill

Windmill

Pennyhill Farm

PH

Bulb Farm

Greenfield Farm

WASHWAY ROAD

Star Cross Farm

The Manor

Mast

A17

DARK LANE

CACKLE HILL LANE

MILL LANE

Cackle Hill

PE12

TOLL'S LANE

Home Farm

Washway House Farm

Cackle Hill Farm

Old River

PENNY HILL ROAD

ASHBURTON CL

HIGHBURY DR

ACADEMY CL

Distillery Farm

A151

PEPPERMINT WAY

Sewage Works

University of Lincoln Holbeach Campus

Holbeach Technology Park

Battle Fields

Town Farm

CIBUS WAY

BUSH MEADOW LANE

WELBOURNE LA EAST

CHERRY TREE LANE

A17

LOW LANE

STOCKWELL GATE

SPRUCE CL

BOSTON RD

MERCURY WAY

HUNGERBROKE GATE

Freeman's Bridge

Holbeach Prim Sch

University Academy Holbeach

CORNFIELDS

HACKNAM

MARKET RASEN

BATTLEFIELDS LANE SOUTH

SPENCER GARDENS

St William CT

KENSINGTON CLOSE

Kingston Gardens

Willow Tree Farm

WELBOURNE LANE SOUTH

HOLBEACH

Holbeach United FC Superstore Carters Park

Cemy

St Catherine CT

Park Lane

THE TENTERS

EDINBURGH WK

NORTH PARADE

MARSHLANDS DRIVE

WILLIERS

GARTH

FOXES LOW RD

THE BRAMBLES

25

SPALDING ROAD

WEST END

HIGH STREET

FLEET STREET

FLEET ROAD

B1515

A151

HIGH OR MAIN RD

SPALDING ROAD

B1515

BROOME WY

MAPLE GROVE

WELBY GDNS

JOHN HARRISON CL

FENLAND WK

WESTERN AV

HIX CL

LANGWITH DR

LUTTLEBURY GD

William Stukeley CE Prim Sch

Holbeach Liby

BACK LA

CHURCH ST

PO

THE CHASE

Park Road

P

PH

ST JOHNS MEWS

Holbeach & District Nature Reserve

RATHKENNY CL

ALLISON AVE

ALLISON AVE

CROSS ST

Whaplode Fen

WIGNALS GATE

HARWOOD AVE

HOLLAND WY

WINDMILL CL

LANGWITH GDNS

HALL HILL RD

STUKELEY RD

STATION ROAD

HARRINGTON GATE

LAWYERS

FLOUR FARROW AV

LYNDIS WK

DAMGATE

Com Ctr

Playing Fields

HALL GATE

THE SIDINGS

OXFORD GDNS

Flour Mill

Mill Farm

CRANMORE LANE

DAISY RD

Holbeach Fen

Manor Farm

THE BOUNDARIES

B1168

FEN ROAD

TUDOR WY

BAILEYS CL

Fleet Fen

34 A B 35 C D 36 E F

B2
1 REAPERS CL
2 MERIDIAN WK
3 WHEATSHEAF CL

C2
1 COLLEGE CL
2 STUKELEY GDNS

D2
1 CROSS ST
2 CHURCH WK
3 ALBERT WK
4 ST MATTHEW'S CL
5 ARTHURS' AVE
6 ALBERT ST
7 CHANCERY LA
8 BARRINGTON CL
9 STUKELEY HALL DR

E2
1 GREENWOOD CL
2 CHAPEL ST
3 ST JOHN'S ST
4 VICTORIA ST
5 WATERSIDE GDNS
6 MATTIMORE DR
7 DRAKES CL
8 HARRINGTON CFT
9 HUNTERS CL

E3
1 THE PADDOCKS
2 HUNTINGDON CL
3 SIR ISAAC NEWTON CL
4 MONDEMONT CL

F3
1 KING GEORGE V AVE
2 STOCKMAN'S AVE
3 ALL SAINTS CL
4 SANDRINGHAM CT

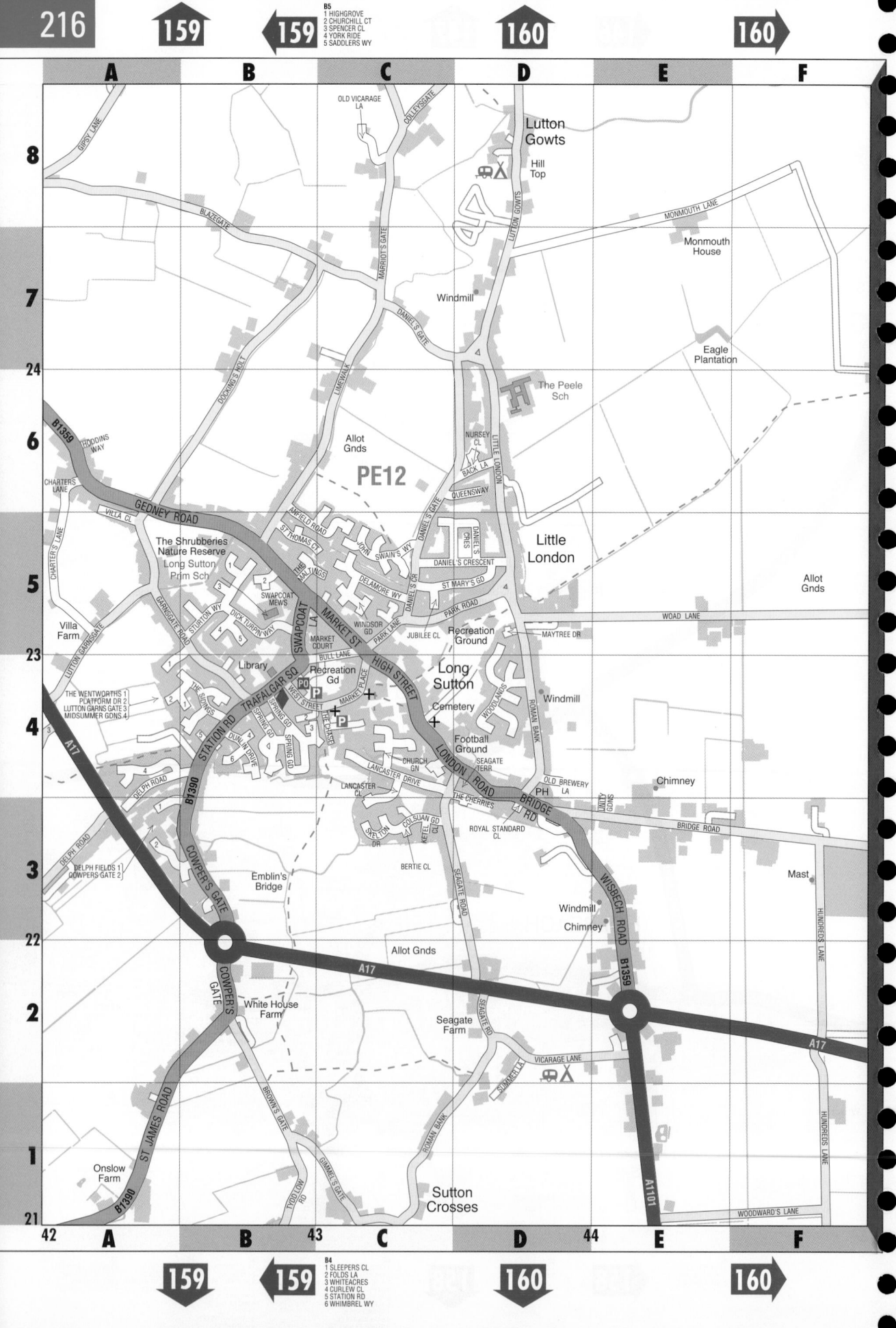

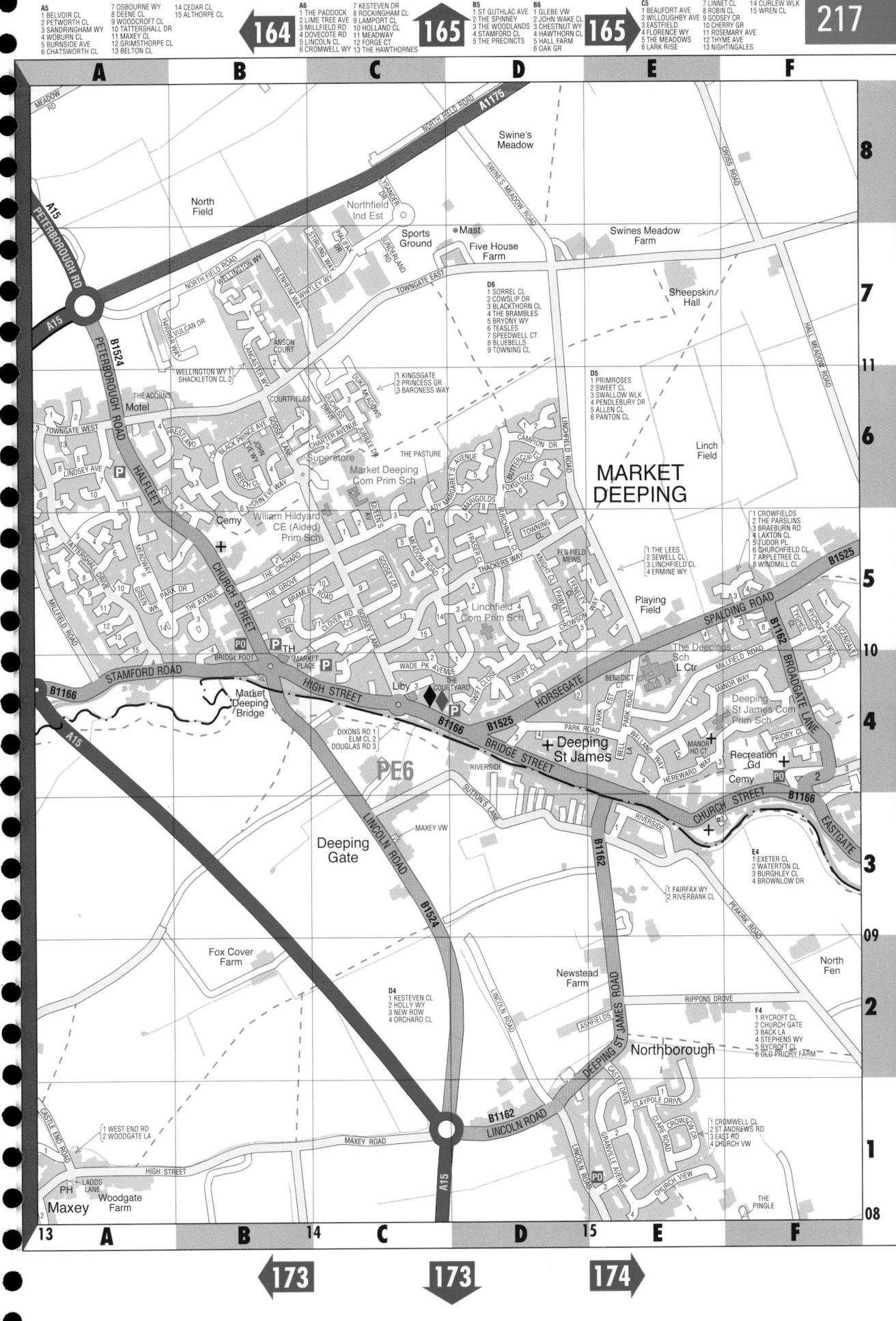

217
A5
1 BELVOIR CL
2 PETWORTH CL
3 SANDRINGHAM WY
4 WOBURN CL
5 BURNSIDE AVE
6 CHATSWORTH CL
7 OSBOURNE WY
8 DEENE CL
9 WOODCROFT CL
10 TATTERSHALL DR
11 MAXEY CL
12 GRIMSTHORPE CL
13 BELTON CL
14 CEDAR CL
15 ALTHORPE CL
164
A6
1 THE PADDOCK
2 LIME TREE AVE
3 MILLFIELD RD
4 DOVECOTE RD
5 LINCOLN CL
6 CROMWELL WY
7 KESTEVEN DR
8 ROCKINGHAM CL
9 LAMPORT CL
10 HOLLAND CL
11 MEADWAY
12 FORGE CT
13 THE HAWTHORNES
165
B5
1 ST GUTHLAC AVE
2 THE SPINNEY
3 THE WOODLANDS
4 STAMFORD CL
5 THE PRECINCTS
B6
1 GLEBE VW
2 JOHN WAKE CL
3 CHESTNUT WY
4 HAWTHORN CL
5 HALL FARM
6 OAK GR
165
C5
1 BEAUFORT AVE
2 WILLOUGHBY AVE
3 EASTFIELD
4 FLORENCE WY
5 THE MEADOWS
6 LARK RISE
7 LINNET CL
8 ROBIN CL
9 GODSEY CR
10 CHERRY GR
11 ROSEMARY AVE
12 THYME AVE
13 NIGHTINGALES
14 CURLEW WLK
15 WREN CL
A B C D E F
8 7 11 6 5 10 4 3 09 2 1 08
13 14 15
MEADOW RD
NORTH FIELD ROAD
A1175
Swine's Meadow
SWINE'S MEADOW ROAD
CROSS ROAD
North Field
A15
PETERBOROUGH RD
Northfield Ind Est
LYSANDER DR
Sports Ground
Mast
Five House Farm
Swines Meadow Farm
STIRLING WAY
HALIFAX DR
SUNDERLAND RD
WHITLEY WY
NORTH FIELD ROAD
WELLINGTON WY
BLENHEIM WAY
TOWNGATE EAST
D6
1 SORREL CL
2 COWSLIP DR
3 BLACKTHORN CL
4 THE BRAMBLES
5 BRYONY WY
6 TEASLES
7 SPEEDWELL CT
8 BLUEBELLS
9 TOWNING CL
Sheepskin Hall
HALL MEADOW ROAD
B1524
PETERBOROUGH ROAD
VULCAN DR
HARRIER WAY
LANCASTER WY
ANSON COURT
WELLINGTON WY 1
SHACKLETON CL 2
1 KINGSGATE
2 PRINCESS GR
3 BARONESS WAY
D5
1 PRIMROSES
2 SWEET CL
3 SWALLOW WLK
4 PENDLEBURY DR
5 ALLEN CL
6 PANTON CL
THE ACORNS
Motel
COURTFIELDS
DUKE MEADOWS
DUCHESS DRIVE
TOWNGATE WEST
PRESTLAND
BLACK PRINCE AVE
JOHN EVE WY
GODSEY LANE
CHARTER AVENUE
JUBILEE DR
CAMPION DR
LINCHFIELD ROAD
Linch Field
LINDSEY AVE
HALFLEET
Superstore
THE PASTURE
LADY MARGARET'S AVENUE
BUTTERCUP CT
Market Deeping Com Prim Sch
FOXGLOVES
MARKET DEEPING
BEECH CL
JOHN EVE WAY
MARIGOLDS
Cemy
Wiliam Hildyard CE (Aided) Prim Sch
QUEEN'S AV
BURCHNALL CL
TOWNING CL
1 CROWFIELDS
2 THE PARSLINS
3 BRAEBURN RD
4 LAXTON CL
5 TUDOR PL
6 CHURCHFIELD CL
7 APPLETREE CL
8 WINDMILL CL
TATTERSHALL DRIVE
MEADWAY
THE ORCHARD
MEADOW ROAD
FRASER CL
THACKERS WAY
KNIGHT CL
FEN FIELD MEWS
1 THE LEES
2 SEWELL CL
3 LINCHFIELD CL
4 ERMINE WY
B1525
GREEN WK
PARK DR
CHURCH STREET
THE GROVE
BRAMLEY ROAD
GODSEY CR
PAWLETT CL
FENELEY CL
Playing Field
MILLFIELD ROAD
THE AVENUE
STILL CL
CLOVER RD
GODSEY LANE
Linchfield Com Prim Sch
CROWSON WAY
SPALDING ROAD
RYCROFT AVENUE
ASCENDALE
TYGHES CL
B1162
BROADGATE LANE
The Deepings Sch L Ctr
MILLFIELD ROAD
PO
P
TH
BRIDGE FOOT
MARKET PLACE
WADE PK AVENUE
Liby
THE COURTYARD
SWIFT CLOSE
SWIFT CL
HORSEGATE
BENEDICT CT
MANOR WAY
STAMFORD ROAD
B1166
HIGH STREET
Market Deeping Bridge
PARK EST
PARK ROAD
Deeping St James Com Prim Sch
DIXONS RD 1
ELM CL 2
DOUGLAS RD 3
PARK ROAD
Deeping St James
BELL LA
WELLAND WAY
MANOR HO CT
PRIORY CL
Recreation Gd
BRIDGE STREET
PE6
RIVERSIDE
HEREWARD WAY
Cemy
SUTTON'S LANE
RIVERSIDE
CHURCH STREET
EASTGATE
MAXEY VW
Deeping Gate
LINCOLN ROAD
E4
1 EXETER CL
2 WATERTON CL
3 BURGHLEY CL
4 BROWNLOW DR
1 FAIRFAX WY
2 RIVERBANK CL
PEAKIRK ROAD
North Fen
Fox Cover Farm
Newstead Farm
D4
1 KESTEVEN CL
2 HOLLY WY
3 NEW ROW
4 ORCHARD CL
LINCOLN ROAD
RIPPONS DROVE
DEEPING ST JAMES ROAD
ASHFIELDS
F4
1 RYCROFT CL
2 CHURCH GATE
3 BACK LA
4 STEPHENS WY
5 RYCROFT CL
6 OLD PRIORY FARM
Northborough
CASTLE DRIVE
CLAYPOLE DRIVE
B1162
LINCOLN ROAD
CLARE ROAD
CROWSON CR
1 CROMWELL CL
2 ST ANDREWS RD
3 EAST RD
4 CHURCH VW
CASTLE END ROAD
1 WEST END RD
2 WOODGATE LA
MAXEY ROAD
GRANVILLE AVENUE
LINCOLN ROAD
HIGH STREET
LADDS LANE
PH
Woodgate Farm
Maxey
CHURCH VIEW
THE PINGLE
173
173
174

Map index references:

C7
1 FOXGLOVE RD
2 MEADOWSWEET
3 SWEETBRIAR
4 TOBIAS GR
5 BLACKTHORN
6 CLOVER GDNS

171

171

D6
1 FIR RD
2 BRAMBLE GR
3 ANGUS CL
4 SORREL CL
5 MORAY CL
6 ASH PL

D7
1 LAVENDER WY
2 BLUEBELL RD
3 BUTTERCUP CL
4 CAMPION CL
5 FOREST GDNS
6 BIRCH RD

E5
1 TENNYSON WY
2 KEATS GR
3 KIPLING CL
4 LUFFENHAM CL
5 LOTTESMORE RD
6 EXTON CL

E6
1 BELVOIR CL
2 WALCOT WY
3 BARNWELL RD
4 ROCKINGHAM RD
5 GLENEAGLES CL
6 FALKIRK CL

7 OBAN CL
8 CROMARTY RD
9 MELROSE CL
10 MONTROSE CL
11 TROON CL
12 SHELLEY CL
13 AUDUS PL

14 LAUGHTON DR
15 BRADSHAW CL
16 CLAPTON CL

F6
1 HARDWICK RD
2 ELTON CL
3 WAVERLEY PL
4 CALEDONIAN RD
5 BURNS RD
6 MASON DRIVE
7 WINTERTON CL
8 JACKSON WAY

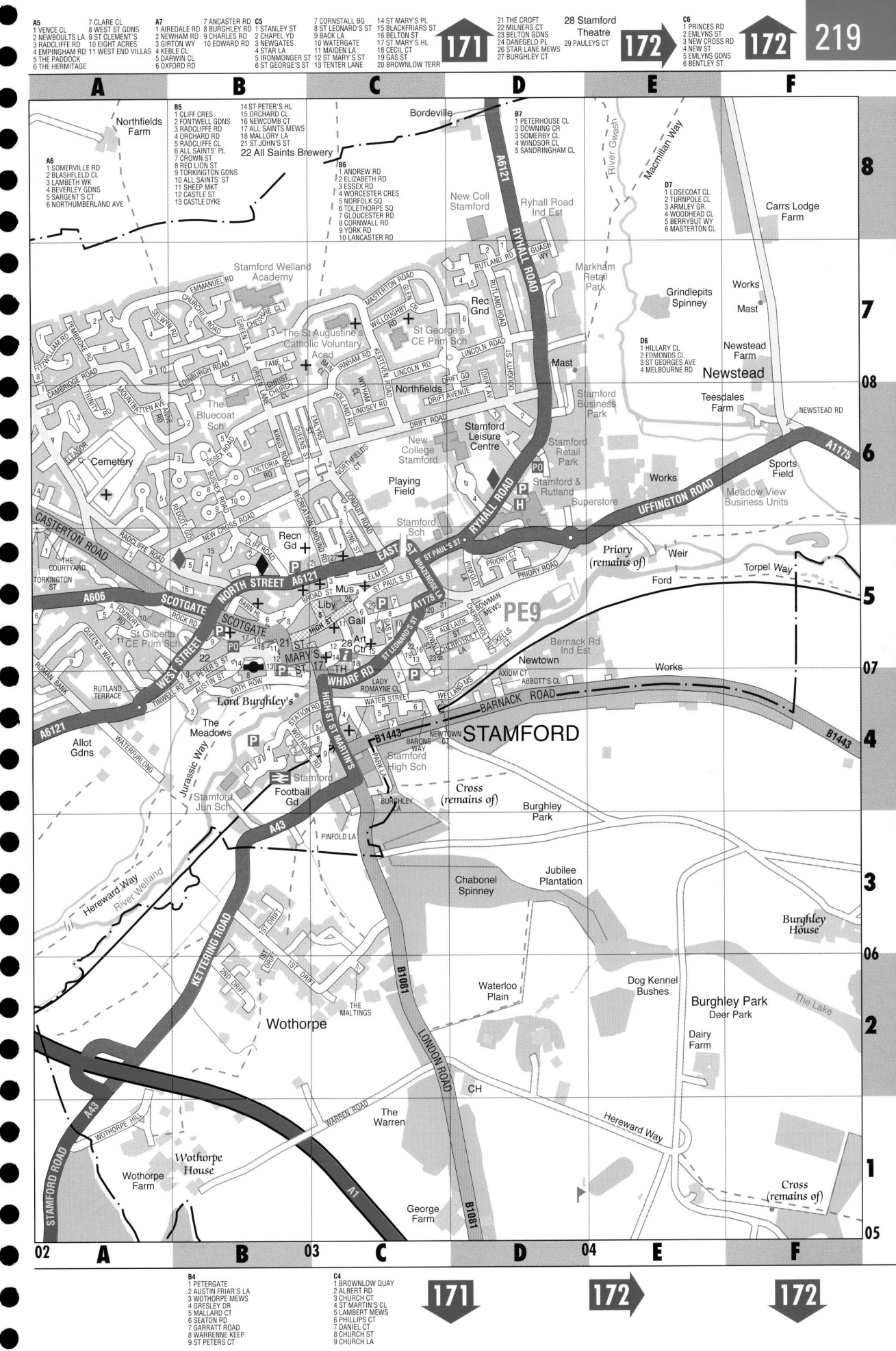

A5
1 VENCE CL
2 NEWBOULTS LA
3 RADCLIFFE RD
4 EMPINGHAM RD
5 THE PADDOCK
6 THE HERMITAGE

7 CLARE CL
8 WEST ST GDNS
9 ST CLEMENT'S
10 EIGHT ACRES
11 WEST END VILLAS

A6
1 SOMERVILLE RD
2 BLASHFIELD CL
3 LAMBETH WK
4 BEVERLEY GDNS
5 SARGENT'S CT
6 NORTHUMBERLAND AVE

A7
1 AIREDALE RD
2 NEWHAM RD
3 GIRTON WY
4 KEBLE CL
5 DARWIN CL
6 OXFORD RD

7 ANCASTER RD
8 BURGHLEY LA
9 CHARLES RD
10 EDWARD RD

B5
1 CLIFF CRES
2 FONTWELL GDNS
3 RADCLIFFE RD
4 ORCHARD RD
5 RADCLIFFE CL
6 ALL SAINTS' PL
7 CROWN ST
8 RED LION ST
9 TORKINGTON GDNS
10 ALL SAINTS' ST
11 SHEEP MKT
12 CASTLE ST
13 CASTLE DYKE

14 ST PETER'S HL
15 ORCHARD CL
16 NEWCOMB CT
17 ALL SAINTS MEWS
18 MALLORY LA
21 ST JOHN'S ST
22 All Saints Brewery

B6
1 ANDREW RD
2 ELIZABETH RD
3 ESSEX RD
4 WORCESTER CRES
5 NORFOLK SQ
6 TOLETHORPE SQ
7 GLOUCESTER RD
8 CORNWALL RD
9 YORK RD
10 LANCASTER RD

C5
1 STANLEY ST
2 CHAPEL YD
3 NEWGATES
4 STAR LA
6 ST GEORGE'S ST

7 CORNSTALL BG
8 ST LEONARD'S ST
9 BACK LA
10 WATERGATE
11 MAIDEN LA
12 ST MARY'S ST
13 TENTER LANE

14 ST MARY'S PL
15 BLACKFRIARS ST
16 BELTON ST
17 ST MARY'S ST
18 CECIL CT
19 GAS ST
20 BROWNLOW TERR

B7
1 PETERHOUSE CL
2 DOWNING CR
3 SOMERBY CL
4 WINDSOR CL
5 SANDRINGHAM CL

21 THE CROFT
22 MILNERS CT
23 BELTON GDNS
24 DANEGELD PL
26 STAR LANE MEWS
27 BURGHLEY CT

D6
1 HILLARY CL
2 EDMONDS CL
3 ST GEORGES AVE
4 MELBOURNE RD

D7
1 LOSECOAT CL
2 TURNPOLE CL
3 ARMLEY GR
4 WOODHEAD CL
5 BERRYBUT WY
6 MASTERTON CL

C6
1 PRINCES RD
2 EMLYNS ST
3 NEW CROSS RD
4 NEW ST
5 EMLYNS GDNS
6 BENTLEY ST

28 Stamford Theatre
29 PAULEYS CT

171 172 172

B4
1 PETERGATE
2 AUSTIN FRIAR'S LA
3 WOTHORPE MEWS
4 GRESLEY DR
5 MALLARD CT
6 SEATON RD
7 GARRATT ROAD
8 WARRENNE KEEP
9 ST PETERS CT

C4
1 BROWNLOW QUAY
2 ALBERT RD
3 CHURCH CT
4 ST MARTIN'S CL
5 LAMBERT MEWS
6 PHILLIPS CT
7 DANIEL CT
8 CHURCH ST
9 CHURCH LA

173
173
174

F5
1 ROWLAND CT
2 FAR PASTURE
3 MIDDLE PASTURE
4 HOMEPASTURE
5 LONG PASTURE
6 CANDIDUS CT

7 DERWOOD GR

A B C D E F

8

OAK RD
CHESTNUT CL
HELPSTON ROAD
HELPSTON ROAD B1443

House
Farm

Arthur Mellows
Village College

HIGH ST   Glinton
PH
Peakirk-cum-Glinton
CE Prim Sch
Cemy

PO

B1443   PEAKIRK ROAD   ST PEGA'S ROAD

CLAREMON WAY
THE WILLOWS
WELMORE ROAD
SCOTTS RD
HOLMES RD

D8
1 PEMBROKE GR
2 ST BENEDICTS CL

Werrington
Lakes

FOXCOVERT ROAD

7

LINCOLN ROAD B1443

C8
1 LINCOLN RD
2 THE GREEN
3 NORTH FEN RD
4 SCHOOL LA
5 RECTORY GDNS
6 WESTBOURNE DR

A15

A15

D7
1 ASHBURN CL
2 NEAVERSON RD

A15

Fox
Covert

KYVERSTONE
SOBRITE WAY
BARBERS
ASH PK
TEMPLE
GRANGE
WOODHALL

06

Works

WATERWORKS LANE

LINCOLN RD

E5
1 KINGSBRIDGE CT
2 THE PADDOCKS
3 GASCOIGNE
4 MERELADE GR

TALLGATE
REDBRIDGE   HODGSON AVENUE
STATSFIELD
ABBOTTS GR
SAPPERTON
WYCLIFFE GR

6

SUNNYMEAD

SOMERVILLE
DAVID'S LANE
TWELVETREE AVENUE
PLEASANT

PARTRIDGE GR

LINCOLN ROAD

5

PE6

WILLIAM LAW
CE Prim Sch

MONKS GR
TWINWRIGHT

WERRINGTON PARKWAY

05

Steeping
Wood

DAVID'S CL DAVID'S GATE
CARDINAL'S GATE
CRANEMOOR
CANDEFIELD
LOXLEY
SWALLOWFIELD
HAZEL CROFT

Werrington
Sports Ctr

Liby

Ken Stimpson
Com Sch   FOXCOVERT
ROAD

4

WOODCROFT ROAD

LC

Gate House
Farm

LAMBEK

FYNSH CT

SOUTHWELL CL
RUSHTON AVE
GREENACRES

PRIORS
GATE

Werrington
PE4

COVENTRY CL

SALISBURY ROAD

LINCOLN ROAD

RIPON
CHURCH STREET
TYLERS
MEWS

CANTERBURY RD
LICHFIELD AV
EDINBURGH AV

BIRWELLS GR
BRINDLE CR

RIVENDALE

04

WOODCROFT ROAD

HURN ROAD

PAPYRUS ROAD

STAVERTON ROAD

WERRINGTON PARKWAY

JOHN WESLEY
ROAD

CARSON DRIVE

LINCOLN ROAD

SHARMAN
LEAS

DUKESMEAD

BENEDICT SQ

BELEOST

BARNES RD

Dukesmead
Mobile Home
Pk
Werrington Gr
Caravan Park
Brookfield
Home Park

3

STAMFORD ROAD

Belham
Wood

F1
1 WATERGALL
2 NORBURN
3 BRETTON WY
4 MARHOLM RD
5 MARHOLM RD

CONNISBY RD

Brookfields
Industrial
Park

2

Poplar
Farm
Manor
Farm
WATER END
P
PH

GASTON RD

Marholm

Pocock's
Wood
Cemetery
Peterborough
Crem

WALTON ROAD

STIRLING WAY

CONNISBY RD

PE3

OLDBROOK

Planet
Ice

MALLARD RD

BRETTON WAY
LINKSIDE

MANCETTER
SQUARE

1

STAXTON CL

Mucklands
Wood   DUNSBERRY

MOWBRAY RD

NEWBURN

GURNARD
LEYS
OUTFIELD

BRETTON WAY

MEAD CL

02

14   A   B   15   C   D   16   E   F

173
224
225

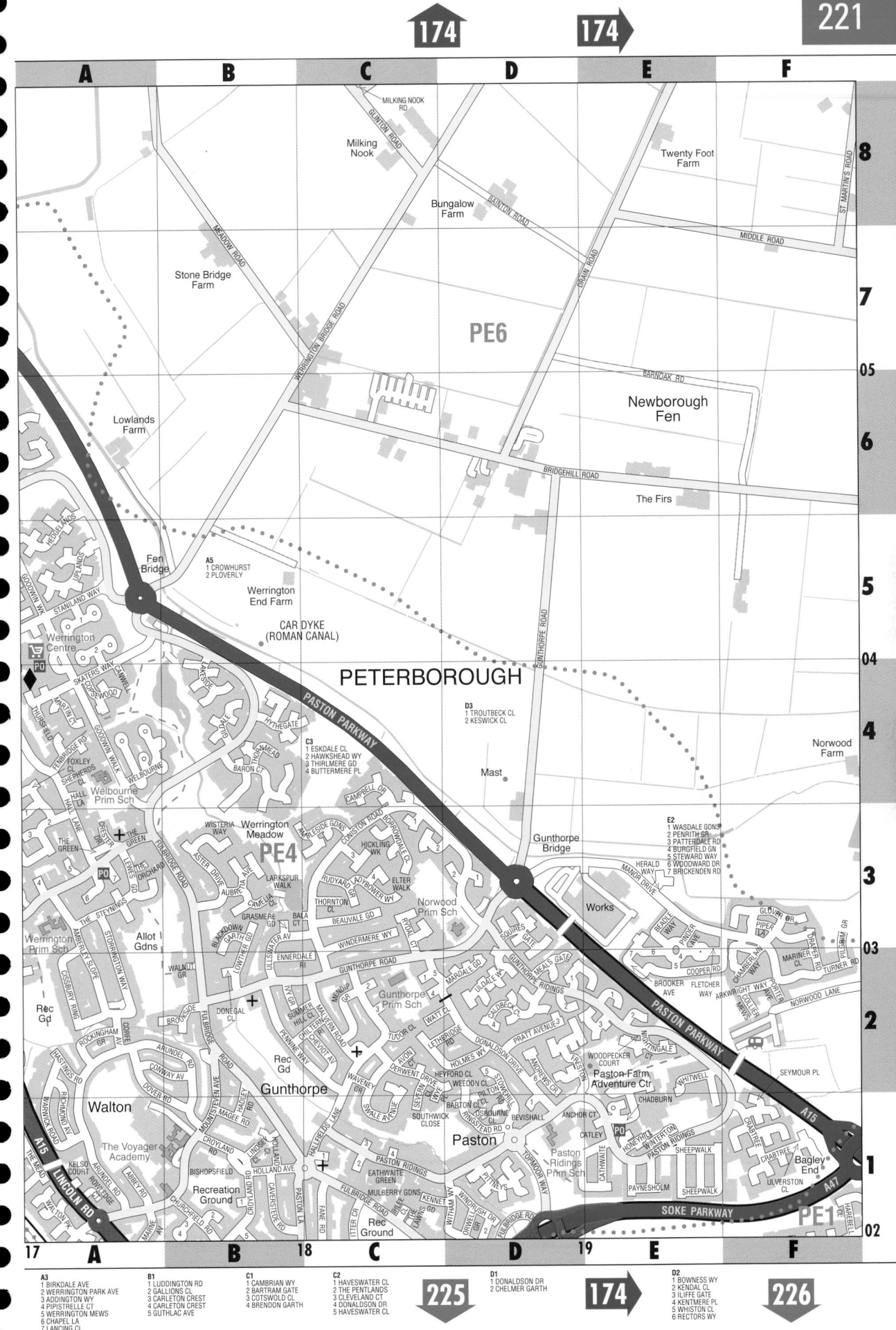

174 174

PE6

Newborough
Fen

PETERBOROUGH

Milking Nook

MILKING NOOK RD

GLINTON ROAD

Bungalow
Farm

RAINTON ROAD

Twenty Foot
Farm

MIDDLE ROAD

ST MARTIN'S RD

DRAIN ROAD

BARNOAK RD

Stone Bridge
Farm

MEADOW ROAD

WERRINGTON BRIDGE ROAD

Lowlands
Farm

BRIDGEHILL ROAD

The Firs

Fen
Bridge

A5
1 CROWHURST
2 PLOVERLY

Werrington
End Farm

CAR DYKE
(ROMAN CANAL)

GUNTHORPE ROAD

Norwood
Farm

Werrington
Centre

D3
1 TROUTBECK CL
2 KESWICK CL

PASTON PARKWAY

C3
1 ESKDALE CL
2 HAWKSHEAD WY
3 THIRLMERE GD
4 BUTTERMERE PL

Mast

E2
1 WASDALE GDNS
2 PENRITH SR
3 PATTERDALE RD
4 BURGFIELD GN
5 STEWARD WAY
6 WOODWARD DR
7 BRICKENDEN RD

Gunthorpe
Bridge

Welbourne
Prim Sch

WISTERIA
WAY

Werrington
Meadow

PE4

Larkspur
Walk

Norwood
Prim Sch

Works

Werrington
Prim Sch

Allot
Gdns

Gunthorpe
Prim Sch

PASTON PARKWAY

Rec
Gd

GUNTHORPE ROAD

Rec
Gd

Gunthorpe

Walton

The Voyager
Academy

Recreation
Ground

Paston

Paston Farm
Adventure Ctr

Paston
Ridings
Prim Sch

Rec
Ground

Bagley
End

LINCOLN RD

A15

SOKE PARKWAY

A47

PE1

A3
1 BIRKDALE AVE
2 WERRINGTON PARK AVE
3 ADDINGTON WY
4 PIPISTRELLE CT
5 WERRINGTON MEWS
6 CHAPEL LA
7 LANCING CL

B1
1 LUDDINGTON RD
2 GALLIONS CL
3 CARLETON CREST
4 CARLETON CREST
5 GUTHLAC AVE

C1
1 CAMBRIAN WY
2 BARTRAM GATE
3 COTSWOLD CL
4 BRENDON GARTH

C2
1 HAVESWATER CL
2 THE PENTLANDS
3 CLEVELAND CT
4 DONALDSON DR
5 HAVESWATER CL

D1
1 DONALDSON DR
2 CHELMER GARTH

D2
1 BOWNESS WY
2 KENDAL CL
3 ILIFFE GATE
4 KENTMERE PL
5 WHISTON CL
6 RECTORS WY

225 174 226

172

A
B
C
D
E
F
Bushey Wood
Gravel Pit
Lady Wood
Dearden Wood
PE9
Wall Spinney
Beech Spinney
Crow Spinney
SUTTON HEATH ROAD
Hereward Way
Sutton Wood
PE6
Mast
A1 Stamford
Sacrewell Lodge Farm
OLD RECTORY DR
RUSSELL HILL
WINDGATE WAY
Northamptonshire STREET ATLAS
Sutton Heath
Sacrewell Farm and Country Centre
OLD NORTH RD
THACKERS CL
Top Field Spinney
Wansford
PE8
A47 Leicester
A47
LEICESTER RD
Mast
PE5
ROBINS WOOD
ROBINS FIELD
BLACK SWAN SPINNEY
SWANHILL
OLD NORTH RD
OLD LEICESTER ROAD
NENE CL
PETERBOROUGH RD
A6118
River Nene
Nene Way
YARWELL RD
BRIDGE END
A1
Wansford
A47
WANSFORD ROAD
Old Hill Farm
Wansford Bridge
THE DRIFT
LONDON RD
Nene Way
PO PH
B671
CHAPEL CT
Stibbington
NENE WAY
Manor Farm
Stibbington Hall
CHURCH LA
OLD GREAT NORTH RD
ROMAN DR
CHURCH LANE
CHURCH LANE
NENE WY
LOVERS LA
GRAEME RD
MANOR ROAD
GRAEME RD
Stibbington House
ELTON ROAD
Field Studies Centre
Sutton
Hereward Way
Lock
Weir
NEW LANE
Toll Bar Spinney
A1 GREAT NORTH ROAD
OLD GREAT NORTH ROAD
Nene Valley Railway
Cambridgeshire STREET ATLAS
A1 Huntington (A1(M), A14)
8
7
01
6
5
00
4
3
99
2
1
98
07
08
09

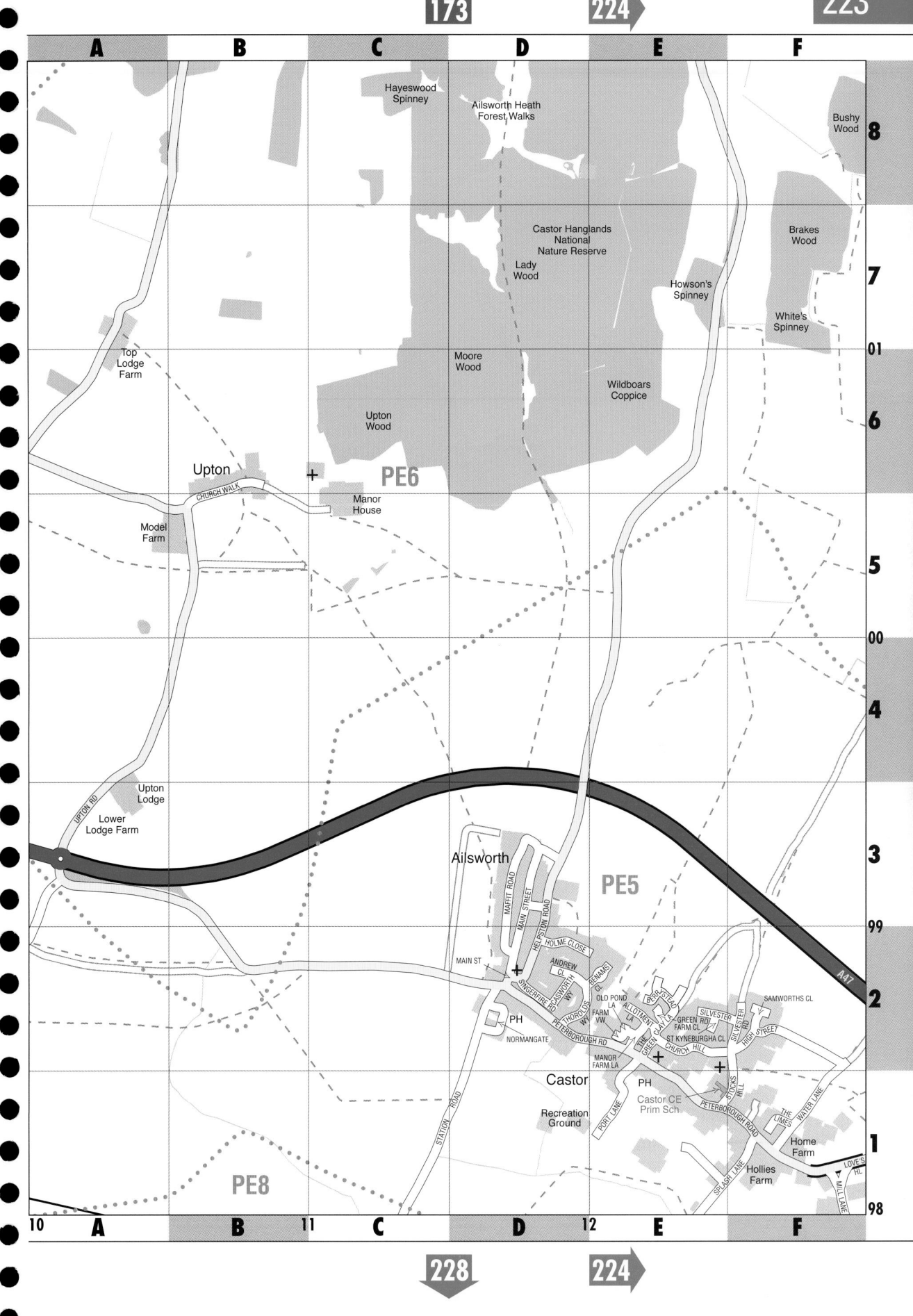

8

7

01

6

5

00

4

3

99

2

1

98

A B C D E F

Hayeswood
Spinney

Ailsworth Heath
Forest Walks

Bushy
Wood

Castor Hanglands
National
Nature Reserve

Brakes
Wood

Lady
Wood

Howson's
Spinney

White's
Spinney

Moore
Wood

Wildboars
Coppice

Top
Lodge
Farm

Upton
Wood

PE6

Upton

CHURCH WALK

Manor
House

Model
Farm

UPTON RD

Upton
Lodge

Lower
Lodge Farm

Ailsworth

PE5

MAFFIT ROAD

MAIN STREET

HELPSTON ROAD

HOLME CLOSE

MAIN ST

ANDREW
CL

BEMARS

SINGERFIRE RD

ACASWORTH
WY

THOROLD

PETERBOROUGH RD

NORMANGATE

PH

OLD POND
LA

FARM
VW

ALLOTMENT
LA

ST KYNEBURGHA CL

THE
GREEN

GREEN CL LA

GREEN RD

Samworths CL

SILVESTER
FARM CL

SILVESTER
RD

HIGH STREET

CHURCH HILL

MANOR
FARM LA

STOCKS
HILL

Castor

PH

Castor CE
Prim Sch

Peterborough ROAD

THE
LIMES

WATER LANE

Home
Farm

STATION ROAD

PORT LANE

Recreation
Ground

SPLASH LANE

Hollies
Farm

MILL LANE

LOVE'S
HL

A47

PE8

10 A B 11 C D 12 E F

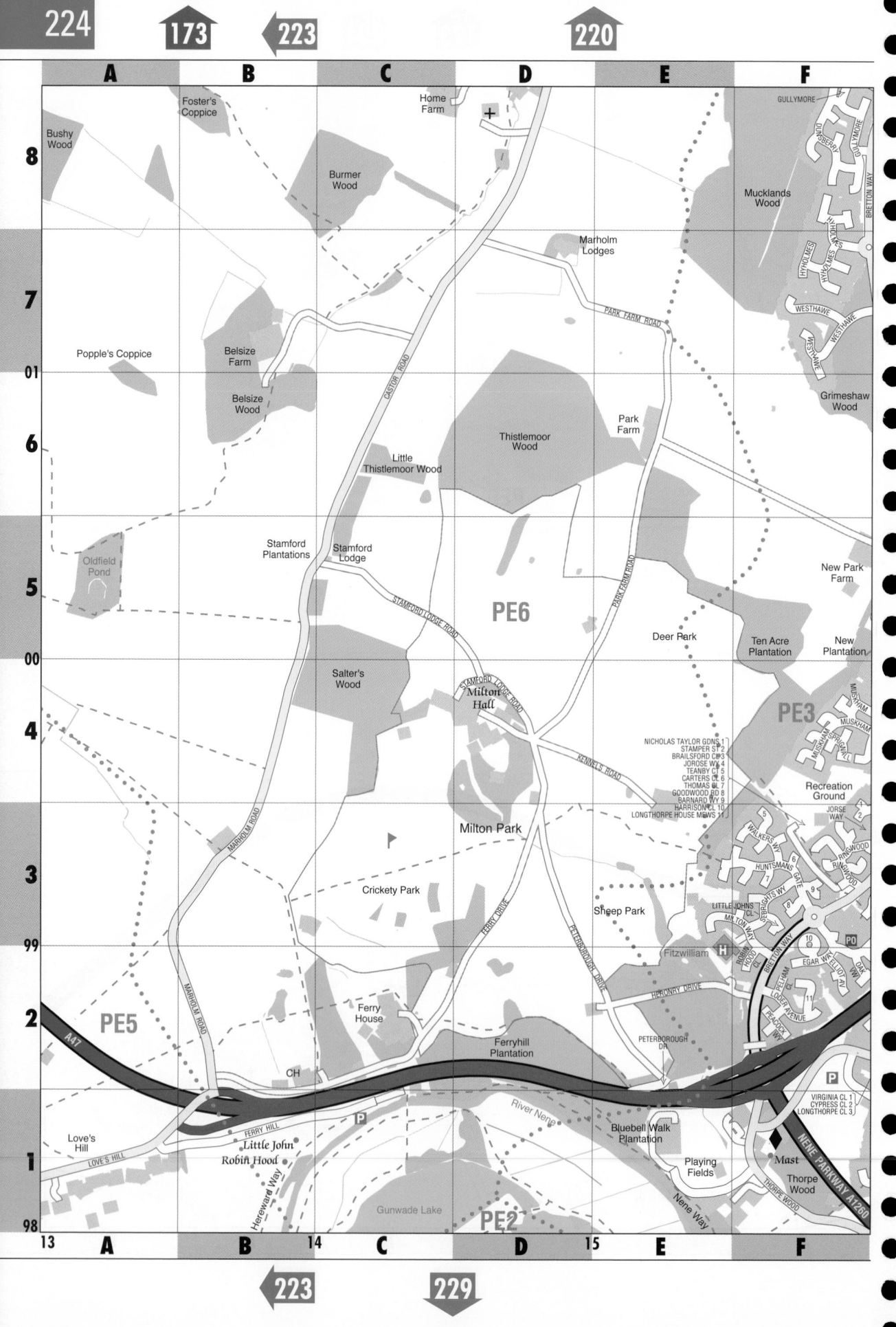

173
223
220

A   B   C   D   E   F

8

7

01

6

5

00

4

3

99

2

1

98

223
229

13   A   B   14   C   D   15   E   F

Bushy Wood

Foster's Coppice

Home Farm

Burmer Wood

GULLYMORE

Mucklands Wood

Marholm Lodges

PARK FARM ROAD

Popple's Coppice

Belsize Farm

Belsize Wood

Grimeshaw Wood

CASTOR ROAD

Little Thistlemoor Wood

Thistlemoor Wood

Park Farm

Oldfield Pond

Stamford Plantations

Stamford Lodge

New Park Farm

STAMFORD LODGE ROAD

PE6

PARK FARM ROAD

Deer Park

Ten Acre Plantation

New Plantation

Salter's Wood

STAMFORD LODGE ROAD

Milton Hall

PE3

NICHOLAS TAYLOR GDNS 1
STAMPER ST 2
BRAILSFORD CL 3
JOROSE WY 4
TEANBY CT 5
CARTERS CL 6
THOMAS CL 7
GOODWOOD RD 8
BARNARD WY 9
HARRISON CL 10
LONGTHORPE HOUSE MEWS 11

KENNELS ROAD

Recreation Ground

JORSE WAY

Milton Park

MARHOLM ROAD

Crickety Park

FERRY DRIVE

Sheep Park

PETERBOROUGH DRIVE

LITTLE JOHNS CL

WALKERS WY

HUNTSMAN'S CL

MILTON WAY

RINGWOOD

SEBRIGHTS WY

Fitzwilliam H

ROBIN HOOD CL

BRETTON WAY

EGAR WY

ELLIOT AV

PELHAM CL

PEACOCK WY

LOUSEF AVENUE

HERONRY DRIVE

PETERBOROUGH DR

PO

PE5

A47

MARHOLM ROAD

Ferry House

Ferryhill Plantation

River Nene

Bluebell Walk Plantation

CH

P

NENE PARKWAY A1260

P

VIRGINIA CL 1
CYPRESS CL 2
LONGTHORPE CL 3

Love's Hill

FERRY HILL

Little John

Robin Hood

LOVE'S HILL

Hereward Way

Gunwade Lake

PE2

Nene Way

Playing Fields

Mast

Thorpe Wood

THORPE WOOD

220 221 226

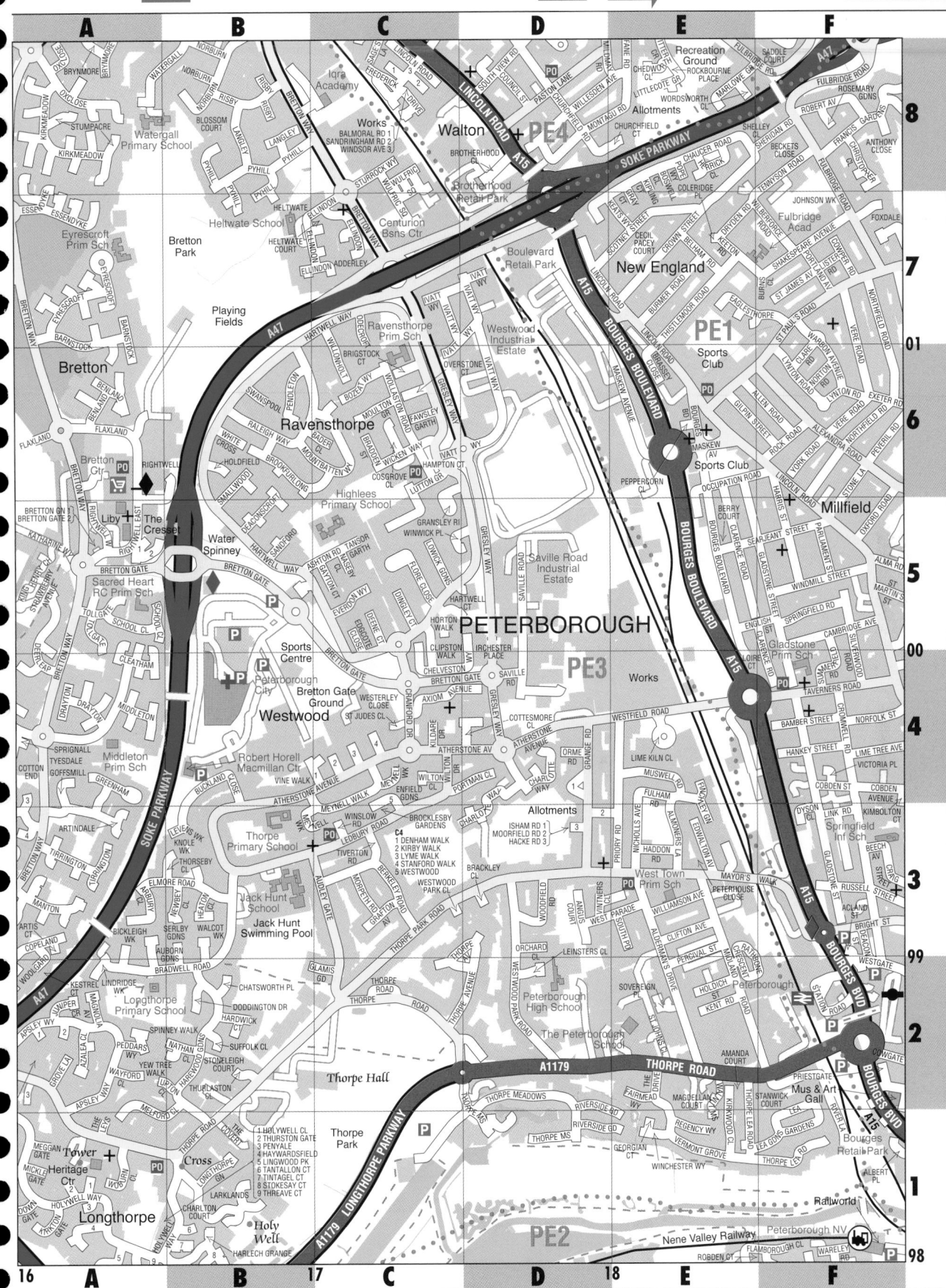
A
B
C
D
E
F
8
7
01
6
5
00
4
3
99
2
1
98
16
17
18
Walton
PE4
Lincoln Road
A15
A47
Soke Parkway
Recreation Ground
Allotments
Iqra Academy
Works
Brotherhood Retail Park
Watergall Primary School
Heltwate School
Centurion Bsns Ctr
Eyescroft Prim Sch
Bretton Park
Playing Fields
Boulevard Retail Park
New England
Fulbridge Acad
Bretton
Ravensthorpe Prim Sch
Ravensthorpe
Westwood Industrial Estate
PE1
Sports Club
Bourges Boulevard
Bretton Ctr
Liby
The Cresset
Water Spinney
Highlees Primary School
Saville Road Industrial Estate
Millfield
Sacred Heart RC Prim Sch
Sports Centre
PETERBOROUGH
PE3
Peterborough City
Bretton Gate Ground
Westwood
Works
Gladstone Prim Sch
Middleton Prim Sch
Robert Horell Macmillan Ctr
Allotments
Springfield Inf Sch
Thorpe Primary School
West Town Prim Sch
Jack Hunt School
Jack Hunt Swimming Pool
Longthorpe Primary School
Peterborough High School
Peterborough
The Peterborough School
Thorpe Hall
A1179
Thorpe Road
Mus & Art Gall
Bourges Retail Park
Thorpe Park
A1179 Longthorpe Parkway
Tower
Heritage Ctr
Cross
Longthorpe
Holy Well
PE2
Nene Valley Railway
Railworld
Peterborough NV

230 226

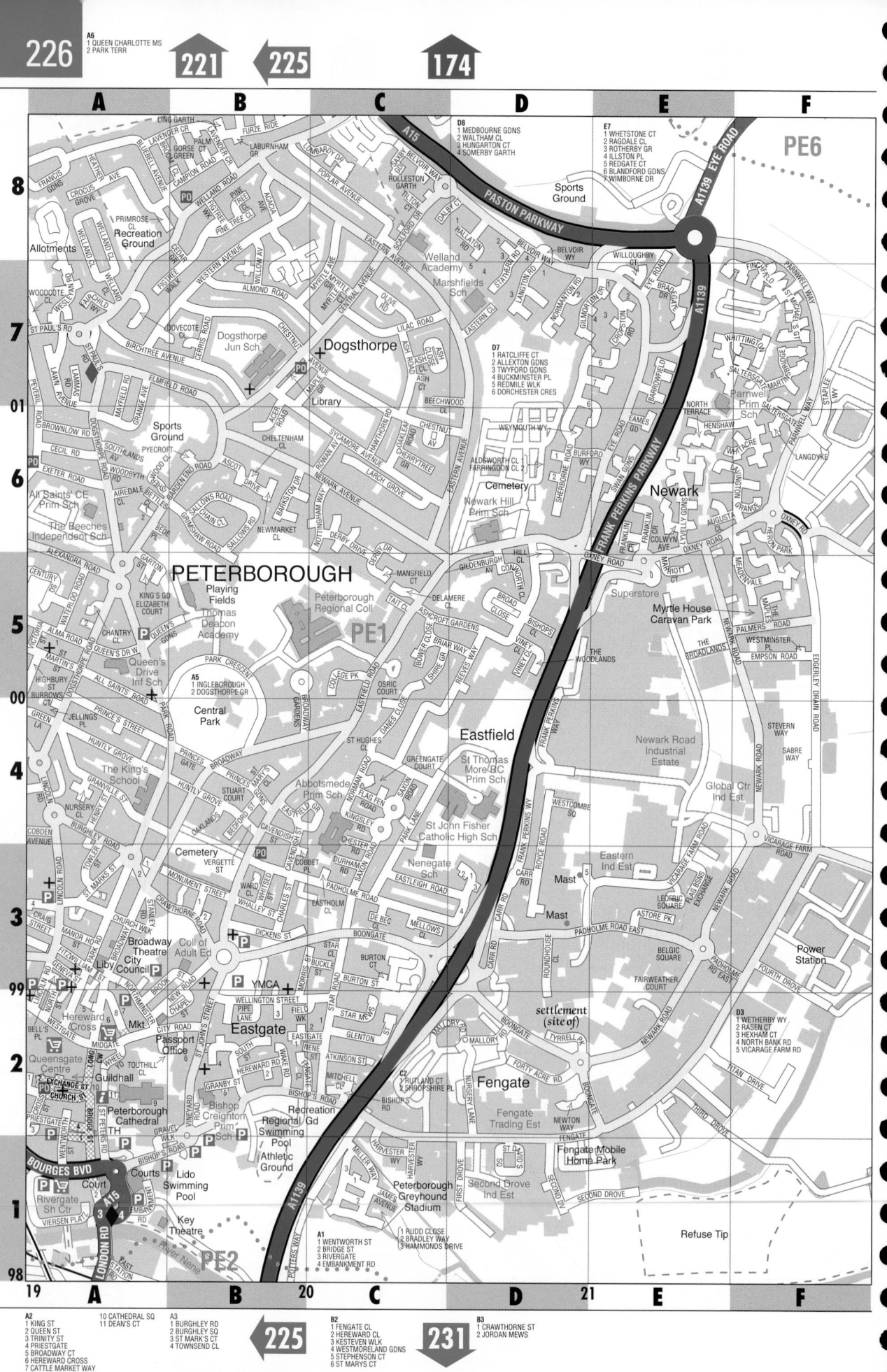

PE6

A B C D E F

D8
1 MEDBOURNE GDNS
2 WALTHAM CL
3 HUNGARTON CT
4 SOMERBY GARTH

E7
1 WHETSTONE CT
2 RAGDALE CL
3 ROTHERBY GR
4 ILLSTON PL
5 REDGATE CT
6 BLANDFORD GDNS
7 WIMBORNE DR

A15

BELVOIR WAY

PASTON PARKWAY

Sports Ground

A1139 EYE ROAD

8

Allotments

Recreation Ground

PRIMROSE CL

Welland Academy
Marshfields Sch

Willoughby

A1139

North Terrace

Parnwell Prim Sch

7

St Paul's Rd

Dogsthorpe Jun Sch

Dogsthorpe

Library

D7
1 RATCLIFFE CT
2 ALLEXTON GDNS
3 TWYFORD GDNS
4 BUCKMINSTER PL
5 REDMILE WLK
6 DORCHESTER CRES

FRANK PERKINS PARKWAY

Whittington

Henshaw

Langdyke

01

Sports Ground

Cemetery
Newark Hill Prim Sch

Newark

6

All Saints CE Prim Sch

The Beeches Independent Sch

Weymouth Wy

Superstore

Myrtle House Caravan Park

Westminster Pl
The Broadlands
Empson Road

5

PETERBOROUGH

Playing Fields

Thomas Deacon Academy

Peterborough Regional Coll

PE1

A5
1 INGLEBOROUGH
2 DOGSTHORPE GR

The Woodlands

Palmers Road

Central Park

Queen's Drive Inf Sch

00

Abbotsmede Prim Sch

St Hughes

Eastfield

Newark Road Industrial Estate

Global Ctr Ind Est

Stevern Way

Sabre Way

4

The King's School

Greengate Court

St Thomas More RC Prim Sch

St John Fisher Catholic High Sch

Nenegate Sch

Westcombe Sq

Vicarage Farm Road

Cemetery

Eastfield Rd

Eastleigh Road

Eastern Ind Est

Power Station

3

Broadway Theatre

City Council

Coll of Adult Ed

YMCA

Wellington Street

Eastgate

settlement (site of)

Fairweather Court

D3
1 WETHERBY WY
2 RASEN CT
3 HEXHAM CT
4 NORTH BANK RD
5 VICARAGE FARM RD

99

Hereward Cross

Mkt

Fengate

Belgic Square

2

Queensgate Centre

Guildhall

Peterborough Cathedral

Bishop Creighton Prim Sch

Recreation Gd
Regional Swimming Pool
Athletic Ground

C2
1 RUTLAND CT
2 SHROPSHIRE PL

Fengate Trading Est

Newton Way

Fengate Mobile Home Park

1

Bourges Blvd

Courts
Court

Rivergate Sh Ctr

Key Theatre

Lido Swimming Pool

A1

A1
1 WENTWORTH ST
2 BRIDGE ST
3 RIVERGATE
4 EMBANKMENT RD

B1
1 RUDD CLOSE
2 BRADLEY WAY
3 HAMMONDS DRIVE

Peterborough Greyhound Stadium

Second Drove Ind Est

Refuse Tip

98

PE2

River Nene

19 A 20 B C 21 D E F

A2
1 KING ST
2 QUEEN ST
3 TRINITY ST
4 PRIESTGATE
5 BROADWAY CT
6 HEREWARD CROSS
7 CATTLE MARKET WAY
8 CATTLE MARKET RD
9 MINSTER PRECINCTS

10 CATHEDRAL SQ
11 DEAN'S CT

A3
1 BURGHLEY RD
2 BURGHLEY SQ
3 ST MARK'S CT
4 TOWNSEND CL

B2
1 FENGATE CL
2 HEREWARD CL
3 KESTEVEN WLK
4 WESTMORELAND GDNS
5 STEPHENSON CT
6 ST MARYS CT

B3
1 CRAWTHORNE ST
2 JORDAN MEWS

225 231

175

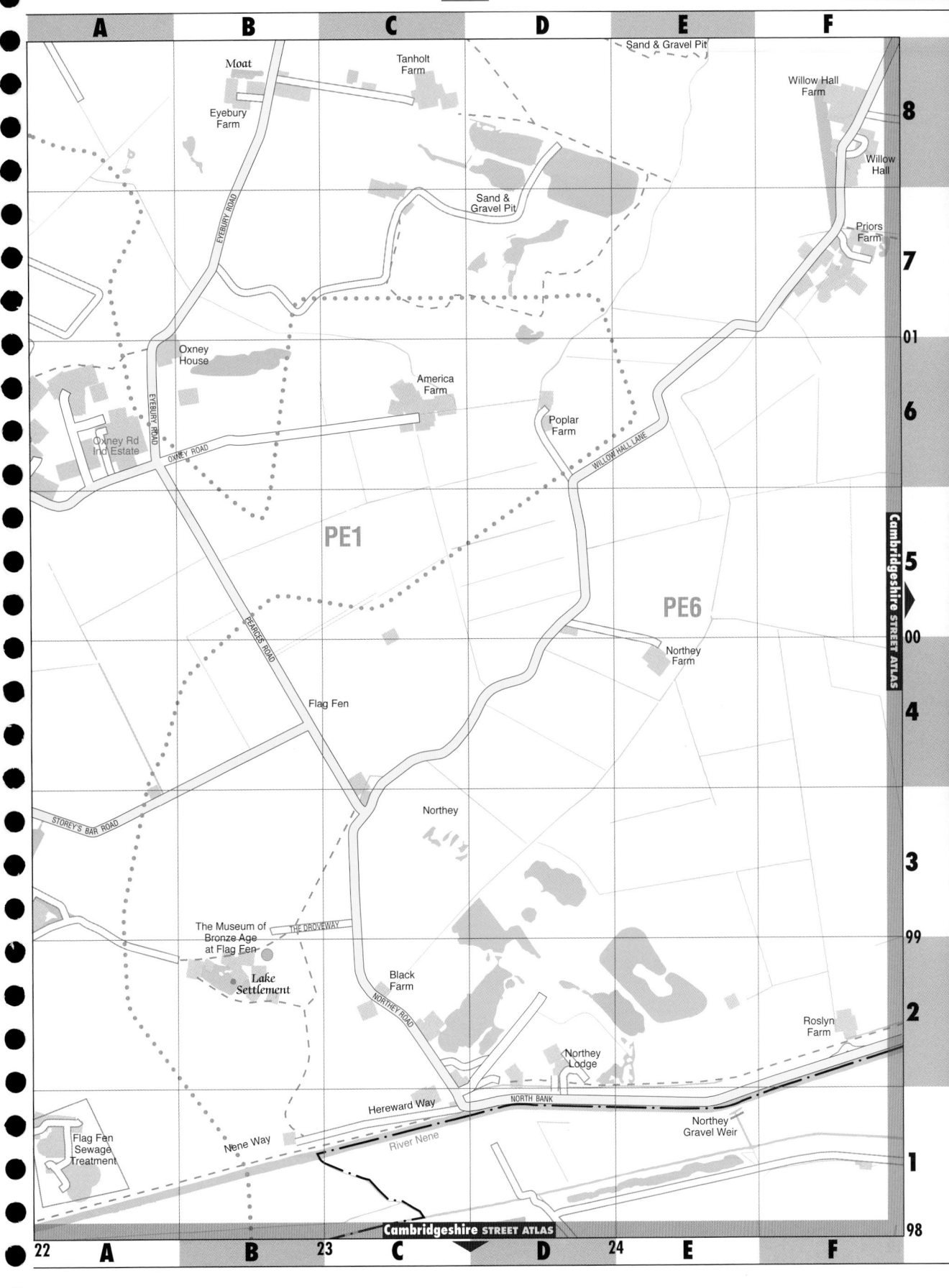
A
B
C
D
E
F
Sand & Gravel Pit
Moat
Tanholt Farm
Willow Hall Farm
Eyebury Farm
8
Willow Hall
Sand & Gravel Pit
EYEBURY ROAD
Priors Farm
7
01
Oxney House
America Farm
6
Poplar Farm
EYEBURY ROAD
Oxney Rd Ind Estate
OXNEY ROAD
WILLOW HALL LANE
PE1
5
PE6
00
Northey Farm
PEARCES ROAD
Flag Fen
4
STOREY'S BAR ROAD
Northey
3
The Museum of Bronze Age at Flag Fen
THE DROVEWAY
99
Black Farm
Lake Settlement
2
NORTHEY ROAD
Roslyn Farm
Northey Lodge
NORTH BANK
Hereward Way
Northey Gravel Weir
Nene Way
River Nene
Flag Fen Sewage Treatment
1
98
Cambridgeshire STREET ATLAS
22
A
B
23
C
D
24
E
F

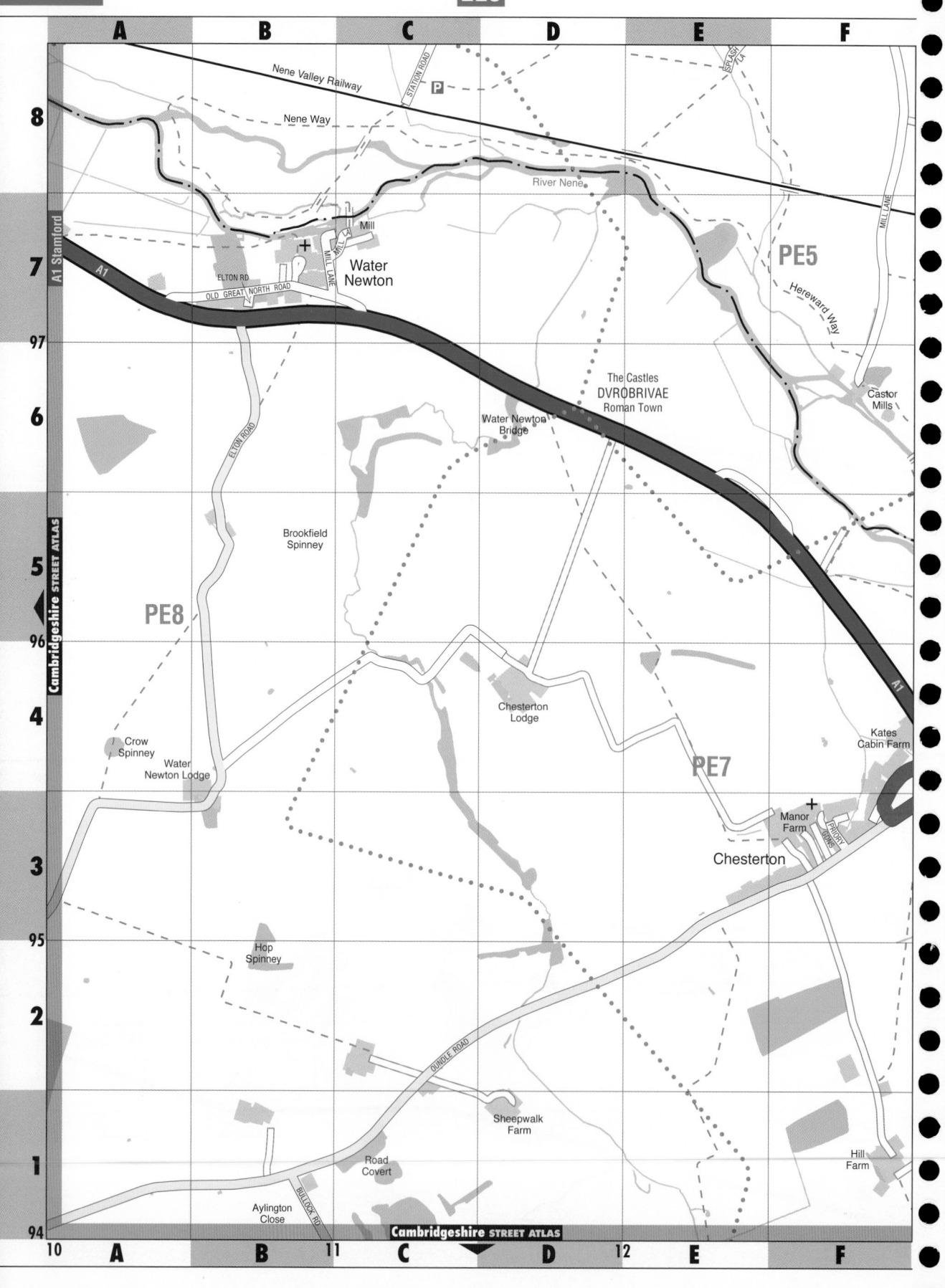

Cambridgeshire STREET ATLAS

Nene Valley Railway

STATION ROAD

P

Nene Way

SPLASH LA

River Nene

A1 Stamford

A1

Mill

MILL LANE

ELTON RD

OLD GREAT NORTH ROAD

Water
Newton

PE5

Hereward Way

Castor
Mills

The Castles
DVROBRIVAE
Roman Town

MILL LANE

ELTON ROAD

Water Newton
Bridge

Brookfield
Spinney

PE8

Crow
Spinney

Water
Newton Lodge

Chesterton
Lodge

PE7

Kates
Cabin Farm

A1

Hop
Spinney

Manor
Farm

FRIDAY LANE

Chesterton

QUIDLE ROAD

Sheepwalk
Farm

Hill
Farm

BULLOCK RD

Road
Covert

Aylington
Close

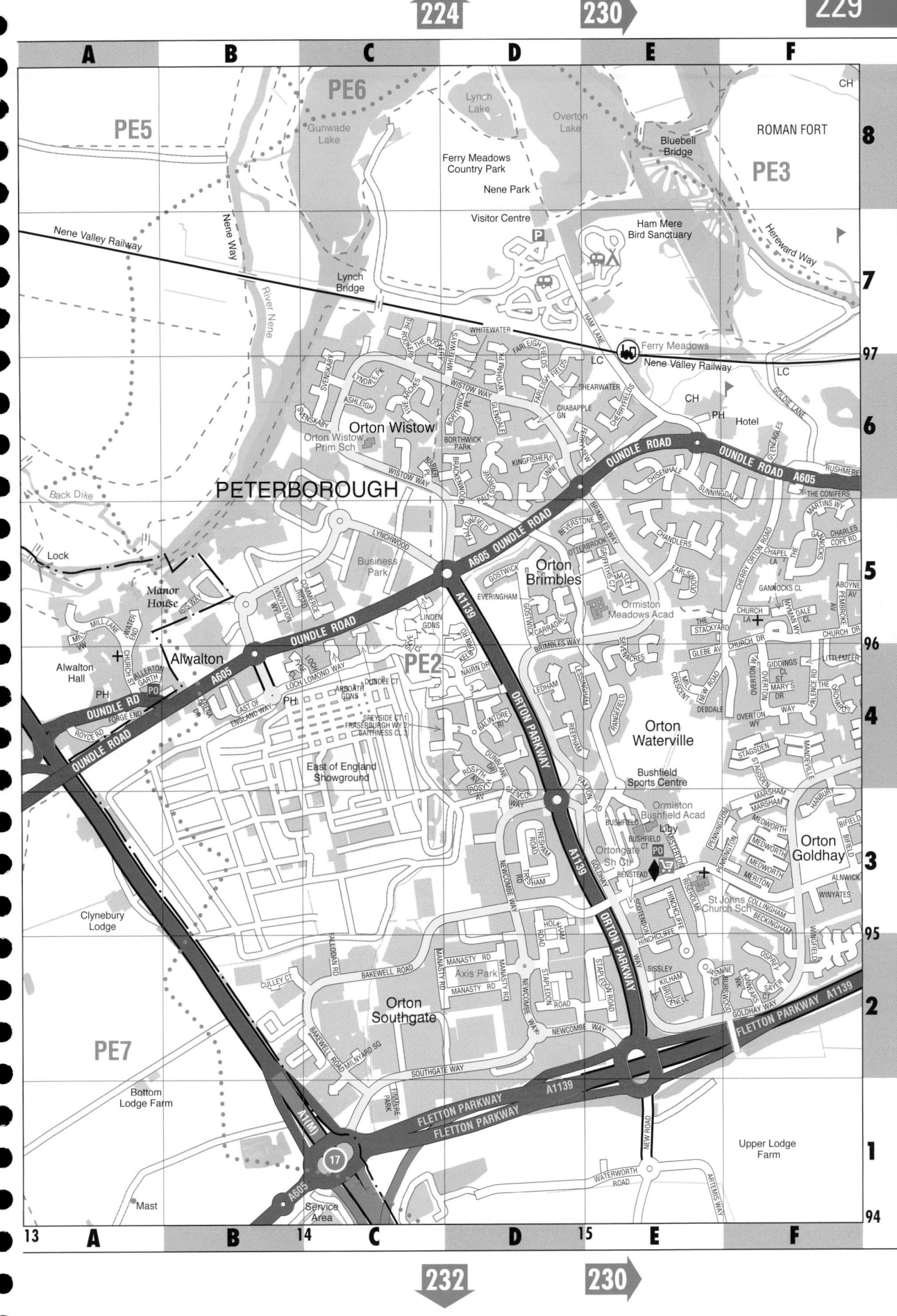

224
230
A
B
C
D
E
F
PE5
PE6
PE3
PE2
PE7
Gunwade Lake
Lynch Lake
Overton Lake
Bluebell Bridge
ROMAN FORT
Ferry Meadows Country Park
Nene Park
Visitor Centre
Ham Mere Bird Sanctuary
Hereward Way
Nene Valley Railway
Nene Way
River Nene
Lynch Bridge
Ferry Meadows
Orton Wistow
Orton Wistow Prim Sch
PETERBOROUGH
Back Dike
Lock
Manor House
Alwalton
Alwalton Hall
Business Park
Orton Brimbles
Ormiston Meadows Acad
OUNDLE ROAD
A605
A1139
ORTON PARKWAY
East of England Showground
Orton Waterville
Bushfield Sports Centre
Ormiston Bushfield Acad
Ortongate Sh Ctr
Liby
St Johns Church Sch
Orton Goldhay
Clynebury Lodge
Axis Park
Orton Southgate
FLETTON PARKWAY
A1(M)
Bottom Lodge Farm
Upper Lodge Farm
Service Area
Mast
Hotel
13
14
15
94
95
96
97
1
2
3
4
5
6
7
8
232
230

Grid columns: A B C D E F
Grid rows: 8 7 97 6 5 96 4 3 95 2 1 94
Lower scale: 16 A 17 B C 17 18 E F

PE3

PE2

PE7

PETERBOROUGH

Woodston

Orton Longueville

Orton Malbourne

Hampton Hargate

Hampton Vale

Major roads/features: A1260, A1179, A605, A15, A1139, LONGTHORPE PARKWAY, NENE PARKWAY, OUNDLE ROAD, FLETTON PARKWAY, LONDON ROAD, THE SERPENTINE, MORLEY WAY, SHREWSBURY AVENUE, Nene Valley Railway, River Nene, Nene Way

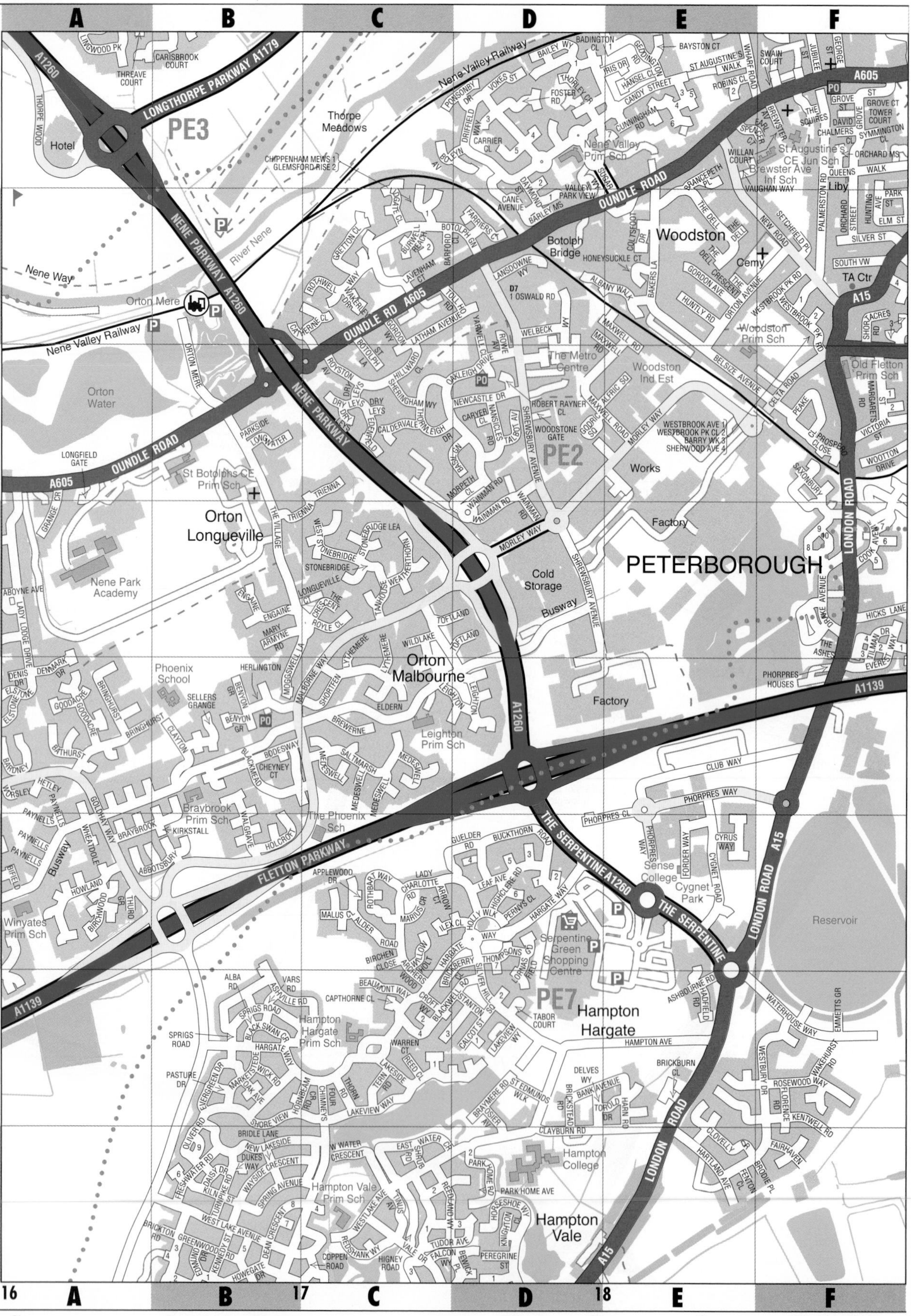

Places: Hotel, Thorpe Meadows, Orton Water, Orton Mere, Nene Park Academy, Phoenix School, Leighton Prim Sch, Braybrook Prim Sch, The Phoenix Sch, Winyates Prim Sch, St Botolphs CE Prim Sch, Nene Valley Prim Sch, Woodston Prim Sch, Cemy, The Metro Centre, Woodstone Ind Est, Cold Storage, Busway, Works, Factory, Serpentine Green Shopping Centre, Sense College, Cygnet Park, Hampton Hargate Prim Sch, Hampton Vale Prim Sch, Hampton College, Reservoir, Old Fletton Prim Sch, St Augustine's CE Jun Sch, Brewster Ave Inf Sch, Liby, TA Ctr

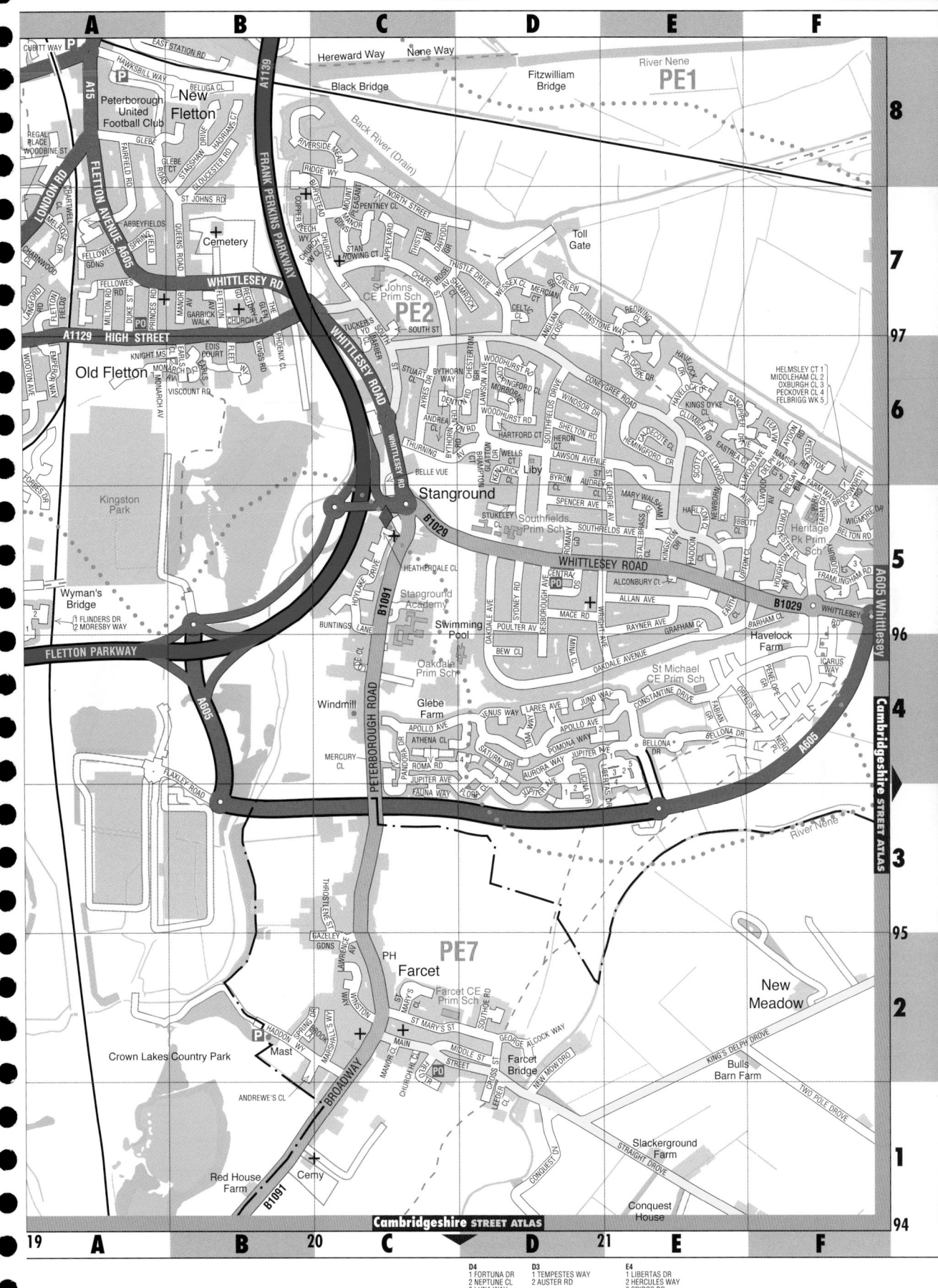

CUBITT WAY
EAST STATION RD
HAWKSBILL WAY
BELUGA CL.
A15
Peterborough United Football Club
New Fletton
Hereward Way
Nene Way
Black Bridge
Fitzwilliam Bridge
River Nene
PE1

FLETTON AVENUE A605
LONDON RD
HADRIANS DRIVE
RIDGE WY
RIVERSIDE MEAD
Back River (Drain)
Toll Gate

Regal Place
WOODBINE ST
CHARTWELL
MELBOURNE
FAIRFIELD RD
GLEBE
SPRING RD
QUEENS ROAD
Cemetery
FRANK PERKINS PARKWAY
A1139
COPPER BEECH
RIDGE WY
MOUNT PLEASANT
NORTH STREET
APPLEYARD
PENTNEY RD
THISTLE DRIVE
WESSEX CL.
MERCIAN
CURLEW
REDWING

ABBEYFIELDS
FELLOWES GDNS
ST JOHNS RD
WHITTLESEY RD
ST JOHNS CE PRIM SCH
PE2
CHAPEL ROSE
SHAMROCK
SOUTH ST
CELTIC CL
ANGLIAN
TURNSTONE WA
PELARGR DR
HAVELOCK DR
HAVELOCK RD
KINGS DYKE

HELMSLEY CT 1
MIDDLEHAM CL 2
OXBURGH CL 3
PECKOVER CL 4
FELBRIGG WK 5

A1129 HIGH STREET
Old Fletton
KNIGHT MS
EDIS COURT
STUART RD
BYTHORN WAY
CHESTERTON
LAWSON AV
WOODHURST RD
CONINGFORD CL
MORBORNE
HARTFORD CT
WINDSOR DR
SHELTON RD
HERON CT
CONEYGREE ROAD
CADECOTE CL
HEMINGFORD CR
CLUMBER GR

VISCOUNT RD
WHITTLESEY ROAD
BELLE VUE
THURNING
BYTHORN RD
GLATTON
KEDRICK CL
WELLS CL
LIby
BYRON CL
ST ANDRES
ST GEORGE AV
LAWSON AVENUE
MARY WALSHAM

Kingston Park
Stanground
B1029
STUKELEY CL
Southfields Prim Sch
SOUTHFIELDS AVE
ROMANY CL
SPENCER AVE
STALLERBRASS
KINGSTON DR
HADDON CL
ALCONBURY CL
Heritage Pk Prim Sch

Wyman's Bridge
1 FLINDERS DR
2 MORESBY WAY
HEATHERDALE CL
Stanground Academy
WHITTLESEY ROAD
PO
CENTRAL
ALLAN AVE
B1029 Whittlesey
A605 Whittlesey

FLETTON PARKWAY
B1091
HOYLAKE DRIVE
BUNTINGS LANE
Swimming Pool
SYDNEY RD
STONEY RD
MACE RD
WRIGHT AVE
RAYNER AVE
GRAHAM CL
BARHAM CL
Havelock Farm

A605
Windmill
PETERBOROUGH ROAD
Oakdale Prim Sch
OAKDALE AVE
POULTER AV
BEW CL
OAKDALE AVENUE
St Michael CE Prim Sch
ICARUS WAY
PENELOPE GR
ORPHEUS DR
FABIAN DR

FLAXLEY ROAD
Glebe Farm
APOLLO AVE
ATHENA CL
VENUS WAY
LIMA WAY
LARES AVE
JUNO WAY
APOLLO AVE
POMONA WAY
CONSTANTINE DRIVE
BELLONA DR
BELLONA DR

MERCURY CL
PANDORA DR
SATURN DR
AURORA WAY
JUPITER AVE
LUCINA DR
LIBERTAS DR
MEDU
A605

JUPITER AVE
FAUNA WAY
FLORA
JUPITER AVE
River Nene

THROSTLENE CL
PE7
Farcet

GAZELEY GDNS
LAWRENCE AVE
PH
Farcet CE Prim Sch
GEORGE ALCOCK WAY
New Meadow

Crown Lakes Country Park
HADDON RD
Mast
WINSTON AVE
MARSHALL
MANOR CL
ST MARY'S ST
ST MARY'S RD
MIDDLE ST
Farcet Bridge
MAIN STREET
CONQUEST DV
KINGS DELPH DROVE
Bulls Barn Farm
STRAIGHT DROVE

ANDREWE'S CL
BROADWAY
CHURCH LA
CROSS ST
LEEDER CL
GEORGE ALCOCK WAY
Slackerground Farm
TWO POLE DROVE

Red House Farm
B1091
Cemy
Conquest House

D4
1 FORTUNA DR
2 NEPTUNE CL
3 LUNA WAY
4 VESTA CL

D3
1 TEMPESTES WAY
2 AUSTER RD

E4
1 LIBERTAS DR
2 HERCULES WAY
3 SPIROS RD
4 ELENA RD
5 VIOLETA WAY

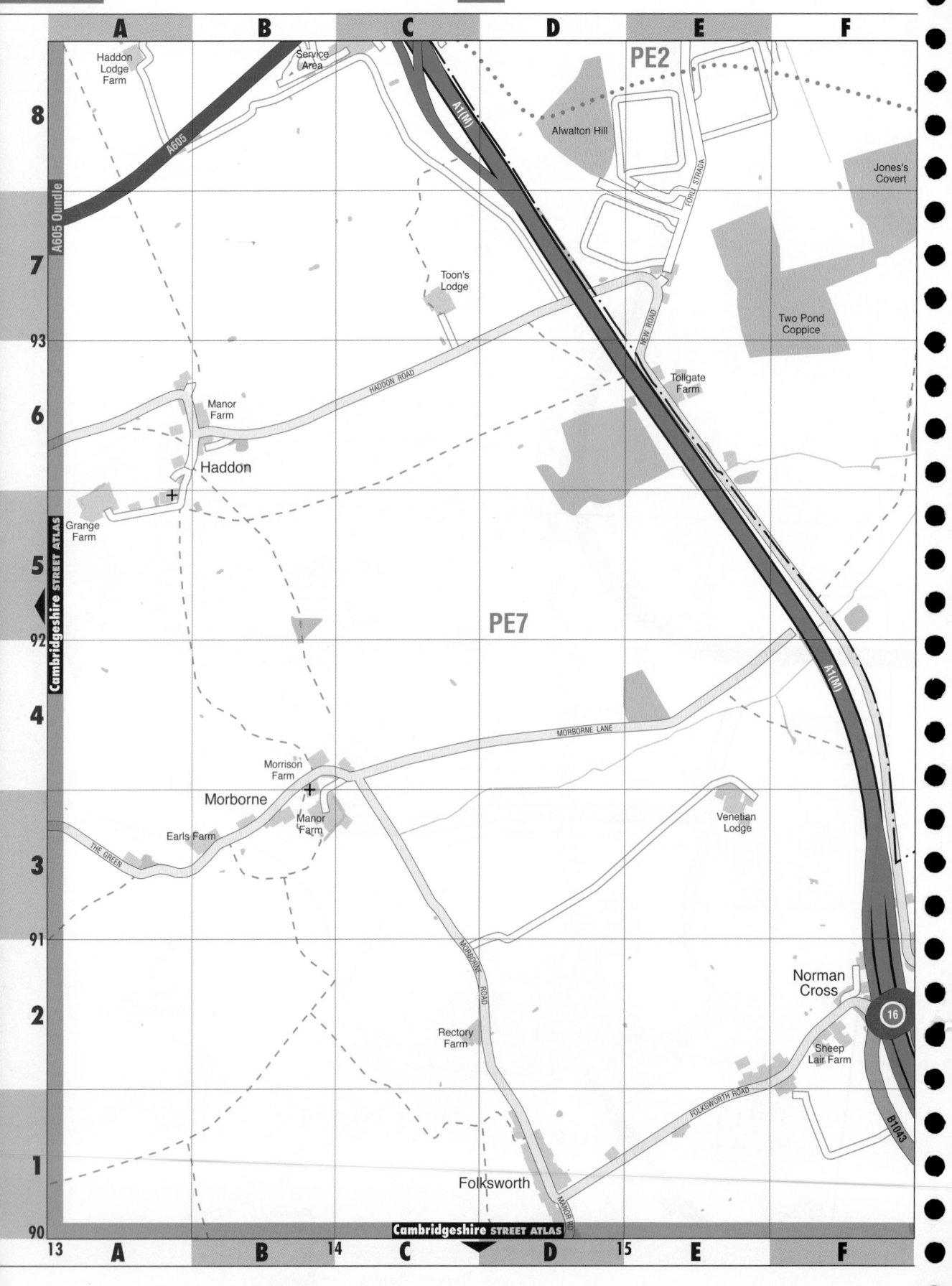

PE2

Haddon
Lodge
Farm

Service
Area

A605

Alwalton Hill

Jones's
Covert

A605 Oundle

Toon's
Lodge

Two Pond
Coppice

HADDON ROAD

Manor
Farm

Tollgate
Farm

Haddon

Grange
Farm

PE7

Cambridgeshire STREET ATLAS

A11(M)

NEW ROAD

FORT STRADA

MORBORNE LANE

Morrison
Farm

Venetian
Lodge

Morborne

Manor
Farm

Earls Farm

THE GREEN

MORBORNE ROAD

Norman
Cross

16

Rectory
Farm

Sheep
Lair Farm

FOLKSWORTH ROAD

B1043

Folksworth

MANOR RD

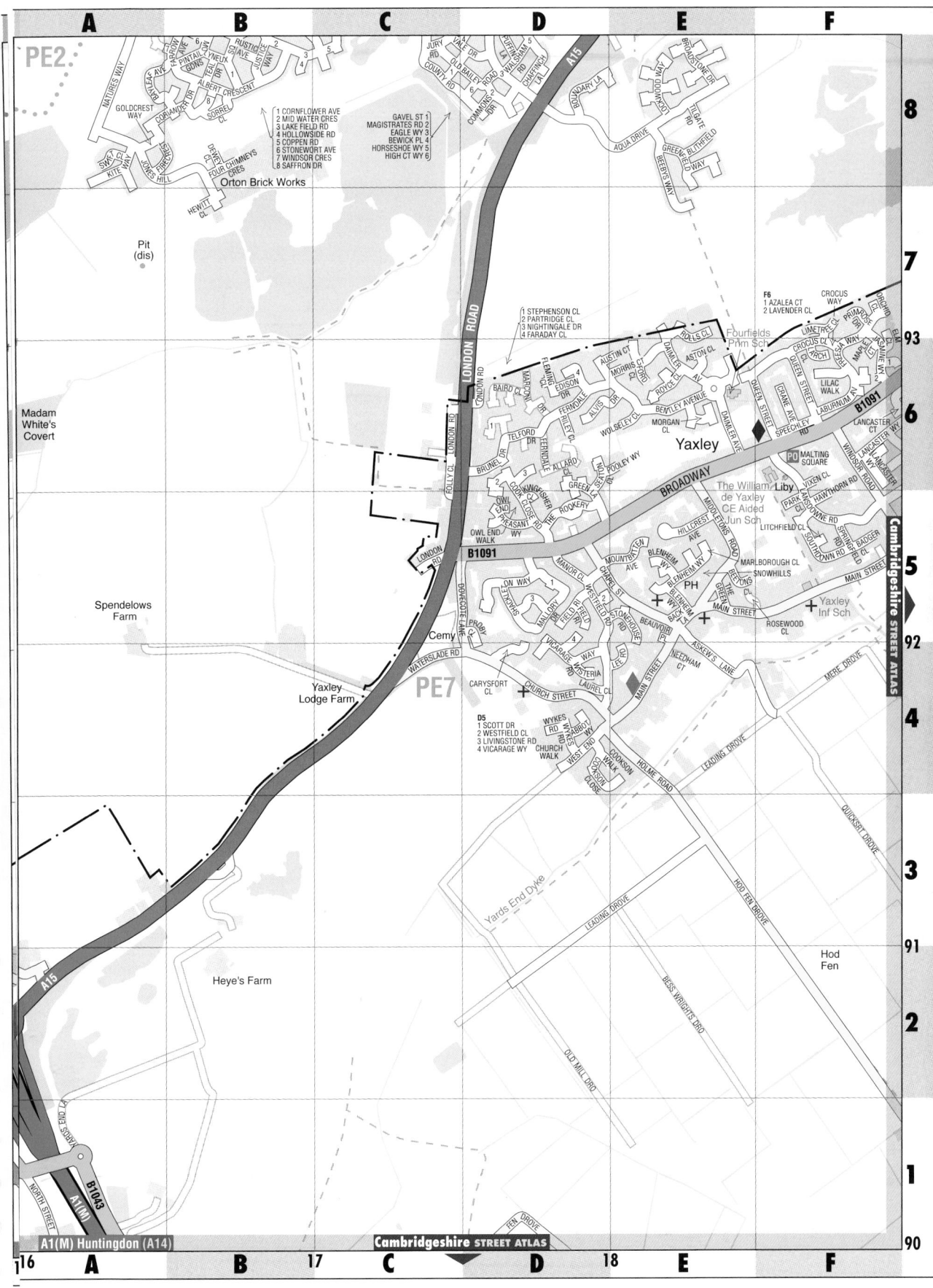

A B C D E F

8

7

93

6

5

92

4

91

2

1

90

PE2

NATURES WAY

GOLDCREST WAY

CORIANDER DR

SWA CL
KITE WY

JONS HILL

DEVOKE WAY
FOUR CRES

SORREL

FOUR CHIMNEYS

HEWITT CL

RUSTIC CL

PINTAIL GDNS

BARLEY AVE

TYNEUX

JUSTICE WAY

ALBERT CRESCENT

Orton Brick Works

1 CORNFLOWER AVE
2 MID WATER CRES
3 LAKE FIELD RD
4 HOLLOWSIDE RD
5 COPPEN RD
6 STONEWORT AVE
7 WINDSOR CRES
8 SAFFRON DR

JURY RD
VALE DR
OLD BAILEY
COMMONS LDR
COUNTY RD

DUFFIELD RD

WALSHAM

HAEFINCH

GAVEL ST 1
MAGISTRATES RD 2
EAGLE WY 3
BEWICK PL 4
HORSESHOE WY 5
HIGH CT WY 6

A15

BOUNDARY LA

AQUA DRIVE

BROADSIDE DR

TAN DOO WOO

TILGATE RD

GREEK BLITHFIELD WAY

BEEBYS WAY

F6
1 AZALEA CT
2 LAVENDER CL

CROCUS WAY

ORCHID

PRIMROSE

JASMINE WY

FREESIA WAY

MAPLE CL

Pit
(dis)

Madam
White's
Covert

Spendelows
Farm

Yaxley
Lodge Farm

Heye's Farm

LONDON ROAD

1 STEPHENSON CL
2 PARTRIDGE CL
3 NIGHTINGALE DR
4 FARADAY CL

LONDON RD

CONDOM RD

FLEMING CL

BAIRD CL

MARCONI DR

EDISON DR

AUSTIN CT

MORRIS CL

DAIMLER DR

ASTON CL

ROLLS CL

Fourfields
Prim Sch

ROYCE CL

BENTLEY AVENUE

CHURCH

QUEEN STREET

CRANE CL

LILAC WALK

LABURNUM

B1091

CRANE ST

SPEECHLEY RD

LANCASTER CT

LANCASTER WY

WINDSOR WY

LANCASTER

TELFORD DR

FERNDALE

RILEY CL

ALVIS DR

WOLSELEY CL

FERNDALE

ALLARD

GREEN STATION

POOLEY WY

MORGAN CL

Yaxley

BROADWAY

DAIMLER AVE

The William
de Yaxley
CE Aided
Jun Sch

Liby

PO MALTING
SQUARE

VIXEN CL

PARK CL

HAWTHORN RD

TOWNE RD

SOUTHGROW

STIRLING RD

LITCHFIELD CL

BADGER

MAIN STREET

FOLLY CL

BRUNE DR

KINGFISHER

COOK CLOSE

THE ROOKERY

OWL END WY
PHEASANT WY

OWL END WALK

LONDON RD

B1091

MANOR CL

HILLCREST AVE

MIDDLETONS ROAD

BLENHEIM WY

BLENHEIM AVE

MOUNTBATTEN AVE

CHAPEL ST

WESTFIELD RD

BLENHEIM CL

PH

MAIN STREET

SNOWHILLS

MARLBOROUGH CL

BELL ONS

GREEN

Yaxley
Inf Sch

ON WAY

SHACKLE CL

MALLORY

FIELD RD

WESTFIELD RD

STONEHOUSE

BEAUVOIR

BACK LA

LEE CL

MAIN STREET

NEEDHAM CT

ASKEW'S LANE

ROSEWOOD CL

PROBY

DOVECOTE LANE

VICARAGE WAY

WATERSLADE RD

CARYSFORT CL

WISTERIA

LAUREL CL

Church Street

PE7

D5
1 SCOTT DR
2 WESTFIELD CL
3 LIVINGSTONE RD
4 VICARAGE WY

WYKES RD

ABBOT CL

CHURCH WALK

WEST END

CHURCH WALK

COOKSON WALK

COOKSON CLOSE

HOLME ROAD

LEADING DROVE

MERE DROVE

QUICKSET DROVE

Yards End Dyke

LEADING DROVE

BESS WRIGHT'S DRO

HOD FEN DRIVE

Hod
Fen

OLD MILL DRO

A15

B1043
A1(M)

NORTH STREET

HARRIS LA

FEN DROVE

Cemy

Cambridgeshire STREET ATLAS

16 A 17 B C 17 D 18 E F

Cambridgeshire STREET ATLAS

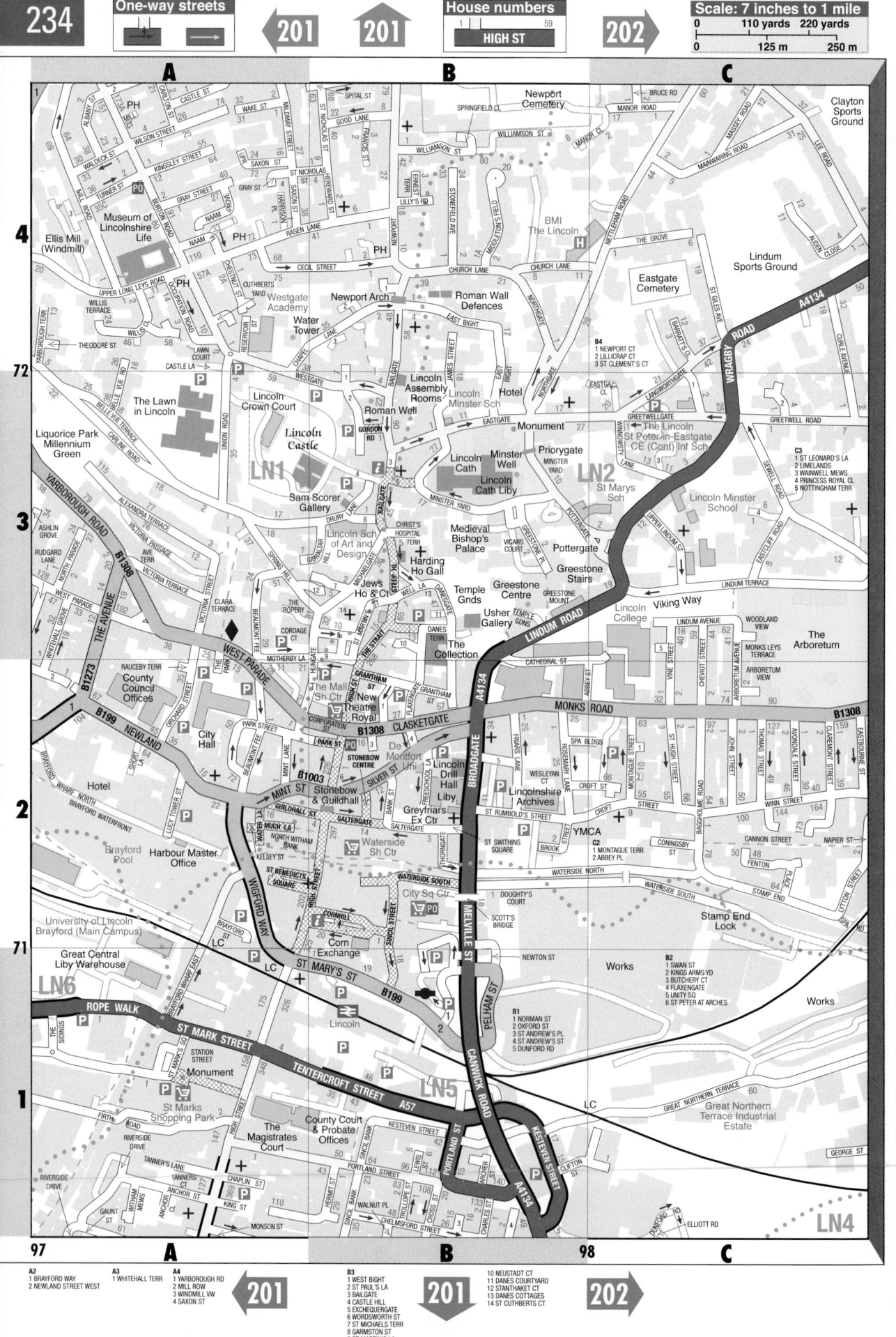

One-way streets
House numbers
HIGH ST
Scale: 7 inches to 1 mile
0 110 yards 220 yards
0 125 m 250 m
201
201
202
A
B
C
4
3
2
1
72
71
97
98
Newport Cemetery
Clayton Sports Ground
Museum of Lincolnshire Life
Ellis Mill (Windmill)
BMI The Lincoln
Lindum Sports Ground
Eastgate Cemetery
Westgate Academy
Newport Arch
Roman Wall Defences
Water Tower
The Lawn in Lincoln
Lincoln Crown Court
Lincoln Assembly Rooms
Lincoln Minster Sch
Hotel
Roman Well
Monument
The Lincoln St Peter-in-Eastgate CE (Conf) Inf Sch
Liquorice Park Millennium Green
Lincoln Castle
LN1
LN2
Lincoln Cath
Minster Well
Priorygate
Lincoln Cath Liby
St Marys Sch
Lincoln Minster School
Sam Scorer Gallery
Lincoln Sch of Art and Design
Medieval Bishop's Palace
Pottergate
Harding Ho Gall
Greestone Stairs
Jews Ho & Ct
Temple Gnds
Greestone Centre
Usher Gallery
Lincoln College
Viking Way
The Arboretum
The Collection
County Council Offices
City Hall
The Mall Sh Ctr
New Theatre Royal
De Montfort Uni
Lincoln Drill Hall Liby
Lincolnshire Archives
Hotel
Stonebow & Guildhall
Greyfriars Ex Ctr
YMCA
Brayford Pool
Harbour Master Office
Waterside Sh Ctr
City Sq Ctr
University of Lincoln Brayford (Main Campus)
Great Central Liby Warehouse
Corn Exchange
Stamp End Lock
Works
LN6
Lincoln
Monument
St Marks Shopping Park
The Magistrates Court
County Court & Probate Offices
LN5
Great Northern Terrace Industrial Estate
LN4
YARBOROUGH ROAD
B1308
THE AVENUE
B1273
NEWLAND
B199
WEST PARADE
CLASKETGATE
MINT ST
B1003
SILVER ST
WIGFORD WAY
ST MARY'S ST
ROPE WALK
ST MARK STREET
TENTERCROFT STREET
A57
CANWICK ROAD
BROADGATE
A4134
MELVILLE ST
PELHAM ST
LINDUM ROAD
WRAGBY ROAD
MONKS ROAD
KESTEVEN STREET
PORTLAND ST
HIGH STREET
NEWPORT
NORTHGATE
EASTGATE
GREETWELLGATE
LINDUM TERRACE
BAILGATE
STEEP HILL
THE STRAIT
UNION ROAD
BURTON ROAD
CHURCH LANE
EAST BIGHT
NETTLEHAM ROAD
LANGWORTHGATE
WATERSIDE NORTH
WATERSIDE SOUTH
GREAT NORTHERN TERRACE
B4
1 NEWPORT CT
2 LILLICRAP CT
3 ST CLEMENT'S CT
C3
1 ST LEONARD'S LA
2 LIMELANDS
3 WAINWELL MEWS
4 PRINCESS ROYAL CL
5 NOTTINGHAM TERR
C2
1 MONTAGUE TERR
2 ABBEY PL
B2
1 SWAN ST
2 KINGS ARMS YD
3 BUTCHERY CT
4 FLAXENGATE
5 UNITY SQ
6 ST PETER AT ARCHES
B1
1 NORMAN ST
2 OXFORD ST
3 ST ANDREW'S PL
4 ST ANDREW'S ST
5 DUNFORD RD
A2
1 BRAYFORD WAY
2 NEWLAND STREET WEST
A3
1 WHITEHALL TERR
A4
1 YARBOROUGH RD
2 MILL ROW
3 WINDMILL VW
4 SAXON ST
B3
1 WEST BIGHT
2 ST PAUL'S LA
3 BAILGATE
4 CASTLE HILL
5 EXCHEQUERGATE
6 WORDSWORTH ST
7 ST MICHAELS TERR
8 GARMSTON ST
9 ST MARTIN'S LA
10 NEUSTADT CT
11 DANES COURTYARD
12 STANTHAKET CT
13 DANES COTTAGES
14 ST CUTHBERTS CT
201
201
202

Index

Place name May be abbreviated on the map

Location number Present when a number indicates the place's position in a crowded area of mapping

Locality, town or village Shown when more than one place has the same name

Postcode district District for the indexed place

Page and grid square Page number and grid reference for the standard mapping

Church Rd [6] Beckenham BR2..........**53** C6

Cities, towns and villages are listed in CAPITAL LETTERS

Public and commercial buildings are highlighted in magenta **Places of interest** are highlighted in blue with a star★

Abbreviations used in the index

Acad	Academy	Comm	Common	Gd	Ground	L	Leisure	Prom	Promenade
App	Approach	Cott	Cottage	Gdn	Garden	La	Lane	Rd	Road
Arc	Arcade	Cres	Crescent	Gn	Green	Liby	Library	Recn	Recreation
Ave	Avenue	Cswy	Causeway	Gr	Grove	Mdw	Meadow	Ret	Retail
Bglw	Bungalow	Ct	Court	H	Hall	Meml	Memorial	Sh	Shopping
Bldg	Building	Ctr	Centre	Ho	House	Mkt	Market	Sq	Square
Bsns, Bus	Business	Ctry	Country	Hospl	Hospital	Mus	Museum	St	Street
Bvd	Boulevard	Cty	County	HQ	Headquarters	Orch	Orchard	Sta	Station
Cath	Cathedral	Dr	Drive	Hts	Heights	Pal	Palace	Terr	Terrace
Cir	Circus	Dro	Drove	Ind	Industrial	Par	Parade	TH	Town Hall
Cl	Close	Ed	Education	Inst	Institute	Pas	Passage	Univ	University
Cnr	Corner	Emb	Embankment	Int	International	Pk	Park	Wk, Wlk	Walk
Coll	College	Est	Estate	Intc	Interchange	Pl	Place	Wr	Water
Com	Community	Ex	Exhibition	Junc	Junction	Prec	Precinct	Yd	Yard

Index of towns, villages, streets, hospitals, industrial estates, railway stations, schools, shopping centres, universities and places of interest

12th Ave DN36 ... 36 F8
1st Drift PE9 ... 219 B2
1st Main Rd DN36 ... 36 F8
2nd Ave DN36 ... 36 F8
2nd Drift PE9 ... 219 B2
4th Ave DN36 ... 36 F8
5th Ave DN36 ... 36 F8
6th Ave DN36 ... 36 F8
7th Ave DN36 ... 36 F8

A

AALPS Coll DN15 ... 8 F3
Aalsmeer Rise [6] PE11 ... 214 A2
Aaron Wy PE20 ... 136 C4
Abberton Mews PE7 ... 233 E8
Abbey Bldgs [19] PE11 ... 214 D4
Abbey Cl Coningsby LN4 ... 207 B5
[6] Skegness PE25 ... 206 A4
[5] Woodhall Spa LN10 ... 97 C6
Abbey Cres [4] PE20 ... 135 C7
Abbeydale Cres NG31 ... 211 A8
Abbey Dr [20] Hatfield DN7 ... 14 D4
[13] Woodhall Spa LN10 ... 97 C5
Abbey Dr E DN32 ... 191 D6
Abbey Dr W DN32 ... 191 D6
Abbeyfield Rd [1] DN7 ... 14 C4
Abbeyfields PE2 ... 231 A7
Abbeygate DN31 ... 191 D7
Abbey Gdns [22] DN7 ... 14 D4
Abbey Gr [23] DN7 ... 14 D4
Abbey La North Ormsby LN11 ... 48 D4
Sedgebrook NG32 ... 128 F4
Swineshead PE20 ... 135 C6
Woodhall Spa LN10 ... 97 C5
Abbey Mews [11] PE6 ... 166 F1
Abbey Park LN11 ... 198 E7
Abbey Pk Mews DN32 ... 191 D6
Abbey Pk Rd DN32 ... 191 D6
Abbey Pl [2] Lincoln LN2 ... 234 C2
[10] Thorney PE6 ... 176 A3
Abbey Rd Alvingham LN11 ... 49 F2
Bardney LN3 ... 83 B4
Bourne PE10 ... 213 D5
Grimsby DN32 ... 191 D6
Hatfield DN7 ... 14 D4
Louth LN11 ... 198 D6
North Killingholme DN39 ... 12 B4
Peterborough PE4 ... 221 A1
Revesby PE22 ... 99 C5
Scunthorpe DN17 ... 184 F6
Sleaford NG34 ... 212 A2
Abbey Rd *continued*
Swineshead PE20 ... 135 C7
Ulceby DN39 ... 12 A1
Abbey Rise [14] DN19 ... 11 D8
Abbey St
Kingston upon Hull HU9 ... 181 C7
Lincoln LN2 ... 234 C2
Abbey Way DN7 ... 14 D5
Abbey Wlk
[10] Crowland PE6 ... 166 F1
Grimsby DN32 ... 191 D7
Abbey Yd [12] PE11 ... 214 D4
Abbotsbury PE2 ... 230 A3
Abbot's Cl [5] PE10 ... 213 E4
Abbots Cres [6] PE11 ... 214 A4
Abbots Dr [1] PE6 ... 175 B8
Abbots Gdns [1] PE12 ... 158 B6
Abbotsmede Prim Sch PE1 ... 226 C4
Abbots Rd DN17 ... 184 F6
Abbot St LN5 ... 201 E1
Abbotsway DN32 ... 191 D6
Abbot's Way [5] PE11 ... 214 A3
Abbott Cl [10] LN8 ... 57 B8
Abbott's Cl PE9 ... 219 D4
Abbotts Gr PE4 ... 220 F6
Abbotts Grange DN36 ... 195 E7
Abbotts Way LN11 ... 198 E6
Abbott's Wy NG24 ... 104 A5
Abbot Way PE7 ... 233 D4
Abel Cl PE6 ... 165 D1
Abel Smith Gdns [7] LN4 ... 81 E2
Abercorn St DN16 ... 183 A2
Aberdeen Cl PE9 ... 218 D6
Aberporth Dr LN6 ... 204 B8
Abingdon Ave LN6 ... 204 C6
Abingdon Cl [15] LN6 ... 204 C6
Aboyne Ave PE2 ... 229 F5
Abraham Cl [5] NG31 ... 129 E5
ABY LN13 ... 75 B5
Aby CE Prim Sch LN13 ... 75 B5
Aby Rd LN13 ... 75 C7
Acacia Ave
Chapel St Leonard PE24 ... 90 D8
Gainsborough DN21 ... 197 D6
Peterborough PE1 ... 226 B8
Scunthorpe DN15 ... 182 C5
Spalding PE11 ... 214 F5
Waddington LN5 ... 205 D1
[3] Wisbech PE13 ... 170 D1
Acacia Cl [12] NG34 ... 212 D2
Acacia Ct [3] DN16 ... 185 B6
Acacia Way Boston PE21 ... 208 C4
Acacia Way *continued*
Messingham DN17 ... 29 C7
Acad PE11 ... 156 E6
Academy Cl PE12 ... 215 E5
Acadia Gr HU13 ... 178 F1
Acasta Wy HU9 ... 5 E8
Accommodation Rd LN9 ... 199 A5
Acer Cl LN6 ... 204 D7
Acer Ct [2] LN6 ... 204 D7
Acer Gr [3] DN17 ... 184 C5
Acer Rd PE1 ... 226 B6
Achille Rd DN34 ... 190 D5
Achurch Cl LN9 ... 199 D1
Acklam Ave [3] PE11 ... 214 F6
Acklam Gr DN32 ... 192 B6
Acklands La [13] NG23 ... 117 D3
Ackrill Cl LN4 ... 207 D5
Acland St
Gainsborough DN21 ... 197 C5
[4] Kingston upon Hull HU3 ... 180 A6
Peterborough PE1 ... 225 F3
Acomb Comm Rd DN7 ... 14 F4
Acorn Avenue LN11 ... 198 E6
Acorn Cl Freiston PE21 ... 126 C4
Grantham NG31 ... 211 C7
Lincoln LN5 ... 205 D7
[19] Sutton on Sea LN12 ... 76 F8
Acorn Ct DN35 ... 192 D2
Acorn Dr LN6 ... 93 A8
Acorns The PE6 ... 217 A6
Acorn Way
[5] Bottesford DN16 ... 185 B2
Hessle HU13 ... 178 B3
Acre Cl LN8 ... 57 D8
Acre Dyke La LN4 ... 82 B4
Acre La Scopwick LN4 ... 95 E1
Threekingham NG34 ... 132 E2
Acres La DN9 ... 26 D7
Acres The [1] PE9 ... 172 D4
Acton Ct [12] DN32 ... 189 C1
Adam Cl [18] LN6 ... 204 D7
Adam Smith St DN31 ... 188 F1
Adamstiles [2] NG32 ... 210 B4
Adams Way [6] DN21 ... 65 E8
Ada Way LN11 ... 198 D7
Adderley PE3 ... 225 C7
Addington Way [3] PE4 ... 221 A3
Addison Cl [4] LN5 ... 107 A8
Addison Dr LN2 ... 202 B6
Addison Pl LN1 ... 65 E3
ADDLETHORPE PE24 ... 90 C3
Adelaide Cl
Gainsborough DN21 ... 197 F2
Adelaide Cl *continued*
[13] Waddington LN5 ... 93 E8
Adelaide Prim Sch HU3 ... 180 D5
Adelaide St
Kingston upon Hull HU3 ... 180 D5
Stamford PE9 ... 219 D5
Adelphi Ct [5] DN36 ... 195 C6
Adelphi Dr DN33 ... 194 E7
Adlard Gr DN36 ... 36 C7
ADLINGFLEET DN14 ... 7 E7
Adlingfleet Rd DN17 ... 7 E6
Adlington Mews DN21 ... 197 F2
Admirals Dr [7] PE13 ... 170 D2
Admiralty Rd [19] LN12 ... 64 B4
Adrian Cl Louth LN11 ... 198 C4
[9] Skegness PE25 ... 206 A4
[9] Swineshead PE20 ... 135 B7
Advent Ct [2] DN39 ... 12 A1
Adwalton Cl [1] NG24 ... 104 C4
Aegir Cl DN21 ... 197 F2
Africa Cl DN34 ... 190 D4
Agard Ave DN15 ... 182 E3
Agnes St [2] NG31 ... 211 B4
Aidan Rd NG34 ... 212 B2
AILBY LN13 ... 75 D4
AILSWORTH PE5 ... 223 D3
Aima Ct [2] LN2 ... 68 C2
Ainsdale Dr PE4 ... 220 F3
Ainslie St DN32 ... 191 E6
Ainsworth Rd [5] DN40 ... 186 B4
Ainthorpe Gr HU5 ... 179 C7
Ainthorpe Prim Sch HU5 ... 179 C8
Aintree Dr PE11 ... 214 B1
Aintree Wy PE10 ... 213 D3
Aire Cl DN40 ... 186 A3
Airedale Cl
[12] Broughton DN20 ... 19 E4
Peterborough PE1 ... 226 A6
Airedale Rd
[1] Scunthorpe DN16 ... 185 D5
[1] Stamford PE9 ... 219 A7
Airedale Way DN31 ... 191 D8
Aire Rd NG31 ... 210 E3
Airfield La LN3 ... 69 E7
Airlie St HU3 ... 180 B5
Airmanship Rd NG34 ... 120 B8
Airmyn Ave [1] HU3 ... 179 E6
Airship Rd NG34 ... 107 C1
AISBY Heydour NG32 ... 131 D5
Pilham DN21 ... 41 D4
Aisby Wlk DN21 ... 197 F3
Aisne Cl LN1 ... 201 E7
Aisne St HU5 ... 180 A8
AISTHORPE LN1 ... 67 C7
Ajax Cl DN34 ... 190 D4
Ajax Ct DN15 ... 182 F5
Akeferry Rd DN9 ... 27 C1
Akeman Cl [10] PE10 ... 213 C6
Akeman Dr [14] LN4 ... 81 A1
Akita Cl [4] PE11 ... 214 A5
Alabala Cl LN4 ... 203 C1
Alabala La LN4 ... 81 F4
Alan Cres DN15 ... 182 F2
Alba Cl DN17 ... 184 D5
Alban Ret Pk PE21 ... 208 B3
Albany Cl Louth LN11 ... 198 D3
Skegness PE25 ... 206 A5
Albany Pl LN11 ... 198 D3
Albany Rd Louth LN11 ... 198 D3
Skegness PE25 ... 206 A5
[21] Wisbech PE13 ... 170 D1
[3] Woodhall Spa LN10 ... 97 D5
Albany St
Gainsborough DN21 ... 197 C6
Kingston upon Hull HU3 ... 180 D8
Lincoln LN1 ... 234 A4
Albany Terr LN5 ... 205 D5
Albany Villas HU13 ... 179 A1
Albany Way PE25 ... 206 A5
Albany Wlk PE2 ... 230 D7
Alba Rd PE7 ... 230 B2
Albatross Dr DN37 ... 190 B7
Albatross Way LN11 ... 198 D8
Albemarle Cl [5] HU15 ... 2 B5
Albemarle St [2] HU3 ... 180 B5
Alberta Cres DN17 ... 184 E3
Albert Ave
Kingston upon Hull HU3 ... 180 A7
Long Sutton PE12 ... 159 E7
[4] Newark-on-Trent NG24 ... 104 B2
[1] Skegness PE25 ... 103 E4
Albert Ave Pools [5] HU3 ... 180 A7
Albert Cl [7] DN32 ... 189 B1
Albert Cres Lincoln LN1 ... 201 D4
Yaxley PE7 ... 233 B8
Albert Ct PE21 ... 208 E5
Albertine Ct [4] DN37 ... 194 C5
Albert Marson Ct [6] DN16 ... 183 B2
Albert Pl Grimsby DN32 ... 189 B1
Peterborough PE3 ... 225 F1
Albert Rd
[7] Cleethorpes DN35 ... 192 F6
Scunthorpe DN16 ... 185 A5

Albert Rd continued
Skegness PE25 206 B3
2 Stamford PE9 219 C4
Albertross Dr DN36 195 E6
Albert St E DN32 189 B1
Albert St W 5 DN32 189 B1
Albert St Boston PE21 208 D5
15 Bottesford NG13 128 A6
Brigg DN20 196 C3
Grantham NG31 211 C2
6 Holbeach PE12 215 D2
Horncastle LN9 199 C3
7 New Holland DN19 4 E2
Spalding PE11 214 E5
Thorne/Moorends DN8 15 B8
Albert Terr 2 Boston PE21 208 E4
Boultham LN5 205 D8
14 Sleaford NG34 212 D4
Albert Wlk 3 PE12 215 D2
Albery Way DN36 195 C7
Albion Cl LN1 201 C6
Albion Cres LN1 201 C6
Albion Ct HU4 179 B6
Albion Hill 8 DN9 27 E6
Albion Pl LN11 198 C5
Albion Rd 2 NG31 211 A5
Albion St 8 Crowland PE6 166 E1
13 Grantham NG31 211 A5
Grimsby DN32 189 B1
Holbeach PE12 215 F2
10 Kingston upon Hull HU1 180 E7
Spalding PE11 214 E5
Albion Terr
4 Misterton DN10 40 A5
Sleaford NG34 212 E4
Albourne Ave DN15 183 A2
Alconbury Cl
13 Birchwood LN6 204 C6
Peterborough PE2 231 E5
Alcorn Gn PE21 209 C4
Aldbro' St HU2 180 F8
Aldburgh Cl 16 LN10 97 C5
Alden Cl DN40 186 C4
Alder Ave 18 DN36 36 C8
Alder Cl 30 Brough HU15 2 C5
3 Lincoln LN6 204 F3
Louth LN11 198 D4
Alderfield Cl 3 PE21 208 E1
Alder Gr PE21 209 C2
Aldergrove Cl 2 LN6 204 C7
Aldergrove Cres LN6 204 C7
Alderlands Cl 6 PE6 175 B8
Alderley Edge DN37 194 C4
Alderman Payne Prim Sch
PE13 177 D7
Alderman's Dr PE3 225 E3
Alderney Way
Immingham DN40 186 C2
Lincoln LN6 205 A1
Alder Pl 27 LN13 75 F2
Alder Rd Hessle HU13 178 B1
Peterborough PE7 230 C3
Sleaford NG34 212 D2
Alderson Mews 5 HU9 181 C7
Alders The DN21 197 F5
Alder View DN33 190 F3
ALDGATE PE9 171 A3
Aldgate Ct 9 PE9 171 A3
Aldred Gdns DN33 191 B1
Aldrich Rd DN35 192 F4
Aldrin Cl Spalding PE11 214 C2
16 Spalding PE11 214 C2
Aldsworth Cl 1 PE1 226 D6
Aldwych Croft 8 DN36 195 C6
Aldwych Ct HU5 179 E8
Aldwych Gdns 11 PE11 214 A2
Alec Rose Gr DN21 197 F3
Alexander Ave NG24 104 A6
Alexander Cl 15 LN4 95 D4
Alexander Dr LN11 198 D4
Alexander Rd Lincoln LN2 202 D8
Scunthorpe DN16 183 C3
Alexandra Cl 8 NG23 117 D4
Alexandra Ct 9 PE25 206 C3
Alexandra Dock N DN31 188 F2
Alexandra Pk 22 LN12 64 B4
Alexandra Rd
Cleethorpes DN35 192 F6
Grantham NG31 210 F3
Grimsby DN31 188 F1
Immingham DN40 186 F6
Louth LN11 198 C6
21 Mablethorpe/Sutton on Sea
LN12 64 B4
Peterborough PE1 225 F6
Scunthorpe DN16 185 B6
Skegness PE25 206 B3
Sleaford NG34 212 C4
Spalding PE11 214 E3
3 Woodhall Spa LN10 97 C6
Alexandra Rd S DN40 186 E6
Alexandra Ret Pk DN31 188 F1
Alexandra St HU3 180 D7
Alexandra Terr LN1 234 A3
Alexandra Terraces 4
PE10 213 D5
Alexandra Wharf DN31 191 D7
Alexandre Ave 2 LN6 204 F1
Alexandria Rd LN8 56 D5
Alfonso St 5 HU3 180 B5
ALFORD LN13 75 E2
Alford Mill Cl 6 LN6 93 B8
Alford Pottery★ LN13 75 E3
Alford Prim Sch LN13 75 F2
Alford Rd 1 Alford LN13 75 F3
Alford Rd continued
Bilsby LN13 76 A3
Farlesthorpe LN13 76 B1
Mablethorpe/Sutton on Sea
LN12 64 A3
Alford St NG31 211 B5
Alford Windmill★ LN13 75 F3
Alfred Ave LN4 95 C4
Alfred Cl 10 NG34 212 B2
Alfred Gelder St 6 HU1 180 F6
Alfred Smith Way 5 LN11 61 F3
Alfred St Boston PE21 209 A3
Gainsborough DN21 197 C5
Grimsby DN31 191 D8
Kingston upon Hull HU3 180 D5
Lincoln LN5 201 E1
Alfreton Ct 2 DN15 182 B2
Alfric Sq PE2 230 D6
ALGAKIRK PE20 136 B2
Algernon St DN32 191 F5
Algers Wlk PE11 214 A5
Algitha Rd PE25 206 C3
ALKBOROUGH DN15 8 C8
Alkborough La DN15 8 D7
Alkborough Prim Sch DN15 8 C8
Allan Ave PE2 231 E5
Allanby St DN15 183 A3
Allandale Cl LN1 201 D8
Allandale View 11 LN1 201 E8
Allanhall Way HU10 178 B8
Allard Cl PE7 233 D6
Allenby Ave DN34 191 A6
Allenby Cl LN2 202 D3
Allenby Cres LN11 49 A2
Allenby Rd LN2 202 D4
Allenby Rd Ind Est LN2 202 D4
Allenby's Chase 14 PE12 160 E4
Allenby Way PE25 206 D8
Allen Cl
7 Billingborough NG34 133 B1
4 Claypole NG23 117 E8
5 Market Deeping PE6 217 D5
Allen Rd Coningsby LN4 207 F6
Fenton NG23 105 C1
Peterborough PE1 225 E6
Allens Bsns Pk LN1 66 F1
Allen's Dro PE13 169 D1
Allerthorpe Cres 19 HU15 2 D5
Allerton Cl PE9 172 D3
Allerton Dr DN40 186 B4
Allerton Garth PE7 229 A4
Allerton Prim Sch DN40 186 B4
Allestree Dr DN33 194 E7
Allexton Gdns 2 PE1 226 D7
Alliance Ave HU3 179 F7
Alliance La HU3 179 F7
ALLINGTON NG32 128 F7
Allington Dr DN37 188 A2
Allington Gdn PE21 209 A7
Allington La NG32 129 B4
Allington Rd NG32 128 F5
Allington with Sedgebrook CE
Prim Sch NG32 129 A7
Allis Chalmers Way 8
PE9 163 D3
Allison Ave PE12 215 E2
Allison Cl 3 DN17 29 D7
Allison Pl 5 LN1 201 D4
Allison Rd
6 Heckington NG34 122 D3
7 Louth LN11 198 C6
Allison St LN1 201 D4
Allotment La PE5 223 E2
All Saints Ave PE13 170 E1
All Saints Brewery★ 22
PE9 219 B5
All Saints CE Jun Sch
HU13 178 F2
All Saints CE Prim Sch
LN6 204 E1
All Saints' CE Prim Sch
PE1 226 A6
All Saints Cl 4 Hessle HU13 3 F4
3 Holbeach PE12 215 F3
7 Moulton PE12 157 F7
Ruskington NG34 108 D2
4 Wainfleet All Saints
PE24 102 D1
All Saints' Cl 17 DN19 12 A8
All Saints Cty Prim Sch
LN5 93 F7
All Saints Gr 4 NG34 212 B6
All Saints La 14 LN2 68 C2
All Saints Mews 17 PE9 219 B5
All Saints' Pl 6 PE9 219 B5
All Saints Rd LN2 202 F6
All Saints' Rd PE1 226 A5
All Saints' St
Kingston upon Hull HU3 180 D8
10 Stamford PE9 219 B5
Allwood Rd 20 LN2 68 D6
Ally's Wy LN4 202 F2
Alma Ave PE25 206 B5
Alma Cl
Kingston upon Hull HU10 178 D7
3 Skegness PE25 206 B5
Alma Martin Way 7 LN3 83 C4
Alma Pk Cl 1 NG31 211 F6
Alma Pk Ind Est
Grantham NG31 211 F7
Londonthorpe & Harrowby Without
NG31 130 C4
Alma Pk Rd NG31 211 F6
Alma Rd PE1 225 F5
Alma St 6 HU9 181 B7
Almond Ave Heighington LN4 81 F4
Lincoln LN6 205 A8
Almond Cl Boston PE21 208 C5
Almond Cl continued
9 Saxilby LN1 66 D2
Almond Cres Lincoln LN6 205 A8
Louth LN11 198 D5
Waddington LN5 205 D1
Almond Ct LN6 205 A8
Almond Gr Brigg DN20 196 B4
Grantham NG31 211 C6
3 Kingston upon Hull HU3 180 D6
3 Scunthorpe DN16 185 B8
Skellingthorpe LN6 200 A4
Stallingborough DN41 23 E6
Almond Rd PE1 226 B7
Almonds Gn LN4 108 C8
Almond Wlk Boston PE21 208 D5
Sleaford NG34 212 D6
Almoners La PE3 225 E3
Alness Cl LN6 204 B8
Alnwick PE2 229 F3
Alnwick Way NG31 210 E6
Altham Terr LN5 205 D7
ALTHORPE DN17 17 D5
Althorpe Cl 15 PE6 217 A5
Althorpe & Keadby Prim Sch
DN17 17 D5
Althorpe Sta DN17 17 D5
Altoft Cl 19 DN37 23 F1
Altyre Way DN36 192 C1
Alverston Ave LN10 97 D5
Alveston Rd DN17 184 D8
Alvey Rd NG24 104 C2
ALVINGHAM LN11 49 E2
Alvingham Ave DN35 192 F3
Alvingham Rd
Keddington LN11 198 E8
Scunthorpe DN16 185 B7
Alvis Cl LN4 205 F2
Alvis Dr PE7 233 D6
ALWALTON PE2 229 B4
Alwyn Rd 10 DN8 15 B8
Amanda Ct PE3 225 E2
Amanda Dr Hatfield DN7 14 D4
Louth LN11 198 C8
Ambassador Wlk PE11 214 A1
Ambergate Sports Coll
NG31 210 D3
Ambergate Wlk NG31 210 E3
Amberley Cl DN33 191 B1
Amberley Cres PE21 208 C4
Amberley Slope PE4 221 A3
Amble Cl LN1 201 E8
Ambleside Cl 4 NG34 212 B2
Ambleside Dr PE11 214 B2
Ambleside Gdns PE4 221 B3
Ambleside Pk LN6 204 F1
Ambrose Ave 3 DN7 14 E4
Ambury Gdns 9 PE6 166 F1
Amcott Ave DN10 40 A4
Amcott Rd DN17 7 F1
AMCOTTS DN17 7 F1
Amcotts Rd DN33 191 A2
Amelia Ct DN36 36 D8
Amery Way 31 PE24 90 D7
Amesbury Ave DN33 194 D7
Amethyst Cl 3 NG34 212 A3
Amethyst Ct DN36 195 D7
Amman Sq 1 NG34 120 D8
Amos Cl DN33 194 D7
Amos Cres 3 DN16 185 D7
Amos La NG23 91 E6
Amos Way 8 PE22 113 B1
Ampleforth Ave DN32 190 F8
Ampleforth Gr HU5 179 D8
Amstel Cl 1 PE11 214 B2
Amsterdam Gdns 9 PE11 214 B3
Amwell Gn 10 DN7 14 D3
Anastasia Cl DN21 197 C7
ANCASTER NG32 120 B2
Ancaster Ave
Chapel St Leonard PE24 90 D7
Grimsby DN33 194 D8
Lincoln LN2 202 B5
Spilsby PE23 100 F8
Ancaster CE Prim Sch
NG32 120 A3
Ancaster Cl LN3 203 E6
Ancaster Ct Horncastle LN9 199 B3
Scunthorpe DN16 185 A5
Ancaster Dr NG34 212 B2
Ancaster Mews 33 PE24 90 D7
Ancaster Rd
1 Bourne PE10 213 E5
16 Mablethorpe/Sutton on Sea
LN12 64 B3
7 Stamford PE9 219 A7
Ancaster Sta NG32 120 A3
Ancaster Valley Nature
Reserve★ NG32 120 A2
Ancholme Ave DN40 186 A3
Ancholme Bsns Pk DN20 196 A4
Ancholme Cl LN1 201 D8
Ancholme Gdns 9 DN20 196 C3
Ancholme Leisure Ctr
DN20 196 A3
Ancholme Rd DN16 185 D6
Ancholme Way DN20 196 B3
Anchorage St 4 DN20 196 B3
Anchor Cl Canal Side DN8 15 A8
Lincoln LN5 234 A1
Anchor Ct PE4 221 D1
Anchor La PE25 90 D4
Anchor Rd Scunthorpe DN16 19 B4
Sutton Bridge PE34 161 C4
Anchor St LN5 234 A1
Anchors Way 7 DN20 196 A3
Ancient La DN7 14 E3
ANDERBY PE24 77 A2
Anderby Cl LN6 204 F6
ANDERBY CREEK PE24 77 C3
Anderby Dr Grimsby DN37 190 D7
Lincoln LN6 204 F6
Anderby Drainage Mus★
PE24 77 C2
Anderby Rd PE24 77 D1
Anderson LN2 68 D5
Anderson Cl
5 Newark-on-Trent
NG24 104 A2
7 Wisbech PE13 170 C1
Anderson La 2 LN1 201 F6
Anderson Rd
2 Hemswell Cliff DN21 55 A8
Scunthorpe DN16 185 C7
Anderson St DN31 191 D7
Anderson Way DN21 52 F5
Andover Cl LN6 204 B8
Andrea Cl PE2 231 C6
Andrew Ave 27 PE24 90 D7
Andrew Cl PE5 223 D2
Andrewe's Cl PE7 231 B1
Andrew Paddock 18 DN20 30 F5
Andrew Rd
9 Humberston DN36 36 D8
1 Stamford PE9 219 B6
Andrews Cl LN11 198 C7
Andrews Cres PE4 221 D2
Andrews Rd 1 DN18 10 A7
Andrews Way 7 DN40 186 A4
Anfield Rd PE12 216 B5
Angel Ct 5 NG32 120 A2
Angelica Dr 1 PE11 214 B6
Angell La PE12 215 E1
Angel Prec The PE10 213 C5
Angerstein Rd DN17 184 F5
Anglesey Cl 20 LN6 204 C7
Anglesey Dr DN40 186 C2
Anglia Cl 13 NG34 212 B2
Anglian Cl PE2 231 D6
Anglian Way 5 LN8 57 E8
Angus Cl 3 PE9 218 D6
Angus Ct PE3 225 D3
ANLABY HU10 179 A6
Anlaby Acre Head Prim Sch
HU4 179 B7
Anlaby Ave 7 HU4 179 B6
Anlaby High Rd HU4 179 C6
Anlaby House Estate
HU10 178 E6
ANLABY PARK HU4 179 C5
Anlaby Pk Rd N HU4 179 B5
Anlaby Pk Rd S HU4 179 B2
Anlaby Prim Sch HU4 179 A6
Anlaby Rd HU3 179 F6
Anlafgate 7 HU10 178 F6
Annandale Rd HU10 178 C8
Anne Rd Stamford PE9 219 A6
11 Sutton Bridge PE12 160 E4
Annes Cres DN16 185 C7
Annesley St 1 DN31 188 F1
Annette Cl 8 PE11 214 B5
Ann Gr DN35 192 D4
Anningson La DN36 195 D7
Annpasture La LN4 207 C8
Ann Wayne Ave 4 LN9 199 B2
Anson Ave LN4 207 D3
Anson Cl Grantham NG31 211 C2
Skellingthorpe LN6 200 A4
Anson Ct PE6 217 B7
Anson Rd LN4 207 D2
Antelope Rd DN18 4 A1
Anthony Cl PE1 225 F8
Anthony Cres LN11 198 C8
Anthony's Bank Rd DN36 193 D1
Anthony Way 3 DN41 23 D6
ANTON'S GOWT PE22 125 B6
Antrim Rd 9 LN5 205 D2
Antrim Way DN33 191 D2
Anvil Cl PE12 148 B1
Anvil Wlk 2 DN15 8 F3
ANWICK NG34 109 B1
Anzio Cres LN1 201 E7
Anzio Terr LN1 201 E7
Anzio Wlk LN1 201 E7
Apeldoorn Gdns 3 PE11 214 B3
APLEY LN8 70 A2
Apley Cl
Gainsborough DN21 197 F3
Lincoln LN2 202 A8
Apley La LN8 70 C1
Apley Rd LN8 70 B3
Apollo Ave
Peterborough PE2 231 D4
Stanground PE7 231 C4
Appian Way 8 Baston PE6 164 E5
11 Bracebridge Heath LN4 81 A1
West Marsh DN31 188 C2
Apple Ave 31 NG24 104 C1
APPLEBY DN15 9 D1
Appleby Cl
5 Beacon Hill NG24 104 B4
Scunthorpe DN17 184 F5
Appleby Ct 17 DN32 189 C1
Appleby Gdns DN20 19 D4
Appleby La DN20 19 D4
Appleby Mill Rd DN16 183 E3
Appleby Wy
15 Birchwood LN6 204 B8
12 Birchwood LN6 204 B8
10 Birchwood LN6 204 B8
Apple Cl LN4 81 F4
Appledore Cl HU9 181 C6
Apple Garth LN5 205 D4
Applegarth Cl 2 DN35 192 D5
Applegarth Rd 2 HU8 181 A7
Appleton Cl 2 PE7 230 C2
Appleton Gate NG24 104 A5
Appleton Way DN16 185 C6
Appletree Cl PE6 217 F5
Apple Tree Cl 19 LN4 95 C4
Apple Tree Ct 14 DN41 23 F5
Apple Tree La DN37 23 F2
Applewood Dr
5 Gonerby Hill Foot
NG31 210 F8
Hampton Hargate PE7 230 C3
Apple Wy Pinchbeck PE11 157 A8
Pinchbeck PE11 214 F8
Appleyard PE2 231 C7
Appleyard Dr 38 DN18 10 E8
Apricot Cl PE1 226 C8
Apsley Way PE3 225 A2
Aqua Dr LN12 64 B2
Aqua Drive PE7 233 E8
Aquila Way PE6 164 E2
Arabis Cl 3 LN2 202 C8
Arakan Way 2 PE10 213 E7
Arbella Rd PE21 209 C4
Arboath Gdns PE2 229 C4
Arboretum Ave LN2 234 C2
Arboretum The★ LN2 234 C3
Arboretum View LN2 234 C2
Arborfield Cl 5 PE6 173 C4
Arbury Cl PE3 225 A3
Arcadia Cres 2 PE25 206 D2
Arcadia Rd PE25 206 D3
Archer Ct
8 Bishop Norton LN8 43 D3
Little London PE11 214 A1
Archer La 12 PE21 208 F5
Archer Rd Branston LN4 81 E2
Waltham DN37 194 D4
Archers Dro PE6 176 D6
Archers La PE20 136 C3
Archer St
3 Bishop Norton LN8 43 D3
Lincoln LN5 234 B1
Archers Way NG33 140 A5
Archibald Wlk PE21 208 B4
Archway Dr LN8 70 C4
Arcon Dr HU4 179 D6
Arcott Dr PE21 208 C5
Arden Cl 6 LN12 64 C3
Arden Moor Way 4 LN6 93 B8
Ardent Rd DN18 4 A1
Arden Village DN35 192 F1
Arena Dr PE2 229 B4
Argyle Ct 6 DN15 183 B3
Argyle St Boston PE21 208 D5
Kingston upon Hull HU3 180 C7
Argyll Way PE9 218 F5
Ariston St DN32 192 B7
Arkley Cl 22 HU15 2 C5
Ark Rd LN11 50 F8
Ark Royal Ct 2 NG34 212 A3
Arkwright St DN21 197 C5
Arkwright Way
Peterborough PE4 221 F2
Scunthorpe DN16 185 F6
Arlington Rd Dunscroft DN7 14 D3
4 Toft Newton LN8 56 D5
Arlington St 2 HU3 180 D6
Armada Cl 16 PE13 170 D2
Armeria Dr 4 DN17 185 A1
Armley Gr 3 PE9 219 D7
Armour Rd DN16 183 E3
Armstrong Pl E 3 DN31 188 E1
Armstrong Pl W 2 DN31 188 E1
Armstrong Rd 12 PE11 214 C2
Armstrong's Cl 2 PE12 157 D7
Armstrong's La PE22 115 B7
Armstrong St DN31 188 E1
Armthorpe La DN3 14 A3
Armtree Rd PE22 124 E7
Arne Cl 10 NG32 120 A3
Arnhem Ave 1 NG34 108 D2
Arnhem Cl LN1 201 E7
Arnhem Dr
10 Caythorpe NG32 119 B7
2 Spalding PE11 214 C5
Arnhem Way Bourne PE10 213 E6
7 Woodhall Spa LN10 97 D5
Arnold Ave NG31 210 E8
Arnold Cl DN37 23 F2
Arnold Ct 11 DN32 189 C1
Arnold La HU3 180 B6
Arnold's Mdw Nature
Reserve★ PE12 214 F2
Arnold St HU3 180 B6
Arran Cl Immingham DN40 186 D2
New Waltham DN36 195 C7
Sleaford NG34 121 A2
Arran Rd PE9 218 D5
Arras Cl LN1 201 E6
Arrow Ct PE7 230 C3
Art Coll Ct DN32 191 F8
Art Coll Mews DN32 191 F8
Artemis Way Haddon PE7 232 F8
Orton Southgate PE2 228 E1
Art Haven The★ NG31 211 B3
Arthur Mellows Village Coll
PE6 220 B8
Arthur Rd DN21 197 D6
Arthurs' Ave 5 PE12 215 D2
Arthur St Grimsby DN31 191 C8
Kingston upon Hull HU3 180 A5
6 Lincoln LN5 201 F1
Arthur Taylor St 1 LN1 201 D3
Artillery Row 13 PE21 209 A5
Artindale PE3 225 A3
Artis Ct PE3 225 A3
Arun Ct 9 PE11 214 A4
Arundel Cl
Gainsborough DN21 197 E6
Kingston upon Hull HU9 181 C8

Arundel Cres PE21 208 B4
Arundel Dr Green Hill NG31 210 E6
Louth LN11 198 A7
Arundel Pl DN35 192 E5
Arundel Rd PE4 221 A1
Arundel St 3 HU9 181 C8
Arundel Wlk DN34 191 A7
Arvina Cl 20 LN6 93 B8
Ascendale PE6 217 F5
Ascot Cl 11 Bourne PE10 213 D3
4 Spalding PE11 156 E3
Ascot Dr
7 Grantham NG31 211 D7
Peterborough PE1 226 B6
Ascot Rd DN37 194 D4
Ascott Cl HU4 179 D5
Ascot Way 7 LN6 93 A8
ASGARBY
Asgarby and Howell NG34 122 B4
Lusby with Winceby LN9 86 F1
Asgarby Rd NG34 122 B2
Asgard Way DN33 191 B2
Ash Ave 19 HU15 2 C6
Ashberry Dr
31 Messingham DN17 29 D7
4 Scunthorpe DN16 185 B6
Ashbourne 6 DN37 194 C4
Ashbourne Cl 3 NG34 212 B2
Ashbourne Ct DN15 182 B3
Ashbourne Rd PE7 230 E2
Ash Buckingham Studio* LN9 85 C5
Ashburn Cl 1 PE6 220 D7
Ashburnham Rd 20 DN8 15 A8
Ashburton Cl PE12 215 E5
ASHBY DN16 185 B5
Ashby Ave LN6 204 F7
Ashby Broadway DN16 185 A6
ASHBY BY PARTNEY PE23 88 D1
Ashby Cl Bracebridge LN5 205 D1
Grimsby DN37 190 D8
Holton le Clay DN36 195 E1
Kingston upon Hull HU4 179 B7
Ashby Ct 2 NG34 212 D6
ASHBY CUM FENBY DN37 35 D3
ASHBY DE LA LAUNDE LN4 108 B6
Ashby Gdns 7 PE12 157 F6
Ashby High St DN16 185 B6
ASHBY HILL DN37 35 C3
Ashby Hill DN37 35 C3
Ashby La DN37 35 D4
Ashby Mdws PE23 88 A1
ASHBY PUERORUM LN9 86 E6
Ashby Rd
Cleethorpes DN35 192 D3
Kingston upon Hull HU4 179 B4
Scunthorpe DN16 183 A1
Spilsby PE23 88 A1
Ash Cl Burgh le Marsh PE24 102 D7
5 Colsterworth NG33 151 E7
Fulbeck NG32 106 C1
Hessle HU13 178 C3
Holbeach PE12 215 C3
Langtoft PE6 164 E2
Lincoln LN6 204 E8
Louth LN11 198 C7
Peterborough PE1 226 C7
Spalding PE11 214 F5
1 Thorney PE6 175 F3
Ashcroft Gdns PE1 226 C5
Ashcroft Rd DN21 197 D2
Ash Ct Cleethorpes DN35 192 D2
5 Donington PE11 134 E2
Peterborough PE1 226 C7
Spalding PE11 214 F6
Ashdale Cl 3 LN4 95 C4
Ashdale Pk 18 HU14 3 A5
Ashdene Cl HU10 178 E7
Ashdown Ave 5 DN15 182 E3
Ashdown Cl 3 DN20 196 E3
Ash Dr
Kingston upon Hull HU10 178 F8
3 Kirton PE20 136 C5
Asheridge LN4 81 E2
Ashes The PE7 230 F5
Ashfield 2 LN1 66 D7
Ashfield Ave 2 DN8 15 A7
Ashfield Ct 20 DN17 16 D7
Ashfield Gr 1 DN7 14 C6
Ashfield Grange 5 LN1 66 C2
Ashfield Pk DN17 184 C5
Ashfield Rd 8 Hatfield DN7 14 C4
Sleaford NG34 212 D5
Thorne DN8 14 F7
Ashfields PE6 217 D2
Ashfield St 3 LN2 202 B3
Ash Gr Bourne PE10 213 C6
Brigg DN20 196 B4
Cherry Willingham/Reepham LN3 203 D5
Gainsborough DN21 197 D6
Grantham NG31 211 D7
Lincoln LN6 204 F2
32 Messingham DN17 29 D7
Scunthorpe DN16 185 B7
Ash Hill Adacemy DN7 14 D3
Ash Hill Cres DN7 14 D4
Ash Hill Rd DN7 14 D4
Ashing La LN2 68 F6
ASHINGTON END PE24 90 B1
Ash La 26 LN5 93 F6
Ashlawn Dr PE21 209 B6
Ashlea 3 DN10 39 F5
Ashleigh PE2 229 C6
Ashleigh Ct 3 DN41 23 F5
Ashley Cl LN12 64 C1
Ashley Dr NG31 210 E8
Ashley Pool La 5 PE6 176 A2
Ashley Rd 2 LN11 198 C5
Ashlin Gr LN1 234 A3
Ash Pk PE4 220 F6
Ash Pl 6 PE9 218 D6
Ash Rd 7 Coningsby LN4 207 D4
Peterborough PE1 226 C7
Ashridge Dr DN32 192 C5
ASHTON PE9 173 A4
Ashton Hall Dr PE21 208 A1
Ashton Rd PE3 225 B5
Ashtons Ct LN5 201 E1
Ashtree Ave DN34 191 A6
Ash Tree Ave 11 LN2 68 D2
Ashtree Cl 1 Belton DN9 16 E2
12 Ruskington NG34 108 E1
Ash Tree Cl
Immingham DN40 186 C5
10 Market Rasen LN8 57 D7
Ash Tree Dr 5 DN9 27 D2
Ashtree Gdns 5 PE9 171 B1
Ash Tree Rd 7 DN8 15 B7
Ash Tree Wy LN5 92 E2
Ash Villa South Rauceby The NG34 121 A3
Ashville Cl PE12 215 C6
Ashville Rd PE7 230 B2
Ashwell Ave 2 HU9 5 E8
Ashwin Gate 2 PE11 145 A8
Ashwood Cl LN9 199 B4
Ashwood Dr 10 DN36 36 D8
Ashworth Cl
6 Beacon Hill NG24 104 B4
Lincoln LN6 204 F5
Askew Ave HU4 179 E4
Askew's Dro PE6 166 D2
Askew's La PE7 233 E4
ASLACKBY NG34 142 D5
Aslackby Rd NG34 142 D3
Aspen Cl Kettlethorpe LN1 65 D2
Kingston upon Hull HU4 179 C3
Aspen Ct Cleethorpes DN35 192 D2
Gainsborough DN21 197 F6
Aspen Dr 4 NG34 212 D2
Aspen Gr DN16 185 B8
Aspen La DN37 23 F2
Aspen Wlk 10 HU15 2 D5
ASPERTON PE20 135 D4
Asperton Rd PE20 135 E4
Asphodel Cl DN36 195 D7
Asquith St DN21 197 B6
ASSERBY LN13 76 D4
ASTERBY LN11 72 E6
Asterby Cl LN2 202 A7
Asterby End LN11 72 E6
Asterby La LN11 72 E5
Asterby Rd DN17 184 F5
Aster Cl LN2 202 C8
Aster Dr PE4 221 B3
Astley Cres 15 DN21 29 C3
Astley St HU3 179 F7
Aston Cl 4 Waddington LN5 93 F7
Yaxley PE7 233 E6
Aston Gn 5 DN7 14 D3
Aston Hall Dr 12 HU14 3 A5
Aston Rd HU10 178 F8
Astore Pk PE1 226 E3
Astor Pl PE11 214 A1
Astral Cl HU13 178 F3
Astral Rd HU13 178 F3
Astral Way 8 LN6 204 C1
Astwick Rd LN6 205 A5
ASWARBY NG34 132 D6
ASWARDBY PE23 87 E5
Aswell St LN11 198 B5
Athelstan Cl 9 NG34 212 B2
Athena Cl PE7 231 C4
Athena Dr DN31 188 C2
Athenian Way 1 DN31 188 A3
Atherstone Ave PE3 225 B4
Atherton Gdns PE11 214 D8
Atherton Way DN20 196 B4
Atholl Ave HU13 178 E3
Athol St HU3 179 F4
Atkinson Ave DN20 196 C5
Atkinson Dr 24 HU15 2 C6
Atkinson La 6 DN37 194 E4
Atkinsons La PE23 101 C6
Atkinson St PE1 226 C2
Atkinsons Warren Nature Reserve* DN15 182 D5
Atkinsons Way DN15 182 F7
Atlantic Pl 8 NG31 211 A3
Atlas Rd DN17 184 F8
ATTERBY LN8 43 D3
Atterby Carr La DN21 43 F4
Atterby La LN8 43 C3
Atton Ave 4 PE11 157 B6
Atwater Cl LN2 202 D7
Atwater Ct 2 LN2 202 D7
Atwater Gr LN2 202 D7
Atwood Cl DN40 186 B5
Auborn Gdns PE3 225 B3
AUBOURN LN5 93 A5
Aubourn Ave LN2 201 F7
Aubourn Hall* LN5 93 A5
Aubretia Ave PE4 221 B3
Aubretia Dr 3 DN17 185 A1
Aubrey Parker Cl 4 LN12 64 C2
Auckland Cres 1 LN4 96 C1
Auckland Rd
Grimsby DN31 189 B2
Scunthorpe DN15 182 F2
Auden Cl LN2 234 C4
Auden Ct 2 LN4 207 B5
Audern Rd DN16 185 A4
Audley Gate PE3 225 C3
Audley St 5 HU2 180 E8
Audus Pl 13 PE9 218 E6
Augusta Cl Grimsby DN34 191 C5
Peterborough PE1 226 E6
Augusta Dr PE13 170 A7
Augusta Oaks DN34 191 C6
Augusta St DN34 191 C6
Augustin Ret Pk NG31 211 A4
Augustus Dr 17 HU15 2 C5
AUNBY PE9 163 B5
AUNSBY NG34 132 A5
Aunsby Rd NG34 132 A7
Aurora Wy PE2 231 D4
Austacre Way LN2 202 F6
AUSTENDIKE PE12 157 E4
Austendike Rd PE12 157 C4
AUSTEN FEN LN11 49 F5
Austen Mews 5 PE11 214 A1
Austen Wlk LN2 202 C6
Austerby PE10 213 E4
Austerby Cl PE10 213 D4
Austerby The PE10 213 E4
Auster Rd 2 PE7 231 D3
Austin Cres 3 DN17 184 F3
Austin Ct PE7 233 D6
Austin Friar's La 2 PE9 219 B4
Austin Garth 5 DN37 23 F1
Austin St PE9 219 B4
AUTHORPE LN11 74 F7
Authorpe Top LN11 74 E6
Autumn Croft Rd 6 NG24 104 B5
Autumn Pk Ind Est NG31 210 F4
Avalon Wy LN11 198 C7
Av Clumber NG24 104 A3
Avebury Gdns PE11 214 F4
Aveland Cl
Aslackby & Laughton NG34 142 E5
5 Bourne PE10 213 C5
Aveland Dr NG34 143 B8
Aveland Way
Aslackby & Laughton NG34 142 D5
3 Baston PE6 164 E4
Avenswood La DN15 182 C6
Avenue A DN21 53 D5
Avenue B DN21 53 D5
Avenue Cannes DN15 182 D5
Avenue Clamart DN15 182 D5
Avenue Farm Rd PE12 160 D6
Avenue Fontenay DN15 182 D5
Avenue Lourdes DN15 182 D5
Avenue Nozay 2 DN20 19 E4
Avenue Rd NG31 211 B4
Avenue Rouen DN15 182 D6
Avenue Terr LN1 234 A3
Avenue The 9 Blyton DN21 41 C5
Burton upon Stather DN15 8 B4
Carlby PE9 163 E4
Deeping St Nicholas PE11 166 C7
East Ravendale DN37 35 C2
Friskney PE22 115 A6
Gainsborough DN21 197 E6
Grantham NG31 210 E4
6 Great Gonerby NG31 129 D5
Grimsby DN37 190 C8
Healing DN41 23 F5
7 Ingham LN1 54 F2
Kingston upon Hull HU10 178 C7
Lincoln LN1 234 A3
Market Deeping PE6 217 B5
8 Newark-on-Trent NG24 104 A4
Nocton LN4 95 B7
Swinderby LN6 92 C6
Avenue Vivian DN15 182 E4
Aviary Cl NG31 211 C5
Avignon Rd PE11 214 A5
Avocet Cl
4 Birchwood LN6 204 D8
4 Essendine PE9 163 D3
Avocet Mews DN16 185 F5
Avon Cl Grantham NG31 210 E3
5 Lincoln LN6 205 A2
Avon Ct PE4 221 C2
Avondale
1 Kingston upon Hull HU4 179 B2
7 Lincoln LN6 204 C1
Avondale St LN2 234 C2
Avon Rd DN16 183 C2
Axholme Acad The DN17 16 D7
Axholme Ave 3 DN17 16 C7
Axholme Ct HU9 181 B5
Axholme Dr 6 DN9 27 D6
Axholme Gn 19 DN8 15 B7
Axholme Line Nature Reserve* DN9 27 C4
Axholme Rd
Scunthorpe DN15 182 D2
2 Westwoodside DN9 27 A2
Axiom Ave PE3 225 C4
Axiom Ct PE9 219 D4
Axis Park PE2 229 D2
Ayam Cl 5 LN2 68 D6
Aydon Rd PE7 231 F6
Aykroft 1 PE10 213 E2
Aylesbury Gr HU5 179 D8
AYLESBY DN37 23 E2
Aylesby Cl 7 LN1 201 E8
Aylesby Gdns 2 DN33 191 B3
Aylesby La DN37 23 F3
Aylesby Rd Aylesby DN37 190 B6
Scunthorpe DN17 184 F5
Aylesford St 7 HU3 180 B5
Aylmer Ave PE24 103 D2
Aynsley Cl 18 LN6 204 C6
Aynsley Rd LN6 204 B6
Ayots Gn 14 DN7 14 D3
Ayr Cl PE9 218 E6
Ayres Dr PE2 231 C6
Ayscough Ave
Spalding PE11 214 D3
7 Stallingborough DN41 23 E6
Ayscoughfee Hall Mus & Gdns* PE11 214 D3
Ayscoughfee Hall Sch PE11 214 D3
Ayscough Gr 9 LN7 33 B4
Ayscough St 4 DN31 188 E1
Aysgarth Ave 18 DN17 29 D7
Azalea Cl PE3 225 A2
Azalea Ct 1 PE7 233 F6
Azalea Rd LN2 202 C8

B

Baatsfjord Cl 3 DN36 195 B7
Babington Row HU9 181 C8
Bacheler St HU3 180 B5
Back Bank Crowland PE12 167 B3
Whaplode PE12 168 A3
Back Field La DN7 14 E4
Backgate PE12 167 B8
Back La 5 Allington NG32 128 F7
Aswarby & Swarby NG34 132 A7
Barnby in the Willows NG24 105 A3
Belvoir NG32 138 D6
Bicker PE20 134 F6
Bilsby LN13 76 A2
Bolingbroke PE23 100 A7
Buckminster NG33 151 A4
Burton Coggles NG33 152 C8
Cammeringham LN1 54 F1
Candlesby with Gunby PE23 89 B1
Caythorpe NG32 119 B7
Claxby with Moorby PE22 99 B7
Claypole NG23 117 E7
Collyweston PE9 171 B1
Colsterworth NG33 151 E7
3 Deeping St James PE6 217 F4
Dunston LN4 95 C6
Eye PE6 175 A1
3 Foston NG32 117 F1
Garthorpe & Fockerby DN17 7 F6
Heighington/Washingborough LN4 81 F4
Holbeach PE12 215 D2
Ingoldsby NG33 141 C5
Leadenham LN5 106 C3
Long Bennington NG23 128 D8
Long Sutton PE12 216 D6
4 Lutton PE12 160 A8
Market Deeping PE6 174 A8
North Clifton NG23 78 C7
North Cockerington LN11 50 A1
Scothern LN2 68 F4
1 Searby cum Owmby DN38 32 D8
4 Skillington NG33 151 A8
4 Stainforth DN7 14 C6
9 Stamford PE9 219 C5
Stickford PE22 100 A3
Wainfleet All Saints PE24 102 A2
Wilsford NG32 120 C2
Winteringham DN15 2 B1
Wood Enderby PE22 98 F6
Yaxley PE7 233 E5
Back Rd Gorefield PE13 169 E2
Murrow PE13 177 E6
Back St Alkborough DN15 8 C8
Buckminster NG33 150 E5
East Stockwith DN21 40 B5
Saltfleetby LN11 51 C1
South Clifton NG23 78 C5
Sproxton LE14 138 F1
Bacon's La 1 PE11 145 C1
Bacon St DN21 197 D2
Bader Cl Peterborough PE3 225 B6
The Willows DN37 190 E8
Bader Way 3 PE25 206 A5
Badgate PE11 134 F2
Bad Gate PE12 169 B6
Badger Cl PE7 233 F5
Badger La PE10 213 C2
Badger's La PE20 136 B7
Badgers Oak 2 LN5 92 F3
Badger Way 1 DN20 19 E4
Badington Cl PE2 230 D8
Badinton La PE9 172 F5
Badminton Way LN11 198 A7
Baffen's La PE11 145 A4
BAG ENDERBY PE23 87 B7
Baggaley Dr LN9 199 A4
Baggholme Rd LN2 234 C2
Baghdad Rd 2 NG34 120 D8
Bagmoor La DN15 8 D3
Bagsby Rd DN9 28 B3
Baildon Cres LN6 205 A3
Baildon Rd DN15 182 D4
Bailey La DN7 14 E6
Baileys Cl PE12 215 D1
Baileys La LN5 92 F5
Bailey St HU10 178 F5
Bailey Way PE2 230 D8
Bailgate 3 LN2 234 B3
Baily's La PE12 147 F2
Bain Cl PE9 219 C7
Baines Ave NG24 104 B2
Baines Cl LN4 207 D5
Baines Rd DN21 197 F4
Bain Rd PE21 208 C3
Bain Rise 7 LN8 59 A7
Bain St LN1 201 D8
BAINTON PE9 172 F5
Bainton Rd Barnack PE9 172 D4
Newborough PE6 221 D8
Baird Cl PE7 233 D6
Bakehouse Ct 5 LN3 69 C3
Baker Ave 8 DN10 39 C1
Baker Cres LN6 204 E7
Baker Dr Nettleham LN2 68 C2
30 Winterton DN15 9 A5
Bakers Cl DN38 21 B5
Bakersfield DN20 196 F7
Bakers La Bassingham LN5 92 E2
Peterborough PE2 230 E7
Baker's La
Candlesby with Gunby PE23 89 A2
Fishtoft PE21 126 C4
Great Steeping PE23 101 E6
Westborough & Dry Doddington NG23 117 E3
Baker St HU2 180 E7
Bakers Way 5 PE10 154 D6
Bakestraw Gate PE12 157 F5
Bakewell Cl 15 NG24 104 B2
Bakewell Ct 1 DN15 182 B3
Bakewell Mews 6 LN6 204 F2
Bakewell Rd PE2 229 C2
Bala Ct PE4 221 B3
Balder Ct 2 DN33 191 C2
BALDERTON NG24 104 C2
Balderton Gate 10 NG24 104 A4
Balderton La NG24 104 D3
Baldock's Mill Heritage Ctr* PE10 213 D4
Baldwin Ave DN16 185 B2
Baldwin Cl PE8 172 C1
Baldwin Dr 1 PE2 230 E8
Baldwin Gr PE10 213 D6
Balfour Pl 3 DN40 186 B4
Balfour St
Gainsborough DN21 197 C5
2 Kingston upon Hull HU9 181 C8
Balintore Rise PE2 229 D4
Balk Rd 8 PE9 163 C1
Balliol Dr DN16 185 B4
Ball's La PE12 159 A6
Balmoral Ave
1 Grimsby DN34 191 A7
Spalding PE11 214 D2
Balmoral Cl
12 Mablethorpe/Sutton on Sea LN12 76 F8
2 Wragby LN8 70 D4
Balmoral Ct DN17 184 F4
Balmoral Dr
7 Beacon Hill NG24 104 C4
Grantham NG31 210 E6
Sleaford NG34 120 F2
Balmoral Rd
Cleethorpes DN35 192 C4
4 Hatfield DN7 14 D4
1 Peterborough PE4 225 C8
Balmoral Way PE12 159 A8
Bamber St PE1 225 F4
Bamburgh Cl NG31 210 E6
Bamford Ave 1 HU9 5 F8
Bamford Cl 6 LN6 204 E2
Banbury Cl PE11 214 D6
Banbury Ct 9 DN31 189 C1
Banbury Rd DN16 183 D2
Bancroft Rd NG24 104 A3
Bangor Cl LN5 205 C3
Bank Ave PE7 230 D2
Bank Dr Ingoldmells PE25 90 F3
5 Wisbech PE13 170 C1
Bank End LN11 50 E8
Bank End Rd DN9 26 A3
Bank La 12 LN7 33 B4
Bank's Ave 4 PE11 214 F6
Banks Cres PE9 218 F6
Bank Side 1 PE21 136 D8
Banks La 4 NG34 122 E2
Banks Rd 6 LN9 199 C4
Banks St 5 LN9 199 C4
Bank St Boston PE21 208 F5
Kingston upon Hull HU3 180 C7
Lincoln LN2 234 B2
Bank The
Parson Drove PE13 177 C7
Skidbrooke LN11 51 B3
Swaton NG34 133 D4
Banner Ct HU4 179 D2
Bannister Cl 3 HU13 3 F4
Bannister Dr HU9 181 C7
Bannister's La PE20 136 C7
Bannister's Row 6 PE13 170 C1
Banovallum Gdns 1 LN9 199 D3
Banovallum Sch LN9 199 C2
Baptist Chapel La 4 DN40 12 F2
Baptist La 3 NG23 91 C4
Barbara Cl 3 DN33 194 E7
Barbara Rd 6 PE25 206 D2
Barber Cl PE2 231 C7
Barberry Ct 3 HU3 180 C5
Barbers Dro 10 PE6 175 C8
Barbers Dro North 8 PE6 175 C8
Barbers Hill PE4 220 F7
Barbican Way DN36 195 C6
Barcroft St DN35 189 E1
Bardling's Dro PE12 169 A7
BARDNEY LN3 83 C4
Bardney PE2 230 A4
Bardney Ave DN16 185 A7
Bardney Cl LN6 204 F6
Bardney Gdns 1 DN34 190 F4
Bardney Linewood National Nature Reserve* LN3 83 C3
Bardney Primary School LN3 83 C4

Bardney Rd Barlings LN3 69 E2
Branston & Mere LN4 82 C3
Wragby LN8 70 C4
Bardots Leisure Ctr LN5 205 C1
Barehams La PE11 145 A7
Barfen La LN13 63 B3
Barff La LN8 43 F2
Barff Mdw LN8 43 E1
Barff Rd LN4 82 B1
Barfields La LN3 68 F1
Barford Cl PE2 230 C7
Bargate Grimsby DN34 191 C5
12 Lincoln LN5 205 E8
Bargate Ave DN32 191 D5
Bargate Gr 3 HU5 179 D8
Bargate La 4 LN9 199 C3
Barge Cl 1 PE11 214 F5
Barge Rd PE12 148 A7
Barham Cl PE2 231 F5
BARHOLM PE9 164 C1
Barholme Ave 7 PE12 160 A8
Barholme Rd PE9 164 D2
Barkestone La NG13 128 A5
Barkham St 7 PE24 102 D2
Barkhouse Cl 4 DN35 192 F5
Barkhouse La 5 DN35 192 F5
Bark St DN35 192 F5
BARKSTON NG32 130 B8
Barkston Cl Bourne PE10 213 E6
29 Newark-on-Trent NG24 104 B2
Barkston Dr PE1 226 B6
Barkston Gdns LN2 202 B7
Barkston Rd NG32 118 D2
Barkston & Syston CE Prim Sch NG32 130 B8
Barkwith Rd LN8 58 F1
Barkworth Cl HU10 178 D6
Barkworth Ct 3 DN37 194 C4
Barkworth Way HU13 178 B3
Bar La 20 LN5 93 F7
Barley Cl Heckington NG34 122 D2
12 Hibaldstow DN20 31 A5
8 Kirton in Lindsey DN21 30 B2
24 Metheringham LN4 95 C4
Barleycroft Rd NG33 152 E8
Barley Ct DN33 191 B1
Barleyfield PE6 164 E2
Barleyfield Cl LN4 81 E4
Barley Gr 4 PE11 166 C6
Barley La LN4 109 E6
Barley Mews PE2 230 D7
Barley Sheaf Ct PE20 124 B8
Barley Way LN9 199 A3
Barley Wy 19 NG24 104 A6
BARLINGS LN3 69 D1
Barlings Ave DN16 185 A7
Barlings Cl 1 Barlings LN3 69 C3
Hartsholme LN6 204 F7
7 Scotter DN21 29 C4
Barlings La LN3 69 C2
Barlode Drain PE22 100 E1
Barmouth Dr DN37 190 E8
Barmston St HU2 180 F8
BARNACK PE9 172 E4
Barnack CE Prim Sch PE9 172 D4
Barnack Est 4 PE24 102 E7
Barnack Hill & Holes National Nature Reserve* PE9 172 D3
Barnack Rd Bainton PE9 172 E4
St Martin's without PE9 219 D4
Barnack Rd Ind Est PE9 219 D5
Barnard Ave DN20 196 B3
Barnard Way 9 PE3 224 F3
Barnard Wlk DN40 186 D3
Barnberry Way PE10 142 D2
BARNBY DUN DN3 14 A4
Barnby Gate NG24 104 A4
BARNBY IN THE WILLOWS NG24 104 F3
Barnby La NG23 104 F1
Barnby Rd NG24 104 B3
Barnby Road Acad Prim Sch NG24 104 A4
Barn Cl 2 Maxey PE6 173 C7
Peterborough PE4 220 F3
Barn End 9 NG33 151 A8
Barnes Cl 1 NG34 212 C6
Barnes Cres
Scunthorpe DN15 182 E4
Skegness PE25 206 A5
Barnes Ct PE9 218 E5
Barnes Dro PE10 154 F4
Barnes Gn 2 DN21 29 C4
Barnes La LN5 106 F7
Barnes Rd
9 Donington PE11 134 E2
Skegness PE25 206 A5
Barnes Wallis Acad The LN4 207 B5
Barnes Way PE4 220 F3
Barnetby La DN20 20 F7
BARNETBY LE WOLD DN38 21 C4
Barnetby Rd
1 Kingston upon Hull HU13 179 A3
Scunthorpe DN17 184 F5
Barnetby Road DN38 21 B2
Barnetby Sta DN38 21 B4
Barnet Dr DN36 195 E7
Barnet Gn 18 DN7 14 D3
Barnett Pl DN35 192 B7
Barnetts La PE11 145 C8
Barneyfield Rd PE22 126 E1
Barnfield Rd 22 NG23 91 D5
Barn Hill PE9 219 B5
BARNOLDBY LE BECK DN37 35 B6
Barnoldby Rd DN37 194 C4
Barn Owl Cl
Corby Glen NG33 152 F7
23 Humberston DN36 36 D8
1 Langtoft PE6 164 F3
Barn Owl Wy LN4 203 B1
Barnside 6 DN20 30 F5
Barnstaple Rd 3 DN17 184 D8
Barnstock PE3 225 A7
Barnston Way 12 DN15 8 B4
Barnswallace Ct 15 LN2 68 D7
Barnwell Rd 3 PE9 218 E6
Barnwell Terr 2 NG31 210 F3
Baron Ave DN36 195 D7
Baron Ct PE4 221 B4
Baroness Rd DN34 190 F6
Baroness Wy PE6 217 C6
Barons Way PE9 219 C4
Barrack Sq NG31 211 C4
Barracks The PE13 169 E2
Barraclough's La
1 Barton-upon-Humber DN18 3 E1
Barton-upon-Humber DN18 3 E2
Barratt's Cl LN2 234 C4
Bar Rd DN10 52 B8
Bar Rd N 3 DN10 52 B8
Bar Rd S 7 DN10 52 B8
Barrett Gr 7 LN2 68 E6
Barrett's Cl PE12 215 D3
Barrick Cl 16 DN19 11 D8
Barrier Bank Cowbit PE12 156 F2
Spalding PE12 214 C1
Barrington Cl 8 PE12 215 D2
Barrington Gate PE12 215 E1
Barrons Cl LN3 203 E7
Barrow Blow Wells Nature Reserve* DN19 4 D1
BARROWBY NG32 210 A5
Barrowby CE Prim Sch NG32 129 B3
Barrowby Gate NG31 210 D4
Barrowby Rd 8 NG31 211 A5
Barrowden Rd PE9 171 A2
Barrowfield PE1 226 E7
Barrowfield Dr 1 PE9 218 E4
BARROW HANN DN19 4 E1
BARROW HAVEN DN19 4 B2
Barrow Haven Reedbed Nature Reserve* DN19 4 B2
Barrow Haven Sta DN19 4 C2
Barrow La HU13 178 D2
Barrow Rd
Barton-upon-Humber DN18 11 A8
New Holland DN19 4 E1
Barrows Gate
3 Beacon Hill NG24 104 A6
North Somercotes LN11 50 D6
BARROW UPON HUMBER DN19 11 C8
Barr's La PE12 168 B4
Barry Ave DN34 190 F3
Barry Wlk 3 PE2 230 F7
Bars La Benington PE22 126 E5
Bicker PE20 135 A5
Bartholemew Cl 1 LN3 83 C4
Bartol Cres PE21 208 D5
Barton Cl
3 Mablethorpe LN12 64 C2
Paston PE4 221 D1
Barton Dr HU13 178 D1
Barton Gate LN11 198 D4
Barton La
Barrow upon Humber DN19 11 C8
Tydd St Mary PE13 169 F8
Barton-on-Humber Sta DN18 3 F1
Barton Outdoor Pursuits Ctr* DN18 3 D2
Barton Rd Burnham DN19 11 C5
5 Wainfleet All Saints PE24 102 D1
Wrawby DN20 196 F6
Barton St Peters CE Prim Sch 22 DN18 3 F1
Barton Sch DN18 11 A8
Bartons La PE23 101 F6
Barton St
Aylesby DN37 23 D2
Barrow upon Humber DN19 11 C8
Fotherby LN11 49 A2
Irby DN37 34 F7
Keelby DN41 23 A4
Ludborough DN36 48 C6
BARTON-UPON-HUMBER DN18 10 F7
BARTON WATERSIDE DN18 3 F2
Bartram Gate 2 PE4 221 C1
Bartrams 3 HU15 2 D6
Basic Slag Rd DN16 183 E2
Basil Gn PE2 230 D6
Baslow Rd DN15 182 B2
Bass Cotts NG34 212 E3
Bassett Cl 2 DN20 19 E3
Bassett Rd DN35 193 A4
Bass Industrial Pk NG34 212 E3
BASSINGHAM LN5 92 F2
Bassingham Cres LN2 201 F7
Bassingham La PE23 88 E3
Bassingham Prim Sch LN5 92 F2
Bassingham Rd LN5 92 F5
BASSINGTHORPE NG33 140 E3
BASTON PE6 164 E4
Baston CE Prim Sch PE6 164 E5
Baston Edge Dro PE10 164 E7
Baston Fen Nature Reserve* PE6 165 A8
Baston Outgang Rd PE6 165 A6
Baston Rd PE6 164 D4
Bateman's Cl 3 PE12 159 D7
Batemans Ct 2 PE24 102 E2
Bates La 4 PE7 230 F5
Bath Gdns PE21 208 F3
Bath La 15 PE11 214 D4
Bath Rd
Bracebridge Heath LN4 81 A2
25 Eye PE6 175 A1
Wisbech PE13 170 D1
Bath Row PE9 219 B4
Bath St 8 Grantham NG31 211 A4
Grimsby DN32 189 C1
Bathurst PE2 230 A4
Bathurst St
8 Kingston upon Hull HU3 180 D5
Lincoln LN2 202 D3
Battery St DN40 186 D4
Battlefields La N PE12 159 A8
Battlefields La S PE12 215 F3
Battle Gn DN9 27 D7
Battle of Britain Meml Flight Visitor Ctr* LN4 207 B3
Baulkin's Dro PE12 159 C1
BAUMBER LN9 72 A1
Baumber Prim Sch LN9 72 A1
Baumber Road LN10 84 D5
Bawtry Cl LN6 204 C8
Bawtry Rd DN7 14 F3
Baxter Cl Coningsby LN4 207 D3
15 Wisbech PE13 170 E1
Baxter Gdns PE11 214 C7
Bayard St DN21 197 C5
Bayes Rd 6 PE25 103 E4
Bayfield Rd 4 LN4 96 B1
Bayford Dr 8 NG24 104 C4
Bayford Gn PE21 208 B4
Bayleaf Ave PE7 233 A8
Bayleaf La DN18 4 A1
Bayons Ave DN33 194 D8
Baysdale Gr NG31 211 B8
Baysdale Rd DN16 185 D5
Baysgarth House Mus* DN18 10 F8
Baysgarth Leisure Ctr DN18 10 F8
Baysgarth Sch DN18 10 F8
Baysgarth View DN18 10 F7
Bayston Ct PE2 230 E8
Bayswater Pl 1 DN33 194 D8
Bayswood Ave PE21 208 F1
BAYTHORPE PE20 135 C8
Baytree Ave DN34 191 A6
Baytree Owl Ctr* PE12 157 D7
Baywood Cl 4 LN6 200 C1
Beach Ave 15 PE24 90 D7
Beach Bank
Pinchbeck PE11 144 E3
Surfleet PE11 145 A3
Beach Holt La DN37 23 D2
Beach La PE11 144 F3
Beachside 10 LN12 77 A8
Beacon Acad DN35 192 C5
Beacon Ave
16 Barton-upon-Humber DN18 10 E8
Cleethorpes DN35 192 D6
Beacon Cl 7 HU13 3 F4
Beacon Ct DN35 192 D6
BEACON HILL NG24 104 B5
Beacon Hill La PE34 161 E3
Beacon Hill Rd
Gringley on the Hill DN10 39 D1
Newark-on-Trent NG24 104 B4
Beacon Hts NG24 104 B4
Beacon La NG31 211 C4
Beacon Pk Cl 4 PE25 206 A6
Beacon Pk Dr PE25 206 A6
Beacon Primary Acad PE25 206 C5
Beacon Rd 7 NG34 107 C1
Beaconsfield Dr 3 NG24 104 C5
Beaconthorpe Rd 4 DN35 192 E7
Beacon View 2 NG13 128 A6
Beacon Way PE25 206 A6
Beacon Wy HU3 180 A3
Beadle Way PE4 221 E3
Beadle Wy PE6 221 E3
Beaford Ct DN17 184 C8
Beagle Cl 16 DN20 19 E4
Beagle La NG34 107 C1
Bean St HU3 180 C6
Bear La 14 PE11 145 C1
Beatrice Rd 11 PE13 170 D2
Beatrice Way 28 PE24 90 D7
Beatty Ave DN33 194 F7
Beaubridge Bsns Pk PE25 206 B3
Beauchamp St 3 DN16 183 B1
Beauchamp Wlk 7 DN16 183 B2
Beauchief Gdns DN16 185 A8
Beaufort Ave 1 PE6 217 C5
Beaufort Cl
Kingston upon Hull HU3 180 D6
Lincoln LN2 202 D8
Beaufort Cres DN35 192 D2
Beaufort Dr Bourne PE10 213 C7
4 Spalding PE11 214 C3
Beaufort Rd LN2 202 D8
Beaufort St DN21 197 B7
Beaulahland 8 DN18 10 A7
Beaulah Villas 9 DN18 10 A7
Beaulieu Ct 6 PE6 175 A1
Beaumaris Way NG31 210 E6
Beaumonde 5 DN36 195 C2
Beaumont Cl 11 PE24 102 E7
Beaumont Ct 3 HU9 181 D7
Beaumont Dr 2 NG31 210 F8
Beaumont Fee LN1 234 A2
Beaumont St DN21 197 D4
Beaumont Way PE7 230 C2
Beauvale Gdns PE4 221 C3
Beauvoir Pl PE7 233 E5
Beaver Cl LN6 200 A5
Beccelm Dr 9 PE6 175 B8
Beck Bank Gosberton PE11 144 C3
Kirton PE20 124 E1
Beck Cl 5 Binbrook LN8 47 C5
13 Keelby DN41 23 A4
1 Ruskington NG34 108 D2
Becke Cl LN3 203 E5
Becket Cl LN4 203 D1
Beckets Cl Grantham NG31 210 F4
New England PE1 225 F8
Beckett Ave DN21 197 E6
Beckett Cl
9 Heckington NG34 122 D3
2 Skegness PE25 206 C1
Beckett Dr PE11 214 C6
Beckett Sch DN21 53 A8
Beckhall LN2 68 D6
Beckhead Cvn Site LN6 204 C1
Beck Hill
6 Barton-upon-Humber DN18 10 F8
Cherry Willingham/Reepham LN3 203 F8
Tealby LN8 46 C1
Beckhole Cl HU3 180 A6
Beckhythe Cl DN33 191 E1
BECKINGHAM
Barnby in the Willows NG24 105 A4
Beckingham DN10 40 B1
Beckingham PE2 229 F3
Beckingham Rd
Coddington NG24 104 C5
Walkeringham DN10 40 A2
Beckingthorpe Dr 19 NG13 128 A6
Beck La Appleby DN15 9 D1
Aubourn Haddington & South Hykeham LN6 93 B7
10 Barrow upon Humber DN19 11 D8
7 Broughton DN20 19 E3
Fulbeck NG32 106 C1
Heighington/Washingborough LN4 81 F4
Ingoldmells PE25 90 E2
Redbourne DN21 30 F2
Scunthorpe DN16 185 B3
6 Welton/Dunholme LN2 68 E6
Welton le Marsh PE23 89 A3
Becklands Ave DN36 195 B6
Beckside 11 Brough HU15 2 D6
Normanby by Spital LN8 55 E7
Rothwell LN7 33 F2
Scopwick LN4 108 C8
Beck Side 5 DN20 30 F5
Beckside Cl DN36 192 E1
Beckside Ct LN11 198 D3
Becks La DN21 29 A3
Beck St Digby LN4 108 E5
Welbourn LN5 106 E4
Becks The 4 LN9 199 C4
Beck Way 5 PE10 164 C8
Beck Wlk 2 DN35 192 E1
Bedale Mews 31 HU15 2 C5
Bedale Pl DN35 192 E3
Bedale Rd 3 DN16 185 D5
Bede Cl NG34 212 B2
Bede Cres PE22 126 F5
Bedehouse Bank PE10 213 E4
Bede House La 3 NG24 104 A4
Bede Pl PE1 226 A6
Bede Rd 3 PE6 164 E5
Bedford Cl NG31 211 F5
Bedford Ct 16 PE6 176 A3
Bedford Pl 1 PE11 214 D3
Bedford Rd
Humberston DN35 193 A1
Kingston upon Hull HU13 178 F3
Bedford Row PE13 170 D8
Bedford St Grimsby DN32 189 C1
2 Lincoln LN1 201 D4
Peterborough PE1 226 B4
Bedford Wy DN15 183 A5
Beebys Way PE7 233 E8
Beechams Mews 5 PE11 214 B3
Beech Ave Bourne PE10 213 B5
Gainsborough DN21 197 D6
Grimsby DN33 191 C3
5 Gunness DN15 17 E6
Kingston upon Hull HU10 178 D8
24 Nettleham LN2 68 C2
Peterborough PE1 225 F3
Scunthorpe DN15 182 B6
Spalding PE11 214 F5
Beech Cl
1 Bracebridge Heath LN4 81 A1
5 Broughton DN20 19 D3
2 Colsterworth NG33 151 E7
4 Coningsby LN4 207 D4
Dunholme LN2 68 E5
3 Gringley on the Hill DN10 39 C1
7 Heckington NG34 122 D3
Kingston upon Hull HU3 180 C5
Market Deeping PE6 217 B6
RAF Cranwell NG34 107 D1
9 Sudbrooke LN2 68 F2
4 Thorney PE6 176 A3
Beech Cres 1 DN7 14 D6
Beechcroft Cl 6 LN6 93 A8
Beechcroft Dr 5 DN21 30 B2
Beechcroft Rd NG31 210 C3
Beech Dr
16 Bottesford NG13 128 A5
6 North Ferriby HU14 3 A4
15 Ryhall PE9 163 C1
3 Welton HU14 2 F5
Beechers Way LN8 57 D7
Beeches Ave DN16 185 B4
Beeches Independent Sch The PE1 226 A6
Beeches La PE22 112 C5
Beeches The
New Waltham DN36 195 E5
Spalding PE11 214 E4
1 Sturton by Stow LN1 66 C7
Beechfield Ct DN34 191 C6
Beechfield Rd 7 DN7 14 C4
Beech Garth 9 DN19 11 C7
Beech Gr
Anlaby with Anlaby Common HU13 178 C3
3 Burton upon Stather DN15 8 B5
Donington PE11 134 E2
Holton le Clay DN36 195 E1
Louth LN11 198 C7
4 Scopwick Heath LN4 108 A7
Stamford PE9 218 D6
4 Swanland HU14 3 C7
Beech Hill Rd HU14 3 C7
Beechings Way 10 LN13 75 E2
Beechings Way Ind Est LN13 75 E2
Beech La 12 Eye PE6 175 A1
20 New Waltham DN36 36 C8
Beech Lawn HU10 178 E6
Beech Rd Branston LN4 81 D2
6 Brough HU15 2 C6
Glinton PE6 220 B8
Beech Rise Sleaford NG34 212 D6
2 South Rauceby NG34 120 E4
Beech St LN5 205 D5
Beech Tree Ave 17 DN8 15 B7
Beechtree Cl 8 NG34 108 E1
Beechway DN16 185 B7
Beech Way DN35 192 D2
Beechwood Ave
Grimsby DN33 190 F3
Immingham DN40 186 C4
Beechwood Cl
16 Kirk Sandall DN3 14 A1
Peterborough PE1 226 C7
6 Wisbech PE13 170 D1
Beechwood Cres 4 DN20 19 E4
Beechwood Ct 22 DN7 14 D3
Beechwood Dr
12 Scawby DN20 30 F8
7 Scotter DN21 29 C3
Beechwood Rd 5 PE13 170 D1
BeechWy PE25 103 C8
Beeden Pk Est NG31 210 C4
Bee Field The LN2 202 F7
Beehive La LN6 79 C1
Beeley Rd DN32 192 C6
BEELSBY DN37 34 E4
Beelsby Rd LN7 34 C5
Beelsby Road DN37 34 D2
Beel's Rd DN41 187 B2
Bee Orchid Way LN11 198 A6
BEESBY LN13 76 A7
Beesby Dr 3 DN35 192 F3
Beesby Rd
Maltby le Marsh LN13 76 A7
Markby LN13 76 B6
Scunthorpe DN17 184 E5
Bees Cnr 1 PE24 102 D2
Bee's La PE13 169 F6
Beeson Gr DN31 188 E1
Beeson St DN31 188 E1
Beeston Dr PE7 231 F5
Beeston Rd 11 NG24 104 A3
Beeton Cl LN11 198 D4
Beetons Cl PE7 233 E5
Beevor St LN6 201 C2
Beggar Hill Messingham Rd DN21 29 D4
Beggar's La PE22 98 F3
Begger's Bush La PE12 157 D7
Beilby St HU3 179 F4
Belcanto Ct 3 PE11 214 A5
BELCHFORD LN9 73 B2
Belchford Rd LN9 72 C1
Belchmire La PE11 145 B5
Beldings Cl PE23 101 F6
Belfry The 5 NG31 211 D7
Belgic Sq PE1 226 E3
Belgrave Cl 11 DN9 16 E1
Belgrave Dr HU4 179 D5
Belgrave Rd Grimsby DN33 191 B2
7 Spalding PE11 214 C2
Belgrave Sq 1 DN15 183 B3
Belgravia Cl LN6 200 E1
Belham Hill Lane LN5 105 E7
Belham Rd PE1 225 E7
Belisana Rd 5 PE11 214 A5
Bellamy Ct HU9 181 C7
Bellamy's La PE14 170 D4
Bellbutts View DN21 29 B3
Bell Cl NG31 210 E7
Bell Ct 5 PE21 208 F1
Bell Dro PE6 175 F6
BELLEAU LN13 75 A5
Belle Isle LN4 110 F6
Belleisle Rd DN34 190 D4
Belle Vue PE2 231 C6
Belle Vue Rd LN1 234 A3

Belle Vue Terr Lincoln LN1 234 A3
21 Thorne/Moorends DN8 15 A8
Bellfield Cl 4 PE11 214 B3
Bellflower Cl 2 LN2 202 C8
Bell Gr LN6 205 C6
Bellingham Rd DN16 185 D7
Bellingham's Dro PE11 166 F7
Bell La 4 Collingham NG23 91 C4
Fosdyke PE20 146 D8
Market Deeping PE6 217 E4
Moulton PE12 157 F7
Scunthorpe DN15 183 A2
BELLMOUNT PE34 161 E4
Bellona Dr PE2 231 E4
Bell's Dro PE12 159 C1
Bell's Pl PE1 226 A2
Bellview Rd 6 NG34 108 E1
Bellwin Dr DN15 8 A1
Bellwood Cres 5 DN8 15 A8
Bellwood Gdns NG31 211 C5
Bellwood Grange 1 LN3 203 E7
Bell Wr Drain Bank
Eastville PE22 101 B1
New Leake PE22 100 E1
BELMESTHORPE PE9 163 D1
Belmesthorpe La PE9 163 D1
Belmesthorpe Rd
Belmesthorpe PE9 163 F1
Greatford PE9 164 A2
Belmont DN36 195 C1
Belmont Cl DN35 192 D3
Belmont Com Prim Sch NG31 211 E6
Belmont Gr 2 NG31 211 D6
Belmont St
Kingston upon Hull HU9 181 D8
Lincoln LN2 202 B3
Scunthorpe DN16 185 A6
BELNIE PE11 145 D5
Belnie La PE11 145 D5
Belper Ct 6 Crosby DN15 182 B2
Grimsby DN32 189 C1
Belsay Dr PE2 231 F5
Belshaw La DN9 16 D1
Belsize Ave PE2 230 E6
Belthorn Rd 2 DN17 7 F1
BELTOFT DN9 17 B1
Beltoft Road DN9 28 A7
BELTON Belton DN9 16 E1
Belton and Manthorpe NG32 130 B6
Belton All Saints CE Prim Sch DN9 16 E2
Belton Ave Grantham NG31 211 C6
Lincoln LN6 204 F6
Belton Cl Boston PE21 209 B5
13 Market Deeping PE6 217 A5
Belton Fields 1 DN9 16 D1
Belton Gdns 23 PE9 219 C5
Belton Gr Grantham NG31 211 B7
1 Grimsby DN33 191 A3
Belton House* NG32 130 B6
Belton La Grantham NG31 211 C6
Great Gonerby NG31 129 E5
Belton Lane Prim Sch NG31 211 D7
Belton Park Rd PE25 206 B6
Belton Pk* NG32 211 F8
Belton Pk Dr 7 LN6 93 C8
Belton Rd Belton DN9 17 A1
Epworth DN9 27 E7
Peterborough PE7 231 F5
Sandtoft DN9 16 B3
Belton St 16 PE9 219 C5
Belton Wlk LN11 198 A7
Belt Rd The DN21 197 F7
Beluga Cl PE2 231 B8
Belvedere Cl PE11 214 B2
Belvedere Dr DN17 184 E7
Belvedere Rd HU13 178 F2
BELVOIR NG32 138 B8
Belvoir Ave
12 Bottesford NG13 128 A5
Grantham NG31 210 F1
Spitalgate NG31 211 E2
Belvoir Castle* NG32 138 B8
Belvoir Cl Bracebridge LN5 205 D1
4 Colsterworth NG33 151 E6
1 Market Deeping PE6 217 A5
1 Stamford PE9 218 E6
Belvoir Cres 2 NG24 104 A3
Belvoir Ct LN11 198 B8
Belvoir Gdns NG31 129 D5
Belvoir High Sch NG13 128 A5
Belvoir La NG32 128 D1
Belvoir Pk Wlk DN35 192 D2
Belvoir Pl 10 NG24 104 B2
Belvoir Rd Bottesford NG13 128 A4
Cleethorpes DN35 192 D2
Croxton Kerrial NG32 138 A6
Belvoir St HU5 180 C8
Belvoir Way Eye PE1 226 D8
Louth LN11 198 B8
Peterborough PE1 226 C8
Belwood Dr 7 DN9 16 E2
Bempton Gr
4 Grimsby DN32 192 A5
Kingston upon Hull HU5 179 D8
Bemrose Way 2 DN31 191 C8
Benams Cl PE5 223 E2
Benbow Way LN1 201 C6
Benderslough Dro PE12 159 C3
Bendike La PE11 145 D4
Benedict Cl 2 HU4 179 A2
Benedict Ct PE6 217 E5
Benedict Rd HU4 179 A2
Benedict Sq PE4 220 E2
BENINGTON PE22 126 F5
Benington Rd PE22 126 E3
Benjamin Adlard Com Sch DN21 197 E2
Benjamin Adlard Prim Sch DN21 197 E2
Benjamins Wlk DN35 192 E1
Benland PE3 225 A6
Benner Rd PE11 214 E8
Benner Rd Ind Est PE11 214 E8
Bennett Dr 28 DN15 9 A5
Bennett Rd
Cleethorpes DN35 192 D7
Louth LN11 198 C8
Scunthorpe DN16 185 C7
Bennetts Mill Cl 10 LN10 97 D5
Bennington Cl
8 Lincoln LN6 205 A7
11 Long Bennington NG23 117 D3
Bennington La NG23 117 E4
BENNIWORTH LN8 59 B1
Benniworth Rd LN8 71 C7
Ben's Gate PE12 159 B5
Benson Cl LN6 204 C6
Benson Cres LN6 204 C6
Benson Ct LN11 48 F4
Benstead PE2 229 E3
Bentinck Cl 6 PE11 214 C6
Bentinck Sq 2 LN2 202 B3
Bentinck St 4 LN2 202 B3
Bentley Ave PE7 233 E6
Bentley Ct HU3 180 A5
Bentley Dr LN4 205 F3
Bentley La 6 DN38 32 E7
Bentley St
Cleethorpes DN35 192 E6
6 Stamford PE9 219 C6
Bentley Way 1 LN4 95 C4
Benton Cl 6 PE12 157 E1
Benyon Gr PE2 230 B4
Berberis Cl 2 PE6 175 F3
Berea The DN34 191 C5
Beresford Ave PE25 206 C2
Beresford Cl 4 PE25 206 C2
Beresford Cres 5 PE25 206 C2
Beresford Dr 5 LN2 68 F3
Beretun Gn 7 DN18 10 E8
Bergen Cl DN36 195 B6
Berilldon Dr LN1 201 C7
Berkeley Ave
Green Hill NG31 210 E6
Lincoln LN6 205 A3
Berkeley Ct 5 NG34 212 E4
Berkeley Dr
4 Bourne PE10 213 C7
Lincoln LN6 205 A3
Berkeley Ind Est DN15 182 C4
Berkeley Inf & Jun Sch DN15 182 D4
Berkeley Rd
Humberston DN35 193 A2
Peterborough PE3 225 C3
Berkeley St
1 Kingston upon Hull HU3 180 D8
Scunthorpe DN15 183 A4
Berkley Ct 4 PE11 214 C5
Berkshire Dr NG31 211 D7
Bermondsey Dr HU5 179 E8
Bernadette Ave HU4 179 B5
Bernard St LN2 202 B4
Berners Rd DN35 193 B1
Bernicia Dr NG34 212 B2
Berrigan Way LN4 81 E1
Berrybut Way 5 PE9 219 D7
Berry Cl 6 NG34 212 D2
Berry Ct PE1 225 E5
Berryfield End 7 NG32 210 A5
Berryman Way HU13 179 A3
Berrystead PE5 223 E2
Berry Way 5 PE25 206 C3
Bert Allen Dr 1 PE22 114 A1
Bertie Cl Long Sutton PE12 216 C3
Swinstead NG33 153 A5
Bertie La 8 PE9 172 C6
Bert's Way 7 NG32 128 F7
Berwick Ct DN40 186 C4
Besant Cl 10 PE22 113 B1
BESCABY LE14 138 B1
Bessemer Way DN15 183 B6
Bess Wrights Dro PE7 233 E2
Bestall Rd DN32 192 C6
BESTHORPE NG23 91 C7
Besthorpe Cty Prim Sch NG23 91 C7
Besthorpe Rd
Besthorpe NG23 91 C6
North Scarle NG23 78 D1
Beswick Cl 5 LN6 204 D7
Bethlehem St DN32 191 D7
Bethlem Cres 9 PE24 102 D1
Bethune Ave HU4 179 A3
Bethune Ave W HU13 179 A3
Bethune Pk Prim Sch HU4 179 B3
Betjeman Cl
1 Bourne PE10 213 D3
Spalding PE11 214 B4
Betony Cl DN15 182 C6
Bette Camplings Cl PE12 159 D1
Bettesworth Rd DN21 54 F8
Bettles Cl PE1 226 A6
Betton Lane Ind Est NG31 211 B6
Betula Gr 3 LN6 204 D7
Betula Way 1 DN17 184 C5
Beverley Cl 7 DN36 195 D1
Beverley Cres DN32 192 A5
Beverley Ct Eye PE6 175 B1
12 Healing DN41 23 F5
Westcliffe DN17 184 D7
Beverley Gdns 4 PE9 219 A6
Beverley Gr Lincoln LN6 204 F3
7 Skegness PE25 206 B3
Beverley Rd HU3 180 D8
Beverstone PE2 229 D5
Bevers Wy DN36 195 D3
Bevishall PE4 221 D1
Bew Cl PE2 231 D4
Bewholme Gr 3 HU9 5 D8
Bewick Pl PE7 233 D8
Bexley Ct 10 DN32 189 C1
BICKER PE20 135 A4
Bicker Dro PE20 134 D6
BICKER GAUNTLET PE20 134 F6
Bicker Prep Sch PE30 135 A4
Bicker Rd PE11 134 F3
Bickleigh Wlk PE3 225 A3
Bidwell La LE15 162 B6
Biergate LN11 49 F7
Bifield PE2 229 F3
BIGBY DN38 21 C2
Bigby Gn DN38 21 B2
Bigby Gr DN17 184 F4
Bigby High Rd DN20 196 D2
Bigby Hill DN38 21 C1
Bigby Rd 6 DN20 196 C3
Bigby Road DN38 21 C4
Bigby St DN20 196 C3
Bilberry Cl 7 PE11 214 B6
Billet La DN15 182 F8
Billet Mill App Rd DN16 19 A4
Billet Mill Rd DN16 183 E1
Billgate La PE24 102 E7
BILLINGBOROUGH NG34 133 A1
Billingborough Dro NG34 143 E8
Billingborough Prim Sch NG34 133 B1
Billingborough Rd
Billingborough NG34 133 B1
Folkingham NG34 132 E1
BILLINGHAY LN4 109 F5
Billinghay CE Prim Sch LN4 109 F6
Billinghay Cottage* 9 LN4 109 F5
Billinghay Ct DN35 192 F3
Billinghay Dales Head LN4 110 B4
Billings Gate LN11 50 E5
BILSBY LN13 76 A3
Bilsby Cl LN2 202 A7
BILSBY FIELD LN13 76 A2
Bilsby Rd 2 LN13 75 F3
Bilsdale Gr HU9 181 F8
Bilsdale Rd DN16 185 E5
BINBROOK LN8 47 B4
Binbrook Cl 8 LN6 204 D7
Binbrook (Controlled) Prim Sch LN8 47 B5
Binbrook La LN8 47 B2
Binbrook Road LN11 60 C6
Binbrook Way DN37 190 E8
Bircham Cres DN21 30 C1
Birch Ave Brigg DN20 196 B4
Grimsby DN34 191 A6
Birch Cl 4 Branston LN4 81 D2
28 Brough HU15 2 C5
11 Coningsby LN4 207 D4
Hessle HU13 178 B3
Kingston upon Hull HU5 179 B7
1 Lincoln LN6 204 F2
Wyberton PE21 136 E7
Birch Croft 31 HU15 2 C6
Birchdale 31 DN18 10 E8
Birch Dr DN17 185 D4
Birchen Cl PE7 230 C3
Birches The
New Waltham DN36 195 E6
8 Westwoodside DN9 27 A2
Birchfield Rd 8 DN9 27 D6
Birch Gdns 28 DN18 3 E1
Birch Gr 28 Alford LN13 75 F2
Gainsborough DN21 197 D6
Spalding PE11 214 F3
Birchin Way DN31 188 D1
Birch La 4 LN9 85 E7
Birch Leigh HU3 180 C6
Birchnell Gdns PE10 213 E4
Birch Rd Louth LN11 198 E5
6 Newark-on-Trent NG24 104 B3
6 Stamford PE9 218 D7
Birchtree Ave PE1 226 A7
Birch Tree Cl 4 DN3 14 A4
Birch Way DN38 21 C5
Birch Way Ind Est DN31 188 D1
BIRCHWOOD LN6 204 D7
Birchwood PE2 230 A3
Birchwood Ave
Birchwood LN6 200 D1
Kingston upon Hull HU5 179 A7
Birchwood Cl 4 NG31 210 F7
Birch Wood Cl 14 DN18 3 E1
Birchwood Jun Sch LN6 204 C8
Birchwood Rd
Scunthorpe DN16 185 A4
1 Sleaford NG34 212 D6
Birchwood Sh Ctr LN6 204 C8
Birchwood View 2 DN21 197 F5
Birdcroft La DN10 40 A3
Birds Dro PE11 145 C4
Bird's Dro Gorefield PE13 169 D1
Sutton St James PE12 169 B8
Birds Holt Cl LN6 200 A3
Birds Wood Nature Reserve* DN9 26 F4
Birkbeck Sch & Com Arts Coll LN11 50 E7
Birkdale Lincoln LN5 205 D1
Birkdale *continued*
9 Waltham DN37 194 C4
Birkdale Ave 1 PE4 221 A3
Birkdale Cl
3 Grantham NG31 211 D7
Heighington/Washingborough LN4 203 E1
Kingston upon Hull HU10 178 B8
1 Skegness PE25 206 D6
8 Spalding PE11 214 C2
8 Woodhall Spa LN10 97 C5
Birkdale Dr 3 DN40 186 D5
Birkdale Rd DN17 184 D3
Birkdale Square DN21 197 E6
Birkdale Way HU9 181 D8
Birketts La LN11 49 D5
BIRKHOLME NG33 152 B6
Birkland La NG23 78 D5
Birkwood PE22 98 E2
Birkwood La PE22 98 E3
Birmingham Cl 5 NG31 210 E5
Birrel St DN21 197 B6
BIRTHORPE NG34 143 A8
Birthorpe Rd NG34 143 A8
BISCATHORPE LN11 59 D3
Biscay Cl 1 PE25 206 A6
Bishop Alexander L.E.A.D. Acad NG24 104 A6
Bishop Blunt Cl 2 HU13 178 F1
BISHOPBRIDGE LN8 44 C1
Bishop Cockin Cl HU13 179 A1
Bishop Creighton Prim Sch PE1 226 B2
Bishopdale Cl NG31 129 F5
Bishop Grosseteste Univ Coll Lincoln LN1 201 F6
Bishop Gurdon Cl 4 HU13 178 F1
Bishop Kempthorne Cl 3 HU13 178 F1
Bishop King Ct 7 LN5 201 F1
Bishop La HU1 181 A6
Bishop La Staithe HU2 181 A6
BISHOP NORTON LN8 43 D3
Bishop Norton Rd LN8 43 E1
Bishops Cl
6 Bourne PE10 213 E4
Louth LN11 198 E6
Peterborough PE1 226 D5
Bishops Ct 3 NG34 212 D5
Bishopsfield PE4 221 B1
Bishops Gate LN1 201 E8
Bishop's La LN8 47 D7
Bishop's Pal The* LN2 234 B3
Bishop's Pl 5 LN2 68 C6
Bishops Rd
Leasingham NG34 121 B7
Lincoln LN2 202 C5
Bishop's Rd PE1 226 A1
Bishops Wlk 5 PE9 172 D3
Bishop's Wlk 1 DN34 191 C6
Bishop Temple Ct HU13 178 F3
Bishopthorpe Rd DN35 192 F3
Bishop Tozer Cl 9 PE24 102 E8
BITCHFIELD NG33 141 B3
Bittern Cl
23 Barton-upon-Humber DN18 3 E1
Kingston upon Hull HU4 179 D2
Bittern Way
3 Birchwood LN6 204 D8
Wyberton PE21 136 F8
BJ's Leisure Ctr PE25 90 E3
Black And Amber Wy 4 HU4 179 E5
Black Bank Ealand DN17 16 F7
Messingham DN17 29 A6
Blackbarn Road PE12 148 D2
Black Bear La PE13 170 F1
Blackberry Cl 9 LN6 93 A8
Blackberry Way 3 NG24 104 C1
Blackberry Wy 25 NG24 104 C1
Blackbourn Cl 20 NG23 91 D5
Blackbourn Rd LN6 205 C6
Blackbrook Rd 4 NG24 104 B5
Blackburn Ave HU15 2 C5
Blackburn Cl 2 NG31 210 D5
Black Dike PE13 169 E6
Blackdown Garth PE4 221 B3
Black Dro Anwick LN4 109 D2
Baston PE6 165 B8
Ewerby & Evedon NG34 122 E8
Midville PE22 100 D2
Thorney PE6 175 F5
Wisbech St Mary PE13 177 B4
Black Drove PE22 114 A8
Black Dyke PE13 169 F4
Blackdykes Rd DN9 28 B4
Blackey La PE22 99 B4
Black Fen La LN4 82 C4
Blackfriargate HU1 181 A5
Blackfriars Ct 5 LN2 202 E6
Blackfriars Rd LN2 202 E6
Blackfriars St 15 PE9 219 C5
Blackfriars Wlk 6 LN2 202 E6
Blackhill La LN9 73 F1
Black Hole Dro PE11 155 F8
Black Horse Dr 8 LN6 93 A8
BLACKJACK PE20 135 E6
Blackjack Rd PE20 135 C6
Black La
Doddington & Whisby LN6 79 E3
Gorefield PE13 169 C2
Blackmead PE2 230 B4
Blackmoor La DN9 27 D3
Blackmoor Rd
Aubourn Haddington & South Hykeham LN5 93 C5
Blackmoor Rd *continued*
Haxey DN9 27 D2
Black Prince Ave PE6 217 B6
Black's Cl 17 LN5 93 F7
Blacksmith Cl 9 DN9 27 D7
Blacksmith Hill DN15 1 E3
Blacksmith La
Boothby Graffoe LN5 94 A2
East Keal PE23 100 D6
2 Harmston LN5 93 F5
Thorpe on the Hill LN6 92 E8
Blacksmith Rd
4 Fiskerton LN3 82 A7
Miningsby PE22 99 E7
Blacksmith Row 1 LN5 92 F3
Blacksmiths Cl 2 DN19 11 C7
Blacksmith's Cnr 5 LN4 207 A5
Blacksmiths Ct 10 LN4 95 C4
Blacksmiths La
North Scarle LN6 78 E1
South Willingham LN8 59 A2
17 Spilsby PE23 88 A1
Welby NG32 130 F5
Blacksmith's La
13 Navenby/Wellingore LN5 107 A7
Norton Disney LN6 92 B2
Blacksmith's Row PE11 156 B7
Black Swan Cr PE7 230 B2
Black Swan Spinney PE8 222 A4
Blackthorn 5 PE9 218 C7
Blackthorn Ave 15 DN36 36 C8
Blackthorn Cl
1 Gainsborough DN21 197 F5
1 Lincoln LN2 202 C8
3 Market Deeping PE6 217 D6
13 Ruskington NG34 108 E1
Scunthorpe DN15 182 C6
Blackthorn Ct 4 HU3 180 D6
Blackthorne Cl 4 NG24 104 B3
Blackthorn La
Boston PE21 209 C5
Cammeringham LN1 54 E1
Cherry Willingham/Reepham LN3 203 E7
Kingston upon Hull HU10 178 F7
Blackthorns The
4 Broughton DN20 19 D4
6 Sleaford NG34 212 D3
Blackthorn Way PE10 213 E5
Blackwell Rd PE7 230 C2
Bladon Est PE21 209 F4
Bladons Wlk HU10 178 D8
Blaides Staithe 1 HU1 181 A6
Blair Wlk DN40 186 E3
Blake Ave DN17 184 E7
Blake Cl 2 HU2 180 E7
Blakeney Lea 4 DN35 192 F1
Blanchard Cl PE10 142 F2
Blanchard Rd LN11 198 E3
Blandford Gdns 6 PE1 226 E7
Blands Hill LN8 47 D5
Blanket Row HU1 180 F5
BLANKNEY LN4 95 D3
Blankney Cl 4 LN1 66 D2
Blankney Cres LN2 201 F8
Blankney Ct 13 DN15 9 A5
Blankney Dro LN10 96 E5
Blankney Moor La LN4 95 E3
Blankney N Dro LN4 96 B5
Blashfield Cl 2 PE9 219 A6
Blasket Rd HU14 3 B4
Blasson Way 12 NG34 133 B1
Blatherwick Rd NG24 104 B4
Blaydon Gr 1 DN34 190 E4
Blazegate PE12 216 B8
BLEASBY LN8 58 A3
BLEASBY MOOR LN3 57 F2
Bleasby Moor Road LN3 57 E2
Bledwick Dro PE13 170 C3
Blenheim Ave HU15 2 C5
Blenheim Cl
17 Hatfield DN7 14 D3
Louth LN11 198 B7
9 Skegness PE25 206 B6
Skellingthorpe LN6 79 F6
Blenheim Ct DN16 185 A2
Blenheim Pl DN35 192 E4
Blenheim Rd
Coningsby LN4 207 C4
Lincoln LN1 201 D4
Moorland Prison DN7 26 A8
Blenheim Square LN1 201 E7
Blenheim St HU5 180 B8
Blenheim Way
Londonthorpe & Harrowby Without NG31 211 D3
Market Deeping PE6 217 B7
Yaxley PE7 233 E5
Blenkin St HU9 181 B7
Blind La Coleby LN5 93 F3
Hough-on-the-Hill NG32 118 E7
4 Maxey PE6 173 C7
22 Waddington LN5 93 F7
Blithfield PE7 233 E8
Bloomfield Ave HU5 179 C8
Bloom La DN15 8 C1
Bloomsbury Ct 1 HU3 180 D6
Bloomsbury Gdns DN33 191 B2
Blossom Ct PE3 225 B8
Blossom Way 1 DN40 186 B3
Blow Row DN9 27 E6
Blow's La PE20 135 F3
BLOXHOLM LN4 108 C4
Bloxholm La Blankney LN4 95 A2

Bloxholm La *continued*
Bracebridge Heath LN4 ..... 81 B1
Nocton LN4 ..... 94 D6
Bloxholm Lane LN4 ..... 108 C5
Bluebell Ave PE1 ..... 226 A8
Bluebell Cl 7 Lincoln LN5 .. 205 C2
Scunthorpe DN15 ..... 183 C3
Bluebell Ct 23 Healing DN41 . 23 F5
8 Owston Ferry DN9 ..... 28 A3
Bluebell Gdns HU13 ..... 3 E4
Bluebell Gr 1 DN20 ..... 196 B4
Bluebell Rd 2 PE9 ..... 218 D7
Bluebells 8 PE6 ..... 217 D6
Bluebells The PE12 ..... 215 A6
Bluebell Wk LN6 ..... 92 D5
Bluebell Wlk PE21 ..... 208 B4
Blueberry Ct HU4 ..... 179 C4
Bluebird Way HU15 ..... 2 C5
Bluecoat Meres Acad NG31 ..... 210 E3
Bluecoat Sch The PE9 ..... 219 B6
Bluegate NG31 ..... 211 A5
Blue Gowt Dro PE11 ..... 214 A7
Blue Gowt La PE11 ..... 214 B7
Blue Horse Ct NG33 ..... 140 A5
Blue St 7 PE21 ..... 208 E4
Bluestone Cl DN32 ..... 192 A8
Bluestone Heath Rd
Scamblesby LN11 ..... 73 A7
Skendleby PE23 ..... 88 D5
South Ormsby cum Ketsby LN11 ..... 74 B3
South Thoresby LN13 ..... 75 A1
Tetford LN11 ..... 73 F3
Ulceby with Fordington LN13 . 88 B8
Welton le Wold LN11 ..... 60 A4
Bluestone La DN40 ..... 186 B4
Bluestone Rise LN11 ..... 198 B4
Bluestone Way 24 LN12 ..... 77 A7
Blundell Ave DN35 ..... 189 E1
Blundell Pk (Grimsby Town FC) DN35 ..... 192 C8
BLYBOROUGH DN21 ..... 42 E5
Blyth Ct 28 DN18 ..... 10 F8
Blyth St 2 HU9 ..... 181 B7
Blyth Way DN37 ..... 23 E2
BLYTON DN21 ..... 41 C5
Blyton Cl 11 LN6 ..... 204 C7
Blyton cum Laughton CE Sch DN21 ..... 41 C6
Blyton Gr 13 LN6 ..... 204 C7
Blyton Rd
12 Birchwood LN6 ..... 204 C7
Laughton DN21 ..... 41 B8
Skegness PE25 ..... 206 C6
Thonock DN21 ..... 197 C8
BMI The Lincoln Hospl LN2 ..... 234 B4
Boardsides Frampton PE20 124 F2
Wyberton PE21 ..... 208 A3
Boating Dyke Way 19 DN8 . 15 A8
Boatswain Croft 7 HU1 .. 180 F5
Bobbin La LN2 ..... 202 E6
Bob Rainsforth Way DN21 197 F6
Bodiam Way DN32 ..... 191 F8
Bodmin Cl DN17 ..... 184 D8
Bodmin Moor Cl LN6 ..... 204 D1
Bog Gate DN14 ..... 6 D8
Boggle La LN8 ..... 45 E5
BOLE DN22 ..... 52 C5
Boleyn Ave PE2 ..... 230 C8
Bolingbroke Castle (remains of)★ PE23 ..... 100 A7
Bolingbroke Rd
Cleethorpes DN35 ..... 193 A3
Louth LN11 ..... 198 B8
Mavis Enderby PE23 ..... 87 B1
Scunthorpe DN17 ..... 184 E4
Bolle Rd LN11 ..... 198 C6
Bolsover Rd
Earlsfield NG31 ..... 210 F1
Scunthorpe DN15 ..... 182 B2
Boltgate La DN17 ..... 7 C3
Bolton Ave LN6 ..... 205 A3
Bolton's La PE25 ..... 90 D2
Bomber Cty Aviation Mus★ DN21 ..... 42 F1
Bon Accord Rd HU13 ..... 178 E1
Bona La PE13 ..... 169 E1
BONBY DN20 ..... 10 C2
Bonby Gr 2 Grimsby DN33 191 A3
Scunthorpe DN17 ..... 184 F5
Bonby La DN20 ..... 10 D3
Bonby Rd DN20 ..... 10 C1
Bond Hays La 3 PE23 ..... 87 A4
Bond St 1 Boston PE21 ..... 208 F4
Kingston upon Hull HU1 ..... 180 F7
Bonemill La NG34 ..... 121 E6
Bonnetable Rd LN9 ..... 199 D3
Bonnyhale Rd DN17 ..... 16 E6
Bonsdale Lane DN21 ..... 41 F5
BONTHORPE LN13 ..... 89 B7
Bonthorpe Rd LN13 ..... 89 B7
Boole Cl LN2 ..... 202 A6
Boongate PE1 ..... 226 C3
Boonground La PE22 ..... 115 A3
Bootham Cl 6 DN7 ..... 14 D4
Bootham Cres 12 DN7 ..... 14 C6
Bootham La DN7 ..... 14 D5
Bootham Rd 11 DN7 ..... 14 C6
Boothby Cl 14 PE20 ..... 136 C5
BOOTHBY GRAFFOE LN5 ..... 94 A2
BOOTHBY PAGNELL NG33 .. 140 E5
Boothby Pagnell Manor House★ NG33 ..... 140 E5
Boothferry Park Halt 1 HU4 ..... 179 E5
Boothferry Rd HU13 ..... 178 B2
Booth Nooking La DN15 ..... 2 A2
Boot La PE20 ..... 136 E3
Borman's La 7 DN36 ..... 36 B1
Boroughfield Rd 9 PE2 .. 230 F5
Borrowdale Cl PE4 ..... 221 C3
Borrowdale Way NG31 ..... 211 B8
Borthwick Pl PE2 ..... 229 D6
Bos App Rd DN16 ..... 185 F7
Boscombe Cl 12 LN6 ..... 204 C6
BOSTON PE21 ..... 209 C6
Boston Aerodrome PE21 .. 125 B2
Boston Coll (De Montfort Campus) PE21 ..... 209 B3
Boston Coll (Rochford Campus) PE21 ..... 209 A4
Boston Ent Pk PE21 ..... 208 A4
Boston Gram Sch PE21 ..... 209 A4
Boston Hawthorn Tree Sch PE21 ..... 209 D4
Boston High Sch PE21 ..... 209 B7
BOSTON LONG HEDGES PE22 ..... 126 B6
Boston Long Hedges PE22 ..... 126 C6
Boston Pioneers Free Sch Acad PE21 ..... 208 F5
Boston Rd
Algarkirk PE20 ..... 136 A3
Frithville PE22 ..... 125 E7
Gosberton PE11 ..... 145 C6
Heckington NG34 ..... 122 E2
Holbeach PE12 ..... 215 C4
Horncastle LN9 ..... 199 C1
Revesby PE22 ..... 99 C3
Sleaford NG34 ..... 212 D4
14 Spilsby PE23 ..... 88 A1
Swineshead PE20 ..... 124 D1
Wainfleet St Mary PE24 ..... 102 D1
Boston Rd N PE12 ..... 215 C5
Boston Rd Pits Nature Reserve★ PE11 ..... 145 C6
Boston Rd S PE12 ..... 215 D3
Boston Road Ind Est LN9 .. 199 C1
Boston Sta PE21 ..... 208 E5
Boston Stump (St Botolph's Church)★ PE21 ..... 208 F5
Boston Trade Pk PE21 ..... 208 F6
BOSTON WEST PE20 ..... 125 B4
Boston West Hospl PE21 .. 208 E4
Boston W Prim Sch PE21 . 208 B5
Boswell Cl PE1 ..... 225 E8
Boswell Dr LN6 ..... 205 A5
Boswell Gr LN6 ..... 204 F5
Boswell Rd LN11 ..... 48 B3
Bosworth Cl 18 DN7 ..... 14 D3
Botany Bay La DN3 ..... 14 B4
Bothwell Gr 3 HU9 ..... 5 E8
Botolph Gn PE2 ..... 230 C7
Botolph St 7 PE21 ..... 209 A5
Botolph's View 1 LN11 ..... 51 C4
Botteford Jun & Inf Schools DN16 ..... 185 A2
BOTTESFORD
Bottesford NG13 ..... 128 A6
Scunthorpe DN16 ..... 185 B3
Bottesford Ave DN16 ..... 185 B5
Bottesford Cl 12 LN6 ..... 204 D8
Bottesford La DN16 ..... 185 B4
Bottesford Rd
Allington NG32 ..... 128 E6
Scunthorpe DN16 ..... 185 B5
Bottesford Sports Ctr DN17 ..... 184 C3
Bottesford Sta NG13 ..... 128 B6
Bottle La PE13 ..... 169 C7
Bottlings The 8 DN20 ..... 196 C3
Bottom St NG32 ..... 128 F7
BOUGHTON NG34 ..... 122 C4
Boughton Ave DN15 ..... 182 F4
Boulevard HU3 ..... 180 B5
Boulevard Acad The HU3 .. 180 B5
Boulevard Ave DN31 ..... 188 E1
Boulevard Gdns DN31 ..... 191 B8
Boulevard Ret Pk PE1 ..... 225 D7
Boulevard The 23 LN12 ..... 64 B3
Boulevard Way DN31 ..... 191 B7
Boulevard Wlk DN31 ..... 191 B8
BOULTHAM LN5 ..... 205 D8
Boultham Ave LN5 ..... 201 D1
Boultham Mere Nature Reserve★ LN6 ..... 201 B3
BOULTHAM MOOR LN6 ..... 205 B6
Boultham Pk Rd LN6 ..... 201 D1
Boundaries The PE12 ..... 215 D1
Boundary La
Aubourn Haddington & South Hykeham LN6 ..... 93 A8
Yaxley PE7 ..... 233 D8
Boundary Paddock 1 LN5 ..... 107 A7
Boundary Pastures NG34 . 212 D3
Boundary Rd DN33 ..... 194 E6
Boundary St LN5 ..... 205 D7
Boundary The PE21 ..... 208 C5
Boundary Way HU5 ..... 179 D7
Boundry Wlk LN8 ..... 56 F3
Bourges Bvd PE1 ..... 225 D7
Bourgess Ret Pk PE3 ..... 225 F1
BOURNE PE10 ..... 213 C7
Bourne Abbey CE Prim Acad PE10 ..... 213 E5
Bourne Acad PE10 ..... 213 E6
Bourne Cl Lincoln LN6 ..... 205 B5
Sleaford NG34 ..... 212 C3
Bourne Dro PE10 ..... 155 A5
Bourne Elsea Pk CE Prim Acad PE10 ..... 213 C3
Bourne Gram Sch PE10 ..... 213 D4
Bourne La 7 NG34 ..... 108 D2
Bourne Outdoor Swimming Pool PE10 ..... 213 D4
Bourne Rd 20
Alford LN13 ..... 75 F2
Baston PE6 ..... 164 E3
Bourne PE10 ..... 213 E2
Colsterworth NG33 ..... 151 E6
Essendine PE9 ..... 163 E3
Folkingham NG34 ..... 142 D8
Morton PE10 ..... 154 C6
Old Somerby NG33 ..... 140 D8
Pinchbeck PE11 ..... 155 F5
Spalding PE11 ..... 214 A3
Swinstead NG33 ..... 153 A5
Thurlby PE10 ..... 164 D8
Bourne Rd Est 6 NG33 ..... 151 E6
Bourne Skills Ctr PE10 ..... 213 D5
Bourne St HU2 ..... 181 A7
Bourne Westfield Prim Acad PE10 ..... 213 B5
Bourne Westfield Prim Sch PE10 ..... 213 B5
Bovill Cl DN31 ..... 191 C7
Bowbridge Gdns 4 NG13 128 A6
Bowbridge La
10 Bottesford NG13 ..... 128 A6
Hawton NG24 ..... 104 A1
Bowbridge Rd NG24 ..... 104 A2
Bowden Dr LN6 ..... 205 A5
Bowditch Rd PE11 ..... 214 E3
Bower Cl PE1 ..... 226 C5
Bowers Ave Grimsby DN31 . 191 B7
3 Louth LN11 ..... 198 D7
Bowfield Cl DN37 ..... 190 D8
Bow Gate PE11 ..... 145 B6
Bowlalley La 9 HU1 ..... 180 F6
Bowl Alley La LN9 ..... 199 C4
Bowling Gn La
Chapel Hill LN4 ..... 110 E5
11 Crowle DN17 ..... 16 D8
Grantham NG31 ..... 211 B3
3 Grimsby DN32 ..... 191 E7
Bowling Gn Rd DN21 ..... 197 B5
Bowling Green Gdns 7 DN21 ..... 30 B2
Bowling La DN35 ..... 192 E6
Bowman Ave PE22 ..... 115 A6
Bowman Cl PE21 ..... 208 D6
Bowmandale 30 DN18 ..... 10 E8
Bowmandale Prim Sch DN18 ..... 10 E8
Bowman Mews PE9 ..... 219 D5
Bowmans Ridge 1 PE23 ..... 87 F1
Bowmans Way NG32 ..... 128 F4
Bowman Way 7 DN40 ..... 186 B3
Bowness Way 1 PE4 ..... 221 D2
Bow Rd HU15 ..... 2 E6
Boxer Rd PE8 ..... 172 B1
Boxgrove Cl 8 PE6 ..... 175 A1
Boyfield Cres 4 PE9 ..... 218 E4
Boyfields 1 PE11 ..... 145 A8
Boynton Cres 9 DN15 ..... 9 A5
Boynton St 1 HU3 ..... 180 C4
Bozeat Way PE3 ..... 225 C6
Brabbs Ave 4 DN7 ..... 14 E4
BRACEBOROUGH PE9 ..... 164 B4
Braceborough Rd PE9 ..... 164 B4
BRACEBRIDGE LN5 ..... 205 D6
BRACEBRIDGE HEATH LN4 ..... 205 E3
Bracebridge Inf Sch LN5 .. 205 E6
BRACEBY NG34 ..... 131 D2
Braceby Rd
Ropsley & Humby NG33 ..... 131 B1
Skegness PE25 ..... 206 B7
Brackenborough Ct LN11 198 C7
Brackenborough Rd
Brackenborough with Little Grimsby LN11 ..... 49 C1
Keddington LN11 ..... 61 C8
Louth LN11 ..... 198 C8
Brackenburry Way PE21 .. 208 E8
Brackenbury Cl LN9 ..... 199 A3
Brackenbury Fields NG33 140 F6
Bracken Cl
Gainsborough DN21 ..... 197 B7
Leasingham NG34 ..... 121 C7
Bracken Ct LN6 ..... 204 B1
Bracken Heen Cl 2 DN7 ..... 14 E4
Brackenhill Rd DN9 ..... 27 E2
Brackenholmes Rd DN15 ..... 9 A2
Bracken La PE24 ..... 90 A7
Bracken Pk DN33 ..... 194 E8
Bracken Pl DN37 ..... 190 C6
Bracken Rd LN6 ..... 92 B7
Bracken's La LN8 ..... 43 C4
Bracken Way LN11 ..... 198 C7
Brackley Cl Bourne PE10 ..... 213 D7
Peterborough PE3 ..... 225 D3
Brackwood PE2 ..... 229 D6
BRACON DN9 ..... 16 F2
Bracon Cl 9 DN9 ..... 16 E2
Bradbury Ave LN5 ..... 205 C2
Bradden St PE3 ..... 225 C6
Bradegate Dr PE1 ..... 226 E7
Bradford Ave DN35 ..... 193 A5
Bradford Cl 10 NG31 ..... 210 D5
Bradford Rd
Boston PE21 ..... 208 D3
Immingham DN40 ..... 186 B4
Bradgrade La 4 HU3 ..... 179 F5
Brading Ave NG31 ..... 210 E4
BRADLEY DN37 ..... 190 E2
Bradley Cl LN11 ..... 198 D3
Bradley & Dixon Woods Nature Reserve★ DN37 . 194 A8
Bradley Dr NG31 ..... 211 A2
Bradley La LE15 ..... 162 B7
Bradley Rd Bradley DN37 .. 194 B6
Grimsby DN37 ..... 190 E2
Bradley St DN32 ..... 191 F7
Bradley Wy PE1 ..... 226 C1
Bradman Cl LN8 ..... 56 F3
Bradman Ct 17 DN32 ..... 189 C1
Bradshaw Cl 15 PE9 ..... 218 E6
Bradshaw's La PE24 ..... 90 C7
Bradshaws Terr PE21 ..... 209 A5
Bradway 9 LN1 ..... 66 D7
Bradwell Cl 19 DN18 ..... 10 E8
Bradwell Rd PE3 ..... 225 A2
Brady St 1 PE21 ..... 208 E6
Braeburn Ave 14 PE13 ..... 170 D2
Braeburn Rd PE6 ..... 217 F5
Braemar Cl
Grantham NG31 ..... 211 C7
1 Middle Rasen LN8 ..... 57 B8
Stamford PE9 ..... 218 E6
Braemar Rd
Cleethorpes DN35 ..... 192 E4
3 Mablethorpe/Sutton on Sea LN12 ..... 76 F8
Braemer Rd NG23 ..... 91 D4
Braeton La DN33 ..... 195 A7
Braids Wlk HU10 ..... 178 B8
Brailsford Cl 3 PE3 ..... 225 A4
BRAITHWAITE DN7 ..... 14 A7
Braithwaite La DN7 ..... 14 A8
Bramar Rd 5 DN7 ..... 14 D4
Brambleberry La PE24 ..... 102 B7
Bramble Cl Billinghay LN4 .. 109 E6
Grimsby DN31 ..... 191 C7
19 Long Bennington NG23 ..... 117 D3
4 Welton/Dunholme LN2 ..... 68 D7
Bramble Ct 24 LN2 ..... 68 D2
Bramble Gr 2 PE9 ..... 218 D6
Bramble Grange 3 PE11 . 214 B5
Bramble Hills PE25 ..... 103 E3
Bramble La DN15 ..... 2 B1
Brambles The
3 Barrow upon Humber DN19 ..... 11 C8
Bourne PE10 ..... 213 D7
Cherry Willingham LN3 ..... 203 B7
Grantham NG31 ..... 211 A2
8 Helpringham NG34 ..... 133 D7
Holbeach PE12 ..... 215 F2
4 Market Deeping PE6 ..... 217 D6
Market Rasen LN8 ..... 45 D1
15 Market Rasen LN8 ..... 57 D8
Newton on Trent LN1 ..... 65 D1
Bramble Way
2 Brigg DN20 ..... 196 B4
Humberston DN36 ..... 192 E1
Bramblewood Cl 6 NG31 210 F8
Brambling Wlk PE10 ..... 143 A3
Brambling Wy DN16 ..... 185 F5
Bramhall St DN35 ..... 192 C7
Bramley Cl
1 Barton-upon-Humber DN18 ..... 3 F1
5 Bourne PE10 ..... 213 C6
8 Fleet PE12 ..... 159 C7
2 Heckington NG34 ..... 122 E2
4 Louth LN11 ..... 198 C5
Bramley Cres DN16 ..... 185 A3
Bramley Ct
Gainsborough DN21 ..... 197 F5
Lincoln LN6 ..... 204 F4
Bramley Gr 1 DN21 ..... 29 C3
Bramley La 6 PE21 ..... 208 E4
Bramley Mdws 7 PE12 ..... 159 D7
Bramley Rd
Market Deeping PE6 ..... 217 B5
11 Wisbech PE13 ..... 170 D1
Bramley Wlk PE25 ..... 206 C6
Bramley Wy DN10 ..... 40 A4
Bramling Way NG34 ..... 212 F4
BRAMPTON LN1 ..... 65 E6
Brampton Ct PE2 ..... 231 D6
Brampton Way DN35 ..... 192 D3
Bramwith La DN7 ..... 14 A6
Brancaster Dr Lincoln LN6 . 205 C8
Skegness PE25 ..... 206 D5
Brancepeth Pl PE2 ..... 230 E7
Branches La PE12 ..... 159 A7
BRAND END PE22 ..... 126 D4
Brand End Rd PE22 ..... 126 E4
Brandesburton St HU3 ..... 180 B7
BRANDON NG32 ..... 118 D7
Brandon Cl 1 NG24 ..... 104 C2
Brandon Rd
Hough-on-the-Hill NG32 ..... 118 E6
Scunthorpe DN15 ..... 182 D2
Stubton NG23 ..... 118 C7
Brandy Wharf Cider Ctr★ DN21 ..... 44 A7
Brandy Wharf Rd DN21 ..... 43 E6
Brankwell Cres DN17 ..... 184 E3
BRANSBY LN1 ..... 66 E6
Bransby Home of Rest for Horses★ LN1 ..... 66 D6
Bransdale Gr HU9 ..... 181 F8
Bransdale Rd 5 DN16 ..... 185 D5
Bransdale Way DN37 ..... 190 E8
BRANSTON
Branston and Mere LN4 ..... 81 E2
Croxton Kerrial NG32 ..... 138 A4
BRANSTON BOOTHS LN4 ..... 82 C4
Branston CE Inf Sch LN4 ..... 81 D2
Branston Cl Lincoln LN6 ..... 205 B4
4 Winthorpe NG24 ..... 104 B7
Branston Cswy LN3 ..... 82 F3
Branston Jun Sch LN4 ..... 81 E2
Branston La LN4 ..... 94 D7
Branston Rd
Branston NG32 ..... 138 A4
Heighington LN4 ..... 81 E3
BRANT BROUGHTON LN5 ..... 105 F5
Brant Broughton CE Methodist Prim Sch LN5 ..... 105 F5
BRANTINGHAM HU15 ..... 2 C8
Brantingham Rd HU15 ..... 2 B7
Brant Rd Fulbeck NG32 ..... 105 F1
Lincoln LN5 ..... 205 D2
Scunthorpe DN15 ..... 182 E2
Waddington LN5 ..... 93 D7
Brassey Cl PE1 ..... 225 E6
BRATOFT PE24 ..... 102 B7
Bratoft Cnr PE24 ..... 102 D7
Bratoft End PE24 ..... 102 C5
Brats La LN8 ..... 47 E5
Bratt Field Rd DN21 ..... 53 F8
Bratt Field South Rd DN21 . 54 A8
BRATTLEBY LN1 ..... 67 C8
Brattleby Cres LN2 ..... 201 F7
Brauncewell Cl 18 NG34 .. 108 D2
Brauncewell Rd 6 NG34 .. 107 C1
Bray Ave 8 LN12 ..... 64 C2
Braybrook PE2 ..... 230 A3
Braybrook Prim Sch PE2 .. 230 B4
Braybrooks Way 1 PE12 .. 157 E1
Bray Cl DN33 ..... 191 B2
Brayfields 3 PE11 ..... 156 F8
Brayford St LN5 ..... 234 A2
Brayford Waterfront LN1 . 234 A2
Brayford Way 1 LN1 ..... 234 A2
Brayford Wharf E LN5 ..... 234 A1
Brayford Wharf N LN1 ..... 234 A2
Braygate La PE23 ..... 100 E5
Braymere Rd PE7 ..... 230 D2
Brazenose La PE9 ..... 219 C5
Brazil St HU9 ..... 181 C8
Breakneck La LN11 ..... 198 A5
Breckland Cl 1 HU3 ..... 179 F5
Brecks La Kirk Sandall DN3 .. 14 A2
Stapleford LN6 ..... 105 C8
Brecon Cl NG31 ..... 210 D8
Brecon Way NG34 ..... 212 B3
Breda Ct 8 PE11 ..... 214 A2
Breedon Dr LN1 ..... 201 D7
Breezemount Ct 2 DN7 ..... 14 C6
Brellows Hill 7 PE34 ..... 161 F3
Bremerhaven Way DN33 .. 190 F3
Brendon Cl NG31 ..... 210 D8
Brendon Garth 4 PE4 ..... 221 C1
Brendon Wlk 5 PE11 ..... 214 C6
Brent Rd LN4 ..... 110 E8
Brentwood Cl HU15 ..... 2 B6
Brereton Ave DN35 ..... 192 C8
Brethergate DN9 ..... 27 B2
BRETTON PE3 ..... 225 A6
Bretton Cl 4 DN7 ..... 14 D3
Bretton Ctr PE3 ..... 225 A5
Bretton Gate 2 PE3 ..... 225 A5
Bretton Gn 1 PE3 ..... 225 A5
Bretton Way Bretton PE3 .. 225 A7
3 Peterborough PE3 ..... 220 F1
Brewerne PE2 ..... 230 B4
Brewers La PE13 ..... 170 A5
Brewery Gdns 2 DN17 ..... 16 D8
Brewery Hill NG31 ..... 211 B3
Brewery La NG34 ..... 143 B8
Brewery Rd DN17 ..... 16 D8
Brewery St 6 PE24 ..... 102 E8
Brewhouse Gall★ NG31 .. 211 A1
Brewster Ave
Immingham DN40 ..... 186 D3
Peterborough PE2 ..... 230 F8
Brewster Ave Inf Sch PE2 . 230 F8
Brewster La PE24 ..... 102 C2
Brewster Rd Boston PE21 .. 209 B4
Gainsborough DN21 ..... 197 F2
Breydon Ct 3 DN15 ..... 8 B4
Brian Ave
Cleethorpes DN35 ..... 192 D3
Scunthorpe DN16 ..... 185 C5
7 Skegness PE25 ..... 206 C4
Waltham DN37 ..... 194 D4
Briar Cl 6 Birchwood LN6 .. 200 C1
5 Lincoln LN6 ..... 93 A8
Skegness PE25 ..... 206 C3
2 Sleaford NG34 ..... 212 D2
4 South Killingholme DN40 .. 12 E3
Briar La Grimsby DN33 ..... 194 D8
Healing DN41 ..... 23 F5
Briars La 6 DN7 ..... 14 C7
Briars The HU13 ..... 178 E3
Briar Way
Peterborough PE1 ..... 226 C5
Scunthorpe DN15 ..... 182 C6
Skegness PE25 ..... 206 C2
Briar Wlk PE10 ..... 213 D7
Briarwood Cl 6 NG31 ..... 210 F7
Brickberry Cl PE7 ..... 230 C2
Brickburn Cl PE7 ..... 230 E2
Brickenden Rd 7 PE4 ..... 221 E2
Bricken Field La LN9 ..... 84 C8
Brickenhole La 7 DN10 ..... 39 F3
Brickings Way 4 DN22 ..... 52 B3
Brick La
North Killingholme DN40 ..... 12 E5
Wrangle PE22 ..... 114 C1
Brickstead Rd PE7 ..... 230 D2
Brickton Rd PE7 ..... 230 B1
Brickyard La Brigg DN20 ..... 20 C3
Folkingham NG34 ..... 142 D8
Hundleby PE23 ..... 87 E1
Mablethorpe & Sutton LN12 .. 76 E8
Melton HU14 ..... 2 F4

Brickyard La *continued*
Navenby LN5 94 A1
Theddlethorpe St Helen LN12 63 F7
Walkeringham DN10 39 E3
Bridge Cl
Kingston upon Hull HU9 181 D6
3 Louth LN11 198 C6
Bridge Dro PE13 177 B7
Bridge End
Colsterworth NG33 151 D7
Wansford PE8 222 A3
Bridge End Cswy NG34 133 F3
Bridge End Gr NG31 211 D2
Bridge End Rd NG31 211 C2
Bridge Foot PE6 217 B4
Bridgegate Dr HU9 181 C6
Bridge Gdns 1 DN31 188 D1
Bridgehill Rd PE6 221 D6
Bridge La Cadney DN20 31 C6
Horkstow DN18 9 F5
Scopwick LN4 108 D8
Bridge Pl 22 LN1 66 D2
Bridge Rd
Aubourn Haddington & South Hykeham LN5 92 F5
Gainsborough DN21 197 D3
Greetham with Somersby LN9 86 F7
Long Sutton PE12 216 D3
4 Sutton Bridge PE12 160 F4
Bridge St N 1 DN32 189 B1
Bridges Rd DN17 184 E7
Bridge St 3 Billinghay LN4 109 F5
2 Boston PE21 208 F4
Brigg DN20 196 A3
Gainsborough DN21 197 C3
Grantham NG31 211 C3
Horncastle LN9 199 B4
Louth LN11 198 B6
Market Deeping PE6 217 D4
Marston NG32 118 D2
19 Nettleham LN2 68 C2
2 Peterborough PE1 226 A1
4 Ryhall PE9 163 C1
Saxilby LN1 66 D2
27 Thorne/Moorends DN8 15 A8
Bridges The 24 DN18 10 F8
Bridge View LN8 56 F8
Bridgeview Sch HU4 179 C4
Bridge Vw 3 HU4 179 C2
Bridgewater Rd DN17 184 D8
Bridle Cl Fishtoft PE21 209 C3
7 Sleaford NG34 212 D2
Bridle La
Carlton-le-Moorland LN5 105 E8
Hampton Vale PE7 230 B1
Bridles The 11 DN19 12 A8
Bridle Way 7 LN8 70 D5
Bridle Way The LN4 95 B7
Bridlington Ave HU2 180 F8
Bridport Wlk DN17 184 C8
Brierholme Carr Rd DN7 14 F5
Brierholme Cl DN7 14 F5
Brierholme Ings Rd DN7 14 F5
BRIGG DN20 196 E4
Briggate Dr 19 DN17 29 D7
Brigg Cl 6 LN6 204 C6
Brigg Dr HU13 178 F3
Brigg Gr 5 LN6 204 C6
Brigg La LN5 105 F8
Brigg Prim Sch DN20 196 B4
Brigg Rd
Barton-upon-Humber DN18 10 E5
Broughton DN20 19 E3
Cadney DN20 31 D7
Grasby LN7 33 A6
Hibaldstow DN20 30 F6
North Kelsey LN7 32 A5
Scawby DN20 30 F8
Scunthorpe DN16 183 D2
South Kelsey LN7 32 A1
Wrawby DN20 196 F5
Brigg Road DN21 29 D4
Briggs La DN7 14 C8
Brigg Sta DN20 196 C2
Brighowgate DN32 191 D6
Brighton St
2 Cleethorpes DN35 193 A5
Kingston upon Hull HU3 180 A3
Bright St
2 Gainsborough DN21 197 C4
Kingston upon Hull HU8 181 B8
Peterborough PE1 225 F3
BRIGSLEY DN37 35 D4
Brigsley Rd DN37 194 D2
Brigstock Ct PE3 225 C6
Brigstock Rd PE13 170 C1
Brimbles Way PE2 229 E5
Brindle Road HU3 179 F4
Brinkhurst Rd PE2 230 A4
Brinkhall Way 9 LN2 68 D7
BRINKHILL LN11 87 C8
Brinkhill Pottery★ LN11 87 D8
Brinkhill Rd LN9 74 D1
Brinkle Spring La LN4 82 A4
Brisbane Cl
5 Skegness PE25 206 A4
12 Waddington LN5 93 E8
Brisbane St HU3 180 D5
Brisson Cl NG31 211 C5
Bristol Arc 16 NG34 212 D4
Bristol Ave PE4 220 F3
Bristol Cl
14 Beacon Hill NG24 104 C5
Grantham NG31 210 E4
Bristol Dr LN6 205 C8
Bristol House Rd NG34 107 C1
Bristol Rd
Kingston upon Hull HU5 179 C8

Bristol Rd *continued*
Scunthorpe DN17 182 C1
Bristol Way NG34 212 B5
Bristow Rd Cranwell NG34 107 E1
3 Cranwell & Byard's Leap NG34 120 E8
Bristows Yd NG32 118 D2
Britannia Cres DN34 190 D5
Britannia Gdns 3 PE11 214 C5
Britannia Terr 4 DN21 197 D3
Briton Ct 11 PE11 214 C2
Brittain Dr NG31 211 C5
Britton Cl DN17 7 D3
Brixham Ct Grimsby DN33 194 E6
7 Kingston upon Hull HU3 180 A5
5 Kingston upon Hull HU3 180 A5
Broach Rd LN5 106 B5
Broadacre Pk 2 HU15 2 D5
Broad Avenue HU13 178 B3
Broadbank LN11 198 B6
Broadbeck 7 DN21 43 D7
Broadbent Theatre★ LN3 69 E8
Broad Cl PE1 226 D5
Broad Dale Cl 4 LN2 68 F3
Broad Dro PE11 144 B5
Broad Dro E PE13 169 E6
Broad Dro W PE13 169 B4
Broad Fen La NG23 104 D1
Broadfield La 8 PE21 208 E4
Broadfield La Ind Est PE21 208 E3
Broadfield St PE21 208 E4
Broadgate Gedney PE12 159 D6
Lincoln LN2 234 B2
Whaplode PE12 168 A3
Broad Gate
Sutton St James PE12 169 A8
Weston PE12 157 C1
Wrangle PE22 114 C3
Broadgate Dro PE12 167 C8
Broadgate La PE6 217 F4
Broadgate Rd
South Witham NG33 151 E2
Sutton St Edmund PE12 168 F3
BROADHOLME LN1 66 C1
Broadholme Rd LN1 66 D1
Broadhurst Rd 18 PE8 172 B1
Broadings La DN22 65 A4
Broad La Adlingfleet DN14 7 B7
Bicker PE20 135 B4
Moulton PE12 157 F6
South Leverton DN22 65 A7
Sutterton PE20 135 F1
Whaplode PE12 146 F1
Broadlands Ave PE10 213 C7
Broadlands Cl 1 DN7 14 D3
Broadlands The PE1 226 E5
Broadley Ave HU10 178 D6
Broadley Cl 6 HU9 181 C7
Broadley Cres LN11 198 E6
Broadley Croft 5 HU15 2 D5
Broadley Way 8 HU15 2 D5
Broad St
5 Grantham NG31 211 A5
Spalding PE11 214 D4
Stamford PE9 219 B5
Broadstone Dr PE7 233 E8
Broadsyke La NG24 105 A4
Broadwater Dr 3 DN7 14 D3
Broadwater La PE12 158 A4
Broadway Ashby DN16 185 B6
Crowland PE6 175 B8
Farcet PE7 231 C1
3 Grimsby DN34 190 D4
Hatfield DN7 14 C3
2 Keelby DN41 23 A5
Lincoln LN2 201 F6
Mablethorpe/Sutton on Sea LN12 77 A8
Peterborough PE1 226 A3
Spalding PE11 214 A2
Yaxley PE7 233 E5
Broadway Cl
11 Bourne PE10 213 C7
4 Lincoln LN2 201 F6
Broadway Ct 5 PE1 226 A2
Broadway Gdns PE1 226 B5
Broadway Nook 1 DN7 14 C3
Broadway The
Morton PE10 154 B7
Woodhall Spa LN10 97 D6
Broadway Theatre★ PE1 226 A3
Broad Wheel Rd PE6 173 B3
Brock Cl 13 Epworth DN9 27 D6
1 Grimsby DN33 191 C2
Brockenhurst Cl LN6 204 B7
Brockenhurst Rd 9 DN7 14 E4
Brocklebank Cl LN5 92 F2
Brocklebank Way NG34 212 C7
BROCKLESBY DN41 22 E6
Brocklesby Ave DN40 186 A4
Brocklesby Cl
Gainsborough DN21 197 F3
5 Kingston upon Hull HU13 179 A3
Brocklesby Gdns PE3 225 C3
Brocklesby Pk Prim Sch DN37 22 D4
Brocklesby Pl DN34 190 E4
Brocklesby Rd
Brocklesby DN37 22 E4
Brocklesby DN41 22 E5
Grimsby DN34 190 E4
Habrough DN40 22 E8
Scunthorpe DN17 184 F4
Ulceby DN39 12 A1
Brocklesby Wlk LN11 198 A7
Brocks Cl 22 PE24 90 D7

Brockton Cl 7 HU3 179 F5
Brodie Pl PE7 230 F1
Brodsworth Rd PE7 231 F5
Bromley Ave 6 NG24 104 A3
Brompton Cl HU10 179 A6
Bromwich Rd HU10 178 F8
Bronzegarth DN32 192 B5
Brookdale Rd DN17 184 D6
Brook Dr 4 LN12 64 C3
Brooke Ave PE9 218 E4
Brooke Cl NG24 104 B3
BROOKENBY LN8 47 B6
Brookenby Bsns Pk LN8 47 B6
Brooker Ave PE4 221 E2
Brookes Cl 31 DN21 30 B1
Brooke St DN8 15 A8
Brookfield Ave LN2 68 D2
Brookfield Cl
Skellingthorpe LN6 200 A5
6 Thorne/Moorends DN8 15 A8
Brookfield Home Pk PE4 220 E2
Brookfield Rd DN33 191 B1
Brookfields Ind Pk PE4 220 F2
Brookfurlong PE3 225 B6
Brook La Farcet PE7 231 B2
Morton DN21 197 F6
Scawby DN20 20 A1
Brooklands 1 DN20 19 E3
Brooklands Ave
Broughton DN20 19 D4
Cleethorpes DN35 193 A5
Brooklands Cl
5 Birchwood LN6 204 C7
3 Collingham NG23 91 D5
Brooklands Rd HU5 179 E8
Brooklands Way 8 LN6 204 C7
Brooklands Wy 4 PE10 213 E5
Brooklyn Dr DN36 193 B1
Brook Rd LN9 199 D2
Brookside
8 Ancaster NG32 120 A3
4 Brough HU15 2 D6
Louth LN11 198 D3
Peterborough PE4 221 B2
Scopwick LN4 108 C8
Brookside Cl
7 Ancaster NG32 120 A3
Ruskington NG34 108 D2
Brook St Grantham NG31 211 A5
Hemswell DN21 42 D2
Kingston upon Hull HU2 180 E7
Lincoln LN2 234 B2
Peterborough PE1 226 A2
Brook Way 5 NG34 108 D2
Broom Cl PE1 226 A8
Broom Ct 24 DN7 14 D4
Broome Way PE12 215 A2
BROOMFLEET HU15 1 B6
Broomfleet Sta HU15 1 B6
Broom Gr DN16 185 B8
Broomhill 8 LN6 204 C8
Broomston La DN9 26 F1
Broomwood Cl 2 NG31 210 F7
Brosley Ave 1 DN3 14 A4
Brotherhood Cl PE4 225 D8
Brotherhood Ret Pk PE4 225 D8
BROTHERTOFT PE20 124 F5
Brothertoft Rd PE21 208 D5
Brotts Rd NG23 78 A3
BROUGH Brough HU15 2 C5
Collingham NG23 91 E1
Brougham St HU3 179 F7
Brough Cl 14 LN6 204 C7
Brough La NG23 91 D2
Brough Prim Sch HU15 2 C6
Brough Rd LN6 105 A8
Brough Road HU15 2 B8
Brough Sta HU15 2 B5
BROUGHTON DN20 19 D3
BROUGHTON COMMON DN20 19 F5
Broughton Gdns LN5 205 D3
Broughton House Coll LN5 105 F4
Broughton Jun Sch DN20 19 E3
Broughton La LN5 93 C3
Broughton Rd
Carlton-le-Moorland LN5 92 E1
Stapleford LN6 105 C8
Broughton's La 1 PE22 126 E3
Browndons St 4 NG31 211 A5
Brownes Rd 7 PE8 172 B1
Browning Cl
3 Kingston upon Hull HU3 180 D8
1 Scunthorpe DN17 184 E6
Browning Ct 4 LN4 207 B5
Browning Dr LN2 202 B7
Browning Rd NG24 104 C3
Brown La NG23 79 A7
Brownlow Cres 3 PE11 145 B1
Brownlow Dr 4 PE6 217 E4
Brownlow Quay 1 PE9 219 C4
Brownlow Rd PE1 226 A4
Brownlow's Dro PE12 167 A8
Brownlow's Hill NG24 104 D5
Brownlow Terr 20 PE9 219 C5
Brown's Church of England Prim Sch NG34 133 C2
Brown's Dro PE20 123 F2
Brown's Gate
Long Sutton PE12 216 B1
Spalding PE11 214 C4
Browns La 13 DN8 15 A8
Browns Orch DN32 191 D6
Brown's Rd 3 PE21 209 A7
Brown St DN31 189 C3
Browntoft La 2 PE11 134 F2

BROXHOLME LN1 66 F5
Broxholme Gdns 2 LN2 201 F8
Broxholme La LN1 66 F3
Broxholme Nature Reserve & Arts Ctr★ LN1 67 F4
Bruce Cl 7 Broughton DN20 19 D3
Lincoln LN2 234 C4
Bruce St DN15 182 F3
Brudenell PE2 229 E2
Brudenell Cl 1 PE6 164 E5
Brulon Cl LN4 207 B6
BRUMBY DN16 185 C8
Brumby Comm La DN17 184 B7
Brumby Comm Nature Reserve★ DN17 184 C7
Brumby Cres 10 LN5 93 F7
Brumby Engineering Coll DN16 185 B8
Brumby Hall Gdns DN17 182 F2
Brumby House Dr DN16 185 A8
Brumby's Terr 4 HU9 181 D7
Brumby Wood La DN15 182 C2
Brumby Wood Nature Reserve★ DN17 182 D1
Brunel Ave 13 NG33 151 D7
Brunel Cl DN16 185 B4
Brunel Ct 12 NG24 104 B5
Brunel Dr Newark NG24 104 B5
Yaxley PE7 233 D6
Brunel Rd PE11 214 E8
Brunslow Cl 8 HU3 179 E5
Brunswick Ave HU2 180 E8
Brunswick Dr PE25 206 C4
Brunswick Gr 5 HU13 178 E2
Brunswick Sq 1 LN4 109 F6
Brunton Way DN36 195 D5
Brush Mdw La PE34 161 E3
Brustrokes Ceramics★ DN37 194 E3
Brutus Ct LN6 93 B8
Bryans Cl 17 NG24 104 C5
Bryant Cl LN9 199 C3
Brynmore PE3 225 A8
Bryony Gdns PE10 213 D7
Bryony Way 5 PE6 217 D6
Buccaneer Way 21 HU15 2 C5
Buchanan Cl LN1 201 D8
Buchanan Rd DN21 54 F8
Buchanan St LN1 201 D8
Buck Beck Way DN36 192 D2
Buck Cl LN2 202 D6
Buckfast Cl DN37 188 A1
Buckfast Ct DN17 184 D8
Buckfast Rd 4 LN1 201 E6
Buckingham Ave DN15 182 F5
Buckingham Cl
Fishtoft PE21 209 C6
15 Mablethorpe & Sutton LN12 76 F8
Buckingham Dr 16 PE24 90 D7
Buckingham Gr DN33 191 B2
Buckingham Rd LN11 198 A7
Buckingham St N DN15 182 F5
Buckingham St S DN15 182 F4
Buckingham St 5 DN15 182 F4
Buckland Cl PE3 225 B4
BUCKLEGATE PE20 136 F3
Bucklegate La PE20 136 F2
Buckle St PE1 226 C3
BUCKMINSTER NG33 150 E5
Buckminster Gdns NG31 210 F2
Buckminster La NG33 151 A7
Buckminster Pl 4 PE1 226 D7
Buckminster Prim Sch NG33 150 F5
Buckminster Rd
Gunby & Stainby NG33 151 A5
Sproxton LE14 150 C7
BUCKNALL LN10 84 A4
Bucknall Ave 4 LN6 205 A7
Bucknall Prim Sch LN10 84 B3
Bucknall Rd LN10 84 C3
Bucknall's Mdw 5 LN12 76 F8
Buckshott Rd PE14 170 E3
Buckthorn Ave
3 Skegness PE25 103 E4
8 Skegness PE25 103 E4
Buckthorn Rd PE7 230 D3
Buddleia Cl DN41 23 E5
Buddleia Dr LN4 81 D3
Bude Cl DN36 195 C7
Bukehorn Rd PE6 175 D4
BULBY PE10 142 B1
Bulby La 1 NG32 106 C1
Bulham La NG23 78 A1
Bull Bank LN11 49 D7
Bulldog Cres LN11 62 B6
Bull Dro PE22 114 B5
Bullen's La PE20 135 C6
Buller Cl 16 NG23 91 D5
Buller St 4 DN32 191 F7
Bullfinch La DN35 192 E1
Bullingham Rd LN2 202 D6
BULLINGTON LN8 69 E4
Bullivant Rd DN7 14 E4
Bull La 1 Ketton PE9 171 A3
Long Sutton PE12 216 C4
North Witham NG33 151 E4
4 Peakirk PE6 174 A5
Bull Moor Rd DN7 15 A4
Bullock Rd
Terrington St Clement PE34 161 F1
Thorney PE8 228 B1
Bullock's Short Gate PE12 159 C4
Bull Pasture PE22 126 D2

Bullpit Rd NG24 104 C3
Bull Ring LN9 199 B4
Bull's Bank PE11 144 E8
Bully Hill LN8 46 D2
Bulpit La LN6 91 F7
Bulwick Ave DN33 194 E7
Bungley La PE20 136 C6
Bunkers Hill Hemswell DN21 42 E1
Lincoln LN2 202 D6
Welton le Wold LN11 60 D6
BUNKER'S HILL LN4 111 E4
Bunkers Hill Cl 2 DN36 36 D4
Bunker's Hill La PE21 136 F8
Bunkers Hill Rd 5 HU4 179 E5
Bunting Road PE21 208 E3
Burchnall Cl PE6 217 D6
Burchnall Dr 4 PE25 90 E3
Burcom Ave 3 DN36 36 D8
Burcott Garth HU4 179 B3
Burcroft Rd 17 PE13 170 C1
Burdett Cl 8 PE25 206 A6
Burdock Rd DN16 185 C4
Bure Cl LN6 204 F3
Burford Way PE1 226 D6
Burgar Rd 11 DN8 15 A7
Burgate 5 DN18 10 F8
Burgess Cl 2 PE21 209 B4
Burgess Dr 4 PE12 159 C7
Burgess Rd Brigg DN20 196 E3
Little Casterton PE9 218 F7
Burgfield Gn 4 PE4 221 E2
BURGH LE MARSH PE24 102 E7
Burgh le Marsh Mus★ 15 PE24 102 E7
Burghley Ave 14 PE8 172 B1
Burghley Cl Birchwood LN6 200 E1
22 Crowland PE6 166 F1
Great Casterton PE9 171 C8
3 Market Deeping PE6 217 E4
3 Nettleton LN7 33 A3
Burghley Cres LN11 198 B7
Burghley Ct
1 Bourne PE10 213 C5
27 Stamford PE9 219 C5
Burghley House★ PE9 219 F3
Burghley La PE9 219 C4
Burghley Pk Cl 8 LN6 204 F1
Burghley Rd
Birchwood LN6 200 E1
1 Peterborough PE1 226 A3
Scunthorpe DN16 185 D7
8 Skegness PE25 206 C1
8 Stamford PE9 219 A7
Burghley Sh Ctr The PE10 213 D5
Burghley Sq 2 PE1 226 A3
Burghley St PE10 213 C5
Burgh Old Rd PE25 206 A6
BURGH ON BAIN LN8 59 D5
Burgh Rd Friskney PE22 115 A7
Orby PE24 89 D1
Skegness PE25 103 C7
Burgin Cl 6 NG32 117 F1
Burgon Cres 3 DN15 9 B5
Burke St (North) 2 DN15 183 A5
Burke St DN15 183 A4
Burland Ct 3 LN4 203 B2
Burleigh Cl NG31 211 F5
Burleigh Gdns 2 PE21 209 A7
Burleigh St HU8 181 C8
Burley Ave DN35 192 F3
Burley Cl DN37 23 F2
Burley Rd 4 PE9 163 C1
Burlies' Gate PE12 159 E4
Burlington Rd PE25 206 B3
Burma Dr HU9 5 D8
Burma Rd DN16 183 F2
Burmer Rd PE1 225 E7
Burmor Cl 8 PE10 213 E4
Burneside Cl LN2 202 B8
Burnet Dr DN16 185 C4
Burnett's Yd LN7 33 C4
BURNHAM DN18 11 C4
Burnham La Kirton PE20 136 F4
Thornton Curtis DN39 11 E4
Burnham Rd
Barton-upon-Humber DN18 11 A6
Epworth DN9 27 E6
Kingston upon Hull HU4 179 B3
New Barnetby DN38 21 C7
Owston Ferry DN9 28 A3
Scunthorpe DN15 182 D2
Burnham Reach 5 DN35 192 F1
Burnham Sq 2 DN9 28 A3
Burnmoor Cl 3 LN6 200 C1
Burn Rd DN15 182 C3
Burns Cl Grantham NG31 211 E6
Peterborough PE1 225 F7
Burns Cres 8 NG34 212 F4
Burns Gdns LN2 202 C6
Burns Gr DN33 191 B3
Burnside DN20 19 D3
Burnside Ave 5 PE6 217 A5
Burns Rd 5 PE9 218 F6
Burns St DN21 197 B6
Burnstone Gdns 4 PE12 157 F7
Burnt Hill La 5 LN11 198 B5
Burrells Cl DN9 27 D2
Burrettgate Rd 4 PE13 170 F1
Burrett Gdns PE13 170 F1
Burrett Rd PE13 170 F2
Burrill La HU15 2 B8
BURRINGHAM DN17 17 E4
Burringham Rd
Burringham DN17 17 E5

Burringham Rd *continued*
Scunthorpe DN17 184 D5
Burr La PE12 156 F3
Burrows Cl 2 Boston PE21 208 E7
Grantham NG31 211 A3
Burrows Ct PE1 226 A5
Burrs The HU15 2 B5
Bursar Prim Sch DN35 192 E6
Bursar St DN35 192 E6
Bursnells La 3 LE14 150 B1
Burswood PE2 229 F2
Burtey Fen Collection The★ PE11 145 B1
Burtey Fen La PE11 145 B2
Burtoft La PE20 135 E2
BURTON LN1 67 D1
Burton Cl PE21 209 B7
BURTON CORNER PE21 209 B7
Burton Ct 2 Louth LN11 198 D4
Peterborough PE1 226 C3
Burtonfield Cl 1 LN3 203 E6
Burton Gravel Pits Nature Reserve★ LN1 67 C1
Burton Hathow Prep Sch LN1 66 F1
Burton La
8 Billingborough NG34 133 B1
Burton Coggles NG33 140 E1
Burton La End LN1 200 C8
BURTON-LE-COGGLES NG33 152 D8
Burton Mews
Heighington/Washingborough LN4 203 D1
5 Lincoln LN1 201 E6
Burton on Stather Prim Sch DN15 8 B4
BURTON PEDWARDINE NG34 122 B1
Burton Rd
Burton upon Stather DN15 8 C4
Heckington NG34 122 C2
Lincoln LN1 234 A4
Spalding PE11 214 B2
Burton Ridge 2 LN1 201 D7
Burton St
14 Gainsborough DN21 197 D3
Peterborough PE1 226 C3
BURTON STATHER DN15 8 B5
BURTON UPON STATHER DN15 8 B4
Burton Way LN9 199 D2
BURWELL LN11 74 B6
Burwell Cl LN2 202 A8
Burwell Dr DN33 191 B3
Burwell Rd Belleau LN11 74 E6
Burwell LN11 74 D7
Burwell Reach PE2 230 C7
Burystead PE2 231 B8
Bush Cl HU4 179 D3
Bushfield PE2 229 E3
Bushfield Ct PE2 229 E3
Bushfield Rd DN16 183 B1
Bushfield Rd Inf Sch DN16 183 A1
Bushfield Sports Ctr PE2 229 E4
Bush Gn La Algarkirk PE20 146 C8
Fosdyke PE20 136 C1
Bush Mdw La PE12 215 A4
Bushy Cl 5 PE7 230 D3
BUSLINGTHORPE LN8 57 A4
Buslingthorpe Rd
Faldingworth LN8 57 A4
Linwood LN8 57 D5
Bustards' La PE14 161 C1
Buston La LN11 61 E3
Butcher La 10 LN11 198 B5
Butchers Sq HU13 178 E1
Butchery Ct 3 LN2 234 B2
Butforth La DN19 11 E8
Butler Pl DN35 192 B7
Butler's Way 14 PE20 135 B7
Butlin Cl 1 PE25 206 A4
Buttercake La PE22 113 F2
Buttercross Cl 2 DN41 23 E6
Buttercup Cl
1 Kingston upon Hull HU9 181 D7
3 Spalding PE11 214 A2
3 Stamford PE9 218 D7
Buttercup Ct PE6 217 D6
Buttercup Dr PE10 213 D3
Buttercup La LN11 198 A6
Buttercup Paddock 4 PE12 158 B6
Buttercup Wy LN6 92 D5
Butterfield Cl 7 DN37 23 F1
Buttergate Hill LN9 71 F3
Buttermere Cl
2 Birchwood LN6 200 D1
East Ella HU4 179 E6
Buttermere Cres 2 DN36 36 C8
Buttermere Pl 4 PE4 221 C3
Buttermere Way 6 DN32 191 F8
Butter Mkt 11 LN7 33 B4
BUTTERWICK PE22 126 F4
Butterwick Cl DN35 192 F3
Butterwick Pinchbeck's Endowed CE Prim Sch The PE22 126 E3
Butterwick Rd
Benington PE22 126 F4
Messingham DN17 29 A7
Buttery Cl LN6 204 F4
Buttfield Rd HU13 178 E1
Butt Gate LN11 50 B8
Butt La Barrowby NG32 210 A6
Goulceby LN11 72 D6
Laceby DN37 23 F2
Norton Disney LN6 92 C2
Theddlethorpe All Saints LN12 63 E7
Walcott LN4 109 C7
Wymondham LE14 150 C2
Buttler Way 3 NG34 212 C3
Butts Hill La 5 DN15 8 C8
Butts La LN5 92 F6
Butt's La LN4 207 B5
Butts Rd DN18 3 F1
Butts The LE14 138 F1
Buxton Ct DN15 182 B2
Bycroft Rd DN21 197 C8
Byfield Rd DN17 184 D6
Bygott Wlk DN36 195 D7
Byland Cl 2 LN2 202 E6
Byland Ct 4 HU9 181 E8
Byland Gr DN37 188 A1
Byrd Rd DN16 185 E6
Byron Ave Grantham NG31 211 E6
Lincoln LN2 202 A6
Byron Cl
1 Newark-on-Trent NG24 104 A3
Peterborough PE2 231 D6
Scunthorpe DN17 184 E6
6 Sleaford NG34 212 F4
Byron Ct 8 NG24 104 C2
Byron Gr DN33 191 C4
Byron Rd LN12 64 B4
Byron Way PE9 218 E5
Bytham Hts 3 NG33 162 E8
Bythams Prim Sch The NG33 153 A2
Bythorne Bank PE13 169 B6
Bythorn Rd PE2 231 C6
Bythorn Way PE2 231 C6
Bywood Pl DN37 190 C6

C

CABOURNE LN7 33 D4
Cabourne Ave LN2 202 B7
Cabourne Ct LN2 202 B7
Cabourne Rd DN33 191 B3
Cabourne Road LN7 33 C7
CACKLE HILL PE12 215 C5
Cackle Hill La PE12 215 C5
Caddle Rd 11 DN41 23 A4
Cade Cl 12 LN2 68 F4
Cade Dro PE12 159 D4
Cade La DN21 53 D6
Cades Field Rd 24 LN12 77 A8
Cadman Way DN21 41 A1
CADNEY DN20 31 D6
Cadney Rd DN20 196 C1
Cadwell Cl 4 LN6 204 C7
Cadwell Pk Motor Racing Circuit★ LN11 73 B8
CAENBY LN8 55 F8
Caenby Cl DN21 197 F3
Caenby Cnr LN8 55 B8
Caenby Rd Caenby LN8 43 F1
Cleethorpes DN35 192 E4
Scunthorpe DN17 184 E5
Caenby St LN1 201 D6
Caesar Cl 7 PE6 164 E5
Caesar Rd LN6 93 B8
Cagthorpe LN9 199 B3
Cairns Way 8 LN5 93 E8
CAISTOR LN7 33 B4
Caistor Ave DN16 185 B4
Caistor By-pass LN7 33 B3
Caistor Cl 7 LN6 204 C7
Caistor CofE and Methodist Prim Sch LN7 33 B3
Caistor Dr
Bracebridge Heath LN4 81 A2
Grimsby DN33 191 B3
Caistor Gram Sch LN7 33 B4
Caistor La LN8 46 C3
Caistor Rd
Barrow upon Humber DN19 11 B6
Barton-upon-Humber DN18 11 A7
Birchwood LN6 204 C7
Cabourne LN7 33 F5
Caistor LN7 32 E4
Laceby DN37 23 E1
2 Market Rasen LN8 57 D8
Middle Rasen LN8 45 D2
Rothwell LN7 33 E2
South Kelsey LN7 32 A1
Swallow LN7 34 A5
Caistor Yarborough Acad LN7 33 C4
Caithness Cl PE2 229 D4
Caithness Rd PE9 218 E6
Calbom Ct LN11 49 B7
CALCEBY LN13 74 E2
Calceby La LN13 74 F3
Calcot St PE7 230 D2
Caldbeck Cl PE4 221 D2
Caldecote Cl PE2 231 E6
Calder Ave DN21 197 F6
Calder Cl Grantham NG31 210 E3
Immingham DN40 186 A3
Calderdale Dr
5 Spalding PE11 214 D5
Spalding PE11 214 D7
Calder Gn 24 DN17 29 D7
Calder Rd Lincoln LN5 205 C2
Scunthorpe DN16 185 D6
Caldervale PE2 230 C6
Caldicot Gdns NG31 210 E6
Caldicott Dr 8 DN21 53 A8
Caleb Hill La
Leake Commonside PE22 113 F3
Old Leake PE22 114 A3
Caledonian Rd 4 PE9 218 F6
Caledonia Pk HU9 181 B5
Callan's La PE10 142 C2
Callerton St East Ella HU3 179 F5
2 Kingston upon Hull HU3 179 F5
Calthwaite Dr 25 HU15 2 D5
Calver Cres DN37 190 D7
Calvert La HU4 179 D7
Calvert Rd HU5 179 D8
Camargue Ave DN37 194 F4
Camarthen Cl 4 NG31 210 E5
Cambian Willows PE13 169 F3
Cambrai Cl LN1 201 E7
Cambrian Cl NG31 210 E7
Cambrian Way
Holton le Clay DN36 195 C3
11 North Hykeham LN6 93 B8
1 Peterborough PE4 221 C1
Cambridge Ave
Lincoln LN1 201 D4
Peterborough PE1 225 F5
Scunthorpe DN16 185 A3
Cambridge Cres 4 LN8 47 B6
Cambridge Dr
Heighington/Washingborough LN4 203 D1
Wisbech PE13 170 C1
Cambridge Gdns 4 PE11 145 B7
Cambridge Mdws 6 NG24 104 C4
Cambridge Pk Sch DN34 191 A5
Cambridge Rd
Grimsby DN34 190 F5
Kingston upon Hull HU13 178 F3
Scunthorpe DN16 185 C6
Stamford PE9 219 A6
Cambridge Rd N 1 LN12 64 B5
Cambridge Rd S 3 LN12 64 B5
Cambridge St
Cleethorpes DN35 192 F6
Grantham NG31 211 B3
Kingston upon Hull HU3 180 D6
Camdale La 8 NG24 104 C1
Camden St 1 HU3 180 B5
Camdon Cl 1 LN5 205 D3
Came Ct 8 LN10 97 D6
Camel Gate PE12 157 B7
Camelia Cl PE4 221 B3
Camellia Gro LN11 198 E3
Camelot Gdns Boston PE21 209 E5
11 Mablethorpe/Sutton on Sea LN12 76 F8
Cameron Dr 3 PE11 214 E3
Cameron La 13 NG24 104 C1
Cameron St 4 NG34 122 E3
Camilla Cl HU9 181 A5
CAMMERINGHAM LN1 54 F1
Camm's La PE22 114 D2
Campain's La PE11 166 C7
Campbell Ave DN16 185 B4
Campbell Cl 4 NG31 210 F5
Campbell Ct HU13 178 E2
Campbell Dr PE4 221 C4
Campbell Gr DN37 190 E8
Campbells Cl PE11 214 B1
Campbells Farm Ave 1 DN15 17 E6
Campbell St DN21 197 B5
Campden Cres DN35 192 D7
Campion Ave HU4 179 B2
Campion Cl 3 PE11 214 B6
Campion Dr PE6 217 D6
Campion Gr 4 PE9 218 D7
Campion Rd PE1 226 B8
Campions Cl DN36 195 D2
Campions' La 11 DN36 36 B1
Campion Way PE10 213 D2
Camp La NG33 141 B1
Campling Pl PE12 215 D7
Campling Way 2 LN12 64 C2
Campney La LN10 83 F1
Campus Way LN6 201 D3
Camshaws Rd 5 LN2 202 F6
Camwood Cres LN6 200 C1
Canada La Caistor LN7 33 C4
Wildmore LN4 111 A4
Canal Cl LN11 198 D7
Canal La DN10 40 B5
CANAL SIDE DN8 15 A7
Canal View 12 DN8 15 A7
Canberra Ave DN7 26 A8
Canberra Cl 5 LN4 207 C4
Canberra Cres
11 Binbrook Tech Pk LN8 47 B6
Grantham NG31 211 D7
10 Manby LN11 62 C6
Canberra Dr 5 LN1 67 F5
Canberra St HU3 180 D5
Canberra Vw
Barrow Haven DN18 4 A1
Barton-upon-Humber DN18 11 A8
Canberra Way LN6 200 A4
Canberra Wy LN4 207 C3
Candidus Ct 6 PE4 220 F5
Candlehouse La 9 LN13 75 F3
CANDLESBY PE23 88 F2
Candlesby Hill Quarry Nature Reserve★ PE23 88 F2
Candlesby Rd
Claxby St Andrew LN13 88 E6
Grimsby DN37 190 C7
Candy Bank DN9 26 B5
Candy St PE2 230 E8
Cane Ave PE2 230 D7
Canister La Frithville PE22 112 C1
Langriville PE22 124 F8
Cannon Cl 16 NG24 104 C5
Cannonhill Dro PE12 167 A8
Cannon Oakes Ct DN36 195 E6
Cannon Peter Hall CE Prim Sch DN40 186 D4
Cannon St
Kingston upon Hull HU2 180 F8
1 Lincoln LN2 202 B3
3 Louth LN11 198 B5
Canon Cook Cl 7 LN1 66 D3
Canon Dr 6 PE9 172 D3
Canon Peter Hall CE Prim Sch The DN40 186 D4
Canonsfield PE4 220 E4
Canon Stevens Cl 11 NG23 91 D4
Canon Tardrew Cl 5 HU13 178 F1
Canon Tardrew Ct HU13 179 A1
Canterbury Cl
Grantham NG31 211 E7
1 Scunthorpe DN17 184 D7
Spalding PE11 214 B4
Canterbury Dr
Grimsby DN34 191 C6
Heighington/Washingborough LN4 203 D1
Skegness PE25 206 D7
4 Sleaford NG34 212 C7
Canterbury Rd
1 Hatfield DN7 14 D4
Peterborough PE4 220 F3
Cant's Dro PE13 177 C4
Canturbury Cl 10 LN10 97 C5
Canty Nook 5 DN38 32 E7
Canwell PE4 221 A4
CANWICK LN4 81 B4
Canwick Ave LN4 205 F4
Canwick Hill LN4 81 A4
Canwick Rd Canwick LN5 81 A4
Lincoln LN5 234 B1
Washingborough LN4 81 D4
Cape Drive HU10 178 D5
Capes Entry PE12 157 A2
Capito Dr 19 LN6 93 B8
Capitol Pk DN8 14 F8
Capper Ave 3 DN21 55 A8
Cappitt Dr 2 PE10 164 C8
Capp's La 19 LN5 93 F7
Capstan Way 17 DN8 15 A8
Captains Beck 9 PE11 145 C1
Captain's Hill NG34 121 B7
Captains Wlk HU1 180 E5
Capthorne Cl PE7 230 C2
Caravan Pk LN6 204 C1
CaraWy Dr LN6 92 D5
Carbis Cl DN36 195 C7
Cardiff Ave DN36 195 C6
Cardigan Rd HU3 179 E6
Cardinal Cl Lincoln LN2 202 D5
New Quarrington NG34 212 A2
Cardinal Ct 3 DN37 194 C5
Cardinals Gate PE4 220 E4
Cardinal Wlk HU13 179 A1
Cardyke Dr 13 PE6 164 E5
CAREBY PE9 163 B7
Careby Road PE9 162 F6
Carew St HU3 179 F7
Carholme Cl 1 PE10 213 D6
Carholme Rd LN1 201 C4
Carisbrook Ct PE3 230 B8
Carisbrooke Cl
2 Lincoln LN1 201 E6
New Waltham DN36 195 D7
Carisbrooke Gr PE9 218 E5
Carisbrooke Manor La DN17 184 A5
Carisbrooke Wlk DN40 186 D3
CARLBY PE9 163 D5
Carlby Rd PE9 164 B3
Carleton Crest 3 PE4 221 B1
Carline Rd LN1 234 A3
Carlisle Cl
6 Grantham NG31 210 D5
1 Lincoln LN6 204 F1
Carlisle Gdns LN9 199 D5
Carlisle St 2 DN21 197 D5
Carlisle Way 9 LN4 81 A2
Carlton Acad LN2 202 E6
Carlton Ave DN41 23 F5
Carlton Bvd LN2 202 D5
Carlton Cl
Humberston DN35 193 B1
8 Leverington PE13 170 B2
Sleaford NG34 212 C3
2 Spalding PE11 214 B1
Carlton Ctr Ret Pk LN2 202 D6
Carlton Ferry La NG23 91 A6
Carlton Gr LN2 201 F7
Carlton La Broxholme LN1 67 A4
Sutton-on-Trent NG23 91 A7
CARLTON-LE-MOORLAND LN5 105 E8
Carlton Mews 9 LN4 203 D1
Carlton Pk LN11 62 C5
Carlton Rd Ancaster NG32 119 E3
Bassingham LN5 92 E2
Boston PE21 208 D5
Grimsby DN34 191 B6
9 Healing DN41 23 F5
Hough-on-the-Hill NG32 119 B5
Manby LN11 62 C6
7 Newark-on-Trent NG24 104 A3
Carlton Rd Acad PE21 208 E5
Carlton Road LN11 62 B3
CARLTON SCROOP NG32 119 D3
Carlton St
Kingston upon Hull HU3 179 F4
Lincoln LN1 234 A4
12 Scunthorpe DN15 183 B3
Carlton Wlk LN2 202 A7
Carlyle Cl DN35 193 A2
Carlyle Wlk LN2 202 B6
Carmel Ave 5 PE2 230 E8
Carmel Gn PE21 208 E2
Carmen Cres DN36 195 C3
Carnaby Gr 2 DN32 192 A5
Carnarvon Ave 1 DN34 191 B4
Carn Cl 3 LN5 205 D2
Carnegie Rd 21 PE8 172 B1
Carnegie St 6 HU3 180 A6
Carnell La 16 NG24 104 C1
Carnforth Cres DN34 191 A5
Carnforth Parade DN34 191 A5
Carnoustie
9 Spalding PE11 214 C2
7 Waltham DN37 194 C4
Carnoustie Cl
Harrowby Est NG31 211 E7
2 Woodhall Spa LN10 97 C5
Carnoustie Ct
Port Sutton Bridge PE12 160 F4
Tydd St Giles PE13 170 A7
Carnoustie Dr LN6 204 B7
Carol Dickson Ct 9 HU3 180 C5
Caroline Cl 12 NG34 212 F4
Caroline Ct 10 PE21 209 A5
Caroline Pl HU2 180 F7
Caroline Rd 5 LN4 95 D4
Caroline St 10 Alford LN13 75 F2
Kingston upon Hull HU2 180 F8
Carpenters Cl LN8 70 C4
Carradale PE2 229 D5
Carral Cl LN5 205 C3
Carram Way LN1 201 C7
Carr Dike La HU15 1 C7
Carr Dyke Bank
Kelfield DN17 28 C5
West Butterwick DN17 28 D5
Carr Dyke Rd DN17 17 D3
Carre's Gram Sch NG34 212 D5
Carre's Sq LN4 109 E6
Carre St NG34 212 D4
Carr Gate LN4 109 F6
Carrhouse Rd DN9 16 D1
Carrier Cl 5 PE3 230 D8
CARRINGTON PE22 112 D6
Carrington Cl
Coningsby LN4 207 D5
2 Spalding PE11 214 B3
Carrington Dr
Deeping St Nicholas PE11 165 F5
8 Humberston DN36 36 D8
Lincoln LN6 204 F7
Carrington Rd
Carrington PE22 112 D3
Moulton PE12 146 C3
Spalding PE11 214 B4
Carrington Rd South PE6 175 C7
Carrington St 6 HU3 180 B5
Carr La 6 Alford LN13 75 F2
Appleby DN15 9 D2
Bishop Norton LN8 43 F3
Blyton DN21 41 B5
Bonby DN20 10 B1
Broomfleet HU15 1 B7
Broughton DN20 196 A6
Burton upon Stather DN15 8 D4
Doddington & Whisby LN6 79 D6
Gainsborough DN21 197 C1
Garthorpe & Fockerby DN17 7 E4
Grimsby DN32 192 B7
Haxey DN9 27 E2
Healing DN41 23 F4
Hibaldstow DN20 31 A6
Horkstow DN18 9 F4
Kingston upon Hull HU1 180 E6
Luddington & Haldenby DN17 7 C1
Misterton DN10 39 F5
Redbourne DN21 30 F3
Skinnard LN5 106 D7
Stallingborough DN41 23 F7
Ulceby DN39 12 B3
West Butterwick DN17 28 C8
Wildsworth DN21 40 F8
Winterton DN15 9 D6
Worlaby DN20 20 B7
Carroll Pl 4 HU1 181 A7
Carron Cl 3 LN3 83 B4
Carron Dr PE4 220 E3
Carr Rd
Gringley on the Hill DN10 39 A4
North Kelsey LN7 31 E4
Peterborough PE1 226 D3
Carrside DN9 27 D6
Carr Side La DN7 14 E2
Carr St
9 Kingston upon Hull HU2 180 F8
Lincoln LN1 201 D4
Carrwood Cres LN4 207 C7
Carson Ave DN34 191 B6
Carson Cl 6 PE24 90 B7
Carson Rd DN21 197 C6
Carter Dr HU13 178 F4
Cartergate DN32 191 C7
Carterplot Rd NG34 123 A2
Carters Cl 6 PE3 224 F3
Carter's Cl LN3 203 B7
Carter's Garth Cl 4 LN11 50 B8
Cartledge Ave DN32 192 B6
Cartmel Gr DN32 192 B6
Cartmel Way 14 PE6 175 A1
Carver Rd Boston PE21 208 D3

Carver Rd *continued*
Immingham DN40 ... 186 D3
Caryer Cl PE2 ... 230 D6
Cary La 3 DN20 ... 196 B3
Carysfort Cl PE7 ... 233 D4
Casewick La 4 PE9 ... 172 F7
Casewick Rd PE9 ... 172 E7
Caskgate St DN21 ... 197 C4
Caspian Cres DN33 ... 191 A2
Cassbrook Dr 2 LN11 ... 49 B8
Cassia Gn 7 LN6 ... 204 C8
Cassons Cl PE12 ... 157 D4
Casson's Rd 1 DN8 ... 15 A8
Casswell Cl 1 DN32 ... 189 D1
Casswell Cres 4 LN11 ... 49 B8
Casswell Dr PE11 ... 145 A7
Castella Dr DN16 ... 183 D3
Casterton Bus & Enterprise Coll PE9 ... 171 C8
Casterton La PE9 ... 218 C4
Casterton Lane PE9 ... 162 E4
Casterton Rd PE9 ... 218 E6
Casthorpe Rd
3 Barrowby NG32 ... 210 A5
Denton NG32 ... 139 A8
Castings Way LN6 ... 204 C3
CASTLE BYTHAM NG33 ... 152 D1
Castle Bytham Rd
Clipsham LE15 ... 162 C7
Swayfield NG33 ... 152 E5
Castle Bytham Road PE9 .. 162 F7
CASTLE CARLTON LN11 ... 62 C2
Castle Cl
3 Bottesford NG13 ... 128 B5
Spalding PE11 ... 214 F6
Castle Cswy NG34 ... 212 C4
Castle Ct 14 DN18 ... 10 F8
Castle Dr Epworth DN9 ... 27 E7
Holbeach PE12 ... 215 E1
Northborough PE6 ... 217 E2
Castle Dyke 13 PE9 ... 219 B5
Castledyke Bank PE22 ... 125 A8
Castle Dyke Bank LN4 ... 111 B4
Castledyke Prim Sch 27 DN18 ... 3 E1
Castledyke S 13 DN18 ... 10 F8
Castledyke W 7 DN18 ... 3 E1
Castle End Rd PE6 ... 217 A1
Castlefields 2 PE11 ... 214 D5
Castleford Ave DN34 ... 191 A4
Castlegate
Castle Bytham NG33 ... 152 D1
Grantham NG31 ... 211 B4
Thornton le Fen PE22 ... 111 F1
Castle Hill 15 Caistor LN7 ... 33 B4
4 Lincoln LN1 ... 234 B3
3 Welbourn LN5 ... 106 E5
Castle Hills Com Art Coll DN21 ... 197 D7
Castle Keep DN20 ... 30 F6
Castle La
Boothby Graffoe LN5 ... 93 E1
Coningsby LN4 ... 207 C5
Lincoln LN1 ... 234 A4
Castle Lane LN11 ... 62 D3
Castle Rd PE21 ... 209 B8
Castle Rise PE9 ... 163 D1
Castle Sports Complex PE11 ... 214 E5
Castle St Boston PE21 ... 208 D6
Grimsby DN32 ... 192 A8
Kingston upon Hull HU1 ... 180 E5
Lincoln LN1 ... 234 A4
Sleaford NG34 ... 212 D4
12 Stamford PE9 ... 219 B5
Castle Terr 5 NG34 ... 212 C4
Castle Terr Rd 4 NG34 ... 212 C4
CASTLETHORPE DN20 ... 20 A1
Castleton Bvd PE25 ... 206 D4
Castleton Cres PE25 ... 206 D4
Castleton Rd DN15 ... 182 B2
Castleview Coningsby LN4 .. 110 E8
Tattershall LN4 ... 97 E1
Castle View LN4 ... 109 D7
Castle View Rd NG13 ... 128 B4
Castle Way LN11 ... 198 A8
Castle Wy 6 Hessle HU13 ... 3 F4
7 Hessle HU13 ... 178 E1
CASTOR PE5 ... 223 D1
Castor CE Sch PE5 ... 223 E2
Castor Hanglands National Nature Reserve* PE6 .. 223 D7
Castor Rd Marholm PE6 ... 173 C1
Marholm PE6 ... 220 B1
Peterborough PE6 ... 224 C6
Casworth Way PE5 ... 223 D2
Catchpole Gr PE22 ... 100 B2
Cater La LN7 ... 44 F7
Cater Way PE21 ... 208 D2
Cates's Cove Cnr PE6 ... 167 F4
Cathedral Ct
13 Hatfield DN7 ... 14 C2
Scunthorpe DN17 ... 185 A6
Cathedral Dr PE11 ... 214 C5
Cathedral Sq 10 PE1 ... 226 A2
Cathedral St LN2 ... 234 B2
Catherine Cl PE2 ... 230 B7
Catherine Gr 6 DN20 ... 19 E3
Catherine St
6 Grimsby DN32 ... 191 F7
1 Kingston upon Hull HU2 .. 180 F7
Catherines Way 15 PE11 ... 145 C1
Cathwaite PE4 ... 221 E1
Catkin Rd 6 DN16 ... 185 B2
Catkin Wy NG24 ... 104 A2
Catley PE4 ... 221 E1
Catling's La PE13 ... 170 C7
Catskin La LN8 ... 46 A3
Catterick Rd PE10 ... 213 B3
Cattistock Rd DN35 ... 192 E3
Cattle Dike PE13 ... 169 E2
Cattle Mkt Rd 8 PE1 ... 226 A2
Cattle Mkt Way 7 PE1 ... 226 A1
Cattle Rd DN10 ... 39 B5
Caughey St HU3 ... 180 D7
Causeway
Burgh le Marsh PE24 ... 102 E7
Wyberton PE21 ... 136 E7
Causeway Bank La LN13 ... 63 F1
Causeway La 3 DN21 ... 52 F6
Causeway Rd LN4 ... 109 E5
Causeway The
6 Northorpe PE10 ... 164 C8
Revesby PE22 ... 111 F7
Thorney PE6 ... 175 E2
Cavalry Ct 2 LN4 ... 95 D4
Cave La HU15 ... 2 A8
Cavell Cl PE3 ... 225 B4
Cavendish Ave 4 NG24 ... 104 A3
Cavendish Cl DN35 ... 193 B1
Cavendish Dr
9 Boston PE21 ... 136 D8
Gainsborough DN21 ... 52 F5
Cavendish Mews 5 LN4 .. 203 D1
Cavendish Pk 10 HU15 ... 2 C5
Cavendish Rd
Scunthorpe DN16 ... 185 A4
Skegness PE25 ... 206 C4
Cavendish St PE1 ... 226 B3
Cavendish Way
1 Grimsby DN32 ... 191 F7
Harrowby Est NG31 ... 211 F7
Spalding PE11 ... 214 C6
Cave Rd HU15 ... 2 B6
Caverstede Rd PE4 ... 221 B1
Cave's Cl 8 PE34 ... 161 F3
Cave's La DN10 ... 39 E3
Cavill Pl HU3 ... 180 D5
CAWKWELL LN11 ... 73 A6
Cawkwell Cl 25 LN12 ... 77 A7
Cawkwell Hill LN11 ... 73 A6
Cawood La PE11 ... 145 B5
Cawthorne Cl 18 NG23 ... 91 D5
Cawthorne Dr HU4 ... 179 C3
CAWTHORPE PE10 ... 154 B5
Cawthra Ct NG32 ... 139 A7
Caxton Theatre & Arts Ctr The* DN32 ... 189 B1
Cayley Rd HU10 ... 178 F6
CAYTHORPE NG32 ... 119 C7
Caythorpe Heath La NG32 119 D7
Caythorpe Prim Sch NG32 ... 119 B7
Caythorpe Rd PE11 ... 134 F2
Cecil Ave PE25 ... 206 C4
Cecil Cl Bourne PE10 ... 213 B4
16 Scotter DN21 ... 29 C3
Cecil Ct 18 PE9 ... 219 C5
Cecile Cres DN15 ... 182 E3
Cecil Pacey Ct PE3 ... 225 E7
Cecil Pywell Ave PE12 ... 215 C3
Cecil Rd PE1 ... 226 A6
Cecil St Gainsborough DN21 197 C5
Grantham NG31 ... 211 C3
Kingston upon Hull HU3 ... 179 F5
Lincoln LN1 ... 234 A4
Cedar Ave
Cherry Willingham/Reepham LN3 ... 203 D5
Lincoln LN5 ... 205 D4
8 Newark-on-Trent NG24 .. 104 A6
Scunthorpe DN15 ... 182 B6
9 Sleaford NG34 ... 212 D6
2 Stainforth DN7 ... 14 D6
Cedar Cl
4 Cleethorpes DN35 ... 192 D2
Gainsborough DN21 ... 197 B7
Kingston upon Hull HU10 .. 178 D7
1 Louth LN11 ... 198 B6
14 Market Deeping PE6 ... 217 A5
6 Market Rasen LN8 ... 57 D7
9 Ruskington NG34 ... 108 D1
6 Scawby DN20 ... 30 F8
2 Scotter DN21 ... 29 C3
13 Sudbrooke LN2 ... 68 F2
Cedar Ct 2 Spalding PE11 .. 214 E3
The Willows DN37 ... 190 E8
Cedar Dr Bourne PE10 ... 213 B6
Holbeach PE12 ... 215 C4
Immingham DN40 ... 186 C5
Cedar Gr PE1 ... 226 B8
Cedar Rd PE9 ... 218 D6
Cedars The
Chapel St Leonard PE24 ... 90 D5
New Waltham DN36 ... 195 E7
Cedarwood Cl 1 NG31 ... 210 F7
Cedarwood Dr HU5 ... 179 B7
Cedric Rd 10 DN3 ... 14 A1
Cekhira Ave 4 PE12 ... 157 E1
Celandine Cl 6 PE11 ... 214 B6
Celta Rd PE2 ... 230 F6
Celtic Cl PE2 ... 231 D7
Cemetery Cres 10 DN37 ... 23 F1
Cemetery La LN7 ... 32 A5
Cemetery Rd Hatfield DN7 .. 14 F4
16 Laceby DN37 ... 23 F1
North Somercotes LN11 ... 50 E8
Scunthorpe DN16 ... 185 B8
Winterton DN15 ... 9 B5
4 Wragby LN8 ... 70 D4
Centaur Rd LN6 ... 201 D2
Centenary Cl
3 Butterwick PE22 ... 126 E3
2 Newark-on-Trent NG24 .. 104 B2
Centenary Way PE12 ... 160 F2
Centenary Wy DN16 ... 183 A1
Central Ave
Ingoldmells PE25 ... 90 F3
Peterborough PE1 ... 226 C7
Central Dr 7 NG34 ... 120 C8
Central Parade DN34 ... 191 A7
Central Pl NG31 ... 211 D5
Central Prom DN35 ... 192 F6
Central Rd LN8 ... 47 A6
Central Sq Brigg DN20 ... 196 C4
Peterborough PE2 ... 231 D5
Central Way DN16 ... 183 D2
Centurion Bsns Ctr PE3 ... 225 C7
Centurion Cl 8 LN5 ... 107 B8
Centurion Way 12 HU15 ... 2 C5
Centurion Wy LN7 ... 33 A4
Century La 1 LN1 ... 66 D3
Century Square PE1 ... 226 A5
Cerris Rd PE1 ... 226 B7
Cervantes Ct 8 PE24 ... 102 E8
Ceylon St 9 HU9 ... 5 D8
Chadburn PE4 ... 221 E1
Chad Varah Prim Sch The LN2 ... 202 B6
Chadwell Springs DN37 .. 194 B4
Chadwick Way LN4 ... 207 D4
Chafer La DN15 ... 8 A4
Chaffinch Cl DN15 ... 182 D5
Chaffinch Dr DN35 ... 192 E1
Chaffinch La PE7 ... 233 D8
CHAIN BRIDGE PE21 ... 208 B3
Chain Bridge Rd PE21 ... 208 B3
Chain Cl PE1 ... 226 B6
Chaintoft La PE11 ... 145 A7
Chaldean Way PE11 ... 214 B6
Chalfont Ave LN12 ... 64 A5
Chalfont Cl HU13 ... 178 D2
Chalfonts The LN4 ... 81 E2
Chalgrove Way LN6 ... 200 E2
Chalk La
Burgh le Marsh PE24 ... 89 F1
Sutton Bridge PE12 ... 160 F3
Withern with Stain LN13 ... 63 A1
Chalk Pit La PE23 ... 88 F2
Chalk Rd PE13 ... 169 D1
Chamberlain Way PE4 ... 221 F2
Chamber's Ct PE11 ... 214 E5
Chamber's Farm Wood Nature Reserve* LN8 ... 83 F8
Chambers St NG31 ... 211 A5
Chamomile Cl DN16 ... 185 D5
Chamomile Wy PE11 ... 214 B6
Champion Way LN12 ... 64 B2
Champneys Cl 6 HU13 ... 178 E1
Chancel Rd DN16 ... 185 A4
Chancel Wlk 13 DN20 ... 19 E3
Chancery Cl LN6 ... 205 B5
Chancery Ct
Kingston upon Hull HU5 ... 179 E8
4 Spalding PE11 ... 214 D3
Chancery La
3 Crowle DN17 ... 16 D7
7 Eye PE6 ... 175 A1
7 Holbeach PE12 ... 215 D2
Chanctonbury Cl 20 LN12 ... 77 A8
Chanctonbury Way 19 LN12 ... 77 A8
Chandlers PE2 ... 229 E5
Chandlers Cl 1 DN36 ... 195 C6
Chandlers Ct HU9 ... 181 C6
Chandos Rd DN17 ... 184 F7
Chanterlands Ave HU5 ... 180 A8
Chantreys Dr 16 HU15 ... 2 C6
Chantry Cl Grimsby DN31 ... 191 C7
Peterborough PE1 ... 226 A5
Chantry La DN31 ... 191 C7
Chantry The 1 PE11 ... 214 A4
Chantry Way 16 HU14 ... 3 B7
Chantry Way E 14 HU14 ... 3 B7
Chapel Baulk DN9 ... 26 E1
Chapel Cl
Barrow upon Humber DN19 .. 11 D7
Chapel St Leonard PE24 ... 90 D8
Cherry Willingham/Reepham LN3 ... 203 F8
8 Misterton DN10 ... 39 F5
Northfield HU13 ... 179 A1
1 South Rauceby NG34 ... 120 E4
2 Westwoodside DN9 ... 27 B2
Chapel Ct
6 Alkborough DN15 ... 8 C8
Brigg DN20 ... 196 C3
17 Hibaldstow DN20 ... 30 F5
Scunthorpe DN15 ... 183 B4
Wansford PE8 ... 222 B2
Chapel Dro PE12 ... 168 B2
Chapel Farm Dr 21 PE24 ... 90 D7
Chapelfield Rd DN19 ... 5 C1
Chapel Garth
Broomfleet HU15 ... 1 B5
16 Tetney DN36 ... 36 D4
CHAPELGATE PE12 ... 159 D7
Chapelgate Gedney PE12 .. 159 D7
Kirton End PE20 ... 136 B7
12 Sutterton PE20 ... 136 A2
Chapel Gate
Sutton St James PE12 ... 159 B1
Whaplode PE12 ... 168 B5
Chapel Gdns
3 Moulton PE12 ... 157 E1
2 Whaplode PE12 ... 158 B7
CHAPEL HILL LN4 ... 110 E5
Chapel Hill Brough HU15 ... 2 D6
Ropsley NG33 ... 131 B1
Whaplode PE12 ... 168 A4
Woolsthorpe by Belvoir NG32 ... 138 D8
Chapel Hill Ct 7 NG34 ... 212 E3
Chapel Hill La HU15 ... 2 E6
Chapel La Addlethorpe PE24 . 90 C3
Amber Hill PE20 ... 124 B5
Anwick NG34 ... 109 B1
Ashby cum Fenby DN37 ... 35 D3
3 Aubourn Haddington & South Hykeham LN5 ... 93 A5
3 Barnetby le Beck DN37 ... 35 B6
4 Barrowby NG32 ... 210 A5
1 Barton-upon-Humber DN18 ... 10 F8
Belchford LN9 ... 73 B2
Branston & Mere LN4 ... 81 E2
Caythorpe NG32 ... 119 B7
Chapel Hill LN4 ... 110 E5
2 Claypole NG23 ... 117 E8
1 Croxton Kerrial NG32 ... 138 D4
5 Donington on Bain LN11 .. 59 E1
Dunston LN4 ... 95 C5
East Kirkby PE23 ... 99 F5
4 Elsham DN20 ... 20 F7
2 Folkingham NG34 ... 142 D8
4 Foston NG32 ... 117 F1
Friskney Eaudike PE22 ... 115 A6
2 Fulletby LN9 ... 86 B8
Gainsborough DN21 ... 197 B8
Glentworth DN21 ... 54 F7
3 Grainthorpe LN11 ... 50 B8
Habrough DN40 ... 12 E1
Hameringham LN9 ... 86 C2
4 Harmston LN5 ... 93 F5
Heckington NG34 ... 122 F1
Heighington/Washingborough LN4 ... 81 E4
2 Helpringham NG34 ... 133 D7
Hemingby LN9 ... 72 B1
Horkstow DN18 ... 10 A5
Huttoft LN13 ... 76 F3
Ingoldsby NG33 ... 141 D5
Keadby with Althorpe DN17 .. 17 C6
3 Ketton PE9 ... 171 A3
Kingston upon Hull HU1 ... 181 A6
2 Leasingham NG34 ... 121 B7
6 Legbourne LN11 ... 61 F3
Lincoln LN1 ... 234 A4
Little Hale NG34 ... 133 E8
Ludborough DN36 ... 48 E6
Ludford LN8 ... 59 A8
Manby LN11 ... 62 C6
6 Mareham le Fen PE22 ... 99 A4
Messingham DN17 ... 29 D7
Minting LN9 ... 84 C8
10 Misterton DN10 ... 39 F5
Navenby/Wellingore LN5 .. 107 A8
13 Nettleham LN2 ... 68 C2
7 Newark-on-Trent NG24 .. 104 D5
Newton PE13 ... 170 B5
Normanby by Spital LN8 ... 55 F7
North Cockerington LN11 ... 49 F1
Northorpe PE10 ... 164 C8
North Scarle LN6 ... 78 E2
Peterborough PE2 ... 229 F5
6 Peterborough PE4 ... 221 A3
Scamblesby LN11 ... 73 A5
10 Scawby DN20 ... 30 E8
14 Sibsey PE22 ... 113 B1
Snitterby DN21 ... 43 D5
South Cockerington LN11 ... 62 A8
17 Spalding PE11 ... 214 D4
Spalford NG23 ... 78 D4
Springthorpe DN21 ... 53 E8
Swallow LN7 ... 34 B5
Tattershall Thorpe LN4 ... 207 C8
Thimbleby LN9 ... 85 B4
14 Thorne/Moorends DN8 ... 15 A8
Toynton All Saints PE23 ... 100 F6
Toynton St Peter PE23 ... 101 A6
4 Tydd St Giles PE13 ... 169 F7
Utterby LN11 ... 48 F4
Welton/Dunholme LN2 ... 68 E6
West/East Butterwick DN17 . 17 D1
Whitton DN15 ... 1 E3
16 Winterton DN15 ... 9 A5
2 Winthorpe NG24 ... 104 B7
Wrawby DN20 ... 20 E4
2 Wymondham LE14 ... 150 C1
Chapel La Staith 1 HU1 ... 181 A6
Chapel Lodge Dr LN8 ... 55 F7
Chapel Mews 8 HU15 ... 2 C6
Chapel Nook La LN5 ... 93 B1
Chapel Pas 16 PE21 ... 208 F4
Chapel Pit Nature Reserve* PE24 ... 90 D8
Chapel Rd Branston LN4 ... 81 E2
4 Broughton DN20 ... 19 E3
Carrington PE22 ... 112 B8
Fillingham DN21 ... 54 F4
Fiskerton LN3 ... 82 A7
4 Habrough DN40 ... 22 E8
Ingoldmells PE25 ... 90 D4
Leake Commonside PE22 ... 113 F3
Sutton St Edmund PE12 ... 168 E4
Terrington St Clement PE34 161 F3
Tumby Woodside PE22 ... 111 E8
Chapel Row Baumber LN9 ... 72 A1
7 Skillington NG33 ... 151 A8
CHAPEL ST LEONARDS PE24 ... 90 E7
Chapel St Leonards Prim Sch
Chapel St Leonard PE24 ... 90 D6
Collingham NG23 ... 91 D4
Chapel St 10 Alford LN13 ... 75 F3
3 Amcotts DN17 ... 7 F1
Beckingham LN5 ... 105 B4
6 Billingborough NG34 ... 133 B1
4 Boston PE21 ... 208 F5
16 Bottesford NG13 ... 128 A6
13 Caistor LN7 ... 33 B4
Chapel St *continued*
4 Crowland PE6 ... 175 B8
12 Crowle DN17 ... 16 D8
6 Epworth DN9 ... 27 E6
Goxhill DN19 ... 12 A8
Haconby PE10 ... 154 D8
2 Holbeach PE12 ... 215 E2
1 Market Rasen LN8 ... 57 D7
7 North Kelsey LN7 ... 32 A4
Peterborough PE1 ... 226 B2
18 Ruskington NG34 ... 108 E2
Scunthorpe DN15 ... 183 B3
Yaxley PE7 ... 233 D5
Chapel Way 6 DN20 ... 196 D3
Chapel Yd 2 PE9 ... 219 C5
Chaplin Cl 22 LN4 ... 95 D4
Chaplin St LN5 ... 234 A1
Chapman Ave
6 Burgh le Marsh PE24 ... 102 E7
Scunthorpe DN17 ... 184 D6
Chapman Cres 4 DN36 ... 36 D8
Chapman Gr 1 DN35 ... 192 F5
Chapman Rd
Cleethorpes DN35 ... 192 D7
2 Sleaford NG34 ... 212 B6
Chapman St
Kingston upon Hull HU8 ... 181 A8
3 Market Rasen LN8 ... 57 E7
Chapnall Cl 18 PE13 ... 170 E1
Chapnall Rd PE13 ... 170 E1
Chappell Rd 3 PE11 ... 166 C6
Chapter Cl LN2 ... 68 C7
Chapter Wk 12 DN20 ... 19 E3
Charing Cl HU3 ... 180 C8
Chariots Way 6 PE6 ... 164 E5
Charity St NG32 ... 119 D4
Charles Ave
11 Ancaster NG32 ... 120 A2
Grimsby DN33 ... 191 D2
3 Laceby DN37 ... 23 E1
Louth LN11 ... 198 D7
12 New Waltham DN36 ... 195 C6
18 Scotter DN21 ... 29 C3
Charles Baines Com Prim Sch DN21 ... 197 F4
Charles Cl Bourne PE10 ... 213 D6
1 Skegness PE25 ... 206 B4
Charles Cope Rd PE2 ... 229 F5
Charles Gate LN11 ... 63 A8
Charles Hume Ct 3 DN32 192 B8
Charles Lovell Way DN17 . 184 D8
Charles Rd
5 Fleet Hargate PE12 ... 159 C7
9 Stamford PE9 ... 219 A7
12 Sutton Bridge PE12 ... 160 E4
Charles Read Acad NG33 . 152 F7
Charles St W LN1 ... 201 D4
Charles St Boston PE21 ... 209 A3
2 Cleethorpes DN35 ... 192 F5
3 Kingston upon Hull HU2 .. 180 F7
Lincoln LN5 ... 234 B1
Louth LN11 ... 198 C6
Newark-on-Trent NG24 ... 104 A4
Peterborough PE1 ... 226 B3
1 Sleaford NG34 ... 212 C4
Wrange PE22 ... 114 C2
Charlestown 12 NG32 ... 120 A3
Charlestown Way HU9 ... 181 C6
Charlesworth St 2 LN1 .. 201 D3
Charles Wright Cl 15 LN12 . 64 B4
Charlette Way 13 PE11 ... 214 B5
Charlock Dr PE9 ... 218 D6
Charlotte Cl 4 LN8 ... 57 E8
Charlotte St 5 HU1 ... 181 A7
Charlotte Wlk 5 PE11 ... 145 A8
Charlotte Wy PE3 ... 225 D3
Charlton Cr 8 PE7 ... 230 B1
Charlton Ct PE3 ... 225 B1
Charlton St DN31 ... 188 E1
Charnwood Cl PE2 ... 231 A7
Charter Ave PE6 ... 217 C6
Charter Cl PE21 ... 208 E7
Charterhouse Ct PE21 ... 208 B5
Charterhouse Dr DN16 ... 185 C4
Charterhouse La 1 HU2 .. 181 A7
Charters Dr 9 NG24 ... 104 A2
Charters La PE12 ... 216 A6
Charter's La PE12 ... 216 A5
Charters The 2 PE9 ... 172 C6
Chartwell Cl PE2 ... 231 A7
Chartwell House Sch PE13 ... 170 A5
Chase Hill Rd DN40 ... 12 E5
Chase St PE13 ... 170 D1
Chase The Boston PE21 ... 209 C3
Cherry Willingham/Reepham LN3 ... 203 F8
Crowland PE6 ... 166 F1
Holbeach PE12 ... 215 E2
Long Sutton PE12 ... 216 C4
9 Metheringham LN4 ... 95 C4
Pinchbeck PE11 ... 156 E8
Ropsley NG33 ... 131 A1
Weston PE12 ... 145 F1
West Walton PE14 ... 170 D4
Whaplode PE12 ... 147 A6
Wisbech PE13 ... 170 C1
Chasm & Northorpe Slipe Nature Reserve The* PE10 ... 165 B8
Chater La PE9 ... 171 A3
Chater Rd 5 PE8 ... 172 B1
Chatham St HU3 ... 179 F7
Chatsfield PE4 ... 220 E6
Chatsworth Ave NG31 ... 211 F5

Chatsworth Cl
4 Lincoln LN2 . . . .**202** C8
6 Market Deeping PE6 . . . .**217** A5
Chatsworth Dr
4 Lincoln LN6 . . . .**204** E2
Louth LN11 . . . .**198** B7
Chatsworth Pl
Cleethorpes DN35 . . . .**192** C4
Peterborough PE3 . . . .**225** B2
Chatsworth Rd PE9 . . . .**218** E6
Chatsworth St HU5 . . . . . .**180** B8
Chatsworth Way 12 DN9 . . . .**27** C2
Chatterton Ave LN1 . . . . . .**201** E8
Chatterton Cres DN15 . . . .**183** A5
Chaucer Ave
12 Mablethorpe/Sutton on Sea
LN12 . . . .**64** B4
Scunthorpe DN17 . . . .**184** D7
Chaucer Cl 1 PE13 . . . . . .**170** B1
Chaucer Dr LN2 . . . .**202** C6
Chaucer Gdns 10 NG34 . . .**212** F4
Chaucer Rd
11 Balderton NG24 . . . . . .**104** C2
Peterborough PE1 . . . .**225** E8
Chaucer's Way PE11 . . . . . .**214** A4
Chauntry Rd 19 LN13 . . . . .**75** F2
Cheal La PE11 . . . .**144** F2
Cheal Rd PE11 . . . .**144** F4
Cheapside
Kingston upon Hull HU8 . . .**181** A8
Waltham DN37 . . . .**194** C4
Cheapside Rd DN36 . . . . . .**36** A4
Cheapside Road Ind Est
DN37 . . . .**195** A2
Chedburgh Cl 1 LN6 . . . . .**204** B6
Chedworth Cl
1 Lincoln LN2 . . . .**202** D7
Peterborough PE4 . . . .**225** E8
Chedworth Rd LN2 . . . . . .**202** D7
Cheese Hill 10 PE20 . . . . .**135** B7
Cheesemans Cl 4 DN37 . . .**194** E4
Cheesemans La DN37 . . . . .**194** E4
Cheethams La LN4 . . . . . .**110** F2
Chelmer Cl LN6 . . . .**204** C4
Chelmer Garth 2 PE4 . . . .**221** D1
Chelmsford Ave DN34 . . . .**191** A5
Chelmsford Dr NG31 . . . . .**210** F4
Chelmsford Pl DN34 . . . . .**191** A6
Chelmsford St LN5 . . . . . .**234** B1
Chelsea Cl LN6 . . . .**200** D2
Chelsea Wlk DN35 . . . .**193** A1
Cheltenham Cl
Peterborough PE1 . . . .**226** B6
Scunthorpe DN16 . . . .**185** C4
Cheltenham Ct 1 PE10 . . .**213** C3
Cheltenham Way
Humberston DN35 . . . .**192** F1
7 Mablethorpe/Sutton on Sea
LN12 . . . .**64** A3
Chelveston Way PE3 . . . . .**225** C4
Chelwood Dr 4 DN33 . . . .**191** B3
Chelwood Rd DN17 . . . . . .**184** F7
Chepstow Cl 1 LN6 . . . . . .**156** E3
Chepstow Dr PE10 . . . .**213** C2
Chepstow Gr DN34 . . . . . .**191** A5
Chequered Flag Karting ★
DN36 . . . .**195** C1
Chequergate 1 LN11 . . . . .**198** B5
Chequers La DN22 . . . .**65** A2
Chequers The DN15 . . . . . .**182** D3
Cheriton Cl 1 LN3 . . . .**83** B4
Cheriton Pk PE10 . . . .**213** D7
Cherries The PE12 . . . .**216** D4
Cherry Ave Branston LN4 . . .**81** D2
Hessle HU13 . . . .**178** C3
Cherry Cl Humberston DN36 .**36** D8
8 Sleaford NG34 . . . .**212** D6
Cherry Cnr PE22 . . . .**113** A5
Cherry Cobb Lane DN37 . . .**35** B5
Cherry Cobb Sands Rd
HU12 . . . .**13** F8
Cherry Dale DN35 . . . .**192** D3
Cherryfields PE2 . . . .**229** E6
Cherry Garth HU3 . . . .**180** A5
Cherry Gr 10 Belton DN9 . . .**16** E1
Lincoln LN6 . . . .**205** A8
10 Market Deeping PE6 . . .**217** C5
Scunthorpe DN16 . . . .**185** B6
Cherry Holt 33 Caistor LN7 . .**33** B4
1 Cherry Willingham/Reepham
LN3 . . . .**203** E5
Cherryholt La PE9 . . . .**219** D5
Cherry Holt La
13 Pinchbeck PE11 . . . . . .**156** E8
Sutterton PE20 . . . .**136** A4
Cherryholt Rd PE9 . . . .**219** D5
Cherry Holt Rd PE10 . . . . .**213** F4
Cherry La
Barrow upon Humber DN19 . .**11** D8
7 Fleet PE12 . . . .**159** C7
21 New Waltham DN36 . . . .**36** C8
Stubton NG23 . . . .**118** B7
Wootton DN39 . . . .**11** E2
Cherry Mount DN16 . . . . . .**185** C4
Cherry Orch
21 Epworth DN9 . . . .**27** E6
Grantham NG31 . . . .**211** D5
Cherry Orton Rd PE2 . . . . .**229** F5
Cherry Paddocks LN3 . . . .**203** B6
Cherry Rd 9 PE13 . . . .**170** C2
Cherrytree Ave PE25 . . . . . .**90** E4
Cherry Tree Ave DN34 . . . .**190** F6
Cherry Tree Cl 4 LN6 . . . .**204** C4
Cherry Tree Cres DN34 . . .**190** F6
Cherry Tree Dr 5 DN7 . . . . .**14** D5

Cherrytree Gr PE1 . . . .**226** C6
Cherry Tree Gr
2 Hatfield DN7 . . . .**14** D5
Spalding PE11 . . . .**214** F5
Cherry Tree La
Holbeach PE12 . . . .**215** D4
23 Nettleham LN2 . . . .**68** C2
Rigsby LN13 . . . .**75** E1
Cherry Tree Rd DN21 . . . . .**197** E5
Cherry Tree Rise DN21 . . . .**29** C4
Cherry Tree's Bsns Pk
DN31 . . . .**188** C2
Cherry Tree Way
3 Coningsby LN4 . . . .**207** D4
17 Metheringham LN4 . . . . .**95** C4
Cherry Way 34 DN17 . . . . . .**29** D7
CHERRY WILLINGHAM
LN3 . . . .**203** E5
Cherry Willingham Com Sch
LN3 . . . .**203** D7
Cherry Willingham Prim Sch
LN3 . . . .**203** D5
Cherry Wlk PE21 . . . .**208** D4
Cherrywood Dr NG31 . . . . .**210** F8
Chesboule La PE11 . . . . . .**144** E5
Chesham Dr 7 PE6 . . . . . .**164** E4
Cheshire Cl PE9 . . . .**219** B7
Cheshire Gr 7 PE25 . . . . .**206** A5
Cheshire La LN6 . . . .**92** E5
Cheshire Rd LN6 . . . .**204** B5
Cheshire Wlk DN37 . . . . . .**190** E8
Chesney Dr DN16 . . . .**185** A3
Chesney Rd LN2 . . . .**202** D7
Chesnut Cl 11 LN2 . . . .**68** F2
Chesnut Dr 12 LN2 . . . .**68** F2
Chesnut Way 4 DN9 . . . . . .**12** A8
Chesswick Ave DN17 . . . . . .**17** D5
Chester Cl Bourne PE10 . . .**213** B3
Heighington/Washingborough
LN4 . . . .**203** D1
8 Skegness PE25 . . . .**206** D7
Chesterfield Rd DN15 . . . .**182** B4
Chester Gdns 8 NG31 . . . .**210** D5
Chester Grange DN33 . . . .**191** E1
Chester Pl DN32 . . . .**192** C5
Chester Rd PE1 . . . .**226** C3
CHESTERTON PE7 . . . .**228** F3
Chesterton Gr PE2 . . . .**231** D6
Chesterton St
East Ella HU3 . . . .**179** F5
8 Kingston upon Hull HU3 . .**179** F5
Chester Way PE21 . . . .**208** C3
Chestnut Ave
7 Donington PE11 . . . . . .**134** E2
Edenham PE10 . . . .**153** C2
Gainsborough DN21 . . . . . .**197** D6
Grimsby DN31 . . . .**191** B7
Holbeach PE12 . . . .**215** C3
Immingham DN40 . . . .**186** C5
Kingston upon Hull HU13 . . .**178** C1
6 Newark-on-Trent NG24 . .**104** A6
Peterborough PE2 . . . .**226** B7
RAF Cranwell NG34 . . . . . .**107** D1
3 Stainforth DN7 . . . .**14** D6
6 Thorne/Moorends DN8 . . .**15** B7
Chestnut Cl
Bottesford NG13 . . . .**128** B6
Digby LN4 . . . .**108** E6
Glinton PE6 . . . .**220** B8
Horncastle LN9 . . . .**199** A5
4 Metheringham LN4 . . . . .**95** C4
7 Peakirk PE6 . . . .**174** A5
18 Scotter DN21 . . . .**29** C3
2 Sleaford NG34 . . . .**212** D3
Swaton NG34 . . . .**133** D4
13 Waltham DN37 . . . . . .**194** C4
Chestnut Cres 2 LN5 . . . . .**92** F3
Chestnut Dr
5 Coningsby LN4 . . . .**207** D4
Louth LN11 . . . .**198** B6
38 Messingham DN17 . . . . .**29** D7
2 Thorney PE6 . . . .**176** A3
Chestnut Gdns PE9 . . . . . .**218** D5
Chestnut Gr
11 Barnetby le Wold DN38 . .**21** B4
2 Broughton DN20 . . . .**19** E4
4 Colsterworth NG33 . . . . .**151** E7
1 Grantham NG31 . . . . . .**210** D2
Waddington LN5 . . . .**205** C1
Chestnut La NG33 . . . .**152** C8
Chestnut Rd
3 Boston PE21 . . . .**209** C2
Lincoln LN6 . . . .**204** F2
Waltham DN37 . . . .**194** C4
Chestnut Rise 1 DN19 . . . .**11** C8
Chestnut St CE Prim Sch
NG34 . . . .**108** F1
Chestnut St Lincoln LN1 . . .**234** A4
5 Ruskington NG34 . . . . .**108** E1
Chestnuts The 7 LN2 . . . . .**68** C2
Chestnut Terr 2 PE12 . . . . .**160** E4
Chestnut Way
6 Binbrook LN8 . . . .**47** C5
6 Bourne PE10 . . . .**213** B6
3 Market Deeping PE6 . . . .**217** B6
Scunthorpe DN16 . . . .**185** B8
Chestnut Wlk 9 DN41 . . . . .**24** A5
Cheviot Ave PE4 . . . .**221** C4
Cheviot Cl
Gonerby Hill Foot NG31 . . . .**210** D1
Sleaford NG34 . . . .**212** A3
6 Thorne/Moorends DN8 . . .**15** A7
Cheviot St LN2 . . . .**234** C2
Chichester Cl 8 DN33 . . . . .**210** E5
Chichester Dr 20 LN7 . . . . .**33** B4
Chichester Rd
6 Binbrook Tech Pk LN8 . . .**47** B6

Chichester Rd continued
4 Bracebridge Heath LN4. . .**81** A4
Cleethorpes DN35 . . . .**192** F4
Chieftain Rd 1 LN6 . . . . . .**205** C8
Chieftain Way 1 LN6. . . . . .**205** C8
Childersgate La PE12 . . . . .**159** D2
Childers' N Dro
Cowbit PE12 . . . .**157** B5
Spalding PE11 . . . .**214** F4
Childers' S Dro
Cowbit PE12 . . . .**157** B4
Pinchbeck PE11 . . . .**214** F2
Chiltern Cl NG31 . . . .**210** E7
Chiltern Cres DN17 . . . . . .**184** D8
Chiltern Dr Spalding PE11 . .**214** E6
Waltham DN37 . . . .**194** D3
Chiltern Prim Sch HU3 . . . .**180** B5
Chiltern Rd 3 LN5 . . . .**205** D3
Chiltern Rise PE4 . . . .**221** B2
Chiltern Way
3 Grimsby DN33 . . . .**194** E8
24 North Hykeham LN6 . . . .**93** C8
Chilton Cl 7 DN40 . . . .**186** B4
China St PE22 . . . .**114** C4
Chingford Ave DN34 . . . . .**191** A4
Chippendale Cl
2 Birchwood LN6 . . . .**204** D6
2 Humberston DN36 . . . . . .**36** D8
Chippendale Rd 3 LN6 . . . .**204** D6
Chippenham Mews 1
PE2 . . . .**230** C7
Chisenhale PE2 . . . .**229** E6
Chivenor Cl 3 LN6 . . . .**200** B1
Cholmley St HU3 . . . .**180** B5
Chopdike Dro PE11 . . . . . .**144** D3
Christ Church Cl PE9 . . . . .**219** B7
Christchurch Rd 10 NG31 . .**211** D7
Christine PE21 . . . .**195** A8
Christopher Cl
5 Heckington NG34 . . . . .**122** E3
Louth LN11 . . . .**198** C6
Peterborough PE1 . . . .**225** F8
Christopher Cres 8 NG32 . .**212** F4
Christopher Dr 8 PE13 . . . .**170** C1
Christopher Rd 6 LN11 . . . .**75** E2
Christopher's La 4 PE10 . .**213** D6
Christ's Hospl Terr LN2 . . .**234** B3
Church Ave
Ashby de la Launde & Bloxholm
LN4 . . . .**108** B5
Humberston DN36 . . . .**36** C8
7 North Ferriby HU14 . . . . .**3** A4
Church Balk DN8. . . . .**15** B8
Church Bank 2 PE34 . . . . .**161** F3
Church Cl 2 Bonby DN20 . . .**10** C2
Donington on Bain LN11 . . . .**59** E2
Grimsby DN32 . . . .**192** B5
Holton le Clay DN36 . . . . .**195** D2
12 Louth LN11 . . . .**198** B5
16 Mablethorpe/Sutton on Sea
LN12 . . . .**77** A8
4 Newborough PE6 . . . . . .**174** E4
12 Sibsey PE22 . . . .**113** B1
11 Sleaford NG34. . . . . . .**212** B2
Stoke Rochford NG33 . . . . .**139** F2
3 Thorne/Moorends DN8 . . .**15** B8
Wrangle PE22 . . . .**114** C1
Church Cres 4 DN9 . . . .**28** A3
Church Ct
Scunthorpe DN15 . . . .**183** B4
3 Stamford PE9 . . . .**219** C4
6 Sudbrooke LN2 . . . .**68** F3
Church Dr Lincoln LN6 . . . . .**201** D1
3 Misterton DN10 . . . .**39** F5
Norton Disney LN6 . . . .**92** C1
Peterborough PE2 . . . .**229** F4
Surfleet PE11 . . . .**145** D3
CHURCH END LN11 . . . .**50** F6
Church End Gedney PE12 . .**159** D7
9 Leverington PE13 . . . . . .**170** D7
Skegness PE25. . . . .**206** B8
Wrangle PE22 . . . .**114** C1
Church End Dro PE11. . . . .**134** F1
Church Farm Cl 28 PE24 . . .**90** D7
Church Farm Mus ★ PE25 **206** B4
Churchfield Cl PE6 . . . .**217** F5
Churchfield Ct PE4 . . . .**225** E4
Churchfield Rd
Peterborough PE4 . . . .**221** B1
Scunthorpe DN16 . . . .**185** B5
Church Fields
Pickworth NG34 . . . .**142** A8
Winterton DN15 . . . .**9** A5
Churchfields Rd NG34 . . . .**142** C8
Churchfleet La PE11 . . . . .**145** B7
Churchgate Gedney PE12 . .**159** D7
14 Sutterton PE20 . . . . . .**136** A2
Church Gate Fleet PE12 . . .**159** B6
2 Market Deeping PE6 . . . .**217** F4
Spalding PE11 . . . .**214** D3
22 Sutton Bridge PE12 . . .**160** E4
Whaplode PE12 . . . .**158** B6
Churchgate Mews 5
PE12. . . . .**159** D7
Church Gdns 15 PE12. . . . .**160** A8
Church Gn Cl PE21 . . . .**216** C4
Church Gn Cl PE21 . . . .**209** F2
Church Gn La
Frampton PE20 . . . .**136** B7
Quadring PE11 . . . .**135** A1
Church Gn Rd PE21 . . . . . .**209** F4
Church Hill Belvoir NG32. . .**138** C6
1 Burgh le Marsh PE24 . . .**102** E7
Castor PE5 . . . .**223** E2
1 Grasby DN38 . . . .**32** E7
Heighington/Washingborough
LN4 . . . .**203** B2

Church Hill continued
Ingham LN1 . . . .**55** A2
Riby DN37 . . . .**23** C2
Spridlington LN8 . . . .**55** F3
Whitton DN15 . . . .**1** E3
Church Hill Cl PE7 . . . .**231** C1
Churchill Ave Bourne PE10 .**213** B4
Bracebridge Heath LN4 . . . .**205** F4
Brigg DN20. . . . .**196** D4
2 Hatfield DN7 . . . .**14** F4
Horncastle LN9 . . . .**199** C2
4 Keelby DN41 . . . .**23** A5
4 Market Rasen LN8. . . . . .**57** D7
Skegness PE25. . . . .**206** B6
2 Skegness PE25 . . . .**206** D7
Churchill Cl 6 LN11. . . . . . .**50** F7
Churchill Ct 2 PE12. . . . . .**216** B3
Churchill Dr
3 Boston PE21 . . . .**209** D4
2 Martin LN4 . . . .**97** B4
Spalding PE11 . . . .**214** D2
Churchill La LN12 . . . .**63** E8
Churchill Rd
Gorefield PE13. . . . .**169** F3
Gorefield PE13. . . . .**169** F3
North Somercotes LN11 . . . .**50** F7
Stamford PE9 . . . .**219** B7
Churchill St HU9 . . . .**181** D7
Churchill Way
Grimsby DN32 . . . .**191** F7
Heckington NG34 . . . .**122** D3
5 Lea DN21 . . . .**52** F6
Church La Addlethorpe PE24 .**90** D4
Algarkirk PE20 . . . .**136** B2
Alvingham LN11 . . . .**49** F2
9 Ancaster NG32 . . . .**120** A2
Appleby DN15 . . . .**9** D1
Aylesby DN37 . . . .**23** E2
Balderton NG24 . . . .**104** C2
7 Bardney LN3. . . . .**83** B4
Baumber LN9 . . . .**72** B1
Benniworth LN8 . . . .**71** E8
Besthorpe NG23. . . . .**91** D7
4 Billinghay LN4 . . . .**109** F5
Blyton DN21 . . . .**41** C5
19 Boston PE21 . . . .**208** F5
Bottesford NG13 . . . .**128** C4
Bourne PE10 . . . .**213** D4
Bourne PE10 . . . .**213** D5
Brant Broughton LN5 . . . . .**105** F5
Brigsley DN37 . . . .**35** D4
4 Brough HU15. . . . .**2** C7
6 Broughton DN20 . . . .**19** E3
Buckminster NG33 . . . .**150** F4
Burton Coggles NG33 . . . . .**152** D8
Cadney DN20 . . . .**31** D6
6 Carlton-le-Moorland LN5 .**105** E8
3 Caythorpe NG32 . . . . . .**119** B7
24 Chapel St Leonard PE24 . .**90** D7
Cherry Willingham/Reepham
LN3 . . . .**203** E5
Clipsham LE15 . . . .**162** B7
Coleby LN5 . . . .**93** F3
6 Collingham NG23 . . . . . .**91** D5
Corringham DN21 . . . .**41** E2
Counthorpe & Creeton
NG33 . . . .**153** A2
Croft PE24 . . . .**102** E5
7 Crowland PE6 . . . .**166** F1
3 Croxton Kerrial NG32 . . .**138** D4
2 Donington PE11 . . . . . .**134** F2
Eagle & Swinethorpe LN6. . .**79** B2
East Keal PE23 . . . .**100** E6
Edenham PE10 . . . .**153** F4
Elkington LN11 . . . .**60** E7
Ewerby & Evedon NG34 . . .**122** C6
2 Fishlake DN7 . . . .**14** D8
1 Folkingham NG34 . . . . .**142** D8
Fotherby LN11. . . . .**49** A2
Friesthorpe LN3 . . . .**57** A2
Friskney PE22 . . . .**114** F6
Frithville PE22 . . . .**125** D8
4 Fulletby LN9 . . . .**86** B8
5 Glentham LN8 . . . .**43** F1
Goulceby LN11 . . . .**72** D6
Grainthorpe LN11 . . . .**50** B7
Grayingham DN21 . . . .**42** E7
Great Casterton PE9 . . . . . .**171** B8
Great Gonerby NG31 . . . . .**210** C8
Great Limber DN37 . . . .**22** D3
Grimsby DN37 . . . .**190** E2
1 Hagworthingham PE23 . . .**87** A4
Harmston LN5 . . . .**93** F5
Haxey DN9 . . . .**27** C2
Heckington NG34 . . . .**122** E1
3 Helpringham NG34 . . . . .**133** D7
8 Helpston PE6 . . . .**173** C4
Holton le Clay DN36 . . . . .**195** D2
Horbling NG34 . . . .**133** B2
4 Horncastle LN9 . . . .**199** B4
Hougham NG32 . . . .**118** C3
Humberston DN36 . . . .**36** B8
Huttoft LN13 . . . .**76** E3
Immingham DN40 . . . .**186** B5
3 Ingham LN1 . . . .**54** F2
Ingoldmells PE25 . . . .**206** C8
4 Keadby with Althorpe
DN17. . . . .**17** D4
Keddington LN11 . . . .**198** B8
3 Keelby DN41 . . . .**23** A4
Kingston upon Hull HU10 . . .**178** C8
Kirkby la Thorpe NG34 . . . .**121** F4
Kirkby on Bain LN10 . . . . . .**98** C5
Kirton PE20 . . . .**136** C5
12 Laceby DN37 . . . .**23** F1
3 Legbourne LN11 . . . .**61** F3
Lincoln LN2 . . . .**234** B4

Church La continued
3 Little Bytham NG33 . . . .**163** A8
Londonthorpe & Harrowby Without
NG31. . . . .**130** D5
Long Bennington NG23 . . . .**117** E2
Luddington & Haldenby DN17. .**7** D4
Lutton PE12 . . . .**160** A8
14 Mablethorpe/Sutton on Sea
LN12 . . . .**77** A8
2 Mareham le Fen PE22 . . . .**98** F4
Marshchapel DN36. . . . . . .**37** B1
17 Metheringham LN4 . . . . .**95** D4
Minting LN9 . . . .**84** C8
5 Misterton DN10 . . . .**39** F5
Misterton LN13 . . . .**89** B6
Moulton PE12 . . . .**157** F7
Navenby LN5 . . . .**107** A8
Newton LN5 . . . .**170** A5
North Carlton LN1 . . . .**67** C4
10 North Kelsey LN7 . . . . .**32** A4
North Kyme LN4 . . . .**109** F3
North Rauceby NG32 . . . . .**120** C5
North Scarle LN6 . . . .**78** E1
North Somercotes LN11 . . . .**50** E6
Old Somerby NG33. . . . . . .**140** E8
Owersby LN8 . . . .**44** B3
5 Owmby LN8 . . . .**55** F6
Peterborough PE2 . . . .**229** F5
Pickworth NG34 . . . .**132** A1
6 Potterhanworth LN4 . . . .**82** B1
Rand LN8 . . . .**70** A5
Ropsley & Humby NG33 . . .**131** B1
Roughton LN9. . . . .**85** B1
Saltfleetby LN12 . . . .**63** B7
Saxby All Saints DN20 . . . .**10** B3
Saxilby with Ingleby LN1 . . .**66** C3
Scamblesby LN11. . . . .**72** F5
Scawby DN20 . . . .**20** A1
Scopwick LN4 . . . .**108** E8
9 Scotter DN21 . . . .**29** C3
Scredington NG34 . . . .**132** F7
Scunthorpe DN15 . . . .**182** E2
Sedgebrook NG32 . . . .**128** F4
Silk Willoughby NG34. . . . .**121** B1
Skegness PE25. . . . .**206** B8
Skidbrooke with Saltfleet Haven
LN11 . . . .**51** B4
Sleaford NG34 . . . .**212** D5
Snitterby DN21. . . . .**43** D5
South Clifton NG23 . . . .**78** C6
South Kyme LN4 . . . .**123** A8
15 South Witham NG33 . . .**151** D2
Spilsby PE23 . . . .**87** E1
Springthorpe DN21 . . . .**53** E8
Sproxton LE14 . . . .**150** C7
Stallingborough DN41 . . . . .**23** D6
9 Stamford PE9 . . . .**219** C4
Sudbrooke LN2. . . . .**68** F3
Swaby LN13 . . . .**74** E3
13 Swineshead PE20 . . . .**135** B7
Tallington PE9 . . . .**172** F6
Tealby LN8 . . . .**46** C1
Tetford LN9 . . . .**73** F1
Tetney DN36 . . . .**36** D3
3 Timberland LN4 . . . .**96** C1
Torksey LN1 . . . .**65** D5
Toynton St Peter PE23 . . . .**101** A6
Twin Rivers DN14 . . . .**7** A8
Tydd St Giles PE13 . . . . . .**169** F7
Tydd St Mary PE13 . . . . . .**160** B1
2 Ulceby DN39 . . . .**12** A1
Ulceby with Fordington LN13 .**88** C7
Utterby LN11 . . . .**48** F3
Waddingham DN21 . . . .**43** D7
21 Waddington LN5 . . . . . .**93** F7
Wainfleet St Mary PE24 . . .**102** B1
Waithe DN36 . . . .**36** A3
Waltham DN37 . . . .**194** E4
Wansford PE8. . . . .**222** D2
Welby NG32 . . . .**130** F3
2 Welton/Dunholme LN2 . . .**68** D6
3 Westborough & Dry
Doddington NG23 . . . .**117** F2
West Keal PE23 . . . .**100** C6
Withern with Stain LN13 . . . .**62** F1
Wood Enderby LN9. . . . . . .**98** F7
Wrangle PE22 . . . .**114** C1
Wyberton PE21 . . . .**136** F8
8 Wymondham LE14. . . . . .**150** C1
CHURCH LANEHAM DN22 . . .**65** B3
Church La Prim Sch
NG34 . . . .**212** D5
Church La Staith 7 HU1 . . .**181** A6
Church Lees NG32. . . . . . .**131** C6
Church Lodge DN21 . . . . . .**53** F1
Church Mdw Dr 20 PE24 . . .**90** D7
Church Mdws PE20. . . . . . .**136** C5
Church Mews
Spalding PE11 . . . .**214** E4
7 Sutterton PE20 . . . .**136** A2
Church Pk 17 LN12 . . . .**77** A8
Church Rd
Auburn Haddington & South
Hykeham LN5 . . . .**93** A5
4 Bicker PE20. . . . .**135** A4
Boston PE21 . . . .**209** B4
4 Butterwick PE22 . . . . . .**126** E3
Friskney PE22 . . . .**115** A6
Harby NG23 . . . .**79** B5
4 Ketton PE9 . . . .**171** A3
Laughton DN21 . . . .**41** C8
Leverington PE13 . . . .**170** E1
3 Mablethorpe/Sutton on Sea
LN12 . . . .**64** A3
North Ferriby HU14 . . . .**3** A4
Old Leake PE22 . . . .**114** A4
Saxilby LN1 . . . .**66** D2
Skellingthorpe LN6. . . . . . .**200** A4

Church Rd *continued*
Stainforth DN7 14 C6
Stickford PE22 100 B3
1 Stow LN1 66 C8
Upton DN21 53 D5
Wigtoft PE20 135 E3
Wisbech PE13 170 B1
Wittering PE8 172 B1
Church Rd N PE25 206 B4
Church Rd S 4 PE25 206 B3
Church Rise 5 PE22 98 F4
Church Row HU8 181 A8
Church Side
3 Alkborough DN15 8 C8
3 Appleby DN15 9 D1
19 Goxhill DN19 12 A8
3 Grasby DN38 32 E7
3 West Halton DN15 8 E7
14 Winterton DN15 9 A5
Church Sq DN15 183 B3
Church St 4 Alford LN13 75 F3
Amcotts DN17 7 F1
Barkston NG32 130 B8
2 Barrowby NG32 210 A5
2 Baston PE6 164 E4
Beckingham DN10 40 A1
4 Billingborough NG34 133 B1
2 Billinghay LN4 109 F5
20 Boston PE21 208 F5
Bottesford NG13 128 A5
7 Brough HU15 2 C7
5 Burgh le Marsh PE24 102 E8
Caistor LN7 33 B3
14 Caistor LN7 33 B4
Candlesby PE23 88 F2
Carlby PE9 163 D5
4 Carlton-le-Moorland LN5 105 E8
Collingham NG23 91 C4
Corby Glen NG33 152 F8
2 Crowle DN17 16 D7
Denton NG32 139 A7
Digby LN4 108 D5
3 Donington PE11 134 E2
Easton on the Hill PE9 171 D3
Elsham DN20 20 F7
1 Epworth DN9 27 E6
6 Fishlake DN7 14 D8
1 Foston NG32 117 F1
Gainsborough DN21 197 C5
Glentworth DN21 54 F6
4 Gosberton PE11 145 B6
16 Goxhill DN19 12 A8
Grantham NG31 211 A5
Grimsby DN32 189 B1
1 Haconby PE10 154 D8
5 Harlaxton NG32 139 C7
Haxey DN9 27 C2
6 Heckington NG34 122 E3
Hemswell DN21 42 D1
7 Hibaldstow DN20 30 F5
Holbeach PE12 215 D2
Kingston upon Hull HU10 178 E6
7 Kirton in Lindsey DN21 30 B1
Long Bennington NG23 117 D3
Louth LN11 198 C5
Market Deeping PE6 217 B5
6 Market Rasen LN8 57 D8
Messingham DN17 29 D7
7 Middle Rasen LN8 57 B8
Misterton DN10 39 F5
20 Nettleham LN2 68 C2
Nettleton LN7 33 B3
Northborough PE6 173 F6
12 North Kelsey LN7 32 A4
North Witham NG33 151 D4
Owston Ferry DN9 28 A3
Peterborough PE2 231 C7
Peterborough PE4 220 F3
Peterborough PE7 229 A4
Pinchbeck PE11 145 C1
17 Ruskington NG34 108 E2
7 Ryhall PE9 163 C1
9 Scawby DN20 30 E8
10 Scothern LN2 68 F4
Skillington NG33 151 A8
10 South Witham NG33 151 D2
Spalding PE11 214 D4
11 Spilsby PE23 87 F1
8 Stamford PE9 219 C4
Sturton le Steeple DN22 52 B2
21 Sutton Bridge PE12 160 E4
1 Sutton on Trent NG23 91 A8
26 Thorne/Moorends DN8 15 A8
9 Thorney PE6 176 A3
Thurlby PE10 164 D7
Willoughton DN21 42 E4
1 Wragby LN8 70 D4
Yaxley PE7 233 D4
Churchthorpe 1 LN11 49 B8
Churchtown 9 DN9 16 E1
CHURCH TOWN DN9 16 E1
Church View
2 Alkborough DN15 8 C8
11 Barton-upon-Humber DN18 10 F8
1 Beckingham DN10 40 A1
13 Bottesford NG13 128 A6
9 Brough HU15 2 C7
Freiston PE22 126 D2
3 Gainsborough DN21 53 A5
8 Great Gonerby NG31 129 D5
Grimsby DN34 190 E7
23 Newark-on-Trent NG24 104 B2
Northborough PE6 217 E1
10 Ruskington NG34 108 E2
Swallow LN7 34 B5
2 Waltham DN37 194 E4
Churchview Cl 5 NG34 122 D3
Church View Cl
3 Belton DN9 16 E1
1 Donington PE11 134 E2
Peterborough PE2 231 B7
Church View Cres LN3 82 B7
Churchway PE22 127 A5
Church Way PE13 160 A1
Church Wlk Bourne PE10 213 D5
Brant Broughton & Stragglethorpe LN5 105 F4
1 Dunham-on-Trent NG22 65 B1
2 Holbeach PE12 215 D2
3 Holton le Clay DN36 195 D2
1 Legbourne LN11 61 F3
1 Manby LN11 62 C6
21 Metheringham LN4 95 D4
1 Owston Ferry DN9 28 A3
Peterborough PE1 226 A3
2 Pinchbeck PE11 156 F8
Sibsey PE22 113 B2
Upton PE6 223 B5
Yaxley PE7 233 D4
Church Wy LN7 33 B3
Church Yd LN1 65 D1
Chuter Ede Prim Sch NG24 104 C2
Cibus Way PE12 215 B4
Cinder La LN11 198 B5
Circle The 4 HU13 178 E2
Circus Approach PE11 214 A1
Cirencester Cl 15 LN6 93 B8
Cissbury Cl 12 LN12 77 A8
Cissbury Ring PE4 221 A2
Cissplatt La Brocklesby DN41 22 F5
Keelby DN41 23 A5
Cisterngate 3 LN11 198 B6
Citadel Way HU9 181 A6
City Rd PE1 226 A2
City Sports Ctr LN6 205 A8
City Sq Ctr LN1 234 B2
Clairbrook Cl 8 HU3 180 A5
Claires Wlk DN17 184 C7
Clampgate Rd PE21 126 C1
Clapgate Pits Nature Reserve★ DN15 19 E5
Clapson's La 32 DN18 3 E1
Clapton Cl 16 PE9 218 E6
Clapton Gate PE12 157 E5
Clara Terr LN1 234 A3
Clare Ave DN17 184 D7
Clare Cl 11 Lincoln LN5 205 D3
7 Stamford PE9 219 A5
Clare Cres DN16 185 A3
Clare Ct 4 Baston PE6 164 E4
Grimsby DN34 191 A5
Claremont Park NG34 212 C6
Claremont Rd
1 Burgh le Marsh PE24 102 E8
Gainsborough DN21 197 E2
Grimsby DN32 192 D6
Claremont St LN2 234 C2
Clarence Cl 2 DN40 186 B3
Clarence Gdns 3 PE11 214 E2
Clarence Rd
Peterborough PE1 225 E5
28 Wisbech PE13 170 D1
3 Woodhall Spa LN10 97 D6
Clarence St
Kingston upon Hull HU1 181 A6
1 Lincoln LN1 201 E6
Clarendon Gdns 1 LN1 201 E8
Clarendon Rd
Grimsby DN34 190 E4
Scunthorpe DN17 184 F7
Skegness PE25 206 A4
Clarendon St HU3 180 D7
Clarendon View LN1 201 E8
Clarendon Way PE6 220 D8
Clare Rd Northborough PE6 217 E1
Peterborough PE1 225 F6
Claricoates Dr 9 NG24 104 C8
Clarina St LN2 202 B4
Clark Ave DN31 191 A7
Clarke Ave LN4 81 F4
Clarke Ct 10 PE21 136 D8
Clarke Rd 11 LN6 93 C8
Clarkes Cl PE22 114 A7
Clarkes Rd 3 DN40 12 E4
Clarke St 2 DN15 183 A3
Clarke Way PE25 206 A4
CLARK'S HILL PE12 159 B3
Clarks La
11 Beacon Hill NG24 104 A5
8 Beacon Hill NG24 104 A5
Clarkson Ave 1 PE12 167 B8
Clarkson Ct 27 PE13 170 D1
Clarkson Infants Sch The PE13 170 E1
Clarksons Dr 3 DN41 23 E6
Clasketgate LN2 234 B2
Clatterdykes Rd PE20 136 E6
Claudette Ave PE11 214 B5
Claudette Way 5 PE11 214 B5
Claudius Rd LN6 93 B8
Clavering St 6 DN31 188 D1
CLAXBY LN8 45 D5
Claxby Rd DN17 184 F5
CLAXBY ST ANDREW LN13 88 E6
Claxby Springs Nature Reserve★ LN13 88 E6
Claxy Bank PE22 114 D6
Clay Bank LN4 123 C7
Clay Bank Rd DN8 15 C6
Clayberg Dr 2 NG34 212 D5
Clayburn Rd PE7 230 D1
Clayden St 4 DN31 188 D1
Claydike Bank PE20 124 B4
Claydon Way DN37 194 F3
Clay Dro PE11 156 C5
Clayfield Rd DN15 182 F6
Clay Hill Rd NG34 212 A3
Clay La
Carlton-le-Moorland LN5 105 D8
Castor PE5 223 E2
Gate Burton DN21 53 B1
Harby NG23 79 C5
Holton le Clay DN36 195 D3
Kirton in Lindsey DN21 30 A1
Newark NG24 104 B4
Norton Disney LN5 92 D2
Scotter DN21 29 C4
Stapleford LN6 105 B7
Tetford LN9 73 F2
Toft Newton LN8 56 C7
Waddingham DN21 43 D7
CLAY LAKE PE11 214 E2
Clay Lake Bank PE12 157 A3
Clay Lake La PE11 214 E2
Claymore Cl DN35 192 E6
Clay Pit La NG34 122 C6
CLAYPOLE NG23 117 F7
Claypole CE Prim Sch NG23 117 F8
Claypole Dr PE6 217 E1
Claypole La NG23 117 E6
Claypole Rd NG23 118 A7
Clayside Wy 10 PE7 230 F5
Clays The LN5 105 D6
Claythorne Dr DN21 197 E4
CLAYTHORPE LN13 75 B6
Claythorpe Rd LN13 75 A6
Claythorpe Wr Mill★ LN13 75 B5
Clayton PE2 230 B4
Clayton Cl 16 PE13 170 E1
Clayton Cres PE12 157 C2
Clayton Rd LN5 205 E6
Clayworth Rd 6 DN10 39 C1
CLEATHAM DN21 30 B3
Cleatham PE3 225 A4
Cleatham Rd DN21 30 B3
Clee Cres DN32 192 C5
Cleefields Cl DN32 192 B5
Clee Ness Dr DN36 193 A1
Clee Rd DN35 192 C5
Cleethorpe Rd DN32 189 B1
CLEETHORPES DN35 192 D5
Cleethorpes Acad DN35 192 D4
Cleethorpes Coast Light Rly & Mus★ DN35 193 B3
Cleethorpes Ctry Pk★ DN35 192 F2
Cleethorpes Discovery Ctr★ DN35 193 B3
Cleethorpes Leisure Ctr DN35 193 A4
Cleethorpes Nature Reserve★ DN35 193 D2
Cleethorpes Showground★ DN35 193 C3
Cleethorpes Sta DN35 192 F7
Clee Village DN32 192 C6
Clematis App LN6 204 C8
Clematis Ave 7 DN41 23 F5
Clematis Cl LN4 81 D2
Clematis Way DN16 185 C4
Clement Ave NG24 104 C2
Clement Cl 2 LN4 81 E2
Clementine Cl 7 PE25 206 B6
Clensey La NG23 117 F5
Clerke St DN35 192 B8
Clevedon Rd DN17 184 D8
Cleveland Ave 26 LN6 93 C8
Cleveland Cl
2 Immingham DN40 186 A4
2 Scunthorpe DN17 184 D8
4 Spalding PE11 214 F4
Cleveland Ct 3 PE4 221 C2
Cleveland Gdns 2 DN31 188 D1
Cleveland St
2 Gainsborough DN21 197 D3
3 Grimsby DN31 188 D1
Kingston upon Hull HU8 181 A8
Cleveland Way 27 DN7 14 D4
Cleve Pl 3 PE6 175 A1
Cley Hall Gdns PE11 214 E4
Cleymond Chase 2 PE20 136 C5
Cliff Ave 22 Nettleham LN2 68 C2
Winterton DN15 8 F5
Cliff Closes Rd DN15 182 D3
Cliff Cres 1 PE9 219 B5
Cliff Dr
Burton upon Stather DN15 8 B5
3 Kingston upon Hull HU13 3 E4
Cliffe Ave 1 NG34 108 D1
Cliffedale Prim Sch NG31 211 A8
Cliffe Rd
Easton on the Hill PE9 171 D2
Gonerby Hill Foot NG31 210 E7
Cliffe View NG34 120 E4
Cliff Gdns DN15 182 F2
Cliff Gr 9 DN18 10 E8
Cliff La Marston NG32 129 D8
Waddingham DN21 43 C6
Washingborough LN4 81 D4
Cliff Nook La
21 Beacon Hill NG24 104 A5
26 Beacon Hill NG24 104 A5
Clifford Rd PE25 206 B4
Clifford's Cl DN20 20 A1
Cliff Rd Fulbeck NG32 119 C8
Hessle HU13 3 E4
Leadenham LN5 106 D2
Scampton LN2 67 F8
Snitterby DN21 43 C5
Spridlington LN8 55 F3
Stamford PE9 219 B5
Cliff Rd *continued*
Welbourn LN5 106 E4
Welton LN2 68 C6
Winteringham DN15 9 A8
Woolsthorpe by Belvoir NG32 128 D1
Cliffside 3 LN5 107 A7
Cliff St DN16 183 C2
Cliff The DN15 182 D3
Cliff Top La 2 HU13 3 E4
Clifton Ave PE3 225 E3
Clifton Ct 2 DN8 15 A8
Clifton Gr 3 PE25 206 D1
Clifton Prim Sch HU2 180 E8
Clifton Rd Boston PE21 209 E4
Grimsby DN34 191 A6
Clifton St LN5 234 B1
Clint La 9 LN5 107 A8
Clinton Dr NG34 212 C2
CLINTON PARK LN4 207 A5
Clinton Terr 3 DN21 197 D3
Clinton Way LN10 97 B5
Clipseygap La PE10 154 B6
CLIPSHAM LE15 162 B7
Clipsham Rd PE9 162 D8
Clipsham Road PE9 162 E6
Clipson Crest 46 DN18 10 E8
Clipston Wlk PE3 225 C5
Clive Ave LN6 205 C8
Clive Sullivan Way
Barton-upon-Humber DN19 4 A4
Kingston upon Hull HU4 179 C1
CLIXBY DN38 33 A7
Clixby Cl DN35 193 A3
Clixby La DN38 32 E7
Cloddy Gate LN11 50 F5
Cloister Cl DN17 184 E6
Cloisters The
Grimsby DN37 190 D7
17 Humberston DN36 36 D8
Welton LN2 68 C7
Cloister Wk 14 DN20 19 E3
Cloot Dro PE6 166 F2
Close The
Barkston NG32 130 A8
1 Colsterworth NG33 151 D7
Easton on the Hill PE9 171 C3
2 Fiskerton LN3 82 A7
2 Goxhill DN19 5 A1
Grimsby DN34 191 C7
Scunthorpe DN16 183 B2
4 Skegness PE25 206 C4
Sleaford NG34 212 B2
5 Sturton by Stow LN1 66 D7
1 Woodhall Spa LN10 97 C6
Closshill La PE21 136 F8
Clouds La Belton DN9 17 B1
West Butterwick DN17 28 C8
Clough La East Halton DN40 12 F6
Firsby PE23 101 F5
Kirton PE20 136 F2
Clough Rd Gosberton PE11 144 D4
Holbeach PE12 215 B7
Clough & Risegate Com Prim Sch PE11 144 D4
Clovelly Dr PE7 230 E1
Cloven Ends 4 PE6 164 F3
Clover Ct DN20 196 B4
Clover Gdns
14 Newark-on-Trent NG24 104 B5
6 Stamford PE9 218 C7
Clover La PE20 135 D4
Clover Rd
6 Bracebridge Heath LN4 81 A1
Market Deeping PE6 217 C5
Misterton LN13 89 A6
Clover Road Ind Est LN13 89 A6
Clover Way PE11 214 B6
Clowes Ct 4 HU13 178 E1
Club Ct NG24 104 B2
Clubhouse Way DN36 195 F6
Clubhurn La PE11 145 D4
Club Way PE7 230 E4
Cludd Ave 5 NG24 104 C4
Clumber Ave NG24 104 A3
Clumber Dr 7 PE11 214 C6
Clumber Pl DN35 192 E5
Clumber Rd PE2 231 E6
Clumber St
Kingston upon Hull HU5 180 C8
Lincoln LN5 205 E7
Clutton's Cl 4 PE6 166 E1
Clyde Ct 1 NG31 210 E2
Clydesdale Cres 1 PE11 214 A2
Clyde St HU3 179 F5
Clyfton Cres DN40 186 B4
Coach House Gdns 8 DN20 30 E8
Coachings The HU13 3 E4
Coach Rd NG32 118 C3
Coachroad Hill DN21 54 F7
Coalbeach La 1 PE11 145 E3
Coalbeach La S PE11 145 E4
Coalport Cl 7 LN6 204 D7
Coal Shore La LN11 37 D1
Coal Yd La NG23 78 C4
Coastguard Rd LN11 38 C2
COATES
North Leverton with Habblesthorpe DN22 65 B8
Stow LN1 54 C2
Coates Ave 27 DN15 9 A5
Coates La LN1 54 B2
Coates Rd DN22 65 B8
Cobbet Pl PE1 226 B3
Cobblers Way 6 NG34 212 E3
Cobbs Hill 13 PE34 161 F3
Cobden Ave PE1 225 F4
Cobden St
1 Gainsborough DN21 197 C4
Kingston upon Hull HU3 179 F7
Peterborough PE1 225 F4
Cob Gate PE12 158 A6
Cobgate Cl 2 PE12 158 B6
Cobham Cl 11 NG34 122 E3
Cobleas NG32 138 D8
Cochran Cl 9 NG31 210 F8
Cockbourn Fen Dike PE12 159 B2
Cockburn Way 6 LN5 93 F5
Cockerels Roost LN1 65 D1
Cocketts Hill NG22 65 A1
Cocketts La 10 DN20 30 F5
Cocklehole Rd PE34 161 B5
Cock Pit Cl HU10 178 C6
Cockthorne La DN15 9 C7
CODDINGTON NG24 104 D5
Coddington CE Prim Sch NG24 104 D5
Coddington La LN6 105 A7
Coddington Rd NG24 104 C3
Coelus St HU9 181 A7
Cogan St HU1 180 E5
Coggle Cl LN11 198 E6
Coggles Cswy PE10 213 D4
Cogglesford Mill★ NG34 212 F5
Coggles Way LN11 61 E3
Coging Cl 8 NG24 104 B2
Cohort Cl 13 HU15 2 C5
Coke Oven Ave DN16 183 F2
Colchester Mews 12 LN6 93 B8
Coldham Rd LN4 207 E6
COLD HANWORTH LN2 56 C2
COLD HARBOUR NG33 130 D1
Cold Harbour La
Carrington PE22 112 B6
Covenham St Mary LN11 49 D5
Grantham NG31 211 C2
Cold Harbour Lane LN11 72 E7
Coldhorn Cres 14 PE13 170 D1
Cold Hurn La PE11 144 F6
Coldrons Wy LN5 105 F5
Coldwater Lane PE24 102 C5
Cole Ave LN5 93 F6
COLEBY Coleby LN5 93 F3
West Halton DN15 8 E6
Coleby CE Prim Sch LN5 93 F3
Coleby Rd DN15 8 E7
Coleby St LN2 202 B3
Colegrave St 14 LN5 205 E8
Cole La PE22 100 B3
Coleman Ave 4 NG24 104 A2
Colenso Terr 3 LN1 201 D4
Coleraine Cl 8 LN5 205 D2
Coleridge Ave DN17 184 D7
Coleridge Ct 5 LN4 207 B5
Coleridge Gdns
Lincoln LN2 202 B7
15 Sleaford NG34 212 F4
Coleridge Gn 3 LN2 202 C7
Coleridge Pl Bourne PE10 213 E3
Peterborough PE1 225 E8
Coleridge Rd NG24 104 C3
Coles Ave LN13 75 E2
Coles Cl PE12 215 E3
Coleshill La 7 HU3 179 F5
Cole's La 1 PE20 135 B7
Cole St DN15 183 B3
Coles Wy NG31 210 F4
Colin Ave DN32 192 B6
Colindale PE21 209 B5
Colin Rd DN16 183 C2
Colins Wy 4 DN21 29 C4
College Ave DN33 194 F8
College Cl
7 Alkborough DN15 8 C8
1 Holbeach PE12 215 C2
Horncastle LN9 199 C2
Lincoln LN1 201 F6
Stamford PE9 171 C8
7 Wainfleet All Saints PE24 102 D1
College Gdns
East Ella HU3 179 F7
2 Grimsby DN33 194 F8
College Pk Horncastle LN9 199 C2
Peterborough PE1 226 C5
College Rd
Barrow upon Humber DN19 11 E7
Cranwell & Byard's Leap NG34 120 E8
Thornton Curtis DN39 12 B6
College St
Cleethorpes DN35 192 E6
Grantham NG31 211 B3
Grimsby DN34 191 C6
1 Kingston upon Hull HU2 180 E7
College Yd DN20 196 B3
Colleysgate PE12 216 C8
Colley St 11 PE21 208 F5
Colleywell Cl 5 DN9 27 A2
Collier Cl 11 HU14 3 A4
Collier Mews PE4 221 F2
Collier Rd 2 DN40 186 D5
COLLINGHAM NG23 91 C4
Collingham PE2 229 F3
Collingham Rd LN6 91 F5
Collingham Sta NG23 91 D4
Collingwood 21 LN6 93 C8
Collingwood Cres
3 Boston PE21 136 D8
Grimsby DN34 190 D4

Collingwood Prim Sch HU3 180 C7
Collingwood St HU3 180 D7
Collins Ave PE9 218 F6
Collinson Ave DN15 182 C3
Collinson La
19 Balderton NG24 104 C1
Newport HU15 1 A8
Collison Gate PE24 102 C2
Collum Ave DN16 185 B6
Collum Gdns 2 DN16 185 B6
Collum House Rd DN16 185 B6
Collum La DN16 185 B6
Collynson Cl 1 HU10 178 E8
Collyns Wy 8 PE9 171 B1
COLLYWESTON PE9 171 B1
Collyweston Rd 1 PE8 172 B1
Colne Cl 1 LN6 204 F3
Colne Ct 6 NG31 210 E2
Colne Valley Visitor Ctr* PE6 227 B2
Colonial St HU2 180 D7
Colonsay Ct DN36 195 C7
Colson Pl DN35 192 B7
Colster Way 3 NG33 151 E6
COLSTERWORTH NG33 151 E7
Colsterworth CE Prim Sch NG33 151 E7
Colsterworth Rd NG33 151 C6
Colsuan Gdns PE12 216 C3
Coltman St HU3 180 C5
Colton Cl 6 PE6 164 E4
Colton St Brigg DN20 196 B4
2 Misterton DN10 39 F5
Coltsfoot Cl 4 DN15 182 C6
Coltsfoot Dr Bourne PE10 213 D2
Bradley DN37 194 B5
Peterborough PE2 230 E7
Coltsfoot Way PE10 213 D2
Columbia Rd DN32 192 A7
Columbus Cl 5 PE11 214 C2
Columbus Way DN33 190 F3
Colvile Rd PE13 170 A5
Colville Ave HU4 179 B6
Colville Terr 3 DN21 197 D4
Colwyn Ave PE1 226 E6
Comber Pl DN32 189 B1
Combe St DN35 192 C8
Comer Cl PE21 209 A5
Comforts Ave DN15 183 A2
Commerce La HU1 180 D4
Commerce Rd PE2 229 C5
Commercial Rd
2 Alford LN13 75 F2
Grantham NG31 211 A3
Kingston upon Hull HU1 180 E5
1 Louth LN11 198 D6
Scunthorpe DN16 183 D3
Spalding PE11 214 E5
Commodore Croft 6 HU1 180 F5
Common Balk LN13 76 C1
Common Dro PE6 166 C3
Common La Bardney LN3 83 C4
Barnby Dun with Kirk Sandall DN3 14 B4
Burgh le Marsh PE24 89 F1
Heapham DN21 53 F7
North Somercotes LN11 50 F8
Old Leake PE22 113 F4
Sturton le Steeple DN22 52 C3
Twin Rivers DN14 7 B6
Welton HU15 2 D4
Woodside DN9 26 E6
Common Mid Rd DN17 16 C8
Common Rd
Broughton DN20 19 E4
Gedney Hill PE12 176 F8
Moulton PE12 146 E3
Parson Drove PE12 176 F6
South Cave HU15 1 C7
Waddingham DN21 43 D6
Whaplode PE12 168 A2
Wrangle PE22 114 B4
Commons Dr PE7 233 D8
Commonside
2 Crowle DN17 16 C8
Westwoodside DN9 27 A2
Common Side Rd PE22 113 E4
Common Way PE13 160 B1
Comper Swift Cl
1 Mablethorpe/Sutton on Sea LN12 77 A7
Sandilands LN12 77 A7
Compton Cl 1 PE25 206 C1
Compton Dr
Faldingworth LN8 56 F3
Grimsby DN34 191 C7
Concast Rd DN16 19 A3
Conduit La NG31 211 A4
Conduit Rd PE9 219 C6
Coney Garth La PE11 145 F5
Coneygree Rd PE2 231 D6
Conference Ct DN16 185 A2
Conference Way 13 PE13 170 D2
Conging St 2 LN9 199 B4
Congreves Cl 3 PE12 160 A8
Conifer Cl
6 Kingston upon Hull HU5 179 C7
2 Scunthorpe DN17 184 C5
Conifers The PE2 229 F6
Conifer Wy PE25 103 C8
CONINGSBY LN4 207 D4
Coningsby Airfield LN4 207 C2
Coningsby Cl Boston PE21 208 D5
Coningsby Cl *continued*
Gainsborough DN21 197 F4
2 Skegness PE25 206 A5
Coningsby Cres LN4 205 F5
Coningsby Dr DN34 191 A5
Coningsby Rd
Coningsby LN4 207 A1
Peterborough PE3 220 E1
Scunthorpe DN17 184 D5
Coningsby St Michaels Prim Sch LN4 207 C4
Coningsby St LN2 234 C2
Conisborough Ave DN36 195 B6
Conisborough Mews 22 HU15 2 D5
Conisbro Croft HU13 178 C2
CONISHOLME LN11 50 D6
Conisholme Rd LN11 50 B7
Coniston Ave 1 DN33 194 E7
Coniston Cres DN36 192 E1
Coniston Dr LN6 205 A2
Coniston Rd PE4 221 C3
Conker Gro LN11 198 E6
Connaught Ave DN32 191 D4
Connaught Dr
4 Chapel St Leonard PE24 90 D7
6 Kirk Sandall DN3 14 A2
Connaught Rd
Gainsborough DN21 197 C6
Scunthorpe DN15 183 A6
Connaught Terr LN5 205 D5
Conquest Dro PE7 231 D1
Consort Ct HU9 181 B5
Constable Ave LN6 205 A6
Constable Cl LN6 205 A5
Constable St HU3 180 C5
Constable Way 23 HU15 2 D5
Constance Ave LN6 204 F4
Constantine Dr PE2 231 E4
Constitutional Ave DN35 192 C8
Convamore Rd DN32 191 F6
Convent La HU3 180 D6
Conway Ave Grimsby DN34 191 A7
Peterborough PE4 221 A2
Conway Cl HU3 180 B5
Conway Dr LN6 205 B2
Conway Sq 3 DN15 182 E3
Conworth Cl PE1 226 D5
Conyard Rd DN35 192 E7
Conyers Ave DN33 191 D2
Cook Ave PE7 230 F5
Cook Cl Rd PE7 233 D6
Cook Dr PE11 214 C2
Cooke Cres 9 LN4 207 D4
Cookridge Dr 31 DN7 14 D4
Cooks La Grimsby DN37 24 B5
4 Nettleton LN7 33 A3
Cook's La PE23 88 E3
Cooks Lock PE21 208 C3
Cookson Cl PE7 233 D4
Cookson Wlk PE7 233 E4
Cook's Rd PE11 145 E7
Coomb Brigg's Prim Sch DN40 186 A3
Cooper Ave PE25 90 E4
Cooper La DN37 23 E1
Cooper Rd Grimsby DN32 192 A7
Paston PE4 221 E2
Coopers Cl PE12 168 B4
Coopers Holt Cl LN6 200 A3
Cooper St Hessle HU13 178 C3
8 Kingston upon Hull HU2 180 F8
Coots Cl PE25 103 C8
Coots La LN13 76 E1
Copeland PE3 225 A3
Copeland Ct 5 NG34 212 C3
Cope St DN32 192 A8
Coppen Rd PE7 233 C8
Copper Beech Cl
1 Gainsborough DN21 52 F6
6 Swanland HU14 3 B6
Copper Beech Way PE2 231 B7
Copper Beech Wlk DN16 185 B3
Copper St LN10 84 B3
Coppice Ave 13 DN7 14 D3
Coppice La 2 DN7 14 D3
Coppice Rd 11 PE9 163 C1
Coppice Side HU4 179 C6
Coppingford Cl PE2 231 D6
Copse Cl DN40 186 C5
Copse Rd DN16 185 B5
Copse The Brigg DN20 196 E2
Grimsby DN33 194 F8
16 Mablethorpe/Sutton on Sea LN12 77 A7
Copsewood PE4 221 A4
Copthill Independent Day Sch PE9 172 C6
Coral Dr 1 DN37 194 C5
CORBY GLEN NG33 152 E8
Corby Glen Com Prim Sch NG33 152 E8
Corby Pk HU14 3 A5
Corby Rd
Burton Coggles NG33 141 A1
Scunthorpe DN16 183 C2
Swayfield NG33 152 D5
Cordage Ct LN1 234 A3
Cordeaux Cl Louth LN11 198 C7
8 Scotter DN21 29 C4
Cordeaux Corner LN11 61 A8
Cordella Cl 1 HU3 180 A5
Corden Cl PE25 206 C1
Corfe Ave PE4 221 A2
Corfe Cl 1 NG31 210 E5
Corfe Wlk DN40 186 D3
Coriander Dr
11 Bourne PE10 213 C6
Coriander Dr *continued*
Yaxley PE7 233 B8
Corinne Cres 3 PE25 206 C3
Corinne Gr 1 PE11 214 A3
Corinthian Ave DN34 191 B6
Corinthian Way HU9 181 D6
Cork La PE24 102 B3
Cork Tree Cres PE21 208 E2
Cormack La 15 NG24 104 C1
Cormorant Dr DN37 190 C8
Corn Cl Fiskerton LN3 82 B7
Horncastle LN9 199 B5
Cornfield Cl
9 Deeping St Nicholas PE11 166 C6
4 Grimsby DN33 194 D8
Cornfield Dr DN21 53 B1
Cornfields PE12 215 F3
Cornfield View 2 NG34 212 C2
Cornflower Ave PE7 233 B8
Cornflower Cl
18 Healing DN41 23 F5
8 Spalding PE11 214 B6
Stamford PE9 218 C6
Cornflower Way 3 LN6 93 A8
Cornhill LN5 234 B2
Cornhill Dr DN18 11 A8
Cornhill La 30 PE21 208 F5
Cornish Cres NG34 133 E7
Cornley Lane DN9 39 D2
Cornley Rd DN10 39 C7
Cornmarket 8 LN11 198 B5
Cornstall Bldgs 7 PE9 219 C5
Cornwall Cl
Grantham NG31 211 C7
12 Scampton LN1 67 E5
Cornwallis Rd LN2 202 D4
Cornwall Rd
5 Keadby DN17 17 D6
Scunthorpe DN16 185 C5
8 Stamford PE9 219 B6
Cornwall St 21 DN21 30 B1
Cornwall Way 8 NG34 108 D2
Cornwell Cl DN33 191 C3
Corn Wlk DN33 191 A2
Corona Dr 3 DN8 15 A8
Coronation Ave
3 Crowland PE6 175 B8
2 Deeping St Nicholas PE11 166 C6
Parson Drove PE12 177 A7
Coronation Cl
1 Louth LN11 198 D7
3 Spalding PE11 157 B6
Coronation Cotts DN35 192 F5
Coronation Cres Coleby LN5 93 F3
3 Epworth DN9 27 D6
Coronation Rd
Cleethorpes DN35 192 F5
Corby Glen NG33 152 E8
Ingoldmells PE25 90 F3
3 Market Rasen LN8 57 D7
9 Stainforth DN7 14 C6
5 Ulceby DN39 12 A1
Woodhall Spa LN10 97 D6
Corporation Bank 12 PE6 166 E1
Corporation Rd
1 Grimsby DN31 188 E1
Grimsby DN31 191 D8
10 Kingston upon Hull HU9 5 D8
4 Scunthorpe DN15 183 A3
Corran Garth 6 HU4 179 A3
Correen Cl 2 LN5 205 D2
CORRINGHAM DN21 41 E2
Corringham CE Prim Sch DN21 41 E2
Corringham Rd DN21 197 F5
Corringham Rd Ind Est DN21 41 A1
Corsair Gr 4 HU3 180 A4
Corwood Cl LN2 202 E7
Cosford Cl LN6 204 B8
Cosgrove Cl
2 Lincoln LN6 205 A6
Peterborough PE3 225 C6
Cosgrove St 5 DN35 192 F6
Costa Row NG23 117 D3
Costello Stadium* HU4 179 C4
COSTON LE14 150 C5
Coston Rd NG33 150 E5
Cot Garth La DN21 53 E3
Cotham Gdns 22 DN41 23 A4
Cotman Rd LN6 205 B6
Cotman Wlk LN6 205 A6
Cotswold Cl 22 Lincoln LN6 93 C8
3 Peterborough PE4 221 C1
Cotswold Dr
Great Gonerby NG31 210 E7
Waltham DN37 194 D4
Cotswold Rd 5 DN8 15 A7
Cottage Beck Rd DN16 183 B2
Cottage Cl 2 DN20 30 F5
Cottage Dr HU10 178 B8
Cottage La Collingham NG23 91 C3
1 Lincoln LN6 205 B4
North Clifton NG23 78 D7
Cottage Paddock The LN6 205 B5
Cottage Yd La DN36 36 C7
COTTAM DN22 65 C7
Cottesmore Cl
Grantham NG31 211 B6
Peterborough PE3 225 D4
Skegness PE25 206 B6
Cottesmore Rd
Birchwood LN6 204 D5
Cleethorpes DN35 192 E2
Kingston upon Hull HU13 178 F2
Cottesmore Rd *continued*
5 Stamford PE9 218 E5
Cottingham Ct
35 Barton-upon-Humber DN18 3 E1
Scunthorpe DN15 183 A4
Cottingham Dr LN2 202 B7
Cotton Dr 7 NG24 104 A2
Cotton End PE3 225 A4
Cotton Rd PE21 208 D6
Cotton Smith Way 1 LN2 68 C2
Coulam Pl 11 DN36 36 D8
Coulbeck Dr DN35 192 D5
Coulby Cl NG23 117 F7
Coulman Rd DN8 15 B8
Coulman St DN8 15 B8
Coulman Street Ind Est DN8 15 B8
Coulson Cl 13 DN20 31 A5
Coulson Dr HU13 178 F2
Coulson Rd LN6 201 D1
Coultas Ct 3 HU3 180 A6
Coult Ave LN6 93 C8
Council Ave HU4 179 E3
Council Rd 19 PE13 170 E1
Council St PE4 225 D8
Council Terr 6 DN18 3 E1
Count Alan Rd PE25 206 D8
Counter Drain Dro PE11 155 E2
Countess Cl DN36 195 D6
Counthorpe La NG33 152 E2
Counthorpe Rd NG33 152 F3
County Rd
3 Hampton Vale PE7 230 C1
Yaxley PE7 233 C8
County Rd S 2 HU5 179 C8
Coupland Cl 5 DN21 197 F5
Coupledyke La PE20 136 D5
Courtfield Cl 10 LN2 68 F2
Courtfields PE6 217 B6
Courtney St HU8 181 B8
Court The PE24 77 C3
Courtyard The
Boston PE21 209 B3
Market Deeping PE6 217 C4
Stamford PE9 219 A5
Cousin Wk DN36 195 D7
Covel Rd NG34 212 B6
Covenham Rd LN11 49 D4
COVENHAM ST BARTHOLOMEW LN11 49 C5
COVENHAM ST MARY LN11 49 C5
Coventry Ave DN34 191 A5
Coventry Cl
7 Grantham NG31 210 D5
Peterborough PE4 220 F3
5 Scunthorpe DN17 184 D7
Coventry Rd 7 DN8 15 B8
Cove Rd DN9 26 F3
Coverley Rd 5 NG33 151 D2
Covert Rd DN16 185 B5
Covert The
Clinton Park LN4 207 C5
Peterborough PE3 225 B1
16 Thurlby PE10 164 C8
Covill Cl 2 NG31 129 D5
Covington 29 HU15 2 C6
Covin's La LN11 49 C8
Coward's La PE11 144 F2
Cowbank La PE24 116 D8
Cowbank Lane PE24 103 D4
COWBIT PE12 157 B1
Cowbit Dro PE11 144 C1
Cowbit Rd PE12 214 D2
Cowbit St Mary's (Endowed) CE Prim Sch The PE12 167 A8
COWBRIDGE PE22 125 E6
Cowbridge Bsns Pk PE22 125 F7
Cowbridge Rd PE20 134 E5
Cowbroads La PE22 113 E2
Cowdale La LN1 66 D6
Cow Dale La DN10 39 C3
Cowdale's Dro PE11 134 F1
Cow Dro LN4 123 B7
Cowes Rd NG31 210 E4
Cowgate Brough HU15 2 D6
2 Heckington NG34 122 E3
Peterborough PE1 225 F2
Cow Gate NG34 143 C8
Cowhams La PE20 146 C8
Cow La Minting LN8 71 B1
Swinderby LN6 92 B5
Tealby LN8 46 C1
Twin Rivers DN17 7 C6
Upton DN21 53 F6
Welbourn LN5 106 E5
Cowle La 1 LN11 62 A3
Cowley Cl 6 PE20 135 C7
Cowley's Rd 10 PE11 134 E2
Cow Marsh La DN36 36 E5
Cowpaddle La LN4 82 A5
Cowpasture La DN22 52 D3
Cow Pasture La DN22 65 A7
Cow Pasture Lane LE15 162 C8
Cowper Ave DN17 184 D7
Cowper Cl DN36 37 B2
Cowper Dr LN2 202 C7
Cowper Rd PE1 225 F7
Cowpers Gate PE12 216 A3
Cowslip Cres 9 PE10 213 D3
Cowslip Ct 26 DN41 23 F5
Cowslip Dr 2 PE6 217 D6
Cowslip La LN11 198 F8
Cox La 7 DN17 16 D8
Cox's Ct 7 DN20 31 A5
Cox's Dro PE6 167 C1
Cox's Hill DN21 197 D5
Cox's Wlk 8 NG31 129 E5
Coxwold Gr HU4 179 E5
Crabapple Gn PE2 229 D6
Crab La PE20 123 C4
Crabley La HU15 1 E7
Crab Marsh PE13 170 C2
Crabtree PE4 221 F1
Crabtree La
Beckingham DN10 52 A8
Mablethorpe & Sutton LN12 77 A7
Saltfleetby LN12 51 D1
Crabtree Rd
Colsterworth NG33 151 B7
Easton NG33 140 A1
8 Hatfield DN7 14 C5
Skillington NG33 139 F1
Crack Holt La PE22 126 F8
Crackle Hill 6 DN9 27 B2
Cradge Bank Rd
Deeping St Nicholas PE11 167 A7
Spalding PE11 214 C1
Cradge Dro PE11 165 E3
Cragg Cl 3 PE20 135 C7
Cragmire La PE22 114 C3
Cragston Ave DN33 191 D3
Craig Cl 3 DN20 19 D3
Craig St PE1 225 F3
Craikbank La DN22 65 A8
Craikhill Ave DN40 186 C4
Craithie Rd DN35 192 E4
Crake Ave DN33 191 C1
Crakedale Rd 9 DN15 9 B5
Crampin Rd 3 DN35 192 E7
Cranberry La PE22 114 F7
Cranberry Way HU4 179 C4
Cranbourne Chase LN6 93 B8
Cranbourne Cl 7 DN35 192 F1
Cranbourne Mews 6 LN4 203 D1
Cranbourne St HU3 180 C8
Crane Ave PE7 233 F6
Crane Cl 1 NG34 120 F8
Crane Gr LN6 205 C7
Cranemore PE4 220 E4
Cranepit La PE11 135 B1
Crane Rd HU9 181 C6
Crane's Gate PE12 158 C1
Cranesgate S PE12 168 C8
Cranford Dr PE3 225 C4
Cranidge Cl 8 DN17 16 D8
Cranmore Dro PE6 165 F1
Cranmore La PE12 215 B1
CRANWELL NG34 120 F8
Cranwell Airfield NG34 120 D7
Cranwell Ave NG34 120 D8
Cranwell Aviation Heritage Centre* NG34 120 D6
Cranwell Cl
2 Beacon Hill NG24 104 B5
6 Kirton in Lindsey DN21 42 F8
4 Skegness PE25 206 A5
Cranwell Dr DN37 190 F8
Cranwell Prim Sch NG34 120 D8
Cranwell St LN5 201 E1
Crapple La DN21 29 C2
Craske La PE34 161 D3
Craven Ave 4 PE20 136 D5
Craven Cl NG32 139 C8
Craven Prim Acad HU9 181 C8
Craven Rd
Cleethorpes DN35 192 B7
4 Hatfield DN7 14 C4
Craven St N HU9 181 C8
Craven St S HU9 181 D7
Craven's La PE20 146 E7
Craven St LN5 205 D8
Crawcroft La LN13 76 E5
Crawford Gdns 3 PE6 175 C8
Crawthorne Rd PE1 226 A3
Crawthorne St 1 PE1 226 B3
Craycroft Rd 3 DN9 27 B2
Craypool La 7 LN2 68 F4
Craythorne La 23 PE21 208 F5
Creamery The 8 NG34 212 D3
Creampoke Cres 8 DN21 55 A8
Crease Dro PE6 175 B7
Creaseyplot La PE20 124 B1
CREETON NG33 153 A2
Creeton Rd NG33 153 A1
Crescent Cl 7 LN2 68 D2
Crescent Mews LN5 93 F4
Crescent St DN31 191 C7
Crescent The
Beckingham DN10 40 B1
Bracebridge Heath LN4 81 A2
15 Brough HU15 2 D6
Easton on the Hill PE9 171 C3
10 Eye PE6 175 A1
Fiskerton LN3 82 B7
Gainsborough DN21 52 F5
Hatfield DN7 14 C5
Holton le Clay DN36 195 C2
Horncastle LN9 199 C3
9 Kirk Sandall DN3 14 A1
Louth LN11 198 B7
13 Mablethorpe/Sutton on Sea LN12 77 A7
Morton PE10 154 B7
12 Nettleham LN2 68 C2
Peterborough PE2 230 C5
Ryhall PE9 163 D1
Sleaford NG34 121 A3
9 Spalding PE11 214 D4
Swayfield NG33 152 E5
Cresent The 3 LN8 70 D4
Cresset The* PE3 225 A5
Cressey St 2 DN31 189 A1

Cre–Dee 247

Cresswell Cl
1 Kingston upon Hull HU2 180 E8
Pinchbeck PE11 214 E8
Cresta Cl LN6 204 D1
Cresta Dr DN17 184 E4
Cresta The DN34 191 C5
Crester Dr PE4 221 A3
Cres The NG32 128 F6
Crew Rd NG23 91 D5
Creyke La 12 HU15 2 D6
Cricketers Way 19 PE13 170 C1
Cridling Pl DN35 192 D4
Cringle Rd NG33 139 F2
Cringleway NG33 140 A5
Crispin Cl
5 Kingston upon Hull HU4 179 A2
13 Lutton PE12 160 A8
Crispin Way DN16 185 B2
Croake Hill NG33 153 A5
Crocus Cl PE7 233 F6
Crocus Gr PE1 226 A8
Crocus Wlk PE11 214 D2
CROFT PE24 102 F4
Croft Bank 1 PE24 102 E2
Croft Cl 3 Croft PE24 102 E2
Sleaford NG34 212 B7
Croft Dr Grantham NG31 211 C3
Kingston upon Hull HU10 178 C6
Crofters Gr DN36 195 C5
Croft La Bassingham LN5 92 F3
Cherry Willingham LN3 203 E7
Coningsby LN4 110 E8
Croft PE24 102 E2
Scunthorpe DN17 184 E2
Croft Lodge 1 DN9 16 E1
Croft Marsh La PE24 102 F3
Crofton Cl LN2 202 D4
Crofton Dr LN2 202 D4
Crofton Rd LN2 202 D4
Croft Pk 4 HU14 3 A5
Croft Rd Croft PE24 102 E3
Finningley DN10 26 A1
Crofts La DN7 14 B6
Croft's La DN9 28 B3
Croft St 2 Horncastle LN9 199 C3
Lincoln LN2 234 B2
Crofts The
7 Humberston DN36 36 C8
Scunthorpe DN16 183 B2
Croft The
6 Beckingham DN10 52 B8
Bourne PE10 213 D6
10 Nettleham LN2 68 D2
21 Stamford PE9 219 C5
23 Thorne/Moorends DN8 15 B7
2 West/East Butterwick DN17 28 D8
Croft View HU10 178 C6
Croft Way PE7 230 C2
Cromarty Rd 8 PE9 218 E6
Cromer Ave Grimsby DN34 191 A5
Mablethorpe/Sutton on Sea LN12 64 D1
Cromer Cl
Harrowby Est NG31 211 E7
4 Lincoln LN6 205 A1
Cromford St 1 DN21 197 D5
Cromwell Ave
6 Gainsborough DN21 52 F6
Grimsby DN31 191 C7
Horncastle LN9 199 C2
4 Scunthorpe DN16 183 B1
2 Woodhall Spa LN10 97 D5
Cromwell Cl Boston PE21 208 D7
2 Heighington/Washingborough LN4 203 A2
2 Kingston upon Hull HU3 180 D8
Northborough PE6 217 E1
Cromwell Cres 3 NG34 212 E4
Cromwell Ct 1 HU10 178 E7
Cromwell Mews 1 PE6 173 C4
Cromwell Pl LN4 207 A5
Cromwell Rd
Cleethorpes DN35 193 A4
Grimsby DN37 188 A1
Peterborough PE1 225 F4
Cromwell St
Gainsborough DN21 197 D2
Lincoln LN2 202 B3
Cromwell View 21 LN7 33 B4
Cromwell Way 6 PE6 217 A6
Crook Bank LN12 63 F6
Crooked Billet St DN21 197 B8
Crookes Broom Ave 32 DN7 14 D4
Crookes Broom La DN7 14 D4
Crookesbroom Prim Acad DN7 14 C4
Crook Hill HU15 2 C8
Crook Mill Rd DN40 12 C4
Crook O Moor Road DN8 16 B7
Crook Tree La DN7 14 F5
Crook Tree Lane DN7 14 E5
Cropper's La PE22 126 E1
Croppers Way PE22 137 E7
Cropston Rd PE1 226 E7
CROSBY DN15 182 D4
Crosby Ave DN15 182 F6
Crosby House Flats DN15 183 B4
Crosby La 1 LN5 106 E4
Crosby Prim Sch
Scunthorpe DN15 183 A4
Scunthorpe DN15 183 A5
Crosby Rd Grimsby DN33 191 B2
Scunthorpe DN15 183 B4
Crosby Row PE12 160 D4
CROSBY WARREN DN15 183 D6
Crosland Rd DN37 190 D8
Cross Bank LN4 96 D8
Crossbeck Rd DN16 185 A4
Crossberry Way 1 PE6 173 B4
Cross Carr Rd DN20 31 B5
Crosscliff Hill LN11 60 A8
Cross Coates Rd DN34 191 A6
Cross Comm La DN22 52 D3
Cross Dro Fleet PE12 168 B2
Holland Fen with Brothertoft PE20 125 B5
Horbling NG34 133 F2
Kirton PE20 136 A5
Tydd St Giles PE13 169 C5
Crossfield Rd
Kingston upon Hull HU13 178 E3
12 Navenby/Wellingore LN5 107 A8
CROSSGATE PE11 145 C1
Cross Gate
Long Sutton PE12 159 F3
Quadring PE11 135 A1
Spalding PE12 157 B6
Tydd St Mary PE13 160 A2
Weston PE12 157 C7
Crossgate Cres 5 PE11 145 C1
Crossgate La 3 PE11 145 C1
Crossgill Cl NG31 211 F5
Cross Hill
Gringley on the Hill DN10 39 C1
Haxey DN9 27 C3
Cross Keys La LN4 207 F4
Cross Keys Yd 5 NG34 212 D4
Cross La 4 Alkborough DN15 8 C8
4 Amcotts DN17 7 F1
Balderton NG24 104 B1
3 Bourne PE10 213 E2
Butterwick PE22 126 F3
Collingham NG23 91 D5
Flixborough DN15 8 B1
Glentham LN8 44 A2
Gringley on the Hill DN10 39 A5
Harby NG23 79 B5
8 Lincoln LN6 93 C8
Long Bennington NG23 117 D1
North Kelsey LN7 32 B5
Pinchbeck PE11 144 F1
Wellingore LN5 106 E6
Crosslands 5 PE11 134 F2
Crossmoor Bank DN14 6 C5
Cross O'Cliff Cl LN5 205 E6
Cross O'Cliff Hill LN5 205 E6
Cross Rd Hatfield DN7 15 B4
Langtoft PE6 165 B4
Market Deeping PE6 217 F8
Sutton St Edmund PE12 169 A4
Tydd St Mary PE13 160 B2
Ulceby DN39 12 B3
Cross Slack 5 DN17 16 D8
Cross Spencer St 10 LN5 205 E8
Cross St
Barnby in the Willows NG24 104 F3
8 Barrow upon Humber DN19 11 D8
4 Brigg DN20 196 C3
Cleethorpes DN35 192 E6
13 Crowle DN17 16 D8
Gainsborough DN21 197 B8
Garthorpe & Fockerby DN17 7 E6
Grimsby DN31 189 B2
1 Holbeach PE12 215 D2
Horncastle LN9 199 C3
Kingston upon Hull HU1 180 E6
Lincoln LN5 234 B1
11 Nettleham LN2 68 C2
Peterborough PE1 226 A2
4 Potter Hanworth LN4 82 B1
Scunthorpe DN15 183 B4
3 Skegness PE25 206 B3
Spalding PE11 214 C3
Sturton le Steeple DN22 52 B3
3 Waltham DN37 194 E4
2 West Halton DN15 8 E8
5 Whaplode PE12 158 B7
Cross Tree Rd 21 DN17 29 D7
Crossways 8 DN7 14 C6
Crossway The DN34 190 E3
Crowberry Dr DN16 185 D5
Crowder Cl LN3 83 B4
Crowdyke Gate PE12 158 B5
Crowfields PE6 217 F5
Crowhall La PE22 127 A4
Crow Hill Ave DN35 192 E6
Crowhurst 1 PE4 221 A5
Crow La Gedney PE12 159 D6
Great Hale NG34 122 F1
Leadenham LN5 106 D3
CROWLAND PE6 166 E1
Crowland Ave
Grimsby DN34 190 F4
Scunthorpe DN16 185 A7
Crowland Dr LN6 204 F7
Crowland Ponds Nature Reserve★ PE6 166 D2
Crowland Rd
14 Crowle DN17 16 D7
Deeping St James PE6 174 D7
Eye PE6 175 A3
CROWLE DN17 16 D7
Crowle Bank Rd DN17 17 C4
Crowle Dr DN33 191 A3
Crowle Moor Nature Reserve★ DN17 6 B1
Crowle Prim Sch DN17 16 C7
Crowle Rd DN17 6 F2
Crowle St HU9 181 D7
Crowle Sta DN17 16 E5
Crown Ave
3 Chapel St Leonard PE24 90 D7
Holbeach PE12 147 C6
Crown Cl
10 Collingham NG23 91 D5
5 Leverington PE13 170 B1
Crown Ct 3 DN22 52 B3
Crown Dr PE11 214 F6
Crown Gdns 22 DN21 29 C3
Crown Hill NG33 141 B8
Crown La
14 Northorpe PE10 164 C8
Tinwell PE9 218 D3
Crown Lakes Ctry Pk★ PE7 231 B2
Crown Lodge PE12 215 C7
Crown Mills 2 LN11 198 D6
Crown St Peterborough PE1 225 E7
Ryhall PE9 163 C2
7 Stamford PE9 219 B5
Crown Wlk Bourne PE10 213 C5
Louth LN11 198 E5
Crow Pk LN6 204 A1
Crow's La PE24 102 C2
Crowson Cres PE6 217 E1
Crowson Way PE6 217 D5
Crowston Wlk 7 DN15 183 B3
Crowther Way 8 HU14 3 B7
Crow Tree Bank DN8 15 D4
Crowtree La LN11 198 A5
CROXBY DN37 34 D1
Croxby Ave DN33 194 F8
Croxby Gr DN33 194 F7
Croxby Lane LN7 34 A2
Croxby Ponds Road DN37 34 C4
Croxby Rd DN37 47 B8
CROXTON DN39 21 F7
Croxton Dr LN6 204 F6
CROXTON KERRIAL NG32 138 D4
Croxton Kerrial CE Prim Sch NG32 138 D4
Croxton La NG32 138 D5
Croxton Rd Croxton DN39 21 F7
Kirmington DN39 22 A5
Sproxton LE14 138 E2
Croyland Rd PE4 221 B1
Croyland Way 15 PE6 166 F1
Crucible Cl LN6 204 D3
Crusader Rd LN6 201 C1
Crystal Dr 1 PE2 230 D8
Crystal St HU3 180 C7
Cubitt Way PE2 231 A8
Cuckoo La
Ashby de la Launde & Bloxholm LN4 107 F7
Hatfield DN7 14 E6
Pinchbeck PE11 145 C2
Cul De Sac The 8 PE22 99 A4
Cul-de-sac The PE22 100 B2
Cullen Cl LN4 109 E5
Culley Ct PE2 229 B2
Cullin Cl 1 LN5 205 D2
Culpins Cl PE11 214 F5
CULVERTHORPE NG32 131 E7
Culverthorpe Hall★ NG32 131 D7
Culverthorpe Rd NG34 132 A7
Culvert Rd PE24 102 B3
Cumberland Ave
Grimsby DN32 191 D5
14 Navenby/Wellingore LN5 107 A7
Cumberland Gdns NG33 152 D1
Cumberland Rd DN35 193 A2
Cumberland St HU2 181 A8
Cumberland Terr 12 LN8 47 B6
Cumberland Way 17 LN1 67 E5
Cumberlidge Cl 10 PE24 102 E7
CUMBERWORTH LN13 89 F8
Cumberworth La 2 LN13 76 F1
Cumberworth Rd LN13 89 C7
Cunningham Rd
1 Moorland Prison DN7 26 A8
Woodston PE2 230 E8
Cunsdike La PE11 145 D5
Cupola Cl LN6 204 C3
Cupola Way DN15 183 A8
Cuppleditch Wy LN11 198 C7
Curle Ave LN2 234 C4
Curlew Cft DN16 185 F5
Curlew Cl 4 PE12 216 B4
Curlew Dr 8 PE12 167 B8
Curlew Gr PE2 231 D7
Curlew Lodge La PE12 160 F8
Curlew Way NG34 212 B3
Curlew Wlk 14 PE6 217 C5
Currie Rd 16 NG24 104 A5
Curry Rd DN34 190 F7
Curtis Cl 13 NG23 91 D5
Curtis Dr Coningsby LN4 207 D4
Heighington LN4 81 E4
Curtois Cl 4 LN4 81 E2
Curzen Cres 8 DN3 14 A2
Curzon Ave DN35 192 D5
Curzon Ct DN35 192 D5
Curzon Est 6 LN4 207 A5
Curzon Mews 3 LN4 203 D1
Curzon St
1 Gainsborough DN21 197 C6
Kingston upon Hull HU3 179 F7
Cushman Cres DN40 186 C3
Customhouse St 2 PE12 160 F4
Custom Rd Frognall PE6 165 E1
Newborough PE6 174 B8
Cut Dike PE22 124 D8
Cut End Rd PE22 137 D7
Cuthbert Ave 6 DN38 21 B4
Cuthbert Cl 15 NG34 212 B2
Cuthbert's La PE20 136 B8
Cuthberts Yd LN1 234 A4
CUXWOLD LN7 34 B4
Cuxwold Rd
3 Scunthorpe DN16 185 C8
Swallow LN7 34 B5
Cydonia App LN6 204 C8
Cygnet Cl 8 NG34 212 B3
Cygnet Pk PE7 230 E3
Cygnet Rd PE7 230 E3
Cynthia Rd DN32 192 C5
Cypress Cl
2 Peterborough PE3 225 A2
9 Sleaford NG34 212 D2
Cyprus St 8 HU9 5 D8
Cyrano Way DN37 190 C7
Cyril Cooper Ct DN32 191 D6
Cyrus Wy PE7 230 E3

D

Daffodil Cl PE11 214 B3
Daffodil Gr PE2 231 C7
Dagger La HU1 180 F6
Daggett Rd DN35 193 A4
Daimler Ave PE7 233 E6
D'aincourt Pk LN4 81 D2
Dairy Cl 1 Gosberton PE11 145 C6
Normanby DN15 8 C3
Dairycoates Ave HU3 180 A4
Dairycoates Rd HU4 179 E3
Dairy Dro PE6 176 E2
Daisy Cl DN16 185 D4
Daisy Ct PE10 213 D3
Daisy Dale PE21 209 A3
Daisy Dr PE7 230 B1
Daisyfield La NG34 212 C5
Daisy Rd PE12 215 C1
Daisy Way LN11 198 A7
DALBY PE23 88 B5
Dalby Ct PE1 226 C8
Dalby Rd LN13 88 C5
DALDERBY LN9 85 D1
Dalderby Cres 16 LN2 68 C2
Dale Ave LN3 203 E6
Dale Cl Peterborough PE2 229 F5
10 Swanland HU14 3 B7
Dale Cres 1 NG24 104 C1
Dalehouse Dr 2 HU10 178 F6
Dale Pit Rd 8 DN7 14 F3
Dale Pk Ave DN15 9 A5
Dale Rd 6 Brough HU15 2 C7
Grantham NG31 211 A7
Swanland HU14 3 B7
Welton HU15 2 E6
Dale St N DN15 182 F5
Dales La DN10 39 A6
Dale's La PE20 135 D5
Dale St Lincoln LN5 202 B2
Scunthorpe DN15 182 F4
Dales The 25 Nettleham LN2 68 C2
Scunthorpe DN17 184 E3
Dalesway HU10 178 B6
Dales Wy LN11 198 C8
Dale View DN33 190 F3
Dale Way 17 NG24 104 C1
Dalewood LN5 205 D2
Dallisons Rd 5 DN20 31 A5
Dallygate NG33 140 A5
Dallygate La NG33 140 B5
Dalmatian Way 14 DN20 19 E4
Dalton Cl NG31 210 E6
Dame Kendal Gr DN33 191 B3
Damgate PE12 215 E1
Dam Gn La 5 HU15 2 C7
Dam La DN39 11 E5
Dam Rd DN18 3 D1
Dams La LN9 73 B2
Danby Hills LN2 68 B1
Danby Rd 16 DN17 29 D7
Dane Cl 15 Broughton DN20 19 E4
31 Metheringham LN4 95 C4
Danegeld Pl 24 PE9 219 C5
Danes Cl PE1 226 C4
Danes Cotts 13 LN2 234 B3
Danes Ctyd 11 LN2 234 B3
Danes Dr 2 HU13 3 F4
Danesfield NG34 132 E2
Danesfield Ave DN37 194 E5
Danesgate Lincoln LN2 234 B3
11 New Holland DN19 4 E2
Danes Rd DN21 197 F5
Danes Terr LN2 234 B3
Danethorpe La NG24 104 D8
Danial Cl PE25 206 C8
Daniel Cres 10 LN4 203 D1
Daniel Ct 7 PE9 219 C4
Daniel's Cres PE12 216 C5
Daniel's Dro PE6 167 D1
Daniels Gate 1 PE11 214 C6
Daniel's Gate PE12 216 C7
Daniel's Reach PE11 214 C7
Danish Ct PE4 220 E4
Danns Hill DN20 10 B3
Dansom La S HU8 181 B8
Danson Cl 19 DN18 10 F8
Danube Rd HU5 179 C8
Danube Sq PE11 214 A4
Danum Cl 11 DN8 15 B8
Danum Rd 6 Hatfield DN7 14 D3
Scunthorpe DN17 184 F8
Daphne Cl 9 LN4 81 E2
Dar Beck Rd DN21 29 C4
Darby Rd DN15 8 B4
Darbyshire Cl NG23 79 B5
Dark La Amcotts DN17 7 F1
Barnby in the Willows NG24 105 A3
Dark La *continued*
Bicker PE20 135 A5
Bitchfield & Bassingthorpe NG33 141 A3
Burwell LN11 74 C6
Holbeach PE12 215 B5
Darley Cl PE8 172 C1
Darley Dale Cres 1 NG31 211 A7
Darley's La PE11 214 A6
Darlton Rd NG22 65 A1
Darnholm Ct DN37 190 E8
Darnholme Cres 15 DN17 29 D7
Darrismere Villas 4 HU3 180 A5
Dart Ave LN6 205 A2
Dartmouth Rd DN17 182 D1
Dartmouth Wlk HU4 179 A3
Darwin Cl
5 Stamford PE9 219 A7
7 Sutton Bridge PE12 160 E4
10 Waddington LN5 93 E8
Darwin Ct Lincoln LN2 202 B5
Little Coates DN34 190 F6
Darwin St
3 Gainsborough DN21 197 D2
6 Kirton in Lindsey DN21 30 B1
6 Kirton in Lindsey DN21 30 B2
Darwn Ct 15 NG33 151 D7
Dashwood Rd 7 LN13 75 E2
Datchet Garth 3 HU4 179 B2
Daubeney Ave LN1 66 D2
Daubney St DN35 189 E1
Davenport Ave HU13 178 D1
Davenport Dr DN35 192 C4
Davey Cl 1 Boston PE21 208 E7
Louth LN11 198 C7
David Ave Lincoln LN1 201 D8
Louth LN11 198 D7
David Chalmers Cl PE2 230 F8
David Dr PE25 206 B6
David Pl DN36 195 C5
David's Cl PE4 220 D4
David's La Benington PE22 127 A5
Peterborough PE4 220 F5
Davidson Dr PE21 208 D2
David St DN32 191 F5
Davie Pl DN35 192 B7
Davisons Ave DN31 191 D8
Davis's Cl HU10 178 C8
Davos Way PE25 206 A7
Davy Ave DN15 182 E4
Davy Cl 3 LN11 61 F3
Davy Cres DN20 196 C5
Davy's La 6 LN4 81 A2
Dawber La
Claxby St Andrew LN13 88 F5
Thimbleby LN9 85 C5
Dawes La DN16 183 D4
Dawes Lane Acad DN15 183 D3
Dawlish Rd DN33 194 E6
Dawnay Dr HU10 179 A6
Dawnhill La DN21 42 E2
Daws Gate Moulton PE12 157 F2
Whaplode PE12 158 A2
DAWSMERE PE12 148 E5
Dawsmere Rd PE12 148 F4
Dawson Ave 1 PE11 214 F6
Dawson City Claypits Nature Reserve★ DN19 5 C4
Dawson Cl Lincoln LN6 204 F6
6 Newborough PE6 174 E4
Dawson Dr 8 PE24 102 E7
Dawson Rd 7 NG34 212 D6
Dawsons La LN3 203 F8
Daybell Cl 20 NG13 128 A6
Daybrook Cl NG32 139 C8
Day Cl 6 Keadby DN17 17 D6
Wrawby DN20 20 E4
Daymond St PE2 230 D8
Day's La PE20 134 F3
Deacon Dr DN15 182 B2
Deacon Rd LN2 202 C5
Deaconscroft PE3 225 B5
Deacon St PE1 225 F3
Dealtry Cl DN21 53 D5
Dean Cl 3 NG34 121 B8
Dean Cres PE7 230 B1
Deane Cl 7 NG23 91 D5
Deane Rd DN40 186 D4
Dean Rd Lincoln LN2 202 C5
Scunthorpe DN17 184 E6
Deans Cl 6 DN10 39 F5
Dean's Ct 11 PE1 226 A2
Deansgate DN32 191 C6
Deansgrove DN32 191 D7
Deansleigh LN1 201 E8
Deansway LN4 81 D3
Dear Love Gate
1 Gedney PE12 160 A8
Lutton PE12 148 D1
Dearne Ct 9 HU15 2 D5
Dear St 11 LN8 57 D8
De Aston Sch LN8 57 E7
De Aston Sq 2 DN15 182 E3
Deaton La DN36 195 C6
Debdale PE2 229 E4
Debdale Rd NG32 210 A5
Debdhill Rd DN10 39 F6
De Bec Cl PE1 226 C3
Decoy Cl 16 PE11 145 C1
Decoy Rd Borough Fen PE6 174 D6
Gorefield PE13 169 D2
Deeke Rd 21 NG24 104 C1
Deene Cl 7 Grimsby DN34 190 D4
8 Market Deeping PE6 217 A5
Deene Ct PE3 225 C5

Deep (Aquarium & Marine Research Centre) The★ HU1 181 A5
Deepdale Dr NG34 121 C7
Deepdale Gr 2 HU9 181 E8
Deepdale La LN2 68 C2
DEEPING GATE PE6 217 C3
Deeping Lakes Nature Reserve★ PE6 174 C7
Deeping Rd Baston PE6 164 E4
Glinton PE6 174 A6
DEEPING ST JAMES PE6 217 D4
Deeping St James Com Prim Sch PE6 217 F4
Deeping St James Rd PE6 217 D2
DEEPING ST NICHOLAS PE11 166 C6
Deeping St Nicholas Prim Sch PE11 166 B6
Deepings Leisure Ctr PE6 217 E4
Deepings Sch The PE6 217 E5
Deep La PE23 87 A5
Deerhurst Way 18 PE6 175 A1
Deerleap PE3 225 A5
Deer Pk Rd 3 PE6 164 F3
Deer Valley Rd 4 PE2 230 E8
Dee St 6 HU3 180 B4
Defender Dr DN37 190 B7
De Gaunt Dr 10 NG34 107 F1
De Gravel Dr 5 NG34 107 F1
De Havilland Rd PE13 170 D1
Deira Cl NG34 212 C1
De la Bere Ave 25 LN12 77 A8
Delacorte Gn PE11 214 A1
De Lacy Ave PE25 206 C8
De Lacy La 6 DN35 192 F6
De Lacy Way DN15 9 A5
Delaine Cl PE10 213 E5
Delamere Cl PE1 226 C5
Delamere Ct DN36 192 F1
Delamore Way PE12 216 C5
De la Pole Ave HU3 179 F7
Delapre Ct 11 PE6 175 A1
Deldale Rd PE21 136 D8
Delfield Rd PE21 136 D8
Delgate Ave 3 PE12 157 E7
Delgate Bank PE12 157 D2
Delhi Sq 3 NG34 120 D8
Delhi St 7 HU9 5 D8
De Ligne Dr 6 NG32 139 C7
Delius Cl HU4 179 B4
Dellfield Ave LN6 200 C1
Dellfield Cl LN6 200 C2
Dellfield Ct 8 LN6 200 C1
Dell The 16 Broughton DN20 19 E3
Peterborough PE2 230 E7
Scunthorpe DN17 184 D5
Delph Ct PE2 231 F6
Delph Fields PE12 216 A3
Delph Rd 18 Lincoln LN6 93 C8
Long Sutton PE12 216 A3
Delph The PE11 155 F4
Delves Way PE7 230 D2
DEMBLEBY NG34 132 A4
Dembleby Rd NG34 132 A5
Demeter House DN20 196 B3
Demeter House Sch DN20 196 C3
De Montfort Univ LN2 234 B2
Denbigh Ct 11 NG23 91 D5
Denby Cl DN15 182 D5
Denby Dale Cl LN6 200 C2
Denby Dr DN35 192 C3
Dene Cl LN6 200 B3
Denefield LN6 200 B3
Denehall Rd 14 DN3 14 A2
Dene La LN4 109 C7
Dene Rd Grimsby DN32 191 E4
Skellingthorpe LN6 200 B3
Denesway HU13 178 D2
Dene The 6 Nettleham LN2 68 C2
Skellingthorpe LN6 200 B3
Denham Cl 2 PE25 206 C2
Denham Wlk 1 PE3 225 C4
Denis Dr PE2 230 A4
Denmark Ct 7 HU9 181 C7
Denmark Dr PE2 230 A4
Dennett Cl PE23 100 F8
Dennor Cl 15 LN12 77 A8
Denshire Ct 5 PE6 164 E4
DENTON NG32 139 B7
Denton Ave NG31 210 F1
Denton CE Sch NG32 139 A7
Denton Cl Grantham NG31 210 F1
28 Newark-on-Trent NG24 104 B2
Denton La Barrowby NG32 128 F3
Belvoir NG32 138 E6
Denton Rd PE2 231 C6
Denton's Way 11 DN20 31 A5
Depot St LN1 201 D3
Derby Ave PE25 206 D1
Derby Cl
1 Grantham NG31 210 E4
23 Grimsby DN32 189 C1
Derby Dr PE1 226 C5
Derby Rd DN15 182 B2
Derby St
Kingston upon Hull HU3 180 D8
13 Lincoln LN5 205 E8
Dere Cl 9 PE10 213 C6
Derringham Ave 5 HU4 179 B6
Derringham St HU3 180 C7
DERRYTHORPE DN17 17 C3
Derrythorpe Rd DN17 17 D4
Derrythorpe Road DN17 17 C2
Derry Way DN33 194 E8
Derwent Ave 18 HU14 3 A4
Derwent Cl LN6 205 A2
Derwent Ct 20 NG24 104 B2
Derwent Dr
1 Humberston DN36 36 C8
Peterborough PE4 221 C2
Derwent Rd
Grantham NG31 210 F3
Scunthorpe DN16 185 E6
Derwent St LN1 201 C4
Derwent Wy
6 Beacon Hill NG24 104 A5
Spalding PE11 214 A4
Derwood Gr 7 PE4 220 F5
Desborough Ave PE2 231 D5
Detuyll St W DN15 182 F5
Detuyll St DN15 182 F5
Devereux Way LN9 199 D2
Devon La 17 NG13 128 A6
Devonshire Ave DN32 191 D4
Devonshire Rd
2 Scampton Airfield LN1 67 E5
Scunthorpe DN17 184 F6
Devon St
Kingston upon Hull HU4 179 F3
8 Lincoln LN2 202 C3
Dewberry Ct HU4 179 C4
Dewey Cl PE7 233 B8
De Wint Ave LN6 205 A5
De Wint Cl Lincoln LN6 205 B5
6 Metheringham LN4 95 C4
De Wint Ct LN6 205 A5
Dewsbury Ave DN15 182 C4
Dexter Ave NG31 210 F3
Deyne Ave DN15 183 A3
Dial Sq 1 DN31 191 E7
Diana Princess of Wales Hospl DN33 191 C3
Diana St DN15 183 A5
Dias Cl PE11 214 B2
Dickens Beck La LN11 49 D5
Dickens Cl PE6 164 E2
Dickens Dr PE9 218 E5
Dickenson Terr 10 DN21 197 D3
Dickens Rd NG31 211 E6
Dickens St
Little London PE11 214 A1
Peterborough PE1 226 B3
Dickinson Cl 11 DN20 30 F5
Dickinson's La 6 DN36 36 B1
Dickon Hill Rd PE22 114 D7
DICKON HILLS PE22 114 D7
Dick Turpin Way PE12 216 B5
DIGBY LN4 108 E5
Digby CE Sch LN4 108 D6
Digby Cl 9 LN6 204 C7
Digby Cnr Nature Reserve★ LN4 108 F5
Digby Gdns DN34 191 A5
Digby Rd LN4 109 B6
Digby St DN15 182 F4
Digby the Tedder Prim Sch LN4 108 B7
Dimmock Cl NG32 139 B7
Dingley Ct PE3 225 C5
Dinna Nook National Nature Reserve★ LN11 51 B7
Dirty La 4 DN7 14 D8
Discovery Cl NG34 212 A3
Disney Ct LN6 92 C2
Ditmas Ave 9 HU4 179 B6
Division Rd 1 HU3 180 B4
Dixon Ave
14 Broughton DN20 19 D3
Dorrington LN4 108 E3
Grimsby DN32 191 E4
Dixon Cl Brigg DN20 196 C4
Lincoln LN6 201 D1
12 Tetney DN36 36 D4
Dixon Dr LN13 75 E2
Dixon Pl 5 NG31 211 A3
Dixon's Dro PE14 170 F4
Dixons Rd PE6 217 C4
Dixon St LN5 201 D1
Dixon Way LN6 201 D1
Dockholme Gate PE11 145 A4
Docking La LN9 199 B8
Docking's Holt PE12 216 B6
Dock Office Row 6 HU1 181 A7
Dock St HU1 180 F6
Dock Terr PE21 209 B3
Dock Twr The★ DN31 189 B3
Doctor's La PE10 143 A2
DODDINGTON LN6 79 E5
Doddington Ave LN6 205 A4
Doddington Dr PE3 225 B2
Doddington Hall & Gdns★ LN6 79 D5
Doddington La
Claypole NG23 117 E7
Stubton NG23 118 B7
Westborough & Dry Doddington NG23 117 E5
Doddington Rd
Birchwood LN6 204 C6
Doddington & Whisby LN6 79 E3
Lincoln LN6 204 F4
Dodswell Gr HU9 5 F8
Doe Cl LN6 92 D5
Dog and Duck La DN21 197 B8
Dog Dro Holbeach PE12 158 C5
Sutton St James PE12 159 A1
Dog Dro N PE12 168 B4
Dog Dro (Nutts Lane) PE12 158 D2
Dog Dro S PE12 168 A2
DOGDYKE LN4 110 E6
Dogdyke Ppg Sta★ LN4 110 D7
Dogdyke Rd Coningsby LN4 207 B2
Wildmore LN4 111 B6
Dog Holes La DN22 52 A1
Dog Kennel Rd DN21 55 A8
Dog Rose Dr PE10 213 D2
DOGSTHORPE PE1 226 C7
Dogsthorpe Gr 2 PE1 226 A5
Dogsthorpe Jun Sch PE1 226 B7
Dogsthorpe Rd PE1 226 A5
Dolby Vale DN33 190 F3
Dole Rd DN17 6 B1
Dole Wood Nature Reserve★ PE10 164 C7
Doll La 1 DN20 20 F7
Doll's Bank PE12 159 A4
Dolman Cres DN17 184 F4
Dolphin La 28 PE21 208 F5
Dolphin St 4 DN35 192 F6
Dominion Cl 3 DN36 195 C6
Donaldson Dr 4 PE4 221 C2
Doncaster Cl 14 PE10 213 D3
Doncaster Gdns 14 LN5 107 A8
Doncaster Rd
Gunness DN15 17 E6
Hatfield DN7 14 D3
Haxey DN9 26 F2
Scunthorpe DN15 182 B3
Stainforth DN7 14 B6
Doncaster St HU3 180 B6
Donegal Cl PE4 221 B2
DONINGTON PE11 134 F1
Donington Cowley Endowed Prim Sch The PE11 134 E2
DONINGTON EAUDIKE PE20 135 A3
Donington La LN11 72 C8
DONINGTON ON BAIN LN11 59 F1
Donington on Bain Sch The LN11 59 E1
Donington Rd Bicker PE20 135 A4
Horbling NG34 133 C2
Kirton PE20 135 F6
Donington Road LN11 60 D4
DONNA NOOK LN11 38 D2
Donna Nook National Nature Reserve★ LN11 38 C2
Donna Nook Road LN11 38 C1
Donnington Gdns DN15 182 F3
Donnington Pk 1 PE13 170 A1
Donnington Rd LN8 59 B2
Donnington St DN32 191 F7
Donville Rd DN17 7 A2
Dooks Cl DN21 29 C1
Doon Garth HU4 179 A3
Dorado Cl 2 HU3 180 A5
Dorchester Ave PE10 213 E3
Dorchester Cres 6 PE1 226 D7
Dorchester Rd DN17 184 C8
Dorchester Way 10 LN6 93 B8
Dore Ave LN6 204 E2
Dormy Ave PE25 206 D8
Dornoch Cl 11 LN10 97 C6
Dorothy Ave
Skegness PE25 206 C3
Waltham DN37 194 E5
Dorothy Cl PE22 113 A1
Dorothy Cres 1 PE25 206 C3
Dorrigan Cl LN1 201 C7
DORRINGTON LN4 108 E4
Dorrington Cl 19 NG34 108 D2
Dorset Cl E 6 DN15 8 B4
Dorset Cl W 5 DN15 8 B4
Dorset Pl 8 LN1 67 E5
Dorset St
Kingston upon Hull HU4 179 F3
7 Lincoln LN2 202 C3
Dorton Ave DN21 197 F4
Dotam's La PE22 126 D4
Dotterel Dr DN16 185 F5
Double Bank PE22 126 D6
Double Bridges Rd DN8 15 B6
Doubledays La PE24 102 D8
Double St PE11 214 D4
Doubletwelves Dro PE20 134 D6
Doughty Cl DN37 194 E5
Doughty Rd DN32 191 E7
Doughty's Ct LN5 234 B2
Doughty St PE9 219 D6
Douglas Ave Grimsby DN31 191 A8
5 Ingoldmells PE25 90 D3
Douglas Cl 10 PE24 102 E8
Douglas Rd
Cleethorpes DN35 192 D8
Market Deeping PE6 217 C4
Doulton Cl 4 LN6 204 D7
Dove Cl
9 Gainsborough DN21 197 F5
Louth LN11 198 D7
7 Sleaford NG34 212 B3
Dovecote
4 Middle Rasen LN8 57 B8
Rippingale PE10 143 A3
Dovecote Cl
Peterborough PE1 226 B7
Snitterby DN21 43 D5
Dovecote La
Aubourn Haddington & South Hykeham LN5 92 F5
Coleby LN5 93 F3
Wainfleet St Mary PE24 102 E1
Yaxley PE7 233 C5
Dovecote Mdws NG34 142 E5
Dovecote Mews 4 DN20 196 F6
Dovecote Rd 4 PE6 217 A6
Dovecotes 3 PE11 145 A8
Dovecot La PE22 127 D6
Dove Ct PE11 214 B5
Dove Dale 5 LN6 204 F2
Dovedale Cl
Grantham NG31 211 B8
2 Winterton DN15 9 A6
Dovedale Dr 6 DN33 194 E8
Dovedale Gr 1 HU9 181 E8
Dovedale Rd DN16 185 D5
Dove Gdns 2 PE2 230 E8
DOVENDALE LN11 60 F1
Dover Cl NG31 210 E6
Dover Rd PE4 221 A2
Dover St Grimsby DN31 191 C8
Kingston upon Hull HU3 180 C8
Doves' La PE22 126 E3
Dove Willow PE6 174 E6
Dowding Mews LN2 202 E4
Dowding Rd LN2 202 E4
Dowdyke Dro PE20 146 B8
Dowdyke Rd PE20 145 F8
Dower Rise 11 HU14 3 B7
Dowgate Cl 2 PE11 214 A3
Dowgate Rd 4 PE13 170 B1
Dowlands Bsns Pk LN11 62 C5
Down Gate PE3 225 A1
Downing Cl DN34 190 F6
Downing Cres
Scunthorpe DN16 185 A3
2 Stamford PE9 219 B7
DOWSBY PE10 143 B4
DOWSDALE PE6 167 D1
Dowsdale Bank
Thorney PE6 176 A8
Whaplode PE12 167 E2
Dowse Ave DN15 182 E3
Dowsing Way PE25 206 A6
Doyle La 2 PE11 214 A1
Dozen's Bank PE11 156 B6
DRAGONBY DN15 8 E1
Dragonby Rd DN17 184 E4
Dragon Fly Cl 1 PE7 230 C2
Drain Bank East Kirkby PE23 99 F3
Newport HU15 1 B8
Drain Bank North PE12 157 A2
Drain Bank South PE12 157 A1
Drain Rd PE6 221 E7
Drainside PE20 136 B5
Drainside S PE20 136 C4
Drakards La PE21 209 A3
Drake Ave Grimsby DN32 192 B6
Heighington/Washingborough LN4 203 B1
Peterborough PE7 230 F5
Drake Cl 14 PE11 214 C2
Drake Rd PE25 103 E4
Drakes Cl
7 Holbeach PE12 215 E2
19 Mablethorpe & Sutton LN12 77 A7
Drakes Mdw LN8 55 E6
Drake St
Gainsborough DN21 197 D2
Lincoln LN1 201 C4
Draper Rd PE4 221 F2
Drapers Pl 13 PE11 214 D4
Draw Dike PE12 159 D1
Drax Ct 6 LN8 57 B8
Draycot 6 LN7 33 A3
DRAYTON PE20 135 C6
Drayton PE3 225 A4
Drayton Rd PE20 135 C7
Drayton The PE20 135 C6
Drew Ave DN32 191 F4
Drewry La 10 DN9 27 A2
DRIBY LN13 74 E1
Driby Hill LN13 75 F2
Driby La LN13 74 F1
Driffield Way PE2 230 D8
Driffil Way 29 DN15 9 A5
Drift Ave PE9 219 C6
Drift Gdns PE9 219 C6
Drift La NG32 119 A1
Drift Rd PE9 219 C6
Drift Rd The LE14 150 F2
Drift The Barrowby NG32 210 A3
Belvoir NG32 138 F5
Buckminster NG33 151 A4
Collyweston PE9 171 B1
Croxton Kerrial NG32 138 F5
Harlaxton NG32 139 C8
Ryhall PE9 163 B3
Skillington NG33 151 A7
Syston NG32 130 A7
Walcott LN4 109 D7
Wansford PE5 222 F3
Drigh Rd 17 LN8 47 B6
Drill Hall La 5 DN21 197 D5
Dring La DN21 41 D7
Drinsey Nook La NG23 66 B1
Drive The
Brocklesby DN41 22 E6
Gainsborough DN21 197 E3
Grantham NG31 210 D3
Ingoldmells PE25 206 E8
7 Kirk Sandall DN3 14 A1
2 Mablethorpe/Sutton on Sea LN12 64 A4
Peterborough PE3 225 E2
Waltham DN37 194 F3
1 Winthorpe NG24 104 B7
Dronfield Ct 3 DN15 182 B3
Drove La Coddington NG24 104 D7
Sleaford NG34 212 A5
Drove Rd Crowland PE12 167 F3
Whaplode PE12 168 A3
Drovers Ct DN21 197 E1
Drovers Rise 1 HU15 2 C6
Drove The
4 Aubourn Haddington & South Hykeham LN6 93 A8
Collyweston PE9 171 B1
Osbournby NG34 132 D5
Sleaford NG34 212 B5
Droveway The PE6 227 B3
Drummond Rd
Bourne PE10 213 E4
Skegness PE25 206 D1
Drury Cl 1 DN37 194 C4
Drury La Bicker PE20 135 A4
Lincoln LN1 234 B3
New Waltham DN36 195 C6
Drury Pk 9 NG23 117 D3
Drury St LN4 95 D4
Drydales HU10 178 C6
Dryden Ave
Balderton NG24 104 C3
Lincoln LN2 202 B6
Dryden Cl NG31 211 D6
Dryden Ct 3 LN4 207 B5
Dryden Rd
Peterborough PE1 225 E7
Scunthorpe DN17 184 D6
DRY DODDINGTON NG23 117 E5
Dry Leys PE2 230 C6
Drypool Way HU9 181 B6
Duchess Dr PE6 217 C6
Duchess St DN32 191 D6
Ducie La DN22 52 C5
Duckpool La LN10 84 B1
Duckthorpe La DN36 37 B2
Dudley Cl 1 PE21 209 B4
Dudley House Sch NG31 211 B4
Dudley Pl DN35 192 D4
Dudley Rd Brigg DN20 196 C3
Grantham NG31 211 B4
Scunthorpe DN16 185 E6
Dudley St DN31 191 C7
Dudley Wlk HU4 179 B3
Duesbery St HU3 180 C8
Dugard Rd DN32 192 B7
Duke Mdws PE6 217 C6
Duke of Bedford Prim Sch PE6 176 A3
Duke Rd PE22 113 F3
Duke's Covert Nature Reserve★ NG32 120 A1
Dukesmead PE4 220 E2
Dukesmead Mobile Home Pk PE4 220 E2
Duke St Boston PE21 208 E4
22 Grimsby DN32 189 C1
Grimsby DN32 192 B8
Peterborough PE2 231 A7
Sleaford NG34 212 E5
14 Stainforth DN7 14 C6
Dukes Wy PE7 230 B1
Dunbar Ave DN36 195 B6
Dunbar Cl 5 DN21 197 E6
Dunblane Dr PE2 229 D4
Duncan Dr 34 DN18 3 E1
Duncombe Gdns 1 DN32 191 F8
Duncombe St DN32 191 F8
Dundee Ct PE2 229 C4
Dundee Dr PE9 218 E6
Dundee St HU5 180 A8
Dunes Family Entertainment Ctr The★ LN12 64 C4
Dunford Rd 5 LN5 234 B1
Dunham Cl LN1 65 D1
DUNHAM ON TRENT NG22 65 B1
Dunham on Trent CE Prim Sch NG22 65 A1
Dunham Rd DN22 65 A3
DUNHOLME LN2 68 E6
Dunholme Cl
Gainsborough DN21 197 E4
11 Welton/Dunholme LN2 68 D6
Dunholme Ct 4 LN2 202 A8
Dunholme Rd
Gainsborough DN21 197 E4
9 Welton/Dunholme LN2 68 D6
Dunholme St Chads CE Prim Sch LN2 68 E6
Dunkirk Rd LN1 201 D6
Dunlin Dr
Long Sutton PE12 216 B4
Scunthorpe DN16 185 F5
Dunlin Rd 2 PE9 163 D3
Dunlop St LN5 201 F1
Dunlop Way DN16 185 E7
Dunmires La DN14 6 E8
Dunmore Cl LN5 205 C3
Dunmow St DN31 188 D1
Dunnegate Way PE11 145 D2
Dunnock Cl 3 DN16 185 B2
Dunns Paddock 3 DN20 20 F7
Dunoon Ct 4 DN37 190 E8
Dunsberry
Marholm PE6 220 D1
Peterborough PE3 224 F8
DUNSBY PE10 143 A1
Dunsby Dro PE10 143 D1
DUNSCROFT DN7 14 C4
Dunstall St DN15 183 A3
Dunstall Wlk DN21 197 F3
Dunstan Dr DN8 15 A8
Dunstan Hill 26 DN21 30 B1
Dunstan Villas 29 DN21 30 B1
Dunster Cl NG31 210 F6
Dunster Rd DN21 197 E6
DUNSTON LN4 95 C5
Dunston Cl 10 LN2 202 A8
Dunston Dr HU13 178 D1
Dunston Fen La LN4 83 D1
Dunston Heath La LN4 94 E5

Dunston Rd
 Kingston upon Hull HU5 ....179 D7
 Metheringham LN4........95 C5
DUNSVILLE DN7 ....14 C3
Dunsville Prim Sch DN7 ...14 C3
Durban Rd DN32 ....192 A7
Durham Ave Grimsby DN34 191 A7
 Sleaford NG34 ....212 C6
 Thorne/Moorends DN8 ....15 A8
Durham Cl Birchwood LN6..200 D2
 Grantham NG31 ....210 C4
Durham Cres LN4 ....203 D1
Durham Rd
 Cleethorpes DN35 ......192 C4
 Hatfield DN7 ....14 D4
 Peterborough PE1 ....226 C3
Durham's Rd PE12 ....148 D5
Dursley Ave DN36 ....195 B6
Dutton Ave PE25 ....206 A4
Dycote La LN5 ....106 D5
DYKE PE10 ....154 D5
Dyke Dro PE10 ....154 E5
Dyke Rd 5 DN36 ....37 C5
Dykes Cl 5 HU13 ....3 F4
Dykes End NG23 ....91 D4
Dyke Windmill & Peremill
 Galery★ PE10 ....154 D5
Dymoke Cl 3 DN21 ....29 C4
Dymoke Dr Grimsby DN37..190 C6
 Horncastle LN9 ....199 C2
Dymoke Rd 6 LN12 ....64 C3
Dysart Rd NG31 ....210 E4
Dyson Ret Pk NG31.......211 A4
Dyson Cl PE1 ....225 F3

E

EAGLE LN6 ....79 C2
EAGLE BARNSDALE LN6....92 C7
Eagle Cl 7 LN12 ....64 A4
Eagle Com Prim Sch LN6 .79 B2
Eagle Dr
 New Waltham DN36 .....195 E6
 3 Sleaford NG34 ....212 B3
 Waltham DN37 ....194 F3
 7 Welton/Dunholme LN2 ..68 D7
Eagle La LN6 ....79 D1
EAGLE MOOR LN6 ....79 C2
Eagle Moor LN6..........79 C3
Eagle Rd
 Doddington & Whisby LN6..79 D3
 North Scarle LN6 ....78 F2
 Spalford NG23 ....78 D4
Eagle Road LN6 ....92 B6
Eaglesthorpe PE1 ....225 E7
Eagle Way Bourne PE10...213 C6
 2 Hampton Vale PE7....230 D1
 Yaxley PE7 ....233 D8
EALAND DN17 ....16 E6
Ealand Rd 3 DN17 ....17 C6
Eames Gdns PE1 ....226 E6
Earl Ave DN36...........195 D7
EARLESFIELD NG31 ......210 F3
Earlesfield La NG31 .....210 F3
Earle's Rd HU9..........181 D7
Earle St HU10 ....178 F5
Earls Cl PE2 ....231 E6
Earls Dr LN5 ....205 D8
Earlsfield Cl LN6 ....204 B5
Earlsfield Ind Est NG31 .139 F3
Earlsgate Gdns 3 DN15....8 F5
Earlsgate Rd DN15 ....8 F5
Earl Spencer Ct PE2 ....230 E8
Earl St Grimsby DN31 ...191 C7
 Scunthorpe DN16 ....183 B1
Earls Wlk 8 DN16 ....183 B2
Earlswood PE2...........229 E5
Earp Ave 21 NG24 ....104 A4
Earth Cl PE2 ....231 E5
Ease La NG23 ....117 F3
Easenby Ave HU10 ....178 C6
Easenby Cl 2 HU14 ....3 C7
Eason Rd 5 DN33 ....191 B2
East Acridge 15 DN18......3 F1
East Ave
 Brant Broughton LN5 ...105 F5
 Grantham NG31 ....210 E3
 1 Stainforth DN7 ....14 C5
East Bank 5 Stainforth DN7 14 C7
 Sutton Bridge PE12 ....160 F5
East Banks 7 NG34 ......212 E4
EAST BARKWITH LN8 .....71 A8
Eastbeck La LN9 ....86 A2
East Bight LN2 ....234 B3
East Boundary Rd DN16..183 F2
Eastbourne St
 Kingston upon Hull HU3..180 A5
 Lincoln LN2 ....234 C1
Eastbourne Way DN33...194 F7
Eastbrook Rd LN6 ....205 A5
EAST BUTTERWICK DN17..28 E8
East Butterwick Road
 DN17..................17 D2
East Camp Rd 3 DN34....120 C8
Eastchurch Rd 4 NG34...120 D8
East Cl 13 NG34 ....108 E2
Eastcliffe Sq 9 NG32...119 B7
Eastcliff Rd LN2 ....234 C3
East Cob Gate PE12 .....157 F6
East Comm La DN16 .....185 B8
Eastcroft 1 LN11 ....66 D3
East Croft 10 LN3 ....203 E7
East Cross St 25 DN21....30 B1
East Dale Dr 3 DN21 .....30 B2
East Dale Rd HU14 ....2 E5
East Dr LN4 ....110 E8
EAST ELLA HU5 ....179 D7

East Ella Dr HU4 ....179 C6
East Elloe Ave PE12 ....215 D3
East End
 1 Burgh le Marsh PE24...102 E7
 Humberside Airport DN39 ..22 A6
 Langtoft PE6............164 F3
East End Cl DN33 ....191 D1
Eastern Ave
 Gainsborough DN21......197 F5
 Peterborough PE1 ......226 C8
Eastern Cl PE1 ....226 D7
Eastern Dr
 11 Balderton NG24 .....104 C1
 RAF Cranwell NG34 ....120 D8
Eastern Ind Est PE1 ....226 E3
Eastern Inway DN34 .....191 A4
Eastern Rd PE12 ....215 F8
Eastern Terr LN5 ....201 D1
Eastern Terr La 13 NG24..104 A4
East Fen La PE22 ....113 B7
EAST FERRY DN21 ....28 B2
East Ferry Rd
 East Ferry DN21 ....28 E3
 Laughton DN21 ....41 B8
 Wildsworth DN21........40 D8
EASTFIELD PE1 ....226 D4
Eastfield
 14 Humberston DN36 ....36 D8
 3 Market Deeping PE6 ..217 C5
 11 Sturton by Stow LN1 ..66 D7
East Field LN5 ....92 F2
Eastfield Ave DN33 .....195 A7
Eastfield Cl
 1 Dunholme LN2........68 E6
 6 Sutterton PE20 ......136 A2
Eastfield Gr PE1 ....226 B4
Eastfield Inf Sch LN11 ..198 D6
Eastfield La Manby LN11 ..62 C7
 Welton LN2 ....68 E7
Eastfield N Ind Est LN11 ..12 F3
Eastfield Prim Acad DN40 186 C2
Eastfield Prim Sch HU4 ..179 D6
Eastfield Rd
 Barton-upon-Humber DN18..10 F7
 Brigg DN20.............196 B3
 Epworth DN9............27 E6
 Firsby PE23 ....101 F7
 Immingham DN40 ....12 F3
 3 Keelby DN41 ....23 A5
 Kingston upon Hull HU4 ..179 D6
 Louth LN11.............198 C6
 40 Messingham DN17 ....29 D7
 North Killingholme DN40...12 E5
 Peterborough PE1 ......226 C4
 Scunthorpe DN16 ....185 C5
 1 Wisbech PE13 ....170 C1
East Field Rd DN7 ....14 C8
Eastfield Rise
 2 Holton le Clay DN36 ..195 D2
 Louth LN11.............198 E7
Eastfields 2 LN8 ....43 D3
Eastfield S Ind Est DN40 ..12 F3
Eastfield St 5 LN2 ......202 B3
Eastfield Way 17 PE13 ..170 D1
EAST FIRSBY LN8 ....55 F4
Eastgate Bassingham LN5 ..92 F2
 Bourne PE10 ....213 E4
 Grimsby DN32 ....191 E8
 Heckington NG34 ......122 E3
 Kingston upon Hull HU13..178 E2
 Lincoln LN2 ....234 B3
 Louth LN11.............198 C6
 Market Deeping PE6 ...217 F3
 Peterborough PE1 ......226 B2
 Scotton DN21...........29 C2
East Gate Bourne PE10...213 E4
 Fleet PE12 ....159 C4
 Moulton PE12 ....158 A7
 Sleaford NG34 ....212 E4
 Whaplode PE12 ....158 C7
Eastgate Cl LN2 ....234 C3
Eastgate Gdns 3 PE12 ..159 C2
Eastgate La PE34.........161 E2
East Gn 30 DN17..........29 D7
East Gr
 12 Barton-upon-Humber
   DN18...................3 F1
 8 Colsterworth NG33 ...151 E6
 Kingston upon Hull HU4 ..179 D4
Easthall Rd LN7 ....32 B4
EAST HALTON DN40 ....12 E6
East Halton Prim Sch
 DN40...................12 D6
East Halton Rd DN40 ....12 E3
East Hann La DN19 ....4 E1
EAST HECKINGTON PE20..123 D3
Eastholm LN2...........202 E7
Eastholm Cl PE1 ....226 C3
Eastholme Gdns 10 DN15 ..8 B8
EASTHORPE NG13 ....128 B5
Easthorpe La NG13 .....128 C5
Easthorpe Rd
 1 Bottesford NG13.....128 B5
 2 Great Gonerby NG31..129 E5
Easthorpe View 2 NG13..128 B5
East Hull Pools★ HU9...181 C8
EAST KEAL PE23 ....99 F5
East Keal Bank PE23....100 C3
East Keal Fen Rd PE23...100 D3
EAST KEAL FEN SIDE
 PE23..................100 C4
EAST KIRKBY PE23 ....99 F5
East La Brattleby LN1 ....67 C7
 Corringham DN21........41 E2
 Morton PE10 ....154 C7
 Stainforth DN7 ....14 C6
Eastlands 4 PE6 ....166 F1

Eastlands Bank PE14 ...161 B1
Eastleigh Cl LN6 ....200 B1
Eastleigh Rd LN6 ....226 C3
East Liberty LN2 ....202 C4
East Lound DN9 ....27 E2
East Lound Rd Haxey DN9 ..27 D2
 Owston Ferry DN9 ....28 A3
EAST MARSH DN32 ....189 B1
East Marsh Rd DN9 ....5 C3
East Marsh St 3 DN31 ..191 E8
East Mid Mere Rd DN40 ..12 F4
East Mill Gate 3 LN3 ...203 E6
Eastmoor Villas DN9 .....27 D3
East Mount 12 HU14 ......3 A4
East of England
 Showground★ PE2.....229 C4
East of England Way PE2 229 B4
EASTOFT DN17 ....7 A3
Eastoft CE Prim Sch DN17 ..7 A3
Eastoft Moors Road DN17..17 A8
Eastoft Rd Crowle DN17...16 D8
 Luddington & Haldenby DN17 ..7 C3
EASTON DN33 ....140 B1
Easton Garford Endowed CE
 Sch PE9 ....171 D3
Easton La DN33 ....140 A2
EASTON ON THE HILL
 PE9...................171 C3
Easton Walled Gdn★
 NG33..................140 B2
East Parade DN20 ....196 C4
EAST RAVENDALE DN37....35 C2
East Ravendale CE Prim Sch
 DN37...................35 C2
East Rd 21 Brookenby LN8 ..47 B6
 Deeping St Nicholas PE11 ..156 C4
 4 Keadby with Althorpe
   DN17..................17 C6
 Navenby/Wellingore LN5..107 B8
 Northborough PE6 ......217 E1
 Sleaford NG34 ....212 F6
 Tetford LN9 ....73 F1
 Tydd St Mary PE13 .....170 C8
East Rd Ind Est NG34 ...212 F5
Eastrea Ct PE2 ....231 E6
East Row LN11 ....50 E4
East St Mary's Gate 2
 DN31..................191 D7
Eastside Rd Grimsby DN31 189 B1
 Scunthorpe DN16 ....183 F2
East St Alford LN13 ......54 F4
 Bole DN22 ....52 C6
 Crowland PE6 ....166 E1
 Grantham NG31 ....211 B4
 Grimsby DN32 ....191 E7
 Helpringham NG34 .....133 C7
 13 Hibaldstow DN20 ....30 F5
 Horncastle LN9 ....199 C4
 5 Kingston upon Hull HU9 181 B7
 Nettleham LN2 ....68 C2
 Rippingale PE10 ....143 A2
 Roxby cum Risby DN15....9 A3
 Stamford PE9 ....219 C5
East Sta Rd PE2 ....231 B4
EAST STOCKWITH DN21 ...40 C5
EAST TORRINGTON LN8 ...58 C2
East View LN4 ....109 D7
Eastview Cl
 Chapel St Leonard PE24 ..90 E6
 Cranwell NG34 ....107 C1
EASTVILLE PE22 ....114 B8
Eastville Rd
 4 Grimsby DN33.........191 A3
 Toynton St Peter PE23 ..101 A6
Eastway 1 LN2 ....68 D2
East Wlk DN15 ....183 B3
East Wold CE Prim Sch
 LN11...................62 A3
Eastwood Ave DN32 .....191 D4
Eastwood Ct 5 DN15 ....182 B2
Eastwood Dr
 2 Boston PE21 ....209 D4
 10 Broughton DN20 .....19 E4
 4 Grantham NG31 ......211 D2
Eastwood Rd PE21 ......209 D5
East Wr Cres DN7 ....230 C1
East Wykeham LN8 ....59 D7
Easy Rd PE11 ....156 E1
Eathwaite Gn PE4 ....221 C1
Eaton Cl HU10 ....178 E5
Eaton Ct DN34 ....191 C6
Eaton Rd Boston PE21...208 E3
 Immingham DN40 ....186 D4
Eau Bank LN11 ....50 D7
Eaudike Rd
 Donington PE20 ....135 A3
 Quadring PE11 ....145 C8
Eau Dike Rd PE22 ....115 A7
Eaudyke Bank 1 PE13...169 F7
Eaugate Rd PE12 ....157 F1
Ebony Gr LN6 ....200 C1
Ebrington Cl 3 LN10.....97 E6
Eccles Cl 3 DN20.......196 F7
Eccleston Rd 15 DN3 ....14 A3
Eco Wy 8 DN7...........14 D5
Eddystone Dr 3 LN6....205 A1
Eden Cl 6 PE21 ....206 C1
Edendale Gdns 3 LN1....201 A3
Edendale View LN1.......201 E8
Eden Dene DN16 ....185 C5
Edenfield PE2 ....230 C6
Eden Field Rd 4 DN3.....14 A1
Eden Gr Rd 8 DN3 ....14 A1
EDENHAM PE10 ....153 F4
Edenham Church of England
 Sch The PE10 ....153 F5
Edenham Rd PE10 ......154 B6
Edensand Rd HU3 ....179 E5

EDENTHORPE DN3 ....14 A1
Edenthorpe Hall Prim Sch
 DN3....................14 A1
Edgar Cl 10 DN21 ....29 C4
Edgar St HU3 ....180 D5
Edgbaston Ave 3 DN17..184 E3
Edgcote CI PE3 ....225 C5
Edge Ave DN33..........191 D2
Edgefield 6 PE12 ....157 E7
Edgehill 10 LN5 ....205 D2
Edgehill Dr 4 NG24 .....104 C4
Edgemere DN15 ....182 B3
Edgerley Drain Rd PE1 .226 F5
Edinburgh Ave
 Peterborough PE4 .....220 F3
 2 Skegness PE20 ......206 B3
Edinburgh Cl 13 PE20...136 C5
Edinburgh Cres
 2 Bourne PE10 ....213 D6
 12 Kirton PE20 ....136 C5
Edinburgh Dr
 Holton le Clay DN36 ...195 C3
 11 Kirton PE20 ....136 C5
 Spalding PE11 ....214 E2
 Wisbech PE13 ....170 C1
Edinburgh Rd
 16 Binbrook Tech Pk LN8 ..47 B6
 2 Grantham NG31 ......211 E6
 3 Ruskington NG34 ....108 C2
 Stamford PE9 ....219 B6
Edinburgh Sq 4 LN5 .....94 A7
Edinburgh St HU3 ......180 A5
Edinburgh Wlk
 Holbeach PE12 ....215 E2
 Pinchbeck PE11 ....156 B7
Edinburgh Wy DN33 .....191 B1
Edington Ct 3 DN21......53 A8
Edis Ct PE2 ....231 B6
Edison Dr PE7 ....233 D6
Edison Way 6 PE21 ....208 F1
EDLINGTON LN9 ....85 B6
Edlington Cl 6 LN5 .....201 F8
Edlington Moor LN10 .....97 D7
Edmonds Cl 3 PE9 ......219 D6
Edmonds Dr 7 PE9 ......171 A3
Edmonds Way 2 DN31 ...191 D8
Edmondthorpe Drift LE14 150 D1
Edmondthorpe Rd LE14..150 C1
Edmund Cl DN21 ....41 D2
Edmund Dr PE7 ....230 B1
Edmunds Rd 3 NG34 ...107 F1
Edna St LN5 ....201 F1
Edwalton Ave
 9 Mablethorpe/Sutton on Sea
   LN12...................77 A8
 Peterborough PE3 .....225 E3
Edward Barker Rd LN4 ...81 F4
Edward Collins Sq 2
 HU9...................181 C7
Edward Cres PE25 ......206 B3
Edward Heneage Prim Acad
 DN32..................191 F7
Edward Jermyn Dr 16
 NG24..................104 A6
Edward Rd
 Gainsborough DN21.....197 D6
 Spalding PE11 ....214 B4
 10 Stamford PE9 ......219 A7
Edward Richardson Prim Sch
 The LN9 ....73 F1
Edwards Rd 3 DN15 ....182 F4
Edward St
 Cleethorpes DN35 .....192 E5
 Grantham NG31 ....211 B2
 Grimsby DN32 ....191 F7
 Kingston upon Hull HU13..178 F1
 1 Lincoln LN5 ....205 B8
 17 Louth LN11 ....198 B5
Edwina Ave 6 PE11 .....156 F8
Edwin Cl 12 NG34 ......212 B2
Edwin Gdns PE10 ......213 B5
Edwin St 13 PE21 ......208 F1
Egar Way PE3 ....224 F2
Egerton Rd LN2 ....202 B5
Egginton Cl HU10 ......178 C7
Egginton St 4 HU2......180 F7
Egret Gr 5 LN6 ....204 D8
Egton Ave 17 DN17......29 D7
Egton St HU8 ....181 A8
Eider Cl 42 DN18 ....10 E8
Eider Gr PE11 ....214 A4
Eight Acres 10 PE9.....219 A5
Eighth Ave DN15 ....8 A1
Elan Cl PE21 ....208 E5
Elba St 8 HU9 ....5 E8
Elbow La PE13 ....177 F8
Elderberry Dr HU4 .....179 C4
Elderberry Way 2 DN35..192 C2
Elder Cl
 2 Bourne PE10 ....213 C6
 Skegness PE25 ....206 A5
 Witham St Hughs LN6.....92 D5
Elderflower Wy 5 PE7...230 B1
Eldern PE2 ....230 C4
Elder's Gate PE12 .....169 E8
Elder St LN5 ....205 D5
Elder Tree Way LN10 .....84 D3
Elderwood Ct 6 HU3....180 D5
Eleanor Cl Lincoln LN5..205 E7
 Stamford PE9 ....219 A6
Eleanor St DN32 ....191 F8
Electric Sta Rd NG24 ..212 C4
Elena Rd 4 PE2 ....231 E4
Eleven Acre La PE20...136 D4
Elgar Rd HU4 ....179 B4
Elgar Way PE3 ....218 F6
Eliot Cl Gainsborough DN21 197 F3
 9 Sleaford NG34 ......212 F4

Elizabeth Ave
 Dogdyke LN4 ....110 D7
 11 Kirk Sandall DN3 ....14 A2
 6 Lincoln LN6 ....93 C8
 Lincoln LN6 ....204 F1
 Wrange PE22 ....114 C2
Elizabeth Cl
 17 Chapel St Leonard PE24 ..90 D7
 23 Crowle DN17 ....16 C7
 Gainsborough DN21.....197 C7
 Glentworth DN21 ....54 F6
 Grimsby DN33 ....194 D7
 1 Scotter DN21 ....29 C4
Elizabeth Cres
 6 Ingoldmells PE25 .....90 E3
 Pinchbeck PE11 ....144 C1
Elizabeth Ct Brigg DN20..196 C5
 18 Chapel St Leonard PE24..90 D7
 Dogsthorpe PE1 ....226 A5
 Sleaford NG34 ....212 D3
Elizabeth Dr
 Billingborough NG33 ...143 B8
 12 Chapel St Leonard PE24..90 D7
Elizabeth Gr PE25 .....206 C5
Elizabeth Rd Boston PE21..209 B5
 2 Stamford PE9 ....219 B6
Elizabeth St 3 DN15 ....183 A4
Elizabeth Way 4 PE10..164 C8
Elkington Rd LN11 ....48 C2
Ella Ct HU10 ....178 C8
Ella Pk HU10 ....178 C8
Ellen Cres PE11 ....214 A3
Ellen Way DN36 ....195 B7
Ellerby Ct PE23 ....100 C6
Ellerby Mead NG33 .....152 D5
ELLERKER HU15 ....2 A8
Ellerker Rd HU15 ....2 B8
Ellers La DN9 ....27 C8
Ellesmere Ave 3 LN2 ...202 D4
Ellesmere Bsns Pk NG31 210 E2
Ellesmere Gr 4 DN7 .....14 D6
Ellesmere Rise DN34 ...190 D3
Ellicar La DN10 ....39 A3
Ellindon PE3............225 B7
Elliot Ave PE3 ....224 F2
Elliot Cl NG31 ....211 E6
Elliott Rd LN5 ....234 C1
Elliott's Way PE9 ....164 B4
Elliott Way 11 PE24 .....90 D7
Ellis Mill★ LN1 ....234 A4
Ellison Ave DN16 ....185 A1
Ellison Boulters CE Prim Sch
 LN2....................68 F4
Ellison Cl 5 LN2 ....68 F2
Ellison St Lincoln LN5...205 D5
 Thorne/Moorends DN8 ..15 A7
Ellis St HU9 ....181 C8
Elliston Prim Sch DN35..192 C8
Elliston St DN35........192 C8
Ellis Way DN32 ....191 E8
Ellis Wy DN20 ....30 F6
Ellmore La LN7 ....32 C3
Elloe Bank PE13 ....169 B2
ELLOUGHTON HU15 ....2 B6
Elloughton Dale HU15 ....2 D8
Elloughton Prim Sch HU15 ..2 B7
Elloughton Rd HU15 ......2 C6
Elloughtonthorpe Way 15
 HU15....................2 D5
Ellwood Ave PE2 ....231 E5
Ellyslande NG33........140 A5
Elm Ave 18 Brough HU15 ..2 C6
 Cherry Willingham/Reepham
   LN3..................203 D5
 Cleethorpes DN35 .....192 E6
 Grimsby DN33 ....191 A6
 13 Mablethorpe/Sutton on Sea
   LN12..................64 B3
 Newark-on-Trent NG24 ..104 A3
Elm Cl Lincoln LN6......204 F2
 17 Long Bennington NG23 ..117 D3
 Market Deeping PE6....217 C4
 13 Saxilby LN1 ....66 D2
 Yaxley PE7 ....233 F7
Elm Cres
 Burgh le Marsh PE24 ..102 D8
 Glinton PE6 ....220 B8
Elmdale 29 DN18 ....10 E8
Elmdene 5 LN2..........68 F4
Elm Dr Ingoldmells PE25..206 D8
 Louth LN11.............198 D7
 Skegness PE25 ....90 E1
 3 Sudbrooke LN2 ....68 F2
Elmer St N 3 NG31 .....211 A4
Elmer St S NG31 ....211 A4
Elmfield Rd PE1.........226 A7
Elmgarth 3 NG34 ....212 F3
Elm Gdns DN35 ....192 E6
Elm Gr Grantham NG31..211 C6
 8 Healing DN41 ....24 A5
 Scunthorpe DN16 ......185 B8
Elmhirst Ave PE25 ......206 D6
Elmhirst Rd 5 DN8........15 B8
Elmhurst La LN9 ....199 B6
Elm La Goxhill DN19 ......5 A1
 7 Laceby DN37..........23 E1
 Low Fulney PE12 ......157 C6
Elmore Cl 6 NG34 ......212 C4
Elmore Rd PE3 ....225 A3
Elm Rd Cleethorpes DN35..192 E6
 Waltham DN37 ....194 E3
Elms Dr HU10 ....178 C8
Elm St Peterborough PE2 230 F7
 Stamford PE9...........219 C5
Elms View 4 NG31......129 D5

Elmswood HU13 178 C2
Elm Terr PE10 213 B6
Elmtree Ave 10 HU14 3 A4
Elm Tree Cl 11 LN8 57 D7
Elm Tree Gr 8 DN8 15 B7
Elmtree Rd NG34 108 D1
Elm Way Brigg DN20 196 B4
Messingham DN17 29 C7
Elmwood Ave 4 PE21 208 F2
Elmwood Cl 6 LN6 200 D1
Elmwood Dr 6 PE25 90 D3
Elm Wy 10 PE25 206 D7
Elsea Dr 3 PE10 164 C8
Elsea Pk Way PE10 213 D2
Elsenham Rd DN31 188 D1
ELSHAM DN20 20 F7
Elsham Cl 7 LN6 204 D8
Elsham Cres LN6 204 D8
Elsham Dr DN37 194 C3
Elsham Gr 1 DN33 191 B3
Elsham Hall Ctry & Wildlife Pk★ DN20 20 F6
Elsham Rd DN20 20 D7
Elsham Rise HU13 178 D1
Elsham Wlk DN21 197 F4
Elsham Wold Ind Est DN20 21 A8
Elsie Davies Cl NG31 211 C7
Elsiemere Wlk 6 HU4 179 B6
Elsom Way LN9 199 A4
Elsthorpe Rd
Edenham PE10 153 E6
Haconby PE10 154 A7
Elstone PE2 230 A4
Elter Wlk PE4 221 C3
Elton Cl Ermine LN1 201 D6
34 Newark-on-Trent NG24 104 B2
2 Stamford PE9 218 F6
Elton Rd Thorney PE8 228 B6
Wansford PE8 222 B2
Elton St 1 NG31 211 A3
Elveley Dr HU10 178 A7
Elvin Cl 3 LN2 201 F6
Elvington Cl 7 LN6 204 B6
Elvington Rd LN6 204 B6
Elwes St DN20 196 C2
Elwyn Pl DN35 192 D2
Ely Cl PE4 220 F3
Ely St Lincoln LN1 201 D4
5 Sleaford NG34 212 C6
Ely Way 5 NG31 210 F5
Embankment Rd 4 PE1 226 A1
Embassy Ctr★ PE25 206 E3
Ember La
Chapel St Leonard PE24 77 B1
Hogsthorpe PE24 90 B8
Embry Rd 22 PE8 172 B1
Emerald Gr 8 HU3 180 A4
Emerson Ave DN7 14 C5
Emery La 15 PE21 208 F4
Emfield Gr DN33 194 E7
Emfield Rd DN33 194 D6
Emily St 8 HU9 181 C7
Eminson Cl 6 DN21 29 C4
Emlyns Gdns 5 PE9 219 C6
Emlyns St 2 PE9 219 C6
Emmanual Rd DN16 185 F6
Emmanuel Ct
3 Scunthorpe DN16 185 C6
Yarborough DN34 191 A6
Emmanuel Dr DN16 185 A3
Emmanuel Rd PE9 219 B7
Emmendingen Ave 2 NG24 104 A6
Emmery Cl 2 DN20 19 D4
Emmetts Gr PE7 230 F2
Emminson Way 1 NG31 210 E8
EMORSGATE PE34 161 E3
Emorsgate PE34 161 E3
Emperor Wy PE2 231 A6
Empingham La PE9 171 A8
Empingham Rd
4 Stamford PE9 219 A5
Tinwell PE9 218 B6
Empire Ct 18 NG34 212 F4
Empringham St 5 HU9 181 D7
Empson Rd PE1 226 F5
Ena St HU3 180 B6
Endcliffe Ave DN17 184 F2
Endeavour Cres 1 HU9 5 D8
Endeavour Ct 5 NG34 212 A3
Endeavour Pk Ind Est PE21 208 A4
Endeavour Way PE20 136 A2
Endell Dr 35 DN21 30 B1
Enderby Cl LN4 203 A2
Enderby Cres DN21 197 E3
Enderby Rd DN17 184 E4
Enderby Rd Inf Sch DN17 184 D4
Endsleigh St 4 HU3 180 A7
Energy Park Way
Grimsby DN31 24 B7
Pyewipe DN37 188 A4
Enfield Ave DN36 195 D5
Enfield Ct PE6 175 B1
Enfield Gdns PE3 225 C4
Enfield Prim Sch DN36 195 D6
Enfield Rd 8 LN11 59 E1
Engaine PE2 230 B5
Engine Bank PE12 157 F2
Engine Dro NG34 134 B4
Engine Dyke PE12 148 B1
Engine La LN11 49 E3
Engine St DN20 196 B3
English Cl HU3 180 E4
English Rd PE6 176 B5
English St
Kingston upon Hull HU3 180 E4
Peterborough PE1 225 E5
Ennerdale Cl
3 Birchwood LN6 200 D1
6 Humberston DN36 192 E1
Ennerdale Rise PE4 221 B2
Enterprise Rd Caistor LN7 33 A4
Mablethorpe/Sutton on Sea LN12 64 A4
Enterprise Way
Grimsby DN32 192 A6
Pinchbeck PE11 214 E8
4 Winterton DN15 8 F5
Ephams La DN41 23 E7
Epperstone Residential Cvn Pk DN36 193 C1
Epsom Cl LN6 204 B8
Epsom Pl DN35 192 F1
Epsom Rd LN6 204 B8
Epsom Wy 17 PE10 213 D3
EPWORTH DN9 27 E7
Epworth Leisure Ctr DN9 27 D6
Epworth Prim Acad DN9 27 D6
Epworth Rd Epworth DN9 28 A8
Hatfield DN7 14 F4
Haxey DN9 27 D3
Owston Ferry DN9 28 A4
Epworth Rd (West) 10 DN7 14 E4
EPWORTH TURBARY DN9 27 C6
Epworth Turbary Nature Reserve★ DN9 27 B6
Epworth View LN1 201 E8
Erebus Cl 7 PE23 101 A8
Eresbie Rd LN11 198 D3
Eresby Ave 13 PE23 87 F1
Eresby Specl Sch The PE23 100 F8
ERMINE LN2 202 B8
Ermine Cl
5 Ancaster NG32 120 A3
Bourne PE10 213 C6
Grantham NG31 211 D5
8 Lincoln LN1 201 E8
Stamford PE9 218 F5
Ermine Cres LN1 67 F6
Ermine Ct 10 LN4 81 A1
Ermine Dr 3 LN5 107 B8
Ermine Prim Acad LN2 202 A8
Ermine Rise PE9 171 B8
Ermine St Ancaster NG32 120 A2
Appleby DN15 9 C1
Winteringham DN15 9 B8
Winterton DN15 9 C6
Ermine Way
Market Deeping PE6 217 E5
Stamford PE9 218 F5
Ernest Terr LN2 234 B4
Eryholme Cres 1 DN15 182 F2
Escart Ave DN32 192 B6
Escombe View LN1 201 D8
Eshings The LN2 68 D7
Esk Cl LN6 204 F4
Eskdale Cl 1 PE4 221 C3
Eskdale Rd NG31 211 A7
Eskdale Way DN37 190 D8
ESKHAM DN36 37 C1
Eskham Cl 1 DN35 192 F3
Eslaforde Gdns 16 NG34 212 F4
ESSENDINE PE9 163 D3
Essendine Rd Ryhall PE9 163 C2
Uffington PE9 172 C8
Essendyke PE3 225 A7
Essex Dr 9 DN15 8 B4
Essex Rd 3 PE9 219 B6
Essex St HU4 179 E3
Essex Way PE10 213 D4
Estate Ave DN20 19 D3
Estate Rd No 1 DN31 188 B2
Estate Rd No 2 DN31 188 B1
Estate Rd No 3 DN31 188 B3
Estate Rd No 4 DN31 188 B3
Estate Rd No 5 DN31 188 B2
Estate Rd No 6 DN31 188 B2
Estate Rd No 7 DN31 188 B1
Estate Rd No 8 DN31 188 B1
Estcourt Prim Sch HU9 181 D8
Estcourt St HU9 181 D8
Estella Way PE11 214 A5
Esther Wy DN33 191 A2
Estuary Way DN31 188 D2
Estwaite Cl LN6 205 B2
Ethel Ct 4 DN15 183 B3
Ethelstone Rd 2 DN34 191 A7
Etherington St DN21 197 D4
Eton Cl LN6 200 D3
Eton Ct DN17 184 F4
Eton Dr DN17 184 F3
Eton Rd
Heighington/Washingborough LN4 203 C1
9 Mablethorpe/Sutton on Sea LN12 64 C2
Eton St Grantham NG31 211 B4
Kingston upon Hull HU3 180 C4
Eton Way PE21 208 B5
ETTON PE6 173 E5
Euclide Rd DN15 8 E4
Eudo Rd PE25 206 D7
Eugate Rd PE6 167 F4
Europa Bsns Pk DN31 188 C2
Europarc Innovation Ctr DN37 24 B6
Europa Way Brigg DN20 196 A4
Immingham DN41 187 B3
Eusden Ct LN4 207 A5
Euston Ave 5 PE11 214 B2
Euston Cl LN6 200 D2
Evans Cl NG23 117 E8
EVEDON NG34 121 F6
Evedon Rd NG34 121 F5
Eve Gdns LN4 203 D1
Evelyn Gr N 1 DN32 192 B6
Evelyn Gr S 3 DN32 192 B6
Evendine Ct DN36 195 E1
Everard Rd PE11 155 C1
Everdon Way PE3 225 C5
Everest Rd DN16 185 C5
Everest Wy PE7 230 F4
EverGn Dr PE7 230 B2
Everingham PE2 229 D5
Everington's La PE25 103 C8
Everthorpe Cl 16 HU15 2 D5
Ever Thorpe Cl 5 HU3 180 C5
Eves Cl 9 PE6 174 E5
Evesham Ave DN34 190 E5
Eve St LN11 198 B6
Evison Cres 2 LN13 75 E3
Evison Ct 12 PE22 113 B1
Evison Way LN11 50 E7
Ewart St LN5 205 D6
EWERBY NG34 122 B6
Ewerby Pond Nature Reserve★ NG34 122 E8
Ewerby Rd NG34 122 A5
EWERBY THORPE NG34 122 D6
Exchange Cl LN6 204 E4
Exchange Pl 5 DN20 196 B3
Exchange Rd LN6 204 E4
Exchange St PE1 226 A2
Exchequergate 5 LN2 234 B3
Exeter Cl 3 Bourne PE10 213 C5
Grantham NG31 210 C5
Heighington/Washingborough LN4 203 E2
1 Market Deeping PE6 217 E4
Exeter Ct 2 Bourne PE10 213 C5
10 Grimsby DN34 190 D4
Exeter Dr 4 Sleaford NG34 212 C6
Spalding PE11 214 E4
Exeter Gdns
10 Bourne PE10 213 C5
Stamford PE9 218 F4
Exeter Rd
Peterborough PE1 225 F6
Scunthorpe DN15 182 F3
8 Wittering PE8 172 B1
Exeter St PE10 213 C5
Exley Sq LN2 202 D6
Exmoor Ave DN15 182 D7
Exmoor Cl LN6 204 D1
Exmoor Rd DN17 184 C8
Exton Cl 6 PE9 218 E5
Eyam Way 3 LN6 204 F1
EYE PE6 175 A1
Eyebury Rd Eye PE6 175 A1
Peterborough PE6 227 A6
Eye CE Prim Sch PE6 175 B1
EYE GREEN PE6 175 B2
Eye Green Ind Est PE6 175 A2
Eye Rd PE1 174 F1
Eyre Ave DN16 185 B5
Eyrescroft PE3 225 A7
Eyrescroft Prim Sch PE3 225 A7
Eyre's La LN6 78 F1

F

Fabian Gr PE2 231 E4
Fagans Way 7 PE25 206 C1
Fainlight Cl 2 PE25 206 D8
Fairburn Cl 9 PE24 90 D7
Fairchild Way PE1 226 A7
Fairfax Cl Boston PE21 208 D7
Gainsborough DN21 197 F2
6 Horncastle LN9 199 D3
2 Toft Newton LN8 56 D5
Fairfax Rd DN31 191 B7
Fairfax St LN5 205 D6
Fairfax Way PE6 217 E3
Fairfield LN4 207 C4
Fairfield Ave
26 Chapel St Leonard PE24 90 D7
Grimsby DN33 194 E7
Fairfield Cl
8 Broughton DN20 19 E3
3 Spalding PE11 214 C6
Fairfield Croft 8 DN9 27 E6
Fairfield Ct 3 DN35 193 A1
Fairfield Dr
29 Barton-upon-Humber DN18 10 F8
39 Messingham DN17 29 D7
Fairfield Ind Est LN11 198 B8
Fairfield Pit Nature Reserve★ DN19 4 D3
Fairfield Prim Sch DN33 194 E8
Fairfield Rd Grimsby DN33 194 E7
Peterborough PE2 231 A8
Scunthorpe DN15 182 C4
Fairfields Holbeach PE12 215 C3
33 Kirton in Lindsey DN21 30 B1
Fairfield St LN2 202 B4
Fairfield View 11 HU15 2 D5
Fairhaven PE7 230 F1
Fair Isle Rise DN40 186 C2
Fairleas LN4 81 E2
Fairmead Way PE3 225 E2
Fairmont Cres DN16 183 B2
Fairmont Rd DN32 192 A7
Fairtree Wlk 24 DN8 15 A8
Fair View Ave DN35 192 E6
Fairview Way PE11 214 C6
Fairway DN37 194 D5
Fairway Ct DN35 193 C1
Fairways PE10 164 A8
Fairways The Kirton PE20 136 C6
Scunthorpe DN15 182 B2
Torksey LN1 65 E5
Fairway The
Kingston upon Hull HU10 178 A8
1 Mablethorpe/Sutton on Sea LN12 64 A4
Fairweather Ct PE1 226 E3
Fakenham Chase PE12 215 E3
Falcon Cl LN6 79 B2
Falcon Ct
9 Grantham NG31 210 E2
Kingston upon Hull HU4 179 D2
Falconers The DN21 30 F2
Falcon Gr 12 DN21 197 F5
Falcon Rd 7 LN4 108 A7
Falcon Way
Hampton Vale PE2 230 C1
13 Sleaford NG34 212 B3
Falcon Wy PE10 213 E3
FALDINGWORTH LN8 56 F3
Faldingworth Cl 8 LN6 204 C7
Faldingworth Com Prim Sch LN8 56 F3
Faldingworth Rd LN8 55 F3
Faldos Way 3 LN12 64 A4
Falkirk Cl 6 PE9 218 E6
Falkland Rd 4 HU9 5 F8
Falklands Cl LN1 201 E8
Falklands Rd PE12 160 D4
Falkland Way DN18 3 F1
Fallodan Rd PE2 229 C3
Fallowfield PE2 229 D5
Fallowfield Rd DN33 194 D7
Fallow Fields 7 PE11 166 C6
Fallow La Foston NG32 118 A2
Nunsthorpe DN33 191 B1
1 Westborough & Dry Doddington NG23 117 F3
Fall's Dro PE6 175 F7
Falls Drove PE6 167 B1
Falsgrave Gr HU5 179 D7
Falstone Ave 12 NG24 104 A3
Fane Cl PE9 219 B7
Fane Rd PE4 221 C1
Fanny Hands La 1 LN8 59 A7
Fannystone Rd DN34 191 B7
Fantail Cl 2 PE11 156 E2
Fantasy Island★ PE25 90 E3
Fantasy World★ DN35 192 F7
Fanthorpe La LN11 198 A7
Faraday Cl PE7 233 D6
Faraday Wlk 9 NG33 151 D7
FAR BANK DN7 14 C8
Far Bank La DN7 14 C8
FARCET PE7 231 C2
Farcet CE Prim Sch PE7 231 C2
Far Comm Rd DN7 15 A3
Fardell Rd DN16 185 D7
Far Dro PE20 124 E2
Farebrother St DN32 191 E6
Far End LN5 94 A2
Far Field Rd 22 DN3 14 A2
FARFORTH LN11 73 D5
Far Holme La 5 NG23 91 A8
Far Hurn Dro LN4 110 B7
Faringdon Rd DN31 189 C2
Far Ings La DN18 3 C1
Far Ings Nature Reserve★ DN18 3 D2
Far Ings Rd DN18 3 D1
Far La Coleby LN5 93 F3
27 Waddington LN5 93 F7
Farlakes Dr 8 PE2 230 F5
Farleigh Fields PE2 229 D6
FARLESTHORPE LN13 76 B1
Farlesthorpe Nature Reserve★ LN13 89 A7
Farlesthorpe Rd
Alford LN13 75 F2
Bilsby LN13 76 A2
Willoughby with Sloothby LN13 89 B8
Farmall Cl 6 DN7 14 D5
Farm Cl 2 Gunness DN15 17 E6
12 Kirk Sandall DN3 14 A1
Farmers Gate PE12 215 B2
Farmhouse Cl 12 NG13 128 A6
Farmhouse Dr 10 PE11 166 C6
Farm House La LN8 45 E4
Farmhouse Mews 11 DN36 195 C6
Farm La 1 DN17 28 D8
Farm View Castor PE5 223 E2
18 Welton LN2 68 D7
Farndale Cres 5 NG31 211 A8
Farndale Way
Grimsby DN31 191 D8
1 Winterton DN15 9 A5
Farnella Cl HU3 180 A5
Far Pasture 2 PE4 220 F5
Farrar Cl 10 NG24 104 B5
Farrier Rd LN6 204 B5
Farriers Ct
Peterborough PE2 230 D7
Scopwick LN4 95 C1
Farriers Fold 18 DN9 27 D2
Farriers Gate 2 NG34 120 F8
Farriers Way Carlby PE9 163 D4
8 Market Rasen LN8 57 E7
2 Tattershall LN4 207 A5
Farrier Way PE11 214 A2
Farringdon Cl 2 PE1 226 D6
Farrington Cres LN6 200 D2
Farrishes La DN18 10 A8
Farrow Ave
3 Hampton Vale PE7 230 B1
Farrow Ave *continued*
Holbeach PE12 215 E1
Yaxley PE7 233 B8
Farrow Rd PE12 168 A4
Farrows Pond 3 DN19 5 A1
Farthingales PE11 214 C6
Farthing Ave DN15 182 E4
Farthings Fold PE10 154 B6
Farthorpe LN9 72 D1
Far Wharf LN6 201 D3
Fauconberg Ave 4 DN33 191 C2
Faulding La DN40 12 F2
Faulding Way DN37 190 C7
Faulkers La PE24 89 E1
Fauna Wy PE7 231 C3
Favell Rd 1 LN4 203 B2
Faversham Ave HU4 179 B6
Fawcett St DN21 197 C5
Fawsley Cl 6 LN2 202 E7
Fawsley Garth PE3 225 C6
FAXFLEET DN14 1 A2
Faxfleet La DN14 1 A3
Fayid La LN4 95 C7
Feale Abbey PE34 161 E1
Featherby Pl 7 LN5 205 E8
Feather La 8 DN19 11 C7
FeatherworksThe★ PE21 209 B3
Felbrigg Wlk PE2 231 F6
Fellands Gate PE22 113 F3
Fellowes Gdns PE2 231 A7
Fellowes Rd PE2 231 A7
Felstead Rd DN34 190 F6
Fenbridge Rd PE4 221 A4
Fenby Cl DN37 190 D6
Fence Bank PE34 161 D1
Fen Cl 24 PE13 170 D1
Fen Ct 1 DN3 14 A1
Fen Dike PE12 159 B3
Fendike Bank PE24 101 F3
Fendike La PE20 135 B5
Fen Dro PE7 233 D1
Fendyke End La PE22 126 E5
Fendyke La PE13 169 F1
Feneley Cl PE6 217 D5
Fen End La PE12 156 F3
Fen Field Mews PE6 217 D5
FENGATE PE1 226 D2
Fengate PE1 226 D1
Fen Gate PE12 157 E2
Fengate Cl 1 PE1 226 B2
Fengate Dro PE12 157 C3
Fengate Mobile Home Pk PE1 226 D1
Fengate Rd
Pinchbeck PE11 214 A8
Walsoken PE14 170 F1
Fengate Trad Est PE1 226 D2
FENHOUSES PE20 135 D7
Fenhouses Dro PE20 135 D8
Fenhouses La PE20 135 C7
Fen La Balderton NG24 104 D2
Bassingham LN5 93 A3
Beesby with Saleby LN13 76 A7
Conisholme LN11 50 C5
Dunston LN4 95 C6
East Keal PE23 100 E5
Grainthorpe LN11 49 F5
Lincoln LN6 205 A1
Long Bennington NG23 117 B6
Mablethorpe & Sutton LN12 64 A1
Maltby le Marsh LN13 63 E1
Mareham le Fen PE22 98 F2
North Somercotes LN11 50 D6
North Thoresby DN36 36 C1
South Carlton LN1 67 C2
Tydd St Giles PE13 169 B5
Fenland Airfield PE12 168 B8
Fenland Ct 19 DN18 3 F1
Fenland Rd
13 Thorne/Moorends DN8 15 B7
Wisbech PE13 170 E1
Fenland Wlk PE12 215 B2
Fennell Rd 5 PE11 156 E8
Fennell Way 3 PE9 218 E4
Fenners Ave DN17 184 E3
Fen Rd
Billinghay LN4 109 F6
Dowsby PE10 143 D4
East Kirkby PE23 99 F4
Frampton PE20 125 B1
Gosberton PE11 144 A4
Heighington LN4 82 A4
Heighington/Washingborough LN4 203 E2
Holbeach PE12 215 D1
Little Hale NG34 133 F8
Metheringham LN4 95 C4
Newton PE13 169 E4
Owmby LN8 55 F6
Pointon & Sempringham NG34 143 D6
Ruskington NG34 108 F2
Stickford PE22 100 C2
Thurlby PE10 154 E1
Timberland LN4 96 C1
Toynton Fen Side PE23 100 F4
Toynton St Peter PE23 101 A4
Wisbech St Mary PE13 177 E2
Fenscape★ PE12 157 B7
Fen Sch NG34 123 C3
Fenside
Halton Holegate PE23 101 C6
Sibsey PE22 113 A2
Toynton All Saints PE23 100 F4
FEN SIDE PE22 100 A1
Fenside Dr 5 PE6 174 E5
Fenside Farm La LN4 95 D6
Fenside Rd Boston PE21 208 C6

Fenside Rd *continued*
Holland Fen with Brothertoft PE21 125 C5
FENTON Fenton LN1 65 E3
Fenton NG23 105 B1
Fenton Cl PE7 230 E1
Fenton Dr PE9 163 E5
Fenton Fields LN1 65 E3
Fenton La DN22 52 C1
Fenton Pl LN2 234 C2
Fenton Rd Fenton NG23 105 B1
Stubton NG23 118 B8
Fenton St DN15 183 B3
Fen View Heighington LN4 81 F4
Peterborough PE2 231 F6
Fenwick Ct
6 Holton le Clay DN36 195 D1
Nunsthorpe DN33 191 B1
Fenwick Rd DN33 191 B2
Fen Wlk DN36 37 C5
Ferens Art Gall★ HU2 180 F6
Ferensway HU2 180 E7
Fernbank 2 DN9 27 D7
Fern Cl
3 Kingston upon Hull HU2 180 F8
Louth LN11 198 C7
Fern Croft 10 DN9 27 E6
Fern Ct HU13 179 A1
Ferndale PE7 233 D6
Ferndale Cl NG33 152 F7
Ferndown 1 DN37 188 A1
Ferndown Dr DN40 186 D4
Fern Dr Market Rasen LN8 57 D8
Pinchbeck PE11 214 C7
Ferneries La 3 DN38 21 B4
Fern Farm La PE34 161 F6
Fern Gr LN3 203 D5
Fernhall Cl 15 DN3 14 A2
Fernhill DN37 190 C7
Fernie Cl 3 PE6 174 E4
Fernland Cl 18 HU15 2 C5
Fernleigh Ave 4 LN4 81 A1
Fernleigh Way PE21 209 B6
Fernwood Mews DN21 197 F2
Ferriby High Rd HU14 3 B5
Ferriby La DN33 191 C2
Ferriby Rd
Barton-upon-Humber DN18 10 E8
Hessle HU13 178 B1
Scunthorpe DN17 184 E5
FERRIBY SLUICE DN18 9 F7
Ferriby Sta HU14 3 A4
Ferries St HU9 181 D7
Ferrous Way LN6 204 C3
Ferry Dr PE6 224 D3
Ferry Hill PE5 224 B1
Ferry La
Holland Fen with Brothertoft PE20 124 D6
Newton PE13 170 B5
North Kyme LN4 109 F2
Skellingthorpe LN6 200 C5
South Kyme LN4 109 F1
Sturton le Steeple DN22 52 D3
Washingborough LN4 203 B2
Winteringham DN15 2 B1
Ferry Mdws Ctry Pk★ PE2 229 D8
Ferry Mdws Sta PE2 229 E7
Ferry Rd Bardney LN3 83 D1
Barrow upon Humber DN19 4 C1
Fiskerton LN3 82 D6
Haxey DN9 27 D1
2 Keadby with Althorpe DN17 17 D4
Kingston upon Hull HU13 178 E1
Langriville PE22 124 D8
Scunthorpe DN15 182 E5
Ferry Rd W DN15 182 A6
Ferryside 2 LN3 82 B6
Ferryside Gdns 3 LN3 82 B6
Ferryview PE2 229 E6
Festival Ave 3 PE25 90 D3
Festival Square PE12 159 C1
Feyzin Dr 40 DN18 10 E8
Ffolkes Dr 12 PE34 161 F3
Field Ave Saxilby LN1 66 D3
6 Tydd St Giles PE13 169 F7
Field Cl 6 Gosberton PE11 145 B6
13 Laceby DN37 23 F1
23 Nettleham LN2 68 D2
14 Ruskington NG34 108 D2
1 Welton LN2 68 D7
Field Dr 4 PE21 136 E8
Fieldfare Cl 8 DN16 185 B2
Fieldfare Croft PE21 208 C6
Fieldfare Dr PE2 231 E6
Field Farm La 3 LN4 95 D4
Field Head 5 DN37 23 E1
Fieldhouse Rd DN36 193 A1
Fielding Way DN21 197 E5
Field La Bardney LN3 83 C5
Eastoft DN17 7 A3
Ewerby & Evedon NG34 122 C6
Friskney PE22 115 A6
Morton DN21 197 A8
2 Normanby by Spital LN8 55 F6
Strubby with Woodthorpe LN13 63 C1
Wroot DN9 26 D5
Field Rd Billinghay LN4 109 E6
Crowle DN17 16 D7
Stainforth DN7 14 C6
Thorne/Moorends DN8 15 A8
Field Reeves Wlk 14 DN9 27 D6
Field Rise PE7 233 D5
Fields Cl 3 DN9 27 D7
Fields End
14 Misterton DN10 39 F5
Ulceby Skitter DN39 12 B2
Fields End Cl 2 PE7 230 D2
Fieldside 6 Blyton DN21 41 C5
11 Crowle DN17 16 D7
Epworth DN9 27 D6
Field Side
Mareham le Fen PE22 98 F4
Thorne DN8 15 A8
Fieldside Cres 1 PE22 99 A4
Fields Rd DN9 27 E2
Field St 6 Boston PE21 209 A5
Kingston upon Hull HU9 181 B7
Field Terr PE7 231 C2
Field The DN32 192 C6
Field View PE22 111 F8
Field Wlk PE1 226 B2
Fife Cl PE9 218 D6
Fifth Ave 19 Brookenby LN8 47 B6
Fixborough Ind Est DN15 8 A1
Grantham NG31 211 F6
Scunthorpe DN17 184 B6
Fifth Dro PE11 144 A4
Fiftyeights Rd DN10 26 B2
Figtree Wlk PE1 226 A7
Fildes St DN31 191 D7
Filey Cl LN6 205 A3
Filey Rd DN32 192 A5
FILLINGHAM DN21 54 F4
Fillingham Cres
Cleethorpes DN35 192 F3
Scunthorpe DN15 182 B3
Fillingham La DN21 53 F3
Finch Cl LN6 204 D8
Finch Dr NG34 212 B3
Finchfield PE1 226 F7
Finchley Ct DN31 191 A8
Finchley Gn PE3 225 E4
Finch Wy LN8 70 D4
Findlay Cres DN36 195 D6
Fingle St 3 DN22 52 B1
Finisterre Ave PE25 206 A6
Finkell St DN10 39 C1
Finkin St NG31 211 A4
Finkle La 11 DN18 3 F1
Finkle St Benington PE22 127 A5
Stainforth DN7 14 C7
Finmere Park PE2 229 C1
Finney Cl LN4 207 D5
Finningley Cl 9 LN6 204 D6
Finningley Rd LN6 204 D6
Finns La NG32 138 C6
Finsbury Dr 3 DN33 191 B2
Finsbury St 13 LN13 75 F2
Fir Ave PE10 213 A5
Firbeck Ave PE25 206 D1
Fir Cl DN16 185 A4
Fircroft NG31 211 C1
Firdale Cl 3 PE6 174 A5
Firebeacon La
Grainthorpe LN11 49 E8
Marshchapel LN11 37 D1
Firecrest PE7 233 AD8
Firethorn Cl 3 HU3 180 D5
Fir Hill Quarry Nature Reserve★ LN11 61 E1
Fir Lane LN7 32 C5
Fir Rd 1 PE9 218 D6
FIRSBY PE23 101 F7
Firsby Cres DN33 191 A2
First Ave Brookenby LN8 47 A6
1 Fixborough Ind Est DN15 7 F1
Grantham NG31 211 E6
Grimsby DN33 191 C4
6 Scampton Airfield LN1 67 E5
Scunthorpe DN17 184 C6
Spalding PE11 214 B4
First Dro Crowland PE6 166 E2
Gosberton PE11 144 C3
Moulton PE12 146 E6
Peterborough PE1 226 D1
Firs The 6 NG34 108 D1
First Holme La 2 NG23 91 A8
First Hurn Dro LN4 110 A6
First La HU10 179 A5
First Marsh Rd PE13 170 C2
Firth Field Rd DN7 14 E4
Firth La DN9 26 D6
Firth Lane DN9 27 C7
Firth Rd LN6 234 A1
Firtree Ave LN6 200 C1
Fir Tree Ave 5 LN5 93 E8
Fir Tree Cl 4 LN2 68 F2
Firtree Dr 6 DN20 20 F7
Fir Tree La NG32 119 F3
Fir Trees The HU10 178 D6
Fish Dock Rd DN31 189 B2
Fishemore Ave HU13 178 F2
Fisher Cl 23 NG23 91 D5
Fishergate PE12 159 B1
Fisherman's Wharf DN31 191 D8
Fishermans Wlk 2 HU3 180 C4
Fisher Pl DN35 192 D7
Fish Groom's La PE11 145 E6
Fishings La DN9 26 A7
FISHLAKE DN7 14 D8
Fishlake Nab DN7 14 C7
Fishmere End Rd
Sutterton PE20 136 A4
Wigtoft PE20 135 F3
Fishmere Gate Rd LN11 51 B1
Fishpond La PE12 215 E2
Fish St 1 HU1 180 F5
FISHTOFT PE21 126 C1
Fishtoft Acad PE21 126 C1
Fishtoft Dro PE22 125 C7
FISHTOFT DROVE PE22 125 D8
Fishtoft Rd PE21 209 B3
Fish Well Cl 3 NG33 151 A8
Fishwick Ave 5 HU13 178 E1
FISKERTON LN3 82 A6
Fiskerton CE Prim Sch LN3 82 B7
Fiskerton Cl 8 DN34 190 F4
Fiskerton Dr LN2 201 F8
Fiskerton Rd
Cherry Willingham LN3 203 C4
Cherry Willingham/Reepham LN3 82 A8
Fiskerton Rd E LN3 203 E4
Fiskerton Way 2 DN31 188 A3
Fitties La 2 DN36 37 C5
FITTON END PE13 169 F3
Fitton End Rd PE13 169 F3
Fitzgerald Ct 3 LN4 207 A6
Fitzjames Cl 2 PE23 101 A8
Fitzwilliam Hospl PE6 224 E2
Fitzwilliam Mews DN35 192 E2
Fitzwilliam Pl 6 LN4 109 F5
Fitzwilliam Rd PE9 219 A7
Fitzwilliam St
10 Mablethorpe/Sutton on Sea LN12 64 B4
Peterborough PE1 226 A3
Five Arches PE2 229 C6
Five Bell La PE20 135 C4
Five House La
Frampton PE20 136 C8
Wyberton PE21 208 B1
Five La Ends NG23 79 C8
Five Mile La Fiskerton LN3 83 B6
Washingborough LN4 82 B5
Five Oaks NG33 141 C7
Flag Bsns Exchange PE1 226 E3
Flag Fen Bronze Age Mus★ PE6 227 B3
Flag Fen Rd PE1 226 C4
Flag La PE12 168 B7
Flamborough Cl
Peterborough PE2 225 E1
6 Skegness PE25 206 A6
Flaminian Way 8 NG32 120 A2
Flarepath The DN20 21 A8
Flavian Rd LN2 202 C8
Flaxengate 4 LN2 234 B2
Flaxland PE3 225 A6
Flaxley La NG24 104 A2
Flaxley Rd
Peterborough PE7 231 A4
St Giles LN2 202 E6
Flaxmill La 6 PE11 145 C1
Flaxwell Way 12 NG34 121 B7
FLEDBOROUGH NG22 78 A7
FLEET PE12 159 C6
Fleet Cl HU13 178 C3
Fleetgate 8 DN18 3 E1
FLEET HARGATE PE12 159 C7
Fleet Rd Fleet PE12 159 B7
Holbeach PE12 215 F2
Fleet Road Ind Est PE12 159 A8
Fleets La LN1 54 A1
Fleets Rd LN1 66 D7
Fleet St Holbeach PE12 215 E2
Lincoln LN1 201 C4
Fleetway DN36 37 A3
Fleet Way PE2 231 B6
Fleetwood Cl 2 DN33 194 E7
Fleetwood Ct LE15 162 A8
Fleet Wood La Prim Sch PE12 159 B6
Fleming Ave NG13 128 B6
Fleming Cl PE7 233 D6
Fleming Ct 1 Boston PE21 208 F1
3 Woodston PE2 230 D8
Fleming Dr 10 NG24 104 A6
Fleming Rd PE11 214 E8
Fleming Wlk HU4 179 D2
Flemish Cres HU3 179 F5
Fletcher Cl
Kingston upon Hull HU13 178 E2
3 Scunthorpe DN15 182 C6
Fletcher Rd DN34 190 F7
Fletcher St NG31 211 A3
Fletcher Wy PE4 221 E2
Fletton Ave PE2 231 A8
Fletton Fields PE2 231 A7
Fletton Parkway PE2 229 F2
Flinders Cl 5 LN4 95 C4
Flinders Dale 16 PE23 101 A8
Flinders Dr PE7 231 A5
Flinders Rd 13 PE11 134 E2
Flinders Way LN3 203 B6
Flinders Wlk PE11 214 C7
Flint Cl PE9 163 D1
Flint Gate 23 PE12 160 E4
Flintham Cl 2 LN4 95 C4
Flint House Rd PE12 147 C3
Flinton St HU3 180 B3
FLIXBOROUGH DN15 8 B1
Flixborough Rd DN15 8 B4
FLIXBOROUGH STATHER DN15 8 A1
Flood Rd The DN21 197 B3
Flora Cl PE7 231 D3
Flore Cl PE3 225 C5
Florence Ave HU13 178 F1
Florence Rd PE7 233 F2
Florence St Grimsby DN32 191 E5
Lincoln LN2 202 B3
Florence Way 4 PE6 217 C5
Florence Wright Ave 6 LN11 198 D4
Floriade Cl 4 PE11 214 B2
Florins Fold NG34 132 F3
Floss La DN22 65 B6
Flottergate Mall DN31 191 D7
Flour Sq DN31 189 A1
Flowerdown Ave 5 NG34 120 D8
Foal Plats La LN13 90 A8
FOCKERBY DN17 7 E5
Fodder Dike Bank
Eastville PE22 114 C7
Midville PE22 113 E7
FOLD HILL PE22 115 A6
Fold Hill Rd PE22 114 A2
Fold La Moulton PE12 157 F7
5 Tydd St Giles PE13 169 F7
Folds La 2 PE12 216 B4
Folgate La PE14 170 F6
FOLKINGHAM NG34 142 C8
Folkingham Cl 11 LN6 204 D8
Folkingham Rd
Billingborough NG34 133 A1
1 Morton PE10 154 C7
Pickworth NG34 142 A8
FOLKSWORTH PE7 232 D1
Folksworth Rd PE7 232 E1
Folly Cl PE7 233 C5
Folly La
Branston & Mere LN4 81 C2
Hough-on-the-Hill NG32 118 F5
North Kelsey LN7 32 C5
North Scarle NG23 91 D8
West Fen PE22 99 E1
Folly's Dro PE13 177 F3
Fontwell Cres 9 LN6 205 A5
Fontwell Gdns 2 PE9 219 B5
Fontwell Park Dr PE10 213 B3
Foote's Dro PE12 167 C8
Forbes Dr PE2 231 A6
Forbes Rd PE21 209 C4
Ford Cl PE7 233 E6
Forder Wy PE7 230 E3
Fordham Dr LN1 201 C7
FORDINGTON LN13 88 C6
Fordington La PE23 88 A5
Ford La 8 Hibaldstow DN20 30 F5
Morton PE10 154 C6
Ford's Ave 17 DN41 23 F5
Ford Way Asterby LN11 72 D6
Horncastle LN9 85 F5
Low Toynton LN9 199 E7
Foredyke Prim Sch HU9 5 D8
Fore La PE20 135 A5
Foreman Way 1 PE6 166 E1
Forest Ave 3 PE10 213 B5
Forest CE Prim Sch PE7 231 C2
Forest Dale PE21 208 F7
Forest Dro PE6 166 C2
Foresters Ct Galleries★ PE20 135 B7
Forester Way HU4 179 D3
Forest Gdns 5 PE9 218 D7
Forest Pines La 11 LN10 97 C5
Forest Way 7 DN36 36 D8
Forest Wy DN36 193 B1
Forge Cl Freiston PE22 126 C4
South Kelsey LN7 32 A1
Forge Cres
3 Pinchbeck PE11 156 E8
Ulceby DN39 12 A1
Forge Ct 12 PE6 217 A6
Forge Dr 10 DN9 27 D7
Forge End PE7 229 A4
Forge La LN8 56 F8
Forge Way Hartsholme LN6 204 C3
Holton le Clay DN36 195 C3
Forkedale DN18 10 E8
Forlander Pl LN11 198 D6
Forli Strada Haddon PE7 232 E7
Orton Southgate PE2 229 E1
Forman's La NG34 109 B1
Formby Cl NG31 211 C7
Forrest Dr 5 PE7 230 F5
Forrester St 1 DN20 196 B3
Forrington Pl LN1 66 E2
Forstedd Hill NG33 153 B5
Forster St DN21 197 C5
Forsyth Cres 6 PE25 206 C2
Forsythia Ave 25 DN41 23 F5
Forsythia Cl 5 LN4 81 D2
Forsythia Dr DN33 191 C2
Fortescue Cl 1 LN4 207 A5
Fortuna Dr 1 PE2 231 D4
Fortuna Sch LN6 204 B7
Fortuna Way DN37 190 C7
Forty Acre HU10 178 F7
Forty Acre Rd PE1 226 D2
Forty Foot La
Humberside Airport DN39 21 F6
Old Leake PE22 113 D3
Forty Stps HU10 178 F7
Forum The LN6 204 F3
Forum Way 7 NG34 212 F3
FOSDYKE PE20 146 D8
FOSDYKE BRIDGE PE12 146 E7
Foss Bank LN1 201 D3
Fossdyke Gdns 18 LN1 66 D2
Fosse Cl 8 PE6 164 E5
Fosse Ct 5 LN4 81 A1
Fosse Dr LN6 205 A3
Fosse La Thistleton LE15 151 B1
Thorpe on the Hill LN6 92 E7
Fosseway 4 DN21 197 F5
Fosse Way Acad LN6 204 F2
Foss St LN1 201 D3
Foster Cl 2 LN4 96 C1
Foster Rd
21 Collingham NG23 91 D5
7 Thorne/Moorends DN8 15 A8
Woodston PE2 230 D8
Fosters Cl 3 LN5 107 A8
Foster's Dro PE10 155 A3
Foster's Gdns 1 LN4 82 B1
Foster St 3 Boston PE21 209 A5
Heckington NG34 122 E3
Lincoln LN5 201 E1
FOSTON NG32 117 F2
Foston by Pass NG32 117 F1
Foston Cres LN6 204 F7
Foston La NG32 128 F7
Foston Rd NG31 210 E3
FOTHERBY LN11 49 A3
Fotherby Rd DN17 184 F4
Fotherby St 3 DN31 189 A1
Fothergill Dr 17 DN3 14 A2
FOUL ANCHOR PE13 170 D8
Foundary Sh Ctr The DN15 183 B4
Foundry La
11 Spalding PE11 214 D4
12 Thorne/Moorends DN8 15 A8
Foundry Rd Bucknall LN10 84 B3
Ryhall PE9 163 C2
Stamford PE9 219 A5
Foundry St LN9 199 C4
Fountain Cl
Kingston upon Hull HU13 178 C3
5 Waltham DN37 194 C5
Fountain Hill DN10 39 E3
Fountain Hill Rd DN10 39 E4
Fountain La 13 PE21 208 F5
Fountain Pl 10 PE21 208 F5
Fountains Ave DN37 188 A1
Fountains Pl PE6 175 B1
Fountain St 22 Caistor LN7 33 B4
Kingston upon Hull HU3 180 D6
Four Acre Cl HU10 178 C6
Four Chimneys Cres
Hampton Hargate PE7 230 C2
Yaxley PE7 233 B8
Fourfields CE Sch The PE20 136 A2
Fourfields Com Prim Sch PE7 233 E6
FOUR GOTES PE13 170 B7
Fourth Ave
2 Fixborough Ind Est DN15 8 A1
Grantham NG31 211 F6
3 Scampton Airfield LN1 67 E5
1 Scunthorpe DN17 184 C6
Fourth Dro Gosberton PE11 144 B4
Peterborough PE1 226 F3
Fourways 6 DN36 36 D4
Fowler Cl LN11 198 D4
Fowler Ct 32 DN15 9 A5
Fowler Rd DN16 185 B8
Foxby Hill DN21 197 E2
Foxby La DN21 197 F2
Foxby Warren DN21 197 E2
Fox Cl Boston PE21 208 C6
Little Coates DN34 190 F6
Fox Covert
2 Aubourn Haddington & South Hykeham LN6 93 A8
19 Hibaldstow DN20 30 F5
Lincoln LN6 204 A1
North Hykeham LN6 204 B1
Sudbrooke LN2 69 A2
Fox Covert La DN10 40 A4
Foxcovert Rd PE6 220 E8
Fox Ct 1 Crowle DN17 16 D8
6 Owmby LN8 55 F6
Foxdale PE1 225 F7
Fox Dale PE9 218 F6
Foxe End 19 LN12 64 B3
Foxendale Hill LN9 72 F1
Foxes Low Rd PE12 215 F2
Foxfield Cl LN6 200 A5
Foxglove Cl
Brigg DN20 196 B4
1 Spilsby PE23 101 A8
Foxglove Ct PE11 214 B6
Foxglove Gdns DN34 190 F6
Foxglove Rd
16 Market Rasen LN8 57 D8
1 Stamford PE9 218 C7
Foxgloves PE6 217 D6
Foxglove Way 5 LN5 205 C2
Fox Headings PE12 158 C1
Foxhill DN37 190 C7
Foxhill Rd DN8 15 B7
Foxhills Ind Pk DN15 182 F7
Foxhills Rd DN15 182 E5
Foxhole La PE22 126 D3
Fox Hollow LN6 92 D5
Foxley Cl PE4 221 A4
Foxley Ct 1 PE10 213 C7
Fox St DN15 182 F3
Foxtail Cl 6 DN33 194 D8
Foxton Wy DN20 196 D5
Foyle Cl LN5 205 D2
Fracknal's Row 3 PE21 208 E6
Framlingham Rd PE7 231 F5
FRAMPTON PE20 136 F6
Frampton Bank PE20 136 B8
Frampton La PE20 124 E2
Frampton Marsh Nature Reserve★ PE20 137 D5
Frampton Pl PE21 208 D4
Frampton Roads PE20 136 F6
Frances Askew Prim Sch HU4 179 F4
Frances Ct 3 DN37 194 C5
Frances Olive Anderson CE Prim Sch DN21 53 A5
Frances St DN15 183 A3
Francis Bernard Cl 4 PE21 208 D3

Francis Chichester Wlk DN21 197 F3
Francis Gdns PE1 225 F8
Francis La LN9 199 C4
Francis St
Kingston upon Hull HU2 180 F7
Lincoln LN1 234 B4
14 Spalding PE11 214 D4
Francklin Wlk 5 PE12 158 B6
Frankland Cl 1 DN20 196 F6
Frankland Pl DN35 192 D7
Franklin Ave PE25 206 D1
Franklin Cl Boston PE21 208 C6
7 Metheringham LN4 95 C4
Franklin Coll DN34 191 B5
Franklin Cres
Peterborough PE1 226 E6
Scunthorpe DN16 185 E6
1 Sleaford NG34 212 D5
Franklin Dr PE11 214 B2
Franklin Gdns 11 PE23 101 A8
Franklin Mews 17 DN18 3 F1
Franklin Rd 3 DN21 29 C4
Franklin St HU9 181 C8
Franklin Way
Humberside Airport DN39 21 F5
North Greetwell LN3 203 B6
Franklin Wy 20 DN19 11 D8
Frank Perkins Parkway PE1 226 E6
Frank Perkins Way PE1 226 D3
Franks Cl 2 PE20 136 D5
Franks La PE13 169 F5
Frank Swaby Ct LN5 205 E6
Frank Walsham Ct DN32 192 A8
Frank Whittle Cl 1 NG34 120 E8
Frank Wright Ct 4 LN2 202 C7
Fraserburgh Way 2 PE2 229 D4
Fraser Cl PE6 217 D5
Fraser St 2 DN32 191 F7
Frederica Rd 12 PE25 103 E4
Frederick Dr PE3 225 C8
Frederick Gough Sch DN16 185 C4
Frederick St
Cleethorpes DN35 192 E6
Grimsby DN31 191 D8
Lincoln LN2 202 C3
Frederick Ward Way DN31 191 D7
Freehold St HU3 180 D7
Freeman Ave 4 HU15 2 C5
Freeman Cl 10 PE8 172 B1
Freeman Ct DN36 195 E2
Freeman Rd LN6 204 D3
Freemans La 6 DN20 10 C2
Freeman's La DN22 52 A2
Freeman St DN32 189 B1
Freeman Way 9 DN32 189 B1
Freeport Wharf DN31 191 E8
Freer Gdns LN11 198 E6
Freeschool La LN2 234 B2
Freesia Way PE7 233 F6
Freeston St DN35 192 B8
Freetown Way HU2 180 E7
Freightliner Rd
Kingston upon Hull HU3 179 F2
Kingston upon Hull HU3 180 A3
FREISTON PE22 126 D2
Freiston Ctr for Environmental Ed★ PE22 126 D3
Freiston Rd PE21 209 B5
FREISTON SHORE PE22 126 F1
French Dro PE6 175 E7
French's Rd PE14 170 F8
Fresh Fields 14 HU15 2 C5
Freshney Bog Nature Reserve★ DN37 190 E7
Freshney Dr 1 DN31 191 C8
Freshney Pl Sh Ctr DN32 191 D7
Freshney Way PE21 208 B3
Freshwater Rd PE7 230 B1
Freston PE4 221 D2
Freyja Croft DN33 191 B2
Friars Gate PE21 208 E4
Friars La LN2 234 B2
Friars Rd DN17 184 E6
Friar Way PE21 208 F6
Friary Rd 1 NG24 104 A4
FRIESTHORPE LN3 57 A2
Friest La 11 PE20 135 A4
FRIESTON NG32 119 B6
Frieston Heath La NG32 119 D6
Frieston Rd NG32 119 B6
Frieston Shore Nature Reserve★ PE22 127 A1
Frinkley La
Honington NG32 119 B2
Hougham NG32 118 D2
Frisby Cl PE6 164 D4
FRISKNEY PE22 115 A6
Friskney All Saints CE (Aided) Prim Sch PE22 115 A6
Friskney Decoy Wood Nature Reserve★ PE22 115 A8
FRISKNEY EAUDYKE PE22 115 B7
FRITH BANK PE21 125 D5
Frith Bank PE22 125 D6
Friths La PE20 125 B1
FRITHVILLE PE22 112 D1
Frithville Prim Sch PE22 112 D1
Frithville Rd PE22 113 A1
Frobisher Ave DN32 192 B6
FRODINGHAM DN16 183 C2
Frodingham Footpath 2 DN15 183 B3
Frodingham Inf Sch DN16 183 B2
Frodingham Rd DN15 183 A4
Frodingham S Rd DN16 183 E2
Frodsham St 8 HU9 5 D8
FROGNALL PE6 165 D1
Frognall PE6 165 D1
Frog's Abbey Gate PE12 158 E4
Frome Cl LN6 204 D5
Front Rd
Tydd St Mary PE13 160 D1
Wisbech St Mary PE13 177 D6
Front St Alkborough DN15 8 C8
Barnby in the Willows NG24 104 F3
Dunston LN4 95 C5
East Stockwith DN21 40 B5
Elsham DN20 20 F7
Gainsborough DN21 197 B7
4 Grasby DN38 32 E7
Normanby by Spital LN8 55 E7
South Clifton NG23 78 C5
Stainton le Vale LN8 46 D5
Tealby LN8 46 C1
Ulceby DN39 12 A1
Frost Cl DN15 2 A1
Frostley Gate PE12 158 F3
Frusher Ave DN33 191 C3
Fryston 28 HU15 2 C6
Fuchsia Croft 2 DN15 182 F2
Fuchsia Dr HU4 179 B2
FULBECK NG32 106 C1
Fulbeck Rd DN16 185 C6
Fulbridge Acad PE1 225 F7
Fulbridge Rd PE4 221 A3
Fulford Cl NG31 211 D8
Fulford Cres
Kingston upon Hull HU10 179 A8
3 New Holland DN19 4 E2
Fulford Way PE25 206 C6
Fulham Pk 1 DN33 191 B2
Fulham Rd PE3 225 E4
Fuller St DN35 192 D8
FULLETBY LN9 86 B8
Fulletby Rd LN9 73 B2
Fulletby Road LN9 199 F7
Fulmar Dr LN11 198 C8
Fulmar Rd LN6 204 D8
Fulmen Cl LN1 201 C7
FULNETBY LN8 69 F6
Fulnetby La LN3 69 E7
FULNEY PE11 157 B6
Fulney Dro PE12 157 B3
Fulney La PE12 157 B6
FULSTOW LN11 49 B8
Fulstow Gr 5 DN33 191 B3
Fulstow Prim Sch LN11 49 B8
Fulstow Rd LN2 202 B8
Fundrey Rd PE13 170 E1
Fun Farm★ PE12 157 D7
Furlongs La Belchford LN9 73 B1
Old Leake PE22 114 A1
Furlongs Rd LN12 77 A8
Furlongs The 17 LN8 57 D8
Furlong Wy NG34 212 B7
Furnace Cl Hartsholme LN6 204 C3
Hartsholme LN6 204 C3
Furndown Ct LN6 204 B7
Furniss Ct 2 DN18 10 E8
Furrow Cl 10 LN2 68 D6
Furrows The PE21 209 C3
Further Old Gate PE12 158 D5
Fury Ave LN11 62 B6
Furze Hill Nature Reserve★ PE23 87 A3
Furze Hills LN9 85 D7
Furze La LN11 62 A5
Furze Ride PE1 226 B8
Fusilier Wy DN21 30 C1
Fussey Gdns DN20 10 C1
Fydell Cres PE21 208 E4
Fydell Ct PE21 208 E6
Fydell St PE21 208 E5
Fyson Way PE20 136 C6

G

Gables The PE10 213 C2
Gabriel Cres LN2 202 E6
Gadd's La PE13 170 A1
Gadwall Wy DN16 185 F5
Gage Ct 4 LN2 202 D6
Gainas Ave DN21 197 C6
GAINSBOROUGH DN21 197 B4
Gainsborough Acad The DN21 197 F6
Gainsborough Central Sta DN21 197 E4
Gainsborough Coll DN21 197 C5
Gainsborough Dr 7 NG24 104 A6
Gainsborough Gdns 2 LN6 205 B7
Gainsborough La DN20 30 F8
Gainsborough Lea Rd Sta DN21 197 D1
Gainsborough Leisure Ctr DN21 197 D6
Gainsborough Model Railway★ 15 DN21 197 D3
Gainsborough Old Hall★ DN21 197 C5
Gainsborough Rd
Blyton DN21 41 B4
Bole DN22 52 A6
Girton NG23 78 C2
Gainsborough Rd *continued*
Hemswell Cliff DN21 54 F8
32 Kirton in Lindsey DN21 30 B1
Kirton in Lindsey DN21 42 D8
Little Casterton PE9 218 F7
Middle Rasen LN8 57 B7
Saundby DN22 52 B7
Saxilby with Ingleby LN1 66 D2
Scotter DN21 29 B3
Sturton le Steeple DN22 52 B3
West Rasen LN8 57 A7
Willingham DN21 53 E4
6 Winthorpe NG24 104 B7
Wiseton DN10 39 A1
Yawthorpe DN21 43 B2
Gainsthorpe Rd E DN21 30 D4
Gainsthorpe Rd W DN21 30 C4
Galba Rd LN7 33 A4
Gallagher Ret Pk DN15 182 A3
Gallamore Ct 5 LN8 57 C8
Gallamore La
Market Rasen LN8 57 D8
6 Middle Rasen LN8 57 C8
Gallamore Lane Ind Est LN8 57 D8
Galland Rd 34 HU15 2 D5
Gallands Cl 19 HU14 3 B7
Galletly Cl PE10 213 D6
Galley Ct HU9 181 C6
GALLEY HILL LN13 75 E6
Gallions Cl 2 PE4 221 B1
Galway Cl 2 PE11 214 A5
Gamage Cl 3 NG24 104 C2
Gamlyn Cl 1 PE11 214 D2
Gannet Ct 3 NG31 210 E2
Gannocks Cl PE2 229 F5
Gannocks The PE2 229 F5
Ganton Way
Harrowby Est NG31 211 E7
Kingston upon Hull HU10 178 F8
Garbutt Pl DN35 193 A4
Garcia Rd DN36 36 C4
Garden Cl PE9 218 E6
Garden Dr DN36 195 C7
Garden End Rd PE1 226 B6
Gardeners Wlk PE21 208 D2
Gardenfield LN6 200 B3
Gardenia Dr DN17 184 F1
Garden St 5 Brigg DN20 196 C3
Grimsby DN31 191 D7
Gardens The
3 Crowland PE6 166 F1
Horncastle LN9 199 C3
Gardiner Ave 7 NG24 104 C1
Garfield Cl LN1 201 D8
Garfield St DN21 197 C5
Garfield View LN1 201 D8
Garfit's La PE21 208 D1
Garford Ct PE6 173 C7
Garford La 8 PE9 171 D3
Garganey Wk DN16 185 F5
Garibaldi St 6 DN32 189 B1
Garmston St 8 LN1 234 B3
Garner's La PE34 161 A4
Garner St DN32 191 E6
Garnet Gr 6 HU3 180 A4
Garnett St DN35 192 D8
GARNSGATE PE12 159 E5
Garnsgate Rd PE12 216 A5
Garratt Cl LN4 81 E4
Garratt Rd 7 PE9 219 B4
Garrick Cl LN5 205 C3
Garrick La DN36 195 C7
Garrick Wlk PE2 231 B7
Garrison Rd HU9 181 C6
Garth La DN31 191 D8
GARTHORPE
Garthorpe LE14 150 A4
Garthorpe and Fockerby DN17 7 F6
Garthorpe Rd DN17 7 C4
Garth Sch The PE11 214 E5
Garth The HU10 179 A4
Garthway 7 DN36 195 D2
Garton Gr
3 Grimsby DN32 192 A5
3 Kingston upon Hull HU5 179 C7
Garton St PE1 226 A5
Gascoigne 8 PE4 220 E5
Gashouse La 3 DN9 28 A3
Gas House La 16 PE12 160 E4
Gas La
7 Navenby/Wellingore LN5 107 A8
Stamford PE9 219 C5
5 Thorney PE6 176 A3
Gas St 3 Horncastle LN9 199 C3
19 Stamford PE9 219 C5
GATE BURTON DN21 53 B2
Gated Rd PE22 99 C7
Gatehouse Rd Goxhill DN19 11 F7
Moortown LN7 32 E1
Gate La DN33 191 D1
Gateroom La PE22 114 E3
Gate Way DN31 188 E2
Gateway The 4 NG24 104 A4
Gatewood La DN7 14 E1
Gatherums The DN35 192 E5
Gatram Rd PE24 90 D6
Gaunt Cl 5 PE12 157 B6
Gauntlet Dro PE20 134 F6
Gauntlet Rd
3 Bicker PE20 135 A4
Grimoldby LN11 62 B6
Gaunt St LN5 234 A1
GAUTBY LN8 84 B7
Gautby Lane LN10 84 A6
Gautby Rd LN8 83 F7
Gautry La DN9 28 B4
Gavel St PE7 233 C8
Gayle Rd LN4 110 E8
Gaysfield Rd 6 PE21 126 C1
Gayton Cl Lincoln LN2 202 A7
Skegness PE25 206 C2
Gayton Ct PE3 225 C5
GAYTON ENGINE LN12 63 C6
GAYTON LE MARSH LN13 62 F3
GAYTON LE WOLD LN11 59 E4
Gayton Rd DN35 193 A3
Gazeley Gdns PE7 231 B2
Geddington Rd PE2 230 E8
GEDNEY PE12 159 D7
GEDNEY BROADGATE PE12 159 D5
Gedney Church End Prim Sch PE12 159 D7
Gedney Cl 13 Bicker PE20 135 A4
Grimsby DN37 190 C8
GEDNEY DROVE END PE12 149 A4
Gedney Drove End Cty Prim Sch PE12 148 F3
GEDNEY DYKE PE12 148 B1
GEDNEY HILL PE12 168 D2
Gedney Hill CE VC Prim Sch The PE12 168 D2
Gedney Hill Gate PE12 168 F7
Gedney Rd PE12 216 A6
Gee St HU3 180 C5
GEESTON PE9 171 A2
Geeston Rd PE9 171 A2
Geipel Cl DN37 194 F5
Gelder Beck Rd DN17 29 D6
Gelder's La PE12 158 A1
GELSTON NG32 118 F4
Gelston Rd NG32 119 A4
Gemsbok Cl 3 HU4 179 D2
Genesis Way
Great Coates DN37 24 B6
Pyewipe DN37 188 A3
Geneva Ave LN2 202 B6
Geneva St PE1 226 A3
Geoff Moulder Leisure Complex★ PE21 209 A4
George Alcock Wy PE7 231 D2
George Ave Gedney PE12 148 F4
4 Keadby DN17 17 D5
Skegness PE25 206 B3
George Butler Cl 23 DN37 23 F1
George Janney Ct 24 DN32 189 C1
George Matthews Gdns 27 PE6 175 A1
George Mews 2 LN7 33 B4
George Sh Ctr The NG31 211 A4
George St
2 Barton-upon-Humber DN18 10 F8
20 Beacon Hill NG24 104 A5
5 Boston PE21 208 E4
Bourne PE10 213 D5
Broughton DN20 19 D3
Cleethorpes DN35 192 F5
Gainsborough DN21 197 B6
Grantham NG31 211 B4
Grimsby DN31 191 D7
Helpringham NG34 133 D7
5 Keadby DN17 17 D5
Kingston upon Hull HU1 180 F6
11 Kirton in Lindsey DN21 30 B1
Lincoln LN5 234 C1
Louth LN11 198 B5
Mablethorpe/Sutton on Sea LN12 64 B3
7 Market Rasen LN8 57 D8
Peterborough PE2 230 F8
Scunthorpe DN15 183 A4
Sleaford NG34 212 C3
Georgette Gdns 7 PE11 214 B5
George Yd 5 HU1 181 A6
Georgian Ct
Peterborough PE3 225 E1
6 Spalding PE11 214 D3
Georgina Ct 27 DN18 10 E8
Gerald's Cl LN2 202 B5
Gerbera Dr 15 NG24 104 B5
German's La PE34 161 D2
Gerrard Mews LN4 203 D1
Gershwin Ave HU4 179 B4
Gershwin La PE11 214 A1
Gertrude St DN32 191 E5
Gervase St DN15 183 A3
Gibbeson St 6 LN5 205 E8
Gibbet La LN8 57 A5
Gibbon La DN8 14 F7
Gibbs Cl 8 PE6 164 F3
Giblin Cotts DN15 182 E5
Gibraltar Hill LN1 234 A3
Gibraltar La 2 DN37 23 F1
Gibraltar Point National Nature Reserve★ PE24 103 E2
Gibraltar Point Visitor Ctr★ PE24 116 D4
Gibraltar Rd Croft PE24 103 D1
5 Hemswell Cliff DN21 55 A8
Mablethorpe/Sutton on Sea LN12 64 B4
Seacroft PE24 116 D5
Gibson Cl Branston LN4 81 E2
1 Sleaford NG34 212 B6
Gibson Cres 9 NG24 104 B2
Gibson Gn LN6 92 E5
Gibson La HU14 2 E4
Gibson La N 6 HU14 2 F5
Gibson Pl 5 PE25 206 A5
Gibson Rd 2 DN7 26 A8
Gibsons Gdn 2 LN11 50 F7
Giddings Cl PE2 229 F4
Giddon's Dro PE6 174 A7
Gilbert Dr PE21 208 A1
Gilberts Gr 4 PE25 206 D8
Gilbert Sutcliffe Ct DN35 192 A2
Gilbert Wy 28 NG24 104 C1
Gilbey Rd DN31 188 D1
Gildale PE4 221 B4
Gildenburgh Ave PE1 226 D5
Gilder Way PE21 209 F2
Gildesburgh Rd LN4 203 B1
Giles Acad The 14 PE22 114 A1
Giles Cl 12 PE22 114 A1
Giles Rd PE11 214 C2
Giles St DN35 192 E6
Gillatts Cl 1 DN20 196 F7
Gill Ct DN33 191 B2
Gillett St HU3 180 B4
Gilliatt St DN15 183 A4
Gilmores La 18 NG24 104 C1
Gilmorton Dr PE1 226 D7
Gilpin Cl PE10 213 E2
Gilpin St PE1 225 E6
Gilstrap Cl 3 NG24 104 B4
Gimmel's Gate PE12 216 C1
GIPSEY BRIDGE PE22 124 F8
Gipsey Bridge Prim Sch PE22 125 A8
Gipsy Dro Friskney PE22 114 D7
Langriville PE22 124 F8
Gipsy La Gedney PE12 216 A8
Holton le Moor LN7 32 C1
Osgodby LN8 45 D3
Owersby LN7 44 F8
Owston Ferry DN9 40 C8
South Kelsey LN7 32 C1
Swineshead PE20 124 A1
Tydd St Mary PE13 160 A2
Wrangle PE22 114 D2
GIPSYVILLE HU4 179 E3
Girdlestone Wlk 2 PE6 166 F1
Girls School La PE22 126 E3
GIRSBY LN8 59 C6
Girsby La LN8 59 B6
GIRTON NG23 78 C1
Girton Cl 3 DN16 185 B4
Girton La NG23 78 D1
Girton Rd DN37 190 F6
Girton Way 3 PE9 219 A7
Gisburn Rd HU13 178 F2
Glade The
8 Mablethorpe/Sutton on Sea LN12 77 A7
New Waltham DN36 195 E7
Gladiator Rd LN11 62 B6
Gladstone Cotts DN21 197 B8
Gladstone Dr 1 DN16 183 C1
Gladstone Prim Sch PE1 225 F5
Gladstone St Bourne PE10 213 C6
Gainsborough DN21 197 C5
Kingston upon Hull HU3 180 C6
Peterborough PE1 225 F3
Gladstone Terr 3 NG31 211 A5
Glaisdale Gdns NG31 211 B8
Glaisdale Gr HU9 181 F8
Glaisdale Rd 2 DN16 185 D5
Glamis Gdns PE3 225 B2
Glamis Pl LN11 198 B6
Glamis Rd HU13 178 F2
Glanford Gr 12 DN19 11 D8
Glanford Pk (Scunthorpe United FC) DN15 182 A2
Glanford Rd Brigg DN20 196 D3
Scunthorpe DN17 184 F3
Glanford Way DN15 182 B3
Glanville Ave DN17 184 F8
Glanville Cres 2 DN17 184 F8
Glasgow St HU3 180 A5
Glastonbury Cl 20 PE6 175 A1
Glatton Dr PE2 231 D6
Gleanings The 5 LN5 107 B8
Glebe Ave PE2 229 E4
Glebe Cl
Burton upon Stather DN15 8 A5
3 Donington on Bain LN11 59 E1
Gorefield PE13 169 E3
Holton le Clay DN36 195 C3
14 Humberston DN36 36 C8
5 Ingham LN1 54 F2
Scopwick LN4 95 C1
5 Sibsey PE22 113 B1
1 Skegness PE25 206 A7
Sleaford NG34 212 A2
2 Spalding PE11 214 A4
Glebe Ct PE2 231 B8
Glebe End LN4 81 A4
Glebe Gdns 2 PE6 175 B8
Glebe Pk 2 NG24 104 B3
Glebe Rd Brigg DN20 196 C4
Cleethorpes DN35 192 E6
Grimsby DN33 191 E1
Humberston DN36 36 C7
Peterborough PE2 231 A8
Scunthorpe DN15 183 B4
Thorne/Moorends DN8 15 B8
Wymondham LE14 150 B1
Glebe Ret Pk DN15 183 B4
Glebe The
Sturton by Stow LN1 66 D8
Upton DN21 53 D5
Glebe View 1 PE6 217 B6
Glebe Way
Barton-upon-Humber DN18 11 A8
5 Sutterton PE20 136 A2
Glebe Wlk 3 PE12 167 B8
Glede Farm Wy LN7 33 B3
Gleedale LN6 204 F1
Gleed Ave PE11 134 E2

Glemsford Rise 2 PE2 230 C7
Glenarm Cres 7 LN5 205 D3
Glen Ave 4 PE11 145 B1
Glenbank Cl LN6 204 F3
Glen Cl NG33 153 A1
Glencoe Cl 2 DN7 14 D4
Glencoe St HU3 179 F6
Glencoe Way PE2 229 D3
Glen Cres
7 Essendine PE9 163 D3
Stamford PE9 219 C7
Glendale PE2 229 D6
Glendon Cl 5 LN5 205 D3
Glendon Gdns PE13 170 C2
Glen Dr PE21 208 B4
Gleneagles
Grantham NG31 211 D8
Peterborough PE2 229 F6
10 Waltham DN37 194 C4
Gleneagles Cl 5 PE9 218 E6
Gleneagles Cres 6 DN19 4 E2
Gleneagles Dr
Skegness PE25 206 D6
1 Sleaford NG34 120 F3
12 Woodhall Spa LN10 97 C5
GLENEAGLES ESTATE
PE25 206 D6
Gleneagles Gr 4 LN4 203 D1
Glenfield Rd DN37 190 D8
Glengary Wy NG34 121 A3
Glen Gdns 2 PE11 145 E3
Glengorm Gdns
Green Hill NG31 210 D6
Green Hill NG31 210 E6
Glen Hall Rise 10 DN19 11 C8
Glenham Dr 4 HU10 178 F7
Glen Ind Est PE9 163 D3
Glenn Ave 3 PE11 214 C4
Glen Rd
Castle Bytham NG33 152 D1
Counthorpe & Creeton NG33 153 A2
3 Wittering PE8 172 B1
Glenrock Pk HU15 2 B6
Glenside NG33 152 E1
Glenside N PE11 156 C8
Glenside S PE11 156 C8
GLENTHAM LN8 43 E1
Glentham Cl LN6 205 B3
Glentham Ct 6 LN8 43 E1
Glentham Rd
Bishop Norton LN8 43 D3
5 Gainsborough DN21 53 A8
Glen The PE2 231 B7
Glenton St PE1 226 C2
GLENTWORTH DN21 54 E7
Glentworth Cres 4 PE25 206 D4
Glentworth Rd DN21 53 F4
Glenwood Dr 2 HU4 179 B6
Glenwood Gr LN6 201 D1
GLINTON PE6 220 D8
Glinton Rd Helpston PE6 173 C4
Newborough PE6 221 C8
Global Ctr Ind Est PE1 226 E4
Gloria Way DN37 190 C7
Glossop Rd DN15 182 B2
Gloucester Ave
Grimsby DN34 191 B4
Scunthorpe DN16 185 B7
Gloucester Cl
Skegness PE25 206 B2
1 Sleaford NG34 212 C7
Gloucester Ct 1 DN15 183 A6
Gloucester Rd
Grantham NG31 210 C5
Peterborough PE2 231 B7
7 Stamford PE9 219 B6
Gloucester St HU4 179 E3
Glover Dr PE4 221 F3
Glover Rd DN17 184 E8
Glovers Ave 8 DN17 17 D4
Glovers La 17 NG24 104 B2
Glynn Rd LN1 201 E8
Glynn View 14 LN1 201 E8
Gn Acres DN37 194 E4
Gndale 45 DN17 29 D7
Gnfinch Cl 15 NG34 108 E1
Gn La Ludborough DN36 48 E6
North End LN11 62 E6
Gnwich Cl 4 DN15 183 A5
Gnwood Rd PE7 230 B1
Gn Wy Cl 6 HU10 178 F7
Goathland Cl HU3 180 A6
Goathland Cl 13 DN37 190 E8
Goble Cl 38 DN18 10 F8
Godber Dr LN4 205 F3
Goddam's La PE12 146 F1
Goddard Cl 37 DN18 10 E8
Goddard Cres 12 PE13 170 D1
Godfrey Ave 6 PE11 145 C6
Godfrey Cl 7 PE6 174 E5
Godfrey Rd 11 DN8 15 A8
Godiva Cl 16 PE6 166 F1
Godiva Cres PE10 213 B5
Godman's La HU10 178 B8
Godnow Rd DN17 16 C6
Godric Sq PE2 230 D6
Godsey Cres 9 PE6 217 C5
Godsey's La PE6 217 B6
Godson Ave 1 NG34 122 D3
Godwin Cl PE10 213 B6
Godwin Rd 13 PE13 170 D1
Goffsmill PE3 225 A4
Goldcrest Cl
2 Birchwood LN6 200 E1
Scunthorpe DN15 182 D6
Goldcrest Way PE7 233 A8
Golden Cup Way DN17 184 C2
Golden Drop 2 PE6 173 C4
Golden Gr PE20 135 C5
Golden Harvest Way 6
PE12 158 B6
Goldenholme La 4 DN22 65 A5
Gold Fen Dike Bank PE22 114 D2
Goldfinch Cl LN6 200 A3
Goldgarth DN32 192 A5
Goldhay Way PE2 229 F2
Goldie La PE2 229 F6
Goldings The 10 DN9 27 D2
Gold La LN13 63 A1
Goldsmith Ct 1 LN4 207 A6
Goldsmith Rd
Grantham NG31 211 D6
8 Newark-on-Trent NG24 104 B3
Goldsmith Wlk LN2 202 C7
Goldson's La PE22 126 F6
Golf Course La DN37 194 F2
Golf Ct PE17 160 F5
Golf Links Dr HU15 2 B6
Golf Rd 4 LN12 64 A4
Gollands La DN9 27 B2
Goltho Hall La LN8 70 B4
Goltho La LN8 70 C4
Goltho Rd LN8 70 B3
Gonerby Hill NG31 210 E8
GONERBY HILL FOOT
NG31 210 F8
Gonerby Hill Foot CE Prim
Sch NG31 210 E8
Gonerby La NG32 129 A7
Gonerby Rd NG31 210 E8
Goochgate PE12 169 A7
Goodacre PE2 230 A4
Goodens La PE13 170 A5
Goodfellows Rd 7 PE11 156 E3
Goodhand Cl DN18 11 A8
Good La LN1 234 B4
Goodliff Rd NG31 210 E2
Goodman Cl 6 NG31 129 E5
Goodson Cl 3 PE21 209 B4
Goodwin Cl 1 NG24 104 B4
Goodwin Dr 8 PE24 90 B7
Goodwin La 32 NG24 104 C1
Goodwin Parade 1 HU3 180 D5
Goodwin Wlk PE4 221 A4
Goodwood DN17 184 D4
Goodwood Cl LN11 198 A7
Goodwood Dr 10 PE10 213 D3
Goodwood La 2 DN35 192 F1
Goodwood Rd 8 PE3 224 F3
Goodwood Way 19 LN6 204 C7
Goole Rd DN14 6 C8
Goosander Cl 24 DN18 3 E1
Gooseacre 33 DN17 29 D7
Goosegate La NG32 118 A2
Goose Gn 10 PE12 160 E4
Goose La PE23 87 D2
Goose's La PE14 161 A1
Gordon Ave PE2 230 E7
Gordon Boswell Romany
Mus★ PE12 214 E1
Gordon Fendick Sch The
PE13 170 D2
Gordon Field 8 LN8 57 D7
Gordon Gdns 1 DN33 194 F8
Gordon Rd LN1 234 B3
Gordon St
Gainsborough DN21 197 D2
4 Kingston upon Hull HU3 180 B5
Gordon Way PE2 230 C7
Goredike Bank PE13 169 C2
GOREFIELD PE13 169 E2
Gorefield Prim Sch PE13 169 F2
Gorefield Rd PE13 169 F2
Gorehall Dr 10 LN2 68 D7
Gore La 8 PE11 214 D4
Goring Pl DN35 192 D7
Gorse Cl Bottesford DN16 185 C4
5 Hatfield DN7 14 C3
4 Woodhall Spa LN10 97 E6
Gorse Dro NG34 133 A6
Gorse Gn PE1 226 B8
Gorse Hill La
Caythorpe NG32 119 A8
Wellingore LN5 107 C7
Gorse La
Gonerby Hill Foot NG31 211 B1
Great Ponton NG31 139 F8
9 Leasingham NG34 121 B7
Scredington NG34 133 A7
Silk Willoughby NG34 121 C1
Gorse Rd NG31 211 D5
Gorse Rise NG31 211 C5
Gorton Rd HU10 178 E7
Gorton St DN31 189 B2
Gorwick La LN1 66 B6
GOSBERTON PE11 145 B6
Gosberton Bank PE11 145 E6
GOSBERTON CHEAL PE11 145 A4
GOSBERTON CLOUGH
PE11 144 D4
Gosberton House Acad
PE11 145 B6
Gosberton Prim Sch PE11 145 B6
Gosberton Rd PE11 145 C4
Goshawk Way LN4 207 C6
Goslings Cnr Wood Nature
Reserve★ LN8 70 E2
Gospelgate LN11 198 B5
Gospel La LN5 106 C3
Gosport Rd DN34 191 A6
Gosport Wlk HU4 179 A4
Gostwick PE2 229 D5
Gote La PE13 169 E3
Gothic Cl 12 LN6 204 D7
GOULCEBY LN11 72 D6
Goulceby Road LN11 60 D1
Gouldeby La LN11 72 D6
Goulton St HU3 180 B3
Gover's Dro PE12 159 A2
Gower Rd HU4 179 B3
Gowt Bank PE22 114 C2
Gowts La PE12 159 E3
GOXHILL DN19 12 A8
Goxhill Ave 4 PE11 134 E2
Goxhill Cl 14 LN6 204 D7
Goxhill Gdns 4 DN34 190 F4
Goxhill Gr 13 LN6 204 D7
Goxhill Prim Sch DN19 12 A8
Goxhill Rd DN19 11 E8
Goxhill Sta DN19 11 F8
Graburn Wy DN18 10 E7
GRABY NG34 142 F4
Grace Ave LN6 204 D3
Grace Cl 4 NG34 212 E3
Grace Cres PE24 77 C3
Gracefield La NG23 78 A4
Grace St LN5 201 F1
Grace Swan Cl
4 Hundleby PE23 87 F1
12 Spilsby PE23 87 F1
Graeme Rd PE5 222 F2
Grafham Cl PE2 231 E4
Grafton Ave PE3 225 C3
Grafton St Grimsby DN32 189 C1
Lincoln LN2 202 B3
Graham Ave HU4 179 C2
Graham Hill Way 4 PE10 213 E4
Graham Rd PE25 206 B4
GRAINSBY DN36 35 F2
Grainsby Ave
Cleethorpes DN35 192 D3
Holton le Clay DN36 195 E1
Grainsby Cl LN6 205 C5
Grainsby La DN36 35 E1
Grains Gate LN11 37 E1
GRAINTHORPE LN11 50 B8
Grainthorpe Sch LN11 50 B7
GRAISELOUND DN9 27 C1
Graizelound Fields Rd DN9 27 D1
Grammar Sch La DN20 196 C6
Grammar Sch Rd DN20 196 C4
Grammar Sch Rd S 3
DN20 196 C3
Grammar Sch Wlk DN16 185 C4
Grampian Cl 14 NG34 212 B3
Grampian Way
Gonerby Hill Foot NG31 210 D8
2 Grimsby DN33 194 E8
Thorne/Moorends DN8 15 A7
Granaries The LN4 108 C8
Granary Cl
22 Metheringham LN4 95 C4
14 Spilsby PE23 87 F1
5 Waddington LN5 93 F6
Granary Croft 7 DN9 27 D2
Granary Ct 12 HU15 2 C7
Granary La LN4 207 A4
Granary Row LN4 207 A4
Granary The DN21 29 C4
Granary Way LN9 199 A3
Granby Ave 5 NG24 104 A3
Granby Dr
5 Bottesford NG13 128 A5
24 Newark-on-Trent NG24 104 B2
Granby Rd LN8 47 B5
Granby St PE1 226 B2
Grand Parade PE25 206 D3
Grand Sluice La 1 PE21 208 F6
Granely Cl LN1 201 C6
GRANGE DN34 191 F5
Grange Ave
13 Barton-upon-Humber
DN18 10 E8
Hatfield DN7 14 D4
24 Laceby DN37 23 F1
Misterton DN10 40 A4
Peterborough PE1 226 A6
1 Scunthorpe DN15 183 A5
Grange Cl 17 Hatfield DN7 14 D4
1 Ingham LN1 54 F2
5 Misterton DN10 40 A5
Grange Cres
Kingston upon Hull HU10 178 E6
Lincoln LN6 205 B3
Peterborough PE2 230 A5
Grange Ct 3 LN5 92 E1
Grange Dr Clinton Park LN4 207 C5
Lincoln LN6 205 B3
Misterton DN10 40 A4
Spalding PE11 214 E4
Stapleford LN6 105 A7
Grange Farm La DN36 195 D6
Grange Field DN20 20 D8
Grangehill Rd PE12 169 B6
Grange Ind Est DN16 185 E7
Grange La Balderton NG24 104 A1
Canwick LN4 81 A4
Covenham St Bartholomew
LN11 49 D6
Garthorpe LE14 150 C4
Heighington LN4 81 E4
Hough-on-the-Hill NG32 118 E6
2 Ingham LN1 54 F2
Keddington LN11 198 E8
8 Manby LN11 62 C6
Nocton LN4 94 F6
North Cockerington LN11 50 A1
North Kelsey LN7 32 A3
Snitterby DN21 43 A5
Stixwould & Woodhall LN10 97 B6
Utterby LN11 49 A4
3 Willingham by Stow DN21 53 E3
Grange La N DN16 185 D7
Grange La S DN16 185 C5
Grange Mdws PE22 113 A1
Grange Paddock 8 NG32 210 A5
Grange Pk 2 Brough HU15 2 C5
17 Kirk Sandall DN3 14 A3
Morton DN21 40 D3
Roughton Moor LN10 98 A7
8 Swanland HU14 3 B6
Grange Prim Sch DN34 190 F5
Grange Prim Sch The
DN16 185 D5
Grange Rd
Bracebridge Heath LN4 205 F2
Gainsborough DN21 41 A1
Garthorpe & Fockerby DN14 7 E8
14 Mablethorpe/Sutton on Sea
LN12 77 A7
4 Metheringham LN4 95 D4
Peterborough PE3 225 D4
8 Ruskington NG34 108 D1
Sutton Bridge PE34 161 B4
10 Wisbech PE13 170 C1
Grange St LN4 109 C7
Grange The 1 NG31 211 A4
Grange Wlk Grimsby DN34 191 A6
6 Misterton DN10 40 A5
Gransley Rise PE3 225 C5
Granson Way LN4 203 A2
Granta Cres NG31 211 C7
GRANTHAM NG31 211 C3
Grantham Ave DN33 191 D1
Grantham Canal Nature
Reserve★ NG31 210 D1
Grantham Coll NG31 211 B4
Grantham Cricket Gd
NG31 211 B1
Grantham & District Hospl
NG31 211 A6
Grantham Dr 2 PE25 206 B3
Grantham Fun Farm The★
NG31 210 F4
Grantham House★ NG31 211 B5
Grantham Mus★ NG31 211 B4
Grantham Prep Sch The
NG31 139 F8
Grantham Rd
Boothby Graffoe LN5 94 A2
Boston PE21 208 A3
Bottesford NG13 128 B5
Bracebridge Heath LN4 205 F2
Carlton Scroop NG32 119 C3
7 Great Gonerby NG31 129 D5
Great Gonerby NG31 210 D8
Harmston LN5 93 F6
Hough-on-the-Hill NG32 119 A4
Ingoldsby NG33 141 C5
Navenby/Wellingore LN5 107 A8
Old Somerby NG33 140 D8
Ropsley & Humby NG33 131 A1
2 Skillington NG33 151 A8
Sleaford NG34 212 B2
Grantham Sandown Sch The
NG31 211 C5
Grantham St LN2 234 B2
Grantham Sta NG31 211 A3
Granthams The 12 LN2 68 E6
Grantham Town FC NG31 210 D3
Grantley St NG31 211 A3
Grants La 29 PE21 208 F5
Grant St Cleethorpes DN35 192 E7
Grimsby DN31 189 D1
GRANT THOROLD DN32 192 A7
Granville Ave
12 Boston PE21 136 D8
Northborough PE6 217 E1
Granville Rd
3 Scunthorpe DN15 183 A6
Scunthorpe DN15 183 A6
Granville St Boston PE21 208 D5
Grantham NG31 211 C3
Grimsby DN32 191 F6
1 Kingston upon Hull HU3 180 A6
Peterborough PE1 226 A4
Granville Terr PE12 160 D4
GRASBY DN38 32 F7
Grasby All Saints CE Prim Sch
The DN38 32 E7
Grasby Cl 4 DN21 53 A8
Grasby Cres DN37 190 D7
Grasby Rd
Great Limber DN37 22 C3
North Kelsey LN7 32 D5
Scunthorpe DN17 184 E5
Grasby Wold La DN38 21 F1
Grasmere Ave PE24 90 E6
Grasmere Cl 3 DN21 197 E6
Grasmere Gdns PE4 221 B3
Grasmere Gr 5 DN36 192 E1
Grasmere Way LN6 200 D1
Grassdale Pk 2 HU15 2 B5
Grassgate La PE14 170 E3
Grassmoor Cl 2 LN6 93 B8
Grassmoor Ct 4 DN15 182 B2
Gravecoat La PE11 144 E6
Gravel Cswy PE6 166 D1
Graveley Cl 4 LN6 204 B6
Gravelhill Dro LN4 109 E7
Gravelholes La DN10 39 F5
Gravel Pit Hill DN20 31 D6
Gravelpit La LN9 199 F2
Gravel Pit La
1 Humberside Airport
DN39 22 A6
Scunthorpe DN17 184 F2
Gravel Pit Rd
Barton-upon-Humber DN18 3 D1
Scotter DN21 29 C4
Gravel Pits La PE24 102 C8
Gravel Rd
Market Deeping PE6 165 D3
Revesby PE22 99 B4
Gravel Wlk PE1 226 A2
Graves Hill LN5 106 F5
Gray Ct PE1 225 E8
Graye Dr LN11 198 D4
GRAYINGHAM DN21 42 D7
Grayingham Rd DN21 42 E7
Grayling Cl 2 DN37 190 D7
Graylings The PE21 208 B6
Grayling Way PE21 208 E3
Gray Rd DN17 184 D6
Grays Ct DN37 190 E8
Gray's Ct 4 LN11 198 B6
Gray's Rd 2 LN11 198 B6
Gray St LN1 234 A4
Gr Ct 12 LN10 97 D5
GREAT CARLTON LN11 62 E4
GREAT CASTERTON PE9 171 B8
Great Casterton CE Prim Sch
PE9 171 C8
Great Casterton Road
PE9 163 B2
Great Cl 1 NG33 151 D2
GREAT COATES DN37 24 B5
Great Coates Prim Sch
DN37 190 E8
Great Coates Rd
Grimsby DN37 190 C8
Healing DN41 23 F5
Great Coates Sta DN37 24 B5
Great Field La 1 HU9 5 E8
GREATFORD PE9 164 B3
Greatford Gdns PE9 164 B3
Greatford Lane PE9 163 E1
Greatford Rd Baston PE6 164 D4
5 Uffington PE9 172 C6
Uffington PE9 172 C7
GREAT GONERBY NG31 129 E5
GREAT HALE NG34 122 F2
Great Hale Dro NG34 123 A2
Great Leighs Bourne PE10 213 B3
4 Bourne PE10 213 C3
GREAT LIMBER DN37 22 D3
Great Northern Ct 12
NG31 211 A4
Great Northern Gdns
PE10 213 D4
Great Northern Terr LN5 234 C1
Great Northern Terr Ind Est
LN5 234 C1
Great N Rd Balderton NG24 117 C8
Empingham PE9 162 B2
Great Gonerby NG32 129 C6
Long Bennington NG23 117 D2
Tinwell PE9 218 D5
Wansford PE8 222 D1
Great Passage St 3 HU1 180 E5
GREAT PONTON NG33 140 A5
Great Ponton CE Sch
NG33 140 A5
Great Stather Cl DN15 8 A5
GREAT STEEPING PE23 101 E7
Great Steeping Prim Sch
PE23 101 E7
Great Steeping Rd PE23 101 D8
GREAT STURTON LN9 71 F3
Great Thornton St HU3 180 D6
GREAT TOWS LN8 47 D1
Great Union St HU9 181 A7
GREBBY PE23 88 D3
Grebe Cl 2 LN6 204 C1
Grebe Mews DN16 185 F5
Greek St HU3 179 F5
Greenacre Cl 7 DN7 14 C2
Greenacres
6 Donington on Bain LN11 59 E1
Peterborough PE4 220 E4
5 Swanland HU14 3 C7
Green Acres HU10 178 C6
Greenacres Dr
Boston PE21 208 D3
5 Bourne PE10 213 D3
Greenaway Ct LN3 203 E6
Green Bank DN8 15 D6
Greenbank Cl PE21 208 D3
Greenbank Dr LN6 205 A5
Green Drift The PE9 172 B3
Green Dro Billinghay LN4 109 F6
Crowland PE6 175 D8
Helpringham NG34 133 F7
Little Hale NG34 134 A7
Thorney PE6 175 F6
Green Dyke PE12 148 D1
Greendyke La PE13 160 A2
Green Farm Cl PE5 223 E2
Greenfield Ave HU13 178 A3
Greenfield Cl 13 DN3 14 A3
Greenfield Dr 9 DN20 31 A5
Greenfield La
Aby with Greenfield LN13 75 D4
Calceby LN13 74 F2
Greenfield Rd
Coningsby LN4 207 D5
3 Sleaford NG34 212 D7
Greenfields
3 Glentham LN8 43 F1
Holbeach PE12 215 F2
22 Nettleham LN2 68 D2
Greenfields Academy
NG31 211 B1
Greenfields La 5 NG34 142 D8
Greenfield Way PE7 233 E8
Greenfinch Dr DN35 192 E1

Greengarth DN17 184 F2
Greengate 11 DN9 27 E6
Green Gate PE22 114 D1
Greengate Ct PE1 226 C4
Greengate La 14 DN19 12 A8
Greengate Rd PE23 88 D3
Greenham PE3 225 A4
Greenhill 8 DN20 19 D3
GREEN HILL NG31 210 E5
Green Hill DN35 192 D3
Greenhill Dr 1 LN8 43 D3
Greenhill Rd DN9 27 C2
Green Hill Rd NG31 210 F5
Greenhoe Rd DN17 184 D3
Green La Algarkirk PE20 136 B3
Aunsby & Dembleby NG34 132 A4
10 Barton-upon-Humber DN18 10 F8
Beckingham LN5 105 C4
Belton DN9 16 D2
Belton & Manthorpe NG32 130 B7
Boston PE21 208 E7
Bottesford NG13 128 B5
Bratoft PE24 102 C7
Brigsley DN37 35 D4
5 Broughton DN20 19 E3
Cherry Willingham LN3 203 D5
Collingham NG23 91 D3
Deeping St Nicholas PE11 166 C8
Dunham-on-Trent NG22 65 B1
Dunston LN4 95 D6
Eagle & Swinethorpe LN6 79 C2
Eaton NG32 138 A2
Gedney PE12 159 A1
Girton NG23 78 C1
Gosberton PE11 145 C7
Grantham NG31 211 D7
Hatfield DN7 14 E1
Hemingby LN9 72 C3
Heydour NG32 131 D5
Hogsthorpe LN13 90 A8
Kingston upon Hull HU13 179 A1
Kirton PE20 135 E6
Lea DN21 52 F5
Leake Commonside PE22 113 F3
Leverington PE13 169 F2
Lincoln LN6 201 D2
Mablethorpe & Sutton LN12 63 F4
Marston NG32 118 D1
Middle Rasen LN8 57 C7
Moulton PE12 146 E1
13 North Kelsey LN7 32 A4
North Somercotes LN11 50 F7
Peterborough PE1 226 A4
Pilham DN21 41 D4
Pinchbeck PE11 145 C2
3 Skegness PE25 103 E4
Spalding PE11 214 C3
Stamford PE9 219 B7
Stickney PE22 113 A7
Stixwould & Woodhall LN10 97 B8
Strubby with Woodthorpe LN13 63 B1
Sutterton PE20 136 A2
Swinderby LN6 92 B5
Thimbleby LN9 85 C5
Threekingham NG34 132 E3
Wainfleet St Mary PE24 102 A1
18 Welton LN2 68 D6
Westborough & Dry Doddington NG23 117 F5
Wigtoft PE20 135 E1
Willoughby with Sloothby LN13 89 C5
Woodhall Spa LN10 97 C5
Wyberton PE21 136 F8
Yaxley PE7 233 D6
Greenlands Ave 10 DN36 195 C6
Green Man La LN4 94 F1
Green Man Rd LN5 94 C1
Greenock Way LN6 204 B7
Green Pastures 4 PE12 158 B7
Green Rd
Aswarby & Swarby NG34 131 F7
Newborough PE6 174 F2
Greenrigg Gdns 1 PE11 214 D5
Greens Cl DN15 183 B3
Green's Rd 4 DN7 14 C3
Green St 1 NG31 129 D5
Greenstiles La HU14 3 C7
Greenstock La PE13 170 A6
Green The
3 Allington NG32 128 F7
Bottesford NG13 128 C4
8 Brough HU15 2 D6
Castor PE5 223 E2
Chapel St Leonard PE24 90 E7
Cherry Willingham/Reepham LN3 203 F8
1 Coddington NG24 104 D5
Collingham NG23 91 C4
Corby Glen NG33 152 E7
Dunston LN4 95 C5
Gainsborough DN21 197 F4
2 Glinton PE6 220 C8
8 Leasingham NG34 121 B8
6 Mablethorpe/Sutton on Sea LN12 64 A4
3 Minting LN9 84 C8
Morborne PE7 232 A3
15 Navenby/Wellingore LN5 107 A7
Peterborough PE4 221 A3
3 Reepham LN3 82 A8
Revesby PE22 99 B4

Green The *continued*
6 Scothern LN2 68 F4
Scotter DN21 29 C3
Spalding PE11 214 E5
4 Swanland HU14 3 B7
23 Thorne/Moorends DN8 15 A8
11 Thorney PE6 176 A3
Thurlby PE10 164 C7
Waltham DN37 194 F2
Welbourn LN5 106 E4
Yaxley PE7 233 E5
Greenway
7 Barton-upon-Humber DN18 3 F1
Waltham DN37 194 E3
2 Welton/Dunholme LN2 68 C7
Greenways 1 HU14 3 A5
Greenway The 1 HU4 179 C6
Greenwich House Sch 8 LN11 198 C6
Green Wlk PE6 217 A5
Greenwood Cl 1 PE12 215 E2
Greenwood Dr PE21 208 F6
Greenwood's Row 5 NG31 211 A4
Greestone Mount LN2 234 B3
Greestone Pl LN2 234 B3
Greestone Strs* LN2 234 B3
GREETHAM LN9 86 D5
Greetham Rd LN9 86 C7
Greetham's La DN32 192 C5
GREETWELL DN20 30 C7
Greetwell Cl LN2 202 B5
Greetwell Ct LN2 203 B8
Greetwellgate LN2 234 C3
Greetwell Hollow Nature Reserve* LN2 202 D5
Greetwell La
1 Lincoln LN2 202 F6
Nettleham LN2 202 F8
Greetwell Pl LN2 202 B5
Greetwell Rd LN2 234 C3
Gregg Hall Cl 2 LN6 205 B4
Gregg Hall Cres LN6 205 B4
Gregg Hall Dr 4 LN6 205 B4
Gregory Cl 1 NG32 139 C7
Gresham Cl 10 NG24 104 C4
Gresham St LN1 201 D4
Gresley Ct 11 NG31 210 E2
Gresley Dr Lincoln LN6 201 D1
4 Stamford PE9 219 B4
Gresley Rd LN11 198 D4
Gresley Way
Immingham DN40 186 F5
Peterborough PE3 225 C6
Gresley Wy DN40 186 E6
Gretton Cl
1 Claypole NG23 117 E8
Peterborough PE2 230 C7
Grevel Cl 6 PE11 214 B5
Greyfleet Bank 7 LN11 51 C4
Grey Friars
9 Grantham NG31 211 A4
Grimsby DN37 190 D7
Greyfriars Cl DN17 184 E6
Greyfriars La 9 PE21 208 F4
Greyfriars Rd 11 DN20 19 E3
GREY GREEN DN9 16 E2
Greyling Cl 5 LN1 201 E8
Greyling View 12 LN1 201 E8
Grey St Gainsborough DN21 197 B6
Kingston upon Hull HU2 180 D7
Greystone Ave HU5 179 E7
Greystones Rd DN21 197 B7
Gride Bank PE22 126 E8
Gride The PE22 113 E1
Griffins Cl 4 PE6 174 E5
Griffiths Ct PE2 229 E5
Grime St DN31 191 E8
Grimmer's Rd 12 PE13 170 E1
GRIMOLDBY LN11 62 B7
Grimoldby Prim Sch LN11 62 C6
GRIMSBY DN31 191 B8
Grimsby Auditorium DN34 190 F8
Grimsby Docks Sta DN31 189 A1
Grimsby Institute DN34 191 C4
Grimsby Leisure Ctr DN34 190 F8
Grimsby Maternity Hospl DN33 191 C3
Grimsby Pool DN33 191 D4
Grimsby Rd 2 Binbrook LN8 47 C5
Brackenborough with Little Grimsby LN11 61 A8
Cleethorpes DN35 192 D8
Fotherby LN11 49 A1
Grimsby DN32 189 D1
Humberston DN36 192 E1
Laceby DN37 190 A2
Louth LN11 198 A6
Swallow LN7 34 B6
Waltham DN37 194 F5
Grimsby Town Sta DN32 191 D7
Grimshaw Rd PE1 226 B6
GRIMSTHORPE PE10 153 E5
Grimsthorpe Castle* PE10 153 D5
Grimsthorpe Cl
Grantham NG31 210 E6
12 Market Deeping PE6 217 A5
Grimston Rd 5 HU10 178 F6
Grindell St HU9 181 D8
GRINGLEY ON THE HILL DN10 39 C1
Gringley Rd DN10 39 E4
Grinter Cl 3 LN6 93 C8
Grocock Cl PE12 146 E2
Groose La PE24 115 D8

Grosvenor Ave
Birchwood LN6 200 D2
Bourne PE10 213 E4
Grosvenor Cres
Grimsby DN32 191 D6
Louth LN11 198 D7
Grosvenor Ct 3 DN7 14 D8
Grosvenor Mews 2 LN4 203 D1
Grosvenor Rd
9 Billingborough NG34 133 B1
Kirton PE20 136 C6
Louth LN11 198 D7
24 Mablethorpe/Sutton on Sea LN12 64 B3
Skegness PE25 206 C4
Wisbech PE13 170 D1
Grosvenor St N DN15 183 A5
Grosvenor St (South) 2 DN15 183 A4
Grosvenor Sq 17 LN5 107 A7
Grosvenor St
Grimsby DN32 191 D6
Kingston upon Hull HU3 180 D8
4 Scunthorpe DN15 183 A4
Grove Cl 10 PE11 145 C1
Grove Cres DN32 192 C6
Grove Ct
3 Gainsborough DN21 197 C6
Woodston PE2 230 F8
Grove Dr 9 LN10 97 D5
Grove End Rd 3 NG31 211 B4
Grovefield La PE22 126 D1
Grove Hill HU13 178 E1
Grove La Peterborough PE3 225 A2
Waltham DN37 194 E4
Grove Leisure Ctr NG24 104 B3
Grovenor Ct 5 DN35 193 A1
Grove Pk DN10 39 F5
Grove Rd 1 Fishlake DN7 14 D8
Mablethorpe/Sutton on Sea LN12 64 C1
Theddlethorpe All Saints LN12 63 D6
Grove St E 5 PE21 209 A5
Grove St W 4 PE21 209 A5
Grove St 14 Boston PE21 209 A5
Heckington NG34 122 E2
5 Kirton in Lindsey DN21 30 B1
Newark-on-Trent NG24 104 B3
Peterborough PE2 230 F8
Groves The HU4 179 B2
Grove The
13 Barrow upon Humber DN19 11 C8
4 Beckingham DN10 40 A1
Edlington with Wispington LN9 85 B6
6 Gainsborough DN21 53 A5
Grantham NG31 210 E3
Lincoln LN2 234 C4
Market Deeping PE6 217 B5
Morton PE10 154 B6
Newton on Trent LN1 65 D1
4 Spalding PE11 214 C6
4 Welton/Dunholme LN2 68 D6
Grove Wood Rd DN10 39 F5
Grove Wood Terr 16 DN10 39 F5
Gr St 14 NG24 104 A3
Grundale HU10 178 C6
Grundy La LN3 57 D2
Grundy's La LN9 84 C8
Grunnill Cl 10 PE25 206 A5
Guanockgate Rd PE12 169 A2
Guash Way PE9 219 D7
Gubbole's Dro PE11 145 A3
Guelder Rd BE7 230 D3
Guernsey Gr DN40 186 C2
Guildford Cl 11 NG31 210 E5
Guildford La LN5 105 F5
Guildford St DN32 192 A8
Guildhall Dr 2 PE11 156 E8
Guildhall Mus* PE21 208 F4
Guildhall Rd HU1 180 F6
Guildhall St
Grantham NG31 211 A4
Lincoln LN1 234 A2
Guild Rd PE13 170 E1
Guile Carr La DN7 14 D5
Guilicarr La LN7 31 F4
Guillemot Dr LN11 198 D8
Guilsborough Rd PE6 175 B2
Guisefield Rd 9 DN9 27 D6
Gulham Rd LN8 44 D5
Gull Bank Whaplode PE12 167 F5
Wisbech St Mary PE13 177 E3
Gull Dro PE13 177 D3
Gull La PE13 170 A2
Gull Rd PE13 177 F2
Gullymore PE3 224 F8
GUNBY
Candlesby with Gunby PE23 89 B1
Gunby and Stainby NG33 151 C4
Gunby Ave LN6 204 F6
Gunby Hall* PE23 89 A1
Gunby La PE23 89 A1
Gunby Pl DN35 192 E4
Gunby Rd
Gunby & Stainby NG33 151 A4
Scunthorpe DN17 184 E5
Gunby Road PE24 89 C2
Gunfleet Cl 18 PE20 135 B7
GUNNERBY DN37 34 F2
Gunnerby Road DN37 34 F2
Gunners Way DN34 190 D4
GUNNESS DN15 17 E6
Gunness & Burringham CE Prim Sch DN17 17 E5
Gunness La Amcotts DN17 17 F8

Gunness La *continued*
Flixborough DN15 182 A7
GUNTHORPE
Owston Ferry DN9 40 D7
Peterborough PE4 221 B1
Gunthorpe Prim Sch PE4 221 C2
Gunthorpe Rd
Newborough PE6 221 D4
Owston Ferry DN9 40 C8
Peterborough PE4 221 C2
Sutton Bridge PE14 160 E1
1 Walpole PE14 170 F8
Gunton's Rd PE6 174 E3
Gurnard Leys PE3 220 E1
Gurnell St DN15 183 A4
Gurry Lane DN9 17 A1
Gurth Ave 6 DN3 14 A1
Guthlac Ave 5 PE4 221 B1
Guthram Ct 11 NG34 107 F1
GUTHRAM GOWT PE11 155 E5
GUYHIRN PE13 177 F2
Guys Head Rd PE12 160 E7
Guy's Head Rd Lutton PE12 149 C1
Sutton Bridge PE12 160 F8
Gwash Cl PE9 163 C1
Gynewell Gr 4 LN2 202 D7
Gypsy La Newton PE13 170 C4
Whaplode PE12 167 F3

H

Haalam Bank LN12 63 C4
Haarlem Ct 5 PE11 214 A2
Habbanya Rise LN4 95 C7
Habblesthorpe Cl 1 DN22 52 C1
Habblesthorpe Rd DN22 52 C1
HABERTOFT PE24 89 E4
HABROUGH DN40 22 E8
Habrough La DN39 22 B6
Habrough Rd
Immingham DN40 186 A3
South Killingholme DN40 12 E2
Habrough Sta DN40 22 E8
Hacconby Dro
Dunsby PE10 144 A1
Haconby PE10 155 A8
Hacconby La PE10 154 C7
HACEBY NG34 131 E3
Hacke Rd 3 PE3 225 D3
Hackness Gr 2 HU5 179 D8
Hack's Dro PE6 164 F6
HACKTHORN LN2 55 E1
Hackthorn CE Prim Sch The LN2 55 F1
Hackthorn Pl 4 LN2 201 F8
Hackthorn Rd LN2 68 D8
HACONBY PE10 154 D8
HADDINGTON LN5 92 F6
HADDON PE7 232 B6
Haddon Cl Birchwood LN6 200 E1
Peterborough PE2 231 E5
Haddon Dr 21 NG24 104 B2
Haddon Rd
Peterborough PE3 225 E3
Peterborough PE7 232 C6
Stamford PE9 218 F6
Haddon St HU3 179 F4
Haddon Way PE7 231 B2
Hadfield Rd
Hampton Vale PE7 230 E2
7 Lincoln LN6 205 A5
Hadleigh Cl NG31 210 F5
Hadleigh Ct DN15 183 A4
Hadleigh Dr LN6 204 F5
Hadleigh Gn 7 DN17 17 D4
Hadleigh Rd DN40 186 D3
Hadley Rd
Peterborough PE4 221 B1
Sleaford NG34 212 E6
Hadrian Dr 10 PE6 164 E5
Hadrians Ct PE2 231 B8
Hadrians Rd 9 LN4 81 A1
Hadrians Wk 12 LN6 93 A8
Haff Cl 2 PE20 135 C7
Haffenden Rd LN2 202 A6
Hagbeach Dro PE12 168 A5
Hagbeach Gate PE12 158 C6
Hagg Cross Roads PE23 87 A4
Hagg La 1 DN17 16 E3
Hagg Rd PE23 87 C6
HAGNABY East Kirkby PE23 100 A5
Hannah cum Hagnaby LN13 76 C6
Hagnaby Abbey LN13 76 C7
HAGNABY LOCK PE22 99 F2
Hagnaby Rd PE23 100 A6
HAGWORTHINGHAM PE23 87 A4
Haig Ave DN16 183 B1
Haigh Ct DN32 191 F5
Haigh St 4 DN35 193 A5
Haile Rd DN36 193 A1
HAINTON LN8 58 F3
Hainton Ave DN32 191 F8
Hainton Cl DN21 197 E3
Hainton Lane LN8 58 C2
Hainton Rd Hainton LN8 58 F3
Lincoln LN6 205 C5
Haith's La 4 DN36 36 B1
Haldane St DN21 197 B5
Hale Cl 4 LN2 202 E7
Hale Hill La Dunsville DN7 14 E1
Hatfield DN7 14 E2
Hale House Rd PE10 153 C2
Hale La PE22 112 F1
Hale Rd Heckington NG34 122 E2
Helpringham NG34 133 E7
Horsington LN10 84 B2
Hales Cl DN16 185 A2

Hales Entry HU9 181 C6
HALESGATE PE12 146 E1
Hales La 6 LN5 107 B8
Haley Cl 6 PE13 170 D2
Half Acre Wood 3 DN17 17 D4
Halfleet PE6 217 A6
Halford Cl 8 NG33 151 D2
Halfpenny Cl 19 LN2 68 D7
Halfpenny La LN11 60 F4
Halfway House La LN6 92 C6
Halfway Houses LN6 92 D5
Halifax App DN20 21 A8
Halifax Cl
4 Skegness PE25 206 B5
3 Skellingthorpe LN6 200 A4
Halifax Dr PE6 217 C7
Halifax Rd Balderton NG24 104 C2
13 Spilsby PE23 101 A8
Halkon Cl DN17 7 D3
Hallam Cl 3 Alford LN13 75 E2
Barrow upon Humber DN19 11 D8
Hallam Gr LN6 205 C7
Hallam Rd 4 HU4 179 C2
Hallam's Dro PE20 123 F2
Hallam's La 3 LN4 96 B1
Hallaton Rd PE1 226 D8
Hall Bank 3 PE13 169 F7
Hallbrook Ct 5 DN16 185 A1
Hall Cl Heckington NG34 122 E3
Ropsley NG33 131 B1
Hallcroft 6 DN39 12 A1
Hallcroft Rd 1 DN9 27 D2
Hall Ct DN17 7 A3
Hall Dr Canwick LN4 81 A4
Grantham NG31 211 C5
Lincoln LN6 205 C7
Swineshead PE20 135 B7
HALL END PE22 114 D1
Hall End Rd PE22 114 C1
Haller St HU9 181 E8
Hall Farm
5 Market Deeping PE6 217 B6
6 Newark-on-Trent NG24 104 D5
Hall Farm Pk* LN7 44 D8
Hallfield Cres NG32 119 C2
Hallfields La PE4 221 C1
Hall Garden LN4 81 A4
Hallgarth DN36 37 B2
Hallgarth Ave DN16 183 B2
Hallgate PE12 159 E8
Hall Gate Fleet PE12 159 B6
Holbeach PE12 215 C1
Moulton PE12 157 F5
Wainfleet St Mary PE24 102 C1
Weston PE12 146 B1
Hall Gate Rd PE12 168 E2
Hall Gdns 8 DN15 9 B5
Hall Hill Rd PE12 215 D1
HALLINGTON LN11 60 F4
Halliwell Cl
5 Kingston upon Hull HU9 5 F8
18 Newark-on-Trent NG24 104 A6
Hall La Algarkirk PE20 136 B3
Benington PE22 126 F5
Branston & Mere LN4 81 D1
Burgh le Marsh PE24 102 E7
Elsham DN20 20 F7
Fiskerton LN3 82 C7
Frampton PE20 136 E6
Gunby & Stainby NG33 151 B5
Hough-on-the-Hill NG32 118 E7
Lenton Keisby & Osgodby NG33 141 E3
Moulton PE12 146 D2
Nettleham LN2 68 B2
Peterborough PE4 221 A4
Stainforth DN7 14 A6
Stenigot LN11 72 D7
Stickney PE22 112 F7
Welbourn LN5 106 E4
West Keal PE23 100 C6
Wrangle PE22 114 D1
Hall Leas Dr 1 LN12 64 C1
Hall Mdw 1 DN20 10 C2
Hall Mdw Rd PE6 217 F7
Hall Orch La 2 LN5 106 E5
Hall Pk Heckington NG34 122 F1
Swanland HU14 3 C7
Hall Pk Rd DN40 186 D5
Hall Pl 7 PE11 214 D4
Hall Rd Buckminster NG33 150 F6
Haconby PE10 154 D8
Heckington NG34 122 E1
Hough-on-the-Hill NG32 118 E7
Londonthorpe & Harrowby Without NG31 211 F4
Hall Rise 7 DN17 29 D7
Halls Ct LN4 95 C6
Halls Hill LN11 72 D6
Halls La 6 Keelby DN41 23 A4
9 North Kelsey LN7 32 A4
Hall's Rd DN10 39 D2
Hall St Crowland PE6 166 F1
Kingston upon Hull HU2 180 D7
16 Navenby/Wellingore LN5 107 A7
Hall Wath LN5 92 E2
Hall Way DN39 21 F5
Hall Wlk 1 HU15 2 D6
Hall Yd 2 Collyweston PE9 171 B1
26 Metheringham LN4 95 C4
Halmer Gate PE11 214 E4
Halmer Gdns PE11 214 F4
Halmer Paddock 6 PE11 214 F5
Haltemprice Leisure Ctr HU10 178 E7
Haltemprice St HU3 179 F5
HALTHAM LN9 98 C6

Haltham Gn DN21 ... 197 F4
HALTOFT END PE22 ... 126 C4
Haltoft End Est PE22 ... 126 C3
Halton Cl
5 Birchwood LN6 ... 204 B8
4 Kirton in Lindsey DN21 ... 42 F8
HALTON FENSIDE PE23 ... 101 C6
HALTON HOLEGATE PE23 ... 101 B8
Halton Holegate CE Prim Sch PE23 ... 101 B7
Halton Pl DN35 ... 192 D4
Halton Rd
Monksthorpe PE23 ... 101 C8
Spilsby PE23 ... 101 A8
Halton Way 3 DN33 ... 191 C2
Halyard Croft 8 HU1 ... 180 F5
Halycon Ave 1 HU13 ... 178 E2
Hambleton La LN8 ... 57 E8
Hambleton Rd PE9 ... 218 E4
HAMERINGHAM LN9 ... 86 C2
Hameringham Rd LN9 ... 87 B2
Hamerton La 1 LN9 ... 199 C3
Hamilton Cl
6 Bourne PE10 ... 213 C7
6 Grimsby DN34 ... 190 D4
Hamilton Gr LN6 ... 200 B3
Hamilton Rd Alford LN13 ... 75 F2
Grantham NG31 ... 211 D6
4 Lincoln LN6 ... 204 D2
Scunthorpe DN17 ... 184 F8
Hamilton St DN32 ... 189 D1
Hamilton Way PE21 ... 208 F3
Hamish Wlk 8 DN40 ... 186 B3
Ham La PE2 ... 229 E7
Hamling Way HU4 ... 179 D2
Hamlyn Ave HU4 ... 179 E7
Hamlyn Dr HU4 ... 179 E6
Ham Mere Bird Sanctuary* PE2 ... 229 E7
Hammerfest Ave DN36 ... 195 B7
Hammerton Rd DN17 ... 184 E4
Hammond Cl PE8 ... 172 C1
Hammond Ct LN12 ... 64 B3
Hammonds Dr PE1 ... 226 C1
Hamont Rd DN32 ... 192 B7
Hampden Cl 1 LN6 ... 200 A4
Hampden Cres 3 DN7 ... 26 A8
Hampdens Cl 10 NG24 ... 104 C5
Hampden Way
Sleaford NG34 ... 121 A2
8 Waddington LN5 ... 94 A7
Hampden Wy LN4 ... 207 D3
Hampshire St HU4 ... 179 E3
Hampson Gdns 18 DN3 ... 14 A2
Hampstead Pk DN33 ... 191 B2
Hampton Ave PE7 ... 230 E2
Hampton Cl
Humberston DN35 ... 192 F1
1 Spalding PE11 ... 214 E2
Hampton Coll PE7 ... 230 D1
Hampton Ct PE3 ... 225 C6
HAMPTON HARGATE PE7 ... 230 D2
Hampton Hargate Prim Sch PE7 ... 230 C2
Hampton La PE22 ... 127 B7
Hampton Rd
2 Hatfield DN7 ... 14 C4
Scunthorpe DN16 ... 185 C8
Hampton St LN1 ... 201 D4
HAMPTON VALE PE7 ... 230 D1
Hampton Vale Prim Sch PE7 ... 230 C1
Hanbury PE2 ... 229 F3
Hanbury Ave NG31 ... 211 A2
HANBY NG33 ... 141 E7
Hanby La 11 Alford LN13 ... 75 F2
Welton le Marsh PE23 ... 89 B4
Hancock Dr 9 LN3 ... 83 B4
Handel Ct DN21 ... 197 D5
Handel House Prep Sch DN21 ... 197 D5
Handley Ct Mews 7 NG34 ... 212 D3
Handley St
Heckington NG34 ... 122 E3
8 Sleaford NG34 ... 212 D4
Hands on History Mus* HU1 ... 180 F6
Hangar La DN36 ... 195 C4
Hangman's Cnr PE6 ... 175 F5
Hangman's La
Edenham PE10 ... 153 F7
Haconby PE10 ... 154 A7
Hankey St PE1 ... 225 F4
Hankinson's Est PE34 ... 161 D1
HANNAH LN13 ... 76 E6
Hannah Cres LN6 ... 92 E5
Hannam Bvd PE11 ... 214 A3
Hannath Rd PE13 ... 170 B8
Hanover Ct HU1 ... 180 E5
Hanover Dr 26 HU15 ... 2 C5
Hanover Gdns DN16 ... 185 C6
Hanover Hill DN21 ... 54 F6
Hanover Sq 5 HU1 ... 180 F6
Hansard Cres 3 LN7 ... 33 B4
Hansards Dr 2 LN8 ... 70 D5
Hansard Way 8 PE20 ... 136 C5
Hansel Cl PE2 ... 230 E8
Hanson Dr 2 LN12 ... 76 F8
Hanson Way DN32 ... 192 B8
HANTHORPE PE10 ... 154 B7
Hanthorpe Rd PE10 ... 154 B7
Ha'penny Bridge Way HU9 ... 181 B5
Harbour Way HU9 ... 181 C6
HARBY NG23 ... 79 C5
Harby Cl Grantham NG31 ... 210 E1
Lincoln LN6 ... 205 B3
Harby Cl *continued*
30 Newark-on-Trent NG24 ... 104 B2
Harcourt Dr HU9 ... 181 C8
HarCt St NG24 ... 104 A4
Harden's La LN9 ... 73 F1
Hardian Wy LN7 ... 33 A4
Harding Cl
9 Mablethorpe & Sutton LN12 ... 64 C1
6 Mablethorpe/Sutton on Sea LN12 ... 76 F8
Harding House Gall* LN2 234 B3
Hardings La PE23 ... 88 B2
Hardings The 20 LN2 ... 68 D7
Hardiway PE21 ... 209 B5
Hards La PE6 ... 165 E1
HARDWICK LN1 ... 66 A2
Hardwick Cl Louth LN11 ... 198 A7
3 Saxilby with Ingleby LN1 ... 66 C2
Hardwick Ct PE3 ... 225 B2
Hardwicke Cl 7 NG31 ... 211 A3
Hardwick La LN1 ... 65 F5
Hardwick Pl 1 LN2 ... 202 A8
Hardwick Plot La PE20 ... 124 C1
Hardwick Rd
5 Kirton PE20 ... 136 C5
1 Stamford PE9 ... 218 F6
Hardwick St HU5 ... 180 B8
Hardy Rd DN17 ... 184 D6
Hardy's Animal Farm* PE25 ... 90 E5
Hardys Ct DN32 ... 192 A6
Hardy's Dro PE10 ... 213 F7
Hardy's La PE6 ... 167 D4
Hardy's Rd DN35 ... 192 F4
Harebell Cl PE1 ... 221 F1
HAREBY PE23 ... 99 F8
Hareby Hill PE23 ... 100 A8
Hareby Rd PE23 ... 86 F2
Hare Cl 9 NG34 ... 122 E2
Harecroft Rd PE13 ... 170 C1
Hare Hill LN7 ... 34 A2
Hare St DN32 ... 191 F6
Harewood Ave 7 DN3 ... 14 A2
Harewood Cl PE21 ... 209 B5
Harewood Cres
Lincoln LN6 ... 205 A3
Louth LN11 ... 198 B7
Harewood Crest 32 HU15 ... 2 D5
Harewood Gdns PE3 ... 225 B2
Harewood Gr 1 DN35 ... 192 F1
Harford Gate PE12 ... 159 D5
Hargate Cl 1 PE12 ... 159 C7
Hargate La PE34 ... 161 E2
Hargate Way PE7 ... 230 D3
Hargate Wy PE7 ... 230 B2
Hargon La NG24 ... 104 B7
Hargrave St DN31 ... 188 D1
Hargreaves Way DN15 ... 183 B6
Harland Rd
9 Brough HU15 ... 2 C6
Lincoln LN2 ... 202 D8
HARLAXTON NG32 ... 139 C7
Harlaxton CE Prim Sch NG32 ... 139 C7
Harlaxton Cl 2 LN6 ... 204 C6
Harlaxton College NG32 ... 139 D7
Harlaxton Dr 4 LN6 ... 204 C6
Harlaxton Manor & Gdns* NG32 ... 139 D7
Harlaxton Rd 3 NG31 ... 210 F3
Harlaxton Road Ind Est NG31 ... 210 F2
Harlech Grange PE3 ... 225 B1
Harlech Way DN32 ... 191 F8
Harlech Wlk DN40 ... 186 D3
Harlequin Dr
10 Mablethorpe/Sutton on Sea LN12 ... 64 B3
6 Spalding PE11 ... 214 A5
Harlestone Ct DN34 ... 190 C4
Harley St HU2 ... 180 E8
Harlow St DN31 ... 188 D1
Harlton Cl PE2 ... 231 E5
HARMSTON LN5 ... 93 F5
Harmston Cl LN2 ... 202 A8
Harmston Pk Ave LN5 ... 93 F4
Harmston Rd LN5 ... 93 A5
Harneis Cres DN37 ... 23 F2
Harness Dr LN4 ... 207 A5
Harn Rd PE7 ... 230 E2
Harold Rd NG33 ... 151 D2
Harold's Bank PE13 ... 169 B2
Harold St DN32 ... 192 A8
Harome Gr HU5 ... 179 C7
Harpe Cl 10 PE11 ... 156 E8
Harpenden Cl 15 DN7 ... 14 D3
Harpendon Dr 16 DN7 ... 14 D3
Harper Garth LN9 ... 85 B5
Harpham Cl DN16 ... 185 F5
Harpham Rd
Gate Burton DN21 ... 53 A1
Marshchapel DN36 ... 37 B2
Marton DN21 ... 65 D8
HARPSWELL DN21 ... 54 E8
Harpswell Cl 7 DN21 ... 53 A8
Harpswell La DN21 ... 42 C1
Harpswell Rd LN2 ... 202 A7
Harrier Ct 3 LN6 ... 204 E8
Harrier Rd 3 DN18 ... 3 F1
Harrier Way PE6 ... 217 B7
Harriet Cl 5 PE12 ... 160 E4
HARRINGTON PE23 ... 87 C7
Harrington LN11 ... 198 E6
Harrington Ave 4 LN6 ... 205 C8
Harrington Croft 8 PE12 ... 215 E2
Harrington Dr 7 PE6 ... 175 C8
Harrington Pl DN16 ... 185 A5
Harrington Rd
Hagworthingham PE23 ... 87 B4
7 South Witham NG33 ... 151 D2
Harrington Rise 13 NG34 ... 107 F1
Harrington St
Bourne PE10 ... 213 D6
Cleethorpes DN35 ... 189 D1
Harrington Way 6 PE6 ... 175 C8
Harris Bvd 12 LN12 ... 64 B3
Harris Cl
9 Newborough PE6 ... 174 E4
11 Skegness PE25 ... 206 A5
Harrison Cl Horncastle LN9 199 C5
10 Peterborough PE3 ... 224 F3
Winteringham DN15 ... 9 A8
Harrison Pl Lincoln LN1 ... 234 A4
North Hykeham LN6 ... 204 D5
Harrison's Dro PE20 ... 124 B2
Harrison's La PE24 ... 101 F4
Harrison St DN31 ... 191 C7
Harris Rd LN6 ... 205 B6
Harris St
3 Kingston upon Hull HU3 ... 179 F5
Peterborough PE1 ... 225 F6
Harris Vw 11 DN9 ... 27 D7
Harris Way NG31 ... 211 A2
Harrold Dro PE12 ... 177 C8
Harrold's Bank PE13 ... 177 D8
Harrolds Cl 3 PE13 ... 170 F1
HARROWBY NG31 ... 211 F4
Harrowby CE (Aided) Inf Sch NG31 ... 211 C6
Harrowby Cl Digby LN4 ... 108 E5
Grantham NG31 ... 211 C6
Harrowby Cres NG31 ... 211 E1
Harrowby Est NG31 ... 211 D6
Harrowby La
Grantham NG31 ... 211 D6
Londonthorpe & Harrowby Without NG31 ... 130 C3
Harrowby Rd NG31 ... 211 C3
Harrow Cl
Gainsborough DN21 ... 197 F6
Heighington/Washingborough LN4 ... 203 C1
Harrow Close 16 NG23 ... 91 D4
Harrow Dr PE25 ... 206 B6
Harrowdyke 6 DN18 ... 10 E8
Harrow Gdns DN17 ... 184 F4
Harrow La DN33 ... 191 B1
Harrow Rd
Deeping St Nicholas PE11 ... 166 C7
6 Mablethorpe/Sutton on Sea LN12 ... 64 B4
Harrow St Grantham NG31 ... 211 B3
Kingston upon Hull HU3 ... 180 B4
Harrows The 15 LN2 ... 68 D6
Harrox Rd 3 PE12 ... 157 F7
Harrox Sq 5 PE12 ... 157 F6
Harrys Dream 3 DN20 ... 19 E3
HARSTON NG32 ... 138 E6
Harston Rd NG32 ... 138 F7
Hartford Ct PE2 ... 231 D6
Harthill Dr HU3 ... 180 C5
Hart La DN15 ... 9 B5
Hartland Ave
Hampton Hargate PE7 ... 230 E1
6 Lincoln LN6 ... 205 A1
Hartley Bridge HU9 ... 181 C6
Hartley St Boston PE21 ... 208 F6
3 Lincoln LN2 ... 202 C3
Hartshead Ave DN15 ... 182 C3
HARTSHOLME LN6 ... 204 E6
Hartsholme Acad LN6 ... 204 F7
Hartsholme Dr LN6 ... 205 A8
Hartsholme Pk LN6 ... 204 F7
Hart St DN35 ... 192 C8
Hartwell Ct PE3 ... 225 D5
Hartwell Way PE3 ... 225 B5
Harvard Cl 1 LN4 ... 203 D1
Harvest Ave 34 DN18 ... 10 E8
Harvest Cl
21 Kirk Sandall DN3 ... 14 A2
23 Metheringham LN4 ... 95 C4
Harvest Cres 2 DN37 ... 194 C4
Harvest Dr NG24 ... 104 B6
Harvester Cl 19 DN9 ... 27 E6
Harvester Way
Crowland PE6 ... 175 B8
Peterborough PE1 ... 226 C1
1 Sibsey PE22 ... 113 B1
Harvest Mews 5 PE11 ... 166 C6
Harvest Rise 2 DN19 ... 11 C8
Harvest Way 3 NG34 ... 212 C2
Harvest Wy 15 PE25 ... 206 A5
Harvey Ave 7 NG24 ... 104 C5
Harvey Cl Bourne PE10 ... 213 B4
11 Wittering PE8 ... 172 B1
Harvey Kent Gdns 4 LN3 ... 83 C4
Harveys Cl PE11 ... 214 F6
Harveys La LN11 ... 198 E6
Harvey St 5 LN1 ... 201 D3
Harvey Wk DN36 ... 195 D7
Harwich Cl 12 LN5 ... 205 D3
Harwood Ave PE12 ... 215 C1
Harwood Dr 1 HU4 ... 179 B6
Hase Wlk HU13 ... 178 E1
Hassall Rd PE25 ... 206 A2
Hassock Hill Dro PE13 ... 169 D3
HASTHORPE LN13 ... 89 C4
Hasthorpe Rd LN13 ... 89 C5
Hastings Dr 4 PE24 ... 102 D2
Hastings Gr HU5 ... 179 E7
Hastings Rd PE4 ... 221 A2
Hatchet's La
20 Beacon Hill NG24 ... 104 A5
2 Newark-on-Trent NG24 ... 104 A6
HATCLIFFE DN37 ... 34 F3
Hatcliffe Cl 2 NG31 ... 211 A8
Hatcliffe Gdns 11 LN2 ... 202 A8
Hatcliffe Rd LN8 ... 47 C8
Hatcliffe Cl 6 DN33 ... 191 B3
HATFIELD DN7 ... 14 D5
Hatfield La DN3 ... 14 A4
Hatfield Rd Hatfield DN7 ... 14 F6
Thorne/Moorends DN8 ... 15 A7
Hatfield & Stainforth Sta DN7 ... 14 C5
HATFIELD WOODHOUSE DN7 ... 15 A3
Hatfield Wr Pk* DN7 ... 14 E5
Hathersage Ave LN6 ... 204 E2
Hathersage Cl NG31 ... 211 A2
Hathersage Ct 3 DN15 ... 182 B2
Hatt Cl 2 PE12 ... 157 F7
HATTON LN8 ... 71 B3
Hatton Cl 3 LN6 ... 205 A7
Hatton Gdns 18 NG24 ... 104 A4
Hatton Gr 7 DN33 ... 191 B3
Hatton Mdws Nature Reserve* LN8 ... 71 A2
Hatton Rd LN8 ... 71 C5
HAUGH LN13 ... 75 B2
HAUGHAM LN11 ... 73 F8
Haugham Pastures LN11 ... 61 E2
Haugham Road LN11 ... 61 B1
Haugh La LN13 ... 75 A3
Hauser Cl 8 NG34 ... 212 B2
Havelock Acad DN32 ... 192 C6
Havelock Dr PE2 ... 231 E6
Havelock Mews DN32 ... 192 C6
Havelock St
Kingston upon Hull HU3 ... 180 A4
Spalding PE11 ... 214 C3
Havelok Cl 4 LN11 ... 198 D4
Haven Ave Brough HU15 ... 2 B6
Grimsby DN31 ... 191 C8
HAVEN BANK LN4 ... 111 B3
Haven Bank Boston PE21 ... 208 E5
6 Skidbrooke with Saltfleet Haven LN11 ... 51 C4
Wildmore LN4 ... 111 B2
Haven Cl 1 Blyton DN21 ... 41 C5
9 Fleet PE12 ... 159 C7
Haven Ctry Pk* PE21 ... 137 C7
Haven Garth 1 HU15 ... 2 B5
Haven Gdns DN31 ... 188 C1
Haven High Acad PE21 ... 208 F7
Haven House Rd PE24 ... 102 F3
Havenhouse Sta PE24 ... 102 F2
Haven Mdws PE21 ... 208 C7
Haven Rd
4 Barton-upon-Humber DN18 ... 3 E1
North Killingholme DN40 ... 13 A6
Haven Side 8 PE24 ... 102 D1
Havenside Nature Reserve* PE21 ... 137 A8
Haven The* PE21 ... 208 F4
Haven The HU9 ... 181 B6
Haven Village 3 PE21 ... 208 F3
Haverfield Rd PE11 ... 214 D3
Haverholme Cl 10 NG34 ... 108 E1
Haverholme Dro PE12 ... 159 D5
Haverlands The 3 NG31 ... 210 E8
Haverstoe Pl DN35 ... 192 C3
Haveswater Cl 1 PE4 ... 221 C2
Hawerby Rd 3 Laceby DN37 23 F1
Wold Newton LN8 ... 47 F8
Hawker Dr LN11 ... 198 D4
Hawking Cl 10 NG33 ... 151 D7
Hawkins Dr 20 PE13 ... 170 E1
Hawkins Gr DN32 ... 192 B6
Hawkins Way 7 DN40 ... 12 E3
Hawksbill Wy PE2 ... 231 A8
Hawksdale Cl 3 NG31 ... 211 A7
Hawkshead Gr LN2 ... 202 A8
Hawkshead Way 2 PE4 ... 221 C3
Hawksmede Way LN11 ... 198 D8
Hawksmoor Cl 2 LN6 ... 204 D1
Hawks Way NG34 ... 212 B3
Hawksworth St 2 DN21 ... 197 D4
Haworth Cl DN15 ... 182 D4
Haworth Way PE21 ... 208 D7
Haw's La PE11 ... 134 F1
Hawthorn Ave Brigg DN20 ... 196 C4
Cherry Willingham LN3 ... 203 B6
Gainsborough DN21 ... 197 D6
Immingham DN40 ... 186 E5
Kingston upon Hull HU3 ... 179 F5
Waddington LN5 ... 205 C1
Hawthorn Bank PE11 ... 214 B1
Hawthorn Chase
Lincoln LN2 ... 202 E7
1 Moulton PE12 ... 157 F6
Hawthorn Cl
Beckingham DN10 ... 52 A8
Healing DN41 ... 23 F6
Heighington/Washingborough LN4 ... 81 F4
4 Market Deeping PE6 ... 217 B6
3 Newborough PE6 ... 174 E5
7 Ruskington NG34 ... 108 E1
Hawthorn Cres 11 PE22 ... 114 A1
Hawthorn Ct 1 HU3 ... 179 F6
Hawthorn Dr
5 Billinghay LN4 ... 109 F6
1 Mablethorpe LN12 ... 64 B3
Sleaford NG34 ... 212 D3
Hawthorne Ave
Cleethorpes DN35 ... 192 D8
4 Grimsby DN33 ... 194 F8
9 Hatfield DN7 ... 14 C2
Louth LN11 ... 198 B6
New Waltham DN36 ... 195 B5
Hawthorne Ave *continued*
4 Scunthorpe DN17 ... 184 F8
8 Wisbech PE13 ... 170 D2
Hawthorne Cl
2 Bracebridge Heath LN4 ... 81 A1
5 Manby LN11 ... 62 C6
6 Scopwick Heath LN4 ... 108 A7
20 Winterton DN15 ... 9 A5
Wootton DN39 ... 11 E2
Hawthorne Cres 3 DN17 ... 184 F8
Hawthorne Ct 4 NG31 ... 210 D2
Hawthorne Gdns 8 DN19 ... 12 A8
Hawt Horne Rd 17 DN36 ... 36 C8
Hawthorne Rise HU13 ... 178 B3
Hawthornes The 13 PE6 ... 217 A6
Hawthorn Gate 26 DN18 ... 10 F8
Hawthorn Gr DN21 ... 197 D5
HAWTHORN HILL LN4 ... 110 F6
Hawthorn Rd Bourne PE10 213 C6
Cherry Willingham LN3 ... 203 B7
4 Old Leake PE22 ... 114 A1
Peterborough PE1 ... 226 C6
Skegness PE25 ... 206 A2
Yaxley PE7 ... 233 F5
Hawthorn Rise 4 DN19 ... 11 C8
Hawthorns The
Allington NG32 ... 128 A6
14 Nettleham LN2 ... 68 D2
Hawthorn Way 4 LN5 ... 92 F3
Hawthorn Wlk 1 LN1 ... 66 D7
Hawthorn Wy
Burringham DN17 ... 17 D4
9 Ingoldmells PE25 ... 90 D3
HAWTHORPE PE10 ... 142 A2
Hawthorpe Rd
Irnham NG33 ... 141 E1
Keisby PE10 ... 141 F3
Hawton Cl 1 DN21 ... 197 E6
Hawton La NG24 ... 104 A2
HAXEY DN9 ... 27 C2
HAXEY CARR DN9 ... 27 B4
Haxey CE Prim Sch DN9 ... 27 D3
Haxey Gate Rd DN10 ... 39 F7
Haxey Grange 9 DN9 ... 27 D2
Haxey La DN9 ... 27 D1
Haxey Rd DN10 ... 39 F6
Haxey Turbary Nature Reserve* DN9 ... 27 A4
Hay Barn Rd PE11 ... 166 C6
Haycroft Ave 4 DN31 ... 191 C8
Haycroft La PE12 ... 159 B7
Haycroft St DN31 ... 191 C7
Haydock Park Dr
Bourne PE10 ... 213 B3
Bourne PE10 ... 213 C3
Haydock Wy 10 LN8 ... 57 E7
Haydon Ave PE25 ... 206 A4
Haydon Cl HU10 ... 178 D8
Haydor Ave LN2 ... 202 A8
Hayes Yd 4 LN1 ... 54 F2
Hayfield Cl
7 Barnby Dun DN3 ... 14 A4
6 Haxey DN9 ... 27 D2
Hayfields The PE11 ... 214 B6
Hay Gn Rd PE34 ... 161 E1
Hay Gn Rd (North) PE34 ... 161 E2
Hay Gn Rd (South) PE34 ... 161 D1
HAY GREEN PE34 ... 161 E1
Hayling Mere 4 DN35 ... 192 F1
Haynes Cl 3 DN8 ... 15 B7
Haynes Gdns 13 DN8 ... 15 B8
Haynes Gn 6 DN8 ... 15 B8
Haynes Gr 1 DN8 ... 15 B7
Haynes Rd DN8 ... 15 B8
Hays Cl 4 DN36 ... 195 C2
Hayside Ave 14 NG24 ... 104 B2
Hayton Cl 2 DN15 ... 9 B5
Hayton Gr HU4 ... 179 D4
Haytons La 2 DN15 ... 9 D1
Haywain Dr 6 PE11 ... 166 C6
Haywardsfield 4 PE3 ... 225 A1
Haze La 5 LN6 ... 204 C1
Hazeland Cl PE10 ... 154 C6
Hazeland Steading PE10 ... 154 C6
Hazel Ave 20 DN17 ... 16 D8
Hazelbarrow Dr HU10 ... 178 F7
Hazel Cl Messingham DN17 ... 29 C7
10 North Hykeham LN6 ... 93 A8
Hazel Croft
4 Immingham DN40 ... 186 A4
Peterborough PE4 ... 220 E4
Hazel Ct 29 HU15 ... 2 C5
Hazel Dr LN9 ... 199 B5
Hazel Gr
4 Bottesford DN16 ... 185 B2
2 Kingston upon Hull HU3 ... 180 D5
Louth LN11 ... 198 E4
Sleaford NG34 ... 212 D6
Stamford PE9 ... 218 D6
Welton/Dunholme LN2 ... 68 C6
Hazelnut Cl 3 PE22 ... 99 A4
Hazelnut Way LN11 ... 198 E6
Hazel Rd 6 DN7 ... 14 C5
Hazel Wk 29 LN13 ... 75 F2
Hazelwood Ave LN6 ... 204 C8
Hazelwood Dr
Bourne PE10 ... 213 B6
Hessle HU13 ... 178 B3
Hazelwood La PE12 ... 159 A7
Hazlewood Dr NG31 ... 210 F7
Headingley Ave 4 DN17 ... 184 E3
Headlands Dr HU13 ... 178 C2
Headland Way
3 Haconby PE10 ... 154 D8
7 Navenby LN5 ... 107 B8

Headquarters Cres 5
NG34 . . . . 120 C8
Heads La HU13 . . . . 178 C1
Headstead Bank DN22 . . . . . 65 B7
Healey Cl 5 NG23 . . . . 91 D4
Healey La LN12 . . . . 63 C4
Healey Rd DN16 . . . . 185 C8
HEALING DN41 . . . . 23 F5
Healing Moated Settlement*
DN4 . . . . 23 F5
Healing Prim Sch DN41 . . . . 23 F5
Healing Rd 5 DN41 . . . . . . 23 D6
Healing Science Acad
DN41 . . . . 23 F5
Healing Sta DN41 . . . . 23 F6
Heanor Ct DN15 . . . . 182 B3
HEAPHAM DN21 . . . . 53 E7
Heapham Cres DN21 . . . . . 197 F4
Heapham La DN21 . . . . 53 F7
Heapham Rd DN21 . . . . 197 E5
Hearfield Terr HU13 . . . . . . 178 E1
Heartsease Way PE10 . . . . 213 E3
Heath Cl 4 LN2 . . . . 68 C7
Heathcote Cl HU10 . . . . 178 F5
Heathcote Rd Bourne PE10 213 E4
Castle Bytham NG33 . . . . . 152 D1
Coningsby LN4 . . . . 207 E5
Heathcroft LN3 . . . . 203 E5
Heather Ave PE1 . . . . 226 A8
Heather Cl 1 Boston PE21 208 D3
7 Woodhall Spa LN10 . . . . . . 97 E6
Heather Ct 9 PE11 . . . . 214 B6
Heatherdale Cl
6 Grimsby DN33 . . . . 194 E7
Peterborough PE7 . . . . 231 C5
Heather Gdns LN6 . . . . 204 E3
Heather Gr DN16 . . . . 185 E5
Heather Rd PE25 . . . . 206 B2
Heather Rd Ind Est PE25 . . 206 B2
Heath Farm Cl NG32 . . . . . . 119 F3
Heath Farm Rd NG31 . . . . . 130 C2
Heathfield Ave
Branston LN4 . . . . 81 E2
Spalding PE11 . . . . 214 F2
Heathfield Cl 9 DN3 . . . . . . 14 A3
Heathfield Ct DN34 . . . . 191 B6
Heathfield Rd NG31 . . . . . . 210 C3
Heath La Ancaster NG32 . . . 119 F3
Boothby Graffoe LN5 . . . . 94 B2
Carlton Scroop NG32 . . . . . . 119 D4
Great Ponton NG33 . . . . 139 D4
Honington NG32 . . . . 119 C2
Leasingham NG34 . . . . 121 C7
Normanton NG32 . . . . 119 F6
Syston NG32 . . . . 130 D8
Wellingore LN5 . . . . 107 C8
Welton LN1 . . . . 67 F6
Wilsford NG32 . . . . 120 B1
Heathland Way DN36 . . . . . 195 E6
Heathlea 11 LN2 . . . . 68 F4
Heath Rd
Bracebridge Heath LN4 . . . . 205 F2
Coleby LN5 . . . . 93 F3
Helpston PE6 . . . . 173 C2
15 Navenby LN5 . . . . 107 A8
5 Nettleham LN2 . . . . 68 C2
Pilsgate PE9 . . . . 172 C3
Scopwick LN4 . . . . 108 B8
Scothern LN2 . . . . 68 D4
Skegness PE25 . . . . 206 B3
Heath's Mdw Nature
Reserve* PE24 . . . . 102 C7
Heath The LN5 . . . . 107 B7
Heaton Cl
2 Beacon Hill NG24 . . . . 104 B4
Peterborough PE3 . . . . 225 B3
Heaton St 1 DN21 . . . . 197 D4
Hebden Moor Way 8 LN6 . . 93 B8
Hebden Rd DN15 . . . . 182 C4
Hebden Wlk NG31 . . . . 211 F6
HECKDYKE DN10 . . . . 40 C7
Heckdyke La DN10 . . . . 40 C7
HECKINGTON NG34 . . . . 122 D3
Heckington Rd NG34 . . . . . 122 C1
Heckington St Andrews CE
Prim Sch NG34 . . . . 122 E3
Heckington Sta NG34 . . . . . 122 E2
Heckington Windmill*
NG34 . . . . 122 E2
Hedda Dr 2 PE7 . . . . 230 D3
Hedgefield Hurn PE11 . . . . 144 F4
Hedge Field Rd NG32 . . . . . 210 A4
HEDGEHOG BRIDGE PE20 . . 124 E5
Hedgehog La PE20 . . . . 124 D4
Hedge La LN6 . . . . 92 D4
Hedgelands
Peterborough PE4 . . . . 221 A5
3 Wisbech PE13 . . . . 170 D2
Hedgerow Cl 5 DN19 . . . . . . 11 C8
Hedgerow La 1 DN20 . . . . . 196 D3
Hedgerows The
Collingham NG23 . . . . 91 D4
10 Sleaford NG34 . . . . 212 C6
Hedon Rd HU9 . . . . 181 B6
HEIGHINGTON LN4 . . . . 81 F4
Heighington Fen LN4 . . . . . . 82 A5
Heighington Rd LN4 . . . . 81 C4
Heimdal Rd DN33 . . . . 191 C2
Helen Cres 8 DN40 . . . . 186 A4
Helene Gr DN32 . . . . 192 B7
Helenship La DN22 . . . . 65 A4
Hell La NG33 . . . . 140 C5
Hellyers Ct HU4 . . . . 179 D2
Helm Dr HU9 . . . . 181 C6
Helmsdale Gdns PE4 . . . . . 220 F2
Helmsley Ct 1 PE7 . . . . 231 F5
Helmsley Gr HU5 . . . . 179 C7
Helmsley Rd
Green Hill NG31 . . . . 210 D6
Green Hill NG31 . . . . 210 E6
Helmsley Way PE11 . . . . . . 214 F4
HELPRINGHAM NG34 . . . . . . 133 E7
Helpringham Rd
Burton Pedwardine NG34 . . 122 B1
Helpringham NG34 . . . . 133 C8
Helpringham Sch NG34 . . . 133 D7
HELPSTON PE6 . . . . 173 C4
Helpston Rd Castor PE5 . . . 223 D2
Etton PE6 . . . . 220 A8
Helsby Rd LN5 . . . . 205 D4
HELSEY PE24 . . . . 89 F7
Helsey La PE24 . . . . 89 F7
Helston Wlk DN17 . . . . 184 C8
Heltwate PE3 . . . . 225 B7
Heltwate Ct PE3 . . . . 225 B7
Heltwate Sch PE3 . . . . 225 B7
Helvellyn Way DN33 . . . . . . 191 D1
HEMINGBY LN9 . . . . 72 B1
Hemingby La Fulletby LN9 . . 86 A8
Horncastle LN9 . . . . 199 C6
Hemingby Rd LN9 . . . . 72 B1
Hemingby Way LN9 . . . . 199 C5
Hemingford Cres PE2 . . . . . 231 E6
Hemington Way 1 PE20 . . 136 C5
Hemmingway Wlk HU13 . . 178 E3
Hempdyke Rd DN15 . . . . . . 182 E4
Hemplands The 9 NG23 . . . 91 D5
Hempstead Rd 2 PE7 . . . . 230 C1
HEMSWELL DN21 . . . . 42 D1
Hemswell Ave
4 Kingston upon Hull HU9 . . . . 5 E8
Lincoln LN6 . . . . 205 A7
HEMSWELL CLIFF LN8 . . . . . . 55 A8
Hemswell Cliff Prim Sch
LN8 . . . . 43 A1
Hemswell Dr DN31 . . . . 190 F8
Hemswell La DN21 . . . . 42 D1
Henderson Ave DN15 . . . . . 182 F4
Henderson Avenue Acad
DN15 . . . . 182 F4
Henderson Cres 2 DN15 . 182 F4
Henderson Way DN15 . . . . . . 9 A5
Heneage Rd DN32 . . . . 191 F6
Hengist Cl 7 NG34 . . . . 212 B2
Henley Ct
2 Gainsborough DN21 . . . . 197 C6
Lincoln LN5 . . . . 205 D8
Henley St LN5 . . . . 205 D8
Henlow Cl
6 Birchwood LN6 . . . . 204 B8
3 Kirton in Lindsey DN21 . . . 42 F8
Henrietta St 2 PE11 . . . . . . 214 C3
Henry Boot Way HU4 . . . . . 179 B1
Henry La LN3 . . . . 83 D4
Henry St Grimsby DN31 . . . 191 C8
Lincoln LN5 . . . . 201 F1
Peterborough PE1 . . . . 226 A4
Scunthorpe DN15 . . . . 182 F3
Henshaw PE1 . . . . 226 E6
Henshaw Ave 2 LN12 . . . . . . 77 A7
Henson Cl
13 Spalding PE11 . . . . 214 C2
5 Wisbech PE13 . . . . 170 D2
Henson Dr
13 Navenby/Wellingore
LN5 . . . . 107 A8
6 Peterborough PE7 . . . . . . 230 F5
Henton Cl 13 NG24 . . . . 104 C5
Herald Wy PE6 . . . . 221 E3
Hercules Dr 7 NG24 . . . . . . 104 A4
Hercules Wy 2 PE2 . . . . 231 E4
Herdgate La PE11 . . . . 145 D2
Hereford Ave DN34 . . . . 191 C5
Hereford Cl 2 NG34 . . . . . . 212 C7
Hereford Sq PE10 . . . . 213 B3
Hereford St HU4 . . . . 179 E3
Hereford Way 8 NG31 . . . . 210 E5
Heren Pl 9 PE11 . . . . 214 A2
Hereward Cl 2 PE1 . . . . 226 B2
Hereward Cross 6 PE1 . . . 226 A2
Hereward Pl DN16 . . . . 185 E7
Hereward Rd
Peterborough PE1 . . . . 226 B2
Spalding PE11 . . . . 214 B4
Hereward St
5 Bourne PE10 . . . . 213 D5
Lincoln LN1 . . . . 234 B4
Hereward Way
11 Billingborough NG34 . . . 133 B1
21 Crowland PE6 . . . . 166 E1
Market Deeping PE6 . . . . . . 217 E4
Herewood Cross Sh Ctr
PE1 . . . . 226 A2
Heritage Pk Prim Sch
PE7 . . . . 231 F5
Herlington PE2 . . . . 230 B4
Herlyn Cres 3 PE25 . . . . 90 E3
Hermes Way NG34 . . . . 212 A3
Hermitage The 6 PE9 . . . . 219 A5
Hermit St LN5 . . . . 234 B1
Heron Cl Grimsby DN32 . . . 192 B4
6 Scunthorpe DN15 . . . . . . 182 C6
Skegness PE25 . . . . 103 C8
3 Surfleet PE11 . . . . 145 E3
Heron Ct PE2 . . . . 231 D6
Heron Dr DN21 . . . . 197 F5
Heron Gate DN16 . . . . 185 F5
Heron Holt 3 DN20 . . . . 19 D4
Heron Pk PE1 . . . . 226 F6
Heronry Dr PE6 . . . . 224 E2
Herons Cl PE9 . . . . 172 F6
Heron St HU3 . . . . 180 B5
Heron View LN6 . . . . 204 E8
Heron Way
43 Barton-upon-Humber
DN18 . . . . 10 E8
Holton le Clay DN36 . . . . . . 195 C3
Spalding PE11 . . . . 214 F2
Wyberton PE21 . . . . 136 F8
Heron Wlk LN6 . . . . 204 C1
Herrick Cl PE1 . . . . 225 E8
Herrick Ct 2 LN4 . . . . 207 A6
Herrick Rd DN17 . . . . 184 D7
Herring La
1 Pinchbeck PE11 . . . . 145 B1
4 Spalding PE11 . . . . 214 D4
Herrington Ave 3 LN2 . . . . 68 C2
Hersey Rd 16 LN7 . . . . 33 B4
Hervey Rd NG34 . . . . 212 C2
Hesketh Cres 11 PE25 . . . . 103 E4
Hesketh Ct LE15 . . . . 162 A8
Hesketh Dr 3 DN3 . . . . 14 A2
HESSLE HU13 . . . . 178 D1
Hessle Ave PE21 . . . . 208 D4
Hessle Ct PE21 . . . . 208 C4
Hessle Dr PE21 . . . . 208 C3
Hessle High Sch HU13 . . . . 178 C2
Hessle Mount Sch HU13 . . 178 C3
Hessle Penshurst Prim Sch
HU13 . . . . 178 F3
Hessle Rd HU4 . . . . 179 D3
Hessle Sta HU13 . . . . 3 E4
Hessle View 4 DN18 . . . . . . 10 E8
Hetley PE2 . . . . 230 A4
Hever Cl NG31 . . . . 210 E5
Hewde La DN15 . . . . 2 A1
Hewitt Cl PE7 . . . . 233 B7
Hewitt's Ave
Humberston DN36 . . . . 192 C1
New Waltham DN36 . . . . . . 195 D8
Hewitt's Avenue DN36 . . . . 195 D8
Hewitt's Cir DN36 . . . . 192 C2
Hewitts Manor
1 Cleethorpes DN35 . . . . . . 192 D2
New Waltham DN36 . . . . . . 195 F7
Hewitt's Windmill* DN21 . . 53 E7
Hewson Rd
5 Humberston DN36 . . . . . . 36 D8
Lincoln LN1 . . . . 201 C4
Hewson's La
33 Barton-upon-Humber
DN18 . . . . 3 E1
Collingham NG23 . . . . 91 D3
Hewson St 23 DN17 . . . . 29 D7
Hexham Ave PE10 . . . . 213 B3
Hexham Ct 3 PE1 . . . . 226 D3
HEYDOUR NG32 . . . . 131 D6
Heyford Cl PE4 . . . . 221 D2
Heynings Cl DN21 . . . . 53 B4
Heysham Cl 8 LN5 . . . . 205 D3
Hey St DN35 . . . . 192 F5
Heythrop Rd 3 DN35 . . . . . 192 E3
HIBALDSTOW DN20 . . . . 31 A5
Hibaldstow Cl
10 Birchwood LN6 . . . . 204 C7
9 Grimsby DN34 . . . . 190 F4
Hibaldstow Prim Sch DN20 31 A5
Hibaldstow Rd LN6 . . . . 204 C7
Hickling Cl
15 Grantham NG31 . . . . 210 E2
Kingston upon Hull HU10 . . . 179 A6
Hickling Wlk PE4 . . . . 221 C3
Hickman Cres DN21 . . . . . . 197 C8
Hickman Ct DN21 . . . . 197 E4
Hickman Gr 2 Blyton DN21 . 41 B5
Collingham NG23 . . . . 91 C5
Hickman St DN21 . . . . 197 C4
Hickory Rd 5 LN6 . . . . 200 C1
Hicks La PE7 . . . . 230 F5
Hidcote Wlk 27 HU15 . . . . . . 2 D5
Hide's La Addlethorpe PE24 . . 90 B1
Skegness PE25 . . . . 103 B8
Higgins Cl LN6 . . . . 204 E7
Higgins Rd 5 LN13 . . . . 75 E2
Higham Way 1 HU15 . . . . 2 D5
High Barn La LN9 . . . . 87 D3
Highbridge La PE11 . . . . . . 145 C6
Highbridge Rd LN11 . . . . 49 F2
High Bridge Rd DN8 . . . . 15 C7
High Broadgate PE13 . . . . . 169 F7
High Bunning La NG34 . . . . 143 A7
High Burgage DN15 . . . . 2 B1
Highbury Dr PE12 . . . . 215 E5
Highbury St PE1 . . . . 226 A5
Highclere Rd PE7 . . . . 230 D3
Highcliffe 5 LN5 . . . . 107 A7
Highcliffe Rd NG31 . . . . 211 B7
Highcliff Gdns DN15 . . . . . . 182 E3
High Cliff Rd DN35 . . . . 193 A6
High Cres PE9 . . . . 171 C8
High Ct Way PE7 . . . . 233 D8
Highdales HU10 . . . . 178 C8
High Dike
Cranwell & Byard's Leap
NG34 . . . . 120 B8
Easton NG33 . . . . 151 E8
Great Ponton NG33 . . . . 140 C4
Navenby/Wellingore LN5 . . . . 94 B1
North Rauceby NG32 . . . . . . 120 A5
Old Somerby NG33 . . . . 130 E2
Waddington LN5 . . . . 93 F8
Welby NG31 . . . . 130 E5
Wellingore LN5 . . . . 107 B6
Wilsford NG32 . . . . 119 F1
High Dyke Rd 2 NG34 . . . . . 107 C1
High Fen PE11 . . . . 144 B4
HIGH FERRY PE22 . . . . 126 A8
High Ferry La PE22 . . . . 113 A1
Highfield Ave
4 Immingham DN40 . . . . 186 B3
4 Lincoln LN6 . . . . 205 B7
Highfield Ave *continued*
4 Mablethorpe/Sutton on Sea
LN12 . . . . 64 C1
Scunthorpe DN15 . . . . 182 E3
Wellow DN32 . . . . 191 E5
Highfield Cl
8 Barnby Dun DN3 . . . . 14 A4
Foston NG32 . . . . 117 F2
Gainsborough DN21 . . . . . . 197 E5
7 Hatfield DN7 . . . . 14 D5
8 North Thoresby DN36 . . . . 36 B1
Osbournby NG34 . . . . 132 C5
Highfield Cres
17 Barton-upon-Humber
DN18 . . . . 10 F8
Croxton Kerrial NG32 . . . . . 138 D3
4 Westwoodside DN9 . . . . . . 27 B2
Highfield Dr
2 Kirton in Lindsey DN21 . . . 30 B1
Stapleford LN6 . . . . 105 A6
Highfield Gr DN20 . . . . 196 C5
Highfield La
Halton Holegate PE23 . . . . . 101 B8
Revesby PE22 . . . . 99 B5
Highfield Rd Bainton PE9 . . 172 A4
7 Donington PE11 . . . . 134 F2
North Thoresby DN36 . . . . . . 36 B1
14 Saxilby LN1 . . . . 66 D2
High Field Rd DN20 . . . . 196 F5
Highfields
6 Barrowby NG32 . . . . 210 A5
1 Barrow upon Humber
DN19 . . . . 11 C7
17 Crowle DN17 . . . . 16 D8
2 Nettleham LN2 . . . . 68 D2
Highfields La DN14 . . . . 7 D4
High Fields La PE11 . . . . . . 156 E8
Highfields Ms 9 NG31 . . . . . 129 D5
Highfields Rise 29 LN4 . . . . . 95 C4
Highfields Sch NG24 . . . . . . 104 B3
Highfield Terr
4 Glentham LN8 . . . . 43 F1
2 Lincoln LN6 . . . . 205 A2
Highfield Wy 23 HU14 . . . . . . 3 A4
High Garth DN17 . . . . 184 F2
Highgate
6 Cleethorpes DN35 . . . . . . 192 F5
Leverton Outgate PE22 . . . . 127 B7
High Gate
Helpringham NG34 . . . . 133 D7
Mablethorpe & Sutton LN12 . . 64 C1
Theddlethorpe St Helen LN12 63 D5
Highgate Cl 3 LN12 . . . . 64 C1
Highgate La
Claxby with Moorby PE22 . . . . 99 B6
Normanby by Spital LN8 . . . . . 56 B7
Owmby LN8 . . . . 55 F6
12 Trusthorpe LN12 . . . . 64 C1
Highgrove
1 Long Sutton PE12 . . . . 216 B5
4 Messingham DN17 . . . . 29 D7
Highgrove Cres PE21 . . . . . 209 C6
Highgrove Gdns PE9 . . . . . . 218 E5
High Holme Rd LN11 . . . . . . 198 B6
High Horse Mus* PE22 . . . 111 D8
High House Rd DN22 . . . . . . 52 A2
High La Croft PE24 . . . . 102 D6
Mareham on the Hill LN9 . . . . 85 F2
Highlands 1 PE9 . . . . 163 C1
Highlands Way PE9 . . . . 218 F5
Highland Tarn DN40 . . . . . . 186 B3
High Leas 1 LN2 . . . . 68 D2
Highlees Prim Sch PE3 . . . 225 C6
High Levels Bank DN8 . . . . . 15 F5
High Leys Rd DN17 . . . . 184 F3
HIGH MARNHAM NG23 . . . . . 78 B5
High Mdw Grantham NG31 . 210 D4
Heighington/Washingborough
LN4 . . . . 203 C1
Westborough & Dry Doddington
NG23 . . . . 117 F5
High Mdws 1 Fiskerton LN3 82 A7
Kingston upon Hull HU10 . . . 178 C8
High or Main Rd PE12 . . . . 215 A2
High Point Ret Pk DN31 . . . 189 A1
High Rd Barrowby NG32 . . . 210 A5
Elloughton-cum-Brough HU15 . 2 D7
Gorefield PE13 . . . . 169 F2
Grantham NG31 . . . . 211 C8
Hough-on-the-Hill NG32 . . . . 119 A5
Londonthorpe & Harrowby Without
NG31 . . . . 130 D4
Moulton PE12 . . . . 158 A7
Newton PE13 . . . . 169 F5
Salmonby LN9 . . . . 86 E8
Weston PE12 . . . . 157 C7
Wisbech St Mary PE13 . . . . . 177 F2
High Ridge Comp Sch
DN15 . . . . 182 E3
High Ridge Sports Hall
DN15 . . . . 182 E3
HIGH RISBY DN15 . . . . 9 A1
High St E DN15 . . . . 183 C3
High St N 16 NG34 . . . . 108 E2
High St S
3 Ruskington NG34 . . . . 108 E1
20 Ruskington NG34 . . . . 108 E2
High St St Martin's PE9 . . . 219 C3
High St W DN21 . . . . 29 B4
High Side PE13 . . . . 169 D2
High St 8 Alford LN13 . . . . . . 75 F3
Alvingham LN11 . . . . 49 F2
Barrow upon Humber DN19 . . 11 D8
Barton-upon-Humber DN18 . . . 3 E1
Bassingham LN5 . . . . 92 F2
Baumber LN9 . . . . 85 A8
1 Beckingham DN10 . . . . 52 B8
Belton DN9 . . . . 16 E1
High St *continued*
Benniworth LN8 . . . . 71 F8
Bicker PE20 . . . . 135 A4
Binbrook LN8 . . . . 47 C4
Blyton DN21 . . . . 41 C5
Boston PE21 . . . . 208 F3
Bottesford NG13 . . . . 128 A5
Branston LN4 . . . . 81 E2
Brant Broughton LN5 . . . . . . 105 F4
Broughton DN20 . . . . 19 D3
Burgh le Marsh PE24 . . . . . . 102 E8
Burringham DN17 . . . . 17 D4
Caistor LN7 . . . . 33 B4
Carlby PE9 . . . . 163 D4
Carlton-le-Moorland LN5 . . . 105 E8
Castle Bytham NG33 . . . . . . 152 D1
Castor PE5 . . . . 223 F2
Caythorpe NG32 . . . . 119 B7
Cherry Willingham/Reepham
LN3 . . . . 203 D5
Cleethorpes DN35 . . . . 192 E6
Collingham NG23 . . . . 91 D4
3 Collyweston PE9 . . . . 171 B1
Colsterworth NG33 . . . . 151 D6
Coningsby LN4 . . . . 207 A4
Corby Glen NG33 . . . . 152 E8
Corringham DN21 . . . . 41 E1
9 Crowle DN17 . . . . 16 D7
Donington PE11 . . . . 134 E2
Eagle & Swinethorpe LN6 . . . . 79 B2
East Ferry DN21 . . . . 28 B2
Eastoft DN17 . . . . 7 A3
3 Easton on the Hill PE9 . . . 171 D3
Elkington LN11 . . . . 60 E7
Epworth DN9 . . . . 27 D7
Eye PE6 . . . . 175 A1
Faldingworth LN8 . . . . 56 F3
Fillingham DN21 . . . . 54 F4
3 Fiskerton LN3 . . . . 82 A7
Flixborough DN15 . . . . 8 B2
5 Fulbeck NG32 . . . . 106 C1
Fulletby LN9 . . . . 86 B8
Gainsborough DN21 . . . . 197 D3
Garthorpe & Fockerby DN17 . . 7 E5
Gate Burton DN21 . . . . 53 A1
Girton NG23 . . . . 78 C1
Glentham LN8 . . . . 43 F1
Glinton PE6 . . . . 220 C8
Gosberton PE11 . . . . 145 B6
Grainthorpe LN11 . . . . 50 B8
Grantham NG31 . . . . 211 A4
Great Gonerby NG31 . . . . . . 129 D5
Great Limber DN37 . . . . 22 D3
Gringley on the Hill DN10 . . . 39 C1
Hagworthingham PE23 . . . . . 87 A4
Harby NG23 . . . . 79 C5
Harlaxton NG32 . . . . 139 C7
Harmston LN5 . . . . 93 F5
Hatfield DN7 . . . . 14 C2
Haxey DN9 . . . . 27 C2
16 Heckington NG34 . . . . 122 E2
Heighington/Washingborough
LN4 . . . . 203 B2
Helpringham NG34 . . . . 133 D7
Hogsthorpe PE24 . . . . 90 B7
Holbeach PE12 . . . . 215 E2
Horbling NG34 . . . . 133 B2
Horncastle LN9 . . . . 199 B4
Humberside Airport DN39 . . . 22 A6
Ingham LN1 . . . . 54 F2
2 Ingoldmells PE25 . . . . 90 E3
Ketton PE9 . . . . 171 A3
Kexby DN21 . . . . 53 E5
Kingston upon Hull HU1 . . . . 181 A5
18 Kirton in Lindsey DN21 . . . 30 B1
Laceby DN37 . . . . 23 F1
Leadenham LN5 . . . . 106 D3
Lincoln LN5 . . . . 234 A1
2 Little Bytham NG33 . . . . . . 163 A8
Long Sutton PE12 . . . . 216 C4
Luddington & Haldenby DN17 . . 7 C4
18 Mablethorpe/Sutton on Sea
LN12 . . . . 64 B4
Market Deeping PE6 . . . . 217 B4
Market Stainton LN8 . . . . 72 A6
Martin LN4 . . . . 96 C2
Marton DN21 . . . . 65 D8
Maxey PE6 . . . . 217 A1
Messingham DN17 . . . . 29 D7
Metheringham LN4 . . . . 95 C4
Misterton DN10 . . . . 39 F5
5 Morton PE10 . . . . 154 C7
Moulton PE12 . . . . 157 F6
12 Navenby/Wellingore
LN5 . . . . 107 A7
Nettleham LN2 . . . . 68 C2
Nettleton LN7 . . . . 33 C2
Newton on Trent LN1 . . . . 65 D1
North Ferriby HU14 . . . . 3 A5
8 North Kelsey LN7 . . . . 32 A4
Northorpe PE10 . . . . 164 C7
North Scarle LN6 . . . . 78 E1
North Thoresby DN36 . . . . 36 A1
Osbournby NG34 . . . . 132 C5
Owston Ferry DN9 . . . . 28 B3
Peterborough PE2 . . . . 231 A6
Pointon & Sempringham
NG34 . . . . 143 B7
Redbourne DN21 . . . . 30 F2
Reepham LN3 . . . . 203 F8
Rippingale PE10 . . . . 142 F2
Ropsley NG33 . . . . 131 B1
Roxby cum Risby DN15 . . . . . . 8 E1
Saxilby LN1 . . . . 66 D2
Scampton LN1 . . . . 67 C6
Scotton DN21 . . . . 29 C1
Scunthorpe DN15 . . . . 183 A3
Sixhills LN8 . . . . 59 A7

High St *continued*
Skegness PE25 206 C3
Skellingthorpe LN6 200 A5
Snitterby DN21 43 D5
South Clifton NG23 78 C5
South Ferriby DN18 10 A7
South Kyme LN4 123 B8
South Witham NG33 151 D2
Spalding PE11 214 E4
7 Spilsby PE23 88 A1
Stamford PE9 219 C5
Staunton NG13 117 A2
Sturton by Stow LN1 66 C7
5 Sutton Bridge PE12 160 F4
Swayfield NG33 152 D5
Swinderby LN6 92 A5
Swineshead PE20 135 B7
Swinstead NG33 153 A5
Upton DN21 53 D5
Waddingham DN21 43 D7
Waddington LN5 93 F7
Wainfleet All Saints PE24 102 D1
Walcott LN4 109 D7
Walesby LN8 46 B5
Walkeringham DN10 39 F3
1 Waltham DN37 194 E4
Welbourn LN5 106 E5
West/East Butterwick DN17 17 D1
Willingham by Stow DN21 53 E3
11 Winterton DN15 9 A5
Wootton DN39 11 E2
Wroot DN9 26 D6
Highstock La PE12 168 D1
High Thorpe Cres DN35 192 D3
High Thorpe Rd LN3 83 D1
HIGH TOYNTON LN9 86 A4
High Wash Dro 2 PE6 166 E1
Highwood Mews DN35 192 E5
Higney Rd PE7 230 C1
Higson Rd 4 LN1 201 D7
Hilary Gr HU4 179 B2
Hilary Rd DN33 194 F7
Hilda Cl 6 NG34 212 B2
Hildas Ave HU5 180 A8
Hilda St 4 Boston PE21 209 A7
Grimsby DN32 189 C1
Hildreds Sh Ctr PE25 206 D3
Hildyard Cl 1 HU10 178 F6
Hildyard St DN32 192 B8
Hiles Ave 6 DN15 9 A5
Hill Abbey LN4 95 D7
Hillary Cl 8 Spalding PE11 214 B2
1 Stamford PE9 219 D6
Hillary Rd DN16 185 B5
Hillary Way DN37 190 E8
Hill Ave NG31 211 B5
Hill Brow HU10 178 B6
Hill Cl PE1 226 D5
Hill Cres DN21 197 F5
Hillcrest NG34 107 C2
Hillcrest Ave
Kingston upon Hull HU13 178 C2
Yaxley PE7 233 E5
Hillcrest Dr 2 DN15 8 A4
Hillcrest Early Years Acad
DN21 197 F4
Hillcrest Gdns 3 PE20 135 B7
Hillcroft 1 LN4 203 A2
Hill Ct NG31 210 D2
HILLDYKE PE22 126 A6
Hill Field 3 PE24 102 D2
Hillfoot Dr DN17 184 E3
Hillgate PE12 168 C2
Hillgate St PE34 161 F3
Hillingford Way NG31 210 E3
Hill La PE20 136 B5
Hillman Cl LN4 205 F3
Hillman Rd HU13 178 F3
Hill Rd DN21 41 E1
Hill Rise 8 Brough HU15 2 C6
Coleby LN5 93 F3
Louth LN11 198 A7
Hill's Ct 9 NG34 212 D4
Hills Dr 14 DN36 36 D4
Hillside 4 Ancaster NG32 120 A2
Beckingham LN5 105 B4
3 Marton DN21 65 E8
Hillside App 5 LN2 202 C3
Hillside Ave Lincoln LN2 202 C3
7 Mablethorpe/Sutton on Sea
LN12 77 A8
Hillside Cl Ufford PE9 172 F2
Ufford PE9 172 F2
Hillside Cres
Barnetby le Wold DN38 21 B5
3 Grantham NG31 211 D2
Hillside Dr
5 Barton-upon-Humber
DN18 10 E8
Grantham NG31 211 D2
Hillside Est NG34 108 F2
Hillside Gdns 25 PE8 172 B1
Hillside Rd
6 Broughton DN20 19 E4
Glentworth DN21 54 F7
Woolsthorpe by Belvoir
NG32 128 D1
Hillstead Cl 13 DN36 36 D4
Hillsyde Ave 11 DN10 39 F5
Hill Terr LN11 198 C4
Hill The 4 Saltfleet LN11 51 C4
Skellingthorpe LN6 200 A4
Worlaby DN20 10 E1
Hill Top 1 LN5 93 E5
Hilltop Ave DN15 182 D5
Hilltop Cl LN6 79 B2
Hilltop Gdns DN17 29 C7
Hill Top La 1 DN21 41 B5
Hill Top Pl DN34 190 D3
Hill View Cl NG31 210 E3
Hill View Rd 14 NG33 151 D2
Hillward Cl PE2 230 C6
Hilmore Rd DN34 190 C4
Hilton Ave DN15 182 B3
Hilton Cl 2 DN9 16 E2
Hilton Ct DN35 193 B1
Hilton's La PE20 136 E1
Hinaidi La LN4 95 C7
Hinchcliffe PE2 229 E2
Hindon Wlk DN17 184 C8
Hine Ave NG24 104 B4
Hinkler St DN35 192 E5
Hinkley Dr DN40 186 B5
Hinman Wlk 9 DN15 183 B3
Hipper La PE20 135 D2
Hither Old Gate PE12 158 D6
Hives La LN6 78 E2
Hix Cl PE12 215 C2
Hix's La PE13 160 A1
Hobart Cl 11 LN5 93 E8
Hobart Rd NG31 211 D7
Hobart St HU3 180 D5
Hobb La 4 DN21 29 C3
Hobbs Gdns PE9 218 E4
Hobhole Bank PE22 126 D8
Hobhole Bank Nature Reserve★ PE21 137 C7
Hob La PE22 125 D6
Hobson Rd 7 HU15 2 C6
Hobsons Gn PE11 214 A5
Hobson Way DN41 187 E2
Hockland Rd 2 PE13 169 F7
Hockle's Gate PE12 159 B7
Hockney Hole La PE12 158 A7
Hodder Cl 1 NG31 210 F3
Hoddesdon Cres 20 DN7 14 D3
Hoddins Wy PE12 216 A6
Hod Fen Dro PE7 233 F2
Hodge Ct 3 HU9 181 C7
Hodgetoft La LN13 63 E1
Hodgson Ave PE4 220 E6
Hodgson St HU8 181 A7
Hodgson Way 3 LN12 77 A8
Hodney Rd 5 PE6 175 A1
Hodson Cl LN6 200 B5
Hodson Gn LN9 199 C4
Hodsons Marsh PE25 103 A1
Hoe Dr 18 LN8 57 D8
Hoekman Dr 3 PE11 214 B2
Hoekman Way PE11 214 B2
Hoffleet Rd PE20 135 C4
HOFFLEET STOW PE20 135 C4
Hogens La PE13 170 A5
Hoggard La DN14 7 E8
Hogg La HU10 178 B8
Hog's Gate PE12 158 A6
HOGSTHORPE PE24 90 B6
Hogsthorpe Com Prim Sch
PE24 90 B7
Hogsthorpe Rd LN13 76 F1
HOLBEACH PE12 215 C3
HOLBEACH BANK PE12 215 C7
Holbeach Bank Acad
PE12 215 D7
HOLBEACH CLOUGH PE12 215 B7
Holbeach & District Nature Reserve★ PE12 215 E2
Holbeach Dro Gate PE12 168 C4
HOLBEACH DROVE PE12 168 B3
Holbeach Hospl PE12 215 B5
HOLBEACH HURN PE12 147 F2
Holbeach Prim Sch PE12 215 D3
Holbeach Rd Spalding PE11 214 F6
1 Spalding PE12 157 B6
HOLBEACH ST JOHNS
PE12 158 E1
HOLBEACH ST MARKS
PE12 147 D6
Holbeach St Marks CE Prim Sch PE12 147 D6
HOLBEACH ST MATTHEW
PE12 148 A7
Holbeach Tecnology Pk
PE12 215 B4
Holbeck Pl 2 DN40 186 B4
Holborn Rd PE11 214 B2
Holborn St HU8 181 B7
Holcroft PE2 230 B3
Holdan Cl DN36 193 A1
Holdenby Cl 3 LN2 202 E7
Holden Dr 9 PE24 102 E7
Holden Way 7 NG31 129 E5
Holderness Rd HU9 181 C8
Holdfield PE3 225 B6
Holdich St PE3 225 E2
HOLDINGHAM NG34 212 C7
Holdingham La NG34 121 E7
Hole Gate PE23 101 C8
Holgate La PE4 220 F7
Holgate Pl 20 Swanland HU14 3 B7
13 Swanland HU14 3 B7
Holgate Rd DN16 185 D8
Holkham Rd PE2 229 D3
Holland Ave
18 Crowle DN17 16 D8
Peterborough PE4 221 B1
Scunthorpe DN15 182 E4
Holland Cl 8 Bourne PE10 213 C5
10 Market Deeping PE6 217 A6
Peterborough PE4 221 B1
Holland Dr 7 Grasby DN38 32 E7
Skegness PE25 206 C1
Holland La PE22 114 F4
Holland Mkt 16 PE11 214 D4
Holland Rd Horbling NG34 133 B3
Spalding PE11 214 E4
Holland Rd *continued*
Stamford PE9 219 C6
Swaton NG34 133 E3
Holland's Chase PE11 156 A6
Holland St HU9 181 D8
Holland Way PE12 215 B2
Hollengs La 1 LN11 59 E1
Holles St 6 DN32 191 E8
Hollies Ave 14 NG24 104 A6
Hollies The PE12 215 E3
Hollin Bridge La DN7 15 A3
Hollingsworth Ave 1
DN40 186 B4
Hollingsworth Cl 5 DN35 192 D2
Hollingsworth La DN9 27 E6
Hollis' Rd NG31 210 F2
Hollowbrook Cl 3 NG34 108 D2
Hollowdyke La NG24 104 C1
Hollowgate Hill DN21 42 E4
Hollowgate La NG23 78 A5
Hollowside Rd PE7 233 B8
Hollows The 4 LN11 61 F3
Holly Cl
Cherry Willingham/Reepham
LN3 203 E5
5 Grantham NG31 211 D2
Horncastle LN9 199 A5
Lincoln LN5 205 D5
2 Newborough PE6 174 E5
Scunthorpe DN16 185 C4
1 Sleaford NG34 212 D2
6 Stallingborough DN41 23 E6
Holly Cres LN11 198 E3
Holly Dr Bourne PE10 213 C7
Hessle HU13 178 D3
Holly Hill 1 HU15 2 E6
Holly Rd PE25 206 A2
Holly St LN5 205 D5
Hollytree Ave 2 HU5 179 B7
Holly Tree Cl 9 LN8 57 D7
Holly Way 2 PE6 217 D4
Hollywell Rd LN5 205 D1
Hollywell Rd (The Rookery) 23
LN13 75 F2
Holly Wlk PE7 230 D3
Hollywood Dr 8 NG31 210 F7
HOLME Holme DN16 19 A1
Holme NG23 91 A2
Holme Ave DN36 195 C6
Holme Cl Brigg DN20 196 D4
Castor PE5 223 D2
Thorpe on the Hill LN6 92 F8
Tinwell PE9 218 D3
Holme Dene 1 DN9 27 C2
Holme Dr
Burton upon Stather DN15 8 B5
Sudbrooke LN2 68 F2
Holme Gdns 7 DN7 14 C7
Holme Hall Ave DN16 185 B3
HOLME HILL DN32 191 F6
Holme La Grassthorpe NG23 78 A2
Holme DN16 185 E2
Marnham NG23 78 A4
Messingham DN17 29 E8
4 Ruskington NG34 108 E1
Scunthorpe DN16 185 B3
Winthorpe NG24 104 B8
HOLME RD PE20 135 F8
Holme Rd PE7 233 E4
Holmes Cl Louth LN11 198 B7
2 Skidbrooke with Saltfleet
Haven LN11 51 C4
Holmes Dr 10 PE9 171 A3
Holmes Field 6 LN5 92 F3
Holmes La
North Somercotes LN11 38 A1
Roxby cum Risby DN15 9 D5
2 Welton/Dunholme LN2 68 E6
Holmes Rd Frampton PE20 124 F1
Glinton PE6 220 D7
Horsington LN10 83 F1
Kirton PE20 136 A8
Stickney PE22 113 A7
Stixwould & Woodhall LN10 84 A1
Holmes Road DN10 40 B2
Holme St DN32 191 E7
Holmes Way
Horncastle LN9 199 D1
Peterborough PE4 221 D2
Wragby LN8 70 C5
Holme Valley Prim Sch
DN16 185 C3
Holme Wlk 6 DN21 197 F5
Holme Wood Ct 5 DN3 14 A1
Holme Wood La
Claxby with Moorby LN9 99 B8
Hameringham LN9 86 B1
Holmfield LN3 82 B7
Holmfirth Rd DN15 182 C4
Holm La NG23 104 F1
Holm Rd DN9 27 B2
Holmshaw Cl 24 DN3 14 A2
Holstein Dr DN16 185 A2
Holt Cl 10 Lincoln LN6 93 C8
9 Wittering PE8 172 B1
Holt La Horncastle LN9 199 D4
Mareham le Fen PE22 99 A3
Holton Ct DN36 195 C1
HOLTON CUM BECKERING
LN8 70 C8
HOLTON LE CLAY DN36 195 D2
Holton-le-Clay Inf Sch
DN36 195 D2
Holton le Clay Jun Sch
DN36 195 E1
HOLTON LE MOOR LN7 45 A8
Holton Mount DN36 195 C2
Holton Rd Nettleton LN7 33 A2
Holton Rd *continued*
South Kelsey LN7 32 D1
Tetney DN36 195 F1
Holt Prim Sch The LN6 200 A3
Holt The DN21 197 F5
Holy Cross Gdns 12 NG32 119 B7
Holydyke DN18 10 E8
Holy Family Cath Prim Sch
DN7 14 C6
Holyoake Rd DN32 192 C6
Holyroad Dr DN15 182 D7
Holyrood Cl PE20 134 E3
Holyrood Wlk PE11 214 E2
Holy Trinity CE Prim Sch
LN4 207 A5
Holywell Cl 1 PE3 225 A1
Holy Well La LN11 49 A4
Holywell Rd PE9 162 E8
Holywell Way PE3 224 F2
Home Beat Dr DN20 19 C3
Home Cl 7 Bourne PE10 213 C7
Bracebridge Heath LN4 205 F3
Kingston upon Hull HU4 179 C5
Home Ct 8 LN5 107 A7
Home Farm Cl
Great Casterton PE9 218 C8
Laughterton LN1 65 D2
Homefarm La NG23 79 A7
Homefield Ave DN33 191 D3
Home Paddock DN37 194 E4
Home Pasture 4 PE4 220 F5
Home Pk 4 NG34 120 F8
Homers La PE22 126 D4
Home St DN15 183 B4
Homestead Garth 11 DN7 14 D4
Homestead Gdns 17 PE10 164 C8
Honeyhill PE4 221 E1
Honeyhill Rd PE13 169 C2
Honeyholes La LN2 68 D6
Honey Pot Cl LN2 202 E7
Honey Pot La NG33 151 F4
Honey Pot Lane Ind Est
NG33 151 F4
Honeysuckle Cl
4 Lincoln LN5 205 C2
14 Mablethorpe & Sutton
LN12 76 F8
18 Sutton on Sea Ln11 76 F8
Honeysuckle Ct
Humberston DN35 192 E1
Peterborough PE2 230 D7
3 Scunthorpe DN16 185 D4
Honeysuckle La 16 LN8 70 D4
Honeysuckle Pl 19 HU15 2 C5
HONINGTON NG32 119 C2
Honington App 5 LN1 201 D7
Honington Cres LN1 201 D7
Honington Rd 2 NG32 130 B8
Honningsvaag Cl DN36 195 B7
Hood Cl NG34 212 A3
Hood Rd DN17 184 D6
Hood St
Kingston upon Hull HU8 181 A8
8 Lincoln LN5 201 F1
Hook's Dro PE13 177 C4
Hooks La LN5 106 E6
Hoop End DN36 36 D4
Hoopers Cl 4 NG13 128 A5
Hoop La LN8 70 E2
Hope Gdns PE21 208 F6
Hope House Sch NG24 104 C3
Hope St Cleethorpes DN35 193 A5
Grimsby DN32 191 F8
Lincoln LN5 201 F1
Hopfield DN20 31 A5
Hopgardens 1 DN21 53 E3
Hopgarth 11 DN9 27 D2
Hop Hills La DN7 14 D5
Hopkins Ave DN17 185 A7
Hoplands Cl DN36 195 E7
Hoplands Rd LN4 207 D5
Hoplands The 4 NG34 212 F4
Hopland's Wood Nature Reserve★ LN13 88 F6
HOP POLE PE11 165 F5
Hopton St LN9 199 B3
Hopwood Cl HU3 180 D8
Hopyard La Bassingham LN5 93 B1
Normanton on Trent NG23 78 A3
Horace St PE21 208 E5
HORBLING NG34 133 C2
Horbling Fen Dro NG34 133 D2
Horbling La PE22 113 A7
Horbling Line Nature Reserve★ NG34 133 B1
Horbury Cl DN15 182 D4
HORKSTOW DN18 10 A5
Horkstow Rd DN18 10 E7
Hornbeam Ave DN16 185 A5
Hornbeam Cl 17 NG34 108 E1
Hornbeam Dr DN41 23 E5
Hornbeam Rd PE7 230 B2
Hornby Dr 20 LN12 77 A7
HORNCASTLE LN9 199 D3
Horncastle Cty Prim Sch
LN9 199 C4
Horncastle Hill PE23 87 A1
Horncastle La
Dunholme LN2 68 B5
Grange de Lings LN1 67 F5
Horncastle Rd Bardney LN3 83 C4
Boston PE21 208 F8
Fishtoft PE21 125 E5
Fulletby LN9 86 A7
Goulceby LN9 72 D5
Horsington LN10 84 D4
Louth LN11 198 A4
Mareham le Fen PE22 98 F4
Horncastle Rd *continued*
Raithby cum Maltby LN11 60 F2
Roughton LN9 85 C2
Tathwell LN11 73 A8
West Ashby LN9 199 C8
Woodhall Spa LN10 97 F6
Wragby LN8 70 D4
Horncastle St Lawrence Sch
The LN9 199 D4
Horne La 3 NG22 65 B1
Horner Cl 1 LN5 205 C2
Horn Lane LE15 162 A1
Hornsby Cres DN15 182 F4
Hornsby Rd NG31 210 E2
Hornsea Parade 4 HU9 181 C8
Hornsey Hill Rd DN21 28 D1
Horn The 7 PE25 206 A7
Horse Fair Gn 25 DN8 15 A8
Horse Fayre 7 PE11 214 A3
Horsegate PE6 217 D4
Horsegate Field Rd DN19 5 B2
Horseham's La PE20 135 A5
Horse Mkt 24 LN7 33 B4
Horsemoor Dro PE12 159 B1
Horsemoor La LN9 72 C2
Horse Pasture La DN22 65 C7
Horsepit La 12 PE11 145 C1
Horseshoe Cl
7 Grimsby DN33 194 D8
12 Ruskington NG34 108 D2
Horseshoe La PE20 136 D5
Horseshoe Rd PE11 214 A2
Horseshoe Terr PE13 170 C1
Horseshoe Way
Hampton Vale PE7 230 D1
Yaxley PE7 233 D8
Horseshoe Yd 11 PE6 166 E1
Horsewells St 1 DN10 39 C1
HORSINGTON LN10 84 C3
Horstead Ave DN20 196 D5
Horton St LN2 202 C3
Horton Wlk PE3 225 C5
Hospital Dro PE12 160 C3
Hospital La PE21 209 A6
Hospital Rd PE12 161 A5
Hotchkin Ave LN1 66 E2
Hotham Dr HU5 179 B8
Hotham Rd HU5 179 A8
Hotham Rd S HU5 179 B8
Hotham St HU9 181 D7
Hotspur Rd DN21 197 C6
HOUGHAM NG32 118 C3
Hougham Rd
Hougham NG32 118 B4
Westborough & Dry Doddington
NG23 117 F5
Hough La
Carlton Scroop NG32 119 C4
Claypole NG23 117 F7
HOUGH-ON-THE-HILL
NG32 119 A5
Hough Rd Barkston NG32 130 B8
Carlton Scroop NG32 119 A3
Hough-on-the-Hill NG32 118 E7
Houghton Ave PE2 231 F5
Houghton Rd NG31 211 C2
Houghton Road Ind Est
NG31 211 C1
Houlden Way 1 NG34 122 E3
Hounsfield Cl
9 Beacon Hill NG24 104 C4
Newark-on-Trent NG24 104 B5
Houps Rd 8 DN8 15 B8
Hourne Ct HU13 178 E2
Hourne The HU13 178 E2
House Ct DN16 185 D4
Househams La LN11 61 F3
Howard Cl PE34 161 F2
Howard Fields Wy LN11 198 A7
Howard Gr DN32 192 B6
Howard Rd 10 LN4 108 A7
Howard's Gdns 1 NG24 104 B2
Howard St LN1 201 C4
Howdale La NG32 119 A3
Howdales LN11 50 D1
Howdales Rd LN11 50 E1
Howden Croft Hill HU15 2 A8
Howe Ct 2 LN2 202 D6
Howegate Dr PE7 230 B1
Howe La
Ashby with Scremby PE23 88 C3
Goxhill DN19 11 F8
HOWELL NG34 122 D5
Howell Fen Dro NG34 122 D5
Howell Rd NG34 122 E3
Howgarth La PE22 114 F5
Howitts Rd 14 NG13 128 A5
Howland PE2 230 A3
Howlett Rd DN35 193 A4
HOWSHAM LN7 32 A6
Howsham La 2 DN38 32 D8
Howsham Lane DN38 32 C7
Howsham Road LN7 31 F6
Howville Ave 2 DN7 14 F3
Howville Rd 1 DN7 14 F3
Hoylake Cl DN21 197 E6
Hoylake Dr
1 Immingham DN40 186 D5
Peterborough PE7 231 C5
Skegness PE25 206 D5
Hoylake Rd DN17 184 D3
Hubba Cres PE20 135 C6
Hubbard Cl 2 NG34 122 D3
HUBBERT'S BRIDGE PE20 124 F2
Hubberts Bridge Sta PE20 124 E2

Hubert's Cl PE12 168 C1
Hub The★ NG34 212 E4
Huckles Way PE25 206 B6
Huddleston Rd DN32 192 B7
Hudson Ave Kirk Ella HU10 178 D5
Scunthorpe DN15 182 E5
Hudson Cl PE23 88 B3
Hudson Ct HU13 178 D1
Hudson Dr LN4 207 E6
Hudson Gr 3 PE7 230 F5
Hudson Rd 4 PE11 214 C2
Hudson's Gdns 5 PE21 209 B4
Hudson St HU3 180 D8
Hudson Way
Grantham NG31 211 A3
12 Skegness PE25 206 A5
Huggin Carr Rd DN7 14 F1
Hughes Ford Way 20 LN1 66 D2
Hugh Hill La DN7 14 E5
Hughson Wlk 3 LN2 68 E6
Hulberry Cl 10 DN41 23 A4
Hull Arena★ HU1 180 E4
Hull Coll
Kingston upon Hull HU1 181 A7
Kingston upon Hull HU2 180 D7
Hull Collegiate HU10 178 D5
Hull & E Riding Mus★ HU9 181 A6
Hull Maritime Mus★ HU1 180 F6
Hull Rd HU13 178 F1
Hull Royal Infmy HU3 180 C6
Hull's Dro PE6 167 D3
Hull Sta HU1 180 E6
Hull Trinity House Acad HU1 180 E6
Hull Trinity House Sch HU1 180 F6
Hull Truck Theatre★ HU2 180 D7
Humber Bank Factories DN41 187 D4
Humber Bank S DN31 189 C2
Humber Bridge Rd DN31 189 C1
Humber Cres
6 Brough HU15 2 C5
Scunthorpe DN17 184 F6
Humberdale Cl 5 HU14 3 B6
Humberdale Dr HU14 3 C5
Humber Dock St HU1 180 F5
Humber Dr 8 PE11 214 A4
Humber Rd
Barton-upon-Humber DN18 3 E1
Immingham DN40 186 A8
North Ferriby HU14 3 A4
Humberside DN15 1 E3
Humberside Int Airport DN38 21 F5
Humber St
3 Cleethorpes DN35 192 F5
Grimsby DN31 189 C1
Kingston upon Hull HU1 180 F5
HUMBERSTON DN35 193 A2
Humberston Acad DN36 36 C8
Humberston Ave DN36 195 E6
Humberston CE Prim Sch The DN36 36 D8
Humberston Cloverfields Acad DN36 36 C8
Humberstone Holt 1 LN11 50 F7
Humberstone Rd DN32 192 A6
Humberston Fitties★ DN36 36 F8
Humberston Pk Specl Sch DN36 36 C8
Humberston Rd
Cleethorpes DN36 192 C3
Tetney DN36 36 C6
Humber Terr DN31 191 C8
Humber View
3 Barton-upon-Humber DN18 10 E8
Kingston upon Hull HU13 178 C2
4 Swanland HU14 3 B6
Humberville Rd DN40 186 D4
HUMBY NG33 141 C7
Humby Rd NG33 141 B8
Hume Brae 6 DN40 186 B3
Hume St 5 DN31 191 C7
Hunchback La PE13 170 E2
HUNDLEBY PE23 87 F1
Hundlehouse La LN4 111 D4
HUNDLE HOUSES LN4 111 C4
Hundle Houses La LN4 111 D4
Hund Oak Dr 9 DN7 14 D4
Hundreds La
Gringley on the Hill DN10 39 A5
Little Sutton PE12 216 F1
Hundreds Rd PE6 175 C6
Hungarton Ct 3 PE1 226 D8
Hungate LN1 234 B2
Hun Gate PE11 145 D3
Hungate Rd NG32 139 A7
Hungerdike Gate PE12 215 A2
HUNGERTON NG32 139 B4
Hungram La LN9 71 E1
Hungry Hill La LN11 62 C5
Hunsley Cres DN32 192 B4
Hunsley Dr 5 DN41 23 E6
Hunstan La PE22 113 F4
Hunston Rd 4 LN10 97 C5
Huntcliff Sch DN21 30 C1
Hunter Ave LN11 62 C6
Hunter Gr 1 HU3 180 A4
Hunter Pl LN11 198 B4
Hunter Rd Brookenby LN8 47 A6
Brough HU15 2 C6
Hunters Cl 9 PE12 215 E2
Hunter's Croft 1 DN9 27 D3
Hunters Dr 13 LN4 95 C4
Hunter's Dr 5 DN10 39 C1
Hunters La Baumber LN9 72 A1
Tattershall LN4 207 C5
Hunters Rd NG24 104 C2
Hunting Ave PE2 230 F7
Huntingdon Cl 2 PE12 215 E3
Huntingdon Cres 8 DN15 8 B4
Huntingdon Pl 5 PE10 213 C3
Huntingdon St HU4 179 E3
Huntingtower Com Prim Acad NG31 211 A3
Huntingtower Rd NG31 211 A3
Hunt Lea Ave
Grantham NG31 210 F1
Lincoln LN6 205 C8
Huntly Gr PE1 226 A4
Huntly Rd PE2 230 E7
Hunt Rd DN16 185 C5
Hunts Cl 7 DN20 19 E4
Huntsgate PE12 159 D4
Hunt's Gate PE12 159 E1
Hunts La 4 DN20 30 F5
Huntsman Cl PE21 209 D2
Huntsmans Chase DN36 195 B7
Huntsmans Gate PE3 224 F3
Hurdletree Bank PE12 158 E4
Hurdman Way PE25 90 E3
Hurd's Farm DN20 20 D8
Hurford Pl DN37 194 D7
Hurle Cres PE21 208 D6
Hurlstone Cl 25 DN3 14 A2
Hurn Bank PE12 147 E2
Hurnbridge Rd LN4 111 A4
Hurn Cl 2 Birchwood LN6 204 B8
7 Ruskington NG34 108 D1
Hurn Dro LN4 110 A8
Hurn La PE22 126 A7
Hurn Rd Holbeach PE12 147 E1
Marholm PE6 220 C3
Hurns End PE22 127 C7
HURN'S END PE22 127 C8
Hurn The
5 Billingborough NG34 133 B1
Digby LN4 108 E6
Hurricane Cl DN36 195 C4
Hurst Cres NG32 210 A4
Hurst La DN17 184 E3
Hurstlea Dr DN36 193 B1
Hurst The 5 PE25 206 A6
Hurstwood Cl LN2 202 D8
Hurton's La LN11 49 C6
Hussey Cl 2 NG34 212 E4
Hussey Twr★ PE21 209 A4
Husthwaite Rd 18 HU15 2 D5
Hutchinson Gdns 5 PE12 157 E7
Hutchinson Rd 2 DN35 192 E7
Huteson La DN15 8 C8
Hutson Dr LN6 204 F2
HUTTOFT LN13 76 E3
Huttoft Bank Pit nature Reserve★ LN13 77 B6
Huttoft Prim Sch LN13 76 F3
Huttoft Rd
17 Mablethorpe & Sutton LN12 76 F8
Thurlby LN13 76 D2
Hutton Cl 3 PE11 214 F2
Hutton Rd DN31 189 B2
Hutt St HU3 180 D7
Hyde Gdns PE6 164 F3
Hyde Pk Cl 6 Lincoln LN6 204 F1
Nunsthorpe DN33 191 B2
Hyde Way NG34 212 C7
Hyholmes PE3 224 F7
Hykeham Rd LN6 205 D6
Hykeham Sta LN6 204 D3
Hymers Ave HU3 180 B7
Hymers Coll HU3 180 B7
Hyperion St HU9 181 A7
Hythegate PE4 221 B4

I

Ibbott Cl PE2 231 E5
Icehouse Rd HU3 180 D6
Icelandic Cl HU3 180 C5
Icknield Cl 17 LN4 81 A1
Ickworth Rd NG34 212 D3
Ida Rd PE25 206 C3
Idas Cl HU9 181 A5
Iddesleigh Rd 4 LN10 97 D6
Idle Bank Epworth DN9 15 F1
Haxey DN9 26 E2
Ihlee Cl PE4 221 C1
Ilex Cl PE7 230 C3
Iliffe Gate 3 PE4 221 D2
Ilkeston Ct 2 DN15 182 B3
Illston Pl 4 PE1 226 E7
IMMINGHAM DN40 186 E4
Immingham Bsns Units DN40 186 D3
Immingham Leisure Ctr DN40 186 C4
Immingham Mus★ DN40 186 C3
Impala Way HU4 179 D2
Imperial Ave DN35 192 C8
Independence Dr 5 PE11 156 F8
Infield La 5 DN22 52 C1
Ingamells Dr LN1 66 E2
Ingelow Ave PE21 208 C6
INGHAM LN1 54 F2
Ingham Cl LN6 205 B3
Ingham Ct LN4 207 E6
Ingham Hall Gdns PE13 177 D7
Ingham La LN1 55 B1
Ingham Prim Sch LN1 54 F2
Ingham Rd Coningsby LN4 207 E6
3 Stow LN1 66 C8
Inghams La 1 DN36 36 D4
Inghams Rd 3 DN36 36 D4
INGLEBOROUGH PE14 170 E5
Ingleborough 1 PE1 226 A5
INGLEBY LN1 66 C4
Ingleby Cres LN2 201 F8
Ingleby Ct 2 PE11 214 F4
Ingleby Gr DN37 190 F8
Ingleby Rd 14 DN17 29 D7
Ingle Ct 2 NG33 151 D7
Ingledew Cl 8 NG34 122 E2
Inglenook Dr 2 DN8 15 B8
Ingleton Ave HU4 179 C6
Inglewood Cl 3 NG24 104 B1
Inglewood Ct DN16 185 A4
Inglewood Dr 4 HU4 179 B5
Ingmires 7 HU15 2 D6
INGOLDMELLS PE25 90 E4
Ingoldmells Prim Sch PE25 90 D4
Ingoldmells Rd PE24 102 E8
INGOLDSBY NG33 141 D5
Ingoldsby Prim Sch NG33 141 D5
Ingoldsby Rd NG33 141 B3
Ingoldsby Road NG33 141 E3
Ingram Cres 9 DN7 14 C4
Ingram Gdns 11 DN20 30 E8
Ingram Gr 10 DN7 14 C4
Ingram La NG23 78 A1
Ingram Pl DN35 192 D2
Ingram Rd Boston PE21 208 D6
Hatfield DN7 14 C3
Ingram Row LN9 199 B3
Ing Rd PE20 134 F4
Ings Bank Hilldyke PE22 126 D6
Leverton PE22 126 E7
Ings Dro
Butterwick PE22 126 D7
Leverton PE22 113 E1
Ings La Belchford LN9 73 B2
Brackenborough with Little Grimsby LN11 49 B4
Bratoft PE24 102 C6
Brough HU15 2 C5
Cumberworth LN13 89 E7
Ellerker HU15 1 F8
2 Hibaldstow DN20 31 A5
Horsington LN10 84 D2
Immingham DN40 186 E3
1 Kirk Bramwith DN7 14 C7
Leverton PE22 126 F7
Little Steeping PE23 101 E5
North Coates DN36 37 A3
North Ferriby HU14 3 A4
Saltfleetby LN11 62 F8
Scamblesby LN11 73 A4
Skidbrooke with Saltfleet Haven LN11 51 A3
South Cave HU15 1 E7
South Somercotes LN11 50 E3
Walkerith DN21 40 C3
Waltham DN37 194 F4
6 West Ashby LN9 85 E7
West Ashby LN9 199 D8
West Stockwith DN10 40 C6
Winterton DN15 9 D7
Ings Rd Benington PE22 126 D8
Gringley on the Hill DN10 39 B3
Kirton in Lindsey DN21 29 F1
Mablethorpe & Sutton LN12 76 E7
INGTHORPE PE9 218 A8
Inhams Cl PE13 177 D5
Inley Dro PE12 169 A8
Inner St NG31 211 B3
Innings The 1 NG34 212 D3
Innovation Way
Alwalton PE2 229 B5
Great Coates DN37 24 B6
Inns Cl LN6 204 E3
Inshops Ctr DN32 189 B1
Intax Mews DN32 191 F6
Invenio Acad DN15 182 E5
Inverness Rd 14 DN7 14 D4
Iona Cl DN21 197 E6
Iona Dr DN36 36 D8
Ipswich Gdns NG31 210 E5
Iqra Acad PE3 225 C8
Irby Cres 9 PE12 158 B7
Irby Ct DN35 192 D3
IRBY IN THE MARSH PE24 102 B6
Irby Pl PE21 208 F5
Irby Rd DN17 184 E5
Irby St PE21 208 E5
IRBY UPON HUMBER DN37 34 D7
Irchester Pl PE3 225 D5
Ireland Wlk HU4 179 B4
Ireton Ave 2 NG24 104 C4
Iris Dr PE2 230 E8
Irish Hill LN11 198 A5
IRNHAM NG33 141 E1
Irnham Rd
Corby Glen NG33 141 C1
Osgodby NG33 141 E2
Stamford PE9 219 C7
Iron Bar Dro PE11 155 F4
Ironestone Cl LN2 202 C5
Ironmonger St 5 PE9 219 C5
Ironstone Rd LN7 45 D8
Irvine Rd 2 DN16 185 C5
Irwin Rd DN21 41 C6
Isaac Newton Prim Sch The NG31 210 F3
Isaac Newton Way NG31 211 F6
Isaac's Hill DN35 192 E6
Isaan Newton Ctr 14 NG31 211 A4
Isham Rd 1 PE3 225 D4
Isherwood Cl PE1 226 A6
Isis Ct HU9 181 B5
Isis Wy PE2 229 B5
ISLAND CARR DN20 196 B2
Island Carr Rd DN20 196 A3
Island Rd DN17 7 E6
Isle Cl 3 DN17 16 D8
Islip Ct 2 LN9 199 D3
Ison Cl 4 NG34 120 E8
Itlings La HU13 178 F1
Itterby Cres DN35 192 C3
Itter Cres PE4 221 C1
Ivanhoe Rd 4 DN16 183 C1
Ivatt Ct 13 NG31 210 E2
Ivatt Way PE3 225 C6
Ivel Cl 6 LN12 64 B5
Ivel Gr 4 LN12 64 B5
Ivery La PE22 114 D4
Ivesdyke Cl 3 PE13 170 B2
Ivy Cl DN7 14 E4
Ivy Cres PE21 208 D3
Ivy Farm Ct 20 DN41 23 F5
Ivy Gr PE4 221 B2
Ivy House La PE24 115 C8
Ivy La Coningsby LN4 207 F1
Grainthorpe LN11 37 E1
Ivywood Cl 14 LN6 204 B8
Ixworth Cl 26 PE6 175 A1

J

Jack Fletcher Cl LN4 81 E1
Jack Haws La 3 PE9 172 D4
Jack Hunt Sch PE3 225 B3
Jack Hunt Swimming Pool PE3 225 B3
Jacklin Cl 5 LN11 50 B8
Jacklin Cres LN12 64 A4
Jacklin Dr 3 LN11 51 C4
Jacklin La DN17 7 C3
Jacklins App DN16 185 A3
Jack Row La DN7 14 B8
Jack Simpson Cl 6 LN9 199 B2
Jacks La 5 PE23 87 F1
Jackson Dr 3 PE20 136 C5
Jackson Mews 6 DN40 186 A4
Jackson Rd 1 DN15 182 E3
Jackson's Field LN8 57 B7
Jacksons La 4 PE24 102 E8
Jackson's Pl DN36 192 D1
Jackson St Grimsby DN31 191 C8
Kingston upon Hull HU3 180 D4
Jackson Wy
8 Stamford PE9 218 F6
Welton HU14 2 E4
Jacobean Rd 4 LN6 204 D6
Jacobs Cl LN11 48 F4
Jacobs Ct 2 PE11 214 C6
Jade Gr 1 HU3 180 A4
Jaguar Dr LN6 204 D1
Jail La PE22 126 F2
James Ave
6 Mablethorpe/Sutton on Sea LN12 64 C2
Peterborough PE1 226 C1
Skegness PE25 206 B6
James Ct
Gainsborough DN21 197 D5
Louth LN11 198 C6
12 Market Rasen LN8 57 E7
Jameson Bridge St 8 LN8 57 D8
Jameson Keep HU13 178 C2
Jameson Rd LN11 48 A4
Jameson St 2 HU1 180 F6
James Pl DN39 12 B1
James Rd Crowland PE6 166 F1
1 Hemswell Cliff DN21 55 A8
Peterborough PE6 175 B7
James St Boston PE21 208 E5
Brigg DN20 196 B3
Grimsby DN31 191 C8
Lincoln LN2 234 B3
Louth LN11 198 C6
Jameston Cl NG31 210 E6
James Watt Rd NG24 104 B6
James Way 9 DN40 186 B3
Jankin La PE34 161 F1
Janton Ct DN36 195 C7
Japan Rd DN21 197 B5
Japonica Hill 3 DN40 186 C3
Jaque's Bank DN8 16 A5
Jarratt Hill La HU15 1 D8
Jarratt St HU1 180 F7
Jarvis Cl LN6 204 F7
Jarvis's Gate PE12 159 C1
Jasmin Cl 9 PE13 170 E1
Jasmine Cl PE10 213 B7
Jasmine Ct 2 Goxhill DN19 12 A8
Peterborough PE2 229 E2
Spalding PE11 214 A2
Jasmine Way
Immingham DN40 186 C3
Yaxley PE7 233 F6
Jasmine Wy 15 LN8 70 D4
Jasmin Rd LN6 204 C8
Jason Rd 5 LN6 205 A5
Javelin Ave 8 LN8 47 B6
Javelin Rd 12 LN11 62 C6
Jefferson Cl 24 PE8 172 B1
Jefferson Dr 23 HU15 2 C6
Jeffery Ave 6 PE13 170 E1
Jeffrey La DN9 16 E1
Jekil's Bank Holbeach PE12 158 C1
Moulton PE12 167 F8
Jekil's Bank *continued*
Whaplode PE12 168 B8
Jekil's Gate PE12 159 A5
Jellicoe Ave LN2 202 D3
Jellicoe Ct DN16 183 C1
Jellings Pl PE1 226 A4
Jenkins Cl Louth LN11 198 C8
5 Skegness PE25 206 A7
Jenkins' La PE22 127 A6
Jenner Ct 2 DN35 192 B8
Jenner Pl DN35 192 B8
Jenning St HU8 181 A8
Jenny Brough La HU13 178 B3
Jenny Brough Mdws HU13 178 B3
Jenny Cl HU13 178 B3
Jensen Mews 2 HU4 179 E5
Jensen Rd LN4 205 F2
Jericho La DN40 12 D7
Jericho Rd 1 NG24 104 B1
Jermyn Mews LN4 203 D1
Jermyn St NG34 212 D4
Jerusalem LN6 79 F5
Jerusalem Rd LN6 200 A4
Jesmond Ave 5 DN17 184 E3
Jesmond View LN1 201 E8
Jessop Cl Beacon Hill NG24 104 B5
Cherry Willingham/Reepham LN3 203 E5
Horncastle LN9 199 C3
9 Leasingham NG34 121 B8
Jessop Way NG24 104 B5
Jiggle's Gate PE12 158 F1
Jill Gr HU13 178 F1
Job's La LN6 79 C1
Jobson Rd LN9 199 D2
Jock Hedge PE24 102 E6
Joel Sq 8 NG34 107 F1
John Adams Way PE21 208 F4
John Blow Prim Sch 13 NG23 91 D4
John Brown Cl LN9 199 A4
John Clare Prim Sch PE6 173 B4
John Cornwell Vc Dr DN36 195 D6
John Coupland Hospl DN21 197 B7
John Eve Way PE6 217 B6
John Fielding Com Specl Sch PE21 209 A6
John Foster Cl 9 NG31 211 D7
John Gold Ave 6 NG24 104 A4
John Harrison CE Prim Sch DN19 11 C8
John Harrison's Cl 3 DN19 11 D8
John Harrison Way PE12 215 B2
John Harrox Prim Sch The PE12 157 F7
John Hunt Primary Sch NG24 104 B2
John Leggott College DN17 184 E8
John Pope Wy 17 NG24 104 A6
John Smith Cl LN13 89 A6
Johnson Ave PE11 214 E2
Johnson Cl 8 Belton DN9 16 E2
3 Skegness PE25 206 A7
Johnson Community Hospl PE11 214 D3
Johnson Ct LN4 207 B6
Johnson Dr
Bracebridge Heath LN4 205 F4
9 Scotter DN21 29 C4
Johnson's Dro PE13 177 B6
Johnson's La 7 DN17 16 D7
Johnsons Rd 6 NG24 104 C1
Johnson St DN35 192 B8
Johnson Way 14 PE24 102 E7
Johnson Wlk PE1 225 F7
John Spendluffe Tech Coll LN13 75 F2
John St Lincoln LN2 234 C2
13 Market Rasen LN8 57 D8
John Swain's Way PE12 216 C5
John Wake Cl 2 PE6 217 B6
John Wesley Rd PE4 220 E3
John Whitgift Acad DN37 190 D8
Jolls La LN9 86 C5
Jolly Comm La LN13 77 A3
Jolly Farmer Bank PE21 126 C3
Jolly Farmer La PE21 126 C3
Jonathan Dr PE25 206 C8
Jonathan Gdns 1 NG34 212 F3
Jones Hill PE7 233 A8
Jonquil Ave DN16 185 D5
Jordan Mews 2 PE1 226 B3
Jordan's Cradge Bank Rd PE11 156 C2
Jorose St 4 PE3 225 A3
Jorose Way PE3 224 F3
Joseph Ogle Cl DN36 195 B7
Joseph St DN31 191 C8
Joshua Way 4 DN21 43 D7
Joy Paine Cl PE21 208 C6
Joy's Bank PE12 158 E1
Jubilee Ave Boston PE21 208 E6
Faldingworth LN8 56 F3
Grantham NG31 211 C5
Jubilee Cl 4 Bardney LN3 83 B4
Cherry Willingham/Reepham LN3 203 E6
Coningsby LN4 207 D5
1 Hogsthorpe PE24 90 B7
17 Kirton PE20 136 C5
Lincoln LN6 204 F1
Long Sutton PE12 216 C5
Martin LN4 96 C2

Jubilee Cl *continued*
8 Morton PE10 154 C7
Scotter DN21 29 B3
1 Spalding PE11 214 C4
Sutton St James PE12 159 C1
Jubilee Cres
Gainsborough DN21 197 D5
Louth LN11 198 C8
Jubilee Ct 6 NG34 212 E4
Jubilee Dr 3 Bardney LN3 83 C4
Market Deeping PE6 217 C6
10 Wragby LN8 70 D4
Jubilee Gr NG34 212 C6
Jubilee Parade 6 PE24 90 D7
Jubilee Pl 45 DN18 10 E8
Jubilee Rd LN11 50 E7
Jubilee St
Peterborough PE2 230 F8
2 Ruskington NG34 108 E1
Jubilee Way Crowland PE6 166 F1
Horncastle LN9 199 B4
Scunthorpe DN15 183 B3
Jude Gate PE22 114 E3
Judge Cl 3 PE21 209 C4
Judy Cross PE11 145 B8
Julian Bower LN11 198 B4
Julian Cl HU5 179 A7
Julian St DN32 192 A7
Julian's Wlk 8 HU10 178 F6
Julia Rd LN4 203 D1
Julia's Mead 12 PE11 214 B5
Julius Wy LN6 93 B8
Junction Rd 10 DN7 14 C6
Junella Cl HU3 180 A4
Jungle Zoo The★ DN35 193 B3
Junior Cadets Rd NG34 120 B8
Juniper Cl
Flixborough DN15 182 C6
10 Leasingham NG34 121 B7
3 Lincoln LN5 205 C2
Spalding PE11 214 F4
Juniper Cres
Peterborough PE3 225 A2
Spalding PE11 214 F5
Juniper Dr 13 LN2 68 F4
Juniper Way
Gainsborough DN21 197 D5
3 Sleaford NG34 212 D2
Juniper Wy LN6 92 D5
Juno Wy PE2 231 D4
Jupiter Ave
Peterborough PE7 231 D3
Stanground PE7 231 C4
Jury Rd PE7 233 C8
Justice Hall La 10 DN17 16 D8
Justice La DN14 7 B8
Justice Wy PE7 233 B8
Justinian Wy 16 LN6 93 B8
Jutland Ct DN36 195 D7

K

Karelia Ct HU4 179 B5
Karen Ave 12 DN41 23 A4
Karsons Way LN2 68 D7
Katherine Cres PE25 206 D2
Kathleen Ave
Cleethorpes DN35 192 D8
Scunthorpe DN16 185 B5
Kathleen Gr DN32 192 C7
Kathleen Rice Cl DN35 192 A8
Kaymile Cl 13 DN36 195 C6
KEADBY DN17 17 D7
Keadby Cl LN6 204 F7
Keal Bank PE22 100 C3
Keal Carr Nature Reserve★ PE23 100 E7
KEAL COTES PE23 100 C4
Keal Hill PE23 100 B7
Kealholme Rd DN17 29 D7
Keaton Cl PE25 206 A5
Keats Ave Grantham NG31 211 E6
Scunthorpe DN17 184 D7
Keats Cl Lincoln LN2 202 C7
17 Mablethorpe/Sutton on Sea LN12 77 A7
Keats Dr NG34 121 E4
Keats Gr 2 PE9 218 E5
Keats Rd 10 NG24 104 B3
Keats Way PE1 225 D7
Keb La DN15 9 D2
Keble Cl 4 PE9 219 A7
Keble Ct 1 LN4 207 B5
KEDDINGTON LN11 198 F8
Keddington Ave LN1 201 E8
Keddington Cres 2 LN11 198 D7
Keddington Rd Louth LN11 198 C7
Scunthorpe DN17 184 F4
Kedlestone Rd NG31 210 F1
Kedleston Rd PE7 231 F6
Keeble Dr LN4 203 D1
KEELBY DN41 23 A5
Keelby Prim Sch DN41 23 A5
Keelby Rd
6 Gainsborough DN21 53 A8
Scunthorpe DN17 184 F5
Stallingborough DN41 23 C6
Keel Dr 9 Bottesford NG13 128 A5
Kirton PE20 136 D5
Keeling St 7 LN11 50 F7
Keepers Cl 2 LN2 68 D7
Keepers Way NG34 212 E3
Keeper's Way 6 DN9 16 E1
Keeton Rd PE1 225 E7
Keightley Rd PE12 147 B5
Keir Hardie Wlk DN32 191 D7
KEISBY PE10 141 F3
Keisby Rd PE10 142 A3
Keith Cres 15 DN37 23 F1
Kelburn Rd PE2 229 D4
KELBY NG32 131 C8
Kelby Rd NG32 120 C1
KELFIELD DN9 28 C4
Kelham Rd
9 Great Gonerby NG31 129 E5
2 Great Gonerby NG31 210 E8
Grimsby DN32 192 D6
Kellet Gate PE12 157 B5
Kells Cl 6 LN5 205 D3
Kell's Dro PE20 124 E1
Kelly Cl 14 PE11 156 E8
Kelsey Ave DN15 182 B3
Kelsey La 1 DN17 17 D4
Kelsey Prim Sch LN7 32 A4
Kelsey Rd LN7 32 C2
Kelsey St LN1 234 A2
Kelso Ct PE4 221 A1
Kelso Dr PE10 213 C3
KELSTERN LN11 48 A1
Kelstern Cl 1 LN6 204 C6
Kelstern Ct 1 DN34 191 A5
Kelstern Rd LN6 204 C6
Kelston Dr 2 HU13 179 A3
Kelthorpe Cl PE9 171 A2
Kemble Cl LN6 204 B8
Kemeshame Ct DN37 194 F4
Kemp Rd Grimsby DN31 189 C3
3 Swanland HU14 3 B6
Kemp St PE6 166 E1
Kempton Cl 3 PE11 156 E3
Kempton Dr 4 DN7 14 C2
Kempton Rd
12 Bourne PE10 213 D3
Kingston upon Hull HU3 179 E6
Kempton Vale DN35 192 F1
Kempton Way NG31 210 F4
Kendal Cl 2 PE4 221 D2
Kendal Ct DN16 185 C6
Kendale Rd DN16 185 E8
Kendal Rd DN40 186 E3
Kendal Way HU5 179 C7
Kendon Gdns DN8 15 B8
Kendrick Cl PE2 231 D6
Kenford Ct DN36 195 C7
Kenilworth Cl 3 LN1 66 D2
Kenilworth Dr LN6 205 C5
Kenilworth Rd
Cleethorpes DN35 192 D4
Grantham NG31 211 F5
Scunthorpe DN16 183 C1
Kenlan Rd 23 PE13 170 D1
Kenleigh Dr PE21 209 D4
Kenmare Cres DN21 197 F2
Kenmar Rd 20 DN37 23 F1
Kenmore Dr 10 LN10 97 C6
Kennedy Ave 21 Alford LN13 75 F2
Skegness PE25 206 C2
Kennedy Cl DN20 196 E3
Kennedy Rd
Bracebridge Heath LN4 205 F3
Holbeach PE12 215 C4
Kennedy St PE7 230 B1
Kennedy Way DN40 186 C4
Kennedy Way Sh Ctr DN40 186 C4
Kennel La
Doddington & Whisby LN6 79 E5
Reepham LN3 203 E8
Kennels Rd PE6 224 D4
Kennel Wlk LN3 203 F8
Kenner Cl 4 LN6 205 A6
Kennet Gdns PE4 221 C1
Kenneth Ave
2 Burgh le Marsh PE24 102 E8
8 Hatfield DN7 14 C2
5 Stainforth DN7 14 C6
Kenneth Campbell Rd 4 DN36 37 C5
Kenneth St 1 LN1 201 F6
Kennington Cl LN2 68 E5
Kennulphs Cl 5 PE6 175 C8
Kensington Cl PE12 215 F3
Kensington Dr 6 PE11 214 B2
Kensington Gdns 7 LN12 64 B3
Kensington Pl DN33 195 A8
Kensington Rd DN15 182 B3
Ken Stimpson Com Sch PE4 220 F4
Kent Ave LN12 63 F5
Kent Cl
Kingston upon Hull HU9 181 C7
3 Sutton Bridge PE12 160 E4
Kent Dr 4 DN20 31 A5
Kentmere Pl 4 PE4 221 D2
Kentra Cl PE13 170 C2
Kent Rd
9 Binbrook Tech Pk LN8 47 B6
Leake Commonside PE22 113 F3
Peterborough PE3 225 E2
Kent St Grimsby DN32 189 B1
6 Lincoln LN2 202 C3
Kentwell Rd PE7 230 F2
Kenwardly Rd HU10 178 E8
Kenwick Cl LN11 198 D3
Kenwick Dr NG31 211 D4
Kenwick Gdns LN11 198 D3
Kenwick Hill
Legbourne LN11 198 E1
Raithby cum Maltby LN11 61 C3
Kenwick Pastures LN11 198 D3
Kenwick Rd LN11 198 D2
Kenya Dr DN17 184 F2
Kenyon Cl
Heighington/Washingborough LN4 81 E4
Kenyon Cl *continued*
8 Thorne/Moorends DN8 15 A8
Kerries Wlk DN17 184 C7
Kerrison View 5 LN2 68 D2
Kerr's Cres NG32 118 D2
Kerry Dr HU10 178 C6
Kerry Pit Way HU10 178 C6
Kesgrave St 1 DN31 189 C1
Kesteven and Sleaford High Sch Selective Acad NG34 212 D4
Kesteven Cl 1 PE6 217 D4
Kesteven Ct
3 Habrough DN40 22 E8
7 Lincoln LN6 204 D2
Kesteven Dr 7 PE6 217 A6
Kesteven Gr 19 DN17 16 D8
Kesteven & Grantham Girls' Sch NG31 211 B5
Kesteven Rd PE9 219 C7
Kesteven St Lincoln LN5 234 B1
1 Sleaford NG34 212 E4
Kesteven Way 7 PE10 213 C5
Kesteven Wlk 3 PE1 226 B2
Kestrel Ave 10 DN21 197 F5
Kestrel Cl
6 Birchwood LN6 204 D8
Clinton Park LN4 207 C6
2 Sleaford NG34 212 B3
Kestrel Ct Grantham NG31 210 F2
Longthorpe PE3 225 A2
Kestrel Dr Bourne PE10 213 E3
Louth LN11 198 D8
Kestrel Rd
8 Scopwick Heath LN4 108 A7
Scunthorpe DN17 184 E6
Kestrel Rise LN6 79 B1
Keswick Cl 2 PE4 221 D3
Ketco Ave PE9 171 A4
Ketel Cl PE12 216 C3
Ketlock Hill La 1 DN22 52 B1
KETSBY LN11 74 D3
Ketsby La LN11 74 C3
Kettering Rd
Scunthorpe DN16 183 C2
Wothorpe PE9 219 B2
Kettlebridge La DN40 12 E6
Kettleby La DN20 20 E3
Kettleby View 3 DN20 196 D4
KETTLETHORPE LN1 65 F2
Kettlethorpe Dr 17 HU15 2 D5
Kettlethorpe Rd LN1 65 E3
Kettlewell St DN32 191 E5
KETTON PE9 171 A3
Ketton CE Prim Sch PE9 171 A3
Ketton Drift PE9 171 C3
Ketton Rd PE9 171 B2
Kew Gdns 3 NG24 104 A2
Kew Rd DN35 192 E6
KEXBY DN21 53 E5
Kexby La DN21 53 C4
Kexby Mill Cl 5 LN6 93 B8
Kexby Rd DN21 54 D6
Kexby Wlk DN21 197 F3
Keyholme La DN36 37 D2
Key Theatre★ PE1 226 B1
Keyworth Dr 10 LN7 33 B4
Khormaksar Dr LN4 95 C7
Kiddier Ave DN37 194 D7
Kidd La HU15 2 D6
Kidgate LN11 198 B5
Kidgate Mews LN11 198 B5
Kilburn Ave 4 HU2 180 F8
Kilburn Cres 1 LN6 205 A6
Kildare Dr PE3 225 C4
Kilham PE2 229 E2
Killarney Cl NG31 211 E7
Killingholme Haven Pits Nature Reserve★ DN40 13 A6
Killingholme Prim Sch DN40 12 E3
Killingholme Rd DN40 12 F2
Kilmister Ct 10 LN8 70 D5
Kiln Ave HU3 179 F4
Kiln Hill 4 LN8 59 A7
Kiln La Brigg DN20 196 B3
Fulbeck NG32 106 C1
Immingham DN41 187 C2
Louth LN11 198 B6
Stallingborough DN41 186 F1
Kiln La Ind Est DN41 187 B3
Kiln La Trading Est DN41 187 C2
Kiln St PE7 230 B1
Kilnwell Rd 12 LN8 57 D8
Kiln Yd LN11 198 C5
Kilverstone PE4 220 F6
KILVINGTON NG13 117 A1
Kimberley Ct 7 DN16 185 D4
Kimberley St HU3 180 C7
Kimberley Terr NG31 210 E7
Kimblewick La PE11 214 A2
Kimbolton Ct PE1 225 F3
Kime Cl NG34 142 C8
Kime Ct PE25 206 C8
Kime Mews PE20 136 D5
Kime's La 6 PE22 98 F4
Kinder Ave LN6 205 A2
Kinderley Prim Sch PE13 169 F6
Kinderley Rd PE13 170 D2
King Charles Cl HU10 178 E7
King Edward Ave 7 LN10 97 C6
King Edward Cr 8 LN10 97 C6
King Edward Rd
Thorne/Moorends DN8 15 A8
2 Woodhall Spa LN10 97 C6
King Edward St Belton DN9 16 E2
4 Grimsby DN31 189 A1
3 Kingston upon Hull HU1 180 F6
King Edward St *continued*
Kirton in Lindsey DN21 30 B1
Scunthorpe DN16 183 A1
Sleaford NG34 212 C3
King Edwards Terr 4 HU15 2 B5
King Edward VI Acad PE23 87 F1
King Edward VI Gram Sch The LN11 198 A5
KINGERBY LN8 44 E3
Kingerby Beck Mdws Nature Reserve★ LN8 44 E5
Kingerby Cl DN21 197 E3
Kingerby Rd
Bishopbridge LN8 44 F1
Scunthorpe DN17 184 E5
Kingfisher Cl
25 Barton-upon-Humber DN18 3 E1
2 Birchwood LN6 204 D8
Brigg DN20 196 A3
Scunthorpe DN15 182 D5
Yaxley PE7 233 D5
Kingfisher Ct 2 PE11 214 F2
Kingfisher Dr
2 Skegness PE25 206 A7
Skirbeck Quarter PE21 208 E3
4 Surfleet PE11 145 E3
Kingfishers PE2 229 D6
King George Ave 1 LN10 97 D6
King Georges Ct 3 DN7 14 C5
King George V Ave 1 PE12 215 F3
King George V Stadium DN32 192 B5
King Henry Chase PE3 225 A5
King John Bank
2 Sutton Bridge PE14 170 F8
Walpole PE14 161 A2
King Johns Rd 6 PE20 135 B7
King John St NG34 212 C4
King Oswald Rd 12 DN9 27 D6
King St E DN21 197 D3
King St La LE14 150 A6
Kings Arms Yd 2 LN2 234 B2
Kings Ave PE25 206 E8
King's Ave Boston PE21 209 C3
Brigg DN20 196 D3
King's Bench St HU3 180 B5
Kingsbridge Ct 1 PE4 220 E5
Kings Cl PE22 112 C8
King's Cl 15 DN7 14 D4
Kingscliffe Rd NG31 211 A8
King's Cres Boston PE21 209 C3
Swineshead PE20 135 B8
Kings Croft 1 DN17 16 E6
Kingscroft Dr 31 HU15 2 D5
King's Cross Cl 2 HU3 180 C6
King's Cswy DN14 6 E8
Kings Ct 19 Kirton PE20 136 C5
Louth LN11 198 E7
Old Bolingbroke PE23 100 A7
9 Scawby DN20 30 F8
Scunthorpe DN15 183 B4
Kingsdale DN17 184 E2
King's Delph Dro PE7 231 E2
Kingsdown Dr PE9 218 E5
Kingsdown Rd LN6 204 B7
Kings Dyke Cl PE2 231 E6
Kingsfield Ct LN5 105 B4
Kingsgate Gedney PE12 159 E7
Market Deeping PE6 217 C6
Kings Gate DN32 192 A7
King's Gdns PE1 226 A5
Kings Hill 2 NG32 119 B7
Kings La 11 NG34 120 C8
Kings Leigh 1 HU3 180 C6
Kingsley Ave PE10 213 B5
Kingsley Cl
4 Barnack PE9 172 D3
6 Brough HU15 2 B5
Kingsley Ct 8 LN4 82 B1
Kingsley Gr DN33 191 C4
Kingsley Rd
14 Mablethorpe/Sutton on Sea LN12 64 B4
North Hykeham LN6 204 B5
Peterborough PE1 226 C4
Kingsley St LN1 234 A4
Kingsline Cl 1 PE6 176 A3
Kings Manor LN4 207 D4
Kings Mews DN35 193 C1
Kingsport Cl 1 HU3 180 A7
Kings Rd Holbeach PE12 215 F3
Immingham DN40 186 E5
Metheringham LN4 95 C4
Peterborough PE2 231 B6
Stamford PE9 219 B6
King's Rd
Barnetby le Wold DN38 21 B5
Humberston DN35 193 B3
Spalding PE11 214 D5
Kings Sch The NG31 211 B5
King's Sch The PE1 226 A4
Kings Sconce Ave 2 NG24 104 A5
King St 1 Billinghay LN4 109 F5
Boston PE21 208 E4
East Halton DN40 12 D7
Gainsborough DN21 197 D3
15 Goxhill DN19 12 A8
2 Keelby DN41 23 A4
10 Kirton PE20 136 C5
Lincoln LN5 234 A1
14 Mablethorpe/Sutton on Sea LN12 64 B3
Market Rasen LN8 57 D8
1 Peterborough PE1 226 A2
Scunthorpe DN15 183 B4
King St *continued*
18 Sutton Bridge PE12 160 E4
Thorne/Moorends DN8 15 A8
Wainfleet All Saints PE24 102 A2
West Deeping PE6 173 A8
Wilsford NG32 120 A1
Winterton DN15 9 A5
Yarburgh LN11 49 E4
Kingsthorpe Cres PE25 206 C1
Kingston Ave
Grantham NG31 210 E4
Grimsby DN34 191 A6
Kingston upon Hull HU13 178 F1
Kingston Cl 7 DN35 193 A1
Kingston Communications Stadium (Hull City AFC Hull RLFC)★ HU3 180 B7
Kingston Dr PE2 231 E5
Kingston International Bsns Pk HU9 5 F8
Kingston Rd
Kingston upon Hull HU10 178 F8
Scunthorpe DN16 185 A7
Kingston Ret Pk HU1 180 E5
Kingston St
Kingston upon Hull HU1 180 E4
Kingston upon Hull HU1 180 E5
Kingston Terr NG34 212 E5
KINGSTON UPON HULL HU1 180 F4
Kingston View 20 DN18 10 F8
Kingston Wharf 4 HU1 180 F5
King Street Ind Est PE6 164 D1
Kingsway Boston PE21 209 B3
Bourne PE10 213 D6
3 Brigg DN20 196 B4
Cleethorpes DN35 193 A5
11 Leverington PE13 170 E1
Lincoln LN5 201 F1
Nettleham LN2 68 C2
Scunthorpe DN15 182 C3
Stainforth DN7 14 C6
Tealby LN8 46 C1
Kings Way LN2 68 C7
Kingsway Sta DN35 193 B4
Kings Wlk 11 NG31 211 A4
KingsWy 3 NG24 104 B2
KINGTHORPE LN8 70 C2
Kingthorpe Rd LN8 70 C1
King William Cl 4 PE34 161 F3
Kinloch Way DN40 186 B2
Kinloss Cl 11 LN6 204 C6
Kinnears Wlk PE2 229 F2
Kinoulton Ct 16 NG31 210 E2
Kinross Rd NG34 120 F2
Kinsbourne Gn 40 DN7 14 D4
Kinsley Wlk 8 DN15 183 B3
Kintore Dr NG31 211 C4
Kipling Ave
Little London PE11 214 A1
4 Scunthorpe DN17 184 D7
Kipling Cl
4 Grantham NG31 211 E6
St Giles LN2 202 B7
3 Stamford PE9 218 E5
Kipling Ct PE1 225 E8
Kipling Dr
4 Mablethorpe/Sutton on Sea LN12 77 A7
14 Sleaford NG34 212 F4
Kiplington Cl 2 HU3 180 A7
Kipling Wlk 1 HU4 179 D2
Kippings The 8 PE10 164 C8
Kirby Ct 5 PE11 214 F4
Kirby Wlk 2 PE3 225 C4
KIRK BRAMWITH DN7 14 A6
KIRKBY LN8 44 F3
Kirkby Bank PE23 99 E3
KIRKBY FENSIDE PE23 99 E4
Kirkby Gr DN33 191 A3
Kirkby Gravel Pit Nature Reserve★ LN4 207 A8
KIRKBY GREEN LN4 108 E8
Kirkby Hill PE23 100 A7
Kirkby La Coningsby LN4 207 D8
Woodhall Spa LN10 97 E6
KIRKBY LA THORPE NG34 121 F5
Kirkby la Thorpe CE Prim Sch NG34 121 F4
Kirkby Moor Nature Reserve★ LN10 98 A5
KIRKBY ON BAIN LN10 98 B5
Kirkby on Bain CE Prim Sch LN10 98 C5
Kirkby Rd
Ewerby & Evedon NG34 122 B5
Scunthorpe DN17 184 E4
Kirkby St
7 Kingston upon Hull HU2 180 F8
Lincoln LN5 201 F1
KIRKBY UNDERWOOD PE10 142 D2
Kirkby Underwood Rd PE10 154 A8
Kirk Cl 4 DN15 182 E4
Kirkdale Cl 4 NG34 121 B8
Kirkden Paddocks DN9 16 C2
KIRK ELLA HU10 178 C8
Kirkenes Cl DN36 195 B6
Kirkgate PE13 169 F7
Kirk Gate Waltham DN37 194 E4
6 Whaplode PE12 158 B7
Kirkgate St PE13 170 E1
Kirk Gdns PE21 208 D7

Kirkham Cl HU13 178 F2
Kirkhouse Gn Rd DN7 14 A8
Kirklands Rd HU5 179 E8
Kirkmeadow PE3 225 A8
Kirk Rd LN4 81 E1
Kirk Rise HU10 178 C7
Kirkside DN37 194 D4
Kirkstall PE2 230 B3
Kirkstall Cl LN2 202 E6
Kirkstead Bridge LN10 97 B4
Kirkstead Cres DN33 191 B3
Kirkstead Ct 8 LN10 97 D5
Kirkstone House Sch PE6 164 E4
Kirkton Gate PE3 225 A1
Kirkway HU10 178 B7
Kirk Way NG34 212 C7
Kirkwood Cl PE3 225 E2
Kirman Cres 5 DN17 184 F3
KIRMINGTON DN39 22 A6
Kirmington CE Prim Sch
DN39 22 A6
Kirmington Cl 8 LN6 204 C6
Kirmington Gdns 3 DN34 191 A7
Kirmington Rd DN39 21 F7
KIRMOND LE MIRE LN8 46 A3
Kirmond Rd LN8 47 A4
Kirness Dro LN4 109 C6
KIRTON PE20 136 D5
Kirton Cl 2 NG24 104 B1
Kirton Distribution Pk
PE20 136 C5
Kirton Dro LN4 110 F1
KIRTON END PE20 136 B6
KIRTON HOLME PE20 135 E8
Kirton Holme Rd PE20 124 E1
KIRTON IN LINDSEY DN21 30 C2
Kirton La Hatfield DN8 14 E7
2 Long Bennington NG23 117 D4
Stainforth DN7 14 D6
Kirton Lindsey Prim Sch
DN21 30 B1
Kirton Lindsey Sta DN21 30 B2
Kirton Prim Sch PE20 136 C5
Kirton Rd Blyton DN21 41 D6
Holme DN16 19 B2
Manton DN21 30 A3
Messingham DN17 29 E6
Scawby DN20 30 C8
Scotter DN21 29 D3
Waddingham DN21 43 B7
Kisgate 10 LN1 66 D7
Kishorn Ct DN40 186 B2
Kisimul Sch LN6 92 A6
Kit Cat La PE20 145 F8
Kite Way PE7 233 A8
Kitty Briggs La NG31 210 E1
Kitwood Cl 4 PE21 209 B4
Kitwood Rd PE21 209 B4
KNAITH DN21 53 A3
Knaith Hall La DN22 52 E3
Knaith Hill DN21 53 A3
KNAITH PARK DN21 53 B4
Knapton Ct LN7 33 B4
Knarr Fen Rd PE6 176 E2
Kneeland 24 LN2 68 D6
Knight Cl Holdingham NG34 212 D7
Market Deeping PE6 217 D5
Knight Ms PE2 231 A6
Knighton Cl PE7 230 D1
Knight Pl 2 LN5 205 E8
Knightsbridge 2 DN36 195 C6
Knightsbridge Rd 41 DN17 29 D7
Knights Cl 5 Belton DN9 16 E2
18 Laceby DN37 23 F1
Leverington PE13 170 B2
Knight's Ct DN16 185 A3
Knight St Grimsby DN32 192 B6
4 Lincoln LN5 205 E8
2 Pinchbeck PE11 145 B1
Knight Terr LN5 205 E8
Knipe Ave PE11 214 C3
KNIPTON NG32 138 C6
Knipton CE Prim Sch
NG32 138 C6
Knipton Cl 31 NG24 104 B2
Knipton La NG32 138 D6
Knipton Rd NG32 138 B4
Knole Wlk PE3 225 B3
Knoll St DN35 192 F6
Knolls The NG32 210 B5
Knoll The NG31 210 D8
Knowle St 20 LN12 64 B3
Knowles Wy 8 LN3 83 B4
Kohima Cl 3 PE10 213 E7
Kooreman Ave 19 PE13 170 D1
Kristen Turton Cl DN36 195 D2
Kristiansand Cl 5 DN36 195 B6
Kyme Rd Boston PE21 208 D6
Heckington NG34 122 E3

L

Labour in Vain Dro LN4 110 A6
Labrador Dr 11 DN20 19 E4
Laburnham Ave DN37 194 D4
Laburnham Cl DN37 194 D4
Laburnum Ave
Gainsborough DN21 197 D6
4 Gunness DN15 17 E6
Yaxley PE7 233 F6
Laburnum Cl
3 Bourne PE10 213 C6
Grantham NG31 211 D5
Lincoln LN6 205 A2
Laburnum Cl *continued*
7 Wisbech PE13 170 E1
Laburnum Cres LN11 198 E4
Laburnum Ct
2 Cherry Willingham/Reepham
LN3 82 A8
Hessle HU13 178 E1
Laburnum Dr
Cherry Willingham/Reepham
LN3 203 D5
Grimsby DN34 190 E7
Ingoldmells PE25 206 D8
3 Kingston upon Hull HU5 179 B7
Morton PE10 154 B7
Laburnum Gdns PE20 136 C5
Laburnum Gr
8 Burton upon Stather
DN15 8 B5
16 Crowle DN17 16 D7
Peterborough PE1 226 B8
Scunthorpe DN16 185 B7
Spalding PE11 214 F5
Laburnum Rd NG34 107 C2
LACEBY DN37 23 E1
LACEBY ACRES DN34 190 C4
Laceby Acres Academy
DN34 190 D4
Laceby Rd Grimsby DN34 191 A4
Laceby DN37 190 C3
Scunthorpe DN17 184 E5
Laceby St LN2 202 B3
Lacey Gdns LN11 198 D6
Lacey Gdns Jun Sch LN11 198 D6
Lacey Gr NG24 104 C2
Lacey's Cl PE22 126 F6
Lacey's Dr PE22 126 F6
Lacey's La PE22 126 E6
Lacy Cl 21 LN2 68 D2
Ladbroke Cl 7 NG34 133 D7
Ladds Cl 6 PE21 209 C4
Ladds La PE6 217 A1
Ladd's Mill Cl 7 LN6 93 B8
LADE BANK PE22 113 F5
Lade Bank Old Leake PE22 113 F5
Wrangle PE22 114 B6
Lady Anne Wy 29 HU15 2 D5
Lady Bower Cl 9 LN6 205 A2
Ladybower Way PE4 221 C3
Lady Charlotte Rd PE7 230 C3
Lady Fen La LN13 76 B1
Lady Frances Cres DN35 192 C5
Lady Frances Dr 1 LN8 57 D8
Lady Jane Franklin Dr 14
PE23 101 A8
Lady La PE24 102 A2
Lady Lodge Dr PE2 230 A5
Lady Margaret's Ave PE6 217 C5
Lady Matilda's Dr PE25 206 C8
Lady Meers Rd LN3 203 E6
Lady Romayne Cl PE9 219 C4
Ladysmith Rd DN32 191 F7
Ladysmith Terr NG31 210 E7
Ladywell Gate 4 HU15 2 E6
Ladywood Rd PE11 214 E6
Lafford Ct NG34 212 B5
Lafford Dr 2 LN4 109 F6
Laforey Rd DN31 188 A3
Lagonda Cl LN4 205 F1
Lagoon Rd DN17 184 B6
Lailey Gr HU13 178 B2
Laing Cl 2 LN3 83 B4
Lake Field Rd PE7 233 B8
Lakeside Anderby PE24 77 C3
Great Coates DN37 24 B6
Peterborough PE4 221 B5
Peterborough PE7 230 C2
Pyewipe DN37 188 A3
Lakeside Dr DN17 184 C5
Lakeside Gr HU4 179 D4
Lakeside Leisure Ctr PE2 230 A5
Lakeside Parkway
Scunthorpe DN16 185 E4
Scunthorpe DN16 185 F5
Lakeside Ret Pk DN16 185 F6
Lakeside Sta DN35 193 B2
Lakeside Vw LN3 82 F6
Lakeview Cl 3 LN6 204 C1
Lake View Rd LN6 205 C6
Lakeview Way PE7 230 C2
Lalrgate Pl DN35 192 F1
Lambert Ave 12 HU15 2 C6
Lambert Bank Fleet PE12 158 D1
Holbeach PE12 168 D8
Lambert Mews 5 PE9 219 C4
Lambert Rd
4 Allington NG32 128 F7
Grimsby DN32 191 D6
Lambes Ct PE4 220 E4
Lambeth Wlk 3 PE9 219 A6
Lamb Gdns LN2 202 B6
Lamb La Benington PE22 127 A4
Newport HU15 1 B8
Lambourn Ct 3 DN35 192 F1
Lambourne Rise DN16 185 A2
Lambourne Way 5 NG34 122 D2
Lambs Row 5 PE21 208 E6
La Milesse Way 1 PE20 135 C7
Lammas Leas Rd 4 LN8 57 E7
Lammas Rd PE1 226 A7
Lammin's La 2 PE22 99 A4
Lamplight Sq NG31 210 F4
Lamport Cl 9 PE6 217 A6
Lampton Gr DN32 191 D6
Lanark St 2 HU5 180 B8
Lancaster App DN40 12 D4
Lancaster Ave
Grimsby DN31 191 B7
Horncastle LN9 199 C5
Lancaster Ave *continued*
Skegness PE25 206 A5
Lancaster Cl
3 Great Steeping PE23 101 D7
Long Sutton PE12 216 C4
Stickney PE22 113 A7
6 Waddington LN5 94 A7
Lancaster Ct
6 Nunsthorpe DN33 191 B2
14 Welton/Dunholme LN2 68 D7
Yaxley PE7 233 F6
Lancaster Dr
6 Coningsby LN4 207 D4
Long Sutton PE12 216 C4
7 Market Rasen LN8 57 E8
Moorland Prison DN7 26 A8
6 Scampton Airfield LN1 67 F5
10 South Killingholme DN40 12 E3
Lancaster Gate DN36 195 C1
Lancaster Gdns 2 NG31 211 D2
Lancaster Gn DN21 54 F8
Lancaster Pl 4 LN5 201 F1
Lancaster Rd
11 Beacon Hill NG24 104 C5
3 Binbrook Tech Pk LN8 47 B6
Gringley on the Hill DN10 39 D1
Scunthorpe DN16 185 A5
10 Stamford PE9 219 B6
Lancaster Sch The LN6 204 C8
Lancaster Way
25 Brough HU15 2 C5
Market Deeping PE6 217 B7
2 Skellingthorpe LN6 200 A4
Yaxley PE7 233 F6
Lancelot Ct HU9 181 C6
Lancelot Way 7 PE11 214 B3
Lancer Ct DN33 191 A2
Lancewood Gdns 3 LN6 204 C8
Lancia Cres LN4 205 F2
Lancing Cl 7 PE4 221 A3
Lancing Way 4 DN33 194 E8
Land Dike LN11 37 A1
Landeck Ave DN34 191 B6
Lander Cr 1 PE7 230 F5
Landing La HU15 1 A7
Landings La DN36 195 C4
Landing The HU15 1 A6
Landmere Gr LN6 200 D1
Land of Gn Ginger 10
HU1 180 F6
Landor Ave 3 DN17 184 D7
Landsdowne Cl 22 LN12 77 A8
Landsdowne Ct PE11 214 F6
Landsdowne Rd 2 PE25 206 C4
Landseer Ave PE24 90 D8
LANEHAM DN22 65 A3
Laneham Rd NG22 65 A1
Laneham St Rampton DN22 65 A5
Scunthorpe DN15 183 A3
Lanes The 10 DN36 36 D4
Lane The
1 Easton on the Hill PE9 171 D3
Ruskington NG34 108 C2
West Deeping PE6 173 B7
Laney Cl LN2 202 C7
Langary Gate Rd PE12 158 E1
Langdale Ave DN33 194 D7
Langdale Cl LN2 202 B8
Langdale Cres NG31 211 A8
Langdyke PE1 226 F6
Langer Cl 5 LN6 204 B6
LANGFORD NG23 91 C1
Langford Gdns NG31 211 B6
Langford La NG23 91 A2
Langford Rd PE2 231 A7
Langford Wlk 1 HU4 179 B7
Langham Rd PE24 90 B7
Langhole Dro PE11 145 B1
LANGHOLME DN9 39 E8
Langholme La DN9 27 B1
Langholme Wood Nature
Reserve★ DN9 39 D8
Langley PE3 225 B8
Langley Cl LN11 198 E4
Langley Dr DN16 185 A2
Langley Pl DN35 193 A4
Langley Rd LN6 204 D2
Langley Wlk DN40 186 D3
LANGRICK PE22 124 E7
LANGRICK BRIDGE PE22 124 E6
Langrick Rd Boston PE21 208 C6
Coningsby LN4 98 C1
Holland Fen with Brothertoft
PE20 124 E4
Langthwaite Cl 20 HU15 2 D5
LANGTOFT PE6 164 F3
Langtoft Drain Rd PE6 165 C4
Langtoft Outgang Rd
PE11 165 D6
Langtoft Prim Sch PE6 164 F3
LANGTON Langton LN9 85 B3
Langton by Spilsby PE23 87 F5
LANGTON BY WRAGBY
LN8 70 F3
Langton Cl Grimsby DN33 191 A3
Horncastle LN9 199 A3
Lincoln LN2 202 B7
Langton Ct PE25 206 C5
Langton Dr Grimsby DN33 191 A3
Horncastle LN9 199 A3
Langton Hill
Horncastle LN9 199 A3
Kingthorpe LN8 70 E2
Langton La LN9 85 C4
Langton Rd
Holton le Clay DN36 195 E2
Panton LN8 71 B6
Peterborough PE1 226 D7
Langwith Dr PE12 215 C2
Langwith Gdns PE12 215 C1
LANGWORTH LN3 69 B3
Langworthgate LN2 234 C3
Langworth Rd LN2 69 B4
Lannimore Cl LN5 205 D3
Lansbury Rd 12 NG24 104 B2
Lansdall Ave 4 DN21 52 F6
Lansdowne Ave
Grimsby DN32 191 D4
Lincoln LN6 205 C5
Lansdowne Dr 21 LN12 77 A8
Lansdowne Rd
8 Navenby/Wellingore
LN5 107 A8
Yaxley PE7 233 F6
Lansdowne St HU3 180 C6
Lansdowne Way PE2 230 D7
Lansdown Link 1 DN35 192 E3
Lansdown Rd 4 DN40 186 B4
Lansdown Way 17 LN10 97 C5
Lantern La HU15 1 B5
Laporte Rd DN40 187 C5
Lapwater La PE12 147 C6
Lapwing Cl LN6 200 A3
Lapwing Wy
2 Barton-upon-Humber
DN18 3 E1
Scunthorpe DN16 185 F5
Larch Ave Allington NG32 128 A6
16 Nettleham LN2 68 D2
Larch Cl 8 Bourne PE10 213 C7
2 Grantham NG31 210 D2
Immingham DN40 186 E5
Ruskington NG34 108 D1
Yaxley PE7 233 F6
Larch Ct 9 DN21 197 E6
Larch Gn NG34 107 D1
Larch Gr Peterborough PE1 226 C6
8 Scawby DN20 30 F8
Scunthorpe DN16 185 B7
Larchmont Cl 10 HU15 2 C6
Larch Rd DN35 192 D2
Larch Way 8 NG34 212 D2
Larchwood Cres LN6 200 D1
Larden Ave DN33 194 E8
Lares Ave PE2 231 D4
Lark Cl 13 LN8 70 D4
Lark Dr 4 LN5 107 A7
Larkin Ave LN3 203 D5
Larklands PE3 225 B1
Lark Rise
6 Market Deeping PE6 217 C5
Scotter DN21 29 B3
Larkspur Ave 6 DN41 23 F5
Larkspur Croft PE21 208 C6
Larkspur Rd LN2 202 D7
Larkspur Wlk PE4 221 B3
Larkspur Wy PE11 214 B6
Larks Rise PE10 154 B7
Larmour Rd DN37 190 D7
Larne Cl 12 LN5 205 C2
Larne Rd LN5 205 D2
Larners Fields 6 LN1 66 C7
Las End 37 DN21 30 B1
Lashbrook Garth HU4 179 B4
Lastingham 30 HU15 2 C6
Latham Ave PE2 230 C7
Latham Ct PE20 124 B8
Latimer Gdns 12 NG34 122 E3
Lattimers Paddock PE9 172 C4
LAUGHTERTON LN1 65 D2
LAUGHTON DN21 41 C8
Laughton Cres LN2 202 A8
Laughton Dr 14 PE9 218 E6
Laughton La DN21 40 D3
Laughton Rd Blyton DN21 40 F5
Boston PE21 208 D6
Laughton Road DN21 29 B1
Laughton Way LN2 201 F7
Laughton Way N LN2 201 F8
Launde Gdns 5 PE9 218 E4
Launder Terr NG31 211 A3
Laundon Rd NG34 132 E3
Laura Ct 5 PE25 90 E3
Laureate Gr PE11 214 B4
Laurel Cl
6 Donington PE11 134 E2
8 Gainsborough DN21 197 E6
Kingston upon Hull HU5 179 B7
Lincoln LN5 205 D5
Yaxley PE7 233 D4
Laurel Dr 7 PE6 176 A3
Laurel Gr LN7 32 A1
Laurel La
Kingston upon Hull HU5 179 D7
Thornton Curtis DN39 11 E4
Laurels Cl 1 DN40 22 E8
Laurel Way DN16 185 D4
Lauridston Cl 9 DN37 23 E1
Laurier St DN35 192 D8
Lauriston Rd NG31 210 F6
Laurold Ave 1 DN7 15 A3
Laval Pl PE21 209 B5
Lavender Cl 6 Lincoln LN5 205 C2
10 Sleaford NG34 212 D2
2 Yaxley PE7 233 F6
Lavender Cres PE1 226 B8
Lavender Dr PE11 214 A2
Lavender Gr DN36 195 B7
Lavender Way
Bourne PE10 213 B7
21 Newark-on-Trent NG24 104 C5
18 Scunthorpe DN15 183 B3
1 Stamford PE9 218 D7
Lavender Wlk 1 HU5 179 C7
Lavenham Ct PE2 230 C7
Lavenham Gr LN6 205 A4
Lavenham Rd DN33 194 D7
Lavington Grange PE1 226 E6
Law Ct 1 PE11 214 B5
Lawley Cl LN2 203 B8
Lawn Ave
Peterborough PE1 226 A7
Skegness PE25 206 D2
Lawn Cres 1 PE25 206 D2
Lawn Ct LN1 234 A4
Lawn in Lincoln The★
LN1 234 A3
Lawn La NG33 152 F2
Lawns The Collingham NG23 91 D5
4 Grimsby DN31 191 C7
Kingston upon Hull HU10 178 D7
Peterborough PE4 221 C1
18 Wisbech PE13 170 C1
Lawnswood HU13 178 D2
Lawnswood Ct DN16 185 A4
Lawn Wood Nature Reserve★
NG33 152 E2
Lawrance Way 10 PE10 164 C8
Lawrence Ave PE7 231 C2
Lawrence Cl 1 LN6 205 B7
Lawrence La 3 NG34 120 C8
Lawrence Rd PE8 172 C1
Lawrence's Dro PE10 164 F8
Lawrence St
25 Beacon Hill NG24 104 A5
Grimsby DN31 191 C8
Law's Cl PE6 174 C5
Lawson Ave Grimsby DN31 191 B7
Peterborough PE2 231 D6
Lawson Ct 15 LN2 68 E6
Lawson Leas 5 NG32 210 A5
Lawyers Cl PE12 215 E2
Laxton Cl PE6 217 F5
Laxton Gdns 7 PE11 156 E8
Laxton Gr DN16 185 A2
Laxton La NG33 152 E7
Laycock Ave 2 DN10 39 C1
Layerthorpe Rd 1 HU4 179 C2
Laythorpe Ave PE25 206 D1
Laythorpe Gdns 2 LN4 207 C4
LEA DN21 52 F5
Leaburn Rd DN17 29 D7
Leadenhall Rd PE12 147 C6
LEADENHAM LN5 106 C3
Leadenham CE Prim Sch
LN5 106 D3
Leading Dro PE7 233 D3
Lea Dr DN32 191 F5
Leaf Ave PE7 230 D3
Leafbridge Way LN6 204 C3
Leafere Way 1 PE13 170 B2
Lea Garth 6 DN17 29 D7
Leagate Cl LN4 207 F6
Leagate Rd Coningsby LN4 207 F6
Langriville PE22 124 F8
Thornton le Fen PE22 111 F1
Lea Gdns PE3 225 F1
Lea Gr 2 LN3 83 C4
LEAKE PE22 127 C8
LEAKE COMMONSIDE
PE22 113 F3
LEAKE FOLD HILL PE22 114 A2
Leakes Row LN11 198 C7
Leake's Row LN11 198 C7
Lealand Cl 1 LN2 202 E6
Lealand Way PE21 209 A2
Leame Cl HU3 180 A7
Leamington Cl 2 DN16 183 C1
Leamington Ct DN16 183 C1
Leamlands La PE12 149 B1
Lea Pk Home Est PE21 209 B4
Lea Rd DN21 197 D2
Lea Rd W DN21 197 D1
Leas Cl DN37 194 E5
Lease La DN40 12 D6
LEASINGHAM NG34 121 B8
Leasingham La NG34 108 D1
Leasingham St Andrews CE
Prim Sch The NG34 121 B7
Leas Rd NG34 122 F2
Leas The NG32 119 B1
Lea The NG34 121 B8
Leaver Gate PE24 102 B2
Leaves Lake Dro PE11 155 E7
Lea View 2 PE9 163 C1
Lebanon Dr 3 PE13 170 E1
Lechler Cl LN2 68 D3
Leconfield Cl 7 LN6 204 C6
Leconfield Rd 16 LN6 204 C7
Ledbury Dr DN36 195 D7
Ledbury Rd PE3 225 C3
Ledham PE2 229 D4
Lee Ave
Heighington/Washingborough
LN4 203 D1
Sutterton PE20 136 B2
Leeder Cl PE7 231 D1
Lee Fair Gdns 1 DN17 184 F2
Leek Hill 18 DN15 9 A5
Leeming Cl 8 LN6 204 D6
Lee Rd Lincoln LN2 234 C4
Yaxley PE7 233 E4
Lee Smith St HU9 181 E7
Lees Rest Houses HU4 179 C6
Lee St LN11 198 B5
Lees The PE6 217 E5
Lees Wlk HU3 180 A7
Legard Ave DN16 185 B6
Legard Dr HU10 178 F6
Legarde Ave HU4 179 C6
LEGBOURNE LN11 61 F3
Legbourne Abbey LN11 61 F3
Legbourne Cl 1 LN1 201 D7
Legbourne Rd LN11 198 E3

Legbourne Road LN11 . . . . 62 C4
Legbourne Wood Nature Reserve★ LN11 . . . . 61 F2
Legends Wy 3 HU4 . . . . . . 179 E5
Leggott Way 8 DN41 . . . . . . 23 E6
Legion Cl 8 HU15 . . . . 2 C5
LEGSBY LN8 . . . . 58 A4
Legsby Ave DN32 . . . . 191 E5
Legsby Pl DN32 . . . . 191 E4
Legsby Prim Sch LN8 . . . . . 58 A4
Legsby Rd LN8 . . . . 57 E7
Leicester Cl LN4 . . . . 203 C1
Leicester Gr NG31 . . . . 210 D5
Leicester Mews PE10 . . . . . 213 B3
Leicester Rd PE8 . . . . 222 C4
Leicester St
Kingston upon Hull HU3 . . . . 180 D8
1 Sleaford NG34 . . . . 212 D4
Leiden Fields 2 PE11 . . . . 214 B2
Leighton PE2 . . . . 230 C4
Leighton Cres 2 LN6 . . . . . 205 B6
Leighton Gr DN33 . . . . 191 C4
Leighton Prim Sch PE2 . . . 230 C4
Leighton Wlk 4 PE12 . . . . 159 D7
Leinsters Cl PE3 . . . . 225 D3
Leiston Ct 21 PE6 . . . . 175 A1
Lemon Wong La LN5 . . . . . 106 C3
Lenham La HU1 . . . . 180 E6
LENTON NG33 . . . . 141 E5
Lenton Gn LN2 . . . . 202 B7
Lenton's La Friskney PE22 . . 115 A5
Leverton PE22 . . . . 126 F6
Lenton Way 2 PE20 . . . . . . 136 D6
Leofric Ave PE10 . . . . 213 B5
Leofric Cl 19 PE6 . . . . 166 F1
Leofric Sq PE1 . . . . 226 E3
Leonard Cres DN15 . . . . . . 182 F3
Leonard St 4 HU3 . . . . 180 D8
Leopold Cl DN16 . . . . 185 A6
Lerowe Rd PE13 . . . . 170 E1
Leslie Ct 5 DN15 . . . . 183 B3
Leslie Manser Prim Sch LN6 . . . . 204 B7
Lessingham PE2 . . . . 229 D4
Lestrange St DN35 . . . . 192 C7
Lethbridge Rd PE4 . . . . 221 D2
Lettwell Cres 1 PE25 . . . . . 206 D1
Levellers Wy 12 NG24 . . . . 104 C4
Levels La Blaxton DN9 . . . . . . 26 A4
Misson DN10 . . . . 39 A7
Leven Rd DN16 . . . . 185 D6
Levens Wlk PE3 . . . . 225 B3
Leveret Chase LN6 . . . . 92 D5
Leverett Rd PE21 . . . . 209 B4
LEVERINGTON PE13 . . . . 170 B3
Leverington Comm PE13 . . 169 F1
Leverington Prim Acad PE13 . . . . 170 B2
Leverington Rd PE13 . . . . . 170 C1
Levers Cl PE21 . . . . 209 F5
Leverstock Gn 38 DN7 . . . . . 14 D4
LEVERTON PE22 . . . . 126 F6
Leverton CE Acad DN22 . . . . 52 B1
LEVERTON HIGHGATE PE22 . . . . 127 A6
Leverton Leisure Ctr PE22 . . . . 127 A7
LEVERTON LUCASGATE PE22 . . . . 127 B6
LEVERTON OUTGATE PE22 . . . . 127 B7
Leverton Rd DN22 . . . . 52 B1
Levington St 2 DN31 . . . . . 189 C1
Lewes Ave NG31 . . . . 210 D5
Lewes Gdns PE4 . . . . 221 A3
Lewis Ave 13 LN12 . . . . 77 A8
Lewis Ct 15 PE11 . . . . 214 C2
Lewis Rd Cleethorpes DN35 192 D8
Coningsby LN4 . . . . 207 D4
Lewis St
Gainsborough DN21 . . . . 197 D3
Lincoln LN5 . . . . 234 B1
Lexington Dr HU4 . . . . 179 C5
Leyburn Rd LN6 . . . . 204 F4
Leyden Cl 6 DN40 . . . . 186 B4
Leyland Ave DN7 . . . . 14 E4
Leys Cl NG32 . . . . 210 B4
Leys Farm Jun Sch DN17 . . 184 F4
Leys La DN15 . . . . 9 B6
Leys Ln 7 DN10 . . . . 39 C1
Leys The
Cherry Willingham LN3 . . . . 203 E6
Peterborough PE3 . . . . 225 A1
Leytonstone La PE10 . . . . . 213 D2
Libertas Dr 1 PE2 . . . . 231 E4
Liberty La HU1 . . . . 181 A6
Liberty Pk 3 HU15 . . . . 2 D5
Lichfield Ave
Peterborough PE4 . . . . 220 F3
Scunthorpe DN17 . . . . 184 C7
Lichfield Cl NG31 . . . . 210 E4
Lichfield Ct DN32 . . . . 192 B6
Lichfield Rd
Bracebridge Heath LN4 . . . . . 81 A2
Grimsby DN32 . . . . 192 B6
12 Hatfield DN7 . . . . 14 D4
Liddell St HU2 . . . . 180 E7
Lidgard Rd DN36 . . . . 193 A1
Lidgate Cl PE2 . . . . 230 C7
Lidgett Cl 10 DN20 . . . . 30 F8
Lidgett The 7 DN9 . . . . 27 D6
Lifeboat Ave PE25 . . . . 206 D1
Lighter-than-Air Rd NG34 . . . . 107 C1
Lighton Ave 4 PE20 . . . . . . 136 C5
Lilac Ave DN16 . . . . 183 C1
Lilac Cl Birchwood LN6 . . . . 204 C8
Bourne PE10 . . . . 213 B6
Lilac Cl *continued*
Wisbech PE13 . . . . 170 E1
Lilac Ct DN33 . . . . 194 D8
Lilac Rd
9 Elloughton-cum-Brough HU15 . . . . 2 C5
Peterborough PE1 . . . . 226 C7
Lilac Wlk PE7 . . . . 233 F6
Lilacwood Dr 5 NG31 . . . . . 210 F7
Lila Dr 1 PE11 . . . . 145 B7
Lilburn Cl 5 NG34 . . . . 121 B8
Lilburn Dr PE11 . . . . 214 C6
Lilford Cl 5 LN2 . . . . 202 E7
Lilford Rd LN2 . . . . 202 E7
Lilley St 6 NG23 . . . . 117 D3
Lillicrap Ct 2 LN1 . . . . 234 B4
Lilly's Carr Nature Reserve★ PE23 . . . . 100 E6
Lilly's Rd LN2 . . . . 234 B4
Lily La 13 NG24 . . . . 104 B5
Lilywood Rd 12 DN20 . . . . . . 19 D3
Lima Wy PE2 . . . . 231 D4
Limber Bridle Road DN37 . . 23 C2
Limber Cl 2 DN21 . . . . 53 A7
Limber Ct DN34 . . . . 191 A6
Limber Hill Binbrook LN8 . . . . 47 D4
Great Limber DN37 . . . . 22 E2
Limber Rd
Great Limber DN41 . . . . 22 E5
Humberside Airport DN39 . . . 22 A6
Swallow LN7 . . . . 34 A7
Limber Vale DN34 . . . . 191 A6
Limburg Dr 7 PE11 . . . . 214 A2
Lime Ave Scunthorpe DN16 . . 19 A3
Wisbech PE13 . . . . 170 D1
Limeberry Pl
7 Birchwood LN6 . . . . 204 B8
9 Birchwood LN6 . . . . 204 B8
Lime Cl
Burgh le Marsh PE24 . . . . . . 102 D7
2 Langtoft PE6 . . . . 164 F3
3 Old Leake PE22 . . . . 114 A1
RAF Cranwell NG34 . . . . 107 D1
Ruskington NG34 . . . . 108 D1
Lime Cres Greetwell LN2 . . . 203 B8
Waddington LN5 . . . . 205 C1
Lime Ct PE11 . . . . 214 E3
Limedale View 2 DN3 . . . . . . 14 A3
Lime Gr Bassingham LN5 . . . . 92 F2
2 Boston PE21 . . . . 209 C2
2 Bottesford NG13 . . . . 128 A5
Caythorpe NG32 . . . . 119 C7
Cherry Willingham/Reepham LN3 . . . . 203 D5
9 Goxhill DN19 . . . . 12 A8
Grantham NG31 . . . . 211 C6
Holbeach PE12 . . . . 215 D3
Holton le Clay DN36 . . . . 195 D1
Humberston DN36 . . . . 36 C7
7 Ingoldmells PE25 . . . . 90 D3
Louth LN11 . . . . 198 C7
Scunthorpe DN16 . . . . 185 B7
Lime Kiln Cl PE3 . . . . 225 E4
Lime Kiln Way LN2 . . . . 202 C4
Limelands 2 LN2 . . . . 234 C3
Lime St Grimsby DN31 . . . . . 191 C8
Kingston upon Hull HU8 . . . . 181 A8
3 Sutton Bridge PE12 . . . . . . 160 F4
Limes The
7 Beckingham DN10 . . . . 40 A1
Castor PE5 . . . . 223 F1
4 Stallingborough DN41 . . . . . 23 D6
12 Wittering PE8 . . . . 172 B1
Limetree Ave DN33 . . . . 191 C3
Lime Tree Ave
Gainsborough DN21 . . . . 197 D5
Kingston upon Hull HU13 . . . 178 F2
2 Market Deeping PE6 . . . . . 217 A6
20 Metheringham LN4 . . . . 95 C4
Peterborough PE1 . . . . 225 F4
Limetree Cl
13 Sleaford NG34 . . . . 212 D2
Yaxley PE7 . . . . 233 F7
Lime Tree Cl
1 Collingham NG23 . . . . 91 D4
6 Fulbeck NG32 . . . . 106 C1
6 Lincoln LN6 . . . . 204 E8
Lime Tree Gr 4 DN8 . . . . 15 A8
Lime Tree Paddock 2 LN2 . 68 F4
Limetree Wlk 1 NG34 . . . . . 122 E2
Limewalk PE12 . . . . 216 C6
Lime Wlk 9 PE22 . . . . 114 A1
Limewood Way 2 LN2 . . . . . 202 F6
Linchfield Cl PE6 . . . . 217 E5
Linchfield Com Prim Sch PE6 . . . . 217 D5
Linchfield Rd PE6 . . . . 217 D6
LINCOLN LN5 . . . . 234 C2
Lincoln Ass Rm★ LN2 . . . . 234 B3
Lincoln Ave LN6 . . . . 205 C8
Lincoln Bishop King CE Prim Sch The LN5 . . . . 201 F1
Lincoln Bvd DN31 . . . . 191 B7
Lincoln Castle★ LN1 . . . . . . 234 A3
Lincoln Castle Acad LN1 . . 201 E7
Lincoln Castle Way DN19 . . . 4 D2
Lincoln Cath★ LN2 . . . . . . 234 B3
Lincoln Christ's Hospl Sch LN2 . . . . 202 B6
Lincoln Cl 4 Crowle DN17 . . 16 D7
Grantham NG31 . . . . 210 D4
5 Market Deeping PE6 . . . . 217 A6
Lincoln Coll LN2 . . . . 234 C3
Lincoln Cres 2 DN21 . . . . . . 42 F8
Lincoln Ct
4 Beacon Hill NG24 . . . . . . 104 A6
Brumby DN16 . . . . 185 B7
Lincoln Cty Hospl LN2 . . . . 202 C4
Lincoln Dr
27 Barton-upon-Humber DN18 . . . . 10 F8
30 Caistor LN7 . . . . 33 B4
3 Scampton Airfield LN1 . . . . 67 F5
5 Waddington LN5 . . . . 94 A7
24 Winterton DN15 . . . . 9 A5
Lincoln Drill Hall★ LN1 . . . 234 B2
Lincoln Gate DN36 . . . . 48 D5
Lincoln Gdns DN16 . . . . 185 A6
Lincoln Gdns Prim Sch DN16 . . . . 185 A6
Lincoln Gn
Kingston upon Hull HU4 . . . . 179 C7
Skegness PE25 . . . . 206 B5
Lincoln La Boston PE21 . . . . 208 E5
Holbeach PE12 . . . . 147 D5
Kettlethorpe LN1 . . . . 65 F3
Osgodby LN8 . . . . 44 F2
Thorpe on the Hill LN6 . . . . . . 92 E8
Lincoln Rd Bassingham LN5 . 92 F2
10 Binbrook Tech Pk LN8 . . . . 47 B6
Brant Broughton LN5 . . . . . . 105 F5
Brant Broughton & Stragglethorpe LN5 . . . . 106 A5
Canwick LN4 . . . . 81 B3
Caythorpe NG32 . . . . 119 B6
Cleethorpes DN35 . . . . 192 C5
Deeping Gate PE6 . . . . 217 C3
Digby LN4 . . . . 108 D6
Doddington & Whisby LN6 . . 204 A6
Dunholme LN2 . . . . 68 D6
Dunston LN4 . . . . 95 B5
Faldingworth LN8 . . . . 56 F3
Fenton LN1 . . . . 65 E3
Fiskerton LN3 . . . . 203 F4
1 Glinton PE6 . . . . 220 C8
Heighington/Washingborough LN4 . . . . 203 A2
Holton cum Beckering LN8 . . . 70 B7
Honington NG32 . . . . 119 C2
Horncastle LN9 . . . . 199 A4
Ingham LN1 . . . . 54 F2
1 Leasingham NG34 . . . . 121 B8
Lincoln LN6 . . . . 204 F1
Louth LN11 . . . . 61 B8
Metheringham LN4 . . . . 95 C4
Middle Rasen LN8 . . . . 57 B7
Moorland Prison DN7 . . . . 26 A8
Nettleham LN2 . . . . 68 B1
Newark-on-Trent NG24 . . . . . 104 A6
Northborough PE6 . . . . 217 D1
Peterborough PE6 . . . . 220 D5
Ruskington NG34 . . . . 108 D2
Saxilby with Ingleby LN1 . . . . . 66 E1
4 Skegness PE25 . . . . 206 C3
Skellingthorpe LN6 . . . . 200 B4
Sleaford NG34 . . . . 212 B7
Stamford PE9 . . . . 219 C7
West Barkwith LN8 . . . . 71 A7
Lincoln Rd Bridge NG24 . . 104 A5
Lincoln Rd Nocton LN4 . . . . . 95 A7
Lincoln St Christopher's Sch The LN6 . . . . 205 B4
Lincoln St Peter at Gowts CE Prim Sch The LN5 . . . . 201 E1
Lincoln St Peter-in-Eastgate CE (Cont) Inf Sch The LN2 . . . . 234 C3
Lincoln's Ave PE12 . . . . 168 C2
Lincoln Sch of Art and Design LN2 . . . . 234 B3
Lincolnshire Archives★ LN1 . . . . 234 B3
Lincolnshire Aviation Heritage Ctr★ PE23 . . . . 99 F5
Lincolnshire Coast Light Rly★ PE25 . . . . 90 D1
Lincolnshire Montessori Sch LN7 . . . . 33 C4
Lincolnshire Rare Breeds Poultry★ LN11 . . . . 61 F8
Lincolnshire Rd Transport Mus★ LN6 . . . . 204 D5
Lincolnshire Showground★ LN1 . . . . 67 E4
Lincolnshire Wolds Rly★ DN36 . . . . 48 F6
Lincoln St
Gainsborough DN21 . . . . 197 C5
Kingston upon Hull HU2 . . . . 180 F8
Lincoln Sta LN5 . . . . 234 B1
Lincoln Way 1 PE11 . . . . . . 214 C5
Linda Cres LN11 . . . . 198 B4
Lindale Gdns DN16 . . . . 185 C7
Lindbergh Dr 17 PE11 . . . . 214 C2
Linden Ave 3 Branston LN4 81 D2
16 Newark-on-Trent NG24 . . 104 A3
Linden Cl 16 DN7 . . . . 14 D4
Linden Ct PE11 . . . . 214 E5
Linden Dene 1 LN6 . . . . 204 D1
Linden Dr PE24 . . . . 102 D7
Linden Gdns PE2 . . . . 229 C5
Linden Rd LN9 . . . . 199 C4
Linden Rise PE10 . . . . 213 D7
Lindens Cl PE13 . . . . 177 A3
Lindens The NG31 . . . . 211 B2
Linden Terr DN21 . . . . 197 D3
Linden Way Boston PE21 . . . 209 A7
Pinchbeck PE11 . . . . 144 D1
Linden Wlk LN11 . . . . 198 C4
Lindholme 5 DN21 . . . . 29 C3
Lindholme Bank Rd DN7 . . . 15 B1
Lindholme Rd LN6 . . . . 204 D5
Lindisfarne Ave DN36 . . . . . 195 B6
Lindisfarne Rd PE6 . . . . 175 A1
Lindisfarne Way NG31 . . . . . 210 E5
Lindis Rd PE21 . . . . 209 C5
Lindley St DN16 . . . . 185 A6
Lindrick Cl 4 NG31 . . . . . . 211 D7
Lindrick Dr DN21 . . . . 197 E6
Lindrick Rd 6 DN7 . . . . 14 F3
Lindrick Wlk 5 DN37 . . . . . 194 C4
Lindridge Wlk PE3 . . . . 225 A2
Lindsey Ave PE6 . . . . 217 A6
Lindsey Cl 6 Bourne PE10 . 213 C5
Gainsborough DN21 . . . . 197 F2
Peterborough PE4 . . . . 221 B1
Lindsey Ct 12 DN9 . . . . 27 E6
Lindsey Ctr 4 DN21 . . . . . . 197 D4
Lindsey Dr Crowle DN17 . . . . 16 D8
6 Healing DN41 . . . . 24 A5
Holton le Clay DN36 . . . . . . 195 C2
Morton DN21 . . . . 197 F6
Lindsey Pl HU4 . . . . 179 D6
Lindsey Rd
Cleethorpes DN35 . . . . 192 F4
Stamford PE9 . . . . 219 C6
4 Uffington PE9 . . . . 172 C6
Lindsey Rise 3 DN33 . . . . . 194 F8
Lindsey St 2 DN16 . . . . 183 C2
Lindsey Way LN11 . . . . 198 D4
Lindsey Wy PE22 . . . . 125 A8
Lindum Ave
3 Immingham DN40 . . . . . . 186 B3
Lincoln LN2 . . . . 234 C3
Lindum Cotts PE13 . . . . 170 B2
Lindum Cres 5 DN20 . . . . . 196 B4
Lindum Gr
Chapel St Leonard PE24 . . . . . 90 E7
2 Crowle DN17 . . . . 16 C7
Lindum Mews LN6 . . . . 204 D2
Lindum Rd
Cleethorpes DN35 . . . . 193 A4
Lincoln LN2 . . . . 234 B3
Lindum Sq 5 PE25 . . . . 206 B5
Lindum St
12 Beacon Hill NG24 . . . . . . 104 A4
Scunthorpe DN15 . . . . 183 B3
Lindum Terr LN2 . . . . 234 C3
Lindum Way 9 PE11 . . . . . . 134 F2
Lindum Wlk 1 LN7 . . . . 32 A4
Linecroft La DN10 . . . . 40 B4
Linga La LN5 . . . . 93 A3
Ling Crft 26 HU15 . . . . 2 D5
Ling Dr 11 DN21 . . . . 197 F5
Lingfield Cl 6 LN1 . . . . 66 D3
Ling Garth PE1 . . . . 226 B8
Linghall La LN4 . . . . 111 E5
Ling House La DN7 . . . . 14 A5
Ling La NG33 . . . . 152 C5
Ling Moor Prim Sch LN6 . . 204 E3
Lings La DN7 . . . . 14 D3
Lingwood Pk 5 PE3 . . . . . . 225 A1
Linkage Coll PE23 . . . . 100 F7
Link Rd PE1 . . . . 225 F3
Links Ave 2 LN12 . . . . 64 B5
Links Cres 4 PE25 . . . . 103 E4
Links Dr DN36 . . . . 195 E6
Linkside PE3 . . . . 220 F1
Links Rd DN35 . . . . 193 A3
Link The
Bracebridge Heath LN4 . . . . 205 F4
Kingston upon Hull HU4 . . . . 179 C5
2 Leasingham NG34 . . . . . . 121 B8
Louth LN11 . . . . 198 E5
2 Navenby/Wellingore LN5 . . . . 107 A7
Linkway 7 DN7 . . . . 14 F3
Link Way PE11 . . . . 214 E4
Linley Cl 4 NG23 . . . . 91 D4
Linley Dr PE21 . . . . 208 E2
Linnaeus St HU3 . . . . 180 C6
Linnet PE2 . . . . 229 D6
Linnet Cl Birchwood LN6 . . . 204 D8
7 Market Deeping PE6 . . . . 217 C5
Scunthorpe DN15 . . . . 182 D6
Linnet Dr PE10 . . . . 143 A3
Linnet Garth DN16 . . . . 185 F5
Linnet Way 11 NG34 . . . . . . 212 B3
Linseed Ave 15 NG24 . . . . . 104 A6
Linthorpe Gr HU10 . . . . 178 E8
Linton 21 HU15 . . . . 2 C6
Linton Cl Freiston PE22 . . . . 137 E7
Westwoodside DN9 . . . . 27 A2
Linton Rise 3 DN15 . . . . 8 A4
Linton St 5 LN5 . . . . 201 F1
LINWOOD LN8 . . . . 57 D5
Linwood Ave 5 DN33 . . . . . 194 F8
Linwood Cl
Gainsborough DN21 . . . . 197 F3
9 Sleaford NG34 . . . . 212 C6
Linwood Rd Lissington LN8 . . 57 D3
Martin LN4 . . . . 96 B3
Linwood Warren Nature Reserve★ LN8 . . . . 58 A6
Lions Wy NG34 . . . . 212 F6
Liquorpond St 11 PE21 . . . . 208 F4
Lisburn Cl 7 LN5 . . . . 205 D2
Lisburn Gr DN33 . . . . 191 D2
Lisle Marsden CE Mid Sch DN32 . . . . 191 E4
Lissett Cl 6 LN6 . . . . 204 B6
Lissingly La LN3 . . . . 57 C4
LISSINGTON LN3 . . . . 57 E2
Lissington Cl 2 LN2 . . . . . . 201 F7
Lissington Rd
Gainsborough DN21 . . . . 197 E3
Wickenby LN3 . . . . 57 C1
Lister Rd Peterborough PE1 225 F7
Scunthorpe DN15 . . . . 182 C3
Lister St Grimsby DN31 . . . . 191 B8
Kingston upon Hull HU1 . . . . 180 E5
LISTOFT PE24 . . . . 89 F7
Listoft La PE24 . . . . 89 F7
Litchfield Cl PE7 . . . . 233 F5
Little Bargate St LN5 . . . . . 205 E8
Littlebeck Cl HU3 . . . . 180 A7
Littlebeck Rd 3 DN36 . . . . . . 36 C8
Little Becks DN37 . . . . 23 F2
Little Belt The DN21 . . . . . . 197 D7
LITTLEBOROUGH DN22 . . . . . 52 F1
Littleborough La DN21 . . . . . 53 A1
Littleborough Rd DN22 . . . . . 52 C2
Littlebury Gdns PE12 . . . . . 215 C2
LITTLE BYTHAM NG33 . . . . . 163 A8
Little Bytham Rd
Castle Bytham NG33 . . . . . . 152 E1
Counthorpe & Creeton NG33 . . . . 153 A2
LITTLE CARLTON LN11 . . . . . . 62 C4
LITTLE CASTERTON PE9 . . . 171 E8
Little Casterton Rd PE9 . . . 218 F8
Little Casterton Road PE9 163 B1
LITTLE CAWTHORPE LN11 . . . 61 E2
Littlechild Dr 4 PE13 . . . . . 170 B2
Little Cl Edenham PE10 . . . . 153 D5
15 Eye PE6 . . . . 175 A1
LITTLE COATES DN34 . . . . . . 190 F7
Littlecoates Prim Sch DN31 . . . . 188 D1
Little Coates Rd DN34 . . . . 190 E4
Little Comm PE12 . . . . 215 B7
LITTLE COMMON PE12 . . . . 215 B8
Littlecote Gr PE4 . . . . 225 E8
Little Dog Dro PE12 . . . . . . 158 C1
Little Dowgate PE13 . . . . . . 170 B1
Little Dro PE20 . . . . 124 C2
Littlefair Rd 6 HU9 . . . . 5 D8
LITTLEFIELD DN34 . . . . 191 B6
Littlefield La
Grimsby DN34 . . . . 191 A6
Marshchapel DN36 . . . . 37 B2
Little Gate La LN4 . . . . 82 A1
Little George St HU8 . . . . . 181 A8
Little Gonerby CE (Aided) Infant's Sch NG31 . . . . . . 211 B5
LITTLE GRIMSBY LN11 . . . . . . 49 B2
Little Grimsby La LN11 . . . . . 49 A1
LITTLE HALE NG34 . . . . 133 E8
Little Hale Dro NG34 . . . . . 133 F8
Little Hale Rd NG34 . . . . . . 122 E1
Little Holme Rd PE34 . . . . . 161 C2
Little Johns Cl PE3 . . . . 224 F3
Little John St DN34 . . . . . . 191 B7
Little La Broomfleet HU15 . . . . 1 C6
6 Collingham NG23 . . . . 91 C4
Gringley on the Hill DN10 . . . 39 C1
Louth LN11 . . . . 198 C5
Surfleet PE11 . . . . 145 B3
5 Welbourn LN5 . . . . 106 E5
Whaplode PE12 . . . . 158 A5
Wrawby DN20 . . . . 196 F6
LITTLE LIMBER DN37 . . . . . . 22 C5
LITTLE LONDON Legsby LN8 . . 58 A5
Long Sutton PE12 . . . . 216 D5
Spalding PE11 . . . . 214 A1
Tetford LN9 . . . . 73 F2
Little London PE12 . . . . 216 D6
Little London La LN8 . . . . . . 58 C6
Little Marsh La PE12 . . . . . . 159 B7
Little Mason St 3 HU1 . . . . 181 A7
Littlemeer PE2 . . . . 229 F4
Little Merebalk La LN9 . . . . 86 B2
Little Michael St DN31 . . . . 191 B7
Littlemoors La PE22 . . . . . . 113 A3
Little Northfields PE9 . . . . 172 E4
LITTLE PONTON NG31 . . . . . 140 A7
Littleport La 3 PE22 . . . . . . 113 B1
Little Ramper PE13 . . . . 170 B4
Little Scrubs Wood Nature Reserve★ LN8 . . . . 70 E1
Little Side Rd PE20 . . . . . . 135 E8
Little S St 16 LN11 . . . . 198 B5
LITTLE STEEPING PE23 . . . . 101 D5
Little Steeping Mud & Stud Cottage★ PE23 . . . . 101 D6
LITTLE SUTTON PE12 . . . . . 160 C5
Little Tathwell LN11 . . . . 61 B1
Little Thorpe La LN6 . . . . 79 F1
LITTLE WELTON LN11 . . . . . . 60 F6
LITTLE WISBEACH NG34 . . . 143 C6
Little Wlk DN21 . . . . 40 B5
Littlewood Rd DN8 . . . . 15 B8
Littleworth Dro
Deeping St Nicholas PE11 . . 156 D1
Heckington NG34 . . . . 122 F4
Spalding PE11 . . . . 156 E2
Sutton St Edmund PE12 . . . . 176 F8
Livermore Gn PE4 . . . . 220 E6
Liverpool Dr LN6 . . . . 200 B2
Liverpool St HU3 . . . . 180 A3
Livesey Rd DN36 . . . . 48 E6
Livingstone Dr PE11 . . . . . . 214 B2
Livingstone Rd Hessle HU13 . 3 F4
3 Yaxley PE7 . . . . 233 D5
Lloyd Pl 10 DN21 . . . . 55 A8
Lloyds Ave DN17 . . . . 184 F8
Lobelia Dr 1 DN17 . . . . 185 A1
LOBTHORPE NG33 . . . . 152 A3
Loch Fyne Cl PE2 . . . . 229 B4
Loch Lomond Way PE2 . . . . 229 C4
Locke Way HU13 . . . . 178 B3
Lockham Gate PE22 . . . . 114 B2
Lockhill DN31 . . . . 189 A2
Lock Hill 30 DN8 . . . . 15 A8
Locking Cl 17 LN6 . . . . 204 C6
Locking Garth LN11 . . . . 49 D5
Lock Keepers Ct HU9 . . . . . 181 C6
Lock Keepers Way LN11 . . . 198 D7
Lock La DN8 . . . . 15 A8

Lock Rd Alvingham LN11 . . . . 49 F2
North Coates DN36 . . . . 37 A3
Locks Cl PE6 . . . . 174 A8
Locksley Christian Sch
LN11 . . . . 62 C6
Locksley Cl
6 Boston PE21 . . . . 208 E7
4 North Somercotes LN11 . . 50 F7
Locksley Way 5 LN11 . . . . . 50 F7
Lockton Cl 2 PE20 . . . . 135 B7
Lockton Ct 10 DN37 . . . . . . 190 E8
Lockton Gr 1 HU5 . . . . 179 D8
Lockwood Bank DN9 . . . . . . 27 E6
Lockwood Cl 12 DN8 . . . . . . 15 B8
Lockwood Ct 1 DN15 . . . . 182 E4
Lockwood St HU2 . . . . 180 F8
Lockwood Way PE7 . . . . . . 233 E8
Lode Cl PE7 . . . . 231 C4
Loder Ave PE3 . . . . 224 F2
Lodge Ave 22 DN18 . . . . 10 F8
Lodge Cl 10 Brough HU15 . . . . 2 C7
Kingston upon Hull HU13 . . 178 F1
6 Welton/Dunholme LN2 . . . 68 D7
Lodge Ct 37 DN7 . . . . 14 D4
Lodge Cvn Pk LN4 . . . . 207 A4
Lodge Dr LN6 . . . . 105 A8
Lodge Gdns HU13 . . . . 178 C2
Lodge La Flixborough DN15 . . . 8 B2
Kirk Bramwith DN7 . . . . 14 A8
Nettleham LN2 . . . . 68 D1
Upton DN21 . . . . 53 D5
Lodge Rd Bourne PE10 . . . . . 213 C7
4 Coningsby LN4 . . . . 207 A5
Kelby NG32 . . . . 131 D8
Scunthorpe DN15 . . . . 182 C2
Tattershall Thorpe LN10 . . . . . 97 E3
Lodge Top Cl LN6 . . . . 204 E5
Lodge Way NG31 . . . . 211 A6
Lodington Ct 5 LN9 . . . . . . 199 D3
Loft Ave DN37 . . . . 190 E8
Loganberry Dr HU4 . . . . 179 C4
Loire Ct PE3 . . . . 225 E4
Lomax Dr 2 NG34 . . . . 212 C6
Lombard St DN34 . . . . 191 A7
Lombardy Dr PE1 . . . . 226 B8
Lomond Gr DN36 . . . . 36 C8
Lomond Rd HU5 . . . . 179 E8
Londesborough St HU3 . . . 180 C7
Londesborough Way 13
LN4 . . . . 95 D4
London Rd Boston PE21 . . . 208 E1
Bracebridge Heath LN4 . . . . 205 F5
Frampton PE20 . . . . 136 D7
Grantham NG31 . . . . 211 B3
Haugham LN11 . . . . 74 A7
Long Sutton PE12 . . . . 216 C4
Louth LN11 . . . . 198 C3
Newark-on-Trent NG24 . . . . 104 B2
5 Newark-on-Trent NG24 . . 104 B2
Osbournby NG34 . . . . 132 C5
Peterborough PE2 . . . . 226 A1
Sleaford NG34 . . . . 212 B1
Spalding PE11 . . . . 214 C2
Tathwell LN11 . . . . 61 C2
Wansford PE8 . . . . 222 B2
Wothorpe PE9 . . . . 219 C2
Yaxley PE7 . . . . 233 C5
LONDONTHORPE NG31 . . . . 130 D4
Londonthorpe La NG31 . . . 211 E8
Londonthorpe Rd NG31 . . . 211 F7
Long Acre 1 LN12 . . . . 64 B4
LONG BENNINGTON
NG23 . . . . 117 D3
Long Bennington CE Prim Sch
NG23 . . . . 117 D3
Longcliffe Rd NG31 . . . . 211 A8
Long Cl La LN3 . . . . 82 B7
Longcroft Dr 1 NG34 . . . . . 107 C1
Long Cswy PE1 . . . . 226 A2
Longdales Pl LN2 . . . . 202 A7
Longdales Rd LN2 . . . . 201 F6
Longden St HU3 . . . . 180 A7
Longdon Cl 6 PE12 . . . . 160 E4
Long Dro Bourne PE10 . . . . 155 B1
Gosberton PE11 . . . . 144 B6
Rippingale PE10 . . . . 143 D3
Thurlby PE10 . . . . 164 E7
Walcott LN4 . . . . 109 E8
Wisbech St Mary PE13 . . . . . 177 D4
Long Edge LN11 . . . . 62 E3
Long Farm La DN22 . . . . 52 E2
Longfellow Dr 7 NG24 . . . . 104 B3
Long Field Dr 2 DN3 . . . . 14 A1
Longfield Gate PE2 . . . . 230 A6
Longfield Rd DN34 . . . . 190 E4
Long Field Rd 23 DN3 . . . . . . 14 A2
Long Gates LN11 . . . . 51 A1
Longhead La PE14 . . . . 170 D3
Longhedge Dro PE20 . . . . . 134 E5
Long Hedge La
Greetham with Somersby
LN9 . . . . 86 C5
Swaby LN13 . . . . 74 E4
Long Hedges PE22 . . . . 126 B6
Long Hollow NG33 . . . . 131 C3
Longhorn Cl DN37 . . . . 194 B4
Longhurst Gdns PE21 . . . . . 208 D7
Long La
Aubourn Haddington & South
Hykeham LN6 . . . . 93 B7
Barnby in the Willows NG24 104 F4
Fleet PE12 . . . . 168 B3
Ingham LN1 . . . . 54 E2
Leadenham LN5 . . . . 107 A2
Moulton PE12 . . . . 157 E5
Long La *continued*
Mumby LN13 . . . . 76 E2
Redmile NG32 . . . . 128 A1
2 Westborough & Dry
Doddington NG23 . . . . 117 F3
Willoughton DN21 . . . . 42 E3
Longlands LN13 . . . . 63 D3
Longleat Dr LN11 . . . . 198 A7
Long Leys Rd LN1 . . . . 201 C6
Longmeadow Rise 18
DN41 . . . . 23 A4
Longmeadows PE10 . . . . 154 B7
Longmeadows Dr DN37 . . . . . 23 F2
Long Pasture 5 PE4 . . . . . . 220 F5
Long Rd
1 Scunthorpe DN15 . . . . . . 182 F4
Terrington St Clement PE34 161 F5
3 Tydd St Mary PE13 . . . . . . 170 C8
Longrigg Wlk 17 PE20 . . . . . 135 B7
Long St 2 Foston NG32 . . . . 117 F1
Great Gonerby NG31 . . . . . . 129 E5
LONG SUTTON PE12 . . . . 216 C4
Long Sutton Butterfly Pk*
PE12 . . . . 216 D6
Long Sutton Prim Sch
PE12 . . . . 216 B5
LONGTHORPE PE3 . . . . 225 A1
Longthorpe Cl 3 PE3 . . . . . 225 A2
Longthorpe Gn PE3 . . . . 225 B1
Longthorpe House Mews 11
PE3 . . . . 224 F2
Longthorpe Parkway PE3 225 C1
Longthorpe Prim Sch
PE3 . . . . 225 A2
Long Toft Prim School
DN7 . . . . 14 C6
Longton Rd 4 DN3 . . . . 14 A2
Longueville Ct PE2 . . . . 230 B5
Longwater PE2 . . . . 230 B6
Long Wood La LN4 . . . . 95 C2
Long Wood Rd DN21 . . . . 41 A1
Lonsdale Cl 20 DN36 . . . . 36 D8
Lonsdale Gr PE10 . . . . 213 E6
Lonsdale Pl 3 LN5 . . . . 201 F1
Lonsdale Rd PE9 . . . . 218 E5
Lonsdale St 5 HU3 . . . . 180 A6
Loop La 1 PE12 . . . . 157 F7
LOOSEGATE PE12 . . . . 158 A8
Loosegate Rd PE12 . . . . 158 A8
Lopham La DN37 . . . . 34 F8
Lord Dr 4 NG31 . . . . 129 E5
Lord Porter Ave 9 DN7 . . . . . 14 C7
Lords La 19 DN19 . . . . 11 D8
Lord's La 6 NG33 . . . . 151 A8
Lord St Gainsborough DN21 197 C4
Grimsby DN31 . . . . 191 B8
4 Sleaford NG34 . . . . 212 C3
17 Stainforth DN7 . . . . 14 C6
Lornas Field PE7 . . . . 230 D2
Lorne Cl 1 HU2 . . . . 180 F8
Lorne St LN5 . . . . 234 C1
Losecoat Cl 1 PE9 . . . . 219 D7
Lothian NG34 . . . . 120 F2
Lotus Cl 7 LN5 . . . . 93 F7
Lotus Ct LN6 . . . . 204 D1
Loughborough Univ of
Peterborough PE1 . . . . . . 226 A3
Lough Rd LN9 . . . . 72 F1
Louisberg Rd DN21 . . . . 54 F8
Louis Dr HU5 . . . . 179 B8
Louis St HU3 . . . . 180 C8
LOUTH LN11 . . . . 198 E6
Louth Academy LN11 . . . . . . 198 B7
Louth Cty Hospl LN11 . . . . . . 198 B6
Louth Kidgate Prim Sch
LN11 . . . . 198 C5
Louth Mus* LN11 . . . . 198 B5
Louth Playgoers Riverhead
Theatre* LN11 . . . . 198 D7
Louth Rd East Barkwith LN8 . . 58 E1
Fotherby LN11 . . . . 49 A3
Grimsby DN33 . . . . 191 D1
1 Holton le Clay DN36 . . . . 195 D2
Horncastle LN9 . . . . 199 C5
LOUTH LN11 . . . . 61 F8
New Waltham DN36 . . . . 195 B5
Skidbrooke LN11 . . . . 50 D2
Skidbrooke with Saltfleet Haven
LN11 . . . . 51 C4
2 West Ashby LN9 . . . . 85 E7
Wragby LN8 . . . . 70 D5
Louth Sta Est (Ind) LN11 . . 198 C6
Louth Trading Est LN11 . . . 198 C7
Lovat Cl HU3 . . . . 180 D5
Loveden Cl 32 NG24 . . . . . . 104 B2
Loveden Ct DN35 . . . . 193 A3
Loveden View 6 NG32 . . . . 119 B7
Love La Caythorpe NG32 . . . 119 C7
Gainsborough DN21 . . . . 197 C6
Louth LN11 . . . . 198 A5
Spalding PE11 . . . . 214 E3
9 Sutterton PE20 . . . . 136 A2
Wrangle PE22 . . . . 114 C4
Lovell Rd DN17 . . . . 184 E3
Lovell Way PE34 . . . . 161 F2
Lovers La PE5 . . . . 222 F2
Love's Hill Castor PE5 . . . . . 223 F1
Peterborough PE5 . . . . 224 A1
Loves La LE15 . . . . 162 A1
Love's La PE20 . . . . 135 C8
Lovett St DN35 . . . . 189 E1
LOW BARLINGS LN3 . . . . 82 E8
Lowbridge La 4 PE11 . . . . . 145 C6
Low Burgage DN15 . . . . 2 B1
LOW BURNHAM DN9 . . . . 27 E5
Low Church Rd 2 LN8 . . . . . 57 C8
Low Comm La HU15 . . . . 2 D4
Lowcroft Ave 3 DN9 . . . . 27 D2
Lowcroft Cl 4 DN9 . . . . 27 D2
Low Cross St 6 DN17 . . . . . . 16 D8
Low Deeps La DN10 . . . . 26 B1
LOWER BASSINGTHORPE
NG33 . . . . 140 E4
LOWER BITCHFIELD
NG33 . . . . 141 A3
Lower Church Rd LN6 . . . . 200 B5
Lowerdale 27 HU15 . . . . 2 C6
Lower High St 9 LN5 . . . . . . 93 F7
Lower Kenyon St 10 DN8 . . . 15 A8
Lower Mdws 23 DN18 . . . . 3 F1
Lower Rd NG32 . . . . 119 A5
Lower Sow Dale Nature
Reserve* PE23 . . . . 100 B8
Lower Spring St 1 DN31 . . 189 A1
Low Farm Dr NG34 . . . . 142 C8
Low Farm La
Owmby DN38 . . . . 32 B8
Somerby DN38 . . . . 21 B1
Lowfield Cl
4 Barnby Dun DN3 . . . . 14 A3
31 Kirton in Lindsey DN21 . . . 30 B1
Lowfield Ct HU10 . . . . 178 F6
Lowfield House HU10 . . . . . 178 F6
Lowfield La
Balderton NG24 . . . . 104 A1
Belchford LN9 . . . . 73 C2
Low Field La HU15 . . . . 2 E5
Lowfield Rd HU10 . . . . 178 E5
Lowfields LN3 . . . . 83 E5
Low Fields Ave 1 PE11 . . . 214 F4
Lowfields La
Allington NG32 . . . . 128 F7
Butterwick PE22 . . . . 126 E5
Lowfields Rd PE22 . . . . 126 E6
LOW FULNEY PE12 . . . . 157 B4
Low Fulney Est PE12 . . . . . . 157 C5
Low Garth DN17 . . . . 184 F2
Lowgate Fleet PE12 . . . . 159 C8
Kingston upon Hull HU1 . . . 181 A6
Lutton PE12 . . . . 160 A8
Low Gate Friskney PE22 . . . 115 A6
Gosberton PE11 . . . . 145 C7
Marshchapel DN36 . . . . 37 C1
Moulton PE12 . . . . 146 C1
Surfleet PE11 . . . . 145 C3
Tydd St Mary PE13 . . . . 160 A1
Lowgate Ave 7 PE20 . . . . . . 135 A4
Lowgate Cres PE12 . . . . 159 E8
Low Gate La 6 PE20 . . . . . . 135 A4
Lowgate Rd
Ashby with Scremby PE23 . . . 88 D2
Conisholme LN11 . . . . 50 C5
Hogsthorpe PE24 . . . . 90 B8
Low Holland La DN22 . . . . . . 52 C2
Lowick Gdns PE3 . . . . 225 C5
Low La Croft PE24 . . . . 102 D6
Holbeach PE12 . . . . 215 F4
Kirk Bramwith DN7 . . . . 14 A6
Middle Rasen LN8 . . . . 45 C1
Rigsby LN13 . . . . 75 F1
Terrington St Clement PE34 161 E3
Wrangle PE22 . . . . 114 B3
Low Levels Bank DN8 . . . . . . 15 D4
Low Leys Rd 6 DN17 . . . . . 184 E3
LOW MARNHAM NG23 . . . . . . 78 A4
Low Mill La PE20 . . . . 136 E1
Lowmoor La LN9 . . . . 85 C3
Low Moor Rd LN6 . . . . 204 E5
Low Pk La LN4 . . . . 81 F4
Low Rd Bardney LN3 . . . . 83 E4
Barrowby NG32 . . . . 210 A4
Besthorpe NG23 . . . . 91 C7
Blyborough DN21 . . . . 42 E6
Croft PE24 . . . . 102 F5
Crowland PE6 . . . . 175 A8
Friskney PE22 . . . . 114 F4
Grantham NG31 . . . . 211 C8
Harmston LN5 . . . . 93 D6
Healing DN41 . . . . 23 F5
Holbeach PE12 . . . . 147 F2
Marshchapel DN36 . . . . 37 A1
Osgodby LN8 . . . . 45 B3
South Kyme LN4 . . . . 123 B8
Spalding PE11 . . . . 214 F4
Wainfleet St Mary PE24 . . . . 102 C1
Walpole Cross Keys PE34 . . . 161 D3
Worlaby DN20 . . . . 20 C8
Wyberton PE21 . . . . 136 E7
LOW RISBY DN15 . . . . 9 A2
Low St
Beckingham DN10 . . . . 40 A1
Billingborough NG34 . . . . . . 133 B1
Collingham NG23 . . . . 91 C4
Dunham-on-Trent NG22 . . . . . 65 A1
Harby NG23 . . . . 79 B5
Haxey DN9 . . . . 27 D2
North Ferriby HU14 . . . . 3 A4
5 South Ferriby DN18 . . . . . . 10 A7
Winterton DN15 . . . . 9 A5
Lowther Gdns PE4 . . . . 221 B2
Lowther St HU3 . . . . 180 A7
Low Thorpe Rd LN3 . . . . 83 D1
LOW TOYNTON LN9 . . . . 199 F6
Low Toynton Cl LN9 . . . . . . 199 D5
Low Toynton Rd LN9 . . . . . . 199 D5
Low Wood La LN6 . . . . 91 F8
Loxley PE4 . . . . 220 E4
Loxley Gn HU4 . . . . 179 B7
Loxley Way 6 HU15 . . . . 2 D5
Loyalty La DN18 . . . . 3 E2
Loyd St HU10 . . . . 178 F6
Lucan Cl 13 PE22 . . . . 113 B1
Lucas Ct 4 DN41 . . . . 23 F5
Lucern Ct LN11 . . . . 198 D6
Lucerne Cl 4 PE11 . . . . 214 B6
Lucetta Gdns 9 PE11 . . . . . 214 B5
Lucian Wlk HU4 . . . . 179 A1
Lucina Dr PE2 . . . . 231 D4
Lucius Cl LN6 . . . . 93 A8
Lucy Twr St LN1 . . . . 234 A2
Luda Terr LN11 . . . . 198 D7
LUDBOROUGH DN36 . . . . 48 D6
Ludborough Pk DN36 . . . . . . 48 E6
Ludborough Rd
13 North Thoresby DN36 . . . . 36 B1
North Thoresby DN36 . . . . . . 48 D8
Ludborough Sta DN36 . . . . . 48 F6
Ludborough Way 6 DN35 192 F3
LUDDINGTON DN17 . . . . 7 D3
Luddington & Garthorpe Prim
Sch DN17 . . . . 7 C3
Luddington Rd
Garthorpe & Fockerby DN17 . . 7 E5
1 Peterborough PE4 . . . . . . 221 B1
LUDFORD LN8 . . . . 59 A8
Ludford CE Sch LN8 . . . . 59 B8
Ludford Cres DN21 . . . . 197 E3
Ludford Dr 9 LN6 . . . . 205 A7
Ludford Rd Binbrook LN8 . . . 47 C4
Sixhills LN8 . . . . 58 F6
Ludford St DN32 . . . . 191 E6
Ludgate Cl DN37 . . . . 194 D4
Ludlow Ave DN34 . . . . 191 A7
Ludlow Cl PE10 . . . . 213 C3
Ludlow Gdns
Green Hill NG31 . . . . 210 E6
4 Quadring PE11 . . . . 145 A8
Ludlow Pl DN35 . . . . 192 E5
LUDNEY LN11 . . . . 50 C6
Ludney La LN11 . . . . 50 C6
Luffenham Cl 4 PE9 . . . . . . 218 E5
Lulworth Ave HU4 . . . . 179 A3
Lulworth Ct DN17 . . . . 184 C8
Lulworth Wlk DN40 . . . . 186 D3
Lumbert Way NG23 . . . . 91 C6
Lumley Ave PE25 . . . . 206 D3
Lumley Cres 3 PE25 . . . . . . 206 D4
Lumley Pl 2 LN5 . . . . 201 F1
Lumley Rd PE25 . . . . 206 C3
Lumley Sq 8 PE25 . . . . 206 C3
Luna Wy 3 PE2 . . . . 231 D4
Lunds The HU10 . . . . 178 C6
Lundy Ct DN40 . . . . 186 C2
Luneburg Pl DN15 . . . . 182 C5
Luneburg Way DN15 . . . . . . 182 C6
Lunedale Rd DN16 . . . . 185 D5
Lunn La 5 NG23 . . . . 91 C4
Lunn's Cres 21 DN18 . . . . . . 10 E8
Lupin Rd LN2 . . . . 202 C8
Lurgan Cl LN5 . . . . 205 D3
LUSBY PE23 . . . . 86 F2
Lusher Way DN21 . . . . 41 A1
Luton Cl 1 LN6 . . . . 200 B1
Luton Rd HU5 . . . . 179 F8
LUTTON PE12 . . . . 160 A8
Lutton Bank PE12 . . . . 148 D1
Lutton Garnsgate PE12 . . . 216 A4
Lutton Gate Rd PE12 . . . . . 168 E4
LUTTON GOWTS PE12 . . . . . 216 D8
Lutton Gowts PE12 . . . . 216 D7
Lutton Gr PE3 . . . . 225 C6
Lutton Lodge La PE12 . . . . 149 B2
Lych Gate 10 DN20 . . . . 19 D3
Lydbrook Rd DN16 . . . . 183 A1
Lydd Cl LN6 . . . . 204 C6
Lydford Rd DN40 . . . . 186 D3
Lydia Ct 3 DN40 . . . . 186 A4
Lygon St DN16 . . . . 183 B1
Lyle Cl 5 LN12 . . . . 64 A4
Lyme Wlk 3 PE3 . . . . 225 C4
Lymington Garth HU4 . . . . 179 A3
Lymn Bank PE24 . . . . 102 C4
Lymn Ct 2 NG31 . . . . 210 E2
Lynchwood PE2 . . . . 229 C5
Lyndale Ave 17 DN3 . . . . 14 A1
Lyndale Pk PE2 . . . . 229 C6
Lynden Ave NG31 . . . . 210 E8
Lyndhurst Ave
3 Grimsby DN33 . . . . 191 D3
Skegness PE25 . . . . 206 B5
Lyndhurst Ct 1 PE25 . . . . . 206 B5
Lyndis Wlk PE12 . . . . 215 E1
Lyndon Bsns Pk LN6 . . . . . . 204 B5
Lyndon Cres LN11 . . . . 198 D8
Lyndon Way Louth LN11 . . . 198 D8
Stamford PE9 . . . . 218 E5
Lyneham Cl LN6 . . . . 204 B7
Lyn Ellis Cl 2 PE21 . . . . . . 209 C4
Lynmouth Cl 1 LN6 . . . . . . 205 A1
Lynmouth Dr DN17 . . . . 184 C8
Lynn Rd
Walpole Cross Keys PE34 . . . 161 C3
Walsoken PE13 . . . . 170 E2
Lynnwell Cl PE25 . . . . 206 A6
Lynton Ave HU4 . . . . 179 B3
Lynton Cl DN15 . . . . 182 D4
Lynton Parade DN31 . . . . . . 191 B7
Lynton Prep Sch DN15 . . . . 183 A4
Lynton Rd PE1 . . . . 225 F6
Lynton Rise DN35 . . . . 192 E4
Lynwood Ave HU10 . . . . 178 E6
Lyric Cl 1 HU3 . . . . 180 C5
Lysaghts Way DN15 . . . . 8 C1
Lysander Dr PE6 . . . . 217 B7
Lytham Cl
8 Heighington/
Washingborough LN4 . . . . 203 D1
Londonthorpe &
Harrowby Without NG31 . . 211 E7
Lytham Dr DN37 . . . . 194 C3
Lythemere PE2 . . . . 230 C4
Lyttleport Cl PE11 . . . . 214 D8
Lytton St LN2 . . . . 234 C2
Lyvelly Gdns PE1 . . . . 226 E6

M

MABLETHORPE LN12 . . . . 64 C3
Mablethorpe Prim Acad
LN12 . . . . 64 A4
Mablethorpe Rd
North Coates DN36 . . . . 37 A3
Theddlethorpe St Helen LN12 . 63 F5
Macarthy Cl DN33 . . . . 191 A2
Macaulay Dr Lincoln LN2 . . . 202 B6
Newark-on-Trent NG24 . . . . 104 B3
Macaulay Prim Acad
DN31 . . . . 191 B8
Macaulay St DN31 . . . . 191 B8
Macaulay Way DN31 . . . . . . 191 C8
Mace Rd PE2 . . . . 231 D5
Machray Pl DN35 . . . . 192 D7
Mackender Ct 4 DN16 . . . . 185 C6
Mackenzie Pl 5 DN40 . . . . . 186 B3
Maclure St DN31 . . . . 189 B2
Macmillan Ave LN6 . . . . 204 C2
Macphail Cres LN1 . . . . 66 E2
Maddison La PE23 . . . . 88 B3
Madeley St HU3 . . . . 180 C4
Madely Cl 4 LN9 . . . . 199 D3
Maegan Way DN35 . . . . 192 E5
Mafeking Terr PE21 . . . . . . 209 A7
Maffit Rd PE5 . . . . 223 D3
Magdalen Cl 4 DN16 . . . . . . 185 B4
Magdalene Rd DN34 . . . . . . 190 F5
Magdalene View NG24 . . . . 104 B4
Magdalen Mus* PE24 . . . . 102 D1
Magdalen Rd PE24 . . . . 102 D2
Magdellan Ct PE3 . . . . 225 E2
Magee Rd PE4 . . . . 221 B1
Magellan Dr 9 PE23 . . . . . . 101 A8
Magellan Way PE11 . . . . . . 214 C2
Magistrates Rd PE7 . . . . . . 233 D8
Magna Cres 15 NG34 . . . . . 122 E2
Magna Mile LN8 . . . . 59 B8
Magnolia Ave PE3 . . . . 225 A2
Magnolia Cl LN4 . . . . 81 D2
Magnolia Dr 5 DN36 . . . . . . 195 D1
Magnolia Rd NG34 . . . . 212 D2
Magnolia Rise 4 DN40 . . . . 186 C3
Magnolia Way DN16 . . . . . . 185 B7
Magnus CE Acad NG24 . . . . 104 A3
Magnus Ct 18 LN6 . . . . 93 B8
Magnus St 9 NG24 . . . . 104 A4
Magpie Cl LN6 . . . . 200 A3
Magpie La 3 DN22 . . . . 52 C1
Magrath Ct 1 DN20 . . . . 196 C3
Maiden Cl 1 DN40 . . . . 186 A4
Maiden Ct 18 LN1 . . . . 66 D2
Maiden Gr 2 NG34 . . . . 212 E3
Maiden La Hogsthorpe PE24 . 90 B7
11 Stamford PE9 . . . . 219 C5
Maidens Rd 10 PE20 . . . . . . 136 A2
MAIDENWELL LN11 . . . . 73 E6
Maiden Well Cl 18 LN5 . . . . 107 A8
Maidenwell La 11 LN7 . . . . . . 32 A4
Maiden Well La 5 LN5 . . . . 107 A8
Maidment Dr LN1 . . . . 201 C7
Maidwell Way DN34 . . . . . . 190 C4
Main App Rd DN16 . . . . 183 C3
Main Ave
Bracebridge Heath LN4 . . . . 205 F3
Scunthorpe DN17 . . . . 184 C6
Maine Ave DN15 . . . . 182 B5
Main Rd Anwick NG34 . . . . . 109 B1
Ashby cum Fenby DN37 . . . . . 35 D3
Barkston NG32 . . . . 130 B8
Belchford LN9 . . . . 73 A2
Benniworth LN8 . . . . 59 B1
Bourne PE10 . . . . 154 C5
18 Brookenby LN8 . . . . 47 B6
Carrington PE22 . . . . 112 C7
Collyweston PE9 . . . . 171 B1
2 Donington on Bain LN11 . . . 59 E1
Dunsby PE10 . . . . 143 B2
East Kirkby PE23 . . . . 99 F5
Etton PE6 . . . . 173 E5
Friskney Eaudike PE22 . . . . . 115 C6
Gedney PE12 . . . . 159 D7
Goulceby LN11 . . . . 72 D6
Gunby & Stainby NG33 . . . . . 151 B5
Haconby PE10 . . . . 154 C8
Heighington/Washingborough
LN4 . . . . 203 B2
Leadenham LN5 . . . . 106 D3
Little Hale NG34 . . . . 122 E1
Little Steeping PE23 . . . . 101 D6
Long Bennington NG23 . . . . 117 D3
Nocton LN4 . . . . 95 B7
North Willingham LN8 . . . . . . 58 D7
Parson Drove PE13 . . . . 177 F8
3 Potterhanworth LN4 . . . . . . 82 B1
Quadring PE11 . . . . 134 F1
Saltfleet LN11 . . . . 51 C4
2 Sibsey PE22 . . . . 113 B1
Sotby LN8 . . . . 71 E5
Spilsby PE23 . . . . 87 F1
Stickford PE22 . . . . 100 B3
Stickney PE22 . . . . 113 B5
Thurlby PE10 . . . . 164 D8
Toynton All Saints PE23 . . . . 100 F6
2 Tydd St Mary PE13 . . . . . . 170 C8
Ulceby with Fordington LN13 . 88 B8
Utterby LN11 . . . . 48 F5
West Keal PE23 . . . . 100 C3
Wigtoft PE20 . . . . 135 E3
Wisbech St Mary PE13 . . . . . 177 A2
Withern with Stain LN11 . . . . . 62 E1
Main Ridge E PE21 . . . . 209 A5
Main Ridge W 9 PE21 . . . . . 209 A5
Main St (Southorpe) PE9 . 172 E2
Main St Ailsworth PE5 . . . . . 223 D2

Main St *continued*
Ancaster NG32 119 F3
Ashby de la Launde & Bloxholm LN4 108 B5
Barlings LN3 69 C3
Barnack PE9 172 D3
Barrowby NG32 210 A5
Baston PE6 164 E4
4 Bishop Norton LN8 43 D3
Bonby DN20 10 C2
Boothby Graffoe LN5 94 A2
Boothby Pagnell NG33 140 F5
Bottesford NG13 128 C4
Broomfleet HU15 1 C6
Brough HU15 2 C6
Buckminster NG33 150 E5
Cadney DN20 31 E6
Careby Aunby & Holywell PE9 163 B7
Carlton Scroop NG32 119 C4
Castor PE5 223 D3
Chapel Hill LN4 110 E5
Claypole NG23 117 F7
Clipsham LE15 162 C7
Crowle DN17 16 E6
Croxton Kerrial NG32 138 D3
Denton NG32 139 A7
Doddington & Whisby LN6 79 D5
Dorrington LN4 108 E3
Dunham-on-Trent NG22 65 B1
East/West Stockwith DN10 40 C5
Edenham PE10 153 F4
Ellerker HU15 2 A8
Ewerby & Evedon NG34 122 C6
Farcet PE7 231 C2
Fenton NG23 105 C1
Fishlake DN7 14 D8
Foston NG32 117 F1
Fulstow LN11 49 B8
Gedney PE12 148 B1
Graiseloud DN9 27 D1
1 Grasby DN38 32 E7
Great Casterton PE9 218 C8
Greatford PE9 164 C2
Gunby & Stainby NG33 151 B4
Hackthorn LN2 55 E1
Haconby PE10 154 D8
Hatfield DN7 14 F3
Honington NG32 119 C1
Horkstow DN18 10 A5
Horsington LN10 84 D3
Hougham NG32 118 C3
Ingoldsby NG33 141 D5
Laneham DN22 65 A3
Mablethorpe & Sutton LN12 64 B1
Mareham le Fen PE22 98 F3
Marston NG32 118 D2
Newark-on-Trent NG24 104 C2
Normanby by Spital LN8 55 F7
North Carlton LN1 67 C4
North Kyme LN4 109 F3
North Leverton with Habblesthorpe DN22 52 B1
North Rauceby NG34 120 E5
Norton Disney LN6 92 C2
Osgodby LN8 45 A3
RAF Cranwell NG34 120 C8
Ryhall PE9 163 D1
Scawby DN20 30 F7
Scopwick LN4 95 D1
Scothern LN2 68 F4
Scredington NG34 132 F7
Southorpe PE9 172 E1
South Rauceby NG34 120 E4
South Scarle NG23 91 E6
Sproxton LE14 138 F1
Sutton on Trent NG23 91 A8
Swanland HU14 3 B7
Syston NG32 130 A7
Thistleton LE15 151 C1
Thorney NG23 78 F7
Thornton Curtis DN39 11 E5
Thorpe on the Hill LN6 92 E8
1 Timberland LN4 96 B1
Torksey LN1 65 D6
Ufford PE9 172 F3
Upton DN21 53 D5
Welby NG32 130 F5
West Ashby LN9 85 E7
Westborough & Dry Doddington NG23 117 E5
Whitton DN15 1 E3
Wilsford NG32 120 C2
Worlaby DN20 20 D8
1 Wymondham LE14 150 C1
Yaxley PE7 233 E5
Mainwaring Cl 5 LN2 68 E6
Mainwaring Rd LN2 234 C4
Maisdike La PE12 159 B5
Maize Ct 9 NG34 212 F3
Malborne Way PE2 230 B4
Malborough Dr 4 LN12 64 A3
Malcolm Ave NG34 107 C1
Malcolm Rd DN34 190 F4
Malcolm Sargent Prim Sch PE9 218 E5
Maldon Dr HU9 181 C6
Malham Ave HU4 179 C6
Malham Cl LN6 200 C1
Malham Dr LN6 200 C1
Malim Way 3 NG31 210 F8
Malkinson Cl
4 West Halton DN15 8 E7
12 Winterton DN15 9 A5
Mallalieu Ct 2 DN15 182 E4
Mallard Ave 6 DN3 14 A4
Mallard Cl Birchwood LN6 200 E1
5 Essendine PE9 163 D3

Mallard Cl *continued*
19 Healing DN41 23 F5
Skellingthorpe LN6 200 A3
Spalding PE11 214 E2
Mallard Ct
10 Grantham NG31 210 E2
4 North Hykeham LN6 204 C1
5 Stamford PE9 219 B4
Mallard Dr 6 LN7 33 B4
Mallard Dro PE11 134 B1
Mallard Mews DN32 191 E6
Mallard Rd
Low Fulney PE12 157 C5
Peterborough PE3 220 E1
3 Scunthorpe DN17 184 E6
Mallards Reach 8 PE11 134 F2
Mallards The 5 PE6 174 A5
Mallard Way Brigg DN20 196 A3
Skegness PE25 103 C7
Malling Wlk DN16 185 B2
Mallory Cl 6 LN6 204 C7
Mallory Dr
3 Spalding PE11 214 C2
Yaxley PE7 233 D5
Mallory La 18 PE9 219 B5
Mallory Rd
1 Ashby de la Launde & Bloxholm LN4 108 A7
Peterborough PE1 226 C2
4 Scunthorpe DN16 185 D5
Mallowfield 2 LN8 57 B8
Mallows La PE22 113 C2
Mall Sh Ctr The LN1 234 B2
Malmesbury Dr 3 DN34 191 C6
Malmsgate La PE20 135 F6
Malm St HU3 180 B6
Malpas Ave 4 DN21 197 D5
MALTBY LN11 60 F3
Maltby Ave DN37 190 C3
Maltby Cl 20 PE8 172 B1
Maltby Dr PE6 164 D4
Maltby La 12 DN18 3 E1
MALTBY LE MARSH LN13 76 A8
Maltby Rd
Scunthorpe DN17 184 E5
Skegness PE25 206 D5
Maltby Way LN9 199 D3
Malten La 8 PE12 158 B7
Malting La PE11 134 E2
Maltings La NG31 210 E7
Malting Sq PE7 233 F6
Maltings The 5 Alford LN13 75 F3
1 Leasingham NG34 121 B7
Long Sutton PE12 216 B5
6 Thorney PE6 176 A3
Wothorpe PE9 219 C2
Maltings Way DN32 191 E8
Maltkiln Cl 17 NG34 212 F4
Maltkiln La
1 Beacon Hill NG24 104 A5
Brant Broughton LN5 105 F5
2 Elsham DN20 20 F7
Malt Kiln La 1 LN5 93 F6
Maltkiln Rd
Barton-upon-Humber DN18 3 F1
Fenton LN1 65 E3
Malton Rd LN6 204 F3
Malus Cl PE7 230 C3
Malvern Ave Grimsby DN33 191 A3
Heighington/Washingborough LN4 203 D2
Spalding PE11 214 E6
Malvern Cl Lincoln LN5 205 D4
15 Lincoln LN6 93 C8
20 Lincoln LN6 93 C8
Sleaford NG34 212 B2
Spalding PE11 214 E6
4 Thorne/Moorends DN8 15 A7
Malvern Dr 5 NG31 210 E8
Malvern Rd
5 Mablethorpe/Sutton on Sea LN12 64 B4
Peterborough PE4 221 C2
Scunthorpe DN17 184 F7
Manasty Rd PE2 229 C2
MANBY LN11 62 D6
Manby Hall Bsns Pk DN40 186 D5
Manby Middlegate LN11 62 D7
Manby Rd
Immingham DN40 186 C6
Legbourne LN11 61 E4
Scunthorpe DN17 184 E4
Manby Rd by Pass DN40 186 D6
Manby Road LN11 62 C4
Manby St LN5 205 D6
Mancetter Sq PE4 220 F1
Manchester Rd 11 LN5 94 A7
Manchester St
Cleethorpes DN35 192 D8
Kingston upon Hull HU3 180 A4
Manchester Way
3 Donington PE11 134 F2
Grantham NG31 210 C5
Mandalay Dr 1 PE10 213 E7
Mandarin Dr PE21 208 E3
Mandela Link 1 DN31 191 C7
Mandeville PE2 229 F4
Mandike Rd PE20 136 C2
Manifold Rd DN16 185 E5
Manlake Ave DN15 9 A5
Manley Ct 1 DN9 27 D6
Manley Gdns Brigg DN20 196 B3
11 Cleethorpes DN35 192 F3
Manley St 4 DN15 183 B3
Mannaberg Way
Scunthorpe DN15 183 A6
Scunthorpe DN15 183 B6
Manners Cl 3 PE9 172 C6

Manners Rd NG24 104 B2
Manners St NG31 211 A6
Manning Rd PE10 213 D5
Manningtree Cl DN32 191 E6
Mann La DN9 16 D2
Manor Ave Grimsby DN32 191 D6
Peterborough PE2 231 B7
Manor Cl 6 Bardney LN3 83 C4
11 Baston PE6 164 E5
East Kirkby PE23 99 F4
Farcet PE7 231 C2
3 Great Gonerby NG31 129 E5
11 Keelby DN41 23 A5
Langtoft PE6 164 E3
7 Leasingham NG34 121 B7
Lincoln LN2 234 B4
14 Metheringham LN4 95 D4
15 Ruskington NG34 108 D2
Ryhall PE9 163 C2
7 Sibsey PE22 113 B1
2 Spalding PE11 214 C1
6 Welbourn LN5 106 E5
13 Wittering PE8 172 B1
Yaxley PE7 233 D5
Manor Cliff 1 LN8 55 F6
Manor Ct 9 Bourne PE10 213 C5
2 Carlton-le-Moorland LN5 105 E8
Grimsby DN32 191 D7
17 Nettleham LN2 68 C2
Nocton LN4 95 B7
1 Stallingborough DN41 23 E6
2 Sudbrooke LN2 68 F3
Manor Ct Rd 7 DN9 27 E6
Manor Dr 12 Baston PE6 164 E5
2 Binbrook LN8 47 C4
3 Bonby DN20 10 C2
4 Brough HU15 2 C6
5 Great Gonerby NG31 129 D5
1 Great Gonerby NG31 129 E5
Halton Holegate PE23 101 B7
7 Harlaxton NG32 139 C7
Holbeach PE12 215 D3
1 Long Bennington NG23 117 D3
Peterborough PE6 221 E3
3 Scawby DN20 30 E8
Skegness PE25 206 B5
8 Skegness PE25 206 B6
10 Skegness PE25 206 B6
2 Sudbrooke LN2 68 F2
Waltham DN37 194 E5
7 Wragby LN8 70 D4
Manor Farm Cl 43 DN17 29 D6
Manor Farm Ct DN33 194 F7
Manor Farm Dr 3 LN1 66 D7
Manor Farm La Castor PE5 223 E2
3 Essendine PE9 163 D3
Manor Farm Rd DN17 184 E6
Manor Gdns Boston PE21 209 A4
8 Hatfield DN7 14 E4
Peterborough PE2 231 C7
Manor Grange PE21 126 C1
Manor Hill LN11 60 A1
Manor Hill Cnr PE12 169 D7
Manor House Ct PE6 217 E4
Manor House La
1 Fulletby LN9 86 B8
Westborough & Dry Doddington NG23 117 E5
Manor House Mus★ LN13 75 F3
Manor House Rd PE12 146 F2
Manor House St
5 Horncastle LN9 199 B4
Peterborough PE1 226 A3
Manor La Aisthorpe LN1 67 C7
4 Barrow upon Humber DN19 11 D8
Bourne PE10 213 C4
Broadholme LN6 66 D1
5 Carlton-le-Moorland LN5 105 E8
Goxhill DN19 11 F8
Grayingham DN21 42 E7
Hougham NG32 118 C3
Threekingham NG34 132 E3
16 Waddington LN5 93 F7
1 Welton/Dunholme LN2 68 D6
Wrangle PE22 114 B2
Manor Leas Acad LN6 205 B3
Manor Leas Cl LN6 205 B3
Manor Paddock 6 NG32 128 F7
Manor Paddocks LN5 92 E2
MANOR PARK DN17 184 D6
Manor Pk 7 LN11 61 F3
Manor Pl NG34 212 C5
Manor Rd Barrowby NG32 210 A5
Bottesford NG13 128 A5
Burton Coggles NG33 152 C8
Carlby PE9 163 E4
2 Collingham NG23 91 D4
Coningsby LN4 110 E8
1 Crowle DN17 16 D7
East Ella HU5 179 B8
Folksworth PE7 232 D1
4 Hagworthingham PE23 87 A4
Hatfield DN7 14 E4
Heighington/Washingborough LN4 203 B1
Kingston upon Hull HU5 179 B8
Kirton PE20 136 B5
Lincoln LN2 234 C4
Northorpe DN21 42 A8
Saxilby LN1 66 D2
Scunthorpe DN16 185 B3
Sleaford NG34 212 B2
5 Stainforth DN7 14 C7
Stretton LE15 162 A6
Swanland HU14 3 B6
Swinderby LN6 92 A5
Twin Rivers DN14 7 E7

Manor Rd *continued*
Wansford PE5 222 F2
Manor Rise LN3 203 F8
Manor St
7 Heckington NG34 122 E3
Keelby DN41 23 A5
8 Kingston upon Hull HU1 180 F6
Ruskington NG34 108 D2
Manor Stables Craft Ctr★ NG32 106 C1
Manor Way
Kingston upon Hull HU10 178 F6
6 Langtoft PE6 164 F3
Market Deeping PE6 217 E4
Manrico Dr LN1 201 C7
Manse Ave LN5 205 D4
Mansell Cl 1 PE11 214 B3
Mansel St 3 DN32 189 D1
Mansfield Ct
4 Grimsby DN32 189 C1
Peterborough PE1 226 C5
Mansfield Rd DN15 182 B2
Mansgate Hill LN7 33 B3
Mansion Ct Gdns DN8 15 A8
Manson Cl 11 DN34 190 D4
MANTHORPE
Grantham NG31 211 A8
Toft with Lound and Manthorpe PE10 164 A7
Manthorpe Dro PE10 164 F8
Manthorpe Drove PE10 164 F8
Manthorpe Rd
Grantham NG31 211 B7
Obthorpe PE9 164 B5
Mantle Gn PE22 115 B6
MANTON DN21 30 B5
Manton PE3 225 A3
Manton Ct DN20 30 F6
Manton La DN20 30 E6
Manton Rd Lincoln LN2 201 F7
Manton DN21 30 B4
MANTON WARREN DN16 30 B8
Mantree Cross DN21 41 A8
Manwaring Way 15 PE20 135 B7
Maple Ave 15 Crowle DN17 16 D7
Grimsby DN34 190 E7
Keelby DN41 23 A4
Kingston upon Hull HU10 178 F8
13 Northorpe PE10 164 C8
2 Scunthorpe DN15 182 C5
10 Wisbech PE13 170 D1
Woodhall Spa LN10 97 C6
Maple Cl Brigg DN20 196 C3
Gainsborough DN21 197 B7
9 Keelby DN41 23 A4
5 Kingston upon Hull HU5 179 C7
Leasingham NG34 121 C7
Louth LN11 198 D7
22 Messingham DN17 29 D7
Thimbleby LN9 199 A5
4 Waddington LN5 93 E8
Maple Ct
Gainsborough DN21 197 F5
Yaxley PE7 233 F6
Maple Dr
5 Bassingham LN5 92 F3
Market Rasen LN8 45 D1
1 Sudbrooke LN2 68 F2
Maple Gdns PE10 213 D6
Maple Gr 22 Healing DN41 23 F5
12 Heckington NG34 122 D3
Holbeach PE12 215 A2
Immingham DN40 186 C5
New Waltham DN36 195 B5
Peterborough PE1 226 C7
3 Scopwick Heath LN4 108 A7
Spalding PE11 214 F4
Maple Rd PE21 209 C2
Maple St LN5 205 D5
Maples The PE1 226 F5
Maple Tree Cl E DN16 183 A1
Maple Tree Cl W DN16 183 A1
Maple Tree Way DN16 183 A1
Maple Walk DN37 23 F2
Maple Way 12 PE11 134 E2
Maple Wlk PE7 230 C2
Maplewood Ave HU5 179 B7
Maplewood Cl NG31 210 F7
Maple Wy PE25 103 C7
Mappleton 14 LN6 93 B8
Marbury Cl 26 LN13 75 F2
March Rd PE13 177 F1
March St 13 DN21 30 B1
Marconi Dr PE7 233 D6
Marcus Cl 13 LN6 93 A8
Marcus St DN34 191 A6
Mardale Gdns PE4 221 D2
Marden Hill PE23 100 D6
Mareham La
Aswarby & Swarby NG34 132 E7
Graby NG34 142 F4
Pointon & Sempringham NG34 142 F7
Sleaford NG34 212 F2
Threekingham NG34 132 F3
MAREHAM LE FEN PE22 99 A3
Mareham le Fen CE Prim Sch PE22 99 A4
MAREHAM ON THE HILL LN9 86 A2
Mareham Rd
Hameringham LN9 86 C2
Horncastle LN9 199 D2
MARFLEET HU9 5 E8
Marfleet Ave 4 HU9 5 D8
Marfleet Cnr 9 DN36 36 B1
Marfleet La HU9 5 E8
Marfleet Prim Sch HU9 5 E8

Margaret Ave 1 DN17 17 D5
Margaret Dr PE21 209 B6
Margaret Gr 1 HU13 178 F1
Margaret Moxon Wy HU1 180 E6
Margaret Pl DN36 195 C6
Margaret St
5 Grimsby DN32 191 F7
Immingham DN40 186 C3
Margrave La
Garthorpe & Fockerby DN17 7 E5
Reedness DN14 6 E7
Marham Cl 4 LN6 204 B8
MARHOLM PE6 220 C1
Marholm Rd
4 Peterborough PE3 220 F1
Peterborough PE6 224 B3
Ufford PE9 172 F2
Marian Ave 22 LN12 64 B3
Marian Rd PE21 208 F7
Marian Way
6 Skegness PE25 206 B3
Waltham DN37 194 B4
Mariette Way 5 PE11 214 B6
Marigold Ave PE10 213 D3
Marigold Cl Lincoln LN2 202 C8
Stamford PE9 218 C6
Marigolds PE6 217 D5
Marigold Wlk
3 Humberston DN35 192 E1
5 Sleaford NG34 212 F3
Marina Cl 28 LN5 93 F7
Marina Rd 15 LN12 64 B3
Marina View
Chapel Hill LN4 110 E5
8 Thorne/Moorends DN8 15 A7
Marine Ave
11 Mablethorpe LN12 64 B3
8 Mablethorpe/Sutton on Sea LN12 64 C1
North Ferriby HU14 3 A4
Skegness PE25 206 D1
Marine Ave W 8 LN12 76 F8
Mariner Cl PE4 221 F2
Mariner Cres LN2 202 A6
Mariner Ct LN2 202 A6
Marine Rd PE11 214 E5
Mariners Arms Flats 2 DN17 17 D6
Mariners Cl HU9 181 C6
Marine Wharf 5 HU1 180 F5
Marine Wlk LN6 200 B5
Marisco Ct 2 LN12 77 A8
Marjorie Ave LN6 205 D8
Mark Ave Horncastle LN9 199 A5
Sleaford NG34 212 F4
MARKBY LN13 76 C5
Market Cl 3 PE24 102 E8
Market Ct 8 Crowle DN17 16 D7
Long Sutton PE12 216 C5
MARKET DEEPING PE6 217 E6
Market Deeping Com Prim Sch PE6 217 C6
Market Hall★ LN11 198 B5
Market Hill
Scunthorpe DN15 183 B4
Winteringham DN15 2 B1
Market La Old Leake PE22 127 C8
Terrington St Clement PE34 161 E2
Market Pl 3 Alford LN13 75 F2
1 Binbrook LN8 47 C4
21 Boston PE21 208 F5
2 Brigg DN20 196 B3
Coningsby LN4 207 A4
2 Epworth DN9 27 E6
Gainsborough DN21 197 C4
4 Grantham NG31 211 A4
4 Horncastle LN9 199 B4
6 Kingston upon Hull HU1 181 A6
36 Kirkby in Lindsey DN21 30 B1
Long Sutton PE12 216 C4
9 Louth LN11 198 B5
Market Deeping PE6 217 B4
10 Market Rasen LN8 57 D8
Owston Ferry DN9 28 B3
4 Sleaford NG34 212 D4
6 Spalding PE11 214 D4
Swineshead PE20 135 B7
4 Wragby LN8 70 D5
MARKET RASEN LN8 57 E8
Market Rasen CE Prim Sch The LN8 57 D7
Market Rasen Dr PE10 213 B3
Market Rasen Race Course LN8 57 F7
Market Rasen Rd
Dunholme LN2 68 E6
Holton cum Beckering LN8 70 B8
Lissington LN3 57 E1
Snarford LN8 56 E1
Welton/Dunholme LN2 68 E6
Market Rasen Sta LN8 57 D7
Market Rasen Way PE12 215 E3
Market Sq 17 PE21 208 F5
Market St Bottesford NG13 128 A5
3 Cleethorpes DN35 192 F6
Gainsborough DN21 197 D4
Grimsby DN31 191 D8
Long Sutton PE12 216 C5
3 Sleaford NG34 212 D4
11 Spilsby PE23 88 A1
31 Winterton DN15 9 A5
MARKET STAINTON LN8 72 B6
Market Stainton La LN8 72 C8
Marketstede PE7 230 B2
Market Way PE11 214 C8

Markham Mews DN37 194 F4
Markham Ret Pk PE9 219 E7
Markhams Orch DN33 194 F7
Markham Way 2 DN20 196 F7
Markillie La PE12 160 A3
Marklew Ave DN34 191 B7
Mark Rise 1 DN21 41 C5
MARLBOROUGH LN5 93 B4
Marlborough Ave
  2 Haxey DN9 27 D2
  Heighington/Washingborough LN4 203 C1
  Kingston upon Hull HU13 178 D2
  2 Spalding PE11 214 E2
Marlborough Cl
  21 Grimsby DN32 189 C1
  5 Lincoln LN2 202 C8
  Yaxley PE7 233 E5
Marlborough Dr 1 DN16 185 B8
Marlborough Rd 11 DN8 15 B7
Marlborough St 11 DN21 197 D3
Marlborough Terr 3 HU2 180 E7
Marlborough Way DN35 192 F1
Marles Cl 9 NG24 104 B5
Marleston La NG24 104 A2
Marlowe Dr LN2 202 B6
Marlowe Gr PE4 225 E8
Marlowe Rd DN17 184 D7
Marlow Rd DN21 197 E6
Marmaduke St 3 HU3 180 C4
Marmion Dr 7 DN15 9 A5
Marmion Rd
  Coningsby LN4 207 E5
  4 Scunthorpe DN16 185 C8
Marne Ave PE4 221 A1
Marne Gdns LN1 201 E6
Marne St HU5 180 A8
Marnham Road NG23 78 A3
Marples Mews DN35 192 F5
Marquess Ct 7 PE10 213 D5
Marquis Ave
  25 Newark-on-Trent NG24 104 B2
  New Waltham DN36 195 D7
Marrat Cl 7 St Giles LN2 202 D6
  St Giles LN2 202 E6
Marratts La NG31 129 D5
Marriot's Gate 6 PE12 160 A8
Marriott Ct PE1 226 E5
Marris Dr 11 DN15 9 B5
Marris Wy 9 LN7 33 A3
Marr La HU15 1 A7
Marron Cl 29 NG24 104 C1
Marsden Dr DN15 182 D3
Marsden Rd DN31 189 D1
Marshall Ave
  Grimsby DN34 191 B7
  Kingston upon Hull HU10 178 E8
Marshall Cl
  3 Fishtoft PE21 126 C1
  8 Laceby DN37 23 E1
Marshall Ct 9 NG24 104 C2
Marshall's Bank PE13 177 D8
Marshall's Way PE7 231 C2
Marshalls Yard DN21 197 D4
Marshall Way 2 DN21 53 A8
Marsham PE2 229 F3
Marsh Ave PE21 209 A2
MARSHCHAPEL DN36 37 B2
Marshchapel Cl 2 DN35 192 F3
Marshchapel Prim Sch DN36 37 B2
Marsh Dro PE11 146 A5
Marshfield Rd 1 DN16 185 C5
Marshfields Sch PE1 226 D7
Marsh La Algarkirk PE20 146 B8
  Barnetby le Wold DN38 21 B4
  Barrow upon Humber DN19 4 C2
  Barton-upon-Humber DN18 3 F1
  Boston PE21 209 A1
  Burgh le Marsh PE24 102 E7
  Carlton-le-Moorland LN5 106 A7
  Cottam DN22 65 C6
  Dunham-on-Trent NG22 65 B1
  Grainthorpe LN11 50 C7
  Kettlethorpe LN1 65 C2
  Middle Rasen LN8 57 B8
  Misterton DN10 40 A5
  New Holland DN19 4 D2
  North Leverton with Habblesthorpe DN22 52 E1
  North Somercotes LN11 38 C1
  Orby PE24 89 E2
  Saundby DN22 52 B7
  Skidbrooke with Saltfleet Haven LN11 51 C5
  South Cockerington LN11 62 B8
  South Killingholme DN40 13 B4
  Stallingborough DN41 23 F6
  Tattershall LN4 97 D1
  Winteringham DN15 2 A1
  Wyberton PE21 136 F8
Marshland High Sch PE14 170 E4
Marshlands Dr PE12 215 F3
Marshland St 10 PE34 161 F3
Marsh Rd 3 Crowle DN17 16 C8
  Gedney PE12 148 C2
  Holbeach PE12 215 F8
  Kirton PE20 137 A3
  Orby PE24 90 B3
  Spalding PE12 157 B7
  Sutterton PE20 146 A7
  Tydd St Mary PE13 160 C1
  Walkeringham DN10 40 B3
  Walpole PE14 170 F8
Marsh Rd *continued*
  Weston PE12 145 F1
Marsh The PE14 170 E8
Marsh Way 3 DN36 37 C5
MARSTON NG32 118 C2
Marston Cl 27 NG24 104 B2
Marston Hall & Gdns* NG32 118 D2
Marston La NG32 129 A7
Marston Moor Rd NG24 104 C4
MARTIN Martin LN4 96 C3
  Roughton LN9 85 B1
Martin Cl
  2 Bottesford DN16 185 B2
  Heighington/Washingborough LN4 81 E4
  Louth LN11 198 D8
  Skellingthorpe LN6 200 A3
Martin Ct PE4 221 A4
Martin Dales Dro 1 LN10 97 B4
Martin N Dro LN4 96 D3
Martin Rd LN4 96 C2
Martinsbridge PE1 226 F7
Martin's Cl 5 DN19 11 D8
Martins Cross Dro PE20 124 C3
Martin S Dro LN4 96 D3
Martins Rd Crowland PE6 167 E4
  Ulceby DN39 12 B1
Martin St LN5 201 F1
Martins Way PE2 229 F5
Martins Wlk 11 LN12 77 A8
Martin Way
  Ingoldmells PE25 206 C8
  New Waltham DN36 195 B6
MARTON DN21 65 D8
Marton Gr
  3 Grimsby DN33 191 A3
  35 Hatfield DN7 14 D4
Marton Prim Sch DN21 65 E8
Marton Rd
  10 Newark-on-Trent NG24 104 A3
  Sturton by Stow LN1 66 B7
  Willingham DN21 53 E2
Marston Thorold's Charity CE Sch The NG32 118 D2
Martyn Rd DN35 192 D7
Marvel St HU9 181 B7
Marvis Cres PE7 230 C3
Marwald La PE13 170 A7
Mary Armyne Rd PE2 230 B5
Mary La LE14 138 B1
Marylebone Wlk 2 DN33 191 B2
Mary Lovell Wy PE22 113 A8
Mary St DN15 182 F3
Mary Sumner Way 3 DN15 182 E4
Mary Walsham Cl PE2 231 E5
Masefield Dr 10 LN12 77 A7
Maskew Ave PE1 225 E6
Mason Cl LN12 77 A7
Mason Dr Scunthorpe DN17 184 E3
  6 Stamford PE9 218 F6
Masons Ct 25 DN18 10 E8
Mason St HU2 180 F7
Masovian La LN8 56 C5
Massey Cl 11 Epworth DN9 27 D6
  Kingston upon Hull HU3 180 A5
Massey Rd LN2 234 C4
Massey St HU3 180 A4
Mast Dr HU9 181 C6
Master Dike PE12 159 D1
Masterton Cl 6 PE9 219 D7
Masterton Rd PE9 219 C7
Mathew Ford Way DN41 23 C7
Mathews St DN35 192 C7
Matilda Rd LN6 201 D1
Matley PE2 229 E5
Matlock Ct DN15 182 B2
Matlock Dr Grimsby DN37 190 F8
  Lincoln LN6 204 E2
Matmore Cl PE11 214 F3
Matmore Gate PE11 214 F3
Mat Pitts La PE24 102 C1
Matthew Flinders Way PE21 208 D3
Matthew Humberstone CE Sch DN35 192 C5
Mattimore Dr 6 PE12 215 E2
Maud Foster Mill* PE21 209 A6
Maud St 2 PE21 209 A5
MAVIS ENDERBY PE23 87 C1
Mavis Enderby Cross Roads PE23 87 D1
Mavis Rd 2 DN17 184 E6
Mawford Cl PE12 146 E2
Mawson Gdns 6 PE24 102 E2
MAWTHORPE LN13 88 F8
Mawthorpe Hill Rd LN13 88 F8
MAXEY PE6 173 C7
Maxey Cl 11 PE6 217 A5
Maxey Ct LN11 198 B6
Maxey Rd Maxey PE6 173 C6
  Northborough PE6 217 C1
Maxey View PE6 217 C3
Maxham's Gn Rd PE6 173 D3
Maximus Rd LN6 93 A8
Maxstead Cl HU13 178 B3
Maxwell Ave LN6 205 C8
Maxwell Ct DN34 190 D5
Maxwell Dr 1 LN12 64 B3
Maxwell Rd PE2 230 D6
Mayall Ct 23 LN5 93 F7
Maybell Cl 5 DN21 53 A7
May Blossom Wlk PE11 214 B3
May Cres LN1 201 D4
Mayfair Ave LN6 205 C7
Mayfair Cres 12 DN37 194 C4
Mayfair Ct DN35 193 A1
Mayfair Dr 4 PE11 214 B1
Mayfair Dr W DN37 190 C8
Mayfair Gdns PE21 209 B7
Mayfield Ave
  Gainsborough DN21 197 B7
  3 South Killingholme DN40 12 F2
  5 Stainforth DN7 14 D6
Mayfield Cl
  3 Grimsby DN33 194 D8
  5 Pinchbeck PE11 156 E8
Mayfield Cres Louth LN11 198 D4
  3 Middle Rasen LN8 57 C8
Mayfield Dr 1 PE25 90 D3
Mayfield Gr 5 PE25 206 B3
Mayfield Rd PE1 226 A6
Mayfield St HU3 180 C8
Mayflower Ave DN40 186 C3
Mayflower Cl
  2 Gainsborough DN21 52 F6
  6 South Killingholme DN40 12 E3
Mayflower Dr NG34 122 D2
Mayflower Mews 9 NG31 211 A3
Mayflower Rd PE21 209 C3
Mayflower Way 2 LN12 64 B3
May Gr HU13 178 D2
Mayland Ave HU5 179 A8
Mayner's Dike PE12 169 F8
Mayor's Wlk PE3 225 E3
Maypole House Sch LN13 88 E8
Maypole St DN21 42 D2
Maysfield Ct 10 DN20 31 A5
Maysfield Dr 6 PE13 170 B2
Mays La LN1 66 E2
May's La PE13 170 A2
May St DN35 192 D8
Maythorpe Cl 3 HU3 180 A7
Maytime Cl 7 PE11 214 A5
Maytree Dr PE12 216 D5
McInnes St 4 LN2 202 C3
McVeigh Ct 13 DN41 23 F5
Mdw Cl 11 LN8 57 E7
Mdw Ct DN21 42 E7
Mdw Lands DN21 40 D3
Mdwlily Ct 14 DN36 195 C6
Mdwsweet La LN6 92 D5
Mdw View Allington NG32 128 A6
  6 Willingham by Stow DN21 53 E3
Mead Cl 6 Lincoln LN6 205 A5
  Peterborough PE3 220 F1
Meadenvale PE1 226 F5
Mead Garth DN15 182 B6
Meadow Ave DN39 12 A2
Meadowbank 5 DN9 16 E1
Meadow Bank PE22 126 F6
Meadow Bank Ave 1 LN3 82 B6
Meadowbank Rd HU3 179 E7
Meadowbrook
  9 Ancaster NG32 120 A3
  4 Ruskington NG34 108 D2
Meadow Cl
  1 Bourne PE10 213 D5
  7 Cherry Willingham/Reepham LN3 82 A8
  1 Colsterworth NG33 151 E6
  5 Goxhill DN19 5 A1
  Lincoln LN6 93 C8
  3 Louth LN11 198 C4
  2 Manby LN11 62 C6
  6 Metheringham LN4 95 D4
  2 Pinchbeck PE11 145 C1
  4 Scothern LN2 68 F4
  Spalding PE11 214 E6
Meadowcroft 7 LN11 59 E1
Meadow Croft
  3 Kirk Sandall DN3 14 A1
  Waltham DN37 194 E5
Meadow Ct Grimsby DN34 190 E7
  15 Hibaldstow DN20 30 F5
Meadowdale Cres 3 NG31 211 A8
Meadow Dr
  Barton-upon-Humber DN18 10 F8
  4 Binbrook LN8 47 C5
  Grimsby DN33 194 D8
  2 Healing DN41 24 A5
  13 Misterton DN10 39 F5
Meadow Dro PE10 213 F7
Meadow End NG31 211 D2
Meadowfield
  4 Middle Rasen LN8 57 C8
  Sleaford NG34 212 C5
Meadowfield Cl 17 LN5 93 E8
Meadow Field Rd 6 DN3 14 A3
Meadow Gardens 15 NG23 91 D4
Meadowgate PE9 172 F5
Meadow Gate PE10 213 D6
Meadowgate La 3 PE11 214 A3
Meadow La
  Aubourn Haddington & South Hykeham LN6 93 B7
  Benniworth LN8 59 B1
  Girton NG23 78 C2
  Leasingham NG34 121 B7
  9 Lincoln LN6 93 C8
  Normanton on Trent NG23 78 B3
  North Cockerington LN11 50 A1
  North Hykeham LN6 93 C8
  North Scarle LN6 78 F1
  Pointon & Sempringham NG34 143 C6
  16 Ryhall PE9 163 C1
Meadowlake Cl LN6 200 D1
Meadowlily Ct DN36 195 C6
Meadow Rd Dunston LN4 95 C5
  Hessle HU13 178 B1
  Langtoft PE6 217 A8
Meadow Rd *continued*
  Newark-on-Trent NG24 104 B2
  Newborough PE6 221 B8
  Scunthorpe DN17 184 C6
Meadow Rise
  5 Barnby Dun DN3 14 A4
  Blyton DN21 41 C6
  1 Gainsborough DN21 53 A5
  7 Saxilby LN1 66 D2
Meadows Cl 7 NG23 117 D3
Meadows La Lincoln LN4 202 E2
  Reepham LN3 69 A1
Meadows Prim Sch The LN5 205 C2
Meadows Rise 1 LE14 150 B1
Meadows The
  2 Beckingham DN10 52 B8
  Burringham DN17 17 D4
  8 Long Bennington NG23 117 D3
  Mablethorpe/Sutton on Sea LN12 64 C2
  5 Market Deeping PE6 217 C5
  Messingham DN17 29 D8
  7 Pinchbeck PE11 145 C1
  Skegness PE25 206 A4
  Westwoodside DN9 27 A2
Meadowsweet 2 PE9 218 C7
Meadow The 29 LN7 33 B4
Meadow Vale 4 DN20 30 F8
Meadow View
  Humberston DN35 192 F1
  6 Morton PE10 154 D6
  Swinderby LN6 92 A5
Meadow View Bsns Units PE9 219 F6
Meadow Way
  Billinghay LN4 109 E6
  Bracebridge Heath LN4 81 A1
  7 Old Leake PE22 114 A1
  Spalding PE11 214 A2
  6 Welton/Dunholme LN2 68 D6
Meadow Wlk
  19 Kirk Sandall DN3 14 A2
  6 Swanland HU14 3 B7
Mead The 11 Laceby DN37 23 F1
  Lincoln LN6 205 A5
  Peterborough PE4 221 A1
Meadway
  Cherry Willingham/Reepham LN3 203 E6
  11 Market Deeping PE6 217 A6
  3 Spalding PE11 214 A4
Mead Wlk HU4 179 C6
Meakers Way LN13 76 F3
Meals Gate PE4 221 D2
Mears Ct 6 PE11 214 A1
Measham Dr 4 DN7 14 D7
Measures Cl 10 PE10 154 D6
Mechanic La 9 HU3 180 D5
Medbourne Gdns 1 PE1 226 D8
Meden Ave 12 HU15 2 D5
Medeswell PE2 230 C3
Medforth La PE21 208 E8
Medieval Village of Gainsthorpe* DN21 30 D4
Medina Gdns LN12 64 B2
Medium Section Rd DN16 19 A4
MEDLAM PE22 112 D7
Medlam Cl PE22 112 C7
Medlam La PE22 112 D7
Medlam Rd PE21 208 C3
Medlar Dr 4 HU15 2 D5
Medlock Cres 5 PE11 214 F5
Medway 7 LN1 66 D7
Medway Cl 3 PE11 145 C6
Medway Cres LN6 205 B2
Medway Pl 5 DN34 191 A5
Medworth PE2 229 F3
Meeres' La PE20 136 A5
Meering Cl 12 NG23 91 D5
Meering La NG23 91 C7
Meers Bank LN12 64 A6
Meeting House La LN5 105 F5
Meggan Gate PE3 225 A1
Meggitt La DN15 2 A1
Megs La 10 LN5 107 A8
Melbourne Ave 4 DN33 191 D3
Melbourne Cl 19 LN6 204 D7
Melbourne Dr 4 PE25 206 A4
Melbourne Rd
  Birchwood LN6 204 C8
  Grantham NG31 211 D7
  4 Stamford PE9 219 D6
Melbourne Way 9 LN5 93 E8
Melbury Wlk DN17 184 C8
Meldrum Dr DN21 197 E1
Melford Cl PE3 225 A2
Melford Ct DN16 185 E5
Melholme La LN11 50 A2
Melior Com Coll DN17 184 D4
Melior Community Acad DN17 184 E7
Mellor Wy DN36 195 D7
Mellows Cl
  Cherry Willingham/Reepham LN3 203 F8
  Peterborough PE1 226 C3
Mellwood View DN9 28 A3
Mel Marshall Wy PE22 114 C2
Melrose Cl
  9 Stamford PE9 218 E6
  6 Woodhall Spa LN10 97 C6
Melrose Dr PE2 231 A7
Melrose La 13 LN6 204 B8
Melrose Rd DN21 197 C6
Melrose St HU3 179 F6
Melrose Way DN37 188 A1
MELTON HU14 2 F5
Melton Bottom HU14 2 F6
Melton Fields 4 HU14 2 F5
Melton Old Rd HU14 2 E5
Melton Rd North Ferriby HU14 3 A5
  Wrawby DN20 20 F4
  Wymondham LE14 150 B1
MELTON ROSS DN38 21 D5
Melton Ross Rd DN39 11 C1
Melville Cl 5 LN4 81 E2
Melville St
  2 Kingston upon Hull HU1 180 E5
  Lincoln LN5 234 B2
Melwood Cl DN9 27 F6
Melwood Hill DN9 27 F6
Melwood View 18 DN9 27 E6
Memorial Gdns LN4 81 E4
Memorial Hall Dr 9 LN5 107 A7
Memorial La PE12 148 B1
Menasha Way DN16 185 E7
Mendip Ave Grimsby DN33 191 C1
  25 Lincoln LN6 93 C8
Mendip Cl
  6 Gonerby Hill Foot NG31 210 E8
  2 Lincoln LN5 205 D3
  2 Spalding PE11 214 B6
Mendip Gr PE4 221 C2
Mendip Rd DN17 184 D8
Menson Dr DN7 14 D4
Mentmore Gdns PE21 208 B4
Mercer Dr LN1 201 D6
Mercer Rd DN21 197 B6
Mercer Row LN11 198 B5
Mercia Cl 14 NG34 212 B2
Mercia Dr 3 NG32 120 A2
Mercia Gdns 2 PE10 213 B5
Mercia Gr 4 PE6 164 E5
Mercian Ct PE2 231 D7
Mercury Cl PE7 231 C4
Mercury Way PE12 215 D3
Merebalk La LN9 86 B2
Mere Balk La LN9 85 A7
Mere Booth Rd PE22 125 A7
Mere Cres DN16 185 D7
Meredith Ave DN17 184 D6
Mere Dro Old Leake PE22 113 F4
  Yaxley PE7 233 F4
Meredyke Rd DN17 7 D3
Mere La Edenthorpe DN3 14 A1
  Heydour NG32 131 D6
  Winterton DN15 9 A7
Merelade Gr 4 PE4 220 E5
Mere Rd
  Branston & Mere LN4 81 E1
  Waddington LN5 93 F7
Meres Leisure Ctr & Swimming Pool NG31 210 D3
Meres Rd NG31 210 C3
Mereway The NG33 141 A5
Meridian Cl 1 PE21 209 D4
Meridian Leisure Centre LN11 198 D5
MERIDIAN POINT DN35 193 B3
Meridian Point Ret Pk DN35 193 B3
Meridian Rd PE21 209 C4
Meridian View LN11 198 B4
Meridian Wlk 2 PE12 215 B2
Meriton PE2 229 F3
Merleswen LN2 68 D6
Merlin Cl PE10 213 E3
Merlin Dr 2 DN20 21 A8
Merlin Rd
  14 Binbrook Tech Pk LN8 47 B6
  Scunthorpe DN17 184 E6
Merrick Cl 13 NG31 129 E5
Merrick St HU9 181 B7
Merriemeade Dr 4 PE25 206 D1
Merrifield Rd 7 PE24 102 E2
Merryweather Ct 7 DN16 185 B2
Mersey Cl PE11 214 B5
Mersey Way DN37 190 D8
Merton Rd DN16 185 A3
MESSINGHAM DN17 29 D7
Messingham La DN20 30 D8
Messingham Nature Reserve* DN17 29 F6
Messingham Prim Sch DN17 29 D7
Messingham Rd
  East Butterwick DN17 28 D8
  Scotter DN21 29 C4
  Scunthorpe DN17 184 F4
Meteor Rd LN11 62 C6
METHERINGHAM LN4 95 D4
Metheringham Airfield Visitor Ctr* LN4 96 A2
Metheringham Cl 1 LN6 204 D7
Metheringham Delph Nature Reserve* LN4 96 D7
Metheringham Fen La LN4 95 E5
Metheringham Heath La LN4 94 E3
Metheringham Prim Sch LN4 95 C4
Metheringham Sta LN4 95 D4
Metro Ctr The PE2 230 D6
Mewburn PE3 220 E1
Mew Gull Dr 27 LN12 77 A7
Mews The HU3 180 C5
Meynell Ave 3 LN6 205 C8
Meynell St DN21 40 D8
Meynell Street DN9 40 D8
Meynell Wlk PE3 225 B3
Meyrick Rd 18 NG24 104 A5
Michael Foale La LN11 198 C7
Michaelgate LN2 234 B3

Michael Moses Wy PE20 135 C7
Mickle Gate PE3 225 A1
Middle Barn Hill DN20 10 D1
Middlebridge Rd DN10 39 B3
Middle Broad Dro PE13 169 D5
Middlebrook Cl 10 LN6 205 A5
Middlebrook La 1 DN8 15 A7
Middlebrook Rd 4 LN6 205 A5
Middleburg St HU9 181 D8
Middlecott Cl 2 PE21 208 F2
Middlecott Sch The PE20 136 C5
Middle Dro Gedney PE12 148 C2
Holland Fen with Brothertoft PE21 208 A7
Kirton PE20 124 D2
Newton PE13 169 E4
Middle Fen Dro PE20 134 D4
Middle Fen La LN4 82 C5
Middlefield 7 PE7 230 D3
Middlefield La
Gainsborough DN21 197 E2
1 Glentham LN8 43 F1
Middlegate LN5 92 F2
Middlegate Cl 12 DN19 11 C8
Middlegate La Bonby DN20 10 C3
Elsham DN20 21 A7
Elsham Hill DN20 20 E8
Orby PE24 89 D2
South Ferriby DN18 10 B7
Middlegate Rd PE20 136 C6
Middlegate Rd E PE20 136 D5
Middlegate Rd (West) 1 PE20 136 D6
Middleham Cl
3 Kingston upon Hull HU9 181 E8
2 Peterborough PE7 231 F5
Middle Holme La 3 NG23 91 A8
Middle La Amcotts DN17 7 E1
Stainton le Vale LN8 46 C4
Sturton le Steeple DN22 52 E3
Thorpe on the Hill LN6 92 F8
Middlemarsh Rd PE24 103 A7
Middle Marsh Rd PE12 146 F7
Middlemere Bank PE22 126 E7
Middlemore Yd 1 NG31 211 B4
Middle Pasture 3 PE4 220 F5
Middleplatt Rd DN40 186 E5
MIDDLE RASEN LN8 57 B8
Middle Rasen Prim Sch The LN8 57 B8
Middle Rd Crowland PE6 166 E1
Newborough PE6 221 E7
Terrington St Clement PE34 161 D4
Tydd St Mary PE13 160 B1
7 Whaplode PE12 158 B7
Middle St Aisthorpe LN1 67 D7
Cammeringham LN1 55 A1
Corringham DN21 41 E2
Croxton Kerrial NG32 138 D4
Dunston LN4 95 C5
Farcet PE7 231 C2
Fillingham DN21 55 A5
Gunby & Stainby NG33 151 B5
5 Lincoln LN6 93 C8
7 Metheringham LN4 95 D4
14 North Kelsey LN7 32 A4
5 Potterhanworth LN4 82 B1
Rippingale PE10 142 F2
Scampton LN1 67 D6
Scotton DN21 29 C1
5 Skillington NG33 151 A8
South Carlton LN1 67 D3
Willoughton DN21 42 E3
Middlesykes La LN11 62 C7
Middlethorpe Prim Sch DN35 192 D3
Middle Thorpe Rd DN35 192 D3
Middleton PE3 225 A4
Middleton Cl 9 DN17 29 D7
Middleton Ct HU5 180 B8
Middleton Prim Sch PE3 225 A4
Middleton Rd
Newark NG24 104 B6
Scunthorpe DN16 185 B4
Middleton's Field LN2 234 B4
Middletons La DN38 32 E7
Middletons Rd PE7 233 E5
Middleton St HU3 180 C8
Middleton Way NG34 121 C7
Middle Wy LN3 203 E5
Midfield Pl 16 DN36 36 D8
Midfield Rd DN36 36 D8
Midfield Way 14 DN41 23 A4
Midgate PE1 226 A2
Mid Gate PE22 113 E3
Midgate (East) PE22 113 E1
Midgate La PE22 113 E1
Midgley Cl HU3 180 C5
Midholm LN3 203 E5
Midia Cl LN1 201 C7
Midland Ind Est DN16 185 D8
Midland Rd
Peterborough PE3 225 E3
Scunthorpe DN16 183 D1
Midsummer Gdns PE12 216 A4
Midthorpe La 3 LN9 85 E7
MIDVILLE PE22 113 E8
Midville Cl 10 LN1 201 E8
Midville La PE22 100 B1
Midville Rd Midville PE22 113 B7
Toynton All Saints PE23 100 F4
Mid Water Cr 5 PE7 230 B1
Mid Water Cres PE7 233 B8
Midway Cl 9 LN2 68 D2
Midway Gr HU4 179 E4
Milcroft Cres DN7 14 D4
Mildenhall Dr LN6 204 B8
Mildmay Rd PE4 225 D8
Mildmay St LN1 234 A4
Mile Dro PE6 173 F5
Mile End Ave 19 DN7 14 D3
Mile La LN12 64 A2
Miles Bank PE11 214 C7
Miles Cross Hill LN13 75 D1
Miles Hawk Cl 26 LN12 77 A7
Milestone La PE11 145 C1
Milfoil La 11 PE12 167 B8
Milford Ct 3 DN32 189 C1
Milford Ct Bsns Pk LN11 198 A8
Milkinghill La PE20 135 A5
Milking Nook Dro PE10 154 F3
Milking Nook Rd PE6 221 C8
Millard Ave DN7 14 D4
Millard Nook 30 DN7 14 D4
Mill Bank PE12 159 A5
Mill Baulk Rd 3 DN10 39 F3
Millbeck Bank HU15 1 E8
Millbeck Dr LN2 202 B8
Millbrook Cl 3 LN6 93 B8
Millbrook La LN8 70 C4
Millbrook Sch DN16 185 B6
Millbrook Way 30 DN18 10 F8
Mill Cl 7 Alford LN13 75 F3
Billinghay LN4 109 E5
5 Brigg DN20 196 A3
4 Croft PE24 102 E2
5 Marshchapel DN36 37 C2
Murrow PE13 177 D5
2 North Leverton with Habblesthorpe DN22 52 B1
7 Peakirk PE6 174 A5
Waltham DN37 194 E3
26 Wisbech PE13 170 D1
Mill Cres Peterborough PE2 229 E4
20 Scotter DN21 29 C3
Mill Croft 3 Scawby DN20 30 F8
1 Scunthorpe DN16 185 D7
Mill Ct Lincoln LN1 234 A4
1 Waddingham DN21 43 D7
Mill Dr NG31 211 C2
Mill Drove Bourne PE10 213 E7
Crowland PE6 175 A8
Deeping St Nicholas PE11 155 D1
Mill Drove North PE12 157 B2
Mill Drove South PE12 157 B1
Millennium Fst Coll PE25 206 B3
Millennium Way PE34 160 F3
Miller Ave DN32 192 C6
Miller Cl 12 DN8 15 B7
Miller La DN8 15 B7
Miller Rd DN21 41 A1
Millers Brook DN9 16 E1
Millers Cl
Heighington/Washingborough LN4 81 E4
4 Sleaford NG34 212 C2
Miller's Cl PE10 143 A3
Millers Ct LN11 198 C6
Millers Dale 2 LN6 204 F2
Millers' Gate PE22 113 A2
Millers Quay 6 DN20 196 A3
Millers Rd LN5 93 F6
Millers Rest PE12 158 C7
Millers Way 6 Alford LN13 75 F3
6 Heckington NG34 122 E2
Miller Wy PE1 226 C1
Mill Farm Est LN4 207 B5
MILLFIELD PE1 225 F5
Mill Field 1 LN12 64 C2
Millfield Ave
Grimsby DN33 191 D3
8 Saxilby LN1 66 D2
Mill Field Cl 6 PE6 173 C4
Millfield Cres NG32 119 B6
Mill Field Ct 11 DN3 14 A3
Millfield Gdns 6 PE6 166 F1
Millfield La E PE20 136 D7
Millfield La W PE20 136 D7
Millfield Prim Acad LN4 81 F4
Millfield Rd
Bratoft PE24 102 C7
3 Market Deeping PE6 217 A6
21 Metheringham LN4 95 C4
7 Morton PE10 154 C7
South Somercotes LN11 50 F5
Thorne/Moorends DN8 15 A8
Mill Field Rd
8 Donington PE11 134 E2
Fishlake DN7 14 C8
Scunthorpe DN16 183 C2
Millfields
22 Barton-upon-Humber DN18 10 E8
18 Caistor LN7 33 B4
Millfields Way 9 DN19 11 C8
Mill Field Terr NG34 212 D5
Millfield The 1 DN20 31 A5
Mill Garth
Cleethorpes DN35 192 D3
Roughton Moor LN10 98 A7
Millgate 10 LN5 107 A7
Mill Gate PE12 158 B1
Mill Gn Rd PE11 214 A7
Millgood Cl LN11 198 D5
MILL HILL PE24 103 B8
Mill Hill Ellerker HU15 2 A8
Friskney PE22 114 F6
Gringley on the Hill DN10 39 B1
Nettleham LN2 68 C2
Mill Hill Cres DN35 192 E5
Mill Hill Dr DN16 185 C3
Millhill La 12 PE20 135 B7
Mill Hill Rd DN7 14 E3
Mill Hill Way LN11 62 A8
Mill House La 1 DN15 9 B5
Millhouse St Rise 5 DN40 186 A4
Mill House Windmill ★ DN17 7 C4
Mill La Addlethorpe PE25 90 D1
Ashby with Scremby PE23 88 D3
Aubourn Haddington & South Hykeham LN5 92 F5
8 Barrow upon Humber DN19 11 C8
Beesby with Saleby LN13 75 F5
Bicker PE20 135 B4
Billinghay LN4 109 E5
Boston PE21 208 E4
Brant Broughton & Stragglethorpe LN5 105 E5
Bratoft PE24 102 C7
Brigg DN20 196 B2
Brough HU15 2 C6
9 Broughton DN20 19 E3
Burgh on Bain LN8 59 D5
Butterwick PE22 126 E4
Caistor LN7 33 C4
Castor PE5 223 F1
7 Croxton Kerrial NG32 138 D4
Donington PE11 134 F2
Donington on Bain LN11 59 D2
Eagle & Swinethorpe LN6 79 C2
East Halton DN40 12 D6
Firsby PE24 102 A7
Fleet PE12 168 C2
Fosdyke PE20 136 D1
Friskney PE22 115 C7
Gainsborough DN21 197 B8
Gorefield PE13 169 E1
Gosberton PE11 145 C6
4 Goxhill DN19 5 A1
Grainthorpe LN11 50 B8
Great Casterton PE9 171 B8
Great Ponton NG33 140 A5
Hackthorn LN2 56 B1
Haxey DN9 27 B2
Heighington/Washingborough LN4 81 E4
Hemingby LN9 72 B1
Heydour NG32 131 B5
Hogsthorpe PE24 90 B7
Holbeach PE12 215 B5
Holton le Clay DN36 36 B4
Horbling NG34 133 B3
Horncastle LN9 199 B4
Huttoft LN13 76 E4
Immingham DN40 186 A4
8 Keelby DN41 23 A4
5 Ketton PE9 171 A3
Kingston upon Hull HU10 178 C6
Kirton PE20 136 A7
Kirton in Lindsey DN21 30 C1
Legbourne LN11 61 F3
Lincoln LN5 201 E1
Little Steeping PE23 101 C6
Louth LN11 198 B7
Maltby le Marsh LN13 75 F8
Manby LN11 62 C7
4 Marshchapel DN36 37 C2
Marston NG32 118 D2
Martin LN4 96 C2
Martin LN4 96 C3
Middle Rasen LN8 57 C7
Minting LN8 71 B2
Mumby LN13 76 F1
Newton PE13 169 F5
North Clifton NG23 78 C7
3 North Kelsey LN7 32 A4
Osgodby LN8 45 A3
Owmby LN8 55 E6
Peterborough PE5 228 F7
Pickworth NG34 132 A1
Roughton Moor LN10 98 A7
Saltfleetby LN11 51 C1
Saxilby LN1 66 D2
Scamblesby LN11 72 F5
Scawby DN20 30 F8
Skegness PE25 206 A8
Skidbrooke with Saltfleet Haven LN11 51 C4
10 South Ferriby DN18 10 A7
South Somercotes LN11 50 D4
South Witham NG33 151 C1
Sturton by Stow LN1 66 C6
Sutterton PE20 135 F2
19 Sutton Bridge PE12 160 E4
Swineshead PE20 135 A8
Tallington PE9 172 F7
Tetford LN9 73 E1
Thorney PE8 228 B7
Tinwell PE9 218 D3
Tydd St Mary PE13 160 B1
Wainfleet All Saints PE24 102 C1
Walkeringham DN10 39 F3
Welbourn LN5 106 F4
Welton LN2 68 E8
Welton le Marsh PE23 89 A3
West Keal PE23 100 B4
West Walton PE14 170 F4
Whaplode PE12 158 B7
Wigsley NG23 78 F4
Wildmore LN4 111 C4
Willoughby with Sloothby LN13 89 C6
Woodhall Spa LN10 97 B5
Wrangle PE22 114 D1
Wrawby DN20 20 E3
Mill La Cl PE24 90 B7
Mill La W HU15 2 B6
Mill Marsh Rd PE12 146 D2
Mill Mere Rd
Corringham DN21 41 D2
5 Waddington LN5 93 F7
Mill Moor Way 3 LN6 204 D1
Millom Way DN32 191 F8
Mill Pl DN35 192 F6
Millport Dr HU4 179 B2
Mill Race DN36 36 E4
Mill Rd Addlethorpe PE24 90 D2
Boston PE21 209 B3
Claypole NG23 117 E7
Cleethorpes DN35 192 E5
Crowle DN17 16 D8
Donington on Bain LN11 59 E2
Hibaldstow DN20 30 E4
2 Keadby DN17 17 D5
Lincoln LN1 234 A4
Luddington & Haldenby DN17 7 C4
Market Rasen LN8 57 D7
Maxey PE6 173 C7
Pilsgate PE9 172 C3
Swanland HU14 3 A6
Walpole PE14 170 F6
Wisbech St Mary PE13 177 D5
Mill Rise
6 Navenby/Wellingore LN5 107 A7
14 Scothern LN2 68 F4
Swanland HU14 3 A6
Mill Row Barrowby NG32 129 B3
2 Lincoln LN1 234 A4
Mills Cl 15 NG23 117 D3
Mills Dr DN7 26 A8
Mills Service Rd DN16 19 A4
Mill St
Kingston upon Hull HU1 180 E6
Ryhall PE9 163 C2
Scamblesby LN11 73 A4
Millstone Cl
Horncastle LN9 199 A3
9 Kirton in Lindsey DN21 30 B2
Millstone La 3 PE9 172 D3
Millstream Rd LN4 81 E4
MILLTHORPE NG34 143 B6
Millthorpe Dro NG34 143 E5
Millthorpe La NG34 142 F5
Millthorpe Rd NG34 143 B5
Mill View
Peterborough PE7 229 A5
5 Waltham DN37 194 E4
Mill View Cl
Addlethorpe PE24 90 D4
Epworth DN9 27 D7
Millview Ct LN9 199 B4
Mill View Ct 12 LN8 70 D4
Millview Gdns 3 DN20 20 E3
Millview Rd
11 Heckington NG34 122 E2
Ruskington NG34 108 D2
Mill View Rd 9 LN8 70 D4
Mill Vw 31 DN18 3 E1
Mill Wy LN11 49 B7
Milman Rd LN2 202 B4
Milne Gn 4 PE20 135 B7
Milners Ct 22 PE9 219 C5
Milner's La 2 PE23 87 F1
Milner St 20 NG24 104 A4
Milnyard Sq PE2 229 C2
Milson Cl
18 Barton-upon-Humber DN18 10 E8
7 Broughton DN20 19 D4
Coningsby LN4 207 D4
Milson Rd 17 DN41 23 A4
Milsons La LN13 75 B6
Milson Wy LN4 207 D4
Milton Cl Branston LN4 81 D2
Cherry Willingham LN3 203 E5
2 Gainsborough DN21 197 E6
Milton Dr PE13 170 B1
Milton Rd
Gainsborough DN21 197 E6
Grimsby DN34 191 B4
Peterborough PE2 231 A7
Scunthorpe DN16 185 B5
Milton St Lincoln LN5 205 E7
Newark-on-Trent NG24 104 A3
Milton Way
Kirkby la Thorpe NG34 121 E4
Peterborough PE3 224 E3
2 Sleaford NG34 212 F3
Mimosa Ct DN16 185 E4
Mina Cl PE2 231 D4
Minden Pl 4 DN21 55 A8
Minerva Cl 18 NG32 120 A3
Minerva Wy LN6 204 C1
MININGSBY PE22 99 D7
Miningsby Rd PE23 99 F8
Minnett's Hill NG32 130 B8
Minnow Cl 1 DN37 190 D7
Minshull Rd DN35 192 F4
Minsmere Cl PE11 214 B5
Minster Dr
Cherry Willingham/Reepham LN3 203 E7
Louth LN11 198 D4
Minster Precincts 9 PE1 226 A2
Minster Rd
15 Misterton DN10 39 F5
Scunthorpe DN15 182 B2
Minster Yd LN2 234 B3
MINTING LN9 84 D8
Minting Cl 9 LN1 201 E8
Minting La LN9 71 D1
Mint La LN1 234 A2
Mint St LN1 234 A2
Mirfield Rd Grimsby DN32 191 F4
Scunthorpe DN15 182 C4
Misson Bank DN9 26 C3
MISTERTON DN10 39 F5
Misterton PE2 229 E3
Misterton Prim Sch DN10 39 F4
Mitchell Cl Eastgate PE1 226 C2
3 Hatfield DN7 14 D5
7 Skellingthorpe LN6 200 A4
Mitchell Dr LN1 201 C6
Mitchell Rd LN4 207 F6
Mitre La 16 PE21 208 F5
Moat House Rd 22 DN21 30 B1
Moat La Bolingbroke PE23 100 A8
Old Leake PE22 114 B1
3 South Killingholme DN40 12 E3
4 Welbourn LN5 106 E5
Moat Rd Scunthorpe DN15 8 C1
Terrington St Clement PE34 161 F1
Moat Wlk NG31 211 E6
Modder St 1 DN16 185 B6
Moggswell La PE2 230 B4
Moira Cl 5 DN7 14 D7
Mole Dro PE12 168 C1
Molinari Ave DN36 36 C4
Mollison Ave DN35 192 F5
Mollison Rd HU4 179 A3
Molyneux Sq
1 Hampton Vale PE7 230 B1
Yaxley PE7 233 B8
Monaco Way PE10 213 A4
Monarch Ave PE2 231 A6
Monarchs Rd PE20 136 A3
Monce Cl LN2 68 C7
Monckton Way LN2 68 D5
Mondemont Cl 4 PE12 215 E3
Money Bridge La PE11 144 F1
Moneys Yd 7 NG34 212 D4
Monic Ave HU13 178 F2
Monkhouse Ct 6 PE11 214 A3
Monks Abbey Prim Sch LN2 202 B4
Monks Ave LN11 198 C6
Monks Cl 4 Hatfield DN7 14 D5
New Quarrington NG34 212 A2
Monks Dr 22 PE6 175 A1
Monks Dyke Rd LN11 198 D5
Monks' Dyke Tennyson Coll LN11 198 D5
Monks Gr PE4 220 E5
Monks Ho La 12 PE11 214 A4
Monks House La 5 PE11 214 A4
Monks Leys Terr LN2 234 C3
Monks Manor Ct LN2 202 B5
Monks Manor Dr LN2 202 B4
Monks Mdw 5 PE6 175 B8
Monks Rd Lincoln LN2 234 B2
Scunthorpe DN17 184 F6
8 Swineshead PE20 135 B7
MONKSTHORPE PE23 101 E8
Monksthorpe La PE23 88 F1
Monks Way LN2 202 C3
Monks Way East HU14 2 F5
Monks Way Ind Est LN2 202 D3
Monks Way West HU14 2 F5
Monks Wlk 4 PE11 214 A4
Monkton 2 HU15 2 D6
Monkwood Cl 17 NG23 91 D5
Monmouth La PE12 216 E8
Monmouth St HU4 179 E3
Monmouth Way NG31 210 E6
Monsal Dale LN6 204 F2
Monson Ct LN5 201 E1
Monson Pk LN6 200 A4
Monson Rd DN21 42 A8
Monson St LN5 234 A1
Mons Rd LN1 201 E6
Mons St HU5 180 A8
Montague St
Cleethorpes DN35 189 D1
Lincoln LN2 234 C2
Montague Terr 1 LN2 234 C2
Montagu Rd PE4 225 D8
Montaigne Cl 3 LN2 202 D7
Montaigne Cres LN2 202 D7
Montaigne Gdn LN2 202 D7
Montbretia Dr 2 DN17 185 A1
Monteith Cres PE21 209 B5
Montgomery Rd
Cleethorpes DN35 192 D5
Skegness PE25 206 A3
Montrose Cl
8 Grantham NG31 211 D7
1 Lincoln LN6 204 E1
10 Stamford PE9 218 E6
Montrose Gr NG34 121 A2
Montrose St 5 DN16 183 B2
Monument Rd
5 Bicker PE20 135 A4
Stixwould LN10 97 D7
Monument St PE1 226 A3
Moody La DN31 188 C3
Moon's Gn 3 PE12 157 F6
Moor Bank PE22 113 C3
Moor Bottom Rd DN17 6 C1
MOORBY PE22 99 B6
Moorby Cl LN1 201 E7
Moorby Rd PE22 98 F6
Moor Closes Nature Reserve ★ NG32 120 A2
Moor Dike Rd DN7 26 A8
Moore Cl NG23 117 F7
Moor Edges Rd DN8 15 B8
Moore's La 1 PE6 175 A1
Moor Farm Nature Reserve ★ LN10 98 A6
Moorfield Rd 2 PE3 225 D3
Moorfields La DN14 6 F7
Moor Gate PE12 159 A4
Moorgate Cl PE10 154 D7

Moor Gn HU4 179 B7
Moorhen Cl
Skirbeck Quarter PE21 208 E3
Witham St Hughs LN6 92 D4
Moorhouse Rd HU5 179 B8
MOORHOUSES PE22 112 A8
Moorhouses Rd PE22 111 F8
Moorings The
Broughton DN20 196 A3
Burton LN1 200 D7
Moor La
Ashby de la Launde & Bloxholm LN4 108 C3
Besthorpe NG23 91 D7
Blankney LN4 95 E4
Braceby & Sapperton NG34 131 E1
Branston & Mere LN4 81 F2
Caistor LN7 33 A5
5 Cherry Willingham/Reepham LN3 82 A8
Hatfield DN8 15 D3
Horsington LN10 84 D2
Kirkby on Bain LN10 97 F6
Laneham DN22 65 A3
Leasingham NG34 121 C7
Lincoln LN6 204 E1
Long Bennington NG23 117 C3
Marlborough LN5 93 A4
Martin LN4 96 A2
North Clifton NG23 78 D6
Potter Hanworth LN4 82 B2
Reepham LN3 69 B1
Roughton LN10 98 B7
South Clifton NG23 78 E5
South Witham NG33 151 B2
Stapleford LN6 105 B8
Thorpe on the Hill LN6 79 E1
Thurlby LN6 92 E4
Wroot DN9 26 C6
Moorland Ave
1 Lincoln LN6 205 A5
4 Walkeringham DN10 39 F3
Moorland Cl
8 Carlton-le-Moorland LN5 105 E8
5 Walkeringham DN10 39 F3
Moorland Cres 5 LN6 205 B6
Moorland Dr DN36 195 C7
Moorland Lane DN9 17 B1
Moorlands 9 DN9 27 A2
Moorlands The 23 LN4 95 D4
Moorland Way
5 Epworth DN9 27 E6
Lincoln LN6 204 F5
Moor Owners Rd DN8 15 D8
Moor Pk 5 NG34 108 D1
Moor Pk Dr 9 LN10 97 C5
Moor Rd Bottesford DN17 184 C2
15 Collingham NG23 91 D5
Crowle DN17 16 C8
Newborough PE6 174 C5
Owersby LN8 45 A5
Snitterby DN21 43 D5
Thorne DN8 15 C7
Walesby LN8 45 E3
Moorside PE22 98 E3
MOOR SIDE PE22 111 D8
Moor Side PE22 111 C8
Moorside Ct LN6 204 E1
Moors La LN8 59 A2
Moors Rd DN15 182 C3
Moor St LN1 201 D4
Moorswood Gate PE12 159 D3
MOORTOWN LN7 32 C2
Moortown Cl 6 NG31 211 D7
Moortown Rd LN7 33 A3
Moorwell Bsns Pk DN17 184 D3
Moorwell Rd DN17 184 E2
Moray Cl 5 PE9 218 D6
MORBORNE PE7 232 B3
Morborne Cl PE2 231 D6
Morborne La PE7 232 D4
Morborne Rd PE7 232 C2
Morborn Rd 4 PE7 230 C2
Mordaunt Ave DN33 194 D7
Morden Cl 12 LN4 95 D4
Morecambe Ave DN16 185 A4
Moreland Ave 1 LN12 77 A8
Moresby Wy PE7 231 A5
Morfield Gr 5 DN9 27 D6
Morgan Cl PE7 233 E6
Morgans Cl 2 NG24 104 D5
Morgan Way 5 DN19 4 E2
Morkery La
Castle Bytham NG33 152 B2
North Witham NG33 151 F2
Morley La 10 PE20 135 A4
Morley Rd DN17 184 F5
Morley's La NG33 152 F7
Morley St 2 DN21 197 C5
Morley Way PE2 230 D5
Morningside Dr PE25 103 C7
Morpeth Cl PE2 230 C6
Morpeth Rd PE3 225 C3
Morpeth St HU3 180 D7
Morpeth Wlk DN34 191 A7
Morris Cl 21 LN2 68 D6
Morris Ct PE7 233 E6
Morris Gdns 2 PE25 206 B5
Morrison Cl 10 LN12 76 F8
Morris Rd HU3 179 E7
Morris St PE1 226 B3
Mortal Ash Hill DN16 19 C2
Mortimer Dr HU10 178 F6
MORTON Morton DN21 197 C8
MORTON *continued*
Morton PE10 154 C6
Thorpe on the Hill LN6 92 C6
Morton Carr DN21 40 C4
Morton CE (Controlled) Prim Sch PE10 154 D7
Morton Cl
Gainsborough DN21 197 B8
Immingham DN40 186 B5
Morton Dr LN6 204 F7
Morton Dro PE10 155 A6
Morton Front DN21 197 B7
Morton La LN6 92 C8
Morton N Dro PE10 155 B7
Morton Rd
Gainsborough DN21 197 C7
Grimsby DN34 191 B7
Laughton DN21 41 B8
Swinderby LN6 92 B7
Morton St HU3 180 C8
Morton Terr DN21 197 C6
Morton Trentside Prim Sch DN21 197 B8
Morton Way LN9 199 C1
Morus Cl PE11 214 E2
Mosscroft La DN7 14 F3
Mossdale Cl NG31 129 F5
Moss Dr PE25 206 C2
Mossop Dr PE6 164 E3
Moss Rd Grimsby DN32 191 E7
Kirk Bramwith DN7 14 A8
Motherby La LN1 234 A2
MOULTON PE12 157 F7
MOULTON CHAPEL PE12 157 E1
Moulton Chapel Prim Sch PE12 157 F1
Moulton Chapel Rd PE12 157 C1
Moulton Cl 1 DN34 190 D4
Moulton Cres 13 NG24 104 B2
MOULTON EAUGATE PE12 167 F8
Moulton Gr PE3 225 C6
Moulton Marsh Nature Reserve* PE12 146 F8
Moulton Mere Bank PE12 157 E3
MOULTON SEAS END PE12 146 E2
Mount Ave
14 Barton-upon-Humber DN18 10 E8
Kingston upon Hull HU13 178 D2
10 Winterton DN15 9 B5
Mountbatten Ave
11 Pinchbeck PE11 156 E8
Stamford PE9 219 A6
Yaxley PE7 233 D5
Mountbatten Cl 5 DN16 185 B4
Mountbatten Dr 2 PE13 170 C1
Mountbatten Way
Bourne PE10 213 E7
Peterborough PE3 225 B6
Mount Ct 6 NG24 104 B2
Mount La
Burton Pedwardine NG34 122 A2
Kirkby la Thorpe NG34 121 F3
Legsby LN8 58 A3
Mountney Pl 9 NG24 104 A6
Mount Olivet LN11 198 A6
Mount Pleasant
9 Alford LN13 75 F2
Binbrook LN8 47 B4
1 Holton le Clay DN36 195 D1
Kingston upon Hull HU9 181 C8
Louth LN11 198 C5
8 New Holland DN19 4 E2
Peterborough PE2 231 C7
Sleaford NG34 212 E5
6 Wainfleet All Saints PE24 102 D2
Waltham DN37 194 D5
Mount Pleasant Cl DN21 53 B1
Mount Pleasant Rd PE13 170 D1
Mount Pleasant Windmill* DN21 30 B2
Mount Rd
Bracebridge Heath LN4 205 F3
Newark-on-Trent NG24 104 B2
Mount Royale Cl DN39 12 A1
Mount St
9 Grantham NG31 211 A5
Lincoln LN1 201 E6
Mountsteven Ave PE4 221 B1
Mount Street Acad LN1 201 E6
Mount The 6 DN3 14 A1
Mount Tumbledown Cl 9 PE12 160 E4
Mount View 5 HU14 3 A5
Mourne Terr 6 LN5 205 D2
Mowbeck Wy NG31 210 F3
Mowbray Cl 3 Haxey DN9 27 D3
16 Skegness PE25 206 A5
Mowbray Ct 23 DN9 27 E6
Mowbray Rd
Bretton PE3 220 D1
14 Thorne/Moorends DN8 15 B7
Mowbray St Epworth DN9 27 E6
Gainsborough DN21 197 C6
Moxon's La 13 LN5 93 F7
Mrs Mary Kings CE (Controlled) Prim Sch LN4 96 B3
Mrs Smith's Cottage* LN5 107 B8
Much La LN1 234 A2
MUCKTON LN11 74 D8
Muckton Rd
Little Cawthorpe LN11 61 E2
Muckton LN11 74 D6
Muckton Wood Nature Reserve* LN11 74 E8
Mucky La DN15 9 C5
Muirfield Grantham NG31 211 D8
11 Waltham DN37 194 C4
Muirfield Cl
Birchwood LN6 204 B7
6 Spalding PE11 214 C2
Muirfield Croft DN40 186 C4
Muirfield Dr PE25 206 D5
Mulberry Ave 3 LN6 204 F2
Mulberry Cl
5 North Thoresby DN36 36 B1
Sleaford NG34 212 D2
Waddington LN5 205 C1
Mulberry Ct 6 PE20 135 B6
Mulberry Dr 21 DN17 16 D7
Mulberry Gdns
Bottesford DN16 185 E4
Paston PE4 221 C1
Mulberry La DN37 23 F2
Mulberry Rd LN8 45 E5
Mulberry Way
Skegness PE25 206 B6
Spalding PE11 214 E3
Mulberry Wlk 11 NG34 122 D3
Mulgrave Cl DN37 190 F8
Mulgrave St S DN15 183 A4
Mulgrave St HU8 181 A8
Mull Way DN40 186 C2
Multon Ings La PE20 136 B7
MUMBY LN13 76 F1
Mumby Cl
22 Beacon Hill NG24 104 A5
12 North Thoresby DN36 36 B1
Mumby Mdws LN13 76 F1
Mumby Rd LN13 76 F2
Mumby's Bridge Rd PE22 98 F2
Munday Way PE13 170 B2
Munstead Wy 28 HU15 2 D5
Munster Ct 6 DN31 189 C1
Munton Fields NG33 131 A1
Murdock Rd LN5 205 E6
Murrayfield Ave 3 NG34 120 F3
Murray St 2 DN31 189 B2
MURROW PE13 177 D5
Murrow Bank PE13 177 D6
Murrow La PE13 177 F5
Murrow Primary Acad PE13 177 D5
Museum of Lincolnshire Life* LN1 234 A4
Musgraves Orch LN2 68 E7
Muskham PE3 224 F4
Musselburgh Way PE10 213 B3
Mussons Cl NG33 152 E7
Muster Roll La PE21 209 A3
Musticott Pl 17 PE13 170 E1
MUSTON NG13 128 C5
Muston La NG13 128 B5
Muston Meadows National Nature Reserve* NG13 128 B3
Muston Rd NG31 210 E2
Muswell Rd PE3 225 E4
Mutton La DN10 39 F1
Myers Cl NG32 120 C1
Myles Way 15 PE13 170 D2
Myrtle Ave PE1 226 C7
Myrtle Ct PE1 226 C7
Myrtle Gr PE1 226 C7
Myrtle House Cvn Pk PE1 226 F5
Myrtle Rd 5 DN7 14 C4
Myrtle Way 16 HU15 2 C5
Myton St HU1 180 E6

N

Naam Gr LN1 234 A4
Naam Pl LN1 234 A4
Nab La DN7 14 C8
Nags Head Pas 10 NG34 212 D4
Nairn Dr PE2 229 D4
Nairn Rd PE9 218 E6
Nandike Cl 4 HU10 178 F6
Nan Sampson Bank DN9 26 B4
Nansicles Rd PE2 230 D6
Napier Pl PE2 229 C6
Napier St LN2 234 C2
Narrow Boats The 3 DN20 196 A3
Narrow La Belchford LN9 73 B2
Twin Rivers DN14 7 C8
Whaplode PE12 158 C4
Narrow Lane DN9 28 A7
Naseby Cl 21
Hatfield DN7 14 D3
Peterborough PE3 225 C5
Naseby Dr DN31 191 B8
Naseby Gr DN31 191 B7
Nash Cl 18 NG34 122 E2
Nash La 2 LN6 204 E1
Natal View LN1 201 D8
Nathan Cl PE3 225 B2
National Ave HU5 179 F8
National CE Jun Sch The NG31 211 B5
National Fishing Heritage Ctr* DN31 191 E8
National Parrot Sanctuary The* PE22 114 D7
Natural World Ctr* LN6 79 F1
Natureland Seal Sanctuary* PE25 206 E4
Natures Way PE7 233 A8
NAVENBY LN5 107 A8
Navenby CE Prim Sch LN5 107 B8
Navenby La
Ashby de la Launde & Bloxholm LN4 107 F6
Bassingham LN5 93 A1
Navensby Cl DN31 188 A2
Navigation House* 8 NG34 212 E4
Navigation La 28 LN7 33 B4
Navigation Way HU9 181 C6
Naylors Dr 5 LN8 57 B8
Naylor's Row 3 HU9 181 B7
Ndola Dr LN9 199 C2
Neale Rd 16 LN6 93 C8
Neals Cres NG31 210 F4
Neal's Gate PE12 158 E2
Neap House Rd
Flixborough DN15 182 A7
Gunness DN15 17 E6
Neatgangs La DN19 5 A3
Neath Rd DN16 183 A1
Neaverson Rd 2 PE6 220 D7
Needham Ct PE7 233 E4
Needham Dr PE12 159 C1
Needham Rd PE10 154 C6
Needhams Mdw LN13 76 B3
Needles The 8 PE25 206 A7
Neile Cl LN2 202 D7
Nelson Cl 5 Crowland PE6 166 F1
4 Skegness PE25 206 A7
Nelson Dr LN4 203 B2
Nelson Gdns 31 PE13 170 D1
Nelson Rd Fiskerton LN3 82 A6
Kingston upon Hull HU5 179 B7
4 Mablethorpe/Sutton on Sea LN12 64 B3
1 Newark-on-Trent NG24 104 A2
Nelson St
Gainsborough DN21 197 C6
Grimsby DN32 189 B1
Kingston upon Hull HU1 181 A5
Lincoln LN1 201 D3
Nelson Way
9 Boston PE21 208 E4
5 Grimsby DN34 190 D4
Nelthorpe Cl 9 DN39 12 A1
Nelthorpe St LN5 201 E1
Nene Cl Bourne PE10 213 E4
Guyhirn PE13 177 F2
10 Ruskington NG34 108 D2
Wansford PE8 222 A3
4 Wittering PE8 172 B1
Nene Ct 4 Grantham NG31 210 E2
3 Spalding PE11 214 F5
Nenegate Sch PE1 226 C3
Nenelands 8 PE12 160 F4
Nene Mdws 1 PE12 160 F4
Nene Parade 9 PE13 170 C1
Nene Park Acad PE2 230 A5
Nene Parkway PE3 224 F1
Nene Pk 6 LN6 204 C1
Nene Rd LN1 201 E8
Nene St PE1 226 B2
NENE TERRACE PE6 175 D6
Nene Terr Rd PE6 175 D7
Nene Valley Prim Sch PE2 230 D8
Nene Way PE5 222 F2
Neptune Cl 2 PE2 231 D4
Neptune St
Cleethorpes DN35 192 E7
Kingston upon Hull HU1 180 D4
Nero Pl PE2 231 F4
Nero Wy LN6 93 A8
Neslam Rd NG34 143 C7
Ness La DN17 7 E6
Netherfield PE12 215 B2
Nethergate DN9 27 B2
Nether La NG32 139 A7
Netherlands Way DN41 187 B3
Netherton Rd HU4 179 B4
Nettlecroft La NG32 119 C6
NETTLEHAM LN2 68 D2
Nettleham CE VA Jun Sch The LN2 68 C2
Nettleham Cl LN2 202 A6
Nettleham Infant Sch The LN2 68 C2
Nettleham Rd Lincoln LN2 234 C4
Scothern LN2 68 E3
Nettleholme 10 DN7 14 D4
NETTLETON LN7 33 A3
Nettleton Cl LN4 81 E2
Nettleton Com Prim Sch LN7 33 A3
Nettleton Dr LN6 92 E5
Nettleton Rd LN7 33 B3
Neustadt Ct 10 LN2 234 B3
Neville Ave PE11 214 F4
Neville Cl
5 Keadby with Althorpe DN17 17 D4
Kingston upon Hull HU3 180 D5
Neville Cres 5 DN15 9 A5
Neville La DN7 14 A8
Neville Rd DN16 183 C2
Neville St DN35 192 D8
Neville Turner Way DN37 194 D4
NEWARK PE1 226 E6
Newark Acad The NG24 104 B3
Newark Air Mus* NG24 104 D6
Newark Ave PE1 226 C6
Newark Hill Foston NG23 117 F1
Great Gonerby NG31 129 D6
Newark Hill Prim Sch PE1 226 D6
Newark Hospl NG24 104 A4
Newark La NG32 119 C4
Newark N Gate Sta NG24 104 A5
Newark & Nottinghamshire Agricultural Society's Showground* NG24 104 C7
NEWARK-ON-TRENT NG24 104 B4
Newark Rd
Barnby in the Willows NG24 104 E3
Bassingham LN5 92 E2
Dry Doddington NG23 117 A5
Fenton LN1 65 D4
Leadenham LN5 106 C3
Lincoln LN6 204 F3
Newark-on-Trent NG24 104 C5
North Rauceby NG34 120 C7
Norton Disney LN6 91 F2
Peterborough PE1 226 E2
Stapleford LN6 105 B8
Swinderby LN6 92 A4
Newark Rd Ind Est PE1 226 E4
Newark Vw NG31 210 D6
Newark Wlk DN40 186 D3
NEW BALDERTON NG24 104 A2
NEWBALL LN3 69 D3
NEW BARNETBY DN38 21 D5
New Beacon Rd NG31 211 C4
Newbey Cl PE3 225 B3
Newbigg 1 Crowle DN17 16 C8
Westwoodside DN9 27 B2
NEW BOLINGBROKE PE22 112 D8
Newbolt Ave 2 DN17 184 D7
Newbolt Cl 1 LN7 33 A3
Newborn Ave DN15 182 E4
Newborn Cl PE2 231 E5
NEWBOROUGH PE6 174 E4
Newborough CE Prim Sch PE6 174 E4
Newborough Rd PE4 174 E1
Newboults La 2 PE9 219 A5
Newbridge Hill LN11 198 C6
Newbridge La LN11 49 E5
New Bridge Rd HU9 181 C8
Newbury Ave DN37 188 A1
Newbury Cres PE10 213 C2
Newbury Gr 2 DN34 190 E4
Newbury Rd
3 Beacon Hill NG24 104 C4
15 Newark-on-Trent NG24 104 C5
Newbury Terr DN37 188 A1
Newby Rd DN31 191 C7
New Cartergate 1 DN31 191 D7
Newcastle Dr PE2 230 D6
Newcastle Rd 4 NG31 210 D5
New Chapel La 8 DN37 23 F1
New Cl DN33 191 C4
New Clee Sta DN31 189 D1
New Cleveland St HU8 181 A8
New College Stamford PE9 219 C6
New Coll Stamford PE9 219 D8
Newcomb Ct
2 Sleaford NG34 212 B7
16 Stamford PE9 219 B5
Newcombe Way PE2 229 D2
Newcomen Way DN15 183 B6
Newcot La LN4 81 F4
New Cres LN3 203 D6
Newcroft La LN11 50 A8
New Cross Rd 3 PE9 219 C6
New Cut PE6 176 D5
Newdike Gate PE12 158 C5
Newdown Rd DN17 184 D3
Newell Lane PE9 162 F5
New End Hemingby LN9 72 B1
5 Wainfleet All Saints PE24 102 D2
NEW ENGLAND Croft PE24 102 E2
Peterborough PE1 225 E7
New England Rd NG33 141 B7
New Est
1 Little Bytham NG33 163 A8
Swinstead NG33 153 A5
New Fen Dike PE12 169 A7
New Fen Dro PE12 168 B1
Newfield Cl 10 DN3 14 A4
Newfield Dr LN4 109 F3
Newfield Rd NG34 212 C5
Newfields PE13 169 D1
NEW FLETTON PE2 231 B8
Newgate La NG31 130 D4
Newgate Rd PE13 169 F6
Newgates 3 PE9 219 C5
New Gdn St 5 HU1 180 F7
New George St HU2 180 F7
New Gn 3 DN7 14 C6
Newhall Rd
13 Kirk Sandall DN3 14 A2
10 Kirk Sandall DN3 14 A2
NEWHAM PE22 112 A1
Newham La PE22 112 A1
New Hammond Beck Rd PE21 208 A3
Newham Rd 2 PE9 219 A7
Newhaven Dr LN5 205 D3
New Haven Terr DN31 188 D1
New Hill NG32 119 A5
NEW HOLLAND DN19 4 E2
New Holland CE Methodist Prim Sch DN19 4 E2
New Holland Rd DN19 4 E1
New Holland Sta DN19 4 E3
New Ings La DN22 52 E3
Newington Ave HU4 179 E5
Newington Prim Sch HU3 180 A4
Newington St HU3 179 F4
New Inn La 3 DN7 14 C7
New La Girton NG23 78 D2
Great Carlton LN11 62 E3

New La *continued*
Leasingham NG34 . . . . 121 B7
Reedness DN14 . . . . 6 E8
Tathwell LN11 . . . . 61 A1
Toynton St Peter PE23 . . . . . . 101 A5
Wansford PE8 . . . . 222 C1
New Lakeside PE7 . . . . 230 B1
Newland LN1 . . . . 234 A2
Newland Ave DN15 . . . . 182 E2
Newland Dr DN15 . . . . 182 D3
Newlands DN21 . . . . 197 E5
Newland St W 2 LN1 . . . . . 234 A2
Newlands Ct DN21 . . . . 197 E5
Newlands Lane DN9 . . . . 28 A7
Newlands Pk DN36 . . . . 193 B1
Newlands Rd
2 Haconby PE10 . . . . 154 D8
Parson Drove PE13 . . . . 177 D7
Surfleet PE11 . . . . 145 F4
Newland View 17 DN9 . . . . . 27 E6
Newland Wlk DN15 . . . . 182 E3
NEW LEAKE PE22 . . . . 114 A8
New Leake Prim Sch PE22 . . . . 113 F7
New Life Chrsitian Acad HU2 . . . . 180 F8
Newlyn Cl
4 Kingston upon Hull HU13 . . . . 179 A2
New Waltham DN36 . . . . 195 C7
Newman Cl 19 PE8 . . . . 172 B1
Newmarch Ct DN33 . . . . 191 B2
Newmarket LN11 . . . . 198 C4
Newmarket Ave 13 PE10 . . 213 D3
Newmarket Cl PE1 . . . . 226 B6
Newmarket St 4 DN32 . . . 191 F8
New Marsh Rd PE12 . . . . . . 149 B3
New Mdw Dro PE7 . . . . 231 D1
NEW MEADOW PE7 . . . . 231 F2
New Michael St 4 HU1 . . . 180 E5
New Mill Field Rd DN7 . . . . . 14 E3
Newnham Cres DN16 . . . . . 185 A4
Newnham Rd 17 NG24 . . . . 104 A5
New Park Pl 3 LN2 . . . . 202 F6
New Pk Est 1 DN7 . . . . 14 D7
Newport LN2 . . . . 234 B4
Newport Ave NG31 . . . . 210 D4
Newport Cl 4 HU3 . . . . 180 D5
Newport Cres
2 Waddington LN5 . . . . 93 F7
1 Waddington LN5 . . . . 93 F7
Newport Ct 1 LN1 . . . . 234 B4
Newport Dr DN15 . . . . 9 A6
Newport St 8 DN18 . . . . 3 F1
Newport Wlk DN40 . . . . 186 D3
Newport Wy PE9 . . . . 172 F2
NEW QUARRINGTON NG34 . . . . 212 A2
New Rd Blankney LN10 . . . . . . 96 F5
Brantingham HU15 . . . . 2 C8
Cleethorpes DN35 . . . . 192 F6
Clipsham LE15 . . . . 162 B7
1 Collyweston PE9 . . . . 171 B1
Croft PE24 . . . . 103 C3
Deeping St Nicholas PE6 . . . 166 D5
5 Easton on the Hill PE9 . . . 171 D3
9 Eye PE6 . . . . 175 A1
Folksworth PE7 . . . . 232 E6
Holbeach St Marks PE12 . . . 147 F6
Laceby DN37 . . . . 35 A8
Langtoft PE6 . . . . 164 F3
Peterborough PE1 . . . . 226 B2
Quadring PE11 . . . . 145 C8
Ryhall PE9 . . . . 163 C1
Scunthorpe DN17 . . . . 184 B6
Silk Willoughby NG34 . . . . . . 121 A1
Spalding PE11 . . . . 214 D4
Staunton NG13 . . . . 117 B2
Sutton Bridge PE12 . . . . 160 F5
Swinefleet DN14 . . . . 6 C4
Thistleton LE15 . . . . 151 D1
Wainfleet All Saints PE24 . . . 102 E2
Waltham DN37 . . . . 194 E4
Worlaby DN20 . . . . 10 D1
New River Dro
Cowbit PE12 . . . . 156 F3
3 Spalding PE12 . . . . 214 C1
New River Gate PE12 . . . . . 168 D8
New Roman Bank PE34 . . . 161 D3
New Row
Gonerby Hill Foot NG31 . . . . 210 E7
3 Market Deeping PE6 . . . . 217 D4
8 Messingham DN17 . . . . 29 D7
Newsham Dr DN34 . . . . 191 A7
Newsham Garth HU4 . . . . . 179 B5
Newsham La DN39 . . . . 22 D8
New St
Aby with Greenfield LN13 . . . . 75 B5
14 Beacon Hill NG24 . . . . . . 104 A4
7 Brigg DN20 . . . . 196 C3
Elsham DN20 . . . . 20 E7
1 Gainsborough DN21 . . . . . 197 C5
Grantham NG31 . . . . 211 A5
Grimsby DN31 . . . . 191 E7
5 Heckington NG34 . . . . . . 122 E2
Helpringham NG34 . . . . 133 D7
6 Louth LN11 . . . . 198 B5
Osbournby NG34 . . . . 132 D5
Sleaford NG34 . . . . 212 E4
4 Stamford PE9 . . . . 219 C6
Newstead Ave
24 Beacon Hill NG24 . . . . . . 104 A5
Cherry Willingham/Reepham LN3 . . . . 203 E5
Holton le Clay DN36 . . . . . . 195 E2
Newstead Cl PE6 . . . . 175 A2
Newstead Rd
Cleethorpes DN35 . . . . 192 E4
Newstead Rd *continued*
2 Mablethorpe/Sutton on Sea LN12 . . . . 64 C3
Newstead PE9 . . . . 219 F6
Ryhall PE9 . . . . 163 D1
Newstead St
Kingston upon Hull HU5 . . . . 180 A8
Quarrington NG34 . . . . 212 C2
Newsum Gdns 23 DN41 . . . . 23 A4
NEWTOFT LN8 . . . . 56 E5
NEWTON Newton PE13 . . . . . 170 A5
Newton and Haceby NG34 . . 132 A3
Newton Abbot Wy 2 PE10 . . . . 213 C3
Newton Bar NG34 . . . . 132 A3
NEWTON BY TOFT LN8 . . . . . . 56 E6
Newton Cl
8 Metheringham LN4 . . . . 95 C4
Swinderby LN6 . . . . 92 A5
5 Wragby LN8 . . . . 70 D4
Newton Ct 6 NG33 . . . . 151 E7
Newton Dr LN3 . . . . 203 C6
Newton Gr DN33 . . . . 191 C4
Newton La Binbrook LN8 . . . . 47 D5
15 Ruskington NG34 . . . . . . 108 E2
Newton Marsh La
Tetney DN36 . . . . 36 F6
Tetney Lock DN36 . . . . 37 A5
NEWTON ON TRENT LN1 . . . . 65 D1
Newton-on-Trent CE Prim Sch LN1 . . . . 65 C1
Newton Pk 10 NG23 . . . . . . 117 D3
Newton Rd DN16 . . . . 185 E6
Newton St
5 Grantham NG31 . . . . 211 B4
3 Kingston upon Hull HU3 . . 180 B4
Lincoln LN5 . . . . 234 B1
Newark-on-Trent NG24 . . . . 104 A4
Newton Terr LN11 . . . . 198 C5
Newton Thorpe Cl HU14 . . . . . 3 B7
Newton Way
5 Colsterworth NG33 . . . . . 151 D7
Sleaford NG34 . . . . 212 D5
Newton Wy PE1 . . . . 226 D2
Newtown 8 Spilsby PE23 . . . 101 A8
Stamford PE9 . . . . 219 D5
New Town 6 PE9 . . . . 171 D3
Newtown Ct
Kingston upon Hull HU9 . . . . 181 E7
Stamford PE9 . . . . 219 C4
Newtown Sq HU9 . . . . 181 E7
New Trent St DN17 . . . . 16 E6
NEW WALTHAM DN36 . . . . . . 195 D7
New Waltham Prim Sch DN36 . . . . 195 C7
New Wlk HU14 . . . . 3 A4
NEW YORK LN4 . . . . 111 C5
New York Prim Sch LN4 . . . 111 C4
New York Rd LN4 . . . . 110 F6
Nicholas Ct 26 DN18 . . . . 10 E8
Nicholas Taylor Gdns 1 PE3 . . . . 224 F3
Nicholas Way DN21 . . . . 41 E2
Nichol Hill 2 LN11 . . . . 198 B5
Nicholls Ave PE3 . . . . 225 E3
Nicholson Rd
3 Healing DN41 . . . . 24 A5
Immingham DN40 . . . . 12 E4
Nicholson St
17 Beacon Hill NG24 . . . . . . 104 A4
8 Cleethorpes DN35 . . . . . . 192 F5
Nicholson Way 7 DN9 . . . . . 27 D7
Nickersons Wlk 7 LN7 . . . . . 33 A3
Nicolette Way 10 PE11 . . . . 214 B5
Nicolgate La DN20 . . . . 196 D4
Nicolson Dr 18 DN18 . . . . . . 10 F8
Nidd's La PE20 . . . . 136 E4
Nightingale Cl
10 Balderton NG24 . . . . 104 C2
35 Barton-upon-Humber DN18 . . . . 10 F8
Scunthorpe DN15 . . . . 182 D5
Nightingale Cres 1 LN6 . . . 204 E8
Nightingale Ct PE4 . . . . 221 E2
Nightingale Dr PE7 . . . . 233 D6
Nightingales 13 PE6 . . . . . . 217 C5
Nightleys Rd DN22 . . . . 65 B5
Nile Dr PE11 . . . . 214 A5
Ninescores La DN9 . . . . 26 B4
Ninth Ave
3 Fixborough Ind Est DN15 . . 8 A1
Grantham NG31 . . . . 211 F5
NINTHORPE PE25 . . . . 206 D6
Nipcut Rd PE6 . . . . 175 C2
Nisa Wy DN15 . . . . 8 C1
NOCTON LN4 . . . . 95 B7
Nocton Cty Prim Sch LN4 . . . 95 C7
Nocton Dr LN2 . . . . 201 F8
Nocton Fen La LN4 . . . . 83 A1
Nocton Rd
7 Potterhanworth LN4 . . . . . 82 B1
Potter Hanworth LN4 . . . . 95 B8
Noel St DN21 . . . . 197 C6
Nooking La DN37 . . . . 23 D2
Nookings Dr 3 DN20 . . . . . . 31 A5
Nooking The DN9 . . . . 27 C3
Nookin The 1 LN5 . . . . 106 E5
Nook The
Croxton Kerrial NG32 . . . . . 138 D3
7 Easton on the Hill PE9 . . . 171 D3
4 Helpston PE6 . . . . 173 C4
Sproxton LE14 . . . . 150 C7
Norbeck La LN2 . . . . 68 C6
Norburn
2 Peterborough PE3 . . . . . . 220 F1
Peterborough PE3 . . . . 225 B8
Norfolk Ave DN15 . . . . 8 B4
Norfolk Bank La HU15 . . . . . . 1 F8
Norfolk Cl 1 LN8 . . . . 47 B6
Norfolk Cres
Bracebridge Heath LN4 . . . . 205 F4
1 Scampton Airfield LN1 . . . . 67 E5
Norfolk Ct 19 DN32 . . . . 189 C1
Norfolk La DN35 . . . . 192 E7
Norfolk Pl 4 PE21 . . . . 208 F6
Norfolk St Ind Est PE21 . . . 208 F7
Norfolk Sq 5 PE9 . . . . 219 B6
Norfolk St Boston PE21 . . . . 208 F6
Kingston upon Hull HU2 . . . . 180 E7
Lincoln LN1 . . . . 201 C4
Peterborough PE1 . . . . 225 F4
Norland Ave HU4 . . . . 179 C6
Norman Ave
5 Boston PE21 . . . . 208 F5
11 Newark-on-Trent NG24 . . 104 A6
NORMANBY DN15 . . . . 8 C3
NORMANBY-BY-SPITAL LN8 . . . . 55 E7
NORMANBY BY STOW DN21 . . . . 53 E1
Normanby Cliff Rd LN8 . . . . 55 D7
Normanby Enterprise Pk DN15 . . . . 182 F8
Normanby Hall Ctry Pk★ DN15 . . . . 8 C3
Normanby Hill LN7 . . . . 45 E7
NORMANBY LE WOLD LN7 . . . 45 F5
Normanby Pk Farming Mus★ DN15 . . . . 8 C3
Normanby Prim Sch LN8 . . . 55 E7
Normanby Rd
Burton upon Stather DN15 . . . . 8 C3
Nettleton LN7 . . . . 33 B2
3 Owmby LN8 . . . . 55 F6
Scunthorpe DN15 . . . . 183 A5
Skegness PE25 . . . . 206 C7
Stow DN21 . . . . 53 F1
Normanby Rise LN8 . . . . 45 E5
Norman Cl
9 Barton-upon-Humber DN18 . . . . 10 F8
30 Metheringham LN4 . . . . . . 95 C4
NORMAN CORNER DN37 . . . 194 C2
Norman Cres 1 DN17 . . . . . 184 F8
NORMAN CROSS PE7 . . . . . 232 F2
Norman Dr Frith Bank PE22 125 D5
7 Hatfield DN7 . . . . 14 D3
Normandy Cl LN11 . . . . 198 E6
Normandy Rd DN35 . . . . 192 D5
Normangate PE5 . . . . 223 D2
Norman Mews 3 PE10 . . . . 213 D5
Norman Rd Grimsby DN34 . . 191 B7
Hatfield DN7 . . . . 14 D3
Peterborough PE1 . . . . 226 C4
Norman St 1 LN5 . . . . 234 B1
NORMANTON
Bottesford NG13 . . . . 128 A7
Normanton NG32 . . . . 119 D5
Normanton La NG13 . . . . . . 128 A6
Normanton Rd
3 Beacon Hill NG24 . . . . . . 104 B5
1 Crowland PE6 . . . . 166 F1
Peterborough PE1 . . . . 226 D7
Normanton Rise HU4 . . . . . 179 C7
Norman Wy LN3 . . . . 83 C5
Nornabell St 1 HU8 . . . . . . 181 C8
Norris Cl 10 NG34 . . . . 122 D3
Norris St LN5 . . . . 201 F1
Norsefield Ave DN37 . . . . . . 194 E5
Nortcote Heavy Horse Ctr★ PE23 . . . . 101 D7
Northam Cl PE6 . . . . 175 B3
Northampton Rd DN16 . . . 183 C1
North Ave PE10 . . . . 153 D6
North Bank Crowland PE6 . . 166 E1
Thorney PE6 . . . . 227 D1
North Bank Rd 4 PE1 . . . . 226 D3
NORTHBECK NG34 . . . . 132 F8
North Beck La PE23 . . . . 87 E1
NORTHBOROUGH PE6 . . . . . 217 E2
Northborough Prim Sch PE6 . . . . 173 F6
Northborough Rd PE6 . . . . 174 C5
Northborough Road PE6 . . 221 E8
NORTH CARLTON LN1 . . . . . . 67 C4
NORTH CARR DN9 . . . . 27 C3
North Carr La DN20 . . . . 9 F3
North Carr Rd
Misterton DN10 . . . . 39 F7
Scotter DN17 . . . . 28 E5
West Stockwith DN10 . . . . 40 B6
North Church Side 12 HU1 . . . . 180 F6
Northcliffe Rd NG31 . . . . . . 211 A7
North Cliff Rd DN21 . . . . 30 C2
NORTH CLIFTON NG23 . . . . . 78 C7
North Clifton Prim Sch NG23 . . . . 78 C6
North Coates Rd DN36 . . . . 37 A4
NORTH COCKERINGTON LN11 . . . . 50 A1
North Cockerington CE Prim Sch LN11 . . . . 50 A1
Northcote Heavy Horse Ctr★ PE23 . . . . 101 D7
NORTH COTES DN36 . . . . 37 A3
North Cotes CE Prim Sch The DN36 . . . . 37 B3
North Cres 7 NG13 . . . . . . 128 A5
Northcroft 4 LN1 . . . . 66 D3
Northcroft La NG23 . . . . 91 C5
North Cswy LN4 . . . . 82 D4
North Ct 10 LN2 . . . . 68 C2
North Cty Prim Sch The DN21 . . . . 197 B6
North Dale Ct 4 DN21 . . . . . 30 B2
Northdale Pk 1 HU14 . . . . . . 3 B7
North Dales Rd LN4 . . . . 82 A5
North Dr 2 Ancaster NG32 120 A3
5 Balderton NG24 . . . . 104 C1
1 Kingston upon Hull HU10 178 E6
RAF Cranwell NG34 . . . . 107 D1
Swanland HU14 . . . . 3 B7
North Dro Bicker PE20 . . . . . 134 E6
Deeping St Nicholas PE11 . . 155 F1
Helpringham NG34 . . . . 133 E7
Lutton PE12 . . . . 148 D1
Quadring PE11 . . . . 144 C8
Swaton NG34 . . . . 133 E4
North Eastern Rd DN8 . . . . . 15 A8
NORTH ELKINGTON LN11 . . . . 48 D1
North Elkington La LN11 . . . 48 E1
NORTH END Alvingham LN11 . 49 E3
Saltfleetby LN11 . . . . 62 F8
Swineshead PE20 . . . . 135 B8
North End 5 Goxhill DN19 . . 12 A8
South Ferriby DN18 . . . . 10 A8
7 Welbourn LN5 . . . . 106 E5
Wisbech PE13 . . . . 170 C1
North End Cres 9 DN36 . . . 36 D4
North End La
2 Fulbeck NG32 . . . . 106 C1
Saltfleetby LN11 . . . . 62 F8
South Cockerington LN11 . . . . 50 F1
South Kelsey LN7 . . . . 32 A2
Sturton le Steeple DN22 . . . . . 52 E4
North End Rd 7 DN36 . . . . . 36 D4
Northern Ave DN20 . . . . 196 C5
Northern Rd NG24 . . . . 104 A5
Northern Road Ind Est NG24 . . . . 104 A5
Northern's Cl NG33 . . . . 151 D5
Northey Rd PE6 . . . . 227 C2
North Farm Rd DN17 . . . . . 184 D3
Northfeild Rd DN21 . . . . 41 B8
North Fen Dro PE20 . . . . . . 134 E4
North Fen Rd
3 Glinton PE6 . . . . 220 C8
Helpringham NG34 . . . . 133 D7
NORTH FERRIBY HU14 . . . . 3 B4
North Ferriby CE Prim Sch HU14 . . . . 3 A5
Northferry La 2 DN9 . . . . . . 16 D1
NORTHFIELD HU13 . . . . 178 F2
Northfield HU14 . . . . 3 B7
Northfield Ave
Kingston upon Hull HU13 . . . 178 E3
3 Sudbrooke LN2 . . . . 68 F3
Northfield Cl
Kingston upon Hull HU10 . . . 178 D6
19 Ruskington NG34 . . . . . . 108 E2
1 Scunthorpe DN16 . . . . 185 C6
11 Tetney DN36 . . . . 36 D4
West Butterwick DN17 . . . . . . 17 D1
Northfield Industrial Est PE6 . . . . 217 C8
Northfield La Amcotts DN17 . . 7 E2
North Clifton NG23 . . . . 78 D7
Thornton Curtis DN39 . . . . . . 11 D5
Willoughton DN21 . . . . 42 C4
Northfield Rd
Ashby with Scremby PE23 . . . 88 D1
Kingston upon Hull HU3 . . . . 179 F6
Messingham DN17 . . . . 185 A1
North Leverton with Habblesthorpe DN22 . . . . . 52 D1
Peterborough PE1 . . . . 225 F7
4 Ruskington NG34 . . . . 108 E2
Sleaford NG34 . . . . 212 A2
Welton LN2 . . . . 68 D7
North Field Rd PE6 . . . . 217 B7
Northfield Rise 1 LN1 . . . . . 66 C2
Northfields Bourne PE10 . . . 213 D7
Stamford PE9 . . . . 219 C6
Northfields Ct PE9 . . . . 219 C6
North Foreland Dr 3 PE25 . . . . 206 D8
North Forty Foot Bank PE21 . . . . 208 A6
NORTHGATE PE11 . . . . 144 D1
Northgate Crossgate PE11 . 145 B1
Kingston upon Hull HU13 . . . 178 E2
Lincoln LN2 . . . . 234 B4
Louth LN11 . . . . 198 B5
North Gate
Gosberton PE11 . . . . 145 A6
Newark-on-Trent NG24 . . . . 104 A5
Pinchbeck PE11 . . . . 144 E1
Sleaford NG34 . . . . 212 D5
Northgate Ct LN11 . . . . 198 B6
Northgate La LN11 . . . . 62 B7
Northgate Sports Hall NG34 . . . . 212 D5
NORTH GREETWELL LN2 . . . 203 B8
North Halls 1 LN8 . . . . 47 C5
NORTH HARBY NG23 . . . . 79 C7
North Heath La NG32 . . . . . 106 D1
North Holme
19 Tetney DN36 . . . . 36 D4
8 Tetney DN36 . . . . 36 D4
North Holme Rd LN11 . . . . 198 B7
NORTH HYKEHAM LN6 . . . . . 204 D2
North Ing Dro PE11 . . . . 134 C4
Northing La LN2 . . . . 68 F5
North Ings La LN13 . . . . 77 A5
North Ings Rd DN7 . . . . 14 E5
Northings The 1 NG32 . . . . 210 B4
North Intake La DN9 . . . . 40 D8
NORTH KELSEY LN7 . . . . 32 A4
NORTH KELSEY MOOR LN7 . . . . 32 D4
North Kelsey Rd LN7 . . . . . . 33 A4
North Kesteven Ctr★ LN6 204 D1
North Kesteven Sch LN6 . . 204 D1
NORTH KILLINGHOLME DN40 . . . . 12 D3
North Killingholme Ind Est DN40 . . . . 12 D4
NORTH KYME LN4 . . . . 109 F4
North Kyme Cty Prim Sch LN4 . . . . 109 E3
North La Coningsby LN4 . . . . 110 E8
Marshchapel DN36 . . . . 37 C2
2 Navenby/Wellingore LN5 . . . . 107 A8
Reepham LN3 . . . . 68 F1
Stainton le Vale LN8 . . . . 46 E5
Swaby LN13 . . . . 74 E4
NORTHLANDS PE22 . . . . 113 A4
Northlands Ave 3 DN15 . . . . . 9 A5
Northlands La PE22 . . . . . . 113 A4
Northlands Rd
Glentworth DN21 . . . . 54 E6
Winterton DN15 . . . . 9 A6
Northlands Rd S 10 DN15 . . . 9 A5
NORTH LEVERTON WITH HABBLESTHORPE DN22 . . . 52 B1
North Leys Rd DN22 . . . . 52 E1
North Lincoln Rd DN16 . . . 183 F2
North Lincolnshire Mus★ DN15 . . . . 183 A2
North Lincolnshire Shopping Pk DN15 . . . . 182 B3
North Lindsey Coll DN17 . . 184 E8
North Marsh Rd DN21 . . . . 197 C6
Northminster PE1 . . . . 226 A3
North Moor Dr 2 DN10 . . . . 39 F3
North Moor La Martin LN4 . . 96 B3
Messingham DN17 . . . . 29 B8
Northmoor Rd DN17 . . . . 6 C1
North Moor Rd
Scotter DN17 . . . . 29 C5
Walkeringham DN10 . . . . 39 F3
North Moss La DN41 . . . . . . 187 B1
Northolme
Gainsborough DN21 . . . . 197 D5
Sutton St Edmund PE12 . . . . 168 E5
Northolme Circ 2 HU13 . . . 178 E2
Northolme Cres
Kingston upon Hull HU13 . . . 178 E2
Scunthorpe DN15 . . . . 182 F3
Northolme Ct LN11 . . . . 198 C7
Northolme Rd HU13 . . . . . . 178 E2
Northon's La PE12 . . . . 215 C3
NORTH ORMSBY LN11 . . . . . . 48 E4
NORTHORPE
Donington PE20 . . . . 134 E3
Northorpe DN21 . . . . 42 A8
Thurlby PE10 . . . . 164 C8
Northorpe Cl LN6 . . . . 204 F7
Northorpe La PE10 . . . . 164 C8
Northorpe Rd
Donington PE11 . . . . 134 D3
Halton Holegate PE23 . . . . . 101 B8
Scotton DN21 . . . . 29 D1
NORTH OWERSBY LN8 . . . . . . 44 E5
North Parade
Gainsborough DN21 . . . . 197 F4
Grantham NG31 . . . . 211 A6
Holbeach PE12 . . . . 215 E3
Lincoln LN1 . . . . 234 A3
Scunthorpe DN16 . . . . 185 D6
Skegness PE25 . . . . 206 D3
4 Sleaford NG34 . . . . 212 D7
North Parade Extension PE25 . . . . 206 E5
North Prom DN35 . . . . 192 E7
North Quay DN31 . . . . 189 C3
North Ramper DN21 . . . . 44 A7
NORTH RAUCEBY NG34 . . . . 120 E5
North Rd Bourne PE10 . . . . 213 D8
Bratoft PE24 . . . . 102 B8
7 Cranwell NG34 . . . . 107 F1
Gedney Hill PE12 . . . . 168 D4
1 Keadby with Althorpe DN17 . . . . 17 C6
Kingston upon Hull HU4 . . . . 179 E4
Leadenham LN5 . . . . 106 D3
Mablethorpe & Sutton LN12 . . 64 B1
Sleaford NG34 . . . . 212 C5
Sturton le Steeple DN22 . . . . . 52 B4
Tattershall Thorpe LN4 . . . . . . 97 F3
Tetford LN9 . . . . 73 F1
Tydd St Mary PE13 . . . . 160 B2
NORTH RESTON LN11 . . . . 62 B2
North Road LN11 . . . . 60 B3
North Scaffold La NG23 . . . . 91 D3
NORTH SCARLE LN6 . . . . 78 F2
North Scarle Miniature Railway★ LN6 . . . . 78 F1
North Scarle Prim Sch LN6 78 E2
North Scarle Rd NG23 . . . . . 91 F8
North Sea La DN35 . . . . 193 A1
North Shore Rd PE25 . . . . . 206 D6
Northside 2 DN9 . . . . 27 C2
Northside La 2 DN22 . . . . . . 52 C1
North's La DN37 . . . . 34 D8
NORTH SOMERCOTES LN11 . . . . 50 F8
North Somercotes CE (Controlled) Prim Sch LN11 . . . . 50 F7
North St
1 Barrow upon Humber DN19 . . . . 11 D8
2 Boston PE21 . . . . 208 F6
Bourne PE10 . . . . 213 D5
Caistor LN7 . . . . 33 B4
Cleethorpes DN35 . . . . 192 F6

North St *continued*
3 Crowland PE6 166 E1
9 Crowle DN17 16 D8
Digby LN4 108 E6
Folksworth PE7 233 A1
Gainsborough DN21 197 C5
7 Grantham NG31 211 A5
Horncastle LN9 199 C4
Kingston upon Hull HU10 178 E6
Middle Rasen LN8 57 B8
Morton DN21 197 C8
8 Nettleham LN2 68 C2
Osbournby NG34 132 C5
Owston Ferry DN9 28 B3
Peterborough PE1 226 A2
Roxby cum Risby DN15 9 A4
Scunthorpe DN15 183 B4
Stamford PE9 219 B5
Sturton le Steeple DN22 52 B3
Thimbleby LN9 85 B5
West Butterwick DN17 17 D1
West/East Butterwick DN17 28 D8
Winterton DN15 9 B6
North Terr PE1 226 E7
NORTH THORESBY DN36 36 B1
North Thoresby Prim Sch DN36 36 A1
North Thoresby Sta DN36 36 C1
Northumberland Ave
13 Scampton Airfield LN1 67 E5
6 Stamford PE9 219 A6
Northumberland Cl DN34 191 B6
Northumbria Rd NG34 212 B2
North Walls HU1 181 A6
North Warren Rd DN21 197 B6
Northway 3 LN11 49 B8
North Way
6 Lincoln LN6 204 D2
Marshchapel DN36 37 B2
NORTH WILLINGHAM LN8 58 D7
NORTH WITHAM NG33 151 D4
North Witham Bank LN1 234 A2
North Witham Rd NG33 151 D3
Northwood Dr
Hessle HU13 178 B3
Sleaford NG34 212 C6
NORTON DISNEY LN6 92 C2
Norton Disney Rd LN5 92 D1
Norton Gr HU4 179 D4
Norton La Bishop Norton LN8 43 C2
Thurlby LN6 92 C4
Norton Rd
Peterborough PE1 225 F6
Scunthorpe DN16 185 B5
Stapleford LN6 105 C8
Norton St NG31 211 A3
Norwell La NG23 91 E1
Norwich Ave DN34 191 A4
Norwich Cl
Heighington/Washingborough LN4 203 E1
3 Sleaford NG34 212 C7
Norwich Dr LN4 81 A2
Norwich Rd PE13 170 E1
Norwich Way 7 NG31 210 E5
Norwood Ave DN15 182 F2
Norwood Cl 3 HU10 178 E7
Norwood La
Borough Fen PE6 174 E1
Peterborough PE4 221 F2
Norwood Prim Sch PE4 221 C3
Norwood Rd
7 Hatfield DN7 14 C5
4 Skegness PE25 103 E4
Norwood St HU3 180 C7
Norwood Yd Cl LN4 96 C1
Nostell Rd DN16 183 D1
Nottingham Rd 1 NG13 128 A5
Nottingham Terr 5 LN2 234 C3
Nottingham Way PE1 226 C6
Novello Garth HU4 179 B4
Nowells La 6 PE10 213 D5
Nuffield Cl 6 DN16 185 B4
Nunburnholme Ave 5 HU14 3 A4
Nunburnholme Pk HU5 179 B7
Nunnerley Pl DN37 194 F5
Nuns Cnr DN33 191 C4
Nuns Rd DN17 184 F6
NUNSTHORPE DN33 191 B4
Nunsthorpe & Bradley Pk Children's Ctr DN33 191 A4
Nunthorpe Cl 36 DN7 14 D4
Nurburgring Gdns PE10 213 B3
Nurseries The LN4 108 E7
Nursery Cl
4 Barton-upon-Humber DN18 3 F1
12 Collingham NG23 91 D4
14 Dunholme LN2 68 E6
Langworth LN3 69 B3
Peterborough PE1 226 A4
10 Saxilby LN1 66 D2
Scunthorpe DN17 184 F3
Nursery Ct 15 Brough HU15 2 C5
Sleaford NG34 212 D2
Nursery Dr PE13 170 E2
Nursery Gdns
25 Alford LN13 75 F2
6 Holton le Clay DN36 195 D2
22 Newark-on-Trent NG24 104 B2
Nursery Gr LN2 202 A6
Nursery La Belvoir NG32 138 C6
Morton DN21 40 D3
Peterborough PE1 226 D2
Nursery Rd Boston PE21 209 B2
Nursery Rd *continued*
Cranwell & Byard's Leap NG34 120 C8
Nursery St 2 LN8 57 D7
Nurses La
Skellingthorpe LN6 200 A5
4 Wymondham LE14 150 C1
Nursey Cl PE12 216 D6
Nutfields Gr 7 DN7 14 C6
Nut La PE22 114 C1
Nutwood View 4 DN16 185 D4

O

Oak Ave 13 Brough HU15 2 C6
Grimsby DN32 191 E4
Hampton Vale PE7 230 B2
5 Scawby DN20 30 F8
11 Welton/Dunholme LN2 68 E6
Oak Cl 8 Ingoldmells PE25 90 D3
Louth LN11 198 E4
14 Sudbrooke LN2 68 F2
5 Woodhall Spa LN10 97 E6
Oak Cres Boston PE21 208 E7
Bourne PE10 213 B6
Cherry Willingham/Reepham LN3 203 D5
Oak Ct Lincoln LN6 205 A5
1 Spalding PE11 214 E3
Oakdale Ave
3 Kingston upon Hull HU10 178 E8
Peterborough PE2 231 D4
Oakdale Cl 4 NG31 211 A8
Oakdale Prim Sch PE7 231 C4
Oakdene Ave 19 LN4 81 A1
Oak Dr
Barton-upon-Humber DN18 10 F8
Kingston upon Hull HU5 179 B7
44 Messingham DN17 29 D7
Oak Farm Paddock LN6 204 C1
Oakfield 16 LN1 66 D2
Oakfield Cl 2 DN20 196 E3
Oakfield Prim Sch DN16 185 A5
Oakfield Rd
26 Balderton NG24 104 C1
Skellingthorpe LN6 200 B5
Oakfield St LN2 202 B3
Oakford Cl DN17 184 D8
Oak Gr
13 Barnetby le Wold DN38 21 B4
3 Barrow upon Humber DN19 11 C7
6 Market Deeping PE6 217 B6
Oakham Ave 5 LN12 64 A3
Oakham Cl NG31 210 E6
Oakham Terr 2 PE21 208 F3
Oakham Wlk DN40 186 E3
Oak Hill LN4 203 B2
Oak House La PE22 126 C4
Oakhurst Cl NG31 211 D2
Oakland Ave 39 DN7 14 D4
Oakland Cl 3 LN1 201 D7
Oaklands
3 Beckingham DN10 40 A1
8 Collingham NG23 91 D4
Eastfield PE1 226 B4
5 Woodhall Spa LN10 97 D5
Oaklands Dr
Kingston upon Hull HU13 178 D3
4 Wisbech PE13 170 E1
Oaklands Pk LN10 98 A7
Oaklands Rd DN40 186 C5
Oaklands The
1 Branston LN4 81 E2
6 Wragby LN8 70 D4
Oakland Way 13 PE11 145 C1
Oakleaf Rd PE1 226 C6
Oakleigh DN16 185 C3
Oakleigh Dr Canwick LN1 201 C6
Peterborough PE2 230 C6
Oakleigh Rd NG31 210 C3
Oakleigh Terr LN1 201 C6
Oakley Dr PE11 214 E6
Oakley Pl PE12 147 F2
Oak Rd Glinton PE6 220 B8
1 Healing DN41 24 A5
Scunthorpe DN16 185 B7
Sleaford NG34 212 D2
Stamford PE9 218 D7
Oakroyd Cres 22 PE13 170 D1
Oakside Pk Ind Est NG34 212 F6
Oaks La DN10 39 F2
Oak Sq 9 PE6 175 C8
Oaks The Balderton NG24 104 C2
15 Nettleham LN2 68 D2
1 Scothern LN2 68 F3
Oak Tree Ave DN21 197 F6
Oaktree Cl 3 PE11 145 B7
Oak Tree Cl
3 Long Bennington NG23 117 D3
7 Market Rasen LN8 57 D7
Oak Tree Dr LN6 92 D4
Oak Tree Mdw LN9 199 C5
Oak Tree Wlk 25 DN17 16 D7
Oak View 13 Dunholme LN2 68 E6
Peterborough PE3 224 F2
Oak Way Cleethorpes DN35 192 D2
3 Heckington NG34 122 D3
Oakwell Cl DN16 185 D4
Oakwood Ave 4 LN6 204 C8
Oakwood Cl HU10 179 A7
Oakwood Dr DN37 190 C7
Oakwood Glade PE12 215 C3
Oakwood Pk PE12 146 E2
Oakwood Rise 2 DN16 185 B4
OASBY NG32 131 C6
Oasby Rd NG32 131 C7
Oasis Academy DN40 186 C4
Oasis Acad Nunsthorpe DN33 191 B4
Oasis Acad Parkwood DN17 184 D8
Oasis Acad Wintringham DN32 191 E4
Oat Dr NG34 212 E3
Oatfield Way NG34 122 D2
Oban Cl 7 PE9 218 E6
Oban Ct 6 DN40 186 C3
Oberon Cl LN1 201 C6
OBTHORPE PE10 164 C6
Obthorpe La PE10 164 C7
Occupation La
Anderby PE24 77 C3
Carrington PE22 99 C1
6 North Kelsey LN7 32 A4
Swanland HU14 3 B8
Occupation Rd
Great Gonerby NG32 129 C6
Lincoln LN1 234 A4
Peterborough PE1 225 E6
Occupation Road LN11 49 C8
Ocean Ave PE25 206 D1
Ocean Bvd HU9 181 B6
Octagon Dr 14 PE13 170 C1
Octavia Cl 23 PE13 170 E1
Octavian Cres 14 LN6 93 A8
Odecroft PE3 225 C7
Odin Ct DN33 191 B2
Off Haydons Ave PE25 206 A4
Ogilvy Dr DN17 184 F3
Ogrey PE10 164 C7
O'Hanlon Ave DN20 196 D3
Old Annandale Rd HU10 178 C8
Old Bailey Rd PE7 233 C8
Old Bakery Yd 12 PE25 206 A6
Old Barn Ct
Fleet Hargate PE12 159 C8
Ludford LN8 59 A7
Old Barn La DN15 9 A4
Old Barracks The NG31 211 C4
Old Black Dro NG34 109 D1
OLD BOLINGBROKE PE23 100 B8
Old Boston Rd LN4 207 D3
Old Bowling Gn 4 LN13 75 F2
Old Brewery La PE12 216 D4
Old Brickkiln La LN5 92 F2
Oldbrook PE3 220 E1
Old Brumby St DN16 185 A8
Old Carpenter's Yd 1 DN7 14 B6
Old Chapel Ct 2 DN21 43 D7
Old Chapel La
2 Burgh le Marsh PE24 102 E7
9 Laceby DN37 23 F1
Old Chapel Rd LN6 200 A4
Old Church La 1 PE23 101 D7
Old Church Rd PE24 90 D4
OLD CLEE DN32 192 C6
Old Clee Prim Sch DN32 192 B6
Old Cobham Orch 15 NG24 104 A3
Old Courts Rd 2 DN20 196 C3
Old Crosby DN15 183 A5
Old Ctyd The 1 DN21 65 D6
Old Dairy 11 DN19 11 D8
Old Dairy Cl 32 DN8 15 A8
Old Dairy Rd 6 LN8 57 E8
Old Dairy The PE21 209 A1
Olde Curiosity Mus★ LN12 64 C3
Olde Farm Ct LN7 32 A1
Old Epworth Rd (East) 1 DN7 14 F4
Old Farm Ct 4 DN37 194 C4
Old Fen Bank
Wainfleet All Saints PE24 101 F2
Wainfleet St Mary PE24 102 A1
Old Fen Dike Gedney PE12 158 F1
Sutton St James PE12 169 B8
Old Fendike Rd PE12 157 B3
Old Fen La Coningsby LN4 207 E1
Pinchbeck PE11 145 A1
Old Fen Rd PE22 115 A8
Oldfield Cl
9 Barnby Dun DN3 14 A4
1 Stainforth DN7 14 B6
Oldfield Cres 16 DN7 14 C6
Oldfield La PE22 127 C6
Old Field La DN7 14 A5
Oldfield Rd 20 DN8 15 B7
Old Fleet DN37 190 C6
OLD FLETTON PE2 231 A6
Old Fletton Prim Sch PE2 230 F6
Old Forge Cl 17 DN10 39 F5
Old Forge Rd 7 DN10 39 F5
Old Forty Foot Bank NG34 123 C1
OLD GATE PE12 159 F3
Old Grammar School Wy 8 LN8 70 D5
Old Great N Rd
Stamford PE9 218 C8
Thorney PE8 228 B7
Wansford PE8 222 C2
Old Haddington La LN6 92 F6
Old Hall Dr HU10 178 C8
Old Hall Gdns 5 NG24 104 C5
Old Hall La 6 PE11 145 D2
Old Hall Spinney NG32 119 C2
Oldham Dr 8 PE11 145 C1
Old Hammond Beck Rd PE21 208 A2
Old Haxey Rd DN10 39 F6
Old Hill The NG32 138 C6
Old Hundred La PE12 167 F2
Old Immingham Road DN41 23 D6
Old Inn La PE12 146 E7
Old Ironside Rd DN16 183 D3
Old Iron Way PE21 209 C5
Old Knarr Fen Dro PE6 176 C2
Oldlane Gate DN14 6 F7
Old La DN14 6 D4
OLD LEAKE PE22 114 A1
Old Leake Prim Sch PE22 114 A1
Old Leicester Rd PE8 222 A3
Old Leys La DN21 43 A3
Old Lincoln Rd
Caythorpe NG32 119 B7
Wragby LN8 70 C5
Old Lynn Rd 2 PE13 170 E1
Old Main Rd
2 Barnetby le Beck DN37 35 B6
East Heckington PE20 122 E2
Fleet Hargate PE12 159 C7
Fosdyke PE20 146 D8
Irby DN37 34 D7
Old Leake PE22 114 B1
Scamblesby LN11 72 F5
Old Manor Dr 13 DN20 30 E8
Old Mill Cres NG24 104 A4
Old Mill Dro PE7 233 D2
Old Mill La
10 Broughton DN20 19 E3
Grimoldby LN11 62 B6
Horncastle LN9 199 C3
Whitton DN15 1 E3
Wrawby DN20 196 F7
Old Mill Pk LN11 198 C6
Old Mkt Ave PE23 100 F8
Old Mkt Pl DN31 191 D7
Old Nick Theatre DN21 197 D4
Old N Rd PE8 222 A3
Old Oak Pl PE10 213 E4
Old Orch NG32 210 A5
Old Paddock Ct
1 Horncastle LN9 199 B4
New Waltham DN36 195 F6
Old Pl 3 NG34 212 F4
Old Plumtree La 3 DN36 36 B1
Old Pond Cl 7 LN6 200 D1
Old Pond La PE5 223 E2
Old Pond Pl 20 HU14 3 A4
Old Post La NG33 151 D6
Old Post Office La
8 Barnetby le Wold DN38 21 B4
Butterwick PE22 126 E4
4 South Ferriby DN18 10 A7
Old Priory Farm 6 PE6 217 F4
Old Quarry The 8 DN38 32 E7
Old Rd Grimsby DN37 190 C8
Healing DN37 24 B5
Old Rectory Dr
1 Tallington PE9 172 F7
Wansford PE8 222 A6
Old Rectory Gdns DN16 185 A6
Old Rectory The★ DN9 27 E6
Old Roman Bank
3 Skegness PE25 206 D6
Terrington St Clement PE34 161 E3
Old Sch Dr 14 DN20 30 F5
Old Sch La
4 Billinghay LN4 109 F6
6 Cranwell NG34 120 F8
Donington on Bain LN11 59 E2
4 Fishtoft PE21 126 C1
2 North Kelsey LN7 32 A4
Scunthorpe DN16 185 B3
Old Sch Mews 12 PE23 88 A1
Old School Cl Brigg DN20 196 C4
Thurlby PE10 164 C7
Old School La 26 NG24 104 A4
Old School Rd PE22 99 E7
Old Sch Yd 17 DN21 30 B1
Old S Eau Bank PE12 168 A1
Old Showfields DN21 197 D6
Old Sluice Rd PE12 215 B8
Old Smithy Ct 1 LN4 207 D4
Old Smithy & Heritage Ctr The★ DN9 23 B3
OLD SOMERBY NG33 140 D8
Old Stack Yd La DN21 41 E3
Old Stack Yd The
Fenton LN1 65 E3
3 Wrawby DN20 196 F6
Old Sta Yd Bottesford NG13 128 B6
Morton PE10 154 D6
Old Thorne Rd DN7 14 E4
Old Train Yd The PE10 213 D4
Old Trent Rd DN21 197 A5
Old Upper Ings La DN22 52 D3
Old Vicarage Dr 5 DN15 9 D1
Old Vicarage La
12 Lutton PE12 160 A8
Lutton PE12 216 C8
Old Vicarage Pk 2 DN20 30 E8
Old Village St DN15 17 E6
Old Wainfleet Rd 1 PE25 206 B3
Old Warp La 11 DN18 10 A7
Old Wharf Ind Est NG31 210 F3
Old Wharf Rd 9 NG31 211 A4
Old Wood 1 LN6 200 C1
Old Wood Cl LN6 200 C1
OLD WOODHALL LN9 85 A2
Old Woodhall Road LN9 84 F2
Oliver Cl 5 NG24 104 A4
Oliver Ct DN31 191 D8
Olive Rd PE1 226 C7
Oliver Rd
Hampton Vale PE7 230 B1
16 Long Bennington NG23 117 D3
Oliver St DN35 192 D8
Olivier Ct HU4 179 E3
Ollard Ave PE13 170 D1
Olsen Rise LN2 202 D6
Omega Bvd DN8 14 F8
On Hill 17 HU14 3 B7
Onslow St HU10 178 F5
Ontario Rd DN17 184 E3
Onyx Gr 2 HU3 180 A4
Oole Rd DN35 192 F6
Oosterbeek Cl 5 PE10 213 E7
Opportune Rd 25 PE13 170 D1
Orangawood Cl 7 NG31 210 F8
Orangeleaf Way DN18 4 A1
ORANGE ROW PE34 161 F3
Orange Row 3 PE34 161 F3
Orange Row Rd 1 PE34 161 F3
Orb La DN15 183 A7
ORBY PE24 89 C2
Orby Bank PE24 89 D3
Orby Gr DN33 191 A3
Orby Holme Field La PE24 89 D3
Orby Rd Addlethorpe PE24 90 B4
Burgh le Marsh PE24 89 D1
Orchard Ave 8 DN21 29 C3
Orchard Cl
4 Barrow upon Humber DN19 11 C7
23 Barton-upon-Humber DN18 10 F8
Bassingham LN5 92 F3
Billinghay LN4 109 E6
11 Birchwood LN6 204 B8
4 Blyton DN21 41 C5
4 Bourne PE10 213 C6
6 Burringham DN17 17 D4
9 Burton upon Stather DN15 8 B5
Cherry Willingham/Reepham LN3 203 D5
11 Donington PE11 134 F2
4 Gonerby Hill Foot NG31 210 E8
Great Hale NG34 122 E1
2 Hatfield DN7 14 C3
6 Helpringham NG34 133 D7
3 Kingston upon Hull HU10 178 F7
1 Kirton in Lindsey DN21 30 B2
Leverington PE13 170 B2
Louth LN11 198 C7
2 Mablethorpe/Sutton on Sea LN12 64 A3
4 Market Deeping PE6 217 D4
12 Messingham DN17 29 D7
25 Metheringham LN4 95 C4
2 Morton PE10 154 C7
4 Moulton PE12 157 F6
Newton on Trent LN1 65 D1
Peterborough PE3 225 D3
9 Pinchbeck PE11 156 E8
8 Scothern LN2 68 F4
5 Scunthorpe DN16 185 B6
2 Sleaford NG34 212 F4
15 Stamford PE9 219 B5
7 Welton/Dunholme LN2 68 D6
Whaplode PE12 215 A7
Orchard Croft
4 Epworth DN9 27 D7
5 Grimsby DN33 194 E7
Orchard Ct 3 Thorney PE6 175 F3
Waltham DN37 194 D4
Orchard Dr
7 Burton upon Stather DN15 8 B5
3 Gunness DN15 17 E6
3 Hatfield DN7 14 C3
12 Heckington NG34 122 E2
Kingston upon Hull HU13 178 E1
2 Rampton DN22 65 A5
Walton Highway PE14 170 F4
Winteringham DN15 2 B1
Orchard Garth 16 LN5 93 E8
Orchard Gdns 4 PE13 170 A1
Orchard Gr Boston PE21 209 B6
1 Hatfield DN7 14 D5
Maxey PE6 173 C7
Misterton DN10 40 A4
Orchard La 12 LN1 66 D2
Orchard Mews PE2 230 F8
Orchard Pk
20 Coddington NG24 104 C5
4 Manby LN11 62 C6
Orchard Rd Barnack PE9 172 E3
5 Fiskerton LN3 82 A7
Kingston upon Hull HU4 179 B5
4 Stamford PE9 219 B5
Orchards CE Prim Sch PE14 170 D2
Orchard St Boston PE21 208 D6
Lincoln LN1 234 A2
Peterborough PE2 230 F7
2 Spalding PE11 214 D3
22 Thorne/Moorends DN8 15 A8
Orchards The
Harrowby Est NG31 211 C6
Immingham DN40 186 B3
8 Middle Rasen LN8 57 B8
Peterborough PE2 229 F4
Orchard The Etton PE6 173 E5
Market Deeping PE6 217 B5
New Waltham DN36 195 C6
Peterborough PE4 221 A3
Washingborough LN4 203 A2
Orchard Way
4 Coningsby LN4 207 C4
5 Cowbit PE12 167 B8
Easton on the Hill PE9 171 C3
1 Mablethorpe/Sutton on Sea LN12 64 A3
3 Market Rasen LN8 57 E8
6 Nettleham LN2 68 D2
Orchard Wy 19 NG24 104 B2

Orchid Cl
17 Newark-on-Trent NG24 104 A3
Yaxley PE7 233 F7
Orchid Rd LN5 205 C2
Orchid Rise DN15 182 F2
Orchid Way PE25 206 A4
Ordoyno Gr 2 NG24 104 C5
Ore Blending Rd DN16 19 A4
Orfeus Dr PE2 231 F4
Orford Ms DN33 191 B1
Orford Rd LN8 47 B5
Oribi Cl HU4 179 C2
Origin Wy DN37 24 B6
Oriole Rd DN17 184 E6
Orion Cl 8 HU3 180 B5
Orion Way 4 DN34 190 D4
Orkney Pl DN40 186 C2
Orme La LN11 198 C6
Orme Rd PE3 225 D4
Ormiston Bushfield Acad PE2 229 E3
Ormiston Maritime Acad DN34 191 B5
Ormiston Meadows Acad PE2 229 E5
Ormiston South Parade Acad DN31 191 D8
Ormonde Cl NG31 211 A3
Ormsby Cl DN35 192 D3
Ormsby House Dr 7 PE22 99 A4
Ormsby Rd
Scunthorpe DN17 184 E5
South Ormsby LN9 74 D1
Ormsby Ring LN11 74 C1
Orton Ave PE2 230 E7
Orton Brick Works PE7 233 B8
ORTON BRIMBLES PE2 229 D5
Ortongate Sh Ctr PE2 229 E3
ORTON GOLDHAY PE2 229 F3
ORTON LONGUEVILLE PE2 230 B5
ORTON MALBOURNE PE2 230 C4
Orton Mere PE2 230 B7
Orton Parkway PE2 229 D4
ORTON SOUTHGATE PE2 229 C2
ORTON WATERVILLE PE2 229 E4
ORTON WISTOW PE2 229 C6
Orton Wistow Prim Sch PE2 229 C6
Orwell Dr 4 PE11 214 A1
Orwell Gr PE4 221 D1
Orwell St DN31 189 C1
Osborne Cl 3 LN1 201 E6
Osborne Dr DN36 195 D1
Osborne Pk 1 PE13 170 C2
Osborne Rd
Immingham DN41 187 B2
Wisbech PE13 170 C2
Osborne St
1 Cleethorpes DN35 192 F6
Grimsby DN31 191 D7
Kingston upon Hull HU1 180 E6
Osborne Way LN9 199 A4
Osborn Way 9 NG34 122 D3
OSBOURNBY NG34 132 C4
Osbournby Prim Sch NG34 132 C5
Osbourne Cl PE4 221 D1
Osbourne Way 7 PE6 217 A5
Ose 3 PE25 206 B6
Oseby La NG34 133 A1
OSGODBY
Lenton Keisby and Osgodby NG33 141 E3
Osgodby LN8 45 A3
Osgodby Prim Sch LN8 45 A3
Osgodby Rd LN8 44 E5
Osier Ave PE7 230 D2
Osier Rd PE11 214 E5
Oslear Cres DN35 192 E5
Oslear's La LN11 73 D5
Oslinc Ostrich Farm★ PE22 99 B7
Osprey PE2 229 F2
Osprey Cl 5 NG34 212 B3
Osprey Dr Healing DN37 24 B5
Scunthorpe DN16 185 F5
Osric Ct PE1 226 C5
Oster Fen La NG23 104 F1
Ostler Cl 8 NG31 210 F8
Ostler Dr PE10 213 B4
Ostler's La DN18 10 A5
Oswald Rd
Scunthorpe DN15 183 A3
1 Woodston PE2 230 D7
Oswin Cl 1 NG34 212 C2
OTBY LN8 46 A4
Otby La LN8 46 A3
Ottawa Rd DN17 184 E4
Otter Ave 11 LN1 66 D2
Otterbrook PE2 229 D5
Otterburn St 6 HU3 180 A5
Otters Cotts LN5 205 D7
Oulton Cl LN6 205 A2
Oundle Cl
Heighington/Washingborough LN4 203 C1
Scunthorpe DN16 185 C3
Oundle Rd
5 Mablethorpe/Sutton on Sea LN12 64 C1
Peterborough PE2 229 E6
Our Lady of Lincoln Cath Prim Sch LN2 202 A7
Ousemere Cl 14 NG34 133 B1
Outer Circ Dr LN2 202 C7
Outer Circ Gn LN2 202 C6
Outer Circ Ind Est LN2 202 D5
Outer Circ Rd LN2 202 D5
Outfield PE3 220 E1
Outfield La PE24 101 F7
Outgang La DN22 65 A6
Outgang The
Brantingham HU15 2 B7
Brantingham HU15 2 C8
Outgate Crowle DN17 16 E7
Leverton Outgate PE22 127 B6
Out Holme La DN36 36 E3
Outwood Acad Brumby DN16 185 B8
Oval App LN2 202 B7
Oval The 5 Brough HU15 2 C5
Grimsby DN33 191 C1
5 Hatfield DN7 14 C5
Kingston upon Hull HU10 178 E8
Lincoln LN2 202 B7
Scopwick LN4 108 B7
2 Scunthorpe DN17 184 E3
Overcoat La DN22 65 B7
Overgate Rd NG33 152 D5
Overstone Ct PE3 225 D6
Overton Ave HU10 178 E8
Overton Cl 4 LN5 107 B8
Overton Ct 9 DN18 3 E1
Overton Rd LN4 207 D4
Overton Way PE2 229 F4
Owen Ave HU13 179 A1
Owen Cl 7 PE9 172 D3
Owe's La LN11 51 A5
Owl Cl LN6 92 D5
Owl Dr PE20 135 B7
Owl End PE7 233 D5
Owl End Wlk PE7 233 D5
OWMBY DN38 32 D7
OWMBY-BY-SPITAL LN8 55 F6
Owmby Cliff Rd LN8 55 C5
Owmby Hill DN38 32 D8
Owmby La LN7 32 C5
Owmby Rd
4 Searby cum Owmby DN38 32 D8
Spridlington LN8 55 F3
Owmby Wold La DN38 21 E1
OWSTON FERRY DN9 28 B3
Owston Ferry Rd DN9 27 F1
Owston Rd DN10 40 B6
Oxburgh Cl
3 Peterborough PE7 231 F5
1 Wisbech PE13 170 C1
Oxby Cl 17 NG34 122 E2
Oxclose PE3 225 A8
OXCOMBE LN9 73 D4
Oxcombe Cl DN33 194 D7
Oxcroft Bank Moulton PE12 157 F1
Whaplode PE12 158 A2
Oxeney Dr 2 LN3 69 C3
Oxfield Dr PE13 169 F3
Oxford Cl LN4 203 C1
Oxford Ct 1 NG34 212 D7
Oxford Gdns PE12 215 D1
Oxford Rd
Peterborough PE1 225 F5
6 Stamford PE9 219 A7
Oxford St Boston PE21 208 F3
Cleethorpes DN35 192 F5
Grantham NG31 211 B3
Grimsby DN32 189 B1
Kingston upon Hull HU2 181 A8
2 Lincoln LN5 234 B1
Market Rasen LN8 57 D8
Scunthorpe DN16 185 D6
Oxlands La PE24 102 B7
Oxmarsh La DN19 4 E2
Ox Moor Pasture Rd DN17 7 B1
Oxney Rd PE1 226 D5
Oxney Rd Ind Est PE1 227 A6
Ox Pasture La DN17 7 C2
Ox Pasture Lane LN9 85 B2
Oyster Ct DN35 192 F5

P

Pacey Cl LN6 92 A6
Pach Wy 30 NG24 104 C1
Packhorse Gdns PE20 135 B6
Packman La HU10 178 B8
Paddington Way PE10 154 D7
Paddock Cl
6 Ancaster NG32 120 A2
13 Bracebridge Heath Ln4 81 A1
Ropsley NG33 131 B1
Paddock Ct 5 DN40 186 C3
Paddock Gn 3 PE11 214 D5
Paddock Gr 6 PE21 208 F4
Paddock La 5 Blyton DN21 41 C5
1 Metheringham LN4 95 D4
West Butterwick DN17 17 C1
Paddock Lane DN9 28 A7
Paddock Rd NG34 120 C8
Paddock Rise
11 Barrow upon Humber DN19 11 C8
Ingoldsby NG33 141 C5
Paddocks The
1 Barnetby le Beck DN37 35 B6
25 Beacon Hill NG24 104 A4
5 Beckingham DN10 40 A1
6 Bottesford NG13 128 A5
7 Burgh le Marsh PE24 102 E7
Canwick LN4 81 A4
Carlton Scroop NG32 119 C3
12 Crowle DN17 16 D7
Gedney PE12 159 E7
Great Hale NG34 122 E1
Paddocks The *continued*
1 Holbeach PE12 215 E3
Kingston upon Hull HU10 178 B7
10 Long Bennington NG23 117 D4
Newton on Trent LN1 65 C1
2 Peterborough PE4 220 E5
Stapleford LN6 105 C8
Swayfield NG33 152 E5
Tinwell PE9 218 D3
12 Wainfleet All Saints PE24 102 D1
4 Willingham DN21 53 E3
Paddock The
8 Allington NG32 128 F7
3 Barkston NG32 130 B8
2 Burton upon Stather DN15 8 B4
4 Cherry Willingham LN3 203 E6
10 Collingham NG23 91 D4
Kingston upon Hull HU4 179 B5
Louth LN11 198 A5
Manby LN11 62 C5
1 Market Deeping PE6 217 A6
2 Marton DN21 65 D8
4 Morton PE10 154 C7
2 North Ferriby HU14 3 A5
7 Owmby LN8 55 F6
16 Ruskington NG34 108 D2
Skellingthorpe LN6 200 A4
Sleaford NG34 212 C4
5 Sleaford NG34 212 F4
5 Stamford PE9 219 A5
16 Sudbrooke LN2 68 F2
3 Swanland HU14 3 C7
Paddock View PE22 100 B2
Paddock Vw DN36 36 C4
Paddock Wy 4 DN7 14 F4
Pademoor Terr DN17 7 A2
Padholme Rd PE1 226 C3
Padholme Rd E PE1 226 D3
Padley Rd LN2 202 E6
Padleys La PE23 100 C4
Padmoor La DN21 53 C5
Padmore Pl 8 PE6 164 E4
Pado La LN13 74 E4
Padstow Wlk DN17 184 C8
Pagehall Cl DN33 191 D1
Paignton Ct DN33 194 E6
Pailing's Ride NG24 104 F7
Pain La PE22 113 E3
Painshall Cl 11 LN2 68 D7
Painters Way 20 LN12 76 F8
Paisley Prim Sch HU3 180 A6
Paisley St HU3 180 A7
Palace Theatre★ NG24 104 A4
Palgrave Way PE11 214 D8
Palma Ct 2 PE24 90 D7
Palm Ct PE1 226 B8
Palmer Ave HU10 178 D8
Palmer Ct 3 NG34 212 B6
Palmer La 15 DN19 11 D8
Palmer Rd
Great Gonerby NG32 129 C6
Lincoln LN2 202 A6
Palmers Rd PE1 226 F5
Palmerston Rd PE2 230 F7
Palm Rd LN5 205 C1
Palmwood Cl 3 NG31 210 F7
Pamela Cl DN40 186 D4
Pamela Rd DN40 186 D4
Pandora Dr PE7 231 C4
Pandyke La PE22 113 F3
Pannel Ct PE6 164 E5
PANTON LN8 71 B5
Panton Cl 6 PE6 217 D5
Panton Rd East Barkwith LN8 71 B8
Hatton LN8 71 B4
Papermill La
Ewerby & Evedon NG34 121 E7
Tealby LN8 46 D2
Pape's La PE24 101 F4
Papyrus Rd PE4 220 D3
Parade The LN3 203 E6
Paradise La 5 Fulletby LN9 86 B8
Northborough PE6 173 F6
Paradise Pl 6 Brigg DN20 196 B3
Horncastle LN9 199 C3
Paradise Row LN9 199 C4
Paragon St HU1 180 E6
Parish Church Prim Sch DN21 197 C5
Parishes Sh Ctr The DN15 183 B3
Parish Mews 3 DN21 197 D5
Parish's La PE22 115 A4
Park Acad PE21 208 E6
Park Ave Allington NG32 128 F7
15 Barton-upon-Humber DN18 10 E8
Billinghay LN4 109 F5
17 Crowle DN17 16 D7
Grimsby DN32 191 E4
Heighington/Washingborough LN4 203 D2
Kingston upon Hull HU13 178 E3
Lincoln LN6 204 F7
Louth LN11 198 E6
21 Mablethorpe/Sutton on Sea LN12 64 B3
Misterton DN10 39 E6
Scunthorpe DN17 184 F3
Skegness PE25 206 D4
Sleaford NG34 212 F4
Spalding PE11 214 C5
3 Spilsby PE23 87 F1
Sutterton PE20 136 A2
Park Cl 1 Gosberton PE11 145 B6
Immingham DN40 186 C4
Lea DN21 52 F5
Spalding PE11 214 C5
Park Cl *continued*
8 Sudbrooke LN2 68 F2
Thorney PE6 176 B3
7 Westwoodside DN9 27 A2
Yaxley PE7 233 F5
Park Cres
Heighington/Washingborough LN4 203 D1
16 Metheringham LN4 95 D4
Newark-on-Trent NG24 104 A6
Peterborough PE1 226 B5
Sleaford NG34 212 F4
Swinderby LN6 92 B6
Thorne/Moorends DN8 15 A7
Thorney PE6 176 B3
Park Ct Scunthorpe DN15 183 B4
2 Weston PE12 157 E7
Parkdale 44 DN18 10 E8
Park Dr Grimsby DN32 191 E5
Market Deeping PE6 217 A5
6 Westwoodside DN9 27 A2
Parker Ave LN5 205 D4
Parker Cl Laceby DN37 23 E2
Stamford PE9 218 E7
Parker Rd Humberston DN36 36 D8
23 Wittering PE8 172 B1
Parkers Cl 12 PE24 102 E7
Parkers La DN16 185 C6
Parker St
16 Beacon Hill NG24 104 A4
Cleethorpes DN35 192 F5
Parkes Cl 4 NG24 104 D5
Park Est PE6 217 E4
Park Farm Cres PE7 231 F5
Park Farm Rd
Peterborough PE6 224 E5
Scunthorpe DN15 182 F7
Park Farm Way PE7 231 F6
Parkfield Ave 14 HU14 3 A4
Parkfield Dr East Ella HU3 179 F7
Kingston upon Hull HU3 179 F6
Parkfield Rd
7 Ruskington NG34 108 E2
13 Ryhall PE9 163 C1
Park Gate 7 PE21 208 F5
Park Gdns PE12 215 E3
Park Hill
Cherry Willingham/Reepham LN3 203 E5
28 Kirton in Lindsey DN21 30 B1
Parkhill Cres 3 DN3 14 A4
Parkhill Rd 2 DN3 14 A4
Parkhill Rise 7 DN15 9 B5
Park Home Ave PE7 230 D1
Park Home Rd PE7 230 D1
Parkin Rd 7 Cowbit PE12 167 B8
Scunthorpe DN17 184 F4
Parkinson Ave 1 DN15 183 A3
Parkinson's Way 5 LN12 64 C2
Park La 12 Alford LN13 75 F3
10 Billinghay LN4 109 F5
Billinghay LN4 109 F5
5 Boston PE21 208 F6
Bracebridge LN5 205 D6
Burton LN1 200 D7
Coningsby LN4 207 C4
Denton NG32 139 A7
2 Donington PE11 134 E2
East Kirkby PE23 99 E5
Ewerby & Evedon NG34 122 B7
Freiston PE22 126 D3
Gorefield PE13 169 F3
Heighington/Washingborough LN4 203 C2
Holbeach PE12 215 E3
Humberston DN35 192 F1
Leverington PE13 170 A3
Long Sutton PE12 216 C5
Manby LN11 62 C6
Peterborough PE1 226 C4
Pinchbeck PE11 145 D3
Redbourne DN21 30 F3
Saxby All Saints DN20 10 A3
1 Scawby DN20 30 F8
1 Skillington NG33 151 A8
Spalding PE11 214 C5
Stamford PE9 219 C4
2 Surfleet PE11 145 D2
Swineshead PE20 135 A7
Westwoodside DN9 27 A2
Wigsley NG23 78 F5
Park La Cl 6 DN7 14 C2
Park La E HU4 179 C6
Parklands
2 Fleet Hargate PE12 159 C7
Mablethorpe/Sutton on Sea LN12 64 B3
1 Mumby LN13 76 F1
4 West/East Butterwick DN17 28 D8
Parklands Ave
New Waltham DN36 195 E6
Nocton LN4 95 B7
Parklands Cl 4 NG24 104 C5
Parklands Cres 11 HU14 3 A5
Parklands Dr
4 Harlaxton NG32 139 C7
10 North Ferriby HU14 3 A5
Parklands Mews HU13 3 E4
Parkland Way LN8 70 C4
Park La Rd 11 DN7 14 C2
Park La W HU4 179 C5
Park-Lea 6 NG34 108 E2
Park Rd 11 Alford LN13 75 F3
1 Allington NG32 128 F7
Boston PE21 208 E2
5 Brough HU15 2 E6
Claxby LN8 45 E4
Park Rd *continued*
Grantham NG31 211 B5
Holbeach PE12 215 D2
2 Horncastle LN9 199 C4
Long Sutton PE12 216 C5
Mablethorpe/Sutton on Sea LN12 64 C1
Market Deeping PE6 217 D4
Peterborough PE1 226 A3
Spalding PE11 214 C4
Swinstead NG33 153 A5
1 Weston PE12 157 E7
5 Willingham DN21 53 E3
Park Rd E LN12 64 D1
Park Rd W LN12 64 C1
Park Road LN9 85 F1
Park Row
Kingston upon Hull HU3 180 D7
Louth LN11 198 E7
Northfield HU13 178 E2
Parks Cl 4 DN39 12 A1
Parksgate Ave LN6 204 F5
Parkside 17 Nettleham LN2 68 D2
Peterborough PE2 230 B6
Parkside Cres PE11 214 C5
Parkside Dr 13 PE24 90 D7
Parkside The 4 NG33 151 D2
Park Springs Rd DN21 197 F2
Park Sq DN15 183 A2
Parks Rd 3 DN7 14 C4
Park St Cleethorpes DN35 189 D1
Grimsby DN32 192 B8
Kingston upon Hull HU3 180 D6
Lincoln LN1 234 A2
11 Messingham DN17 29 D7
Peterborough PE2 230 F7
Swinefleet DN14 6 D8
Winterton DN15 9 B5
PARKS THE DN7 14 C4
Parkstone Gr 28 DN7 14 D4
Park Terr 2 PE1 226 A6
Park The
24 Beacon Hill NG24 104 A4
Coningsby LN4 207 D5
Lincoln LN1 234 A2
Potter Hanworth LN4 95 B8
Park View
25 Barton-upon-Humber DN18 10 F8
Cleethorpes DN35 192 C8
Crowle DN17 16 D6
Kingston upon Hull HU4 179 E4
Mablethorpe/Sutton on Sea LN12 64 C1
10 Messingham DN17 29 D7
15 Northorpe PE10 164 C8
13 Thorne/Moorends DN8 15 A7
Park View Ave LN4 81 D2
Park View Cl 7 DN19 11 C7
Park View Terr DN17 28 C8
Parkway The
Kingston upon Hull HU10 178 E8
Spalding PE11 214 A2
Park Wlk
Easton on the Hill PE9 171 D3
Kingston upon Hull HU4 179 B5
Parkwood Rise 14 DN3 14 A3
Parliament Cl 11 PE25 206 B6
Parliament St
5 Brough HU15 2 D6
7 Kingston upon Hull HU1 180 F6
Peterborough PE1 225 F5
Parnell St 3 DN21 197 C5
Parnwell Prim Sch PE1 226 F7
Parnwell Way PE1 226 F6
Parris Pl DN35 192 D7
Parry Rd 22 LN12 64 B3
Parslins The PE6 217 F5
Parsonage La PE12 159 F1
Parson Dro Billinghay LN4 109 F7
Pinchbeck PE11 144 B2
Parson Dro La PE13 170 B2
PARSON DROVE PE13 177 D7
Parson La LN5 106 C8
Parsons Dr 3 PE21 208 E7
Parson's Dro
Holland Fen with Brothertoft PE20 124 A8
Swaton NG34 133 D4
Parsons Halt 1 LN11 198 C6
Parsons La 18 LN13 75 F2
Parson's La PE12 168 B4
Parthian Ave PE21 136 D8
PARTNEY PE23 88 A3
Partney CE (Aided) Prim Sch PE23 88 B3
Partney Rd PE23 87 C4
Partridge Cl 4 Caistor LN7 33 B4
4 Scunthorpe DN17 184 E6
Yaxley PE7 233 D6
Partridge Dr LN7 33 F2
Partridge Gn LN6 92 D5
Partridge Gr PE4 220 E5
Pashley Rd DN8 15 B7
PASTON PE4 221 D1
Paston Farm Adventure Ctr★ PE4 221 E2
Paston La PE4 221 B1
Paston Parkway PE4 221 C4
Paston Ridings PE4 221 C1
Paston Ridings Prim Sch PE4 221 D1
Pasture Ave 9 DN17 17 D4
Pasture Cl
7 Colsterworth NG33 151 E7

Pasture Cl *continued*
Grantham NG31 211 D1
Pasture Dr
Hampton Vale PE7 230 B2
4 Hampton Vale PE7 230 C1
Louth LN11 198 D4
Pasture Dro PE10 154 F7
Pasture Grove 17 NG23 91 D4
Pasture La Amcotts DN17 7 D1
Bassingham LN5 93 B2
Belvoir NG32 138 C6
Garthorpe & Fockerby DN17 7 D6
Market Rasen LN8 57 E8
Northborough PE6 173 F6
Nunsthorpe DN33 191 B1
Pasture Rd DN21 197 F4
Pasture Rd N DN18 3 F1
Pasture Rd S DN18 4 A1
Pastures Ct 36 DN17 29 D7
Pastures Rd NG32 210 A5
Pasture St DN32 191 E7
Pastures The
12 Cowbit PE12 167 B8
12 Long Bennington NG23 117 D3
Old Somerby NG33 140 E8
1 Rampton DN22 65 A5
12 Welton LN2 68 D6
Pasture The PE6 217 C6
Pasture Wharf Nature Reserve* DN18 4 A2
Patchett Cl DN33 191 B2
Patch Rd LN6 92 D4
Pateley Moor Cl 13 LN6 93 C8
Patman's La PE22 114 E4
Patricks Cl 5 LN7 32 A4
Patrick St DN32 191 E5
Patriot Cl PE11 214 C4
Patten Ave 2 PE24 102 D1
Patterdale Rd
Kingston upon Hull HU5 179 E8
3 Peterborough PE4 221 E2
Paul Cres 4 DN36 36 C8
Paulette Ct 11 PE11 214 B5
Pauleys Ct 29 PE9 219 C5
Paul La 1 DN15 9 D1
Paulsgrove PE2 229 D5
Paul's La LN4 207 C7
Paul's Wlk DN17 184 B7
Pavilion Gdns
3 Scunthorpe DN17 182 F2
5 Sleaford NG34 212 D3
Pavilion Way DN36 195 C7
Pavillion Gdns LN6 205 A4
Paving Way LN6 204 C4
Pawlett Cl PE6 217 D5
Paxton Rd PE2 229 D4
Payne Ave PE13 170 D1
Paynell 23 LN2 68 D6
Paynells PE2 230 A3
Paynesholm PE4 221 E1
Paynter Wlk DN33 191 A2
Peace Haven 2 DN37 194 C5
Peach La NG32 128 F6
Peach Tree Cl 5 DN16 185 D4
Peach Tree Ct 5 HU3 180 D5
Peachwood Cl 4 NG31 210 F8
Peacock Ct 5 NG34 212 E3
Peacock Pl 8 DN21 197 F5
Peacocks Launde NG23 117 E7
Peacock's Rd PE22 112 B1
Peacock St DN17 184 F5
Peacocks The 5 NG23 117 D3
Peacock Way PE3 224 F2
Peak Dale LN6 204 E2
Peake Cl Holdingham NG34 212 C7
Peterborough PE2 230 F6
PEAKIRK PE6 174 A5
Peakirk-cum-Glinton CE Prim Sch PE6 220 C8
Peakirk Rd
Deeping Gate PE6 217 F3
Glinton PE6 220 D8
Northborough PE6 174 A7
Peaks Ave DN36 195 C7
Peaksfield Ave DN32 191 F5
Peaks La Grimsby DN36 191 F2
New Waltham DN36 195 D7
Peaks Parkway
Grimsby DN32 191 E5
New Waltham DN36 192 A1
Pearces La 3 PE10 154 C7
Pearces Rd PE6 227 B5
Pearl Cl 8 PE25 206 C4
Pearl Ct PE12 215 D3
Pea Rm Craft Ctr & Heckington Village Trust Sta Mus* NG34 122 F2
Pearson Prim Sch HU3 180 D8
Pearson Rd DN35 192 F3
Pearson St 5 HU2 180 E7
Peartree Cl 5 LN6 200 D1
Pear Tree Cl
4 Epworth DN9 27 D6
Horncastle LN9 199 C5
Sleaford NG34 212 D2
Waltham DN37 194 D4
Pear Tree Cres 2 PE13 170 B1
Peartree Hill Rd PE12 168 B8
Peartree House Rd PE12 215 F7
Pear Tree La
Covenham St Bartholomew LN11 49 B6
Kirk Bramwith DN7 14 A8
Utterby DN36 48 E5
Pear Tree Rd PE20 136 D5
Peascliffe Dr NG31 211 A8
Peaseholme HU13 178 C1
Peasgate La
Toynton All Saints PE23 100 F6
Toynton St Peter PE23 101 A7
Peashill La NG32 139 B8
Peat Carr Bank DN9 26 C3
Peatlings La PE13 170 C1
Pebble Cl 4 PE12 160 E4
Peck Ave PE21 208 D4
Peck Hill NG33 131 B1
Peckover Cl 4 PE7 231 F5
Peckover Prim Sch PE13 170 C1
Pecks Dro W 4 PE11 214 F2
Peddars Ct 16 LN4 81 A1
Peddars Way PE3 225 A2
Pedlar La LN11 62 A7
Pedley La 15 PE13 170 C1
Peel Castle Rd 10 DN8 15 B7
Peele Sch The PE12 216 D6
Peel Hill Rd 9 DN8 15 B7
Peel St
Kingston upon Hull HU3 180 D8
Lincoln LN5 201 E1
Pegasus Gr 6 PE10 213 E7
Pegasus Rd DN20 21 A8
Pegasus Wy DN37 24 B6
Pelham Ave DN33 191 C1
Pelham Cl
20 Barton-upon-Humber DN18 10 E8
Peterborough PE3 224 F2
7 Sudbrooke LN2 68 F2
Pelham Cres 1 DN41 23 A4
Pelham Dr 1 HU9 181 C7
Pelham Ind Est DN40 186 D6
Pelham La Canwick LN4 81 A4
North Owersby LN8 45 B7
Pelham Pl DN33 191 C1
Pelham Rd
Claxby LN8 45 D6
Cleethorpes DN35 192 D7
Grimsby DN31 191 C7
2 Holton le Clay DN36 195 C2
Immingham DN40 186 B3
1 Skegness PE25 206 C4
Pelham Sq 1 DN35 192 E7
Pelham St LN5 234 B1
Pelham View 3 DN20 30 F5
Pell Pl 7 PE21 209 C4
Pell's Dr 5 PE20 136 D5
Pemberton Dr DN36 195 B6
Pemberton St 1 HU8 181 B7
Pembrey Cl 18 LN6 204 C7
Pembroke Ave
Green Hill NG31 210 D6
Green Hill NG31 210 E6
Peterborough PE2 229 F5
Scunthorpe DN16 185 A3
Yarborough DN34 191 A7
Pembroke Gr 1 PE6 220 D8
Pembroke Rd
Grimsby DN34 191 A5
Stamford PE9 219 A7
Pendeen Cl
6 Gainsborough DN21 197 E6
New Waltham DN36 195 C7
Pendine Cres LN6 205 A1
Pendlebury Dr 4 PE6 217 D5
Pendleton PE3 225 B6
Pendred Ave LN6 92 D4
Pendreth Pl DN35 192 D7
Pendula Rd PE13 170 E1
Penelope Gr PE2 231 F4
Penfold La 1 LN4 203 C2
Pengleton Cl 18 NG33 151 D2
Penistone Ct 2 HU9 181 D7
Pennell St LN5 201 E1
Pennine Cl 9 DN40 186 A4
Pennine Rd 7 DN8 15 A7
Pennine Way
Gonerby Hill Foot NG31 210 E7
Peterborough PE4 221 B2
Spalding PE11 214 E6
Pennington PE2 229 E3
Pennington St HU8 181 B7
Pennistone Pl DN33 191 A2
Pennycress Cl LN2 202 C8
Pennyfield 16 PE11 156 E8
Pennygate PE11 214 A4
Penny Gdns 6 PE20 136 C5
PENNY HILL PE12 215 D6
Pennyhill Cl PE11 214 E6
Penny Hill Rd PE12 215 E3
Penny La LN4 96 C2
Penny Toft La PE11 214 B8
Penrith Gr 2 PE4 221 E2
Penrose Cl 19 LN6 93 C8
Penshurst Ave HU13 178 F3
Penshurst Mews HU13 178 F3
Penshurst Rd DN35 192 D4
Pen St PE21 209 A5
Penswick Gr 6 NG24 104 C5
Pentelow Cl PE13 177 D5
Pentland Dr
23 North Hykeham LN6 93 C8
Sleaford NG34 121 A2
Pentlands The 2 PE4 221 C2
Pentney Cl PE2 231 C7
Penwald Cl 7 PE6 175 B8
Penwald Ct 6 PE6 174 A5
Penway Dr PE11 214 B8
Penwith Dr 2 HU10 178 F7
Penyale 3 PE3 225 A1
Peploe Cres 10 DN19 4 E2
Peploe La 9 DN19 4 E2
Peppercorn Cl
3 Lincoln LN6 201 D1
Peterborough PE1 225 E6
Peppercorn Wlk
5 Grimsby DN32 191 E7
8 Holton le Clay DN36 195 D2
Peppermint Gr 7 PE25 206 D2
Peppermint Way PE12 215 B4
Pepper's La NG34 133 C4
Peppin La LN11 49 A2
Percheron Dr 4 PE11 214 A2
Percival St
Peterborough PE3 225 E2
Scunthorpe DN15 183 A4
Percy St
8 Kingston upon Hull HU2 180 E7
6 Lincoln LN2 202 B3
3 Scunthorpe DN16 183 B2
Peregrine Cl
Kingston upon Hull HU4 179 D2
6 Sleaford NG34 212 B3
Peregrine Pl PE10 213 E3
Peregrine St PE7 230 D1
Peregrine Way LN11 198 D8
Periwinkle Way 3 PE10 213 D3
Perkin Field PE34 161 F2
Perkins Cl 2 DN37 190 F8
Perkins La PE6 173 C6
Permain Cl DN33 191 E1
Perney Cres 17 LN6 93 C8
Pernys Cl PE7 230 D3
Perrin Ave 6 PE25 206 A5
Perry Cl 7 PE11 214 A4
Perry Ct LN4 205 F4
Perry La NG23 91 A7
Perry Rd PE13 170 B2
Perry St HU3 180 A6
Pershore Ave DN34 190 D4
Pershore Way
Birchwood LN6 204 C6
Eye PE6 175 B2
Perth Cl Bourne PE10 213 C3
7 Skegness PE25 206 A4
Perth Rd PE9 218 E6
Perth St W HU5 180 A8
Perth St HU5 179 F8
Perth Way DN40 186 B2
Pescod Sq 27 PE21 208 F5
Petchell Way 2 DN32 191 F8
PETERBOROUGH PE3 225 D5
Peterborough Cath* PE1 226 A2
Peterborough City Hospl PE3 225 B4
Peterborough Cl 10 NG31 210 E5
Peterborough Coll of Adult Ed PE1 226 B3
Peterborough Dr PE6 224 E2
Peterborough Her Ctr* PE3 225 A1
Peterborough High Sch PE3 225 D2
Peterborough Mus & Art Gall* PE3 225 A2
Peterborough NV Sta PE2 225 F1
Peterborough Rd
Castor PE5 223 E1
19 Collingham NG23 91 D5
23 Eye PE6 175 A1
Langtoft PE6 217 A8
Newborough PE6 174 E4
Peterborough PE7 231 C3
Scunthorpe DN16 185 B7
Wansford PE8 222 A3
Peterborough Rd South PE6 175 B7
Peterborough Regional Coll PE1 226 B5
Peterborough Sch The PE9 225 E2
Peterborough Sta PE3 225 F2
Peterborough Way NG34 212 C7
Peter Chambers Way 9 LN12 64 A4
Peterfield Rd 7 PE7 230 B1
Petergate 1 PE9 219 B4
Peterhouse Cl
Peterborough PE3 225 E3
1 Stamford PE9 219 B7
Peterhouse Ct DN16 185 A4
Peterhouse Rd DN34 190 F6
Peter Paine Cl PE22 126 F4
Peter Paine Sports Ctr PE21 208 B5
Peter Seadike La PE11 145 D5
Petersfield Cl LN6 204 B7
Peter's La LN13 63 B2
Peterson Dr
New Waltham DN36 195 D7
New Waltham DN36 195 D7
Peterspoint PE12 160 D3
Petfield Dr HU10 178 F5
Pethley La NG34 143 A6
Petticoat La 15 PE21 208 F5
Pettit Way 6 PE21 209 C4
Petts Cl 5 PE13 170 E1
Petts La PE12 160 F5
Petuaria Cl HU15 2 B6
Petworth Cl 2 PE6 217 A5
Petworth La 6 HU3 179 F5
Peveril Ave DN17 184 F8
Peveril Pl NG31 210 D5
Peveril Rd PE1 225 F6
Pheasant Cl 5 DN17 184 E6
Pheasant Ct 5 LN7 33 B4
Pheasant Gr PE4 220 E5
Pheasant Way PE7 233 D5
Phelps Pl DN32 192 C5
Phelps St DN35 189 D1
Pheonix Ave DN15 182 F6
Philip Ave
Cleethorpes DN35 192 D4
Waltham DN37 194 E5
Philip Ct 4 LN6 204 F1
Philip Gr Cleethorpes DN35 192 D4
Skegness PE25 206 B4
Philips Cres DN15 182 F3
Phillipot Cl 8 NG24 104 B5
Phillips Ct 6 PE9 219 C4
Phillips La 6 DN37 23 F1
Phoenix Cl PE2 231 B6
Phoenix Clayton Sch PE2 230 B4
Phoenix Ct DN21 197 F3
Phoenix La
20 Balderton NG24 104 C1
Balderton NG24 104 C2
10 Crowland PE6 175 B8
Phoenix Parkway DN15 182 E7
Phoenix Sch The PE2 230 C3
Phoenix St 6 DN32 191 D7
Phorpres Cl PE7 230 D3
Phorpres Houses PE7 230 F4
Phorpres Way PE7 230 E3
Photinia Cl 8 LN4 81 E2
Phyllis Ave DN34 191 B7
Phyllis Taylor Gdns DN32 191 D7
Piccadilly 4 DN36 195 C6
Piccadilly Way 1 PE10 154 D6
Pickards Way PE13 170 C1
Pickathorpe La LN11 50 E6
Pickering Ct DN37 190 E8
Pickering Gr 15 DN8 15 A7
Pickering Grange 33 HU15 2 D5
Pickering Rd HU4 179 C3
Pickering's Mdw Nature Reserve* LN2 68 F6
Pickerings The 19 HU14 3 A4
Pick Hill La Grimoldby LN11 62 C8
South Cockerington LN11 50 C1
Picksley Cres DN36 195 D1
PICKWORTH
Pickworth NG34 142 A8
Pickworth PE9 162 E4
Pickworth Lane PE9 162 C3
Pickworth Rd PE9 162 F2
Pickworth's Dro PE10 155 A3
Pidgeon Cote La 20 DN19 12 A8
Pied Bull Cl 8 PE9 171 A3
Pier St 9 HU1 180 F5
Pietermaritz St 4 LN1 201 E8
Pieter Maritz View 15 LN1 201 E8
Pigot Wy 5 LN2 202 D6
Pike Dam La PE12 159 A6
Pilgrim Ave DN40 186 D3
Pilgrim Gr PE4 221 F2
Pilgrim Hospl PE21 209 A8
Pilgrim Rd PE21 209 A4
Pilgrims App DN21 197 F2
Pilgrim Sch The PE20 124 B6
Pilgrim's Cl 5 DN40 12 E3
Pilgrims Way DN40 186 A4
Pilgrim's Way PE11 214 A4
Pilgrims Wy DN21 197 F2
PILHAM DN21 41 D4
Pilham Ct DN21 197 F3
Pilham La DN21 41 C4
Pilley's La PE21 125 F5
Pilmore La PE12 157 B6
Pilots View DN18 3 E2
Pilots Way HU9 181 B5
PILSGATE PE9 172 C4
Pilton Cl PE4 221 D1
Pimpernel Way 2 DN16 185 D4
PINCHBECK PE11 156 E8
Pinchbeck Ave 4 DN16 183 C2
Pinchbeck East CE Prim Sch The PE11 156 E8
Pinchbeck Engine Mus* PE11 145 E1
Pinchbeck Fen Slipe Nature Reserve* PE11 156 A6
Pinchbeck La PE24 102 F4
Pinchbeck Rd
5 Butterwick PE22 126 E3
Spalding PE11 214 D5
PINCHBECK WEST PE11 156 A7
Pinder Ave
Peterborough PE4 221 E3
Peterborough PE6 221 E3
Pinder La 10 PE11 134 F2
Pinder's Dro PE22 114 B5
Pine Cl 14 Balderton NG24 104 C1
Grimsby DN37 188 A1
Holbeach PE12 215 C3
Lincoln LN1 201 E8
12 Newark-on-Trent NG24 104 A6
4 Sleaford NG34 212 D3
Stamford PE9 218 D6
7 Waddington LN5 93 E8
Pine Ct
3 Cleethorpes DN35 192 D2
Spalding PE11 214 F4
Pinefield Ave 7 DN3 14 A3
Pinefield Rd 3 DN3 14 A3
Pine Hall Rd DN3 14 A3
Pine Mdws HU10 178 B8
Pine Pk 3 DN18 3 E1
Pines The DN21 197 F2
Pinetree Ave 11 DN21 29 C3
Pinetree Cl 5 DN20 19 E4
Pine Tree Cl
Peterborough PE1 226 B8
Woodside DN9 26 D6
Pinetrees Ct 4 NG34 212 E4
Pine Wlk 5 Brough HU15 2 C6
4 Healing DN41 24 A5
Pinewood Ave PE8 172 B1
Pinewood Cl
Bottesford DN16 185 A4
5 Bourne PE10 213 B5
Pinewood Cr 8 LN6 204 B8
Pinewood Cres DN33 190 F3
Pinewood Dr NG31 210 F8
Pinewood Gr 2 HU5 179 C7
Pinfold 15 DN9 27 E6
Pinfold Cl
7 Bassingham LN5 92 F3
7 Bottesford NG13 128 A6
8 Collingham NG23 91 D5
11 Northorpe PE10 164 C8
Osbournby NG34 132 D5
Pointon & Sempringham NG34 143 B6
Rippingale PE10 142 F2
Pinfold Gdns 4 DN36 195 D1
Pinfold La Anderby PE24 77 B3
Beesby with Saleby LN13 76 A6
11 Bottesford NG13 128 A6
Fishlake DN7 14 D8
Fishtoft PE21 137 C8
Great Steeping PE23 101 E6
Grimsby DN33 191 D1
Halton Holegate PE23 101 C6
3 Holton le Clay DN36 195 D1
Irby in the Marsh PE24 102 B6
Legbourne LN11 61 E3
Marston NG32 118 D2
Minting LN9 71 C1
1 Misterton DN10 39 F5
18 Newark-on-Trent NG24 104 B2
Pointon & Sempringham NG34 143 B6
8 Ruskington NG34 108 E2
South Rauceby NG34 120 E4
2 Stallingborough DN41 23 D6
Stamford PE9 219 C3
Stickney PE22 113 A6
Swaby LN13 74 E4
Walcott LN4 109 C7
Weston PE12 157 D8
Pinfold Rd Bourne PE10 213 F5
Castle Bytham NG33 152 D1
Pinfold The LN4 108 D5
Pinfold Way 11 NG34 108 E2
Pingle Cl DN21 197 E4
Pingle La Bishop Norton LN8 43 D3
Northborough PE6 173 F6
20 Wellingore LN5 107 A7
Pingle Leys 6 LN8 43 D3
Pingle Nature Reserve The* LN4 207 D5
Pingles The 9 PE10 164 C8
Pingle The
2 Billingborough NG34 133 B1
Northborough PE6 173 F6
Northborough PE6 217 F1
Pingley La DN20 196 D2
Pingley Mdw DN20 196 D2
Pinnacle Cl 11 PE6 175 B8
Pinney's Ct 21 DN41 23 F5
Pinnings La DN21 43 D6
Pinstock La 10 PE12 159 C7
Pintail Cl DN16 185 F5
Pintail Gdns PE7 233 B8
Pinter La DN21 197 F2
Pioneer Way LN6 204 E4
Pioneer Wy PE6 175 B1
Piper La PE4 221 F3
Pipistrelle Ct 4 PE4 221 A3
Pippin Cl Louth LN11 198 C5
Misterton DN10 40 A4
Pippin Ct
10 Beacon Hill NG24 104 A5
3 Scunthorpe DN15 182 C5
Pippin Dr DN16 185 B2
Pippin Gdns PE14 170 F1
Pippin Way DN7 14 D3
Pipwell Gate PE12 146 E1
Pitcairn Ave 1 LN2 202 D6
Pitcher Row La PE20 136 B1
Pit La Gedney PE12 149 A4
Great Ponton NG33 140 B4
Ketton PE9 171 A4
Pitman Ave 23 DN18 10 E8
Pitmoor La 8 DN39 12 A1
Pitomy Dr NG23 91 C5
Pitt La DN10 39 C2
Pittneys PE4 221 D1
Pitts Rd LN4 203 C1
Pitt St HU3 179 F7
Pk House Sch PE6 176 A3
Pk Prim Sch PE21 208 E7
Plains La DN8 15 F3
Plains The PE9 162 D4
Plane St HU3 180 A5
Planet Ice PE3 220 E1
Plank Dro PE6 175 B8
Plantain Cl 1 DN16 185 D4
Plantation Dr 5 HU14 2 F5
Plantation Dr E HU4 179 C6
Plantation Dr W HU4 179 C6
Plantation Rd
Cranwell & Byard's Leap NG34 107 C1
29 Thorne/Moorends DN8 15 A8
Planting Rd NG33 140 B1
Plash Dro PE13 177 F4
Plassey Rd 6 DN21 55 A8
Platform Dr PE12 216 A4
Platts Cl PE11 157 A8
Platts La Bucknall LN10 84 B4
Tetford LN9 73 E1
Platt's La NG32 118 B4
Playgarth Est LN4 108 E4
Playhouse The* NG34 212 D4

Playhouse Yd 2 NG34 212 D4
Playing Field La 2 LN8 59 A7
Playtowers★ DN35 193 B3
Pleasance Way LN11 62 C6
Pleasant Ave LN11 198 D5
Pleasant Pl 6 LN11 198 C6
Pleasant Terr 18 LN5 205 E8
Pleasure Island Theme Pk★ DN35 193 C2
Plimsoll Way HU9 181 B6
Plot La NG23 91 E6
Plough Dr 18 LN8 57 D8
Plough Hill 23 LN7 33 B4
Plough La
1 Cherry Willingham/Reepham LN3 82 A8
5 Fiskerton LN3 82 A7
6 Newborough PE6 174 E5
Ploughmans Ct 3 LN2 202 E6
Ploughmans La 4 LN2 202 E6
Plover Ct 18 Dn18 3 E1
Plover Dr 15 HU15 2 C6
Plover Gr Birchwood LN6 204 E8
Louth LN11 198 C8
Ploverly 2 PE4 221 A5
Plover Rd 1 PE9 163 D3
Plover Sq 7 LN7 33 B4
Plover Wy DN16 185 F5
Plowden Rd HU3 179 F5
Plowright Theatre★ DN15 183 A2
Plumpton Chase PE10 213 C3
Plum Tree Dr 3 DN36 37 C2
Plumtree Hill Rd DN7 14 C7
Plumtree La 2 DN36 36 B1
Plum Tree Way DN16 183 A1
Plymouth Cl
Gainsborough DN21 197 F2
23 Winterton DN15 9 A5
Plymouth Rd DN17 182 C1
Poachers Brook LN6 200 A5
Poacher's Croft 8 DN9 16 E1
Poachers Ct 23 LN1 66 D2
Poachers Gate 4 PE11 145 C1
Poachers Hide 2 PE11 145 B7
Poachers La LN2 68 F3
Poachers Mdw 20 LN2 68 D2
Poachers Rest 3 LN2 68 D7
Pocklington Cres 3 NG24 104 B7
Pocklington Rd 24 NG23 91 D5
Pocklington Way 10 NG34 122 E2
PODE HOLE PE11 156 C5
Pode La PE22 113 F1
Poffinder Wood Rd DN7 14 E7
POINTON NG34 143 B7
Pointon Rd NG34 143 B8
Point Rd PE25 90 F3
Poke Holes Lane LN11 60 A6
Poles Bank DN9 26 E6
Policemans La 2 LN4 203 C2
Pollards The PE10 213 D2
Pollyplatt La LN1 67 E5
Pollyplatt Prim Sch LN1 67 F5
Polton Cl 3 DN7 14 D7
Polton Toft 2 DN7 14 D7
Polyanthus Dr 4 NG34 212 F3
Polygon Wlk 4 NG31 211 F6
Pomona Wy PE2 231 D4
Pond Cl 19 LN2 68 D6
Pond La 4 PE10 213 E2
Pond Side DN39 11 E3
Ponds La HU15 1 A6
Pond St
Great Gonerby NG31 129 D5
8 Harlaxton NG32 139 C7
Ponds Way 10 DN18 3 E1
Ponds Wy 28 DN18 3 E1
Ponsonby Dr PE2 230 D8
Ponton Ave NG31 211 E2
Ponton Rd NG33 140 D5
Poolbank La HU15 2 E5
Pool Cl 4 PE11 214 D5
Pool Dr DN17 184 F4
Poole's La 8 PE23 87 F1
Pooley Way PE7 233 D6
Poolham Lane LN10 84 D1
Pools La 8 PE20 136 A2
Poor Gdn Rd NG34 132 F6
Poor Plat La LN13 62 F3
Poor's End LN11 50 B8
Pope's La Leverington PE13 170 A2
Terrington St Clement PE34 161 E2
Pope Way PE1 225 E8
Poplar Ave Lincoln LN6 201 C3
Mablethorpe/Sutton on Sea LN12 64 A5
Peterborough PE1 226 C8
Poplar Cl
Anlaby with Anlaby Common HU4 179 A5
Boston PE21 208 D2
Ruskington NG34 108 E2
Poplar Cres Bourne PE10 213 B6
Burringham DN17 17 D4
Poplar Ct Lincoln LN6 205 B4
5 Old Leake PE22 114 A1
Spalding PE11 214 B4
Welbourn LN5 106 E4
Poplar Dr Brigg DN20 196 C5
6 Broughton DN20 19 D3
2 Gosberton PE11 145 C6
Humberston DN36 193 B1
Poplar Farm Sch NG31 210 D6
Poplar Gdns DN16 185 B7
Poplar Gr
5 Cleethorpes DN35 192 E7
3 Scotter DN21 29 C3
Poplar La Corringham DN21 41 D2
Gedney Dyke PE12 148 D1
Poplar Rd Bucknall LN10 84 A3
Cleethorpes DN35 192 E7
6 Hatfield DN7 14 C4
2 Healing DN41 23 F5
Poplar Rd Bsns Units DN35 192 E7
Poplars Mobile Homes DN15 182 B5
Poplar St LN5 205 D5
Poplar Wy PE25 103 C7
Popple Dro PE13 169 D1
Popple St HU9 181 B6
Popplewell Cl 3 DN9 16 E2
Popplewell Terr 13 DN9 27 E6
Poppy Cl Boston PE21 208 B4
1 Scunthorpe DN15 182 C6
Spalding PE11 214 B6
Poppyfields The 14 NG23 91 D4
Poppyfield Way DN20 196 B4
Poppy Mews 27 DN41 23 F5
Poppy Pl 6 PE10 213 D3
Poppy Rd LN6 92 D5
Porcher Way PE21 208 C6
Portal Gn 8 PE25 206 A5
Portchester Cl PE2 231 F5
Porter Ave PE4 221 F2
Porter's La 4 PE9 171 D3
Porter St
Kingston upon Hull HU3 180 E5
Scunthorpe DN15 183 A4
Porthcawl Cl 12 NG31 211 D7
Port La PE5 223 E1
Portland Ave
Grimsby DN32 191 E4
Peterborough PE1 225 F7
Portland Dr 6 PE25 206 A7
Portland Manor DN32 191 E4
Portland Pl Grimsby DN32 191 E4
9 Kingston upon Hull HU2 180 E7
Portland St Boston PE21 208 E5
Kingston upon Hull HU2 180 D7
Lincoln LN5 234 B1
Portland Terr 5 DN21 197 D3
Portman Cl PE3 225 C4
Portman Rd DN15 182 E6
Portsmouth Cl 1 NG31 210 F5
Portsmouth Wlk HU4 179 B4
PORT SUTTON BRIDGE PE12 160 F4
Posterngate HU1 180 F6
Postland Rd PE6 166 F1
Post Mill Cl LN6 204 C1
Post Office Hill NG33 151 B5
Post Office La
Ashby cum Fenby DN37 35 D3
Burton Coggles NG33 152 C8
Chapel Hill LN4 110 E5
2 Humberside Airport DN39 22 A6
South Scarle NG23 91 E7
5 Spilsby PE23 88 A1
3 Sutterton PE20 136 A2
Whitton DN15 1 E3
Posts The NG32 129 B3
Potesgrave Way 8 NG34 122 D3
Pot La PE20 146 E8
Pottergate LN2 234 B3
Pottergate Rd
Ancaster NG32 120 A3
Caythorpe NG32 119 E7
Fulbeck NG32 106 E1
Normanton NG32 119 E5
Welbourn LN5 106 F4
POTTERHANWORTH LN4 82 B1
POTTERHANWORTH BOOTHS LN4 82 C2
Potterhanworth CE Prim Sch The LN4 82 B1
Potterhanworth Rd
Branston & Mere LN4 82 A1
Heighington LN4 81 F3
Potter Hanworth LN4 95 B8
Potter Hill Road NG23 91 E3
Potters Cl 2 PE10 213 E4
Potter's Lodge Meadows Nature Reserve★ NG33 152 B2
Potters Way PE1 226 B1
Pottinger Gdns 5 LN7 33 A3
Potts La DN17 16 D7
Poulter Ave PE2 231 D5
Pound Rd LN4 96 C2
Poverty La LN11 61 B2
Powells Cres DN16 185 B6
Powell St PE21 209 C2
Pratt Ave PE4 221 D2
Prebend La LN2 68 C7
Precinct Cres
5 Skegness PE25 103 E4
2 Skegness PE25 103 E4
Precincts The 5 PE6 217 B5
Precinct The DN17 184 D7
Premier Ct 6 NG31 211 A5
Prenton Cl 8 LN6 205 A5
Prescott Ave 11 HU15 2 C5
Prescott Gr 3 DN7 14 D4
Prestland PE6 217 A6
Preston Dr DN20 196 C4
Prestongate HU13 178 E1
Preston La 15 DN18 10 F8
Prestwick Cl
2 Birchwood LN6 200 B1
Londonthorpe & Harrowby Without NG31 211 E7
Pretoria Rd NG31 210 E7
Pretoria St HU3 179 F5
Pretymen Cres DN36 195 C5
Prial Ave LN6 205 B6
Prial Cl LN6 205 C6
Pride Parkway NG34 212 F7
Pridmore Rd NG33 152 E8
Priestfield Dro 1 PE12 159 D7
Priestgate
3 Barton-upon-Humber DN18 10 F8
4 Peterborough PE1 226 A2
Priest Hill La PE23 87 A5
Priestley Cl 7 PE20 136 C5
Priest's House★ PE9 171 C3
Primitive Chapel La 1 DN40 12 F2
Primrose Ave 13 NG24 104 A6
Primrose Cl
8 Healing DN41 23 F5
8 Lincoln LN5 205 C2
7 Morton PE10 154 D6
11 North Hykeham LN6 93 A8
Peterborough PE1 226 A8
9 Skegness PE25 206 A5
Primrose Cres
Boston PE21 208 B4
4 Pinchbeck PE11 156 E8
Primrose Dr
1 Kingston upon Hull HU5 179 C8
Yaxley PE7 233 F7
Primrose La 4 NG34 107 C1
Primroses 1 PE6 217 D5
Primrose St DN21 197 D3
Primrose Way
6 Grantham NG31 211 D2
Humberston DN35 192 E1
Scunthorpe DN15 182 C6
2 Spalding PE11 214 A2
Stamford PE9 218 C7
Prince Albert Gdns 2 DN32 189 A1
Prince Alfred Ave 1 PE25 206 D3
Prince Ave 8 PE24 90 D7
Prince Charles Ave 11 LN8 70 D4
Prince Charles Dr 32 DN18 10 F8
Prince Edward Dr DN40 187 A4
Prince George Rd PE10 213 B4
Prince George St PE25 206 C3
Prince Henry Dr DN40 187 A4
Prince of Wales Cl 12 PE13 170 D2
Prince Philip Dr 37 DN18 10 F8
Princes Ave Grimsby DN31 191 C7
Kingston upon Hull HU13 178 E1
Princes Ct 3 PE10 213 D6
Prince's Dock St 16 HU1 180 F6
Princes Gate PE1 226 B4
Princes Gdns PE1 226 B4
Princes Parade PE25 206 D2
Princes Quay Sh Ctr HU1 180 F6
Princes Rd
Peterborough PE2 231 A7
1 Stamford PE9 219 C6
Prince's Rd DN35 192 E6
Princess Alexandra Ct 1 DN17 184 F3
Princess Anne Rd PE21 209 C6
Princess Ave DN7 14 C6
Princess Dr
34 Barton-upon-Humber DN18 10 F8
Grantham NG31 211 D7
Princess Gr PE6 217 C6
Princess Margaret Ave 28 LN4 95 C4
Princess Rd PE20 136 C4
Princess Royal Cl 4 LN2 234 C3
Princess Sq LN4 109 E6
Princess St Boston PE21 208 D5
1 Immingham DN40 186 C3
Lincoln LN5 201 E1
Princes St Brigg DN20 196 C3
Holbeach PE12 159 A7
Prince's St
Metheringham LN4 95 C4
Peterborough PE1 226 A4
Sutton Bridge PE12 160 E4
Princess Wlk DN21 197 F4
Prince St 13 HU1 180 F6
Prince William Dr 8 PE22 126 E3
Prince William Rd 3 LN8 56 D5
Pringle Cl LN4 207 D5
Pringles The PE22 98 F4
Prins Ave PE13 170 D1
Prins Ct 16 PE13 170 D1
Printing Office La 14 DN17 16 D8
Priors Cl DN36 195 D5
Priors Gate PE4 220 E4
Prior St LN5 201 E1
Priory Acad LSST The LN5 205 E6
Priory City of Lincoln Acad The LN6 205 A8
Priory Cl
Gainsborough DN21 197 F4
Louth LN11 198 C5
Market Deeping PE6 217 F4
35 Newark-on-Trent NG24 104 B2
12 Northorpe PE10 164 C8
11 Ruskington NG34 108 E1
12 Swanland HU14 3 B7
Priory Cres
Scunthorpe DN17 185 A6
Ulceby DN39 12 A2
Priory Ct Boston PE21 209 F5
10 Grantham NG31 211 A4
11 South Witham NG33 151 D2
Stamford PE9 219 D5
Priory Dr 5 LN3 82 B6
Priory Farm Dr 4 HU4 179 D2
Priory Gdns PE7 228 F3
Priory Gr HU4 179 D3
Priory La
6 Barrow upon Humber DN19 11 D8
Dunston LN4 95 D5
Manby LN11 62 C6
Scunthorpe DN17 184 F6
Priory La Jun Sch DN17 184 E6
Priory Lane Community Sch DN17 184 F6
Priory Pk HU4 179 B1
Priory Rd Boston PE21 209 F5
Fishtoft PE21 126 C2
Grimsby DN37 190 D6
Louth LN11 198 C6
Peterborough PE3 225 E3
Ruskington NG34 108 E1
Scunthorpe DN17 185 A6
Spalding PE11 214 D3
Stamford PE9 219 D5
Priory Ruskin Acad The NG31 211 A7
Priory Sch The PE11 214 F4
Priory Way
2 Gainsborough DN21 53 A5
Kingston upon Hull HU4 179 A1
Sleaford NG34 212 A2
Priory Witham Acad The LN6 205 B5
Private La LN8 55 F7
Proby Cl PE7 233 D5
Procters Dr NG23 78 C1
Proctors Cl 6 PE12 159 C7
Proctors Rd LN2 202 D5
Proctor's Way 6 DN20 31 A5
Progress Way NG31 211 A6
Promenade
Chapel St Leonard PE24 90 E5
Cleethorpes DN35 192 F7
Mablethorpe/Sutton on Sea LN12 64 D1
Prospect Ctr 12 HU2 180 E7
Prospect La 8 DN15 8 C8
Prospect Pl
1 Grantham NG31 211 A5
Kingston upon Hull HU9 181 B7
2 Market Rasen LN8 57 E7
Prospect St Horncastle LN9 199 B5
Kingston upon Hull HU2 180 E7
Prospect Terr 8 DN21 197 D3
Prospero Cl PE2 230 F6
Proudfoot La PE12 159 B6
Providence Cres
17 Barton-upon-Humber DN18 10 E8
Kingston upon Hull HU5 179 D7
Providence Pl 3 LN4 207 C4
Providence Row 3 HU3 180 E8
Provost Rd 11 LN11 62 C6
Prunus Ave HU10 178 F8
Pryme Rd DN16 185 C8
Pryme St HU10 178 F6
Prystie Pl DN35 192 D2
Psalter Rd LN13 88 E6
Puddiners La DN14 6 E7
Pudding and Dip La
8 Hatfield DN7 14 D4
Hatfield DN7 14 D5
Pudding Bag La PE9 172 C4
Pudding La PE11 214 E8
Puddingpoke La 8 PE12 160 A8
Puffin La PE7 233 D8
Pulcroft Rd HU13 178 D2
Pullan Cl 9 LN5 205 D3
Pullinger Way LN4 81 E1
Pullman Cl 11 LN4 95 D4
Pullover La PE20 146 E7
Pullover The PE24 90 E7
Pulman St HU3 180 A7
Pulvertoft La 12 PE21 208 F4
Pump Hill DN20 31 D6
Pump La Fenton NG23 105 C1
5 Skidbrooke with Saltfleet Haven LN11 51 C4
Pump Sq 18 PE21 208 F5
Punchbowl La
Boston PE21 208 B7
Holland Fen with Brothertoft PE20 125 B4
Purbeck Rd
5 Grimsby DN33 194 E8
Scunthorpe DN17 182 C1
Purcell Cl 1 NG31 211 D6
Puritan Way PE21 208 C7
Puttock Gate PE20 146 D7
Pyecroft PE1 226 B6
PYEWIPE DN31 188 C4
Pyewipe Bglws DN31 188 E1
Pyewipe Rd DN31 188 E1
Pyhill PE3 225 B7
Pyke Rd LN6 204 D5
Pymoor La PE22 113 B2
Pynder Cl LN4 203 A2
Pyruss Dr HU4 179 B2
Pytchley Wlk DN35 192 E2

Q

QUADRING PE11 145 A8
Quadring Bank PE11 144 E6
Quadring Cowley & Browns Prim Sch PE11 135 A1
QUADRING EAUDIKE PE11 145 C8
Quadring Rd
Donington PE11 134 F2
Quadring PE11 145 B7
Quaker La 7 Boston PE21 208 F4
Spalding PE11 214 A3
Quantock Cl
7 Kingston upon Hull HU3 180 D5
1 Scunthorpe DN17 184 D8
3 Thorne/Moorends DN8 15 A7
Quantock Ct 9 NG34 212 B3
Quantock Gdns DN41 23 E5
Quantock Rd DN33 194 E8
QUARRINGTON NG34 212 B1
Quarry La PE6 173 C7
Quarry Rd LN11 198 C4
Quarryside LN11 198 B4
Quart La DN14 6 D6
Quay La DN14 6 C7
Quayside Ctr★ NG34 212 E4
Quayside E 6 PE10 213 E2
Quayside W 7 PE10 213 E2
Quays The DN21 197 B5
Quebec Rd
Mablethorpe/Sutton on Sea LN12 64 B4
Scunthorpe DN17 184 E3
Queen Charlotte Ms 1 PE1 226 A6
Queen Eleanor Ave NG31 210 C5
Queen Eleanor Prim Sch NG23 79 B6
Queen Elizabeth Ave 3 DN18 10 A7
Queen Elizabeth Gram Sch LN9 199 A4
Queen Elizabeth Rd
6 Humberston DN36 36 C8
Lincoln LN1 201 D8
Queen Elizabeth's Grammar Alford LN13 75 E2
Queen Elizabeth's High Sch The DN21 197 C7
Queen Elizabeth St 1 LN8 70 D5
Queen Elizabeth Way 33 DN18 10 F8
Queen Headland La LN5 92 F1
Queen Mary Ave DN35 192 C7
Queen Mary Ave Inf Sch DN32 192 C7
Queen Mary Rd LN1 201 D8
Queen St Pl 1 LN11 198 C5
Queen's Ave
5 Barton-upon-Humber DN18 3 F1
Market Deeping PE6 217 C6
2 Spalding PE11 157 B6
Queen's Bank PE12 167 C5
Queensbury Way 2 HU14 3 B6
Queens Cres DN17 17 D6
Queen's Cres Lincoln LN1 201 D5
15 Stainforth DN7 14 C6
Queens Ct 3 LN11 198 D4
Queen's Ct 18 DN8 15 A8
Queens Dock Ave 4 HU1 180 F6
Queens Dr 28 DN17 16 D7
Queen's Dr PE25 206 E8
Queen's Drive Infant Sch PE1 226 A5
Queen's Dr W PE1 226 A5
Queen's Est PE24 102 C1
Queensfield
Gainsborough DN21 197 B7
South Kelsey LN7 32 A1
Queensgate Ctr PE1 226 A2
Queen's Gate St HU3 180 B5
Queen's Gdns PE1 226 A5
Queens Parade DN31 191 C7
Queen's Parade DN35 192 F5
Queens Pk Cl 1 LN12 64 C3
Queens Rd
Immingham DN40 187 A4
8 Mablethorpe/Sutton on Sea LN12 77 A8
Peterborough PE2 231 B7
Skegness PE25 206 B4
Spalding PE11 214 F5
Queen's Rd
9 Barnetby le Wold DN38 21 B4
1 Boston PE21 209 A5
Bourne PE10 213 D6
14 Heckington NG34 122 E2
Newark-on-Trent NG24 104 A5
Queen's Royal Lancers Mus The★ NG32 138 C8
Queens St PE9 219 B6
Queen St 6 Bardney LN3 83 B4
5 Bardney LN3 83 C4
Barton-upon-Humber DN18 3 F1
Boston PE21 208 E5
Bottesford NG13 128 A6
Brigg DN20 196 C3
4 Collingham NG23 91 D5
Epworth DN9 27 E6
Gainsborough DN21 197 D3
4 Grantham NG31 211 A3
5 Grimsby DN32 191 E8
Horncastle LN9 199 C3
Kingston upon Hull HU1 181 A5
Kirton in Lindsey DN21 30 B1
Lincoln LN5 201 E1
Louth LN11 198 B5
9 Market Rasen LN8 57 D8
2 Peterborough PE1 226 A2
3 Scunthorpe DN16 183 C2

Queen St continued
Sleaford NG34 . . . . .212 C3
6 Spilsby PE23 . . . . .88 A1
17 Sutton Bridge PE12 . . . .160 E4
Thorne/Moorends DN8 . . . .15 A8
15 Winterton DN15 . . . . .9 A5
20 Wisbech PE13 . . . . .170 D1
Yaxley PE7 . . . . .233 F6
Queen's View Cres DN16. .185 D7
Queensway
Gainsborough DN21 . . . . . .197 F4
1 Grantham NG31 . . . . . . .211 E6
Grimsby DN37 . . . . .190 F8
1 Ingoldmells PE25 . . . . . . .90 E3
Lincoln LN2 . . . . .202 B5
Long Sutton PE12 . . . . . .216 C6
Louth LN11 . . . . .198 E5
8 Mablethorpe/Sutton on Sea
LN12 . . . . .64 B4
Pointon & Sempringham
NG34. . . . . .143 B6
2 Potterhanworth LN4 . . . .82 B1
13 Ruskington NG34 . . . . .108 D2
21 Saxilby LN1 . . . . .66 D2
Scunthorpe DN16. . . . . . .185 C7
Skellingthorpe LN6. . . . . .200 A3
Sturton by Stow LN1. . . . . .66 C6
Queensway Ind Est DN17 .185 E6
Queens Wlk PE2 . . . . . . .230 F8
Queen's Wlk PE9. . . . . . .219 A5
Queenswood Rd DN16. . . .185 C5
Queen Victoria Sq HU1 . .180 F6
Quibell Rd 8 NG24. . . . . .104 A4
Quibell's La NG24. . . . . . .104 A6
Quick La PE12 . . . . .168 A7
Quilter Ave HU4. . . . . . . .179 B5
Quintin Cl LN4. . . . . .205 C1
Quinton Rd DN32. . . . . . .191 E4
Quintus Pl LN6. . . . . .93 B8
Quorn Cl 7 PE6. . . . . . . .174 E4
Quorn Dr 5 LN6 . . . . . . .205 C8
Quorn Gdns 1 LN11. . . . .198 D4
Quorn Mews 4 DN35. . . .192 E3
Quorum The HU4 . . . . . . .179 D3

R

Rabbithill La NG23 . . . . . . .78 D3
Racecourse Rd PE9 . . . . . .171 E3
Racecourse The
Bourne PE11 . . . . .214 A1
2 Spalding PE11 . . . . . . .156 E3
Race La DN39 . . . . .11 C3
Race Lane DN38. . . . . .21 C5
Rachel Cl DN21 . . . . .197 C7
Radcliffe Cl 5 PE9 . . . . . .219 B5
Radcliffe Ct PE25 . . . . . . .185 D8
Radcliffe Rd
7 Healing DN41 . . . . .24 A5
3 Stamford PE9 . . . . . . .219 B5
Raddle Way 8 NG24. . . . . .104 A2
Radford Cl PE8. . . . . .172 C1
RAF Digby Ops Mus ★
LN4. . . . . .108 A7
Ragdale Cl 2 PE1 . . . . . . .226 E7
RAGNALL NG22 . . . . .78 A3
Railway 17 NG33 . . . . . . .151 D1
Railway La PE12. . . . . .160 E3
Railway Pk Cl 1 LN6 . . . .201 D1
Railway Pk Mews LN6. . . .201 D1
Railway Pl 4 DN31. . . . . .189 B2
Railway St
Barnetby le Wold DN38. . . .21 B4
Grimsby DN32. . . . . .189 B1
Kingston upon Hull HU1 . .180 F5
Railway Terr
3 Grantham NG31 . . . . . .211 A3
5 Grimsby DN32. . . . . . .191 D7
Railworld ★ PE3. . . . . . . .225 F1
RailWy Cl PE11. . . . . .214 D6
Rainsbutt Rd DN17. . . . . . . .6 C1
Rainton St 3 PE11. . . . . .214 F4
Rainwall Ct 2 PE20 . . . . .136 A2
Rainwall's La PE20 . . . . . .136 A3
RAITHBY LN11. . . . . .60 F3
Raithby Ave 20 DN41 . . . . .23 A4
RAITHBY BY SPILSBY
PE23. . . . . .87 D2
Raithby Cross Roads PE23 .87 C2
Raithby Gr 6 DN33. . . . . .191 A3
Raithby Hill PE23. . . . . . . .87 D1
Raithby Rd PE23 . . . . .87 D1
Raithby Road LN11. . . . . . .61 A2
Rake Bridge Bank DN7 . . .14 D2
Raleigh Ct 2 PE11 . . . . . .214 C2
Raleigh Dr HU9 . . . . .181 D6
Raleigh Way PE3. . . . . . . .225 B6
Ralph Brown Way 5 LN9 .199 B2
Ralphs La PE20 . . . . .136 C7
Ramblers La 19 DN18 . . . . .3 E1
Ram Bvd DN15 . . . . .182 E7
Ramper La LN1 . . . . .65 E4
Ramper Rd DN22. . . . . .52 B7
Ramper The 6 PE11. . . . . .156 E3
RAMPTON DN22. . . . . .65 A4
Rampton Rd DN22. . . . . . . .65 A4
Ramsay Cl PE25 . . . . .206 C1
Ramsden Ave 8 DN18 . . . . .10 E8
Ramsey Way PE2. . . . . . . .231 F6
Ramsgate LN11 . . . . .198 C6
Ramsgate Rd LN11 . . . . . .198 C6
Ramskir La DN7. . . . . .14 C7
RANBY LN8. . . . . .72 B5

Ranby Rd DN17 . . . . .184 E5
RAND LN8 . . . . .70 A5
Randall Bank PE12 . . . . . .158 A2
Rand Farm Pk ★ LN8. . . . . .70 A5
Rand La LN8 . . . . .70 A5
Randolph Rd PE20 . . . . . .146 D7
Randsfield Ave 20 HU15. . . .2 C5
Rangefield PE2. . . . . .229 E4
Rangell Gate PE12 . . . . . .157 B5
Range Rd NG31 . . . . .211 C5
Rangoon Way 4 PE10 . . . .213 E4
Ransom Ct 4 DN39 . . . . . . .22 A6
Ransome Cl 7 NG24 . . . . .104 B4
Ransome Way 17 HU15 . . . . .2 C6
Ranters Row 8 LN13 . . . . .75 F2
Ranville Cl 11 PE11. . . . . .145 C1
Ranworth Cl 1 PE25 . . . . .206 D7
Ranyard La LN11 . . . . .72 E5
Rase La 5 LN8. . . . . .57 D8
Rasen Cl 3 LN8. . . . . .57 B8
Rasen Ct 2 PE1. . . . . . . .226 D3
Rasen La LN1 . . . . .234 A4
Rasen Rd Tealby LN8 . . . . .46 B1
Walesby LN8 . . . . .45 F1
Rasen Road LN7 . . . . .32 B1
Rason's Ct 8 PE21. . . . . . .209 A5
Rasper Rd Pools Nature
Reserve★ DN40. . . . . . . .186 A8
Rat Abbey DN15. . . . . .9 C4
Ratcliffe Ct 1 PE1. . . . . . .226 D7
Rathbone Cres PE3. . . . . .225 E2
Rathkenny Cl PE12 . . . . . .215 E2
Rats Pen La LN11. . . . . . . .62 C1
Ratten Row PE22. . . . . . . .127 A5
Rauceby CE Sch NG34 . . . .120 E5
Rauceby Dro NG34 . . . . . .120 F3
Rauceby La NG34. . . . . . .120 E5
Rauceby Sta NG34. . . . . . .120 F3
Rauceby Terr LN1. . . . . . .234 A2
Rauceby Warren Nature
Reserve★ 120 F2
Ravel Cl PE9 . . . . .218 F6
Raven Cl 1 DN20 . . . . .19 D4
Ravencroft La 6 DN10. . . . .40 A1
Ravendale 3 DN18. . . . . . .10 F8
Ravendale Cl
Gonerby Hill Foot NG31 . . .211 A8
Holton le Clay DN36 . . . . .195 E1
Ravendale Dr LN2 . . . . . . .202 A7
Ravendale Rd
Cleethorpes DN35 . . . . . .193 A3
Gainsborough DN21 . . . . .197 E3
Ravendale St N 3 DN15. . .183 B3
Ravendale St S DN15. . . . .183 B3
Ravenhill DN35 . . . . .192 D3
Ravens Bank PE12 . . . . . .158 B2
Ravenscar Rd 5 DN37. . . .188 A1
Raven's Dro PE12 . . . . . . .159 A3
Ravensfleet Rd DN21 . . . . .40 C6
Raven's Gate Fleet PE12. . .159 A3
Holbeach PE12. . . . . .158 E2
Ravensmoor Cl 4 LN6. . . .204 E1
Ravenspurn Way DN31 . . . .191 D8
Raven St HU9 . . . . .181 D7
RAVENSTHORPE PE3. . . . .225 C6
Ravensthorpe Prim Sch
PE3. . . . . .225 C7
Ravens View LN6. . . . . .92 A4
Ravenwood LN4. . . . . .203 A2
Rawcliffe Gr HU4. . . . . . . .179 D5
Rawling Way HU3. . . . . . . .180 C5
Rawlinson Ave 27 LN7. . . . .33 B3
Rawnsley Cl 16 LN13. . . . . .75 F2
Rawsons La PE21. . . . . . . .125 E5
Raybrook Cl 5 PE21. . . . . .208 E2
Raymond Mays Way PE10 .213 D2
Raymond Rd DN16 . . . . . .185 C7
Rayner Ave PE2. . . . . .231 E5
Raysor's La PE22. . . . . . . .114 A2
Rayton Cl LN4. . . . . .203 A2
Raywell Cl 1 HU10 . . . . . .178 F7
Raywell Lane HU14 . . . . . . .3 B8
Raywell St HU2. . . . . .180 E7
Reaches The PE6. . . . . . . .175 C3
Read Cl 2 NG24 . . . . .104 C1
Reading Cl LN4. . . . . .203 E1
Reading Gate DN14. . . . . . .6 C4
Reading Rm Yd 2 HU14 . . . .3 A4
Reads La 4 NG33 . . . . . . .151 D7
Read Way LN4 . . . . .207 D5
Reams Cl 4 PE21. . . . . . . .209 D4
Reapers Cl 1 PE12. . . . . . .215 B2
Reaper's Rise 20 DN9. . . . .27 E6
Reaper's Way 8 DN9. . . . . .27 D2
REASBY LN3. . . . . .69 C6
Reasby Rd LN3 . . . . .69 C7
Reckitt Dr HU14. . . . . .3 B6
Recreation Gd Rd PE9 . . . .219 B6
Recreation Rd 2 PE10. . . .213 D5
Recto Ave DN32. . . . . .191 F5
Rectors Way 6 PE4 . . . . . .221 D2
Rectory Gdns
5 Beckingham DN10. . . . . .40 A1
5 Glinton PE6. . . . . .220 C8
Peterborough PE2 . . . . . . .231 B7
Rectory La Addlethorpe PE24 90 C4
Barrowby NG32 . . . . .210 A5
Bottesford NG13. . . . . . . .128 A6
Claypole NG23 . . . . .117 F8
Etton PE6 . . . . .173 D5
3 Fulbeck NG32 . . . . . . .106 C1
Gainsborough DN21. . . . . .52 F5
6 Gedney PE12. . . . . . . .159 D7

Rectory La continued
Glinton PE6 . . . . .220 C8
Harlaxton NG32 . . . . . . .139 C7
Leadenham LN5 . . . . . . .106 C2
1 Mareham le Fen PE22 . . .98 F4
North Witham NG33 . . . . .151 D4
4 Owmby LN8 . . . . .55 F6
2 Peakirk PE6. . . . . .174 A5
Stainton le Vale LN8 . . . . .46 D5
24 Waddington LN5 . . . . . .93 F7
Woolsthorpe by Belvoir
NG32. . . . . .138 D8
Rectory Lea DN21 . . . . .54 F4
Rectory Rd Anderby PE24 . .76 F2
Boston PE21. . . . . .209 B3
Coleby LN5. . . . . .93 F3
Newton LN2 . . . . .170 B5
Ruskington NG34 . . . . . .108 D1
Tydd St Mary PE13 . . . . . .160 B1
Rectory Road LN9. . . . . . . .85 D1
Rectory St Beckingham LN5 105 B4
Epworth DN9 . . . . .27 E6
Red Barn La PE20 . . . . . . .136 B3
Redbourn Cl 7 DN16. . . . .183 B1
REDBOURNE DN21. . . . . . . .30 F3
Redbourne Dr LN2 . . . . . .202 A8
Redbourne Mere DN21 . . . .30 E2
Redbourne Rd
Grimsby DN33. . . . . .191 B3
Hibaldstow DN20. . . . . . . .30 F4
Waddingham DN21 . . . . . .43 C7
Redbourn E Rd DN16 . . . . .19 A6
Redbourne St
Kingston upon Hull HU3 . .180 B5
Scunthorpe DN16. . . . . . .183 C2
Redbourn Terr 4 PE21. . . .208 F3
Redbourn Way DN16 . . . . .183 B2
Redbridge PE4. . . . . .220 E6
Red Cap La PE21. . . . . . . .208 E3
Redcar Cl LN6 . . . . .204 F4
Redcar Gr DN32. . . . . .192 A5
Redcliff Dr 22 HU14. . . . . . .3 A4
Redcliffe Rd NG31. . . . . . .211 B7
Redcliff Rd
Kingston upon Hull HU13 . . .3 E4
Melton HU14 . . . . .2 F5
Redcombe La DN20 . . . . . .196 B4
Redcote Dr LN6 . . . . .204 F4
Redcot Gdns PE9. . . . . . . .219 B6
Redcross St NG31 . . . . . . .211 B5
Redfern Cl HU3. . . . . .180 D5
Redgate Cl 5 PE1. . . . . . .226 E7
Redgate Rd PE13. . . . . . . .170 C8
Red Hall ★ PE10 . . . . .213 D4
Redhall Cl 9 DN3 . . . . .14 A2
Red Hall Dr LN4. . . . . .205 F4
Red Hall Farm La LN4. . . . .205 F4
Redhill La LN8 . . . . .59 A8
Red Hill Nature Reserve★
LN11. . . . . .72 E7
Red House Gdns 9 NG32 . .128 F7
Red La South Ferriby DN18. . .9 F7
Welby NG32 . . . . .130 F5
Redland Cres 1 DN8 . . . . . .15 B8
Red Leas La LN11. . . . . . . .62 A8
Red Lion Sq 19 PE9 . . . . . .219 B5
Red Lion St 9 Bicker PE20 135 A4
6 Boston PE21. . . . . . . .208 F5
3 Spalding PE11 . . . . . . .214 D4
8 Stamford PE9 . . . . . . .219 B5
Redman Cl PE21. . . . . .197 E5
Redmile Cl Bourne PE10 . . .154 D5
Pinchbeck PE11 . . . . .214 C8
Red Mile La PE11. . . . . . . .214 C8
Redmile's La PE4 . . . . .171 A3
Redmile Wlk 5 PE1 . . . . . .226 D7
Red Rd LN8. . . . . .84 B8
Redshank Dr DN16 . . . . . .185 F5
Redshank Way PE7. . . . . . .230 C1
Redstone Ind Est PE21. . . .208 E3
Redstone Rd PE21. . . . . . .208 E3
Redthorne Cl 2 PE21. . . . .214 F5
Redthorn Way NG23. . . . . .117 F7
Redwing Cl
Peterborough PE2 . . . . . . .231 E7
Skellingthorpe LN6. . . . . .200 A3
Redwing Gr 1 LN6. . . . . . .204 D8
Redwood Ave 11 NG34. . . .212 D4
Redwood Cl DN16. . . . . . . .185 D3
Redwood Dr
Cleethorpes DN35 . . . . . .192 D2
Waddington LN5 . . . . . . .205 D1
Reedbush Ave 4 LN2. . . . .202 F6
Reed Cl 7 PE7. . . . . .230 C2
REEDHAM LN4. . . . . .111 C7
Reedham Garth HU4 . . . . .179 A3
Reedham La LN4. . . . . .207 F2
Reedings Cl NG32. . . . . . . .210 B5
Reedings Rd NG32. . . . . . .210 B5
Reedland Way PE7. . . . . . .230 C1
Reedmace Cl 3 PE6. . . . . .174 E4
Redmans Cl 5 PE6. . . . . . .164 F3
REED POINT LN4 . . . . .110 E2
Reed St 7 HU2. . . . . .180 E7
REEPHAM LN3. . . . . .203 F8
Reepham PE2 . . . . .229 D4
Reepham CE (Controlled)
Prim Sch LN3 . . . . .203 F8
Reepham Rd LN3. . . . . .82 A7
Reet 2 DN31 . . . . .189 B1
Reeves Way PE1 . . . . .226 D5
Refinery Rd DN16 . . . . . . .183 F2
Reform Pl 2 NG34 . . . . . .212 C4
Reform St
9 Crowland PE6. . . . . . . .166 E1
Kingston upon Hull HU2 . .180 F7

Reform St continued
Stamford PE9. . . . . .218 F5
Regal Gdns 2 NG33. . . . . .162 E8
Regal Pl PE2. . . . . .231 E1
Regency Ct 13 DN18 . . . . . .3 E1
Regency Gdns NG31 . . . . .211 D5
Regency Way PE3 . . . . . . .225 E1
Regent Ave LN6. . . . . .200 C1
Regent Dr 18 DN17 . . . . . .16 C7
Regent Gdns DN31 . . . . . .191 C5
Regent Rd LN12 . . . . .64 B4
Regent St Sh Arc DN32 . . .191 B7
Regents Cl
6 Collingham NG23 . . . . . .91 D4
3 Scunthorpe DN15 . . . . .183 A5
4 Skegness PE25 . . . . . .206 C1
Regents Pk Cl 17 LN6 . . . .204 F1
Regent St PE11 . . . . .214 C3
Reginald Rd LN5. . . . . . . .182 F5
Regina Wlk 10 PE24. . . . . .90 D7
Reindeer Cl LN9 . . . . .199 A4
Rein The DN9 . . . . .27 A2
Reldene Dr HU5. . . . . .179 B7
Rembrandt Way PE11 . . . .214 B3
Remigius Gr LN2. . . . . . . .202 C7
Remple Ave 2 DN7 . . . . . . .15 A3
Remple Comm Rd DN7 . . . .14 F2
Remple La 3 DN7. . . . . . . .15 A3
Renault Dr LN4 . . . . .205 F1
Rendel St DN31 . . . . .188 F1
Renew's Dro PE6. . . . . . . .166 D3
Renfrew Dr 2 LN5. . . . . . .205 C2
Renfrew Dr NG34 . . . . . . .121 A2
Renfrew Rd LN5. . . . . .205 C2
Renton Ct HU10 . . . . .178 F5
Reporto Ave DN32. . . . . . .191 F5
Repton Cl LN4 . . . . .203 D1
Repton Dr 2 DN16 . . . . . .185 B3
Repton Rd 7 LN12. . . . . . .64 B3
Reservation The NG34. . . .212 F7
Reservoir Rd PE11 . . . . . . .145 F4
Reservoir St LN1. . . . . . . .234 A4
Resolute Cl 6 PE23. . . . . .101 A8
Resolution Cl PE21 . . . . . .208 A4
Responso Ave DN32 . . . . .191 F5
Reston Ct DN35. . . . . .193 A3
Reston Gr 4 DN33. . . . . . .191 B4
Retief Cl LN1. . . . . .201 D8
Retief View LN1 . . . . .201 D8
Retreat The
Easton on the Hill PE9 . . .171 C3
6 Maxey PE6 . . . . .173 C6
REVESBY PE22 . . . . .99 C3
Revesby Abbey PE22 . . . . . .99 C5
Revesby Ave Boston PE21 .208 C4
Grimsby DN34 . . . . .190 F4
Scunthorpe DN16. . . . . . .185 A7
Revesby Bank
Carrington PE22. . . . . .99 B1
Revesby PE22. . . . . .112 B8
REVESBY BRIDGE PE22 . . . .99 C3
Revesby Cl Boston PE21 . . .208 C4
Lincoln LN6 . . . . .204 F6
Revesby Cnr 5 PE22 . . . . . .99 A4
Revesby Ct DN16. . . . . . . .185 A8
Revesby Dr PE25 . . . . .206 A4
Revigo Ave DN32. . . . . . . .191 F5
Revill Cl 5 Claypole NG33 .117 E8
17 Scotter DN21 . . . . . . .29 C3
Reynard Ct DN21 . . . . .53 E3
Reynard St 3 PE23. . . . . . .88 A1
Reynolds Cl 2 HU14. . . . . . .2 F5
Reynolds Dr 1 LN6. . . . . .205 B6
Reynolds Gdns 6 PE12. . . .157 F7
Reynold's Paddock 2 LN5 93 A5
Reynolds Prim Sch DN35 .192 D7
Reynolds St DN35 . . . . . . .192 D7
Rhine Ave 6 PE2. . . . . . . .230 E8
Rhodes Ave 2 NG34. . . . . .212 C3
Rhodes St HU3. . . . . .179 F5
Rialto Ave DN32. . . . . .191 F5
Ribble St 4 HU3. . . . . . . .180 B4
Ribbon Pond Dr NG24 . . . .104 A2
Riber Ct 2 PE21 . . . . .210 E5
Ribes Cl 1 PE7. . . . . .230 D3
Ribston Cl DN16. . . . . .185 A2
RIBY DN37 . . . . .23 C2
Riby Cl 3 DN21 . . . . .53 A7
Riby Cross Roads DN37 . . . .23 C3
Riby Ct DN36. . . . . .195 E2
Riby Rd Cabourne LN7 . . . . .33 D6
Keelby DN41 . . . . .23 A4
Scunthorpe DN17. . . . . . .184 E5
Stallingborough DN41 . . . . .23 C4
Swallow LN7 . . . . .34 A7
Riby Sq DN31 . . . . .189 B1
Riby St DN31. . . . . .189 B1
Richard Busby Way 14
PE12. . . . . .160 A8
Richards Ave LN6 . . . . . . .204 F4
Richards Cl 13 NG34. . . . .122 D3
Richardson Cl
Bourne PE10 . . . . .213 D7
18 Humberston DN36 . . . .36 D8
Richardson Rise DN21 . . . .197 F3
Richard St DN31 . . . . .191 C8
Richard Young Cl 4
PE13. . . . . .170 D2
Richdale Ave 1 DN21 . . . . .30 B2
Richmond Ave PE4. . . . . . .221 A2
Richmond Cl Boston PE21. .209 A5
Caythorpe NG32 . . . . .119 B6
2 Newark-on-Trent NG24 .104 A2
3 Sleaford NG34. . . . . . .212 D2
Richmond Cl 1 PE25 . . . . .206 C2
Richmond Dr
Green Hill NG31 . . . . .210 E5
Lincoln LN6 . . . . .204 F3

Richmond Dr continued
Scunthorpe DN16. . . . . . .185 C4
Skegness PE25. . . . . .206 C1
Richmond Leisure Complex
PE25. . . . . .206 B1
Richmond Rd
Cleethorpes DN35 . . . . . .192 E5
Gainsborough DN21. . . . . .197 F4
Grimsby DN34 . . . . .191 A6
Kingston upon Hull HU13 . .178 E2
Lincoln LN1 . . . . .201 D4
Louth LN11 . . . . .61 B8
10 Trusthorpe LN12 . . . . .64 C1
Richmond Sch The PE25 . .206 C2
Richmond Way PE13 . . . . .170 B2
RIDDINGS DN17 . . . . .184 F4
Rider Gdns PE21 . . . . .209 D2
Rides The 7 PE6. . . . . . . .164 F3
Ridge Cl 14 LN2 . . . . .68 D6
Ridge View 1 Brigg DN20 .196 D4
Ermine LN1 . . . . .201 D8
Fillingham DN21. . . . . .54 F4
Harmston LN5 . . . . .93 F4
Ridge View Rd LN4 . . . . . .205 F4
Ridgeway 13 LN2. . . . . .68 D2
Ridge Way
Peterborough PE2 . . . . . . .231 B8
Scunthorpe DN17. . . . . . .182 E1
Ridgeway Rd HU5 . . . . . . .179 B7
Ridgeway The DN34 . . . . .190 D3
Ridgewell Cl 10 LN6. . . . .204 D8
Ridgewood Ave 14 DN3. . . .14 A1
Ridgewood Dr 5 DN15. . . . .8 A4
Ridings The Bourne PE10 . .213 C3
Kingston upon Hull HU5 . .179 A8
Market Rasen LN8 . . . . . . .57 E7
17 North Ferriby HU14. . . . .3 A4
Ridley Ave PE25 . . . . .206 D2
Rightwell PE3. . . . . .225 A6
Rightwell E PE3 . . . . .225 A5
Rightwell W PE3 . . . . .225 A5
RIGSBY LN13 . . . . .75 D2
Rigsby Wood Nature
Reserve★ LN13 . . . . .75 C3
Rigsmoor Cl 2 LN6. . . . . . .93 C8
Rileston Pl DN16. . . . . . . .185 B2
Riley Cl
Bracebridge Heath LN4 . . .205 F2
Yaxley PE7 . . . . .233 D6
Riley Way HU3 . . . . .179 F7
Rimac Rd LN11. . . . . .51 D2
Rimes La DN22 . . . . .65 A7
Rime's La LN10 . . . . .98 C6
Rimington Rd 4 PE21 . . . .126 C1
Ring Beck La HU15. . . . . . . .2 A8
Ringers La PE13. . . . . .170 B2
Ring Moor Cl 7 LN4. . . . . .109 F5
Ringrose La 4 HU10 . . . . .178 E6
Ringrose St HU3 . . . . .179 F5
Ringstead Rd PE4 . . . . . . .221 D1
Ringstone Chase PE10 . . . .142 F1
Ringwood PE3. . . . . .224 F3
Ringwood Cl
4 Birchwood LN6 . . . . . .200 D1
2 Scunthorpe DN16 . . . .185 B4
Rinks La LN5. . . . . .92 E1
Rinovia Dr DN33. . . . . .191 A2
Rio Dr NG32 . . . . .91 D5
Ripley Ct DN15. . . . . .182 B2
Ripley Dr LN6 . . . . .205 A3
Riplingham Rd HU10 . . . . .178 A8
Ripon Cl
1 Bracebridge Heath LN4. . .81 A2
Grantham NG31 . . . . .210 F5
Peterborough PE4 . . . . . . .220 F3
Scunthorpe DN17. . . . . . .184 C7
11 Skegness PE25 . . . . .206 D7
Ripon Dr NG34. . . . . .212 C6
Ripon Pl 17 LN12 . . . . .64 B3
Ripon St Grimsby DN31 . . .191 C8
Lincoln LN5 . . . . .201 F1
Ripon Way HU9 . . . . .181 C8
RIPPINGALE PE10 . . . . . . .142 F3
Rippingale Rd PE10 . . . . . .142 D2
Rippons Dro PE6. . . . . . . .217 E2
RISBY LN8 . . . . .46 B3
Risby PE3 . . . . .224 F3
Risby Gn LN6 . . . . .204 F7
Risby Rd DN15 . . . . .9 A1
Risdale 26 LN7. . . . . .33 B4
RISEGATE PE11. . . . . .144 F4
Risegate Rd PE11 . . . . . . .144 F4
RISEHOLME LN2 . . . . .68 A3
Riseholme PE2. . . . . .229 E3
Riseholme Coll LN1 . . . . . .67 E4
Riseholme La LN2 . . . . .67 F2
Riseholme Rd
Gainsborough DN21. . . . . .197 F3
Lincoln LN2 . . . . .201 F7
Rise The
16 Navenby/Wellingore
LN5. . . . . .107 A8
8 North Ferriby HU14. . . . .3 A5
Scunthorpe DN17. . . . . . .184 E3
South Ferriby DN18 . . . . . .10 A8
Risewood La NG33 . . . . . . .130 F1
Riston St HU3. . . . . .180 C5
Rivan Gr DN33 . . . . .194 E7
Rivehall Ave 7 LN2. . . . . . .68 D7
Riven Cl DN16 . . . . .185 A8
Rivelin Cres DN16 . . . . . . .185 A7
Rivelin Pl DN16 . . . . .185 A7
Rivendale PE4 . . . . .220 F2
River Bain Rd LN8 . . . . . . .72 C8
River Bank PE12 . . . . .214 C1
Riverbank Cl Althorpe DN17 17 D5
Chapel Hill LN4. . . . . . . .110 E5
Guyhirn PE13. . . . . .177 F2

Riverbank Cl *continued*
Market Deeping PE6 ... 217 E3
Riverbank Rise 17 DN18 ... 3 E1
Riverbank Studios★ PE11 214 E4
River Ct 20 PE11 ... 214 D4
Riverdale 8 LN2 ... 68 D2
Riverdale Rd DN16 ... 185 A7
Rivergate
3 Peterborough PE1 ... 226 A1
3 Spalding PE11 ... 214 D2
Rivergate Sh Ctr PE1 ... 226 A1
River Gr HU4 ... 179 E3
Riverhead LN11 ... 198 D7
Riverhead Rd LN11 ... 198 D6
Riverhead Terr LN11 ... 198 D7
River La Anwick NG34 ... 109 B1
Deeping St James PE6 ... 174 B7
Keddington LN11 ... 198 E7
Moulton PE12 ... 158 A8
Peterborough PE3 ... 225 F2
River Mdw DN20 ... 196 A2
Rivermead LN6 ... 205 C4
Rivermead Cl LN6 ... 205 C4
River Rd West Burton DN22 ... 52 D4
West Walton PE14 ... 170 C4
Riverside 2 Brigg DN20 ... 196 A3
Grantham NG31 ... 211 B4
Market Deeping PE6 ... 217 D4
5 Scotter DN21 ... 29 C4
2 Spalding PE11 ... 214 B5
Riverside App DN21 ... 197 C5
Riverside Cl
14 Bottesford NG13 ... 128 A6
12 Sleaford NG34 ... 212 D4
Riverside Ct Louth LN11 ... 198 D6
South Field HU13 ... 3 E4
Riverside Dr
Humberston DN35 ... 193 C2
Lincoln LN5 ... 234 A1
Riverside Gdns
Parson Drove PE13 ... 177 C7
Peterborough PE3 ... 225 D1
Riverside Ind Est PE21 ... 209 A2
Riverside Mead PE2 ... 231 B8
Riverside Pk
Grantham NG31 ... 211 B6
Spalding PE11 ... 214 E2
Riverside Pk Homes PE21 208 E6
Riverside Rise LN11 ... 198 D7
Riverside Spinney PE8 ... 222 A3
Riverside The 11 NG34 ... 212 D4
Riverside Wlk
8 Bottesford NG13 ... 128 A6
Grantham NG31 ... 211 B4
River Terr 4 PE13 ... 170 C1
Riverton Cl LN1 ... 201 D8
Riverton View LN1 ... 201 D8
Riverview
Church Laneham DN22 ... 65 B4
Long Bennington NG23 ... 117 D4
River View
21 Barton-upon-Humber DN18 ... 10 F8
Northfield HU13 ... 178 F1
Riverview Ave HU14 ... 3 A4
River Way PE21 ... 209 C2
Roadwood La NG23 ... 78 F8
Robden Ct PE2 ... 225 E1
Roberta Cl 10 PE25 ... 206 A4
Robert Ave PE1 ... 225 F8
Robert Barnett Cl 6 HU13 ... 178 E2
Robert Cl DN40 ... 186 B4
Robert Dukeson Ave NG24 ... 104 A6
Robert Rayner Cl PE2 ... 230 D6
Robert's Field Nature Reserve★ PE9 ... 162 F5
Robert's Gr PE25 ... 206 D7
Robertson Ave 6 NG34 ... 121 B8
Robertson Cl 14 LN5 ... 93 F7
Robertson Dr NG34 ... 212 D5
Robertson Rd
3 Grantham NG31 ... 210 F5
Lincoln LN6 ... 204 E1
Roberts St DN32 ... 192 A8
Robert St DN15 ... 183 A3
Robert Tressell Wlk 2 LN2 ... 202 C7
Robey St LN5 ... 205 E8
Robin Cl Bottesford DN16 ... 185 B2
8 Market Deeping PE6 ... 217 C5
12 Sleaford NG34 ... 212 B3
Robin Hood Cl PE3 ... 224 F2
Robin Hood Cres 13 DN3 ... 14 A1
Robin Hood Rd
11 Kirk Sandall DN3 ... 14 A1
Skegness PE25 ... 206 C3
Robin Hood's Wlak PE21 ... 208 E7
Robin Hood's Wlk PE21 ... 208 F6
Robins Cl PE2 ... 230 E8
Robins Cres LN6 ... 92 D5
Robins Field PE8 ... 222 A4
Robinson Ave 4 LN13 ... 75 E2
Robinson Cl DN15 ... 182 E4
Robinson La
Grimsby DN31 ... 189 C2
Louth LN11 ... 198 C5
Robinson Pl LN5 ... 105 F5
Robinson Rd DN40 ... 186 F6
Robinson St E DN32 ... 191 E7
Robinson's Gr 8 DN20 ... 31 A5
Robinson's La 1 DN36 ... 36 B1
Robins Wood PE8 ... 222 A4
Robin Wlk DN37 ... 24 B5
Robson Rd DN35 ... 192 D7
Rochdale Rd DN16 ... 185 A5
Rochester Ave HU4 ... 179 B3
Rochester Cl
8 Bracebridge Heath LN4 ... 81 A2
1 Scunthorpe DN17 ... 184 C7
Rochester Ct
2 Bourne PE10 ... 213 C7
Humberston DN35 ... 193 A1
Rochester Dr
Birchwood LN6 ... 200 D2
9 Grantham NG31 ... 210 E5
Rochford Cres PE21 ... 209 B5
Rochford Twr★ PE21 ... 209 E5
Rochford Twr La PE21 ... 209 D6
Rockbourne Pl PE4 ... 225 E8
Rocket La DN9 ... 27 C4
Rockingham Cl 8 PE6 ... 217 A6
Rockingham Cres DN34 ... 190 D4
Rockingham Ct 9 DN34 ... 190 D4
Rockingham Gr PE4 ... 221 A2
Rockingham Rd 4 PE9 ... 218 E6
Rockley Ct HU10 ... 178 F6
Rock Rd Peterborough PE1 ... 225 F6
Stamford PE9 ... 219 B5
Rock The NG32 ... 138 B4
Roden Wy 2 PE7 ... 230 F5
Rod Mill Rd DN16 ... 183 E1
Rodney Cl 9 HU2 ... 180 E8
Roeburn Wy PE11 ... 214 A4
Roegate La PE12 ... 159 F1
Roeze Cl 14 LN10 ... 97 C5
Rogues Alley PE13 ... 177 C4
Rokeby Ave HU4 ... 179 B5
Rokeby Cl HU4 ... 179 B5
Rokeby Mews HU4 ... 179 B5
Rokeby Pk HU4 ... 179 B5
Rokeby Pk Prim Sch HU4 ... 179 B4
Rolleston Cl 3 LN2 ... 201 F7
Rolleston Garth PE1 ... 226 C8
Rollitt Cl HU10 ... 178 F5
Rolls Cl PE7 ... 233 E7
Roman Bank Bourne PE10 ... 213 E4
Chapel St Leonards PE24 ... 90 E8
Holbeach PE12 ... 215 D8
Huttoft PE24 ... 77 C4
1 Ingoldmells PE25 ... 206 D8
Moulton PE12 ... 146 E2
Newton PE13 ... 170 B4
6 Skegness PE25 ... 206 C3
Spalding PE11 ... 214 F6
Stamford PE9 ... 219 A5
Roman Cl
9 Metheringham LN4 ... 95 D4
Navenby LN5 ... 107 B8
Roman Dr PE8 ... 222 D2
Roman Pavement LN2 ... 202 C4
Roman Rd Moulton PE12 ... 157 D1
Panton LN8 ... 71 B5
Scawby DN20 ... 30 D8
Roman Way
7 Ancaster NG32 ... 120 A2
Aubourn Haddington & South Hykeham LN6 ... 93 A8
Horncastle LN9 ... 199 D3
Riddings DN17 ... 184 F6
Roman Wharf LN1 ... 201 C3
Roman Wy LN7 ... 33 A3
Romany Gdns PE2 ... 231 D5
Roma Rd PE7 ... 231 C4
Romney Cl 3 LN6 ... 205 B6
Romney Ct 6 NG34 ... 212 D5
Romney Dr LN6 ... 205 B5
Romsey Ct DN34 ... 190 D5
Romulus Way 18 LN6 ... 93 B8
Ronald Cl 3 PE25 ... 206 C4
Rood's La PE12 ... 157 C8
Rookery Ave
2 Grimsby DN33 ... 191 D3
Sleaford NG34 ... 212 B3
Rookery Cl LN11 ... 198 D8
Rookery Croft 14 DN9 ... 27 E6
Rookery La Ancaster NG32 ... 119 F2
13 Leasingham NG34 ... 121 B7
Lincoln LN6 ... 205 C6
Wildmore LN4 ... 111 E2
Wymondham LE14 ... 150 B1
Rookery Rd 2 Bicker PE20 135 A4
16 Healing DN41 ... 23 F5
Sutton Bridge PE12 ... 160 D7
Rookery The
14 Collingham NG23 ... 91 D5
Peterborough PE2 ... 229 C7
2 Scawby DN20 ... 30 F8
Yaxley PE7 ... 233 D5
Rooklands 10 DN21 ... 29 C3
Rook's La DN10 ... 39 F6
Roosdyke La PE22 ... 137 D7
Roper's Bridge La PE20 ... 136 A4
Roper's Gate Gedney PE12 159 F8
2 Lutton PE12 ... 160 A8
Roper's La PE12 ... 159 D1
Ropery La 2 DN18 ... 3 E1
Ropery Rd DN21 ... 197 B7
Ropery St Grimsby DN32 ... 191 F7
Kingston upon Hull HU3 ... 180 D4
Ropery The LN1 ... 234 A3
Ropewalk 6 LN8 ... 70 D5
Ropewalk Gall★ DN18 ... 3 F1
Ropewalk The
1 Caistor LN7 ... 33 B4
8 Colsterworth NG33 ... 151 E6
Rope Wlk Lincoln LN6 ... 234 A1
15 Thorne/Moorends DN8 ... 15 A8
ROPSLEY NG33 ... 131 B1
Ropsley CE Prim Sch NG33 ... 131 A1
Ropsley Rd NG33 ... 140 E8
Rosaire Pl DN33 ... 195 A8
Rosalind Ave DN34 ... 191 B7
Rosamond St 7 HU3 ... 180 B4
Rose Ave PE2 ... 231 C7
Rosebank DN21 ... 197 B7
Roseberry Ave
26 Hatfield DN7 ... 14 D4
Skegness PE25 ... 206 D1
Rosebery Ave Boston PE21 208 C5
Lincoln LN1 ... 201 D4
Rose Cottage Gdn Ctr & Tropical Forest★ PE11 ... 156 D8
Rose Cottage La LN5 ... 94 A3
Rose Cres PE12 ... 158 D3
Rosedale Scunthorpe DN17 184 E2
Waltham DN37 ... 194 C5
Rosedale Cl
Cherry Willingham LN3 ... 203 E5
4 Lincoln LN6 ... 204 F3
Rosedale Dr NG31 ... 211 B8
Rosedale Gr HU5 ... 179 D7
Rosefield Cl 27 NG24 ... 104 C1
Rosefields DN21 ... 197 E5
Rosegar Ave PE20 ... 135 F2
Rosegarth St 14 PE21 ... 208 F4
Rose Gdns DN40 ... 186 C4
Rose Gr 1 PE25 ... 206 D5
Rosehill Cl 6 LN1 ... 66 D2
Rosehip Rd 8 PE10 ... 154 D6
Rose La
Beesby with Saleby LN13 ... 75 F5
Pinchbeck PE11 ... 156 E8
Roseland Bsns Pk NG32 ... 117 C1
Westborough NG23 ... 117 C1
Roselea Ave 8 LN2 ... 68 D6
Rose Leigh Way PE11 ... 214 C7
Rosemary Ave
Grimsby DN34 ... 190 F6
11 Market Deeping PE6 ... 217 C5
Rosemary Cres NG31 ... 210 E1
Rosemary Gdns
12 Bourne PE10 ... 213 C6
Peterborough PE1 ... 225 F8
Rosemary La LN2 ... 234 B2
Rosemary Rise NG33 ... 141 D5
Rosemary Way DN35 ... 192 E1
Rose Mdws ... 208 B4
Rosemount Dr DN16 ... 185 B6
Rosemount Grange HU13 178 C3
Rosemount La 5 DN21 ... 43 D7
Rose Pl PE21 ... 209 A3
Roseum Cl LN6 ... 204 E5
Roseveare Ave DN31 ... 191 A7
Roseway 6 DN21 ... 197 D5
Rose Wlk Scunthorpe DN15 183 C3
Upton DN21 ... 53 D5
11 Wisbech PE13 ... 170 C1
Wittering PE9 ... 172 B1
Rosewood Cl
12 Beacon Hill NG24 ... 104 A5
2 Birchwood LN6 ... 204 C8
4 Kingston upon Hull HU5 ... 179 B7
Rosewood Dr 5 NG34 ... 212 D2
Rosewood Way
Hampton Hargate PE7 ... 230 F2
1 Scunthorpe DN16 ... 185 B3
Rosey Row 4 HU9 ... 181 C7
Rosina Gr N 2 DN32 ... 192 B6
Rosina Gr S 4 DN32 ... 192 B6
Roslyn Rd HU3 ... 179 E7
Rosmead St HU9 ... 181 D8
Rosner Dr HU13 ... 178 B2
Rosper Rd DN40 ... 186 A8
Rosper Road Pools Nature Reserve★ DN40 ... 186 A8
Rossall Cl
9 Mablethorpe/Sutton on Sea LN12 ... 77 A7
Scunthorpe DN16 ... 185 C3
Rossa Rd LN13 ... 76 D7
Ross Cl
5 Coddington NG24 ... 104 D5
St Giles LN2 ... 202 D6
Ross Dr PE9 ... 218 E7
Rossetti Ct NG31 ... 211 E5
Rossington Cl
18 Metheringham LN4 ... 95 C4
28 Sandilands LN12 ... 77 A8
Ross La 6 DN15 ... 9 B5
Ross Rd DN31 ... 189 D1
Rostrop Rd LN4 ... 95 C7
Rosyth Ave PE2 ... 229 D3
Rothbart Way PE7 ... 230 C3
Rothbury Rd DN17 ... 184 F7
Rotherby Gr 3 PE1 ... 226 E7
Rothschild Cl PE21 ... 208 B4
ROTHWELL LN7 ... 33 F2
Rothwell Ave 8 DN33 ... 191 B3
Rothwell Cl DN21 ... 197 E4
Rothwell Lane LN7 ... 34 B1
Rothwell Rd Cabourne LN7 ... 33 C3
4 Lincoln LN2 ... 201 F7
Scunthorpe DN15 ... 182 D4
Rothwell Road LN7 ... 34 A3
Rothwell Way PE2 ... 230 C7
Rotten Row
Pinchbeck PE11 ... 156 E8
Theddlethorpe St Helen LN12 ... 63 E5
Rotton Sykes La DN15 ... 1 F2
Rotunda The 8 DN10 ... 52 B8
ROUGHTON LN10 ... 98 B7
Roughton Ct 5 LN2 ... 202 A8
ROUGHTON MOOR LN10 ... 98 A7
Roughton Moor Wood Nature Reserve★ LN10 ... 97 F6
Roughton Rd LN10 ... 98 B6
Roundhouse Cl PE1 ... 226 D3
Roundlands PE20 ... 136 D2
Roundway Grimsby DN34 ... 191 C5
2 Immingham DN40 ... 186 C3
Roundway The HU4 ... 179 C5
Rous Ct PE6 ... 164 E5
Routland Cl 8 LN8 ... 70 D4
Roval Dr DN40 ... 186 A4
Rowan Ave
Peterborough PE1 ... 226 C6
Spalding PE11 ... 214 E5
Rowan Cl
6 Barrow upon Humber DN19 ... 11 C8
16 Keelby DN41 ... 23 A4
10 Wisbech PE13 ... 170 E1
Rowan Cres DN16 ... 185 C3
Rowan Ct
34 Chapel St Leonard PE24 ... 90 D7
3 Goxhill DN19 ... 12 A8
11 Heighington/Washingborough LN4 ... 203 D1
Rowan Dr
5 Healing DN41 ... 23 F5
21 Humberston DN36 ... 36 D8
Silk Willoughby NG34 ... 121 B2
Rowan Rd Lincoln LN6 ... 204 F3
Waddington LN5 ... 205 D1
Rowans The
Gainsborough DN21 ... 197 F5
Holbeach PE12 ... 159 A7
9 Nettleham LN2 ... 68 C2
New Waltham DN36 ... 195 E6
4 Westwoodside DN9 ... 27 A2
Rowan Way
1 Boston PE21 ... 209 A7
Bourne PE10 ... 213 B6
16 Metheringham LN4 ... 95 C4
Rowanwood Dr 7 NG31 ... 210 F7
Rowan Wy NG24 ... 104 A3
Rowdyke Rd PE21 ... 136 F7
Rowe Ave PE2 ... 230 D7
Rowgate Rd LN11 ... 73 A5
Rowland Ct 1 PE4 ... 220 F5
Rowland Rd 4 DN16 ... 183 B2
Rowlandson St 3 DN31 ... 189 B2
Rowland Way PE25 ... 206 A4
Rowledge Ct PE4 ... 221 A1
Rowley Rd PE21 ... 209 A4
Rowmills Rd 2 DN16 ... 185 C8
ROWSTON LN4 ... 108 E7
Rowston Cl DN21 ... 197 C6
Rowston St DN35 ... 193 A5
Roxborough Cl LN6 ... 200 E2
Roxburgh Dr NG34 ... 121 A3
Roxburgh Rd PE9 ... 218 F6
Roxburgh St 1 HU5 ... 180 B8
Roxbury Dr DN7 ... 14 D3
ROXBY DN15 ... 9 A3
Roxby Cl LN6 ... 204 F6
Roxby Cswy DN15 ... 9 C4
Roxby Rd DN15 ... 8 F4
Roxholm Cl 2 NG34 ... 108 D1
Roxholme Rd
Leasingham NG34 ... 121 B8
Ruskington NG34 ... 108 C2
Roxton Ave DN41 ... 23 A5
Roxton Hall Dr 15 HU14 ... 3 A5
Roxton La DN40 ... 23 A6
Roxton Rd DN40 ... 23 A7
Royal Air Force Coll The NG34 ... 120 B8
Royal Arthur Cl 5 PE25 ... 206 C1
Royal Cl 15 PE12 ... 160 E4
Royal Ct DN35 ... 193 B1
Royal Mews HU3 ... 180 C6
Royal Oak Ct
18 Heckington NG34 ... 122 E3
19 Louth LN11 ... 198 B5
Royal Oak La
1 Aubourn Haddington & South Hykeham LN5 ... 93 A5
Martin LN4 ... 96 C2
Royal St DN31 ... 189 A2
Royal Standard Cl PE12 ... 216 D3
Royalty Bank PE22 ... 101 B3
Royal Way PE21 ... 209 F2
Royce Cl PE7 ... 233 E6
Royce Rd
Peterborough PE1 ... 226 D3
2 Spalding PE11 ... 214 F6
Roydon Gr LN6 ... 205 B6
Royle Cl PE2 ... 230 C5
Royston Ave PE2 ... 230 C6
Ruards La DN19 ... 5 A1
RUCKLAND LN11 ... 73 F5
Ruckland Ave LN1 ... 201 E7
Rudd Cl PE1 ... 226 C1
Rudgard Ave LN3 ... 203 E6
Rudgard La LN1 ... 234 A3
Rudham Ave DN32 ... 191 E4
Rudkin Dr 5 NG34 ... 212 D6
Rudyard Cl 7 LN12 ... 77 A7
Rudyard Gr PE4 ... 221 C3
Rue de L'yonne 1 NG23 ... 91 D5
Rue de Nozay 3 DN20 ... 19 E4
Rufford Gn 2 LN6 ... 205 C8
Rufford Rd DN35 ... 192 E4
Rugby Ct 1 NG31 ... 211 B3
Rugby Rd
4 Mablethorpe/Sutton on Sea LN12 ... 64 B4
Scunthorpe DN16 ... 185 A8
Rugby St 5 HU3 ... 180 B4
Rumbold La 3 PE24 ... 102 D1
Runcorn Garth HU4 ... 179 B3
Runcorn Rd LN6 ... 204 B5
Running Post La PE20 ... 135 B4
Runswick Cl LN6 ... 205 A3
Runswick Ct DN32 ... 192 B6
Runswick Rd DN32 ... 192 B6
Runway La DN36 ... 195 C4
Rupert Rd 1 DN33 ... 191 D3
Rural Ave PE11 ... 144 D1
Rushcliffe Rd NG31 ... 211 A7
Rushes The 18 DN18 ... 3 F1
Rush Furlong Nature Reserve★ DN9 ... 27 E3
Rushmere PE2 ... 229 F6
Rushmore Ctry Pk★ LN11 ... 61 F8
Rushton Ave PE4 ... 220 E4
Rushtons Way 12 DN20 ... 30 F5
Rushy Dro PE11 ... 145 C8
Rushy La DN7 ... 14 B8
Ruskin Ave LN2 ... 202 B6
Ruskin Gn LN2 ... 202 B6
RUSKINGTON NG34 ... 108 E2
Ruskington Cl DN37 ... 188 A2
Ruskington Sta NG34 ... 108 E1
Ruskin Rd 13 LN12 ... 64 B4
Ruskin St
2 Gainsborough DN21 ... 197 D2
Kingston upon Hull HU3 ... 180 B6
Russell Ave Lincoln LN6 ... 93 C8
Newark-on-Trent NG24 ... 104 A2
Russell Cl
5 Scunthorpe DN15 ... 183 A5
12 Thorney PE6 ... 176 A3
Russell Cres NG34 ... 212 F4
Russell Ct DN35 ... 193 A1
Russell Dr 2 PE12 ... 167 B8
Russell Hill PE8 ... 222 A6
Russell Rd 7 NG34 ... 121 B8
Russell Read Almshouses 13 NG31 ... 211 A4
Russell St
Kingston upon Hull HU2 ... 180 E7
Lincoln LN5 ... 205 D6
Peterborough PE1 ... 225 F3
32 Wisbech PE13 ... 170 D1
Russell Wlk 2 DN17 ... 29 D7
Russell Wy 15 PE10 ... 213 D3
Russet Cl 4 DN15 ... 182 C5
Russet Dr LN11 ... 198 C4
Russet La DN20 ... 196 F6
Rustic Ave PE7 ... 233 B8
Rustic La DN21 ... 41 C6
Ruston Rd NG31 ... 211 F7
Ruston Way LN6 ... 201 D3
Ruther Cl 2 PE2 ... 230 D8
Rutland Ave
3 Newark-on-Trent NG24 ... 104 A3
Waddington LN5 ... 93 E8
Rutland Cl 13 NG33 ... 151 D2
Rutland Dr DN36 ... 195 C5
Rutland La 15 NG13 ... 128 A5
Rutland Rd
Kingston upon Hull HU5 ... 179 E8
25 Mablethorpe/Sutton on Sea LN12 ... 64 B3
Scunthorpe DN16 ... 185 D7
Skegness PE25 ... 206 D3
Stamford PE9 ... 219 D7
Rutland St 2 DN32 ... 189 D1
Rutland Terr PE9 ... 219 A4
Rutland Way Ryhall PE9 ... 163 C1
15 Scampton Airfield LN1 ... 67 E5
Rycroft Ave PE6 ... 217 F5
Rycroft Cl
1 Deeping St James PE6 ... 217 F4
5 Market Deeping PE6 ... 217 F4
Rycroft St NG31 ... 211 B3
Rydal Ave DN33 ... 194 D7
Rydal Cl LN6 ... 200 D2
Rydal Ct PE4 ... 221 C3
Ryde Ave NG31 ... 210 E4
Rye Cl NG34 ... 212 E3
Rye Cres 3 HU15 ... 2 D5
Ryecroft 11 LN5 ... 205 D2
Rye Ct DN33 ... 191 B1
Ryedale 6 HU15 ... 2 D6
Ryedale Ave 1 DN15 ... 9 A6
Ryedale Cl NG31 ... 211 B8
Ryefield PE6 ... 164 E3
Ryefield La PE12 ... 159 B3
Rye La LN13 ... 75 D5
RYHALL PE9 ... 163 C1
Ryhall CE Prim Sch PE9 ... 163 C1
Ryhall Rd
Great Casterton PE9 ... 171 C8
Stamford PE9 ... 219 D5
Ryhall Rd Ind Est PE9 ... 219 D8
Ryland Bridge LN2 ... 68 E6
Ryland Gdns 10 LN2 ... 68 D6
Ryland Rd LN2 ... 68 D6
Rymac Cres PE25 ... 90 E4
Rymer Pl DN35 ... 193 A4
Ryton Rd PE21 ... 208 B3

S

Sable Cl HU4 ... 179 C2
Sabre Way PE1 ... 226 F4
Sackville Cl DN40 ... 186 D4
Sackville Rd DN40 ... 186 D4
Sackville St 2 DN31 ... 191 C7
Sacred Heart RC Prim Sch PE3 ... 225 A5
Sacrewell Farm & Ctry Ctr★ PE8 ... 222 C5
Sacrewell Lodge Sch
Wansford PE8 ... 222 A6
Wansford PE8 ... 222 A6
Saddleback Rd
Skidbrooke with Saltfleet Haven LN11 ... 51 A3

Saddleback Rd continued
South Cockerington LN11. . . . .50 E1
Saddle Ct PE4. . . . . .225 E8
Saddler Dr PE10. . . . . .154 C6
Saddle Row NG34. . . . . .120 B8
Saddlers Cl Glinton PE6. . . . . .220 D8
Osbournby NG34. . . . . .132 D5
Saddler's Cl LN4. . . . . .95 C4
Saddlers Mead 10 PE11. . . . .214 A2
Saddlers Way
Fishtoft PE21. . . . . .209 C2
5 Long Sutton PE12. . . . . . .216 B5
6 Middle Rasen LN8. . . . . . . .57 E7
Saddler's Way 2 DN9. . . . . . .27 D3
Saddlers Wy 13 LN8. . . . . .57 E7
Sadler Cl 9 PE25. . . . . .206 C1
Sadler Rd LN6. . . . . .204 B5
Saffrondale HU10. . . . . .178 E7
Saffron Dr PE7. . . . . .233 B8
Saffron Wlk 12 PE10. . . . . . . .213 C5
Sage Ct Boultham LN6. . . . . . .205 D8
Lincoln LN6. . . . . .205 D8
Sagefield Cl 5 DN33. . . . . . . .194 D8
Sage's La PE4. . . . . .225 C8
Sail Ct PE21. . . . . .208 C4
Sailors Wharf HU9. . . . . .181 C6
Sainsbury Way HU4. . . . . . . .179 A1
St Abbs Cl 3 HU9. . . . . .181 A5
St Aiden's Rd 5 LN6. . . . . . . .204 E2
St Albans Ave DN31. . . . . . . .191 A8
St Albans Cl
5 Grantham NG31. . . . . .210 D5
16 Hibaldstow DN20. . . . . . . .30 F5
3 Scunthorpe DN17. . . . . . . .184 C7
St Alban's Dr 16 PE6. . . . . . . .175 A1
St Andrews NG31. . . . . .211 D7
St Andrews Ave 2 DN17. . . . .184 F2
St Andrews CE Prim Sch
LN10. . . . . .97 C6
St Andrews Cl LN5. . . . . .201 F1
St Andrew's Cl
4 Helpringham NG34. . . . . .133 D7
Redbourne DN21. . . . . .30 F3
St Andrew's Com Prim Sch
HU10. . . . . .178 C7
St Andrew's Cres 6 NG34 121 B7
St Andrews Ct
Immingham DN40. . . . . .186 A4
4 Timberland LN4. . . . . .96 C1
St Andrews Dr
6 Saxilby LN1. . . . . .66 C2
9 Woodhall Spa LN10. . . . . . .97 D6
St Andrew's Dr
1 Burton upon Stather
DN15. . . . . .8 B4
Grimsby DN32. . . . . .192 B4
Lincoln LN6. . . . . .205 C8
Skegness PE25. . . . . .206 D5
St Andrew's Gdns LN6. . . . . .205 C8
St Andrews Gr 33 DN7. . . . . .14 D4
St Andrews La DN40. . . . . . . .186 B3
St Andrew's Mount HU10. . .178 C6
St Andrew's Pl 3 LN5. . . . . . .234 B1
St Andrews Rd
2 Mablethorpe/Sutton on Sea
LN12. . . . . .64 B4
Northborough PE6. . . . . .217 E1
St Andrew's Rd
6 Butterwick PE22. . . . . .126 E3
Spalding PE11. . . . . .214 C1
St Andrew's St
8 Heckington NG34. . . . . . . .122 E3
16 Kirton in Lindsey DN21. . . .30 B1
4 Lincoln LN5. . . . . .234 B1
St Andrew's Way
8 Barnby Dun DN3. . . . . .14 A3
Epworth DN9. . . . . .27 C4
4 RAF Cranwell NG34. . . . . .120 C8
St Andrews Wlk 5 LN10. . . . . .97 C5
St Annes Ave 8 LN11. . . . . . . .50 F7
St Anne's CE (Cont) Prim Sch
NG31. . . . . .211 C3
St Annes Cl Lincoln LN2. . . . .202 B4
Skegness PE25. . . . . .206 C6
3 Sleaford NG34. . . . . .212 C6
4 Spalding PE11. . . . . .214 C6
St Anne's Com Specl Sch
HU15. . . . . .2 E5
St Anne's Rd
9 Keelby DN41. . . . . .23 A4
Lincoln LN2. . . . . .202 B4
St Anne's St NG31. . . . . .211 C3
St Annes Way LN11. . . . . .214 C6
St Anne's Wlk 13 HU15. . . . . . .2 D6
St Ann's Ave DN34. . . . . .191 B6
St Ann's La PE21. . . . . .208 F3
St Anns Wharf 1 PE21. . . . . .208 F3
St Aubins Cres LN4. . . . . .81 F4
St Audrey Cl PE2. . . . . .231 D6
St Augustine Ave DN32. . . . . .191 E5
St Augustine Cres DN16. . . . .185 B5
St Augustine Rd LN2. . . . . . . .202 F6
Saint Augustine's Cath Vol
Acad PE9. . . . . .219 C7
St Augustines CE Jun Sch
PE2. . . . . .230 F8
St Augustine's CE Sch
PE13. . . . . .170 D2
St Augustine's Wlk PE2. . . . . .230 E8
St Augustine Webster Cath
Vol Acad DN32. . . . . .182 D4
St Augustin Way NG31. . . . . .211 A4
St Barbara's Cres 7 DN15. . . . .8 B4
St Barnabas CE Prim Sch
DN38. . . . . .21 B4

St Barnabas Ct 4 HU3. . . .180 C4
St Barnabas Dr 1 HU14. . . . . .3 C7
St Barnabas Rd DN38. . . . . . . .21 C7
St Bartholomews CE Prim Sch
PE11. . . . . .156 A8
St Bartholomew's Cl 4
DN41. . . . . .23 A4
St Bede Ct HU4. . . . . .179 E5
St Bedes Cath Vol Acad
DN16. . . . . .185 B6
St Bee's Dr 19 PE6. . . . . .175 A1
St Benedict Ct 18 PE6. . . . . . .166 F1
St Benedicts Cl 2 PE6. . . . . . .220 D8
St Benedicts Cl 2 LN6. . . . . . .204 D2
St Benedicts Sq LN5. . . . . . . .234 A2
St Benet's Gdns 2 PE6. . . . . .175 A1
St Bernadettes Cath Prim Vol
Acad DN16. . . . . .185 C6
St Bernards Ave LN11. . . . . . .198 D6
St Bernards Cl LN11. . . . . .198 C6
St Bernard's Cl 13 DN16. . . . .19 E4
St Bernard's Sch LN11. . . . . . .198 C6
St Botolph La PE21. . . . . .230 C6
St Botolphs CE Prim Sch
Peterborough PE2. . . . . .230 B6
Sleaford NG34. . . . . .212 B3
St Botolphs Cl 2 LN1. . . . . . . .66 D3
St Botolph's Cres 8 LN5. . . . .205 E8
St Botolphs Ct 16 LN5. . . . . .205 E8
St Botolphs Gate LN1. . . . . . .66 D3
St Botolphs Infants Sch
LN5. . . . . .205 D8
St Botolphs Mews 31
PE21. . . . . .208 F5
St Botolphs Rd 7 DN16. . . . . .212 C6
St Botolph's Rd DN16. . . . . . .185 C7
St Botolph's Way PE6. . . . . . .176 A2
St Catherine Ct PE12. . . . . . . .215 F3
St Catherines 15 LN5. . . . . . .205 E8
St Catherines Cres DN16. . . .185 A4
St Catherines Ct
Ashby DN16. . . . . .185 D6
Grimsby DN34. . . . . .190 F6
St Catherine's Cl 3 LN5. . . . .205 D7
St Catherine's Dr 3 DN7. . . .14 C2
St Catherine's Gr LN5. . . . . . .205 D7
St Catherine's Rd
Grantham NG31. . . . . .211 B4
Lincoln LN5. . . . . .205 E7
St Chads Ct 8 LN2. . . . . .68 E6
St Chads Gate DN37. . . . . . . .188 A1
St Chad's Rd DN16. . . . . .185 D7
St Chads Wlk S 20 DN37. . . .190 E8
St Charles RC Prim Sch
HU2. . . . . .180 E8
St Christophers Cl 1
NG34. . . . . .107 F1
St Christopher's Rd 11
DN36. . . . . .36 C8
St Claire's Cl 6 LN6. . . . . .204 C8
St Clares Wlk DN20. . . . . .196 C2
St Clement's 9 PE9. . . . . .219 A5
St Clements Cl 27 LN12. . . . . .77 A8
St Clement's Cl 3 LN1. . . . . . .234 B1
St Clement's Dr 4 LN3. . . . . . .82 B6
St Clements Gn PE25. . . . . . . .206 B4
St Clements Rd 17 NG34. . . .108 D2
St Clement's Rd
3 Lincoln LN6. . . . . .204 E2
2 Skegness PE25. . . . . .206 B4
St Clements Way DN36. . . . . .195 C2
St Crispins Cl DN40. . . . . .12 E4
St Crispin's Cl 3 LN6. . . . . . .204 D1
St Cuthberts Ct 14 LN1. . . . .234 B3
St Davids Cl 2 PE25. . . . . . . .206 D6
St David's Cl 2 LN3. . . . . .203 E7
St Davids Cres DN17. . . . . . . .184 E3
St David's Rd LN6. . . . . .204 D2
St David's Sq PE1. . . . . .226 D1
St David's St 13 LN8. . . . . .47 B6
St Denys Ave NG34. . . . . .212 B6
St Deny's Cl 2 DN40. . . . . .12 E3
St Edith Gate 6 LN11. . . . . . . .62 C6
St Edmonds Cl PE24. . . . . . . .115 D8
St Edmunds Cl 3 NG31. . . . .210 D5
St Edmunds Dr DN16. . . . . . .190 F6
St Edmunds Rd NG34. . . . . . .212 C3
St Edmunds Walk PE7. . . . . . .230 D2
St Edmunds Wy 1 PE7. . . . . .230 D2
St Edward's Dr 15 LN2. . . . . . .68 F2
St Edwins Cl 18 DN7. . . . . . . .14 D4
St Edwins Dr 19 DN7. . . . . . . .14 D4
St Faith & St Martin CE Jun
Sch The LN1. . . . . .201 D4
St Faiths CE Inf Sch LN1. . . . .201 D4
St Faith's Cl 1 LN1. . . . . .201 D4
St Firmin's Way PE10. . . . . . .164 D7
St Frances Cl PE25. . . . . .206 B6
St Francis Ave DN31. . . . . . . .191 A8
St Francis Cl 5 LN6. . . . . .204 D2
St Francis Gdns 23 LN12. . . . .77 A7
St Francis Gr 1 DN37. . . . . . . .23 E1
St Francis Specl Sch The
LN1. . . . . .201 E7
St George Ave PE2. . . . . .231 E6
St George's Acad NG34. . . . . .212 C4
St Georges Ave 3 PE9. . . . . . .219 D6
St George's Ave 5 DN7. . . . . .14 C2
St George's CE Com Prim Sch
DN21. . . . . .197 F2
St George's CE Prim Sch
PE9. . . . . .219 C7
St Georges Cl
4 Cranwell NG34. . . . . .107 F1
22 Thorne/Moorends DN8. . .15 B7
St George's Cl LN6. . . . . .204 E2
St George's Cl DN21. . . . . .30 F3
St Georges Dr 3 LN10. . . . . . .97 C5

St George's Hill DN21. . . . . . .54 F7
St Georges La LN2. . . . . .67 F1
St Georges Prim Sch HU3 180 A6
St Georges Rd 21 DN8. . . . . . .15 B7
St George's Rd
Kingston upon Hull HU3. . . . .180 A5
17 Wittering PE8. . . . . .172 B1
St George's St 6 PE9. . . . . . . .219 C5
St George's Way 6 NG31. . . .211 D7
St Gilbert of Sempringham CE
Prim Sch The NG34. . . . . .143 B7
St Gilberts CE Prim Sch
PE9. . . . . .219 A5
St Gilbert's Cl 3 NG34. . . . . .143 B6
St Gilbert's Rd PE10. . . . . . . .213 C6
St GILES LN2. . . . . .202 C7
St Giles Ave Lincoln LN2. . . . .234 C4
1 Sleaford NG34. . . . . .212 F4
St Giles' Ave DN33. . . . . .191 D1
St Guthlac Ave 4 PE6. . . . . . .217 B5
St Guthlac's Cl 8 PE6. . . . . . .166 F1
St Guthlac's Way 1 PE21 126 C1
St Helenas CE Prim Sch
LN13. . . . . .89 A7
St Helens Ave DN33. . . . . . . .191 D3
St Helen's Ave LN6. . . . . .205 B7
St Helen's Cl NG31. . . . . .210 D4
St Helen's Cres DN37. . . . . . .194 D1
St Helen's Dr 14 HU15. . . . . . . .2 D6
St Helen's Rd Brigg DN20. . . .196 D3
7 Lea DN21. . . . . .53 A5
St Helens Way DN21. . . . . .42 E2
St Helier's Rd DN35. . . . . .192 E7
St Hilary's Cl 1 LN6. . . . . . . .204 D2
St Hilda's Ave DN34. . . . . . . .191 B6
St Huberts Dr PE25. . . . . .206 B6
St Hughes Cl PE1. . . . . .226 C4
St Hugh's Ave DN35. . . . . . . .192 E6
St Hugh's Cath Prim Sch The
LN6. . . . . .204 B7
St Hugh's Cl 7 LN3. . . . . .203 E7
St Hugh's Communication and
Interaction Coll 5
DN16. . . . . .183 B1
St Hugh's Cres DN16. . . . . . . .185 C8
St Hugh's Dr
3 Barlings LN3. . . . . .69 C3
Lincoln LN6. . . . . .204 E2
St Hugh's Hospl DN32. . . . . . .191 F4
St Hughs Sch
Scunthorpe DN16. . . . . .183 B1
Woodhall Spa LN10. . . . . .97 D5
St Hugh St LN2. . . . . .234 C2
St Hugh's Terr 13 LN1. . . . . . .66 C7
St Hybald's Gr 2 DN20. . . . . .30 F7
St Ives Cres DN34. . . . . .190 E5
St James Ave
Grimsby DN34. . . . . .191 A6
7 Hatfield DN7. . . . . .14 C2
Peterborough PE1. . . . . .225 F7
St James Cl
19 Crowle DN17. . . . . .16 D7
Kingston upon Hull HU13. . . .179 A5
Newton PE13. . . . . .170 A5
St James Ct
3 Scunthorpe DN15. . . . . . . .183 A3
11 Trusthorpe LN12. . . . . . . .64 C1
St James' Ct 2 DN34. . . . . . . .191 C6
St James Pl
North Hykeham LN6. . . . . . . .204 D3
Scunthorpe DN16. . . . . .185 D4
St James Rd Brigg DN20. . . . .196 D3
Long Sutton PE12. . . . . .216 A1
1 Welton HU14. . . . . .2 F5
St James's Rd 6 DN20. . . . . . .30 E8
St James St HU3. . . . . .180 D5
St James's Way 5 PE11. . . . . .214 D2
St James View LN11. . . . . .198 B4
St James Way 2 PE12. . . . . . .157 E1
St Joan's Dr 5 DN20. . . . . .30 E8
St John Fisher Cath High Sch
PE1. . . . . .226 C4
St John's Ave
6 Cherry Willingham/Reepham
LN3. . . . . .203 E7
1 Lincoln LN6. . . . . .204 E2
St Johns CE Prim Sch
PE2. . . . . .231 C7
St Johns Church Sch PE2 229 F3
St Johns Cl 2 Baston PE6. . . .164 E5
Brigg DN20. . . . . .196 D3
21 Hatfield DN19. . . . . .12 A8
Scampton LN1. . . . . .67 C6
St John's Cl
11 Leasingham NG34. . . . . . .121 B7
6 Morton PE10. . . . . .154 C7
2 Ryhall PE9. . . . . .163 C1
St Johns Ct Grange DN34. . . .191 A5
8 Grantham NG31. . . . . .211 A3
St John's Dr
Corby Glen NG33. . . . . .152 D7
Ingoldmells PE25. . . . . .90 E4
6 Spalding PE11. . . . . .214 B3
St Johns Mews PE12. . . . . . . .215 E2
St John's Prim Sch LN4. . . . . .205 F4
St Johns Rd PE2. . . . . .231 B7
St John's Rd Boston PE21. . . .209 A3
Bracebridge Heath LN4. . . . .205 F2
9 Humberston DN36. . . . . . . .36 C8
Lincoln LN2. . . . . .201 C4
Scunthorpe DN16. . . . . .185 C6
Spalding PE11. . . . . .214 C3
Weston PE12. . . . . .157 C2
15 Wittering PE8. . . . . .172 B1
St John's St
3 Holbeach PE12. . . . . .215 E4
Peterborough PE1. . . . . .226 B2

St John's St continued
21 Stamford PE9. . . . . .219 B5
St John St 1 PE24. . . . . .102 D1
St John's Terr 13 DN21. . . . . .197 D3
St John's Wlk HU13. . . . . .178 F2
St Joseph Dr HU4. . . . . .179 C5
St Joseph's Cath Prim
Voluntary Acad DN35. . . .192 D4
St Judes Cl PE3. . . . . .225 C4
St Julian's Wells HU13. . . . . .178 F2
St Katherines Ms 3 PE7. . . . .230 C2
St Kyneburgha CE Prim Sch
PE5. . . . . .223 E2
St Lamberts Gr 4 PE12. . . . . .157 D7
St Lawrence Acad The
DN15. . . . . .182 E3
St Lawrence CE (Controlled)
Prim Sch DN16. . . . . .200 B4
St Lawrence Dr 9 LN3. . . . . . .83 C4
St Lawrence Rd DN7. . . . . .14 C4
St Lawrence's Pl 2 DN16 185 D7
St Lawrence's Rd DN16. . . . . .185 D6
St Lawrence St 3 LN9. . . . . . .199 B4
St Lawrence Way 3 PE9. . . . . .172 F7
St Leodegar's Cl 2 PE20. . . . .136 D7
St Leonard Cl PE21. . . . . .209 A6
St Leonard's Ave DN31. . . . . .191 A8
St Leonards Dr PE24. . . . . .90 D7
St Leonard's Dr
6 Woodhall Spa LN10. . . . . . .97 D5
11 Woodhall Spa LN10. . . . . .97 D5
St Leonard's La
Lincoln LN2. . . . . .234 C3
South Cockerington LN11. . . . .62 B7
St Leonard's Rd 2 PE13. . . . .170 B2
St Leonard's St 8 PE9. . . . . . .219 C5
St Luke's Cl
Cherry Willingham/Reepham
LN3. . . . . .203 F7
1 Hatfield DN7. . . . . .14 C2
St Luke's Cres 3 DN36. . . . . . .36 C8
St Lukes Ct HU10. . . . . .178 F8
St Luke's Ct 7 DN32. . . . . . . .170 F7
St Luke's Prim Sch DN16. . . . .185 D8
St Luke's St HU3. . . . . .180 C6
St Margaret's Ave PE25. . . . . .206 A6
St Margaret's CE Sch The
LN13. . . . . .63 A1
St Margarets Cl LN13. . . . . . . .76 F3
St Margaret's Cl
17 Laceby DN37. . . . . .23 F1
1 Lincoln LN6. . . . . .205 B4
St Margaret's Cres 6
DN40. . . . . .22 E8
St Margaret's Dr PE22. . . . . . .113 A2
St Margaret's Gdns LN6. . . . .205 A4
St Margarets Mews NG34 190 F6
St Margaret's Pl 2 PE2. . . . . .230 F6
St Margarets Rd 1 PE2. . . . . .230 F6
St Margaret's Wlk
Scunthorpe DN16. . . . . .185 C5
5 Scunthorpe DN16. . . . . . .185 C6
St Mark's Ave 3 LN3. . . . . . . .203 E7
St Mark's Cl
North Hykeham LN6. . . . . . . .204 C8
Skegness PE25. . . . . .206 B6
St Mark's Ct 3 PE1. . . . . .226 A3
St Marks Dr 6 PE6. . . . . .166 E1
St Marks Rd PE13. . . . . .169 E3
St Mark's Rd
Holbeach PE12. . . . . .147 D6
10 Humberston DN36. . . . . . .36 C8
St Marks Sh Ctr LN5. . . . . . . .234 A1
St Mark's Sq
Kingston upon Hull HU3. . . . .180 D4
Lincoln LN5. . . . . .234 A1
St Marks St PE1. . . . . .226 A3
St Mark St
Kingston upon Hull HU8. . . . .181 A8
Lincoln LN5. . . . . .234 A1
St Marks Terr 25 PE21. . . . . .208 F5
St Martins NG33. . . . . .152 E1
St Martins Ave 2 HU4. . . . . . .179 E6
St Martins CE Prim Sch
DN9. .28 A3
St Martins Cl 2 NG34. . . . . . .107 F1
St Martin's Cl
8 Blyton DN21. . . . . .41 C5
4 Stamford PE9. . . . . .219 C4
Stubton NG23. . . . . .118 B7
St Martin's Cres DN33. . . . . . .191 C3
St Martin's La LN1. . . . . .234 B1
St Martins Park 7 DN9. . . . . . .28 A3
St Martin's Pl 6 DN41. . . . . . . .23 A4
St Martins Prep Sch
DN32. . . . . .191 D5
St Martin's Rd
Newborough PE6. . . . . .221 F8
4 Scawby DN20. . . . . .30 E8
1 Wisbech PE13. . . . . .170 E2
St Martin's St Lincoln LN2. . . .234 B1
Peterborough PE1. . . . . .225 F5
St Martin's Way 4 NG32. . . . .120 A3
St Mary Cl 12 PE6. . . . . .166 F1
St Mary's Abbey (Cistercian) ★
PE20. . . . . .135 C2
St Mary's Ave
Barnetby le Wold DN38. . . . . .21 B4
4 Pinchbeck PE11. . . . . . . .156 A5
12 Welton/Dunholme LN2. . . .68 D7
Wittering PE8. . . . . .172 C1
St Mary's Cath Prim Vol Acad
DN20. . . . . .196 C5
St Marys Cl South Field HU13. .3 E4
4 Weston PE12. . . . . .157 D7
St Mary's Cl Bainton PE9. . . . .172 C5
18 Bottesford NG13. . . . . . .128 A6
2 Brough HU15. . . . . .2 C7

St Mary's Cl continued
Farcet PE7. . . . . .231 C2
Grimsby DN32. . . . . .192 C6
Peterborough PE1. . . . . .226 B4
Thorney PE6. . . . . .176 A2
Wilsford NG32. . . . . .120 C1
St Mary's Cres
9 Manby LN11. . . . . .62 C6
5 Stow LN1. . . . . .66 C8
Swineshead PE20. . . . . .135 B6
St Marys Ct 6 PE1. . . . . .226 B2
St Mary's St 5 DN15. . . . . . . .182 C6
St Marys Dr
6 Sleaford NG34. . . . . .212 C6
13 Sutterton PE20. . . . . . . .136 A2
St Mary's Dr 1 Hatfield DN7 14 C2
Peterborough PE2. . . . . .229 F4
St Mary's First & Middle Sch
DN32. . . . . .191 F8
St Mary's Gdns
6 Cowbit PE12. . . . . .167 B8
Long Sutton PE12. . . . . .216 C5
3 Whaplode PE12. . . . . . . .158 B7
St Mary's Hill 17 PE9. . . . . . .219 C5
St Mary's La
4 Barton-upon-Humber
DN18. . . . . .10 F8
Binbrook LN8. . . . . .47 C4
Claxby LN8. . . . . .45 E5
Louth LN11. . . . . .198 A5
St Mary's Mdws 2 PE12. . . . .159 D7
St Mary's Pk LN11. . . . . .198 A6
St Mary's Pl 14 PE9. . . . . .219 C5
St Marys RC High Sch
DN33. . . . . .191 A3
St Mary's Rd Hatfield DN7. . . .14 C2
2 Lincoln LN6. . . . . .204 E2
Skegness PE25. . . . . .206 B6
West Walton PE14. . . . . .170 E4
St Marys Sch LN2. . . . . .234 C3
St Mary's Sq LN9. . . . . .199 B4
St Mary's St Farcet PE7. . . . . .231 C2
Lincoln LN5. . . . . .234 A1
12 Stamford PE9. . . . . .219 C5
St Mary's Way 2 PE22. . . . . . .114 A1
St Marys Wlk 21 HU14. . . . . . . .3 B7
St Mathews Cl 2 LN6. . . . . . . .201 D1
St Matthews Cl 11 PE25. . . . .206 A4
St Matthew's Cl
5 Cherry Willingham/Reepham
LN3. . . . . .203 E7
4 Holbeach PE12. . . . . .215 D2
St Matthew's Dr 13 PE12. . . .160 E4
St Matthew's Rd 12 DN36. . . .36 C8
St Matthew St HU3. . . . . .180 B5
St Mawes Cres DN34. . . . . . . .191 A7
St Mawes Way NG31. . . . . . . .210 D5
St Mellion Dr NG31. . . . . .211 E7
St Michael CE Prim Sch
PE7. . . . . .231 E4
St Michael Cl 25 LN5. . . . . . . .93 F7
St Michael's Ave PE13. . . . . . .170 D1
St Michael's CE Prim Sch
Thorpe on the Hill LN6. . . . . . .92 E8
Thorpe on the Hill LN6. . . . . . .92 E8
St Michael's CE Sch LN11 198 D5
St Michaels Cl 8 LN4. . . . . . .109 F5
St Michael's Cl 16 DN16. . . . .15 B7
St Michael's Cres 5
DN16. . . . . .185 C8
St Michael's Ct 22 DN19. . . . .12 A8
St Michael's Dr 18 DN8. . . . . .15 B7
St Michael's Gate PE1. . . . . . .226 F7
St Michael's La
11 Wainfleet St Mary
PE24. . . . . .102 D1
Wainfleet St Mary PE24. . . . .115 D8
St Michael's Mount 18 HU14 3 B7
St Michael's Rd
Grimsby DN34. . . . . .190 D4
3 Louth LN11. . . . . .198 C5
16 Wittering PE8. . . . . .172 B1
St Michaels Terr 7 LN1. . . . . .234 B3
St Michael's Way 1 NG34 120 C8
St Michaels Wlk NG34. . . . . . .212 C6
St Nectan Cl 9 HU3. . . . . .180 A4
St Nicholas Ave HU4. . . . . . . .179 C2
St Nicholas CE (Controlled)
Prim Sch PE21. . . . . .209 B4
St Nicholas CE Prim Sch
DN39. . . . . .12 A1
St Nicholas Cl
4 Barkston NG32. . . . . .130 B8
Boston PE21. . . . . .209 B3
St Nicholas Ct DN16. . . . . . . .185 E4
St Nicholas Cty Prim Sch
PE12. . . . . .160 A8
St Nicholas Dr DN37. . . . . . . .190 C6
St Nicholas Gdns HU4. . . . . . .179 C2
St Nicholas Rd
Boston PE21. . . . . .209 B3
Thorne/Moorends DN8. . . . . .15 A8
St Nicholas St LN1. . . . . .234 A4
St Nicholas Way
5 Lutton PE12. . . . . .160 A8
9 Spalding PE11. . . . . .214 A5
St Norbert's Cath Prim Sch
DN17. . . . . .16 D7
St Norbett's Cath Prim Sch
PE11. . . . . .214 C4
St Olaf's Dr DN32. . . . . .191 D6
St Olave's Dr 17 PE6. . . . . . . .175 A1
St Paul Rd DN21. . . . . .197 B7
St Paul's Ave 4 LN3. . . . . . . .203 E7
St Paul's Ct PE24. . . . . .102 D7
St Paul's Cl PE13. . . . . .169 E2
St Pauls Com Prim Sch
PE11. . . . . .214 F6

St Pauls Gdns DN16 185 B5
St Paul's Gdns PE10 213 D4
St Paul's La 2 LN1 234 B3
St Paul's Rd
Gainsborough DN21 197 B7
Peterborough PE1 225 F7
Scunthorpe DN16 185 B6
Spalding PE11 214 F5
St Pauls St HU2 180 E8
St Paul's St PE9 219 C5
St Paul St 1 HU2 180 E8
St Pega Cl 17 PE6 166 F1
St Pega's Rd PE6 220 E8
St Peter and St Paul Cath Vol Acad LN6 205 B7
St Peter at Arches 6 LN2 234 B2
St Peter & St Paul CE Prim Sch
Burgh le Marsh PE24 102 D7
Scunthorpe DN17 185 E5
St Peter's Ave
8 Cherry Willingham/Reepham LN3 203 E7
Cleethorpes DN35 192 E6
Kingston upon Hull HU10 178 E6
Lincoln LN6 204 D2
Scunthorpe DN16 185 B3
St Peters CE Aided Jun Sch PE13 170 E1
St Peters CE Prim Sch
Cleethorpes DN35 192 F6
Dunston LN4 95 C6
St Peter's CE Prim Sch
Gringley on the Hill DN10 39 B1
Wymondham LE14 150 B1
St Peters Cl DN21 40 B5
St Peter's Cl
Burgh le Marsh PE24 102 D8
4 Holton le Clay DN36 195 D2
St Peter's Cres 5 DN36 36 C8
St Peters Ct 9 PE9 219 B4
St Peter's Ct 36 DN18 3 E1
St Peter's Dr 4 LN10 97 D5
St Peters Gr 2 DN37 23 E1
St Peter's Gr 14 DN21 29 C3
St Peter's Hill
4 Grantham NG31 211 A4
14 Stamford PE9 219 B5
St Peter's La 7 LN12 64 C2
St Peters Rd
11 Bourne PE10 213 C5
Peterborough PE1 226 A2
St Peter's Rd 12 DN21 29 C3
St Peter's St PE9 219 B4
St Peter's Way PE6 176 A2
St Pierre Ave NG31 211 E7
St Polycarp's Dr PE12 168 B3
St Quintins Cl 5 HU9 181 C8
St Rumbold's St LN2 234 B2
St Sebastians CE (Aided) Prim Sch NG31 129 E5
St Simon's Dr 9 LN3 203 E7
St Stephen's Sh Ctr HU1 180 D6
St Stephens St HU2 180 D6
St Swithins Cl 1 PE20 135 A4
St Swithuns Sq LN2 234 B2
St Thomas' CE Prim Sch PE21 208 F1
St Thomas Ct Boston PE21 208 F2
Long Sutton PE12 216 B5
St Thomas Dr PE21 208 E2
St Thomas Moore RC Prim Sch PE1 226 D4
St Thomas Moore Rd HU4 179 A4
St Thomas More RC Prim Sch HU4 179 A4
St Thomas Rd 2 PE11 214 D2
St Thomas' Rd 13 DN36 36 C8
St Tibba Way 12 PE9 163 C1
St Valentines Way PE25 206 B6
ST VINCENT NG31 211 D3
St Vincent Cl 2 PE25 206 A6
St Vincent's Ave DN15 183 A6
St Vincent's Rd NG31 211 C3
St Wilfrid's Cl 18 LN4 95 D4
St William Ct PE12 215 F3
Salacon Way 16 DN32 189 C1
Saladine Ct 24 DN41 23 F5
Salamander Cl DN31 191 B8
SALEBY LN13 75 F6
Salem St 5 PE11 145 B6
Salisbury Ave 2 LN8 47 B6
Salisbury Cl
1 Grantham NG31 210 D5
Morton DN21 40 D3
1 Saxilby with Ingleby LN1 66 D2
2 Scunthorpe DN17 184 C7
Salisbury Dr
2 Canwick LN4 81 A2
Waltham DN37 194 D4
Salisbury Rd PE4 220 F3
Salisbury St
Gainsborough DN21 197 C7
Kingston upon Hull HU13 178 D1
Salix App 1 LN6 204 C8
Sallie Bank La LN1 65 D2
Sallows Rd PE1 226 B6
SALMONBY LN9 86 E8
Salmonby Rd Salmonby LN9 86 E7
Scunthorpe DN17 184 E4
Salsbury Ave DN34 191 B6
Saltash Rd HU4 179 A2
Saltburn Gr 5 DN32 192 A5
SALTBY LE14 138 F1
Saltby Rd
Croxton Kerrial NG32 138 D3
Sproxton LE14 150 C7
Saltergate Lincoln LN2 234 B2
Peterborough PE1 226 E7
The Willows DN37 188 A1
Salter Gate LN11 51 A1
Saltergate Rd 28 DN17 29 D7
Saltern Dr Spalding PE11 214 B5
Spalding PE11 214 B5
Salters Cl 18 LN4 81 A1
Saltersford Gr NG31 211 D1
Saltersford Rd NG31 211 D2
Saltersgate PE1 226 F7
Salters' La LN11 48 B4
Salters Lane PE9 163 A1
Saltersway NG34 132 F3
Salters Way
14 Donington PE11 134 E2
Gayton le Marsh LN11 62 E3
SALTFLEET LN11 51 B4
SALTFLEETBY ALL SAINTS LN12 51 C1
Saltfleetby CE Prim Sch LN11 63 A8
SALTFLEETBY ST CLEMENT LN11 51 C2
SALTFLEETBY ST PETER LN11 63 B8
Saltfleetby-Theddlethorpe Dunes National Nature Reserve* LN11 51 E3
Saltfleet La PE11 145 B4
Saltfleet Rd Saltfleetby All Saints LN12 51 D1
Theddlethorpe All Saints LN12 63 E8
Saltford Ave 2 HU9 5 F8
Saltgrounds Rd HU15 2 B5
Salthouse La HU1 181 A6
Saltings The 6 PE34 161 F3
Saltmarsh PE2 230 C4
Saltmarsh Ct 2 HU4 179 D2
Saltney Gate PE12 215 A6
Salts Rd PE14 170 F4
Salvesen Rd DN35 189 D1
Salvesen Way HU3 180 A3
Samman Cl HU10 178 D6
Sampey Way 13 NG34 133 B1
Samphire Cl 6 DN36 37 C5
Sampson St DN17 7 A2
Sam Scorer Gall* LN1 234 B3
Samuel Ave DN32 192 B6
Samuel John Wy 13 PE25 206 A5
Samworths Cl PE5 223 F2
Sanbeds La DN9 27 B2
Sanctuary Way DN37 190 C6
Sandars Cl DN9 28 B3
Sandars Rd DN21 53 A8
Sandbank La DN14 7 A5
Sandbank Rd DN14 7 A5
Sandbeck Arc PE25 206 D3
Sandbeck Ave PE25 206 C2
Sandbeck La DN21 41 B6
SANDBRAES LN7 33 A4
Sandcliffe Rd NG31 211 A7
Sanderling Wy DN16 185 F5
Sanders Cl Lincoln LN1 201 D8
15 Mablethorpe & Sutton LN12 77 A7
Meering NG23 91 C8
Sanderson Cl 1 DN16 183 B1
Sanderson's Bank DN10 26 C2
Sanders View LN1 201 D8
Sandfield Cl DN17 184 D5
Sandfield Dr 3 HU15 2 C5
Sandford PE3 225 B5
Sandford St 8 DN31 188 D1
Sandgate Cl DN33 191 B1
Sandhayes La LN8 43 F4
Sandhill La 1 DN22 52 B3
Sandhill Rd DN14 7 B6
SANDHOLME PE20 136 F4
Sandholme La PE20 136 E5
Sandhouse Cres
3 Scunthorpe DN16 183 C1
Scunthorpe DN16 185 C8
Sandhurst Cres 5 NG34 212 B2
Sandhurst Ct 6 LN12 77 A7
Sandhurst Rd
3 Hampton Vale PE7 230 D1
5 Mablethorpe/Sutton on Sea LN12 77 A7
SANDILANDS LN12 77 A8
Sandilands Cl 22 LN12 77 A7
Sandilands Pit Nature Reserve* LN12 77 A7
Sand La Barkston NG32 129 F8
Besthorpe NG23 91 C8
Broadholme LN6 66 D1
4 Broughton DN20 19 D3
Caistor LN7 32 E4
Fenton LN1 65 D3
Great Steeping PE23 101 C7
Hougham NG32 118 C5
Manton DN21 30 A5
Marston NG32 118 E1
Messingham DN17 29 A7
Osgodby LN8 45 B3
Spalford NG23 78 D4
Thorney NG23 79 B8
Torksey LN1 65 E5
Wroot DN9 26 C6
Sandlees La NG34 123 B4
Sandlemere Cl 3 HU3 180 A5
Sandon Cl NG31 211 C5
Sandon Rd NG31 211 B5
Sandown Cl 5 PE11 156 E3
Sandown Dr PE10 213 D3
Sandpiper Dr
Kingston upon Hull HU4 179 B1
Peterborough PE2 231 E6
Sandpiper Wy 21 DN18 3 E1
Sand Pit La DN15 1 C1
Sandpit Rd 14 PE6 176 A3
Sandra Cres LN4 203 D1
Sand Rd DN17 28 B8
Sandringham Ave 29 PE13 170 D1
Sandringham Cl
5 Stamford PE9 219 B7
3 Whaplode PE12 158 B6
Sandringham Cres DN17 184 F3
Sandringham Ct 4 PE12 215 F3
Sandringham Dr
Londonthorpe & Harrowby Without NG31 211 E5
Louth LN11 198 B7
13 Mablethorpe & Sutton LN12 76 F8
Wragby LN8 70 D4
Sandringham Gdns PE21 209 C6
Sandringham Rd
32 Brough HU15 2 C5
Cleethorpes DN35 192 D4
2 Peterborough PE4 225 C8
Sandringham St 2 HU3 180 A6
Sandringham Way 3 PE6 217 A5
Sandringham Wlk 6 PE11 214 D2
Sandringham Wy NG34 212 C2
Sands Cl 3 DN17 17 D5
Sands Ct
1 North Ferriby HU14 3 A4
Rippingale PE10 143 A3
Sandsfield La DN21 197 D2
Sands La Brantingham HU15 1 F7
Brough HU15 2 C6
Carlton-le-Moorland LN5 92 E1
Ellerker HU15 2 A6
Scotter DN21 29 B3
2 South Ferriby DN18 10 A7
SANDTOFT DN8 16 A3
Sandtoft Cl LN6 204 D6
Sandtoft Ind Est DN8 16 B3
Sandtoft Rd Hatfield DN7 15 A4
Sandtoft DN9 16 B3
Sandtone Gdns PE11 214 D5
Sandwell Dr LN6 200 D1
SANDY BANK LN4 111 E6
Sandy Bank Coningsby PE22 98 C1
Sandy Bank LN4 111 E6
Sandy Bank Rd LN4 111 D6
Sandy Cl 1 DN36 37 C5
Sandyford La PE22 113 E3
Sandy Gate Quadring PE11 144 F7
Sutton St James PE12 169 A7
Sandygate Cl NG34 133 C1
Sandygate Cres PE22 113 E3
Sandygate Ct NG34 133 B2
Sandygate La NG34 133 C2
Sandy La Anderby PE24 77 C3
Belchford LN9 73 A2
Calceby LN13 74 F2
Candlesby with Gunby PE23 88 F1
Chapel St Leonard PE24 90 E7
Great Steeping PE23 101 D7
Lusby with Winceby PE23 86 F1
North Willingham LN8 58 C8
Tealby LN8 46 C1
Tydd St Giles PE13 170 A7
5 West Ashby LN9 85 E7
Woodhall Spa LN10 97 E7
Saner St HU3 180 B6
Sansford Gn 5 LN6 205 A6
Santolina Wy HU4 179 C2
SANTON DN15 19 B7
Santon La DN15 19 C7
Sapling Cl 3 NG24 104 B3
SAPPERTON NG34 141 E8
Sapperton PE4 220 F6
Sapphire Cl PE24 89 D2
Sapphire Gr 7 HU3 180 A4
Saracen Cl DN21 197 F2
SARACEN'S HEAD PE12 215 A7
Sarah Gate PE11 145 B8
Sarah's Wlk DN17 184 B6
Sargeants Cl 9 PE22 113 B1
Sargent Cl 4 LN4 95 C4
Sargent's Ct 5 PE9 219 A6
Sargent's Way 15 DN20 31 A5
Sargon Way 3 DN31 188 A3
Sarthe Cl 5 PE20 135 B7
Sassaby Cl HU4 179 C3
Satinwood Cl 10 LN6 200 C1
Satterley Cl LN6 92 D4
Saturn Dr PE2 231 D4
Saunby Gr DN35 192 E7
SAUNDBY DN22 52 B7
Saundby Rd DN22 52 B6
Saundergate La PE21 136 D8
Saundergate Pk 11 PE21 136 D8
Saunders Cl 7 PE2 230 E8
Saunders St 3 DN31 191 C8
SAUSTHORPE PE23 87 E4
Sausthorpe Rd
Partney PE23 88 A3
Sausthorpe PE23 87 F3
Sausthorpe St 9 LN5 201 F1
Savile St HU1 180 F6
Saville Rd PE3 225 D4
Saville Rd Ind Est PE3 225 D5
Saville St LN5 205 D7
Savory Rd 1 PE13 170 D1
Savoy Ct 7 DN36 195 C6
Sawcliffe Ind Est DN15 183 B5
Sawmill La LN8 70 C5
Sawyers Cl 28 NG24 104 A4
SAXBY LN8 55 F5
SAXBY ALL SAINTS DN20 10 A3
Saxby Ave PE25 206 D2
Saxby Cl DN40 186 A4
Saxby Cliff Rd LN8 55 D4
Saxby Gdns PE1 226 C8
Saxby Gr DN33 191 A3
Saxby Hill DN20 10 B4
Saxby Rd Bonby DN20 10 B2
Horkstow Wolds DN18 10 C5
Scunthorpe DN17 184 E5
SAXILBY LN1 66 D3
Saxilby CE Prim Sch LN1 66 E2
Saxilby Rd Lincoln LN1 201 A7
Skellingthorpe LN6 200 A6
Sturton by Stow LN1 66 D6
Saxilby Road LN1 67 A1
Saxilby Sta LN1 66 D2
Saxon Cl
7 Barton-upon-Humber DN18 10 F8
10 Metheringham LN4 95 D4
Spalding PE11 214 F2
Saxon Cres DN35 192 E6
Saxon Ct 2 Blyton DN21 41 C5
Grimsby DN31 188 D2
Scunthorpe DN16 185 B3
Saxondale HU4 179 B7
Saxonfield LN7 33 A4
Saxon Gate 15 PE20 136 C5
Saxon Rd 8 Barnack PE9 172 D3
Peterborough PE1 226 C3
Saxon St 4 LN1 234 A4
Saxon Way
2 Ancaster NG32 120 A2
Bourne PE10 213 C6
17 Caistor LN7 33 B4
3 Horncastle LN9 199 D3
6 Ingham LN1 54 F2
Kingston upon Hull HU13 178 F1
Louth LN11 198 B4
Saxon Wlk 16 PE20 136 C5
Saxon Wy LN3 83 C5
Saxony Way 6 PE11 134 F2
Saxton Cl 6 DN17 184 E6
Sayer Ct PE2 229 F2
Scalby Gr HU5 179 D8
Scald Gate PE22 115 B8
Scale La HU1 181 A6
Scale La Staith 9 HU1 181 A6
Scalesgate Rd PE12 159 B1
Scalford Dr PE1 226 C8
Scallow La DN17 29 D6
Scalp Rd PE21 137 B7
SCAMBLESBY LN11 72 F5
Scamblesby CE Prim Sch LN11 72 F5
Scamblesby Hill LN9 72 E4
SCAMPTON LN1 67 D6
Scampton Airfield LN1 67 E6
Scampton Ave LN6 204 F6
Scampton CE Prim Sch LN1 67 D6
Scampton Cl 3 DN34 191 A5
Scampton Way
Gainsborough DN21 197 E3
Scampton LN1 67 F5
Skegness PE25 206 A5
Scandinavian Way DN41 187 B3
Scanlan Ct LN4 207 F6
Scarborough Bank PE22 100 B1
Scarborough Cl
Green Hill NG31 210 E6
Rippingale PE10 142 F2
Scarborough La LN4 111 B2
Scarborough Rd LN11 61 B8
Scarborough St HU3 180 A4
Scarbrough Ave PE25 206 D4
Scarbrough Espl PE25 206 E3
Scargate La LN4 108 F8
Scarle Cl 1 LN6 205 A2
Scarle La LN6 79 B2
Scarrington Cres HU4 179 B6
Scarrow Cl HU3 180 A7
Scarsdale Wy NG31 211 A1
SCARTHO DN33 194 E8
Scartho Junior Acad DN33 191 D2
Scartho Pk DN33 191 B2
Scartho Rd DN33 191 D2
SCAWBY DN20 30 E8
Scawby Acad DN20 30 E8
Scawby Cres LN6 204 F7
Scawby Rd Brigg DN20 196 A2
Broughton DN20 19 E2
Grimsby DN33 191 A3
Scawby DN20 31 A7
Scunthorpe DN17 184 E5
Sch NG31 129 F4
Schiphol Way DN39 21 E5
Schofield Cl 7 DN19 11 C8
School Cl 1 Maxey PE6 173 C7
Peterborough PE3 225 A5
School Cres Anwick NG34 109 B1
1 Scothern LN2 68 F4
5 Surfleet PE11 145 E3
School Croft DN9 27 B2
School Dr
27 Messingham DN17 29 D7
8 Welton/Dunholme LN2 68 C6
School Hill LE14 150 C7
Schoolhouse La 11 LN11 198 B5
School House La 6 DN10 39 F3
School Houses 9 DN20 19 E4
School La Aby LN13 75 B5
Addlethorpe PE24 90 D3
Appleby DN15 9 D1
1 Baston PE6 164 E4
Beckingham LN5 105 B4
8 Bicker PE20 135 A4
School La *continued*
Binbrook LN8 47 B5
5 Bonby DN20 10 C2
Boothby Pagnell NG33 140 F5
Brattleby LN1 67 C8
Buckminster NG33 150 F5
Butterwick PE22 126 E3
Cabourne LN7 33 D5
Canwick LN4 81 A4
Claypole NG23 117 F8
7 Colsterworth NG33 151 D7
1 Coningsby LN4 207 C4
5 Croxton Kerrial NG32 138 D4
4 Donington PE11 134 F2
East Keal PE23 100 E6
Edenham PE10 153 F4
Fulletby LN9 86 B8
4 Glinton PE6 220 C8
18 Goxhill DN19 12 A8
Grayingham DN21 42 E7
Great Steeping PE23 101 E7
Hainton LN8 58 E3
3 Harmston LN5 93 F5
Heighington/Washingborough LN4 203 C2
5 Helpringham NG34 133 D7
2 Irby DN37 34 D7
Kingston upon Hull HU10 178 C8
9 Lincoln LN6 204 F1
5 Lutton PE12 160 A8
Maltby le Marsh LN13 76 A8
4 Mareham le Fen PE22 99 A4
Marston NG32 118 D2
3 Maxey PE6 173 C7
12 New Holland DN19 4 E2
1 New Holland DN19 4 E2
North Cockerington LN11 49 F1
3 North Ferriby HU14 3 A4
4 North Kelsey LN7 32 A4
North Scarle LN6 78 E1
North Somercotes LN11 50 F7
Old Leake PE22 114 A1
Old Somerby NG33 140 E8
Raithby PE23 87 D2
Redbourne DN21 30 F3
Ropsley NG33 131 B1
Rothwell LN7 33 E2
1 Scampton Airfield LN1 67 F5
Sedgebrook NG32 128 F4
Silk Willoughby NG34 121 A1
Snitterby DN21 43 D5
South Carlton LN1 67 D3
7 South Ferriby DN18 10 A7
Springthorpe DN21 53 E8
2 Sturton by Stow LN1 66 C7
17 Tetney DN36 36 D4
Thistleton LE15 151 C1
Thorpe on the Hill LN6 92 E8
6 Uffington PE9 172 C6
Walcott LN4 109 C7
3 West/East Butterwick DN17 28 D8
2 Willingham by Stow DN21 53 E3
Wilsford NG32 120 C1
School Rd 1 Barnack PE9 172 D3
Newborough PE6 174 E5
10 RAF Cranwell NG34 120 C8
Scunthorpe DN16 185 B6
8 South Killingholme DN40 12 E3
West Walton PE14 170 E4
Winteringham DN15 2 A1
School View 10 NG13 128 A5
School Wlk DN35 192 C5
School Yd Mews DN20 196 C4
Schooner Ct HU4 179 B3
Schrimshaw Ct 6 PE25 206 C4
Schrimshire's Rd DN22 52 A1
Scoggins Way 4 NG34 122 D3
Scoldall La PE11 145 E4
Scolding Dro PE6 176 E5
SCOPWICK LN4 95 D1
Scopwick Pl 3 LN2 201 F8
Scorer St LN5 201 F1
Scotenoon PE2 229 E3
Scotgate PE9 219 A5
SCOTHERN LN2 68 E4
Scothern La 4 Barlings LN3 69 C3
Dunholme LN2 68 E5
Stainton by Langworth LN2 69 B4
10 Welton/Dunholme LN2 68 E6
Scothern Rd LN2 68 D3
Scotia Rd PE21 209 F2
Scotia Way PE21 209 F2
SCOTLAND NG33 141 C5
Scotland La NG33 141 B5
Scotney Dr NG31 211 F5
Scotney St PE1 225 E7
Scott Ave DN17 184 C6
Scott Cl 6 Claypole NG23 117 E8
Grimsby DN37 190 F8
Peterborough PE2 231 E6
Scott Dr 18 Spalding PE11 214 C2
1 Yaxley PE7 233 D5
Scotten Dike Dro PE10 154 E6
SCOTTER DN21 29 B3
Scotter Prim Sch DN21 29 C3
Scotter Rd Laughton DN21 41 C8
Messingham DN17 29 D5
Scunthorpe DN17 182 C1
Scotter Rd S DN17 184 C3
SCOTTERTHORPE DN21 29 B5
Scotterthorpe Rd DN21 29 B4
Scott Gdns LN2 202 C6
Scottlethorpe PE10 153 E4
Scottlethorpe Rd PE10 153 D3

SCOTTON DN21 29 C2
Scotton Comm Nature Reserve★ DN9 27 B1
Scotton Dr 7 LN6 205 A7
Scotton Rd DN21 29 C3
Scott's Cl PE6 164 E3
Scott's Hill 4 NG32 106 C1
Scotts Rd PE6 220 D8
Scott St
Gainsborough DN21 197 C5
Kingston upon Hull HU2 180 F7
SCOTT WILLOUGHBY NG34 132 B4
SCRAFIELD LN9 86 C3
SCRANE END PE22 137 F8
Scrane End East PE22 137 E8
Scrap Bay Rd DN16 19 A3
SCREDINGTON NG34 132 E7
Scredington Rd
Burton Pedwardine NG34 122 B1
Helpringham NG34 133 C7
SCREMBY PE23 88 E2
Scremby Rd PE23 88 C1
SCRIVELSBY LN9 98 E8
Scrivelsby Ct DN35 193 A3
SCRUB HILL LN4 111 B6
Scrub La Authorpe LN11 75 A8
East Halton DN40 12 E5
Withern with Stain LN11 62 D1
Scullery La NG33 141 A5
SCUNTHORPE DN15 183 B5
Scunthorpe CE Prim Sch DN15 183 A4
Scunthorpe General Hospl DN15 182 E2
Scunthorpe Leisure Ctr DN15 183 B3
Scunthorpe Sta DN16 183 A2
Sea Bank PE20 145 F8
Seabank Rd 22 PE13 170 E1
Sea Bank Rd PE24 90 E7
Seabrook Dr DN16 185 A2
SEACROFT PE25 103 E4
Seacroft Cl 13 NG31 211 D7
Seacroft Dr 10 PE25 206 C1
Seacroft Espl PE25 103 E4
Seacroft Rd
Cleethorpes DN35 193 A5
Mablethorpe/Sutton on Sea LN12 64 B3
Seacroft Sq
10 Skegness PE25 103 E4
11 Skegness PE25 116 E8
SEADYKE PE20 136 E3
Sea Dyke PE22 114 B2
Seadyke Rd Kirton PE20 136 E3
Wisbech St Mary PE13 177 F6
Sea Dyke Way 1 DN36 37 C2
Sea End Rd PE22 127 A4
Seafield Rd 5 PE13 170 B2
Seaford Rd DN35 193 B1
Sea Front Rd
10 Skegness PE25 103 E4
9 Skegness PE25 103 E4
Seagate Rd PE12 216 D2
Seagate Terr PE12 216 D4
Seagran Ave
Kingston upon Hull HU13 178 F3
7 Kingston upon Hull HU4 179 A3
Seagull Cl HU4 179 E2
Seaholme Rd LN12 64 B2
Sea La Benington PE22 127 B4
Butterwick PE22 126 F3
Friskney PE22 115 C5
Hogsthorpe PE24 90 C7
Huttoft LN13 77 A4
Ingoldmells PE25 90 E3
Leverton PE22 127 B6
Mablethorpe/Sutton on Sea LN12 77 A7
North Coates DN36 37 B4
Old Leake PE22 114 C1
Saltfleet LN11 51 C5
Theddlethorpe St Helen LN12 63 F7
Wrangle PE22 114 E1
Seal Cr DN36 195 D7
Sealey's La PE13 177 D8
Seal Sanctuary & Nature Ctr The★ LN12 64 B5
Seamer Gr 1 DN32 192 A5
SEARBY DN38 32 C8
Searby Hill DN38 32 D8
Searby Rd Lincoln LN2 202 B8
Scunthorpe DN17 184 E4
Searby Wold La DN38 21 E1
Sea Rd Anderby PE24 77 B2
19 Chapel St Leonard PE24 90 D7
Cleethorpes DN35 192 F6
Seargeants Cl 1 PE6 174 E4
Searjeant St PE1 225 E5
Searson Cl PE9 172 F7
Seascale Wlk DN32 191 F8
Seas End Rd Moulton PE12 146 D1
Surfleet PE11 145 E3
SEATHORNE PE25 206 E8
Seathorne Cres PE25 90 F1
Seathorne Prim Sch PE25 206 D7
Seaton Cl PE7 233 D6
Seaton Gr Grimsby DN32 192 A5
Kingston upon Hull HU4 179 E5
Seaton Rd
Kingston upon Hull HU13 178 F2
Scunthorpe DN17 184 D8
6 Stamford PE9 219 B4
Sea View LN11 51 D3
Sea View Rd PE25 206 D5
Sea View St DN35 192 F5
Seawall La DN36 37 C5
Sebrights Way PE3 224 F3
Second Ave Brookenby LN8 47 A6
Fixborough Ind Est DN15 7 F1
Grantham NG31 211 F6
Grimsby DN33 191 B4
5 Scampton Airfield LN1 67 E5
3 Scunthorpe DN17 184 C6
Spalding PE11 214 A4
Second Dro Crowland PE6 166 E3
Gosberton PE11 144 C3
Peterborough PE1 226 D1
Second Dro Ind Est PE1 226 D1
Second Marsh Rd PE14 170 C3
Secret Gdns 10 LN7 33 A3
SEDGEBROOK NG32 128 F5
Sedgebrook Cl 1 LN2 201 F8
Sedgebrook Rd NG32 128 F6
Sedge Cl
6 Barton-upon-Humber DN18 3 F1
Leasingham NG34 121 C7
Sedgefield Ct PE10 213 B3
Sedge Hole Cl Nature Reserve★ DN9 27 F2
Sedgemoor Cl 3 LN6 204 E1
Sedge Pl 9 PE12 167 B8
Sedgewood Way DN15 182 C6
Seed Cl La 4 DN37 23 F1
Seedlands Cl PE21 209 B7
Sefton Ave PE13 170 E1
Sefton St 2 HU3 180 B4
Segmere St 3 DN35 193 A5
Segrave Gr HU5 179 D8
Selbourne Rd 4 DN34 190 E4
Selby Cl LN6 205 A3
Selby Ct DN17 184 D7
Selby Rd DN8 14 F8
Selby St HU3 180 A5
Selemba Wy NG34 121 A2
Selge Way DN33 190 F3
Selkirk St HU5 180 A8
Sellers Grange PE2 230 B4
Sellwood Ct NG34 212 F7
Sellwood Gdns LN9 199 B3
Selmeston Ct DN34 191 C6
Selwyn Ave 16 HU14 3 A4
Selwyn Ct DN34 190 F6
Selwyn Rd PE9 219 A7
Sempers Cl LN6 92 E8
Sennefleet Rd DN21 29 B4
Sense Coll PE7 230 E3
Sentance Cres PE20 136 C6
Sequana Ct HU9 181 B6
Seraphim App Rd DN16 183 E1
Seraphim Rd DN16 183 F1
Serena Rd 5 PE25 206 D2
Serlby Gdns PE3 225 B3
Serpentine Gn Sh Ctr PE7 230 D3
Serpentine St 1 LN8 57 D7
Serpentine The PE7 230 D3
Service Rd DN37 190 D8
Service Rd 10 6 DN37 188 A1
Service Rd 1 18 DN37 190 E8
Service Rd 12 2 DN37 188 A1
Service Rd 13 4 DN37 188 A1
Service Rd 14 3 DN37 188 A1
Service Rd 15 16 DN37 190 E8
Service Rd 16 DN37 190 E8
Service Rd 17 DN37 190 F8
Service Rd 18 DN37 190 F8
Service Rd 19 4 DN37 190 F8
Service Rd 20 19 DN37 190 E8
Service Rd 2 17 DN37 190 E8
Service Rd 21 1 DN37 190 E8
Service Rd 22 3 DN37 190 E8
Service Rd 23 DN37 190 E8
Service Rd 25 11 DN37 190 E8
Service Rd 26 9 DN37 188 A1
Service Rd 3 15 DN37 190 E8
Service Rd 4 8 DN37 190 E8
Service Rd 5 13 DN37 190 E8
Service Rd 6 14 DN37 190 E8
Service Rd 7 3 DN37 190 F8
Service Rd 8 8 DN37 188 A1
Service Rd 9 7 DN37 188 A1
Service Rd No 1 3 DN32 189 B1
Service Rd No 2 4 DN32 189 B1
Services Rd DN16 183 E2
Setchfield Pl PE2 230 F7
Setterwood Garth 2 HU10 178 E8
Setts Gn PE10 213 C2
Sevayn's Dr 12 NG34 107 F1
Sevenacres PE2 229 E5
Seven Quay Rd DN40 186 E7
Seventh Ave 3 NG31 211 F6
Seventy Acre La DN37 33 F8
Severn Cl PE4 221 C1
Severn Rd PE11 214 F5
Severn St LN1 201 C4
Severn Way 2 DN37 190 F8
Sewell Cl PE6 217 E5
Sewell Rd LN2 234 C3
Sewell's Wlk LN5 201 E1
Sewell Wy 3 PE11 214 A1
Sewer La 3 HU1 180 F5
SEWSTERN NG33 150 F4
Sewstern Cl 15 LN4 81 A1
Sewstern La
Allington NG32 128 E7
Long Bennington NG23 117 E1
Sedgebrook NG32 128 D4
Sewstern Rd
Gunby & Stainby NG33 151 B4
Sewstern Rd *continued*
Wymondham LE14 150 D2
Seymour Ave LN11 198 C4
Seymour La 14 LN13 75 F2
Seymour Pl PE4 221 F2
Seymour St HU3 179 F5
Sezanne Wlk 10 PE11 214 C6
Shackleton Cl
Market Deeping PE6 217 B7
10 Spalding PE11 214 C2
Shackleton Wy PE7 233 D5
Shaddys Wlk LN13 88 E6
Shadows La LN8 43 D1
Shadwell Rise 29 DN18 3 E1
Shaftesbury Ave
Birchwood LN6 200 D2
Grimsby DN34 191 B7
Shaftesbury Mews 6 DN36 195 C6
Shaftesbury Way 2 NG23 91 D5
Shakespeare Ave
Grantham NG31 211 E6
Peterborough PE1 225 F7
4 Scunthorpe DN17 184 C6
Shakespeare Cl 6 HU3 180 D8
Shakespeare St
5 Gainsborough DN21 197 D2
5 Lincoln LN5 205 E8
13 Newark-on-Trent NG24 104 A3
Shakespeare Way PE11 214 A1
Shamfields Rd 3 PE23 101 A8
Shamrock Cl PE2 231 C7
Shamrock Ct LN5 205 E6
Shanklin Dr NG31 210 E4
Shannon Ave LN6 205 A5
Shannon Cl 2 Lincoln LN6 205 A5
11 Spalding PE11 214 A4
Shannon Rd 8 LN4 207 D4
Shardloes LN4 81 E2
Shardloes Rd 9 PE25 103 E4
Sharma Leas PE4 220 E3
Sharmans Cl 11 LN12 77 A7
Sharman Way PE11 214 B5
Sharnbrook Ave 1 PE7 230 C1
Sharpe Cl 35 DN18 10 E8
Sharpe Rd NG31 211 C6
Sharpe's Rd PE6 165 C3
Sharp's Cl PE10 213 B6
Sharp's La PE22 127 A6
Sharp Wlk LN6 93 C8
Shaw Ave 35 HU15 2 D5
Shawbury Cl 10 LN6 204 C6
Shaw Dr DN33 191 E1
Shawfield Cl 10 DN3 14 A3
Shaw Rd Boston PE21 208 C7
Grantham NG31 210 D2
Gringley on the Hill DN10 39 C2
Shaws La Hilldyke PE22 126 C5
Little Sutton PE12 160 B3
Old Leake PE22 127 B8
Shaws Mews LN11 198 B5
Shaw St HU9 181 B7
Shaw Way 4 LN2 68 C2
Shays Dr 1 LN6 205 A7
Shearers Dr 12 PE11 214 A2
Shearman's Wath
Thimbleby LN9 85 C6
West Ashby LN9 199 A8
Shears Ct DN37 194 F4
Shearwater PE2 229 D6
Shearwater Cl
3 Birchwood LN6 200 E1
Louth LN11 198 D8
Shearwater Rd LN6 200 E1
Sheep Cote La DN7 14 D2
Sheep Dip La DN7 14 D4
Sheepdyke La
4 Bonby DN20 10 C2
4 Careby Aunby & Holywell PE9 163 A8
Sheepfold St DN32 191 E7
Sheepgate PE22 127 A6
Sheep Marsh La DN36 37 B3
Sheep Mkt
2 Spalding PE11 214 D4
11 Stamford PE9 219 B5
Sheepwalk
Aubourn Haddington & South Hykeham LN5 92 E5
Peterborough PE4 221 E1
Sheepwash La LN4 81 E4
Sheep Wash Lane NG31 211 B1
Sheffield Pk Ave DN15 182 F5
Sheffield St (East) 1 DN15 183 A4
Sheffield St (West) 4 DN15 182 F4
Sheffield St DN15 183 A4
Sheila Cres 4 PE11 214 A3
Sheldon Gdns HU13 178 A3
Sheldon Rd
Nunsthorpe DN33 191 A2
Nunsthorpe DN33 191 A2
Sheldrake Rd 1 NG34 212 B3
Shelford St DN15 183 A3
Shelley Ave
Grantham NG31 211 D6
Grimsby DN33 191 B4
Shelley Cl
3 Mablethorpe/Sutton on Sea LN12 77 A7
New England PE1 225 F8
12 Stamford PE9 218 E6
Shelley Dr Lincoln LN2 202 B6
7 Sleaford NG34 212 F4
Shelroy Cl DN15 182 C5
Shelton Rd PE2 231 D6
Shenley Cl 11 DN7 14 D3
SHEPEAU STOW PE12 167 F3
Shepeau Stow Prim Sch PE12 167 F3
Shepherds Cl PE4 221 A4
Shepherd's Croft 1 DN9 27 D7
Shepherd's La NG34 133 E7
Shepherd's Wlk PE9 163 D1
Sheppard's Cl
Heighington/Washingborough LN4 81 E4
Heighington/Washingborough LN4 81 E4
Sheppard's Dro PE6 167 B1
Shepperson's Ave PE11 144 F5
Shepton La NG34 142 A8
Sheraton Cl 15 LN6 204 D7
Sheraton Dr 13 DN36 36 D8
Sherborne Rd PE1 226 D6
Sherbourne Cl 16 PE20 135 B7
Sherbrooke St 2 LN2 202 D4
Sherburn Cres DN15 182 D4
Sherburn St
Cleethorpes DN35 192 F4
Kingston upon Hull HU9 181 D8
Sheridan Cl 1 Lincoln LN2 202 C7
16 Newark-on-Trent NG24 104 B2
Sheridan Rd PE1 225 F8
Sheriff Way PE21 208 E7
Sheringham Way PE2 230 C6
Sherwood Ave
Boston PE21 208 E7
Newark-on-Trent NG24 104 A4
4 Peterborough PE2 230 F7
7 Wisbech PE13 170 D1
Sherwood Cl
1 Louth LN11 198 C4
Stamford PE9 218 F5
Sherwood Dr
Kingston upon Hull HU4 179 A7
Spalding PE11 214 D6
Waddington LN5 205 D1
Sherwood Rd
10 Coningsby LN4 207 D4
Grimsby DN34 190 F5
3 Mablethorpe/Sutton on Sea LN12 64 B4
Sherwood Rise 7 NG32 119 B7
Sherwood Vale DN15 182 D3
Shetland Way DN40 186 C2
Shillaker Ct PE10 213 D4
Shipton Rd DN16 185 C5
Shire Ave PE11 214 A5
Shire Cl 6 LN4 109 F6
Shiregate 12 LN4 95 C4
Shire Gr PE1 226 C5
Shire La NG23 117 D8
Shires Orch 6 NG32 138 D4
Shirewood La PE22 99 A5
Shirley Cres DN16 185 B8
Shivean Gate 5 PE12 157 F7
Shodfriars La 4 PE21 208 F4
Shoe La LN9 72 C5
Shoemaker's La DN21 29 E5
Shoff Dro PE11 134 D1
Shoff Rd PE11 134 D1
Sholt's Gate PE12 158 C7
Shop Hill 7 PE22 98 F4
Shop La Goulceby LN11 72 D6
New Barnetby DN38 21 D5
Shore Rd Freiston PE22 126 D2
Garthorpe & Fockerby DN17 7 F5
Shore View PE7 230 B2
Shortacres Rd PE2 230 F7
Short Dro Gosberton PE11 144 C5
Pointon & Sempringham NG34 143 F4
Thurlby PE10 164 E8
Shortfen PE2 230 C4
Short Ferry Rd LN3 82 F6
Shortfield La PE21 209 E8
Short Furrow 9 LN5 107 B8
Short Hollow NG33 131 C1
Short La Fotherby LN11 49 A2
Ingham LN1 54 F3
Lincoln LN1 234 A2
11 West Halton DN15 8 E8
3 Wisbech PE13 170 A1
Shortleys Rd DN22 65 B5
Short's Cnr PE22 112 D3
Short St
2 Cleethorpes DN35 192 F6
4 Spalding PE11 214 C4
Short Wheatley La NG23 91 D3
Shortwood La
Bullington LN8 69 F4
Friesthorpe LN3 57 A2
Shorwell Cl 3 NG31 210 E4
Shotbolt La PE11 214 F8
Shrewsbury Ave PE2 230 D5
Shropshire Rd 9 LN1 67 E5
Shrubberies Nature Reserve The★ PE12 216 B5
Shrub Rd PE7 230 C1
Shrubwood Cl 3 NG34 122 E2
Shuttlefield La PE20 135 F4
Shuttleworth Ct 12 LN6 93 C8
Sibcy La NG24 104 B2
Sibelius Rd HU4 179 B4
SIBSEY PE22 113 B2
Sibsey Ct DN37 188 A2
Sibsey Drain Bank PE22 126 A6
Sibsey Free Prim Sch The PE22 113 A2
Sibsey La 3 PE21 208 F4
Sibsey Rd Boston PE21 209 B8
Fishtoft PE21 125 F5
Sibsey Trader Windmill★ PE22 113 A2
Sibthorpe Dr LN2 68 F2
Sibthorp Gdns LN4 81 A4
Sibthorp St LN5 201 E1
Sickling Gate Rd PE22 115 B7
Sidebar La NG34 123 C4
Side La DN33 195 A7
Side Row NG24 104 A4
Side St 2 NG32 128 F7
Sidings Ct 3 HU15 2 B5
Sidings Rd DN31 191 A8
Sidings The Cranwell NG34 120 E8
Holbeach PE12 215 D1
Horncastle LN9 199 A3
Lincoln LN6 234 A1
Long Sutton PE12 216 B4
2 Louth LN11 198 C6
23 Mablethorpe/Sutton on Sea LN12 77 A8
4 Morton PE10 154 D6
8 Moulton PE12 157 F6
9 Ruskington NG34 108 E1
25 Saxilby LN1 66 D2
Sidlaw Gr LN5 205 C2
Sidney Chase LN1 54 F1
Sidney Cl PE24 90 D6
Sidney Ct 1 DN35 192 B8
Sidney Pl DN35 192 B8
Sidney Rd Grimsby DN34 191 B7
5 Scunthorpe DN17 184 C6
Sidney St
4 Cleethorpes DN35 189 D1
Cleethorpes DN35 192 B8
Grantham NG31 211 A6
Lincoln LN5 205 E8
Sidney Terr 17 LN5 205 E8
Sidney Way DN35 192 B8
Signal Rd NG31 211 C5
Signhills Ave DN35 193 A4
Signhills Infant Acad DN35 193 A4
Silica Cres DN17 184 C5
SILK WILLOUGHBY NG34 121 C1
Silt La PE20 136 E3
Silt Pit La PE21 137 A7
Siltside PE11 144 D4
Silverbell DN16 185 E4
Silver Birch Rise DN16 185 B3
Silvergarth DN32 192 B5
Silver Hill PE7 230 D3
Silverines Mdws Nature Reserve★ LN11 72 E5
Silver La 20 PE9 219 B5
Silversides La DN20 196 A2
Silversides La Cvn Site DN20 196 A2
Silver's La PE13 177 E7
Silver St Bardney LN3 83 C4
Barnetby le Wold DN38 21 B4
Barrow upon Humber DN19 11 C7
Baumber LN9 72 A1
Benniworth LN8 71 F8
Branston LN4 81 E2
Coningsby LN4 207 C4
Gainsborough DN21 197 C4
Holton le Clay DN36 195 D1
11 Kingston upon Hull HU1 180 F6
Lincoln LN2 234 B2
Minting LN9 84 C8
North Clifton NG23 78 C7
Owston Ferry DN9 28 B2
Peterborough PE2 230 F7
1 Ruskington NG34 108 E1
Stainforth DN7 14 C6
Theddlethorpe St Helen LN12 63 E5
3 Waddingham DN21 43 D7
6 Wainfleet All Saints PE24 102 D1
Winteringham DN15 2 B1
Wisbech PE13 170 D1
5 Wragby LN8 70 D5
Silverstone Rd
17 Birchwood LN6 204 C7
5 Bourne PE10 213 E5
Silvertoft La PE20 136 B8
Silverwood Rd
8 Bottesford NG13 128 A5
Peterborough PE1 225 F5
Silvester Rd PE5 223 E2
Silvester St HU2 180 F7
Simons Cl
4 Donington on Bain LN11 59 E1
5 Louth LN11 198 D4
Simon's Gn LN6 205 C6
Simons Pl DN35 192 D7
Simon Weir La PE20 135 D8
Simpson Cl
5 Balderton NG24 104 C2
17 Barrow upon Humber DN19 11 D8
Chapel St Leonard PE24 90 D6
Simpson's Fold Ct DN36 195 B6
Simpson St 16 PE23 88 A1
Sincil Bank LN5 234 B1
Sincil Bank (Lincoln City FC) LN5 201 E1
Sincil Sch The LN5 205 F8
Sincil St LN5 234 B2
Sinclair Cl PE21 208 E8
Sinderson Rd DN36 36 D8
Singerfire Rd PE5 223 D2
Sir Francis Hill Com Prim Sch LN6 205 C8
Sir Isaac Newton Cl 3 PE12 215 E3
Sir Isaac Newton Dr 3 PE21 208 F1
Sirius Acad HU4 179 B4
Sirius Cl 3 HU3 180 B5

Sir John Nelthorpe Sch
DN20. . . . .**196** C3
Sir Robert Pattinson Acad
LN6. . . . .**204** E2
Sir William Robertson High
Sch The LN5 . . . .**106** E4
Siskin Cl PE10 . . . .**143** A3
Siskin Cres DN16. . . . .**185** B2
Sissley PE2 . . . .**229** E2
Sitwell St HU8 . . . .**181** A8
Sixfields Cl LN6 . . . .**205** A7
SIXHILLS LN8. . . . .**58** E6
Sixhills La Little London LN8 .**58** B5
Ludford LN8 . . . .**59** A7
Sixhills Rd LN8. . . . .**58** D6
Sixhills St DN32 . . . .**191** E7
Six House Bank PE11 . . . . .**144** D1
Six Hundreds Dro PE20 . . .**123** E3
Sixth Ave Brookenby LN8 . .**47** B6
Fixborough Ind Est DN15 . . . .**8** A1
2 Grantham NG31 . . . .**211** F6
Scunthorpe DN17. . . . .**184** B6
Skaters Way PE4 . . . .**221** A4
Skayman Fields **7** LN5 . . . .**105** E8
Skegger Beck Rd DN38 . . . . .**21** A4
SKEGNESS PE25 . . . .**206** E4
Skegness Bsns Ctr PE25 . .**206** B3
Skegness Coll of Vocational
Ed PE25 . . . .**206** C2
Skegness & District Hospl
PE25 . . . .**206** B3
Skegness Gram Sch PE25 **206** C4
Skegness Infant Acad
PE25 . . . .**206** C4
Skegness (Ingoldmells)
Aerodrome PE25. . . . .**90** D1
Skegness Jun Sch PE25. . .**206** C4
Skegness Motor Racing
Stadium PE24. . . . .**90** A2
Skegness Rd
Burgh le Marsh PE24 . . . . .**103** A7
Chapel St Leonard PE24 . . . .**90** D6
Ingoldmells PE25. . . . .**90** E3
Partney PE23 . . . .**88** B3
Skegness PE25. . . . .**103** C8
5 Wainfleet All Saints
PE24 . . . .**102** E2
Skegness Ret Pk PE25 . . . .**206** A4
Skegness Sports Ctr PE25 **206** B5
Skegness Sta PE25 . . . .**206** C3
Skegness Wr Leisure Pk★
PE25 . . . .**90** E1
SKELDYKE PE20 . . . .**136** F4
Skeldyke Rd PE20 . . . .**136** D5
Skellingthorpe LN6. . . . . . .**200** D3
Skellingthorpe Rd LN6 . . . .**200** D2
Skells Ct PE9 . . . .**219** D5
Skelton Cl **14** NG34. . . . . . .**122** D3
Skelton Dr PE12. . . . .**216** C3
Skelton Rd DN17. . . . .**184** C7
SKENDLEBY **88** D4
Skendleby Nature Reserve★
LN13. . . . .**88** E6
Skerries Cl **5** LN6. . . . .**205** A1
Skerry La NG13. . . . .**128** C5
SKIDBROOKE LN11. . . . .**51** B3
Skillings La HU15 . . . .**2** C5
SKILLINGTON NG33 . . . .**151** B8
Skillington Rd
Gunby & Stainby NG33 . . . . .**151** B6
Stroxton NG33 . . . .**139** F4
SKINNAND LN5 . . . .**106** C8
Skinnand La LN5 . . . .**106** D7
Skinners La
6 South Ferriby DN18. . . . . .**10** A7
Waltham DN37. . . . .**194** E4
Skinner's La
Middle Rasen LN8 . . . .**45** C1
South Kyme LN4 . . . .**110** B1
Skipmarsh La
Leverton PE22 . . . .**126** E8
Old Leake PE22 . . . .**113** E1
Skippingdale Ind Pk
DN15. . . . .**182** C7
Skippingdale Rd DN15. . . .**182** E6
Skipwith Cres **20** LN4. . . . . .**95** D4
Skipworth Way PE25 . . . . .**206** C8
SKIRBECK PE21. . . . .**209** B3
Skirbeck Dr **15** LN11. . . . . . .**66** D2
Skirbeck Gdns PE21. . . . . .**209** B3
SKIRBECK QUARTER
PE21. . . . .**208** D2
Skirbeck Rd PE21 . . . .**209** A3
Skirmore Rd PE22. . . . .**114** E5
Skirth Rd LN4. . . . .**109** F6
Skitter Rd DN40. . . . .**5** D1
Skye Cl PE2. . . . .**229** C5
Skylark Dr DN16 . . . .**185** B2
Skylarks Cl **6** PE7. . . . . . .**230** D3
Slack The **4** DN17. . . . .**16** D8
Slash La LN9. . . . .**86** D3
Slate Drift **2** PE9 . . . .**171** C2
Slate Farm Cl **7** LN8 . . . . . .**43** D3
Slate Mill Pl NG31. . . . .**211** B5
Slate Mill The NG31 . . . . . .**211** B5
Slay Pit Cl **3** DN7 . . . .**14** F4
Slay Pit La DN7 . . . .**14** F3
Slea Cotts **15** NG34 . . . . . .**212** D4
SLEAFORD NG34. . . . .**212** B4
Sleaford (Aided) RC Prim Sch
NG34. . . . .**212** C4
Sleaford Art Studio★
NG34. . . . .**212** D5
Sleaford Coll NG34. . . . . . .**212** E4
Sleaford Enterprise Pk
NG34 . . . .**212** F6
Sleaford Leisure Ctr
NG34. . . . .**212** E4

Sleaford Lollycocks Field
Nature Reserve★ NG34 . . .**212** E4
Sleaford Mareham Nature
Reserve★ NG34. . . . .**212** E2
Sleaford Rd Ancaster NG32 **120** A2
Barnby in the Willows NG24 . .**104** F5
Boston PE21. . . . .**208** B4
Bracebridge Heath LN4 . . . . .**81** A1
Coningsby LN4 . . . .**207** A4
Cranwell NG34. . . . .**120** F8
East Kirkby PE23 . . . .**99** E4
Folkingham NG34 . . . .**142** D8
Heckington NG34. . . . .**122** D3
Honington NG34 . . . .**119** C2
Leadenham LN5 . . . .**106** D2
14 Leasingham NG34. . . . . .**121** B7
Metheringham LN4. . . . .**95** B4
18 Navenby/Wellingore
LN5. . . . .**107** A7
Newark-on-Trent NG24 . . . .**104** A5
North Kyme LN4 . . . .**109** E2
Ruskington NG34. . . . .**108** E1
Tattershall LN4. . . . .**110** D7
Walcot near Folkingham
NG34. . . . .**132** D2
Sleaford Sta NG34. . . . . . .**212** D3
Sleaford Virtual Mus★ **7**
NG34. . . . .**212** C4
Sledge La LN8 . . . .**59** B8
Sledmere Gr HU4 . . . .**179** E5
Sleepers Cl **1** PE12 . . . . . .**216** B4
Sleights Cl HU3. . . . .**180** A7
Sleights Dr **2** PE14. . . . . . .**170** F1
Sleights La HU15. . . . .**1** B6
Slessor St **2** LN5. . . . .**94** A7
Slipe Dro PE11. . . . .**155** F5
Slipe The PE10. . . . .**213** F4
Slippery Gowt La PE21. . . .**136** F8
Slipway DN35 . . . .**193** A6
SLOOTHBY LN13. . . . .**89** D5
Sloothby High La
Hogsthorpe PE24. . . . .**90** A6
Willoughby with Sloothby
PE24 . . . .**89** E6
Sluice La DN18. . . . .**9** E8
Sluice Rd Holbeach PE12. . .**215** B8
South Ferriby DN18 . . . .**9** F8
Sutton Bridge PE12 . . . .**161** A6
Whaplode PE12 . . . .**147** B4
Small Dro PE12 . . . .**157** E7
Small Dro La PE11. . . . . . .**144** E1
Small End Rd PE22 . . . .**114** E6
Smalley Rd PE21. . . . .**209** D4
Smallwood PE3 . . . .**225** B5
Smeeton Ct **6** NG34. . . . . . .**212** D6
Smeeton's La PE20 . . . .**146** C7
Smithdale Cl **9** PE11. . . . . .**214** C6
Smithfield PE6. . . . .**176** B3
Smith Field **10** DN36 . . . .**36** B1
Smithfield Rd DN16. . . . . . .**185** D6
Smithson Cl **11** NG24 . . . . .**104** B5
Smith St Beacon Hill NG24 . .**104** A4
Lincoln LN5 . . . .**201** E1
Scunthorpe DN15. . . . .**182** F4
Smithy La
7 Barnetby le Wold DN38 . . .**21** B4
Friskney PE22 . . . .**115** A6
Smooting La **4** LN8 . . . .**82** A8
Smooting The LN8 . . . .**46** C1
Smoots The **15** LN5. . . . . . .**107** A8
Smythe La DN22. . . . .**52** D1
Snaffer's La PE12. . . . .**158** C5
Snainton Gr **4** HU5 . . . .**179** D8
Snaith Ave PE20. . . . .**146** D7
Snaith Cl **9** LN6. . . . .**204** B6
SNARFORD LN2. . . . .**56** D1
Snarford Rd LN3 . . . .**69** D8
SNELLAND LN3. . . . .**69** E6
Snelland La LN3. . . . .**69** E6
Snelland Rd LN3. . . . .**69** D7
Snetterton Cl **1** LN6. . . . . .**204** C7
Snipe Dales Ctry Pk★ PE23 **86** F3
Snipe Dales Nature Reserve★
LN9 . . . .**86** E3
SNITTERBY DN21. . . . .**43** D5
Snitterby Carr La DN21. . . . .**43** F5
Snitterby Rd DN21. . . . .**43** D6
Snowberry Gdns **5** LN6. . . .**204** C8
Snow Cl NG34. . . . .**212** C7
Snowden Cl **1** PE6. . . . . . .**175** C8
Snowdon Cl **4** LN5. . . . . . .**205** D3
Snowdonia Ave DN15. . . . .**182** D7
Snowdon Rd **3** NG23. . . . . . .**91** D4
Snowdrop Ave **22** NG34. . . .**104** C5
Snowdrop Cl **10** DN41. . . . . .**23** F5
Snowdrop La LN11. . . . .**198** A6
Snowdrop Pl **8** PE11. . . . . .**214** A5
Snowhills PE7 . . . .**233** E5
Sobrite Wy PE4 . . . .**220** F7
Sods La PE11. . . . .**145** D5
Soff La DN19. . . . .**12** A6
Soggin La LN5. . . . .**106** F5
Soke Parkway PE1 . . . .**221** E1
Soke Rd PE6 . . . .**174** D5
Solent Dr PE11. . . . .**214** B5
Solhem Ave **18** PE21. . . . . .**136** D8
Solomon Ct DN35 . . . .**192** D5
Solway Ave PE11. . . . .**136** E8
Solway Ct **5** DN37. . . . .**190** E8
SOMERBY DN38 . . . .**21** B1
Somerby Cl
8 Moulton PE12. . . . .**157** F7
2 Stamford PE9 . . . .**219** B7
Somerby Dr **3** DN9 . . . .**28** A3
Somerby Garth **4** PE1. . . . .**226** D8
Somerby Gr NG31 . . . .**211** D2
Somerby Hill NG31. . . . . . .**211** C2
Somerby Rd NG31 . . . .**211** E1

Somerby Rd
Gainsborough DN21. . . . . . .**197** F5
Ropsley & Humby NG33 . . . .**141** A8
Scunthorpe DN17. . . . .**184** D5
Somerby Wold La DN38. . . . .**21** C1
Ulceby DN39 . . . .**12** B1
Somercotes Rd LN11 . . . . . .**51** A3
Somerden Rd HU9 . . . .**5** F8
Somerfield Dr **9** LN11. . . . . .**50** F7
SOMERSBY PE23. . . . .**87** A7
Somersby Ave **9** LN12. . . . . .**64** B4
Somersby Cl LN6. . . . .**205** C4
Somersby Ct
15 South LN11 . . . .**198** B5
North Carlton LN1 . . . .**67** C4
Somersby Gn PE21 . . . .**209** B7
Somersby Gr **2** PE25. . . . . .**206** D1
Somersby La NG9 . . . .**86** F6
Somersby St **5** DN31. . . . . .**191** D8
Somersby Way NG31. . . . . .**209** B7
Somersby Wy LN11 . . . .**198** E6
Somerscales St **2** HU3. . . . .**180** E8
Somerset Dr **4** DN15 . . . .**8** B4
Somerset St HU3. . . . .**180** A5
Somerton Cl NG34 . . . .**212** C3
Somerton Dr **3** DN7 . . . .**14** F3
Somerton Gate La LN5. . . . . .**93** D7
Somerton Rd DN40 . . . .**186** D3
Somervell Rd DN16. . . . . . .**185** C4
Somerville PE4 . . . .**220** E5
Somerville Cl **15** LN5 . . . .**93** E8
Somerville Ct **14** LN5 . . . .**93** E8
Somerville Rd **11** PE9 . . . . . .**219** A6
Somes Cl **1** PE9. . . . .**172** C6
Somme La DN1. . . . .**201** E7
Sonia Crest DN40 . . . .**186** B4
Sophia Ave DN33. . . . .**191** C1
Sorbus Cl **3** PE7 . . . .**230** D3
Sorbus Ct **5** HU3. . . . .**180** D6
Sorbus View **4** HU5 . . . . . .**179** C7
Sorby Cl PE25. . . . .**206** E8
Sorrel Cl **3** Binbrook LN8 . . .**47** C5
1 Market Deeping PE6 . . . .**217** D6
4 Stamford PE9. . . . .**218** D6
Yaxley PE7. . . . .**233** B8
Sorrel Ct LN6. . . . .**204** C8
Sorrel Dr PE11. . . . .**214** A5
Sorrel Way Hessle HU13. . . .**178** B1
Scunthorpe DN15. . . . .**182** C6
Soss La DN10 . . . .**40** A5
SOTBY LN8. . . . .**71** E5
Sotby Mdws Nature Reserve★
LN8 . . . .**71** E5
SOTS HOLE LN4. . . . .**96** C7
Soulby La PE22 . . . .**114** C2
Sour La DN7 . . . .**14** E8
Soutergate **13** DN18. . . . .**3** F1
South Airfield Rd NG34 . . . .**120** C8
South Axholme Com Sch
DN9. . . . .**27** D6
South Bank **3** DN17. . . . . . .**17** D6
Southbank La DN22 . . . .**65** A8
SOUTH BRAMWITH DN7 . . . . .**14** A6
South Brick Lines NG34. . . .**120** B8
South Bridge Rd **2** PE9. . . .**181** A5
Southburn Ave HU5. . . . . . .**179** E7
SOUTH CARLTON LN1. . . . . . .**67** D3
South Carr Rd DN20 . . . .**31** A4
South Church Side **14**
HU1. . . . .**180** F6
Southcliffe Rd **19** DN21. . . . .**29** C3
South Cliff Rd **27** DN21. . . . . .**30** B1
SOUTH CLIFTON NG23 . . . . . .**78** B5
Southcoates La HU9. . . . . . .**181** E8
SOUTH COCKERINGTON
LN11 . . . .**62** A8
South Cres
11 Bottesford NG13. . . . . .**128** A5
1 Chapel St Leonard PE24 . .**90** D7
South Cross Moors Road
DN17. . . . .**17** A6
South Dale LN1 . . . .**33** B4
South Dale Cl **3** DN21. . . . . .**30** B2
Southdown LN5. . . . .**205** D1
Southdown Rd PE7 . . . .**233** F5
South Dr
12 Balderton NG24 . . . .**104** C1
4 Stow LN1. . . . .**66** C8
South Dro Bicker PE20. . . . .**134** E4
Helpringham NG34. . . . .**133** E6
Lutton PE12 . . . .**149** A1
Quadring PE11. . . . .**144** A8
Spalding PE11 . . . .**156** E2
SOUTH ELKINGTON LN11. . . . .**60** E7
South Ella Dr HU10. . . . . . .**178** D7
South Ella Farm Ct HU10. . .**178** D6
South Ella Way HU10. . . . . .**178** D7
SOUTH END DN19 . . . .**12** B7
South End Boston PE21. . . .**208** F4
Collingham NG23 . . . .**91** C4
Hogsthorpe PE24. . . . .**90** B6
South Ferriby DN18. . . . .**10** A7
Thorne/Moorends DN8. . . . . .**15** A7
South End La DN22. . . . .**52** E3
Southern Dr HU4. . . . .**179** C5
Southern La LN6. . . . .**92** B4
Southern Lane LN5. . . . . . .**105** E4
Southern Rd DN40 . . . .**186** D4
Southern Way DN40 . . . . . .**186** C7
Southern Wlk DN31 . . . .**191** D8
South Fen Rd Bourne PE10 **213** F4
Helpringham NG34. . . . .**133** D6
SOUTH FERRIBY DN18. . . . . . .**10** B8
South Ferriby Prim Sch
DN18. . . . .**10** A7
Southfield
7 Balderton NG24 . . . .**104** C2
7 Belton DN9 . . . .**16** E1

Southfield continued
4 Kingston upon Hull HU13. . .**3** E4
SOUTH FIELD HU13. . . . .**3** E4
Southfield Ave DN33 . . . . . .**194** F7
Southfield Cl
18 Thorne/Moorends DN8. . .**15** B7
Ulceby DN39 . . . .**12** B1
Southfield Dr
10 Epworth DN9. . . . .**27** D6
2 Louth LN11 . . . .**198** C4
21 North Ferriby HU14. . . . . . .**3** A4
Southfield La
Beckingham DN10 . . . .**52** B8
Fishtoft PE21. . . . .**137** C8
6 Old Leake PE22 . . . .**114** A1
Old Leake PE22 . . . .**127** A8
Willoughton DN21 . . . .**42** D3
Southfield Pl LN9 . . . .**199** C3
Southfield Rd
1 Broughton DN20 . . . .**19** D3
13 Crowle DN17. . . . .**16** D7
Grimsby DN33 . . . .**194** F7
Holton le Clay DN36 . . . . . .**195** D1
North Kelsey LN7 . . . .**31** F3
Scunthorpe DN16. . . . .**185** C5
Thorne/Moorends DN8. . . . . .**15** B7
1 Winterton DN15 . . . .**8** F5
Southfields **8** Binbrook LN8 **47** C4
Bourne PE10 . . . .**213** D4
3 Sleaford NG34. . . . .**212** D3
Southfields Ave PE2. . . . . . .**231** D5
Southfields Cl **10** PE13. . . . .**170** D2
Southfields Dr PE2. . . . .**231** D5
Southfields Prim Sch PE2 **231** D5
South Furlong Croft **22**
DN9. . . . .**27** E6
Southgate
Kingston upon Hull HU13. . . .**178** E1
12 Pinchbeck PE11. . . . . . .**156** E8
Scunthorpe DN15. . . . .**183** B3
South Gate NG34. . . . .**212** D4
Southgate Spinneys **3**
NG34. . . . .**120** E4
Southgate Way PE2 . . . . . .**229** C2
SOUTH GREEN PE34. . . . . . .**161** E2
South Gn PE34 . . . .**161** F2
SOUTH HEATH LN4. . . . .**106** D1
South Holland Ctr★ PE11 **214** D4
South Holland Enterprise Pk
PE11. . . . .**214** E2
South Humberside Ind Est
DN31. . . . .**188** B2
South Hunsley Sch HU14. . . .**2** E5
SOUTH HYKEHAM LN6. . . . . . .**93** B7
South Hykeham Com Prim
Sch The LN6 . . . .**93** B7
South Ing Dro PE11. . . . . . .**134** C1
South Ings La PE24 . . . .**90** B5
South Intake La DN9. . . . . . .**40** C7
SOUTH KELSEY LN7. . . . .**32** A1
South Kesteven Works
DN31. . . . .**210** F3
SOUTH KILLINGHOLME
DN40. . . . .**12** E3
SOUTH KYME LN4 . . . .**123** B8
South La
Kingston upon Hull HU13. . . .**178** E1
Stainton le Vale LN8 . . . .**46** E4
Willingham DN21 . . . .**54** A3
Southland Ct DN17. . . . . . .**188** A1
Southland Dr **5** LN6. . . . . . .**205** B4
Southlands Ave
Gainsborough DN21. . . . . . .**197** B8
Louth LN11. . . . .**198** D3
Peterborough PE1. . . . .**226** A6
Southlands Dr
Grantham NG31 . . . .**211** C4
Morton DN21 . . . .**197** B8
Southlands Gdns DN21 . . . .**197** B8
South Lawn Way HU14. . . . . . .**2** F5
South Lincs Con Ctr
NG31. . . . .**211** A1
South Marsh Rd
Immingham Power St
DN41. . . . .**187** F1
Stallingborough DN41 . . . . . .**23** F7
South Marsh Rd Ind Est
DN41. . . . .**187** F2
South Mkt Pl **7** LN13. . . . . . .**75** F2
Southmoor La
Newton on Trent LN1. . . . . . .**78** D8
Snitterton DN21. . . . .**43** E5
Southmoor Rd Crowle DN17 **16** C8
Newton on Trent LN1. . . . . . .**78** D8
South Moor Rd DN10 . . . . . .**39** F3
Southoe Rd PE7. . . . .**231** D2
Southolme DN21. . . . .**197** D8
SOUTH ORMSBY LN11 . . . . . .**74** D2
Southorpe PE9 . . . .**172** E2
Southorpe La DN21. . . . .**42** A7
Southorpe Paddock Nature
Reserve★ PE9 . . . .**172** E1
South Osbourne Wy
DN40. . . . .**186** D6
SOUTH OWERSBY LN8. . . . . . .**44** E4
South Parade Boston PE21 **208** C4
11 Caythorpe NG32 . . . .**119** B7
Gainsborough DN21. . . . . . .**197** D3
Grantham NG31 . . . .**211** B2
Grimsby DN31 . . . .**191** D8
7 Lincoln LN1. . . . .**201** D3
Peterborough PE3 . . . .**225** E3
5 Saxilby LN1. . . . .**66** D2
Skegness PE25. . . . .**206** D2
South Kyme LN4 . . . .**123** B8
Spalding PE11 . . . .**214** C3
Thorne/Moorends DN8. . . . . .**15** A7
South Pk LN5 . . . .**205** F8

South Pk Ave
Bracebridge Heath LN5 . . . .**205** F8
Lincoln LN5 . . . .**201** F1
South Pk Enterprise Coll
DN17. . . . .**184** D3
South Pk Ind Est DN17 . . . .**184** D3
South Pk Rd DN17. . . . .**184** D3
South Ramper
Bishop Norton DN21. . . . .**44** A5
North Owersby DN21. . . . . . .**44** A6
SOUTH RAUCEBY NG34 . . . .**120** E4
South Rd Bourne PE10. . . . .**213** D4
Chapel St Leonard PE24 . . . .**90** E6
5 Keadby with Althorpe
DN17. . . . .**17** C6
Mablethorpe/Sutton on Sea
LN12. . . . .**64** C1
North Somercotes LN11. . . . .**50** E7
Sturton le Steeple DN22. . . . .**52** C4
Tetford LN9 . . . .**73** F1
SOUTH RESTON LN11. . . . . . .**62** D1
SOUTHREY LN3. . . . .**83** D1
South Ridge Cres **2**
DN17. . . . .**184** F3
South Rise **6** LN8. . . . .**47** C4
South St Mary's Gate **4**
DN31. . . . .**191** D7
South Scaffold La NG23. . . . .**91** E3
SOUTH SCARLE NG23. . . . . . .**91** E6
South Scarle La LN6. . . . . . .**78** E1
South Scarle Rd NG23 . . . . .**91** E6
South Sea La DN36 . . . .**36** D7
South Side DN15 . . . .**2** A1
SOUTH SOMERCOTES
LN11. . . . .**50** E5
South St **12** Alford LN13. . . . .**75** F2
17 Alford LN13. . . . .**75** F2
10 Barnetby le Wold DN38 . . .**21** B4
Bole DN22 . . . .**52** C5
Boston PE21. . . . .**208** F4
Bourne PE10 . . . .**213** D4
Caistor LN7 . . . .**33** B4
1 Cleethorpes DN35. . . . . . .**193** A5
20 Crowland PE6 . . . .**166** F1
Drayton PE20 . . . .**135** C6
Horncastle LN9. . . . .**199** B3
Keelby DN41 . . . .**23** A5
Louth LN11. . . . .**198** B5
Morton DN21 . . . .**197** C8
15 North Kelsey LN7 . . . .**32** A4
Owston Ferry DN9 . . . .**28** B2
Peterborough PE1. . . . .**226** B2
Roxby cum Risby DN15. . . . . . .**8** F3
Scamblesby LN11. . . . .**72** F5
Swineshead PE20. . . . .**135** B7
West Butterwick DN17. . . . . .**28** D8
17 Winterton DN15 . . . .**9** A5
South Terr Boston PE21. . . .**208** F3
4 Louth LN11 . . . .**198** C5
SOUTH THORESBY LN13 . . . . .**75** A3
South Thoresby Rd LN13. . . .**75** A4
South View Anlaby HU4. . . . .**179** B6
Broughton DN20. . . . .**19** D4
Holton le Clay DN36 . . . . . .**195** E1
Humberston DN36. . . . .**193** A1
Peterborough PE2 . . . .**230** F7
Yarborough DN34. . . . .**191** A6
South View Ave
Brigg DN20. . . . .**196** C5
Burringham DN17. . . . .**17** D4
South View Cl **4** PE25. . . . . .**206** D2
Southview Com Prim Sch
PE6. . . . .**166** E1
Southview Gdns LN9 . . . .**73** F1
South View La LN11. . . . .**62** A7
Southview Leisure Ctr
PE25. . . . .**103** C8
South View Rd PE4 . . . .**225** D8
South View **16** LN2. . . . .**68** E6
Southwell Ave
3 Kingston upon Hull HU9. . . . .**5** F8
Peterborough PE4 . . . .**220** E4
Southwell Cl
Barrowby NG31 . . . .**210** C5
11 Caistor LN7. . . . .**33** A3
Southwell Dr
3 Skegness PE25. . . . .**206** D7
5 Skegness PE25. . . . .**206** D7
Southwell Rd **2** PE13. . . . . .**170** D1
Southwell's La **1** LN9. . . . . .**199** C4
Southwell Way PE10. . . . . . .**213** B3
Southwick Cl PE4 . . . .**221** C1
SOUTH WILLINGHAM LN8. . . . .**59** A2
SOUTH WITHAM NG33 . . . . . .**151** E2
South Witham Acad
NG33. . . . .**151** D2
South Witham Nature
Reserve★ NG33. . . . .**151** F2
Southwold Cres DN33 . . . . .**194** E8
South Wood Dr **10** DN8 . . . . .**15** A7
Sovereign Cl
3 Grimsby DN34. . . . .**190** D4
12 Wisbech PE13. . . . .**170** C1
Sovereign Pl PE3. . . . .**225** E2
Sovereign St NG34. . . . .**142** E4
Sow Dale Nature Reserve★
PE23 . . . .**87** A1
Sowers La DN15. . . . .**9** A5
Spa Bldgs LN2 . . . .**234** B2
Spafford Cl **7** DN21. . . . .**65** E8
Spa Hill **9** DN21. . . . .**30** B1
Spain Cl **17** PE21 . . . .**208** F4
Spain La **3** PE21. . . . .**208** F4
Spain Pl **4** DN21. . . . .**209** A4
SPALDING PE11. . . . .**214** E6

Spalding Acad PE11 . . . 214 F4
Spalding Bulb Mus★ PE11 . . . 145 C1
Spalding Comm 6 PE11 . . 214 B1
Spalding Dro Cowbit PE12 . 157 A3
Spalding PE12 . . . 214 E1
Spalding FE Ctr PE11 . . . 214 D4
Spalding Gate PE12 . . . 158 B8
Spalding Gram Sch PE11 . 214 D3
Spalding High Sch PE11 . . 214 F3
Spalding Monkhouse Prim Sch The PE11 . . . 214 A3
Spalding Parish CE Day Sch PE11 . . . 214 E2
Spalding Prim Sch PE11 . . 214 B5
Spalding Rd Algakirk PE20 . 136 B2
Boston PE21 . . . 208 E3
Bourne PE10 . . . 213 E5
Crowland PE6 . . . 167 B3
Deeping St James PE6 . . . 165 D1
Gosberton PE11 . . . 145 C5
Holbeach PE12 . . . 215 A2
Market Deeping PE6 . . . 217 E5
Pinchbeck PE11 . . . 214 C8
Scunthorpe DN16 . . . 185 B8
Wigtoft PE20 . . . 135 E1
Spalding Rd Bsns Pk PE10 . . . 213 F5
Spalding St John the Baptist Prim Sch The PE11 . . . 214 C2
Spalding Sta PE11 . . . 214 C4
SPALFORD NG23 . . . 78 D4
Spalford La LN6 . . . 78 E2
Spalford Rd LN6 . . . 78 E3
Spalford Warren Nature Reserve★ NG23 . . . 78 D2
Spall Cl DN33 . . . 191 A2
SPANBY NG34 . . . 132 F4
Spanby Dr 5 LN6 . . . 205 A7
Spanby La NG34 . . . 132 F5
Spanning Dr 22 LN13 . . . 75 F2
Spa Rd Lincoln LN5 . . . 234 C2
2 Woodhall Spa LN10 . . . 97 D6
Spark's La PE12 . . . 158 A4
Spark St DN34 . . . 191 A7
Sparrowgate Rd PE14 . . . 170 F1
Sparrow La
2 Long Bennington NG23 . . . 117 D3
Marnham NG23 . . . 78 A5
Newball LN8 . . . 69 F2
Sparrow Rd 1 PE7 . . . 230 D1
Spa St LN2 . . . 202 B3
Spaw La 5 LN11 . . . 198 B6
Spayne Rd PE21 . . . 209 A4
Speechley Rd PE7 . . . 233 F6
Speechley's Dro PE6 . . . 174 F7
Speedwell Cl 23 NG24 . . . 104 C5
Speedwell Cres DN15 . . . 182 C6
Speedwell Ct 7 PE6 . . . 217 D6
Speedwell Dr 16 PE10 . . . 213 D3
Speeton Gr HU5 . . . 179 D7
Speight Cl 5 NG24 . . . 104 B7
Spencer Ave
Peterborough PE2 . . . 231 D5
Scunthorpe DN15 . . . 182 F4
Spencer Cl
3 Long Sutton PE12 . . . 216 B5
West Walton PE14 . . . 170 E4
Spencer Gdns
7 Butterwick PE22 . . . 126 E3
Holbeach PE12 . . . 215 F3
Spencer St Grimsby DN31 . . 189 D1
6 Kingston upon Hull HU2 . 180 E7
9 Lincoln LN5 . . . 205 E8
Spence St 10 PE23 . . . 87 F1
Spendla's La PE12 . . . 159 F3
Spendluffe Ave 3 LN13 . . . 75 F3
Spennymoor Cl 1 LN6 . . . 93 B8
Sperrin Cl 5 LN5 . . . 205 D2
Speyer Ave PE11 . . . 214 C5
Speyside Ct 1 PE2 . . . 229 D4
Spice Ave PE21 . . . 136 D8
Spicer's La PE22 . . . 127 B5
Spilby Mdws 12 PE23 . . . 101 A8
SPILSBY PE23 . . . 101 A8
Spilsby Cl 8 LN6 . . . 204 D8
Spilsby Hill PE23 . . . 100 B8
Spilsby Prim Sch PE23 . . . 88 A1
Spilsby Rd Boston PE21 . . . 209 A6
Eastville PE22 . . . 101 A1
High Toynton LN9 . . . 86 B4
Horncastle LN9 . . . 199 E4
Scunthorpe DN17 . . . 184 E5
Spilsby PE23 . . . 101 A8
Thorpe St Peter PE24 . . . 102 B4
Spindelwood Dr 8 PE10 . 213 D3
Spindles The PE10 . . . 213 D7
Spindlewood 1 HU15 . . . 2 C7
Spinnaker Cl HU9 . . . 181 C6
Spinners Cl 3 NG34 . . . 212 E3
Spinney Cl
Immingham DN40 . . . 186 C4
7 Manby LN11 . . . 62 C6
9 Ryhall PE9 . . . 163 C1
Spinney Croft Cl 14 HU14 . . 3 A5
Spinney La 10 Ryhall PE9 . . 163 C1
2 Scopwick Heath LN4 . . . 108 A7
Spinneys The 5 LN2 . . . 68 D7
Spinney The
1 Barnby Dun DN3 . . . 14 A3
13 Barrow upon Humber DN19 . . . 11 D8
Brigg DN20 . . . 196 D2
3 Gainsborough DN21 . . . 197 F5

Spinney The *continued*
3 Grimsby DN31 . . . 191 C7
2 Market Deeping PE6 . . . 217 B5
7 Swanland HU14 . . . 3 B7
7 Winthorpe NG24 . . . 104 B7
Spinney Wlk
Kingston upon Hull HU4 . . . 179 C6
Longthorpe PE3 . . . 225 B2
Spion Kop La PE20 . . . 135 E3
Spirea App LN6 . . . 204 C8
Spire Cl LN1 . . . 201 E7
Spire Gdns 5 NG24 . . . 104 A6
Spire Hull & East Riding Hospl HU10 . . . 178 E5
Spires The 15 PE20 . . . 136 A2
Spire View
1 Bottesford NG13 . . . 128 A6
14 Grantham NG31 . . . 211 A5
1 Kingston upon Hull HU13 178 E1
Sleaford NG34 . . . 212 A2
Spire View Rd LN11 . . . 198 D5
Spirewic Ave PE25 . . . 206 D8
Spiros Rd 3 PE2 . . . 231 E4
Spital Hill
Gainsborough DN21 . . . 197 E5
18 Louth LN11 . . . 198 B5
SPITAL IN THE STREET LN8 . . . 43 B1
Spital La LN8 . . . 55 B8
Spital St LN1 . . . 234 B4
Spital Terr DN21 . . . 197 D4
Spitfire Ave LN11 . . . 62 B6
Spitfire La DN36 . . . 195 C4
Spittal Hill Rd PE22 . . . 126 D4
SPITTLEGATE NG31 . . . 211 A3
Splash La Ailsworth PE5 . . . 228 E8
Castor PE5 . . . 223 E1
Spotfield La PE20 . . . 136 C7
Spout Hill HU15 . . . 2 C8
Spout Yd 6 LN11 . . . 198 B6
Spratt Cl LN9 . . . 199 D1
Spratton Ct DN34 . . . 190 C4
SPRIDLINGTON LN8 . . . 55 F3
Spridlington Rd LN8 . . . 56 D3
Spriggs Cl NG34 . . . 212 C3
Sprignall PE3 . . . 224 F4
Sprigs Rd
Hampton Vale PE7 . . . 230 B2
Hampton Vale PE7 . . . 230 B2
Spring Ave PE7 . . . 230 B1
Springbank DN20 . . . 196 C5
Spring Bank
5 Binbrook LN8 . . . 47 C4
Grimsby DN34 . . . 191 A7
Kingston upon Hull HU3 . . . 180 D7
Spring Bank W HU5 . . . 179 D7
Springbok Cl HU4 . . . 179 D2
Springburn St HU3 . . . 180 A5
Spring Cl 9 LN2 . . . 68 E6
Spring Ct Dunston LN4 . . . 95 C5
Louth LN11 . . . 198 C5
13 Welton/Dunholme LN2 . . . 68 D7
Springdale Cl
Kingston upon Hull HU10 . . . 178 F8
2 Kingston upon Hull HU9 . . . 5 D8
Spring Dr
22 Balderton NG24 . . . 104 C1
9 Balderton NG24 . . . 104 C1
Farcet PE7 . . . 231 B2
Spring End 3 NG31 . . . 129 D5
Springfield PE2 . . . 231 A7
Springfield Ave Brough HU15 2 C6
7 Hatfield DN7 . . . 14 E4
Springfield Cl
6 Branston LN4 . . . 81 E2
Branston LN4 . . . 81 E2
Gainsborough DN21 . . . 197 E4
Lincoln LN5 . . . 234 B4
2 Scunthorpe DN16 . . . 185 C6
Springfield Est LN4 . . . 95 D1
Springfield Inf Sch PE1 . . . 225 F3
Springfield Pk Ind Est NG31 . . . 211 A2
Springfield Prim Sch DN33 . . . 194 D7
Springfield Rd
2 Brigg DN20 . . . 196 D3
Grantham NG31 . . . 211 A2
Grimsby DN33 . . . 191 C1
Kingston upon Hull HU3 . . . 179 F6
Parson Drove PE13 . . . 177 D7
Peterborough PE1 . . . 225 F5
6 Ruskington NG34 . . . 108 D2
Yaxley PE7 . . . 233 F5
Springfield Rise 1 DN20 . 196 E3
Springfields LN8 . . . 46 B1
Springfields Sh & Events Ctr PE12 . . . 157 B7
Springfield Way HU10 . . . 178 E7
Spring Gdns
Gainsborough DN21 . . . 197 D4
Grantham NG31 . . . 211 B2
Long Sutton PE12 . . . 216 B4
13 Louth LN11 . . . 198 B5
Sleaford NG34 . . . 212 C5
Spalding PE11 . . . 214 C3
Spring Gdns E HU4 . . . 179 B6
Spring Gdns S HU4 . . . 179 B5
Spring Gdns W HU4 . . . 179 B6
Spring Gr
Kingston upon Hull HU3 . . . 180 A7
Terrington St Clement PE34 161 F2
Springhead Ave HU5 . . . 179 A7
Springhead Ct HU10 . . . 179 A6
Springhead Gdns HU10 . . . 179 A7
Springhead La HU5 . . . 179 A7
Springhead Prim Sch HU10 . . . 178 E7

Spring Hill 3 Binbrook LN8 . 47 C4
Cherry Willingham/Reepham LN3 . . . 203 F8
Grantham NG31 . . . 211 D3
Lincoln LN1 . . . 234 A3
Spring La Balderton NG24 . . 104 C2
2 Balderton NG24 . . . 104 C2
8 Colsterworth NG33 . . . 151 D7
4 Folkingham NG34 . . . 142 D8
Horbling NG34 . . . 133 B2
14 Laceby DN37 . . . 23 F1
5 Leasingham NG34 . . . 121 B7
4 Wymondham LE14 . . . 150 B1
Springs La DN22 . . . 52 A2
Springs Parade DN20 . . . 196 B3
Springs Rd DN10 . . . 26 C1
Spring St
Immingham DN40 . . . 186 D4
Kingston upon Hull HU2 . . . 180 D7
Spalding PE11 . . . 214 D3
Springs Way DN20 . . . 196 B3
SPRINGTHORPE DN21 . . . 53 E8
Springthorpe Rd
Corringham DN21 . . . 41 E1
Gainsborough DN21 . . . 197 F4
Spring View 4 LN8 . . . 47 C4
Springville Ave HU13 . . . 178 F2
Springway Cres DN34 . . . 191 A7
Springwood Cres DN33 . . . 194 D7
Sprite La LN4 . . . 109 D5
SPROXTON LE14 . . . 150 C7
Sproxton Rd
Buckminster NG33 . . . 150 D6
Skillington NG33 . . . 151 A8
Spruce Cl PE12 . . . 215 C4
Spruce Cres 2 LN4 . . . 81 D2
Spruce La DN39 . . . 12 A1
Spurn Ave DN33 . . . 194 F8
Spurn Lightship★ HU1 . . . 180 F5
Spurr Rd DN39 . . . 21 F5
Spurr The 7 LN5 . . . 107 A7
Spyvee St HU8 . . . 181 A7
Square The
2 Barnack PE9 . . . 172 D3
Barrowby NG32 . . . 129 B3
12 Goxhill DN19 . . . 12 A8
Kingston upon Hull HU13 . . . 178 E1
18 Kirton PE20 . . . 136 C5
4 Leasingham NG34 . . . 121 B7
North Thoresby DN36 . . . 36 B1
5 Ryhall PE9 . . . 163 C1
Toynton All Saints PE23 . . . 100 F6
Squires Gate PE4 . . . 221 D3
Squires Mdw 10 LN11 . . . 50 F7
Squires Rd 18 LN5 . . . 93 E8
Squires The PE2 . . . 230 F8
Squirrel Chase LN6 . . . 92 D5
Stable La 3 DN18 . . . 3 E1
Stables Ct 11 PE13 . . . 170 B2
Stable Way 7 LN8 . . . 57 E7
Stacey Cl 2 PE25 . . . 90 D3
Stackyard The PE2 . . . 229 E5
Stafford Ave NG24 . . . 104 A2
Staffordshire Cres 6 LN6 . . . 204 D7
Stafford St 3 Boston PE21 208 F6
Kingston upon Hull HU2 . . . 180 E8
Stagsden PE2 . . . 229 F4
Stagshaw Dr PE2 . . . 231 B8
STAINBY NG33 . . . 151 C5
Stainby Rd
Buckminster NG33 . . . 150 F5
Gunby & Stainby NG33 . . . 151 C4
Staindale Rd DN16 . . . 185 D5
Stainesway LN11 . . . 198 E7
STAINFIELD Haconby PE10 . 154 A8
Stainfield LN8 . . . 83 B8
Stainfield Rd Kingthorpe LN8 70 B1
Kirkby Underwood PE10 . . . 142 D1
Morton PE10 . . . 154 B7
STAINFORTH DN7 . . . 14 C6
Stainforth Inf Sch DN7 . . . 14 C6
Stainforth Kirton La Prim Sch DN7 . . . 14 D7
Stainforth Moor Rd DN7 . . 15 C3
Stainforth Rd DN7 . . . 14 A5
Stain La LN12 . . . 63 E3
STAINSBY LN9 . . . 86 F6
Stainton Ave 6 DN21 . . . 43 D7
STAINTON BY LANGWORTH LN3 . . . 69 C4
Stainton Cl 5 DN21 . . . 53 A5
Stainton Dr Grimsby DN33 . 191 A3
8 Immingham DN40 . . . 186 B4
Scunthorpe DN17 . . . 184 E4
Stainton Gdns LN1 . . . 201 E7
Stainton La LN2 . . . 69 B4
STAINTON LE VALE LN8 . . . 46 E5
Stallebrass Cl PE2 . . . 231 E5
STALLINGBOROUGH DN41 . . . 23 E6
Stallingborough CE Prim Sch DN41 . . . 23 E6
Stallingborough Rd
Immingham DN40 . . . 186 B2
Keelby DN41 . . . 23 A5
Stallingborough Sta DN41 . 23 E6
STAMFORD PE9 . . . 219 D4
Stamford Bsns Pk PE9 . . . 219 E6
Stamford Cl
4 Market Deeping PE6 . . . 217 B5
Sleaford NG34 . . . 212 C3
Stamford High Sch PE9 . . . 219 C4
Stamford Jun Sch PE9 . . . 219 B3
Stamford Leisure Ctr PE9 219 D6
Stamford Lodge Rd PE6 . . 224 C5
Stamford Mus★ PE9 . . . 219 C5
Stamford Rd Barnack PE9 . . 172 C4
Buckminster NG33 . . . 151 A4

Stamford Rd *continued*
Collyweston PE9 . . . 171 C2
Colsterworth NG33 . . . 151 E5
Easton on the Hill PE9 . . . 219 A1
Essendine PE9 . . . 163 D2
Helpston PE6 . . . 173 C1
Ketton PE9 . . . 218 A2
Marholm PE6 . . . 220 A1
Market Deeping PE6 . . . 217 A4
Tinwell PE9 . . . 218 A6
West Deeping PE9 . . . 173 A7
Stamford Ret Pk PE9 . . . 219 D6
Stamford & Rutland Hospl PE9 . . . 219 D6
Stamfords Art Ctr★ PE9 . . 219 C5
Stamford Sch PE9 . . . 219 C6
Stamford St NG31 . . . 211 B2
Stamford Sta PE9 . . . 219 C4
Stamford Theatre★ 28 PE9 . . . 219 C5
Stamford Welland Acad PE9 . . . 219 B7
Stamford Wlk 25 PE9 . . . 219 C5
Stamp End LN2 . . . 234 C2
Stamper St 2 PE3 . . . 224 F3
Standard La LN5 . . . 93 A2
Standish Ct 4 PE2 . . . 230 D8
Standish Gr PE21 . . . 209 B7
Standish La DN40 . . . 186 B5
Stane Dr 12 LN4 . . . 81 A1
Stanfield Rd 2 DN9 . . . 27 D6
Stanford Cl 1 DN37 . . . 23 F1
Stanford Jun & Inf Sch DN37 . . . 23 E1
Stanford Wlk 4 PE3 . . . 225 C4
STANGROUND PE2 . . . 231 C5
Stanground Acad PE7 . . . 231 C5
Stanholme La DN36 . . . 36 A1
Stanhope Ave 7 LN10 . . . 97 D6
Stanhope Gdns 1 PE21 . . . 209 C4
Stanhope Pl DN35 . . . 192 C7
Stanhope Rd LN9 . . . 199 C4
Stanhope Terr 3 LN9 . . . 199 C4
Stanhurst La DN7 . . . 15 A5
Staniland Acad PE21 . . . 208 D4
Staniland Rd PE21 . . . 208 D3
Staniland Way
1 Humberston DN36 . . . 36 D8
Peterborough PE4 . . . 221 A5
Staniwell Rise DN17 . . . 184 D7
Staniwells Dr 11 DN20 . . . 19 D3
Stanley Ave 5 LN12 . . . 64 B3
Stanley Cl 2 PE24 . . . 102 D2
Stanley Cres LN4 . . . 205 F4
Stanley Dr
11 Sutterton PE20 . . . 136 A2
Sutton Bridge PE12 . . . 160 E4
Stanley Gdns 13 DN7 . . . 14 C6
Stanley Jackson Wy 24 HU15 . . . 2 D5
Stanley Pl 1 LN5 . . . 201 F1
Stanley Rd
Peterborough PE1 . . . 226 A3
Scunthorpe DN15 . . . 182 C3
18 Stainforth DN7 . . . 14 C6
Stanley St
14 Beacon Hill NG24 . . . 104 A5
Bourne PE10 . . . 213 C6
Gainsborough DN21 . . . 197 D2
Grimsby DN32 . . . 189 C1
Kingston upon Hull HU3 . . . 180 C7
Lincoln LN5 . . . 205 D7
1 Stamford PE9 . . . 219 C5
Stan Rowing Ct PE2 . . . 231 C7
Stansfield Gdns DN40 . . . 186 A5
Stansted St 5 DN31 . . . 188 D1
Stanthaket Ct 12 LN1 . . . 234 B3
Stanton Cl 2 PE10 . . . 213 E5
Stanton Rd 4 LN12 . . . 77 A8
Stanton's Pit Nature Reserve★ PE10 . . . 163 C8
Stanton Sq PE7 . . . 230 D2
Stanton St 7 NG31 . . . 211 A4
Stanwick Ct PE3 . . . 225 F2
Stapes Garth 1 LN11 . . . 50 B8
Stapledon Rd PE2 . . . 229 D2
Staplee Way PE1 . . . 226 F7
STAPLEFORD LN6 . . . 105 B8
Stapleford Ave LN2 . . . 201 F8
Stapleford La
Coddington NG24 . . . 104 E6
Collingham NG23 . . . 91 E1
Staple La NG24 . . . 104 B1
Staple Rd DN40 . . . 12 F3
Staples La 12 LN5 . . . 93 F7
Stapleton Wy PE11 . . . 214 D8
Star Carr La DN20 . . . 196 D8
Star Cl PE1 . . . 226 C3
Starella Gr HU3 . . . 180 A4
Star Fen Dro NG34 . . . 123 A4
Starham Rd LN7 . . . 31 C4
Starks La LN8 . . . 58 D7
Stark Wy 3 LN2 . . . 202 D6
Star La Holbeach PE12 . . . 215 C7
4 Stamford PE9 . . . 219 C5
Star La Mews 26 PE9 . . . 219 C5
Star Lode Dro PE11 . . . 144 B1
Star Mews PE1 . . . 226 C2
Star Rd PE1 . . . 226 C2
Stathern Rd PE1 . . . 226 D7
Stathern Wlk NG31 . . . 210 E2
Stather Rd DN15 . . . 8 A1
Stathers Wlk 3 HU10 . . . 178 F6
Station App
6 Ancaster NG32 . . . 120 A3
Boston PE21 . . . 208 E4
Cleethorpes DN35 . . . 192 F7
11 Donington PE11 . . . 134 E2

Station App *continued*
Louth LN11 . . . 198 C6
Station Ave
New Waltham DN36 . . . 195 D6
16 South Witham NG33 . . . 151 D2
Wisbech St Mary PE13 . . . 177 D5
Station Cl 9 NG23 . . . 91 D4
Station Ct 33 Canal Side DN8 15 A8
7 Hatfield DN7 . . . 14 D4
Station Field LN6 . . . 200 B3
Station La Horncastle LN9 . 199 A3
Searby cum Owmby DN38 . . . 32 D7
Station Mews
New Waltham DN36 . . . 195 C6
17 Wragby LN8 . . . 70 D4
Station Rd
Ailsworth PE5 . . . 223 C1
Alford LN13 . . . 75 E2
Algarkirk PE20 . . . 146 B8
Bardney LN3 . . . 83 B4
Barkston NG32 . . . 129 F8
Barlings LN3 . . . 69 B3
Barnack PE9 . . . 172 E4
Beckingham DN10 . . . 52 B8
1 Billingborough NG34 . . . 133 B1
Blyton DN21 . . . 41 C5
Bottesford NG13 . . . 128 A6
Bourne PE10 . . . 155 C3
Branston LN4 . . . 81 E2
Brough HU15 . . . 2 B5
Burgh le Marsh PE24 . . . 102 C8
Burringham DN17 . . . 17 E4
Candlesby with Gunby PE24 . . 89 B1
Careby Aunby & Holywell PE9 . . . 163 A8
Castle Bytham NG33 . . . 152 D1
6 Cherry Willingham/Reepham LN3 . . . 82 A8
Cherry Willingham/Reepham LN3 . . . 203 F8
Cleethorpes DN35 . . . 192 F7
Collingham NG23 . . . 91 D4
Corby Glen NG33 . . . 152 D7
Deeping St James PE6 . . . 174 B7
Digby LN4 . . . 108 E5
Donington on Bain LN11 . . . 59 E1
East Halton DN40 . . . 12 D7
Epworth DN9 . . . 27 D7
6 Essendine PE9 . . . 163 D3
Fulstow LN11 . . . 49 A7
Garthorpe & Fockerby DN17 . . 7 E6
Gedney Hill PE12 . . . 168 C1
Gosberton PE11 . . . 145 A5
Grantham NG31 . . . 211 B3
Grasby DN38 . . . 32 E6
Great Steeping PE23 . . . 101 F6
Grimsby DN37 . . . 190 C8
Gunness DN15 . . . 17 E5
Habrough DN40 . . . 12 F1
Halton Holegate PE23 . . . 101 B8
Harby NG23 . . . 79 B5
Harmston LN5 . . . 93 E5
Hatfield DN7 . . . 14 D4
Haxey DN9 . . . 27 D1
Healing DN41 . . . 23 F5
Heckington NG34 . . . 122 E2
Heighington LN4 . . . 81 E4
Helpringham NG34 . . . 133 D7
9 Hibaldstow DN20 . . . 30 F5
Holbeach PE12 . . . 215 D2
Holton le Clay DN36 . . . 36 B4
Hubbert's Bridge PE20 . . . 124 E1
Keadby with Althorpe DN17 . . 17 D6
6 Ketton PE9 . . . 171 A3
Kingston upon Hull HU13 . . . 178 E1
Kirton PE20 . . . 136 C5
Kirton in Lindsey DN21 . . . 30 B2
Knaith DN21 . . . 53 A4
Legbourne LN11 . . . 61 E3
Lincoln LN6 . . . 204 D3
Little Steeping PE23 . . . 101 D5
5 Long Sutton PE12 . . . 216 B4
Ludborough DN36 . . . 48 E6
16 Mablethorpe & Sutton LN12 . . . 76 F8
20 Mablethorpe/Sutton on Sea LN12 . . . 64 B4
Metheringham LN4 . . . 95 D4
Midville PE22 . . . 113 E8
Midville PE22 . . . 113 E8
1 Misterton DN10 . . . 40 A5
Misterton LN13 . . . 89 A6
Morton PE10 . . . 154 D6
Moulton PE12 . . . 157 F6
Mumby LN13 . . . 76 F1
North Kelsey LN7 . . . 32 B4
Northorpe PE10 . . . 164 C7
North Thoresby DN36 . . . 36 B1
Owston Ferry DN9 . . . 28 A2
Peterborough PE3 . . . 225 F2
Potter Hanworth LN4 . . . 82 A1
Ruskington NG34 . . . 108 E1
Scawby DN20 . . . 30 F7
Scredington NG34 . . . 132 F7
Scunthorpe DN15 . . . 183 A2
Sibsey PE22 . . . 113 C1
Sleaford NG34 . . . 212 D3
South Kelsey LN7 . . . 32 D2
South Killingholme DN40 . . . 13 A5
South Willingham LN8 . . . 59 A1
Stallingborough DN41 . . . 23 E6
Stamford PE9 . . . 219 B4
Stixwould & Woodhall LN10 . 97 A8
Sturton le Steeple DN22 . . . 52 B3
Surfleet PE11 . . . 145 E3
Sutterton PE20 . . . 136 A1
Swinderby LN6 . . . 92 A6
Swineshead PE20 . . . 123 F1

Station Rd continued
Theddlethorpe All Saints
LN12 . . . . 63 D7
Thorney PE6 . . . . 176 A3
Thornton Curtis DN39 . . . 11 F5
Thorpe on the Hill LN6 . . . 79 E1
Thorpe St Peter PE24 . . . . 102 B3
Timberland LN4 . . . . 96 B1
Torksey LN1 . . . . 65 D6
Tumby Woodside PE22 . . . 98 F1
Tydd St Mary PE13 . . . . . 170 C8
Ulceby DN39 . . . . 12 B1
Waddington LN5 . . . . 93 F7
Wainfleet All Saints PE24 . . 102 D1
Walkeringham DN10 . . . . . 40 A3
Waltham DN36 . . . . 195 A5
Waltham LE14 . . . . 138 A1
Whitton DN15 . . . . 1 D3
Wickenby LN3 . . . . 57 B1
Woodhall Spa LN10 . . . . . 97 D6
Station Rd Ind Est PE20 . . . 135 A8
Station Rd N PE34 . . . . . . 161 C2
Station Rd S PE34 . . . . . . 161 C2
Station Rd (West) NG31 . . . 211 A3
Station St Boston PE21 . . . 208 E5
Donington PE11 . . . . . . 134 E2
Lincoln LN5 . . . . 234 A1
Rippingale PE10 . . . . . . 143 A3
1 Spalding PE11 . . . . . . 214 D4
Station Terr LN5 . . . . 106 D3
Staunton Ct LN1 . . . . 201 D3
STAUNTON IN THE VALE
NG13 . . . . 117 A2
Staunton Rd 9 NG24 . . . . 104 A3
Staunton St 3 LN1 . . . . . . 201 D3
Staunt Rd PE22 . . . . 112 E2
Stavanger Cl DN36 . . . . . . 195 B6
Staveley Rd 8 LN13 . . . . . 75 E2
Staverton Cres LN6 . . . . . . 200 B1
Staverton Rd PE4 . . . . . . 220 E3
Staves Ct 5 DN36 . . . . . . 36 D4
Staxton Cl PE6 . . . . 220 A1
Staxton Ct HU9 . . . . 181 D8
Steadfold La PE9 . . . . . . 218 A3
Steadings The
Flixborough DN15 . . . . . . 8 B2
North Scarle LN6 . . . . . . 78 F2
Stealgoose La DN9 . . . . . . 16 F3
Steamer Point Rd LN4 . . . . 95 C7
Steapas Cl 2 PE23 . . . . . . 101 D7
Steeles Dr NG24 . . . . 104 C2
Steepers The 4 LN2 . . . . . 68 D2
Steep Hill LN2 . . . . 234 B3
Steeping Ct LN1 . . . . 201 E8
Steeping Dr DN40 . . . . . . 186 A3
Steeping Rd
Halton Holegate PE23 . . . 101 C6
Thorpe Fendykes PE24 . . . 101 F3
Steeple Leas 15 NG31 . . . 211 A5
Steeple Vw PE11 . . . . . . 214 A1
Stells La PE21 . . . . 208 F3
STENIGOT LN11 . . . . 72 D8
Stenigot Cl 3 LN6 . . . . . . 204 C6
Stenigot Gr LN6 . . . . 204 D6
Stenigot Rd 1 LN6 . . . . . . 204 D6
Stenner Rd LN4 . . . . 207 F6
Stennett Ave 1 PE11 . . . . 156 E2
STENWITH NG32 . . . . 128 D3
Stephen Cl 3 DN39 . . . . . 12 A1
Stephen Cres
16 Barton-upon-Humber
DN18 . . . . 10 F8
Grimsby DN34 . . . . 190 E4
Humberston DN36 . . . . . 36 C8
Stephen Rd NG24 . . . . . . 104 A6
Stephenson Ave
Gonerby Hill Foot NG31 . . 210 F8
Pinchbeck PE11 . . . . . . 214 E8
Stephenson Cl
9 Alford LN13 . . . . . . 75 E2
4 Boston PE21 . . . . . . 208 F1
14 Colsterworth NG33 . . . 151 D7
Heighington/Washingborough
LN4 . . . . 81 E4
Yaxley PE7 . . . . 233 D6
Stephenson Ct 5 PE1 . . . 226 B2
Stephenson Rd LN6 . . . . . 204 D4
Stephenson Way PE10 . . . . 213 D7
Stephenson Wy NG24 . . . . 104 B6
Stephens Way 4 PE6 . . . . 217 F4
Stephen's Way NG34 . . . . . 212 F3
Sterling Cres DN37 . . . . . . 194 C4
Sterne Ave 3 DN20 . . . . . 73 D7
Steve Newton Ave LN9 . . . 199 B2
Stevenson Pl 1 DN35 . . . . 192 D5
Stevenson's Way 33 DN18 . . 10 E8
Stevern Way PE1 . . . . 226 F4
Steward Wy 5 PE4 . . . . . . 221 C2
STEWTON LN11 . . . . 61 E5
Stewton Gdns LN11 . . . . . 198 D4
Stewton La LN11 . . . . . . 198 E4
Steyning La PE20 . . . . . . 135 A7
Steynings The PE4 . . . . . . 221 A3
STIBBINGTON PE8 . . . . . . 222 C2
STICKFORD PE22 . . . . 100 B2
Stickney CE (Aided) Prim Sch
PE22 . . . . 113 A8
Stickney Farm Pk★ PE22 . 112 F8
Stickney La PE22 . . . . . . 112 D7
Still Cl PE6 . . . . 217 B5
Still The PE13 . . . . 170 D1
Stirling Cl 4 DN21 . . . . . . 197 E6
Stirling Ct
14 Grantham NG31 . . . . . 210 E2
Heckington NG34 . . . . . 122 D2
Stirling Dr 12 NG24 . . . . . 104 C5

Stirling Rd PE9 . . . . 218 F5
Stirling St Grimsby DN31 . . 189 D1
Kingston upon Hull HU3 . . 179 F6
Stirling Way
Market Deeping PE6 . . . . . 217 C2
Peterborough PE3 . . . . . 220 B1
4 Skellingthorpe LN6 . . . . 200 A4
STIXWOULD LN10 . . . . 97 B8
Stixwould Rd LN10 . . . . . . 97 C7
Stixwould Rd LN10 . . . . . . 84 C1
Stockbridge Pk 3 HU15 . . . 2 C7
Stockbridge Rd HU15 . . . . . 2 C7
Stocken Hall Mews LE15 . . 152 A1
Stocken Hall Road LE15 . . 162 A7
Stockham Ct DN33 . . . . . . 191 A2
STOCKHOLES TURBARY
DN9 . . . . 16 B2
Stockholes Turbary Rd
DN9 . . . . 16 C2
Stockhouse La PE11 . . . . . 145 B3
Stocking Way LN2 . . . . . . 202 F6
Stockman's Ave 2 PE12 . . 215 F3
Stockmoor La LN8 . . . . . . 57 A8
Stocks Hill 4 Belton DN9 . . 16 E1
Castor PE5 . . . . 223 F1
Ludborough DN36 . . . . . . 48 E6
Stockshill Rd DN16 . . . . . . 185 C6
Stocks La LN8 . . . . 56 F3
Stockwell Gate PE12 . . . . . 215 A4
Stockwell Gr 6 HU9 . . . . . 5 F8
Stockwell Prim Sch HU9 . . . 5 F8
Stockwith Mill ★ PE23 . . . 87 B5
Stockwith Rd Haxey DN9 . . . 27 E1
Walkeringham DN10 . . . . . 40 A3
STOKE ROCHFORD NG33 . . 139 F2
**Stoke Rochford Hall Con &
Leisure Ctr**★ NG33 . . . . . 139 F2
Stokesay Ct 8 PE3 . . . . . . 225 B1
Stokes Dr NG34 . . . . 212 B6
Stoke St 4 HU2 . . . . 180 E8
Stoksley Wlk DN37 . . . . . . 190 F8
Stonebow Ctr LN2 . . . . . . 234 B2
Stonebridge PE2 . . . . 230 C5
Stonebridge Lea PE2 . . . . 230 C5
Stonebridge Rd NG31 . . . . 211 B4
Stone Cl 8 PE12 . . . . 213 C6
Stonecross Rd NG34 . . . . 107 E1
Stone Dr LE15 . . . . 152 A1
Stonefield Ave LN2 . . . . . 234 B4
Stonefield Pk LN2 . . . . . . 68 C7
Stonegate Gedney PE12 . . . 159 D6
Spalding PE11 . . . . 214 E3
28 Thorne/Moorends DN8 . . 15 A8
Stone Gate Cowbit PE12 . . 157 B1
Weston PE12 . . . . 145 F2
STONE HILL DN7 . . . . 14 F4
Stone Hill DN7 . . . . 15 A4
Stone Hill Rd DN7 . . . . . . 15 A4
Stonehouse Rd PE7 . . . . . 233 E5
Stone La
Auborn Haddington & South
Hykeham LN5 . . . . . . 92 E6
Burringham DN17 . . . . . . 17 E4
Humby NG33 . . . . 141 C8
Peterborough PE1 . . . . . 225 F5
Sutterton PE20 . . . . . . 135 F1
6 Waddington LN5 . . . . . 93 F7
Stoneleigh Ct PE3 . . . . . . 225 B2
Stonemasons Ct 4 LN3 . . . 211 B4
Stone Moor Rd 14 LN6 . . . . 93 B8
Stonepit La Marston NG32 . 118 C3
8 Skillington NG33 . . . . . 151 A8
Willingham DN21 . . . . . . 53 F3
Stone Pit La Skendleby PE23 . 88 D4
Stonepit Rd HU15 . . . . . . 2 E6
Stone Pit Lane DN41 . . . . . 23 A3
Stonesby Rd LE14 . . . . . . 138 E1
Stones Cl 4 PE24 . . . . . . 90 B7
Stones La 13 Spilsby PE23 . . 88 A1
West Keal PE23 . . . . . . 100 C5
Stone's La PE24 . . . . 77 C1
Stones Pl 1 LN6 . . . . . . 200 E1
Stone Way NG34 . . . . 212 B6
Stonewell Row LN9 . . . . . 199 C4
Stonewort Ave
2 Hampton Vale PE7 . . . 230 B1
Yaxley PE7 . . . . 233 B8
Stoney La DN36 . . . . 36 D4
Stoney Track NG32 . . . . . . 139 B6
Stoney Way 15 DN36 . . . . 36 D4
Stoney Yd LN6 . . . . 200 A5
Stong's Dro PE11 . . . . . . 144 F8
Stony Cl 10 DN7 . . . . 14 C7
Stonyford Dr 9 DN7 . . . . . 14 C5
Stool Ct B2 DN9 . . . . 16 E1
Storbeck Rd 15 PE13 . . . . 170 D1
Storey's Bar Rd PE6 . . . . 227 A3
Storey's La PE24 . . . . 102 E7
Storrington Way PE4 . . . . 221 A3
Stortford St 7 DN31 . . . . . 188 D1
Story St 11 HU1 . . . . 180 E7
Stothards La 7 DN19 . . . . 12 A8
Stoton's Gate PE12 . . . . . 158 E2
Stour Ct NG31 . . . . 210 E2
Stourton Pl LN9 . . . . 199 B4
Stove Ct LE15 . . . . 162 A8
Stovin Cres DN15 . . . . . . 9 A5
STOW LN1 . . . . 66 B8
Stow Cl DN37 . . . . 190 D8
Stowehill Rd PE4 . . . . . . 221 D2
Stowe Rd PE6 . . . . 164 E2
Stowgarth 36 DN18 . . . . . 10 F8
Stowgate Rd PE6 . . . . . . 174 A8
Stow Hill LE14 . . . . 150 C7
Stow La NG34 . . . . 133 A1
Stow Pk Rd Marton DN21 . . 65 E8
Stow LN1 . . . . 66 B8

Stow Rd Scunthorpe DN16 . . 185 B7
Sturton by Stow LN1 . . . . . 66 C8
Willingham DN21 . . . . . . 53 E2
Wisbech PE13 . . . . 170 E1
St. Peters Orchard 2 DN18 . 3 F1
Strafford St DN21 . . . . . . 197 D2
STRAGGLETHORPE LN5 . . 105 E3
Stragglethorpe La
Caythorpe NG32 . . . . . . 118 E8
Fulbeck NG32 . . . . 105 E2
Strahane Cl LN5 . . . . 205 C3
Straight Dro PE7 . . . . 231 E1
Strait Bargate 26 PE21 . . . 208 F5
Strait The LN2 . . . . 234 B3
Strand Cl
Kingston upon Hull HU2 . . 180 E8
7 Kingston upon Hull HU2 . 180 E8
8 Mablethorpe/Sutton on Sea
LN12 . . . . 64 B3
Strand Community Sch
DN32 . . . . 189 B1
Strand St DN32 . . . . 189 B1
Strand The LN12 . . . . . . 64 B3
Stratford Ave DN34 . . . . . 191 A4
Stratford Dr 5 DN37 . . . . . 183 C1
Stratford Pl 7 PE12 . . . . . 213 C3
Stratten Cl 5 NG34 . . . . . 107 C1
Stratton Pk 1 HU14 . . . . . 3 C6
Strawberry Ave PE3 . . . . 225 A5
Strawberry Cl 13 PE13 . . . 170 C1
Strawberry Fields Dr
PE12 . . . . 147 D6
Strawberry Gdns WY DN9 . . 181 B7
Strawberry Hall La 4
NG24 . . . . 104 A5
Strawberry Hill DN37 . . . . 194 B4
Strawberry St HU9 . . . . . . 181 B7
Strayfleets La PE22 . . . . . 126 D5
Stray Gn 12 NG34 . . . . . . 108 E2
Street La North Kelsey LN7 . 32 B4
North Leverton with
Habblesthorpe DN22 . . . 65 A8
Street Lane Rd 4 DN22 . . . 52 C1
Street Life Mus of Transport★
HU9 . . . . 181 A6
Streetway PE21 . . . . 136 E7
Stretham Way 5 PE10 . . . 213 C7
Stretton Cl 4 LN1 . . . . . . 66 C7
Stretton Rd LE15 . . . . . . 162 B6
Strickland Rd DN17 . . . . . 7 A3
Stricklands Dr 4 PE6 . . . . 175 C8
Strickland St HU3 . . . . . . 180 C4
Stromberg Rd HU10 . . . . . 178 F5
Strong's Bank PE12 . . . . . 158 F4
Strong's Gate PE12 . . . . . 158 F3
Strood Cl NG32 . . . . 139 C8
Stroud Cl 8 PE10 . . . . . . 213 D5
STROXTON NG33 . . . . . . 139 E5
Stroxton La NG33 . . . . . . 139 F5
Stroykins Cl DN34 . . . . . . 190 F6
STRUBBY LN13 . . . . 63 C1
Strubby Airfield LN13 . . . . 75 E8
Strubby Cl
9 Birchwood LN6 . . . . . 204 D8
Cleethorpes DN35 . . . . . 193 A4
Strugg's Hill La PE20 . . . . 136 B3
Stuart Cl Peterborough PE2 . 231 C6
Scunthorpe DN17 . . . . . 184 F2
Stuart Ct PE1 . . . . 226 B4
Stuart St NG31 . . . . 211 C3
Stuart Wortley St 1
DN31 . . . . 189 B2
Stubbs Cl 21 HU15 . . . . . 2 D5
STUBTON NG23 . . . . 118 B7
Stubton Lodge Rd NG23 . . 118 C8
Stubton Rd NG23 . . . . . . 117 F7
Studcross DN9 . . . . 27 D6
Studio Ct 26 LN12 . . . . . 77 A8
Studley St HU8 . . . . 181 B8
Stukeley Cl 2 Lincoln LN2 . 202 E6
Peterborough PE2 . . . . . 231 D5
Stukeley Ct 18 NG24 . . . . 104 A5
Stukeley Gdns 2 PE12 . . . 215 C2
Stukeley Hall Dr
9 Holbeach PE11 . . . . . 215 D2
Holbeach PE12 . . . . . . 215 D2
Stukeley Rd PE12 . . . . . . 215 D2
Stumpacre PE3 . . . . 225 A8
Stump Cross Hill NG34 . . . 212 C1
Stumpcross La PE20 . . . . 135 B6
Stumps La PE12 . . . . 157 B7
Sturdy Hill LN11 . . . . 62 E4
STURGATE DN21 . . . . 53 F8
Sturgate Airfield DN21 . . . 53 E6
Sturgate Cl 15 LN6 . . . . . 204 C7
Sturgate Wlk DN21 . . . . . 197 F3
Sturmer Ct 1 DN16 . . . . . 185 B2
Sturrock Ct 12 NG31 . . . . 210 E2
Sturrock Way PE3 . . . . . . 225 C8
STURTON DN20 . . . . 30 F7
STURTON BY STOW LN1 . . 66 C7
Sturton by Stow Prim Sch
LN1 . . . . 66 B8
Sturton CE Prim Sch DN22 . 52 C2
Sturton Cl 12 LN2 . . . . . . 201 F7
Sturton Gr 2 DN33 . . . . . 191 B4
Sturton La Hatton LN9 . . . . 71 D3
Scawby DN20 . . . . 30 E7
Sturton Way PE12 . . . . . . 216 B5
Sturton Rd Hatton LN8 . . . . 71 C3
North Leverton with
Habblesthorpe DN22 . . . 52 B1
Stow LN1 . . . . 66 C8
STURTON LE STEEPLE
DN22 . . . . 52 B3
Stutte Cl LN11 . . . . 198 E3
Styles Croft 6 HU14 . . . . . 3 C6
Subway St HU3 . . . . 180 B3

Subway The DN16 . . . . . . 19 A4
Sudbeck La 17 LN2 . . . . . 68 D6
SUDBROOK NG32 . . . . . . 119 E3
Sudbrooke Dr LN2 . . . . . . 202 A7
Sudbrooke La LN2 . . . . . . 68 E2
Sudbrooke Rd LN8 . . . . . . 68 F3
Sudbrook Rd NG32 . . . . . . 119 D4
Sudbury Cl LN6 . . . . 205 A5
Sudbury Ct PE7 . . . . 231 F5
Sudbury Pl LN11 . . . . 198 B4
Suddle Way 19 DN41 . . . . 23 A4
SUDTHORPE NG32 . . . . . . 119 C8
Sudthorpe Hill 8 NG32 . . . 106 C1
Suffolk Acre LN4 . . . . . . 207 C4
Suffolk Cl PE3 . . . . 225 B2
Suffolk Cl DN32 . . . . 189 C1
Suffolk Rd 10 LN1 . . . . . . 67 E5
Sugar Way PE2 . . . . 230 D8
Suggitt's Ct DN35 . . . . . . 192 D6
Suggitt's La DN35 . . . . . . 192 D6
Suggitt's Orch DN35 . . . . 192 D6
Sullivan Rd HU4 . . . . 179 B4
Summerdale 28 LN10 . . . . 18 C8
Summerfield Ave DN37 . . . 194 C5
Summerfield Cl
Waltham DN37 . . . . . . 194 C5
16 Wisbech PE13 . . . . . 170 C1
Summerfield Ct 8 NG34 . . 212 D6
Summerfield Dr 4 NG34 . . 212 D6
Summerfield Rd 1 PE1 . . . 225 F4
Summerfields PE22 . . . . . 114 B1
Summergangs La DN21 . . . 197 D1
Summergates La PE24 . . . 102 C2
Summergroves Way HU4 . . 179 B2
Summer Hill DN21 . . . . . . 197 D5
Summer Hill Cl PE4 . . . . . 221 C2
Summer La 16 PE12 . . . . . 216 D2
Summer Lesure La PE12 . . 159 F2
Summer's fld 16 NG24 . . . 104 A5
Sunbeam Ave LN6 . . . . . . 204 D1
Sunbeam Rd HU4 . . . . . . 179 D5
Suncastle★ PE25 . . . . . . 206 E4
Sunderfleet La LN11 . . . . . 51 A5
Sunderland Cl 6 LN6 . . . . 200 A4
Sunfield Cres LN6 . . . . . . 200 D1
Sunfields Cl PE12 . . . . . . 157 C3
Sunflower Cl PE11 . . . . . . 214 B3
Sunflower Way PE21 . . . . 208 B4
Sunningdale
Grantham NG31 . . . . . . 211 C8
Peterborough PE2 . . . . . 229 E6
8 Waltham DN37 . . . . . 194 C4
Sunningdale Ave
Brigg DN20 . . . . 196 C5
Spalding PE11 . . . . 214 C2
Sunningdale Cl
Chapel St Leonard PE24 . . 90 E7
1 Skegness PE25 . . . . . 206 A4
6 Woodhall Spa LN10 . . . 97 C5
Sunningdale Cres 2
PE25 . . . . 206 A4
Sunningdale Dr
Boston PE21 . . . . 208 C6
Chapel St Leonard PE24 . . 90 E7
4 Immingham DN40 . . . . 186 D5
Lincoln LN5 . . . . 205 D8
Skegness PE25 . . . . . . 206 A4
Sunningdale Gr LN4 . . . . . 203 D1
Sunningdale Rd
5 Hatfield DN7 . . . . . . 14 F3
Kingston upon Hull HU13 . 178 F2
Scunthorpe DN17 . . . . . 184 D4
Yaddlethorpe DN17 . . . . 184 D3
Sunningdale Way DN21 . . . 197 E2
Sunnybank 11 DN18 . . . . 10 E8
Sunny Bank HU3 . . . . 180 B7
Sunny Bank Gdns DN10 . . . 39 C2
Sunny Cnr DN33 . . . . 191 D1
Sunnydale Cl 1 PE11 . . . . 145 D2
Sunny Hill 8 DN21 . . . . . . 30 B1
Sunnymead PE4 . . . . 220 E6
Sunway Gr DN16 . . . . . . 185 B5
SURFLEET PE11 . . . . 145 C3
Surfleet Bank PE11 . . . . . 145 F5
**Surfleet Lows Nature
Reserve**★ PE11 . . . . . . 145 D3
Surfleet Prim Sch PE11 . . 145 D3
Surfleet Rd 5 PE11 . . . . . 145 D2
SURFLEET SEAS END
PE11 . . . . 145 F3
Surfside 5 LN12 . . . . 77 A8
Surrey Ct 20 DN32 . . . . . 189 C1
Surrey Garth HU4 . . . . . . 179 B4
Surtees St DN31 . . . . 189 B2
Sussex Ave PE21 . . . . . . 208 B4
Sussex Cl 7 LN8 . . . . . . 47 B6
Sussex Ct DN32 . . . . 189 C1
Sussex Gdns 16 LN1 . . . . 67 E5
Sussex St DN35 . . . . 192 B8
Sussex Rd PE9 . . . . 219 B6
Susworth Rd DN17 . . . . . . 28 C4
Susworth Rd DN17 . . . . . . 28 E4
Sutcliffe Ave DN33 . . . . . 191 A3
Sutherland Way PE9 . . . . 218 F5
Suthers Sch The NG24 . . . 104 C1
SUTTERBY PE23 . . . . 87 E7
Sutterby La PE23 . . . . . . 87 F8
SUTTERTON PE20 . . . . . . 136 A3
SUTTERTON DOWDYKE
PE20 . . . . 146 A4
Sutterton Dro LN4 . . . . . . 110 C1
Sutterton Enterprise Pk
PE20 . . . . 136 A2
Suttling Dales La PE22 . . . 126 B8
SUTTON
Beckingham LN5 . . . . . 105 B3
Sutton PE5 . . . . 222 F2

**Sutton Branch Line Walkway
& Conservation Area**★
LN12 . . . . 76 F6
SUTTON BRIDGE PE12 . . . 160 D4
Sutton Cl
Heighington/Washingborough
LN4 . . . . 203 A1
15 Nettleham LN2 . . . . . 68 C2
SUTTON CROSSES PE12 . . 216 C1
Sutton Ct 2 PE25 . . . . . . 206 C3
Sutton Gate PE12 . . . . . . 159 D1
Sutton Heath Rd 222 D7
Sutton La LN5 . . . . 105 F5
Sutton Mdws PE13 . . . . . 170 C2
SUTTON ON SEA LN12 . . . 76 F8
Sutton on Sea Prim Sch
LN12 . . . . 77 A8
SUTTON ON TRENT NG23 . 91 A8
Sutton Pl Kirk Ella HU10 . . 178 D5
4 Scawby DN20 . . . . . . 30 F7
Sutton Rd Beckingham LN5 . 105 B4
Bilsby LN13 . . . . 76 C4
16 Kirk Sandall DN3 . . . . 14 A3
Mablethorpe/Sutton on Sea
LN12 . . . . 64 C2
Newton PE13 . . . . 170 B6
Sutton St James PE12 . . . 159 D2
Terrington St Clement PE34 . 161 F2
SUTTON ST EDMUND
PE12 . . . . 168 F4
SUTTON ST JAMES PE12 . 159 D1
**Sutton St James Com Primary
School** PE12 . . . . 159 C1
Sutton's La PE6 . . . . 217 D4
Svenskaby PE2 . . . . 229 B6
SWABY LN13 . . . . 74 E4
Swaby Cl Lincoln LN2 . . . . 202 A8
Marshchapel DN36 . . . . . 37 B2
Swaby Cres 4 PE25 . . . . . 206 B4
Swaby Dr DN35 . . . . 192 D3
**Swaby Valley Nature
Reserve**★ LN13 . . . . . . 74 F4
Swadales Cl 11 NG31 . . . . 129 E5
Swain Ct PE2 . . . . 230 F8
Swain's Dro PE13 . . . . . . 170 C8
Swale Ave PE4 . . . . 221 C1
Swale Bank PE11 . . . . . . 144 D5
Swaledale 10 HU15 . . . . . 2 D6
Swaledale Pl 2 DN16 . . . . 185 E6
Swale Dr DN21 . . . . 197 F6
Swale Rd 14 HU15 . . . . . . 2 D5
Swales Rd 12 DN36 . . . . . 36 D8
SWALLOW LN7 . . . . 34 B5
Swallow Ave LN6 . . . . . . 200 A3
SWALLOW BECK LN6 . . . . 205 B5
Swallowbeck Ave LN6 . . . 205 A4
Swallow Cl
Chapel St Leonard PE24 . . 90 D7
4 Gainsborough DN21 . . . 53 C4
1 Sleaford NG34 . . . . . 212 C3
Swallow Ct 6 DN9 . . . . . . 27 D7
Swallow Dr
3 Claypole NG23 . . . . . 117 E8
16 Healing DN41 . . . . . . 23 F5
Louth LN11 . . . . 198 D8
Wragby LN8 . . . . 70 D4
Swallowfield PE4 . . . . . . 220 E4
Swallowfield Dr HU4 . . . . 179 B4
Swallowfields Ct 2 PE25 . 206 A4
Swallow Gate Rd LN11 . . . 51 B2
Swallow Hill PE10 . . . . . . 164 B7
Swallow La
Tydd St Giles PE13 . . . . 170 B8
Wootton DN39 . . . . . . 11 E2
Swallow Rd DN37 . . . . . . 47 B8
Swallow Road DN37 . . . . . 34 E2
Swallow's Cl NG31 . . . . . . 210 E2
Swallow Vale LN7 . . . . . . 34 B7
Swallow Wlk 8 PE6 . . . . . 217 D5
Swanage Wlk HU4 . . . . . . 179 B4
Swan Cl PE11 . . . . 214 F2
Swan Ct 7 DN21 . . . . 197 E6
Swan Dr Skegness PE25 . . 103 C7
6 Sturton by Stow LN1 . . . 66 D7
Swanella Gr HU3 . . . . . . 180 A4
Swan Gdns Newark PE1 . . 226 E6
Parson Drove PE13 . . . . 177 C2
Swanhill PE8 . . . . 222 A4
Swanhole La PE22 . . . . . . 126 D4
Swanholme Cl LN6 . . . . . . 204 E5
SWANLAND HU14 . . . . . . 3 A7
Swanland Butts Cl HU10 . . 178 C6
Swanland Ct 25 DN8 . . . . 15 B7
Swanland Ct 24 DN8 . . . . 15 B7
Swanland Dale HU14 . . . . 3 B8
Swanland Garth 6 HU14 . . 3 A5
Swanland Hill HU14 . . . . . 3 B5
Swanland Prim Sch Acad
HU14 . . . . 3 B6
Swanland Rd HU13 . . . . . 178 C2
Swan Moor Bank PE22 . . . 114 C3
Swannacks View 3 DN20 . 30 F7
Swann St 5 LN2 . . . . 180 E8
Swan's La LN5 . . . . 105 F5
Swanspool PE3 . . . . 225 B6
Swan St 1 Lincoln LN2 . . . 234 B3
Spalding PE11 . . . . 214 D4
Swapcoat La PE12 . . . . . . 216 B5
Swapcoat Mews PE12 . . . 216 B5
SWARBY NG34 . . . . 132 A7
Swarby La NG34 . . . . 132 A7
SWATON NG34 . . . . 133 C3
Swaton La NG34 . . . . 133 C3
SWAYFIELD NG33 . . . . . . 152 D5
Swayne Cl LN2 . . . . 202 D7

Swaythling Cl LN6 204 E5
Sweetbriar 3 PE9 218 C7
Sweet Briar Cl 6 DN37 194 C5
Sweetbriar La PE4 220 F6
Sweet Cl 2 PE6 217 D5
Sweet Dews Gr HU9 181 D8
Sweetlands Way PE11 145 B5
Swen Cl 17 LN2 68 D7
Swift Ave LN11 62 C6
Swift Cl
  Market Deeping PE6 217 D4
  Yaxley PE7 233 A8
Swift Ct 1 PE11 214 F2
Swift Dr DN20 196 A3
Swift Gdns LN2 202 C7
Swift Gn LN2 202 B7
Swift Rd DN17 184 D6
Swiftsure Cres DN34 190 D4
Swift Way PE10 164 B7
Swinburne Cl 9 NG24 104 B3
Swinburne La DN17 184 D7
Swinburne Rd DN17 184 D7
Swin Cl PE20 135 C6
SWINDERBY LN6 92 A5
Swinderby Cl 1 NG24 104 B5
Swinderby Gdns 2 DN34 191 A5
Swinderby Rd
  Collingham NG23 91 E4
  Eagle & Swinethorpe LN6 79 B1
  North Scarle LN6 78 F1
  Norton Disney LN6 92 C2
  South Scarle NG23 91 F7
Swinderby Sta LN6 92 B7
Swindler's Dro PE12 157 C6
Swinefleet Rd DN14 6 B8
Swinegate Grantham NG31 211 A5
  Kingston upon Hull HU13 178 E1
Swine Hill NG32 139 C7
SWINESHEAD PE20 135 B7
SWINESHEAD BRIDGE PE20 123 F1
Swineshead Rd
  Boston PE21 208 A3
  Frampton PE20 124 E1
Swineshead St Marys CE Prim Sch PE20 135 C7
Swineshead Sta PE20 123 F1
Swine's Mdw Rd PE6 217 D8
SWINETHORPE LN6 79 B4
Swingbridge Rd NG31 210 D2
SWINHOPE LN8 47 C7
Swinhope Hill LN8 47 C5
Swinhope Rd
  Binbrook Tech Pk LN8 47 B6
  Thorganby LN8 47 C8
SWINSTEAD NG33 153 A5
Swinstead CE Prim Sch NG33 153 A5
Swinstead Rd
  Corby Glen NG33 152 F7
  Counthorpe & Creeton NG33 153 A3
  Irnham NG33 141 E1
Swinster La DN40 12 E6
Swinthorpe La LN3 69 C7
Switchback LN8 47 C2
Swithin Cl HU13 179 A2
Swynford Cl LN1 65 D2
Sybil Rd 18 PE13 170 D1
Sycamore Ave
  Grimsby DN33 191 C3
  Peterborough PE1 226 C6
Sycamore Cl
  1 Barnetby le Wold DN38 21 B4
  4 Birchwood LN6 204 E8
  Bourne PE10 213 A5
  Branston LN4 81 D3
  2 Broughton DN20 19 D3
  Cherry Willingham/Reepham LN3 203 D5
  Croft PE24 102 E4
  Hessle HU13 178 C3
  Kingston upon Hull HU5 179 C7
  5 Scopwick Heath LN4 108 A7
Sycamore Cres
  5 Birchwood LN6 204 E8
  Scunthorpe DN16 185 E4
Sycamore Ct 3 NG31 210 D2
Sycamore Dr
  7 Gainsborough DN21 197 E6
  Louth LN11 198 E5
  Sleaford NG34 212 D6
  3 Waddington LN5 93 E8
Sycamore Gr LN4 81 A1
Sycamore La 2 LE14 150 B1
Sycamore Rd
  Fordington LN13 88 B6
  16 Ruskington NG34 108 E1
Sycamores The 5 PE11 214 B1
Sycamore View PE12 168 C2
Sycamore Way 16 DN36 36 C8
Sydney Dr 3 PE25 206 A4
Sydney Rd PE2 231 D5
Sydney St
  23 Beacon Hill NG24 104 A5
  Boston PE21 208 D5
Sydney Terr 23 NG24 104 A4
Syd Wilson Ct LN1 201 D7
Syerston Way 5 NG24 104 B5
Syfer Cl 8 LN7 33 A3
Sykemouth Dro PE20 124 C1
Sykes Cl
  6 Kingston upon Hull HU10 178 F6
  15 Swanland HU14 3 B7
Sykes La Goxhill DN19 5 A2
  Newark-on-Trent NG24 104 B2
  Saxilby with Ingleby LN1 66 C3
Sykes St 2 HU2 180 F7
Sylvan Ave 5 LN10 97 D6
Sylvden Dr 24 PE13 170 E1
Sylvester St 12 DN21 30 B1
Symmington Cl PE2 230 F8
Symons Cl 8 HU2 180 E8
Sympson Cl LN2 202 E6
Syne Ave 5 PE25 206 D1
Syringa Gn LN6 200 C1
SYSTON NG32 130 A7
Syston Gr LN5 205 D4
Sywell Cl 16 LN6 204 C6

T

Tabor Ct PE7 230 D2
Tacitus Wy LN6 93 B8
Tadman St HU3 180 D4
Taggs Dr 7 PE25 206 A6
Taining La DN7 14 C8
Tait Cl PE1 226 C5
Talbot Ave PE2 230 D6
Talbot Cl
  20 Navenby/Wellingore LN5 107 A8
  4 Spilsby PE23 101 A8
Talbot Rd
  Immingham DN40 186 D3
  Skegness PE25 206 C4
Talbot Wlk DN16 183 B2
Talisman Dr DN16 185 A2
Tallert Way DN33 190 F3
Tall Gables 2 NG22 65 B1
TALLINGTON PE9 172 E7
Tallington Dry Ski Ctr* PE9 172 F7
Tallington Lakes Leisure Pk* PE9 173 A8
Tallington Rd PE9 172 F6
Tall Trees HU13 178 C3
Tamar Ct 5 NG31 210 E2
Tamar Dr DN36 195 D7
Tamarisk Way DN16 185 D5
Tamar Way 3 LN6 205 A2
Tamar Wlk DN17 184 C8
Tame Ct 4 NG34 212 D5
Tamson Way 5 NG34 212 D5
Tamworth Cl NG31 210 D5
TAMWORTH GREEN PE22 126 E1
Tanglewood PE4 220 F6
Tanglewood Cedar Falls 3 PE11 214 B1
Tanhouse PE2 230 C5
Tanners Ct LN5 234 A1
Tanners' La NG33 152 E8
Tanner's La LN5 234 A1
Tannery Cl Boston PE21 208 E4
  7 Bourne PE10 213 E4
  7 Waltham DN37 194 E4
Tannery La 3 NG34 142 D8
Tansley Ct 1 DN15 182 B2
Tansor Garth PE3 225 C5
Tansy Wy PE11 214 B6
Tantallon Ct 6 PE3 225 B1
Tapin Cl LN1 201 C6
Tarleton Ave 1 LN10 97 E6
Tarleton Cl 2 DN3 14 A2
Tarragon Way PE10 213 C6
Tarrant PE4 220 E6
Tarran Way PE25 206 B5
Tasburgh St DN32 191 F6
Tasman Cl 7 PE11 214 B2
Tasman Rd 5 PE23 101 A8
TATHWELL LN11 61 B2
Tattersall Cl DN17 184 D5
TATTERSHALL LN4 207 A5
Tattershall Ave DN34 190 F4
TATTERSHALL BRIDGE LN4 110 D7
Tattershall Castle* LN4 207 A4
Tattershall Cl 3 NG31 210 E5
Tattershall Coll Bldgs* LN4 207 A4
Tattershall Dr 10 PE6 217 A5
Tattershall Lakes Ctry Pk* LN4 207 A3
Tattershall Prim Sch LN4 207 A5
Tattershall Rd
  Billinghay LN4 109 F5
  Boston PE21 208 D7
  Fishtoft PE21 125 C5
  Kirkby on Bain LN10 98 B4
  Woodhall Spa LN10 97 D5
Tattershall Sta Gall & Pottery* LN4 110 E7
TATTERSHALL THORPE LN4 207 B8
Tattershall Way LN11 198 A8
Tatwin Dr 8 PE6 175 B8
Taunton Cl 2 NG34 212 D7
Taunton Rd
  6 Bourne PE10 213 C3
  Kingston upon Hull HU4 179 A3
Taunton Way DN33 194 E8
Tavella Ct 1 DN9 27 B2
Tavern Cl LN13 89 A6
Taverner Rd PE21 208 D6
Taverners Ct LN11 198 C6
Taverners Rd PE1 225 F4
Tavern La 7 PE24 90 B7
Tavistock Cl 15 PE6 176 A3
Tavistock Rd PE11 214 B2
Tawney St PE21 208 F6
Tawny Owl Cl 22 DN36 36 D8
Taylor Cl 6 Belton DN9 16 E2
  5 Boston PE21 209 D4
  Branston LN4 81 E1
Taylor's Ave DN35 192 E4
Taylor's Dro PE12 159 C1
Taylors Gdn LN11 198 D5
Taylor St DN35 189 D1
TEALBY LN8 46 C1
Tealby Cl
  1 Gainsborough DN21 53 A7
  Immingham DN40 186 A4
Tealby Gr DN33 191 B3
Tealby Rd
  Middle Rasen LN8 57 E8
  Scunthorpe DN17 184 D5
Tealby Sch LN8 46 D1
Tealby St 11 LN5 205 E8
Teal Cl 4 Brigg DN20 196 A3
  Caistor LN7 33 A4
  3 Skegness PE25 206 A6
Teal Dr
  Barton-upon-Humber DN18 10 E8
  Yaxley PE7 233 B8
Teale St DN15 183 A4
Teal Gr 10 PE12 167 B8
Teal Park Rd LN6 204 A3
Teal Pl LN7 33 A4
Teal Rd LN4 110 E8
Team Gate DN37 190 C6
Teanby Ct 5 PE3 224 F3
Teanby Dr 8 DN15 9 A5
Teasel Dr 7 PE10 213 D3
Teasles 6 PE6 217 D6
Tedder Dr 3 LN5 93 F7
Teddy's Farm* LN5 105 C4
Tee La DN15 8 B5
Tees Ct DN37 190 E8
Teesdale Cl LN6 200 C2
Teesdale Rd NG31 211 A7
Telford Dr Newark NG24 104 B6
  Yaxley PE7 233 D6
Telford Pl DN34 191 A7
Telford Wy 12 NG33 151 D7
Temperance Ave 5 DN17 29 D7
Temperance La 2 NG23 91 C4
Temper Rd DN16 185 F8
Temperton's La 5 DN9 28 A3
Tempestes Wy 1 PE7 231 D3
Tempest St LN2 202 B3
Templar Ct DN16 185 B3
Templars Way 2 NG33 151 D2
Temple Bruer Templar Preceptory* LN5 107 C4
Temple Cl 2 Alford LN13 75 E2
  4 Belton DN9 16 E2
  3 Brough HU15 2 E6
Templefield Rd DN21 42 D4
Temple Gdns LN2 234 B3
Temple Goring 1 LN5 107 B8
Temple Grange PE4 220 F6
Temple La Aylesby DN37 23 E1
  6 Welton HU15 2 E6
Templeman Dr PE9 163 E5
Templemans La DN36 36 A1
Templemeads Cl 3 PE10 154 D6
Temple Rd
  Aslackby & Laughton NG34 142 E5
  Welbourn LN5 107 A4
  Westcliffe DN17 184 F6
Temples Ct 3 PE6 173 B4
Temple Terr LN11 198 B6
Templeway Cl 5 NG32 119 B7
Templeway Sq 8 NG32 119 B7
Temple Wlk 2 HU15 2 E6
Ten Acre Dro PE11 135 C1
Ten Acre La
  Pinchbeck PE11 145 C1
  Wyville cum Hungerton NG32 139 B5
Tendley Ave HU3 179 F5
Tenens Way PE21 209 A1
Tennyson Ave
  Grantham NG31 211 E5
  16 Mablethorpe/Sutton on Sea LN12 64 B4
  Sleaford NG34 212 D5
  4 Thorne/Moorends DN8 15 B8
Tennyson Cl Benniworth LN8 59 B1
  Brigg DN20 196 D2
  2 Caistor LN7 33 A3
  12 Mablethorpe/Sutton on Sea LN12 77 A7
  14 Metheringham LN4 95 C4
Tennyson Dr Bourne PE10 213 D3
  22 Welton/Dunholme LN2 68 D6
Tennyson Gdns LN9 199 D2
Tennyson Gn 3 PE25 206 C2
Tennyson High Sch The LN12 64 C3
Tennyson Rd
  Cleethorpes DN35 192 E7
  Louth LN11 198 C4
  17 Mablethorpe/Sutton on Sea LN12 64 B4
  Newark-on-Trent NG24 104 B2
  Peterborough PE1 225 F7
  2 Ruskington NG34 108 E2
  Scunthorpe DN16 185 D7
Tennyson St
  Gainsborough DN21 197 D5
  Grimsby DN31 191 D8
  1 Lincoln LN1 201 D4
Tennyson Way 1 PE9 218 E5
Tennyson Wlk LN3 203 C6
Tennyson Wy 17 PE23 101 A8
Tensing Rd DN16 185 C5
Tentercroft St LN5 234 A1
Tenter La
  6 Navenby/Wellingore LN5 107 A8
  13 Stamford PE9 219 C5
Tenters The PE12 215 E2
Tern Rd PE7 230 C2
Terrace La PE22 99 C5
Terrace The
  Great Ponton NG33 140 A5
  Louth LN11 198 D4
  10 Spilsby PE23 88 A1
Terrington Pl DN35 192 D4
TERRINGTON ST CLEMENT PE34 161 E3
Terry Ave 21 NG24 104 A6
Terry O'Toole Theatre* LN6 204 D1
TETFORD LN9 73 F1
Tetford Hill LN9 73 E3
Tetford Rd LN9 86 A5
Tethering La DN10 39 A2
TETLEY DN17 16 D6
Tetley Rd DN16 185 C7
Tetley View 3 DN17 16 E6
TETNEY DN36 36 D4
Tetney Blow Wells Nature Reserve* DN36 36 E3
Tetney Cl 6 LN1 201 E8
Tetney La DN36 195 E2
TETNEY LOCK DN36 37 A4
Tetney Lock Rd DN36 36 E4
Tetney Marshes Nature Reserve* DN36 37 C7
Tetney Prim Sch DN36 36 D4
Tetney Rd DN36 36 C7
Tewkesbury Dr 4 DN34 191 C6
Thackeray Ct DN37 190 E8
Thacker Bank
  Great Carlton LN12 63 B7
  Three Bridges LN11 62 F6
Thacker La DN7 14 C8
Thackers Cl PE8 222 A4
Thackers La LN4 81 D2
Thacker's Rd PE22 112 B2
Thackers Way PE6 217 D5
Thames Cl 3 PE24 90 B7
Thames Cres 5 PE24 90 B7
Thames Ct DN37 190 E8
Thames Mdw Dr 2 PE24 90 B7
Thames Rd Grantham NG31 210 E2
  Spalding PE11 214 F5
Thames St Hogsthorpe PE24 90 B7
  Louth LN11 198 D6
Thary La PE11 145 E4
Thatch Carr Bank DN9 26 D4
Thatchers Wlk PE22 113 B2
Theaker Ave DN21 197 F5
THEALBY DN15 8 D4
Thealby La DN15 8 E5
Thealby Rd DN15 8 C3
Theatre Royal* LN2 234 B2
THEDDLETHORPE ALL SAINTS LN12 63 D7
Theddlethorpe Prim Sch LN12 63 D6
Theddlethorpe Rd LN12 63 F4
THEDDLETHORPE ST HELEN LN12 63 E8
Theodore Rd DN15 182 E4
Theodore St LN1 234 A4
Theresa Cl 8 PE25 206 A4
Therm Rd HU8 181 A8
Thesiger St
  2 Grimsby DN32 189 B1
  Lincoln LN5 201 F1
Thesiger Wlk 8 DN31 189 B1
THETFORD PE6 164 E5
Thetford Ave 5 PE6 164 E5
THIMBLEBY LN9 85 B5
Thimbleby Hill LN9 85 C5
Thinholme La DN9 27 A1
Third Ave 20 Brookenby LN8 47 B6
  1 Fixborough Ind Est DN15 8 A1
  Grantham NG31 211 F7
  4 Scampton Airfield LN1 67 E5
  2 Scunthorpe DN17 184 C6
  Spalding PE11 214 A4
Third Dro Gosberton PE11 144 B4
  Moulton PE12 146 F7
  Peterborough PE1 226 E2
Third Hill Rd LN4 81 F3
Third La DN37 35 D3
Third Marsh Rd PE14 170 C3
Thirkleby Cres DN32 192 B4
Thirlmere Ave DN33 194 E7
Thirlmere Cl 8 LN6 205 A2
Thirlmere Gdns 3 PE4 221 C3
Thirlmere Way 1 LN6 200 D1
Thirsk Dr LN6 204 F4
Thisle Gdns PE11 214 C4
Thistle Cl LN2 202 C8
Thistle Dr PE2 231 C7
Thistlemoor Rd PE1 225 E7
Thistleton La LE15 151 D1
Thomas Cl 7 PE3 224 F3
Thomas Cowley High Sch The PE11 134 F2
Thomas Ct 13 NG34 212 D4
Thomas Deacon Acad PE1 226 B5
Thomas Gibson Dr LN9 199 D3
Thomas Kitching Way 8 LN3 83 C4
Thomas Mid Cott Dr 20 PE20 136 C5
Thomas Rd
  10 Balderton NG24 104 C1
  Scunthorpe DN17 184 F8
Thomas St Grimsby DN32 191 F7
  Kingston upon Hull HU9 181 B7
  Lincoln LN2 234 C2
  Sleaford NG34 212 D4
Thomas Sully Cl LN9 199 A4
Thompson Cl
  19 Coddington NG24 104 C5
  Skegness PE25 206 C5
  3 Spalding PE11 214 C3
Thompson Dr 25 DN7 14 D4
Thompson Rd DN36 195 D7
Thompsons Gd PE7 230 D3
Thompson's La
  Fosdyke PE20 146 E8
  Hough-on-the-Hill NG32 119 A5
Thompson St 10 DN15 183 B3
Thonock Cl LN2 201 F7
Thonock Dr 7 LN1 66 C2
Thonock Rd DN21 197 D8
Thoresby Pl DN35 192 E4
Thoresby Prim Sch HU5 180 B8
Thoresby Rd Fulstow LN11 49 A8
  Scunthorpe DN17 184 D5
  Tetney DN36 36 D3
Thoresby St HU5 180 B8
THORESTHORPE LN13 75 F4
THORESWAY LN8 46 D7
Thoresway Dr LN2 202 A7
Thoresway Gr 5 DN33 191 A3
Thoresway Rd LN8 46 C8
Thorgam Ct DN31 191 C7
THORGANBY DN37 47 B8
Thorganby Rd
  Cleethorpes DN35 193 A3
  Swinhope LN8 47 C7
Thorlby Haven 12 PE20 135 A4
Thorley Cres PE2 230 D8
Thorn Bank DN9 26 E4
Thornbury Dr DN33 191 B1
Thornbury Rd DN40 186 D3
Thorndales La PE22 113 A5
Thorndike Way DN21 197 E3
Thorndyke Mews 7 DN21 197 D3
THORNE DN8 15 B8
Thorne Brooke Prim Sch DN8 15 B7
Thorne Green Top Prim Sch DN8 15 A7
Thorne King Edward Pri Sch DN8 15 B8
Thorne N Sta DN8 14 F8
Thorne Rd Edenthorpe DN3 14 A2
  Sandtoft DN8 16 A3
  8 Stainforth DN7 14 C7
Thorne S Sta DN8 15 B7
Thorne Swimming Baths DN8 15 B8
Thorne Waste Drain Rd DN8 15 E8
Thorne Way PE20 136 C4
THORNEY Thorney NG23 78 F8
  Thorney PE6 176 A3
Thorney Heritage Mus* PE6 176 A3
Thorney Rd
  2 Crowland PE6 175 C8
  Newborough PE6 174 D5
  Wisbech St Mary PE13 177 C2
Thorney Rd South PE6 175 C8
THORNEY TOLL PE13 177 A2
Thorngarth La 9 DN19 11 D8
Thorngate LN5 234 B2
Thornham's Way 8 HU15 2 C7
Thornhill Cres 4 DN17 184 F3
Thornhill Gdns DN34 191 A7
Thornhill La DN22 52 E1
Thornholme Dr DN16 185 A3
Thorniman La PE20 136 E6
Thorn La DN19 12 A8
Thorn Leigh 3 HU3 180 C6
Thornleigh Dr PE2 230 C6
Thornmead PE4 221 B4
Thorn Rd PE7 230 C2
Thorns La NG32 210 A8
THORNTON LN9 85 C2
Thornton 20 HU15 2 C6
Thornton Abbey* DN39 12 B5
Thornton Abbey Sta DN39 12 A5
Thornton Ave Boston PE21 208 D3
  Scunthorpe DN16 185 A7
Thornton Cl
  3 Heighington/Washingborough LN4 203 A2
  Kingston upon Hull HU13 178 D1
  Langriville PE22 124 F8
  6 Lincoln LN6 205 A7
  Peterborough PE4 221 C3
Thornton Cres
  Cleethorpes DN35 192 E4
  Horncastle LN9 199 C2
Thornton Ct DN36 195 D8
THORNTON CURTIS DN39 11 E4
Thornton Curtis Rd DN18 11 A3
Thornton Gdns 21 DN41 23 A4
Thornton Gr 5 DN34 190 E4
THORNTON LE MOOR LN7 44 E7
Thornton Pl DN40 186 B3
Thornton Rd
  Barrow upon Humber DN19 11 D6
  7 Collingham NG23 91 D4
  Goxhill DN19 11 F6
  Owersby LN7 44 E7
  South Kelsey LN7 32 A1
  Spalding PE11 214 F3
  Thornton Curtis DN39 11 E4
Thornton St
  Barrow upon Humber DN19 11 C7

Thornton St continued
6 Gainsborough DN21 197 D3
Thornton Way LN3 203 E6
Thornwell La 2 PE23 87 A4
Thornwick Ave HU10 178 E8
Thornwick Cl 2 HU3 180 C5
Thorold Ave
5 Cranwell NG34 120 E8
Cranwell & Byard's Leap NG34 107 E1
Thorold Gdns 1 NG32 130 B8
Thorold Pl 1 DN3 14 A2
Thorold Rd NG32 210 A4
Thorold St Boston PE21 208 F6
Grimsby DN31 189 C1
Thorolds Way PE5 223 D2
Thorold Way LN5 93 F4
Thoroton Ave 26 NG24 104 B2
Thoroughfare DN37 35 D3
Thoroughfare La NG24 104 B8
THORPE LN12 64 A1
Thorpe Ave Lincoln LN1 201 D8
Moulton PE12 157 E2
Peterborough PE3 225 C2
Thorpe Bank PE22 101 B3
Thorpe Camp Visitor Ctr* LN4 207 B8
Thorpe Cl 3 NG24 104 D5
THORPE CULVERT PE24 102 A3
Thorpe Culvert Sta PE24 102 B3
Thorpe Dr NG34 120 E2
Thorpe Dro NG34 120 E3
Thorpe Fen PE24 101 E3
THORPE FENDYKES PE24 101 F3
Thorpehall Rd 12 DN3 14 A2
Thorpe La
Aubourn Haddington & South Hykeham LN6 93 A8
Brattleby LN1 67 B7
Eagle & Swinethorpe LN6 79 C1
Tealby LN8 46 B1
THORPE LATIMER NG34 133 C6
Thorpe Lea Rd PE3 225 E2
THORPE LE VALE LN8 47 B1
Thorpe Mdws PE3 225 C2
THORPE ON THE HILL LN6 92 E8
Thorpe Pk Rd PE3 225 C3
Thorpe Pl LN4 207 B6
Thorpe Prim Sch PE3 225 B3
Thorpe Rd
Doddington & Whisby LN6 79 E2
Ewerby & Evedon NG34 122 C6
Peterborough PE3 225 B1
Tattershall LN4 207 C6
THORPE ST PETER PE24 102 B3
Thorpes La 3 NG32 138 D4
Thorpe's La PE12 158 B6
THORPE TILNEY LN4 109 C8
Thorpe Tilney Dro
Timberland LN4 97 A1
Walcott LN4 109 C8
Thorpe Wood PE3 224 F1
Thorsby Cl LN5 205 D1
Thorseby Cl PE3 225 B3
Threadneedle St 9 PE21 208 F5
Threave Ct
Orton Longueville PE3 230 A8
Peterborough PE3 225 A1
Three Bridge La LN11 63 A7
THREE BRIDGES LN11 63 A7
THREEKINGHAM NG34 132 E3
Threekingham Bar NG34 132 D3
Three Leys La DN22 52 B2
THROCKENHOLT PE12 177 B8
Throstlenest PE7 231 C3
Thrumber Marsh La LN13 76 F1
Thrunscoe Prim Acad DN35 192 E5
Thrunscoe Rd 7 DN35 192 F5
Thrush Cl 10 NG34 212 B3
Thurlaston Cl PE3 225 B2
THURLBY Bilsby LN13 76 D2
Thurlby LN5 92 E4
Thurlby PE10 164 C8
Thurlby Cl 4 LN4 203 A2
Thurlby Com Prim Sch PE10 164 C8
Thurlby Cres LN2 202 B8
Thurlby Fen Nature Reserve* PE10 164 F7
Thurlby Rd Bassingham LN5 92 F3
Bilsby LN13 76 B3
Gainsborough DN21 197 E4
Thurlow Ct 1 LN2 202 E7
Thurning Ave PE2 231 C6
Thuro Gr PE2 230 A3
Thursfield PE4 221 A4
Thurstan Cl PE10 213 B6
Thurston Gate 2 PE3 225 A1
Thyme Ave Bourne PE10 213 C5
12 Market Deeping PE6 217 C5
Thyme Ct LN6 205 D8
Tiber Ct 13 PE11 214 A4
Tiber Rd LN6 204 C1
Tichbourne Cl 6 HU3 180 C5
TICKENCOTE PE9 171 A8
Ticklepenny Wlk LN11 198 E7
Tideswell Ct DN15 182 B2
Tigers Wy 6 HU4 179 E5
Tilbury Rd HU4 179 B3
Tilebarn La PE20 134 F7
Tilgate Rd PE7 233 E8
Tilia Cl
Kingston upon Hull HU4 179 B2
Scunthorpe DN16 185 D4
Tilia Gr 10 PE22 114 A1
Tilia Way 5 PE10 213 E2
Till Bridge La Marton LN1 65 F8
Till Bridge La continued
Scampton LN1 67 A6
Stow LN1 66 A8
Tillbridge Rd LN1 66 D7
Tilley Gate LN11 51 B3
Tilling Cl NG31 211 A2
Till Pl PE9 218 E5
Tilman Dr PE7 230 F5
Tilney Ave PE21 208 D6
Tilney The 10 PE12 158 B7
Tilton Ct PE1 226 C8
Timber Hill NG33 151 A4
TIMBERLAND LN4 96 C1
Timberland DN16 185 C4
Timberland Dro LN4 96 E2
Timberland Rd LN4 96 C2
Timberley Dr DN37 190 C7
Time Trap Mus* DN32 191 E7
Timm's La 18 LN5 93 F7
Timms's Dro PE20 134 E8
Timson Ct 5 DN10 52 B8
Tindale Bank Rd DN9 39 C8
Tindall Cl 2 PE13 170 D2
Tindall Way 10 PE24 102 D1
Tinkermere Cl 3 LN2 68 D6
Tinker's Dro PE13 170 D1
Tinker's La Girton NG23 91 C8
2 Waddington LN5 93 F6
Tinkle St LN11 62 C7
Tin La PE10 213 C5
Tinsley Cl NG23 117 F7
Tintagel Ct 7 PE3 225 B1
Tintagel Way DN36 195 C7
Tintern Rise 4 PE6 175 A1
Tintern Wlk DN37 188 A1
Tinus Ave PE7 230 C1
TINWELL PE9 218 D3
Tinwell Rd PE9 219 A4
Tinwell Rd La PE9 218 F4
Tip La PE24 102 B4
Tippett Rd PE9 218 E4
Tirrington PE3 225 A3
Tison Garth HU10 178 F6
Titan Dr PE1 226 E2
Tithe Barn La 9 DN8 15 B8
Tiverton Rd PE3 225 C3
Tiverton St DN35 189 E1
Tivoli Gdns DN32 191 F8
Tobias Gr 4 PE9 218 C7
Tobruk Cl LN1 201 D8
Toby's Hill Nature Reserve* LN11 51 C5
Todd La DN21 41 C4
Todds Cl 1 Swanland HU14 3 C6
18 Tetney DN36 36 D4
Todds Cl 2 DN17 29 D7
Todds La 1 DN15 8 A4
Todd's La HU15 2 A8
Todkill's La 7 PE12 160 F4
TOFT PE10 163 F8
Toft Cl PE24 115 D8
Toft Field La PE22 114 A3
TOFT HILL PE22 98 D5
Toft Hurn 1 PE22 98 F4
Toft La 17 Sleaford NG34 212 D4
Toft Newton LN8 56 E7
Toftland PE2 230 C5
TOFT NEXT NEWTON LN8 56 C7
Tofts Rd 10 DN18 10 E8
Toft Tunnel Nature Reserve* PE10 154 A1
Tolethorpe Hall* PE9 163 B1
Tolethorpe Sq 6 PE9 219 B6
TOLL BAR PE9 218 C8
Toll Bar PE9 171 D8
Tollbar Acad DN36 195 A5
Toll Bar Ave
6 Bottesford NG13 128 A6
New Waltham DN36 195 B6
Tollbar Rd
Great Gonerby NG32 129 B8
Marston NG32 118 C1
Toll Bar Rd Croft PE24 103 D3
Grantham NG31 211 C3
Tollemache Fields 9 NG33 151 D2
Tollemache Rd (North) NG31 139 F8
Tollemach Rd (South) NG31 139 F8
Tollesby La 34 DN7 14 D4
Tollfield Rd PE21 209 B7
Tollgate Peterborough PE3 225 A5
Spalding PE11 214 C4
Toll House Rd PE2 230 C7
Toll's La PE12 215 E5
Tom La NG34 120 E5
Tomline Rd 5 DN41 23 A5
Tomline St DN31 189 B1
Tomlinson Ave 4 DN15 182 E3
Tomlinson Cl 3 LN4 207 A5
Tomlinson Dr DN18 10 E7
Tomlinson Way 5 NG34 108 E2
Tom Otter's La LN1 66 B1
Tom Potts Row HU15 2 E8
Tonbridge 1 DN33 194 E8
Tonbridge Wlk DN33 194 E8
Toneham La PE6 175 F2
Tonglet Cl 3 PE25 206 C1
Tonnant Way DN34 190 D5
Toogood St 6 HU2 180 F8
Tooley La PE22 114 C2
Tooley St Boston PE21 209 A3
Gainsborough DN21 197 D3
Toothill Gdns DN34 190 F6
Toot La PE21 209 D4
Topaz Gr 3 HU3 180 A4
Topham Cres 13 PE6 176 A3
Top La Goulceby LN11 72 C6
Kirk Bramwith DN7 14 A6
Top Lodge Cl LN6 200 B4
Topmoor Way PE4 221 D1
Top Rd
4 Croxton Kerrial NG32 138 D4
Little Cawthorpe LN11 61 E2
Osgodby LN8 45 A2
South Killingholme DN40 12 E3
Thoresway LN7 46 A7
Thorney NG23 78 F7
Winterton DN15 8 F6
Worlaby DN20 10 D1
Top Rd The LN9 99 C8
Topsgate PE12 159 C7
Torbay Dr DN33 194 E6
Torchil Cl HU10 178 C6
Torfrida Dr PE10 213 B6
Torfrid Cl 14 PE6 166 F1
Torgate Ave LN5 92 F2
Torgate La LN5 93 A2
Torkington Gdns 9 PE9 219 B5
Torkington St PE9 219 A5
TORKSEY LN1 65 E5
Torksey Ave LN1 66 C2
Torksey Dr DN33 191 B3
Torksey Ferry Rd DN22 65 B5
TORKSEY LOCK LN1 65 E5
Torksey Pl 3 DN33 191 B3
Torksey St
14 Kirton in Lindsey DN21 30 B1
Rampton DN22 65 A5
Torold Dr PE7 230 D2
Tor-o-Moor Gdns 2 LN10 97 E6
Tor-o-Moor Rd 9 LN10 97 E6
Toronto St 2 LN2 202 C3
Torpel Way 5 PE6 173 C7
Torrington La
East Barkwith LN8 71 A8
Fleet PE12 159 B5
Legsby LN8 58 C1
Torrington Rd Lincoln LN2 201 F8
Scunthorpe DN17 184 C8
Torrington St DN32 191 F5
Torr St DN21 197 D4
Torskey Castle* LN1 65 D5
Tortoiseshell Wood Nature Reserve* NG33 152 B2
Tossey La LN11 50 B2
Tothby Cl 1 LN13 75 E3
Tothby La LN13 75 E2
Tothby Mdws LN13 75 E3
TOTHILL LN11 62 E1
Tothill Cl LN6 204 F7
Totnes Pl Green Hill NG31 210 D6
Green Hill NG31 210 E6
Totnes Rd DN33 194 E6
Tottermire La 5 DN9 27 D7
Touthill Cl PE1 226 A2
Towell Cl PE21 209 B3
Tower Ave
Bracebridge Heath LN4 205 F3
Lincoln LN2 202 D4
Tower Cl
9 Mablethorpe & Sutton LN12 64 B3
Woodhall Spa LN10 97 F7
Tower Cres LN2 202 D4
Tower Ct PE2 230 F8
Tower Dr Lincoln LN2 202 D4
Woodhall Spa LN10 97 F7
Tower Espl PE25 206 D3
Tower Flats 4 LN2 202 D4
Tower Gdns Boston PE21 209 A4
23 Dunscroft DN7 14 D3
1 Lincoln LN2 202 D4
Tower Hill
Kingston upon Hull HU13 178 E1
Westwoodside DN9 27 B2
Tower Hill Dr HU13 178 E1
Tower Hill Mews 2 HU13 178 E1
Tower House La 7 HU12 5 F8
Tower La Harmston LN4 94 B4
Spalding PE11 214 D3
Tower Rd PE21 209 A5
Tower Rd Acad PE21 209 A6
Tower St 14 Boston PE21 208 F5
Gainsborough DN21 197 D5
1 Kingston Dock Village HU9 181 A5
Towers The 2 PE25 206 D5
Tower View
Kingston upon Hull HU10 178 C5
Sleaford NG34 212 B3
Towgood Cl 7 PE6 173 C4
Tow La 5 NG32 117 F1
Towler St PE1 226 A3
Town Bridge 22 PE21 208 F5
Town Dam Dro PE11 144 F8
Town Dam La PE11 134 F2
Town Dro PE11 144 F8
Town End NG32 120 B2
Town Farm Cl 1 PE11 156 F8
Townfield La 5 PE20 135 C7
TOWNGATE PE6 164 F1
Towngate E PE6 217 C7
Towngate W PE6 217 A6
Town Hall Sq DN31 191 E7
Town Hall St 4 DN31 191 E7
Town Hill DN20 19 E4
Town Hill Dr DN20 19 E4
Townhill Sq 24 NG24 104 C1
Towning Cl 9 PE6 217 D6
Townley Cl LN9 199 D1
Town Rd Sleaford NG34 212 B1
Tetney DN36 36 D4
Townsend Cl
Humberston DN36 193 C1
Townsend Cl continued
4 Peterborough PE1 226 A3
Townsend Rd 6 PE8 172 B1
Townsend Way LN4 95 C4
Townside DN40 12 D6
Town St Cottam DN22 65 B6
Immingham DN40 12 E4
South Somercotes LN11 50 E4
Westborough & Dry Doddington NG23 117 F3
TOYNTON ALL SAINTS PE23 100 F6
Toynton All Saints Prim Sch PE23 100 F6
Toynton Cl 3 LN6 205 B4
TOYNTON FEN SIDE PE23 100 F5
Toynton La PE23 101 B6
Toynton Rd DN33 191 B3
TOYNTON ST PETER PE23 101 A6
Trader Bank Frithville PE22 125 F8
Sibsey PE22 113 A2
Trafalgar Ave
Grimsby DN34 190 D5
Skegness PE25 206 D1
Trafalgar Ct
2 Heighington/Washingborough LN4 203 B2
2 Scunthorpe DN15 183 A6
Trafalgar Pk DN36 195 D7
Trafalgar Pl 3 PE21 208 E4
Trafalgar Sq
Long Sutton PE12 216 B4
4 Sutton on Trent NG23 91 A8
Trafalgar St 5 HU3 180 D7
Trafford Est PE14 170 F4
Trafford Pk 25 PE13 170 E1
Trafford Rd
Kingston upon Hull HU10 178 E8
13 Wisbech PE13 170 E1
Trafford St DN15 183 B4
Traffords Way DN20 30 F6
Train Gate 23 DN21 30 B1
Tramway Dr 21 LN12 76 F8
Tranby Ave HU13 178 D2
Tranby Croft HU10 178 C5
Tranby Dr DN32 192 B4
Tranby La
Anlaby with Anlaby Common HU10 178 B5
Swanland HU14 3 C6
Tranby Lodge Gdns HU13 178 C1
Tranby Mdws Pk HU13 178 C3
Tranby Ride HU10 178 C5
Tranmere Cl HU3 180 B5
Transport Rd DN16 183 E2
Travellers Rest Cvn Site NG31 211 B1
Travis Ave 16 DN8 15 B8
Travis Cl 14 DN8 15 B8
Travis Gr 15 DN8 15 B8
Travis St Lawrence CE Prim Sch DN7 14 E4
Traviss Cl 2 DN16 185 B8
Treadgold Ave 10 NG31 129 E5
Treading Bank PE13 169 C4
Treasure La LN11 49 F5
Treece Gdns 10 DN18 3 F1
Tree Cl PE25 206 A5
Trefoil Dr PE25 103 C6
Trehampton Dr 4 DN21 53 A5
Trelawney Cres 2 LN1 201 E8
Trelowen Wy 7 PE2 230 F5
Tremayne Ave 1 HU15 2 C5
Trenchard Cl DN40 186 E5
Trenchard Rd
9 Ashby de la Launde & Bloxholm LN4 108 A7
Cranwell & Byard's Leap NG34 120 D8
3 Mablethorpe/Sutton on Sea LN12 64 B3
Trenchard Sq
2 Scampton Airfield LN1 67 F5
1 Waddington LN5 94 A7
Trent Ct 6 DN37 190 E8
Trentholme Dr 37 DN17 29 D7
Trent La Beacon Hill NG24 104 A5
Besthorpe NG23 91 B7
Girton NG23 78 B1
Newton on Trent LN1 65 C1
South Clifton NG23 78 B5
Trenton Ave HU4 179 B6
Trent Port Rd DN21 65 D8
Trent Rd Grantham NG31 210 D2
Keadby with Althorpe DN17 17 D6
Trentside
Gainsborough DN21 197 B8
Keadby with Althorpe DN17 17 C3
Trent Side DN17 7 F1
Trent St
Gainsborough DN21 197 D3
Scunthorpe DN16 183 B2
Trentvale Ave DN21 197 F6
Trentvale Prep Sch DN17 17 D6
Trent View Ermine LN1 201 D8
Keadby DN17 17 D5
5 Marton DN21 65 E8
Trent Wlk 13 HU15 2 D5
Trent Wy 5 NG24 104 A5
Tresham Rd PE2 229 D3
Trevitt Cl 1 NG34 212 B7
Trevor Cl 26 DN37 23 F1
Trevose Dr 2 LN6 205 A1
Triangle Dr 9 HU14 3 A4
Triangle The 13 HU14 3 A4
Trienna PE2 230 B5
Trinity Acad DN8 15 B8
Trinity Cl 10 Crowland PE6 166 E1
10 Goxhill DN19 12 A8
Trinity Ct 9 DN20 19 D4
Trinity Gr HU13 178 E2
Trinity House La 17 HU1 180 F6
Trinity La LN11 198 D6
Trinity Rd
Cleethorpes DN35 192 E5
Newark-on-Trent NG24 104 A2
Scunthorpe DN16 185 A4
Stamford PE9 219 A6
Wisbech PE13 170 E1
Trinity St Boston PE21 208 E4
Gainsborough DN21 197 D3
14 Grimsby DN31 189 C1
Kingston upon Hull HU3 180 C7
3 Peterborough PE1 226 A2
Trinity Wharf 8 HU1 181 A6
Trinity Wlk 1 DN18 3 F1
Tritton Rd LN6 201 D2
Trollope St LN5 234 B1
Trolleybus Mus at Sandtoft The* DN8 16 A3
Tromso Cl 6 DN36 195 B6
Trondheim Cl DN36 195 B6
Trondheim Way DN41 187 A2
Troon Cl
Grantham NG31 211 D8
7 Heighington/Washingborough LN4 203 D1
11 Stamford PE9 218 E6
9 Woodhall Spa LN10 97 C6
Troon Ct 2 NG34 120 F3
Troon Rd DN7 14 D4
Trotters La 2 NG32 139 C7
Troughton Way 10 PE13 170 B2
Troutbeck Cl
6 Lincoln LN2 202 A8
1 Peterborough PE4 221 D3
Troutsdale Gr HU9 181 F8
Truesdale Gdns PE6 164 E3
Truman Cl LN8 56 F3
Trunch La PE24 90 D5
Trundle La 2 DN7 14 D8
Trunkass La DN37 34 D7
Truro Cl 6 Grantham NG31 210 F5
7 Skegness PE25 206 D7
5 Sleaford NG34 212 C7
Truro Dr LN6 204 B8
Truro Way 2 PE11 214 C4
TRUSTHORPE LN12 64 B2
Trusthorpe Rd 2 LN12 64 C1
Tuckers Nook PE6 173 C7
Tucker's Yd PE2 231 C7
Tudor Ave PE7 230 C1
Tudor Cl Beacon Hill NG24 104 A4
23 Brough HU15 2 C5
24 Humberston DN36 36 D8
Northorpe PE10 164 C7
Peterborough PE4 221 C2
4 Sutterton PE20 136 A2
1 Toft Newton LN8 56 D5
Tudor Cl (Doglands) LN8 56 C5
Tudor Dr 4 Boston PE21 208 E7
Louth LN11 198 C4
Tudor La 24 HU15 2 C5
Tudor Pk LN9 199 D4
Tudor Pl
Market Deeping PE6 217 E5
Market Deeping PE6 217 F5
Tudor Rd LN6 204 D6
Tudor Way PE12 215 D1
Tudworth Field Rd DN7 15 B5
Tudworth Rd DN7 15 A5
Tulip Fields PE12 158 C7
Tulip Rd DN15 183 C3
Tulipwood Ave 11 LN6 200 C1
Tumby PE22 207 F8
Tumby La PE22 98 D2
Tumby Rd LN4 207 E6
TUMBY WOODSIDE PE22 111 F8
Tummel Ct DN40 186 B2
Tunnard St Boston PE21 208 F6
Grimsby DN32 192 B8
Tunnel Bank PE10 213 F3
Tunnel Rd DN20 196 F7
Tupcroft Road DN10 39 F4
Tuplin Road 10 LN12 64 A4
Turbary Rd DN9 27 B6
Turf Moor Rd 4 DN7 15 A3
Turnberry App DN37 194 C4
Turnberry Cl
1 Grantham NG31 211 D7
Heighington/Washingborough LN4 81 E4
4 Sleaford NG34 120 F3
Turnberry Dr 4 LN10 97 C6
Turnberry Ms 18 DN7 14 C6
Turnbury Cl LN6 204 B7
Turner Ave 3 LN6 205 A6
Turner Cl 2 LN5 107 B8
Turner Ct LN6 204 B8
Turner Rd PE4 221 F2
Turner's La 17 HU14 3 A5
Turner St
15 Kirton in Lindsey DN21 30 B1
Lincoln LN1 234 A4
Turnor Cl
5 Colsterworth NG33 151 E6
9 Wragby LN8 70 D5
Turnor Cres NG31 211 C5
Turnor Rd NG31 211 F4
Turnpike Cl
Great Gonerby NG31 210 D1
14 Wisbech PE13 170 E1

Turnpike Rd
 Hampton Vale PE7 . . . .**230** B1
 Ryhall PE9 . . . .**163** C2
Turnpole Cl 2 PE9 . . . .**219** D7
Turnstone Way PE2 . . . .**231** D7
Turpin Cl DN21 . . . .**197** F5
Turves Rd PE6 . . . .**175** A2
Tut Hole PE23 . . . .**100** F7
Tuxhill Rd PE34 . . . .**161** E1
Tweed Cl Horncastle LN9 . .**199** D2
 10 Spalding PE11 . . . .**214** A4
Twelve Foot Bank LN4 . . . .**109** F5
Twelvetree Ave PE4 . . . . . .**220** E5
TWENTY PE10 . . . .**155** C3
Twenty Dro PE10 . . . .**155** C3
Twenty Foot Bank PE10 . . . .**156** C6
Twigmoor Side Road DN17 **29** F7
Twitchell 4 LN1 . . . .**66** D7
Two Plank La PE11 . . . .**214** B6
Two Pole Dro PE7 . . . .**231** F1
Two Sisters Cl 8 PE12 . . . .**160** E4
Twyford Cl 2 NG33 . . . .**151** E6
Twyford Gdns
 3 Dogsthorpe PE1 . . . .**226** D7
 Grantham NG31 . . . .**211** C4
Twyning Pl DN35 . . . .**192** D7
Tydd Low Rd
 Long Sutton PE12 . . . .**160** A3
 Sutton Cross PE12 . . . .**216** B1
Tydd Rd Pinchbeck PE11 . .**156** C6
 Sutton Bridge PE12 . . . . . .**160** E2
TYDD ST GILES PE13 . . . . .**169** F7
TYDD ST MARY PE13 . . . . .**160** B1
Tydd St Mary CE (Aided) Prim
 Sch PE13 . . . .**160** A1
Tydeman Cl DN16 . . . .**185** A2
Tyesdale PE3 . . . .**225** A4
Tyghes Cl PE6 . . . .**217** F5
Tyler Ave DN31 . . . .**191** A7
Tyler Cres 2 PE2 . . . .**126** E3
Tylers Cl 30 PE24 . . . .**90** D7
Tylers Mews PE4 . . . .**220** F3
Tyndal Rd NG31 . . . .**210** F5
Tyne Cl 4 Lincoln LN6 . . . . .**205** A2
 Spalding PE11 . . . .**214** A4
Tynedale Ct 5 DN3 . . . .**14** A2
Tyne St HU3 . . . .**180** B4
Tyne Way 7 DN37 . . . .**190** E8
Tyrrell Pk PE1 . . . .**226** D2
Tyson Cl
 21 Barton-upon-Humber
 DN18 . . . .**3** F1
 Grantham NG31 . . . .**211** C6
Tytton Cl 2 PE21 . . . .**136** D8
Tytton La E PE21 . . . .**136** D8
Tytton La W PE21 . . . .**136** D8

U

UFFINGTON PE9 . . . .**172** C6
Uffington Ave LN6 . . . .**205** A6
Uffington CE Prim Sch
 PE9 . . . .**172** C6
Uffington Cl 10 LN6 . . . .**205** A7
Uffington Rd Barholm PE9 .**164** B1
 2 Barnack PE9 . . . .**172** D4
 Stamford PE9 . . . .**219** E6
UFFORD PE9 . . . .**172** F3
UK Coll DN31 . . . .**191** B8
ULCEBY Ulceby DN39 . . . . .**12** B1
 Ulceby with Fordington LN13 **88** C7
Ulceby Cross LN13 . . . .**88** B8
Ulceby Rd
 Scunthorpe DN17 . . . .**184** D5
 South Killingholme DN39 . .**12** C2
 Wootton DN39 . . . .**11** F3
ULCEBY SKITTER DN39 . . .**12** C2
 Ulceby Sta DN39 . . . .**12** C2
Uldale Cl LN6 . . . .**200** C2
Uldale Way PE4 . . . .**221** D2
Ullswater Ave PE4 . . . .**221** B2
Ullswater Cl 6 LN6 . . . .**205** A2
Ullyatt's Dro PE20 . . . .**124** B3
Ulster Ave DN33 . . . .**191** D2
Ulster Rd DN21 . . . .**197** D6
Ulverston Cl PE1 . . . .**221** F1
Ulverston Rd HU4 . . . .**179** A3
Ulyett La DN7 . . . .**28** C8
Unicorn Row 10 DN21 . . . . . .**30** B1
Union Pl 1 PE21 . . . .**208** F5
Union Rd Lincoln LN1 . . . . . .**234** A3
 Thorne/Moorends DN8 . . . .**15** A8
Union St 2 Boston PE21 . . .**208** F5
 Grantham NG31 . . . .**211** A5
 Holbeach PE12 . . . .**159** A7
 Louth LN11 . . . .**198** B6
 14 Market Rasen LN8 . . . . .**57** D8
Unity Ave HU13 . . . .**178** F1
Unity Gdns PE12 . . . .**216** E3
Unity Rd DN32 . . . .**192** C6
Unity Sq 5 LN2 . . . .**234** B2
Unity Way DN7 . . . .**14** D5
University Acad Holbeach
 PE12 . . . .**215** D3
University Ct 2 NG31 . . . . . .**211** B3
University of Lincoln Brayford
 (Main Campus) LN6 . . . . .**234** A1
University of Lincoln
 Holbeach Campus PE12 .**215** D4
University of Lincoln
 Riseholme Campus LN2 . .**68** A2
Upgate LN11 . . . .**198** B5
Upland Cl LN9 . . . .**199** A5
Uplands PE4 . . . .**221** A5
Uplands Dr NG31 . . . .**211** D6
Upper Burgess St 2
 DN31 . . . .**191** E8
Upper Cl The 8 LN1 . . . .**66** D7
Upper Ings La DN22 . . . .**52** D2
Upper Kenyon St 9 DN8 . . .**15** A8
Upper Lindum St LN2 . . . . .**234** C3
Upper Long Leys Rd LN1 . .**234** A4
Upper Row NG22 . . . .**65** A1
Upper Saxon St LN1 . . . . . .**234** A4
UPPERTHORPE DN9 . . . .**27** B3
Upperthorpe Hill DN9 . . . . .**27** A2
Uppingham Rd 6 LN12 . . . .**64** C1
Upsall Rd 9 PE22 . . . .**126** E3
UPTON Upton DN21 . . . .**53** E5
 Upton PE6 . . . .**223** B6
Upton Cl Peterborough PE2 .**231** E5
 Peterborough PE3 . . . .**225** A2
Upton Rd Knaith DN21 . . . . .**53** B4
 Upton DN21 . . . .**223** A3
Upton Wlk DN21 . . . .**197** F3
Urban St LN5 . . . .**205** D6
Uredale Pl DN16 . . . .**185** E5
Usher Gall ★ LN2 . . . .**234** B3
Usher Gn 2 Lincoln LN6 . . . .**205** B6
 3 Lincoln LN6 . . . .**205** B7
USSELBY LN8 . . . .**45** C4
Utgard Way 4 DN33 . . . . . .**191** B2
UTTERBY LN11 . . . .**48** F4
Utterby Dr DN34 . . . .**191** C5
Utterby Prim Sch The
 DN36 . . . .**48** E5
Uttoxeter Cl PE10 . . . .**213** B3

V

Vacherie La LN4 . . . .**109** F3
Vagarth Cl 15 DN18 . . . .**3** E1
Valda Vale DN40 . . . .**186** A4
Vale Acad The DN20 . . . . . .**196** B4
Vale Ct PE23 . . . .**101** A8
Vale Dr Hampton Vale PE7 .**230** C1
 Yaxley PE7 . . . .**233** D8
Valence Rd PE2 . . . .**229** F4
Valentine Cl Boston PE21 . .**209** C3
 1 Kingston upon Hull HU4 .**179** A2
Valentine Rd LN6 . . . .**201** C1
Vale Rd
 Gonerby Hill Foot NG31 . . .**210** F8
 10 Spilsby PE23 . . . .**101** A8
Valerian Cl 17 LN6 . . . .**93** B8
Vale The HU10 . . . .**178** B7
Vale View NG23 . . . .**117** F5
Vale Wood DN16 . . . .**185** C3
Valiant Rd
 8 Coddington NG24 . . . . . .**104** C5
 Manby LN11 . . . .**62** C5
Valletta St HU9 . . . .**5** E8
Valley Dr HU10 . . . .**178** B7
Valley La
 Long Bennington NG23 . . . .**117** B4
 Swaby LN13 . . . .**74** E4
Valley Pk View PE2 . . . .**230** D8
Valley Rd Grantham NG31 . .**210** C4
 1 Waddington LN5 . . . . . .**93** E8
Valley View 8 NG24 . . . . . .**104** C5
Valley View Dr DN16 . . . . . .**185** A2
Valliant St 7 LN5 . . . .**94** A7
Vampire Rd LN11 . . . .**62** C5
Vancouver Cres DN7 . . . . . .**184** E4
Vanderbank Terr 2 PE9 . . . .**218** E4
Vanessa Dr DN21 . . . .**197** C7
Vanessa Rd LN11 . . . .**198** A4
Vane St HU3 . . . .**180** D7
Van Gogh Dr 8 PE11 . . . . . .**214** B3
Vanguard Ct 4 NG34 . . . . . .**212** A3
Vanwall Dr 8 LN5 . . . .**93** F7
Varah Cl 39 DN18 . . . .**10** D8
Varlow Rd 8 LN7 . . . .**33** B4
Varsity Cl 4 DN7 . . . .**26** A8
Vars Rd PE7 . . . .**230** B2
Vasey Cl LN1 . . . .**66** E2
Vaughan Ave
 Bottesford NG13 . . . .**128** B6
 Grimsby DN36 . . . .**192** B4
Vaughan Rd 1 HU13 . . . .**3** F4
Vauxhall Rd
 12 Boston PE21 . . . .**209** A5
 Bracebridge Heath LN4 . . . .**205** F2
Veall Cl LN4 . . . .**207** C4
Veal St DN31 . . . .**191** C7
Velden Way 5 LN8 . . . .**57** D7
Venables Cl 18 PE24 . . . . . .**102** E7
Venables Way LN2 . . . .**202** D6
Vence Cl 1 PE9 . . . .**219** A5
Venom Rd LN11 . . . .**62** C5
Ventnor Ave NG31 . . . .**210** E4
Ventura Bsns Pk DN31 . . . .**188** D2
Venture Cl PE11 . . . .**157** A8
Venture Way NG31 . . . .**210** D2
Venus Wy
 Peterborough PE2 . . . .**231** D4
 Peterborough PE2 . . . .**231** D4
Verde Cl PE6 . . . .**175** A2
Verdun Cl LN1 . . . .**201** E2
Vere Rd PE1 . . . .**225** F7
Vere St LN1 . . . .**201** F6
Vere Terr DN31 . . . .**191** C8
Vergette Rd PE1 . . . .**220** D8
Vergette St PE1 . . . .**226** B3
Vermont Gr PE3 . . . .**225** E1
Vermuyden Villas DN8 . . . . .**16** A3
Vernatts Gn PE11 . . . .**214** C7
Vernon Ave NG31 . . . .**210** F8
Vernon Rd PE25 . . . .**206** C4
Vernon St LN5 . . . .**201** D1
Veronica Cl 9 PE25 . . . .**206** A7
Vessey Cl 7 NG24 . . . .**104** B2
Vesta Cl 4 PE2 . . . .**231** D4
Vicarage Ave 2 DN20 . . . . . .**196** F6
Vicarage Cl
 5 Collingham NG23 . . . . . .**91** D5
 4 Cowbit PE12 . . . .**167** B8
 Holbeach PE12 . . . .**158** D1
Vicarage Cres 4 DN15 . . . . .**8** B5
Vicarage Cres 18 NG34 . . . .**212** D4
Vicarage Dr LN6 . . . .**200** B3
Vicarage Dro PE20 . . . .**134** D5
Vicarage Farm Rd 5 PE1 . .**226** D3
Vicarage Gdns
 2 Brough HU15 . . . .**2** C6
 11 Elloughton HU15 . . . . . .**2** C7
 1 Littlefield DN34 . . . .**191** C6
 6 Old Leake PE22 . . . .**114** A1
 Scunthorpe DN15 . . . .**182** F2
 1 Wrawby DN20 . . . .**20** E3
Vicarage La
 Beckingham DN10 . . . .**40** B1
 Broughton DN20 . . . .**19** E1
 Cadney DN20 . . . .**31** D6
 3 Carlton-le-Moorland LN5 **105** E8
 Dunston LN4 . . . .**95** C6
 Elsham DN20 . . . .**20** F7
 Grasby DN38 . . . .**32** E7
 Harmston LN5 . . . .**93** F5
 1 Helpringham NG34 . . . . .**133** D7
 1 Immingham DN40 . . . . . .**12** E4
 1 Kingston upon Hull HU13 **178** E1
 4 Long Bennington NG23 . .**117** D3
 Long Sutton PE12 . . . .**216** D2
 11 Lutton PE12 . . . .**160** A8
 21 Nettleham LN2 . . . .**68** C2
 1 Scawby DN20 . . . .**30** E8
 Scopwick LN4 . . . .**95** C1
 9 Scothern LN2 . . . .**68** F4
 4 Sibsey PE22 . . . .**113** B1
 South Clifton NG23 . . . .**78** C5
 Wainfleet All Saints PE24 . .**102** D1
 19 Wellingore LN5 . . . .**107** A7
Vicarage Lawn DN34 . . . . . .**191** C6
Vicarage Pk 4 DN15 . . . .**9** D1
Vicarage Rd
 Great Carlton LN11 . . . .**62** E4
 3 Heckington NG34 . . . . . .**122** E3
 Willoughton DN21 . . . .**42** E4
 Wrawby DN20 . . . .**196** F6
Vicarage View DN37 . . . . . .**22** D3
Vicarage Way 4 PE7 . . . . . .**233** D5
Vicar La 2 HU1 . . . .**180** F5
Vicars Ct LN2 . . . .**234** B3
Vicar's Wlk 6 DN17 . . . .**16** D7
Viceroy Cl 2 HU2 . . . .**180** F8
Viceroy Dr PE11 . . . .**156** F8
Vickers La 4 LN11 . . . .**198** B5
Victor Dr 1 LN6 . . . .**204** C1
Victoria Ave 1 Hatfield DN7 .**14** E4
 Sleaford NG34 . . . .**212** C3
 1 Woodhall Spa LN10 . . . . .**97** D5
Victoria Bank NG34 . . . .**133** B1
Victoria Cl
 Gainsborough DN21 . . . . . .**197** F2
 2 Marshchapel DN36 . . . . .**37** C2
 2 Stainforth DN7 . . . .**14** C5
 Wike Well End DN8 . . . .**15** B7
 3 DN15 . . . .**8** B5
Victoria Dock Prim Sch
 HU9 . . . .**181** B6
VICTORIA DOCK VILLAGE
 HU9 . . . .**181** C5
Victoria Dr 5 DN18 . . . .**3** E1
Victoria Gdns 11 NG24 . . . .**104** A4
Victoria Gr
 Heighington/Washingborough
 LN4 . . . .**203** D1
 Morton PE10 . . . .**154** D7
Victoria Mews 18 PE11 . . . .**214** D4
Victoria Pas LN1 . . . .**234** A3
Victoria Pier ★ HU1 . . . .**181** A5
Victoria Pl 1 Boston PE21 . .**208** F4
 3 Bourne PE10 . . . .**213** E4
 Peterborough PE1 . . . .**225** F4
Victoria Rd
 Barnetby le Wold DN38 . . . .**21** B4
 10 Keelby DN41 . . . .**23** A5
 Louth LN11 . . . .**198** C7
 Mablethorpe/Sutton on Sea
 LN12 . . . .**64** B3
 2 Market Rasen LN8 . . . . .**57** E8
 Scunthorpe DN16 . . . .**185** A5
 Skegness PE25 . . . .**206** B3
 Stamford PE9 . . . .**219** B6
Victoria Ret Pk DN31 . . . .**189** A1
Victoria St S 4 DN31 . . . . . .**191** E7
Victoria St W DN31 . . . .**191** E7
Victoria St
 Billingborough NG34 . . . . . .**133** B1
 3 Billinghay LN4 . . . .**109** F6
 Grantham NG31 . . . .**211** A2
 4 Holbeach PE12 . . . .**215** E2
 Kingston upon Hull HU13 . .**179** A1
 Lincoln LN1 . . . .**234** A3
 Peterborough PE1 . . . .**226** A5
 Peterborough PE2 . . . .**230** F6
 10 Spalding PE11 . . . .**214** D4
 3 Wragby LN8 . . . .**70** D5
Victoria Stables PE10 . . . . .**213** D4
Victoria Terr LN1 . . . .**234** A3
Victoria Way DN31 . . . .**188** D2
Victor St Grimsby DN32 . . . .**189** C1
 Kingston upon Hull HU9 . . .**181** C8
 10 Waddington LN5 . . . . . .**94** A7
Victory Cl 6 PE12 . . . .**157** F6
Victory Ct 1 PE11 . . . .**214** C3
Victory Gdns 23 PE6 . . . . . .**166** F1
Victory Way
 2 Barton-upon-Humber
 DN18 . . . .**3** F1
 8 Grimsby DN34 . . . .**190** D4
 6 Sleaford NG34 . . . .**212** A3
Viersen Platz PE1 . . . .**226** A1
Vigo Cl LN1 . . . .**201** C7
Viking Cl 6 Bourne PE10 . . .**213** C6
 Immingham DN40 . . . .**186** A4
 7 Swineshead PE20 . . . . . .**135** B7
 11 Waddington LN5 . . . . . .**93** F7
Viking Sch The PE25 . . . .**206** B4
Viking Way
 32 Metheringham LN4 . . . . .**95** C3
 7 Northorpe PE10 . . . .**164** C8
 Spalding PE11 . . . .**214** F2
Villa Cl 3 Branston LN4 . . . .**81** E2
 Long Sutton PE12 . . . .**216** A5
Villa Ct DN35 . . . .**192** C4
Village Farm LN5 . . . .**92** F3
Village Farm Dr 5 LN5 . . . . .**66** C7
Village St
 Burton Coggles NG33 . . . . .**152** C8
 Easton NG33 . . . .**139** F2
 Pickworth NG34 . . . .**142** A8
 Sedgebrook NG32 . . . .**128** F4
 Walcot NG34 . . . .**132** C2
 Woolsthorpe by Belvoir
 NG32 . . . .**128** D1
Village The PE2 . . . .**230** B5
Villa La PE20 . . . .**135** B7
Ville Rd DN16 . . . .**185** D6
Vincent Cl 3 HU4 . . . .**179** A2
Vincent Rd DN33 . . . .**191** B2
Vine Cl 13 NG13 . . . .**128** A5
Vine Cres 8 PE21 . . . .**136** D8
Vine Ct 3 NG34 . . . .**133** B1
Vinegarth 3 DN9 . . . .**27** E6
Vinehall Rd 3 DN9 . . . .**27** C2
Vine Rd
 Chapel St Leonard PE24 . . .**90** E7
 2 Skegness PE25 . . . .**103** E4
Vine St Billingborough NG34 **133** C1
 12 Grantham NG31 . . . .**211** A5
 Lincoln LN2 . . . .**234** C2
 Spalding PE11 . . . .**214** D4
 Stamford PE9 . . . .**219** C5
Vine Wlk PE2 . . . .**225** B4
Vineyard Rd PE1 . . . .**226** D5
Viney Cl PE1 . . . .**225** D3
Vinters Way PE22 . . . .**126** E3
Vintners Cl PE3 . . . .**225** D3
Violeta Wy 5 PE2 . . . .**231** E4
Violet Cl
 4 Humberston DN35 . . . . . .**192** E1
 9 Morton PE10 . . . .**154** D6
Virginia Cl
 1 Peterborough PE3 . . . . . .**225** A2
 Willoughby LN13 . . . .**89** A7
Virginia Dr LN11 . . . .**198** E5
Viscount Cl 17 PE11 . . . . . .**156** E8
Viscount Rd PE2 . . . .**231** A6
Viscount Way 6 DN36 . . . . .**36** D8
Vista The 3 PE11 . . . .**214** D3
Visual Arts Ctr ★ DN15 . . . . .**183** C3
Vivian Ave DN32 . . . .**192** B5
Vivian Cl 1 NG31 . . . .**210** F8
Vixen Cl PE7 . . . .**233** F6
Voases Cl HU10 . . . .**178** E6
Voases La HU10 . . . .**178** E6
Vokes St PE2 . . . .**230** D8
Voyager Acad The PE4 . . . . . .**221** A1
Vulcan Cres LN6 . . . .**204** C2
Vulcan Dr
 Market Deeping PE6 . . . . . .**217** B7
 4 Scampton Airfield LN1 . . .**67** F5
Vulcan St 9 LN5 . . . .**94** A7
Vulcan Way DN7 . . . .**15** A1
Vyner Cl 18 LN12 . . . .**64** B3

W

Waby Cl DN37 . . . .**190** D7
WADDINGWORTH DN21 . . . .**43** D7
Waddingham Pl
 5 Habrough DN40 . . . .**22** E8
 New Waltham DN36 . . . . . .**195** D5
Waddingham Prim Sch
 DN21 . . . .**43** D7
Waddingham Rd LN7 . . . . . .**31** F1
WADDINGTON LN5 . . . .**93** F7
Waddington Dr 1 DN17 . .**184** E3
Waddington La NG23 . . . . . .**91** C7
Waddington Pl 4 DN34 . . . .**191** A5
Waddington Rd NG34 . . . . .**212** C2
Waddington Redwood Cty
 Prim Sch LN5 . . . .**93** E8
WADDINGWORTH LN10 . . . .**84** C6
Waddingworth Gr LN2 . . . . .**202** A8
Waddingworth Road LN10 . .**84** C5
Wade Pk Ave PE6 . . . .**217** C4
Waggoners Cl 11 DN21 . . . .**29** C4
Waggoners Way PE10 . . . . .**154** C6
Waggoners Wlk PE22 . . . . . .**113** B1
Waggons Way 4 DN7 . . . . . .**14** C5
Wagoners Wlk 14 PE25 . . . .**206** A5
Waincroft Cl PE24 . . . .**102** E2
Wainer Cl LN6 . . . .**204** C5
WAINFLEET ALL SAINTS
 PE24 . . . .**102** C2
WAINFLEET BANK PE24 . . . .**102** B1
Wainfleet Magdalen CE/
 Methodist Sch PE24 . . . . .**102** D2
Wainfleet Rd Boston PE21 .**209** D7
 Croft PE24 . . . .**102** D1
Wainfleet Rd continued
 Firsby PE23 . . . .**101** F6
 Fishtoft PE21 . . . .**209** D7
 Grimsby DN33 . . . .**191** B3
 Irby in the Marsh DN24 . . . .**102** B6
 Skegness PE25 . . . .**206** A3
 Thorpe St Peter PE24 . . . . .**102** C3
Wainfleet Rd Industrial Est
 PE25 . . . .**206** A2
WAINFLEET ST MARY
 PE24 . . . .**115** E8
Wainfleet Sta PE24 . . . .**102** C1
WAINFLEET TOFTS PE24 . .**115** C8
Wainman Rd PE2 . . . .**230** D5
Wainwell Mews 3 LN2 . . . .**234** C3
Wainwright PE4 . . . .**220** E5
WAITHE DN36 . . . .**36** A3
Waithe La DN37 . . . .**35** E4
Wakefield Ave DN21 . . . . . .**29** D4
Wakefield Cl
 Barrowby NG31 . . . .**210** C4
 10 Bracebridge Heath LN4 . .**81** A2
Wakehurst Rd PE7 . . . .**230** F2
Wake Rd PE1 . . . .**226** B2
Wakerley Dr PE2 . . . .**230** C7
Wakerley Rd DN21 . . . .**29** C3
Wakes Cl 1 PE10 . . . .**213** E4
Wake St LN1 . . . .**234** A4
Walbury Cl 4 LN5 . . . .**205** D2
WALCOT Alkborough DN15 . .**8** B8
 Walcot Near Folkingham
 NG34 . . . .**132** C1
Walcot Bar NG34 . . . .**132** D2
Walcot Cl LN6 . . . .**204** F6
Walcot La NG34 . . . .**142** C8
Walcot Rd Alkborough DN15 . .**8** B8
 Ufford PE9 . . . .**172** F3
WALCOTT LN4 . . . .**109** D7
Walcott Cl LN4 . . . .**109** C7
Walcott Rd LN4 . . . .**109** E6
Walcott St HU3 . . . .**180** C4
Walcott Way 2 PE9 . . . .**218** E6
Walcot Wlk PE3 . . . .**225** B3
Waldeck St LN1 . . . .**234** A4
Walden Gdns 1 LN21 . . . . .**208** E4
Waldo Rd LN4 . . . .**205** F5
Waldorf Rd DN35 . . . .**193** A1
Waldo Way DN15 . . . .**8** C1
WALESBY LN8 . . . .**46** A3
Walesby Cl DN33 . . . .**194** D8
Walesby Hill LN8 . . . .**46** B3
Walesby La LN8 . . . .**46** B2
Walesby Rd
 Market Rasen LN8 . . . .**57** E8
 Middle Rasen LN8 . . . .**45** E1
 Scunthorpe DN17 . . . .**184** E4
Walford Cl 2 NG13 . . . .**128** A5
Walford Dr LN6 . . . .**205** A6
Walgrave PE2 . . . .**230** B4
Walker Ave DN33 . . . .**194** F8
Walker Cl 3 DN15 . . . .**8** E7
Walker Dr 4 DN15 . . . .**9** A5
Walkergate 14 LN11 . . . .**198** B5
WALKERINGHAM DN10 . . . . .**39** F3
Walkeringham Nature
 Reserve ★ DN10 . . . .**39** E3
Walkeringham Prim Sch
 DN10 . . . .**39** F3
Walkeringham Rd
 Beckingham DN10 . . . .**40** A2
 Gringley on the Hill DN10 . .**39** D2
WALKERITH DN21 . . . .**40** B4
Walkerith Rd
 East Stockwith DN21 . . . . . .**40** B5
 Gainsborough DN21 . . . . . .**197** B8
 Morton DN21 . . . .**40** D3
Walker Rd PE6 . . . .**220** D7
Walkers Cl
 4 Bottesford NG13 . . . .**128** C5
 Scunthorpe DN15 . . . .**183** B3
Walker's Cl 5 DN38 . . . .**21** B4
Walkers Ct 20 DN17 . . . .**29** D7
Walker St HU3 . . . .**180** C5
Walkers Way
 Barrowby NG32 . . . .**210** A3
 Peterborough PE3 . . . .**224** F3
 Ulceby DN39 . . . .**12** B2
Walkington Way 18 LN12 . . .**77** A7
Walk La Humberston DN36 . .**36** C7
 Irby DN37 . . . .**34** D7
 Langton by Wragby LN8 . . . .**70** F4
Walks Rd NG34 . . . .**120** F1
Walks The 4 PE9 . . . .**171** B1
Walk The DN21 . . . .**197** F3
Wallace's Dro PE6 . . . .**176** D4
Wallace St 1 PE11 . . . .**214** A1
Wallace Way 3 PE21 . . . . . .**136** E8
Walled Gdn The 5 LN5 . . . .**93** F4
Waller St HU9 . . . .**181** C8
Walliker St HU3 . . . .**180** A6
Wallingfen La HU15 . . . .**1** B8
Wallis Ave LN6 . . . .**205** B4
Wallis Cl DN33 . . . .**191** B2
Wallisgate PE12 . . . .**158** C7
Wallis Rd LN11 . . . .**198** D5
Wallnutt Dr 3 DN9 . . . .**16** D1
Walls Ave 5 PE24 . . . .**102** E7
Wall's La PE25 . . . .**90** E2
Wall St Gainsborough DN21 **197** D3
 Grimsby DN34 . . . .**191** A7
Wallworks Mews NG31 . . . .**211** B4
Walmer St 1 LN2 . . . .**202** C3
WALMSGATE LN11 . . . .**74** C5
Walmsgate DN34 . . . .**191** B4
Walmsgate Gdns DN33 . . . .**191** B4
Walmsgate Pl 3 DN33 . . . . .**191** B4
Walmsgate Wlk DN33 . . . . .**191** B4
Walmsley St HU3 . . . .**180** D7

Walnut Cl Louth LN11 198 E6
5 Newborough PE6 174 E4
14 Ruskington NG34 108 E2
2 Waddington LN5 93 E8
Walnut Cres DN35 192 D2
Walnut Dr 1 DN20 30 F7
Walnutgarth 6 NG34 212 F3
Walnut Gr
3 Colsterworth NG33 151 E7
Peterborough PE4 221 B2
Walnut La DN37 23 F2
Walnut Mews PE3 225 E2
Walnut Pl LN5 234 B1
Walnut Rd
3 Bottesford NG13 128 A5
Kirton PE20 136 C6
Walnut Tree Wy HU4 179 D3
Walnut Way DN17 29 C7
Walpole Bank PE14 170 F7
Walpole Cl PE11 214 D8
WALPOLE CROSS KEYS PE34 161 C3
Walpole Cross Keys Com Prim Sch PE34 161 D2
WALPOLE MARSH PE14 170 F8
Walsall Garth HU4 179 B4
Walsham Rd PE7 233 D8
Walshaw Cl LN4 81 E1
Walsh Gdns 7 DN33 191 B2
Walsingham Ct 3 PE13 170 C1
Walsingham Dr NG33 152 F7
Walsingham Way 13 PE6 175 A1
WALSOKEN PE13 170 E1
WALTHAM DN37 194 D5
Waltham Cl
9 Birchwood LN6 204 C6
2 Dogsthorpe PE1 226 D8
33 Newark-on-Trent NG24 104 B2
Waltham Grange 5 DN35 192 F3
Waltham Leas Prim Sch DN37 194 E5
Waltham Mus of Rural Life★ DN37 194 D3
Waltham Rd
Barnoldby le Beck DN37 194 A3
Birchwood LN6 204 B6
Brigsley DN37 194 C1
Croxton Kerrial NG32 138 A4
Grimsby DN33 194 F8
Waltham St 1 HU1 180 F6
Waltham Windmill★ DN37 194 E3
WALTON PE4 221 A1
Walton Gdns NG31 211 A2
Walton Girls High Sch The NG31 210 F1
Walton Gr DN33 191 C4
Walton Heath Cl 2 NG31 211 D7
WALTON HIGHWAY PE14 170 F3
Walton Pk PE4 221 A1
Walton Rd
7 Leverington PE13 170 B2
Marholm PE6 220 C1
Wisbech PE13 170 E1
Walton St Leisure Ctr HU3 180 A6
Walton St HU3 180 A7
Walton Way 3 NG32 139 C7
Wandell's View HU15 2 C8
Wansbeck Rd 8 NG34 121 B7
WANSFORD PE8 222 A4
Wansford Rd PE8 222 A3
Wanton La PE34 161 F3
Wanton's Cross Gate PE12 159 D2
Wanton's La PE12 159 E2
Wapping La 4 DN21 65 E8
Warblers Cl 22 DN18 3 E1
Warbon Ave PE1 225 F7
Warburton Ct DN32 191 F7
Warburton St 19 NG24 104 A5
Wardall St DN35 192 F6
Ward Cl PE1 226 B3
Ward Cres PE21 209 E4
Wardentree La PE11 157 A8
Wardentree Pk PE11 157 A8
Wardour Dr NG31 211 F5
Ward's La PE22 114 A3
Ward St DN35 192 C8
Wareley Rd PE2 225 F1
Wares Way DN15 182 B3
WARGATE PE11 145 B5
Wargate Field La PE11 145 C5
Wargate Way PE11 145 B6
Waring St LN9 199 B3
Warley Ave 1 DN16 185 C8
Warley Dr DN16 185 C8
Warley Rd DN16 185 C7
Warneford Gdns HU5 180 A8
Warneford Rd DN35 192 D8
Warping Way DN15 182 B3
Warren Cl DN21 197 B6
Warren Ct
Hampton Hargate PE7 230 C2
6 St Giles LN2 202 D6
Warrendale 12 DN18 10 E8
Warren Farm Cl DN40 12 D7
Warren La Wellingore LN5 107 E6
Witham St Hughs LN6 92 D4
Warrenne Cl 21 DN7 14 D4
Warrenne Keep 8 PE9 219 B4
Warrenne Rd DN7 14 D4
Warren Rd
North Somercotes LN11 51 A6
Scunthorpe DN15 183 B5
5 Thorne/Moorends DN8 15 B7
Wothorpe PE9 219 C1
Warren Way NG31 211 F7
Warren Wood Com Sch DN21 197 E2
Warth La PE25 206 A5
Warwick Ave DN33 191 A4
Warwick Cl Bourne PE10 213 C2
9 Grantham NG31 210 D5
4 Hatfield DN7 14 F3
2 Saxilby with Ingleby LN1 66 C2
Warwick Dr 24 DN18 10 E8
Warwick Rd
7 Chapel St Leonard PE24 90 D7
Cleethorpes DN35 192 D4
Louth LN11 198 B8
Newark-on-Trent NG24 104 B2
Peterborough PE4 221 A2
Scunthorpe DN16 183 C1
Warwick St HU9 181 B7
Wascana Cl HU4 179 B3
Wasdale Cl 2 LN6 200 C1
Wasdale Gdns 1 PE4 221 E2
Wash Bank PE12 167 A5
Washdike Dro PE11 135 C1
Washdike La Croft PE24 102 E4
Donington PE11 135 A1
Stoke Rochford NG33 140 A3
Toynton St Peter PE23 101 B6
Wainfleet St Mary PE24 102 C1
Wash Dike La PE22 115 A6
Washdike Rd
Algarkirk PE20 136 B1
Kirton PE20 136 A6
Washdyke La
Belton & Manthorpe NG32 130 A6
Boston PE21 208 B7
Cumberworth LN13 89 E8
Elsham DN20 20 D6
2 Glentham LN8 43 F1
Immingham DN40 186 B5
Leasingham NG34 121 B7
Mumby LN13 76 F1
Nettleham LN2 68 B2
Old Leake PE22 113 F4
Osgodby LN8 45 A3
Washdyke Rd 7 NG32 106 C1
Washdyke Ret Pk DN40 186 C4
WASHINGBOROUGH LN4 203 D2
Washingborough Acad LN4 203 C2
Washingborough Rd
Heighington/Washingborough LN4 81 E4
Lincoln LN4 202 D1
Washinghall La DN17 7 A2
Washington Cl 6 LN4 207 C4
Washington Dr 5 LN8 56 D5
Washington St 4 DN21 197 D2
Wash National Nature Reserve The★ PE12 149 C2
Wash Rd Fosdyke PE20 146 D7
Kirton PE20 136 D4
Washtub La NG23 91 E6
Washway Rd Fleet PE12 159 B8
Holbeach PE12 215 C6
Moulton PE12 146 F4
WASPS NEST LN4 95 E7
Wassand St HU3 180 C4
Wass La LN8 71 E5
Waste Gn La PE20 146 C7
Water Bank DN9 26 E5
Waterbelly La PE20 136 A1
Water End Marholm PE6 220 B1
Peterborough PE7 229 A5
Waterfall Gdns 2 PE6 174 E4
Waterford La LN3 203 D5
Waterfront The PE21 208 F3
Waterfurlong PE9 219 A4
Watergall 1 PE3 220 F1
Watergall Prim Sch PE3 225 B8
Watergate
11 Grantham NG31 211 A5
10 Stamford PE9 219 C5
Water Gate Quadring PE11 145 B8
Sleaford NG34 212 D4
Water Hill LN3 82 B7
Waterhills Ct 31 LN7 33 B4
Waterhouse La HU1 180 E5
Waterhouse Way PE7 230 F2
Watering Dyke Houses LN2 67 F4
Water La
1 Ancaster NG32 120 A2
Bourne PE10 213 D2
Castle Bytham NG33 152 D1
Castor PE5 223 F1
6 Colsterworth NG33 151 E7
Ellougton-cum-Brough HU15 2 D6
Gunby & Stainby NG33 151 B5
5 Hagworthingham PE23 87 A4
Lincoln LN1 234 A2
4 Lincoln LN6 93 C8
1 Long Bennington NG23 117 D4
12 South Witham NG33 151 D2
4 Spalding PE11 214 D2
Threekingham NG34 132 F3
Thurlby LN5 92 E3
Thurlby PE10 164 C8
Tinwell PE9 218 B6
2 West Halton DN15 8 E7
Waterlees Rd PE13 170 D1
Water Lily Way 4 PE10 213 D3
Waterloo Cl 1 NG32 119 B7
Waterloo Dr
4 Grimsby DN33 191 B2
2 Morton PE10 154 D6
Waterloo La LN6 200 B3
Waterloo Paddock LN5 106 D3
Waterloo Rd
Mablethorpe/Sutton on Sea LN12 64 B4
Waterloo Rd *continued*
Peterborough PE1 226 A5
Waterloo St
6 Kingston upon Hull HU2 180 E8
Kingston upon Hull HU2 180 E8
Lincoln LN6 201 D2
4 Market Rasen LN8 57 D8
Waterlow Dr 22 DN15 9 A5
Watermill La 18 LN2 68 C2
Water Mill La PE23 100 F6
Water Mill Rd LN9 199 B4
WATER NEWTON PE8 228 C7
Waters Edge DN20 196 A3
Waters' Edge Ctry Pk★ DN18 3 F2
WATERSIDE DN8 14 E8
Waterside
5 Billinghay LN4 109 F5
4 Louth LN11 198 D7
3 Ryhall PE9 163 C1
Thorne DN8 14 F8
Water Side DN15 2 B1
Waterside Bsns Pk HU13 3 F4
Waterside Cl 10 PE10 213 C7
Waterside Dr 4 DN31 191 D8
Waterside Gdns 5 PE12 215 E2
Waterside N LN5 234 B2
Waterside Rd DN18 3 E2
Waterside S LN5 234 B2
Waterside Sh Ctr LN2 234 B2
Waterside Wy 32 PE24 90 D7
Waterslade Rd PE7 233 C4
Water St PE9 219 C4
Waterton Cl 2 PE6 217 E4
Waterton La DN7 14 D2
Waterton Wy 9 PE7 230 B1
Waterwell La NG32 120 C4
Waterwheel La LN4 81 D2
Waterworks La PE6 220 B6
Waterworks St
1 Gainsborough DN21 197 D2
Immingham DN40 186 D5
Waterworth Rd PE2 229 E1
Watery La Asterby LN11 72 F5
Butterwick PE22 126 F3
Goulceby LN11 72 D6
Lissington LN3 57 D1
Little Cawthorpe LN11 61 E2
Mareham le Fen PE22 98 F4
Swaby LN13 74 E4
4 Welton/Dunholme LN2 68 E6
1 West Ashby LN9 85 E7
Wickenby LN3 70 A8
Watford Ave DN34 190 F4
Watkin St N DN31 188 F1
Watkin St S 2 DN31 188 F1
Watkins La 2 DN22 52 B3
Watling Cl 7 Bourne PE10 213 C6
8 Bracebridge Heath LN4 81 A1
Watson Pk 4 DN10 52 B8
Watsons Croft 5 DN7 14 D6
Watt Ave 11 NG33 151 D7
Watt Cl PE4 221 C2
Watts La LN11 198 C4
Waudby Cl HU13 178 B3
Wauldby Cl 4 HU10 178 E7
Wauldby Road HU15 2 E7
Wauldby View 2 HU14 3 B7
Waumsley Way 1 LN13 75 E2
Wavell Dr LN2 202 E4
Waveney Cl 1 DN15 8 B5
Waveney Gr PE4 221 C2
Waverley Ave LN6 204 F3
Waverley Gdns
3 Leverington PE13 170 B1
Stamford PE9 218 F6
Waverley Pl 3 PE9 218 F6
Waverley St HU1 180 E5
Waverly Cl PE10 154 D7
Waxwing Wy DN37 24 B5
Wayet Rd 6 PE11 156 E8
Wayford Cl PE3 225 A2
Wayside Cl
5 Holton le Clay DN36 195 D2
Scunthorpe DN16 185 A3
Wayside Dr DN36 195 C7
Weatherthorn PE2 230 C5
Weaver Rd LN6 204 B5
Weavers Croft 11 DN9 27 A2
Webb Cl 36 DN18 10 E8
Webster Ave DN15 182 E3
Webster Cl 3 LN6 205 A5
Websters Cl PE6 220 D8
Webster Way NG31 210 E7
Wedgewood Cl 10 LN6 204 D7
Wedgewood Dr 4 PE11 214 B5
Wedgewood Gr 9 LN6 204 D7
Wedgewood Rd LN6 204 D7
Wedland La PE24 102 D3
WEECAR NG23 78 D1
Weedon Cl PE4 221 D2
Weekes Rd DN35 192 F4
WEELSBY DN32 192 A5
Weelsby Ave DN32 191 F4
Weelsby Gr DN32 191 E4
Weelsby Prim Sch DN32 192 A8
Weelsby Rd DN32 191 D5
Weelsby St S DN32 192 A7
Weelsby St
15 Grimsby DN31 189 C1
Grimsby DN32 192 A8
Weelsby View DN36 195 D8
Weelsby Way HU13 178 C2
Weeping Elm Way 6 DN16 185 D4
Weeton Way 5 HU10 178 E7
Wegberg Rd LN4 95 C7
Weir Cl 3 DN9 27 A2
Weir Farm 3 LN2 68 F4
Weir Rd DN9 27 A2
Weirs La PE22 126 D4
Weir St LN5 205 D8
Weir The HU13 178 E1
Welbeck Ave NG24 104 A5
Welbeck Dr PE11 214 C5
Welbeck Pl 3 DN34 190 E4
Welbeck Rd DN35 192 C5
Welbeck St HU5 180 B8
Welbeck Way Louth LN11 198 B6
Peterborough PE2 230 D7
WELBOURN LN5 106 F5
Welbourn Cl NG34 212 C3
Welbourne PE4 221 A4
Welbourne CE Prim Sch LN5 106 E5
Welbourne La PE12 215 C4
Welbourne La E PE12 215 C4
Welbourne Lane South PE12 215 B3
Welbourne's Cl 6 NG23 117 D4
Welbourne's La 7 NG23 117 D4
Welbourn Gdns 9 LN2 202 A8
Welbourn Prim Sch PE4 221 A4
Welbourn Rd LN5 106 A5
Welbourn Wlk HU4 179 B6
WELBY NG32 130 F5
Welby Cl NG34 212 B4
Welby Dr 3 PE11 145 B6
Welby-Everard Ct NG31 211 B4
Welby Gdns
Grantham NG31 211 A6
Holbeach PE12 215 B2
Welby St 6 NG31 211 A4
Weldon Rd DN21 42 E1
Wel Fen La NG23 117 E8
Welham St NG31 211 B4
Welholme Acad DN32 191 F6
Welholme Ave DN32 191 D5
Welholme Rd DN32 191 E6
WELL LN13 88 E8
Welland Acad PE1 226 C8
Welland Ave DN34 190 F4
Welland Bank PE6 166 C1
Welland Cl
9 Beacon Hill NG24 104 A5
Peterborough PE1 226 A7
9 Ruskington NG34 108 D2
1 Spalding PE11 214 C2
Welland Ct 3 NG31 210 E2
Welland Dr Bourne PE10 213 A4
2 Burton upon Stather DN15 8 B5
Welland Hospl PE11 214 F6
Welland Mews PE9 219 C4
Welland Rd
Borough Fen PE1 174 E1
Boston PE21 208 B3
Lincoln LN1 201 D8
Peterborough PE1 226 B8
Spalding PE11 214 D3
2 Wittering PE8 172 B1
Welland Way PE6 217 E4
Wellbeck Cl 4 DN20 196 D4
Wellbeck Rd DN34 190 E4
Wellesley Cl 3 LN8 57 D8
Wellesley Way NG34 120 B8
Wellfield Cl 6 NG33 151 D2
Wellgarth DN32 192 B5
Wellhead La LN4 95 B7
Well High La LN13 75 D1
WELLINGORE LN5 107 A7
Wellingore Rd 5 LN2 201 F8
Wellington Ave
Coningsby LN4 207 D2
11 Mablethorpe/Sutton on Sea LN12 64 B4
Wellington Cl
7 Heckington NG34 122 E2
Skellingthorpe LN6 79 F6
9 South Killingholme DN40 12 E3
Wellington Ct
Grant Thorold DN32 192 A8
Holton le Clay DN36 195 C4
Wellington Dr 1 NG31 211 D2
Wellingtonia Park 4 PE21 208 E1
Wellington La HU3 180 D8
Wellington Rd
2 Beacon Hill NG24 104 A4
Boston PE21 209 B4
Mablethorpe/Sutton on Sea LN12 64 B4
Wellington St Wes HU1 180 E5
Wellington Sq 12 LN5 94 A7
Wellington St
12 Gainsborough DN21 197 D3
Grimsby DN32 191 F8
Kingston upon Hull HU1 180 F5
Lincoln LN1 201 D4
4 Louth LN11 198 C6
Peterborough PE1 226 B2
7 Scampton Airfield LN1 67 E5
Wellington Way
1 Elsham Wold Ind Est DN20 21 A8
Market Deeping PE6 217 B7
1 Skegness PE25 206 A5
Wellington Yd 4 PE23 88 A1
Well La LN2 234 B3
WELLOW DN32 191 E5
Wellowgate DN32 191 D7
Wellowgate Mews DN32 191 D6
Wells Cl Grantham NG31 210 C5
Heighington/Washingborough LN4 203 E1
Peterborough PE4 220 F3
Wells Cl *continued*
5 Skegness PE25 206 D7
Wells Cres DN35 192 E2
Wells Ct PE2 231 D6
Wells Dr
Bracebridge Heath LN4 81 A2
5 Market Rasen LN8 57 E7
Wells La DN22 65 B7
Wells Pl PE21 136 E1
Wells Rd DN37 23 D4
Wells St Grimsby DN31 191 B7
Kingston upon Hull HU3 180 A5
Scunthorpe DN15 183 B4
Well St
5 Bishop Norton LN8 43 D3
Messingham DN17 29 C7
Wellsted St HU3 180 C5
Wells The 18 LN2 68 D6
Wellsyke La LN10 98 A6
Wellsykes Lane LN4 81 D4
Well Turn LN13 75 F1
Well Vale 2 DN33 194 D8
Well Vale Cl 29 PE24 90 D7
Well Vale Ct PE24 90 D6
Welmore Rd PE6 220 D8
Welsdale Rd LN11 59 E2
WELTON Welton HU15 2 E6
Welton LN2 68 C6
Welton Cl 32 DN18 10 E8
Welton Cliff LN2 68 B7
Welton Gdns LN2 201 F8
WELTON HILL LN2 69 A8
WELTON LE MARSH PE23 89 B3
WELTON LE WOLD LN11 60 C6
Welton-le-Wold Nature Reserve★ LN11 60 D7
Welton Low Rd HU15 2 C6
Welton Old Rd HU15 2 E6
Welton Prim Sch HU15 2 D5
Welton Rd Brough HU15 2 C5
Nettleham LN2 68 C3
Welton Road LN11 60 D7
Welton St Mary's CE Prim Sch LN2 68 C6
Welton Wold View 9 HU14 3 B7
Welwyn Cl NG31 210 E1
Wembley Rd LN11 50 F7
Wembley St DN21 197 C4
Wendan Rd 9 DN8 15 A7
Wende The PE11 214 A3
Wendover Cl
19 Humberston DN36 36 D8
Messingham DN17 29 D7
Rippingale PE10 142 F2
Wendover Mews 3 PE10 213 E5
Wendover Rd 13 DN17 29 D7
Wendover Rise DN35 192 E5
Wenlock St HU3 180 C7
Wensleydale Cl 1 NG31 211 A8
Wensleydale Rd DN16 185 E6
Wensum Cl 4 PE11 214 F5
Wentworth Cl
Gainsborough DN21 197 E6
Heighington LN4 203 E1
4 Skegness PE25 206 D6
1 Spalding PE11 214 C1
Willerby HU10 178 F8
Wentworth Cres 2 DN19 4 E2
Wentworth Dr
Dunholme LN2 68 E5
Grantham NG31 211 D8
25 Messingham DN17 29 D7
2 Saxilby with Ingleby LN1 66 D2
Tydd St Giles PE13 170 A7
Wentworth Rd
Grimsby DN34 191 B7
Scunthorpe DN17 184 D2
Wentworth St 1 PE1 226 A1
Wentworths The PE12 216 A4
Wentworth Way
Kingston upon Hull HU9 181 C7
7 Woodhall Spa LN10 97 C5
Werneth Rd DN32 191 F8
WERRINGTON PE4 220 F4
Werrington Bridge Rd PE6 221 B6
Werrington Centre PE4 221 A5
Werrington Ctr PE4 221 A5
Werrington Gr PE4 220 F2
Werrington Gr Cvn Pk PE4 220 F2
Werrington Mews 5 PE4 221 A3
Werrington Parkway PE6 220 C5
Werrington Pk Ave 2 PE4 221 A3
Werrington Prim Sch
Peterborough PE4 221 A3
Werrington PE4 221 A3
Werrington Sports Ctr PE4 220 F4
Werry's La 4 PE10 213 C5
Wesleyan Ct LN2 234 B2
Wesleyan Rd PE1 226 A7
Wesley Ave 5 PE34 161 F3
Wesley Cl 4 Epworth DN9 27 E6
15 Metheringham LN4 95 C4
Sleaford NG34 212 C2
11 Terrington St Clement PE34 161 F3
2 Winterton DN15 9 A5
Wesley Cres 2 DN35 192 E3
Wesley Ct
8 Grimsby DN31 189 C1
8 Kingston upon Hull HU3 180 C5
Wesley Rd Brigg DN20 196 C3

Wesley Rd *continued*
Cherry Willingham LN3 ... 203 B6
Scunthorpe DN16 ... 185 E7
9 Terrington St Clement PE34 ... 161 F3
Whaplode PE12 ... 158 C7
Wesley St 19 DN21 ... 30 B1
Wesley Way LN9 ... 199 D3
Wesley Wy LN6 ... 78 F2
Wesselow Rd LN4 ... 207 F6
Wessex Cl
Peterborough PE2 ... 231 D7
Sleaford NG34 ... 212 B1
West Acridge 16 DN18 ... 3 E1
WEST ASHBY LN9 ... 85 E7
West Ave
Cranwell & Byard's Leap NG34 ... 120 B8
Grantham NG31 ... 210 D3
6 Stainforth DN7 ... 14 C6
West Bank Crowland PE6 ... 166 E1
Saxilby with Ingleby LN1 ... 66 C2
Stainforth DN7 ... 14 B7
West Bank Rd PE12 ... 161 A8
West Banks NG34 ... 212 C4
WEST BARKWITH LN8 ... 70 F7
Westbeck 2 NG34 ... 108 D2
Westbeck La DN21 ... 42 C5
West Bight 1 LN1 ... 234 B3
WESTBOROUGH NG23 ... 117 E3
Westborough La NG23 ... 117 D4
Westborough Way HU4 ... 179 B6
Westbourne Ave 3 HU13 ... 178 E2
Westbourne Dr
22 Crowle DN17 ... 16 D7
6 Glinton PE6 ... 220 C8
Westbourne Gdns 5 PE11 ... 214 D3
Westbourne Gr
6 Grimsby DN33 ... 194 F8
Kingston upon Hull HU13 ... 178 D2
6 Lincoln LN1 ... 201 D3
Westbourne Pk PE10 ... 213 B5
Westbourne Pl 2 NG31 ... 210 E4
Westbourne St 5 HU3 ... 180 A4
Westbrecks La DN22 ... 65 A7
Westbrick Ave 5 HU3 ... 179 F5
Westbridge Rd PE21 ... 208 A3
Westbrook Ave 1 PE2 ... 230 F7
Westbrooke Cl LN6 ... 205 B8
Westbrooke Gr 32 LN7 ... 33 B4
Westbrooke Rd LN6 ... 205 B8
West Brook La NG23 ... 91 D3
Westbrook Pk Cl 2 PE2 ... 230 F7
Westbrook Pk Rd PE2 ... 230 E7
Westburn Ave 4 DN19 ... 4 E2
Westbury Dr PE7 ... 230 F2
Westbury Pk 2 DN35 ... 193 A1
Westbury Rd DN35 ... 193 A1
WEST BUTTERWICK DN17 ... 28 D8
West Butterwick CE Prim Sch DN17 ... 28 D8
West Butterwick Rd DN17 ... 17 C3
WESTBY NG33 ... 140 F3
Westby Rd
Bitchfield & Bassingthorpe NG33 ... 140 F2
Burton Coggles NG33 ... 152 C8
WESTCLIFF DN17 ... 184 E7
Westcliffe NG34 ... 108 B2
Westcliffe Prim Sch DN17 ... 184 D6
Westcliffe Rd
Ruskington NG34 ... 108 C2
21 Scotter DN21 ... 29 C3
Westcliffe St LN1 ... 201 D6
Westcliff Gdns DN17 ... 184 F7
West Coates Rd DN31 ... 188 D2
West Cob Gate PE12 ... 157 F6
Westcombe Sq PE1 ... 226 D4
West Comm Cres DN17 ... 184 F8
West Comm Gdns DN17 ... 184 F7
West Comm La DN17 ... 184 E7
West Comm N Rd DN17 ... 29 A8
West Comm Sports Hall DN17 ... 184 E8
Westcroft Dr 3 LN1 ... 66 D3
West Cross St 24 DN21 ... 30 B1
West Ct 14 DN8 ... 15 A7
Westdale Cres 2 DN21 ... 30 B2
Westdale Dro PE11 ... 134 C2
WEST DEEPING PE6 ... 173 B8
West Dock Ave HU3 ... 180 B4
West Dock St HU3 ... 180 B3
West Dr Coningsby LN4 ... 110 E8
Sudbrooke LN2 ... 68 F3
West Dro PE12 ... 168 C2
West Dro N PE12 ... 168 C3
West Dro S PE12 ... 168 C1
WEST ELLA HU10 ... 178 A8
West Ella Rd
Kingston upon Hull HU10 ... 178 A7
Swanland HU14 ... 3 C7
West Ella Way HU10 ... 178 C7
West Elloe Ave PE11 ... 214 E6
WEST END PE22 ... 126 E6
West End
Burgh le Marsh PE24 ... 102 D8
Garthorpe & Fockerby DN17 ... 7 E5
Gorefield PE13 ... 169 E3
Harlaxton NG32 ... 139 B7
Hogsthorpe PE24 ... 90 B7
Holbeach PE12 ... 215 D2
Ingham LN1 ... 54 F2
Langtoft PE6 ... 164 E3
West End *continued*
7 Spilsby PE23 ... 87 F1
Swanland HU14 ... 3 B6
Walcott LN4 ... 109 C7
Winteringham DN15 ... 2 A1
Yaxley PE7 ... 233 D4
West End Cl
9 Bottesford NG13 ... 128 A6
Laughton DN21 ... 41 B8
West End Cres 9 PE23 ... 87 F1
West End La DN36 ... 37 B1
West End Rd Boston PE21 ... 136 D8
Epworth DN9 ... 27 C8
2 Habrough DN40 ... 22 E8
Kirton PE20 ... 136 B7
Maxey PE6 ... 217 A1
Ulceby DN39 ... 11 F1
Wyberton PE21 ... 208 B2
West End Villas 11 PE9 ... 219 A5
Westerby Ct LN7 ... 32 A1
Westerdale 5 HU14 ... 3 B7
Westerdale Gr HU9 ... 181 E8
Westerdale Rd
2 Grantham NG31 ... 211 A7
Scunthorpe DN16 ... 185 D5
Westerdale Way DN37 ... 190 E8
Westerley Cl PE3 ... 225 C4
Westerly Way 1 PE11 ... 214 A5
Western App 6 NG34 ... 120 D8
Western Ave Brigg DN20 ... 196 C5
Easton on the Hill PE9 ... 171 C3
Holbeach PE12 ... 215 C2
Lincoln LN6 ... 205 C7
Peterborough PE1 ... 226 B7
8 Saxilby LN1 ... 66 C2
Western Cres LN6 ... 205 C8
Western Dr
Balderton NG24 ... 104 C1
11 Barton-upon-Humber DN18 ... 3 E1
9 RAF Cranwell NG34 ... 120 C8
Western Gn DN15 ... 2 A1
Western Outway DN34 ... 191 A4
Western Prim Sch DN34 ... 190 E5
West Fen Drain Bank PE22 ... 112 D1
West Fen Drainside PE22 ... 112 F7
West Fen La PE22 ... 100 A1
Westfield DN21 ... 29 C1
WEST FIELD DN40 ... 12 C6
Westfield App LN2 ... 203 A8
Westfield Ave Boston PE21 ... 208 D4
Greetwell LN2 ... 203 B8
Grimsby DN33 ... 191 C3
Westfield Cl
8 Metheringham LN4 ... 95 D4
2 Yaxley PE7 ... 233 D5
Westfield Dr
Greetwell LN2 ... 203 A8
22 Messingham DN17 ... 29 D7
1 Pinchbeck PE11 ... 156 E8
3 Skegness PE25 ... 206 B4
11 Swineshead PE20 ... 135 B7
Westfield Garth 2 DN17 ... 16 E6
Westfield Gr DN35 ... 192 D6
Westfield La
Collingham NG23 ... 91 B4
Cumberworth LN13 ... 89 D8
Kirk Bramwith DN7 ... 14 B8
North Greetwell LN3 ... 203 C7
West Field La
1 Swanland HU14 ... 3 B6
Thorpe on the Hill LN6 ... 92 E8
Westfield Pk 11 HU15 ... 2 C6
Westfield Rd Bardney LN3 ... 83 D1
Barton-upon-Humber DN18 ... 3 C1
Fishlake DN7 ... 14 B8
13 Goxhill DN19 ... 12 A8
6 Hatfield DN7 ... 14 E4
Kingston upon Hull HU4 ... 179 D5
Newton PE13 ... 169 F5
Peterborough PE3 ... 225 E4
Scunthorpe DN17 ... 184 B6
Waltham DN37 ... 194 C4
2 Wisbech PE13 ... 170 E2
Yarburgh LN11 ... 49 D3
Yaxley PE7 ... 233 D5
Westfield Rise HU13 ... 178 D2
Westfields 1 Alford LN13 ... 75 F2
Easton on the Hill PE9 ... 171 C3
Westfield St 4 LN1 ... 201 D3
Westfield Villas 5 DN7 ... 14 E4
Westfield Way PE6 ... 164 E2
WESTGATE DN9 ... 16 D2
Westgate Grantham NG31 ... 211 A4
Grimsby DN31 ... 188 F1
Kexby DN21 ... 53 E4
Lincoln LN1 ... 234 A3
Louth LN11 ... 198 A5
Peterborough PE1 ... 225 F2
Scotton DN21 ... 29 C1
Sleaford NG34 ... 212 C4
West Gate
9 Ruskington NG34 ... 108 E2
Wainfleet All Saints PE24 ... 101 E2
Weston PE12 ... 157 D2
Westgate Acad LN1 ... 234 A4
Westgate House★ LN11 ... 198 A5
Westgate Pk 3 NG34 ... 212 C4
Westgate Pl 7 LN11 ... 198 B5
Westgate Rd DN9 ... 16 D2
West Gn
Kingston upon Hull HU10 ... 3 C8
29 Messingham DN17 ... 29 D7
West Gr
7 Colsterworth NG33 ... 151 E6
Kingston upon Hull HU4 ... 179 D4
West Grantham Acad St Hugh's The NG31 ... 210 E3
West Grantham Acad St John's The NG31 ... 210 D3
Westhall Cl 11 LN5 ... 92 E1
Westhall Rd 16 LN2 ... 68 D7
WEST HALTON DN15 ... 8 E8
West Halton Hill DN15 ... 8 F7
West Halton La DN15 ... 8 C8
West Hann La DN19 ... 4 C1
Westhaven 2 PE9 ... 171 D3
West Haven Way DN40 ... 186 B8
Westhawe PE3 ... 224 F7
West Hill 1 HU13 ... 3 E4
Westhill Rd DN34 ... 191 A5
Westholm 2 LN3 ... 203 E5
Westholm Cl LN2 ... 202 D8
Westholme Cl 11 DN15 ... 8 B4
Westholme La DN38 ... 21 C5
WESTHORPE PE11 ... 144 F5
Westhorpe Rd PE11 ... 144 F5
Westhouses PE22 ... 112 F5
WEST KEAL PE23 ... 100 C6
West Keal Rd
East Keal PE23 ... 100 D8
Mavis Enderby PE23 ... 87 C1
Westkirke Ave DN33 ... 191 D1
West La Baumber LN9 ... 72 A1
Girton NG23 ... 78 C1
Haltham LN9 ... 98 C6
7 Keelby DN41 ... 23 A4
Skidbrooke with Saltfleet Haven LN11 ... 51 A2
5 Winterton DN15 ... 9 B5
Westlaby La LN3 ... 69 E8
Westlake Ave PE7 ... 230 C1
West Lake Ave PE7 ... 230 B1
Westland Rd
Kingston upon Hull HU10 ... 178 B7
5 Westwoodside DN9 ... 27 B2
Westlands Ave
Grimsby DN34 ... 191 C5
4 Tetney DN36 ... 36 D4
Westlands Rd HU5 ... 179 B8
West Lea DN33 ... 194 F7
West Leys Pk 7 HU14 ... 3 B6
West Leys Rd HU14 ... 3 B6
Westlode St PE11 ... 214 D4
WEST MARSH DN31 ... 188 D1
West Marsh Ind Est DN31 ... 188 F1
West Marsh La
Barrow upon Humber DN19 ... 4 B1
Goxhill DN19 ... 5 A3
West Marsh Rd
Pinchbeck PE11 ... 145 E1
Spalding PE11 ... 214 F6
Westmere Com Prim Sch PE12 ... 160 E4
West Mid Mere Rd DN40 ... 12 D3
West Mill 1 PE9 ... 171 C2
West Mill Gate 2 LN3 ... 203 E6
Westminister Way 2 NG31 ... 210 F5
Westminster Cl DN21 ... 40 D3
Westminster Dr
Grimsby DN34 ... 191 C6
14 Hatfield DN7 ... 14 C2
1 Spalding PE11 ... 214 B1
Westminster Gdns 24 PE6 ... 175 A1
Westminster Ind Est LN6 ... 204 D4
Westminster La 6 PE10 ... 213 B5
Westminster Pl PE1 ... 226 F5
Westminster Rd
5 Broughton DN20 ... 19 D4
Lincoln LN6 ... 204 D4
Westmoor La LN1 ... 65 E2
West Moor Rd 1 DN10 ... 39 F3
Westmoreland Ave 14 LN1 ... 67 E5
Westmoreland Cl 1 DN9 ... 27 A2
Westmoreland Gdns 4 PE1 ... 226 B2
Westmoreland Rd 2 PE12 ... 157 F6
Westoby La DN19 ... 11 C7
WESTON PE12 ... 157 D7
Weston Bypass PE12 ... 157 D7
Weston Gr DN40 ... 186 B5
WESTON HILLS PE12 ... 157 C3
Weston Hills CE Prim Sch PE12 ... 157 D2
Weston Hills Rd PE12 ... 157 B4
Weston Miller Dr 8 PE13 ... 170 D1
Weston St Mary CE Prim Sch PE12 ... 157 E7
Westonville 6 PE9 ... 171 B1
Westover Dr 4 DN15 ... 8 A4
West Parade
Grimsby DN31 ... 191 C7
Kingston upon Hull HU3 ... 180 C7
Lincoln LN1 ... 234 A3
Peterborough PE3 ... 225 D3
Spalding PE11 ... 214 B4
Wisbech PE13 ... 170 C1
West Parklands Dr 9 HU14 ... 3 A5
Westport Rd 1 DN35 ... 193 A1
WEST RASEN LN8 ... 56 E8
WEST RAVENDALE DN37 ... 35 A2
West Rd
Billingborough NG34 ... 133 B1
Bourne PE10 ... 213 B4
Deeping St Nicholas PE11 ... 156 D3
Haconby PE10 ... 154 C8
2 Keadby with Althorpe DN17 ... 17 C6
Pointon & Sempringham NG34 ... 143 A6
3 Ruskington NG34 ... 108 D1
2 Tallington PE9 ... 172 F7
Tetford LN9 ... 73 E1
Thorney NG23 ... 78 F8
West Rd *continued*
1 Tydd St Mary PE13 ... 170 C8
West Riverside DN40 ... 186 E8
West Row 4 PE21 ... 208 E4
WESTRUM DN20 ... 196 C1
Westrum La DN20 ... 196 D2
Westry Cl Barrowby NG32 ... 210 A3
1 Leverington PE13 ... 170 F1
Westry Cnr NG32 ... 210 A4
West St Gdns 8 PE9 ... 219 A5
West St Mary's Gate 3 DN31 ... 191 D7
Westside PE11 ... 214 A1
Westside Ave NG31 ... 139 E8
Westside Rd
Cranwell & Byard's Leap NG34 ... 107 E1
Grimsby DN31 ... 188 F2
West Sq Brigg DN20 ... 196 C4
Brigg DN20 ... 196 C4
West St Alford LN13 ... 75 E2
Barkston NG32 ... 119 A1
Barnetby le Wold DN38 ... 21 B4
Billinghay LN4 ... 109 F6
Boston PE21 ... 208 E4
Bourne PE10 ... 213 C5
Brant Broughton LN5 ... 105 F5
Cleethorpes DN35 ... 192 F6
Clipsham LE15 ... 162 B7
7 Crowland PE6 ... 166 E1
Easton on the Hill PE9 ... 171 C3
Folkingham NG34 ... 142 C8
Gainsborough DN21 ... 197 B8
Hagworthingham PE23 ... 87 A4
Helpston PE6 ... 173 B4
Hibaldstow DN20 ... 30 F5
Horncastle LN9 ... 199 A3
Kingston upon Hull HU1 ... 180 E6
Long Sutton PE12 ... 216 B4
11 Navenby/Wellingore LN5 ... 107 A7
North Kelsey LN7 ... 32 A4
Osbournby NG34 ... 132 C5
1 Roxby cum Risby DN15 ... 8 F3
Scawby DN20 ... 30 E8
Scunthorpe DN15 ... 183 A3
Stamford PE9 ... 219 A4
Swaton NG34 ... 133 C4
Thorne/Moorends DN8 ... 15 A7
2 Timberland LN4 ... 96 B1
West/East Butterwick DN17 ... 28 C8
West Halton DN15 ... 8 E7
Winterton DN15 ... 9 A5
WEST STOCKWITH DN10 ... 40 C6
West Stonebridge PE2 ... 230 C5
West Syke La LN1 ... 66 B7
West Terr DN20 ... 196 B3
West Terr St 10 DN17 ... 16 D7
WEST TORRINGTON LN8 ... 58 A1
West Torrington Rd LN8 ... 57 E3
West View
3 Ancaster NG32 ... 120 A3
5 Bardney LN3 ... 83 B4
Messingham DN17 ... 29 C7
15 North Ferriby HU14 ... 3 A4
Scunthorpe DN17 ... 184 E3
West View Cl 8 DN41 ... 23 A5
West View Cres 25 PE24 ... 90 D7
Westville Rd PE22 ... 112 B2
WEST WALTON PE14 ... 170 E4
Westward Cl DN34 ... 191 C5
Westward Ho DN34 ... 191 C5
Westward Row LN4 ... 207 A5
Westway 18 LN2 ... 68 D2
West Way PE25 ... 206 D7
West Wells La 4 DN10 ... 39 C1
Westwick Dr LN6 ... 205 B7
Westwick Gdns LN6 ... 205 B6
WEST WILLOUGHBY NG32 ... 119 E2
Westwinds Gdns 19 DN15 ... 9 A5
Westwold Rd 25 LN7 ... 33 B4
WESTWOOD PE3 ... 225 B4
Westwood
6 Broughton DN20 ... 19 D4
5 Peterborough PE3 ... 225 C4
Westwood Cl LN6 ... 205 A8
Westwood Dr
Bourne PE10 ... 213 B4
3 Kingston upon Hull HU4 ... 179 B6
Lincoln LN6 ... 205 A8
Westwood Ind Est PE3 ... 225 D7
Westwood Pk Cl PE3 ... 225 C3
Westwood Pk Rd PE3 ... 225 D2
Westwood Rd 1 DN41 ... 23 F5
WESTWOODSIDE DN9 ... 27 A2
Westwoodside CE Prim Sch DN9 ... 27 B2
West Wr Crescen PE7 ... 230 C1
West Wy NG32 ... 128 A6
Wetherby Cl
3 Bourne PE10 ... 213 C7
6 Market Rasen LN8 ... 57 E7
Wetherby Cres LN6 ... 204 F4
Wetherby Way 1 PE1 ... 226 D3
Wetmoor La LN2 ... 56 C1
Wetsyke La 4 NG24 ... 104 C2
Wexford Cl 9 PE10 ... 213 E4
Weydike Bank PE12 ... 159 A4
Weyford Rd 4 DN35 ... 193 A1
Weymouth Cl 10 LN5 ... 205 D3
Weymouth Cres DN17 ... 182 C1
Weymouth Way PE1 ... 226 D6
Whalebone La NG31 ... 140 B7
Whale Dro Holbeach PE12 ... 168 A1
Whaplode PE6 ... 167 E1
Whalley St PE1 ... 226 B3
WHAPLODE PE12 ... 158 A7
Whaplode CE Prim Sch PE12 ... 158 C7
WHAPLODE DROVE PE12 ... 168 B4
WHAPLODE ST CATHERINE PE12 ... 158 C2
Wharfdale Cl 6 DN15 ... 17 E6
Wharfedale Dr 2 LN6 ... 204 F3
Wharfedale Pl 1 DN16 ... 185 E6
Wharfe La
Kirkby on Bain LN10 ... 98 C5
Tattershall LN4 ... 207 D6
Wharf Rd
Crowle DN17 ... 16 D7
Grantham NG31 ... 211 A4
7 Horncastle LN9 ... 199 B4
12 Misterton DN10 ... 39 F5
Peterborough PE2 ... 230 E8
Stamford PE9 ... 219 C4
Wharfside Mews 6 NG34 ... 212 D4
Wharf St 20 PE12 ... 160 E4
Wharf The DN36 ... 37 A5
Wharncliffe Rd DN31 ... 189 C3
Wharncliffe Rd N DN31 ... 189 B3
Wharncliffe St HU5 ... 180 A8
WHARTON DN21 ... 41 B4
Wharton Rd DN21 ... 41 A5
Wharton St DN31 ... 191 B7
Whattoff Way PE6 ... 164 D4
Whatton's Cl NG32 ... 128 F5
Wheatdole PE2 ... 230 A3
Wheatfield Cl
5 Barnby Dun DN3 ... 14 A3
Epworth DN9 ... 27 F6
2 Kingston upon Hull HU4 ... 179 D2
Wheatfield Dr 7 DN37 ... 194 C5
Wheatfield Rd LN6 ... 200 C1
Wheatfields 1 PE12 ... 158 B7
Wheatfield PE6 ... 164 E2
Wheat Gr 8 NG34 ... 212 F3
Wheatgrass La NG32 ... 119 B7
Wheatholme La NG23 ... 78 D6
Wheatley Bank PE14 ... 170 F1
Wheatley La
1 Carlton-le-Moorland LN5 ... 105 E8
Collingham NG23 ... 91 D2
Wheatley Lane LN5 ... 105 E8
Wheatley Rd DN22 ... 52 A3
Wheatmere Dro PE12 ... 157 B5
Wheatsheaf Ave 1 NG24 ... 104 A6
Wheatsheaf Cl
3 Holbeach PE12 ... 215 B2
Sibsey PE22 ... 113 B2
Wheatsheaf Ct 8 PE11 ... 166 C6
Wheatsheaf La 4 NG23 ... 117 D4
Wheatsheaf Way PE9 ... 218 E5
WHEELBRIDGE PE24 ... 103 A2
PE24 ... 116 A6
Wheeldon St 9 DN21 ... 197 D3
Wheeler Cl PE21 ... 209 A4
Wheeler Dr 2 PE21 ... 208 E1
Wheeler Prim Sch 9 HU3 ... 179 F5
Wheeler St HU3 ... 179 F6
Wheelwright Cl PE10 ... 154 C6
Wheelwrights Ct NG34 ... 109 B1
Wheel Yd PE1 ... 226 A2
Whelpton Cl LN9 ... 199 D3
Whetstone Ct 1 PE1 ... 226 E7
Whichcote Rd PE6 ... 174 C7
Whimbrel Chase DN16 ... 185 F5
Whimbrel Way
6 Long Sutton PE12 ... 216 B4
New Waltham DN36 ... 195 D7
Whin Moor La HU15 ... 2 A7
Whins Gate DN17 ... 7 A4
WHISBY LN6 ... 79 E2
Whisby Ct DN36 ... 195 E2
Whisby Nature Pk★ LN6 ... 79 F1
Whisby Rd LN6 ... 204 A4
Whisby Way LN6 ... 204 C5
Whiston Cl 5 PE4 ... 221 D2
Whiston Way 9 DN18 ... 3 F1
Whitacre PE1 ... 226 E6
Whitby Ave PE6 ... 175 B1
Whitby Dr DN32 ... 192 A5
Whitby St HU8 ... 181 B8
Whiteacres 3 PE12 ... 216 B4
Whitebeam Cl
4 Hampton Hargate PE7 ... 230 D3
Kingston upon Hull HU3 ... 180 D5
Whitebread Rd PE20 ... 136 A7
White Bridges 1 PE21 ... 208 E1
White Croft PE3 ... 225 B6
Whitecross Gate PE20 ... 146 D8
Whitecross La NG34 ... 121 F1
White Cross La 4 PE11 ... 145 D2
Whitecross St 12 DN18 ... 10 F8
Whitefriargate HU1 ... 180 F6
Whitefriars Cl 7 LN2 ... 202 E6
Whitefriars Rd LN2 ... 202 F6
White Gate LN9 ... 73 E2
Whitegate Hill LN7 ... 33 C3
Whitehall 5 PE11 ... 145 C6
Whitehall Cres LN4 ... 205 F4
Whitehall Ctry Cotts DN35 ... 192 A1
Whitehall Gr LN1 ... 234 A3
Whitehall Rd 6 DN35 ... 193 A1
Whitehall Terr 1 LN1 ... 234 A3
White Hart La 1 NG23 ... 91 C4
Whitehead Cl 5 LN12 ... 64 B5
Whitehorse La 10 PE21 ... 208 F4
White House Cl
29 Hatfield DN7 ... 14 D4
4 Stainforth DN7 ... 14 C7
White House Garth 19 HU14 ... 3 A5

White House La
Boston PE21 ... 209 D3
3 West Halton DN15 ... 8 E8
White House Mews 16 HU14. 3 A5
Whitehouse Rd 1 NG34 ... 108 E2
White La Harmston LN5 ... 93 F5
Thorne DN8 ... 15 A8
White Leather Sq NG34 ... 133 C1
Whitemoor La NG23 ... 91 C3
WHITE PIT LN13 ... 74 D4
Whitepit Way LN13 ... 74 D4
White Pit Way LN13 ... 75 E3
Whitepost Rd PE6 ... 174 F3
White Rd DN36 ... 48 C8
White Row La LN12 ... 64 C1
Whites La LN5 ... 92 E2
White's Rd DN35 ... 192 F5
White St HU3 ... 179 F5
Whitestone Rd DN17 ... 184 C6
White's Wood Acad DN21 197 F4
White's Wood La
1 Corringham DN21 ... 53 A8
Gainsborough DN21 ... 197 F4
Whitethorn Gr 7 LN6 ... 200 C1
Whitewater PE2 ... 229 D6
Whiteways PE2 ... 229 D6
Whitewell Cl 4 DN21 ... 30 B1
White Wlk HU10 ... 178 C6
Whitfield Rd DN17 ... 184 D6
Whitfield St NG24 ... 104 A4
Whitgift Cl 21 DN37 ... 23 F1
Whitgift Way DN37 ... 190 E8
Whiting Sq PE21 ... 208 F6
Whitley Cl 5 LN6 ... 200 A4
Whitley St 11 LN1 ... 67 E5
Whitley Way PE6 ... 217 B7
Whitman Cl 9 PE9 ... 172 D3
Whitman Rd DN17 ... 184 C6
Whitsed Rd 8 PE6 ... 174 E5
Whitsed St PE1 ... 226 B3
Whittington PE1 ... 226 E7
Whittle Cl
11 Beacon Hill NG24 ... 104 B5
2 Boston PE21 ... 208 F1
Whittle Rd NG34 ... 212 C7
Whittlesey Rd
Peterborough PE2 ... 231 B7
Thorney PE6 ... 175 F1
WHITTON DN15 ... 1 D3
Whitton Rd Alkborough DN15 . 1 C1
Whitton DN15 ... 1 E2
Whitwell PE4 ... 221 E2
Whitworth Way 12 LN8 ... 57 D7
Whomsley Cl 4 NG24 ... 104 B4
Whoofer La DN21 ... 40 E8
Whyalla Cl 2 LN11 ... 50 B8
Whyche The LN4 ... 109 E5
WICKENBY LN3 ... 69 F8
Wickenby Airport LN3 ... 69 F8
Wickenby Cl
6 Grimsby DN34 ... 190 F4
Lincoln LN6 ... 205 A3
Wickenby Cres LN1 ... 201 E7
Wickenby Rd LN3 ... 57 D1
Wickenby Wy PE25 ... 206 B6
Wicken La PE22 ... 113 F3
Wicken Way PE3 ... 225 C6
Wickham Rd DN31 ... 189 C2
Wicklow Ave DN33 ... 194 E8
Wick Rd PE7 ... 230 B2
Wide Bargate 8 PE21 ... 208 F5
Widford Gn 8 DN7 ... 14 D3
Widow Fen La LN13 ... 76 C3
Wigeon Cl 14 PE12 ... 167 B8
Wigeon Wk DN16 ... 185 F5
Wigford Way LN5 ... 234 A2
Wigg La PE24 ... 90 D8
Wigmore Dr PE7 ... 231 F5
Wignal's Gate PE12 ... 215 A2
WIGSLEY NG23 ... 78 F5
Wigsley Cl 7 LN6 ... 204 D6
Wigsley Rd
6 Birchwood LN6 ... 204 D6
Harby NG23 ... 79 B5
North Scarle LN6 ... 78 E3
Wigsley Road NG23 ... 79 A6
WIGTOFT PE20 ... 135 E3
Wigtoft Bank Wigtoft PE20 135 C3
Wigtoft PE20 ... 135 D1
Wigtoft Rd PE20 ... 135 F2
Wigtoft Way PE20 ... 135 E2
Wike Gate Cl 4 DN8 ... 15 B7
Wike Gate Gr 2 DN8 ... 15 B7
Wike Gate Rd DN8 ... 15 B8
WIKE WELL END DN8 ... 15 B7
Wilberforce Dr 6 HU1 ... 180 F7
Wilberforce House★ HU1 181 A6
Wilberforce Rd PE1 ... 225 E7
Wilberforce St HU3 ... 180 D6
Wildfowlers Way PE12 ... 148 F4
Wildlake PE2 ... 230 C5
Wildmore Cl LN4 ... 111 C6
Wildmore Cres PE22 ... 114 F6
Wildshed La PE24 ... 102 D7
WILDSWORTH DN21 ... 40 E8
Wiles Ave 5 PE12 ... 157 E1
Wiles's La PE20 ... 135 B4
Wilford Gr PE25 ... 206 C1
Wilfred Ave NG24 ... 104 B2
Wilkie Cl DN15 ... 182 C3
Wilkie Dr NG34 ... 142 C8
Wilkinson Dr 9 LN8 ... 57 B8
Wilkinson Rd 7 NG32 ... 117 F1
WILKSBY PE22 ... 99 A5
Wilksby La PE22 ... 99 A6
Wilks Rd NG31 ... 211 A2
Willan Ct PE2 ... 230 F8
Willders Garth PE12 ... 215 F2
Willerby Rd HU5 ... 179 C8
Willerton Rd 3 LN11 ... 50 F7
Willesby Rd PE11 ... 214 E5
Willesden Ave PE4 ... 225 D8
Willey's La PE24 ... 90 B8
William Alvey CE Sch
NG34 ... 212 E5
William Barcroft Jun Sch
DN32 ... 192 C7
William de Yaxley CE Aided
Junior Sch The PE7 ... 233 E6
William Farr CE Comp Sch
LN2 ... 68 D6
William Gn Cl 9 LN12 ... 76 F8
William Hildyard CE (Aided)
Prim Sch PE6 ... 217 B5
William Law CE Prim Sch
PE4 ... 220 F5
William Lovell CE Sch
PE22 ... 113 A7
William Mews DN37 ... 194 F5
Williams Cl 1 PE6 ... 174 E5
Williams Dr DN39 ... 12 B1
Williams La 33 NG24 ... 104 C1
Williamson Ave PE3 ... 225 E3
Williamson's Dro LN4 ... 110 A7
Williamson St
Kingston upon Hull HU9 ... 181 C7
Lincoln LN2 ... 234 B4
William St
15 Beacon Hill NG24 ... 104 A4
Cleethorpes DN35 ... 192 E5
2 Grantham NG31 ... 211 A3
Kingston upon Hull HU1 ... 180 E5
24 Saxilby LN1 ... 66 D2
1 Scunthorpe DN16 ... 183 B2
William Stukeley CE Prim Sch
PE12 ... 215 D2
William Tow Cl 7 LN12 ... 76 F8
William Way PE25 ... 206 B2
William Wright Dock HU3 180 C3
Willingham Ave LN2 ... 201 F8
WILLINGHAM BY STOW
DN21 ... 53 F3
Willingham Hill LN8 ... 58 E7
Willingham La LN8 ... 57 F6
Willingham Rd
East Barkwith LN8 ... 58 E1
Fillingham DN21 ... 54 D4
Lea DN21 ... 53 A5
Market Rasen LN8 ... 57 E7
Marton DN21 ... 53 B1
Tealby LN8 ... 58 A7
Willingham St DN32 ... 191 E6
Willington Rd PE20 ... 136 A7
Willing Way DN32 ... 191 F8
Willis Cl LN1 ... 234 A4
Willis Terr LN1 ... 234 A4
Willonholt PE3 ... 225 C7
Willougby Mdw Nature
Reserve★ LN13 ... 89 B6
WILLOUGHBY LN13 ... 89 B7
Willoughby Ave 2 PE6 ... 217 C5
Willoughby Branch Line
Nature Reserve★ LN13 ... 89 A7
Willoughby Chase DN21 ... 197 E1
Willoughby Cl
Corby Glen NG33 ... 152 F7
Helpringham NG34 ... 133 E7
Silk Willoughby NG34 ... 121 B1
Willoughby Ct PE1 ... 226 E8
Willoughby Dr 1 PE23 ... 88 A1
Willoughby Gall The★
NG33 ... 152 F8
Willoughby Gr 5 DN34 ... 190 F4
WILLOUGHBY HILLS PE21 ... 209 E7
Willoughby La
Authorpe LN11 ... 74 F8
Muckton LN11 ... 62 C1
Waddington LN5 ... 205 C1
Willoughby Mdw Nature
Reserve★ LN13 ... 89 B6
Willoughby Mem Trust Gall★
NG33 ... 152 F7
WILLOUGHBY MOOR
NG32 ... 119 F2
Willoughby Rd
16 Alford LN13 ... 75 F2
Ancaster NG32 ... 119 E2
Aunsby & Dembleby NG34 ... 132 B4
Boston PE21 ... 209 A7
Bourne PE10 ... 213 E4
Claxby St Andrew LN13 ... 88 F6
Cumberworth LN13 ... 89 E8
14 Hibaldstow DN20 ... 31 A5
7 Mablethorpe/Sutton on Sea
LN12 ... 64 C1
Scunthorpe DN17 ... 184 E5
Sleaford NG34 ... 120 F3
Stamford PE9 ... 219 C7
Willoughby Road Prim Acad
DN17 ... 184 F4
Willoughby Sch PE10 ... 213 D3
Willoughby St 1 DN21 ... 197 D3
WILLOUGHTON DN21 ... 42 D4
Willoughton Prim Sch
DN21 ... 42 D4
Willoughton Rd 3 PE25 ... 206 D2
Willow Ave
4 Misterton DN10 ... 39 F5
Peterborough PE1 ... 226 B7
Willow Bank Lane DN21 ... 40 C4
Willowbrook Dr DN20 ... 196 E3
Willow Cl 12 Barnetby DN38 . 21 B4
Gainsborough DN21 ... 197 B7
10 Heckington NG34 ... 122 E3
Horncastle LN9 ... 199 A5
6 Laceby DN37 ... 23 E1
Willow Cl *continued*
Ruskington NG34 ... 108 D1
17 Saxilby LN1 ... 66 D2
Scopwick LN4 ... 95 D1
Skellingthorpe LN6 ... 200 B3
Willow Ct
3 Bracebridge Heath LN4 ... 81 A1
Heighington/Washingborough
LN4 ... 203 C2
18 Long Bennington NG23 ... 117 D3
1 Sleaford NG34 ... 212 E3
14 Wragby LN8 ... 70 D4
Willow Dr
14 Barton-upon-Humber
DN18 ... 3 F1
9 Bourne PE10 ... 213 C7
27 Brough HU15 ... 2 C5
2 Coningsby LN4 ... 207 D4
Kingston upon Hull HU10 ... 178 D8
Louth LN11 ... 198 C8
35 Messingham DN17 ... 29 D7
Willow Dro PE6 ... 174 E6
Willowfield Ave 12 LN2 ... 68 D2
Willow Gdns 2 DN19 ... 11 D8
Willow Gr
1 Keadby with Althorpe
DN17 ... 17 D6
7 Scawby DN20 ... 30 F8
Scunthorpe DN16 ... 185 C7
Willow Hall La PE6 ... 227 D6
Willow Holt PE7 ... 230 C3
Willow La Billinghay LN4 ... 109 E6
3 Cranwell NG34 ... 120 F8
Dunston LN4 ... 95 C6
6 Goxhill DN19 ... 5 A1
Grantham NG31 ... 210 F2
Ruskington LN4 ... 109 B3
Willowmead Cl DN15 ... 182 C6
Willow Pk DN37 ... 194 B4
Willow Rd 1 Branston LN4 . 81 D2
Lincoln LN6 ... 204 F2
5 Newark-on-Trent NG24 ... 104 B3
Stamford PE9 ... 218 D7
Willow Row PE11 ... 214 E5
Willow Row Bank LN11 ... 62 F6
Willows Cl PE13 ... 160 A1
Willows Ct LN4 ... 207 A4
Willows Dr PE25 ... 103 C7
Willows La PE22 ... 125 F7
Willows Prim Acad DN37 . 190 E8
WILLOWS THE DN37 ... 190 E7
Willows The
6 Cranwell NG34 ... 107 F1
5 Crowland PE6 ... 166 E1
Glinton PE6 ... 220 D8
Kingston upon Hull HU13 ... 178 E4
Willow Tree Cl DN40 ... 186 D5
Willow Tree Gdns LN6 ... 204 C8
Willow Wlk PE11 ... 214 E5
Willow Wy NG32 ... 128 A6
WILL ROW LN12 ... 63 C5
Will Row LN12 ... 63 C5
Wilmington Dr 18 LN12 ... 77 A8
Wilmore La DN38 ... 32 E7
WILSFORD NG32 ... 120 C1
Wilsford La NG32 ... 120 A2
Wilson Cl
Ingoldmells PE25 ... 90 D3
8 North Ferriby HU14 ... 3 A4
Wilson Ct LE15 ... 162 A8
Wilsons Cl DN15 ... 183 B3
Wilson St
Cleethorpes DN35 ... 192 D8
Gainsborough DN21 ... 197 B5
2 Kingston upon Hull HU10 178 E6
Kingston upon Hull HU10 ... 178 E6
4 Kingston upon Hull HU9 . 181 B7
Lincoln LN1 ... 234 A4
WILSTHORPE PE9 ... 164 C4
Wilsthorpe Rd PE10 ... 164 C6
Wilton Ave 14 PE24 ... 90 D7
Wilton Cl PE3 ... 225 C4
Wilton Dr PE3 ... 225 C4
Wilton Rd DN36 ... 192 D1
Wilton Rd Ind Est DN36 ... 195 F8
Wilton Road Ind Est
DN36 ... 192 D1
Wilton St HU8 ... 181 B8
Wiltshire Ave DN15 ... 8 B4
Wiltshire Rd HU4 ... 179 E2
Wilyman Cl 21 LN12 ... 77 A7
Wimberley Cl 3 PE12 ... 157 D7
Wimberley Way
8 Pinchbeck PE11 ... 156 E8
3 South Witham NG33 ... 151 D2
Wimbishthorpe Cl 3
NG13 ... 128 A6
Wimborn Ave DN34 ... 191 B6
Wimborne Dr 7 PE1 ... 226 E7
WINCEBY PE23 ... 86 E3
Winceby Ave DN31 ... 191 B8
Winceby Gdns LN9 ... 199 D4
Winceby Rd LN9 ... 86 D2
Winchcombe Ave DN34 ... 190 E4
Winchelsea Prim Sch
Ruskington NG34 ... 108 D1
Winchelsea Rd 14 NG34 ... 108 E1
Winchester Ave DN33 ... 191 A3
Winchester Cl
3 Bracebridge Heath LN4 ... 81 A2
6 Skegness PE25 ... 206 D7
Winchester Ct 9 LN6 ... 93 B8
Winchester Dr
Bottesford DN16 ... 185 C3
Heighington/Washingborough
LN4 ... 203 C1
6 Mablethorpe/Sutton on Sea
LN12 ... 64 A3
Winchester Rd
Grantham NG31 ... 210 E4
13 Hatfield DN7 ... 14 D4
8 Wainfleet All Saints
PE24 ... 102 D2
Winchester Way
Peterborough PE3 ... 225 E1
Sleaford NG34 ... 212 C7
Winchilsea Ave 19 NG24 ... 104 A4
Wincolmlee HU2 ... 181 A7
Windass Ct HU13 ... 178 E1
Windermere Ave
4 Grimsby DN33 ... 194 E7
Lincoln LN6 ... 205 A2
Windermere Cres DN36 ... 192 E1
Windermere Rd LN2 ... 202 D8
Windermere Way PE4 ... 221 C3
Windgate Way PE8 ... 222 A6
Windlass Cl 16 DN8 ... 15 A8
Windle Dr PE10 ... 213 E2
Windlesham Ave DN33 ... 194 D7
Windmill Cl Holbeach PE12 215 B2
Market Deeping PE6 ... 217 F5
4 Waddington LN5 ... 93 F6
Windmill Dr
Burgh le Marsh PE24 ... 102 D8
13 Heckington NG34 ... 122 E2
Windmill Gdns 3 PE13 ... 170 E2
Windmill La 5 Alford LN13 . 75 F2
Gosberton PE11 ... 144 F6
Windmill St PE1 ... 225 F5
Windmill View 3 LN1 ... 234 A4
Windmill Way HU13 ... 178 F1
Windrush Dr PE4 ... 221 D1
Windsmoor Rd 15 LN8 ... 47 B6
Windsor Ave
Holbeach PE12 ... 215 F2
Kingston upon Hull HU10 ... 178 E7
3 Peterborough PE4 ... 225 C8
Windsor Bank PE21 ... 209 A3
Windsor Cl Collingham NG23 91 D4
6 Keelby DN41 ... 23 A5
1 Sleaford NG34 ... 212 B2
4 Stamford PE9 ... 219 B7
6 Sudbrooke LN2 ... 68 F2
Windsor Cr 4 PE7 ... 230 B1
Windsor Cres Boston PE21 209 A4
1 Crowle DN17 ... 16 C7
4 Ingoldmells PE25 ... 90 D3
Scunthorpe DN17 ... 184 F2
Yaxley PE7 ... 233 B8
Windsor Ct
3 Bourne PE10 ... 213 C3
7 Grimsby DN31 ... 189 C1
12 Hatfield DN7 ... 14 C2
Windsor Dr 19 Caistor LN7 . 33 B4
Grantham NG31 ... 211 E5
Peterborough PE2 ... 231 D6
Spalding PE11 ... 214 D2
Wisbech PE13 ... 170 D2
Windsor Gdns PE12 ... 216 C5
Windsor Gr 1 DN19 ... 5 A1
Windsor La DN17 ... 16 C7
Windsor Mews LN11 ... 198 C5
Windsor Pk Cl 5 LN6 ... 204 F1
Windsor Rd
Cleethorpes DN35 ... 192 C5
Crowle DN17 ... 16 C7
Louth LN11 ... 198 B8
Yaxley PE7 ... 233 F6
Windsor Terr 11 PE21 ... 209 A5
Windsor Way
Barnetby le Wold DN38 ... 21 B5
Broughton DN20 ... 19 E4
Wine Hill La LN11 ... 51 B5
Winfrey Ave PE11 ... 214 D4
Wingate Parade DN37 ... 190 E8
Wingate Rd DN37 ... 190 D8
Wingate Way PE10 ... 213 E7
Wing Dr PE21 ... 209 C4
Wingfield PE2 ... 229 F3
Wingfield Ct NG31 ... 210 F1
Winn Ct DN35 ... 192 E5
Winniffe Gdns LN2 ... 202 D7
Winn La 4 LN9 ... 86 B8
Winnowsty La LN2 ... 234 C3
Winn St Lincoln LN2 ... 234 C2
2 Scunthorpe DN16 ... 183 B2
Winship Cl 4 HU3 ... 180 C5
Winslow Dr DN40 ... 186 B5
Winslow Gate PE12 ... 159 B8
Winslow Gr 2 DN34 ... 190 F4
Winslow Rd
4 Boston PE21 ... 209 C4
Peterborough PE3 ... 225 C3
Winsover Rd PE11 ... 214 B3
Winston Ave DN34 ... 191 B6
Winston Dr PE25 ... 206 B6
Winston Gdns PE21 ... 209 A7
Winston Rd PE23 ... 100 F8
Winston Way
5 Brigg DN20 ... 196 D4
Farcet PE7 ... 231 C2
Winterbeck Cl 5 NG13 ... 128 A6
Winterdale Cl 7 NG24 ... 104 B5
Wintergold Ave PE11 ... 214 A5
WINTERINGHAM DN15 ... 2 A1
Winteringham Foreshore
Nature Reserve★ DN15 ... 2 B1
Winteringham La DN15 ... 8 E8
Winteringham Prim Sch
DN15 ... 2 A1
Winteringham Rd DN15 ... 9 B6
Wintern Ct DN21 ... 197 D2
Winter's La
9 Long Bennington
NG23 ... 117 D4
Long Sutton PE12 ... 160 A3
WINTERTON DN15 ... 9 A5
Winterton PE1 ... 221 E1
Winterton CE Inf Sch DN15 .. 9 A5
Winterton Cl 7 PE9 ... 218 F6
Winterton Com Acad DN15 .. 9 A6
Winterton Rd
Roxby cum Risby DN15 ... 8 F2
Scunthorpe DN15 ... 183 B4
Winteringham DN15 ... 9 B8
WINTHORPE
Langford NG23 ... 104 B8
Skegness PE25 ... 206 C8
Winthorpe Ave PE25 ... 206 D8
Winthorpe Cl 17 LN6 ... 204 D7
Winthorpe Gr 16 LN6 ... 204 D7
Winthorpe Prim Sch
NG23 ... 104 C8
Winthorpe Rd
Birchwood LN6 ... 204 D7
Grimsby DN33 ... 191 B3
Kingston upon Hull HU13 ... 178 F3
4 Kingston upon Hull
HU13 ... 179 A3
8 Newark NG24 ... 104 B7
Winthorpe Way
Ingoldmells PE25 ... 206 D8
Skegness PE25 ... 90 E1
Winton Gdns 17 LN5 ... 107 A8
Winton Rd 11 LN5 ... 107 A8
Wintringham 26 HU15 ... 2 C6
Wintringham Rd DN32 ... 191 E6
Winwick Pl PE3 ... 225 C5
Winyates PE2 ... 229 F3
Winyates Prim Sch PE2 ... 230 A3
Wire Hill La LN8 ... 70 E5
Wirral Ave 7 DN34 ... 190 F4
WISBECH PE13 ... 170 B1
Wisbech Rd
Long Sutton PE12 ... 216 E1
Thorney PE6 ... 176 A3
Walpole PE14 ... 161 C1
Walsoken PE14 ... 170 E2
Wisbech St Mary PE13 ... 177 A2
Wisdom Cl 23 NG24 ... 104 C1
Wiseholme Rd LN6 ... 200 B2
Wiseman's Gate 1 PE12 ... 157 D7
Wiske Ave 7 HU15 ... 2 D5
WISPINGTON LN9 ... 84 E6
Wispington Road LN9 ... 84 E7
Wistaria Rd PE13 ... 170 E1
Wisteria Ave LN4 ... 81 D2
Wisteria Dr DN41 ... 23 F5
Wisteria Rd PE7 ... 233 D4
Wisteria Way Bourne PE10 213 B7
Scunthorpe DN16 ... 185 E4
Werrington PE4 ... 221 B3
Wistow Gr HU4 ... 179 D5
Wistow Way PE2 ... 229 D6
Witchford Cl 2 LN6 ... 204 B6
Witchford Rd 3 LN6 ... 204 B6
Witham HU9 ... 181 B7
Witham Ave PE22 ... 125 D5
Witham Bank Dogdyke LN4 110 D8
Timberland LN10 ... 97 C3
Witham Bank E 4 PE21 ... 208 E6
Witham Bank W PE21 ... 208 E6
Withambrook Pk NG31 ... 211 F7
Witham Cl
7 Beacon Hill NG24 ... 104 A5
Lincoln LN6 ... 205 D5
11 Ruskington NG34 ... 108 D2
Stamford PE9 ... 219 C6
Witham Cres PE10 ... 213 A4
Witham Ct 2 Boston PE21 . 208 E6
Lincoln LN6 ... 201 D1
Witham Dr
6 Burton upon Stather
DN15 ... 8 B5
Chapel Hill LN4 ... 110 E5
Witham Gdns PE21 ... 208 E6
Witham Gn PE21 ... 208 E6
Witham Hall Prep Sch
PE10 ... 163 D7
Witham/Haven Mouth Nature
Reserve★ PE22 ... 137 F6
Witham Mews LN5 ... 234 A1
WITHAM ON THE HILL
PE10 ... 163 D7
Witham Pl Boston PE21 ... 208 E5
Grantham NG31 ... 211 C2
Witham Prospect Sch LN6 . 92 B2
Witham Rd
Gunby & Stainby NG33 ... 151 C4
5 Long Bennington NG23 ... 117 D4
Spalding PE11 ... 214 A4
Thistleton LE15 ... 151 C1
Woodhall Spa LN10 ... 97 B5
WITHAM ST HUGHS LN6 ... 92 D5
Witham St 3 PE21 ... 208 F5
Witham Town PE21 ... 208 E6
Witham View LN4 ... 203 A2
Witham Vw LN3 ... 82 F6
Witham Way
Peterborough PE4 ... 221 D1
Westborough NG23 ... 117 F3
WITHCALL LN11 ... 60 C2
WITHERN LN13 ... 63 A1
Withern Rd DN33 ... 191 A3
Withington St 1 PE12 ... 160 E4
WITTERING PE8 ... 172 B1
Wittering Airfield PE8 ... 171 F1
Wittering Cl 5 LN6 ... 204 D6
Wittering Ford Rd PE8 ... 172 C1
Wittering Prim Sch PE8 ... 172 B1
Wittering Rd PE9 ... 172 D3

Witty St HU3 . . . . .180 A3
Wivell Dr [1] DN41 . . . . .23 A5
Wlker Cl [22] NG24 . . . . .104 A4
Woad Farm Rd PE21 . . . . . . .209 B4
Woad La Fishtoft PE22 . . . . . .137 C2
  Grimsby DN31 . . . . .188 A2
  Long Sutton PE12 . . . . .216 E5
Woburn Ave LN1 . . . . .201 E6
Woburn Cl Louth LN11 . . . . . .198 B7
  [4] Market Deeping PE6 . . . .217 A5
  Peterborough PE3 . . . . .225 A1
Woburn Dr Grantham NG31 211 F5
  Thorney PE6 . . . . .176 A2
Woburn Gr [1] LN10 . . . . .97 C5
Woburn St HU3 . . . . .179 F4
Woffindin Cl [12] NG10 . . . . . .129 E5
Woldcarr Rd East Ella HU3 .179 F7
  Kingston upon Hull HU3 . . .179 F6
WOLD NEWTON LN8 . . . . . . .47 F7
Wold Rd
  Barrow upon Humber DN19 . .11 D7
  Burnham DN18 . . . . .10 F4
  Kingston upon Hull HU5 . . .179 C8
  Wootton DN39 . . . . .11 C2
  Worlaby DN20 . . . . .10 E1
Wolds Cl [5] DN17 . . . . .16 D7
Wolds Leisure–De Aston
  Sports Ctr LN8 . . . . .57 E7
Wolds The DN21 . . . . .43 D6
Wold The DN38 . . . . .21 E3
Wold View [1] Brigg DN20 . .196 B4
  [25] Burgh PE15 . . . . .2 C6
  Caistor LN7 . . . . .33 C4
  Fotherby LN11 . . . . .49 A2
  Holton le Clay DN36 . . . . . .195 C2
  [3] Nettleham LN2 . . . . .68 D2
  Rothwell LN7 . . . . .33 F2
Wolf La PE13 . . . . .169 F1
Wolfreton Ct
  [3] Anlaby HU10 . . . . .178 E6
  Anlaby HU10 . . . . .178 E6
Wolfreton Dr HU10 . . . . .178 E6
Wolfreton Garth HU10 . . . . .178 D8
Wolfreton La HU10 . . . . .178 F8
Wolfreton Mews HU10 . . . . .178 F7
Wolfreton Rd HU10 . . . . .178 C7
Wolfreton Sch HU10 . . . . . . .178 C7
Wolfreton Villas [5] HU10 . .178 F7
Wolla Bank Nature Reserves★
  PE24 . . . . .77 D1
Wollaston Rd
  Cleethorpes DN35 . . . . .192 E6
  Peterborough PE3 . . . . .225 C6
Wolseley Cl PE7 . . . . .233 D6
Wolsey Dr [6] DN19 . . . . .11 C7
Wolsey Rd NG24 . . . . .104 A6
Wolsey Way LN2 . . . . .202 D8
Womersley Rd DN35 . . . . . . .189 C2
Wong Gdns NG32 . . . . .210 A4
Wong Row [10] NG31 . . . . . .211 A5
Wongs La PE24 . . . . .102 B7
Wong The LN9 . . . . .199 B3
Woodale Cl [2] DN15 . . . . . .182 C6
Woodapple Ct [4] DN41 . . . . .23 E6
Woodbank
  [1] Deeping St Nicholas
  PE11 . . . . .166 C6
  Skellingthorpe LN6 . . . . . . .200 A8
Woodbine Ave DN20 . . . . . .196 C4
Woodbine Contemporary
  Arts★ PE12 . . . . .168 A3
Woodbine St PE21 . . . . .231 A8
Woodbridge Rd NG34 . . . . . .212 E6
Woodbridge Rd Ind Est
  NG34 . . . . .272 E6
Woodbridge Way [15] LN10 . .97 C5
Woodburn Cl LN1 . . . . .201 E8
Woodburn View [13] LN1 . . .201 E8
Woodbyth Rd PE1 . . . . .226 A6
Wood Carr La DN9 . . . . .16 C2
Wood Cl DN33 . . . . .194 F7
Woodclose Rd DN17 . . . . . . .184 D6
Woodcock La LN1 . . . . .200 C8
Woodcock St HU3 . . . . .180 A4
Woodcote Cl PE1 . . . . .226 A7
Woodcroft [7] PE6 . . . . .217 A5
Woodcroft Rd
  Marholm PE6 . . . . .220 A3
  [4] Saxilby LN1 . . . . .66 C2
Woodcross Ave DN16 . . . . . .185 D4
Wood Dr HU14 . . . . .3 A4
Wooden Beck Hill DN10 . . . .39 E2
Wood End NG31 . . . . .131 A1
WOOD ENDERBY PE22 . . . . .98 F6
Wood Enderby La LN9 . . . . . .98 D6
Wood Farm Cl [12] LN7 . . . . .33 A3
Woodfield [7] PE9 . . . . .171 B1
Woodfield Ave LN6 . . . . .200 C1
Woodfield Cl
  [9] Birchwood LN6 . . . . . . .200 C1
  [15] Humberston DN36 . . . . .36 D8
  Spalding PE11 . . . . .214 F2
Woodfield La HU13 . . . . .178 C1
Woodfield Rd
  Gainsborough DN21 . . . . . .197 F5
  Peterborough PE3 . . . . .225 D3
Woodford Gdns PE13 . . . . . .169 E3
Woodgarr Ave [4] DN17 . . . . .17 D6
Woodgate PE6 . . . . .173 C4
Woodgate La
  Beckingham LN5 . . . . .105 C4
  Kingston upon Hull HU5 . . .179 F8
  Maxey PE6 . . . . .173 D6

Woodgate La continued
  Maxey PE6 . . . . .217 A1
Woodgate Rd
  Kingston upon Hull HU5 . . .179 F7
  Leverington PE13 . . . . .170 A2
  [7] Moulton PE12 . . . . .157 E1
Woodgates Cl [13] HU14 . . . . .3 A5
Woodgates La HU14 . . . . .3 A6
Woodgates Mount [3] HU14 . .3 A5
Woodhall Cl PE21 . . . . .208 C5
Woodhall Cres [9] LN1 . . . . .66 C2
Woodhall Dr Lincoln LN2 . . .201 F8
  Waltham DN37 . . . . .194 C4
Woodhall Rd
  Horncastle LN9 . . . . .199 A3
  Roughton LN9 . . . . .85 C3
  Stixwould LN10 . . . . .97 C7
Woodhall Rise PE4 . . . . .220 F6
WOODHALL SPA LN10 . . . . . .97 E5
Woodhall Spa Cottage Mus★
  LN10 . . . . .97 D6
Woodhead Cl [4] PE9 . . . . . .219 D7
Woodhill Ave DN21 . . . . .197 E6
Woodhill Cl [2] HU10 . . . . . .178 E7
Wood Hill Rd DN21 . . . . .29 B3
Woodhill Rise HU13 . . . . .178 C2
WOODHOUSE DN9 . . . . .16 E3
Woodhouse Gn Rd DN7 . . . . .14 B8
Woodhouse La
  [2] Belton DN9 . . . . .16 E3
  Hatfield DN7 . . . . .14 D2
  Holbeach PE12 . . . . .159 A8
  Moulton PE12 . . . . .146 E1
Woodhouse Prim Sch DN7 .15 A4
Woodhouse Rd DN16 . . . . . .185 E8
Woodhouse St HU9 . . . . .181 D7
Woodhurst Rd PE2 . . . . .231 D6
Wood La Bardney LN3 . . . . . .83 B4
  Beckingham DN10 . . . . .52 A8
  Croxton Kerrial NG32 . . . . . .138 A6
  Fishlake DN7 . . . . .14 D8
  Gringley on the Hill DN10 . . .39 C2
  [1] Lincoln LN6 . . . . .93 A8
  Little Cawthorpe LN11 . . . . .61 F2
  Louth LN11 . . . . .198 D4
  Norton Disney LN6 . . . . .92 B3
  Quadring PE11 . . . . .135 C1
  South Kyme LN4 . . . . .109 F1
  South Kyme LN4 . . . . .123 B8
  South Scarle NG23 . . . . .91 F7
  Sturton le Steeple DN22 . . . .52 A3
  Thurlby PE10 . . . . .213 C1
Woodland Ave
  [8] Bourne PE10 . . . . .213 B5
  [22] Brough HU15 . . . . .2 C6
  [19] Crowle DN17 . . . . .16 D8
  Gainsborough DN21 . . . . . .197 B7
  Skellingthorpe LN6 . . . . . . .200 B2
Woodland Chase DN21 . . . . .197 E5
Woodland Cl [13] PE22 . . . . .114 A1
Woodland Dr
  [8] Broughton DN20 . . . . . . .19 D4
  [5] Elsham DN20 . . . . .20 F7
  Grantham NG31 . . . . .211 F7
  Kingston upon Hull HU10 . . .178 C6
  [6] Woodhall Spa LN10 . . . . .97 E6
Woodland End HU4 . . . . .179 C5
Woodland Lea [2] PE13 . . . . .173 B4
Woodland Park HU13 . . . . . .178 B1
Woodlands Langford NG24 104 B8
  Long Sutton PE12 . . . . .216 D4
  [5] Louth LN11 . . . . .198 C6
Woodlands Acad PE23 . . . . . .87 F1
Woodlands Ave
  Immingham DN40 . . . . .186 C5
  [15] Keelby DN41 . . . . .23 A4
  [6] Spilsby PE23 . . . . .87 F1
Woodlands Cl
  [5] Barrow upon Humber
  DN19 . . . . .11 C7
  Potter Hanworth LN4 . . . . . .95 B8
Woodlands Dr
  [1] Colsterworth NG33 . . . .151 E7
  Grantham NG31 . . . . .211 C4
Woodlands Inf Sch LN6 . . . .200 C1
Woodlands La [14] HU15 . . . . .2 C6
Woodlands Prim Sch
  DN33 . . . . .191 A2
Woodlands Rd HU5 . . . . .179 B7
Woodlands Rise [7] HU14 . . . .3 A5
Woodlands The
  [11] Beacon Hill NG24 . . . . .104 C4
  [3] Market Deeping PE6 . . . .217 B5
  Peterborough PE1 . . . . .226 E5
  [1] Stallingborough DN41 . . . .23 D6
Woodland View
  [2] Barnetby le Wold DN38 . .21 B4
  Lincoln LN2 . . . . .234 C3
  Scunthorpe DN15 . . . . .182 C3
  [15] Spilsby PE23 . . . . .101 A8
Woodland Way [16] DN9 . . . .27 E6
Woodland Wlk [1] DN35 . . . .192 E1
Woodlea Cl DN7 . . . . .14 D2
Woodmans Cl [15] NG34 . . . .122 D3
Woodman's Ct [2] PE22 . . . . .98 F4
Woodmill Bank PE12 . . . . . .159 F2
WOODNOOK NG33 . . . . .140 C7
Woodpecker Cl LN6 . . . . .200 A3
Woodpecker Ct PE4 . . . . .221 E2
Woodpecker Way PE11 . . . . .42 E8
Wood Rd [24] LN13 . . . . .75 F2
Woodrow PE PE13 . . . . .191 D1
Woodrow Pl PE11 . . . . .214 B4

Woodrush Rd [6] LN2 . . . . . .202 C8
Woods Cl [14] NG23 . . . . . . .117 D3
WOODSIDE DN9 . . . . .26 D6
Woodside Boston PE21 . . . . .208 E1
  Branston & Mere LN4 . . . . . .81 D2
  Kingston upon Hull HU13 . . .178 D1
  [7] Swanland HU14 . . . . .3 C7
Woodside Ave NG34 . . . . . . .212 D6
Woodside Cl [1] PE10 . . . . . .164 C8
Woodside Ct NG34 . . . . .212 D7
Woodside Dr DN17 . . . . .184 C5
Woodside E PE10 . . . . .164 D8
Woodside Falconry &
  Conservation Ctr★ LN3 . 69 D3
Woodside La LN4 . . . . .69 D3
Woodside Rd PE20 . . . . .136 B5
Woods La Drayton PE20 . . . .135 C6
  [2] South Killingholme DN40 . .12 F2
Wood's La
  Kingston upon Hull HU1 . . .180 E5
  [3] Pinchbeck PE11 . . . . . . .145 D2
Woodsley Ave DN35 . . . . . . .192 E5
Woods Mdw [1] DN20 . . . . . .30 F6
Wood St [3] DN32 . . . . .191 F8
Woods Terr DN21 . . . . .197 C7
Woodstock Cl [27] NG24 . . . .104 A4
Woodstock Rd DN16 . . . . . . .183 D5
Woodstock St [4] LN1 . . . . . .201 D4
WOODSTON PE2 . . . . .230 E7
Woodstone Gate PE2 . . . . . .230 D6
Woodston Ind Est PE2 . . . . .230 E6
Woodston Prim Sch PE2 . . .230 E7
WOODTHORPE LN13 . . . . . . .75 D7
Woodthorpe Ave PE21 . . . . .209 C4
Woodvale Ave LN6 . . . . .204 C6
Woodvale Cl [14] LN6 . . . . . .204 C6
Wood View Bourne PE10 . . . .213 C5
  [1] Messingham DN17 . . . . .29 D7
  [3] Swanland HU14 . . . . .3 B7
Woodville Gdns E [3]
  PE21 . . . . .208 D3
Woodville Gdns W [2]
  PE21 . . . . .208 D3
Woodville Rd PE21 . . . . .208 D4
Woodward Dr [6] PE4 . . . . . .221 E2
Woodward's La
  Little Sutton PE12 . . . . .160 B3
  Long Sutton PE12 . . . . .216 F1
Woodwards The [1] NG24 . .104 B3
Woodyard The [4] NG32 . . . .119 B7
Woolcroft Cl [2] PE13 . . . . . .170 A1
Woolfellhill Rd PE6 . . . . .174 F1
Woolgard PE3 . . . . .225 A3
Woolley's La
  Castle Bytham NG33 . . . . . .152 A4
  North Witham NG33 . . . . . . .151 F4
Woollin Ave DN17 . . . . .185 A6
Woolpack Mdws LN11 . . . . . .50 F7
Woolram Wygate PE11 . . . . .214 C5
WOOLSTHORPE BY BELVOIR
  NG32 . . . . .128 D1
WOOLSTHORPE-BY-
  COLSTERWORTH NG33 . .151 D7
Woolsthorpe La
  Belvoir NG32 . . . . .138 D7
  Bottesford NG13 . . . . .128 C4
Woolsthorpe Manor★
  NG33 . . . . .151 D7
Woolsthorpe Rd [3] NG33 . .151 D7
Woolwich Dr [2] HU4 . . . . . .179 B2
WOOTTON DN39 . . . . .11 F3
Wootton Ave PE2 . . . . .231 A6
Wootton Cl DN17 . . . . .184 C8
Wootton Dr PE2 . . . . .230 F6
Wootton Rd Grimsby DN33 191 A3
  Wootton DN39 . . . . .11 F2
  Worlaby DN20 . . . . .10 F1
Wootton St Andrews CE Prim
  Sch DN39 . . . . .11 E3
Worcester Ave DN34 . . . . . . .191 A4
Worcester Cl
  [11] Birchwood LN6 . . . . . . .204 D7
  [7] Bracebridge Heath LN4 . .81 A2
  [5] Louth LN11 . . . . .198 C5
  Scunthorpe DN16 . . . . .185 A2
Worcester Cres [4] PE9 . . . . .219 B6
Worcester Rd
  Grantham NG31 . . . . .210 D4
  [4] Wisbech PE13 . . . . .170 D1
Wordsworth Cl
  [3] Grantham NG31 . . . . . . .211 E6
  Peterborough PE4 . . . . .225 E8
Wordsworth Ct
  [5] Grimsby DN33 . . . . .189 C1
  [13] Sleaford NG34 . . . . . . .212 F4
Wordsworth Dr NG24 . . . . . .104 A3
Wordsworth Gr [2] PE10 . . .213 D3
Wordsworth Rd
  North Greetwell LN3 . . . . . .203 C6
  Scunthorpe DN17 . . . . .184 D6
Wordsworth St [6] LN2 . . . .234 B3
Workhouse La
  Algarkirk PE20 . . . . .136 B1
  Hogsthorpe PE24 . . . . .90 C7
Workington Ave [8] HU4 . . .179 B6
WORLABY Maidenwell LN11 . .74 A4
  Worlaby DN20 . . . . .20 D8
Worlaby Acad DN20 . . . . .20 D8
Worlaby Rd DN33 . . . . .191 B1
World's End Rd PE13 . . . . . .160 A1
Worldwide Way DN41 . . . . . .187 C2
Wormgate PE21 . . . . .208 F5
Worship St HU2 . . . . .180 F7
Worsley PE2 . . . . .230 A4

Worsley Cl
  [1] Holton le Clay DN36 . . .195 C2
  Immingham DN40 . . . . .186 D4
Worsley Rd DN40 . . . . .186 D4
Worthington La NG32 . . . . . .128 D1
Worthington Rd [6] NG24 . .104 C2
  [7] Swanland HU34 . . . . .3 C7
Wortley's La PE21 . . . . .208 A2
Wortley St DN16 . . . . .183 A2
WOTHORPE PE9 . . . . .219 B2
Wothorpe Hill PE9 . . . . .219 A1
Wothorpe Mews [3] PE9 . . .219 B4
Wothorpe Rd PE9 . . . . .219 B4
WRAGBY LN8 . . . . .70 E5
Wragby Prim Sch LN8 . . . . . .70 D5
Wragby Rd Bardney LN3 . . . .83 C4
  Holton cum Beckering LN8 . . .70 C7
  Lincoln LN2 . . . . .234 C3
  Lissington LN3 . . . . .57 E2
  Reepham LN3 . . . . .68 F1
  Scunthorpe DN17 . . . . .184 D5
  Stainfield LN8 . . . . .83 B6
Wragby Rd E
  Greetwell LN2 . . . . .203 A8
  Reepham LN3 . . . . .68 E1
Wragby St [3] DN32 . . . . . . .191 F7
WRAGHOLME LN11 . . . . .50 A8
Wragholme La LN11 . . . . .50 A8
Wragholme Rd LN11 . . . . . . .50 A8
WRANGLE PE22 . . . . .114 C1
WRANGLE BANK PE22 . . . . .114 C4
Wrangle Bank PE22 . . . . . . .114 B4
WRANGLE LOWGATE
  PE22 . . . . .114 C2
WRANGLE LOW GROUND
  PE22 . . . . .114 D4
Wrangle Prim Sch PE22 . . .114 C2
WRAWBY DN20 . . . . .20 E4
Wrawby Rd Brigg DN20 . . . .196 D4
  Scunthorpe DN17 . . . . .184 E5
Wrawby St Mary's CE Prim
  Sch DN20 . . . . .20 E4
Wrawby St DN20 . . . . .196 C3
Wray Cl [9] DN37 . . . . .194 C5
Wray St [20] DN21 . . . . .30 B1
Wren Cl
  Deeping St Nicholas PE11 . .166 B6
  [1] Healing DN41 . . . . .23 F5
  [15] Market Deeping PE6 . . .217 C5
  Scunthorpe DN16 . . . . .185 B2
  [4] Sleaford NG34 . . . . .212 B3
Wren Cres DN33 . . . . .191 B2
WRESSLE DN20 . . . . .19 F4
Wressle Rd DN20 . . . . .19 E3
Wright Ave PE2 . . . . .231 D5
Wright's Dro PE6 . . . . .175 B7
Wrights Gdns DN10 . . . . .40 A3
Wrights La [5] LE14 . . . . . . .150 C1
Wright's La Friskney PE22 . .115 A5
  Sutton Bridge PE12 . . . . . . .160 E4
Wright St HU2 . . . . .180 E7
Wrightsway LN2 . . . . .202 D5
WROOT DN9 . . . . .26 C6
Wroot Rd DN9 . . . . .26 A3
Wroot Road DN9 . . . . .27 A6
Wroot Travis Charity Prim Sch
  DN9 .26 D5
Wroxall Dr NG31 . . . . .210 E4
Wroxham Ave DN34 . . . . . . .190 E5
Wroxham Cl [7] LN6 . . . . . . .205 A4
Wrygarth Ave [7] HU15 . . . . .2 C5
Wulfram Dr NG31 . . . . .211 E2
Wulfric Sq PE3 . . . . .225 C8
Wyatt Ave [3] DN20 . . . . .19 D3
Wyatt Cl LN4 . . . . .96 B2
Wyatt Rd LN5 . . . . .205 D7
Wybeck Rd DN15 . . . . .183 A6
Wybers Way DN37 . . . . .190 D7
WYBERS WOOD DN37 . . . . .190 C6
Wybers Wood Prim Sch
  DN37 . . . . .190 C8
Wybert Cres [6] PE21 . . . . . .136 D8
Wybert La PE21 . . . . .136 F8
WYBERTON PE21 . . . . .136 D8
Wyberton Low Rd [1]
  PE21 . . . . .208 F2
Wyberton Prim Sch PE21 .136 E7
Wyberton Roads PE20 . . . . .137 A7
Wyberton W Rd PE21 . . . . . .208 C2
Wyche Ave [3] PE6 . . . . .166 F1
Wycliffe Gr PE4 . . . . .220 E5
Wydham Pk PE2 . . . . .229 D6
Wye Pl PE4 . . . . .221 C1
Wye Valley Rd [3] PE2 . . . . .230 E8
Wygate Mdws PE11 . . . . . . .214 B5
Wygate Park Acad PE11 . . .214 B4
Wygate Park Academy
  PE11 . . . . .214 A5
Wygate Pk PE11 . . . . .214 A5
Wygate Rd PE11 . . . . .214 B4
Wyggeston Ave [22] NG13 . .128 A6
Wyggeston Rd [21] NG13 . . .128 A6
WYKEHAM PE12 . . . . .145 F1
Wykeham La
  Burgh on Bain LN8 . . . . .59 C6
  Weston PE12 . . . . .145 F1
Wykes La PE11 . . . . .135 A2
Wykes Rd Donington PE11 . .135 B1
  Yaxley PE7 . . . . .233 D4
Wyke St HU9 . . . . .181 D7
Wyke The [8] PE11 . . . . .214 A3
Wyke Wy HU15 . . . . .2 E5
Wylson Cl [5] NG34 . . . . . . .120 F8
Wyman Way PE2 . . . . .229 F5
Wymark View DN33 . . . . . . .190 F3
Wymersley Rd HU5 . . . . . . .179 A8
WYMONDHAM LE14 . . . . . . .150 B1

Wymondham Drift LE14 . . . .150 D1
Wyndham Cl NG31 . . . . .211 C5
Wyndham Rd [9] DN36 . . . . .195 C6
Wyndham St HU3 . . . . .180 C7
Wynmoor Rd DN17 . . . . .184 F7
Wyredale Rd DN16 . . . . .185 D5
Wyside Cres PE7 . . . . .230 B1
Wythes La PE21 . . . . .126 C2
Wyton Cl [8] LN6 . . . . .204 B6
Wyvern Cl [16] DN17 . . . . . . .16 D8
WYVILLE NG32 . . . . .139 C4
Wyville Rd Grantham NG31 210 E1
  Hungerton NG32 . . . . .139 B4
  Little Ponton & Stroxton
  NG31 . . . . .139 E8
Wyvill Wlk LN6 . . . . .204 F7

Y

YADDLETHORPE DN17 . . . . .184 E3
Yale Cl LN4 . . . . .203 D1
YARBOROUGH DN34 . . . . . . .191 A7
Yarborough Cl [3] DN36 . . . .195 C2
Yarborough Cres
  [17] Broughton DN20 . . . . . .19 E4
  Lincoln LN1 . . . . .201 E6
Yarborough Ct DN15 . . . . . .182 B2
Yarborough Dr [3] DN31 . . .191 D8
Yarborough Leisure Ctr
  LN1 .201 E7
Yarborough Prim Sch
  DN34 . . . . .190 F7
Yarborough Rd
  Boston PE21 . . . . .136 E8
  Brigg DN20 . . . . .196 D3
  Grimsby DN34 . . . . .190 F6
  Keelby DN41 . . . . .23 A5
  [1] Lincoln LN1 . . . . .234 A4
  Scunthorpe DN16 . . . . .19 A4
  [9] Skegness PE25 . . . . .206 A6
Yarborough Rise LN7 . . . . . .33 C4
Yarborough Terr LN1 . . . . . .234 A4
YARBURGH LN11 . . . . .49 E4
Yarburgh Rd LN11 . . . . .49 E2
Yarde The [2] PE10 . . . . .213 E2
Yardley Way [2] DN34 . . . . . .190 D4
Yards End La PE7 . . . . .233 A1
Yarmouth Ave
  Grantham NG31 . . . . .210 D4
  [3] Kingston upon Hull HU4. .179 A3
Yarnsworth Rd [6] NG24. . . .104 A2
Yarra Rd DN35 . . . . .192 F6
Yarrow Rd DN34 . . . . .190 F7
Yarwell Cl PE2 . . . . .230 D7
Yarwell Rd PE8 . . . . .222 A3
Yawling Gate Rd PE22 . . . . .114 F5
YAWTHORPE DN21 . . . . .42 A2
YAXLEY PE7 . . . . .233 E6
Yaxley Infant Sch PE7 . . . . .233 F4
Yew Cl HU13 . . . . .178 D3
Yew Dr DN16 . . . . .185 B2
Yew Gro [19] DN36 . . . . .36 C8
Yews La DN37 . . . . .23 E1
Yew Tree Cl [1] PE10 . . . . . . .213 C6
Yewtree Dr HU5 . . . . .179 B7
Yew Tree Gr [1] PE21 . . . . . .209 C2
Yew Tree Way [1] NG24 . . . .104 C5
Yew Tree Wlk PE3 . . . . .225 A2
York Ave Lincoln LN1 . . . . . .201 D4
  Scunthorpe DN16 . . . . .185 B4
York Cl LN4 . . . . .203 D1
York Dr [33] HU15 . . . . .2 C5
Yorke Dr NG24 . . . . .104 A5
York Gdns
  [2] Gosberton PE11 . . . . . . .145 B6
  [30] Wisbech PE13 . . . . . . .170 C1
York House Rd [6] NG34. . . .120 C8
York Pl DN35 . . . . .192 C4
York Rd
  [5] Binbrook Tech Pk LN8 . . .47 B6
  Bourne PE10 . . . . .213 C3
  Brigg DN20 . . . . .196 D4
  Hatfield DN7 . . . . .14 D4
  Kirton in Lindsey DN21 . . . . .30 C1
  Mablethorpe/Sutton on Sea
  LN12 . . . . .64 D1
  Peterborough PE1 . . . . .225 F6
  RAF Cranwell NG34 . . . . . . .107 C1
  Sleaford NG34 . . . . .212 C6
  [9] Stamford PE9 . . . . .219 B6
  Wisbech PE13 . . . . .170 D1
York Ride [4] PE12 . . . . .216 B5
York St (Boston United FC)
  PE21 . . . . .209 A5
Yorkshire Moors Bottom Road
  DN17 . . . . .16 B8
Yorkshireside DN17 . . . . .7 A3
York St Boston PE21 . . . . . .209 A4
  Grimsby DN31 . . . . .191 C8
York Terr [3] DN10 . . . . .40 A5
York Way
  [5] Bracebridge Heath LN4. . .81 A2
  Grantham NG31 . . . . .210 C5
York Wy [4] PE25 . . . . .206 D7
Youlgrave Ave [6] LN12 . . . .77 A8
Younger's La PE24 . . . . .103 A8
Young Pl DN35 . . . . .192 B7
Youngs Ave [9] NG24 . . . . . .104 C1
Youngs Cl [18] NG24 . . . . . .104 C5

Z

Zara Cl PE21 . . . . .209 C6
Zetland St HU3 . . . . .180 A5